HANDBOOK OF

TRADE POLICY
FOR
DEVELOPMENT

HANDBOOK OF

TRADE POLICY

FOR

DEVELOPMENT

Edited by

ARVID LUKAUSKAS
ROBERT M. STERN
GIANNI ZANINI

OXFORD
UNIVERSITY PRESS

OXFORD
UNIVERSITY PRESS

Great Clarendon Street, Oxford, OX2 6DP,
United Kingdom

Oxford University Press is a department of the University of Oxford.
It furthers the University's objective of excellence in research, scholarship,
and education by publishing worldwide. Oxford is a registered trade mark of
Oxford University Press in the UK and in certain other countries

© Oxford University Press 2013

The moral rights of the authors have been asserted

First Edition published in 2013

Impression: 1

Published in the United States of America by Oxford University Press
198 Madison Avenue, New York, NY 10016, United States of America

British Library Cataloguing in Publication Data
Data available

Library of Congress Control Number: 2013941641

ISBN 978-0-19-968040-5

Printed and bound in Great Britain by
CPI Group (UK) Ltd, Croydon, CR0 4YY

Links to third party websites are provided by Oxford in good faith and
for information only. Oxford disclaims any responsibility for the materials
contained in any third party website referenced in this work.

1006960406

Preface and Acknowledgments

This volume is comprised of chapters prepared originally for a comprehensive two- to three-week-long Trade Policy for Development Executive Course designed and offered jointly by Columbia University's School of International and Public Affairs School (SIPA) and the World Bank Institute (WBI). Incorporating also contributions from other trade specialists and the World Bank's International Trade Department, the chapters have been updated, revised, and undergone editorial review.

Although there are many textbooks that cover international trade, there is a glaring lack of books that survey contemporary trade theory, policy, and negotiations in a concise, up-to-date manner from an interdisciplinary perspective. This volume provides a comprehensive overview of the issues that dominate both academic discourse and the policymaking arena. For the most part, it emphasizes the economic and development implications of trade policy and negotiations (be it at the unilateral, multilateral, or regional fronts). But it also ensures adequate coverage of the international trade architecture and the institutional and practical aspects of policymaking and negotiations. The treatment of each issue is rigorous, yet highly accessible to anyone with a basic background in economics, law, and international political economy, as the editors asked the contributors to limit their technical presentations to avoid turning away potential readers. Moreover, the three main disciplines relevant to trade policy, economics, law, and political science are well represented in this volume.

Our hope is that this volume may be widely adopted for courses on international trade or international political economy in both graduate and undergraduate programs in departments of economics, political science, schools of public policy, and law schools. Policymakers, negotiators, middle-level government officials, external advisors, and many academics in both developed and developing countries who are engaged or interested in trade reforms or in multilateral or regional/bilateral trading arrangements will find this volume to be an important and comprehensive reference source for all the key issues.

The editors wish to acknowledge Columbia/SIPA and the WBI for generous financial and logistical support for this project. We owe special thanks to Judith Jackson for her efforts in handling all of the manuscripts and preparing them for publication.

June 28, 2013
Arvid Lukauskas
Robert M. Stern
Gianni Zanini

Contents

PART IV: IMPLEMENTING AND NEGOTIATING TRADING ARRANGEMENTS FOR THE TWENTY-FIRST CENTURY

LIST OF FIGURES

List of Tables

LIST OF BOXES

List of Abbreviations

AB	Appellate Body
ACP	Africa, the Caribbean, and the Pacific
ACWL	Advisory Centre on WTO Law
AD	Anti-Dumping
ADR	Alternative Dispute Resolution
AFAS	ASEAN Framework Agreement on Services
AFL-CIO	American Federation of Labor and Congress of Industrial Organizations
AFTA	ASEAN Free Trade Area
AGOA	African Growth and Opportunity Act
AMAD	Agricultural Market Access Database
AMS	Aggregate Measure Of Support
ANZCERTA	Australia New Zealand Closer Economic Relations Trade Agreement
APEC	Asia-Pacific Economic Cooperation
APEDA	Agricultural Product Export Development Authority
AROWTO	Agreement on Rules of Origin
ASEAN	Association of South East Asian Nations
AVEs	*Ad valorem* Equivalents
BACI CEPII	International Trade Database
BITs	Bilateral Investment Treaties
BM	Bonded Manufacturing
BOP	Balance of Payments
BSE	Bovine Spongiform Encephalopathy
CACM	Central American Common Market

CAFTA	Central America Free Trade Agreement
CARICOM	Caribbean Community
CARIFORUM	Caribbean Forum of African, Caribbean, and Pacific States
CB	Consumer Burden
CBD	Convention on Biological Diversity
CBO	Congressional Budget Office
CC	Change at the Chapter level
CES	Constant Elasticity of Substitution
CET	Common External Tariff
CGE	Computable General Equilibrium
CH	Change at the Heading level
CI	Change at the Item level
CIF	Cost, Insurance, and Freight
CITES	Convention on International Trade in Endangered Species of Wild Fauna and Flora
CME	Central European Media
CME	Competitive Market Equilibrium
CMEA	Council for Mutual Economic Assistance
CODEX	Codex Alimentarius
COMESA	Common Market for Eastern and Southern Africa
COMTRADE	United Nations Commodity Trade Statistics Database
CPC	Central Protection Classification
CROC	ommittee on Rules of Origin
CS	Change at the Subheading level
CSE	Consumer Subsidy Equivalent
CTC	Change-of-Tariff Classification
CTE	Consumer Tax Equivalent
CTEWTO	Committee on Trade and Environment
CTESS	Council for Trade in Services Special Sessions
CUs	Customs Unions

CVD	Countervailing Duty
DDA	Doha Development Agenda
DECRG	Development Research Group (World Bank)
DFQF	Duty-Free and Quota-Free
DOT	Direction of Trade
DOTS	Direction of Trade Statistics
DSB	Dispute Settlement Body
DSM	Dispute Settlement Mechanism
DSU	Dispute Settlement Understanding
DTIS	Diagnostic Trade Integration Studies
DTT	Double Taxation Treaties
DUP	Directly Unproductive [rent seeking]
EAP	Extensible Authentication Protocol; East Asia and Pacific
EBA	Everything But Arms
EC	European Community
EC	Exchequer Cost
ECOWAS	Economic Community of West African States
ECSC	European Coal and Steel Community
EDIFACT	Electronic Data Interchange for Administration, Commerce, And Transport
EEC	European Economic Community
EFTA	European Free Trade Association
EGS	Environmental Goods And Services
EIC	Export Inspection Council
EPA	Economic Partnership Agreement
EPAs	Export Promotion Agencies
EPZs	Export Processing Zones
ERPs	Effective Rates of Protection
ETI	Enabling Trade Index (World Economic Forum)
EU	European Union

FAO	Food and Agriculture Organization
FATS	Foreign Affiliates Trade in Services
FDI	Foreign Direct Investment
FE	Foreign Exchange Displacement
FPE	Factor Price Equalization
FTA	Free Trade Area
FTAA	Free Trade Area of the Americas
GAP	Good Agricultural Practices
GATS	General Agreement on Trade in Services
GATT	General Agreement on Tariffs and Trade
GCNet	Ghana Community Network
GDP	Gross Domestic Product
GI	Geographical Indications
GMOs	Genetically Modified Organisms
GMP	Good Manufacturing Practices
GNP	Gross National Product
GNTB	Group of Eminent Persons on Non-Tariff Barriers
GPA	Government Procurement Agreement
GPO	Global Pareto Optimum
GSIM	Partial-Equilibrium Models
GSP	Generalized System of Preferences
GSSE	General Services Support Estimate
GTAP	Global Trade Analysis Project
GTAP	Global Analysis and Trade Project
HACCP	Hazard Analysis and Critical Control Point
HS	Harmonized System
HWP	Harmonization Work Program
ICC	International Chamber of Commerce
ICJ	International Court of Justice

ICSID	International Center for Settlement of Investment Disputes (World Bank Group)
ICT	Information and Communication Technology
ICTSD	International Centre for Trade and Sustainable Development
IDB	Integrated Data Base
IIAs	International Investment Agreements
ILO	International Labor Organization
IMF	International Monetary Fund
IPPC	International Plant Protection Convention
IPPC	International Convention on Plant Health
IPRs	Intellectual Property Rights
ISI	Import Substitution Industrialization
ISO	International Organization for Standardization
ISPs	Internet Service Providers
IT	Information Technology
ITA	Information Technology Agreement
ITC	International Trade Centre
ITO	International Trade Organization
IUCN	International Union for Conservation of Nature
LAC	Latin America and Caribbean
LAFTA	Latin American Free Trade Association
LCR	Latin America and the Caribbean Regions
LDCs	Least-Developed Countries
LPI	Logistics Performance Index
LPI	Logistics Performance Index (World Bank)
LSMS	Living Standards Measurement Surveys
MA	Market Access
MAM	Market Access Map (International Trade Centre)
MEA	Multilateral Environmental Agreement

MENA	Middle East and North Africa
Mercosul/Mercosur	South American trade bloc
MERCOSUR	Mercosur: *Mercado Común del Sur* (Spanish), or Mercosul: *Mercado Comum do Sul* (Portuguese)
MFA	Multi-Fibre Arrangement
MFN	Most Favored Nation
MNCs	Multinational Corporations
MPL	Marginal Product of Labor
MPS	Market Price Support
MPT	Marginal Product of Land
MRLs	Maximum Residue Levels
MSITS	Manual on Statistics of International Trade in Services
MTR	Multilateral Trade-Resistance
NAFTA	North American Free Trade Agreement
NAMA	Non-Agricultural Market Access
NBER	National Bureau of Economic Research
NGO	Non-governmental Organization
NIE	Newly Industrialized Economies
NT	National Treatment
NTBs	Non-Tariff Barriers
NTMs	Non-Tariff Measures
OECD	Organisation for Economic Co-operation and Development
OIE	International Office of Epizootics
OLS	Ordinary Least Squares
OPEC	Organization of Petroleum Exporting Countries
OTDS	Overall Trade-Distorting Domestic Support
OTRI	Overall Trade Restrictiveness Index
PBRs	Plant Breeders' Rights
PD	Prisoner's Dilemma
POL	Petroleum, Oil, and Lubricant

PPF	Production Possibilities Frontier
PPMs	Process and Production Methods
PRI	Institutional Revolutionary Party (Mexico)
PRODY	Index developed by Hausmann, Hwang, and Rodrik (2005)
PSE	Producer Subsidy Equivalent
PSV	Producer Subsidy Value
PTAs	Preferential Trade Areas/Arrangements
PTT	Postal Telegraph and Telephone or Public Telephone and Telegraph
QR(s)	Quantitative Restriction(s)
RAM	Recently Acceded Members
RASFF	Rapid Alert System for Food and Feed
RCA	Revealed Comparative Advantage
ROO	Rules-of-Origin
RTAA	Reciprocal Trade Agreements Act
RTAs	Regional Trade Agreements
SAARC	South Asian Association for Regional Cooperation
SACU	South African Customs Union
SADC	South African Development Community
SAM	Social Accounting Matrix
SCM	Subsidies and Countervailing Measures
SDRs	Special Drawing Rights
SDT	Special And Differential Treatment
SITC	Standard International Trade Classification, Rev. 4 (United Nations)
SMEs	Small and Medium Enterprises
SPARTECA	South Pacific Regional Trade and Economic Cooperation. Agreement
SPS	Sanitary and Phyto-sanitary
SS	Stolper–Samuelson Theorem
SSG	Special Safeguard
SSM	Special Safeguard Mechanism
STE	State Trading Enterprises

STOs	Specific Trade Obligations
SVE	Small and Vulnerable Economies
TAAG	Trade-at-a-Glance
TBT	Technical Barriers to Trade
TCI	Trade Complementarity Index
TCRO	Technical Committee on Rules of Origin
TE	Tariff Equivalent
TEDs	Turtle Exclusion Devices
TNCs	Transnational Corporations
TPOs	Trade Promotion Organizations
TPRs	Trade Policy Reviews
TRAINS	Trade Analysis and Information System
TREM(s)	Trade-Related Environmental Measure(s)
TRI	Trade Restrictiveness Index
TRIMS	Trade-Related Investment Measures
TRIPS	Trade-Related Aspects of Intellectual Property Rights (WTO)
TRIST	Tariff Reform Impact Simulation Tool
TRQs	Tariff Rate Quotas
TRS	Time Release Studies
TSE	Total Support Estimate
TTRI	Tariff Trade Restrictiveness Index
UEMOA	West African Economic and Monetary Union
UN	United Nations
UN CEFACT	United Nations' Centre for Trade Facilitation and Electronic Business
UNCITRAL	United Nations Commission on International Trade Law
UNCTAD	United Nations Conference on Trade and Development
UNEP	United Nations Environment Programme
UNFCCC	United Nations Framework Convention on Climate Change
UR	Uruguay Round

URAA	Uruguay Round Agreement on Agriculture
US ITC	International Trade Commission
USD	United States Dollars
VER(s)	Voluntary Export Restraint(s)
VoIP	Voice Over Internet Protocol
WCO	World Customs Organization
WIPO	World Intellectual Property Organization
WITS	World Integrated Trade Solution
WTI	World Trade Indicators
WTO	World Trade Organization
WWI	World War I
WWII	World War II

List of Contributors

Soamiely Andriamananjara	World Bank
Paul Brenton	World Bank
Olivier Cadot	University of Lausanne and World Bank
Steve Charnovitz	George Washington University
Simon J. Evenett	University of St. Gallen
Carsten Fink	World Intellectual Property Organization
Ana Frischtak	Debevoise & Plimpton
Jean-Marie Grether	University of Neuchatel
Spencer Henson	Guelph University
Andrew Grainger	Nottingham University
Bernard Hoekman	World Bank
Robert Howse	New York University
Steven Jaffee	World Bank
Geoffrey A. Jehle	Vassar College
Tim Josling	Stanford University
Pravin Krishna	Johns Hopkins School of Advanced International Studies
Mary E. Lovely	Syracuse University
Arvid Lukauskas	Columbia University
Edward D. Mansfield	University of Pennsylvania
Aaditya Mattoo	World Bank
Jean-Christophe Maur	World Bank
Gerard McLinden	World Bank
Patrick A. Messerlin	Science-Po

Devashish Mitra	Syracuse University
Richard Newfarmer	World Bank
Arvind Panagariya	Columbia University
Francisco L. Rivera-Batiz	Columbia University
Salomon Samen	World Bank
T. N. Srinivasan	Yale University
Robert M. Stern	University of Michigan and UC—Berkeley
Wendy E. Takacs	University of Maryland, Baltimore County
Joel P. Trachtman	Tufts University
Gianni Zanini	World Bank

CHAPTER 1

....

INTRODUCTION AND OVERVIEW

....

ARVID LUKAUSKAS, ROBERT M. STERN, AND GIANNI ZANINI

I. INTRODUCTION

....

THIS volume focuses on trade policy for development; that is, it attempts, wherever possible, to consider trade policy issues from the perspective of developing and emerging market countries.

For some time now, emerging market countries have been growing faster than developed countries. Moreover, developed countries have emerged from the recent financial crisis as financially fragile, politically paralyzed, facing unfavorable demographic trends, and increasingly lacking competitiveness. As a result, the ongoing shift of dynamism away from developed countries toward emerging markets, particularly in Asia, has accelerated. This transformation has occurred in large part because these countries have used trade as a means of modernizing and accelerating their growth. Over time, these countries may consequently take on a more significant role in governing the international trade regime and issues of special significance to them may grow more central to policy discussions.

The current global trade environment at the time of final review of this chapter (June 2013) is challenging and perhaps at a major tipping point. While the global financial crisis raised the specter of a global turn toward protectionism, of the sort that accompanied the financial and economic crises of the 1930s, thus far protectionist pressures have been fairly well contained. But the threat of trade wars, especially involving China, is very real, especially if global growth remains sluggish. Progress on concluding the Doha Round of multilateral trade negotiations is at an impasse, so that the momentum of liberal trade reform is at a standstill.

Preferential Trading Arrangements (PTAs) continue to multiply. There are some who believe that PTAs complement global efforts to liberalize trade and will eventually put pressure on countries to renew multilateral reform; but others fear that this will only undermine it.

The trade agenda has expanded over time from focusing primarily on "at the border" issues to encompassing, since the end of the Uruguay Round in 1994, "behind the border" issues. More recently, efforts to link new issues, such as labor rights and the environment, to multilateral negotiations have gained traction. But there has been resistance from emerging economies and developing countries to include these topics in the multilateral framework of the World Trade Organization. Nonetheless, these issues have become incorporated in PTAs, especially those negotiated by the United States and European Union.

As the subsequent chapters in this volume make clear, there is much to be done in understanding, designing, implementing, and evaluating the complex of trade policies that are of immense importance especially for emerging market and developing countries. Our hope is that this volume will serve to move ahead with the range of issues involved.

II. Overview

The chapters in the book are organized as follows. Part I deals with an overview of the global trading system. Part II provides theoretical background material. Part III is devoted to trade policy and trade liberalization. Part IV covers implementation and negotiation issues in modern trading arrangements, whether preferential or multilateral.

Part I: The Global Trading System

The global trading system has become increasingly complex over time due to profound economic and political trends. In recent decades, technological advances that have lowered communication, logistical, and transportation costs have made it possible for nations to trade a broader range of goods and services at a continually growing rate. These developments have also enabled firms to become truly global, engaging in multifaceted economic activities in real time using subsidiary units separated by vast distances, many of which involve the movement of goods across national borders, a surprisingly large percentage of this being intra-firm trade. More generally, many industrial sectors are organized around complex global supply chains often encompassing multiple lead firms, contractors, and subcontractors. The modern vertically-integrated firm, the epitome of twentieth-century efficiency, has begun to deconstruct, leading to what some scholars have termed "modular production networks" in which lead firms no longer conduct manufacturing on their own, but subcontract it out to foreign specialist firms, which in turn may base their plants in other countries.[1] The complicated flow of goods and services supporting these intricate networks almost defies description.

Prior to World War II, even during periods of relatively free trade such as the late nineteenth century, most countries carefully managed their commercial relations, and trade liberalization was based largely on a web of bilateral agreements, although most agreements, like the famous 1860 Cobden–Chevalier treaty between the United Kingdom and France, included a most favored nation (MFN) clause extending agreements to third parties. There was no international institution analogous to the WTO to oversee trade relations. During World War II, nations began the process of creating a truly multilateral, institutionalized system based on three norms or principles, namely, economic liberalism, non-discrimination, and reciprocity. The drive toward multilateralism was motivated as much by political as economic rationales. On the economic side, the victorious Western powers wanted to maximize the potential gains from trade by extending trade liberalization to as many countries and sectors as possible. On the political side, multilateralism was viewed as a strategy for strengthening the prospects of peace among major nations. Trade would make the welfare of one country dependent upon that of others, making it less likely that nations would go to war. For the United States, the most ardent advocate of multilateralism, freer trade was a critical element in its overall security strategy. Trade (as well as financial and monetary ties) among Western nations would strengthen their collective security vis-à-vis the Soviet threat by increasing the West's prosperity and deepening its economic and political integration.

In Chapter 2, Robert Stern examines the underlying norms, architecture, and functions of the multilateral trading system and its institutions, notably, the General Agreement on Tariffs and Trade (GATT) and its successor, the WTO. In the early post-World War II years, the core principles of non-discrimination and reciprocity largely shaped international trade relations, and their application was instrumental in guiding nations to significantly reduce tariffs on manufactured goods. By 1994, with the conclusion of the Uruguay Round, however, several developments began to challenge the prevailing framework. Chief among these were the proliferation of preferential trade agreements and the efforts by developed nations to broaden the trade agenda to include efforts to promote convergence on a wide range of internal political, social, and economic issues, often dubbed "behind the border" measures, such as competition and government procurement policies. Stern argues that the latter trend represented a new paradigm for trade relations, pitting those who believe that the emergence of an integrated world economy should be governed by a set of common rules, against those who contend that each country should retain the right to determine "how far it wants to adjust its domestic laws and practices in order to accommodate its trading partners and to gain a comparable adjustment from them."

---

[1] For example, see Sturgeon (2002).

Stern examines various objections to the WTO, such as its exclusion of labor standards ("it does too little") and environment ("it does too much"), lack of transparency, and tendency to be dominated by corporate interests, but finds that overall it "serves an extremely useful purpose, and that it serves it surprisingly well." Nonetheless, he expresses concern that the expansion of the boundaries of the WTO, just noted, may result in overextension and less effectiveness. Two conditions should be respected in evaluating efforts to expand its scope: the "positive economic nationalism" that prompts governments to meet legitimate economic and social goals that improve the welfare of their populations, and respect for the institutions that comprise national markets, which are embedded in social norms and in the organizational characteristics of business firms.

As noted, one of the distinguishing features of the post-World War II trade environment has been the explosive growth of PTAs. In Chapter 3, Pravin Krishna provides the analytical tools for evaluating the economic effects of PTAs on member and non-member countries (later chapters by Edward Mansfield and Jean-Christophe Maur examine other aspects of preferential trade). Krishna demonstrates that PTAs have ambiguous welfare effects, with net benefits largely depending on whether they are trade creating or trade diverting. Contrary to conventional wisdom, he argues that claims in favor of geographic proximity or regionalism's economic benefits as a basis for extending trade preferences are not supported theoretically or empirically. This suggests that other factors, such as the wish to forge closer political ties, probably also motivate countries to seek regional PTAs. Krishna argues that PTAs can be designed in ways that limit trade diversion and augment their welfare-enhancing effects. Specifically, members should completely eliminate internal barriers while aiming to continue to import the same amounts of goods from the rest of the world as they did before the PTA was created. WTO rules do not ensure these results; instead, they practically guarantee the diversion of trade to higher cost sources of supply. Devising rules to completely eliminate trade diversion is difficult, but requiring preferential partners to simultaneously lower external barriers (perhaps through pro rata reduction of external tariffs) while reducing internal barriers would be a step in the right direction. In addition, adequate rules of origin (ROO) are required to prevent agents from importing goods into the PTA through the lowest tariff member country and then trans-shipping them into higher tariff member countries. Krishna cautions, however, that ROO are easily abused by politicians who seek to curry favor with final and intermediate goods suppliers.

One of the most widely debated topics surrounding PTAs is whether they distract from or support multilateral trade liberalization. Are preferential and multilateral liberalization complements or substitutes? Can they provide a more efficient and rapid means of achieving global free trade than multilateralism? The academic literature that Krishna surveys is divided on these issues. One reason that preferential trade might impede progress toward global free trade is that PTAs that divert trade are more likely to garner internal political support. Trade-diverting PTAs decrease the likelihood of subsequent multilateral trade opening since liberalization would eliminate the rents that such PTAs create for producers.

If the WTO were to require PTAs that have open membership (where any country willing to accept the PTA's rules could become a member), the prospects of preferential agreements leading to global free trade would be enhanced. Adoption of this rule is unlikely, however, given that entry into trade blocs is normally a slow, often difficult, process, and no existing PTA has open membership.

Part II: International Trade Theory

International trade theory provoked intense debates among some of the most famous economists in history and, for at least the past two centuries, their competing views have contributed directly to the way that states have managed their external commercial relations. Trade theory is less controversial today, with leading economists offering or accepting mostly complementary perspectives to explain the causes, consequences, and features of trade patterns and behavior of market participants. This volume concentrates on two main areas of trade theory: neo-classical theory, as epitomized by the Heckscher–Ohlin model and its offshoots, and a more recent body of work built upon analysis of economies of scale and product differentiation.

In Chapter 4, Arvind Panagariya analyzes the Ricardian theory of comparative advantage and its reformulation in the leading modern theory of international trade: Heckscher–Ohlin. Although almost 200 years old, the intuition behind Ricardo's concept of comparative advantage, presented in the *Principle of Political Economy and Taxation* (1817), remains central to our thinking about international trade. Building on arguments developed by Adam Smith in his forceful critique of mercantilism, Ricardo developed the first fully articulated theory of international trade. While economists universally accept the logic of comparative advantage—indeed, it is often hailed as one of the greatest achievements in economic reasoning—many non-specialists view it with suspicion. In particular, skeptics often ask whether a nation that has an absolute disadvantage in all products can have a comparative advantage in any products.[2] Panagariya examines the logic of comparative advantage, demonstrating that if a country specializes in the good that it produces relatively more efficiently and trades it for the good it produces relatively inefficiently, it will benefit, as well as the proposition that free trade will leave both countries better or at least as well off as in its absence.

The core concept of comparative advantage has formed the basis for much modern trade theory grounded in the influential Heckscher–Ohlin model (1933) (see Ohlin, 1967, and Leamer, 1995). This model overcame some of the limitations of the Ricardian approach by allowing for two factors of production (as opposed to only labor) and increasing (rather than constant) opportunity costs of production. Panagariya

---

[2] This line of questioning, a central pillar of some strains of dependency theory, became highly influential, particularly among policymakers in developing countries, who viewed trade as constituting "unequal exchange." For a leading example, see Amin (1977). Nowadays, it still survives as the fear of politicians and manufacturers in both developed and developing countries that they just cannot compete with China.

illustrates the central finding of the model—which is that each country exports the good that uses its abundant factor more intensively and imports the good that uses its scarce factor more intensively—as well as the key theorems (Stolper–Samuelson, Rybczynski, and Factor Price Equalization) derived from the basic framework. The Heckscher–Ohlin framework generated an ambitious research agenda, especially in the 1960s and 1970s, which led to many important hypotheses about patterns of trade and their effects on relative factor prices, income distribution, and levels of income. This body of work formed the basis for the textbook international trade model taught to legions of economic students.

Despite its prominence as a theory of international trade, the Heckscher–Ohlin model has garnered only limited support in empirical studies. In particular, a large share of trade is accounted for by the exchange of similar goods among similar industrial countries and, furthermore, much of the trade among developed countries can be classified as intra-industry trade, patterns that are at odds with the predictions of Heckscher–Ohlin. Other theories of trade emerged to explain the anomalies in the empirical record or take advantage of advances in other areas of economics, such as industrial organization. The 1980s, for instance, saw the emergence of the "new trade theory," a body of work which took as its starting point the observations that most firms operate under increasing returns to scale and there are differentiated products. Under such assumptions, trade takes place in imperfectly competitive markets. One of the implications drawn from this body of work—that governments may have a solid theoretical basis to engage in an activist strategic trade policy—was in sharp contrast to the neo-classical view that governments should adopt a laissez-faire trade policy, since comparative advantage is primarily determined by a slow-changing variable, namely, a country's factor endowments.[3]

In Chapter 5, Mary Lovely and Devashish Mitra explore perhaps the most important class of alternative models of trade that have emerged, those based on economies of scale. Lovely and Mitra present four different types of scale economies, derived from distinctions drawn on two dimensions. The first centers on whether scale economies are internal to an individual firm or external to it, the second on whether geographic concentration of production is necessary for costs to fall as the scale of activity increases (that is, whether scale economies are national or international in scope). The authors find that the conclusions that can be drawn regarding the effect of trade and the role of policy are sensitive to the form of scale economy and the structure of the market. For instance, if scale economies are internal to the firm, then the market for its goods will be imperfectly competitive and likely to be dominated by large competitors; depending on the extent of entry barriers, these large firms may be able to act as price makers in international markets. On the other hand, if scale economies are external to firms, they are likely to act as price takers, and no firm will dominate the market. Lovely and Mitra also show that the increasingly global scope

---

[3] For an influential volume on strategic trade, see Krugman (1986).

of some industries, such as automobiles, is being driven in part by the fact that these industries are characterized by scale economies that are international in scope, and firms have taken advantage of the fall in trade barriers and costs to make good use of these traits.

Part III: Trade Policy and Trade Liberalization

Advocates of free trade once urged developing and emerging market countries to liberalize their trade as much and as soon as possible. They contended that trade opening improves the allocation of resources and reduces deadweight losses, thereby improving efficiency and promoting economic growth. Greater trade spurs innovation and increases in productivity largely by forcing a country's firms to compete against the most competitive firms in world markets and exposing them to best practice. In recent years, however, influential scholars such as Dani Rodrik and Joseph Stiglitz have urged caution in prescribing rapid trade liberalization for the developing world.[4] They suggest that trade opening only promotes growth when other key economic policies are adequate and institutions are strong. They worry that import surges after liberalization can devastate key sectors, and so worsen unemployment and slow growth. The historical record also leads them to conclude that strategic use of trade barriers to protect "infant industries" may be necessary if developing countries are to ever be able to transform their economies and catch up with industrialized countries. Moreover, sectoral liberalization may be dangerous if developed countries retain barriers to products that are important to the developing world, as is still the case in agriculture for instance. Certainly, developing countries should act cautiously until developed countries open up vital sectors, thus permitting the former to have a realistic chance of finding sufficiently deep markets for their exports. Movement in this direction has been slow because progress on the development agenda of the Doha Round of multilateral negotiations has been stymied repeatedly.

These observations and in-depth studies of successful country cases have led to a more cautious set of policy prescriptions. Even most strong proponents of free trade now urge gradual, not rapid, liberalization in order to permit domestic firms to adjust to increased competition and allow factors of production to shift to more efficient uses in a less disruptive manner. Moreover, they stress that liberalization must be accompanied by complementary reforms in order for it to succeed; this involves creating more flexible labor and financial markets, better infrastructure, stronger regulatory institutional structures, and achieving greater macroeconomic stability. In addition, most scholars and practitioners also recognize that governments must compensate the losers of trade opening if it is to be politically viable. Regrettably, creating a viable safety net is often difficult given the fiscal constraints that many governments already face.

---

[4] For example, see Rodríguez and Rodrik (2001) and Stiglitz and Charlton (2005).

Part III of this volume analyzes various dimensions of trade policy with this debate as the backdrop. In Chapter 6, Geoff Jehle examines the primary instruments of national trade policy, often termed commercial policy, and thereby introduces the core analytical concepts and framework on which many of the chapters in Part III rely. The real world significance of the various instruments has changed markedly over the course of economic history. Quotas, once widely used, were replaced by tariffs in most areas of trade after the General Agreement on Trade and Tariffs was signed, though they re-emerged years later in a somewhat disguised form as negotiated market shares (e.g. "Voluntary" Export Restraints or VERs). As policymakers in many countries reduced tariffs to very low levels for many products, they turned to a dizzying variety of non-tariff measures (NTMs) to erect protectionist barriers, leading observers to complain of the rise of a "New Protectionism" during the 1970s. Among the most important of these are a myriad of safety regulations, including sanitary and phyto-sanitary (SPS) measures. And, in a somewhat surprising turn of events, export taxes and embargos have come into use again. In particular, governments in countries that export agricultural goods have recently imposed them in response to dramatic increases in food prices as they have sought to safeguard supplies of key products.

Jehle focuses on the implications of various trade policy instruments for aggregate national social welfare, the distribution of rents among various groups—notably, producers, consumers, and the government—and the relative value of using trade policy instruments versus other means of government intervention to achieve various policy objectives. He carefully demonstrates the distortions that various types of protectionist barriers create in the domestic economy. In many cases, the protectionist impact of a trade measure is greater than one would anticipate by examining only nominal rates of protection. Indeed, the typical cascading tariff schedule found in many countries implies very high rates of effective protection for producers of finished goods. As Wendy Takacs shows in her chapter, high effective rates of protection generated by overlapping policy measures are at the heart of protectionist trade regimes.

In Chapter 7, Soamiely Andriamananjara, Olivier Cadot, and Jean-Marie Grether discuss the data and statistical instruments available for applied trade policy analysis. Advances in computing, better data collection and dissemination, and the development of a variety of analytical and statistical tools now equip trade analysts with the means to create a rigorous portrait of the policy-relevant features of a country's trade patterns and the consequences of its policy choices. Applied analysis is not only useful for researchers seeking to investigate the effects of various trade policies; as the authors state, if policymakers had access to accurate statistical information and assessments, policy decisions would be made in a better informational environment and many mistakes would be avoided.

The authors examine the practical data and implementation issues for the most widely used tools and indicators of policy and trade performance, enabling the reader to understand how these models are constructed and what can and cannot be gleaned from them. Among the topics covered are methods for presenting a picture of a country's trade performance and standard measures of its trade policy stance, the econometric techniques that can be used to assess *ex post* the effects of trade policies on trade flows and on key domestic economic aggregates, and the principal attributes of the tools used in the *ex ante* assessment of trade policy, first in partial equilibrium settings, then in general equilibrium ones.

Arvid Lukauskas explores the political underpinnings of protectionist barriers and their removal in Chapter 8. Barriers to trade are generally at most second-best instruments for achieving domestic policy goals as they create dead-weight losses that reduce aggregate social welfare. The only objective that is best advanced through protectionist measures is to improve the terms of trade when a country has sufficient market power to affect world prices, a policy that can improve national welfare (but worsen that of the rest of the world). Despite this, protectionism of various sorts has been a constant throughout history. Why then has protectionism been so pervasive? Lukauskas argues that political factors fundamentally influence commercial policy design and implementation, including the decisions to impose or remove barriers to trade such as tariffs, quotas, and other forms of non-tariff barriers. Protectionism hurts some groups but favors others, so some private actors will always have an interest in the implementation of trade barriers; those who favor protection typically face less severe collective action problems in organizing to influence commercial policy, so they often prevail. Nevertheless, the "supply" side of trade policy, determined by the complex balancing act among competing interests that politicians undertake when designing strategy, is equally important. Trade liberalization is most likely to occur when protected industries themselves no longer desire trade barriers or politicians determine that the political costs of protectionism have become too high. To be successful, however, liberalization must be accompanied by complementary reforms in other economic policy areas, particularly those concerning factor markets.

Lukauskas also shows that the international political and economic context in which trade takes place is critical for understanding trade policy. The structure of the "trade game" generates a powerful set of constraints and incentives that policymakers must consider when formulating strategy. Governments have ample reason to be cautious in removing trade barriers, so much so that widespread protectionism has characterized economic relations among states throughout most of history. As Stern finds in Chapter 2, once created, multilateral institutions such as the WTO can help states overcome the collective action problems inherent in opening up trade on a global basis, as they facilitate communication among countries as well as monitoring and enforcing trade agreements. Deepening globalization has also increased the costs of maintaining highly protected markets, giving public officials a stronger incentive to undertake trade reform.

In Chapter 9, Patrick Messerlin examines the Doha Development Agenda or Doha Round launched in 2001 to achieve major reform of the multilateral trading system with an emphasis on improving the trading prospects of developing countries and, thereby, promoting their economic development. The Doha Round has dragged on for years with only episodic progress and, as of (mid 2013), still has no clear end date in sight. Messerlin structures his analysis by considering four general questions about trade rounds, which he then applies specifically to the Doha Round: (1) What is the value of a trade round? (2) Should nations link trade negotiations with broader goals, such as economic development in the case of the Doha Round? (3)What is the main objective of a trade round? Is it necessarily to achieve further trade liberalization or can it be something else, like the "binding" of past liberalizations? (4) How can countries use rounds to negotiate effectively on trade in services given the inherent difficulties, such as the fact that services are rarely protected by measurable barriers?

Messerlin argues that if the Doha Round were completed along the lines originally envisaged, it would be very valuable. It would bring welfare gains in the order of US$300 to US$700 billion and deliver legally-binding commitments that would prevent countries from increasing their applied tariffs up to currently bound rates, an outcome that would provide badly needed certainty to the business community. In sum, the value of a completed Doha Round would compare favorably with previous Rounds. Messerlin suggests that linking trade negotiations with broader issues is counter-productive; in the case of the Doha Round, it impeded progress in the early years of the Round, as developed and developing countries had widely divergent views of what trade policies were needed to promote development. This constrained negotiators by requiring them to subject all negotiations to a divisive development goal and generated excessive expectations that have resulted in disappointment and acrimony.

The ambiguity about the central objectives of the Doha Round has also complicated the negotiating process; indeed, it made finding a negotiating "technology"—a complete set of liberalization and exception formulas acceptable to all WTO members— a critical task that consumed much of the period between 2004 and 2008. The 2008 mini-Ministerial draft texts, which are the most likely basis for a final agreement, indicate that the Doha process has "clearly slanted toward...a 'binding Round'," although this issue remains unsettled. Finally, the political economy and regulation-based nature of protection in services makes further liberalization among all WTO members unlikely at this time. Service exporters have less incentive to push for opening, and import-competing providers can more easily block reform than in the case of liberalization of trade in goods. Yet deeper liberalization of services would require countries to adopt difficult, pro-competitive regulatory reforms in the future—as well as trust in the capacity of others to carry them through to completion. Consequently, Messerlin concludes that the most likely means of achieving a deal in services in the Doha Round is to concentrate on binding unilateral liberalizations undertaken previously through a plurilateral approach involving the largest WTO members.

In Chapter 10, Wendy Takacs analyzes the features of protective trade regimes and their reform. Governments implement a wide variety of overlapping and often contradictory trade-related measures to promote particular industrial sectors. Takacs examines some of the most commonly used instruments—export controls on raw material inputs, domestic content requirements, barriers to imports, and compensatory export requirements—both in general terms and through a set of short case studies highlighting their application. Although these measures seek to accomplish different goals— stimulate expansion of industries that use a raw material (export controls on raw

materials) versus encouraging local production of inputs (domestic content requirements)—they have in common the fact that they alter the effective rate of protection
for different sectors and thereby influence the allocation of national resources and economic benefits.

Takacs illustrates the consequences of export controls through a case study on
export licensing requirements on raw cashmere in Mongolia. She shows that the
requirements failed to achieve the stated goal of augmenting the country's total export
earnings. Moreover, they had profound distributional impacts (such as lowering the
income of one of the country's most disadvantaged groups, herdsmen), a fact that
highlights the potential significance of political economy factors in explaining their
adoption. Similarly, she demonstrates the effects of domestic content requirements and
compensatory export restrictions in conjunction with import barriers for final goods
through an analysis of their application to the automobile industry in the Philippines.
Governments often implement these trade measures in an overlapping and contradictory fashion, so it can be difficult to determine the final impact on various groups.
Local input producers generally benefit, but the net effect on final goods producers
can be either positive or negative, depending on the degree of import protection they
are afforded; consumers of final products, however, are unambiguous losers, and
dead-weight national welfare losses are typically substantial, reflecting the multiple
distortions these policies introduce in markets.

Takacs claims that ascertaining how the various components of a complicated protective regime interact is critical for designing a successful trade reform program. One
of the most common problems with trade reforms is that they may lead to unintentional or inadvertent dramatic increases or reductions in the effective rate of protection for particular activities. This is most likely to happen if the government adopts a
"piecemeal" approach, abolishing or liberalizing some parts of the protective regime
while leaving other parts unchanged. In the case of Peru, a trade reform program that
replaced a complete ban on automobiles with an *ad valorem* tariff but kept domestic
content requirements in place, resulted in a large and unintended drop in the effective
rate of protection for the industry; as a consequence, domestic automobile production
quickly collapsed.

In Chapter 11, Tim Josling explores in detail how market access, export competition, domestic support, and health and safety regulatory policies affect world agricultural trade. These policies create significant distortions in world markets for agricultural
goods and are particularly detrimental to the interests of many developing countries.
Agricultural trade policy is consequently hotly contested, and negotiating new disciplines for the sector has become a critical part of the on-going Doha "development"
agenda. Josling examines the Doha negotiations on agricultural trade (the place of
agriculture in the broader Doha agenda is analyzed by Patrick Messerlin in Chapter 9),
highlighting the major issues and the likely impact of the envisaged new modalities on
both developed and developing countries, including those that import as well as those
that export various farm products. Although the welfare gains from liberalization are
substantial, he suggests that one of the most important motivations behind the Doha

Round may be the desire to lock in or "bind" autonomous policy changes undertaken for largely domestic political or economic reasons.

Josling's review of agricultural trade policies reveals their remarkable complexity. Tariff levels on agricultural goods, for instance, vary markedly not only across countries, but also within countries by sector and even by specific good. Moreover, the same good, particularly in sensitive sectors such as meat, dairy, sugar, and cereals, can face very different tariff levels if it is covered by a tariff-rate quota, depending on whether in-quota or over-quota rates apply. Export promotion and domestic support policies are, if anything, even more complicated and frequently in flux. For example, domestic support policies used to rely on price supports but have shifted toward direct payments "decoupled" from production decisions. Some of these changes reflect continuing efforts to protect sensitive sectors when existing policies come under attack, but they may actually increase the chances of reaching a multilateral agreement on agricultural policy rules. Josling also notes that the justification for protection has changed over time, from support of poor farmer incomes or food security in previous decades to, more recently, environmental stewardship and climate change mitigation, including the development of agriculture product-based alternatives to fossil fuels. The convoluted nature of many agricultural trade policy measures also means that the domestic benefits and costs of liberalization can be difficult to estimate. Consumers are generally clear winners, but the effect on different classes of producers is ambiguous and must be determined in each specific country context.

In Chapter 12, The Economics of Service Trade, Aaditya Mattoo and Gianni Zanini note that international trade and investment in services are an increasingly important part of global commerce. Advances in information and telecommunication technologies have expanded the scope of services that can be traded cross-border. Many countries now allow foreign investment in newly privatized and competitive markets for key infrastructure services, such as energy, telecommunications, and transport. More and more people are traveling abroad to consume tourism, education, and medical services, and to supply services ranging from construction to software development. In fact, services are the fastest growing components of the global economy, with trade and foreign direct investment (FDI) in services having increased faster than in goods over the past two decades.

International transactions, however, continue to be impeded by policy barriers, especially to foreign investment and the movement of service-providing individuals. All countries, and developing ones in particular, are likely to benefit significantly from further domestic liberalization and the elimination of barriers to their exports. Indeed, estimated income gains from a reduction in protection to services are multiples of those from trade liberalization in goods. The increased dynamism of open services sectors can make the difference between rapid and sluggish growth.

The benefits from service liberalization, however, are by no means automatic. Significant challenges exist in introducing genuine competition, building the regulatory institutions that are needed to remedy market failures, appropriately sequencing service sector reforms, and establishing mechanisms that promote the availability of essential services—especially among the poor.

Mattoo and Zanini discuss how international transactions are conducted in services and the sources of data on these transactions. They then present some evidence on the pattern of services trade, which launches a conceptual discussion on what can be said about the determinants of the pattern of services trade. After this, they turn to the normative issues, discussing how services reform can promote efficiency and growth at the sectoral level and economy wide, and the fact that the benefits and sustainability of services liberalization may be diminished by flaws in reform programs. They argue that domestic policy reforms should recognize the importance of increasing competition among service providers, strengthening regulation to remedy market failure, creating appropriate sequencing of reforms, and putting in place policies that widen access to services for the poor and remote. For the benefit of the more technical reader, the Appendix to this chapter contains a graphic presentation of the economic effects of barriers on trade in services.

In Chapter 13, Arvind Panagariya makes a vigorous case for trade liberalization. He reviews recent evidence on the relationship between trade openness and economic growth and finds strong confirmation of the view often advanced by economic historians that "trade is an engine of growth." Specifically, the fastest growing ("miracle") countries in the 1980s and 1990s were those that experienced rapid increases in both exports and imports; on the other hand, countries with the worst growth record ("debacles") typically had slow growth in exports and imports. This leads him to conclude that "sustained growth cannot be achieved without rapid growth in trade, which requires either low or declining barriers to trade." Moreover, Panagariya finds little evidence that growth debacles were associated with import surges as some critics of trade liberalization, like Joseph Stiglitz, have contended. Panagariya complements his large empirical study with several brief case studies. His comparison of Indian and South Korean trade policies highlights the point that, even if the latter's growth was driven by the government's efforts to coordinate investment activities, as free trade skeptics often emphasize, the country succeeded because these efforts took place in the context of outward-oriented trade policies; India attempted similar policies but failed because it adopted a fiercely inward orientation.

In Chapter 14, Salomon Samen examines the policy practices and institutions that can promote export development and diversification in developing countries. He contends that many of the most tested and successful measures for export expansion and diversification involve considerable government intervention, in the form of export-oriented trade and industrial policy measures, to correct market failures that are pervasive in developing countries. He reviews a number of the most successful practices and institutions in the developing world, especially in East Asia, in order to develop a set of policy recommendations for countries seeking to expand or diversify their exports.

Surveying the range of government practices intended to promote exports, Samen notes that the least controversial are "permissive" policies that aim to remove an anti-export bias created by other government policies (such as high tariffs). Among the most important of these are special import regimes, which include measures such as duty drawbacks, bonded manufacturing, and export processing zones, designed to allow exporters to gain access to imported inputs at world prices. More controversial are "positive" policies, particularly "selective" (as opposed to "functional") ones that explicitly aim to shift resources to specific firms, sectors, or activities in an attempt to expand and diversify exports. ("Functional" policies attempt to remedy market failures without influencing resource allocation between specific activities, for instance, by improving physical infrastructure and general skills/human capital.) Favored sectors tend to be involved in industrial activities facing large information externalities, coordination failures, or poor institutional environments; intervention proponents argue that these market failures would slow export growth in these sectors to undesirable levels without concerted government action. Samen contends that the empirical record clearly demonstrates that successful exporters have used a mixture of permissive and positive policies to accelerate their export growth and diversification. Moreover, the distinctions between "permissive" and "positive" as well as "functional" and "selective" policies are blurred in practice, so policymakers need to be flexible and non-ideological in their efforts to design the correct combination of policies to fit their particular circumstances.

In Chapter 15, Francisco Rivera-Batíz examines the impact of international trade in goods and services on poverty and income distribution. He considers leading theories on the various connections involving trade, poverty, and inequality and presents a careful analysis of the indicators used to measure trends in these variables. He then reviews the available evidence on these relationships and also analyzes the diverse effects that trade and trade policy may have on the socioeconomic status of various groups in society. Rivera-Batíz reports empirical support for the view that trade liberalization is associated with reductions in poverty, but notes that this finding is somewhat sensitive to the poverty threshold used, and that other factors, including other economic reforms, have also contributed to reductions in poverty, making it hard to distinguish the impact of trade specifically. Increased trade, however, is associated with a period of rising income inequality within countries, in part because since the 1980s it has been associated with skill-biased technical change that increases demand for high-skilled labor relative to unskilled workers; since skilled labor has much higher wages than unskilled workers, this may result in higher inequality. In contrast, trade has not had a systematic effect on poverty or inequality on the basis of gender, although its impact in individual countries has been substantial. For instance, in countries where the percentage of women in the agricultural labor force is relatively high, trade has been associated with a deterioration of the relative economic status of women.

The international movement of the factors of production, namely, capital and labor, may serve as a substitute for international trade in goods and services. The causes and effects of capital mobility on economic policymaking have been widely studied, but those of migration are far less appreciated.

In Chapter 16, Francisco Rivera-Batíz explores recent trends in international migration. International migration has increased markedly in the past few decades, and currently approximately 214 million people reside in countries other than their birth-place. Rivera-Batíz examines the causes of these migration flows and the consequences for the migrants themselves as well as for the source and recipient countries. This growth is due to several forces, including: the relaxation of immigration policies in high-income economies; the sustained and sometimes widening gaps in income and employment opportunities between high-income and developing countries; demographics that cause low or negative population growth rates in recipient countries and high rates in source countries; reduced transport costs and rising regional economic integration; and the growth of closely-knit networks of household members across source and destination countries.

Rivera-Batíz reports that, in general, the effect of immigration on host countries is positive because it generates increased investment and sectoral adjustments that create employment opportunities and offset any significant negative effects of immigrants on wages and employment of natives; this is particularly true when immigrants and natives belong to different sectors of the labor market (e.g., unskilled versus skilled). This find-ing, though conditional on several factors, runs counter to popular perceptions that have fueled anti-immigration sentiment in many countries, such as the United States and Spain. For source countries, one area of particular controversy involves the emigra-tion of skilled labor (the "brain drain"). Many scholars worry about the effect of this emigration on the sending country's economy, contending that it deprives it of skilled labor needed for essential services (e.g., teachers and nurses), tax revenue, savings, and human capital. These risks are real, but Rivera-Batíz suggests that emigration may also provide positives, notably, a steady flow of remittances and access to international net-works that enhance scientific and technological capabilities. The chapter concludes with a brief discussion of the current and potential future role played by the WTO in the management of labor flows, as part of the General Agreement on Trade in Services, not-ing that coordinated international migration policies would be helpful in managing the impacts of immigration flows.

Part IV: Implementing and Negotiating Trading Arrangements for the Twenty-First Century

This final section of the Handbook covers a variety of topics that are pertinent to the trading arrangements that exist currently and that may form the basis for design-ing new arrangements for years to come. The topics include aspects of deep inte-gration in preferential trading arrangements, rules of origin, and an assessment of North American Free Trade Agreement (NAFTA) and Mercosur. In addition, there are topics of importance for the multilateral trading system, including: safeguards, anti-dumping, and subsidies in international trade law; services trade agreements and negotiations; food safety standards; intellectual property rights; international invest-ment agreements; dispute settlement; competition law; public procurement; trade facilitation; trade and environment; and trade and labor standards.

In Chapter 17, Jean-Christophe Maur addresses issues of deep integration in PTAs. This chapter should be read in conjunction with Chapter 3 by Pravin Krishna. Among the issues that Maur considers are: the sources of economic gains, if any, by liberalizing preferential policies; the results and policy lessons of economic and political economic theory; concerns of trade creation and diversion and new barriers to trade; and whether preferential liberalization creates a stumbling or building block for further liberalization. Maur notes that, in the last 20 years, growth in the number of PTAs has been unabated. Even more strikingly, their scope has broadened while their number has increased. The ambition of recent PTAs beyond tariff liberalization is illustrated by the general growth of agreements that include deep integration provisions. Deep integration provisions include some areas partially covered or being negotiated in the WTO (e.g., services trade, investment, trade facilitation, standards, intellectual property, government procurement) as well as other areas that can often be found in North–South PTAs like competition, labor, or environment. Many of these new changes in PTAs encompass what has been called a WTO-plus agenda, on disciplines already included in the WTO, but often expanding on them in depth and breadth and seeking enforceability. A second and important dimension is that PTAs also incorporate numerous areas that are not covered by the WTO.

The growth of deep integration in both quantity and scope is thus posing a challenge for policymakers as they must cover an increasingly large and complex set of issues—of different natures—with limited administrative resources, both for negotiation and implementation. This means that countries should either increase their negotiating capacity or prioritize the areas where they want to see reform (or likely both). Moreover, PTAs increasingly address policy areas that are entirely new to many developing countries signing up to them. This is a sharp difference from traditional trade agreements, which are chiefly about dismantling barriers to trade (in a way making it actually easier to administer trade policy). Furthermore, these are areas of reform where there is no simple and single template as is the case for tariff elimination. This raises questions as to what the content of agreements should be: should they restrict themselves to common universal principles or explore specific solutions to the issues that signatories face? While offering opportunities for countries wishing to reform their trade and business environment, this set of new issues also raises numerous challenges and policy dimensions that did not exist before. This will be especially the case when commitments included in agreements are not a priority interest of the conceding partner.

Maur emphasizes that deep integration differs from traditional integration agreements both in its motives and modalities of implementation. Deep integration captures intuitively the fact that the external dimension (chiefly market access, but also access to efficient inputs) is only one part of the picture. The domestic dimension is the other paramount facet of the integration challenge of modern PTAs. This chapter identifies several important general characteristics of modern PTAs that should be taken into account by policymakers. The first and main message is that *mercantilism is not the right way to think about deep agreements*. Whereas the focus on market access has the unintended consequence of leading to an optimal and mutually beneficial free-trade outcome when tariffs are concerned, this is largely insufficient when dealing with the regulatory policies found in modern PTAs. One reason is that deep integration is not achieved through the complete elimination of trade barriers since other regulatory objectives must be met—the mercantilist logic does not pay heed to them, just market access. The usual reciprocity mechanism of trade liberalization may not work any longer because it becomes very difficult to separate clearly measures that promote market access and measures that pursue legitimate regulatory objectives.

Secondly, the political-economy considerations are of a different nature when regulatory issues are at stake as consumers may fear that liberalization will affect their well-being. But the discriminatory aspects of preferential integration can be complex when similar treatment may be provided on an MFN basis to third parties, as is often the case. Since deep integration tends to be multilateral in nature, pursuing liberalization through PTAs, which may be faster and deeper than multilaterally, should then be beneficial and should provide a building block towards free multilateral trade.

Maur notes that trade policies can no longer be conceived by assuming separability from other policies. Deep integration is as much about trade as it is about other dimensions of economic management and public policy. The liberalization question cannot be divorced from the consideration of these other objectives. Thus, policymakers need to carefully think about *why* and *how* trade agreements should serve these objectives in the specific context of PTAs as well how the various objectives interact. PTAs thus capture a broader paradigm than traditional agreements. All these consideration have important implications on how developing countries especially should approach and implement deep PTAs.

Finally, Maur notes that a focus on implementation is vital. Deep integration agreements should be understood as "living agreements," where the process of integration is as important as agreeing on rules of liberalization. First, because of the attention that must be devoted to enforcement questions as, in many cases, enacting the legislation is only a start. Compliance with law requires a regulatory infrastructure, a legal infrastructure, and information systems. Second, regulatory practice tends to evolve with business practices, technology evolutions, and improvements over time. Third, since the text of the PTAs is only one starting element of the process of integration, implementation aspects must also be carefully examined to see whether or not liberalization is effective. Monitoring and accountability matter. This is a more complex process than verifying that trade barriers are effectively dismantled, and one for which information is often not readily available. In general, implementation in PTAs is not a very transparent process. Fourth, the nature and operation of common institutional arrangements that will govern the PTA and their relation to national ones should be as much a part of the design as negotiations over rules.

Paul Brenton addresses issues of preferential rules of origin in Chapter 18. The justification for preferential rules of origin is to prevent trade deflection, or simple trans-shipment, whereby products from non-preferred countries are redirected through a free-trade partner to avoid the payment of customs duties. Hence the role of preferential rules of origin is to ensure that only goods originating in participating countries enjoy preferences. Therefore, preferential rules of origin are integral parts of PTAs. The nature of rules of origin and their application can have profound implications for trade flows and for the work of customs agencies. Rules of origin can be designed in such a way as to restrict trade and therefore can and have been used as trade policy instruments. The proliferation of free trade agreements (FTAs) with accompanying preferential rules of origin is increasing the burden on customs agencies in many countries with consequent implications for trade facilitation.

Brenton first explains what is meant by origin and examines various methods for determining substantial transformation. He then discusses the current situation with regard to non-preferential rules of origin, where a concerted attempt, although one which has yet to bear fruit, has been made at the WTO to harmonize the rules regarding wholly obtained products and substantial transformation. He thereafter elaborates on the definition of preferential rules of origin for which, to date, there has been no attempt to achieve harmonization and for which there are no real and effective multilateral disciplines, and then looks at the rules of origin in existing free trade and preferential trade agreements. He reviews the economic implications of rules of origin, discusses the links between rules of origin and the utilization of trade preferences, and estimates of the costs of complying with rules of origin. He also analyzes the use of rules of origin as a tool of economic development.

He offers a number of conclusions. Specifying generally applicable rules of origin, with a limited number of clearly defined and justified exceptions, is appropriate if the objective is to stimulate integration and minimize the burdens on firms and customs in complying with and administering the rules. Unnecessary use of a detailed product-by-product approach to rules of origin is likely to lead to complex and restrictive rules of origin and to constrain integration. Producers should be provided with flexibility in meeting origin rules, for example, by specifying that *either* a change of tariff requirement *or* a value added rule can be satisfied. When change of tariff classification is used, the level of the classification at which change is required should, as much as possible, be common across products. Change at the heading level seems most appropriate as a principal rule. Preferences granted by OECD countries would be more effective in stimulating exports from developing countries if they were governed by less restrictive rules of origin. Ideally, rules of origin for these schemes should be common. Producers in developing countries should be able to gain preferential access to all developed country markets if their product satisfies a single origin test. Finally, restrictive rules of origin should not be used as tools for achieving economic development objectives, as they are likely to be counter-productive. The potential benefits of trade agreements amongst developing countries can be substantially undermined if those agreements contain restrictive rules of origin.

In Chapter 19, Edward Mansfield reviews the proliferation of preferential trading arrangements (PTAs) and then focuses on the analysis of the NAFTA and Mercosur. He begins by examining the run-up to each agreement and the factors that prompted its establishment. He then discusses the institutional design and the effects of each agreement. He concludes by addressing some future challenges facing NAFTA and Mercosur and by using these cases to draw some more general lessons about the political economy of PTAs. Within NAFTA, Canada, Mexico, and the USA face ongoing problems with illegal immigration and illegal drug trafficking. In the wake of 9/11, these issues have become linked to national security concerns, making them even more sensitive. These countries also face a series of environmental challenges, including US–Mexican water allocation issues; problems associated with deforestation, soil erosion, and the water supply in Mexico; and logging and energy issues in the USA and Canada. From an economic standpoint, the looming problem facing NAFTA is agriculture. The agricultural challenges facing NAFTA are hardly unique. In almost every major regional and multilateral forum, they are crucially important. But these issues could be a source of considerable stress on the arrangement.

Mercosur faces important challenges as well. One concern is its institutional form insofar as Mercosur appears to be structured between a free trade area and a customs union with few mechanisms for institutionalization. Import-competing interests remain politically powerful, especially in Brazil, and will need to be kept at bay for the arrangement to succeed. Mercosur is in the process of trying to expand. Adding states with policy positions that diverge significantly from the four original members could damage the PTA. Mercosur has started negotiating PTAs with the members of the Southern African Customs Union: Egypt, Israel, Jordan, Morocco, and Turkey, among others.

The experiences of NAFTA and Mercosur also suggest various broader lessons about the political economy of PTAs. First, both of these institutions have been marked by the existence of one particularly large country, the USA in the case of NAFTA and Brazil in the case of Mercosur. Smaller participants have bridled at their dependence on the US and Brazilian markets and the tendency for these regional hegemons to discount the interests of other member states, creating strains on each of the arrangements. Second, despite these strains, the experiences of NAFTA and Mercosur suggest that PTAs help to defuse conflicts and stabilize political relations among members. Third, both NAFTA and Mercosur illustrate how PTAs can be used to foster economic and political reform in participating countries. NAFTA and Mercosur have limited the ability of member states to roll back various economic reforms, since doing so would violate the regional agreements. Fourth, while these PTAs have reinforced certain economic reforms, they have also been marked by various industries (for example, agriculture in NAFTA and autos in Mercosur) that were initially granted exceptions to the open trade regime. Both arrangements illustrate how states can use PTAs to improve their bargaining position in international negotiations. These cases illustrate the importance of a PTA's institutional design, insofar as both NAFTA and Mercosur have fairly sparse designs. Mercosur's institutions are especially weak. This feature has preserved the autonomy of member states, since they do not answer to a regional authority. However, this design feature has also limited the effectiveness of both PTAs in responding to certain intraregional issues. The problem is especially acute for Mercosur.

In Chapter 20, Joel P. Trachtman addresses issues of safeguards, anti-dumping, and subsidies in international trade law. Since the establishment of the GATT in 1947, states have determined that it is desirable to maintain the right to impose "contingent protection" in order to reverse their liberalization under certain circumstances. Obviously, if the right to engage in contingent protection is not constrained enough, then the concessions made by states in international trade negotiations would have little value. So the international system is finely balanced between enforcement of liberalization commitments and permission to derogate from liberalization commitments.

It might be argued that the permission to derogate from liberalization commitments under appropriate circumstances may play a role in inducing greater liberalization commitments. That is, trade negotiators may be willing to make greater liberalization commitments under conditions of uncertainty regarding the effects of liberalization, when they know that they can derogate from these commitments in the event that they turn out to be unexpectedly burdensome. It might further be argued that at least the safeguard mechanism represents a kind of international legal facility for "efficient breach," insofar as it allows states to back away from their commitments, if they are willing to provide compensation (under certain circumstances).

The contingent measures tend to ignore the consumer benefits that may arise from the imported goods at issue. Especially in the case of dumping and subsidization, there may be a transfer of economic welfare from the exporting state to the importing state, with consumers in the importing state experiencing the greatest benefit. Yet attitudes towards dumping, subsidization, and safeguards tend to assume that imports of inexpensive goods cause harm that is greater than the benefits that accrue. They also tend to assume, without necessarily finding empirical or theoretical support, that dumping or subsidization may allow exporters to capture market share that will be difficult to regain. This is a mercantilist perspective, although in some contexts, it is possible that the mercantilist perspective may be validated by a strategic trade theory analysis.

Trachtman provides a discussion of core definitions and concepts that form the basis of his more detailed treatment of safeguards, dumping, and subsidies, and the determination of serious injury, material injury, and causation. He discusses the implementation, political economy, and economic rationales associated with each of the instruments, and their links to international law and policies. He concludes with some observations on the policy and negotiating implications for developing countries with regard to the use and design of the different instruments.

In Chapter 21, Aaditya Mattoo and Gianni Zanini address service trade agreements and negotiations. They note that services were included in the multilateral trade architecture of the WTO in the form of the General Agreement on Trade in Services (GATS). Services have also featured prominently in the process of WTO accession, and they are increasingly important in the large and growing network of regional, and especially, of North–South trade agreements. Further, international trade in services has assumed added significance from a broader global policy perspective in the aftermath of the recent global financial and economic crisis. In the multilateral negotiations under the Doha Development Agenda and also in most traditional South–South regional agreements, however, services have received surprisingly little attention. The neglect of services can be costly. The potential gains from reciprocal liberalization of trade in services are likely to be substantial, and progress in services is necessary for a positive negotiating outcome in other areas. For international negotiations to be fruitful, however, countries must recognize mutual interests in reciprocal liberalization, supported by broader international cooperation.

The chapter covers the GATS' scope, general obligations, rules on protection, and the unfinished agenda related to safeguards, subsidies, and government procurement. Also addressed is the growing trend towards preferential agreements, which may provide greater opportunities for achieving deeper integration of particular services sectors. A subsequent section provides a brief overview of the achievements to date (or lack thereof) of the current Doha negotiating round. Finally, an assessment is provided for what international services trade negotiations have to offer with respect to unilateral liberalization, and the context—multilateral, regional, bilateral—in which they are most likely to produce outcomes that support economic development.

Chapter 22 by Spencer Henson and Steven Jaffee addresses the role that public and private safety standards play in influencing exports from developing countries, with a particular focus on the impact of SPS standards on trade in agricultural and food products. Food safety standards are singled out for analysis because of their constraining role on the efforts of developing countries to access higher value markets for agricultural exports, and because they illustrate well the ways in which the WTO Agreements have attempted to discipline the use of standards as non-tariff barriers to trade (NTBs), the complex and inter-related ways in which standards influence trade, and the particular issues and concerns for developing countries.

The chapter starts by outlining the nature of standards and the institutional forms they take, before focusing specifically on food safety standards. It then describes the ways in which food safety standards are evolving, and the drivers that are directing such changes. Alternative perspectives on the trade effects for developing countries of food safety standards are then examined, before proceeding to the related challenges in the areas of establishing associated management capacity, costs of compliance, and scope for SPS diplomacy. Finally, the scope and need for a strategic perspective on compliance with standards in international trade is explored. Throughout, country and product-specific examples are provided as illustration.

The key issues identified in the chapter are, first, that standards have become a critical institutional mechanism through which markets are governed and increasingly form a basis of competitive strategies among market participants. This is particularly evident with food safety standards in both national and international markets for agricultural and food products. Thus, food safety standards are associated with modes of quality-based competition, while compliance has become a critical capacity at the firm and national levels. Second, in many high value markets for agricultural and food products, food safety standards are evolving rapidly due to a wide range of inter-related demand and supply-side drivers. In particular, there is a shift towards quality meta-systems that define broad parameters for effective food safety controls and that are associated with systems of certification. At the same time, private food safety standards have come to play a more prominent role, working alongside and sometimes interrelated with public standards. Thus, for many agricultural and food products, compliance with prevailing food safety standards rather than high domestic support or tariffs in the importing countries is the predominant challenge for developing countries attempting to maintain and/or enhance exports of agricultural and food products.

Third, seeing food safety standards mostly as "barriers to trade," whereby the costs of compliance and associated impact on competitiveness act to prevent market entry and/or exclude developing country exporters from high-value markets, will not be the most fruitful approach. If it can be acknowledged that developing countries are often "standards takers" rather than "standard makers," standards can be used as catalysts for processes of capacity upgrading and competitive positioning in high value markets. Fourth, the challenges faced by developing countries in the context of evolving food safety standards relate to weaknesses in food safety management capacity. The sheer scale of the upgrading needed, especially in most low-income countries, suggests the need to prioritize. In many cases there is a hierarchy of food safety management functions that are most efficiently established and enhanced in an iterative manner. Indeed, the chapter defines a pyramid that distinguishes between lower and higher levels of capacity. Even in countries where overall capacity is weak, "islands" of enhanced capacity that support internationally competitive exports of particular agricultural and food products can often be identified or created and then nurtured with government and donors' support.

Finally, in responding to the changing standards landscape, leveraging "standards as catalysts" is greatest when countries and exporters can be proactive. Thus, with compliance and capacity upgrading being both a challenge and an opportunity to gain competitive advantage in key markets, proactivity by the public and private sectors of developing countries is recommended.

In Chapter 23, Carsten Fink addresses the Agreement on Trade-Related Aspects of Intellectual Property Rights (TRIPS), which is one of three pillar agreements setting out the legal framework in which the WTO has operated since the end of the Uruguay Round. Due to the growth of trade in knowledge and information-intensive goods, the economic implications of imitation, copying, and counterfeiting have become in many industries at least as relevant for international commerce as conventional border restrictions to trade. Developed countries, which host the world's largest creative industries, were the key advocates for comprehensive minimum standards of protection and enforcement of intellectual property rights (IPRs). By contrast, many developing countries, which saw themselves mostly as consumers of intellectual property, felt that stronger standards of protection would serve to limit access to new technologies and products, thereby undermining their development prospects. The chapter reviews the main instruments used to protect intellectual property, the key economic trade-offs of stronger IPRs, the basic provisions of the TRIPS Agreement, recent IPRs developments affecting access to medicines in developing countries, and the intellectual property disciplines found in free trade agreements.

The key messages in the chapter are as follows. First, IPRs protect creations that result from intellectual activity in the industrial, scientific, literary, and artistic fields. IPRs instruments encompass patents, copyrights and neighboring rights, trademarks, geographical indications, layout designs for integrated circuits, plant breeders' rights, and trade secrets. Second, IPRs seek to resolve certain failures of private markets. Patents, copyrights, and related forms of protection aim at stimulating inventive and creative activities. Trademarks and geographical indications offer information about the origin of goods to consumers. Third, for developing countries, stronger IPRs can bring about benefits in terms of increased trade, foreign direct investment, and technology transfer. However, these benefits mainly accrue to middle-income countries, and the size of benefits depends on complementary policy reforms, notably improvements in other aspects of the investment climate. Fourth, the main cost of stronger patents, copyrights, and related rights is the market power conveyed to IPRs holders, leading to prices above marginal production costs for the duration of protection. For small developing economies with little inventive and creative capacity, stronger IPRs may lead on balance to rent transfers to foreign title holders.

Fifth, the TRIPS Agreement is binding on all members of the WTO and enforceable through the WTO's dispute settlement system. It sets minimum standards of protection for all IPRs instruments, but also leaves governments important flexibilities to design IPRs regimes to suit domestic needs. Sixth, the pharmaceutical patent rights recognized by TRIPS have raised concerns that the greater pricing power by pharmaceutical companies would adversely affect access to medicines in poor countries. To address these concerns, WTO members have reaffirmed the right of governments to use compulsory licenses to override the exclusive rights conferred by patents. In addition, a special importing mechanism was created in 2003 that allows developing countries with insufficient pharmaceutical manufacturing capabilities to import generic drugs. Seventh, discussions on TRIPS in the Doha Round have focused, among other things, on strengthening the protection of geographical indications and promoting the appropriate use of genetic resources and traditional knowledge. However, disagreements among WTO members have so far prevented the adoption of new rules or mechanisms in these two areas. Finally, many "new generation" FTAs negotiated in past years—especially by the United States, the EU, and EFTA—feature TRIPS-plus standards of IPRs protection. TRIPS-plus provisions relate to all of the different IPRs instruments and the mechanisms available to enforce exclusive rights. Their acceptance by developing countries cannot be explained by expected economic benefits, but has to be understood as a quid pro quo for preferential market access for their agricultural and manufactured goods to developed country markets.

The investment provisions in bilateral investment treaties (BITs) and PTAs are rapidly putting in place a worldwide network of basic regulation covering a sizeable portion of FDI. In Chapter 24 Ana Frischtak and Richard Newfarmer review recent trends regarding provisions that grant foreign investors greater predictability on the policy framework regulating FDI in BITs and PTAs. They enumerate the purported benefits of increased investment flows and consider the costs associated with disputes lodged under these agreements.

These agreements typically provide for transparency, non-discrimination among foreign and domestic investors, and guarantees against expropriation. Some agreements may prevent contracting parties from imposing trade-related investment measures (TRIMS) on foreign investments, such as local content requirements and local hiring requirements. Finally, nearly all provide for some sort of dispute settlement. Ironically, many of these agreements contain far more ambitious provisions—such as investor-state dispute resolution—than those proposed at the outset of the Doha Round and that countries collectively have resisted.

There is tentative evidence that provisions in these arrangements have on average contributed to increased investment flows, but these findings are by no means universal. Studies indicate that investment provisions can help some stable countries with otherwise less developed property rights or those initiating reforms, and they appear to be most helpful in attracting foreign investment when undertaken in combination with multilateral or preferential trade agreements. However, the mixed results of the evidence and the several unanswered questions of available research underscore the wisdom of avoiding sweeping assertions of benefit and instead tailoring the policy recommendations to each country. One reason is that according investor protections under these agreements has come at considerable cost for some countries. The number of cases that investors lodge against governments in developing countries has risen geometrically along with the size of damages claimed. That said, actual awards have typically been a fraction of total claims, and governments have won a significant minority of dispute cases. The process of investment dispute resolution could be made more efficient and equitable through reforms that improved transparency, the appointment of arbitrators, and more tightly worded rights and obligations under the contracts. The situations in countries such as Indonesia after the East Asia crisis of 1997–98 and Argentina in 2001–02 underscore the need to include provisions that accommodate unanticipated macroeconomic shocks through more flexible force majeure arrangements.

Robert Howse provides a manual for dispute settlement resolution in the WTO in Chapter 25. He traces the legacy of the GATT and sets out the key elements and purposes of the WTO dispute settlement understanding, including examples of the softwood lumber and shrimp–turtle cases. He next provides an overview of all the individual steps or stages that can occur in a WTO dispute, from the commencement of proceedings to the enforcement stage, making reference to the relevant legal provisions, deadlines, and practices of the participating actors and institutions. He also provides a discussion of how legal findings are determined and interpretations applied, and the different stages of panel and Appellate Body reports and procedures in dealing with the treatment of disputes. He concludes with a discussion of the challenges and opportunities for developing countries in using the WTO Dispute Settlement Mechanism effectively. These challenges include litigation costs that challenge the resources of poorer countries, lack of in-house governmental expertise in WTO law and dispute settlement, problems of coordination of private sector interests, and effective mechanisms for partnerships between government and the private sector in WTO litigation and the limits of retaliation (withdrawal of concessions) as an effective means of achieving compliance.

Chapter 26 by Simon Evenett discusses and summarizes the main findings of published analyses of the competition-related provisions in RTAs. This account provides a basis for the description of the various options for policymakers that are interested in including competition principles and measures in RTAs. Evenett concludes that the scope of competition principles, the values advanced, and the measures and sectors covered have broadened considerably since 2000. Thus, many RTAs now include not just chapters devoted to competition law and its enforcement, but have sought to entrench competition principles in the overall objectives of such accords and in the implementation of a number of laws with potentially significant economic impact.

Evenett notes that, ideally, it would be desirable to have evidence concerning the costs of implementation and, where relevant, any costs associated with inappropriate use of competition provisions in RTAs, as well as the benefits of these different provisions. Much of the empirical evidence concerning competition law that does exist relates to the effects of national enforcement regimes. To the extent that competition provisions in RTAs plausibly improve the enforcement record and, therefore, the deterrent effect of national competition law, then an indirect case for competition provisions in RTAs can be made. But lacking a strong evidential base, Evenett suggests that it would be better instead to continue to explore what is feasible and commit to undertaking evaluations of existing competition provisions on a more regular basis so as to add to the empirical base to guide policymaking.

In Chapter 27, Bernard Hoekman and Simon Evenett address issues of international discipline on government procurement. As they note, although a large portion of government expenditure is devoted to salaries, pensions, and redistribution (e.g., transfer payments), government entities of all types spend considerable sums on a wide range of products as inputs into the production of public goods and services—education, defense, utilities, infrastructure, public health, and so on. The state thus has considerable influence over the allocation of resources in market-based economies. The purchases by the entities concerned are governed by various procedures and mechanisms that aim to ensure that the specific objectives of each agency or activity are achieved while minimizing costs to taxpayers. Such procedures and mechanisms constitute government procurement policy.

Given that government procurement often involves large projects and is an important interface between the public and private sectors, many countries have made attaining efficiency in public purchasing a priority. However, there is often a tension between the focus on efficiency ("value for money") and other policy objectives that are pursued by governments in the context of procurement. Insofar as procurement policies favor domestic firms and products, they can impede international commerce. The desire to discriminate against foreign suppliers in public purchases was the major reason that government procurement was excluded from the original GATT in 1947. It was not until the completion of the Tokyo Round of multilateral trade negotiations in 1979 that an agreement on disciplines for government procurement practices was introduced into the world trading system. During the Uruguay Round of multilateral trade negotiations, the coverage of the Government Procurement Agreement (GPA) was expanded, but participation remains voluntary (binding only those countries willing to sign it) and limited to mostly OECD countries.

In the chapter, Evenett and Hoekman discuss prevailing international disciplines on government procurement practices through the lens of economic analyses of the trade-related aspects of procurement reform; the political forces that encourage or retard such reforms; and developments in the WTO and in other international fora. They conclude that public purchasing practices are one of the few major policy areas where WTO members continue to have discretion to discriminate at will against foreign suppliers. Limitations on the ability to discriminate only apply if governments decide to sign the GPA (or enter into PTAs that include disciplines in this area). But even for signatories of the GPA, the proportion of goods and services contracts awarded to foreign firms is generally quite small. Thus, there is considerable room for expanding access to national procurement markets. How significant those opportunities are is not known, in part because *de jure* discrimination may not be binding, but the potential for greater trade in this area is clearly substantial, given the size of government procurement markets and the prevalence of discrimination. This explains the interest that many current signatories of the GPA have in seeing membership expand.

The question then is whether there are situations where it makes economic sense to discriminate. If not, then engaging in multilateral negotiations has few downsides, although it may also generate few upsides insofar as the prospects of boosting exports to foreign government agencies are limited. Recent bilateral and regional trade agreements that cover procurement in a significant manner suggest that the GPA falls short in addressing the preconditions for governments to feel comfortable with making binding commitments to liberalize their procurement rules. More ambitious bilateral and regional agreements go beyond a focus on discrimination and procedural rules (e.g. transparency) to include mechanisms for technical assistance and capacity building, for cooperation aimed at convergence of procedures, for periodic review and allowance for adjustments in the rules of the game, and make better allowances for pursuit of the non-economic objectives of governments.

In Chapter 28, Andrew Grainger and Gerard McLinden address the nexus of trade facilitation and development. Countries have progressively lowered tariffs, established regimes to encourage foreign investment, and pursued opportunities for greater global and regional integration. But this progress has been undermined by the high costs and administrative difficulties associated with outdated and excessively bureaucratic border clearance processes, which are now for most developing countries regarded as more important barriers to trade than tariffs. Inefficient border processing rules and institutions and inadequate trade infrastructure result in high transaction costs, long delays in the clearance of imports, exports, and transit goods, and present significant opportunities for administrative corruption. They essentially undermine a country's competitiveness in the international marketplace. The potential benefits to be derived from implementing trade facilitation measures are therefore significant.

Trade facilitation has been recognized as an important development issue in recent years, as is reflected in increased levels of investment in trade facilitation reform by governments and donors alike. The importance of trade facilitation is also reflected in the numerous border management related provisions incorporated in various bilateral and regional trading agreements, as well as in a desire by many countries to seek enhanced multilateral rules on trade facilitation in the context of the WTO. Trade facilitation has furthermore become a key component of the global "Aid for Trade" initiative. Essentially, there is now widespread agreement amongst all countries that trade facilitation reform is a win–win agenda. Nonetheless, many developing and least developed countries face significant capacity and resource constraints that prevent them from improving their trade logistics and trade facilitation infrastructure and institutions.

Grainger and McLinden note that much of the reform effort for trade and customs procedures has been focused on customs agencies. The wider trade environment and linkages with the non-customs border agencies have received little, if any, attention from the development community. While improving the performance of customs administrations remains a high priority for many countries, evidence suggests that it is often responsible for no more than a third of regulatory delays. For traders, it matters little whether the problems they face are the result of poor customs procedures, inadequate infrastructure, or anti-competitive transport regulation. They all contribute to excessive transactions costs, delays, and unpredictability in the supply chain. This highlights the need to focus attention on reforming and modernizing border management agencies other than customs (including health, agriculture, quarantine, police, immigration, standards, etc.). Achieving meaningful trade facilitation gains therefore requires comprehensive "whole of border" reform initiatives and effective cooperation and information sharing among all border management agencies.

Chapter 29 by Steve Charnovitz deals with trade and environment. He notes that, as a result of the "trade and environment" debate beginning in the early 1990s, there is now much greater understanding of these linkages. Trade officials at the WTO and in national capitals are much more aware of the linkages between trade and environment and say that they are committed to avoiding conflicts. Similarly, there is greater recognition by environmental officials as to how trade restrictions can be overused or misused in the pursuit of environmental goals. There have been several initiatives undertaken to head off or resolve tensions between importing and exporting countries at the interface of environment or health, on the one hand, and trade on the other. Nonetheless, it can be said that so long as the policies in one country can impose externalities on other countries, and so long as prices in the market are not fully reflective of environmental costs, there will be a need for international governance to manage the trans-border conflicts that will inevitably ensue.

Charnovitz states that the optimal analytical tools for thinking through the challenges of trade and the environment would include theories and practice of trade economics, environmental economics, trade law, environmental law, public choice, international relations, and organizational behavior. His chapter emphasizes the legal dimension. He provides instruction on the various provisions of WTO law that address the environment. He also discusses the important environmental issues to be addressed in the Doha Round of multilateral negotiations, the environmental provisions of RTAs, and the environmental policy and negotiating implications for developing countries.

T. N. Srinivasan addresses issues of trade and labor standards in Chapter 30. His chapter focuses on four questions. (1) If a country has lower standards for labor rights, do its exports gain an unfair advantage? Would this force all countries to lower their standards (the "race to the bottom")? (2) If there is a "race to the bottom," should countries only trade with those that have similar labor standards? (3) Should WTO rules explicitly allow governments to take trade action as a means of putting pressure on other countries to comply? (4) Is the WTO the proper place to discuss and set rules on labor—or to enforce them, including those of the International Labor Organization (ILO)?

He discusses definitions of labor standards in the literature ranging from the so-called "core" labor standards of ILO conventions to others that include hours of work, minimum wage, and other conditions of work. He considers the question whether the standards should be viewed as *universal* and *eternal* norms that ought to apply *in any country* and *at any time* or whether they are spatially and temporally context specific, such as for example, the stage of economic development of a country and its implication for the choice of standards in international agreements. The analytics of labor standards in economic theory are presented in the chapter and, in more technical terms, in appendices.

Srinivasan examines the analytical and response questions of the WTO by asking whether there are cross-border spillovers and externalities with respect to labor standards. Also considered is the possible use of trade policy interventions to prevent a race to the bottom and concerns in high-income countries over how low labor standards in poor countries, particularly child labor, can be framed in terms of purely altruistic considerations. He argues that there are alternatives that are better from the perspectives of high-income countries and the workers in poor countries than the use of trade sanctions in expressing such concerns. He further questions whether trade and labor standards should be linked in the WTO.

The key messages that Srinivasan draws from his chapter are as follows: (1) The assertion that increasing competition from trade with developing countries with low labor standards is a threat to the prevailing higher labor standards in developed countries has weak analytical foundation and empirical support. The case based on it for including a social clause in trade agreements conditioning market access to enforce agreed labor standards has no merit. (2) Most countries of the world have signed and ratified conventions covering the ILO's core labor standards. Expanding the definition of labor standards to go beyond these to include minimum wages or hours of work is not appropriate. (3) The claim of universality and eternity for a narrow set of rights proposed to be included in the social clause is not only overblown but is also ahistorical. It is most appropriate to view these and the broader rights in the covenants as *universal* in their aspiration while their attainment would be conditional on national and temporal contexts, including the stage of development of a nation. (4) Labor standards can be modeled analytically as an activity that diverts resources from production from a producer perspective, while influencing welfare from a consumer perspective. It can be shown that labor standards will differ across countries in a competitive equilibrium. As long as there is *international cooperation* in the sense of a consensus on minimum standards and a willingness to make income transfers and impose optimal domestic taxes and subsidies, there is no need for a social clause or for the departures from free trade. (5) If the use of first-best transfer-tax subsidy policies is precluded, a second-best role for trade policy could arise: trade policy instruments could be used to raise labor standards, if not welfare, in poor countries, as long as there is international cooperation. (6) The demand for a social clause or a trade–labor standard linkage based on low labor standards conferring competition is not new. Yet the issue is alive, particularly in preferential trade agreements already negotiated. (7) Efficiency in the assignment of mandates to international institutions would strongly suggest specialization: that the WTO's mandate is confined to trade matters and the ILO's to labor issues, with coordination, if needed, in dealing with any overlap. A postscript was added to take into account research completed after the chapter was first drafted.

III. Conclusion: Where Do We Go From Here?

The global trading system and policy agenda continue to evolve in myriad ways. In this concluding section, we identify several broad issues that merit watching in the next decade or so as well as some conjectures about likely outcomes.

What Will Happen to the Trade Regime?

Will developing countries be able to exert greater influence over global trade institutions? Until the Doha Round, developed countries had largely been able to shape the rules and processes of multilateral institutions to advance their interests. This was perhaps most clearly seen recently in the ability of the United States and Europe to enlarge the trade policy agenda to include "behind the border" issues during the Uruguay Round. By requiring all countries to approve the Uruguay Round agreements as a "single undertaking," these actors managed to oblige developing countries to accede to a bold expansion of commitments in policy areas that had once been treated as voluntary. Will the increasing economic and political importance of developing and emerging market countries translate into greater influence in the WTO? If so, what sort of agenda will these countries promote?

This is not the first time that scholars have predicted a shift in power toward the developing world, nor the first time that developing countries have sought to influence global economic arrangements. The call for a New International Economic Order in the 1970s and efforts to act collectively, such as the formation of the Group of 77, received ample attention but ultimately proved largely ineffectual. Developing and emerging market countries today do seem to have gained the power to block developed country initiatives, albeit at the cost of sacrificing progress on issues important to them. But they are unlikely to be able to promote a new trade agenda unless some countries individually gain much greater economic or political weight. In the event that they do, there is no guarantee that these "representatives" will speak on behalf of other developing or emerging market countries. Much has been made of the rise of the BRICs (Brazil, Russia, India, and China) and their potential impact on global governance structures. Yet the BRICs show little unity on key issues apart from an expressed desire for more influence over international economic affairs. For instance, in the critical area of agricultural trade, Brazil has pushed for deeper liberalization whereas China and India have remained largely opposed.

Does the difficulty in completing the Doha Round augur a permanent difficulty in moving forward at the multilateral level? Given the lack of significant progress in multilateral negotiations, it is possible that PTAs, which in many ways have become the *de facto* vehicle for trade agreements in recent years, will become the preferred vehicle. As the political economy of PTAs is often very different than multilateral agreements, this development has the potential to transform the political dynamics surrounding trade policy within nations as well as a different negotiating process between countries. Alternatively, if PTAs become the template for future multilateral accords—perhaps because nations try to codify at the global level what they have achieved at the bilateral or regional level—the scope of multilateral agreements may become more expansive, including items that have been excluded from global talks.

How Will the Trade Agenda Evolve?

Will efforts to promote deeper harmonization of national economic structures continue, perhaps extending to areas that are still not included in the trade agenda, such as environment and labor rights, or will there be a reaffirmation of economic nationalism? On the one hand, if the integration of national economies deepens as part of an inexorable wave of globalization, diminishing the importance of national borders for economic activity, it seems likely that there will be tremendous pressure on government officials to harmonize national policies on a much broader range of policies that affect trade and finance. As already noted, some PTAs include provisions such as environmental and labor standards, and their continued growth may be the channel by which these issues become part of the multilateral framework. On the other hand, the backlash against a perceived loss of sovereignty may grow, especially if the pain of economic adjustment brought on by convergence of national policies is felt more keenly by influential actors.

REFERENCES

Amin, S. (1977), *Imperialism and Unequal Development*. New York: Monthly Review Press.

Krugman, P. (ed.) (1986), *Strategic Trade Policy and the New International Economics*. Cambridge, MA: MIT Press.

Leamer, Edward E. (1995). *The Heckscher-Ohlin Model in Theory and Practice*. Princeton Studies in International Finance. Volume 77. Princeton, NJ: Princeton University Press.

Ohlin, Bertil (1967), *Interregional and International Trade*. Harvard Economic Studies. Volume 39. Cambridge, MA: Harvard University Press.

Rodríguez, F., and Rodrik, D. (2001), 'Trade Policy and Economic Growth: A Skeptic's Guide to the Cross-National Evidence' *NBER Macroeconomics Annual 2000*, Volume 15. Boston, MA: MIT Press.

Stiglitz, J., and Charlton, A. (2005), *Fair Trade for All: How Trade Can Promote Development*. Oxford: Oxford University Press.

Sturgeon, T. (2002), 'Modular Production Networks: A New American Model of Industrial Organization' *Industrial and Corporate Change*, 11(3): 451–96.

PART I

THE GLOBAL TRADING SYSTEM

CHAPTER 2

THE MULTILATERAL TRADING SYSTEM

ROBERT M. STERN

I. Introduction

THIS chapter first traces the evolution of the global trading system from the nineteenth century to the present-day GATT/WTO arrangements, calling attention to the key roles of reciprocity and non-discrimination and taking note of how the system is now challenged by the new paradigm of global market integration. In Section II, the main features of the WTO are described, the boundaries of the WTO identified, and how the expansion of these boundaries may result in the over-extension and weakening of the effectiveness of the WTO is discussed. Section III concludes.

II. The Global Trading System: Yesterday and Today[1]

> "I don't think they play at all fairly," Alice began in a rather complaining tone, "and they all quarrel so dreadfully one can hardly hear oneself speak—and they don't seem to have any rules in particular; at least, if there are, no one attends to them..."
>
> (Lewis Carroll, *Alice's Adventures in Wonderland*, 1946, p. 112)

To a reader in the nineteenth century, that might well have seemed a fair description of global trading relations at the time rather than of a game of croquet in the Queen of Hearts' court. It was only over the course of the nineteenth century that the beginnings

---

[1] This section has been adapted from Brown and Stern (2006).

of some order, as we know it today, began to emerge. Industrialization was taking hold in several countries, and it generated an intensified search for foreign markets and sources of supply. Governments in Europe were faced with calls to lower tariff barriers on imported inputs and to negotiate reductions in tariffs protecting foreign markets. But in a nationalistic world of vying states—as is still the case today—governments were not about to ease access to their markets in the absence of some quid pro quo.

The way forward was found in the adoption of two instruments of policy—reciprocity and non-discrimination—which set off a wave of trade liberalization. These two ideas enabled countries to surmount their innate distrust of each other and to engage in mutually beneficial and generalized reductions in tariff barriers. Reciprocity—meaning contingent and equivalent concessions—assuaged the fear of governments that they might not be receiving at least as much from others as they were giving themselves, and non-discrimination reassured them that they were enjoying the same treatment as had been won by other competing states. Neither of these ideas was a sudden intellectual invention; they had long been known in human affairs. But their application to trade relations was comparatively new and did much to advance global trade liberalization.

Historians usually identify the signing of the Anglo–French Treaty of 1860 as the landmark that signaled the new era of trade relations. Besides the need for a political gesture of friendship, the immediate cause of the signing of the Treaty was a decision by the French government to follow Britain's policy of trade liberalization. The French leaders were persuaded at the time by the popular, but mistakenly simplistic and mono-causal, belief that Britain's superior industrial performance owed much to its free trade policy. However, in undertaking to reduce tariffs on British manufactures, the French government sought some concession from Britain in order to win the support of its export interests in getting the lower tariffs passed through Parliament. Although Britain had already nailed the flag of free trade to its mast—and firmly, but exceptionally, believed that others in their own interest should also reduce their tariffs unilaterally—it accommodated the French political need.[2] Further, when other European countries anxiously sought comparable access to the French market, France offered them the same tariff rates that it had set for Britain. The inclusion of such a most favored nation (MFN) clause in commercial treaties thereafter became common practice among the European states. It also had the advantage of preventing treaties from being in a constant state of flux with tariff schedules having repeatedly to be renegotiated bilaterally.

What emerged in industrializing Europe from the struggle of countries to gain market access for their exports of manufactured goods was a network of bilateral, commercial treaties linked together through the MFN clause. While this was a step toward more predictable trade relations, however, the system was not notable for its stability. Apart from Britain—which adhered with almost religious fervor to free trade—most

---

[2] For a full account of the Anglo–French negotiations, see Hinde (1987). For a history of multilateral trade relations over the period 1850 to 2000, see Brown (2003).

European countries found their treaty obligation hard to live with. After a drift toward freer trade in the 1850s and 1860s, most countries later assumed more protectionist stances. Commercial treaties were frequently denounced or renegotiated, and some lengthy and bitter trade wars broke out. Still, while every country valued the freedom to make unilateral decisions about its national trade barriers, all were driven reluctantly to accept constraints on their behavior in order to gain access to others' markets.

The outbreak of World War I in 1914 and the political upheaval engendered in its aftermath disrupted trade relations for some years. Nevertheless, in the peace conferences following the war, the avowed goal of governments was to restore the pre-1914 order in international monetary, financial, and trade relations. But economic conditions militated against a restoration of the minimal levels of mutual trust necessary for agreements. In the unstable monetary conditions of the early 1920s, countries engaged in currency depreciations that were seen by others as competitive and that, in line with economic thinking of the time, made the negotiation of tariff reductions pointless. For a while, in the later 1920s, restoration of the gold standard made the outlook appear more hopeful for trade relations. But the differences in tariff levels between the high and low tariff countries were sizable, and governments could not agree on a common formula for tariff cutting. The onset of the Depression in the 1930s and the early responses to it, with tariff increases and currency devaluations, put an end to any hopes for more normal trade relations.

Some countries, led by Germany, resorted to bilateral barter or clearing arrangements that were necessarily discriminatory. Others, like Britain, sought to revive trade through the creation of preferential trading areas. In these circumstances of worldwide inadequacies in domestic demand, trade relations largely ceased to be conducted within a multilateral framework based on non-discrimination.

It is notable that the United States played virtually no part in the evolution of trade relations before World War I and remained largely aloof from international trade affairs in the inter-war years. American manufacturing and marketing skills had become internationally evident as early as the 1890s, but the United States remained for many years principally an exporter of primary commodities. It was fortunate that agricultural exports generally met with low trade barriers before World War I, so there were few restraints on the US pursuit of a high tariff policy on imported manufactures. Indeed, the US Congress could then interpret reciprocity as the negotiation of reductions in foreign tariffs under the threat of increases in American tariffs. MFN treatment was also offered only conditionally so that to qualify for a new MFN tariff rate, all trading partners had to offer equivalent tariff reductions.

However, by the 1920s the interest of US manufacturing industries in foreign markets had grown substantially with the share of manufactures having risen to nearly two thirds of total exports. A latecomer in the world of trade relations, it was only then that the United States began gradually to accommodate itself to the accepted international norms. With the adoption of the Fordney–McCumber Tariff Act in 1922, the principle of unconditional MFN treatment was adopted. And in 1934, the passage of the Reciprocal Trade Agreements Act made reciprocity—understood as equivalence in concessions—the accepted means of gaining improved access to foreign markets.

The New Era of the General Agreement on Tariffs and Trade (GATT) and the World Trade Organization (WTO)

Following World War II, which ended in 1945, the United States launched its grand design to establish an orderly multilateral framework for international monetary, financial, and trade relations. The ideas of non-discrimination and reciprocity again became central to the global arrangements for trade. But now, they were formally embodied in a multilateral agreement, the General Agreement on Tariffs and Trade (GATT). Two factors reinforced the great importance given by US policymakers at the time to the principle of non-discrimination. One was the conviction of the Roosevelt Administration's Secretary of State, Cordell Hull, that the trade discrimination practiced internationally in the 1930s exacerbated the bitter political rivalries in a period that had finally terminated in war. The other was the more commercial reason that US manufacturers particularly resented the British imperial preferences erected in the early 1930s.

The ideas of non-discrimination and reciprocity have contributed substantially to the progressive reduction of trade barriers on manufactured goods among the core industrialized countries, including North America, Western Europe, and Japan, since the end of World War II. The core countries, until very recently, dominated trade relations within the framework of the GATT, and their central focus was on the reduction of industrial tariffs. The degree to which these tariffs were reduced can be seen for selected countries in Figure 2.1 for the period from 1913 to the conclusion of the Uruguay Round. In the early years of the post-World War II GATT negotiating rounds, these tariff reductions were negotiated bilaterally on a reciprocal basis. Later, in the Kennedy Round in the 1960s, reciprocity was expressed in the adoption of a common tariff formula that replaced or supplemented bilateral negotiations. In principle, the core countries likewise adhered largely to non-discrimination in their trade with each other. But subsequently, in practice, they deviated substantially in the 1970s and 1980s by resorting to measures outside the framework of the GATT. These measures mainly took the form of voluntary export restraints or orderly marketing agreements. While their incidence fell more on Japan and some of the newly industrializing countries in East Asia and elsewhere, this evasion of GATT rules became so prevalent that it seriously undermined the respect for the system on which its existence depended. It was partly for this reason that governments during the Uruguay Round negotiations (1986–94) agreed to eschew these practices and so reaffirm adherence to non-discrimination.

Thus, up to and even including the Uruguay Round, it could be fairly said that the ideas of reciprocity and non-discrimination largely shaped international trade relations.

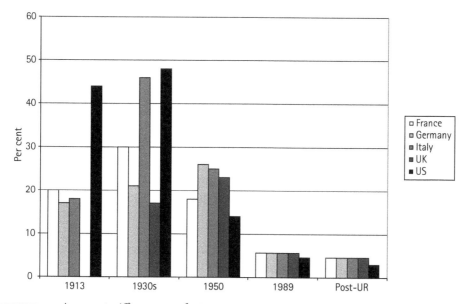

FIGURE 2.1 Average tariffs on manufactures

Source: Crafts (2000, Table 2.4, p. 28).

But events brought about changes during and after the Uruguay Round. Reciprocity lost some of its relevance and clarity as a guiding principle; and, in the face of the proliferation of free trade agreements (FTAs), non-discrimination in trade relations among states appeared to fade into the background.

Reciprocity and the Changing Character of Trade Negotiations

Two changes taking place during and since the Uruguay Round have muddied the nature of reciprocity as an idea guiding multilateral trade relations. The first is that, at the behest of the industrial countries, the content of trade negotiations has been substantially broadened; and the second is that the developing countries—thanks largely to their emergence as significant exporters of manufactures—have become influential participants in these negotiations.

Among the major industrial countries, the negotiation of improved market access for service industries and for capital remained based on a clear recognition of reciprocity. Countries agreed to a mutual widening of markets, yielding potential advantage to producers and investors on all sides. In this regard, even the new Uruguay Round agreement on the protection of intellectual property rights (IPRs) only reaffirmed a mutually advantageous form of cooperation that had long been in place.

For the developing countries, however, the question of reciprocity was more complex and uncertain. Developing countries had earlier sought a special status within the GATT, claiming that the industrial countries should reduce their trade barriers to the developing countries in line with the principle of non-discrimination, but without reciprocity by the developing countries. The exceptional status of the developing countries was taken further in the 1970s when the industrial countries introduced the Generalized System of Preferences; and it was also given formal recognition during the Tokyo Round in the late 1970s when clauses relating to Special and Differential Treatment were incorporated into the GATT. Further, particular groups of developing countries were given additional, preferential access to industrial countries' markets. The other side of the coin was that the industrial countries felt free to disregard the spirit of the GATT whenever it proved politically expedient to do so. They did not hesitate to practice extensive discrimination against specific exports from developing countries, most egregiously when they imposed restrictions on textiles and apparel in the 1960s, which burgeoned into the Multi-Fibre Arrangement (MFA).

Before the launching of the Uruguay Round in 1986, however, these unequal relations had begun to change. Many developing countries had made progress in modernizing their economies through industrialization; and they were all influenced, to a varying degree, by the worldwide shift in beliefs about economic policy that, among other things, favored more outward-oriented growth. Indeed, several developing countries had unilaterally lowered their trade barriers and most had become members of, or sought membership in, the GATT.

During and after the Uruguay Round, some "rebalancing" in trade relations began to take place, though it remains highly controversial whether the negotiations satisfied the condition of reciprocity. While developing countries generally did not fully reciprocate in tariff reductions, they agreed, in principle, to the opening up of market access to service industries and to limitations on the conditions that could be imposed on foreign direct investment (FDI). These were both concessions that appeared to largely benefit producers and investors in the industrial countries. When the new international rules on IPRs were added to the list, the grounds for questioning the reciprocal character of the negotiations appeared substantial to many observers.

But there is another and less obvious reason why the idea of reciprocity has lost much of its clarity. This is because the Uruguay Round also gave weight to rules—like those relating to subsidies and FDI—that, while certainly bound up with issues of market access, also impinged directly on domestic policies and practices. Together with revisions of domestic laws and regulations required by the liberalization of the service industries, these initiated what some commentators have dubbed the "deeper integration" of markets. They marked the beginning of a new development in trade relations in which actual or proposed trade rules could penetrate more deeply into the management of national economic and social affairs.[3] Some of the issues later raised by

[3] See Whitman (2004) for a discussion of the issues involving the deeper integration of markets, including pertinent references to the writings of Sylvia Ostry and others.

the industrial countries for inclusion in the Doha Round negotiations have borne the same stamp.

While some developing countries may have tacitly accepted these changing rules, others have voiced serious misgivings. As in all countries, the desire to protect entrenched domestic interests for internal political reasons has doubtless been an active consideration. But there are other, more valid, reasons. Of central concern are the limitations that these changes imposed on the development policies that these countries were pursuing. Since the early years after World War II, most developing country governments have used their powers to establish national firms in non-traditional sectors. They have created investment opportunities for the domestic business community (or political elite) through the use of a range of measures including tariffs, subsidies in one form or another, quantitative restrictions, and limitations on foreign investment. There is considerable concern accordingly that the freedom to pursue such development policies has been jeopardized by some of the rules adopted in the Uruguay Round.

Some of these new rules were apparently extending the principle of national treatment beyond its traditional, and limited, meaning through added restrictions on the freedom of governments to discriminate in favor of national firms by means of domestic measures. In effect, the leading industrialized country governments were collectively seeking to create an international framework of rules and procedures within which their own markets could be more closely integrated with each other. It was, in more popular terms, aiming to establish a "level playing field" in which the firms of each country would ideally compete everywhere on the same terms. The incipient framework drew on the ideas that guided the industrialized countries in the management of their own domestic markets, and in particular, on those of the leading power, the United States.

This represents a new paradigm in trade relations. It is advocated by those who lean toward a cosmopolitan view of the global economy, one that sees the emergence of an increasingly integrated world market governed by common rules that regulate transactions in this single market. It is a view that coincides with exporting interests, and especially those of multinational corporations. But almost all countries also have national aims that they are not willing to surrender in order to accommodate their trading partners. Some of these aims are rightly dismissed by cosmopolitan proponents as essentially being obstructive rent-seeking activities, agricultural protectionism and anti-dumping measures being cases in point. But, it needs to be understood that there is a global diversity in aims and policies. Many of these aims and policies have deep roots in national societies, and it can be argued that they should therefore be afforded legitimacy. This is a reality that is reflected in the historically more familiar view of the world as composed of separate nation states, each with its own national market. In this view, it is for each country to decide—in the light of its own social norms and economic aims—how far it wants to adjust its own domestic laws and practices in order to accommodate its trading partners and to gain a comparable adjustment from them.[4] It is a view that has long been the basis for achieving the reciprocal liberalization of trade.

III. Establishing the World Trade Organization (WTO)[5]

The World Trade Organization (WTO) was created in 1995. It is the successor to, and incorporates within it, the GATT, which, as already noted, was a treaty among Western market economies that came into effect at the end of World War II. In the GATT, member countries agreed to rules about when they might increase trade barriers, especially tariffs, in order to prevent them from using trade policies that harm other countries. The GATT was also a forum for negotiation to reduce trade barriers. As noted in Table 2.1, the GATT oversaw eight rounds of multilateral trade negotiations, culminating in the Uruguay Round that created the WTO. As a consequence, as already noted in Figure 2.1, average tariffs on manufactures have been reduced to relatively low levels. The WTO also took on issues that the GATT had not covered, including trade in services, tariffication in agriculture, and intellectual property protection. In 2001, the WTO inaugurated a further round of multilateral trade negotiations that was entitled the Doha Development Agenda in ostensible recognition of the objective of focusing trade liberalization to enhance the interests of the developing countries. The WTO is thus designed to continue the move toward freer trade that was started under the GATT, but the so-called Doha Round is currently in limbo because of unresolved differences in the negotiating positions of its member countries.

The most important change in the WTO, compared to the GATT, may be its dispute settlement mechanism (DSM). The GATT permitted countries to complain about other countries violating its rules. Each complaint was handled by a "panel" of experts who issued a report that, if adopted unanimously by GATT members, would require the offending party to either change its behavior or be subject to sanctions. However, unanimity meant that the offending party could block a report, in effect giving every country veto power over findings against itself. The surprise was that this ever worked at all, which it did.

The WTO reversed this bias, requiring instead a unanimous decision to block a report, and it therefore made the DSM much more effective. It also made other improvements, including the right to appeal. The various stages of the DSM are depicted in Figure 2.2. The intent was to provide viable enforcement for WTO rules, and it appears to have worked. Thus, it can be seen in Figure 2.3 that the DSM has been used much more often than under the GATT. The numbers of DSM complaints and dispositions

---

[4] See Whalley (2005) for a perceptive analysis of how different social values might interact and change in the process of increasing international economic interdependence.

[5] This section has been adapted from Deardorff and Stern (2003).

Table 2.1 Rounds of GATT/WTO multilateral trade negotiations

No.	Years	Name	Accomplishments	Countries
1	1947	Geneva	Reduced tariffs	23
2	1949	Annecy	Reduced tariffs	13
3	1951	Torquay	Reduced tariffs	38
4	1956	Geneva	Reduced tariffs	26
5	1960–61	Dillon	Reduced tariffs	26
6	1964–67	Kennedy	Tariffs and anti-dumping	62
7	1973–79	Tokyo	Tariffs and NTBs, framework agreements	102
8	1986–94	Uruguay	Tariffs, NTBs, rules, services, intellectual property, textiles, agriculture, dispute settlement, created WTO	123
9	2001 to date	Doha	To cover reduction/removal of: agricultural tariffs, export subsidies, and domestic supports; tariffs on manufactures; and services barriers, clarification of various WTO rules and agreements	150

Source: "The GATT Years from Havana to Marrakesh" <http://www.wto.org>.

from 1995–2005 and the percentages of complaining and responding country are indicated in Pelzman and Shoham (2007, pp. 20–21). The United States and the European Community have been involved in the most DSM actions, but several other countries have been major users as well. Just as importantly, large countries such as the United States have stopped going outside the GATT with their most important complaints.

Inevitably, however, the DSM has not worked to everyone's satisfaction. The WTO restricts policies that harm other countries, not only deliberately, but also inadvertently, as when policy restricts the options of another country's citizens. A contentious example was the "shrimp–turtle" case. A US law protected sea turtles from death in the nets of shrimp fishermen by prohibiting imports of shrimp caught without "turtle exclusion devices" (TEDs). Since it is impossible to tell from looking at a shrimp how it was caught, the law restricted imports from certain countries. These countries took the case to the WTO, which decided against the United States. In effect, this decision struck down US law, an intrusion into sovereignty that offended environmentalists and others. There have been other, similar, examples.[6]

---

[6] The details of the DSM cases and decisions can be found on the WTO official website <http://www.wto.org>. See Devereaux, Lawrence, and Watkins (2006) for a description and analysis of a number of important case disputes involving the United States, including hormone-treated beef, bananas, film, steel, cotton, and genetically modified organisms (GMOs); also, see the periodic issues of the *World Trade Review*.

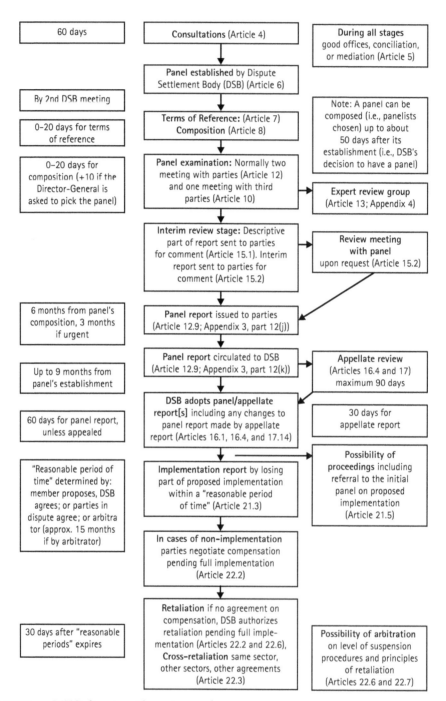

FIGURE 2.2 WTO dispute settlement procedure

Source: <http://www.wto.org>.

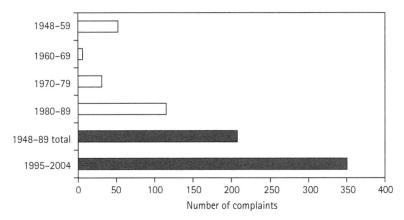

FIGURE 2.3 Complaints submitted to GATT/WTO by member countries about other member countries, 1948–2004

Source: Devereaux, Lawrence, and Watkins (2006, Vol. 2, p. 11).

The potential of the WTO to intrude in national affairs was also increased by its expanded coverage. This can be seen in Table 2.2, which indicates the scope of the WTO regime. The GATT was limited to trade in goods, even excluding certain sectors such as agriculture and textiles/apparel. The latter was covered instead by the GATT-sanctioned Multi-Fibre Arrangement (MFA), restricting developing country exports to developed countries. The WTO changed all that, or at least it promised to. The Uruguay Round scheduled the elimination of the MFA, though the most difficult liberalization was postponed ("backloaded") ten years. First steps were also taken in agriculture, converting existing non-tariff barriers (NTBs) to tariffs (tariffication) so as later to negotiate them downward. And trade in services was covered in a parallel agreement to the GATT, the General Agreement on Trade in Services (GATS).

The WTO also expanded into new areas. Most prominent is the TRIPS (Trade Related Intellectual Property) Agreement covering intellectual property—primarily patents, copyrights, and trademarks. In addition, the WTO includes (as the GATT had before, actually) some small ways that countries may use trade policies for environmental purposes. However, the one area—much discussed—where the WTO has *not* been extended is labor standards and rights. This is the case despite the pressures from many interest groups in developed countries favoring the use of trade policies for this purpose. The resistance from the developing world, including corporations who employ labor there, has prevented labor standards from even being discussed in the WTO.

Whom Does It Help or Hurt?

With its expanded role, the WTO potentially affects many groups. But fundamentally it is still, like the GATT, a force for increased trade, and thus for much of globalization. The WTO has not, yet, done much on international capital movements, although its

Table 2.2 The boundaries to the WTO regime

Core disciplines

- Most favored nation (MFN) treatment
- Market access based on reciprocity
- Prohibition of quantitative import restrictions
- Customs valuation and procedures
- Transparency (especially in standards)
- Safeguards
- Anti-dumping
- Dispute settlement

Present disciplines requiring modification to take legitimate national interests into account

- Domestic subsidies
- TRIMS
- TRIPS
- Government procurement

Preferential trading arrangements that do not inhibit global trade (Article XXIV)

- Customs unions
- Free trade arrangements
- Sectoral arrangements
- Developing country preferences

National regulations for health, safety, and consumer protection

- Countries set their own national standards, without protectionist intent

National regulations wholly beyond WTO boundaries

- Labor and environmental standards
- Regulations affecting service industries exempt from market access negotiations
- Competition policy

Source: Brown and Stern (2006: 268).

agreement on financial services will lower transaction costs for movements of financial capital. But it has done much to facilitate international trade. Those who gain and lose from the WTO, then, are also those who gain and lose from globalization.

That is, as in the case of globalization, the reduction of trade barriers will bring about the increased movement of goods and capital across national borders and international markets will become more integrated. Participants in domestic markets will find themselves either competing with their counterparts in foreign markets, taking advantage of them, or both. Consumers in particular will stand to gain. That is, everybody in a country stands to gain from trade in their role as consumers of goods and services. For many reasons—including comparative advantage, economies of scale, increased competition, and access to a greater variety of products—a country's average consumer, with an average income, is better off with trade than without.[7] That is, the average person's income will buy a larger, more desirable bundle of goods and services with trade than without, increasing their material standard of living. This proposition, called the "gains from trade," has been shown theoretically in all sorts of economic models. With only a few exceptions—which economists generally view as unlikely to reverse the broad conclusion in practice—it applies to all countries comparing trade to not trading at all. The argument extends to further degrees of openness, as well as to other kinds of openness such as international movement of capital. Thus, the fundamental case for trade liberalization and globalization is that it raises the average person's standard of living.[8]

While this benefit applies to the average person, with average income, income is not in reality equally distributed, and increased trade may not benefit everybody. A fundamental result of trade theory, the Stolper–Samuelson (SS) Theorem, identifies winners and losers from trade in terms of the national abundance and scarcity of factors of production, such as labor and capital, from which they derive their incomes. Owners of abundant factors tend to gain more than average from trade, while owners of scarce factors are made unambiguously worse off.[9] More general models allow for additional sources of gain from trade and suggest that even owners of scarce factors may gain, in which case SS says only that they gain less than average. But the possibility remains that they actually lose.

So trade theory tells us that, indeed, there may be losers as well as gainers from trade liberalization and globalization. Who are the losers? In countries like the United States, with its abundance of capital, education, and land, the scarce factor is clearly labor. It is not that the United States has a small labor force. Rather, the United States has even more of everything else. In this relative sense, the United States is especially scarce in those workers without a great deal of education, what can simply be called labor. Therefore, international trade theory tells us that the group in the United States most likely to lose from trade liberalization and globalization, or at best to gain less than everyone else, is

---

[7] This statement is literally correct only if the word "average" refers to the simple arithmetic mean of incomes—that is, total income divided by total population. Given the very skewed distribution of income, this does *not* necessarily mean that the majority of consumers are better off, since in principle the rich could enjoy a disproportionate share of the gains. However, in practice the vast majority of consumers are likely to gain from trade, the losers being only the small minority whose incomes fall disproportionately due to direct competition from imports.

[8] This conclusion is, strictly speaking, theoretically valid only for countries that are too small to influence world prices by changes in their trade. For large countries, the "optimal tariff" is positive, allowing them to benefit somewhat at the world's expense. While this argument might apply to a country the size of the United States, US levels of protection in sectors where it is highest are well above this "optimal" level, and in any case this argument for protection bears scant resemblance to what opponents of trade liberalization and globalization have in mind.

[9] The formal details are provided in Stolper and Samuelson (1941).

labor. This is hardly a surprise. The opposition to trade liberalization and globalization by organized labor in the United States shows that they are well aware of this. The surprise may be that economists, who tend to favor trade, would agree.

It follows from this also that trade may increase income inequality in advanced countries. Because labor has lower income than those with income from other sources, and because trade lowers the relative wage, it may make the poor relatively poorer. Leaving aside the legitimate question of whether an increased return to some other factors, such as the return to education, may actually increase the opportunity to escape poverty by becoming skilled, it is possible that, in the short run at least, trade liberalization and globalization may increase inequality in rich countries like the United States. In fact, there are empirical studies that suggest that increased trade may account for a portion (although much less than half) of the increased inequality observed in the United States since 1980.

Why, then, is it claimed that there are gains from trade? The reasoning derives from the confidence based on both theory and experience that the winners gain more than the losers lose, enough so that policy could potentially compensate them, leaving everyone better off. In the long run, with some mobility across population groups and with programs to permit the whole population to share in the country's income, most people can expect to be better off with increased trade than without.[10]

SS also applies to developing countries, but in these cases typically the scarce factor is different. Being relatively poor, developing countries can be viewed as the mirror image of the United States, with labor abundant and most other factors scarce, especially capital and education. These belong to the elite, who therefore lose from trade, according to SS. Labor in developing countries can be expected to gain. Since labor in developing countries is far poorer than labor in developed countries, increased trade and globalization can be expected to reduce income inequality worldwide, even while it may increase inequality within rich countries.

Are there other gainers and losers from trade, besides the owners of abundant and scarce factors? Yes, and many of them are obvious. Due to trade, some industries expand and others contract. Many people are invested in "industry specific" capital, human and/or physical, in particular industries—skills and equipment that are useful only within an industry. These people gain or lose along with their industries, and some can find the basis for their livelihoods destroyed, a serious cost that public policy can usually only partially acknowledge. For some, these costs can continue for months or even years, as they relocate, retrain, reinvest, and otherwise readjust. Others, especially those later in life, may never recover. International trade theory does not in any way dismiss these costs as unimportant or even as smaller than other gains. Economists therefore usually favor only gradual movement toward freer trade,

---

[10] Also in the long run, economic wellbeing depends most on how rapidly countries grow. Here the role of trade is less well understood, but in recent decades countries have grown more rapidly with trade than without.

so that these adjustment costs can be accommodated within the routine ups and downs of markets.[11]

Nonetheless owners of contracting industry-specific factors are a major source of concern in response to increased trade and globalization. These include, for example, US owners and workers in textile and apparel firms, factory workers in developing countries who have been employed during the periods when self-sufficient industrialization was being pursued, and Mexico's small farmers of corn (maize) who now compete with more productive farms in the midwest United States. These are only a few of the many groups throughout the world who have reason to be concerned about the effects of increased trade and globalization because of their dependence on industry-specific factors.

It is not only whole industries that expand and contract due to trade and globalization. Within an industry, particular firms also win and lose, and firms that have prospered in a protected domestic market may not be the same ones that do well in a globalized economy. Anticipating in advance the identities of winners and losers may be impossible, but once the process is underway, particular firms will try to speed it up or slow it down, depending on how well they deal with its competitive pressure.

This discussion of gains and losses by particular firms and by specific factors is appropriate primarily to the short run, because in the longer run, people relocate, retrain, and otherwise readjust to changing circumstances. Gains and losses to abundant and scarce factors, in contrast, last longer, continuing even after factors have moved from failing firms and contracting industries into new and expanding ones. However, this is not the end of the story. Over even longer time horizons, the total of a country's factors changes with economic growth. It is reasonable to ask, then, who gains and who loses from trade in the *very* long run, as sizes of countries and their rates of economic growth may change.

An easy answer to who gains and who loses from trade in the very long run is: "Not us." Keynes said that "in the long run we are all dead," and he was probably right. Thus, whoever may be the long run gainers and losers from trade liberalization and globalization, they will be subsequent generations, not the present generation. That makes it more difficult to predict how future generations will fare, since we know less about them than we do about the present generation. In a dynamic economy like the United States, the owners of tomorrow's capital, land, and human capital may not be the descendents of those who own these factors today. Therefore, even without economic growth, the best bet for helping future generations is to maximize total income. Trade liberalization and globalization do exactly that. Therefore, there may be a basis for confidence that "everyone" in future generations will benefit from it as trade and globalization continue to grow and spread.

---

[11] In Brown, Deardorff, and Stern (1992), for example, the employment reallocation effects of the NAFTA for the United States were estimated and found to be much smaller than the normal turnover within US industries in any one year.

Allowing for economic growth, this conclusion becomes still more likely, although the theoretical basis for it is less certain than the aggregate gains from trade liberalization in the shorter run. Economists do not in fact have a solid theoretical grasp of how trade affects economic growth, perhaps because growth itself is less well understood than the economics of static markets. Instead, there exists a variety of models of growth, and even more ideas of how trade may interact with growth. Some predict only that trade permits a country to grow larger than it otherwise would; others suggest that trade lets countries grow faster indefinitely. And there are also models where trade may be bad for growth.

But empirical evidence is much clearer that trade and globalization are good for growth. Since the end of World War II, most countries that restricted their trade have failed to grow significantly, while those that stressed export expansion have done much better. After a few successful countries demonstrated the benefits of trade for growth—especially the "four tigers" of Hong Kong, Singapore, South Korea, and Taiwan—other countries opened their markets and grew faster as well. This process has had setbacks, but few economists today doubt that open markets are beneficial for growth, even if the underlying conceptual connections are not entirely clear.

If so, the case is even stronger that, in the very long run, entire populations gain from increased trade and globalization. Those who are hurt in the short run may lose relative to others. But because they will have a smaller slice of a larger pie, they may well be better off absolutely. That will surely be true if increased trade and globalization permit countries not just to grow to larger size, but to continue growing at faster rates indefinitely. In that case, present and future generations will benefit.

With its expanded role, the WTO will thus affect many groups. But fundamentally it is still, like the GATT, a force for increased trade, and thus for much of globalization. Thus, the preceding discussion about gains and losses to abundant and scarce factors, to industry-specific factors, and to factors unable to move or retrain applies to the WTO. Because the WTO now extends to previously excluded sectors—textiles, apparel, agriculture, and services—those principles will apply especially strongly to them. For example, developed-country textile workers, who have been protected for decades, have particular reason now to be concerned with the end of the MFA, whereas developing-country textile workers in some countries may have corresponding reason to be hopeful.[12]

More generally, however, the WTO has an important institutional role beyond just fostering trade: to constrain countries from using trade policies that will hurt each other and themselves. Without such constraints, two things would guide countries' uses of trade policies. First, large countries would be able to use policies to gain at small countries' expense. Second, weak and misguided governments would be able to use policies to benefit themselves and their "cronies," and domestic political forces would likely lead them to

---

[12] For owners of textile firms in developing countries, it is more complicated. Developed-country firms may move production abroad. Some developing-country firms have prospered, using export licenses under the MFA to make extraordinary profits. But with the elimination of the MFA and increased competition, especially from such large, low-cost producers as China and India, many developing-country firms and workers will face difficulties in adjusting.

do so. The WTO, with its rules and its DSM for enforcement, helps to prevent both of these unfortunate outcomes. It protects weak countries from strong countries, and also weak countries from themselves. This is true not only for small countries, but especially for countries that are poor. Thus, even though the WTO was mostly designed by rich countries and even corporations, its greatest beneficiaries may well be in the developing world.

Who loses from the WTO? Again, some of the losers are simply those who lose most from trade, and here the most vulnerable are again the relatively unskilled workers in developed countries. It makes perfect sense that organized labor in developed countries should be skeptical of the benefits from the WTO, for theory predicts that greater trade will indeed hurt their members, at least relatively.

Aside from the foregoing, the rules of the WTO will also hurt those who would wish to break them. If there are large countries that seek to use their economic size at other countries' expense, then they will be frustrated by the WTO. Fortunately, there is little evidence in recent decades that the most powerful countries have sought to do this. More likely losers, therefore, are those who seek to use trade policy for other legitimate purposes but run afoul of the WTO, as in the shrimp–turtle case. In this case, those who seek to halt environmental degradation naturally wish to use trade policies to pursue their aims, since few other policies work across borders. Yet to do so risks violating the strictures of the WTO. Environmentalists have therefore sometimes been hamstrung by WTO rules, and they believe that they—or the environment—are hurt by the WTO.

It is true that the WTO makes the objectives of environmentalists harder to attain. Policies impose costs, and some are borne by other countries when one country unilaterally uses trade policies for environmental purposes. The WTO gives those costs more weight than if countries could act alone. This means that a lower level of environmental protection will result when these costs are factored in. This is as it should be, however, since global policy decisions should be based on global costs and benefits, including all aspects of all peoples' lives, not just the environment or one country. Environmentalists, whose role is narrower, will indeed make less progress when their interests are balanced against those of others.

Environmentalists might say, "Fine, but the WTO does not just balance other interests against the environment; it rules the environment out of court. All we want is for environmental concerns to be heard in the WTO." In fact, the WTO does include several environmental clauses, so even here the question is one of balance. How much of a role should environmental concerns play in justifying trade policies? Arguably, the current system has not done badly. The problem with using trade policies for environmental and other purposes is that they too easily push the cost onto others. The WTO has forced their advocates to find fairer ways to achieve those purposes. For example, the shrimp–turtle dispute led, more quietly, to shrimp fishermen being equipped with TEDs at developed countries' expense. It could be said that this was the right solution all along.

There are other issues, besides the environment, whose advocates want to use trade policies, including human rights and labor standards. For both, the United States especially has used trade policies in the past to deny trade preferences for some developing country trading partners that are allegedly pursuing abusive labor policies. Some US groups view the WTO as an enemy of human rights and labor standards. This conclusion may not be justified, but, as with the environment, as the WTO interferes with policies that would otherwise be available to pursue these ends, the ends themselves will not be attained as fully as some groups desire.

In the case of human rights, the WTO does permit some use of trade policies, such as the economic sanctions that were used against Rhodesia in 1965 and against South Africa in 1985. Formally, these were permitted under GATT Article XXI, based on actions under the United Nations Charter for purposes of peace and security.[13] The WTO does not permit unilateral sanctions for human rights, however.

In the case of labor standards and labor rights, the issue is more complex, partly because it is so difficult to separate the moral from the economic, and partly because of different views of what labor standards mean economically.[14] Some labor standards, such as the prohibition of slave labor and exploitative child labor, are clearly moral issues. Others, such as minimum wage, are economic. And still others, such as working conditions and child labor with the approval of caring parents, are somewhere in between. It is hard to say where to draw the line and who should draw it.[15]

Economically, most labor standards affect the cost of labor, even when not explicitly about wages. But their effects depend on how one believes that wages are determined. From the perspective of competitive markets, which guides most economists on this issue, labor standards are mostly about the remuneration of labor in poor versus rich countries, and higher labor standards in the former primarily benefit the latter, putting developing country workers out of work. Another view, however, is that all labor remuneration is at the expense of capital, so that higher labor standards merely reduce profits. This second view makes most sense if employers have market power, something that trade liberalization and globalization are in fact likely to undermine. But not everyone believes market economics, and there are plenty of subscribers to this second view among opponents of the WTO. In their view, by excluding labor standards as a basis for trade policy, the WTO helps capitalists and hurts workers—everywhere. But modern economics suggests that only developed-country workers may be hurt, while the true beneficiaries of the WTO are the developing-country workers that labor standards are ostensibly meant to help.

The latter view is voiced prominently by most economists and by most leaders of developing countries. They perceive labor standards, when enforced by trade sanctions, as thinly disguised protection for developed-country labor. The WTO thus excludes labor standards as part of its broader role of protecting the weak from the strong. Thus,

---

[13] See Jackson and Davey (1986: 917).

[14] The line between human rights and labor standards is not always clear. The right to organize and a safe workplace are both on most lists of labor standards, but they might also be regarded as human rights.

[15] For more on labor standards, see Brown and Stern (2007).

at the 1996 GATT Ministerial Meeting in Singapore, it was decided that issues of labor standards should be handled by the International Labor Organization, which was established in the 1920s with the express purpose of improving labor rights and working conditions but without resort to the use of trade sanctions to punish alleged violations of worker rights.

Other Objections to the WTO

Even among those who conclude that it is appropriate for the WTO to limit its jurisdiction on issues of the environment and labor standards, however, the WTO does nonetheless have some limitations. One is its lack of transparency. The proceedings of the DSM panels are generally closed and make only limited use of information from non-government sources. Some observers regard this mechanism as non-democratic, and they fear its capture by corporations with financial stakes in the outcome. They would like interested NGOs to be able to provide more input to the process, and perhaps to have the panelists themselves selected by a process that NGOs could influence.

The complaint about non-democratic procedures is ironic, however, since the WTO works by consensus among mostly democratic governments, whereas NGOs are by definition self-appointed special interests. More important, however, is a concern of developing countries, that opening the DSM to greater public scrutiny and influence would cause its capture by precisely these special interests, at developing-country expense. Nonetheless, even defenders of the WTO recognize that the DSM's procedures may be counter-productive. It has thus become increasingly common in DSM cases to permit NGOs and others to file "friend of the court briefs." Some observers also argue that a more permanent body should replace the panels themselves, instead of being assembled case by case. If so, then greater public input to selection of that body might be natural.

A further concern has long been that a few rich countries dominate the WTO, developing countries having little role. This is true in spite of—or even because of—its formal reliance on consensus. With over 150 member countries, however, consensus is not practical, and therefore a smaller group has typically sought agreement among themselves, thereafter coming to the larger group for approval. This smaller group, sometimes referred to as the "green room group" after the room in which they have sometimes met at WTO headquarters in Geneva, has been assembled on an ad hoc basis by the Director General and has included both developed and developing countries based on their interest in the issues being addressed. However, many developing countries—especially smaller ones—have been excluded and not formally represented, not by design because there was no design, but by default. Exactly how to change this aspect of WTO governance is not clear, but it requires careful consideration.

As already noted, a common objection to the WTO is that it overrules domestic laws. This is true, for that is its purpose. The GATT was a treaty among countries to prevent them from using certain laws and policies that would adversely affect each other. The WTO continues that purpose. However, while the original GATT dealt only with tariffs, over time the GATT/WTO has expanded to many other policies whose main purposes are not international. Critics object that the WTO undermines domestic policies, not just tariffs. Presumably, countries might well want to reconsider membership if they find WTO rules too onerous, but to date no countries have found it in their interest to leave the organization.[16]

A final concern of many WTO critics is that it is dominated by large corporations. This is true and probably inevitable, since it is large corporations that do most trade. Corporations have both the incentive and the resources to influence policies, and they do, both within countries and internationally. This means that the WTO has elements that would not be there without corporate lobbying, and some of these elements are undesirable. For example, anti-dumping statutes are economically nonsensical and pernicious, and yet the GATT has always permitted them, for the obvious reason that many corporations want them. More recently, in response to corporate lobbying the Uruguay Round added intellectual property rights to the WTO, in spite of strong resistance from developing countries that ultimately was overcome by the promise of market opening in textiles and apparel.

The WTO, then, is not a perfect organization. It could be improved, but many of its flaws will inevitably remain, because they are there in response to political realities. Overall, it seems clear that the WTO serves an extremely useful purpose, and that it serves it surprisingly well.

One indication that the WTO is not too far off the mark comes from its opponents. Although they share unhappiness with the WTO, some say that it does too much, others that it does too little. Environmentalists usually complain that it does too much, ruling against national efforts to improve the environment, and they want it weakened or destroyed so that national policies can proceed unhindered. Labor activists, on the other hand, complain that it does too little, not enforcing labor standards around the

---

[16] A troubling feature of the WTO for some countries is that imports may not be restricted based upon the process by which they were produced. The WTO permits countries to exclude goods deemed harmful to health or the environment, for example, but only based on observable characteristics of the products themselves. In practice, countries often want to exclude imports that were produced by a process that has harmed the environment, has violated labor standards or human rights, has adverse health consequences for consumers, or may be otherwise undesirable. These are often legitimate concerns, and if the process could be inferred from a product characteristic at the border, the WTO might permit their exclusion. However, the problem with exclusion based on process is that there is no way to observe the process at the border when goods are being imported. Countries must therefore in practice exclude imports based on where they were produced, excluding all imports from any country that does not effectively ban the offending process. Permitting restrictions based on process runs the risk of imposing particular production techniques on countries, and thus of undermining their comparative advantage. For these reasons, the WTO has maintained its position that process-based import restrictions are unacceptable.

world. They want the WTO to take on more issues, and interfere more with national policies.

IV. Issues of National Sovereignty and the Boundaries of the WTO[17]

As already noted, world trade liberalization made great strides after World War II on the basis of the two major pillars of multilateralism: reciprocity and non-discrimination (MFN). Until the Uruguay Round (UR: 1986–94), the periodic GATT negotiations focused on the reduction of external trade barriers to make gains in reciprocal and non-discriminatory market access. During and since the UR, these underpinnings of the multilateral system have lost their primacy. Over the course of the UR, there was an extension of trade rules, directed most notably toward the liberalization of domestic markets for services and investment and toward the protection of IPRs. Following the conclusion of the UR, efforts were made to include the so-called Singapore issues of competition, investment, government procurement, and trade facilitation on the agenda of the WTO Doha Development Agenda negotiations. Attempts have also been made to incorporate labor and environmental standards into the WTO. All of these developments reflect the idea not simply of promoting trade liberalization among separate national markets, but of furthering global market integration through the convergence of national market regulations. To some degree, the break away from non-discrimination through the proliferation of FTAs in the past decade only accentuates the movement away from trade liberalization based on reciprocal gains in market access.

It can be argued that the existing and proposed extensions of the WTO into domestic rule-making may be misguided. That is, the central role of the WTO should be viewed as facilitating commercial relations among its member nations. It is by no means clear, therefore, that the WTO should be an instrument to shape national markets and institutions so that they will conform to some idealized model of how a global economic system should work. The point is that there are boundaries to the extent to which WTO disciplines can, or should, superimpose themselves on commercial conduct in national markets.

The Boundaries to the WTO Regime

To clarify the scope of the WTO, Table 2.2 provides a categorization of the various actual or proposed disciplines of the WTO regime. These include: (1) core disciplines;

---

[17] This section has been adapted from Brown and Stern (2006).

(2) disciplines that may require modification to take legitimate national interests into account; (3) preferential trading arrangements that do not inhibit global trade; (4) national regulations involving health, safety, and consumer protection; and (5) national regulations that lie wholly beyond WTO boundaries. While not included explicitly, allowance needs to be made under the foregoing disciplines/boundaries for provision of Special and Differential treatment to low income or least developed countries.

In considering the WTO boundaries, there are two conditions to bear in mind: (1) the positive economic nationalism that legitimately motivates most governments to pursue policies that are sincerely believed to improve the material wellbeing of their populations and sustain their social cohesion; and (2) the institutions surrounding national markets that are embedded in social mores and the particular structure of business organization. When WTO rules and procedures are pushed beyond the boundaries set by these conditions, they may sour trade relations and erode the general consent to the core disciplines on which the effectiveness of the WTO rests.

To expand further on the application of WTO boundaries, we now elaborate on the interpretation of these conditions,[18] addressing subsequently how the WTO "playing field" may be best delineated and the role of the WTO in dealing with preferential trading arrangements.

Economic Nationalism

Economic nationalism is widely used as a pejorative term. It manifests itself frequently in international economic relations and policies and is usually rightly denounced by trade specialists as a regression into mercantilism. There is a long history of beggar-thy-neighbor policies in international economic affairs, and the guardians of economic rationality are justly wary of nationalist rhetoric. But that should not blind them to the reality that nationalist sentiment is a powerful force that also has positive economic consequences. The great revolution in rising expectations, which first began within some Western countries in the eighteenth and nineteenth centuries, has since swept around the world; and politically vocal people everywhere expect that their own national governments will take measures to improve their material wellbeing. Though the great majority of countries now have capitalist systems, beliefs about how governments could best accomplish this purpose vary widely; and they have changed within countries over time. But what has remained ever present is the responsibility that peoples place on their governments—as the highest political authority in their societies—to seek gains in national wellbeing. As illustrated below, such economic nationalism sets limits that have to be respected in multilateral rule making.

Domestic Subsidies and Industrial Policies

Among today's established industrial countries, governments broadly see themselves as fulfilling their responsibility if they are able to maintain technological leadership—at

---

[18] Issues of delimiting the WTO boundaries are also addressed in Hoekman (2002, 2004, 2005) and Sutherland et al. (2004, esp. pp. 61–72).

least in some sectors—or, at worst, not fall behind other countries in the endless race toward economic betterment. Accepting that private enterprises should make most economic decisions in response to market prices, they see their responsibility largely as the support of education, provision of infrastructure, and promotion of general scientific and technological research and development. Such economic nationalism has been reflected in the WTO mainly through its rules on subsidies. While government subsidies to individual firms or industries are often seen as contraventions of "fair" trade because they may distort market prices, subsidies of general research and development are not so viewed. The lines between specific and general subsidies, however, are not always clear-cut. For example, in very large-scale industries like the aircraft industry, EU subsidization of the Airbus and US defense procurement favoring Boeing have been an ongoing source of bilateral friction. Yet, until recently, the EU and US policies broadly remained in place, although they are now under challenge in the WTO dispute settlement procedure. Other manifestations of economic nationalism stem from cross-border mergers and acquisitions that may threaten the independence of national corporations regarded as "national champions." But they have so far not been constrained in this area by the WTO since it has no agreement on competition policy.

Most developing country governments have been no less powerfully motivated by economic nationalism. In the earlier post-World War II years, indeed, the sense of national pride—enhanced by new won independence—occasioned widespread nationalization of foreign enterprises and stressed the development of nationally owned enterprises. While most governments have since shed their hostility toward foreign investment, they have not lost their determination to foster the expansion of a rising indigenous industrial sector. Countries that have made substantial progress in industrialization have generally made extensive use of policies intended to provide inducements to, and financial and technical support for, national firms to encourage expansion of production and introduction of new products and processes. By such means, they have sought to benefit from learning spillovers, and to overcome coordination failures that might otherwise impede their economic growth. However, such policies—pursued on the nationalist grounds that they promote indigenous development and evidently effective in the circumstances—are perhaps not consistent with the rules of the GATT/WTO as these rules now stand. But it is noteworthy that national policies have for the most part been considered to lie within the purview of governments and have not been challenged in the GATT/WTO. Efforts to restrict domestic subsidies that constrain industrial policies should therefore be carefully circumscribed in the WTO.

TRIMS and TRIPS

In the UR negotiations, agreements on "trade related" investment measures (TRIMS) and IPR (TRIPS) protection were incorporated into the WTO. These are clear examples of the extension of international rule making into areas of domestic policy.

The TRIMS Agreement fell short of what its sponsors—mainly the United States—sought. They had hoped for an agreement on foreign investment that, when taken together with the GATS (which accorded foreign investors the right of establishment in service industries), would succeed in gaining less restricted access to the markets of other countries for their corporate investors. They also hoped that, once their investors had been granted access, such foreign investment would enjoy full national treatment. These aims were not realized. However, developing countries had to accept some restrictions on their freedom to apply conditions on FDI. They were no longer permitted to impose local content requirements on foreign enterprises to mandate their meeting particular levels of local procurement, or stipulate that foreign enterprises meet trade balancing requirements. Underlying TRIMS is an evident conflict between the legitimate economic nationalism of developing countries in pursuing measures intended to advance their own development and the commercial interests of multinational corporations.

The TRIPS Agreement addresses longstanding issues of foreign piracy and counterfeiting of patents, copyrights, and trademarks that have always been of concern to the owners of these IPRs. In the earlier stages of their own industrialization, the now industrialized countries were generally neglectful of foreign-owned IPRs. Freewheeling imitation and reverse engineering of foreign products and processes were the principal means of gaining new technology (Chang, 2002). However, as these countries themselves began to generate technological innovations, they acquired an interest in the reciprocal recognition of IPRs. What TRIPS accomplished was an extension of such mutual recognition to all WTO members. For a great many developing countries, however, the element of reciprocity has been largely absent from the agreement, since they have had few IPRs for which they might seek recognition abroad. On the other hand, the agreement has restricted their freedom to copy and apply new technologies at will. Further, utilization of new technologies patented elsewhere will require payment of royalties or fees, implying a transfer of financial resources from poor to rich countries.

Defenders of the new discipline point to the potentially beneficial development effects. Their argument is that, as the rights of patent holders are now more secure, corporations may be more willing to set up production in countries where they formerly feared that their patented processes would be surreptitiously stolen and copied. But against this is the check that the discipline imposes on the unrestrained transfer of technology. WTO members have, at least, recognized this in the special provisions agreed to in regard to pharmaceutical patents and the treatment of HIV/AIDS, malaria, and tuberculosis.[19]

It can be argued that the TRIMS and TRIPS Agreements may well lie outside the appropriate boundaries for many WTO developing-country members. Also, it may be argued that the broader investment measures, that were part of the Singapore agenda and that were shelved following the September 2003 WTO Cancun Ministerial, should be permanently shelved. Furthermore, the transition period for TRIPS conformance could be made open ended for developing countries until such time as they themselves

---

[19] A well informed and balanced assessment of IPRs and development is provided in the report of an international group of experts appointed by the UK government (Commission on Intellectual Property Rights, 2002).

will benefit—both internally and through the reciprocal recognition of rights—by implementing the domestic laws and institutions needed to carry out the enforcement procedures of the Agreement.

Government Procurement

In the course of the Tokyo Round in the late 1970s, a plurilateral agreement on government procurement was negotiated to become effective in 1981, with a number of industrial country signatories. There are presently 28 signatory governments. The agreement was designed to make the procedures and practices of government procurement more transparent and non-discriminatory, as between domestic and foreign suppliers. The emphasis is on tendering practices and covers both designated national and local government entities, with specified threshold values for the contracts involved. While the number of signatory countries has expanded, it is noteworthy that comparatively few developing countries have become signatories. The reason apparently is that the procurement agreement is viewed as being overly intrusive in challenging the rights of governments to maintain control over the award of contracts and programs for public procurement.

It may be the case that existing procurement policies in many countries are inefficient, costly, and subject to rent seeking, so that measures to reform these policies may therefore be in a country's national interest. But it is not clear why such reform should be carried out under WTO auspices, especially since a substantial amount of public procurement may stem from pursuit of a variety of social and political objectives and programs that are at the foundations of domestic government policies and may only tangentially be trade related. It is not surprising, therefore, that many developing countries were opposed to inclusion of government procurement, one of the Singapore issues, as part of the Doha Development Agenda negotiations. As in the case of investment policies, government procurement was shelved following the Cancun Ministerial Meeting.

Markets and Institutions

It is obvious that national markets function within a framework of laws, regulations, and more informal, but well embedded, practices; and that the framework differs widely among countries. Some obvious forces that account for the differences are the social mores of each country, its political institutions, and the particular forms of organization of its firms and industries as its capitalist system has evolved. These have never prevented transactions across national frontiers. As long as traders share some core similarities in modes of commercial conduct, they have been able to trade advantageously with each other. It has been enough that they share respect for private property rights and contractual arrangements, and that they accept some judicial procedure for resolving disputes. But in a world of nation states, traders have also found that the differences in laws, institutions, and social practices may impede their access to foreign markets. This has driven the search in the GATT/WTO for common rules that would ensure greater similarity in competitive conditions. Firms in the leading economic powers have deemed dissimilarities from their own national conditions to give rise to "unfair" competition and have called for a "level playing field." This has been powerfully supported, at the intellectual level, by an idealized neo-classical model of markets that presupposes universal institutional conditions associated historically with the development of capitalism in the United States or Great Britain.

There are, however, limits on the extent to which nations can be expected to conform to multilaterally established rules that may challenge their own social mores or forms of business organization. To be effectively applied at home, rules have to be compatible with the prevailing beliefs and practices within which the domestic market functions. Rules that are in conflict will not be accepted or, if formally accepted, will not be enforced or will be enforced only weakly. Certainly, some distinction has to be drawn here between laws, regulations, and practices that are deeply embedded and those that lie more on the surface or merely benefit rent seekers. Cumbersome and outmoded customs procedures, for instance, may not reflect any deeply held beliefs, and their reform may be impeded only by bureaucratic inertia. There is no objective test by which to determine where the line lies, but there are some reforms proposed as appropriate for the WTO that may exceed the appropriate boundaries.

Competition Policy

Competition policy is a case in point in which the diversity in forms of business organization among countries limits the possibility or desirability of common rules. There are many variants of capitalism as it has evolved in the unique political, social, and economic circumstances of each country. Perhaps two of the most striking circumstantial differences are the relations between the state and private enterprises and the interrelations among firms themselves. In most English speaking industrial countries, for example, the relationships between private enterprises and government have historically been more adversarial and arms length in comparison with the more cooperative relations in many other countries. Likewise, there are many differences in the competitive or cooperative relations among firms that are socially regarded as acceptable. These give rise to differences in market practices that foreign producers may see as impediments to trade.

An example is the Structural Impediments Initiative that was prominent in US–Japan relations in the 1980s and 1990s, and that involved US pressure on Japan to change longstanding business practices and institutions that allegedly constrained access of US exports and FDI in the Japanese market. The WTO was involved in two prominent cases dealing with US access to Japan's domestic market in automobiles and film. The United States decided to drop the automobiles complaint and was on the losing side of the WTO dispute settlement decision to deny the Kodak film complaint.[20] In retrospect, the US actions may have been ill advised to begin with. It also appears that the Japanese

---

[20] For an analysis of the Kodak–Fuji film dispute between the United States and Japan, see Devereaux, Lawrence, and Watkins (2006, Vol. 2, pp. 143–191).

Government instituted measures on its own in recognition of the national need for institutional and policy reform in a number of sectors.

Arguments similar to the foregoing can be applied to developing countries. It can be argued accordingly that competition policy may lie outside the appropriate boundaries of the WTO regime. This was another of the Singapore issues that was shelved following the September 2003 WTO Cancun Ministerial Meeting.

Labor Standards

Labor standards are a further case in point. As noted in the earlier discussion, there have been strong political pressures from organized labor and social activists to seek the incorporation of labor standards in the WTO. But it may suffice to note that the case for inclusion of labor standards in the WTO rules, on grounds of economic welfare, is widely regarded as very weak, both logically and empirically. The best contribution that the WTO can make to raising labor standards is accordingly to facilitate the expansion of world trade since, almost everywhere, as economic growth has taken place and incomes have risen, working conditions have sooner or later improved.

Nonetheless, the proponents favoring inclusion of labor standards in trade agreements have been powerfully reinforced in their claim to the high moral ground by arguing that, whatever the economic consequences, it is morally wrong to condone poor labor standards in other countries. No one would contest the right of individuals or groups to advocate the norms of their society or to call for economic sanctions when the most egregious violations of human rights are being committed. In the present context, however, the issue is whether industrial nations, by virtue of their power, should, as a condition of trade, insist that other countries respect particular labor standards that they themselves value and that are interwoven with the levels of individual and social wellbeing, which thanks to their long history of economic growth, they now enjoy.

Many developing countries see this demand as presumptuous and politically self-serving, as the governments of industrial countries appear to be placating domestic groups that either represent sectional interests or are not well informed. But there is a more pragmatic reason for rejection of this position, which is that it is very likely to be ineffective. The transplant of social norms from one society to another is exceedingly difficult to accomplish. Everywhere, changes in domestic regulations embodying new norms of behavior take place in response to demands from coalitions of politically influential groups within the country. External leverage applied through trade threats may possibly tilt the balance in favor of reform, but by itself will rarely bring about any lasting change in prevailing social beliefs and practices. What the inclusion of rules about labor standards in the WTO would most likely accomplish is its entrapment in disputes about policies that countries regard as wholly domestic affairs.

Environmental Standards

The arguments just made concerning labor standards may apply to domestic environmental standards, which will depend on prevailing social beliefs and practices and differences in per capita incomes between nations. Just as with labor standards, the determination of environmental standards should therefore lie outside the boundaries of the WTO.

Health and Safety Standards and Consumer Protection

Another problematic policy area for the WTO is the range of measures that governments may design and implement with regard to health and safety standards and consumer protection. In this connection, EU policies regarding imports of hormone-treated beef and products containing genetically modified organisms (GMOs) provide an apt illustration of the limits of WTO policies.[21] The issues here concern the rights of nations to establish their own national health and safety standards, including the restriction of imports deemed to contravene national standards. Such standards can be and have been used for protectionist purposes, and there may not always be a firm scientific basis to warrant certain standards. But so long as governments believe it is in the national interest to protect public health, the right to do so should be respected. Depending on how scientific evidence evolves, governments may then decide over time to moderate their restrictions, as, for example, the EU has been doing recently with GMOs. This suggests accordingly that the rules and decisions of the WTO should not be rigidly applied in cases in which public health is at issue, and there is a consensus lacking regarding the available scientific evidence for the production and processing of the products involved.

The Playing Field

So, if we accept the limits described above, how is the WTO's playing field to be defined? The role of the WTO is to provide a framework in which governments can negotiate and monitor the reduction of impediments to trade that serve no larger purpose than the protection of sectional interests within individual countries. Such impediments cannot be legitimately defended on the kinds of grounds discussed above. They serve only to lower economic efficiency within the countries in which they are practiced and deprive producers in other countries of wider market access. The world abounds in these impediments, and their gradual reduction is the raison d'être of the WTO. Drawing the line between these impediments and those that have larger purposes is the task of the WTO rules.

As already mentioned, agricultural impediments illustrate this point. Even if, for example—as the EU, Japan, and other nations assert—the subsidization of agriculture has broad social as well as economic aims, it is an inefficient way of accomplishing the social purposes as well as meeting economic needs. The economic case against agricultural subsidization as serving sectional interests and lowering national efficiency appears to be well founded. A similar case can be made against the resort to anti-dumping measures that are the policy of choice by protectionist interests

---

[21] The US–EU WTO disputes hormone-treated beef and GMOs are analyzed in Devereaux, Lawrence, and Watkins (2006, Vol. 2, pp. 31–96 and pp. 283–344).

in developed countries and have become increasingly widespread in developing countries.

Sectional interests are, of course, everywhere and governments are rarely independent of them. For individual governments, trade negotiations based on reciprocity have the advantage that they pit export interests against sectional protectionist interests. Negotiations force governments that want wider market access abroad to liberalize at home. It is a great benefit of the WTO that, in bringing countries together around the negotiating table, pressures are openly and internationally placed on protectionist domestic interests.

Many issues are not clear-cut and rules can never be drawn that are always unambiguous or that foresee changing circumstances. A mechanism for dispute settlement is consequently essential, but it should not be called upon to adjudicate on policy issues. Its business is the interpretation of existing rules, not the formation of policy. So, in the rules-making process, it is important that new rules should enjoy widespread consent.

Free Trade Agreements

We need finally to consider how the WTO boundaries should be defined with respect to FTAs. FTAs often manifest the "realpolitik" that motivates nation states in pursuing national self-interest in their external relations. Many FTAs that have been negotiated involve neighboring countries that already trade extensively with each other, so that there has been comparatively little trade diversion, except perhaps in some labor-intensive sectors such as textiles and clothing.

Except for US FTAs, most other FTAs are confined mainly to the bilateral removal of tariffs and quotas. US FTAs are more invasive in seeking to extend the integration of markets to cover many non-trade issues and to impose conformity with US institutions and policies. Nonetheless, FTA members are still bound by WTO rules, which may help to explain why we have not witnessed the formation of major trading blocs as some analysts postulated might occur. It may be the case furthermore that FTAs are becoming generalized as both large and small countries seek to expand their arrangements to help offset preferences provided in previously negotiated FTAS. But there are some large countries like Brazil, China, and India that are latecomers to the FTA process and are not likely to become partners in FTAs with the major industrialized countries. It may well turn out then that these large developing countries will become bulwark supporters of the WTO multilateral system.

There is, however, some role for the WTO to play in encouraging the greater openness of existing FTAs by expanding FTA membership, thereby moving the trading system closer to multilateralism. It might thus become possible to dispense with the rules of origin and remove the distortions that have been created by the many overlapping FTAs that now exist. Continuing pursuit of multilateral trade negotiations will also serve to erode preferential trade margins incorporated into FTAs and offer countries greater benefits than they may obtain from FTAs.

V. CONCLUSION

This chapter has reviewed the development of the present-day global trading system. It was noted that the success of the GATT system prior to the Uruguay Round was based on the twin pillars of reciprocity and non-discrimination. But during and since the conclusion of the UR, there has been a pronounced shift toward the pursuit of conformity in domestic regulatory policies and institutions covering a variety of institutions, business practices, and social mores. It can be argued this expansion of the boundaries of the WTO into domestic areas may be misguided.

Countries cooperate with each other through the WTO in order to benefit mutually from international specialization. To this end, they negotiate reductions in trade barriers and agree on supporting rules of conduct to verify compliance. Businesses, after all, have a legitimate concern that reductions negotiated on their behalf should not be effectively annulled by domestic measures later taken by trading partners. But this does not mean that the WTO should be taken as a vehicle for the dissemination of values or economic beliefs that are not widely shared. The criterion of success for WTO rules is that they should be widely, and willingly, accepted as necessary to promote mutually advantageous trade relations. If this is not so, the cooperation on which the system rests is vitiated.[22]

To be sure, there are strong differences in views about where the WTO boundaries should lie. But too much energy can be poured unproductively into debate about the boundaries. Within the WTO boundaries, there is great scope for further multilateral action to lower trade barriers and widen markets. There are many trade barriers that do not bear close scrutiny as rational measures either from a national or an international viewpoint. They can neither be defended as measures integral to national growth or development policies nor embedded in social values or in the longstanding structure of business organization. Unbiased analysis would reveal that they are no more than the abuse of governmental powers to protect special interests.

But where does the drive to confront these interests and remove the protectionist barriers come from? In recent decades in the developing world, it has come sometimes from governments committed to a radical shift in economic policies that have privatized and deregulated at home and liberalized external trade. More generally, over time, in both industrial and developing countries, it has come incrementally through pressure from their own export interests to negotiate for improvements in market access abroad. Reciprocity has demanded, however, that countries face up to at least some of their own protectionist interests and remove barriers.

Thus, reciprocity in the reduction of barriers to trade in goods and services remains the key to further trade liberalization. There are many other actions that the WTO can, and does, take to facilitate trade and smooth trade relations. But its task should not be the integration of national markets into one grand global market. By the same token, the

---

[22] For further elaboration on this point, see Brown and Stern (2007).

rise of FTAs has been eroding the principle of non-discrimination. While market forces and particularly the resistance of some of the major emerging economies may gradually result in restoration of respect for non-discrimination, the WTO could play a key role in convincing the countries that are parties to FTAs to change the nature and structure of these arrangements to move the trading system closer to the multilateral ideal and to continue pursuit of multilateral trade negotiations that will benefit countries even though preferential margins will be eroded.

References

Brown, A. G. (2003), *Reluctant Partners: A History of Multilateral Trade Cooperation, 1850–2000*. Ann Arbor: The University of Michigan Press.

Brown, A. G., and Stern, R. M. (2006), 'Global Market Integration and National Sovereignty,' *The World Economy* 29(3):257–79.

Brown, A. G., and Stern, R. M. (2007), 'Concepts of Fairness in the Global Trading System' *Pacific Economic Review,* 12(3):293–318.

Brown, D. K., Deardorff, A. V., and Stern, R. M. (1992), 'A US-Mexico-Canada Free Trade Agreement: Sectoral Employment Effects and Regional/Occupational Employment Realignments in the United States' in National Commission for Employment Policy, *The Employment Effects of the North American Free Trade Agreement: Recommendations and Background Studies*, Special Report, October.

Brown, D. K., and Stern, R. M. (eds). (2007), *The WTO and Labor and Employment* Williston, VT: Edward Elgar Publishing Inc.

Carroll, L. (1946), *Alice's Adventures in Wonderland* London: Penguin.

Chang, H.-J. (2002), *Kicking Away the Ladder: Development Strategy in Historical Perspective.* London: Anthem Press.

Commission on Intellectual Property Rights. (2002), *Integrating Intellectual Property Rights and Development Policy*, Report of the Commission on Intellectual Property Rights, London.

Crafts, N. (2000), 'Globalization and Growth in the Twentieth Century' International Monetary Fund, Research Department, Working Paper WP/00/44, March.

Deardorff, A. V., and Stern, R. M. (2002), 'What You Should Know about Globalization and the WTO' *Review of International Economics*, 10(3): 404–23.

Devereaux, C., Lawrence, R. Z., and Watkins, M. D. (2006), *Case Studies in US Trade Negotiations, Volume 2: Resolving Disputes.* Washington, D.C.: Institute for International Economics.

Hinde, W., and Cobden, R. (1987), *A Victorian Outsider,* New Haven and London: Yale University Press.

Hoekman, B. (2002), 'Strengthening the global trade architecture for development: the post Doha agenda' *World Trade Review,* 1:23–45

Hoekman, B. (2004), 'Overcoming Discrimination Against Developing Countries: Access, Rules and Differential Treatment' Centre for Economic Policy Research, Discussion Paper No. 2694 (October).

Hoekman, B. (2005), 'Operationalizing the Concept of Policy Space in the WTO: Beyond Special and Differential Treatment' *Journal of International Economic Law 8*: 405–24.

Jackson, J. H., and Davey, W. J. (1986), *Legal Problems of International Economic Relations* 2nd Edition. St. Paul, MN: West Publishing Co.

Pelzman, J. and Shoham, A. (2007), 'WTO Enforcement Issues' *Global Economy, Journal* 7(1), Article 4.

Stolper, W., and Samuelson, P. A. (1941), 'Protection and Real Wages' *Review of Economic Studies,* 9:58–73.

Sutherland, P., (Chairman) et al. (2004), *The Future of the WTO: Addressing institutional challenges in the new millennium.* Geneva: WTO.

Whalley, J. (2005), 'Globalization and Values' CESifo Working Paper Series No. 1441 (April).

Whitman, M. (2004), 'From Trade Liberalization to Economic Integration: The Clash between Private and Public Goods' in Ryten, J. (ed.), *The Sterling Public Servant: A Global Tribute to Sylvia Ostry.* Montreal & Kingston: McGill-Queen's University Press.

CHAPTER 3

....

PREFERENTIAL TRADE AGREEMENTS

....

PRAVIN KRISHNA

I. INTRODUCTION

....

A cornerstone of the Geneva-based multilateral organization, the General Agreement on Tariffs and Trade (GATT), and its more recent incarnation, the World Trade Organization (WTO), is the principle of non-discrimination: member countries may not discriminate against goods entering their borders based upon the country of origin. However, in a nearly singular exception to its own central prescript, the WTO through Article XXIV of the GATT, permits countries to enter into preferential trade agreements with one another. Specifically, under Article XXIV, countries may enter into preferential trade agreements by liberalizing "substantially" all trade between themselves while not raising trade barriers on outsiders.[1] They are thereby sanctioned to form Free Trade Areas (FTAs), whose members simply eliminate barriers to internal trade while maintaining independent external trade policies, or Customs Unions (CUs), whose members additionally agree on a common external tariff against imports from non-members. Additional derogations to the principle of non-discrimination now include the Enabling Clause, which allows tariff preferences to be granted to developing countries (in accordance with the Generalized System of Preferences) and permits preferential trade agreements among developing countries in goods trade.

The early post-war years saw the formation of a relatively small number of PTAs and multilateral approaches to trade liberalization—through negotiations organized by the GATT—that made substantial progress in reducing international barriers to trade. More recently, however, preferential trading has come into vogue. Hundreds of PTAs are currently in existence, with nearly every member country of the WTO belonging to at least one PTA. Among the more prominent PTAs currently in existence are the North

---

[1] Article XXIV's provisions are discussed in greater detail in Section V.

American Free Trade Agreement (NAFTA) and the European Economic Community (EEC). Mercosur (the CU between the Argentine Republic, Brazil, Paraguay, and Uruguay) and the ASEAN (Association of South East Asian Nations) Free Trade Area (AFTA) are both examples of PTAs formed under the Enabling Clause.

That a country liberalizing its trade preferentially against select partners is doing something distinct from multilateral liberalization (where it eliminates tariffs against all imports regardless of country of origin) should be easy to see. What this implies for the liberalizing country is a little more difficult to understand. Even a good half century after the economic implications of trade preferences were first articulated by Viner (1950), the differences between preferential and multilateral liberalization (or free trade areas versus free trade) remain a nuance that most policy analysts (and occasionally even distinguished economists) appear to miss.

It is with a discussion of these issues concerning the distinction between preferential and non-discriminatory trade liberalization that we begin the analytical section of this chapter, which is intended as a brief and accessible primer on the economics of PTAs.[2] Specifically, Section II develops the classic analysis of Viner (1950) and demonstrates the generally ambiguous welfare effects of preferential trade liberalization. Section III discusses the role that geographic proximity ("regionalism") may play in this discussion. The design of welfare-improving preferential trade agreements is discussed in Section IV. Section V discusses GATT/WTO regulations concerning PTA formation and asks how the existing provisions compare with the welfare-improving designs for PTAs described in Section IV. Section VI discusses the arguments made in the theoretical literature on the question of the impact of PTAs on the multilateral system. Section VII concludes.

II. Welfare Analysis

Trade Creation and Trade Diversion

Does preferential trade liberalization in favor of particular trading partners have the same welfare consequences as non-discriminatory trade liberalization in favor of all imports? Does a simple proportion of the welfare benefits of non-discriminatory free trade accrue with preferential liberalization?

A thorough answer to these questions would require the reader to take a deep plunge into the abstruse world of the second-best (whose existence and complexities were indeed first discovered and developed by analysts working on the economics of PTAs). But the idea may be introduced in a rudimentary fashion using the following "textbook"

---

[2] For more comprehensive treatments, see Krishna (2005), Panagariya (2000), and Schiff and Winters (2003).

representation of Viner's analysis: Consider the case of two countries, A and B, and the rest of the world W. A is our "home" country. A produces a good and trades it for the exports of its trading partners B and W. Both B and W are assumed to export the same good and offer it to A at a fixed (but different) price. Initially, imports from B and W are subject to non-discriminatory trade restrictions: tariffs against B and W are equal. Imagine now that A eliminates its tariffs against B while maintaining its tariffs against W. This is preferential tariff reduction as opposed to free trade, since the latter would require that tariffs against W be removed as well. It is very tempting to think that this reduction of tariffs against B is a step in the direction of free trade, and therefore that this ought to deliver to country A a proportionate fraction of the benefits of complete free trade. But Viner (1950) showed that this need not (and generally would not) be the case. Indeed, while a complete move towards free trade would be welfare-enhancing for country A, Viner demonstrated that the tariff preference granted to B through the FTA could in fact worsen A's welfare.

Figures 3.1 and 3.2 illustrate preferential tariff reform as respectively welfare-enhancing and welfare-worsening. The y-axes denote price and the x-axes denote quantities. M_A denotes the import demand curve of country A. E_B and E_W denote the price at which countries B and W are willing to supply A's demand; they represent the export supply curves of B and W respectively. In Figure 3.1, B is assumed to be a more efficient supplier of A's import than is W: E_B is drawn below E_W, and its export price P_B is less than W's export price P_W. Let "T" denote the non-discriminatory per unit tariff that is applied against B and W. This renders the tariff-inclusive price to importers in A as $P_B + T$ and $P_W + T$ respectively. With this non-discriminatory tariff in place, imports initially equal M_0 and the good is entirely imported from B. Tariff revenues in this initial situation equal the areas (1+2). When tariffs against B are eliminated

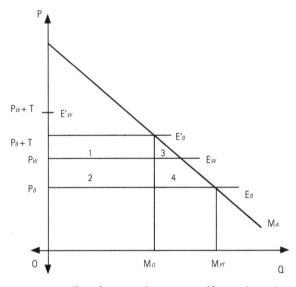

FIGURE 3.1 Trade creating tariff preference: change in welfare = (3 + 4)

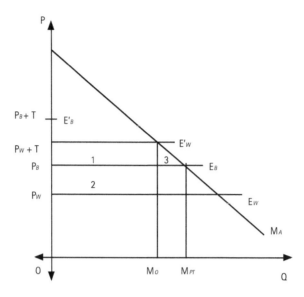

FIGURE 3.2 Trade creating tariff preference: change in welfare = (3 + 4)

preferentially, imports rise to M_{PT}. Imports continue to come entirely from B (since the import price from B now, P_B, is lower than the tariff-inclusive price of imports from W, $P_W + T$). The tariff preferences granted to B simply increase the volume of imports. This increase in the volume of trade with the country whose exports were initially being purchased by A anyway (i.e., with the more efficient producer) when tariffs against it are preferentially reduced is referred to as "trade creation." Trade creation here can be shown to be welfare improving. The increase in benefit to consumers (consumer surplus) in A following the reduction in consumption prices from $P_B + T$ to P_B equals the areas (1 + 2 + 3 + 4). No tariff revenue is now earned, and so the loss of tariff revenue equals areas (1+2). The overall gain to A from this preferential tariff reduction equals areas (1 + 2 + 3 + 4)–(1 + 2) = areas (3 + 4), a positive number. The trade-creating tariff preference is thus welfare-enhancing.

   In demonstrating that the tariff preference we have considered is welfare improving for the home country, A, we have assumed that the partner which receives this tariff preference, B, is the more efficient supplier of the good. Figure 3.2 reverses this assumption, making W, the rest of the world, the more efficient supplier of the good. E_W is thus drawn below E_B. Initial imports are M_0. The tariff revenue collected is equal to the areas (1 + 2). When tariffs are eliminated against B, the less efficient partner, the tariff-inclusive price of imports from W is higher than the tariff-exclusive price from B (this need not necessarily be the case, it is simply so as drawn). This implies that all trade is now "diverted" away from W to B. What is the welfare consequence of this trade diversion? The increase in consumer surplus is equal to the areas (1 + 3) since consumers now pay a price equal to P_B for this good. The loss in tariff revenue is (1 + 2). The overall gain to A equals the area (3 – 2), which may or may not be positive. Thus a trade diverting tariff preference may lead to a welfare reduction.

Box 3.1 Trade Diversion

Yeats (1998) investigated the question of trade diversion within PTAs by performing an evaluation of trade patterns within Mercosur. To describe the orientation of Mercosur trade, goods were characterized using two measures. The first measure is a "regional orientation" index, which is the ratio of the share of that good in Mercosur exports to the region to its share in exports to third countries. The second measure is the "revealed comparative advantage" measure, which is the ratio of the share of a good in Mercosur's exports to third countries to its share in world exports (exclusive of intra-Mercosur trade). Yeats then compares the change in goods' regional orientation index between 1988 and 1994 (before and after Mercosur) with their revealed comparative advantage ranking. The results of his study are striking (see attached table from Yeats (1998)). As he notes, the goods with the largest increase in regional orientation are goods with very low revealed comparative advantage rankings. Specifically, for the 30 groups of goods with the largest increases in regional orientation, only two revealed comparative advantage indices above unity. That is, the largest increases in intra-Mercosur trade have been in goods in which Mercosur countries lack comparative advantage, suggesting strong trade-diversionary effects.

The preceding examples illustrate a central issue emphasized in the academic literature on the welfare consequences of preferential trade. Preferential trade liberalization towards the country from whom the good was imported in the initial non-discriminatory situation creates more trade and increases welfare; preferential liberalization that diverts trade instead may reduce welfare. Subsequent analysis also developed examples of both welfare-improving trade diversion and welfare-decreasing trade creation in general equilibrium contexts broader than those considered by Viner. However, the intuitive appeal of the concepts of trade creation and trade diversion has ensured their continued use in the economic analysis of preferential trade agreements, especially in policy analysis (see Panagariya (2000) for a comprehensive survey).

Empirical evaluation of the relative magnitudes of trade creation and trade diversion is a challenging exercise, requiring careful econometric specification and large volumes of data. Furthermore, any results obtained by studying particular PTAs do not carry over to other contexts, as the specific patterns of production and trade in other PTAs will certainly result in quite different magnitudes of trade creation and diversion. Some interesting studies (see Box 3.1 on Yeats (1998)) nevertheless point to the practical relevance of the adverse consequences of trade diversion with preferences in international trade.

Internal Terms of Trade and Revenue Transfer Effects

The Vinerian analysis illustrated in Figures 3.1 and 3.2 has assumed that the home country is small relative to both the partner country and the rest of the world, with the exportable from the partner and the rest of the world being perfect substitutes. Specifically, when consumption is switched from the rest of the world to the partner country, the partner country is assumed to be able to satisfy all of the demand of the home country.

What happens if B is so small that after receiving the tariff preference from A it is unable to satisfy all of A's demand for its importable? This implies that A continues to import some amount from the rest of the world W (which we assume for the moment is so large that it is able to handle all of the changes in A's demand without letting this affect its supply price) even after granting preferential access to B. Here, it can be shown that the home country loses unambiguously. The following example, provided by Panagariya (2000), illustrates. In Figure 3.3, the export supply curve of country B is shown to be rising. The tariff-inclusive supply curve faced by the home country is E_B^T. Total consumption of the importable initially is M_0 and imports from B are M_B^T. A tariff preference in favor of B simply shifts the effective export supply curve to E_B and the imports from B to M_B. Total imports stay at M_0. The domestic price of the importable in the home market in A is set by W (which continues to supply to A) and is the same as before (i.e., it stays at E_W^T). The outcomes in this case are quite stark. Since consumption of the importable continues to be at M_0, there is no change in consumer surplus in the home country. There is, however, a direct tariff revenue loss since no tariff revenue is now earned on imports from the partner. The loss in tariff revenue (which is equal to the overall loss to A) equals the areas $(1 + 2 + 3 + 4)$. In what can effectively be seen as a tariff-revenue transfer to B, a gain of areas $(1 + 2 + 3)$ accrues to B in the form of an increase in producer surplus. Thus, preferential tariff liberalization leads to a loss in welfare for the liberalizing country, a (smaller) gain in welfare for its partner and a net loss of area (4) to the union as a whole.

In general, in the context of an exchange in tariff preferences negotiated under a preferential trade agreement, we may expect that tariff revenue losses to the home country

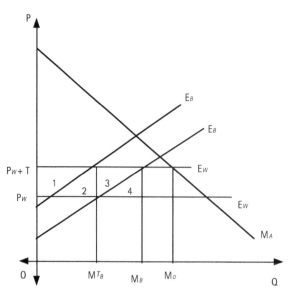

FIGURE 3.3 Change in welfare for home $= -(1 + 2 + 3 + 4)$
          Change in welfare for partner $= (1 + 2 + 3)$
          Change in welfare for union $= -(4)$

in some sectors are made up for by gains in other sectors in which the home country gets preferential access to its partner's markets. Who gains more will depend upon the extent of tariff preferences exchanged and specific market circumstances (shapes of the supply and demand curves). The outcome is uncertain.

External Terms of Trade

Thus far, we have focused our discussion on the welfare consequences of preferential trade liberalization for the countries undertaking the liberalization. While we have not explicitly considered this so far, it should be easy to see that changes in demand by PTA members for the rest of the world's exports could lower the relative price of these exports (i.e., worsen the rest of the world's terms of trade). In general, the overall effect on the external terms of trade may be seen as a combination of income and substitution effects. The former represents the effect of real-income changes due to the PTA on demand for imports from non-members, and the latter reflects the substitution in trade towards partner countries (and away from non-members) due to the preferences in trade. In the case of a real-income reducing PTA, both effects would combine to lower demand from the rest of the world. This is also the case when substitution effects dominate the income effect.[3] (See Box 3.2.) The rest of the world experiences deterioration in its terms of trade and is therefore adversely impacted.

Box 3.2 Terms of Trade Effects

Some indication of how the terms of trade may change for non-member countries in practice is provided by the empirical analysis of Chang and Winters (2002), who examine the impact of Mercosur (specifically, the exemption in tariffs that Brazil provided to its Mercosur partners) on the terms of trade (export prices) of countries excluded from the agreement. Theory would suggest that trade diversion would worsen the terms of trade of excluded countries, and this indeed is what they find. Specifically, their analysis reports significant declines in the export prices of Brazil's major external trading partners (the United States, Japan, Germany, and Korea) to Brazil (relative to their export prices to the rest of the world) following Mercosur (see attached figure from Chang and Winters (2002)). These associated welfare losses sustained by the excluded countries are significant as well—amounting to roughly 10 per cent of the value of their exports to Brazil.*

---

*For instance, the United States is estimated to lose somewhere between $550–600 million on exports of about $5.5 billion with Germany losing between $170–236 million on exports of about $2 billion.

---

[3] See Mundell (1964) for an analysis of how such extra-union terms of trade effects may complicate matters further for the tariff-reducing country, whose terms of trade with respect to the rest of the world may rise or fall following a preferential reduction in its tariffs against a particular partner. On this point see also the recent analysis by Panagariya (1997).

Scale Economies and Competition

It is sometimes argued that preferential trade integration can be beneficial when an industry is characterized by economies of scale (with average costs of production falling as quantity produced rises). Since a trade bloc combines the markets of its member countries, this larger market size may allow such an industry to achieve a more efficient scale of operation. Equally, when there are a small number of firms operating within the individual member countries and exerting their market power, trade integration will induce a greater degree of competition between these firms. Overall, we may end up with an outcome in which, due to the increased (combined) market size of the trade bloc, there is a greater exploitation of scale economies (with each firm producing at lower unit cost) as well as greater competition (reflected in lower unit prices).

It may be noted that the argument stated above is not without qualification. While we have described the existence of scale economies and the number of firms competing in a market separately in the preceding discussion, it should be clear that the number of firms itself may well be influenced by the production cost structure. In the extreme case, when there are large economies of scale, a number of small firms (operating at inefficiently high costs) may be replaced by a single firm which serves the entire trade bloc, exploiting scale economies and producing at very low costs. Since this single firm is now a monopoly, however, the economy suffers from the costs of monopoly distortion in the absence of government regulation of this industry. It may also be noted that gains from increased competition would only be higher in the case of unilateral (non-discriminatory) liberalization as this would involve competition between all of the firms in the world, not merely those belonging to member countries of a trade bloc (see Schiff and Winters (2003)).

III. Geography and Preferential Trade Agreements: Is Regionalism 'Natural'?

The previous section discussed some reasons why economists have been divided on the wisdom of preferential trade arrangements (PTAs). Following Viner's (1950) demonstration that the net welfare effects of PTAs are unpredictable and possibly negative, many attempts have been made to refine the theory and identify member country characteristics that would ensure welfare improvement and thus eliminate the welfare ambiguities associated with preferential trade. However, these efforts yielded results that did not have any greater and direct operational significance than did Viner's (1950). This is to say that they did not yield any direct insights on what partner country characteristics would make trade creation rather than trade diversion a likely outcome.

More recently, however, increasing emphasis has been placed on geographic proximity as a criterion for membership in a PTA. Regionalism in preferential trade has been argued by some authors (see, for instance, Wonnacott and Lutz (1987), Krugman (1991), and Summers (1991)) as being key to generating better economic outcomes, with regional trading partners described as "natural trading partners" in the context of preferential trade. The question of natural trading partners is immensely interesting for policy reasons. Many existing preferential trading arrangements are indeed regional. In addition, many extensions of existing arrangements along regional lines, such as the possible expansion of the North American Free Trade Area (NAFTA) to include Chile, Argentina, and other South American countries, or that of the European Union (EU) to include other regional countries, have been debated and discussed in policy circles.

To evaluate the argument for geographic proximity as a membership criterion, we may start by noting that this argument itself rests on two economic hypotheses. First, that trade creation is greater and trade diversion lower when the initial volume of trade between the partners is higher (and trade with the rest of the world is lower) and second, that geographically proximate countries have larger volumes of trade with each other.

As Bhagwati (1993)) and Bhagwati and Panagariya (1996) have pointed out, however, these are not robust principles. For instance, the contention that geographically proximate countries trade more with each other is generally only valid conditionally. That is to say, it is only after we "control" for a variety of other variables such as income levels of the partner country that we are able to say that trade is higher between countries that are closer to each other. Importantly, however, the choice of partners in a PTA need not be conditioned on these same variables—diluting the relevance of proximity in discussions over trade preferences. An example may serve to clarify this point. In a hypothetical world, where Japan's income and Mexico's income levels are equal (i.e., "controlling" for income) US trade with Mexico may well be higher than trade with Japan. As it stands however, Japan has a much higher income level than does Mexico. Its trade volume with the US is also much higher. Thus, even if initial trade volumes were to be used as a criterion by the US for choosing PTA members, the distant country (Japan) ought to be a preferred partner.

Furthermore, it is incorrect to suggest that preferences towards the more significant partner are more likely to result in trade creation. Panagariya (1996) offers a very clear argument on this point. Thus consider the economy illustrated in Figure 3.3. Recall that trade preferences towards country B result in a loss of welfare for the liberalizing country A. Importantly, note that the losses (areas 1 + 2 + 3 + 4) are greater, the greater is the initial volume of trade. Thus, with changing internal terms of trade, the argument that greater initial volumes of trade result in larger increases in welfare is directly contradicted.

Finally, it should be noted that the argument concerning trade creation and larger initial volumes of trade is not robust—even when the internal terms of trade do not change. To see this, note that welfare gains with trade policy changes generally depend upon substitutions at the margin (changes in trade volumes—with partners and the rest of the world) as well as the initial levels of trade. This raises two issues. First, the relevant substitution elasticities do not generally depend on the initial volumes of trade. Differences in trade elasticities may therefore offset any differences in initial trade volumes. Second, and more importantly, significant trading partners generally also compete to a greater extent with the rest of the world than do less significant trading partners. For example, Japan is a more significant trading partner of the USA than is Ecuador, but it also competes in a wider range of markets and in larger volumes, say with EU suppliers, than Ecuador, which competes in a narrower and economically less significant set of markets. Importantly, while trade creation may be larger with significant partners, so may trade diversion (in the preceding example, this implies that trade preferences granted by the USA to Japan will divert larger volumes of trade—away from the EU—than trade preferences towards Ecuador). The empirical analysis of Krishna (2003) finds evidence of just these effects in US data. In an econometric investigation of US trade, aimed at estimating trade creation and trade diversion effects under (hypothetical) trade preferences towards a variety of countries, trade creation and trade diversion are found to be correlated in their magnitudes. Net welfare gains (i.e., gains from trade creation net of trade diversion losses) are therefore found to be wholly uncorrelated with distance. In sum, arguments for regionalism in trade preferences do not appear to have a robust basis in economic theory and are, thus far, not supported by empirical analysis.

IV. Necessarily Welfare Improving Preferential Trade Areas

The generally ambiguous welfare results with trade preferences provoked an important question in the economic literature relating to the design of necessarily welfare-improving PTAs. A classic result due to Kemp and Wan (1976) and Ohyama (1972) provides a welfare-improving solution for the case of CUs. Starting from a situation with an arbitrary structure of trade barriers, if two or more countries freeze their net external trade vector with the rest of the world through a set of common external tariffs and eliminate the barriers to internal trade (implying the formation of a CU), the welfare of the union as a whole necessarily improves (weakly) and that of the rest of the world does not fall. The logic behind the Kemp–Wan theorem is as follows. By fixing the combined, net extra-union trade vector of member countries at its pre-union level, non-member countries are guaranteed their original level of welfare. Since there is no diversion of trade in this case, the welfare of the member countries is also not adversely affected. The PTA thus constructed has a common internal price vector, implying further a common external tariff for member countries. The Kemp–Wan–Ohyama design, by freezing the external trade vector and thus eliminating trade diversion, offers a way to sidestep the complexities and ambiguities inherent in the analysis of PTAs.

The Kemp–Wan–Ohyama analysis of welfare-improving CUs does not extend easily to FTAs since member-specific tariff vectors in the case of FTAs imply that domestic prices will differ across member countries. Panagariya and Krishna (2002) have, nevertheless, recently provided a corresponding construction of necessarily welfare-improving FTAs in complete analogy with the Kemp–Wan CU that freezes the external trade vector of the area, with the essential difference that the trade vector of each member country with the rest of the world is frozen at the pre-FTA level. Since, in FTAs, different member countries impose different external tariffs, it is necessary to specify a set of rules of origin (ROO) to prevent a subversion of FTA tariffs by importing through the lower-tariff member country and directly trans-shipping goods to the higher-tariff country (which, if allowed, would bring the FTA arbitrarily close to a CU). The Panagariya–Krishna solution requires that all goods with any value added within the FTA are to be traded freely. Goods that enter the FTA as final goods are to be wholly prevented from trans-shipment by suitable ROO.

Theory thus suggests that ensuring welfare improvement requires that, along with elimination of internal barriers, external tariff vectors should eliminate trade diversion—member countries should continue to import the same amounts from the rest of the world as they did initially. In the next section, we examine how these theoretical prescriptions compare with WTO rules concerning the formation of PTAs.

V. PTA Implementation and the WTO

The preceding discussion of necessarily welfare-improving CUs and FTAs provided a precise description of the tariff vectors that ought to be implemented in these agreements. Specifically, internal barriers are to be completely eliminated and the external tariff vector in both cases (i.e., the CU or the FTA) should eliminate trade diversion—member countries should continue to import the same amounts from the rest of the world as they did initially. Can these tariffs be implemented in practice? And where do existing GATT/WTO provisions stand in relation to the theoretical specification?

Article XXIV of the GATT, which permits the formation of PTAs, also originally stipulated broadly that internal preferences needed to be complete (i.e., that internal barriers between the members were to be completely eliminated), and that external trade barriers were not to be more restrictive than initially. As we will discuss below, a number of questions arose in connection with GATT regulations regarding both internal and external tariffs—some having to do with their economic merit, others to do with implementation and possible abuse given the ambiguous and imprecise wording adopted in the original text of the GATT. As we will discuss further, while the more recent "Understanding on the Interpretation" of Article XXIV issued by the GATT in 1994 clarified some of these issues, other questions still remain.

Internal Barriers to Trade

On internal barriers to trade, two questions arise. The first relates to coverage: do GATT regulations require a removal of all internal barriers? The second relates to timing: how much time do countries have to comply with the rules? On the former issue, it should

be clarified that while the putative intent of the GATT was to require that internal barriers be eliminated completely, the actual text of the GATT only required that restrictions be eliminated on "substantially all trade." The ambiguous phrasing through the use
of the qualifier "substantially" opened up a number of possibilities for abuse. Whether
"substantial" should have been taken to imply a full 100 per cent or something smaller
was not clear and has not yet been clarified. In this context, it is worth noting that, for
a given level of external tariffs, member country welfare is not necessarily maximized
with zero internal barriers.[4] From a purely economic standpoint, given the level of
external tariffs, welfare may well be maximized by maintaining some particular level of
internal restrictions. It may therefore be potentially argued that the ambiguous phrasing permitting non-elimination of internal barriers allowed member countries to aim at
welfare-maximizing outcomes. This is, however, quite unlikely. Any retention of internal
barriers within PTAs is probably better explained by selective protectionist motivations
on the part of country governments. Separately, it may be imagined that non-member
countries would have an incentive to monitor and ensure the full dismantling of internal
trade barriers within PTAs. However, it is also quite likely that the welfare of countries
outside the union is higher when the discrimination against them is lower (i.e., when
internal preferences are less than complete). *Ex post*, the external monitoring incentive
is therefore minimal. On the question of the timing and the phasing out of internal barriers to trade, GATT rules, rather than requiring an immediate removal of internal barriers in a PTA, allowed for this to take place within a "reasonable length of time," once
again permitting substantial ambiguity in understanding and room for abuse.[5]

External Barriers to Trade

On external tariffs, the original GATT requirement was that external barriers were
not be more restrictive than initially. For FTAs, since countries retain individual tariff
vectors, this could be taken to imply that no tariff was to rise. For CUs, since a common external tariff was to be chosen, and initial tariffs on the same good likely varied across countries, the tariff vector would necessarily change for each country.
The expectation was then that the "general incidence" of trade barriers would not be
higher or more restrictive than before. Given the imprecise phrasing, there was once
more substantial ambiguity as to what is implied: should the common external tariff
equal the un-weighted mean of initial tariffs in the member countries? Should it be
the trade-weighted mean? Or something else? As Dam (1970), Bhagwati (1993), and

---

[4] It is important to keep in mind here that the elimination of internal tariffs maximizes the welfare of
member countries for a given level of external trade (as in Kemp–Wan) and not for a given level of the
external tariffs. With fixed tariffs, member country welfare may well be maximized with internal tariffs
that are non-zero.

[5] The more recent "Understanding on the Interpretation" of Article XXIV issued in 1994 clarifies that
the "reasonable length of time" should exceed 10 years in only "exceptional cases."

several others have noted, it is clear that Article XXIV's ambiguity in this regard left plenty of room for opportunistic (i.e., protectionist) behavior by member countries against non-members. The 1994 "Understanding on the Interpretation" of Article XXIV issued by the GATT provided substantial clarity on the issue of measurement and choice of the common external tariff—indicating that the GATT secretariat would compute weighted average tariff rates and duties collected in accordance with the methodology used in the assessment of tariff offers in the Uruguay Round of trade negotiations and examine trade flow and other data to arrive at suitable measures of non-tariff barriers. While this relieves, at least partially, the issue of measurement of external barriers and the comparison with barriers in place initially, the economic concern regarding trade diversion is not addressed. Clearly, leaving external barriers at their initial level and removing internal barriers does not eliminate trade diversion (as theoretically required in the Kemp–Wan and Panagariya–Krishna constructions of welfare improving PTAs). Indeed, with this configuration, trade diversion is practically guaranteed.

Having pointed to the deficiencies in existing GATT regulations in relation to the elimination of trade diversion, it may be noted that picking or designing tariff vectors *ex ante* that would ensure zero trade diversion, good by good, is a rather difficult task; the necessary measures of the exact sensitivity of external trade flows to external barriers of the CU or the FTA would be hard if not impossible to estimate accurately. So there is little prospect of identifying the exact trade diversion-eliminating Kemp–Wan tariff vector and implementing it in practice.[6] Nevertheless, designing other disciplines to minimize diversion is less difficult; one can certainly say that lowering external barriers simultaneously with the formation of a CU or an FTA is likely to lower the degree of trade diversion (by minimizing the substitution away from the goods supplied by the rest of the world to within-union goods). McMillan (1993) has suggested as a test of admissibility of any PTA the measurement (estimation) of whether that PTA will result in less trade with the rest of the world.[7] In a similar spirit, Bhagwati (1993) has suggested that the requirement of a simultaneous pro rata reduction of external trade barriers with the progressive elimination of internal barriers could replace the current requirements.

Rules of Origin

In FTAs, importers have a potential incentive to import goods into the bloc through the member country imposing the lowest tariff on that good and then to trans-ship that good into higher tariff member countries by availing themselves of the duty free

---

[6] See, however, the paper by Srinivasan (1997), which attempts to identify and characterize the Kemp–Wan tariff vector in the context of a particular economic model.

[7] Of course, the Kemp–Wan and Panagariya–Krishna schemes both require that the PTA trade exactly the same amount as before. A PTA that trades no less, as in the McMillan test, is not necessarily welfare improving, as Winters (1997) has argued. Since, in practice, at least some traded goods are not covered by the common external barriers of a CU, ROO are often used in CU as well.

treatment within the bloc. To prevent this circumvention of the independent tariffs desired by member countries, however, FTAs need to be supported by rules of origin (ROO), which specify the circumstances under which a good may be given duty free treatment within the union.

The discussion in the previous section has provided a welfare-theoretic basis for very simple ROO—goods that undergo any genuine value added transformation within the union must be allowed to move duty free within the union. For any good entirely produced outside the union, trade deflection is to be prevented by imposing effectively on direct imports and also any trans-shipped units, the external tariff that is chosen by the member country where the good is eventually consumed. ROO are more complex in practice, however. ROO are differently concerned (depending on the good) with the fractional content of the good that is required to be produced within the union for the good to qualify for duty free status.[8] More importantly, while the putative intention of ROO is simply to prevent deflection of trade, it has been argued that these rules have been used more flexibly as instruments of commercial policy (see, for instance, Krishna and Krueger (1995)).

That the opportunity to set ROO would be abused to achieve other ends should come as no surprise to anyone even moderately familiar with the political economy of trade policy determination. While one may hope for FTA rules to be designed by welfare-maximizing governments concerned with the enhancement of internal efficiency and equity towards non-members, in practice, the ROO are determined in intensely political contexts in which a variety of additional factors influence policy. Governments are under great pressure to deviate from the high path of choosing ROO simply to prevent trade deflection toward fixing rules that favor politically active and aggressive constituencies in the economy. Because, in an FTA, there are no internal tariffs and because external tariffs themselves cannot be raised to further disadvantage non-member countries, it has been argued that in order to please their constituencies and protect them from the economic changes that come about due to the entry into the FTA, governments manipulate ROO to protect both domestic suppliers of final and intermediate goods.[9] This may happen in the following ways:

- *Protection for final good suppliers*—Consider a final goods supplier in a member country facing greater competition from suppliers in other member countries due to the impending elimination of internal barriers of trade within the FTA. Consider further that this foreign competition uses in its production intermediates from outside of the FTA. Due to the political pressures brought to bear on the domestic government, whether it is from capitalists, affected voters, or displaced workers,

---

[8] See the papers by Estevadeordal and Suominen (2005) and Krishna (2003) for a detailed discussion of the different ways in which ROO are specified in practice.

[9] Of course, it may be just such protection that enables a government to generate enough political support for the FTA in the first place, as Duttagupta and Panagariya (2001) have argued.

that government will have reasons to negotiate intra-union content criteria severe enough to push those competing goods out of the duty free category. In so doing they will insulate the home country supplier from greater competition, but also undermine the intended competitive enhancement from joining an FTA.

- *Protection for intermediate goods suppliers*—Governments can negotiate for ROO that specify a high degree of domestic (i.e., within-bloc) content, significantly diverting demand from goods produced with foreign intermediates to goods produced using intermediates from within the FTA.

However this use of ROO undermines the two key rules imposed by the WTO on its members for FTA formation. While complete internal liberalization is sought by the WTO, this is negated by the selective use of ROO. Further, while the WTO requires that trade barriers against non-members not be raised by FTA members, the use of stringent ROO would divert imports of intermediates away from non-member exporters even if external tariffs are maintained at the same level as before.[10]

To what extent ROO are used to prevent trade deflection and to what extent they are politically motivated commercial policy instruments is ultimately an empirical question. While empirical research in this area is still in its infancy, Cadot, Estevadeordal, and Suwa-Eisenmann (2003) have recently provided some interesting results. They examine directly the possible use of ROO to achieve protection for final goods producers and the creation of a captive market for intra-union suppliers of intermediate goods, as we have discussed above. Specifically, they measure the effects of ROO on Mexican imports to the US market, to find that ROO are a large enough negative influence on intra-union trade flows as to offset the tariff preferences granted by the trade agreement. Further, the creation of a protected market for intermediate goods producers also appears to be a key determinant of the ROO chosen.

Non-Trade Issues in Preferential Integration

Some proponents of preferential integration have argued (see, for instance, Lawrence (1996)) that PTAs achieve "deep" integration. That is, rather than simply achieving trade liberalization, as in multilateral liberalization contexts, PTAs involve "deep" integration through coordination, or harmonization, of other non-trade policies such as competition policies, environmental policies, labor standards, product standards, and investment codes. It is further argued that such harmonization of policies will be efficiency enhancing and beneficial to member countries.

The proposition that harmonization of policies is uniformly beneficial to all member countries in a PTA has been met with skepticism by others (see, for instance, Panagariya

---

[10] Ironically, however, highly severe ROO may result in greater imports from the rest of the world than before owing to the preference of importers to pay the external tariff rather than comply with demanding domestic content standards.

(1999)), who note that there are good reasons for diversity in domestic policies and standards and that harmonization is not an automatically welfare-enhancing policy. Thus, for instance, the choice of optimal pollution levels and labor standards depends generally on the income level. While every country may prefer lower pollution, countries may reasonably disagree on what the optimal pollution levels are, what costs they should bear to lower pollution, and where these efforts are best directed (for instance, developed countries may prefer to lower water pollution, while air pollution may be a greater concern for richer countries). Similarly, countries may disagree on minimum wage levels, worker safety issues, and the merits of permitting voluntary child labor. Thus, while harmonization may indeed bring some forms of efficiency enhancement, it is far from clear that such harmonization of policies will be beneficial overall or that any benefits will accrue uniformly to all the member countries. A practical concern is that under the guise of "deep integration" the larger and more powerful countries in a PTA negotiation may be able to extract concessions not merely in trade but in other "non-trade" matters as well.

VI. Preferential Trade Agreements and the Multilateral Trade System

Will PTAs expand successively to eventually include all trading nations? Will preferential liberalization prove a quicker and more efficient way of getting to global free trade than a multilateral process?

These questions concerning the interaction between preferential trade liberalization and the multilateral trading system are important and complex, involving economic considerations and complex political factors as well. Recently, several attempts have been made in the economic literature to understand the phenomenon of preferential trade and its interaction with the multilateral trading system—taking into account the domestic determinants (political and economic) of trade policy.

Grossman and Helpman (1995) and Krishna (1998) both model the influence of powerful producers in decision making over a country's entry into a PTA, and while the models and analytic frameworks differ in detail, they come to a similar and striking conclusion, that PTAs that divert trade are more likely to win internal political support. This is so because governments must respond to conflicting pressures from their exporting sectors, which gain from lower trade barriers in the partner, and their import-competing sectors, which suffer from lower trade barriers at home, when deciding on whether to form or enter a PTA. As Krishna (1998) argues, trade diversion effectively shifts the burden of the gain to member country exporters from member country import-competing sectors and onto non-member producers, who have little political clout inside the member countries. Krishna (1998) also argues that such PTAs will lower the incentives for any subsequent multilateral liberalization—producers in trade diverting PTAs may oppose multilateral reform since this would take away the gains from benefits of preferential access that they enjoyed in the PTA that diverted trade to them. Under some circumstances, the incentive for further multilateral liberalization is completely eliminated.

Levy (1997) models trade policy as being determined by majority voting and where income distributional changes brought about by trade lead to different degrees of support (or opposition) by different members of society. Here too, bilateral agreements could preclude otherwise feasible multilateral liberalization if crucial voters (or more generally voting blocs) enjoyed a greater level of welfare under the bilateral agreement than they would under multilateral free trade.

Both sets of papers discussed above argue that bilateral agreements could impede progress towards multilateral free trade and thus undermine the multilateral trade system. Baldwin (1995), on the other hand, argues that PTA expansion could have "domino" effects—increasing the size of a bloc increases the incentive for others to join it (as they then gain preferential access to increasingly large markets).

Open Membership Rules

How might the current momentum for preferential trade agreements be translated into the goal of global free trade? One proposal that has been discussed in the literature is for the WTO to mandate that PTAs be built on the principle of open membership; any country that is willing to accept the rules of a given trade bloc should be allowed to join that bloc.

How might open membership rules alter the effects of PTAs? In this connection, Yi (1996), using advances in endogenous coalition theory, has compared theoretical outcomes with PTAs under two regimes, "open" membership and "unanimous" membership. Under open membership rules, any country interested in joining an existing PTA is able to do so while under unanimous membership, a new country may join only if all existing members agree to admit the new member. The differences in outcomes are striking. Global free trade is an equilibrium outcome with open membership rules, but this generally does not obtain under unanimous membership. Intuitively, while some within-union members may have reasons not to expand membership (for reasons similar to those we have discussed before), outsiders who have had trade diverted away from them will generally be tempted to join, especially as a union expands and yet greater trade is diverted away from them. While unanimous membership rules will stop the expansion of the bloc well before global free trade is reached, open membership will accelerate the movement to global free trade. While these results have been rigorously demonstrated only in the context of the specific theoretical structure assumed by Yi (1996), they have strong intuitive appeal. That open membership rules will bring us closer to global free trade can also be seen to hold in a variety of different formulations of the problem. Baldwin (1995), demonstrates how PTAs create a "domino" effect, with their expansion inducing ever more countries to join. In his framework, as in Krishna (1998), the binding constraint that prevents PTAs from expanding until global free trade is achieved is the incentive of member countries to keep non-members out.

A popular contention in support of PTAs has been that, by circumventing the multilateral process that requires consensus among large numbers of countries, they offer the opportunity of quick liberalization. If this indeed were the true motivation for bilateral agreements between countries, then open membership rules clearly allow the opportunity for even greater liberalization while binding the world trading system closer to the valued principle of non-discrimination. If membership in a PTA is left open, non-members that suffer from trade being diverted away from them have the opportunity to reverse or reduce these losses by entering the PTA themselves. Since non-members that face the greatest costs from the original preferences are the ones most likely to join, the system evolves in a less discriminatory fashion.

Open membership thus appears to be a valuable complement to the preferential integration process. Nevertheless, open membership in combination with preferential trade integration does not imply that discrimination is eliminated—clearly outsiders at any point in time will still face discriminatory trade barriers. Nor does open membership guarantee a faster path to global free trade than the multilateral process. Finally, as a practical matter, it may be noted that no trade bloc in existence has adopted such liberal membership policies. Entry into existing trade blocs is a slow and carefully negotiated process. As Panagariya (1999) notes "The Canada-U.S. Free Trade Agreement was concluded almost a decade ago and, taking into account NAFTA, its membership has grown to only three so far."

VII. Conclusions

PTAs, while conceived originally as minor exceptions to the GATT's central principle of non-discrimination, and only to be permitted under strict conditions, now number in the hundreds. The resulting jumble of trade preferences threatens to skew in highly inefficient ways the allocation of productive resources internationally, and to deeply undermine the non-discriminatory architecture of the GATT that has been responsible for so much of post-war trade liberalization.

References

Baldwin, R. (1995), 'A Domino Theory of Regionalism' In Baldwin, R., Haaparanta, P., and Kiander, J. (eds.) *Expanding Membership of the European Union*, Cambridge: Cambridge University Press.

Bhagwati, J. (1993), 'Regionalism and Multilateralism: An Overview' In deMelo, J., and Panagariya, A. (eds.), *New Dimensions in Regional Integration*, Cambridge: Cambridge University Press.

Cadot, O., Estevadeordal, A., and Suwa-Eisenmann, A. (2003), 'Rules of Origin as Export Subsidies' Mimeo.

Chang, W., and Winters, A. (2002), 'How Regional Trade Blocs Affect Excluded Countries: The Price Effects of MERCOSUR' *American Economic Review*, 92: 889–904.

Dam, K. (1970), *The GATT: Law and International Economic Organization*, Chicago: University of Chicago Press.

Duttagupta, R., and Panagariya, A. (2001), 'Free Trade Areas and Rules of Origin: Economics and Politics' Mimeo.

Estevadeordal, A., and Suominen, K. (2005), Rules of Origin in Preferential Trade Arrangements, *Economia*, 5(2): 63–103.

Grossman, G., and Helpman, E. (1995), 'The Politics of Free Trade Agreements' *American Economic Review*, 85(4): 667–90

Kemp, M., and Wan, H. (1976), 'An Elementary Proposition Concerning the Formation Of Customs Unions' *Journal of International Economics*, 6: 95–97.

Krishna., P. (1998), 'Regionalism and Multilateralism: A Political Economy Approach' *Quarterly Journal of Economics*, 113(1): 227–51.

Krishna, P. (2003), 'Are Regional Trading Partners Natural?' *Journal of Political Economy*, 111(1): 202–26.

Krishna, P. (2005), *Trade Blocs: Economics and Politics*, New York: Cambridge University Press

Krishna, K., and Krueger, A. (1995), 'Implementing Free Trade Agreements: Rules of Origin and Hidden Protection' in Deardorff, Levinsohn and Stern (eds.) *New Directions in Trade Theory*, Ann Arbor: University of Michigan Press.

Krugman, P. (1991), 'The Move To Free Trade Zones' In *Policy Implications of Trade and Currency Zones*, Kansas City: Federal Reserve Bank of Kansas City, 7–41.

Lawrence, R. (1996), *Regionalism, Multilateralism and Deeper Integration*, Washington D.C.: Brookings Institution.

Levy, P. (1997), 'A Political Economic Analysis of Free Trade Agreements' *American Economic Review*, 87(4): 506–19.

McMillan, J. (1993), 'Does Regional Integration Foster Open Trade? Economic Theory and GATT's Article XXIV' in Anderson and Blackhurst (eds.) *Regional Integration and the Global Trading System*, New York: St. Martin's Press.

Mundell, R. (1964). 'Tariff Preferences and the Terms of Trade' *Manchester School of Economic Studies*, 32(1):1–13.

Ohyama, M. (1972), 'Trade and Welfare in General Equilibrium' *Keio Economic Studies*, 9: 37–73.

Panagariya, A. (1996), 'The Free Trade Area of the Americas: Good for Latin America?' *World Economy*, 19(5): 485–515.

Panagariya, A. (1997), 'Preferential Trading and the Myth of Natural Trading Partners' *Japan and the World Economy*, 9(4): 471–89.

Panagariya, A. (1999), 'The Regionalism Debate: An Overview' *The World Economy*, 22(4):455–76.

Panagariya, A. (2000), 'Preferential Trade Liberalization: The Traditional Theory and New Developments' *Journal of Economic Literature*, 38: 287–331.

Panagariya, A., and Krishna, P. (2002), 'On the Existence of Necessarily Welfare Improving Free Trade Areas' *Journal of International Economics*, 57(2): 353–67.

Schiff, M., and Winters, A. (2003), *Regional Integration and Development*, World Bank, Oxford: Oxford University Press.

Srinivasan, T.N. (1997), 'Common External Tariffs of a Customs Union: The Case of Identical Cobb Douglas Tastes' *Japan and the World Economy*, 9(4): 447–65.

Summers, L. (1991), 'Regionalism And The World Trading System' In *Policy Implications of Trade and Currency Zones*, Kansas City: Federal Reserve Bank of Kansas City.

Viner, J. (1950), *The Customs Unions Issue*, New York: Carnegie Endowment for International Peace.

Winters, A. (1997), 'Regionalism and the Rest of the World: The Irrelevance of the Kemp-Wan Theorem' *Oxford Economic Papers*, 49(2): 228–34.

Wonnacott, P., and Lutz, M. (1987), 'Is There A Case For Free Trade Areas?' In Jeffrey Schott (ed.) *Free Trade Areas and US Trade Policy*, Washington D.C.: Institute for International Economics.

Yi, S. (1996), 'Endogenous Formation of Customs Unions under Imperfect Competition: Open Regionalism is Good' *Journal of International Economics*, 41(1–2): 153–77.

Yeats, A. (1998), 'Does MERCOSUR's Trade Performance Raise Concerns about the Effects of Regional Trade Arrangements?' *The World Bank Economic Review*, 12: 1–28.

PART II

INTERNATIONAL TRADE THEORY

CHAPTER 4

COMPARATIVE ADVANTAGE: THE RICARDIAN AND HECKSCHER–OHLIN THEORIES

ARVIND PANAGARIYA[*]

God did not bestow all products upon all parts of the earth, but distributed His gifts over different regions, to the end that men might cultivate a social relationship because one would have need of the help of another. And so He called commerce into being, that all men might be able to have common enjoyment of the fruits of earth, no matter where produced.

(Libanius in *Orations* (III) in the 4th century)[1]

I. ADAM SMITH: FROM "MERCANTILE SYSTEM" TO FREE TRADE

ADAM SMITH (1776) called the system of political economy that dominated Europe during the sixteenth, seventeenth, and eighteenth centuries the "mercantile system."[2] The central premise underlying this system was that the wealth of a nation, like that of individuals, was synonymous with its stock of gold. This premise had two immediate implications. First, a country could get richer by exporting more than it imported since it would then be a net recipient of gold. And second, international trade was a zero-sum game in which the benefits of the recipient of gold were exactly offset by the losses of the sender.

---

[*] The author is Professor of Economics and Jagdish Bhagwati Professor of Indian Political Economy at Columbia University.

[1] Quoted in Irwin (1996) who, in turn, cites Grotius ([1625] 1925: 199) as the source.

[2] In the last chapter of Book IV, he briefly contrasts the mercantile system with the "Agricultural Systems" of Political Economy that represent the produce of land as the principal source of the revenue and wealth of a country.

An obvious question that these implications raise is: why did countries that expected to run a trade deficit and therefore lose gold chose to trade at all? The answer is that to some degree a movement towards autarky—a situation of no trade—did happen when countries faced a trade deficit. A country would impose all kinds of restrictions on imports from another country with which it had a bilateral trade deficit. It also imposed restrictions on the imports of commodities that it could domestically produce.[3] Countries chose not to adopt a complete state of autarky partly in recognition of the fact that this was a physically impossible proposition. Despite restraints imposed by the governments, goods and gold would flow in and out of the country. Additionally, countries wanted to trade with the countries with which they could generate a surplus so as to accumulate gold.

The mercantile system favored policies that seemingly helped to maximize exports and minimize imports.[4] It encouraged duty drawback on imported goods used in exports and also exemption from local taxes on the goods destined to foreign markets. It also viewed favorably positive import subsidies on inputs used in exports. But imports for domestic consumption were discouraged, especially when similar goods were domestically produced. On the export side, export subsidies were seen favorably. The system also encouraged export restrictions on inputs so that the producers of final goods could buy them cheaply to generate high value added exports.

Smith provided a unified and systematic critique of the mercantile system and went on to expound his free trade doctrine. In the *Wealth of Nations*, which was divided into Books I–V, he devoted almost the entirety of Book IV to this task.[5] The first element in his critique was that a nation's wealth is measured, not by gold, but by the value of the annual produce of the country. He argued that the restrictions on and stimuli to trade advocated by the mercantile system must be judged by their impact on the value of this produce. He then reasoned that these interventions necessarily lowered rather than raised the value of the domestic produce. To quote him,

> What is prudence in the conduct of every private family can scarce be folly in that of a great kingdom. If a foreign country can supply us with a commodity cheaper than we ourselves can make it, better buy it of them with some sort of the produce of our own industry employed in a way in which we have some advantage.... According to the supposition, that commodity could be purchased from foreign countries cheaper than it can be made at home. It could, therefore, have been purchased with a part only of the price of the commodities, which the industry employed by an equal capital would have produced at home, had it been left to follow its natural course. The industry of the country, therefore, is thus turned away from a more to a less advantageous employment, and the

[3] See Smith (1776: 396).

[4] I say "seemingly" because we now know that there is no guarantee that these policies would necessarily give rise to a surplus in the balance of trade when all effects are taken into account.

[5] Out of nine chapters in Book IV, only Chapter IX is devoted to the Agricultural System.

exchangeable value of its annual produce, instead of being increased, according to the intention of the lawgiver, must necessarily be diminished by every such regulation. (Smith 1776: Vol. I, p. 401–2)

Later in Book IV, Smith attacked the mercantile system from a slightly different angle. He argued that consumption is the sole goal of all production. Therefore, producer interests should be promoted only so far as they also serve the interests of consumers. He then went on to reason, "In the restraints upon importation of all foreign commodities which can come into competition with those of our own growth or manufacture, the interest of the home consumer is evidently sacrificed to that of the producer" (Smith 1776: Vol. II, p. 155). Regarding export subsidies, he stated, "It is altogether for the benefit of the producer that bounties are granted upon the exportation of some of his production. The home consumer is obliged to pay, first, the tax which is necessary for paying the bounty, and secondly, the still greater tax which necessarily arises from the enhancement of the price of the commodity in the home market" (Smith 1776: p. 155).

   In concluding the critique, Smith came down particularly hard on manufacturers who received the greatest protection at the cost of all others. It is worthwhile here to quote the concluding paragraph of his Chapter VIII in Book IV in its entirety:

   It cannot be very difficult to determine who have been the contrivers of this whole mercantile system; not the consumers, we may believe, whose interests have been entirely neglected; but the producers, whose interest has been so carefully attended to; and among the latter class our merchants and manufacturers have been by far the principal architects. In the mercantile regulations, which have been taken notice of in this chapter, the interest of our manufacturers has been most peculiarly attended to; and the interest, not so much of consumers, as that of some other producers, has been sacrificed to it. (Smith 1776: 156)

II. THE RICARDIAN THEORY OF COMPARATIVE ADVANTAGE

Although Smith (1776) provided a decisive critique of the mercantile system, his argument fell far short of providing a well-articulated theory of international trade. Such a theory required demonstrating that when two or more countries engaged in free trade, each of them is at least as well off in its presence as in its absence. In particular, it was not clear from Smith's discussion how a country that required more resources (say, labor) per unit of output of every commodity than its competitors abroad would successfully compete against the latter in at least some commodity. The credit for this demonstration is given to David Ricardo (1817) via the famous principle of comparative advantage, although others contributed to it around the same time as well.[6] In the following, I offer a detailed exposition of this principle using the modern tools of trade theory. I will develop these tools from the ground up as we proceed.

Because the principle of comparative advantage is subtle, we begin with a deliberately simple example. We will add many real world complications later and show that the principle and its underlying logic are robust. An interesting anecdote puts this point in perspective. Mathematician, Stanislaw Ulam, once teased economics Nobel Laureate, Paul Samuelson, by asking whether there was *any* idea in economics that was unobvious and yet universally true. Samuelson had to think hard but in the end opted for the principle of comparative advantage as the answer. He reasoned that being based on a mathematical relationship, the principle easily passes the test of universal validity. And centuries of assertions by politicians, journalists, and policy analysts directly contradicting the principle testify to its unobvious nature.

Imagine a simple world consisting of just two countries called Home Country (HC) and Foreign Country (FC). Suppose further that there are only two commodities called Corn (C) and Shirt (S), which can be produced using only one factor of production, labor.[7] All Shirts are identical and all Corn is homogeneous in all respects. Table 4.2 summarizes the technology (labor–output ratios) of production for each C and S available in HC and FC. A key feature of the Ricardian theory is that it assumes different technologies across countries for the same commodity. Indeed, this is the main feature distinguishing the two countries, though they may also differ in size. Table 4.2 also shows the total supply of labor available in each country. Armed with this example, we can proceed to distinguish between absolute and comparative advantage, derive the efficient pattern of specialization, and demonstrate the gains from trade to both countries.

Comparative Advantage, Specialization, and Efficiency

According to Table 4.2, the absolute labor costs per unit are lower in HC for both goods: 2 < 12 and 4 < 6. We refer to this as stating that the HC has an *absolute* advantage in the production of both goods. But more subtly, labor cost per unit of C *relative* to that of S is lower in HC than FC: 2/12 < 4/6. We refer to this as stating that HC has a

---

[6] As Irwin (1996: 90–91) discusses in detail, Ricardo's famous example of the exchange of wine and cloth between England and Portugal, which spanned just three paragraphs, was "awkwardly placed" in chapter 7 of his book and there is some doubt as to whether he truly understood it himself. Moreover, Robert Torrens (1815) had anticipated him although he did not provide a fully-fledged example. According to Irwin, James Mill (1821) provided a much clearer statement of the principle of comparative advantage underlying Ricardo's example.

[7] If the example already appears unrealistic, you can assume land is also required but it is available in unlimited quantity. This ensures that land is freely available and the costs depend only on labor, which is scarce. You may think of Shirt production as requiring the production of cotton, its conversion into thread, the conversion of thread into fabric, and of fabric into shirt. In calculating the labor requirement for Shirt, we include the requirements for each of these stages of production.

comparative advantage in the production of C. Alternatively stated, per unit cost of S relative to C is lower in FC than HC: 6/4 < 12/2. Therefore, using the terminology just introduced, we can say FC has a comparative advantage in S. The obvious but important point is that as long as the *ratio* of technology coefficients across countries is different for the two commodities, each country will necessarily have a comparative advantage in one commodity. We will show that this feature of technology is sufficient to establish the gains from trade to each country. In the one exceptional case in which the ratio of the technology coefficients across countries is the same in the two commodities, comparative advantage is undefined and trade does not generate strictly positive benefits. But it also does not hurt either country.

To demonstrate these results most simply, let us begin by assuming that each country initially produces the basket that it consumes. That is to say, each country is initially in autarky (i.e., a state of no trade). Now let each country produce more of the good in which it has a comparative advantage as just defined. This would amount to letting HC produce more of C and FC more of S. Specifically, suppose we let HC produce 1 extra unit of C, moving 2 units of labor from S to C. This entails reducing the production of S by a ½ unit (see Table 4.3).

To ensure that the worldwide output of S does not fall, let FC produce an extra ½ unit of this good. This requires moving three workers from C to S in FC, reducing the output of C by a ¼ unit. The net effect of these changes on world output is a ¾ extra unit of C with no less of S. We have increased the world output using the same technology and resources as before. We can now divide the extra output of C between HC and FC and make them both better off relative to autarky.

How were we able to increase the world output using the same technology and resources as before? The answer is improved allocation of the world's resources. In HC, we sacrifice only a ½ unit of S to produce 1 extra unit of C (in the economist's jargon,

Table 4.1 Technology and factor endowments

Country	Labor per unit of		Total Labor
	Corn (C)	Shirt (S)	
Home Country (HC)	2	4	100
Foreign Country (FC)	12	6	300

Table 4.2 Specialization leading to increased world output

Country	Change in the output of	
	C	S
HC	+1	-1/2
FC	-1/4	+1/2
World	+3/4	0

the *opportunity cost* of producing an extra unit of C in HC is a ½ unit of S). In FC, the opportunity cost of an extra unit of C is 2 units of S. Worldwide efficiency dictates that we let HC produce most or all of the world supply of C. Symmetrically, we must sacrifice 2 units of C to produce an extra unit of S in HC. In FC, the required sacrifice is only a ½ unit of C. We should let FC produce most or all of S. As we move more and more of the production of C to HC and of S to FC, we improve the allocation of the world's resources. That is to say, as each country specializes towards its good of comparative advantage, world efficiency improves. The world production expands and creates the potential for each country to benefit from it.

This analysis assumes no international mobility of labor. It is sometimes asserted that the principle of comparative advantage breaks down in the face of such international mobility of the factors of production. This is an erroneous conclusion, as demonstrated in detail in Box 4.1.

The Production Possibilities Frontier

At this point, we may introduce a geometrical tool of analysis called the Production Possibilities Frontier (PPF). Holding the technology and factor endowments fixed, the PPF shows the maximum quantity of a good the country can produce for each given quantity of the other good. The PPF represents the country's maximum production capacity, taking technology and factor endowments as given. A change in either technology or factor endowments would shift the PPF.

Given only one factor of production and the constant labor–output ratios in our model, the construction of the PPF is relatively simple. In Figure 4.1, we measure the quantity of C (Q_C) produced in HC on the horizontal axis and of S (Q_S) on the vertical axis. From Table 4.2, HC has 100 units of labor. If it were to produce 0 units of C thereby employing the entire labor force in S, it could produce a maximum of 25 units of S. We

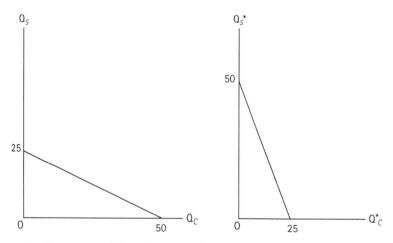

FIGURE 4.1 Production possibilities frontiers of HC and FC

Box 4.1 International Labor Mobility, Comparative Advantages, and the Gains from Trade

In an influential op-ed in the *New York Times*, Charles Schumer and Paul Craig Roberts (2003) asserted that, in a world with factor mobility, the principle of comparative advantage breaks down. The resulting trade somehow turns into a zero-sum activity with some countries gaining at the expense of the others. But this is not correct.

For one thing, factor mobility had existed even when Ricardo (1817) and Mill (1821) wrote about comparative advantage. The phenomenon became pervasive during the First Globalization extending from 1870 to World War I. It is implausible that international factor mobility escaped the attention of Ricardo and all others who wrote about the principle of comparative advantage subsequently!

But more importantly, it is also readily shown that the gains from trade do not depend on the absence of factor mobility. We can demonstrate this in the Ricardian model. Thus, consider Table 4.1, which offers three possible examples assuming the familiar Ricardian structure of two goods (X and Y), two countries (A and B), and one factor of production (labor).

Table 4.3 Comparative advantage and factor mobility

Country	Output per person year					
	Example 1		Example 2		Example 3	
	X	Y	X	Y	X	Y
A	8	4	4	2	4	2
B	2	2	2	4	2	1

In Example 1, A has an absolute advantage in both goods but comparative advantage in X. Denoting by FT and NT the level of welfare under free trade and no trade (autarky), respectively, we know from the conventional Ricardian theory that FT ≥ NT for each country with strict inequality applying to at least one country. In the trading equilibrium, real wages are higher in A so that allowing labor to move internationally results in the workers migrating from B to A. If only a part of B's labor force is allowed to migrate, the inequality FT ≥ NT still holds for the nationals of both countries at the post-migration labor endowments. If all labor in B moves to A, the gains-from-trade issue is of course rendered irrelevant.

In Example 2, A has an absolute advantage in X and B in Y. Consequently, A also has a comparative advantage in X and B in Y so that FT ≥ NT continues to apply. In this case, it is possible for trade to equalize real wages, eliminating the incentive to migrate. If the real wages remain different, however, labor mobility will still be partial and the gains from trade will characterize the trade equilibrium under international factor mobility.

In Example 3, A has an absolute advantage in both goods but comparative advantage in none. With the opportunity costs being the same in A and B, there is no scope for trade so that opening to trade is neither beneficial nor harmful: we then have FT = NT. The real wages being higher in A than B, however, labor in B has an incentive to migrate to A. If such migration is permitted, it benefits migrants without hurting the workers in A. But we continue to have FT = NT at the post-migration labor endowments.

Source: Bhagwati, Panagariya, and Srinivasan (2004).

mark this point on the vertical axis of the left-hand panel in Figure 4.1. Conversely, if the country chose to produce none of S and deployed all its labor force in C, it could produce a maximum of 50 units of C. This point is shown on the horizontal axis of the left-hand panel in Figure 4.1. If the country allocates the labor force partially to S and partially to C, possible output combinations lie on the line joining the two extreme points we just derived. The downward sloping solid line in the left-hand panel of Figure 4.1 shows these combinations and represents the PPF of HC.

Two properties of the PPF may be noted. First, it is negatively sloped (i.e., it slopes down rather than up). This is because at any point in time, the economy has limited resources. With all resources fully employed as is true along the PPF, if it wants to produce more of one good, it must sacrifice the output of the other good. More resources for one sector can only come from the other sector. This will not be true, for example, if part of the labor force was unemployed. But in that case, we would be *inside* and not *on* the PPF. Second, the slope of the PPF is ½. This number should be familiar: it is what we had called the opportunity cost of C in terms of S. The slope of the PPF tells us the amount of S (the good on the vertical axis) we must give up to produce one extra unit of C (the good on the horizontal axis).

We can construct the PPF of FC similarly. The downward sloping solid line in the right-hand panel in Figure 4.1 represents this PPF. We distinguish the variables associated with the FC by an asterisk with Q_S^* and Q_C^* denoting the quantities of S and C produced in FC. The slope of FC's PPF is 2, indicating that the opportunity cost of producing C is 2 units of S in FC.

The Autarky Equilibrium under Perfect Competition

Our earlier demonstration of improved world efficiency as a result of specialization according to comparative advantage was a *possibility* result: if specialization along comparative advantage lines can be effected, world efficiency can be improved and both countries made better off. The real question is how to bring about such specialization. If there was a well-functioning centrally-planned global government, it could accomplish such specialization by fiat. But the world economy is run not by a global government but by markets. How can we be sure that the market will bring about specialization in the right direction (i.e., HC in C and FC in S rather than the opposite)? We next turn to this important question and demonstrate that as long as perfect competition prevails in all markets, free trade leads to the efficient outcome.

Let us begin by first introducing the autarky equilibrium (i.e., the equilibrium with no international trade) under perfect competition. Denote the wage in HC in the local currency by w. Then the average and marginal cost of production of C is 2w and that of S, 4w. Perfect competition leads to price being equated to the marginal cost. Therefore, we have

$$P_C = 2w, P_S = 4w, \quad \text{and} \quad P_C/P_S = \frac{1}{2} \tag{4.1}$$

Thus, the *relative* price of C in terms of S equals the opportunity cost of production of C. Analogously, for FC, we have

$$P_{C^*} = 12w^*, P_{S^*} = 6w^*, \quad \text{and} \quad P_{C^*}/P_{S^*} = 2 \tag{4.2}$$

These equations tell us the relative prices of C in terms of S in HC and FC in the autarky equilibrium. Unsurprisingly, the relative price of C is lower in HC despite the lower *absolute* productivity of its labor in C, reflecting the fact that it is comparative rather than absolute advantage that determines relative prices. Although we will conduct much of the analysis in this chapter in terms of relative prices, I will explain below how we could translate the prices in terms of a common currency.

Given the limited information, this is as far as we can go. In particular, to determine the precise production and consumption baskets, we must specify the demand conditions. We will return to this issue below. Presently, we proceed to illustrate the gains from trade in the simplest possible manner.

The Free Trade Equilibrium

Let us now allow the two countries to trade freely. Let the producers sell where they find the highest price and consumers buy where they find the lowest price. Since transport costs only add to complication but offer no extra insight, assume them to be zero. Focus on the market for C. Consumers in both countries want to buy C in HC and producers in both countries want to sell C in FC. This raises the price of C in HC and lowers it in FC. The international price settles somewhere between the two autarky prices. Letting P_C^I/P_W^I denote the international relative price of C, we have $\frac{1}{2} \leq P_C^I/P_S^I \leq 2$ with strict inequality on at least one of the two sides.

Without taking into account the demand conditions, we cannot say precisely where the international price ratio would settle. I will return to this issue below. Here, let us proceed in the simplest terms possible by *assuming* that the price ratio settles at 1, that is, $P_C^I/P_S^I = 1$.

In HC, the opportunity cost of producing C is a ½ unit of S while the international price of C is 1 unit of S. Given this difference, all resources in HC move into producing C. HC produces 50 units of C. Given $P_C^I/P_S^I = 1$, it can exchange these 50 units along a line with slope 1. This line is shown by the dotted line in the left-hand panel of Figure 4.2 and represents the economy's "consumption possibilities curve." Precisely where the country consumes along this line depends on the demand conditions (not specified so far) but it is clear that its opportunities to consume are better than under autarky.

In FC, the opportunity cost of C is 2 units of S. With the international price of C being only 1 unit of S, no producer finds it profitable to produce C there. FC specializes completely in S and produces 50 units of it. It can exchange these 50 units of S along a line with slope equaling 1. Therefore, the dotted line in Figure 4.2 shows the consumption possibilities curve of FC. As long as the international price ratio is strictly between the two autarky price ratios, both countries positively benefit from trade.

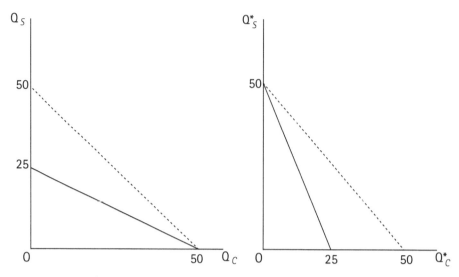

FIGURE 4.2 Gains from trade to both HC and FC

The reader can by now see that the *distribution* of the gains from trade between HC and FC depends on the precise location of the international price ratio or what we may call the terms of trade. The closer the terms of trade to HC's autarky price the smaller the gains to HC and the larger the gains to FC. In one special but important case, if the international price ratio coincides with the autarky price of HC, all the gains accrue to FC. The larger is HC and the smaller is FC, the greater the likelihood of this case. Thus, contrary to common assertions by politicians and confused policy analysts, the smaller a country relative to the rest of the world, the more it stands to benefit from trade.

Real Wages

The gains from trade in the Ricardian model can be seen not just in terms of increased consumption possibilities but also increased real wages. Under autarky, the relationship between the wages and goods prices are given by equations (4.1) and (4.2). A slight rearrangement allows us to write these equations as

$$w/P_C = 1/2, \qquad w/P_S = 1/4 \tag{4.1'}$$
$$w^*/P_C^* = 1/12, \qquad w^*/P_S^* = 1/6 \tag{4.2'}$$

The first equality in these equations gives the wage under autarky in terms of C and the second in terms of S. As expected, the real wages are determined entirely by productivity. For example, 2 units of labor per unit of C are equivalent to a productivity of a ½ unit of C per unit of labor. Hence the real wage in terms of C in HC turns out to be exactly ½. The information from equations (4.1') and (4.2') is summarized in Table 4.4 in the rows marked "HC: Autarky" and FC: Autarky," respectively. As one would expect, given its absolutely higher productivity in each commodity, HC also enjoys a higher real wage in terms of each commodity relative to FC.

The next important question concerns the real wage under free trade. A key distinguishing feature of the free trade equilibrium is that it is characterized by complete specialization. Taking HC first, it produces only C in the free trade equilibrium. Therefore, denoting the HC wage under free trade by w, we now have the marginal cost-pricing condition with respect to C only:

$$P_C^I = 2w \tag{4.3}$$

Analogously, FC only produces S so that the marginal cost-pricing there only yields,

$$P_S^I = 6w^* \tag{4.4}$$

From (4.3), the wage in HC in terms of C, the good it produces and exports, remains ½ as under autarky. Likewise, the wage in FC in terms of S, the good it produces and exports, remains 1/6 as under autarky. This information is incorporated into Table 4.4.

The story is different in each country with respect to the wage in terms of the import good, however. Continuing to assume $P_C^I/P_S^I = 1$ as the international price ratio under free trade, we can combine this price equation with (4.3) to obtain $w/P_S^I = ½$ and with (4.4) to obtain $w^*/P_C^I = 1/6$. Therefore, I record a real wage of a ½ in terms of S in HC and 1/6 in terms of C in FC in Table 4.4. A comparison of wages in Table 4.4 shows that the workers in each country enjoy a real wage under free trade that is equal to that under autarky in terms of the export good and strictly higher in terms of the import good. As long as they spend a part of their wage on the import good, they are necessarily better off under free trade than under autarky.

The final point we may note is that although each country is able to offer higher real wages to its workers under free trade than autarky, given its higher productivity, HC continues to enjoy higher real wages than FC. Comparing the wages between HC and

Table 4.4 Real wages under autarky and free trade

Country	Real wages in terms of	
	Corn (C)	Shirt (S)
HC: Autarky	1/2	1/4
HC: Free Trade	1/2	1/2
FC: Autarky	1/12	1/6
FC: Free Trade	1/6	1/6

FC under free trade, we see that their ratio is $(1/2)/(1/6) = 3$. That is to say, the wage in HC is three times that in FC.

In summarizing the results in Table 4.4, we can make three observations. First, low absolute productivity is not a barrier to reaping the benefits from trade. The lower wage in FC (which is nevertheless higher than its autarky wage) allows it to compete with HC in S even though its productivity in that good is absolutely lower. Second, low wages in FC are not a barrier to HC from reaping the benefits of free trade. The higher productivity of HC in C allows it to compete with FC in that good despite the latter's lower wage. Finally, the higher wage in HC relative to FC under free trade does not represent *exploitation* of the workers in FC: the higher wage in HC is *not at the expense of* FC since the real wage in FC has also gone up as a result of trade. These are some central messages of the theory of comparative advantage that have been repeatedly misunderstood by commentators through the centuries (see Box 4.2).

Determination of the International Price Ratio

In demonstrating the gains from trade, I *assumed* that the international price ratio was $P_C^I/P_S^I = 1$. We can now briefly consider how this price ratio can actually be derived. This requires an explicit introduction of the demand conditions. To do this most simply, assume that the consumers everywhere divide their expenditures between the two goods equally. This means the total expenditure in the world is divided equally between the two commodities. Letting D with appropriate commodity subscript denote the national demand, we have,

$$P_C^I (D_C + D_C^*) = P_S^I (D_S + D_S^*) \quad \text{or}$$
$$(D_S + D_S^*)/(D_C + D_C^*) = P_C^I/P_S^I \tag{4.5}$$

This equation relates the *relative* world demand to the relative price facing the consumers. In equilibrium, the relative world demand must equal the relative world supply. Given our previous analysis, our conjecture is that HC would specialize completely in C and produce 50 units of it. Likewise, we expect FC to specialize completely in S and produce 50 units of it. If our conjecture is right, the relative world supply would be 50/50 = 1. Equating the demand and supply, we obtain $P_C^I/P_S^I = 1$ as the international price. We must finally verify if our conjecture of complete specialization by HC in C and FC in S is correct at this international price. The answer is in the affirmative: at $P_C^I/P_S^I = 1$, perfect competition would lead HC to specialize completely in C and FC in S.

To explain why this verification is essential, suppose our demand assumption was such that the relative demand for S was much stronger than in (4.5). Specifically, suppose the consumers spend three times as much on S as on C. Formally, assume

Box 4.2 Some Common Fallacies

Misconceptions and myths about the benefits of trade abound. Sometimes these myths even contradict one another. I consider below some of the myths that have appeared and reappeared in the writings of prominent authors proving the non-obvious nature of the principle of comparative advantage.

Fallacy 1: Low Productivity Countries Have Nothing to Gain From Trade

The commonest form in which this argument is made is that productivity in a country may be so low that it may be unable to compete in any product in the world market. This is an argument commonly made with respect to many African countries today. The principle of comparative advantage illustrates the falsehood of this assertion. Absolute advantage is not what determines the ability of a country to export. Instead it is comparative advantage. In the end, the ability to compete depends not just on productivity but also the wage rate. Low productivity countries can always compete in at least some product due to their lower wages.

It is only if countries fix the real wages at excessively high levels that they may price themselves out of the market. Alternatively and more commonly, countries price themselves out by letting the home currency overvalue. Trade economists often identify overvaluation as a tax on exports and almost always include depreciation of the currency in the trade liberalization packages.

It bears reminding that in the context of the Ricardian theory, when low productivity countries compete in the world markets on account of their low wages, they are not lowering the wages below the autarky levels. On the contrary, real wages actually rise as the country enters trade. It is only in comparison to the high productivity countries that the country's wages remain low.

Fallacy 2: High Wage Countries Cannot Compete with Low Wage Countries

This is the "pauper labor" argument that remains highly popular in the developed countries despite centuries of explanations to the contrary by trade economists. The argument here is the flip side of the previous one: poor countries have such low wages that rich countries cannot compete against them. The complaint is heard most loudly currently in the context of exports of manufactures from China and of software from India. Once again, within the context of the Ricardian theory, rich countries can compete despite their high wages because of their high productivity.

Often the rich countries' complaints about the inability to compete against the low-wage countries have their origins in the inability to compete in certain specific sectors in which a country lacks comparative advantage in the first place. For example, within the context of the Heckscher–Ohlin theory, rich countries would lack comparative advantage in the unskilled labor-intensive goods. The complaints of low-wage countries being a threat in the United States have often to do with the threat to industries such as apparel in which they lack comparative advantage in the first place.

(Continued)

Box 4.2 *Continued*

Fallacy 3: Small Countries Have Nothing To Gain From Trade

Here the focus is not so much on productivity as on the size of the country relative to the world markets. The assertion is that tiny countries cannot withstand competition in the world markets and that if they engage in free trade, foreign goods will destroy all their industries. Our analysis of the Ricardian theory tells us just the opposite. The terms of trade are set closer to the autarky terms of trade of the larger countries. As a result, they tend to benefit less from trade. Instead, it is the small countries that can trade at the autarky prices of the larger countries that benefit more.

Small countries can expand their exports by proportionately large amounts without the prices of these goods declining. In contrast, if large countries expand their exports by proportionately large amounts, they would find the prices of these goods drop dramatically. At a more practical level, countries such as Singapore, Hong Kong, Taiwan, and the Republic of Korea could expand their exports very rapidly during the 1960s and 1970s without significant decline in their prices. Being small, they also did not have to fear protectionist backlash in the importing countries. This is in contrast to China today, which is constantly under threat of protectionist backlash in the United States and the European Union.

$$(D_S + D_S^*)/(D_C + D_C^*) = 3. \, P_C^I/P_S^I \tag{4.6}$$

Assuming complete specialization, the relative supply will still be 1 so that the solution to the world price would be 3. $P_C^I/P_S^I = 1$ or $P_C^I/P_S^I = 1/3$. But this price of C is too low for even HC to produce any of C. Both HC and FC would want to specialize in S. But this is not possible since that would be incompatible with our demand assumption. In this case, the equilibrium price of C would have to be the lowest possible that does not eliminate the production of C altogether. This price is the autarky price of HC. As long as P_C^I/P_S^I is ½, HC will still produce some C. Thus, in equilibrium, $P_C^I/P_S^I = ½$ with FC specializing completely in S and HC producing both C and S.[8] An interesting feature of this case is that FC walks away with all the gains from trade. HC neither gains nor loses from trade.

III. The Heckscher–Ohlin Theory

While the Ricardian theory is a powerful instrument for demonstrating the gains from trade and dispelling many common myths about international trade, and can also be extended to incorporate many features of reality—many goods, many countries, transport costs, and non-traded goods—it has at least two important limitations. First, being dependent on constant opportunity costs as illustrated by the straight line PPF, it exhibits a strong tendency for complete specialization in production. Second, and much more

---

[8] The reader may verify that HC would produce 20 units of C and 10 units of S and FC 50 units of S.

importantly, it allows for only one scarce factor of production. Conceptually, this feature entirely limits the ability of the model to capture the income distribution effects of freeing up trade. Its prediction is that trade benefits one and all. But much of the conflict over trade liberalization arises on account of the beneficial effects of trade on some and harmful effects on others even if the overall effect is beneficial in the sense that the benefits of the winners can potentially offset the losses of the losers.

The Heckscher–Ohlin (H–O) theory overcomes these limitations of the Ricardian theory. Among other things, it has the following important features: (i) it explains the patterns of trade based on the differences in factor endowments rather than the differences in technology that are central to the Ricardian theory; (ii) it allows for two factors of production, thereby allowing an analysis of the income distribution effects of opening to trade and other exogenous changes; and (iii) it is characterized by increasing opportunity costs and therefore admits the possibility of incomplete specialization by both countries.

The Model

We begin by considering the H–O model in its simplest form. There are two factors of production, labor and land (L and T), two goods (C and S), and two countries (HC and FC). Goods are distinguished according to *factor intensity* and countries according to *factor abundance*, with these concepts defined below. Both countries are assumed to have access to the same technology.

Initially, we assume a fixed coefficients technology meaning that labor and land must be combined in a fixed proportion regardless of their prices. This technology assumes that there is no possibility of substituting one factor for the other through, for example, more extensive or intensive cultivation of land. Later, we will allow for such substitution such that if land becomes more expensive and labor cheaper, the land–labor ratio falls. Table 4.5 summarizes the basic information for HC. Note that we now use the symbol "a" with appropriate product and factor subscripts to denote the input–output ratio and also use a numerical example. For example, a_{TC} denotes the land–output ratio in C. According to the specific numerical value shown, Corn uses 4 units of land per unit of Corn production. But it also requires 1 unit of labor. That is to say, 1 unit of Corn is produced using 4 units of land *and* 1 unit of labor.

Table 4.5 The Heckscher–Ohlin theory: the input–output ratios and factor endowments

Factor of production	Factor use per unit of		Total endowment (HC)
	C	S	
Land	a_{TC} (4)	a_{TS} (2)	T (100)
Labor	a_{LC} (1)	a_{LS} (2)	L (60)

We say that C is *land intensive* relative to S if $a_{TC}/a_{LC} > a_{TS}/a_{LS}$. That is to say, C is defined as land intensive if it uses more land per worker than does S. The concept is entirely *relative*: we compare the ratio of factor usage in one commodity to that in the other. Given the specific numbers shown in Table 4.4, $a_{TC}/a_{LC} = 4/1 = 4$ and $a_{TS}/a_{LS} = 2/2 = 1$ so that C is land intensive. You can readily verify that this necessarily implies that S is labor intensive.

We also define HC to be *land abundant* (or labor scarce) relative to FC if $T/L > T^*/L^*$. According to Table 4.5, $T/L = 100/60 = 5/3$. To keep matters simple, we will assume FC to have the same amount of land as HC but more labor, say, 80 units. This leads to $T^*/L^* = 100/80 = 5/4$ indicating that HC is land abundant and FC labor abundant. Alternatively, we can say that HC is automatically labor scarce and FC land scarce. We may think of HC as the United States and FC as China. Given HC and FC are assumed to have access to the same technology, the technology coefficients shown in Table 4.5 apply to both of them.

The Production Possibilities Frontier [PPF] in HC

Suppose for a moment that we have as much land as we want and that labor is the only constraining factor of production. Then, we can produce a maximum of $L/a_{LC} = 60$ of C or $L/a_{LS} = 30$ of S or a combination of C and S on the (flatter) line marked LL' in Figure 4.4. Algebraically, this line is given by

$$a_{LC} Q_C + a_{LS} Q_S = L \quad \text{or} \quad Q_C + 2Q_S = 60 \qquad (4.7)$$

Next, suppose we have as much labor as we want and land is the only constraining factor. Then we can produce a maximum of $T/a_{TC} = 25$ of C or $T/a_{TS} = 50$ of S or a combination of C and S on the (steeper) line marked TT' in Figure 4.3. Algebraically, the line is

$$a_{TC} Q_C + a_{TW} Q_W = T \quad \text{or} \quad 4Q_C + 2Q_S = 100 \qquad (4.8)$$

Observe that the land constraint is steeper than the labor constraint because C is land intensive and Q_C is measured along the horizontal axis.

LL' represents the PPF provided land is not required in production and TT' if labor is not required. But we assume that both factors are required for production. Therefore, the only feasible output combinations are those along the solid lines shown by LQT' where Q is the point of intersection of LL' and TT'. An immediate conclusion from this shape of the PPF is that the opportunity cost in the H–O model is not constant everywhere. The opportunity cost of C rises as we move from segment LQ to QT'. The opportunity cost along each flat segment is constant because only one factor along it is scarce with the other one freely available due to unemployment. Along the flat segment, only the fully employed factor matters and we are effectively in the constant costs world of the one-factor model. Along LQ (excluding point Q) land is unemployed, while along

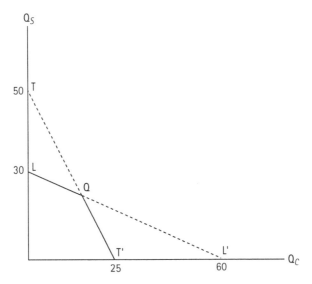

FIGURE 4.3 The PPF in the H–O Model under fixed coefficients technology

QT' (again, excluding point Q) labor is unemployed. Only at Q are both factors fully employed.

Unemployment along the flat segment is due to the assumed lack of substitutability in production. If substitution between labor and land were allowed (as is true in reality), we could adjust the land–labor ratio and utilize the unemployed factor fully and get some extra output. For example, consider point L. Here land is not fully employed. Given the total endowment of 60 workers and land–labor ratio of 1, S is able to employ only 60 units of land. But what if technology was more flexible and we could economize on the use of labor. For example, we could make cultivation of cotton (used in Shirt production) more extensive and spread the workers more thinly on land and bring the remaining 40 units of land under cultivation. This fuller employment of land would allow us to squeeze a few more units of Shirt (or Corn or both). Of course, this logic applies to all points along flat segments LQ and QT' (except Q) where one factor is unemployed. This logic leads to the conclusion that once we take the substitution possibilities into account, the PPF will lie everywhere outside TQL except at Q. Seen this way, Q is not special but instead represents the more general case of full employment along the PPF.

Figure 4.4 incorporates the substitution possibilities and shows MQN as the PPF. With full employment of both factors, the PPF is bowed out. The absolute value of the slope of the PPF reflects the marginal opportunity cost of production of the good on the horizontal axis (C) in terms of the good on the vertical axis (S). Given the bowed out shape of the PPF, this slope rises in absolute value as we produce more and more of C, reflecting the rising opportunity costs of production of the latter. That is to say, as we move from point M towards N along the PPF, for each extra unit

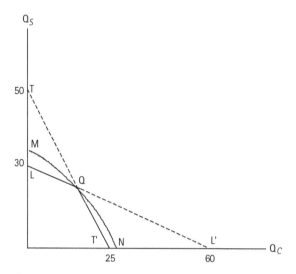

FIGURE 4.4 PPF with increasing opportunity costs everywhere

of C, we must sacrifice larger and larger quantities of S. The reason is that the more we move towards point N, the more labor per unit of land we must employ in each of C and S to avoid moving labor out of employment. Given diminishing scope for substitution at the margin, this calls for ever increasing sacrifice of S for each extra unit of C.

The Production Equilibrium and Relative Supply

The PPF is, of course, a technical relationship. It shows the maximum production possibilities, given technology and factor endowments. Precisely where along the PPF production takes place depends on the relative price. Under perfect competition, producers equate the marginal cost to the price. In relative terms, this condition implies

$$P_C/P_S = MC_C/MC_S \qquad (4.9)$$

But recall that the marginal cost of C in terms of S is nothing but the slope of the PPF in absolute terms. Therefore, the production equilibrium is obtained at the point where the price is tangent to the PPF. This is shown in the left-hand panel of Figure 4.5.

It is important to remember that the slope of the price line represents the price of the good on the *horizontal* axis in terms of the good on the vertical axis, just as the slope of the PPF represents the marginal cost of the good on the horizontal axis in terms of that on the vertical axis. Once this is understood, it is evident from Figure 4.5 that as the

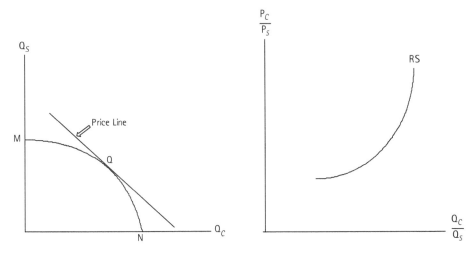

FIGURE 4.5 Production equilibrium and the relative supply

price of C rises, we move towards N on the PPF and the supply of C relative to S rises as well. Conversely, as the price of C falls, the relative supply of C falls. This relationship is shown on the right-hand panel in Figure 4.5.

The Rybczynski Theorem and The PPF in FC

Temporarily, let us return to the fixed coefficients technology shown in Table 4.5 and reproduce the initial full employment point Q in HC in Figure 4.6. Recall that FC is

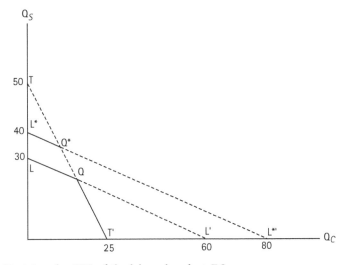

FIGURE 4.6 Deriving the PPF of the labor abundant FC

assumed to have the same technology as HC. In addition, we have assumed FC to have the same amount of land as HC but more labor (80 units). Therefore, the land constraint of FC is the same as of HC. But its labor constraint lies outside that of the latter. Drawing this constraint in Figure 4.6, we obtain point Q* as the full-employment point in FC.

Comparing Q and Q*, we observe something surprising. FC has more labor but the same amount of land as HC. Intuitively, we might have thought that the extra labor will be used partially in the production of C and partially in the production of S. But that is not how it works out. Instead, FC produces much more of S and absolutely less of C than HC. Trade economists like to state this dramatic outcome as:

> *Rybczynski Theorem*: Holding other things fixed, an increase in the supply of a factor leads to a proportionately larger increase in the output of the good using that factor more intensively and an absolute decline in the output of the other factor.

The reader may wish to convince herself that given the coefficients in Table 4.5, the only way to achieve full employment of both resources in FC is for the latter to produce more of S and less of C than HC.

As previously explained, the kinked PPFs in Figures 4.3 and 4.6 result from the assumption of no substitutability between labor and land. The PPFs are smooth if substitution is permitted. But even then, *at a given price*, if FC has more labor than HC and the same amount of land, it produces more of S and less of C than HC. This is shown in the left-hand panel of Figure 4.7 by points Q and Q*.

The Heckscher–Ohlin Theorem

We have just established that *at a given price*, the proportion of Q_S to Q_C is larger in FC than HC. Equivalently, at a given price ratio, the proportion of Q_C to Q_S is smaller in FC than HC. Therefore, when we draw the relative supply of FC along with that of HC in the right-hand panel of Figure 4.7, it lies to the left of the latter. FC is labor abundant relative to HC. Therefore, at each price, it produces a relative larger quantity of the labor intensive commodity S or, equivalently, a relative smaller quantity of the land intensive commodity C.

We are now in a position to derive the pattern of trade in this model. Suppose the demand pattern in HC and FC is the same in the sense that, for each commodity ratio, they consume the two commodities in the same proportion. We can then represent the demand conditions in the right-hand panel of Figure 4.7 by the same relative demand curve. The curve slopes downward since a decline in the relative price of C increases the relative demand for it.

From the right-hand panel in Figure 4.7, it is evident that under autarky, the land-intensive good C is cheaper in the land-abundant HC than FC. Therefore, when

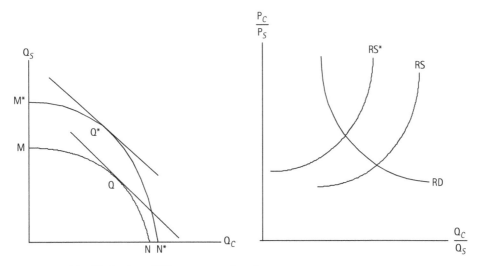

FIGURE 4.7 The Heckscher–Ohlin pattern of trade

trade opens, land abundant FC exports labor intensive good C, and labor abundant FC exports labor intensive good S. We write this important result as:

> *The Heckscher–Ohlin Theorem*: Each country exports the good that uses its abundant factor more intensively and imports the good that uses its scarce factor more intensively.

Factor Prices

So far, we have kept the factor price effects of trade in the background. But just as in the Ricardian theory, when trade changes the goods prices, it also changes the factor prices with one important complication. We now have two factors of production, labor and land, and the returns rise to one of them and fall to the other. Trade now brings about a conflict between the owners of the two factors.

To see how this works in the simplest terms, consider HC, which imports the labor intensive good S and exports the land intensive good C. This pattern of trade lowers the relative price of the labor intensive good S. This causes the output of S to shrink and that of C to rise along the PPF. Since S is labor intensive, at the *original* factor prices, it releases more labor per unit of land than the ratio in which C absorbs these factors. Temporarily, we have excess supply of labor and excess demand for land. This pushes the wage down and the rental price on land up. Denoting the wage by w and the return on land by r, w/r declines. What is more surprising, however, is that the wage declines proportionately more than the decline in the price of S. Thus, the wage declines not only in terms of C but also in terms of S. On the other hand, r rises in terms of both

S and C. Workers are unambiguously worse off (regardless of whether they spend most of their income on S or C) and landowners are unambiguously better off. This result is known as:

> *Stolper–Samuelson Theorem*: A decrease in the price of a good makes the factor used more intensively in that good unambiguously worse off and the factor used more intensively in the other good unambiguously better off.

The striking result that w falls in terms of both goods requires some further explanation. The important link is provided by the relationship between w/r and the labor–land ratios in S and C on the one hand and that between the latter and the marginal products of the factors on the other. The fall in w/r induces firms to substitute labor for land. That is to say, firms increase labor per unit of land. But the increase in labor per unit of land lowers the marginal product of labor (MPL) and raises the marginal product of land (MPT). The former change represents a fall in the real return to labor and the latter a rise in the real return to land.

To make this point explicitly, consider the return to labor. According to an important result in economics, firms in each sector employ labor up to the point where the value of marginal product (i.e., price times the marginal product) of labor equals the wage rate. That is to say,

$$w = P_C.MPL_C = P_S.MPL_S \quad \text{or} \quad w/P_C = MPL_C \quad \text{and} \quad w/P_S = MPL_S \quad (4.10)$$

As just noted, the decline in w/r raises the labor–land ratio in each good, which in turn lowers the marginal product of labor. But from the above relationships, the fall in each marginal product implies that w/P_C and w/P_S both fall. That is to say, the purchasing power of the wage falls in terms of both goods. No matter how workers spend their incomes, they are left worse off. Symmetrically, we can show that r/P_C and r/P_S both rise. The owners of land are made unambiguously better off. Stated differently, trade unambiguously hurts the scarce factor and benefits the abundant factor.

Factor Price Equalization

Given identical technologies in HC and FC, by equalizing the goods prices, trade also equalizes factor prices internationally. Recall that under autarky, S is more expensive in HC. Since S is labor intensive, the higher price of S makes the wage in HC higher than in FC and the return to land lower. When trade opens, according to the Stolper–Samuelson theorem, w falls and r rises in HC while the opposite happens in FC. The factor prices converge between the two countries. Indeed, it can be shown that they do not just converge but equalize. Due to its technical nature, I do not reproduce the proof of the Factor Price Equalization (FPE) here. But it is important to make note of the result to understand some of the current policy debates in which some participants talk of US wages being determined in Beijing (see Box 4.3).

Box 4.3 Trade and Wages

Since the late 1970s, the wages at the bottom of the income distribution in the United States have either not risen or risen very little. The wages at the top of the income distribution have risen very rapidly. Many studies divide the workforce into skilled and unskilled workers and find that from the late 1970s to early 1990s, the ratio of skilled to unskilled wages rose by nearly 30 per cent. A major academic and policy debate has ensued on the reasons of this increase in wage inequality.

Critics of liberal trade policies argue that increasing trade with poor countries such as China and India has caused the wage inequality. The intellectual foundations of this argument come from the Heckscher–Ohlin model, specifically the Stolper–Samuelson Theorem. Thus, suppose the two factors of production in this model are skilled and unskilled labor. Suppose further that skilled labor is the abundant factor and unskilled labor scarce factor in the United States relative to the poor countries such as China and India. Then trade results in the United States importing unskilled labor-intensive goods and exporting skilled labor-intensive goods. In turn, this would drive down the price of unskilled labor-intensive goods and also the real and relative return to unskilled labor. Those terrified by competition with India and China even argue that the wages in Boston would eventually be determined in Beijing meaning that the Factor Price Equalization theorem would drive US wages to Chinese levels.

Trade economists disagree with this diagnosis and argue that trade with the poor countries cannot explain the bulk of the increase in the wage inequality. They cite four reasons in support of their position.

- Trade works to lower the unskilled wage by lowering the relative price of unskilled labor-intensive goods. But a study by Lawrence and Slaughter (1993) pointed out that the relative price of unskilled labor-intensive goods had actually risen since the late 1970s. By itself this point is not decisive, however. In principle, trade may have lowered the relative price of unskilled labor-intensive products but other factors such as sharply declining costs of skilled labor-intensive products may have reversed this decline. Lawrence and Slaughter only looked at the *ex post* change in the prices but did not decompose them according to the sources of the change.
- Extra imports from the developing countries during the relevant period account for less than 2 per cent of the total expenditure in the United States. This is the point made by Krugman (1995). He argues that such a small proportionate expansion of trade simply cannot explain the large increase in wage inequality. This is clearly an important point.
- During this period, wage inequality rose in many developing countries as well. If the simple-minded Stolper–Samuelson Theorem was driving the outcome, developing countries should have experienced a decrease in wage inequality. Given that they export unskilled labor-intensive goods, the Stolper–Samuelson Theorem should have driven their real and relative unskilled wages up. This did not happen.
- Technical change that shifted labor demand in favor of skilled labor and away from unskilled labor provides a far more compelling explanation for increased wage inequality in both rich and poor countries. Technological change has been concentrated in skilled labor-intensive goods and it has also move progressively towards greater use of skilled labor. This change has shifted the demand in favor of skilled labor in both rich and poor countries and led to increased wage inequality in both regions.

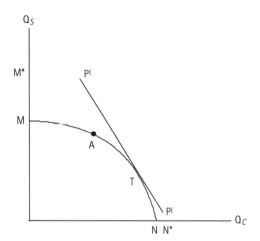

FIGURE 4.8 The gains from trade in the H-O Model

The Gains from Trade Once Again

The analysis in the previous section may raise some doubts regarding the overall gains from trade. It may appear that since one factor wins and the other loses, we cannot tell whether the country as a whole gains or loses. This is an incorrect inference, however. We can show that trade is overall beneficial in the sense that it allows each country to achieve a consumption basket that dominates its autarky consumption basket.

Figure 4.8 demonstrates the point for HC. In the absence of trade, this country produces and consumes at point A. After trade opens, it takes advantage of the higher international relative price of the land intensive good and moves to producing more C and less S. In the trading equilibrium, it produces at T and consumes somewhere along the price line P^IP^I. Observe that in the trading equilibrium, the country has the autarky consumption (and production) basket available to it but it is fully dominated by what is available along P^IP^I.

REFERENCES

Bhagwati, J., Panagariya, A., and Srinivasan, T. N. (2004), 'The Muddles over Outsourcing.' June 30, mimeo, Columbia University (revised version published in the *Journal of Economic Perspectives* 18(4): 93–114).

Grotius, H. (1625), *De Jure Belli Ac Pacis Libri Tres* [The Law of War and Peace]. Translated by Kelsey, F. W. Oxford: Clarendon Press.

Irwin, D. (1996), *Against the Tide*, Princeton: Princeton University Press.

Krugman, P. (1995). 'Growing World Trade: Causes and Consequences.' *Brookings Papers on Economic Activity* 1: 327–62.

Lawrence, R. Z., and Slaughter, M. J. (1993), 'International Trade and American Wages in the 1980s: Giant Sucking Sound or a Small Hiccup?' *Brookings Papers on Economic Activity*, Volume 2, Microeconomics: 161–226.

Mill, J. (1821), *Elements of Political Economy*, London: Baldwin, Cradock & Joy.

Ricardo, D. (1817), *On The Principles of Political Economy and Taxation*, London: John Murray.

Smith, A. (1776), *The Wealth of Nations Volumes I and II*. Everyman's Library with introduction by Seligman, E. R. A. London: J. M. Dent & Sons Ltd.

Torrens, R. (1815), *Essays on the External Corn Trade*. London: J. Hatchard.

CHAPTER 5

TRADE AND THE GAINS FROM TRADE IN THE PRESENCE OF DECREASING COSTS AND IMPERFECT COMPETITION

MARY E. LOVELY AND DEVASHISH MITRA

I. INTRODUCTION

THE concept of comparative advantage is both general and useful. Most of the reasons for trade, including differences in productivity and factor proportions, are special cases of comparative advantage. Comparative advantage helps us understand why the developed countries, on balance, export manufactured goods to the less-developed countries in exchange for primary products. Comparative advantage also helps us understand how a country's trade patterns change as its factor endowments grow. For example, as the available stock of capital per worker rose in Hong Kong, Taiwan, and Korea between 1960 and 1990, the share of their exports accounted for by manufactured goods rose as production patterns changed. Indeed, exports of manufactured goods from middle-income countries are one of the fastest growing segments of international trade.

Comparative advantage alone, however, cannot explain all aspects of international trade. Essentially, comparative advantage implies that countries trade to exploit their differences. On this basis, we would not expect to see a large share of trade accounted for by the exchange of similar goods among similar industrial countries.[1] As Table 5.1 shows, however, trade patterns do not match this prediction. In 2005, almost half of world trade was accounted for by trade among

---

[1] Two-way trade in homogeneous goods can be explained by imperfect competition alone, as in the Brander and Krugman (1983) model, but even here increasing returns play a role in justifying the assumption that only one firm in each country produces the good.

developed countries. The volume of trade between developed countries and developing countries was much smaller, with developing country exports to developed countries accounting for only 20 per cent of total trade flows. These shares have not changed much over the past decade, as seen by comparing across the three panels of Table 5.1.

Another important feature of modern trade flows is that a large share of trade among developed countries can be classified as *intra-industry trade*: two-way trade in a wide variety of goods, such as steel and automobiles. Two-way trade in the same product would appear to be senseless if the products are entirely similar and trade is costless. However, such trade may enhance a country's wellbeing for several reasons. First, if two-way trade in the same product reduces the market power of local firms, it may raise the welfare of domestic consumers. A second reason may be that the products are differentiated as seen by the user, whether that is a consumer or a firm that

Table 5.1 Percentage distribution of exports by major trading groups (US$ billion)

(a) 1995

Exporter	Importer					
	Developed countries		Developing countries		Total	
Developed countries	2420	(52%)	854	(18%)	3274	(70%)
Developing countries	780	(17)	594	(13)	1374	(30)
Total	3200	(69)	1448	(31)	4648	(100)

(b) 2000

Exporter	Importer					
	Developed countries		Developing countries		Total	
Developed countries	2896	(49%)	959	(16%)	3855	(66%)
Developing countries	1193	(20)	813	(14)	2006	(34)
Total	4089	(70)	1771	(30)	5861	(100)

(c) 2005

Exporter	Importer					
	Developed countries		Developing countries		Total	
Developed countries	3222	(49%)	1048	(16%)	4270	(64%)
Developing countries	1314	(20)	1045	(16)	2359	(36)
Total	4536	(68)	2093	(32)	6629	(100)

Source: United Nations, World Economic and Social Survey, 2004. Table A-14. Economies in transition are excluded.

uses the product as an input. Such *product differentiation* is welfare enhancing when variety raises consumer wellbeing or firm productivity. For example, Japanese and German automobiles are not the same in the eyes of consumers and trade gives them wider choice.

If comparative advantage alone cannot fully explain these important phenomena, how can we explain them? This chapter explores a variety of models that seek to provide an answer to that question. The models economists use to study these phenomena all share a common feature: they assume that productivity rises as the scale of production increases. We say that such technologies exhibit *increasing returns to scale*. When there are *scale economies*, an equi-proportional increase in all inputs increases output to a greater proportion. For firms that face an increasing returns technology, the average cost of production declines as output increases.

Scale economies capture many important features of real-world production. In 2007, the value of world merchandise trade exceeded US$13.6 trillion.[2] Of these exports, the largest volumes were in chemicals, machinery and transport equipment, textiles, and metals. Of these four industries, three are industries for which there are large fixed costs, indicating that scale economies play an important role in world trade flows. It is also clear, however, that the scale economies exhibited by these industries are not all alike. While chemical production requires large investments in physical plants, transport equipment is highly clustered in supplier networks, indicating the presence of agglomeration economies. These technological differences matter both for how we analyze these industries and for the conclusions we draw regarding the effect of trade on domestic economies.

Study of scale economies allows us to address the familiar questions of trade theory from a new perspective. Are scale economies a reason for two countries to trade, even if they are otherwise identical? Does such trade produce gains for both partners or for only one? What effect does this trade have on domestic factor rewards? Additionally, we are able to address new questions that arise because of the scale economies themselves. Is two-way trade in the same product beneficial or wasteful? Is it better to specialize in some goods rather than others and, thus, is there a beneficial role for policies that target specific industries through import tariffs or production subsidies?

Because the answers to these important questions depend on the nature of the production technology and on the nature of market competition, our inquiry is naturally one of various cases. To organize our discussion, we next introduce a typology of scale economies. We will use this typology to organize some of the most important results found in the literature. In each case, our focus will be on providing an explanation for significant features of real-world trade flows and on the effect of these flows on domestic welfare. Lessons for policy emerge from this discussion.

---

[2] See The World Trade Organization, "World Trade Developments in 2007," Table 1.7. <>

II. A Typology of Scale Economies

Table 5.2 provides a typology of scale economies drawn from Ethier (1995: 51). The first distinction we make about technology is whether scale economies are internal to an individual firm or external to it. Scale economies are *internal to the firm* if the firm's average costs depend on the firm's size. Scale economies are *external to the firm* (but internal to the industry) if the firm's average costs depend on the size of the industry but not on the size of the firm. In this case, an expansion of the firm with the industry unchanged in size will have no effect on the firm's average costs. One or both types of scale economies may be present in an industry.

If scale economies are internal to the firm, a firm can lower its average costs and raise its profit by increasing output. The market will be *imperfectly competitive* if the seller realizes that its output decisions affect the price it receives. In this case, one or more firms will dominate the market as they increase sales at the expense of smaller competitors. Firms' market power may be limited even when scale economies are internal to the firm, however. Entry barriers may be low so that actual entry or the fear of potential entry forces the firm to price its product at average cost. Alternatively, if scale economies are external to the firm, the firm will not recognize that its production decisions influence average costs in the industry. In this case, the firm may act as a price taker and no one firm will dominate the market.

The second distinction we can make about technology is the geographic scope of the scale technologies. Is geographic concentration of production necessary for costs to fall as the scale of activity increases? To take advantage of large plant size, production must expand at that plant. If a firm benefits from a concentration of specialized labor, firms must concentrate in one location so that workers will be attracted to the same area. In each of these cases, scale economies are *national in scope* because average costs depend on the size of the geographically concentrated industry.

Alternatively, scale economies are *international in scope* if average costs depend on the size of the international industry. The extent of such economies is influenced by trade

Table 5.2 Types of scale economies

	Internal to the firm	External to the firm
National scale economies	Concentration of production in a large, efficient plant	A large industry supporting an industrial labor force and extensive infrastructure
International scale economies	Research and development by a multinational firm	Extensive division of labor in an industry with low barriers to trade and communication

Source: Ethier (1995: 51).

costs, broadly defined. If transportation costs and trade barriers are high, an industry will be concentrated in one country. However, if trade costs are insignificant, stages of production can be located where production costs are lowest, with parts easily shipped from place to place. The North American automobile industry took advantage of low transport costs and the 1965 USA–Canada Automotive Agreement by dividing its production across the border, producing large gains in production efficiency. More recently, as trade costs and tariffs have fallen, the automobile industry has become increasingly global in scope. Japanese, European, and American firms routinely source parts from many regions, such as the rapidly growing economies of East Asia. Similarly, as communication costs have fallen, the information services industry has spread far beyond the countries in which these services are marketed, as in the case of backroom financial services in Ireland and call centers in India. These scale economies depend on the size of the world market, not on geographic concentrations of production.

We consider below each type of scale economy described in Table 5.2. We find that the conclusions that can be drawn regarding the effect of trade and the role of policy are sensitive to the form of scale economy and the structure of the market under review. We begin with the study of internal economies of scale.

III. Internal Scale Economies I: Oligopoly

National Champions and Strategic Trade Policy

When large firm-level fixed costs act as a barrier to new entrants, there are just a few firms in an industry and we call the resulting market structure "oligopoly." Because there are only a few firms in the industry and because they earn extraordinary profits, these firms are often highly visible and one or more may emerge as "national champions," firms considered of special importance for a local population. This oligopoly provides a reason for trade because a foreign firm may enter to capture rents, leading to two-way trade in the same good.

Under perfect competition, each firm produces a homogeneous good whose market price it takes as given. Oligopolistic firms, on the other hand, behave strategically with respect to each other, and their actions are taken factoring in the reactions by their rivals. There are two basic types of oligopoly settings one can analyze. One setting occurs when firms strategically choose the quantity they supply, a situation known as Cournot competition. An alternative setting occurs when firms strategically choose price, a situation called Bertrand competition. For the purposes of our analysis of oligopoly, we will focus on the Cournot case. We will also restrict the total number of firms in an industry to just two. This case is called Cournot duopoly.

The duopoly case is not unrealistic. Examples of duopolies are Coke and Pepsi, Boeing and Airbus, and more recently Bombardier from Canada and Embraer from

Brazil. Because there are only two firms in the market, each firm has some monopoly power that it can use to generate some rents or profits for itself. However, a firm's profit will be determined not only by its own actions, but also by the actions of its rivals. We use game-theoretic analysis to make our predictions about the actions that the two firms will end up choosing. The concept we will use to predict the outcome of this game is called the "Nash equilibrium," where each of the two firms chooses the level of sales that maximizes its profits, given the sales level chosen by its rival. Note that, in this simple setting, both firms act at the same time, with full information about its rival. So the outcome predicted, which is a Nash equilibrium, is one where each firm ends up doing the best it can, given the action of the other.

If one firm can move in setting its quantity before the other, it has an advantage and acts as what we call a "Stackelberg leader." The other firm is called a "Stackelberg follower." The Stackelberg leader understands its rival's options and picks its own sales anticipating the reaction of the follower. Because it acts first, the leader is able to guide the market to the level of sales that gives it the maximum profits.[3] This point is different from the simultaneous move Nash equilibrium because the Stackelberg leader is able to take the first-mover advantage and earn higher profits.

Brander and Spencer (1985) show that government intervention can mimic the effect of a first-mover advantage, even if the two firms are moving simultaneously in setting their quantities. Such profit shifting can be engineered by an interventionist government announcing a subsidy to its own firm prior to the setting of quantities by the two competitors. If the subsidy is chosen appropriately, even though the competitors act simultaneously, the outcome is the same as that resulting from a Stackelberg leader–follower game with no government intervention, where the leader is the same firm that is being subsidized in the simultaneous move game.

In Figure 5.1, we see a possible arrangement of the reaction functions of two firms, namely Firm 1 from Country 1 and Firm 2 from Country 2. The reaction functions are drawn as downward sloping since an increase in output by the rival firm leaves a smaller residual market, inducing the home firm to supply a smaller quantity to the market, keeping prices and profits at the level that maximizes its own profits.[4] The intersection of the two reaction functions is point N, which is the Nash equilibrium of the quantity-setting Cournot game described above. Let's assume, as is likely, that Firm 1 would earn higher profits if it sold more and Firm 2 sold less. Specifically, let point S indicate the point on Firm 2's reaction function where Firm 1 maximizes its profits. Point S is, therefore, the Stackelberg equilibrium. A subsidy given to Firm 1 by the government of Country 1 will shift Firm 1's reaction function (as shown by the dotted line), and a large enough subsidy will move it to the position where it intersects

---

[3] Firm A's reaction function shows the quantity it should sell to maximize its own profits, given each possible quantity produced by Firm B. Similarly, Firm B's reaction function shows its optimal response to each possible quantity chosen by Firm A. The Nash equilibrium is the intersection of these two reaction functions.

[4] The relative slopes of the two reaction functions should be as given in the figure, as this is required by the stability condition of the equilibrium (the explanation for which is beyond the scope of this chapter).

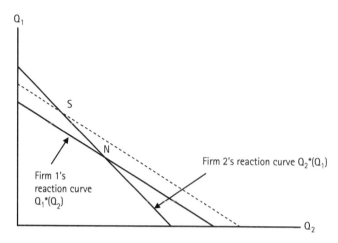

FIGURE 5.1 Firm reaction functions in a Cournot game

Firm 2's reaction function at point S, where profits are higher for Firm 1 and lower for Firm 2 as compared to those at point N. In this case, a subsidy is able to shift profits from Firm 2 to Firm 1. Clearly this is an argument for aggressive industrial policy or strategic trade policy that promotes "profit-shifting" from the foreign firm to the domestic firm.

An example discussed by Krugman and Obstfeld (2006) makes this point very clearly for firms facing a simple dichotomous decision. Suppose two aircraft manufacturers, Boeing and Airbus, are deciding whether or not to design and build a new aircraft. The rows in Figure 5.2a correspond to alternative decisions by Boeing, while the columns correspond to alternative decisions by Airbus. In each box, the lower left-hand entry represents Boeing's profits if those particular actions are taken, while the upper right-hand entry represents the profits of Airbus. This game has two possible Nash equilibria, in each of which one firm decides to produce, while the other firm decides not to produce. Clearly, when Boeing decides to produce, the profits to Airbus from not producing equal 0 and are greater than the -5 profits from producing. Therefore, Airbus's optimal response when Boeing decides to produce is not to produce. When Airbus decides not to produce, Boeing can make profits equal to 100 which is greater than the 0 that it would receive if it decides not to produce. Therefore, Boeing producing and Airbus not producing is a Nash equilibrium. By a similar argument Boeing not producing and Airbus producing is also a Nash equilibrium.

Let us now look at Figure 5.2b where we assume that the European Union provides Airbus with a subsidy of 25 if it produces the new aircraft. Arguing along the lines similar to the above, we see that there is only one Nash equilibrium once the EU offers the subsidy, where Airbus produces and Boeing does not produce. Thus, the subsidy gives Airbus an advantage and can increase Airbus's profits from 0, as explained in the previous case, to 125 in this new situation. So a subsidy of 25 is able to generate an increase in profit of 125, which clearly may increase aggregate welfare in the European Union.

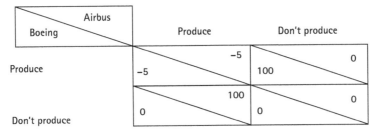

FIGURE 5.2a Hypothetical payoff matrix for two-firm competition

Boeing \ Airbus	Produce	Don't produce
Produce	−5 / −5	100 / 0
Don't produce	0 / 100	0 / 0

FIGURE 5.2b Payoff Matrix for two-firm competition with a production subsidy to Airbus

Boeing \ Airbus	Produce	Don't produce
Produce	−5 / 20	100 / 0
Don't produce	0 / 125	0 / 0

While the above analysis provides arguments for strategic trade policy, there are other factors to consider in assessing the benefits of subsidies. First, for the government to correctly determine the amount of subsidy needed to increase its home firm's profits, it needs to have very accurate information on the payoffs facing both firms. This information is private knowledge and usually not available to the government. Second, the analysis assumes that the rival's government is totally passive. One can easily imagine a situation where, in a stage prior to the firms' decisions, the two governments decide whether or not to subsidize their respective firms. This will lead to a Nash equilibrium between the two governments in setting up subsidies, and research has shown that this might make both countries worse off compared to the no intervention situation, because both firms receive subsidies but neither firm has a strategic advantage from this. Finally, this analysis looks at one industry in isolation of all other industries. This is unrealistic as subsidies involve moving resources from one part of the economy to another and therefore involve opportunity costs that need to be factored into our analysis.

Strategic trade policy can also take the form of research and development (R&D) subsidies or tariffs or quotas for an industry that has high costs of production but significant learning potential so that with experience in production, costs fall. This can turn comparative disadvantage into comparative advantage and has been termed by Krugman (1984) as "import protection as export promotion." Regardless of the exact form of the scale economies or the strategic policy used, the cautions given above apply to any attempt to shift profits to home firms. The experience of Canada and Brazil in the regional jet market is instructive.

Case Study: Regional Jets

Both Embraer and Bombadier are manufacturers of regional jets and are located in Brazil and Canada, respectively. In the last five years of the 1990s the sales of regional jets increased fivefold, with the USA the biggest buyer of these aircrafts. Regional jets are ideal for flights that cover distances of less than a thousand miles, and they fit nicely into the airline industry's attempts to reduce costs by decreasing capacity to low-traffic markets. During this time period, both the Brazilian and Canadian governments provided various types of subsidies and concessional loans to promote their respective firms. Each government also purchased a significant number of aircrafts as an indirect way of subsidizing the producer. The net impact of these policies by both governments was an increase in the sales and profits of both Embraer and Bombadier. However, the opportunity costs of the subsidies were far greater, and they had to be borne by the taxpayers in the form of higher taxes. This is a case of strategic trade policy where both governments were active and they ended up hurting each other. These governments also filed complaints against each other at the WTO and the practices of both governments were declared WTO-illegal.

National Champions and Reciprocal Dumping

National champions are typically highly visible firms with significant market shares. Besides the aircraft duopolies noted above, we can add the names of Kodak and Fuji, Sony and Magnavox, and Lenovo and Hewlett Packard. When national champions enter markets abroad, they are often accused of dumping, defined as selling a product in a foreign market at a price below that charged in the home market. Although such behavior is widely viewed as predatory, economists argue that it can be a consequence of profit maximization by a firm practicing price discrimination. There need not be any attempt by the foreign firm to drive the domestic firm out of business. Rather, price discrimination arises naturally in the presence of transport costs and differences in the characteristics of the two markets.

Let us consider two firms, namely Firm 1 and Firm 2 located in Country 1 and Country 2, respectively. These firms produce exactly the same good. In the absence of any trade between the two countries, each of these firms is a monopolist in its own country and charges a monopoly price. Let us assume that there is a transport cost that is less than the difference between the monopoly price and the per unit cost of production. If trade between these two countries is permitted, each firm will want to sell into the other market. The high price charged by the home monopolist allows the foreign firm to cover its production and transportation costs while still earning a profit on its export sales. Thus Firm 1 will sell into Country 2's market and Firm 2 will sell into Country 1's market, while continuing to serve their respective domestic markets. When we look at each firm's costs, however, we see that each firm receives higher net revenue from each sale in its home market than it does on sales into the foreign market, an outcome we term "reciprocal dumping." This two-way trade in the same product is caused by imperfect competition and it arises out of profit maximization.

Product Cycles

Many of the products that earn economic rents exhibit product cycles, that is, innovation and growth in the market leads to sharply declining costs. In this case, the economies of scale are "dynamic" as productivity goes up through "learning by doing" (i.e., average costs of production are decreasing in the total cumulative output of the good produced over the years), and this knowledge of producing more efficiently can be transferred from one country to another. We can use our models to understand this process.

Suppose a firm in an advanced economy, through investments in R&D, comes up with a new product. Initially, the cost of production of the product is high, as the knowledge and skills required to produce it are scarce. Also the scale of production starts out small. As more of the good is produced, consumers develop a taste for the product and demand for it expands. This expansion in demand leads to an expansion in the scale of production and under economies of scale leads to a fall in the cost of production. The methods of production become standardized and the skills required to produce this good keep decreasing. This reduction in skill requirements may eventually allow production of this good in the developing world where wages are lower. Thus, over the life cycle of this product, we have a developed country exporting the product to the rest of the world and then, with standardization of technology, all developed countries exporting the good to developing countries, and finally with a reduction in skill requirements, we have developing countries exporting the good to the developed world. By this time, another new product may be starting its life cycle in an advanced economy that is exporting it to the rest of the world.

Case Study: Product Cycles in Textiles and Computer Chips

There are many products that exhibit this cyclical development. The textile industry is one commonly cited example. Mass-scale industrial production of textiles started in England during the Industrial Revolution, when raw materials came from its poor eastern colonies. Over time, the technology spread to countries like the United States. Within the USA, textile production first started in the northeast and then spread further south. In the modern era, the technology for textile production became fairly standard and the skill requirements were low. Most production moved to East Asia and South East Asia, where unskilled labor is cheaper and so the cost of goods that are intensive in the use of unskilled labor is lower.

Another example of a product cycle is the case of computer chips. Technology moves very rapidly in the production of these chips. While advances in technology are made in the richest countries, over time the production of each generation of chips becomes

Case Study: *Continued*

standardized and moves to lower-wage locations in Asia. By that time, further product innovation has taken place in the richer countries.

IV. INTERNAL SCALE ECONOMIES II: MONOPOLISTIC COMPETITION

To this point we have considered all goods produced within an industry to be perfect substitutes. An alternative to this assumption of *homogeneous goods* is to assume that an industry produces products that are close, but not perfect, substitutes. Examples of *differentiated goods* are Californian chardonnay and French pinot gris, or the Toyota Highlander and the Ford Explorer. Consumers benefit from the variety that differentiated products provide, either because they are able to find the variety that is most preferable (e.g., the consumer prefers the firmer ride offered by the Ford Explorer to that offered by the Toyota Highlander) or because they enjoy variety in consumption (e.g., chardonnay with chicken, pinot gris with fish).

Differentiating one variety from another requires the firm to devote real resources to product design and marketing. These expenditures are fixed costs because they do not vary with the number of units sold by the firm. These fixed costs imply that the firm's production technology is subject to increasing returns to scale: the firm's average cost falls as it sells more units. Fixed costs explain why we do not observe an endless number of product types. For example, while one may choose certain features when buying a new automobile, such as color and special equipment, there is a limit to the degree of customization one observes in most markets. Fixed costs limit the number of product varieties available in a market of a given size.

In markets for differentiated products, each firm's product is somewhat different from those offered by other firms. Consequently, a firm can raise its price without losing all its customers; it faces a downward sloping demand curve for its unique product variety. By facing a downward sloping demand curve, the firm can set its price above marginal cost without driving its sales to zero. However, because new firms may enter the market whenever positive profits are to be made, competition restrains the extent to which firms can exploit the monopoly power they possess for their unique varieties. This market structure is termed monopolistic competition because it combines some elements of monopoly (downward sloping demand curve) with elements of perfect competition (many firms with free entry and exit).

The equilibrium for an industry that is monopolistically competitive is shown in Figure 5.3a.[5] The demand curve as seen by each firm is labeled *d*. Its downward slope

---

[5] This section uses the diagrams of monopolistic competition and trade developed by Feenstra and Taylor (2008).

indicates that the firm can sell more of its unique variety only if it lowers its price. The marginal revenue curve associated with demand curve d is labeled MR The marginal revenue curve lies below the demand curve because the extra revenue earned by selling one more unit requires the firm to drop its price on all units sold, as in the standard monopoly case. Also shown on this figure are the marginal cost curve MC, which we assume is flat, and the average cost curve AC. Due to the presence of fixed costs, the firm's average cost lies above marginal cost and falls as the quantity produced increases.

An important aspect of monopolistic competition is that each firm's sales depend on the prices of other varieties, which are close substitutes. The firm's demand curve d shows how many units it can sell at each price, assuming the prices of all other varieties do not change. This curve is very elastic since a drop in the price of one variety will attract customers away from other firms. However, we can consider another demand curve, D/N, which shows the quantity demanded from each firm when all firms in the industry charge the same price. The demand curve is steeper than the d curve because when all firms drop their price at the same time, any particular firm will not attract as many customers as it would if it alone had reduced its price.

Figure 5.3a illustrates equilibrium in a market without trade. To maximize its profit, each individual producer offers the quantity Q^A to the domestic market, which is the quantity for which marginal revenue equals marginal cost. The price at which the market will absorb this quantity is P^A, a point on the demand curve d. Although this price exceeds marginal cost, note that it is equal to the firm's average cost. Entry of new firms made the demand curve faced by incumbent producers more elastic (entry shifts d, the demand curve faced by an incumbent, to the left and makes it flatter), a process that only ends when firms are earning zero monopoly profits and further entry is deterred. There are no monopoly profits when price equals average cost, as at point A. Finally, note that point A is also on the industry demand curve, D/N.

How would trade affect the number of varieties and the price offered to consumers? Krugman (1979) provides an answer to this question that can be seen easily with the

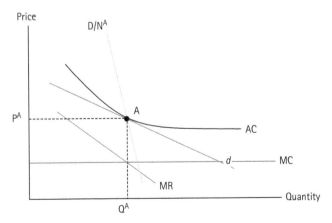

FIGURE 5.3a Equilibrium in a monopolistically competitive market without trade

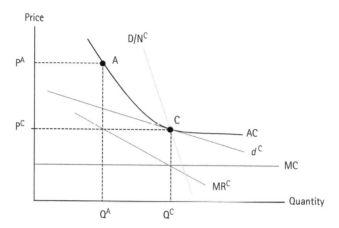

FIGURE 5.3b Equilibrium in a monopolistically competitive market with trade

aid of Figure 5.3b. Suppose that we allow trade between two identical countries, Home and Foreign, both of which have a monopolistically competitive industry selling a differentiated good. Because these countries are identical, there is no basis for comparative advantage. Nevertheless, there is the possibility of mutually gainful trade.

Because the two countries are identical, they will have the same number of firms when trade begins. However, the number of consumers available to each firm doubles. Because we are doubling the number of firms and the number of consumers, the industry demand curve, D/N is exactly the same as before. In other words, the point A is still on the demand curve D/N, as shown in Figure 5.3a. Nevertheless, the market has been changed by the entry of foreign varieties. With more varieties to choose among, consumers are more sensitive to price. The demand for each individual variety becomes more elastic (flatter) than the old demand curve. As a result, each firm has to choose a new profit maximizing level. The new marginal revenue curve, corresponding to the new flatter demand curve, is also flatter and each firm responds by lowering price and expanding output. Not all firms can do this given the size of the market, however, and the increased competition. The new equilibrium will occur when firms just break even, that is, when price equals average cost. This new equilibrium occurs at a point like C, in Figure 5.3b, where the now flatter demand curve facing each firm is tangent to the average cost curve.

This analysis indicates that there are two sources of gains from trade for consumers. First, increased foreign competition has led to a drop in price and, therefore, to an increase in consumer surplus. This drop in price is possible because of scale economies: the fewer firms remaining produce at a higher level of output and, thus, experience a rise in productivity. Second, the total number of varieties available to consumers, domestic plus foreign, is larger than that available in the absence of trade. If consumers value variety, this is a separate source of gains for them. More choices for consumers enhance their wellbeing. Against these gains, however, must be set the short-run dislocation that results from the exit of some domestic firms in the face of competition from foreign firms.

V. National External Economies of Scale

In this section, we consider the effects of trade when the scale economies are external to the firm but national in scope. This type of scale economy may result from labor market pooling, in which workers with special skills concentrate in one location, or from opportunities for infrastructure investment as a country's industrial sector expands. We use a simple model to illustrate the main implication of trade in this context. Because scale economies are external, average costs in all firms decline as the industry expands. Individual firms, of which we assume there are many, take prices as given and do not act as if industry costs are influenced by their own behavior.

Consider an economy that can produce two goods, automobiles and bread, using labor alone. Bread (B) is produced with constant returns to scale, its output being just a multiple of its labor input. Automobiles (A) are produced with external increasing returns to scale because the average labor input needed declines as total domestic automobile production increases. To focus solely on production differences, we assume that consumer's preferences are identical everywhere and that consumers spend a fixed share of income on each commodity.

The production possibility frontier (PPF) for this economy, which shows the maximum number of autos the economy can produce for any given amount of bread production, is provided in Figure 5.4. The PPF is bowed in, reflecting decreasing average costs in the automobile sector.[6] This shape contrasts with the bowed-out shape of the PPF familiar from the standard neoclassical (Heckscher–Ohlin) model, in which the opportunity cost of one good in terms of the other increases as we move along the PPF. Here,

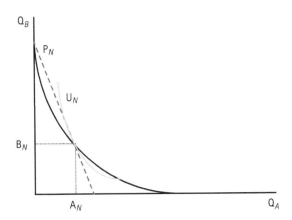

FIGURE 5.4 No-trade equilibrium, automobile production exhibits scale economies

---

[6] Note that with only one factor, labor, there is no difference between industries in factor intensity. As we know from the Ricardian trade model, if both industries produce with constant returns and use only labor, the PPF is a straight line. Thus, the bowed-in shape of the PPF in Figure 5.4 can be attributed to the assumption of increasing returns rather than constant returns.

the opportunity cost of automobiles, defined as the units of bread that must be foregone to produce one more auto, falls as we produce more automobiles.

If there is no trade, where along the PPF will the economy produce? Equilibrium requires that firms in both sectors just break even, so that there is no entry or exit of firms. Therefore, an equilibrium allocation of labor between the two sectors is one where price equals average costs in each industry. Additionally, equilibrium requires that consumers demand the quantities of goods produced at those prices. Such an equilibrium is depicted in Figure 5.4. The slope of the line labeled P_N (indicating the relative price of autos with no trade), shows the relative price of automobiles, the price ratio P_A/P_B. This price ratio equals the average costs of automobile production divided by the average costs of bread production at the production points labeled A_N and B_N. Note that the line labeled P_N cuts through the PPF, rather than being tangent to it. This relationship reflects the fact that automobile firms do not set prices at marginal costs, which would imply negative profits for firms with increasing returns-to-scale technology. Rather, the average price of autos exceeds the marginal cost of autos and the relative price of autos (shown by the slope of P_N) exceeds the ratio of the marginal cost of autos to the marginal cost of bread (shown by the slope of the PPF at the production point (A_N, B_N)).

The curve labeled U_N shows a community indifference curve, which is tangent to the line labeled P_N. We can think of these curves as indicating combinations of goods A and B which provide the same level of utility, in this case U_N, to an average consumer. The tangency of the price line with the community indifference curve implies that the bundle consisting of the quantity A_N of automobiles and the quantity B_N of bread is the production point on the PPF that is most preferred by consumers at that price. Note, however, that the slope of the PPF and the slope of the indifference curve are not the same because goods are priced at average instead of marginal cost.

Can trade between two identical economies with these characteristics be mutually gainful? The answer is not as simple as in the case of constant returns to scale, for which aggregate gains from trade are assured. With increasing returns to scale, there is a possibility of gains for both countries because international trade allows production of the increasing-returns good, automobiles, to be concentrated in one country. Because of declining average costs, this specialization can lead to lower automobile prices for consumers in both countries. However, as we shall see, there is also the possibility that one of the countries would be worse-off with trade than without it. Such an outcome is not possible with constant returns to scale.

A trading equilibrium in which both countries gain from trade is depicted in Figure 5.5. Here we assume that the Home economy produces only automobiles and that the Foreign economy produces only bread. Note that there is no feature of the model that determines which country will end up specializing in automobiles. In this sense, the pattern of trade is indeterminate if the cause of trade is increasing returns to scale. Concentration of autos in one country lowers the relative price of autos with trade (shown as P_W) below the price prevailing in both countries in autarky. Despite specializing in the good whose price has fallen, Home workers are better off. The

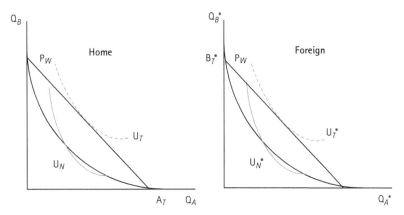

FIGURE 5.5 A trading equilibrium in which both countries gain from trade

higher productivity they achieve in auto making as a result of higher scale more than compensates for the lower price they receive. Foreign workers enjoy a lower price for autos in exchange for each unit of bread they produce. Consequently, workers in both countries are able to consume a bundle that they prefer to the bundle they could afford without trade.

Let us now consider two economies that are identical in all ways except that Home has a larger labor force than Foreign. Because the size of the national industry determines efficiency, the larger country may be more likely to specialize in the increasing-returns industry because it would have the lower relative price of autos in autarky. Essentially, with demand conditions the same in the two countries, Home's larger scale leads to lower average costs in the auto industry and a lower relative price for autos in the autarky equilibrium. Perhaps surprisingly, Home's lower autarky relative price for autos need not guarantee that it will be the automobile exporter.[7] However, if the two countries begin to trade with each other before workers in each country are able to adjust to the larger market, the relative price of autos will fall in the smaller country and its auto sector will shrink. The Home country will be the exporter of autos. Two possible outcomes emerge for the distribution of gains.

In the first case, one economy (say, Foreign) is very small compared to its trading partner, and both countries will gain from trade. The small country is unable to take advantage of scale economies in the absence of trade. Its autarky relative price for autos is very high compared to the autarky relative price of its large partner. With trade, the small country specializes in the constant returns to scale good, while the large country produces both bread and autos. The small country enjoys a lower relative price for autos with trade than it did without trade as the large country operates its industry on a much larger scale. The outcome for the small country is similar to that depicted in panel A of

---

[7] The dynamics of getting from no trade to free trade are not intrinsic to the model and the outcome could be altered by policy interventions along the way. Even when Home is larger than Foreign, an equilibrium could occur with Foreign specialized in automobile production.

Figure 5.5, with gains from trade for both countries. Small countries, in this scenario, are able to take advantage of scale economies present in the international economy that they would not be able to achieve on their own.

Now we consider a case in which the two economies are close in size. Again, suppose that the Home economy is the larger economy and that it is completely specialized in automobiles. Suppose, further, that demand for autos is high, so that the relative price of autos is high, but not high enough to permit production in the Foreign country, which will have a very small scale of activity and thus high costs. As shown in Figure 5.6, both economies will be completely specialized but the situation no longer resembles the case shown in Figure 5.5. The higher price of automobiles makes the gains from trade even larger for the country that specializes in autos. For the country specializing in bread, however, the higher price of autos is a terms of trade deterioration. Indeed, the terms of trade can be so adverse that the country's welfare with trade may be lower than the welfare it achieved without trade. In this case, the larger country reaps all the gains from trade while the somewhat smaller country loses from trade. Such a situation can never happen if trade is based on comparative advantage instead of scale economies.

If demand is high enough so that the somewhat smaller economy produces some autos, it may still lose from trade if it operates its auto industry at a sufficiently small scale. Home is able to run its industry at a large, efficient scale. Foreign cannot sell its autos for a higher price than Home, so its wages must be low to compensate for its low labor productivity. In this sense, we can conclude that the possibility of losses from trade arises when trading partners are close in size. However, some initial condition, such as the location of the original innovation or favorable local policy, may determine the direction of trade and the possibility of losses makes a case for intervention.

National, external scale economies give us a different view on the advantages of free trade, particularly for middle-income countries engaged in manufactured goods trade. If trade might or might not be beneficial and if the country that benefits is not predetermined, why not use trade or industrial policies to ensure that your country enjoys the

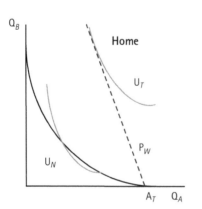
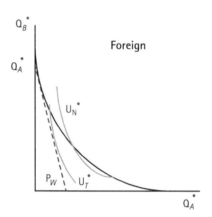

FIGURE 5.6 A trading equilibrium in which home gains and foreign loses from trade

higher productivity and wages that come from larger scale? These views have been used to justify policies that protect manufacturing industries in the hope of realizing scale economies as the industry grows.

The idea behind tariff protection or even export subsidization is to make the home industry more efficient by grabbing market share from foreigners, a process called "production shifting." Such arguments are sophisticated justifications for "infant industry" protection. If production shifting is successful, the foreign economy is left worse-off and, thus, the policy is basically a "beggar-thy-neighbor" one. However, unlike the optimum tariff argument, in which a country uses its tariff policy to improve its own terms of trade at the expense of its partners, production shifting need not leave the world as a whole worse-off. Indeed, if it succeeds in simply switching the location of production, it may change the identity of the gaining and losing country without any effect on world welfare.

Despite the beauty of the theory, there are few concrete examples of cases where countries have successfully engineered production shifting of this sort. Another reason to doubt the usefulness of trade protection as a mechanism for raising domestic productivity is that trade flows do not match those predicted by the theory. If trade is caused by national economies of scale, we should see trade characterized by extensive industrial specialization and *inter-industry* trade. Instead, we find large volumes of trade within broad industry classifications, that is, we see extensive *intra-industry* trade. National scale economies alone cannot help us to explain these important flows.

VI. INTERNATIONAL EXTERNAL ECONOMIES OF SCALE

Our analysis of national scale economies assumed that products were homogeneous; that is, that all products produced in an industry were identical no matter which country produced them. However, many products are differentiated, as discussed above for the case of internal scale economies. Not just consumer goods are differentiated. Producer goods are also differentiated as modern production processes require a large number of specialized inputs. Suppose we consider these inputs to be differentiated business services. In this case, firms gain from increased variety, in a manner similar to our discussion of differentiated consumer goods. Moreover, if we assume that the external economy firms enjoy from a larger industry scale is independent of the location of that industry, trade in differentiated producer goods benefits both trading partners. Put another way, if producers in Europe benefit from specialized producer services, even if these services are produced by IBM in New York or Wipro in Bangalore, they cannot lose from the opening of trade. Our conclusion regarding the possibility of losses from trade no longer holds. When scale economies are international in scope, trade is mutually gainful. Producers in both countries gain when the industry expands and both countries experience a rise in productivity.

Case Study: National and International Scale Economies in the Global Automobile Industry

Policies pursued by Malaysia and Thailand, two members of the Association of Southeast Asian Nations (ASEAN) Free Trade Area, illustrate opposing views of how best to gain from trade in a sector characterized by multiple forms of scale economies: the automotive industry.[8] Both countries produce and export passenger motor vehicles and motor vehicle parts, but have pursued quite different policies to promote domestic production and exports. While Thailand welcomed foreign participation in the industry, Malaysia heavily subsidized domestic production. Both countries developed their industries behind high tariff walls.

ASEAN was formed in 1967 by Indonesia, Malaysia, the Philippines, Singapore, and Thailand, with a vision of promoting stability and security in the region. Brunei joined in 1984, Vietnam in 1995, Laos and Myanmar in 1997, and Cambodia in 1999. The ASEAN Free Trade Area (AFTA) was formed in 1992, with the intent to lower tariffs on industrial and agricultural goods to between 0 and 5 per cent by 2008. AFTA was designed to create a larger market and more attractive environment for foreign direct investment. The elimination of regional trade barriers would allow companies to source parts freely within the region, stimulate greater economies of scale, and promote greater production efficiency. Consumers were promised lower prices and a wider choice of products.

In the automotive industry, the elimination of regional trade barriers fit Thailand's strategy of building a niche in the globally fragmented production chain. Beginning in the early 1980s, Thailand pursued a private sector-led automotive industrial policy. Its automotive manufacturing is fueled by foreign investment. Joint ventures and licensing arrangements with Japanese and US automakers have made Thailand a center for vehicle production as well as for the development and manufacture of parts and components. Japanese vehicles assembled in Thailand dominate its domestic market. Thailand's tariff on completely built vehicles from outside the ASEAN region was set at 80 per cent, with Thailand eager to reduce intra-ASEAN trade barriers to their current level of 0–5 per cent. This combination of policies led to rapid growth in Thai exports of vehicles and parts after 2000, as seen in Figures 5.7a and 5.7b.

In contrast, Malaysia pursued an inward-oriented strategy centered on development of national car companies. Its first national car company, known as PROTON, began in 1985 as a joint venture between a domestic Malaysian firm, which held a 70 per cent share, and the Japanese company, Mitsubishi. The Malaysian government heavily subsidized the development of its domestic automobile industry. Its strategy of transforming the country from a vehicle importer and assembler to a car manufacturer has provided employment and considerable national pride, but these achievements have required substantial financial support and preferential treatment by the national government.

The domestic industry has also benefited from high tariffs on imported vehicles, ranging from 140–300 per cent on completely built vehicles as well as quota restrictions through

---

[8] This case study draws on the longer discussion of AFTA and the auto sector provided by Tran (2001).

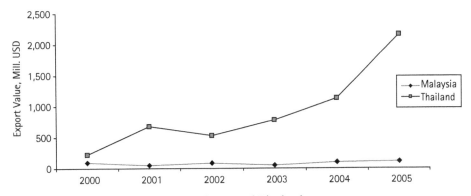

FIGURE 5.7a Motor vehicle exports, Malaysia and Thailand

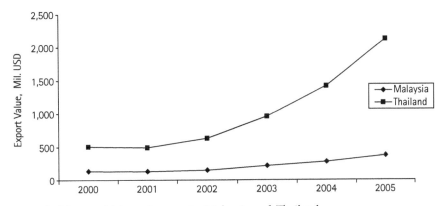

FIGURE 5.7b Motor vehicle parts exports, Malaysia and Thailand

Source: UN Comtrade Database.

Case Study: *Continued*

import licensing. By the end of the 1990s, Malaysia's national cars dominated its domestic market. Despite concerns that domestic manufacturers would not be able to compete successfully with international automotive giants, by 2006 Malaysian intra-regional tariffs were 0–5 per cent and its external tariffs were 20–35 per cent. Nevertheless, Malaysian exports of vehicles and parts remain small, as seen in Figures 5.7a and 5.7b.

International Internal and External Economies of Scale: Offshoring and Outsourcing

Firms may find that costs decline as output rises worldwide, not just at home. For example, headquarter activities can serve a worldwide operation, allowing the firm to lower average costs by expansion. A new literature has developed seeking to explain when firms will decide to leverage the cost advantage available by expanding their operation abroad rather than simply buying imported goods and services. As will be argued below, offshoring, fragmentation, and outsourcing involve the interaction and comparison of different types of implicit and explicit costs, some of which are fixed and do not vary with output. Hence, there are important economies of scale to consider.

We follow Helpman (2006), who uses "outsourcing" to refer to "the acquisition of an input or service from an unaffiliated company." We will call the sourcing of inputs (goods and services) from foreign countries "offshoring," which includes offshore outsourcing, as well as foreign direct investment (FDI). While offshore outsourcing involves inter-firm (arm's length) trade, FDI involves intra-firm trade. Both offshore outsourcing and FDI have grown very rapidly over the past 20 years. And, even though outsourcing and offshoring might not mean the same thing, there is a large overlap between the two, which may explain why the two terms are used so interchangeably.

Jones and Kierzkowski (2001) provide us with a very simple explanation for the increased fragmentation we have witnessed over time. Suppose the overall production process can be divided into a number of fragments of different factor intensities. To minimize the cost of each fragment, production will be divided across countries in accordance with each location's factor prices. However, even as fragmentation lowers the marginal cost of production, by for example shifting the most labor-intensive tasks to low-wage countries, it will simultaneously raise the fixed cost of production because the various parts of the production process must be linked across production locations. When the market for these goods expands, fragmentation is encouraged because these fixed management and communication costs can be spread over more units. Essentially, by allowing the fixed costs to be divided over more sales, economic growth permits firms to reap the benefits of lower marginal costs through offshoring. The opening of new markets, especially the densely populated Asian markets, is another factor that has encouraged fragmentation. In the last three decades, the integration of China and then India has expanded the size of the global market, again encouraging fragmentation. Liberalization of policies toward foreign direct investment in these and many other economies has also permitted firms to fragment production while maintaining control. It is interesting to note, however, that this explanation for recent fragmentation trends implies that it will slow down as differences across countries in factor prices, especially wages, narrow as a result of fragmentation itself.

From this simple theory of fragmentation, we move to the more sophisticated theory of outsourcing that draws heavily on the contract-theory literature. While we understand the factors that drive firms to divide the production process into several fragments, we next ask which fragments should be produced "in-house" and which should involve arm's length transactions. Since production of many final goods requires highly customized and specialized intermediate parts, the quality of the work done by input suppliers may not be verifiable by a third (outside) party. Therefore, it will be impossible for the final-good producer and the input supplier to write a complete contract that fully specifies the price–quality relationship and, thus, that can be enforced by a judicial system. In such cases, the final-good producer and the input supplier may have to bargain, after each has made a relationship-specific investment, over how the profits of their joint effort will be divided. If either party believes it will not be fully compensated for its investment in the production relationship, it may fail to invest enough to maximize the profit from their joint efforts. This failure to invest optimally is termed a "hold up problem" and it may be caused by the input supplier or by the final-good producer whenever a complete contract cannot be written.

Helpman (2006) argues that "intermediate inputs under the direct control of the final good producer suffer less from agency problems than intermediate inputs that require the engagement of suppliers," implying that using an arm's length transaction makes it harder for the firm to achieve the right level of investment in the total production process. Helpman also argues that the bargaining power of the final good supplier is higher when it owns the foreign subsidiary than under outsourcing, because ownership brings some control over inputs and the final-good producer can recover some of its value if bargaining fails. This is good from the point of view of getting the resources provided by the final-good producer as close to the optimum as possible, but it adversely affects the level of activity of the input producer, which now has no ownership stake. Thus, incentives are closer to optimal with integrated production, such as would occur if the final-good producer builds a foreign subsidiary, in the case of goods and services that require intensive use of headquarter services (provided by the final-good producer) in their production, while arm's length outsourcing is better in the case of goods whose production is intensive in the use of specialized inputs (provided by the intermediate-good producer).

This line of reasoning leads to some conclusions that are potentially empirically testable. If (1) headquarter services are capital intensive and input production is labor intensive, and if (2) the two fragments have to be combined in the same country to produce a specific tradable-intermediate input used in the production of a given non-tradable-final good (and there are many different intermediate and final goods), then we should see, controlling for other things, a positive correlation between the share of intra-firm imports of a country and the capital abundance of the exporting country (Antras, 2003 and Helpman, 2006). Note that intra-firm imports occur when a parent trades with a foreign subsidiary, while inter-firm imports are correlated with offshore outsourcing from an arm's length supplier. With intra-firm trade, inputs are being produced in the same multinational firm as the final output. This is not so with offshore outsourcing. Thus, according to this theory, in less capital-abundant countries, such as China and India, we should see relatively more offshore outsourcing than offshoring through FDI. Of course, legal institutions are going to be weaker in these countries than in the more capital-abundant countries, and that will push firms away from arm's length suppliers. Contract enforcement is going to be weaker, as courts are going to be congested due to low judge–population ratios in these countries.

What Triggers Offshoring?

Based on casual empiricism, we believe that temporary shocks can trigger this process, but the effects of such shocks can be permanent. A few home-grown Indian IT groups, namely companies such as Wipro, TCS, and Infosys, have become powerful players in the market for offshore IT services. After getting their big break by subcontracting to overloaded Western firms during the Y2K software crisis at the turn of the millennium, they are now beginning to "expand beyond core IT maintenance and support work into helping multinationals, for instance, to roll out new software applications" (*The Economist*, December 11, 2003). The Y2K crisis can be viewed as a temporary shock which increased the net benefits to American firms from outsourcing, due to a shortage of programmers in the USA. A complementary force was technological change in the form of falling costs of computing and telecommunications equipment. These forces, along with the Y2K crisis, led firms in the USA to outsource to India, which had a vast available pool of programmers. This outsourcing kept increasing well after the Y2K problem became a thing of the past. The fact that a temporary shock had a permanent effect on offshore outsourcing suggests, as we explain below, the existence of external economies. There are also fixed costs of outsourcing that imply the existence of internal economies of scale as a result of outsourcing.

Mitra and Ranjan (2005) argue that as more firms from the developed world offshore their production activities to a developing country, the productivity of workers in that developing country increases. The possible explanations, as explained below, for this increase in productivity are the standard ones for external economies, based on labor market pooling, knowledge spillovers, and learning by doing. Northern firms choose between offshoring their input production to a developing country or, at the other extreme, staying fully domestic. As more firms offshore, productivity of labor in this activity in the developing country increases. Thus, it does not pay a firm to offshore to that country unless and until quite a few other firms offshore, and if all firms wait for several other firms to offshore, offshoring may not take place at all. A temporary shock such as the Y2K crisis makes it much more profitable, at least in the short run, for firms to outsource to a developing country such as India. As these firms enter India, output of the Indian IT industry expands, as a result of which American firms learn more about the skills of Indian software engineers, and at the same time Indian software engineers are able to absorb some new technical knowledge from the American firms. Due to the demand for software engineers, a more efficient labor market in software technology emerges together with the development of better infrastructure for information technology (IT) and the emergence of many more training institutes that produce software engineers. So even when the Y2K shock becomes a thing of the past, offshore outsourcing continues. Thus, a temporary shock has a permanent effect.

Case Study: Exporting of Business Services

Figure 5.8, drawn from Mitra and Ranjan (2005), shows recent computer and business services insourcing (exports) and outsourcing (imports) for India and Ireland.[9] While in India, things were initiated by the Y2K crisis and the dotcom bubble, in Ireland in addition

[9] Here insourcing is from the point of view of India, which is outsourcing from the point of view of other countries such as the United States into India.

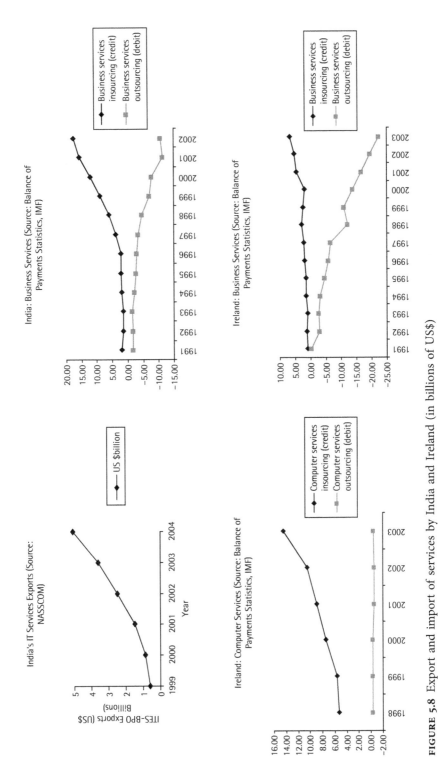

FIGURE 5.8 Export and import of services by India and Ireland (in billions of US$)

Case Study: *Continued*

certain tax breaks given in the late 1990s were responsible for the surge in the exports of business and computer services.

Figure 5.9 shows us the movements in software exports as a share of sales for India for the period, 1993–2002. After remaining roughly constant until 1997, this share contin- ued to rise. As we see from Figure 5.8, the growth in these exports has not been reversed in India or in Ireland so far even though the Y2K and the dotcom bubble were tempo- rary shocks, and the tax breaks to insourcing into Ireland were very partially reversed in response to protests from other European countries. Another interesting thing to note here is that outsourcing (imports) of these services from these countries to other countries shows a declining trend.

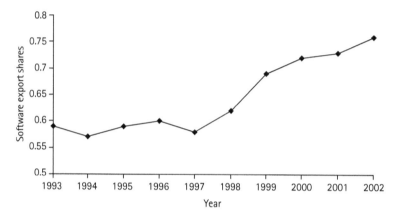

FIGURE 5.9 Indian software exports as a share of software sales

Source: Arora and Gambardella (2005).

VII. Firm Heterogeneity and International Trade

The new literature on scale economies and international trade emphasizes firm het- erogeneity in productivity. In other words, different firms in the same industry have different productivity levels. This is a significant departure from older models in the international trade literature that have assumed homogeneous or symmetric firms. However, these older models cannot help us understand some important empirical facts. First, we find that firms exporting their products are generally more productive than firms that produce only for the domestic market. This has clearly been shown for French firms by Eaton, Kortum, and Kramarz (2004). Second, using the same French dataset, they find that the population of firms exporting is not a random sample from the population of all firms. Third, the more export destinations a firm services, the higher is its productivity.

Melitz (2003) provides a model, with heterogeneous firms, that offers an explanation for these empirical regularities. Firms are heterogeneous because they differ in their productivity levels. If there are fixed costs of servicing each export market, only high productivity firms will be able to pay these fixed costs and profitably export. In addition, because there are fixed production costs even for the firms that decide only to service the domestic market, increased competition from foreign firms will raise the minimum productivity level needed for any firm to survive. As a consequence of this weeding out of less productive firms and growth in the most productive firms, trade liberalization raises average productivity for the industry as a whole. This "Melitz effect" provides an additional source of gains from trade.

Case Study: The Bangladeshi Apparel Industry

An interesting application of the Melitz (2003) model is the apparel industry in Bangladesh. This case study is based on recent econometric work done by Demidova, Kee, and Krishna (2006), who study firm-level exports of woven and non-woven apparel from Bangladesh to the European Union (EU) and the United States. The United States has much higher tariffs than the EU on apparel exports from Bangladesh. While the rules of origin are equally stringent in the case of woven apparel in both the United States and the EU, the EU has much more relaxed rules for non-woven apparel. Demidova, Kee, and Krishna take advantage of all the above variations in policy across the two regions and across the two kinds of apparel. They find that firms in Bangladesh that export to the United States generally also export to the EU, and these firms are more productive (have lower costs of production) than firms that only export to the EU. This finding is consistent with a model in which the ability of firms to jump fixed exporting costs depends on their productivity level.

VIII. Conclusion

Roughly half of world trade today is between developed countries, while only 20 per cent is accounted for by trade between the developed and the developing world. Thus most of world trade cannot be explained by comparative advantage arising from differences in country characteristics. However, trade between similar countries can be explained by a variety of models with one common feature, namely increasing returns to scale or scale economies in production. In this chapter, we have tried to make these modern theories of trade accessible to the non-technical reader to the extent possible. After discussing the various possible types of scale economies, we started with an in-depth analysis of trade arising from scale economies that are internal to the firm. Such increasing returns normally arise from fixed costs in production. These are costs that need to be incurred even to produce the smallest possible unit of output and do not need to be replicated to produce subsequent units. These costs often act as entry barriers, leading to oligopolistic market structures, in turn leading to the scope for strategic trade policy, in the form of export subsidies, R&D subsidies, and import tariffs. Such models also help us understand the existence of segmented markets arising from transport costs, in turn leading to the phenomenon of reciprocal dumping.

Innovation by firms is also an important feature of oligopolistic market structures. However, knowledge created through innovation gets transferred from one country to another, leading to "product cycles." In other words, a good, after significant passage of time, starts being produced in the low-wage South (developing world). This has been true for textiles and more recently in the case of computer chips.

In this chapter, we also discussed monopolistic competition models with internal increasing returns. A firm produces a variety, and in doing so incurs a fixed cost. The presence of fixed costs results in a limited number of varieties produced. It is the size of the market that limits the number of varieties. Economic integration through trade expands market size and increases welfare. We explained this theory pioneered by Krugman using diagrams and economic intuition.

We also covered external economies. In this case, the increasing returns are internal to an industry within a country but are external to the firm. While such economies of scale can also explain trade between similar countries, such trade is not necessarily welfare improving for all trading countries. In this context, we also evaluated the policy of infant industry protection. This was followed by a discussion of international economies of scale. We also discussed here an application of the global automobile industry.

Another application of international internal and external economies is offshoring, which in many cases takes the form of offshore outsourcing. We emphasized that offshoring takes place through the fragmentation of the production process, where each fragment of the production process has a fixed cost associated with it. As a result, there is a limit to the extent of fragmentation and the degree to which production is fragmented will depend on market size and differences in relative endowments across countries. We ended our discussion of offshoring and outsourcing by reviewing the modern contract-theory based literature on outsourcing and its empirically testable predictions, followed by the factors that have recently triggered offshoring. Once again, there are increasing returns involved here and the returns to scale are dynamic. This dynamic aspect leads to permanent effects on the extent of offshoring of temporary shocks such as the Y2K and the dotcom bubble.

We ended our chapter with an intuitive discussion of the well-known and extremely well-cited Melitz theory of international trade in the presence of internal increasing returns under firm heterogeneity. We discussed the "Melitz effect" of trade on productivity. Trade leads to the weeding out of less productive firms and to resource reallocation to the relatively more productive firms. This leads to an increase in industry-level productivity. We concluded by studying an application of the Melitz model to the Bangladeshi apparel industry.

Throughout this chapter, we have tried to illustrate the predictions and usefulness of the various theoretical models using examples and case studies. While the introduction of imperfect competition and scale economies into the discussion of why countries trade and how trade affects welfare leads us to a variety of situations and outcomes, consideration of these factors sheds light on many fundamental sources of trade conflicts.

Careful consideration of each situation allows the analyst to see beyond the immediate effect of import competition on the domestic industry and toward the broader issues at stake for the society. They also aid our understanding of the political economy of trade protection, a subject central to following chapters.

REFERENCES

Antras, P. (2003), 'Firms, Contracts, and Trade Structure' *Quarterly Journal of Economics,* 118(4): 1375–1418.

Arora, A., and Gambardella, A. (2005), *From Underdog to Tigers: The Rise and Growth of the Software Industry in Some Emerging Economies,* Oxford: Oxford University Press.

Brander, J. A., and Spencer, B. J. (1985), 'Export Subsidies and International Market Share Rivalry' *Journal of International Economics,* 17 (February): 83–100.

Brander, J. A., and Krugman, P. (1983), 'A "Reciprocal Dumping" Model of International Trade' *Journal of International Economics,* 15 (November): 313–21.

Demidova, S. A., Kee, H. L., and Krishna, K. (2006), 'Do Trade Policy Differences Induce Sorting? Theory and Evidence from Bangladeshi Apparel Exporters' NBER Working Paper No. W12725.

Eaton, J., Kortum, S. and Kramarz, F. (2004), 'Dissecting Trade: Firms, Industries, and Export Destinations' *AER Papers and Proceedings,* 94: 150–54.

Ethier, W. J. (1995), *Modern International Economics,* Third Edition, New York: WW Norton.

Feenstra, R. C., and Taylor, A. M. (2008), *International Economics,* New York: Worth Publishers.

Helpman, E. (2006), 'Trade, FDI, and the Organization of Firms' *Journal of Economic Literature,* 44: 589–630.

Jones, R. W., and Kierzkowski, H. (2001), 'A Framework for Fragmentation' In Arndt, S. and Kierzkowski, H. (eds.) *Fragmentation: New Production Patterns in the World Economy,* Oxford: Oxford University Press.

Krugman, P. (1979), 'Increasing Returns, Monopolistic Competition, and International Trade' *Journal of International Economics,* 9(4): 469–79.

Krugman, P. (1984), 'Import Protection as Export Promotion: International Competition in the Presence of Oligopoly and Economies of Scale' In Kierzkowski, H. (ed.) *Monopolistic Competition and International Trade,* Oxford: Oxford University Press.

Krugman, P., and Obstfeld, M. (2006), *International Economics: Theory and Policy,* Seventh Edition, Boston, MA: Pearson Addison Wesley.

Melitz, M. J. (2003), 'The Impact of Trade on Intra-Industry Reallocations and Aggregate Industry Productivity' *Econometrica,* 71(6): 1695–1725.

Mitra, D., and Ranjan, P. (2005), 'Y2K and Offshoring: The Role of External Economies and Firm Heterogeneity' NBER Working Paper No. 11718.

Tran, E. (2001), 'The ASEAN Free Trade Area (AFTA) and the Malaysian National Car Project' Case No. HKU144, Center for Asian Business Cases, School of Business, The University of Hong Kong.

PART III

TRADE POLICY
AND TRADE
LIBERALIZATION

CHAPTER 6

INSTRUMENTS OF TRADE POLICY

GEOFFREY A. JEHLE

I. INTRODUCTION

GOVERNMENTS implement a variety of policies targeting international trade—both imports and exports—and they do so for a variety of reasons. In this chapter, we examine the principal instruments of trade policy used by modern governments. Our goal will be to understand the impact each one has on the allocation of resources and on the distribution of welfare to consumers, producers, and government in the country that employs it.

II. IMPORT TARIFFS

The Many Types of Tariffs

Ad valorem and specific tariffs

A tariff is a tax on imports. An *ad valorem* tariff is expressed as a per cent of the imported good's value or price: a 10 per cent tax on the price of imported tomatoes is an example of an *ad valorem* tariff. A specific tariff is expressed as a fixed amount of money per unit of the good: a charge of $20 per 100 pounds of imported tomatoes is an example of a specific tariff. Of course, each type of tariff can be directly converted into an equivalent tariff of the other type. For example, if the price of imported tomatoes is $200 per 100 pounds, the 10 per cent *ad valorem* tariff is equivalent to the $20 specific tariff—each requires the importer to pay a customs duty of $20 on one 100 pounds of tomatoes. As part of the "July 2004 Package" of the Doha Development Agenda, member countries of the World Trade Organization (WTO) have now agreed to work toward converting all non-*ad valorem* tariffs to their *ad valorem* equivalents and to henceforth base negotiations on those. In this chapter, we will always speak in terms of *ad valorem* tariffs. Of course, because of their ready convertibility, conclusions regarding *ad valorem* tariffs will apply to specific ones too, as well as to combinations of the two.

Tariffs can be discriminatory or non-discriminatory by source. Any tariff that applies only to the goods of a particular nation or group of nations is a discriminatory tariff. For example, tariffs on Italian shoes, or on Egyptian cotton, would both be discriminatory tariffs. By contrast, a non-discriminatory tariff is one that applies to all goods of a certain category, regardless of their country of origin. Tariffs on shoes, and cotton, regardless of source, would be non-discriminatory tariffs. Early General Agreement on Tariffs and Trade (GATT) rules, and current WTO rules, generally forbid member countries from explicit discrimination among other members' goods. If a member extends some tariff preference to imports from another member, that same preference must be extended to imports of the same goods from all members. Some major exceptions to this so-called "most favored nation" (MFN) rule have been allowed, though. Some significant regional trading arrangements—such as the European Union—are allowed to offer tariff preferences to member states that are not offered to WTO members outside the union. Some of the original Commonwealth Preferences, giving members of the British Commonwealth special access to the British market, have been preserved by the Lomé Convention even after Britain's entry into the European Union. In addition, the United Nations Conference on Trade and Development (UNCTAD) continues to promote special access for goods from many developing countries into developed countries' markets on special, preferential terms, and this has been accepted into the Development Agenda of the Doha Round.

A protective tariff is one applied to shield a domestic industry from the competition of foreign suppliers. A revenue tariff, by contrast, is one applied purely to raise revenue for the government. Many years ago, a great many tariffs were revenue duties: it was comparatively easy to identify incoming ships, trains, and other vehicles at border crossings and levy the tax. Today, income and other forms of taxation provide by far the largest share of government tax revenues in most developed countries, so the majority of tariffs in those countries are protective duties. In many less-developed countries, though, tariffs remain an important source of government revenue.

Nominal and Effective Rates of Protection

When domestic production of an import substitute requires the use of imported inputs that are themselves subject to tariffs, the nominal rate of tariff applied to final-good imports may differ quite substantially from the overall extent of protection afforded domestic producers of the import substitute. The effective rate of protection is an estimate of the overall extent to which domestic value added in production is protected by the country's entire tariff structure as it affects the imported final good and all intermediate goods in the production process. Calculating effective rates of protection is a tedious business, and it is often of necessity based on arguable assumptions about the underlying production process. Nonetheless the exercise can be illuminating and can provide policy makers with sobering and important information. It is easy to see, for example, that while tariffs on a final good tend to advantage domestic producers of the good, tariffs on their imported inputs essentially serve as taxes on those same producers. It is therefore quite possible that a haphazard or uncoordinated tariff structure—thought to be encouraging domestic producers—may, instead, actually serve to *discourage* domestic production of that good if the rate of effective protection afforded by the entire tariff structure is negative. Quite apart from the wisdom of implementing those tariffs in the first place, such a situation is, at the very least, usually at odds with the policymakers' intentions.

Tariffs Today

The post-war drive for broad trade liberalization, starting with the GATT and continuing through the WTO, has led to significant worldwide reduction in tariffs. Table 6.1 reports average rates of tariff, in their *ad valorem* equivalent, across broad WTO member groupings in 2008. For comparison, earlier figures are included in parenthesis. Over roughly the past two decades, tariff rates have declined very broadly—sometimes

Table 6.1 Tariff rates by WTO member grouping, 2008

	Average				Percentage of lines greater than 15%
	Simple	Weighted	Std. dev.	Max. rate	
High-income Members					
Effective Applied Rate	2.5	1.3	6.2	555	2.4
MFN Rate	3.2	2.3	7.5	555	2.7
Preferential	0.8	0.8	6.2	500	0.9
(1988 Effective Applied Rate)	(4.3)	(3.3)			
Developing Members					
Effective Applied Rate	7.2	4.3	20.3	3,000	18.8
MFN Rate	9.3	6.3	22.7	3,000	24.9
Preferential	2.2	1.5	7.3	254	6.2
(1988 Effective Applied Rate)	(18.9)	(16.4)			
Least-developed Members					
Effective Applied Rate	13.1	9.7	11.1	200	54.0
MFN Rate	13.3	10.4	9.7	200	48.1
Preferential	4.8	2.1	9.7	100	29.2
(1989 Effective Applied Rate)	(105.4)	(88.4)			

Source: UNCTAD TRAINS database at <http://r0.unctad.org/trains_new/index.shtm>.

significantly. However, while rates of tariff are generally lower than they were in the past, there remains considerable diversity across product lines (so-called tariff lines), and across countries. While developing and least developed WTO members have always had higher average rates of tariff, covering a broader range of products, even among developed countries some products continue to be subject to extremely high rates of protection. Hence, a good distance has yet to be traveled in the drive for worldwide trade liberalization.

Tariff Incidence in the Small Country

To explore the impact of tariffs more closely, we begin with the case of a small country. For our purposes, a country is considered small in the world market for some good, regardless of that country's population or geographic size, if its domestic consumption, domestic production, and imports of the good have only negligible effects on world market conditions, especially the good's price.

Throughout this chapter, we will assume that the domestic markets in our analysis are perfectly competitive, with many small consumers and many competing producers of the same homogeneous good. Even when these are not wholly accurate descriptions of the relevant market structure, assuming competitive markets is a useful simplification that leads us, in many cases, to similar conclusions to those we would reach through application of more complex methods needed to analyze imperfectly competitive markets.

Figure 6.1 depicts domestic market demand and domestic market supply for some good at different market prices. With no access to world markets, the equilibrium market price and the quantity of the good produced and consumed in this small country would be found at the intersection of market demand and market supply. However, in

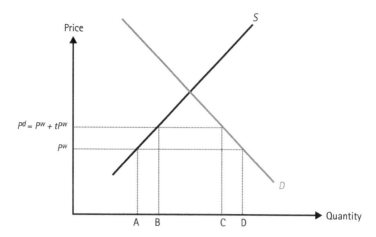

FIGURE 6.1 A tariff's impact on resource allocation

a regime of free trade, if buyers and sellers residing in this country have costless access to the larger world market on which this good currently trades at world price P^w, and if (as we will assume) domestic buyers regard the imported item as indistinguishable from the domestic good, no consumer would be willing to pay more than P^w for a unit of this good and, so, no domestic producer could sell above that price. In Figure 6.1, we can see from the domestic market demand curve that, at a price of P^w, buyers would demand a total of D units. At that same price, we can see from the domestic supply curve that domestic producers would be willing to produce only A units. The difference between domestic demand and domestic supply at P^w—the quantity represented by the line segment AD—measures the quantity of imports. Notice that any good a country imports is necessarily one for which there is *excess demand* in the domestic market at the prevailing world market price.

How Tariffs Affect Resource Allocation

If an *ad valorem* tariff rate of $t > 0$ (in decimal form) is imposed on imports of this good, then under this tariff policy a unit of the foreign-produced good, valued on the world market at P^w, would be subject to import taxes of tP^w. Initially, buyers in the tariff-imposing country would be faced with a choice: buy a unit of the domestic good for the prevailing price P^w, or buy a unit of the imported good, which importers could sell for no less than $P^w + tP^w$ and still break even. Any sensible buyer would want to buy the domestic item at the now-cheaper price.

But what effect would such actions—taken by large numbers of buyers simultaneously—have on market conditions and the allocation of resources in the tariff-imposing country?

Before the tariff was imposed, home-country buyers, in all, were prepared to buy more units of the good at P^w than home-country producers were prepared to sell at that price, the difference being made up by imports. But now, as home-country buyers turn away from the costlier import and turn toward the domestic good, they will soon find there is not enough to satisfy all buyers at the prevailing price. This excess demand from domestic buyers will then cause the price of the domestic good, P^d, to rise above P^w, as buyers bid against each other for the available quantity. This rise in the domestic price, set off by imposition of the tariff, will then, itself, set in motion powerful market forces affecting both domestic producers and consumers.

As the price they must pay for the domestic good begins to rise, consumers will tend to reduce their purchases, economizing on this increasingly expensive item. This is called the consumption effect of the tariff. At the same time, the rising price of the domestic good makes it now more profitable for domestic producers to increase production in existing plants, to bring new plants into production, and perhaps even for new firms to enter the market. The extent to which the tariff increases domestic production of the import substitute is called the protective effect of the tariff. In Figure 6.1, imposition of this tariff should see the domestic price of the good, P^d, begin to rise above P^w. As it does, domestic consumers move up the market demand curve, and the total number of units they demand will begin to decline leftward from D; at the same time, however, domestic producers move up the market supply curve and domestic production will increase rightward from A.

Both the decrease in domestic consumption and the increase in domestic production caused by the rise in P^d work to reduce excess demand for the domestic good and so, over time, tend to slow the rise in its price. When will that process stop entirely? A moment's thought will convince you that as long as the price of the domestic good, P^d, is less than the price of the imported item, inclusive of tariff, $P^w + tP^w$, domestic consumers will continue to turn to domestic sources and, as long as these remain in excess demand in the domestic market, P^d will continue to rise. If the tariff were sufficiently high that $P^w + tP^w$ exceeded the price at which domestic demand and supply intersect in Figure 6.1, then P^d would rise to the level of that point of intersection and the total quantity demanded by domestic buyers would be willingly supplied by domestic producers at that price. There would then no longer be pressure on domestic price to rise as all those who wish to buy the good at that price would find a willing domestic supplier. In this scenario, imports would have been completely choked off. A tariff with this effect is called a prohibitive tariff. If, however, the rate of tariff were not prohibitive, and $P^w + tP^w$ were, say, as indicated on the vertical axis in Figure 6.1, then P^d would rise only to that level and no further. Why no further? Because if P^d were to rise above $P^w + tP^w$, domestic buyers would once again find imports cheaper than the domestic good and so switch their purchases back to the imported item. Foreign exporters would be willing to sell at that price, too, since they collect $P^w + tP^w$ per unit from home country buyers, pay the home country government tP^w in tariff duties, and receive, net, the world price per unit, P^w. We conclude that, for all but prohibitive tariffs, the domestic price of the protected good must rise by the full extent of the tariff, so that in the post-tariff market equilibrium,

$$P^d = P^w + tP^w. \tag{6.1}$$

This is illustrated in Figure 6.1.

Stepping back to compare the pre-tariff equilibrium with the full post-tariff equilibrium, what effects has the decision to implement this non-prohibitive tariff had on the allocation of resources in the tariff-imposing country? Some are seen in Figure 6.1, and we've noted them already: as the price of the domestic good rises, increased domestic production from A to B is encouraged, and decreased domestic consumption from D to C results. The quantity of imports falls, too, from AD before the tariff to BC after. In addition, the government now collects tariff revenue that it did not have before. This is called the revenue effect of the tariff.

But some of the effects of this tariff are unseen. For example, as firms increase output from A to B, additional labor is hired and employment in the protected industry will rise; additional capital, raw materials, and other domestic resources will be drawn into the protected industry too. These resources will have to come from somewhere: to the extent that they are induced away from other productive uses elsewhere in the economy, we can expect that output and employment in those other industries will decline. We will not pursue the full implications of these unseen effects right now: but it is wise to keep an awareness of them in the back of the mind.

How Tariffs Affect Peoples' Welfare

Tariffs cause prices to change, and people are affected as a result. But just how a person is affected depends importantly on who they are. Consumers of the import and the domestic good are generally made worse off by tariffs: they must pay higher prices for the goods they purchase—whether that is the imported item or the domestically produced one. Both will rise in price with the tariff. On the other hand, domestic producers of the good will generally be better off: higher prices for their product, and higher levels of employment and production, usually translate into higher earnings and profit for the firms' owners. The government, too, gains some advantage from the tariff: as long as the tariff does not choke off all imports, the government will have a new source of revenue—the tariff (tax) revenue on the remaining volume of imports.

That tariffs can redistribute welfare in this manner—away from consumers and toward domestic producers and the government—is an important consequence of tariffs and, indeed, may often be the motivating reason a government will decide to impose them. Perhaps the imported good is considered by government to be a frivolous luxury item, only consumed by the idle rich. Then some justification may be felt in imposing the tariff precisely because it redistributes welfare away from those consumers toward others. Perhaps, instead, domestic producers of the good are a favored group: political backers of the regime in power, for example, or perhaps merely just a sympathetic group—poor village women producing simple manufactured or agricultural goods, for example. In such cases, the motivation to impose the tariff may simply be an affirmative desire to help the favored group, with no particular desire to discourage anyone's consumption or harm anyone else. Nonetheless, the tariff will help some and it will harm others—there will be winners *and* losers. This simple fact should give the policymaker pause to consider the distributional effects of the tariff in their entirety.

What's Wrong with Tariffs

Granting that there will be winners and losers when a tariff is imposed, what can we say about its welfare effects on the tariff-imposing country "as a whole?" To answer this, we need some way to measure the impact of tariffs on those that are affected, and we need some agreement on how the different costs borne by some and benefits enjoyed by others will be added up, or aggregated, into an overall assessment of the impact on society as a whole. Economists commonly use consumer surplus to measure the welfare effects on consumers, and producer surplus to measure the effects on domestic producers. Consumer and producer surplus measures, and their relation to social welfare, are described in the Appendix to this chapter. In the discussion to follow, it is assumed the reader is familiar with that material.

In Figure 6.2, which reproduces the elements of Figure 6.1, the distributional effects of the tariff can be clearly seen. The tariff, causing domestic price of the good to rise from P^w to $P^w + tP^w$, causes consumer welfare, measured by consumer surplus, to fall

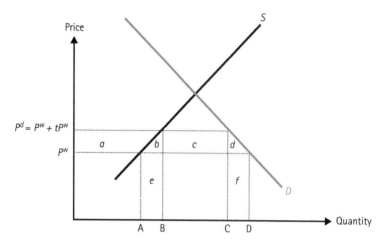

FIGURE 6.2 A tariff's impact on welfare

by an amount equal to sum of areas $a + b + c + d$. That same price rise, however, causes the welfare of domestic producers, measured by producer surplus, to rise by an amount equal to area a. In addition, the government now collects tariff revenue it did not have before, and if we presume that each such dollar is used by the government to benefit *someone* in society by a dollar, we must also reckon that revenue on the "plus" side of the social ledger. In Figure 6.2, the area marked c measures the full extent of the tariff revenue collected by the government: tP^w (the height of box c) is collected on each of BC units imported (the width of the box c), giving total tariff revenue equal to the product, $tP^w(AB)$.

If we are content to treat a dollar's gain, or loss, to any one person in society as having the same social importance as a dollar's gain or loss to anyone else—a strictly utilitarian criterion of social welfare—then how do the winners' gains and losers' losses all add up? It is easy to see in Figure 6.2 that if consumers lose $a+b+c+d$, while producers gain a and the government gains revenue of c, there is still a net loss to society equal to the sum of areas $b+d$. This is called the dead-weight loss due to the tariff—it is welfare that someone in society *could* be enjoying if it weren't for the tariff—and it measures the magnitude of the net social loss from the tariff that will be borne, period after period, while the tariff is in place.

How, intuitively, can we understand the sources of this net social loss? First, notice that there are two distinct components to it: area d and area b. Let's focus on area d first. Recall that one effect of the tariff is to cause consumers to reduce their purchases from D to C. The total value of those units to consumers—their total willingness to pay for them—is equal to the area under the demand curve, or $d + f$. Before the tariff, those CD units of domestic consumption were imported from the foreigner at P^w per unit, or for a total outlay of only f. Area d, then, measures the net gain consumers were able to enjoy when, before the tariff, they consumed something worth $d + f$ to them while paying only f to have it. With the tariff, that consumption of CD is no more and, so, neither is the net benefit someone in society enjoyed from it. Now focus on area b. Recall that the other effect of the tariff was to encourage increased production of the domestic good by an additional AB units. Before the tariff, those AB units of domestic consumption were, instead, imported from the foreigner for P^w per unit, or a total outlay of domestic resources equal to area e. Producing those AB units domestically requires the use of domestic resources—land, labor, capital, and other resources—and those have a dollar value equal to the whole of the area under the supply curve, or $b+e$. Area b, then, measures the amount of *additional* domestic resources now devoted to that bit of domestic consumption over and above what had to be expended before the tariff. Economists call area d the consumption-side inefficiency introduced by the tariff and area b the production-side inefficiency.

We've argued that area $b+d$ must be regarded as a net social loss, "if we are content to treat a dollar's gain, or loss, to any one person in society as having the same social importance as a dollar's gain or loss to anyone else." But what if the policymaker has very good reasons not to hold this view? Suppose, for example, there is a broad social consensus that domestic producers, as a historically disadvantaged group in this society, merit extra weight in the social calculation; that a dollar's gain in welfare to that group should be given greater importance than a dollar's loss in welfare to consumers of this good in the overall social evaluation. Policymakers often have perfectly valid distribution preferences of this sort, and welfare redistribution is a very common objective of government policy. Since tariffs redistribute welfare, why not use them to help achieve those distributional goals whenever possible? The answer is simple: tariffs are an inefficient means of redistributing welfare. Because the dollar value of the welfare loss to consumers is greater than the dollar value of the welfare gain to producers and the government by the amount $b + d$, consumers end up paying that much more than they should have to in order for the government to achieve the goal of transferring welfare in the amount $a + c$. If, instead of implementing a tariff, government were to simply impose a lump-sum tax on consumers equal in total dollar amount to area $a + c$, then transfer that amount to producers and anyone else it favored, the recipients would be just as well off as they were going to be under the tariff policy, but consumers—still able to consume the imported good at P^w—would suffer a welfare loss of only $a+c$ and so be better off than they would have been under the tariff policy by $b + d$. Because tariffs distort prices faced by consumers and producers they introduce consumption-side and production-side inefficiencies, making the cost of achieving the distributional objective greater than it needs to be. For more discussion of the dead-weight loss and its relation to social welfare, see the Appendix to this chapter.

Tariff Incidence in the Large Country

The analysis of tariffs in the case of a large country is similar to that of a small country, but there are also important differences. Regardless of its geographic size, a country is considered a large country in the world market for some good if its

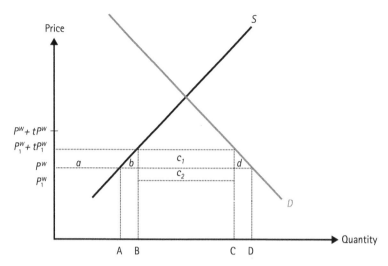

FIGURE 6.3 Tariff incidence in a large country

domestic consumption, domestic production, and imports of it can have noticeable effects on world market conditions, especially market price.

The Terms of Trade Effect

As we've seen, tariffs reduce domestic consumption and encourage domestic production, thereby reducing the volume of a country's imports. When those imports are an important component of total world demand for the good, that drop in imports will shift the world demand curve for the good and cause its equilibrium world price to fall. This terms of trade effect can mitigate the adverse effects of the tariff on the tariff-imposing country, essentially by shifting a portion of the burden onto its trading partners.

To see this more clearly, consider Figure 6.3, which depicts domestic market demand and supply for a large-country importer of some good. Under free trade, the initial world price is again P^w, domestic consumption is at D, domestic production at A, with imports of AD. If an *ad valorem* tariff of $t > 0$ were imposed, and if the fall in this country's imports were to have no effect on world market price, let us suppose that the domestic price of the good would rise to $P^w + tP^w$. However, if the decrease in import demand from the tariff-imposing country causes world market price for the good to fall to, say, P_1^w, then the domestic price of the good in the tariff-imposing country will only rise to $P_1^w + tP_1^w$ before equilibrium is restored with domestic consumption of C, domestic production of B, and imports of BC. As we've seen before, this tariff discourages domestic consumption, encourages domestic production, and reduces the country's volume of imports.

The distributive effects of this tariff are similar to those we've seen in the small country: the increase in domestic price caused by the tariff redistributes welfare from consumers to producers and the government. Here, consumer welfare is again reduced by $a + b + c_1 + d$, producer welfare again increases by a, and government again earns new revenue of $c_1 + c_2$. The tariff again introduces a consumption-side inefficiency of d and a production-side inefficiency of b, but this time there is no net loss to society. In fact, social welfare *increases* overall as a result of this tariff! How can that be? Notice that, this time, part of the tariff revenue the government collects—that part of total tariff revenue, labeled c_2, that lies below the level of the original price P^w—is, in effect, no new burden for domestic consumers, who only see the price they pay rise from P^w to $P_1^w + tP_1^w$. Instead, it is a new type of burden being imposed on the country's trading partners. Foreign producers, who previously received P^w per unit on those BC units now receive only P_1^w. Domestic consumers may pay a total tariff bill equal to the whole of areas $c_1 + c_2$, but only the portion above P^w is a new net burden on them: the portion below the level of P^w can be regarded as a transfer of welfare from foreign producers, to domestic consumers, and then from domestic consumers to the government. In Figure 6.3, the size of that transfer from the country's trading partners more than offsets the efficiency losses $b + d$, resulting in a net welfare *gain* for the tariff-imposing country.

The Optimal Tariff

One should not regard the case we've just described as rare or unusual. Quite often, when a country's import volumes have some impact on the world price, it should be able to craft some tariff that is welfare improving. Of course, policymakers could get it wrong—so this does not mean that just *any* rate of tariff will raise welfare in the large country. But there will often be at least one rate for which the tariff revenue extracted from the country's trading partners more than compensates for the production-side and consumption-side inefficiencies it causes. Since there may be more than one such rate, the one which maximizes the country's net gain is called the optimal tariff.

By distorting market prices at home and abroad, one country's optimal tariff always introduces consumption-side and production-side inefficiencies into the world economy. And while we've seen that those it causes in the tariff-imposing country itself are more than outweighed by that country's tariff revenue gains, those tariff revenue gains are at the expense of producers somewhere else. The world as a whole must therefore lose when any country imposes an optimal tariff.

But should any one country's policymakers be more concerned about world welfare than they are about their own national welfare? If an optimal tariff can raise your country's welfare, shouldn't you impose one? Doesn't the imperative of advancing the nation's interest compel it?

Perhaps, but it would be wise to think carefully before doing so. Because when the tariff-imposing country gains only at the expense of its trading partners, those trading partners may not just sit idly by. In fact, there may be good reasons for them to retaliate with tariffs of their own.

Retaliation

When two or more countries' welfare are interdependent—when the actions of any one of them can affect the others, as well as themselves—all the elements of a strategic game are present. In such situations, rational "players" must think carefully about how others are likely to respond to actions they take, and how that, in turn, can affect them.

		Country 2	
		Free trade	Optimal tariff
Country 1	Free trade	100, 100	80, 120
	Optimal tariff	120, 80	90, 90

FIGURE 6.4 Tariffs and retaliation

Figure 6.4 is the payoff matrix for a typical "tariff game" between two large countries. Each country may either elect a regime of free trade, with no tariffs, or it may implement its optimal tariff. We've seen that if one country implements an optimal tariff while its trading partner acquiesces and continues with a policy of free trade, the tariff-imposing country's welfare will rise and that of its trading partner will fall. It is easy to imagine that if, instead, the trading partner were to retaliate and impose an optimal tariff of its own, that country could recoup some of its losses, albeit at the expense of the other country. The entries in the payoff matrix reflect this thinking. The first number in each cell is some index of national welfare in Country 1, the row player, and the second some index of national welfare in Country 2, the column player.

Let's look carefully at the strategic situation facing each of these countries as they contemplate what their trade policy should be. If Country 1 believes Country 2 will continue to pursue free trade even if Country 1 imposes an optimal tariff, Country 1 can raise its welfare from 100 to 120. If, instead, Country 1 believes that Country 2 will impose its optimal tariff, Country 1 would suffer welfare of only 80 if it adhered to free trade. But it could recoup some of its loss, and have welfare of 90, if, instead, it retaliated with an optimal tariff of its own. Notice that no matter what Country 1 thinks Country 2 will do, its own best course of action is always the same: it should impose an optimal tariff! Of course, the same is true of Country 2: no matter what it thinks Country 1 will do, its own best course of action is always to impose an optimal tariff too. Game theorists would say imposing an optimal tariff is a strictly dominant strategy for each of these countries because no matter what the other player does, that strategy is always the player's very best course of action. Rational players, when they have them, can be expected to use their strictly dominant strategies, so the outcome of this game seems easy to predict: each country will impose an optimal tariff and each will receive welfare of 90.

But notice something interesting about this outcome: both countries are worse off than they would be if they had both resisted the temptation and stayed with a policy of free trade: each would have then had welfare of 100, instead of only 90. Recognizing this, rational players should then, instead, elect free trade, right? They would both be better off if they did. But if either one in fact elects free trade, the other can do even better by imposing an optimal tariff, getting welfare of 120! If either thinks its rival might just do such a thing, it is better off protecting itself with its own optimal tariff, getting welfare of 90, rather than suffering 80. But if they both think and act this way, the outcome is, again, that each imposes an optimal tariff on the other and both are again worse off than they would be if they had both elected free trade! This sorry state of affairs is called a

Prisoner's Dilemma: while there may be mutual gains to be had by cooperating to support a regime of free trade, the logic of national interest makes those gains seemingly impossible to attain.

Difficult, perhaps, but not impossible. One way around this Prisoners Dilemma would be to change the payoffs countries see in the choice between free trade and protection. Indeed, one can regard much of the post-war effort to create institutions such as the GATT and WTO, and to write the rules for membership in them, as an effort to do just that. Negotiations that result in mutually agreed upon rules and sanction regimes are often able to modify the structure of incentives from those so starkly apparent here, by increasing the gains from cooperation and reducing the gains from unilateral action. In so doing, they hope to align the incentives of individual member countries to find it more in their national interest to play their part in the cooperative outcome with benefits for all.

III. IMPORT QUOTAS

A quota is a quantitative restriction on trade. Under an import quota, the government sets an upper limit on the quantity of some good that may be imported in a given period—say, a limit of 40 tons of wheat per year. With a quota, no tax is collected on imports directly, as with a tariff. However, the quota will have very similar effects as a tariff does on resource allocation and the distribution of welfare. But there are a few key differences, too.

How Quotas Affect Resource Allocation and Welfare

The domestic market for an imported good is depicted in Figure 6.5. Under free trade, imports are available on the world market at P^w and this small country imports the quantity AD. Now suppose the government implements a quota on imports, mandating that no more than BC < AD units be admitted. Because domestic consumers demand D units at the free trade price P^w, while domestic producers provide only A at that price, once imports are restricted to something less than AD, there will be excess domestic demand for the good at the world price P^w. The domestic price will therefore begin to rise above P^w as frustrated buyers begin trying to outbid one another for the available quantity. As the domestic price begins to rise, domestic producers will increase production and domestic consumers will reduce their consumption. Price will continue to rise until the total quantity demanded by consumers at the prevailing price is matched by the quantity domestic producers are willing to supply at that price, plus imports of no more than BC, as is the case at P^d.

Through these indirect effects on domestic price, a quota, like a tariff, encourages increased production of the import substitute, and draws additional resources of land, labor, and capital into the protected sector, as domestic producers respond to the

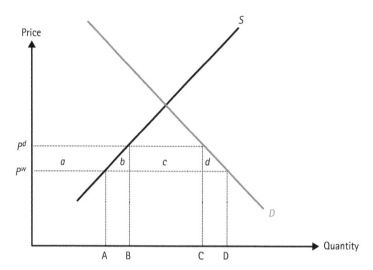

FIGURE 6.5 A quota's impact on resource allocation and welfare

good's rising price. Here, the protective effect of the quota is AB. There is a consumption effect, too, as consumers also respond to the good's rising price, reducing their total purchases by CD.

It is easy to see in Figure 6.5 that the quota of BC units ultimately has exactly the same effects on domestic production, domestic consumption, and the allocation of resources to the protected sector as would an appropriate *ad valorem* tariff. Specifically, a tariff rate of $(P^d - P^w)/P^w$ would raise domestic price to $P^w + ((P^d - P^w)/P^w)P^w = P^d$, giving precisely the same ultimate effects on production and consumption. In this sense, there is said to be tariff and quota equivalence in the ultimate effects each of them has on the allocation of resources.

Tariff and Quota Equivalence?

The rise in price following imposition of the quota redistributes welfare, too, very much like a tariff. But there are some important differences.

As price rises from P^w to P^d, consumer surplus falls by $a + b + c + d$, while producer surplus rises by a. Putting aside for the moment what we should make of area c, there will again be net national welfare losses of b and d, as there were with the tariff, because quotas introduce the same sort of production-side and consumption-side inefficiencies as tariffs do.

Under a tariff, that part of the loss that is consumer surplus measured by area c was compensated for by an equal increase in tariff revenue collected by government. With a quota, the government does not collect any tax revenue of this sort. Instead, it allocates rights to import—import licenses—and how those rights are allocated directly affects the distribution of welfare.

Suppose, for example, that the government simply awards a license to import one unit of this good to some importer. That individual could purchase one unit of the good abroad at the world price P^w, import it into the country and sell it at the prevailing domestic price P^d, earning a profit—or, more precisely—an economic rent—equal to $P^d - P^w$. If licenses for a total of BC units are simply given to importers—say in proportion to the quantities each imported before the quota was imposed—then total rents earned by all importers so favored would be equal in amount to area c. In this scenario, the quota redistributes welfare from consumers to domestic producers and to those lucky enough to secure import licenses at no cost.

But why should government simply give away such a valuable item? If, instead, it were to auction off those import licenses, importers, and others, would have an incentive to bid for them. Since each unit of the good purchased abroad and then sold on the domestic market under the quota regime would earn economic rent of $P^d - P^w$, bidders would bid up to precisely that amount in order to obtain the right to import a unit. If the rights to BC units were auctioned for their full value to bidders, the government could earn revenue from the sale of the full set of licenses equal in amount to the whole of area a! Under this method of allocating import licenses, the distributional, as well as the allocative, effects of the quota are fully equivalent to those of an appropriate *ad valorem* tariff: the quota redistributes welfare from consumers to domestic producers and the government, with a net reduction in national welfare overall due to the production-side and consumption-side inefficiencies caused by the quota.

There are others ways in which tariffs and quotas are not entirely "equivalent." For one, the protective effect of a non-prohibitive *ad valorem* tariff remains unchanged as changing economic conditions in the tariff-imposing country affect domestic demand

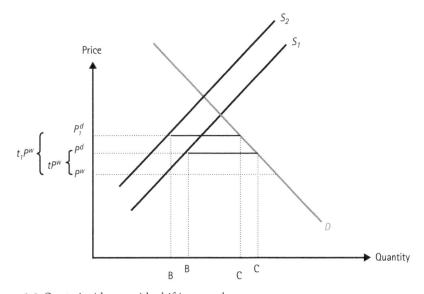

FIGURE 6.6 Quota incidence with shifting supply

and/or supply of the protected good—and this is not so with quotas. The *de facto* rate of protection under a quota will usually change whenever domestic demand and/or domestic supply of the good change. Figure 6.6 illustrates the point. There, a given quota restriction in the amount BC has a *de facto* rate of protection equal to an *ad valorem* tariff of *t* when domestic market supply is S_1. If supply shifts to S_2—due, say, to an increase in input prices, bad weather or some other supply-side shock—the domestic price of the protected good will rise further—this time to P_1^d—giving a *de facto* rate of protection equal to that of a larger *ad valorem* tariff, $t_1 > t$. Finally, though we will not explore the issue in detail here, we should also note that tariffs and quotas may have quite different effects when the domestic market is not perfectly competitive. For example, when a domestic monopoly produces the import substitute, a tariff forces that firm to act much like a competitive firm in the larger world market, but when a quota is used, the domestic monopoly remains free to exercise its monopoly power over whatever is left to it of the domestic market after the quota.

IV. EXPORTS

Until now we've focused on policies directed at imports. Policymakers can, and do, implement policies that affect the country's exports as well. In the United States, Article 1, Section 9 of the Constitution contains an explicit prohibition against export duties of any kind, but many other countries employ them. Russia taxes its petroleum exports and Indonesia taxes its palm oil exports. Export subsidies, particularly agricultural export subsidies, have been contentious issues in trade relations between the US and EU, and between developed and developing countries more broadly. The analysis of export taxes and export subsidies, formally very similar to that of tariffs, is often a bit less easily grasped right at first, so we will proceed carefully. Like tariffs, export taxes and export subsidies can be *ad valorem*, specific or both. Each will have an *ad valorem* equivalent, however, so we'll treat all cases with a close look at the impact of *ad valorem* export taxes and *ad valorem* export subsidies alone.

Export Taxes

Figure 6.7 depicts domestic demand and supply in the market for some exportable good in a small country. In the absence of any opportunity to trade with others, the domestic market clearing price would be at the intersection of market demand and supply, well below the world price, P^w. Under free trade, this country would therefore export the good. At the world price P^w, domestic producers want to sell D units while at that same price domestic consumers only want to purchase A. Domestic producers will find willing buyers abroad, however, and in the free trade equilibrium exports total AD units.

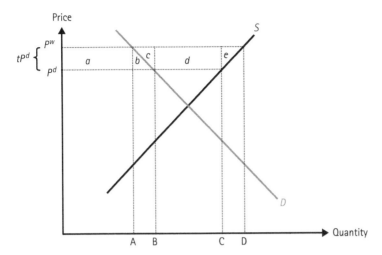

FIGURE 6.7 Incidence of an export tariff

Following imposition of an *ad valorem* export tariff (tax) of $t > 0$, domestic producers of the exportable good are faced with a choice: they can ship the good abroad and pay a tax on it, or they can sell it in the domestic market tax-free. At first, the choice is simple: if the good is selling at the same price in the domestic market and in the export market, net receipts would be lower for sales abroad by the amount of the tax, so firms will tend to ship fewer units abroad and shift their sales to the domestic market. As many firms act in this way, the quantity of output redirected toward the domestic market will cause the domestic price of the good to *fall*. That this must happen is clear, once we recall that the good was originally in excess supply domestically: at the world price P^w, domestic buyers were unwilling to buy all that domestic producers wanted to sell at that price. After imposition of the export tax, then, increased domestic sales by firms seeking to avoid the tax on their exports must force down the domestic price of the good. But just how far will the domestic price, P^d, fall? If it were to fall far enough, it would at some point become profitable for producers to go ahead and pay the tax on exports if they can earn the higher world price, P^w, on those sales. Specifically, if $P^d > P^w - tP^d$ the firm earns more on a unit sold at home than it would on a unit taxed upon export at its domestic value, P^d, and sold abroad at the world price P^w. Hence, the firm would sell that additional unit at home, putting greater downward pressure on P^d. By contrast, if $P^d < P^w - tP^d$, the firm earns more by redirecting that unit abroad, earning more, post-tax, than it would from domestic sales, putting upward pressure on P^d. We may conclude, therefore, that pressure for the domestic price to change will cease only when neither such situation is present: that is, only when $P^d = P^w - tP^d$. This can be rearranged and expressed, instead, as follows:

$$P^d + tP^d = P^w \tag{6.2}$$

Equation (6.2) tells us that the export tax must cause the domestic price of the good to fall by the full extent of that *ad valorem* tax. That is the situation depicted in Figure 6.7.

It is easy now to see the impact the export tax has on resource allocation in the exporting country. As the domestic price falls following imposition of the tax, domestic consumers increase consumption from A to B units. At the same time, domestic producers reduce production from D to C, releasing resources of labor, land, and capital. In the post-tax equilibrium, the country's exports have declined from AD to BC. The government collects tax revenue from the export tariff of $tP^d(BC)$, an amount equal to the area marked d.

The distributional effects of the export tax are easily seen in Figure 6.7, too. With reduced production at lower prices, domestic producers of the exportable lose producer surplus of $a + b + c + d + e$. With greater consumption at a lower price, consumers gain consumer surplus of $a+b$. As we've noted, the government gains new revenue of d. The export tariff, then, redistributes welfare from domestic producers to domestic consumers and the government. But notice that producers' losses are not fully offset by these countervailing social gains: there is a net social loss of $c + e$. We may understand the net national welfare loss as arising from two sources: the redirection of firms' sales from exports toward the domestic market, and the reduction in total production caused by the tax.

We've seen that the price decrease causes domestic consumption to rise by AB units. Originally, domestic firms were able to sell those units to foreign buyers for $b + c$ in revenue more than they now fetch from domestic buyers. All of that revenue loss cannot be reckoned a social loss, however, because domestic consumers now have AB units more consumption, on which they enjoy new consumer surplus of b. Only c, then, can be regarded as a net social loss from the redirection of sales away from exports and toward the domestic market.

We've also seen that the price decrease causes domestic production to fall by CD units overall. Under free trade, firms earned gross revenue on those units equal to the entire area of the rectangle with base CD and height P^w. The value of society's resources devoted to that amount of production—the land labor and capital used by exporting firms—totaled an amount equal to the area beneath the market supply curve above CD. With the export tax, the firms' lost revenue on those units exceeds the value of the resources that were used to produce them by an amount equal to area e, and so that must be reckoned a net loss to society from the overall reduction in output.

Export Subsidies

Everyone knows that if you tax something, you'll get less of it; and if you subsidize it you'll get more of it. The same is true of exports. But exports are not the only thing affected when government decides to subsidize them.

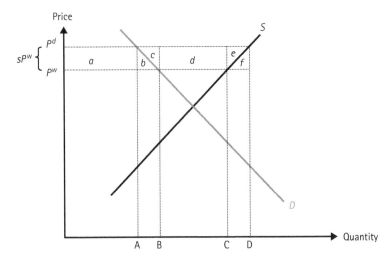

FIGURE 6.8 Incidence of an export subsidy

Figure 6.8 depicts the domestic market for an exportable good. With free trade at a world price of P^w, domestic production is at C, domestic consumption at B and exports are BC.

If an *ad valorem* subsidy of $s > 0$ is granted to exports, domestic producers are faced with a choice: they can ship the good abroad and receive a subsidy on it, or they can sell in the domestic market at the prevailing market price and forego the subsidy. Once again, the choice is simple at first: if the good is selling at the same price in the domestic market and in the export market, net receipts would be higher for sales abroad by the amount of the subsidy, so firms will tend to ship more units abroad and shift sales away from the domestic market. As output is redirected toward the export market, the domestic price of the good must begin to *rise* as home-country buyers who want the good must be willing to pay what sellers can earn, instead, by exporting: if $P^d < P^w + sP^w$, no firm will sell to a domestic buyer so, in the end, equilibrium in the domestic market will only be restored when

$$P^d = P^w + sP^w \qquad (6.3)$$

Equation (6.3) tells us that an export subsidy must cause the domestic price of the good to rise by the full extent of that *ad valorem* subsidy. That is the situation depicted in Figure 6.8.

As the domestic price of the exportable rises following imposition of the subsidy, domestic consumers reduce consumption from B to A units, while domestic producers increase production from C to D, drawing more domestic resources of labor, land, and capital into the production of the exportable good. In the post-subsidy equilibrium, exports will rise from BC to AD and the government must make subsidy payments of $sP^w(\text{AD})$, an amount equal to the sum of areas $b + c + d + e + f$.

The distributional effects of an export subsidy are exactly opposite to those of the export tax. With increased production at a higher price, domestic producers of the exportable gain producer surplus of $a + b + c + d + e$. With lower consumption at a higher price, consumers lose consumer surplus of $a+b$. To support this policy, the government must commit revenue equal to $b + c + d + e + f$ to pay firms the subsidy. The export subsidy, then, redistributes welfare away from domestic consumers and the government toward domestic producers of the exportable good. But notice that the losses to consumers and the government are greater than the gains to domestic producers: there is, this time, a net social loss equal to $b + f$. Once again, that net social loss arises from two sources: the firms' sales redirected away from the domestic market and toward exports, and the increase in total production encouraged by the subsidy.

We've seen that the price increase causes domestic consumption to decline by AB units. Originally, consumers were able to buy those from domestic producers at P^w and enjoy a consumer surplus of b on them. That is lost with imposition of the export subsidy and, instead, those AB units are now exported, giving a net social welfare loss equal to b on those units.

That same price increase induces firms to increase total production for export by CD units, on which the government pays a subsidy of $e + f$ to domestic firms. Only area e of that, though, is received as new producer surplus by the firms: the remainder, area f, therefore represents a net loss to society.

V. THE LERNER SYMMETRY THEOREM

To this point, we have tended to focus on the impact of policy in one market. Economists call that a *partial equilibrium* perspective. But economies are complex networks of interconnected and interdependent markets. It is rarely the case that some impact felt in one market will fail to have repercussions in others. A *general equilibrium*, or economy-wide, perspective would consider *all* the ramifications in all directly and indirectly affected markets whenever a policy is implemented.

As it turns out, a full general equilibrium analysis of the policies we've considered so far would not, in the end, cause us to change the basic conclusions of our partial equilibrium analysis. We can be grateful for this because forging that general equilibrium analysis would require a heavy investment in additional analytical machinery with few new insights for the effort. But there is one important exception.

An Economy-Wide Perspective

No economy has unlimited resources. In fact, it is precisely *because* a country's resources are limited, while needs and wants are not, that individuals, firms, and governments must make choices about how to use the country's resources. A production possibility frontier (PPF), like that depicted in Figure 6.9, illustrates the type of

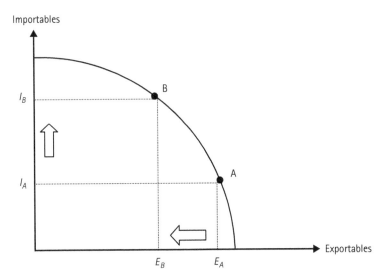

FIGURE 6.9 Lerner Symmetry Theorem and the PPF

trade-off that must be made when resources are limited. On the horizontal axis, different quantities of exportable goods the country can produce are given. On the vertical axis are different amounts of importables it could also produce at home. Points like A and B that lie along the frontier indicate the greatest quantity of importables the economy can produce if it is also going to produce the corresponding amount of exportables, given available technology and the economy's limited resources of labor, land, and capital.

The PPF in Figure 6.9 illustrates an important fact of economic life, and a basic consequence of scarcity: if a country is going to produce more of one thing it must necessarily produce less of something else. Imagine a movement along this country's PPF from A to B. If production of importables rises from I_A to I_B, some of society's resources will have to be directed away from producing exportables, causing the production of those to fall from E_A to E_B.

Now with a moment's reflection, you will recall that import tariffs cause domestic production of importables to rise. In the world of Figure 6.9, such a policy must therefore also cause domestic production of exportables to decline! But then another thought occurs: export taxes cause domestic production of exportables to decline. In the world of Figure 6.9, the resources thereby released must eventually cause the production of importables to rise!

But the "symmetry" actually goes much deeper than this.

Rational consumers and producers throughout the economy make their decisions about how much to buy and sell, respectively, according to the prices they face. In a market economy, resources will therefore be allocated between alternative uses according to *relative prices*. If the price of one good rises relative to the price of another, consumers will buy less of the former and more of the latter. As consumers shift their purchases, producers will produce more of the one good to meet that rising demand and less of the other facing declining demand. Hand in hand, as spending patterns change and production patterns change, some of the economy's resources of land, labor, and capital are systematically redirected from one use to another. Any given set of *relative* prices is therefore associated with some *particular* allocation of society's resources among their alternative uses.

In equation (6.1) we noted that an *ad valorem* tariff of t on importables will cause the domestic and world market prices to differ by the full extent of the tariff. If we let P_I^d and P_I^w stand for the domestic and world prices of importables, respectively, we can re-write this relationship as follows:

$$P_I^d = P_I^w + tP_I^w = P_I^w(1+t).$$

In the absence of any taxes or subsidies on exports, the domestic price and world price of exportables would be the same. If P_E represents that common price, the *relative price of importables* in the tariff-imposing country's home market would be

$$\left(\frac{P_I}{P_E}\right)^d = \left(\frac{P_I}{P_E}\right)^w (1+t) \tag{6.4}$$

But suppose, instead, the country were to impose an *ad valorem* export tax of t, instead of a tariff on imports. In equation (6.2) we observed that the domestic price of exportables would ultimately differ by the full extent of the tax. If we let P_E^d and P_E^w be the domestic and world prices of exportables, respectively, we can rewrite this relationship as follows:

$$P_E^d + tP_E^d = P_E^w,$$

or

$$P_E^d(1+t) = P_E^w,$$

or

$$P_E^d = P_E^w \left(\frac{1}{1+t}\right).$$

Because there is no tariff on imports, the domestic price and world price of importables would be the same, so if P_I represents that common price, the *relative price of exportables* in the country's home market would be

$$\left(\frac{P_E}{P_I}\right)^d = \left(\frac{P_E}{P_I}\right)^w \left(\frac{1}{1+t}\right).$$

This same expression can be written more usefully if we simply take the reciprocal of each side and rewrite it this way:

$$\left(\frac{P_I}{P_E}\right)^d = \left(\frac{P_I}{P_E}\right)^w (1+t). \tag{6.5}$$

Notice that equation (6.5) and equation (6.4) are exactly the same!

This is the Lerner Symmetry Theorem: If we take a long-run, economy-wide perspective, we will eventually see that an *ad valorem* tariff on importables at the rate *t* will have exactly the same effect on the relative prices of importables and exportables as will an *ad valorem* export tax at the same rate. Since relative prices govern production, consumption, and the overall allocation of resources in the economy, the implications of this theorem are clear: an import tariff and an export tax will have exactly the same effects on the overall allocation of resources within the country adopting them.

Anti-export Effects of Tariff Protection

The Lerner Symmetry Theorem encourages policymakers to think broadly about the economy-wide implications of their actions, and it raises awareness of some unintended consequences of actions they might take.

For example, suppose the PPF in Figure 6.9 is that of a country planning to pursue an export-led program of growth and development. If, at the same time, it protects its domestic producers of importables with an import tariff, it will clearly be working against its own plan. The import tariff, raising the domestic relative price of importables, and so encouraging resources to flow into greater production of importables, must also, at the same time, lower the domestic relative price of exportables, causing resources to be drawn away from that sector, and output to fall. These anti-export effects of tariff protection must be taken into consideration in any full assessment of the consequences of tariff protection.

VI. TARIFF PREFERENCES FOR DEVELOPING COUNTRIES

Developing countries have long sought access to developed-country markets on preferential terms, and WTO rules accept the principle of enhanced market access—so called "special and differential treatment" for developing country exports—as an important tool of growth and development. In 2001, the European Union, in its "Anything But Arms" initiative, amended its Generalized Scheme of Preferences to grant duty free and

quota free access into EU markets of *all* products, except arms and ammunition, originating in 48 less-developed countries.

To illustrate the impact such policies have on developing and developed countries,
consider Figure 6.10, depicting market demand and market supply in a developing
country's domestic market for one of its exportable goods. In the absence of any special
access, this country's exports will be sold at the world price, P^w. Domestic consumption
will be at B, production at C and the volume of exports will be BC.

Let us suppose that some developed country initially maintains a non-discriminatory
ad valorem tariff at the rate t on trade with the rest of the world, and that, therefore,
the prevailing domestic price of this good in the developed country's home market is
$P^w + tP^w$. If special, tariff-free access to this country's protected home market is now
granted to the developing country depicted in Figure 6.10, exporters there, now able
to earn a higher price on sales in the developed country, will redirect sales away from
the world market, and away from the domestic market, toward that developed country. As a result, the domestic price of the exportable good in the developing country
will rise to the level of market price in the protected, developed country's market,
$P^w + tP^w$. As price rises in the developing country, domestic consumption declines
from B to A, domestic production increases from C to D, and exports expand from
BC to AD.

The allocative effects in the developing country of enhanced access for their exports
to protected developed country markets are exactly the same as those resulting from an
export subsidy. The distributional effects—both gross and net—are different however.

With preferential access, producers of the developing country's exportable are made
better off: their producer surplus rises by $a + b + c + d + e$. Consumers in the developing
country are made worse off: their consumer surplus falls by $a + b$. With an export subsidy, the developing country's government would have had to make subsidy payments

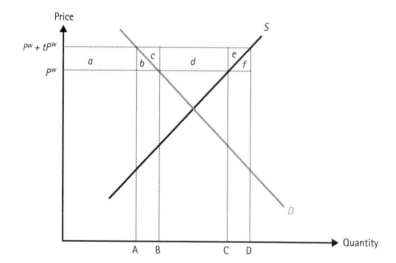

FIGURE 6.10 Tariff preference to a developing country

of $b + c + d + e + f$ to have the same allocative effects, and we noted before that that would mean net losses in overall social welfare for the developing country totaling $b+f$. But with preferential access, the developing country government makes no such subsidy payments. Instead, the whole of $b + c + d + e + f$ represents a transfer from consumers in the developed country to producers in the developing country. This more than compensates for the consumption-side inefficiency, b, and the production side inefficiency, f, giving a net welfare gain in the developing country of $c + d + e$.

Notice, though, that the net welfare gain in the developing country—$c + d + e$—is smaller than the transfer from developed country consumers—$b + c + d + e + f$. This suggests that direct aid, say in the form of a transfer payment from the developed country government in the amount $c + d + e$, could provide the same net increase in developing country welfare at lower cost to the developed country, and without introducing the production-side and consumption-side inefficiencies that attend the practice of enhanced access. Of course, broader policy issues often arise in the debate on "trade vs. aid," and while these are outside the scope of the present chapter, they will be taken up in more detail in others.

VII. Production Subsidies

We've seen that tariffs, quotas, export taxes, and export subsidies will always redistribute welfare among producers, consumers, and the government, and will in most cases also give rise to a net dead-weight loss in social welfare, at least in the small country. But tariffs help spur increased domestic production of import substitutes, and that may form part of an overall development plan. Export subsidies encourage increased production of exportables, and that, too, may be part of an overall development plan. However, subsidies to production, rather than taxes or subsidies to trade, will generally be able to achieve the intended objective at lower social cost.

To see why, consider first the left-hand panel of Figure 6.11, and suppose that the objective of policy is to increase domestic production of this importable good from A to B. One way of doing so would be to implement a tariff sufficient to cause the domestic price of the good to rise to P^d. As we've seen, such a policy would redistribute welfare away from consumers toward producers and the government, but it would also result in an overall deadweight loss in social welfare equal to the sum of areas b and d, due, respectively, to the production-side and consumption-side inefficiencies the tariff introduces.

But suppose, instead, the government were to offer a direct per unit subsidy to domestic producers of this good sufficient to shift the market supply curve out (or down) to S_s. At the world price P_w, plus a per unit subsidy, domestic producers would find it in their interest to increase production from A to B. That additional production absorbs additional domestic resources worth an amount equal to the area beneath the original market supply curve between A and B. Because those same AB units could have been

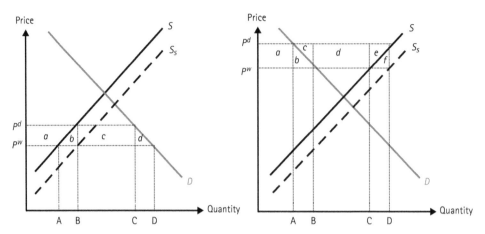

FIGURE 6.11 The Bhagwati–Ramaswami Rule

purchased from abroad in exchange for domestic resources totaling only the area of the rectangle with base AB and height P_w, there is still a production-side welfare loss equal to area b. But the policy of subsidizing production has no effect on the price consumers pay—they continue to pay the world price P_w, and consumption remains at D. As a result, there is no consumption-side loss. Assuming that the subsidy is financed by a non-distorting lump-sum tax on consumers (or anyone else), the overall effect of the subsidy policy is to achieve the same production objective as the tariff, but without the consumption-side cost.

A similar analysis applies in comparing export subsidies with subsidies to the production of exportables, regardless of whether they are sold at home or abroad. In the right-hand panel of Figure 6.11, the world price of some exportable good is P^w, domestic production is at C, domestic consumption at B, and exports are BC. If the government wanted to encourage production of this exportable good, it could implement an export subsidy that would have the effect of causing the domestic price to rise to P^d. We've seen that such a policy redistributes welfare from consumers and the government toward producers, but results in a net loss in social welfare equal to the sum of areas b and f, due, again, to the consumption-side and production-side inefficiencies, respectively, that this type of policy introduces.

But suppose, instead, the government were to offer a direct per unit subsidy to domestic producers, regardless of whether they sold in the domestic market or abroad. If the subsidy were sufficient to shift the market supply curve out (or down) to S_s, then at the prevailing world price P^w, plus a per unit subsidy, domestic producers would find it in their interest to increase production from C to D. That additional production absorbs additional domestic resources worth an amount equal to the area beneath the original market supply curve between C and D. Domestic producers sell those CD units abroad at P^w, earning revenues equal only to the area of the rectangle with base CD and height P^w, so there is still a production-side welfare loss equal to area f. But the policy of subsidizing production again has no effect on the price consumers pay—they continue to pay the world price P^w, and consumption remains at B. As a result, there is no consumption-side loss. Again assuming that the subsidy is financed by a non-distorting lump-sum tax on consumers (or anyone else), the overall effect of the subsidy policy is to achieve the same production objective as the export subsidy, but without the consumption-side cost.

The principle behind the argument we've given here is quite a general one, with applicability to many other situations that arise in trade policy. As a very general rule, whenever trade policy of some kind can be used to achieve some production-level or consumption-level objective, there will always be an alternative policy taxing or subsidizing production or consumption directly that will achieve the desired goal at a smaller welfare cost. This is known as the Bhagwati–Ramaswami Rule, and the intuition for it is fairly simple. Trade—whether imports or exports—is always the difference between domestic production and domestic consumption of a good. When trade policy is used to influence domestic production (consumption) it will unavoidably also affect domestic consumption (production) of the same good. But subsidies or taxes, on either production or consumption, affect only the activity at which they are directed, without affecting the other. As a result, production-side objectives can be achieved without the consumption-side costs, and consumption-side objectives can be achieved without the production-side costs that always accompany the use of trade policy.

VIII. Other Non-Tariff Barriers

Policymakers always feel pressure from powerful interests opposed to freer trade. If those seeking protection can organize and exert political pressure more effectively than those who stand to lose from protection, government may find that pressure hard to resist. Yet today countries are increasingly bound together in a world trading system that has officially embraced the principle of freer trade. Through the GATT, and the WTO, countries have committed themselves to a variety of tariff rationalization and reduction programs. Policymakers caught between the international drive toward freer trade and the pressure for protection have found creative ways to have their cake and eat it too: ways they can avoid direct abrogation of their international obligations, while at the same time yielding in some degree to domestic interests seeking protection.

The UNCTAD system for tracking trade control measures includes 316 different types in all, only 32 of which are directly tariff-related measures. The rest—fully 91 per cent of all types of trade barriers that have been officially identified, categorized, and tracked—are non-tariff barriers to trade or NTBs. Import (and export) quotas are important NTBs, of course, but there are many others, and they take many different forms. Some are nominally related to national defense; some to protecting wildlife; some aim to curb drug abuse; some to ensure minimum local content; and the list goes on. Table 6.2 provides a broad overview, by different country groups, of the extent to which the principal (core) NTBs are used across tariff lines. While there is considerable variation in the proportion of tariff lines subject to NTBs, both across and within the broad country

Table 6.2 Percentage of tariff lines subject to core NTBs

Country group	Years	Average				Percentage with greater than 15% coverage
		Simple	Weighted	Std. dev.	max.	
High-income Non-OECD (7)	1994–2001	17.7	18.2	13.7	43.5	57.1
High-income OECD (9)	1996–2001	29.0	29.5	8.1	36.9	88.9
Developing countries (65)	1992–2001	15.7	18.9	16.9	69.7	38.5
Low income (20)	1993–2001	6.2	10.0	8.9	40.2	5.0
Middle income (45)	1992–2001	20.0	22.9	17.9	69.7	53.3

Source: Ng, F. K. T., "Frequency Coverage Ratio of Non-Tariff Barriers (NTBs) by Country," World Bank Trade Research.

groupings, it is clear from the data that NTBs affect a great deal of international trade. Here, we will look at just two of the most important types of NTBs.[1]

Anti-Dumping Actions

Under WTO rules, a firm can be accused of dumping if it charges a lower price in its export market than it does in its home market for the same good. In competitive world markets, firms have no power to unilaterally set price: market demand and market supply do that. Dumping is therefore something that can only occur "naturally" in markets that are dominated by relatively few firms with enough market power to set their own prices. In addition, the firms must be able to separate their home and export markets, otherwise resale of the product from the low-price to the high-price market would make it impossible for the firm to charge different prices.

When dumping occurs it is generally regarded as "unfair trade" (though many economists do not see it this way). WTO rules allow countries that can demonstrate "material injury" to their domestic producers caused by dumping from foreign firms to take anti-dumping actions in response. These will typically involve authorization for a departure from general non-discrimination rules allowing the injured party to impose additional or anti-dumping duties on imports of the good

---

[1] During the 1970s and 1980s, some countries negotiated Voluntary Export Restraint (VER) and Voluntary Import Expansion (VIE) agreements with major trading partners. "Results-based" NTBs like these, at odds with longstanding principles of the GATT and the WTO aimed at building a "rules-based" world trading system, are no longer commonly used.

from the specific country whose firm is deemed guilty of dumping. These duties, though, are generally not to exceed the minimum necessary to offset the damage done by the dumping.

It is relatively easy to initiate anti-dumping actions, so they are often the policy of choice for protectionist influences. Table 6.3 gives some idea of the frequency with which such actions have been taken by WTO members over the period 1995–2008. The US initiated quite a few anti-dumping actions against other industrialized countries over this period, but both the US and the EU initiated many more against developing countries than they did against each other. Developing countries, too, have initiated a large number of anti-dumping actions against other developing countries over the same period. India has initiated by far the most anti-dumping

Table 6.3 The anti-dumping Top 20, 1995–2008

Top 20 initiators		Top 20 Targets	
Country	Number	Country	Number
India	564	China	677
United States	418	Korea	252
European Union	391	United States	189
Argentina	241	Taiwan	187
South Africa	206	Indonesia	145
Australia	197	Japan	144
Brazil	170	Thailand	142
China	151	India	137
Canada	145	Russia	109
Turkey	137	Brazil	97
Korea	108	Malaysia	90
Mexico	95	Germany	83
Indonesia	73	European Union	69
Egypt	65	Ukraine	61
Peru	64	South Africa	58
New Zealand	53	Italy	46
Colombia	43	Singapore	44
Malaysia	43	Spain	44
Thailand	39	Turkey	44
Israel	32	UK	44

Source: WTO data compiled by <antidumpingpublishing.com>.

actions of any nation, and China has been the most frequent target by a very large margin.

Economists are of many minds on the issue of dumping. If the dumping is predatory in nature—intended by the foreign firm to drive domestic firms out of business so that the foreign firm would then be free to exercise greater monopoly power—dumping would be something to oppose. If, however, a foreign firm sells at a high price in its home market and a lower price in its export market because competitive or other market conditions in the export market require it to do so, there seems no good reason to oppose it.

SPS Measures

Economist Robert Baldwin has likened the long post-war process of multilateral negotiations under the GATT and WTO, and the success they've had in reducing traditional forms of trade restrictions such as tariffs, quotas, and subsidies, as something akin to draining a swamp. As the water level has been made to steadily recede, it has revealed all the, "snags and stumps of non-tariff barriers that still have to be cleared away" (Baldwin, 2000). Many of the most gnarly stumps and nettlesome snags are now found in the different ways that countries regulate sanitation and protect the health of their plant and animal life. Is a regulation that imported wine be "cooked" to a certain temperature before being admitted into the USA a legitimate means of safeguarding California agriculture from French parasites, or is it a way of reducing the complexity, and so the allure, of the French product so that fewer buyers will want to buy it? Is a ban on the importation of poultry from countries not free of Newcastle disease a legitimate means of protecting the health of poultry and the public in Britain—the only country free of the disease—or is it an unfair means of protecting British poultry farmers from competition on the European continent?

Where public health and safety of the food supply are involved, a country's vital interests can truly be at stake. However, the potential for anti-competitive mischief in the abuse of a country's sovereign right to establish its own Sanitary and Phyto-sanitary Measures (SPS) measures is also obvious. Recent trade disputes between the EU and US over genetically modified food products have been among the most highly publicized examples of the difficulties, and the mutual suspicion, cross-country differences of this sort can create. But it is also a very real problem for developing countries. Agricultural exports from developing countries, where enforcement of domestic SPS measures may not yet be uniform and fully up to international standards, can be an easy target for agricultural interests in the importing countries around which to rally public and political support for protection.

Recognizing the legitimate demands of both importing and exporting countries, and the potential for abuse, member countries in the WTO have worked to harmonize cross-country SPS measures, to make them more transparent and to forge agreement on what shall constitute "good science" in determining the legitimacy of new or existing regulations in this area. Developed countries have been subject to the provisions of the SPS Agreement since 1995, developing countries since 1997, and least-developed countries since 2000. This remains, however, an important area of ongoing discussion and negotiation.

IX. Summary

We have examined the principal instruments of trade policy, paying special attention to the impact each has on resource allocation and the distribution of welfare. Much of what has been discussed is summarized in Table 6.4.

Some broad patterns emerge from our analysis. In the case of a small trading country, restrictions on trade will tend to favor some at the expense of others but, as a general rule, result in a net dead-weight loss in national welfare as each introduces production-side and consumption-side inefficiencies compared to free trade. This suggests strongly that when distributional goals are the ultimate objectives of policy, using trade policy instruments in pursuit of those objectives is inefficient. More direct means of redistribution that do not distort market prices from their free trade levels, and so do not lead to the associated production-side and consumption-side inefficiencies, should be able to achieve those same objectives at lower social cost. When the objective of policy is not redistribution, but instead to encourage production, trade policy will again be an inefficient means of achieving the objective since it affects both consumption and production at once. In such cases, subsidies to production will achieve the same production goal with no consumption-side effect, and so lower social cost.

There are, however, some qualifications. For the most part, we have assumed competitive world markets on which the trading country has no appreciable market power. One important exception we considered is the optimal tariff in the case of a large country: by exploiting its market power on the world market, a large trading country may be able to turn its terms of trade in its favor sufficiently to ensure an overall national welfare gain. This comes at the expense of its trading partners, however, and so is likely to provoke retaliation. Ensuing tariff wars will generally be welfare reducing for all.

There are other qualifications and extensions to our analysis that arise when home country and world markets are imperfectly competitive. In such cases, opportunities for strategic behavior by firms, and by governments, can qualify and even reverse some of our conclusions about the effects of certain policy instruments. A careful analysis of these exceptions is beyond the scope of this chapter, but will be taken up in others.

Table 6.4 Impact of trade policy on resource allocation and welfare

Target	Instrument	Resource Allocation		Distribution				
		Consumption	Production	Consumer welfare	Producer welfare	Government revenue	Net welfare	
Imports								
	Tariff							
	Small country	↓	↑	↓	↑	↑	↓	
	Large country	↓	↑	↓	↑	↑	↑	(a)
	Quota	↓	↑	↓	↑	?	↓	(b)
	VER (importing country)	↓	↑	↓	↑	None	↓	(c)
	Anti-dumping duties	Same as tariff						
Exports								
	Export tax	↑	↓	↑	↓	↑	↓	
	Export subsidy	↓	↑	↓	↑	↓	↓	
	Tariff preferences	↓	↑	↓	↑	None	↑	(d)
	VIE (importing country)	↓	↑	↓	↑	↓	↓	(e)
Production								
	Production subsidies							
	Importables	None	↑	None	↑	↓	↓	(f)
	Exportables	None	↑	None	↑	↓	↓	(g)

Notes:

(a) Transfer from foreign producers to government. May provoke retaliation, with welfare loss.

(b) Government revenue depends on method for allocating licenses.

(c) Transfer from importing country consumers to exporting country producers.

(d) Transfer from importing country consumers to exporting country producers.

(e) Transfer from importing country producers and government to exporting country producers.

(f) Smaller welfare loss than tariff with equivalent protective effect.

(g) Smaller welfare loss than export subsidy with equivalent effect on production.

Appendix

Consumer and Producer Surplus

To weigh costs and benefits from alternative policies, economists require some sort of dollar-denominated measure that can be aggregated and compared across individuals affected by those policies. Two commonly used measures of this sort are consumer surplus and producer surplus.

Consumer Surplus

By consumer surplus we mean the excess value a consumer attaches to having a unit of a good over and above what she has to pay for it. Consumer surplus thus measures, in dollars, the net welfare gain a consumer realizes from buying a unit of the good.

Figure 6.A1 depicts an ordinary market demand curve for some good. Typically, we would read the demand curve "over and down," asking, "at such and such price, how many units of the good will consumers want to buy?" We could, instead, though, read it "up and over," asking, "what is the maximum price some consumer would be willing to pay for some particular unit of the good?" If we ask the consumers depicted in Figure 6.A1 that question about the first unit, someone would answer, "P_1." Then P_1, and so, also, the area of the rectangle with base 1 unit in width and height P_1, measures some consumer's maximum willingness to pay for the very first unit of this good consumed. This maximum willingness to pay is the total value that the consumer attaches to having one unit of the good.

With one unit being consumed, we could ask consumers how much one of them would be willing to pay to have another. According to the demand curve, P_2, and so again also the area of the rectangle with base 1 unit and height P_2, would measure some (perhaps other) consumer's willingness to pay for that second unit. We could ask it again of our consumers for the third

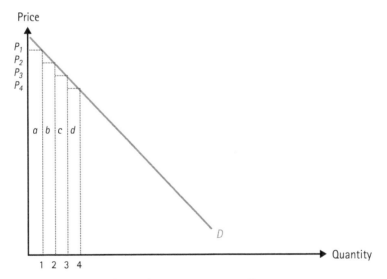

FIGURE 6.A1 Area under the demand curve measures willingness to pay

unit, and the fourth unit in turn. Each time, the rectangle with base 1 unit and height first P_3, then P_4, would measure some consumer's maximum willingness to pay for successive units of the good. But then an amount of money equal to the *sum* of the areas of those rectangles, or $a + b + c + d$, must measure the willingness of some *group* of consumers to pay for a *total* of four units of this good.

If we were now to simply change the scale of measurement along the horizontal axis, making the distance between successive units of the good smaller and smaller, before too long the area of the rectangles $a + b + c + d$ in Figure 6.A1 would become indistinguishable from the whole area beneath the market demand curve, up to four units. By this same reasoning, and with appropriately chosen scales, we may therefore regard the entire area underneath a market demand curve, up to any number of units, Q, as a measure of the total willingness to pay for a total of Q units by consumers as a group. As a result, economists often regard the area under a demand curve as a measure of the total value consumers as a group attach to having a total of Q units to consume.

But consumers must usually pay something for what they get to consume. Suppose our consumers are allowed to buy Q_1 units at a fixed price, P, per unit. Their total outlay is $P*Q_1$, or the area of the rectangle marked b_1 in Figure 6.A2. Getting something worth a_1+b_1 in exchange for payments of b_1, leaves consumers as a group better off, net, by the amount of area a_1. This is consumer surplus on this transaction and, as you see, it always measures, in dollar-terms, the *net gain* that consumers as a group realize from the transaction concerned.

If consumers were free to buy as much or as little of this good as they chose, the demand curve tells us they would want to buy a total of Q_2 units—the point on the market demand curve at price, P. Notice that the additional $Q_2 - Q_1$ units cost consumers an additional outplay equal to area b_2, but those units have a value to those consumers totaling $a_2 + b_2$, so consumers as a group enjoy an additional, or incremental consumer surplus on those new units equal to a_2.

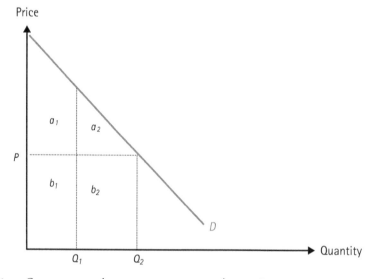

FIGURE 6.A2 Consumer surplus measures consumers' net gain

Producer Surplus

On the other side of any market transaction, firms provide goods to consumers in exchange for money payment. By producer surplus we mean any amount a firm earns in that transaction over and above the minimum that would have been necessary to make it just willing to agree to the transaction. Producer surplus thus measures, in dollars, the net welfare gain a producer realizes from a transaction.

Producer surplus can be seen on familiar graphs too. In Figure 6.A3, the market supply curve of a large number of perfectly competitive firms is depicted and, normally, we would read that supply curve "over and down," asking how many units all firms together would offer for sale at some fixed price per unit. We could, though, read it "up and over," instead, asking, for any given unit of the good, what is the minimum payment some firm would be willing to accept to provide it. If we ask that question of the firms depicted in Figure 6.A3 about the first unit, one of them would answer, "P_1." Then P_1, and so also the area of the rectangle with base 1 unit and height P_1, measures the minimum payment some firm would require in order to be willing to provide that first unit. By a process now familiar, we could ask, in turn, the minimum some firm would require in order to provide the second, then the third, then the fourth units. Stepping back, and asking instead the minimum payment our group of firms as a whole would require in order just to be willing to provide a total of four units for sale, we know what the answer would be: the whole of the area $a + b + c + d$. If, again, we were to simply change the scale of measurement along the horizontal axis, making the distance between successive units of the good smaller and smaller, before long the area of the rectangles $a + b + c + d$ would become indistinguishable from the area underneath the firm's supply curve, up to four units. By this same reasoning, and with appropriately chosen scales, we may therefore regard the entire area underneath a market supply curve up to any number, Q, units of the good as measuring the minimum total payment firms as a group would require in order to be just willing to supply Q units.

In Figure 6.A4, then, the minimum firms as a group would require in order to provide Q_1 units is measured by the area b_1. But what would any firm consider in determining the minimum payment it needed in order to provide one or more of those Q_1 units? Surely, such a payment

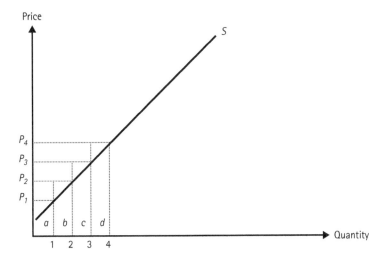

FIGURE 6.A3 Area under the supply curve measures resource cost

would need to cover the cost of any labor, capital, or other resources the firm must acquire to produce the output it provides. That area b_1, therefore, must also measure the total cost of all resources that all firms, and so society, must devote to producing those Q_1 units.

Now suppose that firms are able to sell Q_1 units at a price of P per unit. The total revenue earned by firms would be P^*Q_1 or area a_1+b_1 in Figure 6.A4. Receiving payment of a_1+b_1 in exchange for something the firm would be just willing to sell for b_1 leaves the firm better off, net, by the amount of area a_1. This is producer surplus on this transaction and, as you see, it always measures, in dollars, the *net gain* that firms as a group realize from the transaction concerned.

If firms were free to sell as much or as little as they chose, the supply curve tells us they would want to sell a total of Q_2 units—the point on the market supply curve at price, P. Notice that firms would be willing to supply the additional $Q_2 - Q_1$ units for an additional payment equal to area b_2, the cost of the additional resources needed to produce that increment in output. But firms receive an additional payment totaling $a2 + b_2$, so they enjoy an additional, or incremental producer surplus on those new units equal to a_2.

Social Welfare

With separate measures of consumer welfare and producer welfare in hand, we could form a simple measure of overall *social welfare* arising from transactions in a single market by taking the sum of consumer and producer surplus:

$$SW = CS + PS. \tag{6.A.1}$$

Figure 6.A5 illustrates. Suppose that for some reason—perhaps due to government rules and regulations restricting buyers' and sellers' behavior—only Q_1 units of a good are bought and sold in some market at a price of P per unit. From those transactions, consumers enjoy Q_1 units of the good, worth a total of $a_1 + b_1 + c_1$ to them. They must pay producers $b_1 + c_1$, giving consumer surplus of a_1. Producers receive revenues of $b_1 + c_1$ for the Q_1 units on which they must expend resources worth c_1 to produce, giving producer surplus of b_1. Notice that the sum of consumer and producer surplus—the whole of area $a_1 + b_1$—measures the total of net benefits received by many different individuals in society—some of them consumers and some of them producers—as a result of the transactions described. We may regard that sum as the total of net gains to someone in society from the underlying activities of producing, selling, and consuming those Q_1 units of the good, over and above the value of society's resources that were expended in the process. The division of this sum between consumer surplus and producer surplus is easy to see in the figure, and so it is easy for us to see how these net gains are distributed between consumers and producers of this good in society.

We can use these methods to compare different market outcomes from an overall social point of view: one market outcome can be judged better than another from the viewpoint of society as a whole if the *sum* of net benefits to consumers and producers—the sum of consumer and producer surplus—is larger in the one market outcome than it is in the other.

In Figure 6.A5 suppose that new government policies cause the number of units produced and consumed to rise to Q_2, while market price remains at P. Consumer surplus on those Q_2 units at that price totals $a_1 + a_2$. Producer surplus totals $b_1 + b_2$. The sum of consumer and producer surplus is now $a_1 + a_2 + b_1 + b_2$. Since this is larger than it was when only Q_1 units were produced and consumed, the total of all net gains to consumers and producers throughout society is now higher than it was before. In that sense, the market outcome providing Q_2 units can be judged better for society as a whole than the one providing only Q_1 As a general rule, the very same principles enable us to judge any market outcome as better than any other from

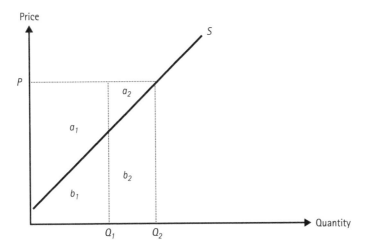

FIGURE 6.A4 Producer surplus measures producers' net gain

a social point of view if the sum of consumer and producer surplus is higher in the one than it is in the other.

The careful, and skeptical, reader will have noticed that when the social value of market outcomes is compared in this way, we treat a dollar's net welfare gain to any one person in society—any consumer or any producer—has having the same significance to society as a dollar's net welfare gain to any other person in society—whether consumer or producer. Similarly, we treat a dollar's net welfare *loss* to some person as representing no loss in the welfare of society as long as some other person—anyone else—enjoys a dollar's net welfare gain at the same time.

The sum of consumer and producer surplus, used as an index of social welfare, does, in fact, bring decidedly utilitarian moral values to the exercise: individuals are treated in a completely symmetric way, with no favorites, and the welfare of society as a whole is being reckoned by the simple sum of net benefits to all its members. For some economists, and some policymakers, this is the view they take and defend: individuals either should, as a moral proposition, or must, as a practical one, be treated equally in this manner when making public policy. Others will not be comfortable with this point of view, taking, instead, the position that the distribution between advantaged and disadvantaged individuals within society is, and ought to be, an important concern of those making policy. Even if one takes this position, though, the sum of consumer and producer surplus still provides an important and useful guide to selecting among different policies that impinge on markets.

To see why, look again at Figure 6.A5. The policy that implements output level Q_1 gives total surplus of $a_1 + b_1$. The policy implementing output level Q_2 gives total surplus greater than that by $a_2 + b_2$. Since the size of the overall social welfare "pie" is bigger in the second case than it is in the first, it must be possible when the second policy is implemented to ensure that everyone has a slice of that larger pie that is no smaller than the one they would have had under the first policy, and still there will be pie left over to divide among people in any way desired. Economists call such a change as we're describing—one where no one is made any worse off and at least some are made better off—a *Pareto improvement* in welfare. Whenever the sum of consumer and producer surplus is increased, there is always the potential for a Pareto improvement in welfare. Of course, turning the potential for Pareto improvement into an actual Pareto improvement

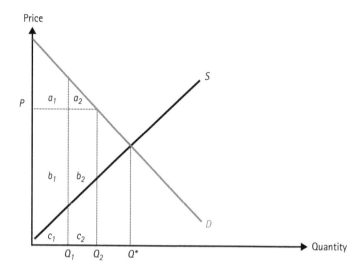

FIGURE 6.A5 Social welfare as the sum of consumer and producer surplus

will often require some form of redistribution—say though lump-sum taxes or subsidies—to also be part of the policy package.

But what if the sum of consumer and producer surplus is as large as it can possibly be? In Figure 6.A5, when output is at Q^* the sum of producer and consumer surplus will be maximized—equal in amount to the entire area between market demand and market supply to the left of Q^*. If the welfare "pie" is as big as it can possibly be, there will be no way to give any one person a larger slice without, at the same time, giving someone else a smaller slice. Further Pareto improvements in welfare will be impossible. Economists call such situations *Pareto efficient*.

Notice that output level Q^* in Figure A5 is the equilibrium level of output we would expect to arise from unhindered market trading between buyers and sellers—the *laissez-faire* market outcome—if this were a properly functioning competitive market. (We've not drawn in the equilibrium market price that would prevail because that is not important at the moment.) It is no coincidence that the equilibrium level of output in a competitive market is Pareto efficient. In fact, economists call that very important property of competitive markets The First Welfare Theorem of competitive economics!

The First Welfare Theorem helps you understand why economists are often reluctant to recommend any kind of policy that interferes with properly functioning competitive markets. If such market equilibria maximize the sum of consumer and producer surplus, and so are Pareto efficient, then *any* policy intervention that changes the market outcome in *any* way can only, at best, redistribute welfare toward some and away from others: and, more often than not, it will also cause the overall level of welfare—the size of the social welfare "pie"—to shrink. When that happens, no matter what the policymaker's distributional objectives might be, the economist would argue that they can be better met—with lower net welfare cost to society—by leaving the market equilibrium alone and addressing those distributional objectives directly, though an appropriate system of lump-sum taxes and subsidies.

For our work in this chapter, it is wise, though, to ask how the arguments and methods presented here must be amended if government does involve itself in the market. For example, if the government were to introduce a tax causing the price consumers pay to rise, and the price producers receive to fall, both consumer and producer surplus would fall. But should we necessarily conclude that overall social welfare declined, too? After all, the government now collects tax revenue it did not have before, and it will presumably do something with that revenue. If we take the view that a dollar of tax revenue collected by government will find its way, somehow and somewhere, to benefit someone in society by a dollar, then all we have to do is include those government revenues as an equal part of the overall social calculation. In cases where government plays a role, then, we would simply expand the index of social welfare in equation (6.A.1) to include any net government revenues collected, R, as follows:

$$SW = CS + PS + R.$$

This is the index of social welfare we use throughout the chapter.

REFERENCE

Baldwin, R. 'Regulatory Protectionism, Developing Nations and a Two Tier World Trade System.' Brookings Trade Forum, 2000, The Brookings Institution, Washington, DC, pp. 237–94.

CHAPTER 7

TOOLS FOR APPLIED GOODS TRADE POLICY ANALYSIS: AN INTRODUCTION

SOAMIELY ANDRIAMANANJARA, OLIVIER CADOT, AND JEAN-MARIE GRETHER

I. INTRODUCTION

NOT so long ago, the analysis of trade policy required not just a sound knowledge of theory and analytical tools, but also familiarity with cranky software and a willingness to replace missing data with heroic assumptions. The picture has changed dramatically over the last quarter-century. The availability and quality of trade statistics have improved under the combined effort of researchers and statisticians at United Nations Conference on Trade and Development (UNCTAD), the World Bank, and other institutions. Software has also become more user-friendly, making the calculation of complex indices easier even with minimal computing skills.

Thus, there is no excuse anymore for staying away from formal analysis, whether it be calculating descriptive indices or estimating statistical relationships. This chapter presents a palette of tools which, taken together, enable the analyst to produce a rigorous yet "readable" picture of the policy-relevant features of a country's trade and the consequences of trade policy choices. All these tools have been proposed and explained in the literature. For instance, Michaely (1996), Yeats (1998), Brülhart (2002), Hummels and Klenow (2005), Hausmann, Hwang, and Rodrik (2005), Shihotori, Tumurchudur, and Cadot (2010), or Cadot, Carrère, and Strauss-Kahn (forthcoming) have discussed the indices presented in Section II of the chapter. Kee et al. (2008, 2009) discuss in detail the construction of trade restrictiveness indices discussed in Section III. The gravity equation has been discussed in many papers and contexts. The collection of essays in Francois and Reinert (1997) gives a thorough analytical discussion of the *ex ante* simulation tools presented in Section IV, and Jammes and Olarreaga (2006) discuss the World Bank's SMART model. Nonetheless, most of these readings remain difficult and leave a gap between the needs of a theoretical or classroom discussion and those of the practitioner.

This chapter discusses practical data and implementation issues for the most widely used among the various tools. Relying extensively on two recent publications (Bacchetta et al. (2012) and Cadot (2011)), and starting with the simplest descriptive methods, we move progressively to more analytical ones, but always keeping the exposition at a level comprehensible to the non-academic practitioner. The last part of the chapter, devoted to *ex ante* simulation analysis (in partial and general equilibrium), however, remains difficult. The construction of simulation models requires advanced mastery of both economic theory and appropriate programming languages, such as GAMS, and remains largely beyond the capability of the beginner analyst, although specialized training programs are regularly given around the world. The models are inherently complex and sensitive to assumptions. Thus, our aim in that part of the chapter is limited: essentially, to enable the reader to get a feel for how these models are constructed and to be in a better position to understand what can be asked from those models and what cannot.

Given space limitations, there is necessarily a trade-off between depth and breadth. We have chosen to err on the "depth" side, not by going into deep discussions of the underlying concepts—those can be found in the original papers and in standard trade textbooks—but rather by discussing practical implementation issues of relevance to the novice practitioner. The price to pay for this is that we had to limit the number of indices and approaches we cover.

The chapter is organized as follows. Section II discusses how to present a panorama of a country's trade performance, and how to present standard measures of its trade-policy stance. Section III presents some of the econometric techniques that can be used to assess, *ex post*, the effects of trade policies on trade flows and the domestic economy. Section IV presents the key features of some of the tools used in the *ex ante* assessment of trade policy, first in partial equilibrium settings, then in general-equilibrium ones. Section V concludes.

II. Analyzing Merchandise Trade Flows and Policy: Descriptive Tools

The material presented in this section draws extensively on Bacchetta et al. (2012) and Cadot (2011).

Trade Flows

Data

Data issues are key. The analyst should choose the type of data in accordance with the type of analysis to be performed. If it is to be performed at the aggregate level (all products together), the International Monetary Fund (IMF)'s Direction of Trade Statistics

(DOTS) is a good source of data. However, if it is to be performed at the product ("disaggregated") level, the best source is UNCTAD's COMTRADE database, which contains data on bilateral trade between all countries for over 5,000 commodities at the most detailed level.[1] For aggregate data, the IMF DOT statistics is a possible option. The CEPII, a Paris-based think tank, also compiles a bilateral trade database, BACI, which reconciles import and export data, dispensing the analyst from using a technique called "mirroring" which we will discuss below.[2]

Disaggregated data comes in various nomenclatures. The most widely used is the Harmonized System (HS). The HS system has four levels with each product coded with a multiple-digit code, with more digits for more detailed levels: 21 sections, 99 chapters ("HS2"), 1,243 headings (HS4) and 5,052 sub-headings (HS6). More disaggregated levels (e.g. HS8 for the EU and HS10 for the USA) are not harmonized and require careful scrutiny as categories before use.[3] As is well known, at high levels of disaggregation (in particular HS6), the HS system has the peculiarity that it is very detailed for some sectors like textile and clothing, but much less so for others like machinery. As a result, the economic importance of subheadings can vary considerably and care should be exercised when using simple averages (more below). However this oft-mentioned bias should not be overstated: as Figure 7.1 shows, the share of each HS section in the total number of HS6 lines is highly correlated with its share in world trade.

The main alternative classification system is the Standard International Trade Classification (SITC) Rev. 4 (adopted in 2006) which has five levels of disaggregation, also by increasing number of digits. Although SITC subgroups (4/5 digits) number about as many (1,023) as HS4 headings, they do not match perfectly, so concordance tables must be used (see Annex II.5 of United Nations (UN), 2006). The SITC classification's finest disaggregation (SITC4/5) is not quite as disaggregated as HS6 (as said, it resembles more HS4), it goes back in time to the 1960s, whereas the HS system goes back only to 1988 (1992 for some countries, most notably the formerly planned economies). Thus, if one needs long time series, SITC is better; if one needs fine disaggregation, HS is better. A number of alternative classifications exist in which goods are classified under different logics. The (UN) has devised "Broad Economic Categories" (BEC) by end use: capital goods (01), raw materials (02), semi-finished goods (03), and final goods (04). This classification is useful, for instance, to assess "tariff escalation" (higher tariffs on final goods than on other categories, a practice that is used to protect domestic downstream transformation activities and is frequent in developing countries). Rauch (1999) has devised an alternative

---

[1] COMTRADE data are available online through the World Bank's World Integrated Trade Solution (WITS) portal <https://wits.worldbank.org/WITS/wits/restricted/login.aspx>. Users only need to register online; from then on access is free.

[2] The BACI database can be freely downloaded from CEPII's web page at <http://www.cepii.fr/anglaisgraph/bdd/baci.htm>.

[3] For the EU, Eurostat publishes HS 8 data; HS 10 data are not available to the public. For the USA, the National Bureau of Economic Research (NBER) provides a clean HS 10 database compiled by Robert Feenstra and updated by Feenstra, John Romalis, and Jeffrey Schott (2002).

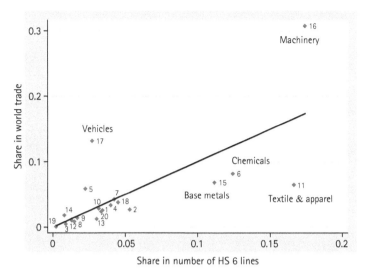

FIGURE 7.1 HS section shares in HS6 lines and in world trade

Notes: 131 countries, average 1988–2004. Section 11 is textile & apparel, section 16 is machinery, section 17 is transport equipment.

Source: COMTRADE.

classification of goods according to their degree of differentiation, from homogenous to reference-priced to fully differentiated.[4] The former uses HS codes, the latter SITC codes. Rauch's classification is useful for many purposes; for instance, competition is likely to take different forms on homogenous vs. differentiated-good markets (price-based for the first, quality, service, or technology-based for the second).

Measurement

One might think that trade flows are about the easiest thing to measure since merchandises must be cleared at customs. Unfortunately, the statistics that measure them are surprisingly erratic. Country A's measured imports from B seldom match B's measured exports to A, and the latter are typically reported with large errors because customs do not monitor exports very closely. The problem is not limited to developing countries, as Figure 7.2 illustrates.

If the same values were reported by importing and exporting customs, all points would lie on the diagonal. Instead, there is substantial dispersion. Because trade values are measured in thousands of dollars and converted into logs in Figure 7.2, a point with

---

[4] Details on the BEC classification can be found in UN (2003). Rauch's classification can be found on Jon Haveman and Raymond Robertson's web page <http://www.macalester.edu/research/economics/page/haveman/trade.resources/tradedata.html>.

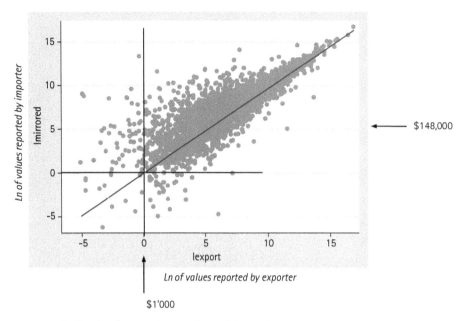

FIGURE 7.2 Switzerland's exports vs. mirrored imports

Note: The horizontal axis measures the log of Switzerland's export values (to the world) as reported by Swiss customs for 2008. The vertical axis measures the log of the world's import values from Switzerland, as reported by the customs of importing countries. Each point represents a commodity at the HS6 level.

Source: COMTRADE.

coordinates (0,5) means that Swiss customs reported the export value of $1,000 ($e^0 = 1$, which means a thousand dollars) whereas importing customs report the import value as $148,000 ($e^5 = 148$). The problem is not limited to small values: HS 270400 has an export value of almost zero and a mirrored import value of over $8 million.

Thus, whenever possible, partner-import data should be used in lieu of direct export data, a technique called "mirroring." That is, rather than requesting data as "reporter = Switzerland, partner = World, flow = exports" one should request data as "reporter = world, partner = Switzerland, flow = imports."

There is a caveat, however. When the importing country is a low-income country with poor statistical capabilities, even import data can be erratic, in which case one might prefer using export data from source countries. Thus, for example, instead of looking at Zambia's imports from the EU, one might prefer looking at EU exports to Zambia. This is particularly important if one has reason to suspect under-reporting of imports (smuggling or under-declaration).

Discrepancies between importer and exporter data are reconciled formally using a variety of techniques (mirroring, interpolating, or direct information) in BACI. The price to pay for the intensive data work involved is that BACI trails COMTRADE with an approximate one-year lag.

In addition to trade values, COMTRADE reports trade volumes (in tons, units, etc.) from which unit values can be recovered by dividing values by volumes. Unit values can be useful, for example, to convert specific tariffs into *ad valorem* tariffs. They are, how-ever, very erratic because volumes, which are measured less precisely than values, are in the denominator. When they are under-reported, unit values can become absurdly large. In addition, unit values vary—and should vary—across countries because of com-position problems. Schott (2004) shows that they are correlated with the exporter's GDP per capita, as goods exported by richer countries are likely to embody higher quality or technology even if classified under the same heading as those exported by poorer coun-tries. They should therefore be used very cautiously.

Trade Composition

The sectoral composition of exports may have an impact on future growth if some sec-tors are "growth engines"—although this conjecture is controversial.[5] Moreover, there may be sector-specific constraints to growth.[6] The geographical composition shows whether a country's exports are predominantly directed at dynamic markets and may help guiding export promotion policies. It is also useful to analyze the benefits of regional integration, an issue that is gaining prominence.

The simplest way of portraying the sectoral orientation of a country's exports is in the form of a "radar screen," as in Figure 7.3.[7] Notice the drastic reorientation of Nepal's exports toward India. This calls for an explanation, which we provide in Section III.

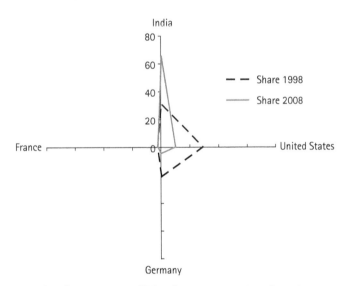

FIGURE 7.3 Geographical orientation of Nepal's exports, 1998 and 2008

Source: COMTRADE.

[5] On this, see Hausmann, Hwang, and Rodrik (2005).
[6] On this, see McKinsey Global Institute (2010).
[7] When displaying a graph of this type, sectoral aggregates have to be selected carefully (more detail in the categories that matter for that country), and so must the scale. When one sector/product greatly dominates the picture, it will be more readable on a log scale. Log transformations are often useful to prevent outliers from obfuscating the picture.

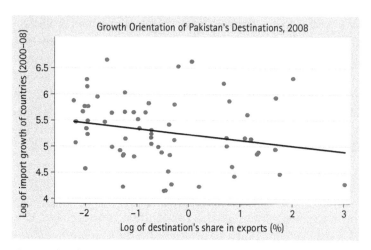

FIGURE 7.4 Geographical orientation of Pakistan's exports

Source: COMTRADE.

A scatter plot of market growth against export shares can also help to highlight "demand-pull" effects. The idea of the scatter plot is to show the import growth rate of each destination country over a ten-year period and to plot it against the destination's share in the home country's total exports. If the cloud of points (and the regression line that summarizes it) has a positive slope, more important destinations have faster import growth; that is, the geographical positioning of the country's export portfolio is favorable. If its slope is negative, by contrast, the positioning is unfavorable; this is the case illustrated in Figure 7.4. In Pakistan's case, this negative orientation may reflect the combination of proximity with slow-growing countries in the Gulf and Central Asian region and the country's failure to integrate with India, a fast-growing market.

The idea behind this scatter plot can be used with product shares rather than destinations (growth would then be defined as world trade growth for that product), or even with product-destination combinations. If the orientation is unfavorable in the product space, the government may think about providing incentives to diversification at the extensive margin. However, one should not over-interpret this type of data without careful micro-analysis, as some exporters may do well even in stagnant markets if they position themselves in dynamic niches.

When one is interested in the convergence of trade and production patterns between a developing ("Southern") country and "Northern" trade partners, a useful indicator is Grubel and Lloyd's intra-industry trade (IIT) index,

$$GL_k^{ij} = 1 - \frac{\left| X_k^{ij} - M_k^{ij} \right|}{X_k^{ij} + M_k^{ij}}$$

where X_k^{ij} is i's exports to j of good k and the bars denote absolute values. The standard interpretation of the GL index runs between zero (for inter-industry trade) to one (for intra-industry trade). Intra-industry trade is consistent with the monopolistic competition model of trade. As countries develop, the GH index rises as income and industrial patterns of specialization tend to converge.[8]

However, GL indices should be interpreted cautiously. First, the GL index rises mechanically with aggregation so, to be comparable, two GL index values must have been calculated at the same level of aggregation. Moreover, a high GL index value may reflect "vertical trade," something that is distinct from monopolistic competition and reflects again the existence of cross-border value chains, a form of trade that has been spreading. For instance, France exports car parts (powertrains, gearboxes, breaking modules) to Morocco, which then exports assembled cars to France. Calculating the GL index at a relatively aggregated level where automobiles are not distinct from car parts will produce a high index value. But this intra-industry trade is really "Heckscher–Ohlin trade" driven by lower labor costs in Morocco (assembly is more labor-intensive than component manufacturing).

Margins of Expansion/Diversification

Export diversification, in terms of either products or destinations, can be at the intensive margin (a more evenly spread portfolio) or at the extensive margin (more export items). Diversification is measured (inversely) by indices like Herfindahl's concentration index (the sum of the squares of the shares) or Theil's (more complicated but pre-programmed in Stata). Concentration indices calculated over active export lines only measure concentration/diversification at the intensive margin. Diversification at the extensive margin can be measured simply by counting the number of active export lines. In general, countries diversify at both the intensive and extensive margins in a first phase of economic development (roughly until a Gross Domestic Product (GDP) per capita of about $24,000 at purchasing-power parity), after which they tend to re-concentrate (see Figure 7.5).

Should diversification be a policy objective in itself? Diversification is often justified to avoid the so-called "natural resource curse" (a negative correlation between growth and the importance of natural resources in exports), but the evidence supporting the natural-resource curse conjecture is controversial.[9] Diversification reduces export and GDP volatility, although the concept of "export riskiness" is a relatively unexplored one.[10] Extensive-margin diversification reflects "export entrepreneurship" which is useful evidence on how favorable is the country's business environment.

One drawback of measuring diversification by just counting active export lines (as in Figure 7.5) is that it fails to distinguish between a case where the new export is coffee or rolled/flaked grains of oats: both add one export line. Hummels and Klenow (2005) propose a new formula for the extensive margin where new export lines are weighted

---

[8] In this regard, one may prefer to use marginal IIT indices, discussed in Brülhart (2002).

[9] Export breakthroughs can sometimes *raise* concentration, see Easterly, Resheff, and Schwenkenberg (2009). On the natural resource curse, see, e.g., Brunnschweiler and Bulte (2009) and the contributions in Lederman and Maloney (2009).

[10] The World Bank is working on a concept of "export riskiness" for foodstuffs, using econometric analysis of counts of sanitary alerts at the EU and US borders. Di Giovanni and Levchenko (2010) propose a more general measure of riskiness based on the variance–covariance matrix of sectoral value added.

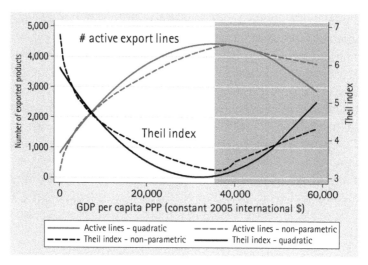

FIGURE 7.5 Export concentration and stages of development

Source: Cadot, Carrère, and Strauss-Kahn (forthcoming).

by their share in world trade. Then, starting to export a $100,000 worth of coffee counts more than starting to export the same amount of oat flakes, because the former is more important in world trade (and therefore, presumably, has a stronger expansion potential).

Formally, let K^i be the set of products exported by country i, X_k^i the dollar value of i's exports of product k to the world, and X_k^w the dollar value of world exports of product k. The (static) intensive margin is defined by Hummels and Klenow as

$$IM^i = \frac{\sum_{K^i} X_k^i}{\sum_{K^i} X_k^w}$$

In words, the numerator is i's exports and the denominator is world exports of products that are in i's export portfolio. That is, IM^i is i's market share in what it exports. The extensive margin (also static) is

$$XM^i = \frac{\sum_{K^i} X_k^W}{\sum_{K^W} X_k^W}$$

where K^w is the set of all traded goods. XM^i measures the share of the products belonging to i's portfolio in world trade. Both measures are illustrated in Figure 7.6.

The picture shows that Pakistan, for instance, broadened its export portfolio (an expansion at the HK extensive margin), but that it failed to consolidate its market shares in products that it already exported at the beginning of the period.

Costa Rica, by contrast, managed to diversify at *both* the intensive and extensive margins after Intel's investment in 1996. This may seem surprising—one would have

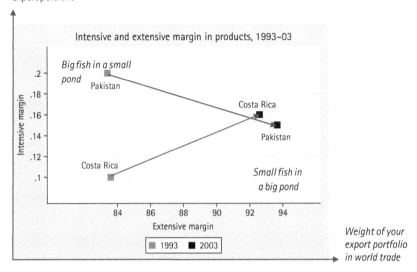

FIGURE 7.6 Evolution of intensive and extensive margins, Pakistan and Costa Rica

Source: COMTRADE.

expected the country to move from big fish in the (relatively) small pond of banana exporters to small fish in the larger pond of semiconductor exporters. Yet it became "bigger fish in a bigger pond." The reason for this paradox is simple: Costa Rica was *already* exporting semiconductors, albeit in very small quantities, before Intel. This highlights another golden rule: always look at the raw numbers, not just indicators. It is very easy to get puzzled or misled by indicators, and the more complicated the trickier things become.

Export expansion can also be defined at the intensive margin (growth in the value of existing exports), at the extensive margin (new export items, new destinations), or at the "sustainability margin" (longer survival of export spells). A useful decomposition goes as follows. Using notation already introduced, let base year exports be

$$X_0 = \sum_{K_0} X_{k0}$$

and terminal exports

$$X_1 = \sum_{K_1} X_{k1}$$

The variation in total export value between those two years can be decomposed into

$$\Delta X = \underbrace{\sum_{K_0 \cap K_1} \Delta X}_{} + \underbrace{\sum_{K_1 \backslash K_0} X_k}_{} + \underbrace{\sum_{K_1 \backslash K_0} X_k}_{}$$

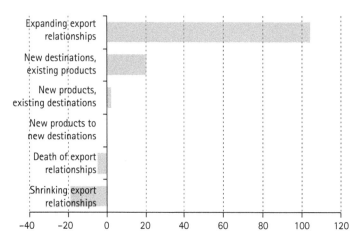

FIGURE 7.7 Decomposition of the export growth of 99 developing countries, 1995–2004

Source: Brenton and Newfarmer (2009).

where the first term is change at the intensive margin, the second is the new-product margin, and the third is the "product death margin." The decomposition highlights that export growth can be achieved by raising exports of existing products, by adding new products, or by reducing the number of failures. The new-product margin, which is conceptually equivalent to the extensive margin, is measured here by the dollar value of new exports, not by their number.

Further decompositions can be constructed in a similar way by combining products and destinations. Empirically, the new-product margin's contribution to overall export growth is generally small (Figure 7.7). This is partly due to the way the margin is constructed: Products appear in the extensive margin only the first year they are exported; after that, they are absorbed in the intensive margin. Thus, unless they are immediately exported on a large scale (which can be the case for large greenfield investments but is rare), the extensive margin's contribution to overall export growth is small by construction. A second reason is that most new exports fail rapidly: the median survival of an export spell (meaning a product-destination combination, where the product is at the HS6 level) is about two years for developing countries. There is a lot of export experimentation, but also a lot of failure. Reducing the "infant mortality" of exports is one way of raising the contribution of the extensive margin to export growth.[11]

Export Expansion Potential

Suppose that it is easier for a producer to expand into new markets with existing products than to start exporting new products. Based on this idea, Brenton and Newfarmer (2009) proposed an index of export market penetration, defined—at the product

[11] The World Bank is currently exploring the causes of Africa's low export survival. Surveys highlight the unavailability of credit as a key binding constraint not just to export entrepreneurship but to the survival of existing export relationships.

level—as the share of potential destination markets that the country actually reaches (i.e., the ratio of the number of i's destination countries for product k relative to the number of countries importing product k from anywhere). This type of information is useful background for trade promotion interventions.

When the issue is *regional* export expansion potential (e.g., to be expected from a preferential agreement), one useful index is Michaely's (1996) bilateral trade complementarity index (TCI). Intuitively, it is best thought of as a correlation between country A's exports *to the world* with country B's imports *from the world*. A is likely to have a comparative advantage in products that it exports substantially to the world (i.e., without the help of tariff preferences); if they are products in which B has a comparative *dis*advantage (because it imports a lot of it), well then A and B should marry.

Formally, the TCI is not a statistical correlation but an (algebraic) indicator. Let m_k^A be product k's share in A's imports from the world and x_k^B its share in B's exports to the world; both should be at the HS6 level of disaggregation. The formula is

$$C^{AB} = 100\left[1 - \sum_k \left|m_k^A - x_k^B\right|/2\right]$$

and can easily be calculated in Excel. The higher the index, the higher the scope for non-diversion (efficient) trade expansion between A and B. Note that there are two indices for each country pair, one taking A as exporter and one taking it as importer. Sometimes the two indices are quite different. The country in a bloc whose *import* pattern fits with its partners' exports will act as a trade engine for the bloc; the one whose *export* pattern fits with its partners' imports will benefit (in political economy terms) from the agreement.

Table 7.1 shows two illustrative configurations with three goods. In panel (a), i's offer does not match j's demand as revealed by their exports and imports respectively. Note that these exports and imports are by commodity but to the world, not to each other.

Comparative Advantage

The current resurgence of interest for industrial policy sometimes confronts trade economists with demands that they are loath to respond to, such as providing guidance to pick winners. In general, there is little to rely on to predict the viability of an infant industry, beyond comparative advantage. But even identifying comparative advantage is tricky. The traditional measure is Balassa's Revealed Comparative Advantage (RCA) index, a ratio of product k's share in country i's exports to k's share in world trade. Formally,

$$RCA_k^i = \frac{X_k^i / X^i}{X_k / X}$$

where X_k^i is country i's exports of good k, $X^i = \sum_k X_k^i$ its total exports, $X_k = \sum_i X_k^i$ world exports of good k, and $X = \sum_i \sum_k X_k^i$ total world exports. An RCA over one in

Table 7.1. Trade complementarity indices

	Dollar amount of trade			
	Country i		Country j	
Goods	X^i_k	M^i_k	X^j_k	M^k_j
1	0	55	108	93
2	0	0	0	0
3	23	221	35	0
Total	23	276	143	93

	Shares in each country's trade				Intermediate calculations			
	Country i		Country j		Cross-differences		Absolute values	
Goods	x^i_k	m^i_k	x^j_k	m^j_k	$m^j_k - x^i_k$	$m^i_k - x^j_k$	$\|m^i_k - x^j_k\|/2$	$\|m^j_k - x^i_k\|/2$
1	0.00	0.20	0.76	1.00	1.00	-0.56	0.50	0.28
2	0.00	0.00	0.00	0.00	0.00	0.00	0.00	0.00
3	1.00	0.80	0.24	0.00	-1.00	0.56	0.50	0.28
Sum	1.00	1.00	1.00	1.00	0.00	0.00	1.00	0.56
Index value							0.00	44.40

good (or sector) k for country i means that i has a revealed comparative advantage in that sector. RCA indices are very simple to calculate from COMTRADE at any degree of disaggregation and are readily available in WITS (see footnote 1). But Balassa's index simply records country i's current trade pattern; it cannot be used to say whether or not it would make sense to support a particular sector.

An alternative approach draws on the PRODY index developed by Hausmann, Hwang, and Rodrik (2005). The PRODY approximates the "revealed" technology content of a product by a weighted average of the GDP per capita of the countries that export it, where the weights are the exporters' RCA indices for that product (adjusted to sum up to one). Intuitively, a product exported by high-income countries is likely to be more technology intensive than one exported by low-income countries.

A recent database constructed by UNCTAD extends that notion to revealed factor intensities. Let $k^i = K^i/L^i$ be country i's stock of physical capital per worker, and let H^i be a proxy for its stock of human capital per worker, say the average level of education of its workforce, in years. These are *national factor endowments*. Good j's revealed intensity in capital is

$$k_j = \sum_{I^j} \omega^i_j k^i$$

where I^j is the set of countries exporting good j and the weights ω are RCA indices adjusted to sum up to one.[12] For instance, if good j is exported essentially by Germany and Japan, it is revealed to be capital intensive. If it is exported essentially by Vietnam and Lesotho, it is revealed to be labor intensive. Similarly,

$$h_j = \sum_{I^j} \omega_j^i H^i$$

is product j's revealed intensity in human capital. The UNCTAD database covers 5,000 products at HS6 and over 1,000 at SITC4-5 between 1962 and 2007 (last updated in December 2010).[13]

Trade Policy

Tariff and Non-Tariff Barriers Data

Developed by UNCTAD, the Trade Analysis and Information System (TRAINS) database provides data on tariff and non-tariff barriers (NTBs) to trade for 140 countries since 1991. Tariffs reported in TRAINS are of two sorts. First, Most-Favored Nation (MFN) tariffs—that is, non-discriminatory tariffs applied by any WTO member to all of its partners—are reported under the code MHS. Second, applied tariffs, which may vary across partner countries depending on preferential trade agreements, are reported under the code AHS. In both cases, tariffs are reported at the HS6 level.

Information on a wide range of NTBs is also collected and reported in TRAINS, but the only year with complete coverage is 2001. Data on NTBs are organized and reported in TRAINS in the form of incidence rates ("coverage ratios") at the HS6 level. That is, each NTB is coded in binary form at the level at which measures are reported by national authorities (1 if there is one, 0 if there is none) and the incidence rate is the proportion of items with 1s in each HS6 category. UNCTAD's original (1994) coding has unfortunately become obsolete, as it featured old-style measures—quantitative restrictions and the like which have largely been phased out, while grouping into catch-all categories many measures that are important now, such as product standards.

In 2006, UNCTAD's Group of Eminent Persons on Non-Tariff Barriers (GNTB) started working on a new classification, more appropriate to record the new forms taken by non-tariff measures (NTMs) (and closer to the WTO's). The new classification, adopted in July 2009, is shown at the broadest level of aggregation (one letter)

---

[12] Adjustments based on the World Bank's agricultural distortions database (Anderson et al., 2008) were also made to avoid agricultural products subsidized by rich countries (say, milk) to appear artificially capital- and human-capital intensive.

[13] At <http://ro.unctad.org/ditc/tab/research.shtm>.

Box 7.1 The 2009 Multiagency Non-Tariff Measure List

A000   Sanitary and phytosanitary measures
B000   Technical barriers to trade
C000   Preshipment inspection and other formalities
D000   Price control measures
E000   Licences, quotas, prohibitions, and other quantity control measures
F000   Charges, taxes, and other para-tariff measures
G000   Finance measures
H000   Anti -competitive measures
I000   Trade related investment measures
J000   Distribution restrictions
K000   Restriction on post -sales services
L000   Subsidies (excluding certain export subsidies classified under P000, below)
M000   Government procurement restrictions
N000   Intellectual property
O000   Rules of origin
P000   Export related measures

---

level in Box 7.1. It provides better disaggregation of NTMs, at one letter and one digit (64 categories), one letter and two digits (121 categories), or even one letter and three digits (special cases). It covers a wide range of measures, some of which are clearly behind the border (like anti-competitive measures, which include arcane measures like compulsory national insurance). It has not been widely used yet, and some ambiguities will need to be dealt with. But it provides the basis for a new wave of NTM data collection run jointly by UNCTAD, the World Bank, and the African Development Bank, to replace TRAINS with up-to-date NTM information.[14]

NTBs are typically coded in binary (one/zero) form, which gives no indication on the severity of the measures. For instance, a quota that is only mildly binding is coded like one that is very severely binding. There is no perfect way of dealing with this problem, and the severity of NTBs must be estimated econometrically through correlation with trade flows.

The WTO's Integrated Data Base (IDB) is a tariff database at the tariff-line level, covering 122 Member Countries' MFN and bound tariffs since 2000. Information on *ad valorem* equivalents of specific tariffs[15] as well as preferential tariffs is not exhaustive. Access to the IDB is free for government agencies of member countries.

---

[14] As of early 2011, the data-collection campaign has covered about 30 countries. Best coverage is for Latin America.

[15] An *ad valorem* tariff is expressed as a percent of the good's CIF price. A specific tariff is expressed as local currency units per physical unit of the good (say, 75 euros per ton). Specific tariffs can be converted into *Ad valorem* Equivalents (AVEs) using prices (trade unit values). But the result will obviously fluctuate with those prices: when they go down, the AVE goes up, when they go up, the AVE goes down (which incidentally illustrates the fact that specific tariffs impose time-varying distortions on the domestic economy).

The Agricultural Market Access Database (AMAD) is a cooperative effort of Agriculture Canada, the EU Commission, the US Department of Agriculture, the Food and Agriculture Organization (FAO), Organisation for Economic Co-operation and Development (OECD), and UNCTAD. It covers data on agricultural production, consumption, trade, unit values, tariffs, and quantitative restrictions including "tariff-quotas" (low tariffs up to a certain quantity, higher tariffs beyond that quantity).

Based on TRAINS, the MACMAP database was developed jointly by CEPII and by the ITC in order to provide a comprehensive and consistent set of AVEs of all tariffs, whether already in *ad valorem* form or in specific form (of the form, say, of "x dollars or euros per ton"—see the discussion below). MACMAP also includes a treatment of tariff-rate quotas (the original data being from AMAD). For instance, suppose that a tariff rate of 20 per cent is levied on imports within a quota of 10,000 tons a year, and a tariff of 300 per cent on any additional quantities, if applicable. Import volume data are compared with the quota to determine if it is binding. If yes, the 300 per cent "out-of-quota" tariff is used; otherwise, the in-quota tariff of 20 per cent is used. The methodology is discussed in detail in Bouët et al. (2005).

The Global Anti-Dumping (GAD) database provides detailed information on all anti-dumping measures notified by the WTO. The data includes determination and affected countries, product, measure type, date, duty rate, and revocation dates; sometimes it also includes information on companies involved.[16]

Direct measures of trade costs are collected by the World Bank in the Logistics Performance Index (LPI) and in Doing Business. Both are survey-based indices, that is, reflecting perceptions, and have been developed as tools to raise awareness rather than to be used for statistical analysis, although they may be used for that purpose. The LPI includes assessments by international freight forwarders of the quality of the logistics environment of a country (border processes, infrastructure, and logistic services such as trucking, warehousing, brokerage, and so on). Doing Business covers a wide array of issues, but one of its dimensions, trading across borders, specifically covers trade-related costs using assessments by local freight forwarders, shipping lines, customs brokers, port officials and banks of the documentation, cost, and time needed to complete procedures for importing or exporting a 20-foot container. Both the LPI and the Doing Business's "cost of trade" aggregate information into rankings. Table 7.2 illustrates the case of Pakistan.

The information in the LPI and the Doing Business' export cost (which excludes maritime freight) should be somewhat related (negatively). Across countries, the correlation is indeed negative and significant at 1 per cent, but it is noisy, as shown in Figure 7.8.

Given the imperfect correlation between the two, it is a matter of judgment which one to use. A natural criterion is the number of respondents per country, as one should treat carefully perception-based indices built from small samples. On the Doing Business's

---

[16] The database can be downloaded free of charge from the World Bank's research site at <http://econ.worldbank.org/ttbd/gad>.

Table 7.2 LPI and Doing Business (Trading Across Borders): Pakistan 2010

(a) Doing Business: Trading Across Borders			
Documents to export (number)	9.0	8.5	4.3
Time to export (days)	22.0	32.4	10.5
Cost to export (US$ per container)	611.0	1,364.1	1,089.7
Documents to import (number)	8.0	9.0	4.9
Time to import (days)	18.0	32.2	11.0
Cost to import (US$ per container)	680.0	1,509.1	1,145.9

(b) LPI	Score	Rank
Customs	2.05	134
Infrastructure	2.08	120
International shipments	2.91	66
Logistics competence	2.28	120
Tracking & tracing	2.64	93
Timeliness	3.08	110
Overall LPI	*2.53*	*110*

Source: World Bank, Logistics performance index (<http://info.worldbank.org/etools/tradesurvey/>); Doing Business Survey (<http://www.doingbusiness.org/rankings>).

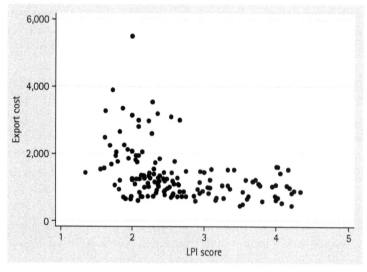

FIGURE 7.8 Doing Business's export cost vs. LPI across countries

Source: World Bank, Logistics performance index <http://info.worldbank.org/etools/tradesurvey/>; Doing Business Survey <http://www.doingbusiness.org/rankings>.

country/topic page, this number is shown in the "local partners" tab. In Pakistan, for instance, the *Trading Across Borders* module had 13 respondents.

Analyzing Tariff and Non-Tariff Barriers

Tariff schedules are typically defined at the HS6 or HS8 levels, meaning that there are at least around 5,000 different tariffs and possibly more. Aggregating them can be done in two ways: by simple averaging or by using import shares as weights. The first method is straightforward to calculate. Under the second one, the average tariff is given by

$$\bar{\tau} = \sum_k w_k \tau_k$$

where k indexes imported goods and $w_k = M_k / M$ is good k's share in the country's overall imports (the Greek letter τ is used in place of t to avoid confusion with time indices). The advantages and drawbacks of the two methods are illustrated in Table 7.3, in which a country imports three goods: good one, whose tariff varies between 0 and 440 per cent going down the table; good two, with a tariff of 40 per cent, and good three, with a tariff of 5 per cent. Each tariff has equal weight in a simple average. This gives excessive weight to good 3, although its imports are very small. For example, if tariffs are at 40 per cent for both goods 1 and 2, the simple average (28.3 per cent) is "pulled down" by good 3, although the large majority of imports are in fact affected by a 40 per cent tariff. By contrast, the weighted average is at a more reasonable rate of 39.75 per cent, which suggests that the weighted average should be preferred.

Table 7.3 Simple vs. trade–weighted average tariffs

Good 1		Good 2		Good 3		Total	Simple	Weighted
Tariff	Imports	Tariff	Imports	Tariff	Imports	imports	average	average
0	1'000	40	670	5	10	1'680	15.0	15.99
50	670	40	670	5	10	1'286	31.7	44.46
100	368	40	670	5	10	1'048	48.3	60.75
150	223	40	670	5	10	903	65.0	66.81
200	135	40	670	5	10	81.	81.7	66.16
250	82	40	670	5	10	362	98.3	62.19
300	40	40	670	5	10	730	115.0	57.29
350	40	40	670	5	10	710	131.7	52.72
400	18	40	670	5	10	698	148.3	48.97
450	11	40	670	5	10	6.11	165.0	46.11
500	7	40	670	5	10	687	181.7	44.03

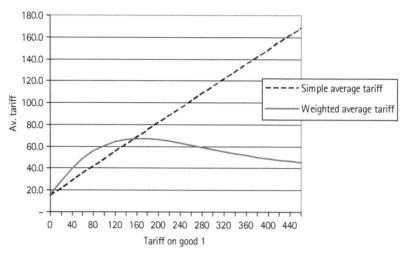

FIGURE 7.9 Bias of trade-weighted average tariffs

However, there is more to the story. If a tariff on a good increases, its imports decrease, and then so does its weight. At the limit, when tariffs become prohibitive, the weight becomes zero. Thus, weighted averages tend to "under-represent" high tariffs, a bias which is illustrated by Figure 7.9.

One way to circumvent the problem is to use different weights, such as free-trade imports (but which are not observed), or world imports (as suggested by Leamer (1974), but then the particular trade structure of each country is not captured anymore). An alternative compromise is proposed by the MACMAP database, where weights are given by imports of the corresponding income group of the country. Still another possibility is to report a variety of tariff measures: simple and weighted averages, minima, maxima, and standard deviations, with the last three measures reported by HS section or overall, but calculated on HS6 data rather than from aggregates, to avoid underestimation. Again, the choice of HS sections is a compromise between total aggregation (large information loss) and excessive disaggregation (loss of synthetic value).

Because tariffs are typically imposed not just on final goods but also on intermediates, the protection offered to local value added may not be correctly represented by nominal rates of protection: the final tariff protects domestic transformation, whereas the intermediate ones penalize it. Ideally one would want to report Effective Rates of Protection (ERPs), by which is meant the percentage increase in local value added when moving from world prices to domestic prices (i.e., the increase in the "price" of domestic transformation induced by the array of tariffs on the final good and all imported intermediates). However the calculation of ERPs involves the use of input–output matrices typically recorded in nomenclatures other than trade ones and at highly aggregated levels. The resulting calculations therefore reflect many approximations of aggregation biases, while being fairly cumbersome to do.

As for NTBs,[17] their effect can be assessed in several ways (see the survey in Deardorff and Stern, 1997). The simplest is to code their presence in binary form, as in TRAINS, and to calculate the percentage of imports that are affected. An example of this approach is OECD (1995). This calculation, known as an "NTB coverage ratio," is vulnerable to the same bias as that of trade-weighted average tariffs. Namely, when an NTB—say, a quota—on one good is very stiff, imports of that good become very small, and, mechanically, so does the good's weight in the final calculation.

An alternative consists of calculating the AVEs of NTBs using price-based methods (see e.g., Andriamananjara et al., 2004).[18] A particularly simple approach is the "price gap" method spelled out in Annex V of the WTO's Agricultural Agreement. It compares the domestic price of the NTB-affected good with either its landed price before import licenses are purchased or its landed price in a comparable but otherwise unrestricted market. In practice, this is typically where problems start. Consider for instance the EU market for bananas prior to the elimination of the tariff quota in 2006. One possible comparator country was Norway, which is about the same distance from producing countries but had no QR in place. However, Norway being a small market, prices were likely to be higher than in a large-volume market like the EU, biasing the price gap calculation downward. Alternatively, the US could be used as a comparator country, but distances to the US being typically shorter and distribution networks not really comparable, it was not clear that US prices really represented the counterfactual prices that would obtain in the EU in the absence of the tariff quota. The last problem is that price data are available for only about 300 products, a small proportion of the 5,000 products at the HS6 level.

Kee, Nicita, and Olarreaga (2009) proposed a more elaborate two-step approach. Step 1 consists of estimating import-demand equations across countries, product by product (at the HS6 level), giving around 5,000 equations to estimate on about 80 observations each. Step 2 consists of retrieving their AVEs algebraically using import-demand elasticities themselves estimated econometrically in Kee, Nicita, and Olarreaga (2008). This is probably the most complete and reliable method currently available. Kee et al. used it to construct an aggregate trade-restrictiveness index which we discuss below. Their results show that "core" NTB use and (unsurprisingly) agricultural support rise with income levels, suggesting that, as countries grow, they tend to substitute non-tariff for tariff barriers.

A final route to assessing the effect of NTBs on trade flows consists of using all the information available in the variation of trade volumes across pairs of countries to construct a statistical counterfactual based on the so-called "gravity equation," to which we will turn to below (for an example of this approach, see e.g., Mayer and Zignano, 2005).

---

[17] Sometimes the acronym "NTM" is preferred to "NTB" in order to avoid a normative connotation.

[18] These methods are based on a well-known equivalence theorem, namely that under perfect competition, a quota of, say, a thousand units has the same price and welfare effects as a tariff reducing imports to a thousand units. It should be kept in mind, however, that the equivalence breaks down under domestic market power, on which the researcher is unlikely to have reliable information.

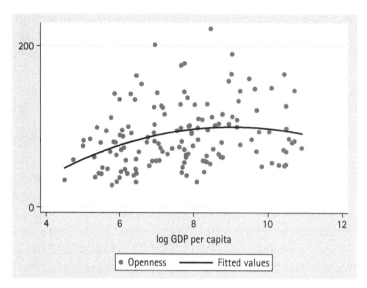

FIGURE 7.10 Trade and per capita GDP

Note: The vertical axis is measured in percent of GDP. The curve is fitted by OLS using a quadratic polynomial. The turning point is around exp(9) which is US$8,000 at PPP.

Source: Authors' calculations from COMTRADE and WDI.

Measuring Overall Openness

As is well known, Adam Smith's and David Ricardo's general prescription in favor of free trade is based on essentially static efficiency arguments. Empirically, the static welfare losses involved in trade protection vary considerably, from large in small countries (see e.g., Connolly and de Melo, 1994) to small in large countries (see e.g., Messerlin, 2001). Perhaps, more importantly, trade openness is statistically associated with higher growth (see e.g., Wacziarg and Welsh, 2008). Thus, assessing a country's openness is crucial and, indeed, international financial institutions use a variety of indices of trade openness or restrictiveness. The problem is, of course, to control, as much as possible, for non-policy influences on observed openness, and that is where difficulties start.

The degree of openness is the most frequent indicator of a country's integration in world trade. By defining country i's total exports, total imports and GDP by X^i, M^i and Y^i respectively, the openness ratio of country i is given by:

$$O_t^i = \frac{X_t^i + M_t^i}{Y_t^i}$$

and is calculated for a large sample of countries and years in the Penn World Tables (PWT).[19] The subscript t indexes time, if the index is traced over several years.

---

[19] The data are on the PWT's site at <http://pwt.econ.upenn.edu/php_site/pwt_index.php>.

Can we use O^i as is for cross-country comparisons? The problem is that it is correlated, *inter alia*, with levels of income, as shown in the scatter plot of Figure 7.10 where each point represents a country. The straight line is fitted by ordinary least squares and therefore gives the best "straight-line" approximation to the relationship between GDP per capita and the ratio of foreign trade to GDP. Countries below the line can be considered as trading less than their level of income would "normally" imply.

Thus, at the very least, income levels should be taken into account when assessing a country's openness. Many further adjustments to the relationship in Figure 7.10 can be made, leading to openness measures estimated as residuals from cross-country regressions of O^i on geographical determinants of trade. This approach goes back to the work of Leamer (1988) and is illustrated in Figure 7.11 for Nepal.

Beyond the relationship between openness and incomes, policymakers may be interested in assessing the overall stance of a trade policy, which can affect, for instance, the disbursement of structural adjustment or other funds from international financial institutions. This, however, involves a double aggregation problem: across goods and across instruments. In order to overcome the difficulties involved in this aggregation, economists have constructed indices based on observation rules to determine how open a country's trade policy is. In a celebrated study, Sachs and Warner (1995) proposed a binary classification of countries (1 for "open" ones, 0 for closed ones) according to five criteria: average tariffs above 40 per cent, NTB coverage ratios above 40 per cent, trade monopolies, black market premium on foreign exchange above 20 per cent for a decade, or a centrally planned system. However, Rodriguez and Rodrik (1999) showed that the trade dimension of the Sachs–Warner (SW) index was hardly correlated with growth, as most of its explanatory power came from the last three (non-trade) criteria. The IMF has also proposed a Trade Restrictiveness Index (TRI) which goes from one (most open) to ten (least

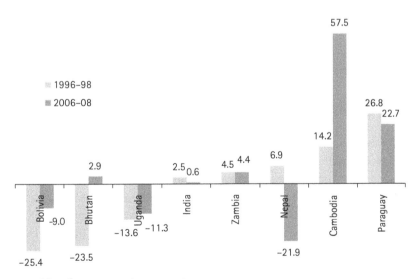

FIGURE 7.11 Nepal's openness in comparison

Source: COMTRADE.

open). This index, which has been used in several IMF research papers, corresponds to the average score of each country along a variety of different dimensions such as average tariff, proportion of tariff lines covered by QRs, and so on (see IMF, 2005 for details).

An alternative approach, more directly grounded in theory, has been proposed by Kee, Nicita, and Olarreaga (Kee et al., 2009). They draw from Anderson and Neary (1994, 1996), who proposed a Trade Restrictiveness Index (TRI) defined as the uniform *ad valorem* tariff on imports that would be equivalent to the set of existing tariff and non-tariff measures in terms of the importing country's *welfare*. Kee et al.'s Overall Trade Restrictiveness Index (OTRI) is the uniform *ad valorem* tariff on imports that would result in the same *import volume* as the set of existing tariff and non-tariff measures. That is, country *i*'s OTRI τ^{i*}, which is a single number, solves

$$M^i = \sum_k M_k\left(\tau_k^i\right) = \sum_k M_k\left(\tau^{i*}\right)$$

where k indexes goods at the HS6 level, τ_k^i stands for the *ad valorem* equivalent of country *i*'s barriers (tariff and non-tariff) on imports of good k, and $M_k\left(.\right)$ is an import-demand function estimated econometrically across countries. A mirror image of the OTRI measure, from the exporter's side, has been proposed by the same authors. It is called the market access OTRI, or MA-OTRI, and defined as the uniform *ad valorem* tariff equivalent to the set of existing measures affecting a country on its export market. Estimates of all three indices for a large number of countries are freely available on the web. They suggest that both the OTRI and the MA-OTRI measures tend to decrease with income,[20] levels.

III. *Ex Post* Analysis

The Material Presented In This Section Draws Extensively on Bacchetta Et Al. (2012).

Revisiting Trade Flows with the Gravity Equation

It has long been known that the size of bilateral trade flows between any two countries follows a law, dubbed the "gravity equation" by analogy with physics, whereby countries trade more, *ceteris paribus*, the closer they are, the larger they are, and the more similar they are, the latter two in terms of their GDPs.[21] Whereas empirics predated theory in this instance, the robustness of the gravity relationship is attributable to the fact that it is a direct implication of the monopolistic competition model of trade and which has established itself as the workhorse of trade analysis between industrial countries.

---

[20] At <http://www.worldbank.org/trade/otri>.

[21] A clear and concise introduction to the gravity equation can be found in Head (2003). A thorough treatment for the advanced reader is in Chapter 5 of Feenstra (2004).

According to the gravity equation, the logarithm of bilateral trade between two countries is related to the log of their respective GDPs, a composite term measuring barriers and incentives to trade between them (typically the log of the distance between their capitals), and additional terms to control for obstacles to trade between these countries and the rest of the world.

The rationale for including these last terms, dubbed "multilateral trade-resistance" (MTR) terms by Anderson and van Wincoop (2003) who argued for their inclusion, is that if the two countries have strong links with the rest of the world (e.g. Austria and Switzerland), there will be less trade between them than if they are isolated (e.g. Tajikistan and Uzbekistan). Several alternative ways of proxying MTR terms are possible. One is to use iterative methods to construct estimates of the price-raising effects of barriers to multilateral trade (Anderson and van Wincoop, 2003). A simpler alternative is to control for each country's "remoteness" by using a formula that measures its average distance to trading partners. An even simpler, and widely used, method consists of using country fixed effects for importers and exporters.[22]

In sum, the gravity equation in its baseline form is as follows. Let V_t^{ij} denote country j's total imports from i at time t (we keep the convention of writing country indices as superscripts and putting the source first and the destination second), and $\ln V_t^{ij}$ its natural logarithm. Let D^{ij} be the distance between the two. Let also I^i be a dummy variable equal to 1 when the country is i and 0 otherwise. The equation is:

$$\ln V_t^{ij} = \alpha_0 + \alpha_1 \ln GDP_t^i + \alpha_2 \ln GDP_t^j + \alpha_3 \ln D^{ij}$$
$$+ \alpha_4 I^i + \alpha_5 I^j + \sum_{\tau=1}^{T} \alpha_{5+\tau} I_\tau + u_t^{ij}. \tag{7.1}$$

Note that, because all variables are in logs, the coefficients can be interpreted as elasticities. That is, a coefficient estimate $\hat{\alpha}_2 = 1$ indicates an income elasticity of (aggregate) imports equal to unity.

To this baseline formulation can be added any controls and variables of interest. Thus, estimation requires data on bilateral trade, GDPs, distances, and possibly other determinants of bilateral trade, including contiguity (common border), common language, colonial ties, exchange rates, and so on. There is a wealth of databases from which the researcher can draw for these variables.

Bilateral merchandise trade flows can be found in the IMF's DOTs, in COMTRADE, or in the CEPII's BACI. They are typically expressed in current dollars. GDPs in current dollars, converted at current exchange rates, can be found in the IMF's International Financial Statistics (IFS). GDPs at Purchasing Power Parity (PPP)[23] can be found in the

---

[22] "Fixed effects" are dummy (binary) variables that "mark" an individual in a panel in which individuals are followed over several periods. In a gravity equation, one such variable will be set to 1 whenever the exporting country is, say, Kazakhstan, and 0 otherwise. Another one will be set to 1 whenever the importing country is Kazakhstan and 0 otherwise, and so on for each country. In a cross-section with n countries, if one-way trade flows are not combined, there are 2n2 country pairs (the unit of observation), but only 2n such fixed effects, so estimation is still possible.

[23] An explanation of how PPP exchange rates are constructed is given in Annex I.

World Bank's World Development Indicators (available online by subscription or on CD-ROM) together with a wealth of other indicators, in the Penn World Tables (PWT).[24]

The gravity equation can be used in various ways to estimate the effect of trade policy on merchandise trade flows. At the aggregate level, gravity equations have been used extensively to assess, *ex post*, the effect of Regional Trade Agreements (RTAs), one of the seminal contributions in this area being Frankel, Stein, and Wei (1995). The crudest way to do so is to include in the set of gravity regressors a "dummy" (0/1) variable marking pairs of countries linked by RTAs. However, as discussed in Carrère (2006), this methodology is fraught with problems, including the fact that RTAs are likely to be endogenous to trade flows (countries that are natural trading partners are more likely to form RTAs if governments decide to form them on welfare grounds). In estimating a gravity equation, several estimation issues should be kept in mind. First, results may differ depending on whether or not zero trade flows (about half the country pairs every year) are included in the dataset. If not, OLS can be used, but the results may be biased. If they are, a ML estimator, Poisson or Tobit, is better. More sophisticated approaches include Heckman's selection model that corrects for the fact that non-zero trade flows are not random, or Helpman, Melitz, and Rubinstein's (2008), which "purges out" the effect of firm heterogeneity.

The gravity equation has been less frequently used at the disaggregated level, but it can also be put to work for sectoral studies. Suppose that we observe, around the world, both tariffs and quotas on the market for a homogenous good, say bananas. The estimates on those can be used to retrieve directly a tariff equivalent of the quotas. Specifically, let τ_t^{ij} and Q_t^{ij} be, respectively, any tariff and quota imposed by j on i in the good in question (here bananas), and other variables be as before. Omitting a few additional explanatory variables like the exchange rate, a gravity equation estimated at the sectoral level looks like this:

$$\ln V_t^{ij} = \beta_0 + \beta_1 \ln GDP_t^i + \beta_2 \ln GDP_t^j + \beta_3 \ln D^{ij}$$
$$+\beta_4 \ln\left(1+\tau_t^{ij}\right) + \beta_5 Q_t^{ij} + FE + TE + u_t^{ij} \tag{7.2}$$

where FE and TE stand respectively for the "fixed effects" I^i and I^j in (7.1) and for its "time effects" I_τ. Note that one has been added to the tariff because, the equation being in logs, zero tariffs would send the log to minus infinity whereas $\ln(1)=0$. Estimates from (7.2) can then be used to retrieve the tariff equivalent of the quota. Let us use hats over variables for estimated coefficients and predicted trade values. Letting Z stand for everything but $\hat{\beta}_5 Q_t^{ij}$ in (2), we have

$$\ln \widehat{V}^{ijt} = Z + \hat{\beta}_5 Q_t^{ij}. \tag{7.3}$$

[24] PWT Mark 6.1 is freely available on the web at <http://pwt.econ.upenn.edu/php_site/pwt_index. php>. It can also be found with a different data-extraction interface at the CHASS center of the University of Toronto at <http://datacentre2.chass.utoronto.ca/pwt/>. Country codes are not identical across databases, but concordance tables can be found on Jon Haveman's page at <http://www. macalester.edu/research/economics/PAGE/HAVEMAN/Trade.Resources/Concordances/OthMap/ country.txt>.

Note that Q_t^{ij} is equal to one if a quota applies and zero otherwise. Thus, the predicted difference in trade between a country pair *with* a quota and the same country pair *without* the quota would be

$$\ln \widehat{V}_{t,\text{quota}}^{ij} - \ln \widehat{V}_{t,\text{no quota}}^{ij} = Z + \hat{\beta}_5(1) - \left[Z + \hat{\beta}_5(0) \right] = \hat{\beta}_5. \tag{7.4}$$

Using again Z as shorthand for everything except $\hat{\beta}_4 \ln(1 + \tau_t^{ij})$ in (7.2), a similar calculation can be performed for the effect of a tariff at rate τ_t^{ij} compared to no tariff at all:

$$\ln \widehat{V}_{t,\text{tariff}}^{ij} - \ln \widehat{V}_{t,\text{no tariff}}^{ij} = Z + \hat{\beta}_4 \ln(1 + \tau_t^{ij}) - \left[Z + \hat{\beta}_4 \ln(1) \right] \tag{7.5}$$
$$= \hat{\beta}_4 \ln(1 + \tau_t^{ij}).$$

A tariff equivalent of quota Q_t^{ij} is a tariff that has the same effect on trade flows. This is equivalent to equating the left-hand sides of (7.4) and (7.5). But if their left-hand sides are equal, so are their right-hand sides; thus, the tariff equivalent $\tilde{\tau}$ of quota Q_t^{ij} satisfies

$$\hat{\beta}_4 \ln(1 + \tilde{\tau}) = \hat{\beta}_5$$

or

$$\tilde{\tau} = \exp\left(\hat{\beta}_5 / \hat{\beta}_4\right) - 1.$$

This simple calculation can be easily programmed after the estimation of the gravity equation, yielding an *ad valorem* tariff equivalent to the quota.

Analyzing a Policy's Distributional Effects

If the textbook treatment of trade policy is usually cast in terms of its welfare effects, policymakers are often as much if not more interested in its *distributional* effects. From a conceptual point of view, the distributional effects of trade have been extensively discussed as part of the so-called "trade and wages" debate, where the issue was essentially whether Stolper–Samuelson effects were responsible for the observed increase in the skill premium in Northern countries. That debate was settled with the observation that most of that increase was within industries rather than across and was thus likely to be due to technical progress more than trade.

A considerable literature has been exploring the effects of trade on poverty and inequality, especially in developing countries (see Koujianou-Goldberg and Pavcnik, 2004, for a survey). Tracing the effects of, say, trade liberalization on poor rural households is typically difficult because, even if prices were measured correctly at the border through trade unit values (which is already unlikely, see above), the pass-through of border-price changes to changes in the domestic producer and consumer prices effectively faced by poor rural households is difficult to assess. A good treatment of this question can be found in Nicita (2004). Here we will illustrate something less ambitious, namely how to measure the regressivity or progressivity of a trade policy.

A variety of tools can be used to analyze quantitatively whether a given trade policy is regressive ("anti-poor") or not, that is if it hurts poor households more than rich ones. We will limit the presentation here to a simple and frequent treatment of this important policy question, but note beforehand that it may be quite demanding in terms of data requirements.

Consider for instance a farming household that consumes and produces n products indexed by k, and let $w_k^i\left(Y^i\right)$ and $W_k^i\left(Y^i\right)$ stand for their respective shares in the household's expenditure and income, with the argument in parentheses meant to highlight that those shares are themselves likely to vary with income levels (goods whose budget shares go down with income are "necessities," and crops grown at lower income levels may, e.g., require lower input use). Let μ_k be the income elasticity of good k, and observe that tariffs on goods produced by households *protect* them, whereas tariffs on consumption goods *tax* them. If tariffs on production goods are positively correlated with income elasticities, they are pro-rich because they protect disproportionately the goods produced by rich households (think, e.g., of crops grown predominantly by large and high-income farmers); if tariffs on consumption or intermediate goods are positively correlated with income elasticities, by contrast, they are pro-poor, because they tax disproportionately goods consumed by the rich.

Formally, one can construct a production-weighted average tariff for each household as

$$\overline{\tau}^{i,\mathrm{prod}} = \sum_{k=1}^{n} W_k^i \tau_k$$

where τ_k is the tariff on good k, and a consumption-weighted average tariff as

$$\overline{\tau}^{i,\mathrm{cons}} = \sum_{k=1}^{n} w_k^i \tau_k$$

Note that the sets of goods produced and consumed need not overlap; an urban, salaried household would simply have zero production weights on all goods. The net effect of the tariff structure on household i is then the difference between the two:

$$\overline{\tau}^i = \sum_{k=1}^{n} \left(W_k^i - w_k^i\right)\tau_k$$

All three can be plotted against income levels in order to get a picture of the regressive or progressive nature of tariffs. One way of doing this could be to simply regress $\overline{\tau}^i$ on income levels. However, nothing guarantees that the relationship between the two will be linear or even monotone, as it may well have one or several turning points. As an alternative to linear or polynomial regression, one may fit what is known as a "smoother" regression, which essentially runs a different regression for each observation, using a sub-sample centered around that observation.[25] The result is a "regression curve" on which no particular shape is imposed and which can therefore have as many

---

[25] Although it sounds involved, this procedure is in practice very simple because it is pre-programmed as the "ksm" command in Stata.

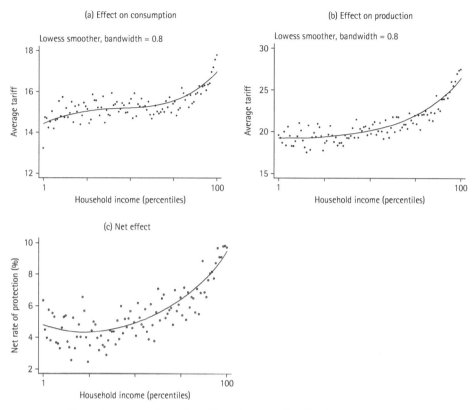

FIGURE 7.12 Smoother regression of tariffs on income distribution

Source: Ethiopia Diagnostic Trade Integration Study (unpublished).

turning points as needed to fit the data. In addition, for readability, households are typically grouped into centiles and the smoother regression is run on the average incomes of the centiles rather than on individual household incomes. An example of the result is shown for Ethiopia in Figure 7.12.

Note that if the smoother regression is very easy to run, the real difficulty in the exercise is to get data on consumption and production shares. This requires the use of household surveys, which are typically very large datasets requiring substantial cleaning before use.

IV. *Ex Ante* Assessment of Trade Policy Changes

In addition to the descriptive statistics and *ex post* type of analyses described above, trade policy analysts also make use of *ex ante* (or simulation) modeling techniques to assess the likely (overall and sectoral) impact of trade policy changes. These are tools that help analysts and policymakers to evaluate and quantify the potential economic effects of various trade policy alternatives. Generally, they help answer *"What if"* types of questions (or counterfactual/anti-monde). Using information on the observed state of the world, they ask how things would be different if a variable (usually a policy instrument) is altered. *Ex ante* models are useful distillation of economic theory that can provide a handle on the often complicated interactions between different economic variables in a consistent and tractable way. When properly designed and constructed, simulation models offer a coherent framework built upon rigorous economic theory that can provide empirical support (or even justification) for a chosen trade policy.

Simulation models can be structured either in a partial or in a general equilibrium setting. A partial equilibrium model generally only focuses on one part or one sector of an economy and assumes that changes in that sector have no, or minimal, impact on other sectors. It takes into account neither the linkages between sectors, nor between income and expenditures. In contrast, a general equilibrium analysis explicitly accounts for all the links between the different elements of a considered economy. These elements may be household, branches of activity, factors of production, and so on. Such analysis imposes a set of conditions on these elements in a way that basic economic identities and resource constraints are always satisfied. For instance, an expansion in a given sector would be associated with a contraction in another sector, since the existing factors of production will move to the expanding one and away from the contracting one.

The choice of appropriate model depends on the nature of the policy being studied, the availability of resources and information, and the variables of interest to policymakers. Whatever their exact nature, however, a number of key elements are common across models and are necessary to make them useful for conducting rigorous quantitative trade policy analysis: economic theory, data (endogenous and exogenous variables), and behavioral parameters.

This section briefly introduces these elements and presents the basic steps required in solving the model. It then presents the main features of the two types of simulation models typically used in trade policy analysis (partial equilibrium and computable general equilibrium models) with the modest goal of familiarizing the reader with the different concepts.

Required Elements for Applied Trade Policy Modeling

A crucial element in a simulation model is that it should be based on solid *economic theory*. This is embodied in a series of mathematical representation of the different economic linkages, constraints, and behavior assumptions of the model's economic agents (market structure, profit maximization, utility optimization . . .) that the analyst wants to capture in the models. They will reflect the key assumptions that are used to simplify the reality into the model.

Next, for the model to be a useful empirical tool, the analyst needs to use good quality real world data. An *ex ante* model starts with a series of observed variables that are assumed to represent an initial equilibrium state of the world. The system is then *shocked* by changing one (or a few) *exogenous* variable and solved until it produces a new equilibrium and new values for the *endogenous* variables of the model.[26] As will be discussed in greater detail below, the choice of exogenous (vs. endogenous) variables determines the *general* or *partial* equilibrium nature of the model, in parallel with the model's *economic closure*. The model closure is characterized by a set of assumptions about some basic identities or constraints that have to hold for the model to reach equilibrium (such as market clearing conditions—demand equals supply, or income equals expenditures).

The final key elements required in conducting *ex ante* trade policy modeling are the *behavioral parameters*. Those parameters reflect how economic agents respond to changes in their environment (e.g., price or income). They can include various price (and cross-price) elasticities, income elasticities, substitution elasticities (among different goods or varieties of goods or factors), and others. These elasticities are generally taken from the existing literature or are estimated independently by the researchers outside the framework of the model (e.g., Donnelly, Johnson, Tsigas, and Ingersoll (2004) and Kee, Nicita, and Olarreaga (2008) provide a set of very useful import and substitution elasticities, respectively).

Required Steps for Applied Trade Policy Simulations

Prior to the actual policy experiment or simulation, an *ex ante* model is generally benchmarked using the observed data and the behavioral parameters—that is, the model is initially calibrated so that its equilibrium replicates observed data. This process (also called *parameterization, initialization,* or *calibration*) involves using the observed data and model parameters to determine the values of a number of unobserved variables (or the *calibration parameters*) in the model.[27] These variables are assumed to incorporate information that is not readily observable and are used as fixed exogenous variables in the simulation steps.

Given the resulting calibration parameters, a policy experiment (or other experiments) can be conducted by first assuming that the parameterized model is in equilibrium. Then the value of an exogenous (policy) variable of interest is shocked to capture the questions that the analyst would like to address. And finally, the model is solved to reach a new equilibrium—by allowing prices to adjust to satisfy some predefined *equilibrium conditions*. Most trade related simulation models rely on what is called *comparative statics* methodology to evaluate the impact of a policy experiment: the effect of the shock is then computed by comparing the new equilibrium values to the observed

---

[26] Stated differently, exogenous variables (also called shock or policy variables) are the variables that are taken as given and assumed to be unaffected by an economic shock applied to the model, while endogenous ones are those whose values respond to changes in the model.

[27] For instance, if the demand function is expressed as $\ln Q = A - b \ln P$, where $\ln Q$ is the demanded quantity, b is the price elasticity, and $\ln P$ is the price, the value of the intercept A is calibrated using the information on price, quantity, and elasticity, and is computed as $A = \ln Q/b \ln P$. The parameter A is the calibration parameter in this case.

data (the initial equilibrium)—two equilibrium states of the world are compared.[28] The impact of the trade policy experiment on any given endogenous variable is then simply measured as the difference between the initial and the final equilibrium value of that variable.

Partial Equilibrium Simulations (Focused Sectoral Analysis)

In a partial equilibrium model, a particular commodity or market is studied, and the linkages with other sectors (income or substitution effects, or spillover) are ignored (i.e., they are assumed exogenous). Any trade policies deal with only this commodity or market. The condition for solving the model is simply to equate demand and supply in that particular market. This type of model can ideally be used when the effects on the rest of the economy are small. That is, either the sector itself is small (limited income effects), or there are limited links with other parts of economy (limited backward and forward linkages).

This approach has a number of attractive features. The main advantage is its minimal data requirement. Usually, it requires only a few trade flow and trade policy data for the sector being studied and a set of (price or substitution) elasticities that are usually easy to collect from databases like COMTRADE or TRAINS. Also, due partly to the minimal data requirement, the analysis can be conducted at a disaggregated or detailed sectoral level, which solves a number of the aggregation biases discussed earlier. For example, it allows the study of the effects of the liberalization of "brown rice" imports by Madagascar, a level of aggregation that is neither convenient nor possible in the framework of a general equilibrium model. This also resolves a number of "aggregation biases." By the same logic, the partial equilibrium approach may allow the analysis of the likely impact of trade agreements, like the Doha Round, more accurately, as the negotiations are conducted at a very disaggregated level. This approach also has the virtue of being transparent and relatively easy to implement and solve. In fact, a typical partial equilibrium model generally consists of a small number of equations representing the demand and supply sides, and solving the model simply entails allowing the price to adjust to equate demand and supply. Modeling is thus straightforward and results can usually be easily explained.

The partial equilibrium approach also has a number of disadvantages that have to be kept in mind while conducting any analysis. Since it is only a "partial" model of the economy, the analysis is only done on a pre-determined number of economic variables. This makes it sensitive to a few (perhaps wrongly estimated) behavioral elasticities. Due to their simplicity, partial equilibrium models may also miss important interactions and feedbacks between various markets. In particular, the partial equilibrium approach

---

[28] An alternative to the comparative statics approach (comparing two equilibrium states of the world) is a more dynamic approach, which involves either comparing two equilibrium (steady state) rates of growth, or tracking the adjustment process of given variables between two equilibrium states of the world. The latter usually involve relatively complicated assumptions on the behavior of the model's economic agents (in terms of saving and investment, capital accumulation, and technological changes, for instance).

tends to neglect the important inter-sectoral input/output (or upstream/downstream) linkages that are the basis of general equilibrium analyses. It also misses the existing constraints that apply to the various factors of production (e.g., labor, capital, land...) and their movement across sectors.

Given limitations in the data and the abstract nature of such models, the user should interpret the results with caution. The numbers that come out of the simulations should only be used to give a sense of the order of magnitude that a change in policy can mean for economic welfare or trade. However, the model has detailed commodity and country coverage and it can be helpful in indicating the relative magnitudes of the effects of policy changes on welfare, trade, and prices in the comparison of various policy scenarios.

The most commonly used partial equilibrium models are SMART, Tariff Reform Impact Simulation Tool (TRIST), and GSIM. All three are currently structured to analyze trade policy changes as changes in tariffs and taxes. New versions are currently being developed to enable the joint analysis of changes in tariffs and in the *ad valorem* equivalent of non-tariff measures (see Cadot and Jammes, 2011).

Overview of SMART: A Commonly Used Partial Equilibrium Approach

In what follows, we provide as an illustration a brief overview of SMART, a simple and widely used partial equilibrium simulation tool that is included in WITS (using COMTRADE and TRAINS databases). It allows the researcher to investigate the impact of unilateral/preferential/multilateral trade reforms at home or abroad on various variables, including trade flows (import, exports, trade creation, trade diversion), world prices, tariff revenue, and economic welfare. It is based on a relatively simple demand and supply equilibrium for a given good.

On the (export) supply side, the setup in SMART is that different countries compete to supply the given good (export to) a given home market. The focus of the simulation exercise is on the composition and volume of imports into that market. Export supply of a given good (say bananas) by a given country supplier (say Ecuador) is assumed to be related to the price that it fetches in the export market and the degree of responsiveness of the supply of export to changes in the export price is given by the "*export supply elasticity*."[29]

On the demand side, SMART relies on the Armington assumption to model the behavior of the consumer. This assumes imperfect substitutions between different import sources (different varieties)—that is, goods (defined at the HS6 digit level) imported from different countries, although similar, are imperfect substitutes (e.g., bananas from Ecuador are an imperfect substitute to bananas from Saint Lucia). Within the Armington assumption, the representative agent maximizes its welfare through

---

[29] In the simplest version of SMART, the elasticity is assumed to be infinite—that is, the export supply curves are flat and the world prices of each variety (e.g., bananas from Ecuador) are exogenously given. The more complex version of SMART introduces upward sloping export supply functions (i.e., finite elasticity).

a two-stage optimization process. First, given a general price index, the consumer chooses the level of total spending/consumption on a "composite good," (say aggregate consumption of bananas). The relationship between changes in the price index and the impact on total spending is determined by a given "*demand elasticity*." Then, within this composite good, the consumer allocates the chosen level of spending among the different "varieties" of the good, depending on the relative price of each variety (say, choose more bananas from Ecuador, and less from Saint Lucia). The extent of the between-variety allocative response to change in the relative price is determined by the "*Armington substitution elasticity*."

In the SMART modeling framework, a change in trade policy (say a preferential tariff liberalization) affects not only the price index/level of the composite good but also the relative prices of the different varieties. Through the export-supply elasticity, the import-demand elasticity, and the substitution elasticity, it will lead to changes in the chosen aggregate level of spending on that good, as well as changes in the composition of the sourcing of that good. Both channels affect bilateral trade flows.

SMART reports the results of any trade policy shock on a number of variables. In particular, it reports the effects on trade flows (i.e., imports from the different sources). It also decomposes those trade effects into trade creation and trade diversion.[30] SMART also calculates the impact of the trade policy change on tariff revenue, which is computed simply as the (*ad valorem*) tariff rate multiplied by the value of the flow. Finally, the framework estimates the change in welfare due to the policy experiment. This is computed as the sum of the change in the tariff revenue and the change in consumer surplus (or consumer welfare), which is broadly defined as the difference between the consumer's willingness to pay (marginal value) and the amount actually paid.

Computable General Equilibrium Models

Compared to the partial equilibrium approach, Computable General Equilibrium (CGE) models tend to be very complex and are usually not readily accessible to non-specialists. They capture complicated inter-sectoral vertical and horizontal, backward and forward economic linkages. Indeed, CGE models are based on the fact that the different markets in a given economy are linked and changes that take place in one market have effects on other markets that should be documented as they can feed back to the original one. One of the key features distinguishing CGE from PE is the use of a Social Accounting Matrix (SAM) to capture these various linkages.[31] Since they can take into account cross-sectoral reallocation of factors of production, CGE models are useful

---

[30] Trade creation is defined as the direct increase in imports following a reduction on the tariff imposed on good k from country i. If the tariff reduction on good k from country i is a preferential tariff reduction (i.e., it does not apply to other countries), then imports of good k from country i are going to further increase due to the substitution away from imports of good g from other countries that become relatively more expensive. This is the definition of trade diversion in the SMART model.

[31] The SAM helps account for all these interactions in a systematic and balanced way. It is built upon the circular-flow conception of the economic system where each expenditure must be matched by a corresponding receipt or income.

tools for studying economy-wide impact and for identifying winners and losers under a policy change. This section briefly discusses the general structure and organization of trade related CGE models.[32]

On the *production* side, most CGE models are characterized in terms of the outputs, the inputs (intermediate goods and factors of production), and the production technologies. The nature of the technology that transforms the inputs into the final output is captured by a number of *fixed input–output coefficients* (or shares), as well as some *substitution elasticities* among inputs and factors of production. Firms maximize their profits using price information to decide how much of each good to produce, using how much of each input. This determines the supply of (final and intermediate) goods and the demand for inputs (including both intermediate goods and factors of production).[33]

On the *consumption* side, most CGE models focus on a representative household, which is also assumed to be the owners of factors of production (land, labor, and capital). The income that it receives from rent (land), wages (labor), and interest (capital) is spent on consumption of goods (and services), on taxes collected by the government, and/or on savings. The representative household maximizes it utility by allocating its (disposable) income among the goods and services available at the going market price. Assuming full employment, the household's endowments of factors of production are supplied to firms at the going factor market prices—this determines the supply of factors of production and the demand for goods and services.

Governments, in CGE models, collect taxes and tariffs, disburse subsidies, and purchase goods and services. It is in this sector, using these policy instruments, that the policy experiments are usually triggered.

So far we have described the behavior of firms, consumers, and government in an economy in autarky. International trade is usually introduced in CGE models by linking the original economy with other countries with their own sets of firms, consumers, and governments. The substitutability between imports and domestic products may be driven by the Armington assumption described above. That is, goods imported from different sources, although similar, are different varieties that are imperfect substitutes. The choice of the representative consumer of how much to allocate to the purchase of each variety depends on the relative prices and the Armington substitution elasticity.

Just as it imports, a country also exports differentiated product(s) to other countries. Each country is the unique supplier of its differentiated variety and the amount supplied depends on the prevailing world prices (which are in turn determined by some global trade balance condition between export supply and import demand). Under these assumptions, trade policy changes in a country can affect the world prices and the terms of trade (the ratio of a country's export and import prices) and thus the welfare of all other countries.

---

[32] The interested non-expert reader is referred to Piermartini and Teh (2005) for an excellent detailed overview of CGE approaches for trade policy modeling.

[33] Revenue from sales of goods is used to pay for intermediate inputs and factors of production.

The CGE model is solved by allowing the prices (including goods and factor prices) in the system to adjust so that all equilibrium conditions are satisfied: demand for goods equals their supply, demand for imports equals supply of exports, and demand for factors of production equals the available endowments. Given the new sets of prices, the new equilibrium level of different price dependent variables can be determined: consumption, production, imports, exports, factor allocation, tax revenues, and so on. From those, in turn, some measure of the welfare impact of the trade policy experiment can be computed.[34] See Box 7.2 for a description of the gains from trade, market structure, and other characteristics of the Michigan CGE model of world production and trade.

Box 7.2 Gains from Trade, Market Structure, and the Michigan Model

While many CGE models assume a perfectly competitive market structure, a number of analysts have explored other types of market structure. As is well established in the CGE literature, adopting different market structures can yield significantly different simulation results and can even change the "gains from trade" concept that is captured by the model. An important model that illustrates this issue is the Michigan Model (that can be accessed at <www.Fordschool.umich.edu/rsie/model/>). It incorporates some aspects of trade with imperfect competition—namely increasing returns to scale, monopolistic competition, and product variety. Agriculture is assumed to be perfectly competitive (with product differentiation by country of origin) while all other sectors covering manufactures and services are monopolistically competitive.

Consumers and producers use a two-stage procedure to allocate expenditure across differentiated products. In the first stage, expenditure is allocated across goods without regard to the country of origin or producing firm. At this stage, the utility function is Cobb–Douglas, and the production function requires intermediate inputs in fixed proportions. In the second stage, expenditure on monopolistically competitive goods is allocated across the competing varieties supplied by each firm from all countries. In the perfectly competitive agricultural sector, since individual firm supply is indeterminate, expenditure is allocated over each country's sector as a whole, with imperfect substitution between products of different countries. The aggregation function in the second stage is a Constant Elasticity of Substitution (CES) function. Use of the CES function and product differentiation by firm imply that consumer welfare is influenced both by any reduction in real prices brought about by trade liberalization, as well as increased product variety.

To determine equilibrium prices, monopolistically competitive firms maximize profits by setting price as an optimal mark-up over marginal cost (perfectly competitive firms set price equal to marginal cost). The numbers of firms in sectors under monopolistic competition are determined by the zero profits condition. The free entry condition in this context is also the basic mechanism through which new product varieties are created (or eliminated). Each of the new entrants arrives with a distinctly different product, expanding

---

[34] The most widely used measure of welfare impact is the equivalent variation (EV) which is defined as the amount of income that would have to be given to (or taken away from) the economy before the policy change to leave the economy as well off as the economy would be after the policy change.

Box 7.2 *Continued*

---

the array of goods available to consumers. Free entry and exit are also the means through which countries are able to realize the specialization gains from trade. In this connection, it can be noted that in the commonly used (Global Trade Analysis Project (GTAP)-type) model based on nationally differentiated products and the Armington assumption, production of a particular variety of a good cannot move from one country to another. In such a model, there are gains from exchange but no gains from specialization. However, in the Michigan Model with differentiated products supplied by monopolistically competitive firms, production of a particular variety is internationally mobile. A decline in the number of firms in one country paired with an expansion in another essentially implies that production of one variety of a good is being relocated from the country in which the number of firms is declining to the country in which the number of firms is expanding. Thus, there is both an exchange gain and a specialization gain from international trade.

Source: Kiyota and Stern (2008).

While very powerful and potentially very useful, CGE models have a number of limitations that need to be kept in mind. First, unlike partial equilibrium, CGE models tend to be resource intensive, requiring a lot of information and computing power. They tend to be very complicated and inaccessible to non-experts. Their complexity can sometimes be overwhelming and their usefulness restricted when policymakers do not have a clear understanding of what they are, what they do, and how their results should be interpreted. To properly interpret the results, one needs to comprehend the economic assumptions and mechanisms underlying the model, and how sensitive the results are to those.

Most commonly used trade CGE models are static in nature and fail to capture the effect of a trade policy change on the dynamic aspects of an economy. It has to be recognized though that a policy change such as the establishment of a FTA is likely to directly affect dynamic phenomena such as capital flows, demographics, and growth rates. An effort is currently being made along these lines in the network of the GTAP.

V. CONCLUSIONS

By now the reader will have had a "*tour d'horizon*" of some of the most widely used techniques in trade and trade policy analysis. A last piece of advice: when embarking on the formal analysis of trade statistics, the beginner analyst should remember the following "good habit" principles:

Always take a thorough look at the data to track mistakes, aberrations, missing values, and so on. This should start with simple procedures like Stata's "summarize" command, but also include plots of all sorts to verify that the data are what the analyst expects it to be. Failure to do this at the outset often means having to redo the analysis at a later point; use the carpenters' maxim, "measure twice, cut once."

Indices, ratios, and variables of interest should always be put in perspective. This means that they should be expressed in ways that make them comparable (e.g., purchasing power parity for cross-country comparisons), but also that parasitic influences should be controlled for as much as possible (e.g., openness should not be assessed without controlling for income levels, geography etc.).

Robustness of results should be a constant worry. In *ex post* analysis, this means, for example, running the regression of interest with different estimation methods and trying various specifications; in *ex ante* analysis this means verifying how results vary when key parameters (elasticities etc.) vary.

Results should not be over-sold; as the experienced analyst discovers, numbers, however hazardous the way in which they were arrived at, tend to take on a life of their own and do not need over-selling. As a matter of fact the media and even restricted policy circles tend to over-focus on eye-catching results, so there can never be too many caveats.

These are no more than common-sense pieces of advice. Together with judicious use of techniques such as those described in this chapter, they nevertheless guarantee that the analysis' client will get a fair picture of what the numbers can say and what they cannot. If all policymakers could have access to statistical information processed in this way, thoroughly but honestly, policy decisions would be made in a better informational environment and many mistakes would be avoided.

References

Anderson, J., and Neary, P. (1994), 'Measuring the Restrictiveness of Trade Policy' *World Bank Economic Review,* 8: 151–69.

Anderson, J., and Neary, P. (1996), 'A New Approach to Evaluating Trade Policy' *Review of Economic Studies,* 63: 107–25.

Anderson, J. E., and van Wincoop, E. (2003), '"Gravity with Gravitas: A Solution to the Border Puzzle' *American Economic Review,* 93: 170–92.

Anderson, K.Valenzuela, E. and Sandri, D. (eds.) (2008), *Fifty Years of Distortions to the World's Agricultural Prices,* Washington DC: The World Bank.

Andriamananjara, S., Dean, J., Ferrantino, M., et al., (2004), 'The Effects of Non-Tariff Measures on Prices, Trade, and Welfare: CGE Implementation of Policy-Based Price Comparisons,' mimeo.

Bacchetta, M. C. Beverelli, O. Cadot, M. Fugazza, J.-M. Grether, M. Helble, A. Nicita and R. Piermartini (2012), *A Practical Guide to Trade Policy Analysis,* Geneva: World Trade Organization.

Bouët, A., Decreux, Y., Fontagné, L., et al. (2005), 'A Consistent, Ad-valorem Equivalent Measure of Applied Protection across the World: The MacMap-HS6 Database,' CEPII Working Paper 2004-22 (updated September 2005)Paris: CEPII

Brenton, P., and Newfarmer, R. (2009), 'Watching More than the Discovery Channel to Diversify Exports,' in Newfarmer, R., Shaw, W., and Walkenhorst, P. (eds.), *Breaking into New Markets,* Washington, DC: The World Bank.

Brülhart, M. (2002), 'Marginal Intra-Industry Trade: Towards a Measure of Non-Disruptive Trade Expansion,' in Lloyd, P.-J., and Lee, H. H. (eds.), *Frontiers of Research on Intra-Industry Trade*. New York: Palgrave Macmillan.

Brunnschweiler, C., and Bulte, E. (2009), 'Linking Natural Resources to Slow Growth and Violent Conflict.' *Science,* 320: 616–17.

Cadot, O. (2011), *A Guide to Trade Data Analysis*, Washington, DC: The World Bank.

Cadot, O., Carrère, C., and Strauss-Kahn, V. (2011), 'Export Diversification: What's Behind the Hump?' *Review of Economics and Statistics,* 93(2): 590–605

Cadot, O., and Jammes, O. (2011), 'Partial-Equilibrium Modelling of the Effect of Changes in Non-Tariff Measures,' mimeo, The World Bank.

Carrère, C. (2006), 'Revisiting the Effects of Regional Trade Agreements on Trade Flows with Proper Specification of the Gravity Model.' *European Economic Review,* 50: 223–47.

Connolly, M., and de Melo, J. (1994), *The Effects of Protectionism on a Small Country*, Washington, DC: The World Bank.

Deardorff, A. and Stern, R. (1997), 'Measurement of Non-Tariff Barriers,' Economic Department Working Papers #179, OECD. Also published by University of Michigan Press.

Di Giovanni, J., and Levchenko, A. (2010), 'The Risk Content of Exports: A Portfolio View of International Trade,' NBER working paper 16005.

Donnelly, W. A., Johnson, K., Tsigas, M., and Ingersoll, D. (2004), 'Revised Armington Elasticities of Substitution USITC Model and the Concordance for Constructing Consistent Set for the GTAP Model,' USITC Office of Economics Research Note No. 20001-A.

Easterly, W., Resheff, A., and Schwenkenberg, J. (2009), 'The Power of Exports,' World Bank Policy Research Working Paper 5081.

Feenstra, Robert C. (2004), *Advanced International Trade: Theory and Evidence*, Princeton NJ: Princeton University Press.

Feenstra, R., Romalis, J., and Schott, J. (2002), 'U.S. Imports, Exports, and Tariff Data, 1989–2001,' NBER Working Paper #9387.

Francois, J. and Reinert, K. (eds.) (1998), *Applied Methods for Trade Policy Analysis*, Cambridge: Cambridge University Press.

Frankel, J.Stein, E., and Wei, S.-J. (1995), 'Trading Blocs and the Americas: The Natural, the Unnatural, and the Super-Natural.' *Journal of Development Economics,* 47: 61–95.

Hausmann, R., Hwang, J., and Rodrik, D. (2005), 'What You Export Matters,' NBER working paper 11905.

Head, K. (2003), 'Gravity for Beginners.' Prepared for UBC Econ 590a students, January.

Helpman, E., Melitz, M., and Rubinstein, Y. (2008), 'Estimating Trade Flows: Trading Partners and Trading Volumes.' *Quarterly Journal of Economics,* 123: 441–87.

Hummels, D., and Klenow, P. J. (2005), 'The Variety and Quality of a Nation's Exports.' *American Economic Review,* 95: 704–23.

IMF (2005), 'Review of the IMF's Trade Restrictiveness Index,' Background Paper to the Review of Fund Work on Trade; mimeo, IMF.

Jammes, O., and Olarreaga, M. (2006), 'Explaining SMART and GSIM,' mimeo, The World Bank.

Kee, H. L., Nicita, A., and Olarreaga, M. (2008), 'Import Demand Elasticities and Trade Distortions.' *Review of Economics and Statistics,* 90(4): 666–82.

Kee, H. L., Nicita, A., and Olarreaga, M. (2009), 'Estimating Trade Restrictiveness Indices.' *Economic Journal,* 574: 172–99.

Kiyota, K., and Stern, R. M. (2008), 'Computational Analysis of APEC Trade Liberalization,' RSIE Discussion Paper No. 578, University of Michigan

Koujianou-Goldberg, P., and Pavcnik, N. (2004), 'Trade, Inequality, and Poverty: What do We Know? Evidence from Recent Trade Liberalization Episodes in Developing Countries', NBER Working Paper #10593.

Leamer, E. (1974), 'Nominal Tariff Averages with Estimated Weights' *Southern Economic Journal*, 41: 34–46.

Leamer, E. (1988), 'Measures of Openness,' in Robert Baldwin (ed.), *Trade Policy Issues and Empirical Analysis*, Chicago: Chicago University Press.

Lederman, D., and Maloney, W. (2009), *Natural Resources: Neither Curse nor Destiny*, Washinton, DC: The World Bank.

Mayer, T., and Zignano, S. (2005), 'Border Effects of the Atlantic Triangle' *Revista Integración y Comercio, Integration and Trade Journal*, 22: 39–59.

McKinsey Global Institute (2010), *How to Compete and Grow: A Sector Guide to Policy*, London: McKinsey & Company.

Messerlin, P. (2001), *Measuring the Cost of Protection in Europe: European Commercial Policy in the 2000s*, Washington DC: Peterson Institute for International Economics.

Michaely, M. (1996), 'Trade Preferential Agreements in Latin America: An Ex Ante Assessment,' World Bank Policy Research Working Paper No. 1583.

Nicita, A. (2004), 'Who Benefited From Trade Liberalization in Mexico? Measuring the Effects on Household Welfare,' *Essays on Trade Liberalization and Poverty*, unpublished dissertation, University of Geneva.

OECD (1995), 'Patterns and Pervasiveness of Tariff and Non-Tariff Barriers to Trade in OECD Member Countries,' ECO/CPE/WP1/GE(96)/3, Paris.

Piermartini, R., and Teh, R. (2005), 'Demystifying Modeling Methods for Trade Policy,' WTO Discussion Papers, No. 10.

Rauch, J. (1999), 'Networks Versus Markets in International Trade' *Journal of International Economics*, 48: 7–35.

Rodriguez, F., and Rodrik, D. (1999), 'Trade Policy and Economic Growth: A Skeptic's Guide to the Cross-National Evidence,' NBER Working Paper No. 7081.

Sachs, J., and Warner. A. (1995), 'Economic Reform and the Process of Global Integration' *Brookings Papers on Economic Activity*, 1: 1–118.

Schott, P. (2004), 'Across-product versus Within-product Specialization in International Trade' *Quarterly Journal of Economics*, 119: 647–78.

Shihotori, M., Tumurchudur, B., and Cadot, O. (2010), 'Revealed Factor Intensities at the Product Level,' Policy Issues in International Trade and Commodity Studies No. 44, UNCTAD.

United Nations (2006), 'Standard International Trade Classification, Revision 4,' ST/ESA/STAT/SER.M/34/REV.4.

Wacziarg, R., and Welsh, K. H. (2008), 'Trade Liberalization and Growth: New Evidence' *World Bank Economic Review*, 22: 187–231.

Yeats, A. (1998), 'What Can Be Expected from African Regional Trade Agreements?' World Bank Policy Research Working Paper No. 2004.

CHAPTER 8

THE POLITICAL ECONOMY OF PROTECTIONISM

ARVID LUKAUSKAS

I. INTRODUCTION

Do governments formulate trade policies solely on the basis of economic rationality? The evidence indicates overwhelmingly that they do not. Though public officials usually claim that their commercial policies are designed to advance the national interest, a closer examination reveals that they often favor select narrow groups at the expense of aggregate social welfare. In many countries, politics intrudes into trade policymaking in profound ways, and the resultant policies are often characterized more by political than economic efficiency. This chapter explores various dimensions of the political economy of trade policymaking, illuminating how political factors fundamentally influence commercial policy design and implementation, including the decisions to impose or remove barriers to trade such as tariffs, quotas, and non-tariff barriers.

I begin by examining the numerous economic rationales proffered for implementing protectionist measures. Are these rationales a sound basis for erecting import barriers? If so, then we might reasonably expect our analysis of trade policy to remain firmly in the realm of economics. Policymakers might occasionally deviate from a trade policy that promotes the national interest, but by and large they are seeking to obtain legitimate economic goals using appropriate tools when they impose trade barriers. Unfortunately, it appears that import barriers are usually a second-best solution to the problems that policymakers claim to be remedying. Moreover, the rationales offered often seem like an excuse for politicians to implement policies that are primarily intended to benefit a narrow set of constituents or themselves.

The next section explores the politics of protectionism. It relies on the premise that protectionism hurts some groups but benefits others, so some private actors have a vested interest in securing or retaining trade barriers. Trade policy analysis frequently focuses on this "demand" side of protectionism, that is, the pressure that social actors apply on public officials to regulate trade. The "supply" side of trade policy, that is, the complex balancing act among competing interests that public officials must undertake in designing strategy, is equally important though often overlooked.

I then analyze the international political and economic context in which trade takes place. The structure of the "trade game" generates a powerful set of constraints and incentives that policymakers must also consider when formulating trade strategy. States have ample reason to be cautious in removing trade barriers, so much so that widespread protectionism has characterized economic relations among states and liberal trading orders have only flourished in two historical periods.

Over the course of the last 50 years, many countries, starting in the developed world, have slowly dismantled their import barriers and adopted relatively free trade policies. The final section examines the factors that have led policymakers to liberalize trade as well as implement the complementary reforms needed to achieve success. While political economists generally agree why public officials impose protectionism, they are more divided on why they seek to liberalize trade.

II. Rationales for Protectionism

This section analyzes the most important arguments advanced for protecting domestic markets. Are any of these valid reasons for imposing import barriers? If so, then we might think of policymakers as seeking legitimate social goals through the best available commercial policy instruments. If, on the other hand, policymakers routinely design trade policy that hurts the public interest, we will be forced to consider other explanations for why public officials so often implement protectionism.

The arguments for protectionism are divided into two groups. *Domestic rationales* focus on the desired effects of protection on attaining various objectives within the home country. These objectives may be economic, such as addressing domestic market failures, or non-economic, such as promoting national security. *International rationales* concern government efforts to use trade barriers to affect the country's economic relations with other nations. Naturally, some arguments for protection straddle this domestic/international divide, so the categories should not be viewed too rigidly. Moreover, this is not an exhaustive list of rationales, though other common motives for protection resemble the ones examined here.

Domestic Rationales

Infant Industry

The infant industry argument is one of the oldest and most frequently cited rationales for protectionism, dating back at least to the late eighteenth century and the writings of Frederick List and Alexander Hamilton. If government officials believe a domestic industry lies within the country's long run comparative advantage, they may choose to

protect it temporarily to give domestic firms time to catch up to more competitive foreign firms.[1] Firms will presumably develop in a sheltered domestic market until they are
able to lower their production costs to the level of their rivals and become ready to compete in international markets.[2] Alternatively, the infant industry argument is sometimes
applied to situations in which protection prevents an otherwise viable domestic industry from going bankrupt due to an exogenous shock, such as a productivity increase
that allows a foreign firm to lower its costs with respect to its rivals. Temporary protection permits an increase in output and reduction in future costs sufficient to allow the
domestic firm to survive. In either case, once the industry has achieved long-run comparative advantage or adjusted to a shock, the government should lift import barriers
and allow domestic and foreign firms to compete on an equal footing.

To be successful the supply curve of the targeted industry should shift out endogenously due to innovation or other improvements in productivity (e.g., learning by
doing effects). Figure 8.1 illustrates this point. The increase in production from Q_O to
Q_T should be due to more efficient operations (supply curve shifts out to S') that permit
the domestic firm to produce Q_T at world prices (P_W); it should not be due solely to the
incentive to produce Q_T created by the rise in prices to P_T (world price plus tariff).

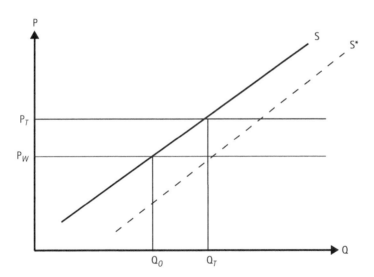

FIGURE 8.1 Infant industry effect on supply

[1] Infant industries often receive other forms of government assistance to complement protectionist
measures. In particular, governments use the instruments of industrial policy, such as subsidies to
production or research and development, tax credits or exemptions, employment credits, privileged
access to scarce factors of production or permits, and provision of credit at below market rates, to
promote the rapid growth of infant industries.

[2] The high profits that firms earn in the protected domestic market may also be used to cross-subsidize
their efforts to expand exports at lower prices; this was a central feature of trade policy in several Asian
countries, such as Japan and Korea. See World Bank (1993).

The infant industry argument assumes that some sort of market failure or distortion prevents the industry from developing without government assistance. If an industry has a long-run comparative advantage, one would expect efficient capital markets to be willing to lend to firms until they develop sufficiently to become profitable. Capital market failures, however, may mean that firms need to earn profits in each reporting period to avoid bankruptcy, because financial entities do not lend to firms to cover current losses against the expectation of future profits. Alternatively, if the industry generates positive externalities for the rest of the economy (e.g., technological spillovers) for which it is not fully compensated, the industry might be insufficiently funded in the absence of government assistance. In both instances, however, import protection is a second-best policy for assisting the industry. From an efficiency standpoint, the optimal policy would be to provide firms with a subsidy on output, since this would allow firms to realize their long-run comparative advantage or enable society to capture positive externalities without provoking the consumption costs of a tariff or quota.[3] In the next section, we examine these costs in detail.

Most developed countries have applied the infant industry argument during their early stages of economic development, suggesting that despite its efficiency costs, the policy played a key role in their modernization. During the nineteenth century, for instance, the United States protected nascent industries like textiles from stiff British competition behind high tariffs walls. In the post-World War II period, many developing countries adopted the infant industry argument through a strategy of import substitution industrialization. This strategy was based on the belief that developing countries could and should develop their own industries in key sectors behind protectionist walls to avoid reliance on imports. The features of import substitution industrialization and its mixed record of success are discussed in the appendix at the end of the chapter.

The proper economic criterion for assessing the ultimate success of an infant industry policy is not whether the protected industry is able to increase its production, become profitable, or compete effectively in international markets. Instead, it is whether the present discounted value of the benefits generated by protecting the industry (principally, its future profits, adjusted for inflation) exceed the consumption and production costs generated by protectionism. This criterion, called the Mill–Bastable test, is generally difficult to meet. Costs occur from the start and are likely to be quite high; benefits, on the other hand, will appear only in the future. Consequently, the revenue stream, properly discounted for inflation, will have to be considerable to offset the immediate costs of the policy.

In fact, the infant industry strategy has generally not fared well in practice. In many instances, protected firms, enjoying guaranteed profits and believing that the government will be reluctant to remove import barriers (since it fears the loss of jobs and

---

[3] The first-best policy to address a *domestic* market failure is a *domestic* intervention, such as the use of a production subsidy, as opposed to a commercial policy instrument. As shown later, an import barrier (e.g., an optimum tariff) is the best instrument only in instances where a foreign distortion exists (e.g., when a country has monopoly power in international markets).

output that might arise), have little incentive to improve their productivity. Therefore, several years after the implementation of import barriers firms are often no closer to competing internationally than they were at the start. More importantly, as the industry becomes established, its political power and ability to resist policy changes it does not like grows, a point we turn to later. More successful use of an infant industry policy, such as in East Asia, has hinged upon the government's ability to push firms to meet performance targets, especially in the area of exports.[4]

National Defense and Security

Protecting industries that produce goods critical for national defense or to confront national emergencies is a popular rationale for imposing import barriers, particularly in developed countries. The reasoning is that the country must be able to generate its own supply of such goods to prevent being cut off at critical times, such as in the event of war. A related argument is to restrict the export of goods that might aid potential adversaries in improving their military capability. The United States in conjunction with its allies, for example, set up CoCom in 1949 to limit or prohibit the export of sensitive goods to Eastern Bloc countries. Some policymakers in the United States wished to push this policy a step further by restricting the export of any good that might aid in the economic development of rival countries.[5]

Governments, especially in developing countries, also cite national security concerns or the need to safeguard political independence as a motive for protecting "strategic" sectors, such as finance, communications, energy, and food, from import competition or foreign direct investment. National leaders fear that foreign producers may come to dominate these sectors and make decisions based on calculations of short-term profit, not on what is in the best long-term national interest. In the ongoing Doha Round negotiations, food security has emerged as an important issue in talks aimed at liberalizing agricultural trade. Some developing countries have contended that if they open their markets fully, domestic agriculture may be decimated by foreign competition, and domestic production of key foodstuffs will diminish to dangerous levels. In the event of external shocks that reduce the global supply of foodstuffs, the country's populace may be left without adequate provisions of food, contributing to starvation or malnourishment.

The national defense argument is easily abused. Many industries are likely to deem themselves as essential to national defense and will demand protection. In addition, this argument ignores the possibility that critical goods can be stored in advance or be purchased from friendly countries in the event of hostilities or another emergency. Governments can also subsidize production of critical goods that are deemed

---

[4] See the appendix of this chapter for a brief discussion of this point.

[5] Governments also restrict trade with other countries to achieve such political objectives as sanctioning a corrupt or repressive regime, promoting better human rights, or punishing international transgressions. In recent years, Cuba, Iran, Iraq, and South Africa have been the targets of US trade sanctions.

to be at risk of shortfalls to ensure sufficient supply and maintain productive capacity. Moreover, evidence is scarce that foreign firms make decisions that are more detrimental to the national interest in so-called strategic sectors. Foreign owned banks, for example, have a better track record than domestic banks in most developing countries and often improve financial efficiency and stability.

Government Revenue

Governments may implement tariffs (or export taxes) to raise revenue to finance spending. Tariffs are attractive in countries that find it difficult, for administrative or political reasons, to raise revenue through other means of taxation, such as income, value-added, or sales taxes, since collecting duties on foreign goods is relatively easy and straightforward. Nonetheless, governments face a limit on how much revenue they can obtain in this fashion: high tariff levels suppress imports and prohibitive tariffs generate no revenue at all. Historically, tariff duties have been an important source of revenue in many countries, including most advanced industrial countries, well into the twentieth century. They remain a highly significant revenue source for many developing (but not developed) countries today; for instance, in 1995, trade tax revenue as a percentage of GDP in non-OECD countries was 4.3 per cent.[6]

As tariffs generate consumption and production dead-weight costs, they are not the best means of raising revenue, especially when the government's financing needs are large, as is the case for the majority of contemporary states. Broad-based taxes, such as income, value added, or sales taxes, are less distortionary, enabling governments to raise significant amounts of revenue without generating excessive dead-weight losses. As a result, most governments rely less on tariff revenue as their financing needs become greater and they develop the administrative capacity to implement more efficient forms of direct taxation.

Income Redistribution

Trade barriers affect the distribution of income, so protection might be advocated on the grounds that it favors disadvantaged social groups and thereby promotes greater income equality. The validity of this argument depends in part on the theoretical trade model used. In the Heckscher–Ohlin model, per the Stolper–Samuelson theorem, protectionism increases the income of the relatively scarce factor of production and reduces that of the abundant factor. If labor is the scarce factor, for instance, trade barriers will increase the income of workers relative to that of holders of capital; since factors of production are assumed to be perfectly mobile, this process will happen quickly.[7] Nonetheless, trade

---

[6] The percentage for OECD countries was only 0.4 per cent. The importance of trade tax revenue was highest in Africa, where it totaled 5.5 per cent of GDP. For details, see Ebrill, Stotsky, and Gropp (1999).

[7] Favoring labor is perhaps the most common goal of efforts to use trade barriers to redistribute income in advanced industrial societies.

barriers generate dead-weight losses, so any redistribution that occurs takes place at the expense of social welfare.

In the Ricardo–Viner model, on the other hand, the ability to use commercial policy to effect redistribution across factors of production is limited. This model posits that factors of production are specific to a particular industry in the short (and perhaps medium) run and, thus, have little mobility across activities. In the short run, both the scarce and abundant factors of production in the protected industry will benefit at the expense of those in the unprotected sectors; only in the long run may the scarce factor of production in both industries become relatively better off.

In either model, therefore, commercial policy is at most a second-best instrument for achieving redistributive goals. Superior policies to influence income redistribution are a lump sum transfer to disadvantaged groups or a tax policy that discriminates in their favor since these are more accurate and have short-run effects. In addition, though these measures may create distortions of their own, they do not cause consumption and production losses that lower aggregate national income to the extent that protectionist barriers do.

Protection of Jobs

The desire to protect jobs is a strong motive for protection in many developed countries. Domestic firms confronting increased imports typically have to decrease their costs and/or level of production, and workers may lose their jobs as a result (unless wages are able to adjust downwards). If imports are from countries where wages are lower, demands for import barriers will intensify since domestic workers will claim that they cannot compete against foreign workers earning less. The use of import barriers to protect jobs is most likely in countries where state-owned industrial firms are large employers and labor unions are strong.

The loss of jobs due to import competition certainly imposes costs, such as relocating or retraining workers. Compensating workers who become unemployed through a lump-sum payment or public employment training is a far better means of managing the disruptive effects of trade. These policies do not generate the consumption or production costs associated with trade barriers and do not hinder the ability of trade to create new jobs throughout the economy, which are often more numerous than those lost to trade competition.[8] In fact, empirical estimates of the cost of saving jobs by imposing protection indicate that it is a very costly proposition. For example, Hufbauer, Berliner, and Elliot (1986) found that consumer losses due to protectionism per job saved in the United States were over $100,000 in more than half of the sectors that they examined and reached $1,000,000 in the case of specialty steel. Finally, the contention that firms paying workers higher wages cannot compete effectively against firms paying less for the

---

[8] Coughlin, Chrystal, and Wood (1988) note that the jobs saved by protectionism are typically more visible than those lost because of it in export sectors, creating the perception that import barriers save jobs.

same work is fallacious. If the difference in worker productivity is greater than the difference in wages, than higher paid workers are actually more competitive.[9]

International Rationales

Terms of Trade

The terms of trade argument applies when a country is such a large consumer or supplier of a good that it has the ability to affect world prices through the imposition of a tariff or export tax, respectively, and, thereby, improve its terms of trade (that is, offer fewer exports for the same amount of imports). In principle, a country can calculate the level of tariff or export tax—the optimum tariff—that would maximize the terms of trade benefit from restricting trade. The optimum tariff reduces the volume of trade, creating both consumption and production dead-weight losses for the country but, under certain circumstances, the terms of trade benefit can outweigh these losses.

The terms of trade argument applies to very few situations, since countries rarely possess the market power to alter world prices; even if they do, this power will be limited to a small number of goods. For a small developing country, the optimal tariff is typically zero. The only exception might be where a country has a near monopoly in the production of an essential primary product. In this case, an export tax could improve the country's terms of trade allowing it to obtain more imports for the same amount of exported good. In principle, a group of countries producing the same commodity could act as a cartel to limit its production, which would have the same effect as imposing an export tax. But such collusion is extremely hard to achieve in practice and we can point to perhaps only one successful case in the 1970s: the Organization of Petroleum Exporting Countries (OPEC), which limited the supply of oil driving up its price.

Calculating the optimum tariff in a world of constantly changing market conditions is no easy task and failure to apply the correct level of tariff or export tax will likely cause more harm than good. Moreover, applying a tariff to improve one's terms of trade may provoke retaliation on the part of other countries, potentially leading to a trade war. In the event of retaliation, the country imposing an optimal tariff is likely to be worse off than in a situation of free trade.

Balance of Payments

In recent years, demands for protection in order to improve a country's balance of payments have become commonplace, especially in the United States where record trade

---

[9] Say workers in country A earn $10 per hour while comparable workers in country B earn $2 per hour. Country A workers, however, are able to produce 10 units per hour whereas country B workers produce only 1 unit per hour. Though country A workers are five times as expensive, they are ten times more productive; therefore, unit labor costs are actually lower in country A ($1/unit) than in country B ($2/unit).

deficits have been recorded repeatedly, especially with respect to China. Trade barriers are intended to eliminate balance of payments deficits by suppressing imports.

Commercial policy is, however, an ineffective means of addressing trade deficits. Import barriers are at best slow-acting policy instruments, as the volume of imports does not usually drop immediately in response to higher prices. Once in place, trade barriers are difficult to remove, even when the balance of payments concerns that engendered them have eased. More importantly, while trade barriers reduce imports, they also cause exports to decrease by a similar amount, generating no significant change in the net balance of payments. Thus, deficits are best managed by other means, particularly, through macroeconomic policy adjustments that balance savings and investment as well as government spending and taxation.

Strategic Trade

The theoretical justification for engaging in a strategic trade policy when international markets for a product are characterized by oligopoly and firms face decreasing average costs has been analyzed in detail elsewhere in this volume. As Krugman (1984) has shown, governments implementing a strategic trade policy can employ import barriers as well as subsidies to target priority sectors for promotion. Although the theoretical case for strategic trade policy is plausible, its practical relevance in economic terms is limited, and it would be difficult to implement because of informational problems. Moreover, the risk that such a policy would fall victim to politics is high in most countries, so that decisions about who receives government assistance become based more on political rather than economic criteria. In addition, if rivals also implement a strategic trade policy in retaliation, the prospects for welfare gains are poor.

III. The "Political Economy" Explanation for Protectionism

The economic arguments advanced for imposing import barriers are often problematic. Trade barriers are the first-best instruments when a country has monopoly power in international markets and wants to improve its terms of trade, but they are not the best for achieving domestic economic goals. Indeed, import barriers, even if they achieve their objective, typically lower aggregate social welfare, imposing both consumption and production losses, and hurt economic efficiency. If this is the case, why do governments implement tariffs? Are there reasons for protectionism derived solely from the domestic political context?

The "political economy" explanation for protectionism concentrates on the motives that drive private groups to seek trade barriers and the political calculations that encourage politicians to impose them. It takes as its starting point the distributional effects of protectionist barriers. Tariffs, quotas, and non-tariff barriers create societal winners and losers who have a vested interest in seeking or opposing protectionist barriers. Nonetheless, analysis that views commercial policy as simply reflecting the *demands* of dominant social groups or emerging from the struggle among competing interest groups for influence will be incomplete; the factors that influence the *supply* of protection by politicians are equally important. Below, we look at three separate forms of protectionism—tariffs, quantitative restrictions, and non-tariff barriers—to highlight important though subtle differences in the political economy of each.

Tariffs

Distributional Consequences of Tariffs

Tariffs can take a variety of forms, but in all cases they are essentially a government duty or tax on an imported good that raises its domestic price. For instance, an *ad valorem* tariff of 50 per cent increases the price of an imported good with a world price of $100 to $150 in the domestic market.

The price increase caused by a tariff has several distributional impacts that can be seen in Figure 8.2.[10] The imposition of a tariff causes the price to increase from P_W to P_T, causing imports to fall from (D_W-S_W) to (D_T-S_T) as the amount of the good supplied domestically increases from S_W to S_T. The big losers from tariffs are consumers, who pay more for the good; in addition, they may be limited to a smaller variety of goods or be forced to settle for goods of inferior quality. In the diagram, the loss of consumer surplus is equal to the area of A + B + C + D. The government obtains tariff revenue equivalent to area B. Among private actors, domestic producers are the big beneficiaries from tariffs, as their profits increase; indeed, tariffs may make it possible for domestic producers to expand their businesses or avoid bankruptcy. Consequently, the shareholders, managers, and employees of import-competing firms will experience an increase in their incomes. In the diagram, producer surplus increases by area A. Areas C and D represent dead-weight losses. Since tariffs increase the domestic price of the good, some resources currently used by non-protected industries will flow to the protected one, attracted by the possibility of higher relative prices. This lowers economic output since scarce factors of production are now being utilized by less efficient final users; that is, the social return on capital and labor in these sectors will be lower.

Finally, tariffs hurt export industries though one cannot discern this point directly from the figure. The domestic relative price of importable (and, most likely, non-tradable) goods will increase relative to that of exportable goods (whose price

---

[10] This analysis assumes a small country and perfect competition. The impact of a tariff is similar for a large country facing perfectly competitive markets, though the relative magnitude of the various distributional effects varies. If the terms of trade effect is sufficiently large, then the net impact on social welfare may be positive, not negative as in the small country case. See Feenstra (2004), chapter 7, for a discussion. Another chapter in this volume analyzes the case of tariffs in imperfectly competitive markets.

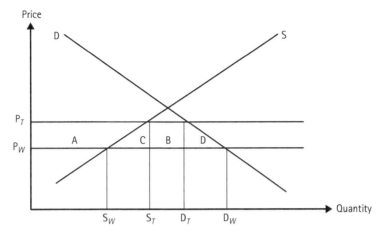

FIGURE 8.2 Effects of a tariff

continues to be set in world markets); in effect, tariffs act like a tax on exportable goods.[11] This will draw resources away from export industries into protected ones, increasing production of importables and lowering that of exportables. In addition, export industries that use the protected good as an input into their production will see their costs increase and, consequently, may lose competitiveness in international markets. Finally, tariffs contribute to exchange rate appreciation by lowering the demand for foreign currency; an appreciated exchange rate makes it more difficult for export industries to compete in world markets (and contributes to the lower domestic price of exportable goods).

Societal Demand for Tariffs

Based on the preceding analysis, producers of import-competing goods should seek tariffs as they increase producer surplus; consumers, on the other hand, should oppose them as they reduce consumer surplus.[12] It is not sufficient, however, to identify the interests of various actors and assume they will be able to act upon them. One might suppose, for instance, that politicians would resist pressure for protectionism because the social losses from tariffs exceed their benefits, and the number of actors who benefit

---

[11] This is the central insight of the Lerner Symmetry Theorem: an *ad valorem* tariff on importables has exactly the same effect on the relative price of importables and exportables as an *ad valorem* export tax at the same rate.

[12] Most of the literature on the political economy of tariffs relies on the Ricardo–Viner model in analyzing the formation of trade policy coalitions among private actors. Thus, authors assume that the fortunes of labor and capital in the same industry improve or decline together with changes in commercial policy. This means that trade policy coalitions will tend to form along sectoral, not factor or class lines, as the Heckscher–Ohlin model predicts. Only a few studies of the political economy of commercial policy use the Heckscher–Ohlin (e.g., Rogowski, 1989) or the increasing returns to scale models as the basis of their analysis.

from tariffs is much smaller than those harmed. Yet, this is usually not the case. Actors, such as consumers, may share a common objective yet be unable to organize adequately to pursue it effectively. In the political economy literature, this is called the dilemma of collective action. Thus, policy analysis requires examining how well groups are able to organize into effective lobby groups and overcome their collective action problems. We also need to explain which groups government officials will choose to respond to and why.

Historically, the identity of winners and losers from tariff policy has been strikingly similar across nations and time: producer interests generally have won out over consumer interests, and the producers of finished goods have enjoyed higher tariffs than those of primary or intermediate goods.[13] The most persuasive explanation for this pattern, based on the interest group approach, suggests that tariffs are implemented because those who favor them are well organized and able to apply effective pressure on policymakers while those hurt by tariffs are less well organized and unable to oppose them. Producers tend to be small in number and relatively concentrated, more so in the case of finished than intermediate goods. Their stake in protectionism is high and easy to identify; in some instances, the imposition of a tariff may mean the difference between bankruptcy and solvency for firm owners and, for workers, between having and losing a job. Therefore, producers face small collective action problems in organizing and are often willing to expend considerable amounts of money and time to lobby governments on tariff policy. Moreover, their decision on which politicians to support will be determined largely by candidates' stances on tariff policy. Consumers of most goods, on the other hand, are large in number and often not geographically or otherwise concentrated; thus, their costs of organization are high. In addition, consumers are typically poorly informed of the features and consequences of commercial policy. Although the aggregate effect of a tariff on consumer welfare is large, an individual's stake in whether it is imposed is relatively small. That is, a tariff will increase the cost of consumption, but not affect welfare significantly unless the good is an important element of the overall consumption bundle and the price increase is very large. Consequently, consumers are unlikely to become effective lobbyists of government officials on tariff policy. Furthermore, their voting decisions will probably be based on candidates' positions on public policy issues other than commercial policy.

A variety of factors may influence the intensity of social demands for protectionism. It is well documented, for instance, that demands for protectionism increase when macroeconomic conditions deteriorate (Cassing, McKeown, and Ochs, 1986). When the economy is vibrant, import-competing industries tolerate competition from abroad because they are earning solid profits. With economic distress, however, firm profits drop and become more uncertain. Under these conditions, domestic firms feel the competition from foreign producers more keenly and will seek protection from imports. During the mid 1970s and 1980s when the global economy struggled through a prolonged period

---

[13] In advanced industrial countries, governments also tend to protect industries that use unskilled labor more heavily than others.

of "stagflation," levels of protectionism, especially in the form of non-tariff barriers, jumped dramatically, leading to a slowdown in the growth of global trade.

Endogenous Tariffs

Thus far, we have focused on the demand side for protection. But why do politicians supply protectionism? Do they merely respond to lobbying from societal groups or do politicians have reasons of their own to implement protection?[14] What calculations do politicians undertake to determine which industries to protect and the level of tariffs?

Most of the political economy literature on tariff policy has been developed using the "economic theory" of politics. This view posits that politicians design trade policy to further their own private interests, the most important of which is to ensure their own political survival. With this goal in mind, public officials implement policies to favor groups that offer them the greatest political support, whether directly in the form of votes or contributions that can be used by politicians to win votes.

Two basic approaches to explaining the pattern and extent of tariffs have emerged. The first is based on the median voter model (Mayer, 1984). In this approach, trade policies are conceived as being set through a majority vote of the populace. The policy that emerges represents the preferences of the median voter if each voter has a unique best policy (i.e., preferences are "single-peaked"). Although the view of the political process implied in this model is overly simplified, it has found empirical support in studies that seek to explain the variance in and pattern of protectionism across countries (Dutt and Mitra, 2002).

The second approach is the "protection for sale" model, named after an influential paper by Grossman and Helpman (1994). Two important variations exist within the protection for sale approach. In the first, opposing parties announce their proposed trade policies during an electoral campaign. Producer-lobby groups supply resources (notably, campaign contributions) to the party whose commercial policy platform promises them the highest payoff. The parties in turn use the resources to sway general voters (some of whom will be hurt by the proposed policies). In the second, the focus is on the incumbent government, which designs commercial policy to maximize political support. In an effort to shape trade policy, producer-lobbies make offers of prospective contributions to politicians depending on the tariffs they chose. In this process, government officials place more weight on the interests of organized groups than unorganized ones, since they are the most effective lobbyists and are best able to deliver contributions.

---

[14] Whether society or state dominates in determining public policy is a classic issue in the social sciences and no consensus exists on which view is best. Most of the political science literature on trade policy assumes that state officials are primarily responding to societal demands, and the analysis presented here will proceed along these lines. A few authors, however, argue that state officials have their own economic and political agenda and attempt to design trade policies according to their preferences. In this view, the nature of domestic political institutions, in particular, the degree of autonomy and insulation that they afford policymakers, is an important variable to consider when examining the sources of trade policy. On the issue of state versus society in explaining foreign economic policy generally, see Ikenberry, Lake, and Mastanduno (1988).

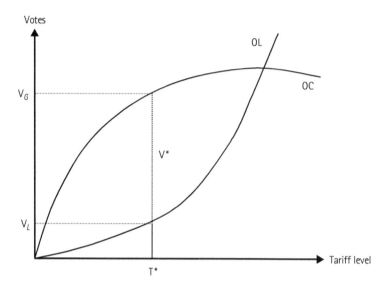

FIGURE 8.3 Endogenous tariff

Grossman and Helpman suggest that the first approach is most useful for explaining the broad contours of commercial policy (whether a country is protectionist or free trade), whereas the second, which they employ, is best at explaining its specific characteristics (particularly, which industries receive the most protection). The protection for sale model has found empirical support in several studies of the United States (Goldberg and Maggi, 1999) and other countries (reviewed by Gawande and Krishna, 2003).

In the Grossman and Helpman model, a rational governing party sets levels of protection to maximize the number of votes it can obtain. This means that it must maximize a weighted sum of total contributions from producers, which it can use to sway voters, and consumer welfare. The higher the tariff it supports, the greater the level of contributions it can obtain from producer-lobbies. Nonetheless, the higher the tariff it imposes, the greater the opposition it will face from general voters, who may decide to vote incumbent politicians out of office if consumer welfare drops sufficiently. The opposition of general voters arises because high tariffs result in obvious redistribution away from consumers to producers, higher prices for items in their consumption bundle and, most generally, greater inefficiency that will act as a drag on national economic performance.

This result can be shown graphically in Figure 8.3.[15] The votes gained through contributions offered by those that desire tariffs are shown in curve "OC" ("contribution effect"). The votes lost due to the disaffection of general voters because of the consumption and production dead-weight losses generated by the tariff are shown by curve "OL" ("distortion effect"). Politicians will choose a tariff that maximizes the difference between votes gained (V_G) because of the contribution effect and votes lost due

[15] This figure is adapted from Magee, Brock, and Young (1989).

to the distortion effect (V_L); that is, they will choose a tariff T^* that generates V^*. The country's tariff schedule will reflect the politically optimal choice of a tariff for each import-competing good.

Although scholars developed the endogenous tariff model based on the US political context, it can be applied, with some caveats, to countries with different political institutions. In other democracies, politicians have to calculate how their commercial policies will affect their electoral support. But countries differ greatly in the extent to which politicians rely on contributions and, thereby, the extent to which producers can influence elected officials through this channel. Also, different electoral rules influence politicians to place greater or less emphasis on appealing to narrow interest groups (such as producers) or general voters in seeking electoral support (Lukauskas, 1997) affecting the balance they strike between the two types of constituencies. The endogenous tariff model may also useful for thinking about commercial policy in a non-democratic regime, as politicians in authoritarian contexts must also weigh the political support they receive from the general citizenry as opposed to producer interests; without votes to measure support, however, it is difficult to formalize the political calculations involved using this model.

Of course, government officials may also seek tariffs in order to enjoy the revenue they yield, especially in countries where it is difficult to raise revenue through other less distortionary forms of taxation. As already noted, tariffs have been an important source of government revenue in many countries. Imposing tariffs is an attractive means of raising revenue because it permits politicians to lower the rate of direct taxation of firms and households, which is administratively or politically difficult in many countries.

Why Not Subsidies?

Subsidies often accomplish the same purpose as a tariff but more efficiently; they are usually the first-best instrument for domestic policy objectives as they produce fewer distortions or dead-weight losses for the economy. For example, a government may impose import barriers to promote an infant industry; alternatively, it can provide the industry with a production subsidy sufficient to offset the cost advantage of foreign firms, enabling consumers to continue to enjoy the good at world prices.[16] Although subsidies are often a superior instrument, their use is far less frequent than that of import barriers. Governments seeking to promote an infant industry or aid a struggling mature industry typically opt for protectionism. One reason for this choice is that subsidies require a direct and immediate expenditure by the government whereas a tariff generates revenue for the state. The government might recoup much of the cost of the subsidy through taxes collected on the industry (or other parts of the economy that experience faster growth), but the immediate expenditure may be infeasible due to fiscal or political constraints. In many developing countries, chronic fiscal deficits or the

---

[16] As in the case of an infant industry tariff, the subsidy should be eliminated once domestic firms have improved their productivity or cost structure and can compete on an equal footing with their foreign counterparts.

inability to use monetary instruments to finance subsidies limit their use. Furthermore, raising the additional revenue needed for a subsidy may create distortions in factor or product markets.

Second, the costs of a subsidy are explicit and the recipients are easy to identify. In contrast, the costs of protectionism are far more difficult to quantify, and the ultimate winners and losers from trade barriers (especially, quantitative restrictions and non-tariff barriers) may be difficult to ascertain. Public officials (and the beneficiaries of commercial policy) often prefer to conceal government support for specific producers in order to prevent public resentment.

Finally, in some countries, singling out an industry or firm for a budget outlay (as opposed to tariff protection) raises issues of fairness and may incite claims for government subsidies from other industries. Rodrik (1986) argues that subsidies generate more lobbying than tariffs because they are allocated to specific firms, giving individual firms a strong incentive to pressure government officials. Tariffs, on the other hand, provide protection for all firms in the industry regardless of individual lobbying efforts, creating a free-rider problem that reduces lobbying.

Quantitative Restrictions

Quotas and other quantitative restrictions (such as voluntary export restraints or orderly marketing arrangements) have similar though not identical distributional consequences as tariffs. The exact identity of the beneficiary of quotas will vary depending on the particular instrument employed and the means by which quota rents are allocated. In general, producers, whether domestic or foreign, benefit in the form of higher profits, at the expense of consumers, who not only pay higher prices but also see the supply of the good in question diminish.

Figure 8.4 illustrates the effects of imposing a quota.[17] The diagram closely resembles Figure 8.2, which examined the consequences of a tariff, and this highlights the basic similarity in the impact of quotas and tariffs. At P_W, imports equal $D_W - S_W$. If the government imposes a quota limiting imports to M_Q ($D_Q - S_Q$), the domestic price rises to P_Q. Consumer welfare declines due to the price increase and the corresponding loss of consumer surplus equals A + B + C + D. Domestic producers enjoy an increase in producer surplus equal to area A. As in the tariff case, quotas generate dead-weight production and consumption losses indicated by B and D.

Area C corresponds to the rents generated by the quota. Those with access to the good in international markets pay P_w for the good, but are able to sell it domestically for P_Q. The identity of the beneficiary will vary considerably depending on the nature and

---

[17] Once again, we assume a small country and perfect competition. The domestic distributional effect is similar for a large country, except quota rents become larger. An analysis of the impact of a quota under imperfect competition is beyond the scope of our discussion. See Feenstra (2004), chapter 8, for a discussion.

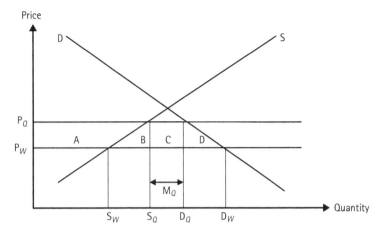

FIGURE 8.4 Effects of a quota

implementation of the quantitative restriction. The government can appropriate quota rents by auctioning off import licenses to the highest bidder, thereby capturing most of C (in which case, the quota has the same distributional effects as a tariff). Instead, government officials may allocate the import licenses to private groups according to various economic criteria, such as in proportion to previous imports or according to demonstrated ability to process imports, and rents will accrue to the firms that receive quota allotments. Alternatively, they may distribute them in direct exchange for political support or bribes. In this way, quotas (or any policy instrument that creates scarcity of highly desirable goods) can become an important tool for the support or rent-maximizing politician seeking to attain personal goals. If the quantitative restriction occurs in the form of a voluntary export restraint (VER) agreement or orderly marketing arrangement, in which foreign countries "agree" to limit their exports to the country, quota rents will mainly accrue to foreign firms (or governments).[18]

The imposition of quotas is also prone to creating what Bhagwati (1982), building on the seminal paper by Krueger (1974), first called directly unproductive rent seeking (DUP). As import rights or licenses are valuable, private actors will expend considerable time and resources lobbying government officials to obtain them. This lobbying results in income gains for the recipients of licenses (though not for non-recipients) but, unfortunately, it contributes nothing to national economic output. Empirical estimates of DUP costs have varied considerably. Early calculations assumed that competition for import licenses and the like would be open and intense, contributing to high DUP expenditures, potentially equivalent to the quota rents generated (area C in Figure 8.4). Bhagwati and Srinavasan (1980), however, pointed out that well-connected actors are likely to prevail in these competitions (what the authors call

[18] This feature of VERs makes them particularly easy to implement, since in effect, the home government bribes foreign governments and firms to accept restrictions on trade that are actually profitable.

the "brother-in-law theorem"), deterring other actors from expending resources to seek these rents. In any case, DUP costs are significant enough to be another reason to avoid policy instruments like quantitative restrictions that artificially create scarcity of highly desired goods.

The problems with quantitative restrictions have led most trade economists to argue in favor of replacing quantitative restrictions with equivalent tariffs. Even at the same level of protectionism, tariffs impose fewer social costs (such as DUP) and governments capture revenue as opposed to rents accruing to other groups. Tariffs are also more transparent and fair. In practice, conversion of quantitative restrictions into tariffs has been a central focus of the multilateral trade regime, such as recent efforts to replace quotas on agricultural goods with tariffs.

Non-Tariff Barriers

The distributional consequences of non-tariff barriers (e.g., safety regulations, customs procedures, government procurement practices, and domestic content rules) are similar to those of tariffs and quotas, but the identity of winners and losers as well as their general welfare effects are often more difficult to determine. Their impact on prices and quantities imported (or exported) are more ambiguous and difficult to define a priori. As noted previously, the use of non-tariff barriers increased dramatically starting in the mid 1970s as governments sought to find ways to increase levels of protectionism during a period of economic distress without violating their formal commitments to lower tariff levels through the GATT.

Non-tariff barriers are attractive to governments and their beneficiaries for various reasons. First, government officials can claim that the intent of a non-tariff barrier is not protectionism, but rather advancing a legitimate public policy goal. For example, a regulation requiring foreign goods to meet national safety standards could conceivably address a real public safety concern but have the unintended consequence of reducing imports. Then again, the safety regulation may simply be a ruse to disguise protectionist intent. Deciding whether the regulation is legitimate is often extremely difficult, as the science involved may be controversial and countries may have widely different public safety standards. For instance, in 1989, the European Union began prohibiting the import of US beef products from cattle treated with hormones, claiming that the long-term health consequences of consuming such beef products were unknown. The United States, however, contended that no scientific evidence supported these claims and that the real motivation of this safety regulation was to keep out US meat that is cheaper and of higher quality than European beef.[19]

---

[19] The WTO ruled in favor of the United States in 1997 and 1998, but the dispute is ongoing. The EU refused to lift its ban and the US imposed counter-measures in the form of increased customs duties on various EU products. In 2004, the EU sought to lift US counter-measures, claiming that it had acquired new evidence that proved it was justified in prohibiting US beef on safety grounds.

Second, since the effects of non-tariff barriers are often difficult to discern, the government may be able to assist even large, unpopular firms without incurring the same level of public resentment. Private groups that believe they will encounter opposition in obtaining relief from foreign competition through tariffs may be able to obtain protection through non-tariff barriers.

It seems likely that disputes surrounding the protectionist effects of various domestic rules, regulations, and practices will remain salient. Since the end of the Uruguay Round, the trade agenda has expanded from focusing primarily on "at the border issues" to encompassing "behind the border" issues as well. There will be tremendous pressure on governments, particularly in developing countries where standards often deviate more from international norms, to harmonize a much broader range of national policies that affect trade.

IV. International Political Economy of Trade

Policymakers design trade policy based not only on domestic economic and political factors but also on what other states are doing or are expected to do. For instance, if its trading partners have protectionist barriers in place, a country may not open its markets to foreign goods and services even though the intellectual case for unilateral free trade is very strong. Import-competing industries will point to closed foreign markets as further justification for imposing barriers to trade at home; exporters may argue that the carrot of opening domestic markets should be employed as a lever to pry open foreign markets. Indeed, appeals for a "level playing field" or "fair trade" are an almost constant refrain in discussions of national trade policy.

With the important exception of hegemonic states, to be discussed later, even a cursory examination of the historical record indicates that states often demand some sort of reciprocity, whether it be in the form of bilateral, regional, or multilateral agreements (formal or informal) as a condition for removing their own trade barriers. The world has only witnessed two sustained periods of open national markets and relatively free trade, that is, during the late nineteenth century and the post-World War II era. Other historical periods have been characterized by heavily protected markets and carefully managed trade.

Why have states found it difficult to achieve free trade despite its demonstrable mutual benefits? One reason is certainly the domestic politics of trade policy that was analyzed in the previous section, in which policymakers impose protectionism to garner support from key societal actors. Even in the absence of these domestic political obstacles, however, states confront collective action problems as they decide whether to cooperate to achieve mutually beneficial free trade. In making this choice, states act strategically, attempting to ascertain how other actors are likely to behave if they adopt one course of action or the other. A powerful heuristic device for understanding situations in which actors interact strategically is game theory. The prisoners' dilemma (PD) game is particularly useful in identifying the incentives that states face when they decide whether to remove or maintain trade barriers.[20]

Figure 8.5 depicts a simple PD trade game between two countries.[21] The countries must decide whether to remove import barriers (e.g., by signing a bilateral treaty), thereby establishing more open trading relations. Each country can *cooperate* by lowering barriers or *defect* by maintaining them. If both countries defect, the status quo is sustained and the payoff for each is zero [payoff = 0, 0].[22] If both actors cooperate, they each achieve gains from greater trade flows [5, 5]. If country A defects but country B cooperates [8, −2], country A gains due to its greater volume of exports to country B (plus economies of scale effects from higher levels of production), while still enjoying protected home markets; on the other hand, country B loses due to higher import competition from country A plus the costs incurred from shifting resources

Country B

		Cooperate	Defect
	Cooperate	5, 5	−2, 8
Country A			
	Defect	8, −2	0, 0

Cooperate = Remove trade barriers
Defect   = Maintain trade barriers

FIGURE 8.5 Prisoners' dilemma trade game

[20] On the classic PD game, see Axelrod (1984).

[21] In the following analysis, states are assumed to be unitary, rational actors. Policymakers formulate and act upon a set of national goals derived from an appreciation of the constraints and opportunities provided by the structure of the game that they are playing without considering the domestic political consequences. More complicated "two-level" games posit that leaders play linked games in the international and domestic spheres simultaneously.

[22] The payoff to country A is shown first, that of country B second. The payoffs indicated here represent the returns to each country from the decision to cooperate or defect, based on the action chosen by the other actor. The values were selected to illustrate the *relative* payoffs to each actor of different courses of action.

to its export sector in anticipation of country A's opening (but whose markets actually remain closed). If country B defects while country A cooperates, the outcome is reversed [−2, 8] and country B gains at country A's expense. Given this payoff structure, the only rational course of action for each country is to defect, since no matter what course of action the other chooses, defecting leaves it better off (if country B defects, country A is better off defecting [0>−2]; if country B cooperates, country A is again better off defecting [8>5]). Thus, the two countries will defect leaving them with the status quo, even though they would both benefit by cooperating and reaping the gains from trade.

The PD game shows that it is not sufficient for countries to have an objective interest in achieving a cooperative outcome, such as the removal of trade barriers; the structure of their interaction may impede them from realizing a mutually advantageous result. In this case, countries have both a defensive (avoiding the "sucker's payoff" [−2, 8]) and offensive (exploiting rivals [8, −2]) motive for imposing trade barriers. Achieving more open trade is even more difficult if the gains from trade are asymmetric. If country A gains less in relative terms from trade (say the payoff to mutual cooperation is [2, 5]), it might be reluctant to eliminate protectionism even though it gains absolutely, particularly if country B is a strategic rival. Some international relations scholars, in fact, contend that states with security concerns accord more weight to the relative gains of trade than the absolute gains (Grieco, 1990); they do not want to provide an economic edge that another state may transform, through the ability to increase defense spending, for example, into a military or strategic advantage.

So, how do states overcome the prisoners' dilemma in the area of trade, especially in situations involving many states with multiple issues and asymmetric payoffs? One answer is that a single powerful state may be able to solve the collective action problem for all. According to hegemonic stability theory, first advanced by Kindleberger (1973), the existence of a hegemon (a single dominant state in the international system) is a necessary condition for establishing a free trade regime; without a hegemon, the international trading system will witness repeated defections by states that lead to its closure. At first glance, the theory is consistent with the evidence: the two periods of robust free trade in the modern era have coincided with the existence of hegemonic states. The United States, as a hegemon, promoted a free trade order after World War II and Great Britain did so in the second half of the nineteenth century.[23] In contrast, the lack of a hegemon during the interwar period undermined the international trading system. The hegemon provides an open trading order because it benefits sufficiently that it is willing to bear the full cost of its provision. Focusing on the post-World War II case, the United States sought a liberal

---

[23] The free trade orders established by Great Britain and the United States have important differences. Of particular interest here, a dense web of bilateral agreements among leading nations characterized free trade under "Pax Britanica"; no international institutions emerged with the purpose of facilitating multilateral trade. In contrast, one of the founding principles of "Pax Americana" was to encourage multilateral trade in order to promote both economic prosperity and more peaceful relations among states. The post-World War II period has been notable for the expansion of multilateral institutions in a wide variety of functional areas.

trading order because it had more competitive industries and expected them to dominate world trade (and initially they did). The United States bore most of the short-term costs of providing the new trading order. It opened its markets unilaterally at first, took the lead in establishing international institutions such as the GATT, and provided ample economic and military assistance to bolster the economies of other Western countries.[24] Although other countries had an incentive to free ride on the liberal order, by keeping their markets protected, they slowly removed barriers to trade as they developed the capacity to compete effectively in global markets; the United States also made further trade liberalization contingent upon reciprocity.

Although they recognize that a hegemonic state is helpful for establishing a free trade regime, other scholars have contended that multilateral institutions, such as the General Agreement on Tariffs and Trade (GATT) and its successor the World Trade Organization (WTO), enable states to overcome the collective action problems that they face in establishing open trade, even in the absence of a hegemon. Although a single-play PD will lead to mutual defection always, in reality, many games are repeated indefinitely, greatly increasing the prospects for cooperation.[25] Multilateral institutions create a platform for iterated play and address some of the problems that plague actors in the PD game. First, they provide a forum for communication, allowing states to exchange information and engage in consultation and negotiation on trade issues; having an established venue also reduces the transaction costs that might otherwise make such exchanges too difficult. Second, they aid states in setting standards for what constitutes cooperation and defection in the area of trade policy, making it easier for states to monitor trading partners and determine when cooperation has broken down. Early detection of bad behavior on the part of other states will give policymakers greater confidence that they can limit their losses from defection by other states. Third, multilateral institutions establish mechanisms for dispute settlement and enforcement. Disputes may be resolved before they damage trade relations and violators can be sanctioned if they persist in following proscribed trade policies. Better monitoring and enforcement are especially important for small states that fear predatory behavior on the part of more powerful states. Finally, multilateral institutions make it harder for states to "backslide" during bad economic times, since rules specify when a country can renegotiate its trade commitments (Barton, Goldstein, Josling, and Steinberg, 2006).

---

[24] Other states made tariff concessions to the United States in signing the GATT agreement in 1947, but they lacked meaning until their currencies became convertible in the late 1950s. British trade liberalization in the nineteenth century was largely unilateral, though it negotiated many trade treaties with key partners.

[25] If the PD game is played repeated times, the prospect of gains from iterated cooperation or the "shadow of the future" can lead to greater cooperation, not immediate defection. A strategy of "tit-for-tat," in which an actor cooperates as long as the other player does (but defects if the other defects), has been shown by Axelrod (1984) to lead to sustained cooperation. Nevertheless, if the endpoint of the game is known in advance, the shadow of the future fades away and actors have an incentive to defect from the first play.

V. Political Economy of Trade Reform

Over the course of the last 50 years, starting in the developed world, many countries have slowly adopted relatively free trade policies. The process of trade reform involves more than just lowering the degree of protectionism; it also includes making import barriers more transparent, less complex, and more uniform across sectors.[26] Eliminating import barriers would seem to present a serious political challenge. Private groups favoring protectionism are well organized and politically influential; their stake in protectionism is high, so that they are likely to devote considerable resources to maintaining the status quo. In addition, tariffs may generate significant government revenue, and public officials often use the controls associated with non-tariff barriers or quantitative restrictions to advance their own political interests. Private groups hurt by protectionism, on the other hand, are typically poorly informed or organized; they are likely to incur higher costs in seeking to abolish protectionism than those they suffer because of protectionist barriers. Finally, the gains from trade liberalization are typically much smaller than the amount of redistribution it engenders.[27] Thus, politicians embarking on trade reform will have to sell a policy that causes substantial shifts of income among groups, shifts which are often politically unpopular, to achieve relatively small improvements in national income. Given these political obstacles, where is the impetus for reform likely to come from? Societal actors? State officials? External pressures to liberalize?

If governments implement protectionism in response to societal demands, as hypothesized above, then the impetus for trade liberalization might stem from protected industries themselves when they no longer favor barriers to trade. Protected industries, for instance, may come to view import barriers as detrimental to their interests. Milner (1988) suggested that the growing interdependence among nations and the "internationalization" of production has affected the preferences of firms with extensive international linkages (especially, multinational firms engaged in significant intra-firm trade). These firms once embraced protectionism, but now oppose it because it raises their costs of doing business across national borders. The growing use of outsourcing as a core business strategy will only add to the incentive for global firms to favor lower levels of protectionism (at least for all products other than their own).

Private actors hurt by protectionism are another potential force behind trade liberalization. Among those who are most likely to press for the removal of import barriers are exporters, industrial import users, businesses providing trade-related services, and retailers of imported products. Exporters, for instance, would benefit from the elimination of the bias that protectionism creates against exportable goods. In addition, in an effort to gain access to foreign markets, they may press for the lowering of domestic protectionist barriers since trade opening often occurs through reciprocal

---

[26] For more on the key issues of trade reform, see Chapter 10 in this volume by Wendy Takacs.

[27] See Rodrik (1994). The redistribution to efficiency gains ratio is higher the lower the existing degree of protectionism.

concessions. Nevertheless, these groups normally face collective action problems in organizing to lobby the government to liberalize trade. Although their stake is moderately high, they tend not to be very concentrated in either business or geographical terms. Post-World War II multilateralism improved the ability of exporters to influence trade policy. The nature of multilateral trade negotiations, in which countries agreed to make tariff concessions on a variety of products in an exchange for better foreign market access for its key goods, meant that it became harder for import-competing groups to resist trade opening, as concessions were part of a broader, multisector deal, and mobilized exporters by providing a greater stake and voice in trade policy (Gilligan, 1997). For their part, consumers face almost insurmountable collective action problems in opposing protectionism and are unlikely to be an organized force behind liberalization.

Politicians will pursue trade liberalization when they determine that the political costs of protectionism have increased or its benefits have declined. In Figure 8.3, this occurs when the "OL" curve shifts up or the "OC" shifts down, lowering the politically optimal level of tariffs (that is, T^* moves toward the origin). The most likely cause for a decline in the political utility of protectionism is weakening economic performance, which exposes the social costs of protectionist policies. In the absence of an economic crisis, leaders usually avoid major reform because demand for it is low and altering the status quo is costly.[28] During a crisis, on the other hand, private groups favoring trade liberalization, like exporters or heavy users of imported inputs, have a greater incentive to seek the removal of import barriers. General voters may not express their dissatisfaction with protectionism directly, but they will withdraw their support for incumbent politicians if economic conditions deteriorate. Incumbents will worry that political entrepreneurs may be able to use poor economic conditions as an issue to mobilize dissatisfied voters and build support for themselves. When faced with political opposition and competition, government officials will be more motivated to discover ways to improve economic performance, including lowering inefficient barriers to trade.

In exceptional cases, a change in domestic political institutions can also promote trade liberalization by altering the cast of trade policymakers or the incentives that they face when they design strategy. In the United States, the Reciprocal Trade Agreements Act (RTAA) of 1934 shifted authority over trade policy from the Congress to the executive branch. This institutional change occurred in the wake of the infamous Smoot–Hawley Act of 1930, which dramatically raised tariffs across a wide range of products and contributed heavily to a sharp drop in the volume of US and global trade as the Great Depression deepened. US legislators were highly protectionist because their incentive was to appeal to fairly narrow sectoral interests in their voting districts. The president,

---

[28] Rodrik (1994) contended that because the amount of redistribution provoked by trade liberalization is typically much higher than its efficiency gains, politicians in the developing world undertook trade opening only as part of a broader set of structural reforms in response to deep economic crises that reduced distributional concerns to second-order importance.

on the other hand, was accountable to a broad, heterogeneous national electorate; therefore, the executive branch had a stronger motivation to design trade policies that promoted better overall economic performance. Of course, such institutional changes are not exogenous; they are endogenously chosen by relevant actors in response to changes in the economic, political, or social environment. Congress, for instance, passed the RTAA because it recognized, based on the devastating results of the Smoot–Hawley Act, that its members were overly vulnerable to the logrolling of sectoral interests, and that recovery of the US economy and the nation's long-term trading interests lay in increasing global trade and growth.

Finally, the impetus for trade liberalization may stem from external pressure. This pressure may be direct and specific, in the form of demands from other states or international economic institutions, like the World Bank or International Monetary Fund, to open up markets as a condition for receiving a loan or other forms of assistance. Trading partners sometimes threaten to withhold bilateral aid or close their markets if the government does not remove import barriers (at least in certain sectors); the United States, for example, applied such pressure repeatedly on Japan in the 1980s and 1990s, with mixed results. Trade reform is a central element in structural adjustment programs funded by the World Bank and International Monetary Fund. In response, government officials often proclaim, especially to a domestic political audience, that they have no choice but to initiate trade liberalization or lose badly needed external funds. The evidence suggests, however, that direct external pressure for trade reform is frequently not very effective; policymakers, for instance, routinely ignore the demands for structural adjustment found in conditionality packages. If anything, the causality may be the reverse: leaders who are committed to trade liberalization seek to enter into agreements in order to initiate or consolidate reforms that they believe will generate substantial domestic political opposition.

External pressure may also take a more indirect form. In a globalizing world, government officials may decide that the costs of remaining protectionist are much higher as they risk missing out on new opportunities and becoming marginalized. Countries interested in obtaining the advantages of membership in multilateral trade institutions like the WTO, for instance, have had to agree to at least some additional trade opening as part of their accession; of course, once members, countries typically have to continue to accept new liberalization measures adopted by these institutions. The proliferation of preferential trade agreements has also been a powerful force: the fear of becoming marginalized is especially strong if neighboring countries or other traditional trading partners are entering into such agreements.

Tariff Uniformity

Some scholars and international organizations, like the World Bank, have proposed the introduction of a uniform tariff as an important step in trade reform. Moreover, the positive experience of Chile with tariff uniformity since the late 1970s has sparked interest among several countries, particularly in Latin America. Proponents of uniform tariffs argue that they promote greater equality in effective rates of protection across sectors and, thus, remove the pernicious consequences that cascading tariff structures have on resource allocation. In addition, they improve administrative simplicity and transparency, thereby reducing the opportunity for corruption. The most important effect, however, may be their ability to reduce lobbying for tariffs by interest groups. As Panagariya and Rodrik (1993) show, a uniform tariff increases the severity of collective action problems among those seeking protection, as the tariff obtained through one sector's activities becomes available to all sectors; this greatly reduces the incentive for groups to lobby policymakers.

Complementary Reforms

In order for trade reform to succeed, governments usually must concomitantly implement other structural reforms. For trade to foster growth, factor markets must become less rigid and more responsive to price signals, allowing labor and capital to move freely throughout the economy to where they bring the highest return. In the area of labor markets, policymakers often will need to reduce controls on the firing and hiring of workers. In many countries, restrictions on layoffs make it difficult for firms to adjust to changing market conditions, for instance, by reducing their workforce in the face of greater import competition.[29] Similarly, firms whose business is expanding due to trade opportunities may resist hiring new workers if they will not be able to dismiss them if market conditions change. In India, for example, firms employing more than 100 people cannot fire workers without obtaining government permission; most observers feel that this has proved to be an obstacle to growth in some manufacturing sectors. Governments can also mitigate the adjustment costs borne by workers who must switch jobs by providing training that equips them to take advantage of new employment opportunities and by supplying a safety net (notably, unemployment compensation) for workers in transition. More generally, the government's ability to compensate or aid the losers from liberalization may be critically important to diminishing any undesirable distributional consequences from trade opening (such as harm to low-income groups); this may have the additional benefit of reducing political resistance to the reform process.

Similarly, policymakers will need to take measures to ensure that financial markets are better able to finance new business opportunities once they arise. Recall that one of the primary rationales for infant industry protection is that capital market failures make it necessary for firms to earn profits immediately because financial entities do not lend to firms to cover current losses; efficient capital markets should be willing to lend to promising firms until they develop sufficiently to become profitable. Governments can also take steps to deepen markets for leasing and used machinery and perhaps modify rules regarding depreciation of capital stock in order to facilitate the mobility of capital across sectors.

---

[29] These restrictions tend to increase the level of protectionism in the first place, since for many firms lobbying the government for protection from import competition is their only strategic alternative to bankruptcy.

If tariffs have been an important source of government revenue, trade liberalization will require policymakers to find alternative sources of revenue to finance government spending. This usually involves fiscal policy reform, including increasing income, value added, or sales taxes, a politically unpopular step that also demands enhancing the government's administrative capacity. More generally, the state's institutional capacity must grow as well, notably by passing more clearly defined property rights, promoting better rule of law, improving the legal system, and creating a more impartial judiciary to enforce contracts and adjudicate disputes.

VI. Conclusion

Governments do not design trade policy solely on the basis of economic rationality; political considerations are always present and often dominate policymaking, frequently to the detriment of aggregate national welfare and the distribution of income. This chapter has explored how domestic politics influence the design and implementation of commercial policy, including decisions to implement or remove barriers to trade such as tariffs, quotas, and non-tariff barriers. Politicians usually claim that they are erecting import barriers in order to promote the national interest when they are actually seeking to benefit a narrow set of constituents or themselves. Protectionism hurts some groups but favors others, so that some private actors always have an interest in the implementation of trade barriers. Nevertheless, the "supply" side of trade policy, the complex balancing act among competing interests that politicians undertake when designing strategy, is equally important. The factors that lead governments to liberalize trade and implement the complementary reforms needed to achieve success are more difficult to pinpoint. The most likely domestic causes of trade liberalization are when protected industries themselves no longer desire trade barriers or politicians determine that the political costs of protectionism, in the form of votes lost due to lower consumer surplus, have increased. Deepening globalization has also increased the costs of maintaining highly protected markets, giving public officials a stronger incentive to undertake trade reform.

The international political and economic context in which trade takes place is also critical for understanding trade policy. The structure of the "trade game" generates a powerful set of constraints and incentives that policymakers must consider when formulating national strategy. Governments have ample reasons to be cautious in removing trade barriers, so much so that widespread protectionism has characterized economic relations among states throughout most of history. Historically, the existence of a hegemonic state, like the United States, has been required for states to create a liberal trading order. Nonetheless, multilateral institutions, such as the WTO, once created, can help states overcome the collective action problems inherent in opening up trade on a global basis, as they facilitate communication among countries as well as monitoring and enforcement of trade agreements.

APPENDIX

The Infant Industry Argument In Practice: Import Substitution Industrialization and Export-Led Growth Experiences

In the post-World War II era, most developing countries pursued a generalized application of the infant industry principle by adopting the development strategy called import substitution industrialization (ISI). The goal of ISI was to increase the percentage of industrial goods supplied domestically by protecting import-competing industries and granting them time to develop. Governments used various means to protect industry, including tariffs, quotas, and non-tariff barriers. Protection was cascading (or escalating), meaning that tariffs were much higher for goods requiring more advanced levels of processing so that finished goods (such as consumer products) had higher levels than inputs (such as raw materials); this led to very high levels of effective protection for manufacturing.

ISI was motivated by the doctrine of "structuralism," developed by the Argentine economist, Raul Prebisch (1950). Structuralism contended that developing countries would become locked into an inferior position in the international division of labor if they integrated themselves too quickly into the global economy. Specifically, they would be relegated to producing primary products and low-order manufacturing as opposed to high value added skills or capital intensive goods. In addition, structuralism suggested that the terms of trade for developing countries would decline over time if they were mainly primary product producers. Similarly, economic historian Alexander Gerschenkron (1962) hypothesized that developing countries, as late industrializers, confronted tremendous challenges going up against already competitive firms in developed countries. The state would have to lead development by concentrating available capital and expertise in priority sectors and by socializing the risk that private investors face.

Countries that adopted an ISI strategy initially did well, experiencing historically high rates of growth. From 1950 to 1973, for instance, GDP growth rates in ISI countries averaged about 6 per cent, with GDP/capita growth rates of about 3.5 per cent. GDP growth slowed dramatically after 1973, however, and several serious economic problems emerged or worsened. ISI increased the relative price of non-tradable goods (notably, services and domestic manufacturing) to tradable goods (mainly, agriculture and labor-intensive manufacturing), creating a bias against exports. In addition, overvalued exchange rates raised the foreign currency price of exportable goods, making them less competitive in international markets. As a consequence, many ISI countries experienced a sharp drop in exports, contributing to large and persistent balance of payment deficits (since imports remained high). Agriculture suffered in particular because many government policies acted as a tax on the sector. Government officials controlled agricultural prices at low levels in an effort to channel resources into industry and farmers had to pay higher prices for manufactured goods and inputs into agricultural production. Consequently, most ISI countries experienced a sharp decline in agricultural production, so much so that many countries had to import agricultural products in order to feed their populations.

ISI policies were also detrimental to overall economic efficiency, as Little, Scitovsky, and Scott (1970) detail. Factors of production flowed into protected sectors, where trade barriers virtually guaranteed high profits. Thus, scarce resources shifted to inefficient final users (hence, the need for protection in the first place) from more efficient sectors, where perhaps the country had a long run comparative advantage. In addition, overvalued exchange rates and other government controls (particularly, interest rate ceilings and minimum wages in the formal sector) encouraged firms to adopt overly capital intense modes of production. This further contributed to the inefficient use of factors of production, leading to, among other things, low employment growth.

Moreover, in most cases, infant industries did not improve their productivity or become internationally competitive. Without competition from abroad, they had little incentive to innovate or lower their costs. In general, increases in industrial production were due to high effective rates of production that afforded them a guaranteed market for their goods, not from a shifting out of their supply curve or success in international markets. Many firms incurred huge operating losses, which governments usually felt compelled to cover. Thus, infant industries frequently turned out to be a huge drain on government finances on a yearly basis. Unfortunately, protected industries became fierce opponents of any efforts to alter the status quo; in many countries, their political influence enabled them to block badly needed structural reforms (such as trade liberalization) for extended periods of time.

Korea and Taiwan followed ISI in the 1950s but soon abandoned it (Taiwan around 1958, Korea in the period from 1962–68) to adopt an export-led development strategy.[30] By the time these states dropped ISI, they had become proficient at labor-intensive manufacturing (e.g., clothing and shoes). To industrialize further and generate more value added, policymakers decided that they would have to move into capital- or skill-intensive sectors and they targeted several of these for intense growth and development. The government gave infant industries protection from import competition, but expected them to increase their production rapidly by expanding their exports aggressively. High, secure profits earned in protected domestic markets subsidized the export push and enabled priority sectors to capture economies of scale.[31] Government assistance (in the form of subsidies, import rebates, or tax credits) was made contingent on firms meeting export targets. In addition, the government designed policies to offset the negative effects of protection. For instance, firms that met export targets received a rebate on import duties imposed on inputs into their production process; thus, they paid world (not tariff inflated) prices for their inputs, allowing them to compete with foreign producers.

The results of the export-led growth strategy were astounding. From 1965 to 1990, the GDP per capita of Korea and Taiwan grew at an annual rate of 6.6 and 7.1 per cent, respectively. This was more than two times faster than the rest of Asia, three times faster than Latin America and South Asia, and twenty-five times faster than Sub-Saharan Africa. Korean and Taiwanese exports expanded dramatically as well, growing annually at 21 and 16 per cent, respectively; exports as a percentage of GDP jumped from 8 to 28 per cent and 19 to 45 per cent, respectively. These results indicate that condemning the infant industry argument out of hand may be premature.

Why was infant industry policy far better in Korea and Taiwan than in other countries? Virtually everyone agrees that the strategy of export promotion backed by a state willing to apply negative sanctions was critical. The emphasis on export performance meant that firms confronted stiff international competition and had to meet the test of highly competitive markets; firms that did not improve their productivity or achieve best practice fell out of government favor. Political institutions were also central. In Korea, policymakers enjoyed autonomy because strong leaders backed them; bureaucrats had a high level of competence and prestige, based on merit and a shared sense of corporate identity and coherence. This

---

[30] On the features of the East Asian experience, see World Bank (1993).

[31] Firms charged lower prices for exported goods than those supplied to the domestic market. This price discrimination led to numerous charges of dumping against Korean and Taiwanese firms in the United States and Europe and contributed to protectionist pressures in those countries.

helped them to remain de-politicized and not prone to capture by special interest groups. In addition, policymakers created quasi-institutionalized links to key social groups, notably business organizations or large industrial conglomerates, establishing what sociologist Peter Evans (1995) has called "embeddedness." In Korea, for instance, the government established direct, intimate links with business groups, especially the *chaebol*, to aid in formulating and implementing industrial policies. Policymakers supplied subsidized credit, information about international market opportunities, and assurances about the intent of government policy; this helped to socialize investment risk and mitigate market failures stemming from information uncertainty. The *chaebol*, for their part, provided first-hand information about the marketplace (including feedback on the success of existing policies). These iterated contacts led to the creation of trust and the result was better policy formulation and implementation because key social actors were involved in the policymaking process.

References

Axelrod, R. (1984), *The Evolution of Cooperation*. New York: Basic Books.

Barton, J., Goldstein, J. Josling, T. and Steinberg, R. (2006), *The Evolution of the Trade Regime: Politics, Law, and Economics of the GATT and WTO*. Princeton NJ: Princeton University Press.

Bhagwati, J. (1982), 'Directly-unproductive, profit-seeking (DUP) activities' *Journal of Political Economy*, 90: 988–1002.

Bhagwati, J. and Srinavasan, T. N. (1980), 'Revenue seeking: a generalization of the theory of tariffs' *Journal of Political Economy*, 88: 1069–87.

Cassing, J., McKeown, T. and Ochs, J. (1986), 'The political economy of the tariff cycle' *American Political Science Review*, 80: 843–62.

Coughlin, C., Chrystal, K. A., and Wood, G. (1988), 'Protectionist trade policies: a survey of theory, evidence and rationale' *Review—Federal Reserve Bank of St. Louis*, 70: 12–26.

Dutt, P., and Mitra, D. (2002), 'Endogenous trade policy through majority voting' *Journal of International Economics*, 58: 107–34.

Ebrill, L., Stotsky, J. and Gropp, R. (1999), 'Revenue implications of trade liberalization' International Monetary Fund, Occasional Paper 180. Washington, DC.

Evans, P. (1995), *Embedded Autonomy: States and Industrial Transformation*. Princeton, NJ: Princeton University Press.

Feenstra, R. (2004), *Advanced International Trade: Theory and Evidence*. Princeton, NJ: Princeton University Press.

Gawande, K., and Krishna, P. (2003), 'The political economy of trade policy: empirical approaches' in Choi, E. K. and Harrigan, J. (eds.), *Handbook of International Trade*. Oxford: Blackwell.

Gerschenkron, A. (1962), *Economic Backwardness in Historical Perspective*. Cambridge, MA: Belknap Press of Harvard University Press.

Gilligan, M. (1997), *Empowering Exporters: Reciprocity, Delegation, and Collective Action in American Trade Policy*. Ann Arbor: University of Michigan Press.

Goldberg, P., and Maggi, G. (1999). 'Protection for sale: an empirical investigation' *American Economic Review*, 89: 1135–55.

Grieco, J. (1990), *Cooperation among Nations: Europe, America, and Non-Tariff Barriers to Trade*. Ithaca, NY: Cornell University Press.

Grossman, G., and Helpman, E. (1994), 'Protection for sale' *American Economic Review,* 84: 833–50.

Hufbauer, G., Berliner, D., and Elliot, K. (1986), *Trade Protection in the United States: 31 Case Studies.* Washington, DC: Institute for International Economics.

Ikenberry, G. J., Lake, D., and Mastanduno, M. (1988), 'Introduction: approaches to explaining American foreign economic policy' in Ikenberry, Lake and Mastanduno (eds.), *The State and American Foreign Economic Policy.* Ithaca, NY: Cornell University Press.

Kindleberger, C. (1973), *The World in Depression, 1929–1939.* Berkeley, CA: University of California Press.

Krueger, A. (1974), 'The political economy of the rent-seeking society' *American Economic Review,* 64: 291–303.

Krugman, P. (1984), 'Import protection as export promotion: international competition in the presence of oligopoly and economies of scale' in Kierzkowki, H. (ed.), *Monopolistic Competition and International Trade.* Oxford: Oxford University Press.

Little, I., Scitovsky, T., and Scott, M. (1970), *Industry and Trade in Some Developing Countries: A Comparative Study.* New York: Oxford University Press.

Lukauskas, A. (1997), *Regulating Finance: The Political Economy of Spanish Financial Policy from Franco to Democracy.* Ann Arbor: University of Michigan Press.

Magee, S., Brock, W., and Young, L. (1989), *Black Hole Tariffs and Endogenous Policy Theory: Political Economy in General Equilibrium.* New York: Cambridge University Press.

Mayer, W. (1984), 'Endogenous tariff formation' *American Economic Review,* 74: 970–85.

Milner, H. (1988), *Resisting Protectionism.* Princeton, N. J.: Princeton University Press.

Panagariya, A., and Rodrik, D. (1993), 'Political economy arguments for a uniform tariff' *International Economic Review,* 34: 685–703.

Prebisch, R. (1950), *The Economic Development of Latin America and its Principal Problems.* New York: United Nations.

Rodrik, D. (1986), 'Tariffs, subsidies and welfare with endogenous policy' *Journal of International Economics,* 21: 285–99.

Rodrik, D. (1994), 'The rush to free trade in the developing world: Why so late? Why now? Will it last?' in Haggard, S., and Webb, S. (eds.), *Voting for Reform: Democracy, Political Liberalization, and Economic Adjustment.* New York: Oxford University Press.

Rogowski, R. (1989), *Commerce and Coalitions: How Trade Affects Domestic Political Alignments.* Princeton, NJ: Princeton University Press.

World Bank (1993), *The East Asian Miracle: Economic Growth and Public Policy.* New York: Oxford University Press.

CHAPTER 9

....

THE DOHA ROUND

....

PATRICK A. MESSERLIN

I. INTRODUCTION

....

IN 2013, almost all observers agree that the Doha Round is in a comatose state and will be for a very long time, possibly forever. However, this chapter provides evidence that the Doha negotiations did a good job between 2001 and 2008, and that a successful conclusion of the Round was within reach in May–June 2008—leaving to the concluding section of the chapter a brief review of the reasons behind the Doha collapse.[1] A detailed description of the negotiations over such a long period goes far beyond the scope of a chapter, and would require a book.[2] Rather, this chapter focuses on the four key questions faced by the Doha Round, and indeed by every future Round.

First, what is the "value" of a Round? The long negotiating process has fueled the wide perception that the Doha Round was not worth it. Section I shows that this perception is wrong by looking at the three alternative dimensions capturing the value of a Round; (1) a Doha Round concluded by 2010–11 would have been as productive as the previous Rounds; (2) the existing draft texts of a Doha Agreement would have brought welfare gains amounting to roughly US$300 to US$700 billion if one includes all the topics under negotiation; and (3) the Doha Round would have had a unique capacity to deliver legally binding commitments, that is, to provide the certainty so crucial to the business community (Wallenberg, 2006). This capacity is reflected by the costs that a definitive failure of the Doha Round would impose on world trade (a fall of 8 to 10 per cent) and on the world Gross Domestic Product (GDP) (a loss of US$900 billion).

Second, should one tightly link trade negotiations with broader concepts—development in the case of the Doha Round (it could be climate change in the next Round)?

---

[1] Strictly speaking, there is no Doha Round as such. The negotiations are being held under an awkward title—the "Doha Development Agenda" (DDA)—as explained below. However, for simplicity sake, this chapter will use both the terms DDA and Doha Round.

[2] See, in particular, Ismail (2009) from an insider perspective and Blustein (2009) from an outsider perspective. See also the huge amount of detailed information provided on a regular basis by a few websites, in particular of the World Trade Organization (WTO) and International Centre for Trade and Sustainable Development (ICTSD).

Section III argues that this is a costly and ultimately disappointing approach. It has absorbed the first four years of the Doha Round (from the 1999 Seattle Ministerial to the 2003 Cancun Ministerial) with little, if any, result. It has generated excessive expectations ending up in unnecessary disillusionment. Last but not least, it is still imposing costly constraints on the current negotiations. A Round is above all a negotiating process. That does not mean that development (or climate change) concerns should not be present in the minds of the trade negotiators. But the multilateral trade framework has enough means to address such concerns, without injecting them directly into the core of the negotiations.

Third, what is the objective of a Round? The answer seems obvious: trade liberalization. But the Doha Round shows that this answer is not precise enough. In sharp contrast with the previous Rounds, the Doha Round has been preceded by years of unilateral and preferential liberalization. Should then the Round deliver additional liberalization, or should it mostly consolidate ("bind" in the WTO jargon) the huge stock of past liberalizations? Section IV shows that this question puts the focus on the "technology" to be used by trade negotiators. Developing such a technology has been the main task of the trade negotiators from the July 2004 Framework and the 2005 Hong Kong Ministerial to the July and December 2008 mini-Ministerials. The resulting 2008 "draft texts" are generally seen as the "best estimates" of a possible Doha Round Agreement.[3]

Fourth, how can one negotiate on services, a still largely uncharted territory of the Doha Round despite the fact that services represent 50 to 70 per cent of the GDP of the WTO Members? Section V argues that there are good reasons—the specificity of protection in services and, more importantly, the political economy of liberalization in services—to believe that multilateral negotiations in services will be largely confined to binding unilateral liberalizations undertaken before a Round. Taking into account these factors suggests that a plurilateral approach involving only the ten or so largest WTO Members may be the necessary pre-requisite for concluding a Doha deal in services.

The concluding section addresses briefly two issues which are likely to dominate the world trade debate after the failure of the Doha Round. First, to what extent has the current global economic crisis strengthened the chances of concluding the Doha Round? Second, which improvements does the crisis suggest for the WTO machinery itself—as distinct from a Round?

II. THE "VALUES" OF THE DOHA ROUND

How should the "value" of the Doha Round (as of any Round) be assessed? There are several dimensions—that complement each other—to this question. First is to compare the outcome of the Doha Round with the outcomes of the Rounds held under the aegis

---

[3] For simplicity sake, this chapter refers to the draft texts of the July and December mini-Ministerials as the 2008 draft texts.

of the General Agreement on Trade and Tariffs (GATT) during the last 60 years. Such a long-term comparison shows a surprisingly good performance of the Doha Round on the one issue that is common to all these Rounds, that is, tariff cuts on industrial products. A second dimension is provided by the estimated impact of a successful Doha Round on world welfare, the traditional measure of economists. This approach shows that most of the gains from the Doha negotiations come from its wide scope of issues, much broader than the scope of its GATT predecessors. Lastly, the value of the Doha Round mirrors another specific feature. As it occurs after a long period of unilateral liberalization by many countries, its capacity to deliver "certainty" by legally binding all these unilateral commitments in a multilateral setting is a source of potentially huge benefits.

The Value in "Productivity" Terms: The Doha Round and Its Predecessors

Most observers assign a low value to the Doha Round because of the endless negotiations. However, using the length of the negotiations as an input for assessing an outcome in terms of the value of the Doha Round is not appropriate. Rather, one needs to have some sense of the "productivity" of the Doha Round. The most obvious, albeit crude, measure of a "Round productivity," is the average worldwide tariff cut agreed on during a Round divided by the number of year of negotiations for the Round (Messerlin, 2007). This measure has the additional merit of allowing a comparison with all previous Rounds.

Table 9.1 provides the length of the negotiations (in months) of the nine Rounds, the average tariff cut agreed during each of these Rounds, and the productivity for each Round defined as the average tariff cut by year of negotiations. It assumes that the Doha Round is concluded by December 2010, and that the worldwide tariff cut that it delivers is the lowest tariff cut mentioned in the December 2008 draft text (like the Swiss25 coefficient, see Section IV).

Table 9.1 provides three key results. First, the Doha Round would deliver roughly the same average tariff cut by year of negotiations (5 percentage points) compared to all its predecessors but the Geneva-I and Kennedy Rounds. This result is all the more remarkable because large tariff cuts at the start of a trade liberalization process (as in the Geneva-I Round) seem much easier than cutting, 60 years later, the remaining tariffs of industrial sectors which have been able to develop the political clout to keep their protection largely intact during all these years.[4]

---

[4] That said, the welfare gains provided by the tariff cuts of the Doha Round are likely to be smaller than those provided by the tariff cuts of the first Rounds because the latter were mostly imposed on high tariffs. This aspect is taken into account in the second way to define the value of a Round.

Table 9.1 Comparing the "productivity" of the Rounds, 1947–2010

Rounds	Dates	Length (months)	Tariff cuts [a]	"Round productivity"	Number of All	members G77
Geneva-I	1947	8	26.0	39.0	19	7
Annecy	1949	8	3.0	4.5	20	8
Torquay	1950–51	8	4.0	6.0	33	13
Geneva-II	1955–56	16	3.0	2.3	35	14
Dillon	1960–61	10	4.0	4.8	40	19
Kennedy	1963–67	42	37.0	10.6	74	44
Tokyo	1974–79	74	33.0	5.4	84	51
Uruguay	1986–94	91	38.0	5.0	125	88
Doha [b]	2001–10	120	50.0	5.0	146	98

Notes:
Average cuts in bound industrial tariffs.
Assuming that the Doha Round will conclude in December 2010, with the implementation of a Swiss25 tariff reduction for the emerging economies and a Swiss10 for the developed countries (for details, see Section IV).

Source: Updated from Messerlin (2007).

Second, the size of the WTO membership or its structure (the share of developing countries in the total WTO membership) has no visible impact on the productivity of a Round. Leaving aside the Geneva-I and Kennedy Rounds, the Round productivities are surprisingly stable over the years.[5] Such a result, confirmed by experienced negotiators (Groser, 2007), reflects the fact that GATT Rounds are dominated by large countries. Up to the Uruguay Round concluded in 1995, once the United States and European Community were close to agreement on the key issues at stake the other members were strongly induced to join the emerging agreements, though of course they tried their best to influence the final outcome (if only at the margin).

Last, two Rounds (Geneva-I and Kennedy Round) have had outstanding productivity. The case of Geneva-I is easy to explain. The immediate post-World War II years witnessed redundant tariffs, pervasive quotas, and exchange rate constraints, all factors that made it easy to decide a first set of large tariff cuts. By contrast, the high productivity of the Kennedy Round is puzzling at a first glance, and seems mostly due to improved negotiating "technology" (see Section IV).

---

[5] The Kennedy Round witnessed a doubling of the GATT membership and was the first Round with a majority of developing members—and yet it was the second most productive Round.

The Value in Terms of Welfare Gains: The Wider Scope of the Doha Round

The preceding assessment of the value of a Round has two limits. It does not necessarily reflect well the welfare gains (the preferred measure of economists) delivered by a Round. And it ignores the fact that the Doha Round has a much wider scope of issues than its GATT predecessors since, in addition to tariffs imposed on industrial goods (an issue dealt with by all the Rounds), it also covers tariffs imposed on agricultural products, non-tariff barriers imposed on industrial goods, barriers to trade and investment in services, and trade facilitation—to mention the most important topics.

The potential world welfare gains to be delivered by the Doha Round are thus a combination of the welfare gains of all these various components (and of improved rules, if any). As of today, no modeling exercise is able to take into account all these components, if only because of a lack of adequate data. Available estimates are limited to the tariffs in the goods sector, and hence substantially underestimate the value of the whole Doha Round. Before leaving this narrow context of tariff cuts in agricultural and industrial goods, it is worth mentioning two studies (Laborde, Martin, and van der Mensbrugghe, 2009a, 2009b), which suggest global welfare gains amounting to US$160 billion from trade liberalization in goods alone, even after allowing for all the exceptions to liberalization (see Section IV). Such gains are substantially larger (up to twice) the gains generally mentioned. The reason is that these two exercises use much more disaggregated trade and tariff data. Hence, they take into account high tariffs as compared to the previous exercises, since cutting high tariffs is the main source of welfare gains.[6]

Getting a better sense of such a value thus requires an ad hoc approach that calculates the welfare gains associated with each of the four components covered by the Doha Round, without trying to integrate them into one global and interactive approach. Such a piecemeal approach provides the following results (Adler et al., 2009). Tariff cuts in agricultural and industrial goods would have an estimated impact of trade gains on GDP amounting to roughly US$100 billion. Full liberalization (tariffs and non-tariff barriers) in three industrial sectors (chemicals, electronic, and environmental goods) would generate an impact of similar size (US$100 billion). A modest liberalization in services would also have an impact of similar size (US$100 billion).

Lastly, the potential gains from improvement in trade facilitation (which covers all the trade costs, such as transit, border fees and formalities, trade regulations, etc.—all issues related to the Doha Round because they have a substantial component of services) would amount to US$385 billion of gains. An alternative way to express the importance of trade facilitation in the Doha Round context is to say that reducing trade costs by 2 to 4 per cent would have the same effect on trade volumes as a successful Doha Round (Hoekman, Martin, and Mattoo, 2009; Hoekman and Nicita, 2010).

In sum, the welfare gains from a successful Doha Round (defined on the basis of the 2008 draft texts) would range from US$300 to US$700 billion.

---

[6] Economic analysis shows that welfare losses are a function of the square of the tariffs.

The Value in Terms of Certainty: The Doha Round as a "Binding Round"

Coming back to the context of trade in goods, looking at the applied tariffs for assessing the value of the Doha Round overlooks another aspect of the value of a Round—indeed, the most important aspect of GATT for its founding fathers. GATT/WTO negotiators conclude agreements in terms of "bound" tariffs. WTO members can apply tariffs that are lower than their bound tariffs, but the bound tariffs are the only ones that, according to WTO rules, an importing country cannot raise without compensating its affected trading partners. In short, bound tariffs are the only ones that deliver the legal certainty that the business community values so much.

Table 9.2 shows that the average applied tariff of the 34 countries that account for roughly 90 per cent of world trade and GDP under WTO rules is roughly 7 per cent in the manufacturing sector for 2007.[7] Such a moderate level mirrors the substantial unilateral tariff cuts that were implemented in the 1990s and early 2000s by many developing and emerging countries, following China's successful liberalization. To a much smaller extent, it also mirrors the tariff cuts generated by preferential trade agreements.[8] In short, there are less and/or smaller tariffs to cut left to the Doha Round (and to its successors, see the concluding section).[9]

Delivering certainty is particularly important in the case of the Doha Round because the 1990s and 2000s have witnessed substantial liberalizations that are not yet bound. Table 9.2 shows that, out of the 34 largest economies, only 8 impose applied tariffs at their bound level (Messerlin, 2008). The 26 other largest economies—more than one-fourth of world trade and GDP, and growing at rates twice those of the USA or the EC—have bound tariffs higher than their applied tariffs, often by 20 to 40 percentage points. Hence, these economies are potential major defaulters in tariff matters at any time and with no penalty. Moreover, the "tariff water" (the difference between bound and applied tariffs) is likely to be higher for the high tariffs, meaning that binding such tariffs would bring even greater welfare gains in terms of certainty.

---

[7] These numbers leave aside only three large economies: Algeria (not yet a WTO Member); Russia (still negotiating WTO accession, but imposing an average tariff of 10.5 per cent), and Vietnam (still implementing WTO accession, with a targeted average bound tariff of 10.4 per cent at the end of its accession period).

[8] Preferential agreements have a limited impact for a host of reasons: most of them are recent, are on a bilateral basis, have complex rules limiting their impact on trade flows, and so on. Such agreements are estimated to amount to 10 per cent only of the liberalization effort (World Bank, 2005).

[9] This evolution explains that the successive estimates of the welfare gains to be delivered by the Doha Round negotiations in goods have declined as time progressed. The gains calculated in the mid-2000s are smaller than those calculated a few years before. For instance, they would amount to an increase of world welfare of 0.5 per cent (Polanski, 2006) compared to a 1.5 per cent increase calculated a few years before (World Bank, 2002). This decline largely reflects two decades of unilateral industrial tariff cuts by many countries.

Table 9.2 Bound and applied tariffs of the 34 largest WTO members, 2008

WTO members	Gross billions US$ [a]	Domestic billions US$ [b]	Product real growth [c]	Total imports US$ [a]	Industry simple average bound tariff (%)	Industry applied tariff (%)	Industry average tariff water [d]	Industry imports US$ [a]	Agriculture simple average bound tariff (%)	Agriculture applied tariff (%)	Agriculture average tariff water [d]	Agriculture imports US$ [a]
The 8 largest "true" WTO members												
EU27 [e]	14554	12634	2.1	1697	3.9	3.8	0.1	1016	15.1	15.0	0.1	124
United States	13202	13202	2.7	1918	3.3	3.2	0.1	1348	5.0	5.5	-0.5	104
Japan	4340	4131	1.6	580	2.4	2.6	-0.2	297	22.7	22.3	0.4	65
China	2668	10048	9.8	791	9.1	9.1	0.0	579	15.8	15.8	0.0	51
Canada	1251	1140	2.5	358	5.3	3.7	1.6	280	14.5	17.9	-3.4	24
Taiwan	365	n.a.	2.8	203	4.8	4.6	0.2	138	18.4	17.5	0.9	10
Hong Kong	190	267	4.7	336	0.0	0.0	0.0	305	0.0	0.0	0.0	12
Macao	14	20	12.9	5	0.0	0.0	0.0	3	0.0	0.0	0.0	1
All	[f] 78.1	[f]	2.9	[f] 67.1	4.1	3.9	0.3	[f] 67.1	13.1	13.4	-0.4	[f] 62.7
The next 26 largest WTO members												
Brazil	1068	1708	2.9	96	30.8	12.5	18.3	66	35.5	10.3	25.2	6
India	906	4247	7.3	175	36.2	11.5	24.7	85	114.2	34.4	79.8	7
Korea	888	1152	4.6	309	10.2	6.6	3.6	178	59.3	49.0	10.3	19
Mexico	839	1202	2.2	268	34.9	11.2	23.7	222	44.1	22.1	22.0	19
Australia	768	728	3.1	139	11.0	3.8	7.2	106	3.3	1.3	2.0	8
Turkey	403	662	4.6	140	16.9	4.8	12.1	93	60.1	46.7	13.4	8
Indonesia	364	921	4.9	80	35.6	6.7	28.9	53	47.0	8.6	38.4	7
Norway	311	202	2.2	64	3.1	0.6	2.5	50	135.8	57.8	78.0	5
Saudi Arabia	310	384	3.4	70	10.5	4.7	5.8	56	20.0	7.6	12.4	9

	(a)	(b)	(c)	(d) bound			(d) applied				(e/f)
South Africa	255	567	4.1	77	15.7	7.6	8.1	55	40.8	9.2	31.6	4
Argentina	214	618	3.1	34	31.8	12.3	19.5	30	32.6	10.2	22.6	1
Thailand	206	604	5.0	131	25.5	8.2	17.3	87	40.2	22.1	18.1	7
Venezuela	182	203	3.8	34	33.6	12.7	20.9	29	55.8	16.4	39.4	4
Malaysia	149	301	4.7	131	14.9	7.9	7.0	101	76.0	11.7	64.3	9
Chile	146	208	4.2	38	25.0	6.0	19.0	23	26.0	6.0	20.0	3
Colombia	136	363	3.9	26	35.4	11.8	23.6	22	91.9	16.6	75.3	3
Singapore	132	144	4.6	239	6.3	0.0	6.3	175	36.5	0.1	36.4	7
Pakistan	129	406	5.1	30	54.6	13.8	40.8	17	95.6	15.8	79.8	4
Israel	123	179	1.6	50	11.5	5.0	6.5	36	73.3	19.7	53.6	4
Philippines	117	463	4.6	54	23.4	5.8	17.6	40	34.6	9.6	25.0	4
Nigeria	115	169	5.5	22	48.5	11.4	37.1	18	150.0	15.6	134.4	3
Egypt	107	352	4.2	21	27.7	9.2	18.5	10	96.1	66.4	29.7	5
NewZealand	104	110	3.2	26	10.6	3.2	7.4	19	5.7	1.7	4.0	2
Peru	93	188	4.7	15	30.0	9.7	20.3	10	30.8	13.6	17.2	2
Kuwait	81	67	5.5	16	100.0	4.7	95.3	13	100.0	4.0	96.0	2
Bangladesh	62	320	5.6	16	34.4	14.2	20.2	10	192.0	16.9	175.1	3
	[f]	[f]		[f]				[f]				[f]
All	17.5	26.5	4.1	26.2	27.6	7.9	19.7	27.1	65.8	19.0	46.8	24.8

Notes: (a) at current exchange rates. (b) at purchasing power parity exchange rates. (c) annual growth rates of real GDP over the 2000–06 period. (d) the tariff water is the difference between the average bound and applied tariff. (e) EU27 is counted as one WTO Member. (f) in percentage of the World total.

Source: WTO Secretariat, Trade Profiles, (<http://www.wto.org>). Author's computations.

It is difficult to estimate the "value of binding" aspect of the Doha Round because it requires one to define the "default" policies that the 26 countries listed in Table 9.2 could implement, if these countries decided to increase their applied tariffs up to their bound rates. World trade is estimated to decline by 8 to 10 per cent (Bouët and Laborde, 2009; Australian Productivity Commission, 2009) and the world GDP by US$900 billion (2 per cent)—strongly suggesting that the value of binding of the Doha Round is its most outstanding contribution to the world trade regime.

This conclusion is reinforced by the fact that such estimates do not take into account two key factors. First, they do not reflect the fact that the unexpected magnitude of the current economic crisis has increased the value of binding of the Doha Round to the extent that it has substantially increased the risks of default. Second, the above estimates ignore the opportunity costs imposed on the world trade regime by the fact that trade officials are so busy with the Doha negotiations that they have no time to look at other pressing major issues, such as the relations between climate change and trade policy (a point briefly discussed in the concluding section).

III. Wasted Early Years (2001–04) and Long-Lasting Mistakes

The Doha Round is generally seen as very similar to GATT Rounds. This apparent continuity hides major differences that have made the launch of the Round very difficult, and are still imposing costs on its negotiating process.

The core of these differences is as follows. GATT was deeply conscious of the fragility of the world trade regime that it established, and of its many limits—a narrow membership, a scope limited to industrial goods, the absence of a robust litigation process, and so on. In sharp contrast, the WTO was conceived with a boundless confidence in the new regime. It seemed that no issue could escape the WTO reach—services, trade-related intellectual property rights, strong litigation, the principle of linking together all the topics discussed during a Round (the so-called "Single Undertaking"), and so forth. Including new topics and new disciplines was simply seen as a matter of time.

These major differences reflect the very different environments prevailing when the two fora were conceived. The GATT birth witnessed a deep fragmentation of the world economy, divided between market-oriented (not necessarily free trade inclined) countries, autarkic centrally planned economies, and developing countries fascinated by import substitution policies. By contrast, the WTO birth witnessed the fall of the Berlin Wall, the unilateral liberalization of former centrally-planned Central European economies (in such a very bold way, as in Czechoslovakia or Estonia, that it eroded the reluctance to more liberalization that characterized the EC approach until the Uruguay Round) and, last but not least, the even bolder market opening of China that led a notable group of developing countries to become supporters of the GATT "liberal" trade regime, including its traditional leading opponents (Brazil and India).

This boundless confidence in the WTO machinery has been the source of severe difficulties in launching the Doha Round. It largely explains the failure of the Seattle Ministerial (1999). It induced the WTO members to link trade negotiations and "development" in a tight rhetoric during the 2001 Doha Ministerial. After a short-lived success, this rhetoric has been a source of bitter disillusionment at the 2003 Cancun Ministerial. Finally, it has imposed costly constraints that the Doha negotiators still have to abide by, as explained below.

Launching a New Round: The Failure of the Seattle Ministerial (1999)

During the GATT years, launching a Round was done on an ad hoc basis, if and when a leading GATT member (*de facto* the USA) felt that time was ripe for making further progress in opening markets. In sharp contrast, the launch of the Doha Round was pre-committed by the 1995 Uruguay Agreement that explicitly scheduled the launch of talks on agriculture and services by 2000. The choice of the year 2000 deserves remark. It was before the full implementation of two highly contentious Uruguay Round agreements—the opening of developed country markets in clothing and textiles by 2005, and the enforcement of the developing country obligations in trade-related intellectual property rights (TRIP) by 2010. Opening a new Round when key concessions of the previous Round were not even close to being fully enforced was a sure recipe for serious trouble.

Troubles were quick to emerge, with the collapse of the Seattle WTO Ministerial in 1999. During this Ministerial, the USA and the EC were still in the mid-1990s mood, and wanted to expand the WTO to new topics, particularly trade and labor. At the same time, developing countries were becoming increasingly divided. At one end of the spectrum, the emerging economies were building an offensive agenda adapted to their mounting export capacities, targeting in particular the USA and EC reluctance to open their markets in agriculture, in some industrial sectors (those still highly protected against goods exported by the developing countries), and in services (including labor movement). At the other end of the spectrum, the least-developed economies (LDC) were hanging on to their exemptions from GATT/WTO disciplines. These divisions were increased by the rapidly fading hopes of many developing countries of benefiting from the scheduled increased openness of the textiles and clothing markets in developed countries, because of the fast and strong rise of China's productive capacities in these products.

All these difficulties were greatly magnified when non-governmental organizations (NGOs) discovered the WTO's capacity to attract media attention, a feature ignored by the GATT. Many NGOs appointed themselves champions of the developing countries, often advocating simplistic solutions to such complex issues as the true impact of the Uruguay Round TRIP Agreement on drugs, or the need of more "policy space" for the developing countries (see below). It took a few years for the trade negotiators of developing countries to reassert themselves, and make clear that they did not need help from NGOs often based in, or funded by, developed countries.

Development: The Rallying Cry at the Doha Ministerial (2001)

Following the Seattle debacle, the WTO negotiators put the negotiating process back on track in less than two years.[10] Such haste had a price. The 2001 Doha Ministerial fell short of launching a fully fledged "Doha Round." Rather, it launched a DDA with an initially very ambiguous status—for a long time it was not even clear whether the DDA discussions were mere exploratory talks or true negotiations. More crucially, injecting the "development" term directly into trade negotiations created serious problems. It was driven by two very different reasons.

First was a fairly usual feature of the GATT negotiating process that consists in including in a Round all the topics of interest for all the participants, before dropping some of them and concluding the deal with the "surviving" topics. The rationale for such an approach is to enlarge the possibilities of trade-offs among participants in order to facilitate the final shaping of the deal.[11]

The second reason was quite new. It was the realization of how it has become easy for developing countries to block WTO negotiations, as illustrated at the Seattle Ministerial. This capacity was generated by the principle of a "Single Undertaking" much more than by the sheer number of developing country WTO members.[12] The Single Undertaking principle states that concluding a Round requires the agreement of all the members on all the topics under negotiation. Ironically, this rule was imposed by the developed countries (most notably, the USA) during the Uruguay Round in order to force developing countries to make commitments on new trade issues (services and TRIPs) as a trade-off for the commitments in textiles, clothing, and agriculture that developed

---

[10] This rapidity was in part related to the 9/11 terrorist attacks. But, it was also (mostly?) pre-determined by the WTO approach that was much less conscious of the fragility of the trade regime than GATT. In this respect, it is worth noting that four years were necessary to recover from the failed attempt to launch a Round in 1982 and to launch what became the Uruguay Round at the 1986 Punta-del-Este conference.

[11] This negotiating technique reached a climax when the Uruguay Round negotiators "traded" better access to the textile and clothing markets of the developed countries with the implementation by developing countries of stricter laws and regulations in TRIPs.

[12] That the number of development countries is not a key parameter is suggested by the fact that, by the late 1960s, developing countries represented more than half the GATT membership. By the way, it should be remembered that there is no official list of developing countries in the WTO. Being such a country is a decision left to each WTO member. Proxy lists are the membership of the G77 Group of non-aligned countries, or of the countries with medium or low GDP per capita. Neither list includes developed countries that still tend to consider themselves as developing countries in the WTO forum (Singapore, Korea, etc.).

countries were ready to take. A few years later, this principle was backfiring and working in favor of the developing countries—now in the position to force the developed countries to take into account the developing countries' requests if they wanted to see their own requests accepted.[13]

Development: Bitter Disillusionment at the Cancun Ministerial (2003)

The success of "development" as a rallying cry for the Doha negotiations was short lived. Before explaining the reasons for such a fate, it should be made clear that the ultimate objective of countries is growth and development, not trade per se. Trade policy is a necessary instrument for achieving such objectives, but not a sufficient one: many other domestic policies are needed. That said, trade policy has many ways to take on board development concerns (as illustrated in Section III). Explicit and multiple references to a broad development goal may then be more harmful than helpful, as illustrated by the first years of negotiations.

The main reason is that, behind the apparent consensus on the words "Development Agenda," WTO members were quick to re-discover their disagreements on the relative role of trade policy and other policies in development.

For developed WTO members, development was seen as requiring all the aspects of modern governance, from market opening to the so-called Singapore issues—competition law and policy, transparency in public procurement, disciplines in investment—and to issues such as labor and environmental regulations. In particular, the EC was pushing hard for making the Singapore issues part of the final Doha deal. The 2003 Cancun Ministerial resulted in the abandonment of this approach.

By contrast, most developing countries interpreted "development" as a way to restore and reinforce the notions of "special and differential treatment" (SDT) and "policy space." The Uruguay Round negotiations on GATT Article XVIII (the key legal basis for SDT) almost succeeded in reducing the notion of SDT to the narrow dimension of longer periods of implementation. By contrast, the late 1990s witnessed the increasing recognition that development does require some policy space.

The key question is then: which type of policy space? Economic analysis insists on a policy space centered on domestic policies, such as regulatory reforms, domestic taxes, and subsidies in markets of goods, services, and factors of production. It repeatedly shows that policy space narrowly defined as trade barriers (tariffs or non-tariff barriers) is rarely the appropriate instrument to deal with the vast majority of development issues.

---

[13] At the end of the Uruguay Round, developed countries were able to impose the Single Undertaking on developing countries by creating a new institution (the WTO), leaving those developing countries willing to benefit from the opening of the developed country markets in textiles and clothing no other option than to join the WTO. Such "blackmail" is not an available option in the Doha Round.

Table 9.3 Negative coalitions: the Doha Round "gruyère"

	Negotiations in	
	Agriculture	NAMA
LDC	32	32
Small and vulnerable economies (SVE) [a]	38	37
Recently acceded members (RAM)	10	10
Other groupings with wide exceptions [b]	4	11
Total	84	90
All WTO members [c]	127	127
Core negotiating countries [d]	43	37

Notes: (a) excluding RAM and other groupings. (b) Countries with Low Binding Coverage in non-agricultural market access (NAMA) and Net Food Importing Countries in agriculture. (c) Counting the EC as one WTO Member. (d) The WTO Members not pertaining to a negative coalition.

Source: WTO NAMA and Agriculture Chair texts, TN/MA/W/103/Rev.3, TN/AG/W/$/Rev.4, December 6, 2008.

Despite this clear message, the Doha negotiators of most developing countries have continuously pushed the notion of policy space to provide the freedom to impose trade barriers. This has led them to build "negative" coalitions, the main objective of which is not to get market opening concessions from other WTO members, but to get exceptions from the ongoing negotiations and future WTO disciplines on access to their own markets.

Table 9.3 presents these negative coalitions: the more than three-decade old LDC and the new SVE and RAM.[14] In addition, many members have succeeded in creating groupings with wide exceptions in manufacturing and agriculture. Altogether, these negative coalitions include roughly 84 to 90 members which are totally or substantially exempted from the possible results of the Doha Round.

In short, the current Doha negotiations fully involve only 40 members or so, half of them being developing and emerging economies (out of a total WTO membership amounting to 127 members, the EC being one member). As these 40 members represent more than 80 per cent of world trade and GDP, the Doha Round looks like a "gruyère" full of small holes.

The Doha negotiators often claim that this situation does not create sub-categories of negotiating members among developing countries. But, of course, it does. Negative

---

[14] SVE are developing WTO members that, in the period 1999–2004, had an average share of (a) world merchandise trade of no more than 0.16 per cent, (b) world trade in NAMA of no more than 0.1 per cent, and (c) world trade in agricultural products of no more than 0.4 per cent.

coalitions reduce or eliminate the incentives for small developing countries to partic-ipate actively in the Doha negotiations, hence blocking them out since most of these small countries are wary of further liberalization. Ironically, they can be seen as a prag-matic solution to the Single Undertaking constraint offered by the small countries to the large WTO members.

From a development perspective, negative coalitions have two opposing faces. For their own members, they are disastrous. They impose self-inflicted damages on the "opting out" countries since they substantially reduce potential trade among all their members and between them and the rest of the world. By contrast, negative coa-litions are positive for the large developing and emerging economies. From a diplo-matic perspective, such coalitions represent a large reservoir of small allies while, at the same time, they leave the large developing and emerging economies free to focus their offensive interests on trade with developed economies, without harming their economic interests much since negative coalitions represent too small a share of world trade and GDP.

Development: A Source of Long-Lasting Constraints on the Doha Negotiating Process

Amidst all these expectations and disillusionment, the WTO negotiators have come up with four concrete guidelines defining "development-friendly" negotiations.

First, paragraph 16 of the 2001 Doha Declaration states: "*The negotiations shall take fully into account the special needs and interests of developing and least-developed country participants, including through less than full reciprocity in reduction commitments (...)*" (author's emphasis). The "*less than full reciprocity*" provision does not make economic sense from a development perspective if one remembers that the Doha negotiations deal with bound tariffs. Almost all the developing countries—with the notable exception of China—have much higher bound tariffs than developed countries. If they want to boost their growth by guaranteeing access to their markets, developing countries should thus cut their bound tariffs more than the developed countries. Cutting bound tariffs more severely than developed countries does not necessarily mean that developing countries would cut their current applied tariffs, or that they could not have longer implementa-tion periods than the developed countries—two simple and common ways to take into account the relative fragility of the development process within the trade negotiating framework.

Second, paragraph 24 of the 2005 Hong Kong Declaration states: "*(...) we instruct our negotiators to ensure that there is a comparably high level of ambition in market access for Agriculture and NAMA.*" This statement links the liberalization of the industrial mar-kets of the developing countries to the liberalization of the agricultural markets of the developed economies. From a purely economic perspective, this second criterion seems neutral. But, combined with the "*less than full reciprocity*" provision, it could constitute a strong incentive for creating a large and powerful "unholy coalition" between developed countries reluctant to liberalize their agriculture and developing countries reluctant to liberalize their industry.

Third, the Doha negotiators have imposed on themselves a "sequencing" in the timing of the negotiations: agreements on agriculture and NAMA should precede serious negotiations in services. This sequencing reflects the widely held view among developing countries that development is associated with the growth of the goods sectors and not the services sectors. It also mirrors the intrinsic difficulties in negotiating liberalization in services (in the WTO forum or elsewhere). For instance, how to measure the concessions that a country is ready to give in some services and those that the trade partners are ready to offer in other services? In goods, the technique is well oiled: it is generally based on comparing the country's trade-weighted tariff cuts with the trade-weighted tariff cuts offered by the country's trading partners. In services, such an approach is impossible because there are no tariff equivalents of the barriers to trade in services. The constraint on sequencing has greatly contributed to the sidelining of services, a counter-productive situation for the whole Doha Round since services are such a large share of domestic GDP in all the countries.

Lastly, development has been an excuse for not requesting any commitment from the LDC—the so-called "Round for free" for the LDC. Sadly, developed countries led by the EC have supported such a view as a way to get LDC support for their own agenda. A "Round for free" imposes a heavy cost on the LDC. From an economic perspective, it deprives them of the progressive liberalization that they need to increase their growth and development. From a negotiating perspective, the "Round for free" has allowed developed countries not to offer the LDC fully free access to their own markets, but to limit their commitments to offer a "duty free-quota free" (DFQF) to only 97 per cent of their tariff lines (at the 2005 Hong Kong Ministerial). Such a proposal is of very limited interest for the LDC that export only a few goods, often covering less than 3 per cent of the tariff lines.

IV. On Track At Last (2004–08) and Improving the Negotiating Technology

The Doha negotiators have spent endless hours trying to define the "modalities" of the negotiations—that is, the broad framework of the Doha Agreement in terms of cuts in trade barriers, exceptions to agreed cuts, time schedules of the cuts, and so on. Such a debate has often been confused and seen as a waste of time. This criticism is justified only to a limited extent. It ignores the fact that the Doha negotiators have faced two unprecedented challenges.

First, they have had to relax tight initial constraints—the constraint subjecting every aspect of the trade negotiations to a divisive "development" goal, and the constraint of the Single Undertaking. They needed four years to complete these tasks—by eliminating some topics ("Singapore issues"), by generating some broadly agreed criteria for taking into account the development goal, and by progressively allowing "negative" coalitions of many small WTO members.

Second, and even more crucially, the Doha Round has been preceded by years of unilateral and preferential liberalization undertaken by many countries, mostly in industrial goods. This situation, unknown in previous Rounds, raised a key question: how to take into account these liberalizations in the Doha Round?

Both unprecedented challenges must be addressed to improve the technology of multilateral trade negotiations in order to address the following question: how to liberalize and make exceptions in a forum as large as the WTO that makes country-specific solutions inadequate and hence requires generic solutions under the form of "formulas." It took four years to provide answers to this question—starting from the early efforts to design the (imperfect) liberalization formula in agriculture in the July 2004 Framework and the 2005 Hong Kong Ministerial (both events were the turning points of the Doha Round, and witnessed the return to the pure logic of trade negotiations) to the 2008 mini-Ministerials "draft texts," which provide a complete set of formulas, often presented as the "best estimates" of what a fully-fledged outcome of the Doha Round in trade in goods could be.

The remarkable productivity of the Kennedy Round (see Table 9.1) reveals the importance of the negotiating technologies in a Round. Before the Kennedy Round, GATT negotiations on tariff cuts relied mostly on offers and requests expressed on a tariff line by tariff line basis, a very cumbersome process. The Kennedy Round made a technological leap-frog by substituting a liberalization formula to the offer-and-request approach undertaken until then, enabling the Kennedy negotiators to be the most productive of GATT history (Baldwin, 1986).

But, liberalization formulas require exception formulas that provide to each negotiating country the degree of freedom needed by its government in order to get the domestic political support necessary for the signature and the ratification of the agreement.[15] The Kennedy Round did not generate such exception formulas for two reasons. First, exceptions against exports from other developed countries have been provided *ex post* under the form of many non-tariff barriers (voluntary export restraints, subsidies, or anti-dumping measures) forcing the following Round (the Tokyo Round) to try to discipline all these measures. In addition, the Kennedy Round negotiators did not need to discuss exception formulas against developing countries' exports simply because, in sharp contrast with the current Doha Round, these countries were not interested in defending their offensive interests, while the then emerging economies (Japan, Hong Kong, Korea, Singapore, and Taiwan) realized quickly the large rents they could get from voluntary export restraints and similar measures imposed *ex post* on their exports by developed countries.

---

[15] In the Doha Round parlance, exception formulas are described as "deviations" from the liberalization formula or as "flexibilities." This section uses the term "exception formulas" for deviations defined in a systematic way and for a broad range of WTO members. It keeps the term "flexibilities" for exceptions specific to a very small group of countries or to individual countries.

The Doha negotiators have thus been the first to have to look for a whole set of liberalization *and* exception formulas acceptable to the whole WTO membership. If they could rely on the previous Rounds for designing the liberalization formula in manufacturing, they are the pioneers for the liberalization formula in agriculture and for the exception formulas for all the goods. In this respect, future WTO Rounds will have to draw lessons from the Doha negotiating technology—its successes and its failures.

Negotiations in Manufacturing (NAMA)

Contrary to a wide belief, the discussions on NAMA have been as difficult as those on agricultural products. (NAMA is an awkward expression allowing one to exclude the food industry from negotiations on industrial goods and to include it in the "agricultural" negotiations.[16]) But, contrary to the case of agriculture, the Doha negotiators have benefited from the use of an efficient liberalization formula tested by previous Rounds. Difficulties were thus concentrated on defining the desirable role of the Doha Round since this definition determines, to a large extent, the type and magnitude of the exception formulas.

The Choice of an Efficient Liberalization Formula

The 2005 Hong Kong Ministerial confirmed the use of the "Swiss formula" as the key liberalization formula in NAMA. A Swiss formula defines the post-Round tariff (T) for a product as a function of two parameters only: the initial tariff (t) imposed on the product and the reduction coefficient (c, hereafter the "Swiss coefficient").[17] More precisely, it takes the following form: $T = (ct)/(c+t)$. The Swiss coefficient has an interesting feature: it gives the highest possible post-Round tariff. For instance, a Swiss formula with a coefficient of 25 implies that the highest possible post-Round tariff will be 25 per cent.

The efficiency of the Swiss formula has three dimensions: economic (items 1 to 3 below) domestic politics (item 4) and negotiating tactics (items 5 to 8).[18] More precisely, the Swiss formula:

1. Cuts high tariffs more deeply than small tariffs, hence delivering most of the gains to be expected from freer trade (such gains come mostly from cutting high tariffs).

---

[16] Note that fish products are part of the NAMA negotiations, not those on agriculture.

[17] For simplicity's sake, what follows uses the term "tariff" as equivalent to "tariff rate."

[18] An interesting variant of this basic formula is $T = ct/(c^\alpha + t^\alpha)^{1/\alpha}$ where "α" is a "political" coefficient (to be negotiated) aiming to reduce tariff cuts in the low tariff range and hence to boost political support—a feature that could be particularly useful for negotiating on agricultural products (see below). I would like to thank Jean Messerlin for having suggested this variant.

2. Reduces the dispersion among tariffs, hence the magnitude of the distortions generated by tariffs in the domestic economy—contributing to a more efficient allocation of resources of the country.
3. Enlarges the tax base (when high tariffs are high enough to prevent or sharply inhibit imports), hence can maintain or even increase public revenues.
4. Does not change the ranking of the existing tariffs (since it cuts all of them by the same factor), hence minimizing the conflicts among domestic firms about the new tariff schedule under negotiation.
5. Makes the Swiss coefficient the only element to be negotiated because initial tariffs are given, except in case of specific tariffs (see next item).
6. Requires a shift from specific tariffs (tariffs in the domestic currency by physical quantities of the products in question) to *ad valorem* tariffs (tariffs in per cent of the world price), which are much more transparent, especially when world prices are volatile.
7. Makes it easy to calculate the post-Round tariff structure, hence reducing uncertainty for foreign and domestic negotiators and operators.
8. Allows a differentiated approach to trade liberalization by offering the possibility of modulating the Swiss coefficients according to countries' specific needs.

All these points present the Swiss formula as a good illustration of the intrinsic capacity of trade negotiations to be pro-development, without the need to make multiple specific references to a "Development Agenda." For instance, the Swiss formula combines cuts of the high tariffs (high welfare gains for the liberalizing country) and the capacity of public budget to support the domestic policy space (public investment, domestic subsidies, etc.). It removes an implicit bias against developing countries that tend to export products with lower unit values than developed countries' exports, a bias that is magnified when importing countries are using specific tariffs instead of *ad valorem* tariffs. By providing immediate, almost costless, information on post-Round tariffs, the Swiss formula is friendly to the small negotiating teams of most developing countries. Last but not least, the possibility of having different Swiss coefficients for different countries allows one to take easily into account the various levels of development of the WTO members.

That said, it took several years for many Doha negotiators from developing countries to recognize these pro-development features and to back the use of the Swiss formula.

The Painstaking Definition of the Target of the NAMA Negotiations

Should the Doha Round focus on currently applied tariffs, and cut those tariffs in order to provide "new additional market access?" Or should it focus on cuts in bound tariffs (bringing them down to the level of the existing applied tariffs) and consolidate the substantial cuts of applied tariffs already delivered by the unilateral and preferential tariff liberalizations of the 1990s and 2000s?

Negotiators from the developed countries favor the first target, while those of the developing countries favor the second goal. However, the business community of the developed countries has been more ambivalent than their own negotiators. In the early years of the Doha Round, the European business community issued a statement saying that post-Doha tariffs should not exceed 15 per cent (Businesseurope, 2001) a position *de facto* consistent with the second goal since this figure is often lower than the average current applied tariff on industrial products in many developing countries. By contrast, the US business community has been insisting on cuts in currently applied tariffs. As time has gone on, the European business community has become increasingly less comfortable with its initial position. The reason for this is the slowness of the negotiating process, which implied that tariffs lower than 15 per cent would be enforced only by 2020 (if the Doha Round were concluded by 2010) and not by 2010, as initially expected by the European business community.

That said, the 2008 mini-Ministerial draft text on NAMA appears clearly slanted towards the second target—a "binding Round." This outcome was quite predictable (Messerlin, 2007) and it would bring substantial welfare gains (see above Section III). However, as of January 2010, the question of the ultimate goal of the Doha Round was not yet completely settled because there is still a strong opposition in some quarters, in the USA mainly.

Table 9.4 summarizes the main components of the current draft text. There are four Swiss coefficients, one for the developed countries and three for the developing countries (leaving aside the LDC which have no commitment). It is important to underline that the higher the Swiss coefficient chosen by the developing countries is (the more limited the liberalization is), the more likely trade between developing countries is hurt. This is because the pre-Doha high tariffs of most developing countries protect mostly

Table 9.4 The liberalization and exception formulas in NAMA, December 2008

	Developed members	Developing members shall chose one of the three following Swiss coefficients				
A. Liberalization formula						
Swiss coefficient	Swiss8	Swiss20		Swiss22		Swiss25
B. Exception formulas	No	Option A	Option B	Option A	Option B	No
coverage (tariff lines)	exception	14% max	6,5% max	10% max	5% max	exception
coverage (trade value)	allowed	16% max	7,5% max	10% max	5% max	allowed
tariff cuts		half of the agreed formula	keeping tariffs unbound or no cut	half of the agreed formula	keeping tariffs unbound or no cut	

Source: WTO NAMA Chair, TN/MA/W/103/Rev.3, December 6, 2008.

domestic industries that operate also in other developing countries because of similar comparative advantages. In short, the Swiss formula allows each developing country to make a policy choice that can be "development friendly" or not (developed countries have a pro-development Swiss coefficient).

Figure 9.1 provides a graphic illustration of the various agreed liberalization formulas. The horizontal axis gives the range of the pre-Doha tariffs (from 0 to 270 per cent, the highest tariff observed in the six emerging economies analyzed in more detail in Table 9.5). The vertical axis gives the corresponding post-Doha tariffs for the various Swiss coefficients. It shows that the target of the European business community (no tariffs higher than 15 per cent) will not be met only if the pre-Doha tariffs in the developing countries are very high—higher than 40 per cent (with a Swiss25) or than 60 per cent (with a Swiss20).

This observation raises the following questions: how frequent and how high are the "peak" tariffs—defined as tariffs higher than 15 per cent? Answering these questions requires more detailed information provided in Table 9.5 for five major emerging economies and Korea.

Before looking at peak tariffs, Table 9.5 sheds some light on the average post-Doha tariff by country, a crude indicator of the global impact of the Doha draft text. The average post-Doha bound tariffs would be smaller by 1 to 2 percentage points than the currently average applied tariffs. In short, the view of the Doha Round as a "binding" Round should not hide the fact that the current draft text provides notable additional access to the markets of the major emerging economies. To put this result into perspective, the post-Doha average bound tariffs would range from 7.5 to 14.5 per cent, meaning that a couple of emerging economies noted would have caught up to the level of bound openness of the developed WTO members in the mid 1990s—in 1995, the EC average bound NAMA tariff was 6.5 per cent (WTO Trade Policy Review, 1998).

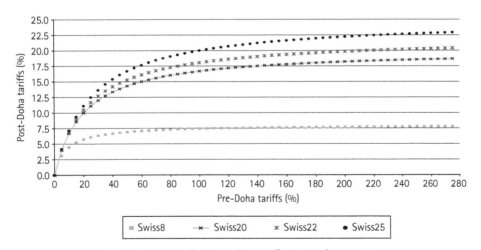

FIGURE 9.1 Comparing the pre- and post-Doha tariffs, December 2008

Table 9.5 Pre–Doha and post–Doha bound and applied tariffs, selected emerging economies

	Current tariffs [a]		Post–Doha bound tariffs		
	bound	applied	Swiss20	Swiss22	Swiss25
India					
Average tariff	36.5	15.4	12.7	13.5	14.5
Maximum tariff	150.0	100.0	17.6	19.2	21.4
Number peaks	4544	4375	70	178	2176
Average peaks	36.8	16.1	17.0	16.5	15.6
Mexico					
Average tariff	34.8	13.3	12.7	13.4	14.5
Maximum tariff	50.0	50.0	14.3	15.3	16.7
Number peaks	4564	1988	0	76	175
Average peaks	35.0	20.3	–	15.3	16.0
Brazil					
Average tariff	30.8	12.6	11.9	12.6	13.6
Maximum tariff	55.0	35.0	14.7	15.7	17.2
Number peaks	4526	1793	0	5	5
Average peaks	31.1	18.3	–	15.7	17.2

	Current tariffs [a]		Post–Doha bound tariffs		
	bound	applied	Swiss20	Swiss22	Swiss25
South Africa					
Average tariff	15.6	7.7	7.5	7.9	8.4
Maximum tariff	60.0	43.0	15.0	16.1	17.6
Number peaks	2579	1201	5	118	265
Average peaks	23.3	23.6	15.0	15.3	16.3
Indonesia					
Average tariff	35.3	6.7	12.4	13.1	14.2
Maximum tariff	100.0	80.0	16.7	18.0	20.0
Number peaks	4411	713	8	20	2976
Average peaks	36.6	16.5	15.7	16.2	15.4
Korea					
Average tariff	9.7	6.7	5.5	5.7	6.0
Maximum tariff	262.3	259.8	18.6	20.3	22.8
Number peaks	566	80	2	2	2
Average peaks	25.9	25.8	18.4	20.1	22.5

Notes: (a) Year 2001 for bound tariffs, 2004 or 2005 for applied tariffs, except for India (2001).

Source: WITS data for the years 2004 or 2005. Author's computations.

Turning to peak tariffs, Table 9.5 provides two key results. First is in terms of frequency of the peak bound tariffs. Today, such tariffs are very common in the tariff schedules of all the countries examined, except Korea. By contrast, peak-bound tariffs would become a rarity with a Swiss20 coefficient, and barely notable (less than 200 tariff lines) with a Swiss22 coefficient. They would remain a substantial factor with a Swiss25 coefficient only for India and Indonesia. Second, the peak tariffs would be drastically cut. The average peak tariff for these six countries would decrease from 25–35 per cent before the Doha Round to 15–18 per cent once the draft text was fully implemented. Even more dramatically, maximum-bound tariffs would be slashed from 55–150 per cent to 15–23 per cent. Finally, the average of the post-Doha bound peak tariffs for these countries would range from 15 to 17 per cent, except for Korea (but only for two tariff lines). In other words, the Businesseurope target of "no tariff higher than 15 per cent" is largely achieved.

The last liberalization formula targets a specific group of countries—the LDC. In 2005, the Hong Kong Ministerial called upon developed countries (and developing countries on a voluntary basis) to grant, on an autonomous basis, duty-free and quota-free (DFQF) market access for NAMA products originating from least-developed countries. Although the draft text opens up the possibility that this DFQF access should cover all the products originating from all the LDC, it makes the DFQF a mandatory commitment for only 97 per cent of all the LDC exports—a threshold that would still easily allow the maintenance of high tariffs on the few key exports of most LDC thanks to the exception formulas.

The Exception Formulas: Building "Sanctuaries" of Highly Protected Products

The Doha negotiators have been much less well inspired when designing the exception formulas. As shown in Table 9.4, such formulas are available only for the developing or emerging countries choosing the Swiss20 or Swiss22 coefficients. In each case, there are two options that have the same structure—reduced tariff cuts on a notable range of products (option A) or no cuts on a narrower range of products (option B). How to assess these two options from an economic perspective?

Option A opens the door to the use of Swiss40 or Swiss44 coefficients, meaning that the highest post-Doha tariffs on the products under option A would be 40 or 44 per cent. Such tariffs are very high. But, one should also recognize that developed countries, such as the EC or the USA, still apply similar tariffs, but on a relatively limited number of products (textiles, clothing, leather, and footwear in the USA, and chemicals and photographic products in the EC). The risk generated by option A thus flows essentially from its relatively wide coverage in terms of products (450 to 650 tariff lines in HS6 terms).

Option B allows unbound tariffs or no tariff cuts. As a result, it creates much more severe risks of highly protected "sanctuaries." Since tariffs under option B remain untouched while the rest of the tariffs will be substantially cut, tariff dispersion (possibly escalation) will be amplified—making, from an economic perspective, option B much more costly than option A for the country adopting it (and for the exporting trading partners). From a political economy perspective, such exceptions will be very difficult to eliminate in the next Rounds because vested interests will have huge incentives to keep such high barriers—sanctuaries of highly protected sectors in largely liberalized economies are very hard to eliminate, as best illustrated nowadays by the agricultural sector in developed economies).

The 2008 mini-Ministerial draft text tries to limit such risks with the so-called "anti-concentration" clause that aims at avoiding the exclusion of entire sectors from tariff cuts. This clause imposes that at least 20 per cent of tariff lines (9 per cent of the value of imports) in each HS tariff chapter will be subject to the full formula tariff reduction. However, the impact of such a clause is ambiguous to say the least for two reasons. First, HS chapters vary a lot in terms of number of tariff lines and economic importance. Second, this clause makes it easier for developing countries protecting a wide range of inefficient economic activities to continue to protect them, compared to countries protecting a narrow range of industrial activities.

In addition to these exception formulas, the draft text provides for five country-specific exceptions. However, these exceptions are much less important for the world-trade regime than the above mentioned exception formulas because they involve mostly the "negative coalitions" of small countries—and hence cover a very small share of world trade. That is:

1. LDC shall be exempt from tariff reductions (the "Round for free"), and they are only expected to substantially increase their level of tariff bindings.
2. SVE (the largest is the Dominican Republic) shall bind all their tariff lines, with an average bound tariff level not exceeding 30 per cent or less, depending on the current average bound tariff of the country.
3. The New RAM (the largest ones are Ukraine and Vietnam) shall not be required to undertake tariff reductions beyond their accession commitments. This exception has no serious negative impact because the accession negotiations have imposed on these countries moderate to low bound tariffs (for instance, the average bound tariffs after full implementation of the accession protocol will be 5.1 and 10.4 per cent in Ukraine and Vietnam, respectively).
4. The developing countries with initial low binding coverage (the largest one is Nigeria) would be exempt from making tariff reductions through the formula, but they would be requested to bind 75 to 80 per cent of their tariff lines, at an average level that does not exceed 30 per cent.
5. In order to soften the impact of multilateral tariff cuts on the exports of developing countries benefiting from preferences (in other words, in order to minimize the consequences of preference erosion), the EC and the USA would cut more slowly a limited number of tariffs on products of key interest for a few developing countries (Bangladesh, Cambodia, Nepal, Pakistan, and Sri-Lanka).

Major Pending Issues in Nama: Sectoral Initiatives and Non-Tariff Barriers

NAMA negotiations are dealing with two other main issues. First, "sectoral initiatives" aim at full liberalization in well defined industrial sectors. Sixteen sectors have been initially listed: cars, bicycles, chemicals, electronics, fish, forestry products, gems and jewels, raw materials, sport equipment, healthcare, pharmaceuticals and medical devices, hand tools, toys, textiles, clothing and footwear, and industrial machinery. Many of these sectors face serious problems, from many NTBs to addiction to anti-dumping cases to sharp downturns during the great economic crisis. As a result, in most of these sectors, the current negotiations would seem to have a hard time reaching the "critical mass" needed for concluding a deal. The sectors for which a deal still seems possible are chemicals, electronic and electric products, and environmental products.

The second major pending issue in NAMA focuses on the elimination of NTBs such as technical barriers to trade, sanitary measures, and so on, or at least on the creation of procedures capable of solving the NTB-related trade conflicts. The 2008 mini-Ministerial draft text includes legal texts submitted by various WTO members. Some of these texts focus on horizontal (non-sectoral) solutions, such as the procedures for the facilitation of solutions to NTBs. Other texts are "vertical" (*de facto* sectoral) solutions, such as how to handle NTBs in the chemical sector or how to manage labeling in textiles, clothing, footwear, and travel goods.

However, a decision on whether all these proposals on sectoral initiatives and NTBs would move forward to fully-fledged text-based negotiations remains to be taken, and probably will be taken only at the extreme end of the negotiations.

The Negotiations in Agriculture[19]

The term "agriculture" in the Doha Round is a (deliberate?) misnomer. It hides the fact that the products covered by the Doha negotiations are of two very different sorts: the farm products produced by farmers, and the food products produced by manufacturing firms, be they cooperatives or private firms. This misnomer raises a crucial—always hidden—question: who will be the ultimate beneficiary of the post-Doha protection—the farmers or the food industry? It is an important question because the interests of these two groups of producers are divergent in trade policy matters. An increase (in relative terms) of the protection of farm products would reduce the profits of the domestic food producers (it increases the relative costs of their farm inputs). A relative decrease of the protection of farm products would increase the profits of the food producers and their ability to substitute foreign farmers for domestic farmers.

Tensions between these two sectors are most visible in the developed countries where the food sector is well developed. Evidence provided below suggests that, in such

---

[19] See the companion chapter on agriculture by T. Josling (2013).

countries, the major beneficiaries of the Doha Round would be the food producers—not the small farmers despite the fact that such farmers are the only group in agriculture that public opinion in developed countries would like to see protected. This is not so surprising: the farm sector represents barely 2 to 4 per cent of the GDP in developed countries, while the share of the food sector is more than double.

By contrast, the tensions between domestic farm and food sectors are more limited in many developing countries if only because the domestic food sector is less developed. Agriculture as defined as the farm sector is the major item of the Doha negotiations for most developing countries. It represents 40 per cent of GDP, 35 per cent of exports, and 50–70 per cent of total employment in the poorest developing countries (12, 15, and 15–40 per cent, respectively, in the other developing countries). Three-quarter of the world's poorest people live in rural areas, the proportion in the poorest countries being as high as 90 per cent.

That said, only a minority of developing countries is likely to specialize in agriculture in the long run. But most of them need to go through a period where they can accumulate wealth and skills in farm-related activities, before shifting to manufacturing and services. In other words, agriculture in the Doha Round is not solely a problem for major farm exporting countries such as Argentina, Brazil, or Thailand. It also is critically important for the poorest developing countries, which are often dependent on a very small number of farm commodities, such as sugar, cotton, or rice, that are highly subsidized and protected by developed countries.

The Uruguay Round Heritage

The Uruguay Agreement on Agriculture was a breakthrough because it brought the farm and food sectors back into the WTO legal framework, after five decades of a general waiver. But it has had two severe limitations.

First, it did not significantly lower the effective level of OECD farm support below the mid 1990s. The estimated share of total support (from consumers and taxpayers to farmers in OECD countries) in farm value added was 84 per cent in 1986–88 and still 78 per cent in 2000–05.[20] The years 2007–08 witnessed a significant drop of this share to 60 per cent. But, this largely mirrors the boom in world farm prices during these two years, an evolution that has already been reversed. Meanwhile, the number of active OECD farmers has declined more sharply since the mid 1980s, and it will continue to do so in the coming years because of the age structure of farmers. As a result, the total support per farmer has risen in OECD countries, sending the wrong signal to the remaining farmers.

Second, the Uruguay Agreement on Agriculture has *de facto* granted a reverse "special and differential treatment" (SDT) to developed WTO members by allowing many exceptions for agricultural products in WTO disciplines that are routinely enforced for industrial products. The Agreement imposed generous caps on export subsidies (such

---

[20] These calculations rely on the assumption that value added amounts to 60 per cent of production at farm gates.

subsidies were not even countervailable until the so-called Uruguay "Peace Clause" lapsed in January 2004). It allowed production subsidies that have a notable impact on trade flows in amounts much greater than the amounts effectively disbursed, creating a phenomenon of "subsidy water" quite comparable to the "tariff water" observed in industrial tariffs. The Uruguay Agreement also allowed the wide use of "specific" tariffs (denominated as a fixed sum of money per unit of product, contrary to the *ad valorem* tariffs expressed as a percentage of the world price). Specific tariffs are automatically more protective when world prices decrease, that is, precisely when protection is sought by farmers. Finally, the Uruguay Agreement introduced a generous use of tariff rate quotas (restrictions combining a lower (in-quota) tariff for a specified volume of imports and a higher (out-quota) tariff for imports above this volume) despite the many shortcomings of this instrument (see below).

Initial Mistakes: From the 2001 Doha Mandate to the 2004 Framework

The Doha negotiators have split their discussions into the same three components used by the Uruguay Agreement: tariff cuts (market access), domestic support (subsidies, whether direct or indirect, such as those through guaranteed prices), and export subsidies. From 2001 to August 2003, the WTO Members spent most of their time bickering over how to define an export subsidy, which kind of formula to use for tariff cuts and for cuts in domestic support, whether the existing "boxes" (defining acceptable and non-acceptable domestic support) should be kept unchanged or redefined. Very little came out of these discussions, except for the choice of an inefficient liberalization formula (the "tiered" formula) for cutting tariffs that happened to be a major flaw (see below).

In August 2003, a few months before the Cancun Ministerial, the EC and the USA tabled a joint paper that was expected to start the real negotiations by providing figures on the cuts in tariffs, domestic support, and export subsidies that these two countries were ready to envisage. The paper did not provide these figures, and it was badly received. This EC and USA tactical mistake has had two consequences. In the short run, it disbanded the USA and EC coalition, led to the collapse of the 2003 Cancun Ministerial, and, more generally, gave a severe blow to the USA and EC leadership in the WTO. In the longer run, it changed the dynamics of the negotiating process by solidifying the "Trade G20" coalition around three major developing economies (Brazil, China, and India).[21] The various attempts by the US and EC negotiators to disband this coalition by discouraging actual or potential members to join it were short-lived, and they were counter-productive because they could not really change the coalition size (almost entirely dependent on the three core countries and their few natural allies) while creating deep resentment among the countries on which pressures were exerted.

[21] That made the WTO forum the first official witness of a process that culminated in 2009 with the emergence of the "Leaders G20" at the level of presidents and prime ministers.

The collapse of the USA–EC coalition was the starting point of a long negotiating process leading to concrete proposals, starting with the so-called July 2004 Framework. It is beyond the scope of this chapter to describe the tortuous path between the 2004 Framework and the draft text of the 2008 mini-Ministerials. Rather, what follows presents the 2008 draft text that includes solidified figures in terms of liberalization and exception formulas.

Tariff Cuts (Market Access)

Tariff cuts are the most crucial aspect of the negotiations in agriculture (Anderson, Martin, and Valenzuela, 2005). By limiting the wedge between world and domestic prices, small tariffs impose strong disciplines on domestic support (they make such a policy very expensive) as well as on export subsidies (they reduce incentives to provide them).

Unfortunately, the potentially high disciplining effect of tariff cuts has been impaired by the Doha negotiators' choice of a "tiered" liberalization formula. Table 9.6 summarizes the Doha draft text on market access. It shows the four tiers and the respective cutting formulas for two groups of countries (developed and developing).[22]

Such a formula is much less efficient than a Swiss formula from the three perspectives of international negotiations, domestic politics, and economics. From a negotiating perspective, the tiered formula requires defining many parameters (the thresholds defining the various "tiers," the tariff cuts to enforce in each tier, etc.) compared to one Swiss coefficient. This complexity is mirrored by the fact that it took as much time to define one formula in agriculture for the developing countries as compared to three in NAMA. From the point of view of domestic politics, a tiered formula has awkward discontinuities that can displace the pre-Doha and post-Doha ranking of domestic activities in terms of tariff level. Such a feature is very likely to trigger strong conflicts among the involved vested interests at the very final stage of the negotiations.[23]

Last but not least, from an economic perspective, a tiered formula cuts (much) less deeply peak tariffs and more strongly small and moderate tariffs than a Swiss formula, hence generating (much) smaller welfare gains than a Swiss formula. This is illustrated in Figure 9.2 that uses the EC tariff schedule for farm and food products as an illustrative schedule.[24]

Figure 9.2 shows that most of the post-Doha tariffs in the fourth tier will remain (much) higher than those allowed by a Swiss42 (in the hypothetical case of a developed country) or by a Swiss130 (in the hypothetical case of a developing country). The opposite situation is observed for the three first tiers. In short, a tiered formula would leave

---

[22] For simplicity's sake, Table 9.6 does not show the five-tier liberalization formula for the RAM.

[23] Such discontinuities appear at the points connecting two different tiers. For instance, a pre-Doha tariff of 49.9 per cent would be cut to a post-Doha tariff of 21.4 per cent, whereas an initial tariff of 50.1 per cent would be cut to a post-Doha tariff of 18.0 per cent. The respective figures for initial tariffs of 74.9 and 75.1 per cent would be 26.9 and 21.4 per cent.

[24] Figure 9.2 relies on the *ad valorem* equivalents of the specific tariffs, particularly numerous in agriculture. The 2008 draft text provides the detailed procedure to be followed for calculating such equivalents since they are very sensitive to many factors, particularly the reference period and exchange rate chosen.

Table 9.6 Liberalization and exception formulas in agricultural tariffs, December 2008

Developed countries		Developing countries [a]	
definition of the tiers	tariff cut (%)	definition of the tiers	tariff cut (%)

A. Liberalization formulas

Developed countries		Developing countries [a]	
1.- Time period: 5 years		1.- Time period: 10 years	
2.- tiers	tariff cuts (%)	2.- tiers	tariff cuts (%)
>75%	70.0	> 130%	47.0
50–75%	64.0	80–130%	43.0
20–50%	57.0	30–80%	38.0
0–20%	50.0	<30%	33.5

3.- Target: a minimum average cut of 54% taking into account exceptions.

3.- Target: a maximum average cut of 36% taking into account exceptions.

4.- Applies to "old" recent Members (RAM)

4.- Target for 45 small members: a maximum average cut of 24%.

B. Exception formulas

Sensitive products	Sensitive products
1.-coverage [b] 4,0%	1.- coverage [b] 5.3–8.0%

2.- tariff cuts   normal cuts reduced by 33, 50, or 66%

2.- tariff cuts   normal cuts reduced by 33, 50, or 66%

3.- sensitive tariffs are allowed to have tariffs above 100%.

3.- sensitive tariffs are allowed to have tariffs above 100%.

4.- "paid" by opening tariff-quotas amounting to 3–4% of domestic consumption.

4.- "paid" by opening tariff-quotas amounting to 3–4% of domestic consumption.

5.- coverage could be extended by 2% if more than 30% of the products are in the top band of the liberal. formula.

5.- Country-specific flexibilities for a dozen of countries (plus LDC, SVE, RAM).

6.- No country-specific flexibilities.

Special products	Special products
Not available	1.- coverage [b] 12% in 2 tranches of

7% (min) & 5% (max)

2.- tariff cuts none for 5% tranche

3.- Target: an average tariff cut of 11%

4.- Specific conditions for SVE and RAM

Special safeguard (SSG)
To be scrapped

Special safeguard mechanism (SSM)
New instrument still under discussion.

Notes: (a) RAM have their own liberalization formulas based on five tiers. (b) Coverages are defined in terms of tariff lines.

Source: WTO Agriculture Chair text, TN/AG/W/$/Rev.4, December 6, 2008.

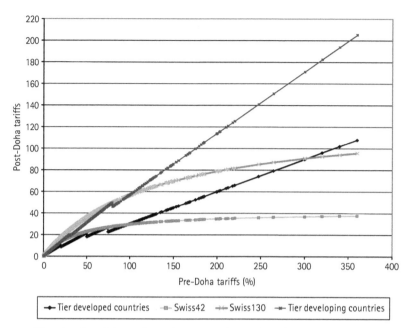

FIGURE 9.2 The tiered and Swiss formulas: a simulation based on the EC tariff schedule

bigger distortions in domestic and world agricultural markets, and hence would allow the survival of more numerous and powerful lobbies fighting for high tariffs in Rounds following the Doha Round.

That said, which sector—farm or food—would remain the most protected in the post-Doha period? A precise answer requires calculations based on the countries' tariff schedules. Table 9.7 provides the result of such detailed calculations, again taking the EC tariff schedule as an illustrative case. It clearly shows the food sector as the winner. Such a result mirrors the tariff escalation solidified during the Uruguay Round, when high tariffs were granted to food producers for "compensating" them for their expensive sources of farm products. Hence, it should also be expected for the other (developed) countries.

Table 9.7 provides several other interesting results. Its section A covers all the farm and food products. It shows the Swiss coefficients that would provide the same average tariff as the tiered formulas described in the draft text. These coefficients are substantial (28.5 for developed countries and 87 for developing countries) with, interestingly, the Swiss coefficient for developed countries not too far away from the highest Swiss coefficient in NAMA for developing countries. As noted above, the Swiss formula would rebalance tariff cuts—cutting more food tariffs and fewer farm tariffs, a result more consistent with government pledges to protect small farmers than the Doha draft text. Section B of Table 9.7 focuses on the "peak" tariffs imposed on the farm and food products in the EC schedule of tariffs. It shows that peak tariffs are relatively similar for both types of products, but are much more frequent in the food sector than in the farm sector (65 per cent of the number of tariff lines vs. 25–30 per cent, respectively). Interestingly,

Table 9.7. The Post-Doha winners: the food vs. the farm sectors

	Number of tariff lines	Uruguay Bound tariffs [a] (%)	Post-Doha bound tariffs [b]			
			Developed country		Developing country	
			tiered formula	Swiss28.5	tiered formula	Swiss87
A. All tariffs						
Farm commodities	117	19.7	7.8	7.8	12.2	12.7
Horticultural products	273	13.6	6.0	7.3	8.7	10.2
Semi-processed food products	488	12.6	4.9	5.3	7.8	8.2
Processed food	1120	32.6	12.3	11.9	20.0	19.4
All farm and food products	1998	24.3	9.4	9.4	15.0	15.0
B. Peak tariffs (tariffs higher than 15 per cent)						
Farm commodities	42	48.9	18.8	17.3	30.0	30.1
Horticultural products	73	34.5	14.1	14.8	21.6	23.5
Semi-processed food products	93	51.9	18.5	17.0	31.6	30.1
Processed food	711	47.8	17.5	15.7	29.1	26.9
All farm and food products	919	47.2	17.4	15.8	28.8	27.1

Source: Table 6 (formulas) and the EC tariff schedule used as an illustrative schedule. Author's computations.

the Swiss formula would have roughly the same rebalancing effect on the peak tariffs than on all the agricultural tariffs.

Turning to the exception formulas, Table 9.6 above summarizes the three main types of exception formulas included in the 2008 draft text: sensitive products, special products, and the SSM.

Sensitive Products

All WTO members would be entitled to define "sensitive" products for political reasons, up to 4 per cent (developed countries) to 5.3–8 per cent (developing countries) of the tariff lines (roughly 80 to 160 tariff lines at HS6 digit). They are eligible for reduced tariff cuts, but these reduced cuts have to be "paid" for by the introduction of tariff rate quotas (TRQ) amounting to 3 to 4 per cent of domestic consumption. It is hard to predict the tariff lines that will be selected. Those with the current highest out-quota tariffs seem good candidates. But, in developed countries, the competition between vested interests will be strong because the number of tariff lines under TRQ will decrease between the post-Uruguay and the post-Doha regimes (for instance, from 251 to 71 in the EC case). Things are even more complicated because there are additional constraints (for instance, the provisions on tariff escalation or on tropical products, see below) to be taken into account. Simulations for the EC suggest that the EC would still be able to achieve the target imposed by the draft text of a minimum average tariff cut of 54 per cent, although the average tariff on sensitive products would only decrease from 112 to 86 per cent (Kutas, 2010).

At first glance, TRQ look like an attractive device because they give the impression of allowing a careful management of the trade opening process. But the reality is quite the opposite, as already witnessed by the TRQ regime introduced under the Uruguay Agreement. The major flaw of TRQ is the difficulty in predicting their ultimate impact because it requires a knowledge of supply and demand reactions that are rarely available to market operators. This uncertainty is compounded by the lack of adequate data at the disaggregated HS6 level. For instance, negotiators have been forced to lay down a complex procedure to calculate the "domestic consumption" (the parameter on which to apply the thresholds of 3 to 4 per cent) at such a disaggregated level when only imports and exports are available, whereas production figures are available at a much higher level of aggregation.

Such an uncertainty opens the door to surprising outcomes. First, TRQ could be a device freezing market entry (contrary to their stated goal) as has been observed under the Uruguay Agreement. Second, if the domestic demand becomes smaller than the TRQ quota, domestic prices reflect the low in-quota tariff, and domestic producers are more exposed to freer trade than expected by the negotiators. Third, TRQ could also favor an increase of imports, including (surprisingly) in the out-quota shares such as in the EC bovine or poultry meat under the post-Uruguay regime (Kutas, 2010). Lastly, if the domestic demand exceeds the quota, domestic prices reflect the high out-quota tariff, generating huge rents. But, who would get such rents? The answer depends on several parameters, but foreign exporting firms or domestic importing (food) firms—not domestic farmers—are the most likely recipients of such rents.

Special Products

Only developing WTO members would be entitled to define special products when they feel that trade liberalization of these goods would affect the country's "food security, livelihood security and rural development." The potential coverage for such products is quite wide—up to 12 per cent of the tariff lines, roughly 240 tariff lines at HS6 digit level. Special products are eligible for much reduced tariff cuts, or even no tariff cut at all. They are not to be "paid" for by TRQ.

Special Safeguard Mechanism

Last but not least, the Doha draft text introduces a last type of exception formula under the form of a conditional SSM made available only to developing and recently acceded countries. As any safeguard, the SSM requires the definition of the threshold allowed to trigger the measure and the type and magnitude of the safeguard measure. Discussions on these issues have failed (Wolfe, 2009), and have become the official reason for the collapse of the whole Doha negotiations in the July 2008 mini-Ministerial.

By contrast, the Doha draft text scraps the SSG created by the Uruguay Agreement for developed Members, hence contributing to the elimination of the "reversed SDT" enjoyed by the developed countries under the Uruguay Agreement.

A Provisional Conclusion on Exception Formulas

Combined with the tiered formula, all these exception formulas would shape a very uneven Doha liberalization. Farm and food products with low or moderate pre-Doha tariffs and not subjected to one of the three exception formulas would be liberalized. But, a substantial number of products—those with pre-Doha high tariffs or subjected to one of the three exception formulas—would remain tightly protected, particularly in the case of the developing countries (because of the special products and SSM formulas). In short, the Doha Round Agreement based on the current draft text is unlikely to open markets of critical interest for the WTO members. In particular, trade between developing countries will remain highly constrained.

Domestic Support

The 2008 draft text introduces two layers of cuts in trade-distorting support. First are the cuts in the three different "boxes" inherited from the Uruguay Round Agreement, that is:

- The Amber Box ("aggregate measure of support" or AMS) covers the domestic support that is the most distorting because it is tightly linked to prices (price support mechanisms) and/or to production.
- The *de minimis* Box covers measures of similar nature as those of the Amber Box, but in smaller amounts (they should not exceed 5 to 10 per cent of farm production).
- The Blue Box includes domestic support considered as less distorting than the Amber Box because it is subjected to some restrictive conditions (such as imposing production limits curbing potential over-production on direct payments based on the number of animals or on the area planted).

All the cuts defined within each of these boxes are defined at two levels: the country's aggregate agricultural output, and the level of the country's outputs of specific products. This two-level system aims at preventing the circumvention of the Doha disciplines on the global domestic support through transfers between different products.

The second layer of cuts in domestic support is based on a new concept created by the Doha negotiators—the "overall trade-distorting domestic support" (OTDS), which is the sum of the Amber, *de minimis*, and Blue Boxes. Hence, it defines cuts in the permitted amounts of the three boxes combined.

All these cuts are achieved by a mix of tiered formulas (the EC being the only country in the highest tier, the USA and Japan pertaining to the second tier, and the other developed and a few developing countries pertaining to the lowest tier) and caps that they should not to go beyond. Rather than describing all these cuts and caps in detail (see the 2008 WTO Agriculture Chair text for a detailed description) it is more interesting to get a sense of the impact of the Doha draft text on the OTDS and on the Amber Box (which constitute the bulk of domestic support) in the case of the EC and of the USA, the two major providers of subsidies.

Table 9.8 presents the bound commitments taken by the EC and USA in the 1995 Uruguay Agreement, the effective support granted in 2004, and the estimated support for 2013. It suggests three major observations. First, the base level used by the Doha negotiators is the Uruguay bound commitments, as in the tariff negotiations. Second, the applied level of support in 2004 is much lower (roughly half) than the bound level agreed in the Uruguay Round. In other words, the "water" in EC and US domestic support to agriculture is as substantial as the "tariff water" of the core developing and emerging countries in NAMA. Third, the EC and US Doha commitments defined by the 2008 draft text represent roughly a cut by half of the applied domestic support in 2004, but they are in line with the applied domestic support estimated for 2013. In sum, the Doha Round would essentially bind the EC and US farm policies expected to prevail by 2013.

This last observation requires an important caveat. It does not mean that the whole support to EC and US farmers will be sharply cut, but only subsidies tightly linked to prices and quantities. The EC and USA remain free to shift Amber and Blue support to the Green Box. Such a shift would be an improvement to the extent that Green subsidies have a smaller impact on agricultural trade than the Amber and Blue support. But, the magnitude of this smaller impact remains a debatable matter. After all, Green subsidies would still induce farmers to produce more than in the total absence of support. In short, it is harder to assess the true liberalization impact of the Doha draft text on farm support than it is to assess the impact of the Doha draft text on NAMA.

Expressing domestic support in percentage of agricultural output is interesting because such an expression is relatively similar to a tariff. Based on the average value added in agriculture for the years 1995–2000, Table 9.8 shows that the Doha commitments would reduce the share of domestic support in agricultural output value to 12–14 per cent in the USA and EC—a percentage close to the NAMA average tariff of emerging economies such as Brazil or India (see Table 9.5). These estimates suggest that the criterion of "a comparably high level of ambition in market access for Agriculture and NAMA" imposed by the negotiators in the context of a "Doha Development Agenda" has been met.

The December 2008 draft text includes many other provisions on domestic support, but examining them in detail goes beyond the scope of a chapter. What follows flags those that are the most important.

Table 9.8 The liberalization formulas in farm support, December 2008

	Support in billion US dollars [a]		Support in % of agricultural output [b]	
	US	EC15 [c]	USA	EC15
1. Overall Trade-Distorting Domestic Support				
The Uruguay bound commitments	55.0	149.0	47.4	70.6
Effective OTDS (2004)	23.0	78.0	19.8	37.0
Estimated OTDS (2013) [d]	12.4	30.0	10.7	14.2
The Doha draft text (December 2008)				
Base levels	48.2	149.0	41.6	70.6
Formula cuts (in %)	70	80	-	-
Commitments	14.5	29.8	12.5	14.1
2. Amber Box (Aggregate measure of support, A , AMS)				
The Uruguay bound commitments	19.1	90.7	16.5	43.0
Effective Amber Box (2004)	13.0	42.0	11.2	19.9
Estimated Amber Box (2013) [d]	6.9	24.3	5.9	11.5
The Doha draft text (December 2008)				
Base levels	19.1	90.7	16.5	43.0
Formula cuts (in %)	60	70	-	-
Commitments	7.6	27.2	6.6	12.9

Notes: (a) Figures for the EC are expressed in Euros in the Chair text, and are translated in US dollars on the basis of an exchange rate of US$1.35 per Euro prevailing in December 2008. (b) Average value added in agriculture for the years 1995–2000. (c) Past figures for the OTDS for the EC 27 are roughly 106% higher than those for the EC15. OTDS for 2013 is estimated for the whole EC27. (d) Support for 2013 is estimated by Kutas (2010) for the EC and by Orden, Blandford and Josling (2011) for the USA.

Source: WTO Agriculture Chair text, TN/AG/W/$/Rev.4, December 6, 2008. Author's computations.

- Almost all the commitments define precise time schedules for implementation and substantial down-payments for the first year of implementation. The implementation time schedule and down-payments differ greatly for developed and developing countries, mirroring the special and differential treatment enjoyed by developing countries.
- Caps on post-Doha support are defined with respect to the support actually provided in 1995–2000 (the product specific Amber Boxes) or to the amount of production (*de minimis* box, Blue Box).
- The Uruguay Blue Box (direct payments based on the number of animals or on the area planted are subjected to production limits ensuring to curb somewhat over-production) would be complemented by a new Blue Box (direct payments based on a fixed amount of production in the past).

The domestic support component of the draft text deserves three final remarks. First, the "Green" Box (support deemed not to distort production or prices or, at least, to cause minimal distortions) provisions will be tightened for developed countries, but made laxer for developing countries in order to allow such countries to purchase farm prod-ucts for stockpiling, fighting hunger, and rural poverty, and/or buying from low-income farmers (even at prices higher than market prices).

Second, there are special provisions for cotton, a product that has attracted signifi-cant media attention since the early 2000s. Trade distorting domestic support for cotton (Amber Box) would be cut more substantially than for the other agricultural products while the Blue support for cotton would be capped at one-third of the normal limit for other farm products.

Finally, there are provisions in favor of the farmers of certain developing countries that have indirectly benefited from OECD domestic support via preferential access to protected OECD markets, as best illustrated by Mauritius (sugar) or certain African or Caribbean countries (bananas) in the EC markets. Such preferential access has allowed these farmers to sell their products on the EC markets at European prices that were much higher than world prices. The Doha draft text allows for a slower lib-eralization for products with such longstanding preferences. The list of the products concerned is still under discussion.[25] Such provisions are ambiguous, to say the least, from a development perspective. Ending past preferences by establishing a (transi-tory) preferential regime disregards the crucial fact that the farmers of the developing countries free riding on OECD support have been favored for decades to the detri-ment of the competing farmers of the developing countries excluded from such OECD domestic support.

Export Measures

Export measures have been among the least difficult topics to negotiate. An (incom-plete) draft text imposing their complete elimination by 2013 was one of the main out-comes of the 2005 Hong Kong Ministerial. There are several reasons for such a situation. First, export subsidies per se have been almost exclusively granted by the EC (85 per cent of all export subsidies in the mid 1990s) hence putting a lot of pressure for reform on just one WTO member. Second, export subsidies have a bad reputation in many cor-ners: they are seen as a source of unfair international competition, as inefficient in terms of food aid, as tightly related to public monopolies (state trading enterprises (STE)), and so on. As a result, they have been under constant attack from all sides, from foreign exporters to NGOs to domestic and/or foreign consumers, to domestic competition authorities, and so on. Finally, they are often perceived as subsidies targeted to large food multinationals—most observers forget that, in fact, the multinationals "pay back"

[25] In the same vein, in December 2009, an agreement between the EC and the Latin American producers of bananas that did not have preferential market access to the EC during the last 60 years has put an acceptable end to this five decade-long dispute.

these subsidies to farmers when they buy farm products at prices (much) higher than world prices.

Under all these pressures, the EC has undertaken a unilateral liberalization of its export subsidies since the mid 1990s. EC export subsidies have decreased from 8 billion Euros (the EC commitment in the Uruguay Round Agreement) to roughly 3 billion in 2003 and less than 2 billion in 2006—mirroring again a huge "subsidy water." In 2007–08, EC export subsidies had almost disappeared because of the boom in world prices in farm products, while less than 0.6 billion Euros for 2009 (half the 2008 amount) have been included in the EC 2009 budget.

However, the 2008–09 economic crisis witnessed a reversal of this long term decline, particularly in dairy products where the EC accounts for a large share of international trade (from 20 to 35 per cent, depending on the product). Another factor raises some doubts on the ease with which a total elimination of export subsidies would be achieved by 2013: if the total amount of export subsidies has declined, the quantities of exports still eligible has declined more slowly, suggesting the survival of a strong demand for such an instrument in some farm niches.

That said, the main difficulties met by the 2008 draft text were related to the definition and treatment of export measures deemed "equivalent" to export subsidies, such as food aid, export credits, guarantees and insurance, exporting state trading enterprises, export restrictions, and taxes. Until recently, such instruments have not represented a substantial amount of money. Available estimates suggest that the share of exports subsidized by such instruments represent 2 (EC) to 5 (USA) per cent of total agricultural exports, and that the subsidy equivalent of all these instruments was smaller than 7 per cent (Hoekman and Messerlin, 2006).[26]

The 2008 draft text confirms the elimination of export subsidies by 2013, and it imposes the same provisions on export credits with repayment periods beyond 180 days. Moreover, it aims to ensure the progressive convergence of disciplines to be imposed on export credits, export credit guarantees, or insurance programs with repayment periods of 180 days or less (these programs should be self-financing, reflect market consistency, and be of a sufficiently short duration so as not to effectively circumvent commercially oriented disciplines). It requires the elimination of the trade distorting practices favored by the STE, with future disciplines curbing potential monopoly power (which could circumvent the disciplines on export subsidies) government financing, and under-writing of losses. Lastly, the 2008 draft text aims at eliminating commercial displacement beyond an adequate level of food aid through the creation of a "safe box" for *bona fide* food aid in case of emergency, and through the adoption of effective disciplines on

---

[26] These small figures are explained by the fact that the subsidy equivalent of an export credit is not the total amount of credit granted, but only the subsidized component created by the difference between the market and preferential interest rates. Similarly, what is at stake with the exporting STEs is not their whole activities, but the export subsidy equivalent provided by government financing and/or underwriting of losses.

in-kind food aid, monetization, and re-exports so that there can be no loopholes for continuing export subsidization.

Major Pending Issues in Agriculture

The above description of topics included in the 2008 draft text is not exhaustive. There are, among others, specific provisions on tariff escalation (when tariffs on processed products are higher than those on raw materials, with a view to reducing such escalation when it is large enough to hinder processing for export in the country producing the raw materials) tariff simplification (with a view to minimizing the number of specific tariffs) tropical products (with a view to having faster and deeper tariff cuts on such products), TRQ administration (shall TRQ be possible only for products already under a TRQ regime, and what will be the TRQ regime if it could be imposed on new products), and inflation (a topic covering price increases that could make void committed limits and those that could create difficulties for developing countries facing sharp rises in food prices). As these provisions deal with complex issues, they tend to be written in general terms that still remain largely open to discussion in the months to come.

Besides this host of provisions, there are two major pending issues. As noted above, the conditions for using the Special Safeguard Mechanism have not been agreed on yet. The reason why negotiations have failed—the possibility, or not, to impose a SSM duty higher than the post-Doha bound tariff for the product in question—does not make much sense. Such a possibility is routinely used in anti-dumping, anti-subsidy, and safeguard measures in NAMA. For instance, it is not uncommon that anti-dumping duties on industrial products are ten times higher than bound tariffs.

The other major pending topic is geographical indications (GI), which are ruled by the Uruguay TRIPs Agreement, but mostly concern agricultural products.[27] They witness the opposition of the WTO members (the so-called W52 sponsors led by the EC) that favor a high level of GI protection based on a multilateral and mandatory register for wines, spirits, and an undefined number of additional products, and the WTO Members that favor a voluntary database on GI. Of course, the stricter the mandatory conditions imposed by the register, the stronger the implicit degree of monopoly created by the register.

GI is a typical case of inertia in trade negotiations. This topic was already part of the Uruguay negotiations. It continues to be tabled by the EC even though it is questionable that a strong GI regime is in the EC's own interests. For instance, the last decade has given ample proof that a strong GI regime did not help the French wine sector.

---

[27] Article 22.2 of the Uruguay TRIPs Agreement requires members to provide the legal means (i.e., GIs) to prevent the use of any means *"in the designation or presentation of a good that indicates or suggests that the good in question originates in a geographical area other than the true place of origin in a manner that misleads the public as to the geographical origin of the good,"* as well as any use *"which constitutes an act of unfair competition."* In contrast with patents, GIs do not aim at promoting innovation, but at giving information on "reputation."

Under the strong French GI regime for wines, some French vineyards have performed very well, but others very poorly—suggesting that "something else" other than strong GI is key for success in the modern wine business. Evidence from the last decade suggests that GI can have severe perverse effects (freezing the production technology, generating over-production, deteriorating quality, generating systematic misinformation, and ignoring changes in consumers' tastes).[28] By contrast, evidence suggests that what counts is the existence of large wine companies (such as in Champagne) capable of meeting an ever changing demand while delivering the required level of quality and reputation via trademarks.

V. Uncharted Territory: Services

Until 2008, the Doha negotiations in services showed little progress, despite the fact that services represent 50 to 70 per cent of the GDP of the WTO members, and are of prime importance for running an efficient economy.

The one-day "Signalling Conference" during the July 2008 mini-Ministerial was the first event suggesting that things could move. Negotiators from 31 countries listed their offers to open domestic services markets, and their requests to get better access to foreign services markets. The day was unanimously considered a success, many participants showing an unexpected appetite for negotiating improved market access in services.

However, since then, negotiations in services seem to be back in limbo, a situation that raises two different questions. Are there some intrinsic difficulties in negotiating in services that could explain such slow progress, beyond the mere sequencing constraint? If there are such intrinsic difficulties, what then could be the role of a multilateral Round in opening markets in services?

The Intrinsic Difficulties in Liberalizing Services

A frequently mentioned source of intrinsic difficulties is the fact that services are generally protected by regulations, rarely by tariffs or barriers that would be easily measurable such as tax differentials. A second source of difference, largely ignored but probably more crucial, is the relative weakness of the political economy of liberalization in services compared to what happens in goods.

---

[28] The negative consequences of strict GI have been recently illustrated by a fraud lasting over two years (on 18 millions of bottles), in which the over-production of syrah and merlot noir in Southern France (Aude) has been sold in the USA markets as pinot noir (*Le Figaro*, 20 February 1, 2010, Cahier 2, page 1).

Regulations vs. Tariffs

As services are rarely protected by measurable barriers, negotiations in services cannot be based on liberalization formulas comparable to those available for industrial or agricultural products. There are two additional difficulties.

First, protection in services is embedded in regulations the main initial objective of which was not to protect domestic services providers against foreign firms, but rather to protect certain domestic providers against other domestic providers. For instance, regulations limiting the entry of foreign retail firms running large outlets are the late by-product of the decision, taken two or three decades ago, to protect domestic small shop-keepers from domestic large stores. A corollary of this key feature is that most of the gains from more liberalization in services would come from non-discriminatory market opening, that is, liberalization with respect to foreign *and* domestic services providers.

Second, opening markets in services is rarely limited to the mere dismantlement of the existing barriers. Rather, it generally requires the adoption of a flow of pro-competitive regulatory reforms in the future. As a result, negotiating market access to foreign markets in services is a bet on the willingness and the capacity of the trading partners to deliver such a sequence of future reforms. This process is made even more complicated because countries compete with each other on regulatory matters in a dynamic way, with the improvement of the regulatory framework in a services sector by a WTO member triggering improvements of the regulatory framework of the service in question by other WTO members. Of course, all these future interactions cannot be easily written down in a schedule of concessions on a year by year basis. Rather, trust in the reform capacity of the trading partners becomes a crucial factor deciding the willingness of a country to negotiate.

WTO negotiations are not well equipped to deal with such a fluid and dynamic process. They are handicapped by the fact that the WTO is a wide forum where members are extremely heterogeneous in their capacity to deliver credible flows of regulatory reforms in the future. In this context, unilateral or preferential liberalizations seem more suitable.

However, the WTO handicap in terms of negotiating new market access in services does not extend to the binding of existing market access since binding relies on regulatory reforms already in place, and on the proven willingness to open the markets in the past. In short, the dominant role of regulations seems simply to slant WTO negotiations in services more systematically towards a "binding" approach that is the case in goods.

The Political Economy of Liberalization in Services

However, there is evidence that even the consolidation of past unilateral liberalizations has not attracted much attention from the Doha negotiators (Gootiiz and Mattoo, 2009; Messerlin and van der Marel, 2009). Which could then be the additional factor(s) inhibiting WTO negotiations on binding unilateral or preferential liberalizations?

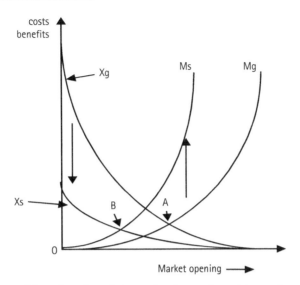

FIGURE 9.3 Costs and benefits of market opening in goods and in services

What follows suggests that the usual political economy of export interests (eager to push for opening the domestic markets in order to get foreign markets more open) and import-competing interests (eager to keep domestic markets protected) is markedly weaker in services than in goods.

Figure 9.3 presents a very simple framework for comparing the political economy of the costs and benefits of trade liberalization—the balance of forces between domestic exporters and domestic import-competing interests—in the case of goods (g curves) and of services (s curves). The Xg curve shows the declining benefits that exporters of a product face as and when a market is opening. It illustrates net benefits, that is, the opportunities lost by the exporters when the market is closed minus the difficulties to be faced by these exporters when they get effective access to the market. The Mg curve illustrates the rising costs that the import-competing producers of a product face when their domestic market is opening. Hence, in the case of goods, the political "equilibrium" between the two lobbies (exporters and import-competitors) is A. What follows uses the Xg and Mg curves and the A point as benchmarks for assessing what happens in services.

In the case of goods, Figure 9.3 generally shows domestic exporters of certain goods (say steel) and domestic import-competing firms producing other goods (say clothing). In the case of services, Figure 9.3 would more often illustrate the situation within the same service sector for several reasons: services are more prone to differentiation than goods, services negotiations are more systematically sectoral than those in products (if only because it is easier to compare offers and requests in the same sector), and so on.

Looking first at the export side, several reasons reduce net benefits from market open-ing in services compared to goods (for a description of these reasons within a negotiat-ing framework, see Adlung (2009)). These reasons prevail at the different stages of the opening process—negotiation, market entry, and comparative advantages.

First, negotiating costs tend to be higher in services than in goods. Trade negotia-tors have to invest in the knowledge of the service sector at stake and to learn about the regulations, contrary to goods where they need to know only the level of the bound and applied tariffs. In such a context, they often have to work with the agencies in charge of regulating and monitoring a service, and these agencies are unlikely to facilitate negotia-tions that could challenge their power or threaten their survival.

Second, the market entry phase requires the exporters of the service to adjust their strategies to the regulations and practices in their export markets. The available empiri-cal literature suggests that such costs are (much) higher in services than in goods (Shepherd and Miroudot, 2009) once again making exporters of the service less sup-portive of market opening.

Lastly, comparative advantages are fuzzier to grasp in services than in goods, even though services liberalization tends to be sectoral. For instance, liberalizing distribu-tion services between France and Germany may induce German retailers, efficient in medium-sized outlets (such as Aldi), to enter the French retail market. To do so, Aldi has to build medium-sized outlets in France, to hire French staff, and adapt to the whole French regulatory environment, meaning that Aldi may lose some of its comparative advantages in terms of capital costs, labor skills, and favorable regulations in Germany. This is quite different from what happens generally in manufacturing, where exporting goods do not require building new factories and hiring workers in the export market, and adjusting whole operations to abide by foreign regulations (a German car exporter would expand its German units of production, increase its German workforce, and would continue to operate mostly under German law). All these risks are compounded by the fact that, services liberalization being often sectoral, Aldi may be exposed to counter-offensives from French competitors in another segment of the retail market (for instance, the French retailer, Carrefour, may try to enter the German hypermarket seg-ment) precisely when Aldi tries to enter the French market.

To sum up, the three above described forces go in the same direction—reducing the net benefits from market opening. As a result, the Xs curve for exporters in services lies below the benchmark Xg curve for goods.

Turning to the import side, the Ms curve for services would lie above the Mg curve for goods for reasons echoing those on the export side. First, import-competing ser-vice providers will need to face adjustment costs in their domestic market. But, because of the more frequent sectoral feature of services liberalization, they may also have to pay costs for entering some segments of the foreign exporters' market. Second, services often involve regulatory agencies that are likely to support the import-competing vested interests. Thus, the two forces described above go in the same direction: the Ms curve for import-competing services lies above the Mg curve for goods.

The political economy global equilibrium in services would be located at the left of point A (say B) meaning a more limited market opening (see the horizontal axis) in services than in goods. Note that, on the vertical axis, the equilibrium level of costs and benefits in services associated with point B could be higher or lower than the level associated to the point A.[29]

What Then Could Have Been Reasonably Expected From The Doha Negotiations?

The Report on the successful 2008 "Signalling Conference" does not provide any precise information on the offers and requests evoked (it does not even mention the names of the countries specifically interested in each service). However, it sheds some qualitative light on the intensity and scope of the services to be liberalized among WTO members that are summarized in the two first columns of Table 9.9.[30]

Column 1 gives a sense of how many participants manifested a serious interest in negotiations during the Signalling Conference. Column 2 focuses on the interest shown for two modes: mode 3 on the right of establishment and mode 4 on the movement of natural persons. These two modes were the most contentious during the Uruguay Round negotiations (WTO Secretariat, 2000) and, during the Doha Round negotiations, services providers have repeatedly underlined their crucial role. Altogether, the two columns reveal a willingness to negotiate, with a high number of participants interested in each service, a high occurrence of offers and requests on mode 3, and even a willingness to include mode 4 (by far the most contentious aspect of international negotiations in services because it is often misperceived as a source of illegal immigration).

Columns 3 and 4 rely on an older source of information, namely the EC and US offers tabled in 2005 before the Hong Kong WTO Ministerial. These offers were notoriously limited, reflecting the highly uncertain state of negotiations in manufacturing and agriculture at this time. However, even if these offers do not provide adequate information on the magnitude of the offers tabled in 2008, they are useful because they give a first sense of the services in which the EC and the USA were already ready to move in 2005. This is particularly the case for the EC offers that tabled notable additional commitments, be it in terms of widening (binding the most recent ECMS at the level of EC 1995 commitments) or deepening (offering new commitments for the EC as a whole in terms of market access or national treatment).[31] The US offers present a less clear picture, with no notable proposals for two-thirds of the services sectors, as shown by column

---

[29] Interestingly, the fact that the political economy may be weaker in services than in goods has no clear-cut *ex post* impact on the adjustment costs to liberalization. For instance, the labor force that French distributors have to fire could be easily re-employed by the German distributors.

[30] Table 9.9 relies on Messerlin and van der Marel (2009).

[31] The information in columns 3 and 4 relies on calculated indicators measuring how much the EC and the USA were willing to move (in terms of widening and deepening and for the four modes of supply) for each service listed in their offers. Weights have been given to each mode of supply by service in order to reflect their relative economic importance when aggregating the various modes. These weights are those used by the World Bank's World Trade Indicators for calculating the bound-level regulatory constraints.

Table 9.9 Revealing the willingness to negotiate in services

Services	Signalling Conference 2008 NbrWTO Mmmbers 1	GATS mode underlined 2	2005 offers: market opening EC 3	moves US 4	Size of sectors (US$ bn) 5	Crisis resilience 6
Business Services	Virtually all	4	yes	no	4,918	High
Communication Services	Substantial	3	yes	yes	737	High
Distribution Services	Substantial	3	yes	no	3,809	-
Environmental Services	Substantial	3	some	no	-	-
Construction & Related Engineering	Substantial	3&4	some	no	1,715	High
Transport Services	Substantial	3	some	some	1,282	Low
Financial Services	Notable	3	yes	small	1,770	Low to High
Educational Services	Notable	3&4	no	yes	1,444	-
Tourism and Travel Related Services	A few		yes	no	774	Low
Health and Social Services	A few	3&4	no	no	1,483	-
Recreational, Cultural & Sporting	-	-	small	no	1,217	-
Energy	Substantial	3	—	some	-	-

Notes: Column 1 reports the number of WTO members having expressed interest in negotiating the service mentioned. The TNC Chairman's Report includes a separate paragraph for audiovisuals, with two WTO members expressing interest. Column 2 reports the explicit mention of modes 3 and 4 for the service at stake. Columns 3 and 4: see text. Column 5 gives the total size in billions of US$ (PPP) in the USA, EC, and Top 8 group markets by service. Note that Recreational Services includes the Personal, Community and other Social sector, while Educational Services include R&D services. Column 6 reports the resilience of services to the current economic global crisis as reported by Mattoo and Borchert (2009). Crisis resilience is low in financial services, and high in insurance.

Source: Columns 1 and 2: TNC Chairman's Report of July 30, 2008; Column 3: WTO (2005a); Column 4: WTO (2005b); Column 5: OECD (2006); Column 6: Mattoo and Borchert (2009).

4. Finally, it should be underlined that the market opening moves in columns 3 and 4 would not necessarily occur in the entire broad sector: they may be observed in some sub-sectors only.

Columns 5 and 6 provide important information from an economic perspective. Column 5 gives the market size of the services listed in billions of US dollars (at the purchasing power parity exchange rates) for a group of ten countries.[32] Market sizes are a key factor determining the magnitude of consumer welfare gains and of firms' opportunities, hence the likelihood and magnitude of the negotiation success. That the size of the agricultural and industrial markets for the ten countries amounts to roughly US$7,900 billion gives a good sense of the size of the market at stake in services.

In particular, Table 9.9 suggests three services sectors (business services, communications, and distribution) as a particularly rich potential source of negotiating successes.

VI. Concluding Remarks

Since 2007, the world economy has been under great stress—first because of burgeoning commodities prices, then because of the "great economic crisis". This turbulence raises two questions with a quite different time line.

The Great Economic Crisis and the Doha Round

The great fear of a significant slippage in protection during the peak of the crisis did not materialize—(Messerlin, 2010). During these 18 months, none of the key countries that could have easily (from a WTO legal perspective) increased its applied tariffs to the higher bound levels (see Table 9.2) has done so.[33]

This happy surprise could have had a positive impact on the Doha deal. By not increasing their applied tariffs up to their (much) higher bound tariffs during the current crisis, the key emerging and developing economies have shown their revealed preference: they have kept unchanged their applied tariffs for their *own* benefit. This behavior undercut their claim that they provide a huge favor to developed countries when cutting their bound tariffs, hence that they should get generous exception formulas. Consequently, negotiators from the key developing and emerging countries should have abandoned such a claim, and agreed on tightening somewhat the exception formulas, particularly the option B in NAMA.

However, it takes two to tango. Such a restraint on their current requests by the key developing and emerging economies should have been met by a similar restraint by the developed WTO members on their own requests. In particular, developed countries should have abandoned their claims for additional market access (deeper cuts in the applied tariffs than those already agreed by the developing and emerging economies) and agreed on the Doha Round as the "binding Round."

---

[32] The ten countries (Brazil, Canada, China, EC, Japan, India, Korea, Mexico, Russia, and the USA) produce more than 80 per cent of the value added in the dozen or so services sectors with available information in National Accounts. For details, see Messerlin and van der Marel (2009).

[33] The only country showing signs of reversal was Russia (not yet a WTO member).

It remains that restraints in agriculture and NAMA negotiations from both sides could not have been enough to conclude the Doha Round. There was a need for an additional, mutually beneficial, booster that only services can provide. Services can attract the support of the business community much more than any other conceivable trade-related issue (such as intellectual property rights, norms, non-tariff barriers, public procurement, rules, etc.). They are the largest source of opportunities for firms for three reasons: their sheer size (50 to 75 per cent of GDP), their ubiquitous presence (even manufacturing or agro-business firms have a significant share, often about 50 per cent, of their turnover in services), and their high level of protection—services are on average twice more protected than goods (Shepherd and Miroudot, 2009). The sheer binding of the services liberalization of the last 15 years would have provided sizable gains for consumers all over the world. It could have been provided by starting exploratory talks on services in a much smaller forum than the WTO, before repatriating them in the WTO if these talks were promising (Messerlin and van der Marel, 2009). For instance, such talks could be limited to the largest world economies—roughly ten, a group small enough to keep negotiations manageable and large enough to cover more than 80 per cent of world production in services. Such talks could start by a transatlantic, transpacific (APEC), or Eurasian dialog—it does not really matter because as soon as such a dialog starts, dynamic forces will expand it to the other, not yet involved, large economies. Indeed, there are current efforts to initiate such negotiations in Geneva. But, it is far from clear whether the process will be based on a discriminatory or a non-discriminatory approach.

Why the Doha Round Failed

Five years after the promising 2008 Ministerial, it is now clear that the Doha Round has failed. Have the many, often very narrow, points discussed in this chapter been the reason for such a failure?

It does not seem to be the case. Trade negotiators are skilled experts in managing such detailed hurdles. Something else—much bigger—had to occur to stop the Doha process.

First was the political blindness of the business sector (particularly in the USA) which preferred "no agreement to a bad agreement." The problem with such a motto is that it does not define what a bad agreement is. Is a pragmatic "binding" Doha Round a bad agreement? Business' answer was yes. But, there is a popular say that "better is the worst enemy of good." By asking too much, there was a risk of getting nothing. As the crisis is still far from resolved in 2013, the bomb of protectionist pressures unbalanced by some progress in liberalization is still with us (Bouet and Laborde, 2009).

Second, and probably even more crucially, Spring 2008 was a decisive moment when the US negotiators decided to put aside the WTO track and to "go preferential." In September 2008, the USA jumped in and begun to lead the negotiations on the Trans-Pacific Partnership, conceived as a "platinum" trade agreement, a kind of WTO version 2.0. The key reason for such a choice was the rivalry between the USA and China on what should be the world global governance—its key disciplines and regulations. The Doha Round failure was simply the first collateral casualty of this rivalry.

References

Adler, M., Brunel, C., Hufbauer, G. C. and Schott, J. J. (2009), 'What's on the Table? The Doha Round as of August 2009' Working paper 09-6. Peterson Institute for International Economics, Washington, DC.

Adlung, R. (2009), 'Services Negotiations from a WTO/GATS Perspective: In Search of Volunteers' WTO Secretariat. WTO, Geneva.

Anderson, K., Martin, W. and Valenzuela, E. (2005), 'Why Market Access is the Most Important of Agriculture's "Three Pillars" in the Doha Negotiations' Trade note 26. World Bank. Washington, DC.

Baldwin, R.E. (1986), 'Toward More Efficient Procedures for Multilateral Trade Negotiations' *Aussenwirtschaft* 41(Heft II/III): 379–94.

Baldwin, R. (2009), 'The Great Trade Collapse: Causes, Consequences and Prospects.' London, VoxEU.org.

Blustein, P. (2009), 'Misadventures of the Most-Favored Nations: Clashing Egos, Inflated Ambitions and the Great Shambles of the World Trading System.' New York: Public Affairs.

Bouët, A., and Laborde, D. (2009), 'The Potential Costs of a Failed Doha Round' Discussion paper 886. IFPRI, Washington, DC.

Businesseurope (formerly UNICE) (2001) <http://www.businesseurop.eu> (search for the page on WTO).

Gootiiz, B. and Mattoo, A. (2009), 'Services in Doha: What's on the Table?' Mimeo. August. World Bank. Washington, DC.

Groser, T., 2007, 'Saving the Doha Round: The Need for Political Leadership' Conference on "Saving the Doha Round and Delivering on Development," Ministry of Trade, New Delhi. Mimeo. July 4.

Hoekman, B., and Messerlin, P. (2006), 'Removing the Exception of Agricultural Export Subsidies' in Anderson, K., and Martin, W. (eds.) *Agricultural Trade Reform and the Doha Development Agenda*. Basingstoke, UK: Palgrave Macmillan.

Hoekman, B., Martin, W., and Mattoo, A. (2009), 'Conclude Doha: It Matters!' Policy research working paper. World Bank, Washington, DC.

Hoekman, B. and Nicita, A. (2010), 'Assessing the Doha Round: Market Access, Transaction Costs and Aid for Trade Facilitation' *Journal of International Trade and Economic Development*, 19(1): 65–79.

Ismail, F. (2009), 'Reforming the World Trade Organization: Developing Countries in the Doha Round.' CUTS International and Friedrich Erbert Stiftung, Geneva.

Josling, T. (2013), 'Protection, Subsidies and Agricultural Trade' in Arvid Lukauskas, Robert M. Stern, and Gianni Zanini (eds.), *Handbook of Trade Policy for Development*. Oxford: Oxford University Press (forthcoming).

Kutas, G. (2010), 'Impact of the Doha Round on the European agricultural sector' PhD thesis. SciencesPo, Paris.

Laborde, D., Martin, W., and van der Mensbrugghe, D. (2009a), 'Implications of the 2008 Doha draft agricultural and non-agricultural market access modalities for developing countries' Mimeo. IFPRI/World Bank, Washington, DC.

Laborde, D., Martin, W., and van der Mensbrugghe, D. (2009b), 'Measuring the Benefits of Global Liberalization with a Consistent Tariff Aggregator' Mimeo. IFPRI/World Bank, Washington, DC.

Mattoo, A. and Borchert, I. (2009), 'The Crisis-Resilience of Services Trade' Policy research working paper, World Bank: Washington, DC.

Messerlin, P. (2007), 'The Doha Round: Where Do We Stand?' Working Paper. September. <http://gem.sciences-po.fr>. Groupe d'Economie Mondiale (GEM) at SciencesPo, Paris.

Messerlin, P. (2008), 'Walking a Tightrope' German Marshall Fund and Groupe d'Economie Mondiale (GEM) Working Paper. June. Washington, DC, and Paris.

Messerlin, P. (2010), 'A Significant Slippage in Protectionism? Not Yet' in Evenett, S., Hoekman, B., and Cattaneo, O. (eds.) *Effective Crisis Response and Openness: Implications for the Trading System*. World Bank and CEPR. Washington and London.

Messerlin, P., and Van der Marel, E. (2009), 'Leading with Services: The Dynamics of Transatlantic Negotiations in Services' GEM Working Paper. September. <http://gem. sciences-po.fr>. Groupe d'Economie Mondiale (GEM) at SciencesPo. Paris.

Orden, D., Blandford, D., and Josling, T. (2011), *WTO Disciplines on Agricultural Support: Seeking a Fair Basis for Trade*. Cambridge: Cambridge University Press

Polanski, S. (2006), 'Winners and Losers: Impact of the Doha Round on the Developing Countries' Carnegie Endowment Report, Washington, DC.

Shepherd, B. and Miroudot, S. (2009), 'Leveraging in Services to Consolidate the Global Economic Recovery: An Agenda for the G20' GEM policy brief. July <http://gem. sciences-po.fr>. Groupe d'Economie Mondiale (GEM) at SciencesPo, Paris.

Wallenberg, M. (2006), 'Business and Trade Liberalization, address to the ECIPE Launch Conference' November 7, ECIPE, Brussels <http://www.ecipe.org>.

Wolfe, R. (2009), 'The Special Safeguard Fiasco: The Peril of Inadequate Analysis and Negotiations' *World Trade Review*, 8(4): 517–44.

World Bank (2002), 'Global Economic Prospects 2005: Making World Trade Work for the World's Poor.' World Bank, Washington, DC.

World Bank (2005), 'Global Economic Prospects 2005: Trade, Regionalism and Development.' World Bank, Washington, DC.

CHAPTER 10

PROTECTIVE REGIMES AND TRADE REFORM

WENDY E. TAKACS

I. INTRODUCTION

GOVERNMENTS have often attempted to protect or encourage particular industries using a combination of trade policy instruments, including import tariffs, export taxes, import and export quotas or licensing regulations, trade subsidies, domestic content requirements, and compensatory export requirements. These protective regimes often became very complicated, with overlapping and sometimes contradictory policy measures piled on top of one another as governments attempted to achieve numerous objectives simultaneously, including stimulating manufacturing production, encouraging backward linkages, reducing imports to save foreign exchange, and promoting exports.

Some of the measures, such as high tariffs and quantitative import restrictions, encouraged domestic production in an industry by increasing its product's domestic price. Other measures, such as export controls on raw material inputs to the industry, protect the industry by keeping the cost of its inputs low. Yet other measures, such as regulations requiring the use of domestically produced inputs, or requirements that firms export to earn foreign exchange to pay for their imported inputs, increase the cost of inputs to the firms. The cumulative net effect of a web of overlapping and sometimes contradictory policy measures can sometimes be difficult to untangle.

This chapter attempts to clarify the economic impact of certain policy instruments often employed as part of protective regimes to promote particular activities or particular sectors of the economy: export controls on raw material inputs used by the industry or sector, domestic content requirements specifying minimum percentages of inputs that must be sourced locally, compensatory export requirements requiring the industry to export to earn foreign exchange to pay for imported inputs, and, of course, import restrictions on the product produced by the industry.

Governments adopt *export controls on raw materials* to protect natural resources from perceived or threatened over-exploitation, to moderate high prices of products produced using the raw materials as inputs, or to promote domestic processing of native raw materials to encourage exports of "higher value added" products. An export restriction that constrains exports of a raw material will drive down the price of that material on the domestic market and encourage production in industries that use the material as an input.

Domestic content (or local content) requirements force firms to use a predetermined minimum amount or minimum proportion of locally produced components when they assemble products for sale on the domestic market. Domestic content requirements are usually imposed by governments in an attempt to foster economic development by encouraging "backward linkages" to broaden manufacturing and industrial activity. But these regulations increase production costs for firms subject to them because imported components are normally less expensive (and possibly of better quality) than the locally produced inputs that firms are required to use instead.

Governments that impose domestic content requirements often also impose "*compensatory export requirements.*" These regulations mandate that firms using imported inputs must export to earn sufficient foreign exchange to "compensate" for a proportion of the foreign exchange spent on imported inputs. Complying with compensatory export requirements also increases production costs for firms, because they often must export at a loss to export sufficient quantities of components or products to satisfy the export requirements.

Export controls on raw materials, domestic content requirements, and compensatory export requirements all affect production costs by either decreasing or increasing the cost of inputs for firms. Any policy measure that decreases or increases the cost of inputs into a production process will increase or decrease the *effective rate of protection* to that production activity. To provide an analytical framework for the different protective regimes discussed here, Section II explains the concept of the effective rate of protection, presents a partial equilibrium graphical approach to the analysis of effective rates, and provides illustrative numerical examples.

Section III focuses on export controls on raw material inputs. It explains the impact of raw material export controls on the price, production, and exports of the controlled raw material input and the processed output that uses the raw material as an input. It also investigates the impact of raw material export controls on total foreign exchange earnings from exports of both the raw material and the higher value added processed good. The discussion also identifies the losses to raw material producers, the gains to both firms processing raw materials and recipients of export licenses, and the sources of the efficiency losses ("dead-weight losses") that constitute the net welfare cost of raw material export controls. The analysis is then applied to a case study of export licensing restrictions on raw cashmere in Mongolia. This example reveals the potential magnitude of the losses and income transfers involved. It also demonstrates that export controls on raw materials imposed to promote higher value added exports may fail to achieve the objective of increasing the country's total export earnings.

Section IV focuses on a quite different type of protective regime involving domestic content and compensatory export restrictions. It explains why these regulations benefit domestic firms producing inputs, but increase input costs for firms producing final goods. Whether the final goods producers benefit from or are hurt by the entire protective regime depends upon the severity of the barriers to imports of the final good that virtually always accompany domestic content restrictions. Section IV also presents a case study of domestic content and compensatory export restrictions on the automobile industry in the Philippines, an example of an industry that was subject to both of these requirements simultaneously.

An understanding of how the various components of a complicated protective regime interact is important in designing a trade reform program. If some parts of the protective regime are abolished or liberalized while others remain unchanged, effective rates of protection can change in unexpected and unintended ways. If import restrictions on inputs are liberalized without simultaneously liberalizing restrictions on final products, effective rates of protection to protected processing activities increase, rather than decrease. This is the opposite of the intention of a trade liberalization program. In contrast, if protection to final products is liberalized without also liberalizing measures that keep input prices high, effective rates of protection to processing activities can drop drastically or even become negative. Section V points out problems that can arise during trade reform programs if the government follows a "piecemeal" approach and liberalizes some restrictions, but not others that affect the same industry. This final section summarizes the implications of the analysis in this chapter for the design of trade reform programs.

II. Nominal and Effective Rates of Protection

Discussion of the concepts of nominal and effective rates of protection provides a useful starting point for analyzing the impact of complicated protective regimes because it focuses attention on the importance of the relationship between the degree of protection to the output of a production process and the rate of protection to intermediate inputs used to produce that final good. A graphical approach to analyzing the effective rate of protection introduced by Corden (1971) provides a convenient framework to identify the magnitude of the efficiency losses and income transfers among consumers, the government, producers of inputs, producers of final goods, and recipients of import or export licenses (if quantitative restrictions or licensing requirements are used to restrict imports or exports).

Nominal and Effective Rates Defined

The *nominal rate of protection* is the percentage by which trade restrictions or trade barriers increase the domestic *price* of a product above the world market price. The simplest and most straightforward example is an *ad valorem* tariff in which the amount of duty owed the government is a percentage of the value of the product. For example, if the tariff rate on a product is 50 per cent, and its world market price is $100, the importer will have to pay 50 per cent of $100 or $50 to import the good, so the full cost of the product to the importer will be $150 (the $100 to buy it plus the $50 import duty). If importing itself is a competitive industry the domestic price will equal the cost of $150 so the percentage increase in the price will exactly equal the percentage tariff rate. For example, if the only trade barrier limiting imports of cloth is a 20 per cent import tariff, the price of cloth in the internal market would be expected to be 20 per cent above the world market price, and the *nominal* rate of protection to the cloth industry would be 20 per cent.

With other forms of import restrictions, such as import quotas, import licensing, technical barriers to trade, costly customs procedures, or advance import deposit requirements, the nominal rate of protection is less clear than in the case of a simple *ad valorem* tariff. However, each of these non-tariff trade restrictions will push up the cost of importing or otherwise increase the domestic price of the imported good. The *nominal rate of protection* resulting from these non-tariff trade barriers will equal the percentage by which the domestic *price* exceeds the world market price because of the restriction.

In contrast, analysis of the *effective rate of protection* focuses on *production processes* rather than on particular products. For example, the various stages of production of a cotton dress begin with the *growing* of the cotton, then proceed through successive production processes: the *ginning* of the cotton to separate the fiber, then the *spinning* of the fiber into yarn, then the *weaving* of the yarn into cloth, and finally the *cutting and sewing* of the cloth into a garment. Analysis of the *effective rate of protection* focuses on the *value added* in each stage of the production process. The *value added* at a stage of production is the difference between the value of the output of that process and the total value of the *intermediate inputs* used as inputs in that stage of production. Intermediate inputs are products that are produced by one stage of production that become inputs into the next stage. For example, the production of yarn uses fiber as an intermediate input. The weaving of cloth uses the yarn as an intermediate input. The production of a garment uses cloth as an intermediate input, and probably also thread, buttons, and zippers.

By definition, the *effective rate of protection* is the percentage by which *value added* in a production process exceeds what value added would have been under free trade as a result of the protective regime. To determine the effective rate of protection to *cloth weaving*, one must compare the value added in cloth weaving under the set of trade policies that exist, with what the value added in cloth weaving would have been under free trade. The percentage difference between these two amounts of value added is the effective rate of protection.

What is important for the effective rate of protection is the impact of the protective structure on the difference between the price of cloth and the price of the intermediate input, yarn. Trade barriers that raise the price of the output (while the prices of inputs remain the same) increase the value added in processing (and increase the *effective* rate of protection to the processing activity). Trade barriers that raise the prices of inputs

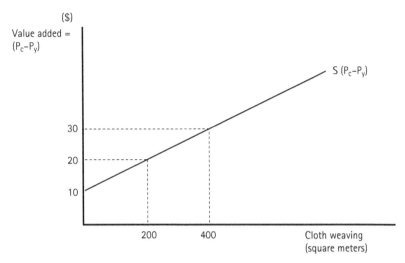

FIGURE 10.1 Supply of 'weaving' as a function of value added

(while the price of the output remains the same) decrease the value added in processing (and decrease the *effective* rate of protection to the processing activity).

Links Between Input and Output Markets

It is reasonable to assume that the firms weaving cloth into yarn will be willing to weave more yarn into more cloth the higher the value added in the process of cloth weaving (that is, the larger the difference between the price of a unit of cloth (P_C) and the cost of the yarn needed to produce a unit of cloth (P_Y)). Figure 10.1 shows this relationship. The line labeled $S(P_C-P_Y)$ is the supply curve of weaving activity as a function of the value added in weaving (P_C-P_Y). In the case shown in Figure 10.1, if the value added in the weaving process were $20 per square meter, the weaving industry would be willing to weave 200 square meters of cloth. At a higher value added per unit of $30, the industry would be willing to weave 400 square meters of cloth.

Figure 10.2 develops a partial equilibrium supply and demand diagram for yarn and for cloth that captures the input–output relationship and the supply of weaving activity.[1] One important feature of Figure 10.2 is that the horizontal axis simultaneously measures the quantity of cloth output and the quantity of yarn input. The "units" of cloth and of yarn are chosen so that one "unit" of yarn is used to produce one "unit" of cloth. If 5 grams of yarn are used as an input to produce 1 square meter of cloth, then the "units" of yarn are defined as 5-gram packages of yarn, and the "units" of cloth are defined as 1 square meter. In this framework, by definition, one unit of yarn is used to produce one

---

[1] This approach is based on Corden (1971) chapters 2 and 3.

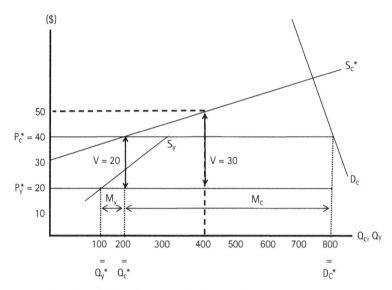

FIGURE 10.2 Markets for cloth and yarn under free trade

unit of cloth. On the horizontal (quantity) axis, the number "100" would simultaneously measure 100 square meters of cloth and 100 "5-gram packages" of yarn.

Free Trade Equilibrium

Suppose that the country in question is a small country that cannot influence world prices, and that the country follows a free trade policy in that it imposes no restrictions on imports or exports of either yarn or cloth. The free trade equilibrium prices, quantities produced and demanded, and quantities traded are shown in Figure 10.2. Suppose that the price of yarn in the world market (P_Y^*) is \$20, and the price of a unit of cloth in the world market (P_C^*) is \$40. The supply curve of the domestic yarn industry is shown by the curve S_Y. At the free trade price of yarn of \$20, domestic yarn producers would supply 100 units of yarn. Under free trade, the cloth weavers can obtain as much yarn as they like at the world market price of \$20. They can buy at that price from domestic yarn producers or import yarn from the world market.

The supply curve of cloth under free trade, S_C^*, shows the quantity of cloth the cloth weavers would supply at various prices for cloth (provided that the price of yarn remains at the free trade price of \$20). S_C^* is constructed by adding the vertical measure of the value added (from Figure 10.1) at which cloth weavers would be willing to weave each quantity of yarn into the equivalent quantity of cloth to the underlying price of yarn (P_Y^*=20). For example, we know from Figure 10.1 that cloth weavers would be willing to weave 400 units of yarn into 400 units of cloth if the value added per unit were \$30. Given a yarn price of \$20, the value added would be \$30 if the price of cloth were \$50. Thus at a price of cloth of \$50, domestic cloth weavers would supply 400 units of cloth (using, as inputs, 400 units of yarn). If the world market price of cloth (P_C^*) were $40, while the world market price of yarn remains at $20, then the value added in weaving under free trade $V^*=P_C^*-P_Y^*=20$. Figure 10.1 shows that if the value added were $20, the weaving industry would weave 200 units of yarn into 200 units of cloth, so the quantity of cloth supplied would be 200.

The demand curve for cloth, D_C, shows that the quantity demanded by domestic consumers under free trade at the world price of $40 would be 800. The quantity supplied by the domestic cloth weavers would be 200. The quantity of cloth imported must then be 600, equal to the difference between the quantity demanded of 800 and the quantity supplied of 200. Given that the units have been defined so that one unit of yarn is used to produce one unit of cloth, under free trade the domestic weavers would demand 200 units of yarn to weave the 200 units of cloth, 100 of which would be produced by the domestic yarn industry and 100 of which would be imported.

Tariffs on Yarn and Cloth and the Effective Rate of Protection to Cloth Weaving

Trade restrictions that change output prices or input prices will cause value added to deviate from what it would be under free trade and generate a positive (or possibly negative) effective rate of protection. To illustrate, suppose as a starting point that a 50 per cent *uniform* tariff rate is imposed on imports of both yarn and cloth. The domestic price of yarn would increase to $30 (=$20+ $20*0.5), and the domestic price of cloth would increase to $60 (=$40+$40*0.5). Figure 10.3 illustrates the impact of the higher cost of yarn, due to the tariff on yarn, on the supply curve of cloth. The behavior of the weavers in terms of the quantity of yarn they are willing to weave into cloth, as a function of the value added in cloth production, (shown in Figure 10.1) remains the same. But the increase in the cost of yarn needed to produce one unit of cloth from $20 to $30 implies that the supply of weaving as a function of the value added must be added vertically to a yarn price of $30 rather than the free trade yarn price of $20. The $10 increase in the cost of yarn needed to produce a square meter of cloth shifts the supply curve of cloth upward by $10. The tariff on *yarn* shifts the supply curve for *cloth* upward to S_C'. Along the higher S_C' supply curve, at a price for cloth of $60, the weaving industry would weave 400 units of yarn into 400 units of cloth.

The *effective* rate of protection is calculated as the percentage increase in *value added* as a result of the protective structure. The uniform 50 per cent tariff structure increased value added in cloth weaving to $30, which is the difference between the $60 price of cloth with the 50 per cent tariff on cloth and the $30 cost of yarn with the 50 per cent tariff on yarn. Recall that value added in cloth weaving under free trade was $20. The effective rate of protection, the percentage increase in value added due to the tariff structure, would thus be (30–20)/20= 10/20=0.5 = 50 per cent. Figure 10.3 illustrates that the cloth weaving industry would expand production from 200 to 400 due to the higher value added provided by the protective regime. This example also illustrates the general rule

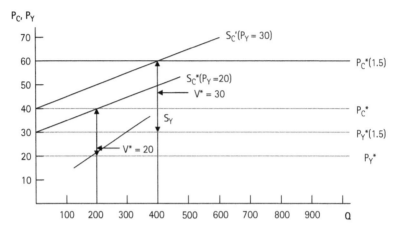

FIGURE 10.3 Supply of cloth and yarn, 50 per cent uniform tariff

that if the nominal tariff rate on the output equals the nominal tariff rate on the inputs, the effective rate of protection equals the nominal tariff rate.

Figures 10.4, 10.5, and 10.6 illustrate the impact of various other combinations of yarn and cloth tariff rates on the cloth supply curve, the effective rate of protection to cloth weaving, and the amount of cloth supplied by the domestic industry. In Figure 10.4, a 50 per cent tariff on yarn shifts the cloth supply curve up to $S_C'(P_Y=30)$ as in the previous figure, but in this case the 100 per cent tariff on cloth increases the domestic price of cloth to $80. Under this tariff structure, value added in cloth weaving would be $50, and the effective rate of protection would equal (50–20)/20=150 per cent. In this example the tariff on cloth (100 per cent) is higher than the tariff on yarn (50 per cent) and as a result the effective rate of protection (150 per cent) exceeds the nominal tariff rate on cloth (100 per cent). The general rule is that if the tariff on the output exceeds the tariffs on the inputs, the effective rate of protection exceeds the nominal tariff rate. Note also that the increase in the effective rate of protection to cloth weaving encouraged greater processing of yarn into cloth and increased cloth production.

Figure 10.5 illustrates the opposite case in which the tariff on cloth is lower than the tariff on yarn. A 100 per cent tariff on yarn increases the domestic price of yarn to $40, and shifts the cloth supply curve upward to $S_C'(P_Y=40)$. The 50 per cent tariff on cloth increases the domestic price of cloth to $60. The result is a value added in cloth production of $20, the same as under free-trade. The effective rate of protection would be ($20–$20)/$20=0. Cloth production would be the same as under free trade, because the effective rate of protection is zero. The tariff on cloth (50 per cent) is lower than the tariff on yarn (100 per cent) and the effective rate of protection (0 per cent) is lower than the

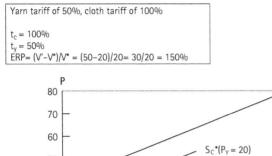

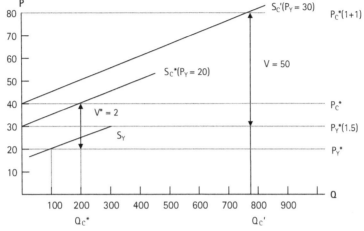

FIGURE 10.4 Supply of yarn and cloth, ERP

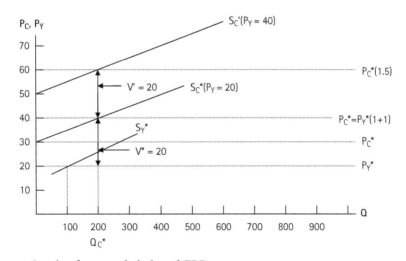

FIGURE 10.5 Supply of yarn and cloth and ERP

nominal tariff rate on cloth (50 per cent). This example illustrates the general rule that if the tariff on the output is lower than the tariff on the inputs, the effective rate of protection is less than the nominal tariff rate on the output.

Figure 10.6 depicts an extreme case in which the tariff rate on cloth is so much lower than the tariff rate on yarn that the effective rate of protection to cloth weaving becomes negative. The 50 per cent tariff on cloth increases the domestic cloth price to $60, but the 150 per cent tariff on yarn increases the domestic yarn price to $50. Under this tariff structure the value added in cloth weaving would be $10, lower than under free trade. The effective rate of protection would be ($10–$20)/$20 = –1/2 = negative 50 per cent. The negative effective rate of protection reduces the production of cloth below its free trade level.

The important point to note from the graphical representations of these numerical examples is that an increase in the cost of inputs used to produce a good will shift the supply curve of the good upward by the amount of the increase in the price of the inputs per unit of output. Policies that increase the cost of intermediate inputs to firms will shift their supply curves upward (and leftward), thus will decrease the supply of goods using those intermediates as inputs and discourage their production. Moving in the opposite direction, policy measures that reduce the cost of inputs to an industry will shift the supply curve of the final product downward by the amount of the decline in the cost of the input package and thus encourage production of the final good. The following sections use this analytical approach to investigate the impact of trade policy

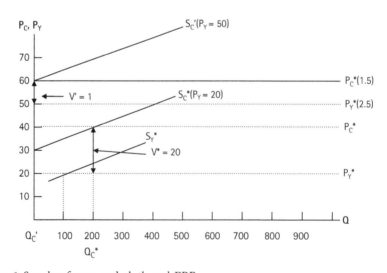

FIGURE 10.6 Supply of yarn and cloth and ERP

measures often used by governments of developing countries or transitional economies (and sometimes used by industrial countries) to protect particular industries or sectors of the economy.[2]

III. Export Controls on Raw Materials

Background

Governments may have a variety of objectives that lead them to impose export controls on raw materials. They may be interested in conserving natural resources or avoiding a detrimental social impact of high prices for products made from the raw materials. For example, the United States imposed export controls on logs in the mid 1970s out of concern that high lumber prices would reduce homebuilding and increase unemployment in the construction industry. Another reason a government may impose an export control is to influence the world market price of the export good. If a country is a significant supplier of the product in the world market, the government may limit exports to decrease total world supply and thus drive up world market price and improve the country's terms of trade. Governments may also limit or even ban exports of raw materials to encourage domestic processing of the materials so that the country exports higher value added products and earns more foreign exchange. This section examines the case in which the government's main objective is to promote domestic processing and increase export earnings.

Export controls can take the form of export taxes, export bans, export quotas, or export licensing regulations. The analysis below presents the case of an export quota, but the major economic impacts will be similar to other forms of export restrictions. First, Figure 10.7 examines the impact of an export quota on the domestic price, domestic production, and domestic consumption of an export good. The analysis is then extended to the more complicated case of the impact of a raw material export quota not only on production and exports of the raw material itself, but also on production and exports of the processed good. The goal is to explain the distortions and costs of protection that arise in both the raw material and final good markets when raw material exports are restricted. The last subsection applies this method of analysis to a case study of Mongolian export controls on raw cashmere.

---

[2] As noted, the analysis is based on a partial equilibrium approach that abstracts from inter-industry effects and assumes fixed input–output coefficients. Taking these considerations into account requires a general equilibrium approach that may yield quite different measures of effective rates of protection. In this connection, see Deardorff and Stern (1984), who use a computational general equilibrium (CGE) model to estimate changes in the structure of protection resulting from trade liberalization in the Tokyo Round of multilateral negotiations.

Impact of an Export Restriction

An export restriction (export tax, export quota, or restrictive export licensing) lowers the price of the export good on the domestic market, reduces the quantity produced, and increases the quantity demanded in the domestic market. Suppose that a country exports logs to the world market, but it is a small exporter, so the quantity that it exports will not affect the world market price. The internal market for logs in the country is shown in Figure 10.7.

The demand curve for logs on the part of domestic users of logs is D_L. S_L is the domestic log suppliers' supply curve. Suppose that the world market price of logs is P_L^*. At that price, the quantity of logs supplied by the logging industry (Q_L^*) would exceed the quantity of logs demanded internally D_L^*. The difference would equal the quantity exported under free trade (X_L^*).

Suppose that the government imposes a "binding" export quota restriction that does not allow exports to exceed a quantity X_L', less than the X_L^* units that had been exported under free trade. Once the quota is imposed, the equilibrium price of logs in the domestic market will be determined where the difference between the quantity demanded and the quantity supplied equals the amount that can be exported, X_L'. The price of logs will fall in the domestic market until a new equilibrium price P_L^D is reached where $Q_L'-D_L'=$ X_L'. As the price falls from P_L^* to P_L^D, the quantity demanded increases from D_L^* to D_L' and the quantity produced by the domestic industry falls from Q_L^* to Q_L'.

The export quota makes domestic producers worse off because they sell less at the lower price. The welfare impact on the producers is a loss of producer surplus equal to area *aefh* in Figure 10.7. Domestic consumers, on the other hand, gain from buying at the lower domestic price, so their consumer surplus increases by area *abgh*. Area *abgh* represents a transfer from producers to consumers. Area *cdfg* represents "quota rents,"

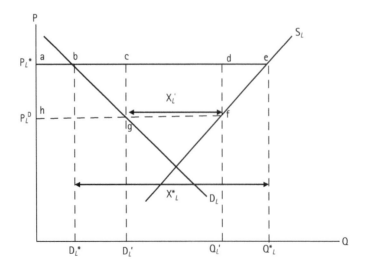

FIGURE 10.7 Impact of an export restriction

the windfall gain to whoever is able to export the limited quantity that can be exported under the quota restriction. The individuals or firms able to export could buy logs in the domestic market at the lower price P_L^D and sell them in the world market at the price P_L^*. This area *cdfg* could also be thought of as "export tax equivalent revenue" because it would equal the export tax revenue the government would have received if the export restriction had been a tax of $(P_L^*-P_L^D)$ per unit exported.

Exactly who receives the benefits from these windfall gains or quota rents will be determined in large part by how the quota limitation is administered. One possibility would be that the export quota is administered on a "first-come first-served" basis, so that those exporters who arrive at the border first will be able to export, until the quota ceiling is reached. Additional exports would not be allowed once the quota limit is reached. A "first-come first-served" rule can create a chaotic situation as potential exporters race to the border at the beginning of each quota period. For this reason governments usually administer export quotas by issuing export licenses or permits to selected exporters. The quota rents then tend to go to the recipients of export licenses because they have the right to export a predetermined amount of the restricted good.

The portion of area *aefh*, the loss to producers, represented by areas *bcg* and *def* are the net social welfare losses ("dead-weight losses") created by the export restriction. Area *def* is the dead-weight loss on the production side that arises because producers respond to the falling price of logs by reducing output. If there had been no quota restriction they would have sold each of the extra logs produced between Q_L' and Q_L^* for the world market price, P_L^*, a price higher than what it would cost to produce each of these extra units along the supply curve. This dead-weight loss area *def* represents a sacrifice of profits to the producers, but also represents a loss to the country because the country could have obtained a higher price on the world market for each extra unit exported than the real resource cost of producing it. Area *bcg* represents the dead-weight loss on the consumption side, because the export quota diverts the units between D_L^* and D_L' (which under free trade would be exported) toward the domestic market. Buyers in the domestic market would only have been willing to pay an amount equal to the height of the demand curve for each these units. Domestic buyers do not value these units as highly as the price at which they could have been sold in the world market. The net welfare cost of the export quota to the country imposing it is the sum of the dead-weight losses *bcg+def* plus any portion of the windfall gains *cdfg* that does not go to nationals of the country imposing the export quota.

Impact of an Export Restriction on an Input on the Markets for Inputs and Final Products

Export controls on raw material or intermediate inputs increase the effective rate of protection to processing industries by lowering the prices of inputs, thus increasing the value added in processing the inputs to produce a final product. They also create distortions and efficiency losses. Export controls on raw materials benefit processing firms at the expense of the producers of the raw material inputs. This section develops a model that links the markets for inputs and final products to identify the nature of the transfers and net costs generated by export restrictions on inputs.

Suppose that a raw material input I (such as raw cashmere, the application considered in the next section), is used to produce a final product F (such as cashmere sweaters). Suppose that the input and the processing industries are perfectly competitive and that the country in question is too small to have any influence on world prices, so it can buy or sell both the input and the output in the world market at given prices.

To link the markets for the input and the final good, as in the discussion of the effective rate of protection above, define the units of the input and the output so that one unit of input is used to produce one unit of the final product. Figure 10.8 shows the equilibrium in the markets for both the input and the final product under a free trade regime. The lower diagram is the market for the input. The units along the horizontal axis measure the quantity of "packages" of inputs, where each "package" is the amount of raw material used to produce one unit of the final product. The price measured along the vertical axis is the price per "package" of inputs. The supply curve of the perfectly competitive producers of the raw material input is S_I. If the price of the raw material input in the world market is $P_I{}^*$, the raw material producers would supply $Q_I{}^*$.

The upper diagram shows the market for the output. The willingness of the producers to process the raw material into the final product as a function of the value added in processing is shown by the curve $S(V)$ in the upper diagram. The processing industry's supply curve of the final good under free trade would be the vertical sum of the $S(V)$ curve and the cost of the input needed per unit of final product under free trade ($P_I{}^*$). This final product supply curve under free trade is labeled $S_F{}^*$. It lies exactly $P_I{}^*$ above the $S(V)$ curve at all output levels. Assume again that the country exporting the final good is small and cannot affect the given world market price of the final good of $P_F{}^*$. If the demand curve for the final product on the domestic market is D_F, and there are no trade restrictions on the final good, then the quantity demanded of the final product by consumers under free trade would be $D_F{}^*$, the quantity produced would be $Q_F{}^*$, and exports of the final good would be $X_F{}^*$.

Given that the units of the input and output are defined so that one unit of input is needed to produce one unit of output, if $Q_F{}^*$ units of final product are produced, then the same number of units of input are demanded by the processing industry, so, in the lower diagram, $D_I{}^*$ units of input would be demanded by the domestic processing industry under free trade. The difference between the units of input produced under free trade ($Q_I{}^*$) and the units demanded by the processing industry ($D_I{}^*$) would be the quantity of the raw material input exported ($X_I{}^*$). Under a free trade regime, export earnings from raw material exports would be $P_I{}^*X_I{}^*$ (the rectangular area $qdru$ in the lower diagram of Figure 10.8) and export earnings from final goods exports would be $P_F{}^*X_F{}^*$ (the rectangular area $vnyz$ in the upper diagram).

Suppose that the government imposes an export quota on the raw material input that constrains exports to a maximum quantity $X_I{}'$ that is lower than the quantity $X_I{}^*$ exported under free trade. As in the log export control example above, the binding

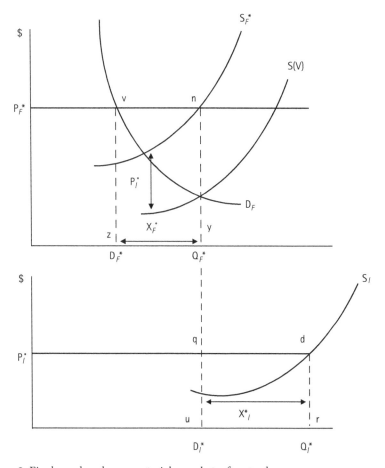

FIGURE 10.8 Final good and raw materials markets: free trade

export restriction will drive down the price of the raw material input in the domestic market until the price reaches a level at which the quantity supplied minus the quantity demanded equals the quantity allowed to be exported under the quota.

The complication in this case is the linkage between the market for the input and the market for the final good. Given that the quantity of the raw material input demanded depends upon the output of the processing industry, and given that the position of the processing industry supply curve depends upon the price of the raw material input, the new equilibrium would be determined jointly in both markets. The impact of the export control is shown in Figure 10.9. As P_I falls in the raw materials market, a smaller amount of raw material input cost would be added vertically to the S(V) curve in the upper diagram of the final goods market. The supply curve of the final good would shift downward as the price of the raw material input falls (which in effect also moves it rightward). At the given world market price P_F^*, the equilibrium output of the final good would increase. Given the one-to-one linkage between the quantity of final good produced and the quantity of raw material demanded, as the final good output increases from Q_F^* to Q_F', the amount of the raw material input demanded increases from D_I^* to D_I'. The equilibrium price of the raw material input will settle at P_I^D, where the quantity supplied along S_I minus the quantity of input demanded D_I' $(=Q_F')$ equals the raw material export quota limit X_I'.

The impact of the export control on the input is to encourage greater domestic production of the final good, and thus divert some of the raw material that had been exported under free trade (D_I' minus D_I^*) toward domestic processing. But the lower price of the input on the domestic market reduces domestic production from Q_I^* to Q_I'. Exports of the raw material input decrease for two reasons. Less is produced, and some of what is still produced is no longer exported, but instead processed domestically and then exported.

Limiting exports of the raw material results in a loss to the producers of the raw material, a gain to the processors of the raw material into the final good, and, overall, a net welfare loss to the country from distortions in both raw material and final good production. These impacts can be identified in Figure 10.9.

In the raw material input market in the lower diagram of Figure 10.9, the decline in the market price of the input reduces producer surplus by area *adge*. This area represents a loss of producer surplus for the raw material or input producers. This loss in producer surplus can be subdivided into three parts: (1) part of it (area *abfe*) represents the lower revenue for the total amount of input supplied to the processing industry; (2) a second part (area *bcgf*) represents lower revenue to the producers on the remaining export sales; and (3) the third part (area *cdg*) represents the profits which would have been made on export sales of the units of input that are no longer produced at the lower price. Each of these parts of the loss to raw materials producers is discussed in turn below:

(1) The raw material producers' loss of revenue on sales to domestic processors can be subdivided into a gain to the processing industry and a dead-weight loss from the distortion in production of the output of the final good. Note first that the area *abfe* in the lower diagram equals area *hijl* in the upper diagram. Part of this area (the part shown by area *hikl*) represents an increase in producer surplus for the processing industry. But the remaining part (area *ijk)* represents a dead-weight loss due to "overproduction" in the processing industry. The artificially low input price encourages expansion of the processing industry, but the *full* cost of production of each the units of the final good between Q_F^* and Q_F' exceeds the price received for it on the world market of P_F^*. The full production cost would evaluate the input at the price at which it could have been sold in the world market. Another way to see the source of this deadweight loss triangle *ijk* is to note that (because S_F^* is vertically parallel to S_F') area *ijk* equals area *min*. The height of the supply curve S_F^* shows the full marginal cost of producing each unit of the final good, and that cost exceeds the world price P_F^* for the extra units produced. Thus the export control creates two distortions: the dead-weight loss from reduced production in the input market (area *cdg*) and the deadweight loss from overproduction in the final good market (area *ijk* = area *min*).

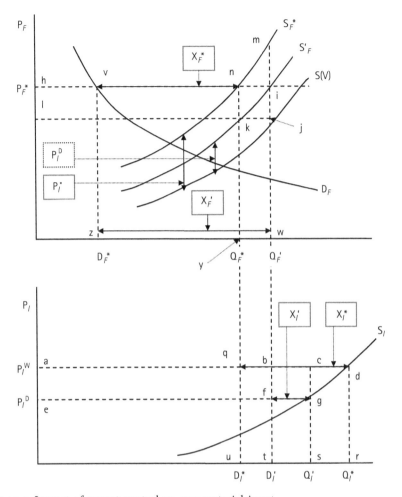

FIGURE 10.9 Impact of export control on raw material input

(2) Another part of the loss to the raw material producers is the lower price received on remaining export sales (area *bcgf*). The market price of the input internally will fall to P_I', but whoever is able to export within the quota limit can sell the input at the higher world market price of P_I^*. The windfall gains from exporting (the quota rents) will go to whoever actually is able to produce in the domestic market and sell abroad (or buy on the domestic market and resell abroad). Export licenses might be allocated directly to producers, but they might be allocated to intermediaries, government trading companies, or even to importers abroad, depending upon how the export quota system is designed and operated.

(3) The third part of the loss to producers (area *cdg*) is a net welfare loss that arises from the distortion to production in the input market. At the lower domestic input price after imposition of the export quota, producers of the input produce less, but the units that they do not produce at the lower price (that is, the units between Q_I^* and Q_I') could have sold on the world market for P_F^*, more than the

marginal cost of production, the height of S_I. The profits that could have been earned from the extra export sales will simply not materialize, so this area also represents a deadweight loss.

Often, when the government imposes export controls on raw materials, its objective is to increase export earnings. The expectation is that the raw material input that cannot be exported will be processed by the domestic industry and then exported as a higher priced, higher value added final good. The net gain in export earnings from increased export sales of the final good and reduced export sales of the raw material would be the difference between the gain in export earnings from increased exports of the final good (area *niwy*) minus the loss of export earnings from decreased sales of the raw material export (area *cdrs* + area *qbtu*).

Case Study: Mongolian Raw Cashmere Export Controls

In the early 1990s Mongolia began dismantling central planning and began shifting toward a more market-oriented economy. Under central planning all international trade had been conducted by government authorities. In the transition to a market economy, international trade was liberalized to allow individuals and enterprises to engage in international trade. The government established an import tariff, and established export licensing requirements for a variety of products, mostly intermediate goods and raw materials. As of August of 1992, the products under export licensing requirements included scrap copper, scrap iron, scrap aluminum, scrap steel, meat, wheat, children's clothes and shoes, timber, live animals, wool, camel wool, sheepskin, goatskin, and raw cashmere. The analysis below concentrates on the export controls on cashmere.

Cashmere fiber comes from cashmere goats, which are raised by the country's nomadic families, who in the early 1990s constituted about half of the total population. One of the early measures undertaken by the government in its transition toward private ownership of economic activity and a market-based economy was to privatize the herds of sheep, goats, and other animals, and shift actual ownership of the herds to the herdsmen who raised and cared for them.

Government officials cited numerous reasons for maintaining export controls on raw cashmere. One primary motivation was to ensure a supply of raw cashmere for the two domestic factories processing raw cashmere into knit goods (sweaters, gloves, scarves, and other knit products). Another objective was to increase foreign exchange earnings by promoting exports of higher value added knit goods rather than cashmere in its raw form. There was also a concern that the private individuals newly engaged in the cashmere trade did not know how to trade cashmere and would sell it at too low a price or not be paid for it.

Rough calculations of the magnitude of the transfers and net welfare costs to the economy from the raw cashmere export controls in Mongolia are presented in Takacs (1994c). These calculations included the size of the areas in Figure 10.9 that represent the loss to the herdsmen, the transfer to recipients of export licenses, the transfer to the processing industry, the dead-weight production losses in raw cashmere production and the cashmere goods processing industry, and the impact on raw cashmere and processed goods

Case Study *Continued*

export earnings. In the absence of estimates of the degree of responsiveness of raw cashmere production to the price of raw cashmere and the response of cashmere processing to the value added in processing, the calculations are based on a range of possible degrees of responsiveness.[3] The results are presented in Table 10.1.

A number of features of these estimated impacts of the cashmere export controls are noteworthy. One surprise is the estimated *negative* net impact of the raw cashmere export controls on total export earnings from raw cashmere and processed cashmere goods. At first glance this result is perplexing, because exporting higher value added goods rather than raw materials might be expected to increase export earnings. But it is possible that

Table 10.1 Estimated impact of Mongolian cashmere export licensing requirements (US$ per year)

Elasticity of supply of cashmere	0.5	1	0.5
Elasticity of supply of garments	1	1	3
Loss to cashmere producers *(adge)*	5,362,424	5,576,364	5,362,424
Efficiency loss in cashmere production *(cdg)*	213,940	427,881	213,940
Gain to garments industry *(hikl)*	870,000	870,000	578,287
Efficiency loss in garments production *(min=ijk)*	145,857	145,857	437,570
Decline in raw cashmere exports *(qbtu+cdrs)*	5,048,857	8,050,979	9,142,326
Increase in garment export earnings *(niwy)*	2,770,878	2,770,878	8,312,635
Change in total export earnings *(niwy−[qbtu+cdrs])*	−2,277,979	−5,280,101	−829,691
Transfer to export license recipients *(bcgf)*	4,132,627	4,132,627	4,132,627
Total efficiency loss *(min+cdg)*	359,797	573,738	651,510
Increase in garments production (units)	79,055	79,055	237,165

[3] The sudden shift from a centrally planned system to a market-oriented economic system implied that production of raw cashmere, and possibly also processing (which in the early 1990s was still controlled by the government) were operating on an entirely different basis than in the past. Historical data on prices and production would not have reflected the probable response of the new owners of the livestock, and possibly the new behavior of the processing industry in the new environment.

Case Study *Continued*

the extra value added by processing the raw cashmere that is diverted from exports to domestic processing (the amount $D_I'-D_I^*$ in Figure 10.9) could be less than the value at world market prices of the raw cashmere no longer produced at the lower price P_I' (the amount $Q_I^*-Q_I'$ in Figure 10.9). In the case of Mongolian cashmere, the raw cashmere may have been sufficiently expensive on the world market that, under plausible assumptions regarding the degree of responsiveness of raw cashmere supply and processing activity, the value of the reduction in production at world market prices $(Q_I^*-Q_I')$ exceeded the increase in the value of the cashmere diverted to domestic production and then exported. This would occur if area *niwy* were less than the sum of area *cdrs* and area *qbtu*. A second noteworthy feature of the Mongolian example is the estimated size of the transfer to export license recipients. About three-quarters of the calculated loss to the herdsmen appeared to be transferred to export license recipients. In the absence of information on who, exactly, received the licenses, it is not possible to tell who gained or indeed whether the herdsmen lost this revenue. To the extent that licenses were issued directly to the herdsmen, they would not lose these quota rents. But this result seems unlikely. It is more likely that intermediaries bought the cashmere from the herdsmen, then exported it, possibly across the border to China. The government agency that had exported cashmere to western countries under central planning was also still engaged in exporting cashmere and may have captured part of the windfall gains. The processing industry also gained, but their gain represented only 10 to 16 per cent of the loss to the raw cashmere producers.

One last interesting feature of the calculations is the extremely small size of the calculated efficiency losses (dead-weight losses) compared to the magnitude of the transfers to the processors and license recipients. The total estimated dead-weight losses (in raw cashmere production and in cashmere processing) range from only 4 per cent to almost 12 per cent of the herdsmen's losses. It seems that in this case the magnitude of the transfer "rectangles" dwarfed the size of the efficiency loss "triangles."

IV. Domestic Content and Compensatory Export Requirements

Export controls on raw materials are designed to encourage expansion of the industry or industries that use the raw material as an input. Domestic content (or local content) requirements, act in the opposite direction: they are designed to encourage local production of inputs by requiring use of domestically produced inputs in products sold on the domestic market. These restrictions favor the producers of inputs and disadvantage producers who use the inputs to produce final goods. Domestic content and compensatory export requirements drive *up* the cost of inputs to firms processing those inputs. These measures are intended to promote production of the inputs, and normally must be accompanied by other types of trade restrictions on the processed output to compensate for the higher input costs.

Background

Domestic content (or local content) requirements are regulations that require firms to use at least a specified minimum amount of domestically produced inputs in the production process. Developing countries often impose these local content requirements on their motor vehicle industries, but these regulations have also been used to promote household appliance and computer assembly operations. Local content requirements may mandate a minimum percentage of value added, a minimum percentage of the value of parts, and/or may require inclusion of certain specified parts, such as tires, batteries, headlights, or engines for motor vehicles.

Many Latin American countries used domestic content requirements in an attempt to force "backward linkages" in their import-substitution industrialization policies (see Baranson, 1969; Munk, 1969; Mericle, 1984; and Jenkins, 1985). But even developed countries such as Canada and Australia had such regulations for a time (Lloyd, 1973). Domestic content requirements tended to spawn motor vehicle assembly operations in which firms imported packages of components, called "kits," from associated vehicle manufacturers abroad and combined them with local components to produce finished vehicles. For example, a "kit" might contain a car body, fenders, engine, and transmission, which an assembler would combine with locally produced chassis, glass, upholstered seats, carpeting, brakes, radiator, and other necessary parts. Local content requirements normally were accompanied by very restrictive trade barriers on assembled vehicles, such as total import bans or very high tariffs.

As development strategies shifted from import-substitution industrialization toward more export-oriented strategies of development, many countries superimposed export incentives on the underlying local content requirements. Brazil (Mericle, 1984) and for a time Argentina (Jenkins 1985) offered tax exemptions and waivers of other requirements for firms with certain levels of exports. At one time, Argentina linked approval of expansion of domestic production to fulfillment of export targets. In Mexico, the Philippines, and Uruguay, export promotion was even more explicit. Firms importing kits to assemble vehicles were required to show that their foreign exchange earnings from exporting automobile industry products was at least a specified percentage of the value of their imported kits.

The protective regimes created by prohibitively high trade barriers on fully assembled vehicles coupled with domestic content and compensatory export requirements are frequently so complicated that it is difficult to disentangle their ultimate impact. The local content requirements unambiguously help domestic parts industries because these regulations increase the demand for locally produced parts. The assembly industry may be helped or hurt by the protective regime. On the one hand, firms in the local motor vehicle assembly industry benefit from import bans or high tariffs on assembled vehicles, but, on the other hand, they are forced to use more expensive and possibly lower quality, locally produced parts.

Compensatory export requirements also impose higher costs on firms assembling vehicles. To obtain permission under the system to import components from abroad, they must export a sufficient volume of qualifying products to earn the required amount of foreign exchange. Assuming that the firms assembling vehicles would not have been exporting in the absence of the export requirements, or would not have been exporting as large a volume of exports, they usually must absorb losses on export sales to be able to export sufficient volumes to qualify to receive permits to import kits. These extra costs are sometimes quite explicit. In Uruguay, for example, firms assembling motor vehicles could buy export invoices from unrelated firms exporting products that qualified as "automotive industry exports" and present these to the authorities to fulfill their export requirements.[4] In Mexico, Chrysler arranged for its Mexican assembly operations to transfer funds to its US assembly operations that used parts exported from Mexico to cover the higher cost of the Mexican parts.[5]

Exactly which domestic firms benefit from the increased demand for their products due to the compensatory export requirements depends on the details of what products qualify as "compensatory exports" under the plan. When (as in Uruguay and the Philippines) "motor vehicle industry products" are the only qualifying exports, the compensatory export requirements further boost demand for locally produced parts. Compensatory export requirements effectively act like an export subsidy for the industries whose products qualify as compensatory exports.

In actual practice, on balance the entire protective regime of trade restrictions on fully assembled vehicles, domestic content restrictions, and compensatory export requirements normally does boost both domestic assembly and domestic component production and does benefit both the assembly operations and parts producers, but at a high cost to the domestic buyers of motor vehicles. The restrictions on imports of assembled vehicles increase domestic production, but this extra production costs more than the cost of the vehicles imported from abroad. Consumers pay higher prices for vehicles that are often of significantly lower quality than similar models imported from abroad. Domestic component production is artificially increased by the local content and compensatory export requirements, and that production takes place at higher real resource cost than the prices at which the components could have been obtained in the world market.

Despite the fact that the intention of the WTO Agreement on Trade Related Investment Measures (TRIMs) was to phase out domestic content and compensatory export requirements, the final declaration of the 1995 Hong Kong WTO Ministerial meeting allowed the least developed countries to continue existing regulations temporarily, and to introduce new measures, initially limited to five years, but renewable, subject to the decision of the Committee on Trade in goods (World Trade Organization, 1995). Thus protective regimes of this kind are likely to continue in the least-developed countries for some time.

---

[4] See Takacs (1994b: 65).
[5] See Bennett and Sharpe (1985: 186).

Economic Impact of the Protective Regime

The major impacts of trade restrictions on assembled vehicles plus domestic content and compensatory export requirements can be explained using an approach similar to that used above to analyze effective rates of protection and the export restrictions on raw materials. Fundamentally, the protective regime consists of some form of import restriction on assembled vehicles that increases the selling price of the output of the assembly industry, coupled with domestic content and compensatory export requirements that drive up the cost of inputs into the automobile assembly process.

To analyze the impact of the entire protective structure, one must again look at the interrelationship between the market for the final product and the market for the inputs into the production process. Figure 10.10 depicts the market for components, and Figure 10.11 depicts the market for assembled vehicles. These two markets are linked not only by the normal input–output relationships, but also by the domestic content and compensatory export requirements. Suppose that the assembly industry is protected by a ban on the importation of assembled vehicles, and that it is subject to both domestic content requirements and compensatory export requirements. Assume that these domestic content and compensatory export requirements are binding (that is, use of locally produced parts would be lower and exports of locally produced parts would be lower in the absence of the restrictions). Assume also that the country imposing these requirements is too small to affect the world market prices of vehicles or components, so the import price of assembled vehicles (P_A^*) and of components (P_C^*) can be taken as given in the world market.

To assess the costs of the protective regime, start by determining what the equilibrium prices and quantities of assembled vehicles and components would be under free trade. With no trade barriers on either imports of assembled vehicles or components,

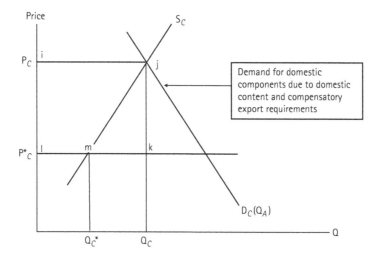

FIGURE 10.10 The market for components

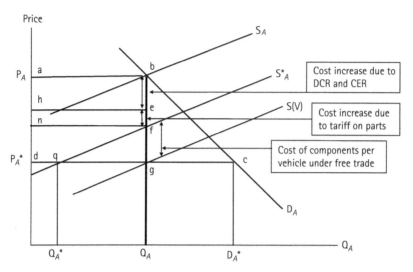

FIGURE 10.11 The market for assembled vehicles

and no other restrictions on the operations of the assembly industry, the local prices of both assembled vehicles and motor vehicle parts would equal their prices in the world market.

Figure 10.10 depicts the components market. S_C is the supply curve of the components industry. Under free trade, the price of components would equal $P_C{}^*$, the world price of components, and components producers would supply quantity $Q_C{}^*$. These would be used by local assemblers, who would import any additional needed components at the world market price $P_C{}^*$.

Figure 10.11 shows the market for assembled vehicles. The demand curve for assembled vehicles in the domestic economy is shown by D_A. On the supply side, assume that a competitive domestic industry assembles vehicles using imported and local components. Assume also that the assembly industry is willing to assemble more vehicles as the value added per unit increases. The curve labeled S(V) in Figure 10.11 shows the quantity of vehicles the industry would be willing to assemble at various amounts of value added per unit (measured vertically). Under free trade, firms assembling vehicles would have access to components at the world price $P_C{}^*$. The free trade supply curve of vehicles on the part of the domestic assembly industry would be $S_A{}^*$, the vertical sum of the cost of components per vehicle at world market prices and the value added per vehicle that assemblers would require to be willing to supply each output level. At the free trade price $P_A{}^*$, the domestic industry would assemble $Q_A{}^*$ units, consumers would purchase $D_A{}^*$ units, and $(D_A{}^*-Q_A{}^*)$ assembled vehicles would be imported.

A motor vehicle protective regime incorporating domestic content and compensatory export requirements and trade barriers limiting imports of assembled vehicles would change equilibrium prices in both the market for components and the market for assembled vehicles. Suppose that the government imposes local content and compensatory export requirements that are "binding," that is, they require assemblers to use more domestic components and export more auto-industry products than they would in the absence of the restrictions. These binding requirements would create a minimum demand for locally produced components, shown by $D_C(Q_A)$ in Figure 10.10. The total demand for components depends on Q_A, the number of vehicles assembled, so the exact position of the demand curve for components depends on Q_A. An increase in the number of vehicles assembled would shift the demand curve for domestic components to the right. The extra demand for components created by the restrictions would drive the price of components up to P_C. The higher components prices increase the cost of domestic components and, given that domestic parts prices exceed world market prices, assembly-industry firms will incur losses exporting parts to the world market.

In the market for assembled vehicles, the higher cost of components due to the protective trade regime would shift the supply curve of assembled vehicles upward to S_A in Figure 10.10. The size of the upward shift equals the increase in the cost the domestic components per vehicle. The cost of components to firms assembling vehicles increases for three reasons: (1) components cost increase due to the local content requirements and the higher components price P_C; (2) the cost of imported components increases because, to comply with the compensatory export requirements, firms must export auto-industry products to the world market. But because domestic parts prices exceed world market prices, they can only be exported at a loss; and (3) any tariff on imported parts also increases the cost of components to assembly firms. This total cost increase per vehicle is shown by the vertical distance *bf* in Figure 10.11, of which the distance *be* is due to the domestic content and compensatory export requirements, and the distance *ef* is due to any tariff on imported parts.

Protective regimes for motor vehicle industries also contain measures to protect the assembly operations. Suppose that, in this example, the government imposes a complete ban on imports of assembled vehicles. In that case, the domestic price of a vehicle would no longer be determined by the world market price, but will be determined in Figure 10.11 by the domestic market equilibrium price P_A, the price at which the quantity of vehicles supplied by domestic assemblers (along the supply curve S_A) equals the quantity demanded by domestic consumers along D_A.

The costs of the entire protective regime can be assessed using the free trade equilibrium as a benchmark for comparison. Welfare costs arise due to distortions in the markets for both assembled vehicles and components. The welfare cost of the protective regime to buyers of motor vehicles is reflected in area *abcd*, the reduction in consumer surplus as compared to free trade. The consumer loss *abcd* can be subdivided into transfers to the assembly industry, transfers to components manufacturers, transfers to the government, and deadweight losses due to the distortion of consumers' decisions on vehicle purchases and due to inefficient production in the assembly and component industries. Consumers reduce their purchases of motor vehicles by $D_A{}^*-Q_A$, resulting in area *bcg* dead-weight loss in consumption. Area *nfqd* represents an increase in profits to domestic assembly operations due to the net effect of the entire protective regime. It represents the increase in producer surplus due to the increase in the assembled vehicle price ($P_A-P_A^*$) *net* of the increase in input costs per vehicle (distances *be* + ef). Area *fgq* represents a production deadweight loss, the extra cost of assembling $Q_A-Q_A^*$ vehicles within the country rather than buying them on the world market at P_A^*.

Given the upward shift in the assembly-industry supply curve from S_A^* to S_A (an upward shift of the distance *be*) due to the domestic content and compensatory export requirements, area *abeh* represents the extra cost of components to assemblers because of the existence of these restrictions. The increased cost to domestic assemblers of area *abeh* is in part a transfer to domestic manufacturers of components and in part a deadweight efficiency loss. To see how the area is divided, note that area *abeh* in Figure 10.11 equals area *ijkl* in Figure 10.10. Area *ijml* represents a transfer to the domestic component manufacturers in the form of higher profits, and area *jkm* represents a dead-weight loss due to higher domestic production cost for components (the height of the components supply curve), compared to the price of components in the world market, for the extra output ($Q_C-Q_C^*$) produced. The area *hefn* is tariff revenue on components imports, a transfer from consumers (who pay higher prices for the vehicles) to the government, via the assembly industry. The net effect, ignoring transfers, is a consumption loss of *bcg*, and production dead-weight losses of *fgq* (in Figure 10.11) and *jkm* (in Figure 10.10) in the assembly and components industries, respectively.

The various elements of the protective regime affect domestic assembly operations in different, and potentially contradictory, ways. Import restrictions on fully assembled vehicles drive up vehicle prices and encourage greater output from domestic assembly operations, whereas the domestic content and compensatory export requirements (and any tariff on components imports) increase costs and discourage domestic assembly activity. On balance, the effective rate of protection provided to domestic assembly operations could be either positive or negative depending upon the net impact of all the regulations. Note that, in contrast to export restrictions on raw materials considered in the previous section, which increase the effective rate of protection to the processing industries by *lowering* input prices, domestic content and compensatory export requirements drive *up* the costs of inputs and reduce the effective rate of protection to the processing or assembly industries. Trade barriers on imports of the final product are thus necessary to maintain domestic vehicle production.

Case Study: Motor Vehicle Protective Regime In The Philippines

The origin of the trade restrictions on motor vehicles in the Philippines (and the origins of the Philippine motor vehicle industry itself) can be traced back to a shortage of foreign exchange in 1949 that prompted the government to impose foreign exchange controls. The foreign exchange control measures denied foreign exchange for the importation of "non-essential items." Motor vehicles were on the list of "non-essential items." By 1951, firms started assembling passenger cars in the Philippines from imported sets of components, called "kits." Another foreign exchange crisis in 1973 prompted the government to impose local content requirements and continue the ban on importing fully assembled

Case Study: *Continued*

vehicles. In 1984, the program was further extended to add export requirements. Firms assembling motor vehicles had to earn foreign exchange by exporting to partially compensate for the foreign exchange spent on import kits. At first, firms could export any product to comply with the compensatory export requirements. But in 1987 the regulations were revised yet again to increase the percentage of local content of parts and components and phase in minimum percentages of compensatory exports that had to be automotive industry products. Between 1989 and 1993, the percentage of compensatory exports that had to be automotive industry products increased from 20 per cent to 100 per cent.

The details of the protective regime varied over time as the regulations were revised, but as of 1990 (the year for which the estimated impacts of the protective regime discussed below were calculated) the protective regime included a ban on the importation of assembled motor vehicles, and requirements that domestic assembly operations use (depending on the type of vehicle) between 13.5 and 54.8 per cent locally produced parts. The compensatory export requirements mandated that firms assembling cars had to export products totaling at least 50 per cent of the value of their imported components. Truck producers were required to export products equal to at least 25 per cent of the value of their component imports.

The economic impact of the Philippine motor vehicle protective regime was estimated by calculating the approximate magnitudes of the areas identified in the analysis above as costs to consumers, transfers to the assembly and components industries, and dead-weight losses. These calculations were based on the actual values of the policy parameters (percentage of local content required, percentage of value of imported components that had to be balanced by exports) and observed or assumed values of other variables and parameters for the Philippine motor vehicle industry. The full model and detailed explanation of the data sources can be found in Takacs (1994a). Table 10.2 summarizes the results.

The estimated cost of the protective regime to purchasers of motor vehicles in 1990 was about 5.2 billion pesos (US$215 million) per year. This loss amounted to approximately 40 per cent of the value of vehicle sales in the Philippines and was roughly equivalent to almost US$3,800 per vehicle.

Component manufacturers would be expected to unambiguously benefit from the protective regime, because all of the measures act to increase demand for locally produced parts. Domestic content requirements mandate the use of specific amounts of local content. The stipulation that compensatory exports must be of automotive industry products further increases the demand for domestically produced parts. The ban on the importation of assembled vehicles sustains domestic assembly operations and thus the demand for components. The estimates indicate that the gains to the component manufacturers from the protective regime were in the range of about 9 per cent of the value of motor vehicle sales.

In principle, assembly operations can either be hurt or helped by this type of protective regime, depending upon the severity of the local content and compensatory export requirements compared to the restrictiveness of the barrier to imports of assembled vehicles. The estimates for the Philippines indicated that in 1990 the impact of the ban on imports of assembled vehicles created net gains to the assembly industry of

(Continued)

Case Study: *Continued*

about 14 per cent of the value of domestic sales, an even larger gain than that of the component producers. Given the import ban, the domestic price of vehicles depends on the interaction of domestic supply and demand, so the magnitude of the gains to the assembly industry would be expected to fluctuate with the state of the economy. During economic downturns when consumer demand, especially for durable goods, is low, the gains would be expected to be considerably smaller. During the economic downturn in the early 1980s, for example, Philippine associates of Ford, Isuzu, and Toyota all shut down operations.

The dead-weight efficiency losses appeared to be relatively large (US$50 million per year), equivalent to about US$895 per vehicle. These efficiency losses include the dead-weight losses in consumption plus the dead-weight losses in production in both the components and assembled vehicle industries. They corresponded to about 10 per cent of the value of sales. These estimates are only approximate, but they indicate that the

Table 10.2 Motor vehicle industry protection in the Philippines: losses and transfers from protective regime, 1990

	CARS (millions of pesos)	(As % of sales)	TRUCKS (millions of pesos)	(As % of sales)	TOTAL (millions of pesos)	(As % of sales)
Consumer loss *(abcd)*	3,231	40%	1,997	40%	5,228	40%
Efficiency loss (consumption) *(bcg)*	476	6%	294	6%	770	6%
Transfer to assembly industry *(nfqd)*	955	12%	831	17%	1,786	14%
Efficiency loss (assembly) *(fgq)*	108	1%	148	3%	256	2%
Transfer to components Industry *(ijml)*	831	10%	376	8%	1,207	9%
Efficiency loss (components) *(jkm)*	165	2%	60	1%	225	2%
Transfer to producers *(nfqd+ijml)*	1,786	22%	1,207	24%	2,993	23%
Total efficiency loss *(bcg+fgq+jkm)*	749	9%	502	10%	1,251	10%
Loss per vehicle:	(Pesos)	(US$)	(Pesos)	(US$)		
Consumer loss	93,840	3,860	90,506	3754		
Efficiency loss	21,754	895	22,740	935		

Case Study: *Continued*

Philippine motor vehicle protective regime imposed substantial costs on consumers and resulted in significant net welfare losses.

The Philippines motor vehicle protective regime case study also provides insights into the impact of liberalizing some restrictions in a complicated protective regime while leaving others intact. One question that arose when analyzing the protection afforded to the Philippines motor vehicle industry was what the impact would be if the non-tariff trade barriers affecting the industry (namely, the ban on imports of assembled vehicles and both the domestic content and compensatory export requirements) were abolished, but the tariffs on imported vehicles and imported kits were left unchanged? There was a tariff on imported vehicles, but that tariff rate was irrelevant as long as imports were banned. Calculations of the impact on consumers, the assembly industry, and component manufacturers are shown in Table 10.3.

The results indicate that abolishing the import ban and domestic content and compensatory export requirements at prevailing tariff rates would have benefited consumers and the assembly industry, at the expense of the component manufacturers. The consumer losses are reduced by about 7 per cent; the transfer to the components industry falls by about 48 per cent, and the transfer to the assembly industry increases by about 21 per cent. The assembly industry gains because even though assembled vehicle prices fall, the cost of

Table 10.3 Motor vehicle industry protection in the Philippines: impact of removing DCR and CER at prevailing tariff rates, 1990

	CARS (millions of pesos)	% change	TRUCKS (millions of pesos)	% change	TOTAL (millions of pesos)	%change
Consumer loss	−142	−4%	−221	−11%	−363	−7%
Efficiency loss (consumption)	−48	−10%	−70	−23%	−118	−15%
Transfer to assembly industry	+367	+38%	+16%	+2%	+383	+21%
Efficiency loss (assembly)	+94	+87%	+6	+4%	+100	+39%
Transfer to components Industry	−367	−44%	−191	−51%	−578	−48%
Efficiency loss (components)	−104	−63%	−43	−71%	−147	−65%
Transfer to producers	+1	0	−175	−14%	−174	−6%
Total efficiency loss	−58	−8%	−107	−21%	−165	−13%
Tariff revenue gain	1,136		552		1,688	

(Continued)

Case Study: *Continued*

inputs falls even more significantly. The component manufacturers would unambiguously lose from the removal of domestic content and compensatory export requirements.

V. Implications for the Design of Trade Reform Programs

What lessons for the design of trade liberalization programs might be drawn from the application of the concept of the effective rate of protection, the analysis of the particular protective regimes considered here, and the case studies of protective regimes for cashmere in Mongolia and motor vehicles in the Philippines?

Effective Rates and Tariff Structure

One insight from the concept of the effective rate of protection is that the incentive to engage in particular economic activities depends upon the relationship of the degree of protection afforded the output of a production process compared with the degree of protection to the intermediate inputs used. If tariff structures include a very wide range of tariff rates, a combination of high tariffs on outputs and low (or zero) tariffs on inputs could generate extraordinarily high effective rates of protection to certain activities. In contrast, low tariffs on outputs and high tariffs on inputs (or very high prices of inputs due to non-tariff barriers) could create negative effective rates of protection to certain activities. Export activities in particular are vulnerable, because firms selling into the world market must sell at world market prices.

These considerations have led to the recommendation that trade reform programs aim for greater uniformity in tariff rates. Some countries (for example, Chile) have adopted a completely uniform tariff structure with the same percentage tariff rate on all imports. Another alternative is to move toward a tariff structure with only a few rates that escalate slightly with degree of processing. For example, a 5 per cent tariff on raw materials, 10 per cent tariff on intermediate goods, and a 15 per cent tariff on final goods. This form of tariff structure would provide some degree of effective protection to domestic firms but avoid extreme variability in effective rates of protection across different activities in the economy.

"Piecemeal" Policy Reforms

The objective of a trade liberalization program is to reduce the degree of protection to relatively inefficient, relatively high cost economic activities to encourage a country's scarce resources to move out of protected sectors into activities that are relatively efficient and in which the country can compete internationally. Moving resources out of protected import-competing sectors into export-oriented sectors will expand international trade and allow the country to attain higher real income and greater overall consumption possibilities.

The protective regimes for a particular sector may be quite complicated and may involve overlapping, interacting, and possibly contradictory elements. When a protective regime is made up of many different policy instruments (such as tariffs and quantitative restrictions on inputs and outputs, exchange control measures, domestic content and compensatory export requirements) a trade reform program must be designed in a way that avoids unintentional or inadvertent drastic increases or reductions in the effective rate of protection to particular activities during the reform process.[6]

Piecemeal policy reforms that liberalize part of a protective regime, while leaving other restrictions intact, run the risk of, at one extreme, decimating an industry, and, at the other extreme, increasing rather than decreasing the protection afforded to a domestic industry. Such a result would be contrary to the goal of reducing protection and encouraging a movement of resources out of protected sectors. One example of the potential problems from piecemeal reform arose in the Peruvian reform program during the early 1990s. The trade liberalization program abolished what had been a complete ban on the importation of assembled automobiles and replaced it with a 50 per cent *ad valorem* tariff. Domestic content requirements, however, were not liberalized at the same time. Firms assembling motor vehicles found themselves in a difficult position. They were forced to compete with imported vehicles, but the domestic content requirements kept the cost of their inputs high. This piecemeal liberalization disadvantaged the assembly industry to the point that only 16 motor vehicles (all trucks) were assembled in Peru during the first 2 months of 1991. At that time, the government was contemplating a further reduction of the tariff on imported vehicles to 25 per cent. Calculations of the effective rate of protection to motor vehicle assembly in Peru indicated that if the domestic content regulations remained intact and tariffs were further reduced, the effective rate of protection to vehicle assembly would have been approximately *negative* 50 per cent. This extreme result did not in the end materialize because the domestic content requirements were abolished before the tariff was further reduced (UNDP/World Bank Trade Expansion Program, 1992).

The opposite problem can also occur. The ultimate goal of a trade reform program is to encourage resources to move out of relatively high cost sectors. Gyrations in incentives during a reform program risk wasting scarce investment resources if, during the reform process, piecemeal reforms temporarily *increase* the effective rate of protection and encourage high cost activities to expand rather than contract. This result may occur more often than would be expected, because reform programs often begin by liberalizing trade in capital goods and intermediate inputs. Then, after a period of time, the trade liberalization is extended to final consumer goods. Reducing import barriers on inputs,

---

[6] This is all the more reason for using a general equilibrium approach rather than distinct partial equilibrium analysis. To do this, of course, requires the construction of a computational generalized equilibrium model, which is by no means an easy task.

followed (with a lag) by liberalization of trade in outputs would temporarily increase the effective rate of protection to final goods and encourage expansion of final goods production. A movement of resources *into* previously protected final goods industries is the opposite of the movement that is desired as the end result of a trade reform program. In the case of the Philippines, presented above, the impact of removing the import ban and domestic content and compensatory export requirements at prevailing tariff rates provides another example of piecemeal reform. This change would have caused an expansion of domestic motor vehicle assembly operations and would have resulted in gains to the assembly industry at the expense of parts manufacturers.

Tariffs vs. Non-Tariff Trade Barriers

Trade reform programs normally also include measures to abolish discretionary quantitative trade restrictions on imports and exports or convert them into import tariffs or export taxes. One advantage of import tariffs and export taxes over quantitative trade restrictions is "transparency." The nominal rate of protection afforded by an *ad valorem* tariff is clear. The protective effect of import or export quotas, import or export bans, or import or export licensing is difficult and possibly costly to assess.

With quotas and licensing arrangements it is also unclear who receives the "quota rents." The Mongolian cashmere case study indicated that by far the largest impact of the export licensing restrictions was to transfer income from producers of cashmere to export license recipients. If the form of the export restriction had been an export tax rather than export licensing, it would have been much more likely that the losses to cashmere producers would have been captured as government revenue and could have been used for public purposes. As is the case in general with quotas and licensing systems, it is not clear who actually received the "quota rents," and thus who actually benefited from the potential losses to the herdsmen.

The potential of tariffs to generate revenue for the government is also illustrated by the analysis of the impact of abolishing the import ban, domestic content requirements, and compensatory export requirements in the motor vehicle sector in the Philippines. The estimated annual government revenue gains from removing the import ban to allow imports of vehicles at prevailing tariff rates exceeds 1.5 billion pesos.

VI. Concluding Observations

The concept of the effective rate of protection is useful when analyzing complicated protective regimes involving input–output relationships. Protective regimes for particular industries often contain a variety of measures that affect the prices of both final goods and intermediate inputs within the industry. Increases or decreases in input prices affect the incentive to supply final goods. The analytical approach to effective rates provides a useful framework to examine and estimate the net welfare costs of protective regimes and the magnitude of the transfers among consumers, producers of final goods, producers of inputs, governments, and recipients of quota licenses if the protective regime involves quantitative trade restrictions.

The exact impacts of complicated protective regimes involving input–output relationships may be difficult to assess and are sometimes counterintuitive. For example, in the case of Mongolia's export controls on raw cashmere, one of the objectives of the restrictions was to increase export earnings by exporting finished cashmere garments rather than raw cashmere. Estimates of the impact of the protective regime, however, indicated that restricting raw cashmere exports to encourage domestic processing and exports of higher value added finished goods may well have reduced export earnings. Lower domestic cashmere prices would reduce raw cashmere production and exports of raw cashmere. If the value added by processing the raw cashmere diverted to domestic production by the export restriction was lower than the value of the reduction in raw cashmere exports, total export earnings from cashmere garments and raw cashmere taken together would fall.

Another observation that emerges from the case studies is that the magnitude of transfers among groups may well be significantly larger than the efficiency losses. The groups that lose, such as consumers in general in low-income countries or raw material producers in the case of export controls on raw materials, may well be the groups in society that are less well-off to begin with. In Mongolia, export licensing restrictions on raw cashmere probably reduced the incomes of nomadic herdsmen, who produced raw cashmere, while the gains appeared to go primarily to export license recipients and the cashmere processing enterprises. In the case of motor vehicle sector protective regimes, the recipients of the largest transfers from consumers may well be the firms assembling vehicles (which quite possibly involve foreign investment).

REFERENCES

Baranson, J. (1969). 'Automotive Industries in Developing Countries' World Bank Occasional Papers 8, Washington, DC.

Bennett, D. C., and Sharpe, K. E. (1985), *Transnational Corporations versus the State: The Political Economy of the Mexican Auto Industry*. Princeton, NJ: Princeton University Press.

Corden, W. M. (1971), *The Theory of Protection* Oxford: Clarendon Press.

Deardorff, A. V. and Stern, R. M. (1984), 'The Effects of the Tokyo Round on the Structure of Protection', in Baldwin, R. E. and Krueger, A. O. (eds.) *The Structure and Evolution of Recent Trade Policy*. Chicago: University of Chicago Press.

Jenkins, R. (1985), 'The Rise and Fall of the Argentine Motor Vehicle Industry' in Kronish, R., and Mericle, K. S. (eds.) *The Political Economy of the Latin American Motor Vehicle Industry*. Cambridge, MA: MIT Press.

Lloyd, P. J. (1973), *Nontariff Distortions of Australian Trade*. Canberra: Australian National University Press.

Mericle, K. S. (1984), 'The Political Economy of the Brazilian Motor Vehicle Industry' in Kronish, R., and Mericle, K. S. (eds.) *The Political Economy of the Latin American Motor Vehicle Industry*. Cambridge, MA: MIT Press.

Munk, B. (1969), 'The Welfare Costs of Content Protection: The Automotive Industry in Latin America' *Journal of Political Economy*, 77: 202–16.

Takacs, W. E. (1994a), 'Domestic Content and Compensatory Export Requirements: Protection of the Motor Vehicle Industry in the Philippines' *World Bank Economic Review*, 8(1): 127–49.

Takacs, W. E. (1994b), 'Domestic Content Restrictions and Compensatory Export Requirements in the Automobile Sector' in Connolly, M., and de Melo, J. (eds.) *The Effects of Protection on a Small Country: The Case of Uruguay*. Washington, DC: The World Bank, 64–80.

Takacs, W. E. (1994c), 'The Economic Impact of Export Controls: An Application to Mongolian Cashmere and Romanian Wood Products' Policy Research Working Paper 1280 The World Bank (March).

UNDP/World Bank Trade Expansion Program (1992), *Peru: Trade Expansion Program Country Report*. Washington, DC: The World Bank

World Trade Organization (1995), 'Hong Kong Ministerial Conference Declaration Annex F Agreement on Trade-Related Investment Measures,' Paragraph 84 WT/MIN (05)/DEC 22Dec.2005.

CHAPTER 11

....

PROTECTION, SUBSIDIES, AND AGRICULTURAL TRADE

....

TIM JOSLING

I. INTRODUCTION

....

THE objective of this chapter is to provide an introduction to the significance for world agricultural trade of the level of protection from imports afforded agriculture in developed countries, along with the subsidies to exports and to the production of farm products in those countries. A major focus will be on their possible impact on developing countries, including those that import as well as those that export farm products. This topic has particular relevance at present as new disciplines on these policies are being negotiated in the Doha Round: they have been identified as a vital part of the Doha Development Agenda (DDA).

The chapter is organized in six sections. Section II presents the background to protection and subsidies in developed countries, including the arguments for domestic support and subsidies, the gradual reform of these subsidies over the past 20 years, the "multilateralization" of the reforms in the Uruguay Round, and the current Doha Round debates about the next stage in reducing protection. Section III discusses the current levels of protection at the border in developed countries, in particular the level of tariffs for agricultural products in the main trading countries and the evidence of tariff escalation and tariff dispersion, the level of tariffs by commodity, including products of interest to developing countries, and a comparison of agricultural tariffs with levels of non-agricultural tariffs. This section continues by discussing the scope of preferential access and agricultural products—including non-reciprocal access into developed country markets and reciprocal access under regional and bilateral trade agreements, and the existence of contingent or safeguard protection, including the Special Safeguard for agriculture. The section concludes with a discussion of the extent of export subsidies for agricultural products—including credit guarantees, state assistance through marketing boards, and abuse of food aid.

Section IV focuses on the current levels of subsidies given to agricultural producers, including the levels of trade-distorting subsidies in developed countries and the change towards policies with less direct trade impact. Section V brings in other trade impediments linked to developed country agricultural policies, such as the use of health and safety measures as trade barriers and the trade-related aspects of the protection of intellectual property, specifically in the form of Geographical Indications. Section VI introduces the multilateral disciplines on developed country agricultural policies embodied in the Uruguay Round Agreement on Agriculture (URAA), and in particular the limitations on Amber, Blue, and Green Box subsidies and the negotiations in the Doha Round to reduce these subsidies.

Section VII discusses the empirical estimates of the gains from the removal of subsidies and protection, including the studies of the gains from tariff reductions in the Uruguay Round and from the further reductions envisaged in the DDA studies on the impact of export subsidies and of the proposals for elimination of such subsidies in the DDA, and studies of specific trade impacts of subsidies, in particular the categories of subsidies notified to World Trade Organization (WTO), and of the proposals for domestic support reduction in the DDA. A short concluding section rounds out the chapter.

II. Background to Agricultural Protection in Developed Countries

Agricultural subsidies and border protection in developed countries have been a controversial component of the discussions among countries on the problems of agricultural trade. At present they are the center of the difficulties that countries are experiencing in finishing the Doha Round of WTO trade negotiations. The border protection and the subsidies work hand-in-hand to shelter domestic producers from unfettered competition from abroad. These measures, and others related to health and safety regulations, make up the bulk of the impediments to trade from developed countries into the industrial country markets and influence the nature of the competition faced in other markets.

This section discusses the context of agricultural policies, examines the merits of some of the common arguments for protection and subsidies, and suggests where these arguments may be a justification for measures in place for other reasons. It describes in brief the nature of changes in these policies over time, and the modification to the objectives of such policies in response to social and political pressures. Emphasis will be on policies of the USA and the EU, though Japan and the non-EU countries of Western

Europe also have high levels of protection for agricultural products and extensive subsidy schemes to promote domestic production.

Most agricultural policies build in a preference for domestic food production over imported produce. The ostensible reasons for this preference range from concerns about the instability of world markets to the undesirability of undue dependence on foreign sources of supply. In reality, with a reliable global network of commodity markets and trading companies established for agricultural products, it is difficult to conceive of the USA and Europe being seriously inconvenienced by too high a dependence on agricultural imports.

Other arguments for agricultural protection also look somewhat dated. One such argument has been based on the need to maintain the incomes of small and family farms through price support. The notion that rural areas in industrial countries need protection to relieve poverty is less credible in a situation where most of the benefits of price support go to large farmers who, in both the USA and the EU, earn average or above average incomes. Though poverty exists, the marginal farmers tend to be more affected by non-farm policies such as the availability of jobs, training, and social services than by the price of commodities.

In the mid 1980s, it became apparent that much of the effect of farm policies was in essence to offset the influence on world prices of the policies of other (developed) countries. Thus, the world markets for sugar and dairy products as well as for beef and cereals were depressed by price support policies that encouraged continued production despite shrinking demand. The low prices in turn appeared to give backing to the support policies, as evidence that world market prices were "unreliable" as an indicator of the value of a commodity. The inclusion of agriculture fully in the Uruguay Round was a result in part of the recognition of this circularity.

However, the policies of the major developed countries have not gone away. They have changed steadily towards a new "model" with its own political justification and claim for legitimacy. The new concept that has become significant in developed country farm policies is the notion that farming is vital to the production of social and environmental benefits, as well as the sequestration of carbon in growing crops. It is claimed that the sales of farm commodities in themselves do not recompense the farmer for these benefits. Allied to this trend toward environmental stewardship and climate change mitigation as a reason for supporting agriculture is the tendency to emphasize quality and safety attributes of food (above and beyond the public responsibility for safe food supplies). This leads to tighter food safety regulations, more information on production and processing methods on the label, and more control over the food system by supermarkets that try to react to consumer demands. Protectionism can hide behind such product and process standards, and may increase the hurdles that developing country exporters have to overcome.

An even more recent rationale for agricultural commodity programs is to promote the use of such commodities as corn, soybeans, and sugar as feedstock for bio-fuels, notably ethanol and bio-diesel. This movement has been spurred by the higher price for oil in recent years and the instability in many of the regions that contain oil reserves. Though it is too early to say whether this trend will continue, it has already begun to transform the nature of the debate about the use of farmland and the conflict between the production of food and fuel from scarce agricultural resources.

Along with the new rationales for agricultural policies have come new instruments. The most significant trend has been toward the use of direct payments. These payments are made to farmers or farm operators on the basis of some criterion not directly related to current production or output. They are said to be "decoupled" from production decisions. But they are of course "coupled" to some criteria, and may still be output-increasing. The most common mechanism for determining these payments is past participation in support programs, and they are often introduced as a way of severing the link between price and income support. But what starts out as a compensation payment can turn into an entitlement. The direct payments also provide a means for making a link between income support objectives and environmental practices: direct payments increasingly include cross-compliance conditions tied to environmental practices.

The trend toward "decoupled" payments in place of price supports has had an important side effect. It has made possible the negotiation of rules for agricultural policy at the multilateral level. The same domestic reforms also make bilateral and regional trade agreements easier to conclude, though agriculture is still treated in most such agreements as a sensitive sector subject to specific safeguards, long transition periods, and specific exceptions. Multilateral and bilateral trade rules rarely drive domestic reform, but can complement them by incorporating constraints that in effect "lock in" domestic policy changes. The current WTO Doha Round is in effect attempting to lock in reforms made in the last decade in the EU and the USA, as well as the autonomous tariff reductions that have been undertaken by many developing countries.

III. Protection at the Border

Protection at the border, raising the price of competing imports or lowering the price abroad of domestic exports, is the bedrock of agricultural support policies. Even where the instruments of policy include different types of domestic subsidy, the overall price level is controlled by imports (or by export subsidies), and the cost of the domestic programs is effectively contained. The tariff level is even important for commodities that are exported: in those cases where exports are subsidized, without border protection those exports would find their way back onto the domestic market and depress the price.

This section will give a description of the levels of protection at the border in the major trading countries, emphasizing the relatively high tariffs in this sector. It will consider the levels of tariffs for particular agricultural products in the main trading countries, and for agricultural products in comparison with non-agricultural tariffs.

Market Access

Market access includes the tariffs on imports as well as non-tariff barriers and safe-guards. The evaluation of tariff levels across countries and across commodities has become easier since the Uruguay Round, as a result of the conversion of non-tariff import barriers (quotas, licenses, etc.) to tariffs. However, certain problems remain.

- As a part of the conversion of non-tariff barriers to tariffs (known as tariffication) countries were allowed to establish tariff rate quotas (TRQs) that carried a lower (or zero) level of duty. Imports above the TRQ bore the full Most Favored Nation (MFN) tariff. Thus a simple comparison of tariffs can be misleading if market access for a commodity is through TRQs at a lower tariff rate.
- Many of the bound duties for agricultural products are set not in *ad valorem* terms but as specific tariffs. The *ad valorem* equivalent (AVE) of these tariffs therefore changes with the world price. Conversion of specific to *ad valorem* tariffs has to be done to obtain comparisons across countries.[1]
- Countries may apply tariff rates that are lower than the bound rates. This difference between bound and applied rates can be very substantial. In the Uruguay Round, developing countries were allowed to use "ceiling bindings" rather than calculate tariff equivalents. These typically tend to be at high levels, of 100 per cent or more, across wide ranges of agricultural products. Applied tariffs are much more closely connected to the country's needs for imports and to the control of its domestic price level.[2]
- A further complication with simple tables of tariffs is that most countries now are a party to some regional, bilateral, or other preferential trade agreement. The level of access from partners under these agreements is often quota controlled for sensitive commodities, but in general is still better than for other countries, for whom MFN tariffs would apply.

As a result of these complications, the assembly of a comprehensive data set for examination of protection levels is a major task. This task was undertaken in 1999 by a consortium of institutions that pooled their expertise to compile the Agricultural Market Access Database (AMAD), and this has formed the basis for much of the work in this area since that time.[3] The AMAD database includes a common set of data on tariffs, tariff-rate quotas, and import levels compiled from the market access commitments

---

[1] In the Doha Round, a negotiated formula has been used for the calculation of AVE of specific tariffs, for the purposes of defining commitments on market access.

[2] This "binding overhang" also makes it difficult to calculate the impact of various proposals for market access improvement in the Doha Round.

[3] The institutions are Agriculture and Agri-Food Canada; the EU Commission; the UN Food and Agriculture Organization (FAO), the Organisation for Economic Co-operation and Development (OECD), the World Bank, United Nations Conference on Trade and Development (UNCTAD), and USDA-ERS. For more details, see the website at <www.AMAD.org>.

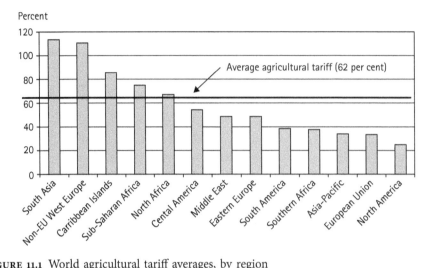

FIGURE 11.1 World agricultural tariff averages, by region

Source: Gibson et al., 2001.

undertaken by WTO members. Calculations are possible of AVE and aggregations from the dataset. Currently 50 countries are included in the AMAD database.

Tariff Levels

In one of the first comprehensive comparative analysis of post-Uruguay Round tariff rates by country and commodity, Gibson et al. (2001) estimated the global average bound rate of post-Uruguay Round agricultural tariffs at 62 per cent.[4] Regional average tariffs for WTO members range from an *ad valorem* tariff equivalent of 25 per cent to 113 per cent (Figure 11.1). With the exception of the high tariff region of non-EU Western Europe (104 per cent), the highest tariffs are in developing county regions: Africa, the Caribbean, and South Asia have average tariffs ranging from 71to 113 per cent—all above the global average of 62 per cent. The OECD economies with agricultural tariffs below the global average include Canada (24 per cent), the EU (30 per cent), Japan (33 per cent), Mexico (43 per cent), and the USA (12 per cent).

The average level of protection by country tells part of the story, but exporting countries are affected by barriers against particular commodities. Levels of protection by tariffs differ by commodity, with those on tropical beverages being generally low and those on temperate zone farm products being high. Many of these products are of export

---

[4] Their analysis is based on tariff data from first version of AMAD that included 40 WTO members. The 62 per cent simple (unweighted) average of post-Uruguay Round bound agricultural tariffs includes the AVE of specific tariffs, which are in some cases very high and whose values depend on prices. It also includes the over-quota tariff in tariff-rate quota regimes.

interest to developing countries, including cereals, sugar, rice, citrus fruits, tree oils, and livestock products.

Gibson et al. (2001) aggregated agricultural commodities into 46 groups and found that average tariffs for these groups varied from 50 per cent to 94 per cent. While there are countries with low levels of tariffs, there are few commodities that are not subject to high import tariffs by some countries. The average tariff for 18 of the commodity groups (including tobacco, dairy, meats, sugar, sweeteners, and several categories of vegetables, grains, grain products, and breeding animals) exceeded the average for all products. Tariffs on the remaining 28 commodity groups fell below the 62 per cent average tariff. Even the commodity groups with the lowest tariffs (coffee, fiber, several fruit categories, spices, and live horticulture) have a high degree of protection, with an average tariff of 50 per cent.

The full impact of these high tariff levels on trade depends on how the tariffs are distributed across countries. Variations in levels across countries and commodities are striking. Non-uniform tariffs introduce relative price distortions within countries that can worsen resource misallocation. Similarly, a wide dispersion of tariffs for the same commodity across countries distorts trade and lowers the efficiency and responsiveness of world markets. One aspect of this tariff dispersion is the existence of tariff peaks, often used to give secure protection to agricultural and labor intensive manufactures. There is evidence that these tariff peaks have been increasing in recent years. Tariff peaks on agricultural products from developing to developed countries doubled over the period 1994–2005, and accounted for 30 per cent of all tariff peaks (UNCTAD, 2006: 77).

OECD tariff protection is very high in many sectors including dairy (116 per cent), grains (78 per cent), livestock (82 per cent), and sugar and sweeteners (64 per cent), but low in others, notably tropical products where there is no domestic production. These are the sectors in which some OECD countries use tariffs higher than 100 per cent, and in which notified tariff rate quotas are concentrated. Because tariff peaks for sensitive commodities characterize OECD tariff profiles, there is a large dispersion, or variation, in tariffs across commodities. Non-OECD countries tend to have higher average tariffs than OECD countries, but with less variation across commodity groups. They have high protection for the same commodities as OECD countries, except that tobacco, rather than dairy, has the highest average tariff. Non-OECD countries use very high tariffs more than OECD countries. Many of the highest were not subject to reduction under the URAA because they were established as ceiling bindings. However, many developing countries have applied tariff rates that are considerably lower than the bound rates in the WTO schedules. For example, the 1998 average applied rate for agricultural tariffs for Latin American countries, at 13 per cent, is less than one-third of the average bound rate of 45 per cent.

The AMAD database is an invaluable compilation of tariff and TRQ data but it is focused on the agricultural sector and emphasizes MFN tariffs. For the purposes of getting a more detailed picture of agricultural protection at the border, and in order to be able to model the implications of this protection, one needs data on all traded products and where possible on the tariffs that are levied on bilateral trade flows. To assemble such a database clearly is a major undertaking, but a group of researchers led by Tom Hertel at Purdue has developed such a database initially for the purpose of facilitating the construction of Computable General Equilibrium (CGE) models to look at trade policy issues, particularly in the agricultural sector. The project is called the Global Analysis and Trade Project (GTAP) and has found widespread support from institutions and other researchers in the field (Hertel, 1997). Though the GTAP database is often linked with the models that can be constructed simply through the software available (with different levels of aggregation and different policy assumptions) it also stands alone as a useful compilation of trade and other parameters and variables.[5] The current database, GTAP 7, is based on the year 2004, with account taken of policy changes resulting from the full implementation of the Uruguay Round agreements, the accession of China and Taiwan in 2001, and the further enlargement of the EU to include 25 countries.[6]

The GTAP database gives an indication of the relative level of protection in agriculture compared with that in non-agricultural product markets. Table 11.1 shows the relative applied tariffs in 2001 for agriculture, textiles, and manufactured goods, distinguished by the source of imports. Among developed importers, agricultural tariffs on goods coming from other developed countries are 18 times the level of manufactured goods tariffs, and on goods coming from developing countries the gap is nearly as wide.[7] Developing importers show the same pattern. Imports of agricultural goods from developed and developing countries face tariffs of "only" twice those of manufactures, suggesting that there is somewhat less discrimination against agricultural goods, or alternatively that manufactured imports are not favored as much.

Also common in agricultural trade is the use of specific tariffs, charged as a particular monetary amount per unit rather than as a percentage of the value of the product. The protection effect of the specific tariff increases with lower world prices. They also discriminate against lower-priced shipments of the same good. Over 30 per cent of the tariff lines in agriculture in the USA, the EU, Japan, and Canada contain specific or other non-*ad valorem* tariffs (Aksoy and Beghin, 2004).

There is also a concern, especially among developing countries, that tariff structures often reflect tariff escalation—low rates on intermediate inputs (such as bulk farm products) and high rates on final products (such as processed foods). This results in high effective rates of protection for value added, and less opportunities for economically viable processing in the countries producing the raw material.[8]

Tariff escalation is a major problem for the agricultural and food system. The location of processing is important for economic development, particularly since the growth in trade is concentrated in processed products. But the pattern of tariff escalation is itself

---

[5] Another widely used database that has information on both tariff and non-tariff trade barriers for agricultural products is the Trade Analysis and Information System (TRAINS) database maintained by UNCTAD.

[6] With the accession of Romania and Bulgaria, the EU now has 27 members.

[7] This of course includes imports of tropical beverages that generally carry small or zero tariffs.

[8] Value added refers to the contribution of primary factors (labor, capital, and land) to a sector's output and can be roughly calculated by subtracting the costs of intermediate inputs from the value of production.

Table 11.1 Average applied import tariffs, by sector and region, 2001 (per cent, AVE)

Exporting region	Importing region		
	High-income countries[b]	Developing countries[a]	World
Agriculture and food			
High-income countries[b]	18	18	18
Developing countries[a]	14	18	16
Textiles and wearing apparel			
High-income countries[b]	8	15	12
Developing countries[a]	7	20	9
Other manufactures			
High-income countries[b]	1	9	4
Developing countries[a]	1	7	3

[a] These import-weighted averages incorporate tariff preferences provided to developing countries, unlike earlier versions of the GTAP database.
[b] High-income countries include the newly industrialized East Asian customs territories of Hong Kong, Korea, Singapore, and Taiwan as well as Europe's transition economies that joined the EU in April 2004.

Source: Anderson, Martin, and van der Mensbrugghe (2006).

significant. Gibson et al. (2001) find that in both the USA and the EU, tariffs have a U-shaped distribution over commodity categories that are classified by level of processing. Rates of protection are higher on bulk commodities than on intermediate products and highest on consumer-ready items.[9] This suggests that first-stage processors of raw materials do not get much benefit, and may actually have negative protection from tariffs, but those further up the processing chain may benefit considerably. Japanese tariffs are highest on bulk products, indicating that the tariff structure penalizes its own processing sector, while Canada appears to exhibit the same type of tariff escalation as the EU and the USA, with the tariff structure protecting processing activities. There is evidence that tariff escalation is more pronounced in commodities such as meat, sugar, fruit, coffee, cocoa, and hides and skins (UNCTAD, 2006: 77). These commodities have a particular importance to developing country exporters.[10]

[9] However, the category of consumer-ready items includes some unprocessed products such as apples and bananas.
[10] Comparing tariffs across broad commodity groups is only a rough indicator of the extent of tariff escalation since it does not capture input–output relationships among commodities. More research is needed to estimate more precisely the extent of tariff escalation, especially in the context of general equilibrium modeling.

Tariff Rate Quotas

TRQs were introduced to open up markets controlled by non-tariff border measures. They have, however, become a controversial aspect of the trade regime for agricultural products. Although tariff rate quotas cover only 6 per cent of tariff lines, they are prevalent in sensitive sectors such as meat, dairy, sugar, and cereals. In all, 1,371 tariff rate quotas have been notified to the WTO, covering a wide variety of bulk and processed products. TRQs are used primarily by developed countries: only 37 of the 137 WTO members use them. Abbott and Morse (2000) examined tariff rate quotas for 14 developing countries and found only a few cases of binding quotas. Many countries applied tariff rate quotas as a simple tariff (no higher over-quota tariff was levied, and hence the quota was ineffective). Eastern European countries also appear to be using tariff rate quotas frequently as simple tariffs, enforcing only 65 per cent of their tariff rate quotas. Iceland and Norway account for 322 tariff rate quotas, but 90 per cent of them are administered as simple tariffs. In fact, quota restrictions are applied for only half of the tariff rate quotas notified to the WTO. As a result, enforcement is concentrated in a relatively small number of developed countries that use them to protect sensitive products.

Although tariff rate quotas were designed to increase market access for commodities that previously faced quantitative barriers, high in-quota and over-quota tariffs imply that tariff rate quotas can still be an impediment to trade. Across all WTO members, the average over-quota tariff is 123 per cent, suggesting that the tariff rate quotas work in much the same way as the quantitative restrictions that they replaced. Five countries have average over-quota tariffs of at least 150 per cent, and in certain instances the over-quota tariffs exceed 1,000 per cent (for example, the Japanese tariff on dried peas). Across WTO members, the simple average in-quota tariff is 63 per cent, similar to that for all types of agricultural tariffs—or even lower, at 50 per cent if a few very high tariffs are excluded. High in-quota tariffs have led to low quota fill rates, often below 65 per cent. In addition, tariff rate quotas have been administered in different ways, causing exporters to argue for more uniformity. Tariff rate quota regimes may provide less market access than the architects of the URAA wished.

Tariff Preferences

One major consideration in interpreting tariff schedules and averages is the widespread network of preferences. The total number of such discriminatory trade regimes notified to the WTO is above 300, involving almost all of the 153 WTO members. Very few countries are not signatories to one or more of such agreements, and many are members of more than one. Incorporating the array of tariff preferences into databases has been a formidable challenge. The latest version of the GTAP database has incorporated some

Table 11.2 Trade-weighted average bound tariffs and average applied agricultural tariffs in 2001, selected countries (percentage)

Country	Average Bound Tariff	Average Applied Tariff
Australia	5.9	3.0
Canada	19.6	9.7
Japan	62.1	34.6
United States	6.2	2.7
EFTA	70.8	28.6
EU	20.5	11.8

Source: Jean, Laborde, and Martin (2006: 91).

important improvements made possible by a French institute CEPII, which includes the impact of preferences its MacMaps database.[11]

The impact of taking into account tariff preferences in comparing tariffs is illustrated in Table 11.2. The table compares the average bound rate with the average applied rate, including preferences. The applied tariff in developed countries is only about one half the bound rate even though the MFN rate is typically very close to the bound rate. So countries that do not qualify for preferential access will suffer a loss of competitiveness in these markets.

Agricultural Safeguards

Among the other innovations in the market access rules of the URAA, those that relate to safeguards had a particularly significant role in convincing those countries that were reluctant to open markets that severe disruption can be avoided. The URAA allows countries to apply special safeguard duties to counter import surges for products whose border protection was "tariffied" and included in the country schedules. The special agricultural safeguard provision allows the imposition of an additional tariff when certain criteria are met: a specified rapid surge in imports (volume trigger) or, on a shipment-by-shipment basis, a fall in the import price below a specified reference price (price trigger). For the volume trigger, higher duties apply only until the end of the year in question. For the price trigger, an additional duty can be imposed only on the shipment concerned. Additional duties cannot be applied to imports within tariff rate quotas. Box 11.1 discusses the use of this safeguard.

[11] More information can be found at the CEPII website <www.cepii.fr>.

Box 11.1 Special Agricultural Safeguards

Of the 137 WTO members that notified tariff rate quotas, only 38 reserved the right to use special safeguards in their URAA schedule of commitments. The share of agricultural tariff lines covered by special safeguards ranges from less than 1 per cent for many developing countries to 9 per cent for the USA, 12 per cent for Japan, 31 per cent for the EU, 49 per cent for Norway, 59 per cent for Switzerland, and 66 per cent for Poland. The number of tariff items that could potentially be protected by special safeguards ranges from 10 for Australia to 961 for Switzerland.

The coverage across product categories reflects the degree of sensitivity to liberalization in each economy. Product coverage is concentrated in dairy for the USA; cereals for Japan; and meat, dairy products, fruits, and vegetables for the EU. The USA declared coffee and tea to be covered by special safeguards to prevent the entry of sugar in dry or powdered beverage preparations. Norway and Switzerland reserve the right to use special safeguards across almost all products.

Despite the broad coverage across products, few special safeguard actions have been taken.[1] Since 1995 only the EU, Japan, and the USA have notified special safeguard actions in almost all years. Of 436 price-based actions reported during 1995–99 the USA accounted for more than a half, Poland for a third, and the EU for about a tenth. Price-based actions tended to be directed at relatively small volumes of imports from specific sources. Of 213 volume-based actions the EU and Japan combined accounted for more than 90 per cent, with the EU alone accounting for almost 60 per cent. The EU used the volume-based special safeguards for fruits (particularly citrus) and vegetables (particularly tomatoes).

In practice the special safeguard provision appears to have been used to balance internal markets by Japan, the EU, and the USA. The US application of price-triggered special safeguard duties on relatively small quantities of individual dairy product imports signaled to exporters that their products would face routinely applied special safeguard duties when trying to gain access to the US market. The EU used the special safeguard, in concert with other policies and regional agreements, to balance internal markets for perishable fruits and vegetables by restricting imports. Only Poland seems to have resorted to special safeguards on several occasions to counteract inflows of products. The USA has used the price trigger to place duties on dairy products, peanuts, and sugar-containing powder and dry beverages. Overall, the special safeguard provisions of the URAA appear not to have been used as a haven for countries seeking to avoid their liberalization commitments.

---

[1] However, for a period after implementation of the URAA, international and national prices for many agricultural products were high by historical standards and so would not have triggered efforts to limit imports.

Export Competition

Many observers consider the rules on export competition to be the most important element of the URAA, by establishing effective constraints on agricultural policies that generated surpluses that had no ready market abroad and hence affected world trading conditions. Implementation of the rules on export competition became an important test for the effectiveness of the URAA.

Based on this criterion, the URAA appears to have worked rather well, though it should be noted that export subsidies were high in the base period and the first few years of the URAA saw higher world prices and thus lower export subsidies. Above all, the URAA prohibited any new export subsidies and increases in existing export assistance programs. The number of countries that are able to grant export subsidies and the products that they can subsidize are now limited. These limits have generally been observed: there has only been one case in which a country flagrantly exceeded its commitments on the volume of subsidized exports or budgetary outlays or granted export subsidies on products not specified in its schedule. The operation of the export competition rules has been without major controversy, with the important exceptions of the cases of Canadian dairy policy, EU sugar policy, and US cotton policy where the respondent member was found (*inter alia*) to have breached its export subsidy commitments.

But these data give a misleading picture of the extent of export subsidies. Overall, WTO members used less than 40 per cent of their allowable export subsidy outlays on aggregate from 1995 to 1998. Many agricultural policy developments underlay this phenomenon, and high world market prices for some agricultural commodities during the URAA implementation period (in particular for cereals in 1995 and 1996) also helped. Moreover, there was "water" in the export subsidy commitments, as the base period chosen for setting the constraints was characterized by particularly large expenditures. Nonetheless, based on the aggregate quantitative experience with the export subsidy commitments, this part of the URAA appears to have been implemented with few problems.

Export Subsidies

Though the URAA has curbed export subsidies, they remain a major factor in world commodity markets. Between 1995 and 2000, WTO members spent more than $42 billion subsidizing exports, with the EU accounting for nearly 90 per cent, Switzerland for 5 per cent, and the USA for less than 2 per cent (Table 11.3). The EU is the largest user of export subsidies in both value and volume terms.[12] According to WTO notifications, the EU spent an average of $6 billion annually from 1995 to 1998 on export subsidies, though expenditures fell in 2000 with firmer prices (and weaker currencies).

Export subsidies are focused on relatively few commodities. Total expenditures on export subsidies by WTO members have been greatest for dairy products—accounting for 34 per cent of all export subsidy expenditures from 1995 to 1998. Among individual commodities, beef has the largest subsidy expenditure at 21 per cent, averaging

---

[12] The EU and Switzerland rely on export subsidies more than most WTO members because they support producers through high internal prices, which stimulate production above domestic needs and commercial export possibilities. Both also employ import barriers to keep cheaper imported products out of the domestic market. The size of export subsidies changes with fluctuations in world prices and exchange rates, as the price gap between the domestic and world price is the per unit export subsidy.

Table 11.3 Total expenditure on export subsidies by country, 1995–2002 (US$ millions)

Country	1995	1996	1997	1998	1999	2000 1/	2001 1/	2002 1/
European Union	6,495.9	7,071.2	4,856.7	5,989.0	5,853.7	2,516.6	2,297.1	3,269.5
United States	25.6	121.5	112.2	146.7	80.2	15.3	54.6	31.5
Switzerland	83.9	77.9	99.9	76.9	126.2	44.0	32.0	NA
Norway	454.6	392.1	294.5	292.8	268.9	187.7	138.4	137.1
Rest of World	263.7	225.0	200.4	175.7	190.5	160.9	55.0	108.8
Total	7,323.6	7,887.6	5,563.6	6,681.0	6,519.5	2,924.5	2,577.1	3,547.0

Source: US Department of Agriculture, Economic Research Service calculations based on WTO notifications.

$1.4 billion a year. Grains, sugar, and processed products together accounted for 35 per cent of expenditures.

From 1995 to 1998, the EU subsidized nearly all of its exports of coarse grains, butter and butter oil, beef, and skim milk powder and much of its wheat and other dairy exports. Switzerland subsidizes exports of breeding cattle and horses, dairy products, fruit, potatoes, and processed products. Dairy products account for 65 per cent of Swiss subsidy expenditures and nearly 80 per cent of subsidized export volume—averaging nearly $230 million and 59,000 tons per year. Nearly 98 per cent of US export subsidy expenditures have been for dairy products, just under 2 per cent for poultry, and less than 1 per cent for coarse grains.

The URAA did not explicitly restrict per unit subsidies; consequently, the size of subsidies has varied greatly across countries and commodities. Subsidy expenditures on a dollar per ton basis have been largest for such high value products as alcohol, wine, and fresh flowers. However, those commodities account for less than 1 per cent of subsidized export expenditures and subsidized export volume. In terms of sectors, dairy has had the largest subsidies per ton. Such subsidies would be expected to have decreased over the implementation period of the URAA, because both permissible volume and value limits were declining. Generally, export subsidies have trended downward recently, due both to market conditions and exchange rates and to reductions in the difference between domestic and world prices.

Export Credits

Export subsidies are not the only policies to distort commodity export markets. Subsidies given through advantageous credit terms have also come under scrutiny. The Uruguay Round was unable to deal with this issue, and subsequent negotiations in the

OECD did not bear fruit. This has become an important element in the Doha Round, as the EU has insisted that the use of export credits (mainly by the US) be disciplined if the EU is to relinquish its use of export subsidies.

Short-term export credit is important to many international transactions. Governments are commonly involved in export credit activity, both for agriculture and other commodities. This "officially supported export credit," as it is termed by the OECD and the WTO, can include state agencies (including state traders) that offer credit, interest rate subsidies offered by government, government assumption of default risk for private loans, and publicly supported or subsidized insurance offered to private lenders. For agricultural commodities, default risk guarantees are the most common form of officially supported export credit. Insurance schemes and credit offered by state trading agencies are also used. Explicit interest rate subsidies are uncommon.

Officially supported export credit can act as a subsidy if the terms of the loans are more favorable than those available in the market. For example, if the interest rate does not fully reflect country risk premiums, a subsidy element is present. The extent of the subsidy depends on interest rates relative to market rates (appropriately reflecting risk), fees charged, down payments required, and the term of the loan. The longer the term for a given interest rate, down payment, and fee structure, the greater the subsidy element. Since risk premiums reflect default risk (at least in theory), the subsidy element of programs that involve default risk guarantees can be gauged from the extent to which government budgetary outlays are required to pay off guarantees. More information on export credits is given in Box 11.2.

Box 11.2 Export Credit Programs

A detailed OECD (2000) study on officially supported export credit programs indicates that the use of export credits in agricultural markets increased from $5.5 billion in 1995 to $7.9 billion in 1998. Credits represented 3.6 per cent of the value of total agricultural exports in 1995 and 5.2 per cent in 1998. That expansion was likely to have been caused by deteriorating financial market conditions, especially the Asian financial crisis in 1997. Interest rates increased substantially during 1998, reflecting the continuing financial crisis.

Few countries used export credits to any significant extent. Only four countries had subsidies that exceeded 1 per cent: 6.6 per cent in the USA, 3.8 per cent in Norway, 3.8 per cent in France, and 1.2 per cent in Canada. The distortions to trade patterns due to export credits are therefore likely to be relatively small.

Less than half of the loans offered under officially supported export credit programs are for a term of more than one year, and more than 96 per cent of these are from the USA, which accounts for 88 per cent of the estimated subsidy value of these programs. The EU accounts for 7 per cent of export credit subsidies, Canada for 4 per cent, and Australia for 1 per cent. Thus, the potential use of export credits as subsidies is largely a US issue. Since the URAA, the US has relied largely on export credits rather than direct export subsidies, whereas the EU has relied on direct export subsidies.

(Continued)

Box 11.2 *Continued*

Bulk cereals are the most important commodity group that benefit from subsidized export credits. More than one-third of subsidies in 1996–97 went to cereals, and up to 14.5 per cent (in 1997) of cereal exports received credit subsidies. However, officially supported export credit programs exist for a wide variety of commodities. The OECD report also notes that most subsidized credits are applied to trade between its member countries. The least developed countries accounted for only 0.2 per cent of export credits, and food-importing developing countries for only 8.9 per cent. For this reason the OECD concludes that disciplines on agricultural export credits would not greatly harm poorer food importing countries. The OECD suggests that this is indirect evidence that liquidity constraints for such countries are not being relieved. However, the study shows increasing use of export credits during the Asian financial crisis, when liquidity constraints were likely to be binding.

IV. Domestic Subsidies to Agriculture

Developed country farm subsidies have risen on the agenda in discussions of agricultural trade. The problem that such subsidies posed for a more open trade system was recognized in the Harbeler Report (1958) presented to the General Agreement on Tariffs and Trade (GATT). The OECD countries began to pay more attention to domestic subsidies in the early 1980s, and by the time of the Uruguay Round in 1986, it was generally agreed that domestic support was a key contributor to distortions in world markets, and that disciplines in this area had to be a part of any trade policy reform.

This section will discuss the prevalence of subsidies, their level, and changes over time. The measurement of the level and the effect of subsidies conferred by the variety of domestic programs has always been problematic. The Harbeler Report mentioned this as a difficulty that had to be surmounted before effective multilateral control could be established. An attempt to measure agricultural protection in developed countries was made in the context of an FAO program on international agricultural adjustment (FAO 1973, 1975) and updated through 1985. This work was built around the Producer and Consumer Subsidy Equivalents (PSEs and CSEs) that calculated the subsidy (or tax) equivalent of the collection of policies in place. The method was adopted by the USDA, which calculated PSEs for a different group of countries and published these estimates from 1985 to 1992, and, as described in Box 11.3, the OECD, which has published PSEs regularly from 1986 until the present (OECD, 2009). A somewhat different measure of the level of subsidies was introduced through the WTO Aggregate Measure of Support (AMS) notifications, made by each member that entered domestic support commitments in their schedules (mostly developed countries) from 1995 to the present date.

Box 11.3 Producer Subsidy Equivalent (PSE)

The first systematic attempt to monitor developed country farm policies was undertaken in the context of a study on international agricultural adjustment, the way in which the agricultural economy of the world adjusted as countries interacted with each other through trade and aid and influenced each other through their domestic policies (FAO, 1973, 1975). The project was motivated by the realization that these policies were having a profound impact on world markets for agricultural goods. The 1973 paper lays out the rationale for monitoring such policies and the links with the issues of trade liberalization in the GATT. Two main indicators were developed: the PSE, and the Consumer Tax Equivalent (CTE).[1] Several measures were developed as potentially useful for trade talks, including the tariff equivalent ((TE), calculated as a weighted average of PSE and CSE) and the Foreign Exchange Displacement (FE) of the policies, designed to indicate the magnitude of the external impact of a country's agricultural policies.[2] The report was presented to the FAO Conference in 1973 as part of the plans for a regular monitoring of IAA. The 1975 paper revised the method and terminology somewhat, and developed the link with trade negotiations. The consumer indicator was relabeled the CSE and its sign changed.

---

[1] These measures were expressed in both per unit and percentage terms. In addition, the actual values of the transfers were calculated as the Producer Subsidy Value (PSV) and the Consumer Burden (CB), along with the Exchequer Cost (EC) and the effective protection. These were grouped as "domestic performance measures."

[2] Two further indicators were also presented in that report, one the ratio of the TE to the PSE represented the extent to which the transfers captured in the PSE are trade distorting, and the other the ratio of the FE to the PSV reflecting the external impact per unit of transfer.

OECD Trade Mandate

The Organisation for Economic Co-operation and Development has a longstanding interest in agricultural policies and more recently in their trade impacts. In 1982, the OECD Ministerial Council committed itself to the task of tackling the problems of agricultural policies and their effects on trade (Legg, 2003). Ministers approved a Mandate that required the Secretariat to analyze "approaches and methods for a balanced and gradual reduction in protection for agriculture and the fuller integration of agriculture within the open multilateral trading system." In doing so they were to conduct an examination of national policies that have a significant impact on international trade. The 1987 report (National Policies and International Trade) was the result of this endeavor (OECD, 1987). The OECD began to monitor domestic agricultural policies of its members and calculate subsidy equivalents for the major commodities. The focus of the OECD work was on the need to reform domestic policies in part to avoid trade impacts but also to improve domestic policy targeting.

The OECD methodology, as it has developed over time, now comprises a three-part classification of policy measures. The PSE itself is made up of Market Price Support (MPS) and Budgetary Payments; the General Services Support Estimate (GSSE), including research and development, infrastructure, marketing and promotion payments, and inspection services; and any transfers from taxpayers to consumers. The total of these three items is known as the Total Support Estimate (TSE). This is equivalent to the sum of transfers to consumers and producers less any budget revenues, such as from import tariffs.

The OECD PSEs represent the most ambitious attempt to date in monitoring agricultural policies. The PSE dataset is both the longest series of quantitative policy indicators (in any sector) and the most inclusive in terms of countries and commodities. It is also unique in that government officials and statisticians take part in the overs ight of the estimates, giving the resulting estimates an implicit degree of approval. As a result it has widespread acceptance among governments and the media, and is the most frequently used measure for modeling policies and constructing models with policy variables.

The development of the total PSE for the OECD countries is shown in Figure 11.2. There has been remarkably little trend in the measure over the past 20 years. The variations correspond closely to world price fluctuations, which affect the level of market price support, a major component of the PSE. However, the real value of the transfers is declining, as is the percentage of total farm receipts. Though the level of domestic subsidies has remained high over the past decade, the nature of those subsidies has been changing in a way that should reduce the trade impacts. Figure 11.2 shows the level of PSE fluctuating between $230 and $280 billion over the past 20 years. However, the share of farm receipts that come from these transfers has declined steadily, if not dramatically, from 40 per cent to 30 per cent. In the current Doha Round, the further reduction of trade distorting agricultural subsidies has become a major objective.

The PSE by country shows considerable differences: Figure 11.3 gives the subsidy levels at the beginning and end of the period for 17 OECD members. The highest levels of protection are in Japan and Korea as well as in Iceland, Norway, and Switzerland.

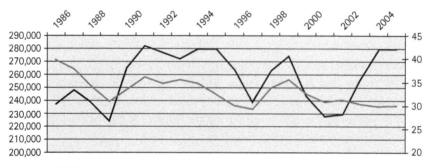

FIGURE 11.2 OECD producer support estimate, 1986–2005 (US$ million and percentage of farm receipts)

Source: See <www.oecd.org>.

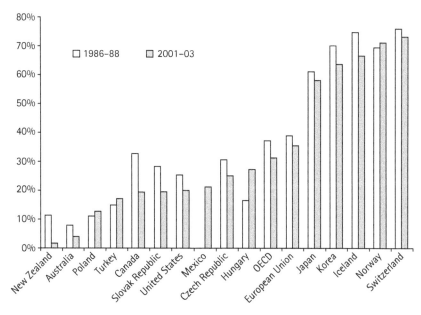

FIGURE 11.3 Agricultural producer support in high-income countries, by country, 1986–2003 (percentage of total farm receipts from support policy measures)

Notes: Czech Republic, Hungary, Poland, and the Slovak Republic data are for 1991–93 in the first period. Austria, Finland, and Sweden are included in the OECD average for both periods but also in the EU average for the latter period.

Source: PSE estimates from the OECD's PSE database (see <www.oecd.org>).

WTO AMS Notifications

The World Trade Organization also monitors agricultural policies of member countries. The Uruguay Round Agreement on Agriculture included the provision for monitoring compliance with commitments to reduce domestic support that was deemed to be trade distorting. The commitments were expressed as an AMS, known popularly as the Amber Box, calculated according to agreed procedures laid down by the Committee on Agriculture (WTO, 1995). Though based loosely on the OECD PSEs, the concept of the Amber Box is somewhat different from the PSE, as it is based largely on budgetary payments and the implied transfer of administered domestic prices relative to a fixed reference price. Thus, it includes some support that would otherwise be captured in the price effects of border measures (in effect double counting this support, as it is also monitored in market access and export subsidy commitments) but it excludes many elements of subsidy that are included in the PSE. Thus, total domestic support as measured by the WTO includes the exempt transfers in the green and blue boxes, the special and differential treatment category for developing countries, a *de minimis* exemption, and the AMS, in turn comprised of market price support and (non-exempt) budgetary payments.

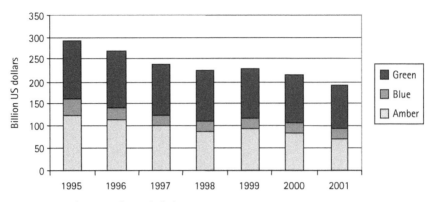

FIGURE 11.4 Trends in total notified domestic support

Source: Economic Research Service, USDA (2006).

The trend in the notified levels of AMS has also been downward. For the period over which there have been comparable notifications for the major developed countries (1995–2001: Figure 11.4) the total AMS (Amber Box) fell from $123 to $74 billion.[13]

An interesting dimension is added to this picture if the subsidies to the processing industry are included. This has been attempted with the GTAP database by Anderson, Martin, and Valenzuela (2006). Table 11.4 shows the magnitude of such subsidies in 2001. Included in the table is a column of support to primary agriculture, as reported by the OECD for member countries. The total, at $228 billion, includes $140 billion in market price support. The GTAP database includes somewhat smaller figures for this support to agriculture. But the GTAP data allow calculation of support to processed agricultural products, and this amount is as high as the OECD estimate for primary agriculture. So the total support for both agriculture and the processing sector is almost $500 billion. Only 20 per cent of this is in the form of direct subsidies: the majority is paid through the support of market prices, much of that by means of tariffs.

IV. PROTECTION THROUGH REGULATIONS

Another type of protection has come from regulations that discriminate against imports through the operation of rules ostensibly designed to prevent the importation of agents that could spread disease in plants or animals or harm human health. Such regulations

[13] Both the USA and the EU have brought their notifications more up to date (to 2006). This shows that the AMS has continued to decline for the EU but the USA has been considerably closer to its agreed limit. An IFPRI study has made unofficial estimates of the "missing" domestic support notifications through 2008 for the USA, EU, Japan, China, India, Brazil, the Philippines, and Norway (see the website at <www.IFPRI.org>).

Table 11.4 Government support to primary agriculture and processed food sectors, by region and policy instrument, 2001 (US$ billion)

	OECD estimates of support to primary agriculture	GTAP database estimates of support to primary agriculture			GTAP database estimates of support to processed agriculture			GTAP database estimates of support to all countries' agriculture and food (% in brackets)
	OECD countries	OECD countries	Non-OECD countries	All countries	OECD countries	Non-OECD countries	All countries	
Direct domestic subsidies	89	90	7	97	0	0	0	97 (19%)
–Fully coupled to prodn	37							
MPS	139	46	76	122	198	82	280	402 (81%)
–Export subsidies	na	3	1	4	26	0.1	26	30 (6%)
–Import tariffs	na	43	75	118	172	82	254	372 (75%)
All support measures	**228**	**136**	**83**	**219**	**198**	**82**	**280**	**499 (100%)**

Source: OECD (2004) for column 1, and Anderson, Martin, and Valenzuela (2006) from the GTAP database (see <www.gtap.org>).

are of course a normal aspect of trade, but on occasions can be used to protect the incomes of local producers rather than the health and safety of consumers, animals, and plants.

This section will address the question of trade barriers through such regulations and health and safety measures (SPS) as well as technical barriers (TBT) and intellectual property protection (Geographical Indications (GIs)), as they impact agricultural and food trade and developing country exports.

The central element of the multilateral rule system for food trade is the SPS Agreement that deals with trade restrictions used in support of measures designed to ensure human, animal, and plant health. An accompanying agreement, the TBT Agreement, relates to technical regulations not designed to deal with health issues. The primary function of the SPS Agreement was to clarify the meaning of Article XX of the GATT. That article established the right of countries to use trade measures if they are necessary to protect animal, plant, and human health. The SPS Agreement reaffirms that right but elaborates on the procedures that countries should follow to be sure that they are not unduly restricting market access for other countries. As such, it sets up a framework for national SPS measures so that countries may be certain that they are operating such policies in a way that does not infringe on the rights of trade partners; and it offers a "notification and review" process that allows countries to challenge those measures that appear to infringe on the rights of themselves and others.

The increase in transparency is a major aspect of the reduction of transactions costs for the food industry, and constitutes a significant improvement in the multilateral food system. As Josling, Roberts, and Orden (2004) put it:

> The WTO's notification requirements constitute the cornerstone of the transparency provisions that are intended to facilitate decentralized policing by trading partners to ensure compliance with the SPS and TBT Agreements' substantive provisions. All of the major agricultural exporting and importing countries now routinely notify proposed measures. Each notification indicates, among other things, what the proposed measure is, which product or products it is applied to, if it is based on an international standard, and when it is expected to come into force. This increased transparency contributes to the smooth functioning of the world trading system by facilitating both compliance and complaints by trading partners. Compliance is aided when advance notice of new or modified measures provides an opportunity for firms to change production methods to meet new import requirements, thereby minimizing disruptions that such changes can cause to trade flows.

The negative inducements in the case of food safety regulations were designed to dissuade countries from using SPS measures to protect the incomes of domestic farmers. The most significant of these provisions are:

- Prohibition on SPS measures that are not developed by the use of risk assessment and are not part of a consistent program to maintain an "acceptable level of risk."

- Multilateral standards agreed in the standard setting bodies are deemed to be based on risk assessment and therefore should be applied, where such standards exist, unless the country concerned can show with scientific evidence that such a deviation is necessary.

The combination of these two strictures implies a regime for health and safety standards based on risk management principles widely accepted and understood in the scientific community, rather than reacting to the pressures put on regulatory agencies by interested parties.

Positive inducements are designed to give national standards bodies the confidence that the new regime involves credible commitments. They include:

- Setting up of the SPS Committee and the obligation to notify changes in regulations to the Committee before they come into operation.
- The opportunity to challenge the regulations of other countries in the Committee as a way of defusing conflicts.
- Establishing a source of information for exporters on importer SPS regulations.

Moreover, the SPS Agreement attempts to guide countries in their use of harmonized or mutually agreed standards.

- Regarding harmonization, it endorses in particular the use of the standards developed by Codex Alimentarius (CODEX) and the procedures followed by the International Plant Protection Convention (IPPC) for the tracking and control of plant diseases and the International Office of Epizootics (OIE) for similar monitoring of animal diseases. While not requiring countries to use such multilateral standards, the SPS Agreement has had the effect of raising the profile of the three standards bodies, in effect by making the use of their standards and procedures *de facto* consistent with the provisions of the Agreement.
- Regarding equivalence, the SPS Agreement also promotes the use of "equivalence" of regulations negotiated between importers and exporters and "regionalization" of SPS measures, whereby parts of countries can be declared free of particular diseases and be granted access to importing country markets.

The TBT Agreement is not quite as strict in some respects as the SPS Agreement: it does not require a risk assessment and does not insist on scientific evidence as the main criterion for justification of a measure. Additionally, it does not explicitly name specific international standards organizations as the basis for accepted domestic standards—leading in some cases to uncertainty as to what constitutes an international standard. But the TBT Agreement is not by any means without constraints. It provides that technical regulations should be applied in a non-discriminatory way, should be used only in pursuit of legitimate objectives, and should be least trade disruptive, taking into account the risks of not fulfilling the objective of the regulation. Risks should therefore be assessed, but in the broader context of a set of objectives that is not limited to health and safety issues. These legitimate objectives could include national security considerations and prevention of deceptive practices, as well as environmental protection.

Some important aspects of agricultural and food production and marketing were included in the TRIPS. The key elements were the obligation to set up protective regulations to apply within each country's borders. For agriculture these include:

- The protection of patents for biotechnology, specifically new plant material created by gene transfer.
- The establishment of Plant Breeders Rights, but with some flexibility for countries as to how to grant that protection.
- The protection of GIs, though again allowing countries a wide range of instruments to effect that protection.

The inclusion of the protection of GIs in the negotiations in the Uruguay Round on trade-related intellectual property issues has essentially transformed GI issues from national, bilateral, or plurilateral matters to the multilateral stage.

The TRIPS Agreement incorporates GIs by requiring member states to "provide the legal means for interested parties to prevent" the use of any means "in the designation or presentation of a good that indicates or suggests that the good in question originates in a geographical area other than the true place of origin in a manner that misleads the public as to the geographical origin of the good," as well as any use "which constitutes an act of unfair competition."

Wines and spirits are singled out for a more comprehensive level of protection. This additional protection was at the request of the EU, and is generally considered to have been a concession by exporters who were unconvinced by the need for such measures in return for restraints on EU subsidies. It is stipulated that each member shall provide legal protection for geographical indications "even where the true origin of the goods is indicated or the geographical indication is used in translation or accompanied by expressions such as 'kind', 'type', 'style', 'imitation' or the like." No mention is made of misleading the public or unfairly competing as the presumption is that no such conditions are required for GI protection for wines and spirits. Moreover, the scope for allowing "generic" exceptions, where a geographical name has become widely used for a type of product regardless of origin, is much narrower for wines and spirits.

The intention of the TRIPS, in the area of GIs, was to increase the level of protection given to such property rights within the global trade system. The Agreement itself gives two avenues to pursue this aim. Countries are mandated to push ahead with a multilateral register of wines and spirits and Members are committed to "enter into negotiations aimed at increasing the protection of individual geographical indications." The more significant issue in the longer run is whether to extend the additional benefits given to wines and spirits to other agricultural and food products. Certain countries have been anxious to provide that extra protection in order to be able to develop market reputations that would increase producer income. As with wines, this would shift the emphasis away from the prevention of deception towards the control of competition from other producers. The wines and spirits register is the source of some controversy, and countries have not been able to agree on its status. The extension of protections given to wines and spirits to other foods and beverages is still further off.

VI. Negotiated Limits to Protection and Subsidies

Multilateral rules governing agricultural trade were introduced in the Uruguay Round in 1995. These replaced the unsatisfactory treatment of the sector in the GATT Articles, which in effect provided loopholes for most of the instruments of protection that had been introduced by countries over the years. These rules have made the types and levels of protection more apparent: the reduction of the protection is one of the main tasks of the current Doha Round. This section outlines the nature of the limits to subsidies and to protection as negotiated in the Uruguay Round, and relates this to the current trade negotiations in the DDA and through bilateral agreements and to the ongoing autonomous reforms in farm policy

Domestic farm policy, and the border measures that accompany it, have not historically been subject to significant constraints under the rules of international trade. The GATT covered agricultural as well as manufactured trade, but made two significant exceptions to the general principles in the case of primary products. One was to provide an exception to the rule that all import barriers should be in the form of customs duties by allowing quotas and licenses in cases where the domestic production of an agricultural product was subject to supply control (Article XI:2 (c)). Many countries relied on this clause to restrict imports by quantitative trade barriers when domestic markets were being managed. A prominent example was the quotas imposed by the USA under Section 22 of the Agricultural Adjustment Act (as amended), which mandated quantitative restrictions on imports of a number of goods whenever domestic programs were "materially interfered with" by imports.

The other exception was to specify different rules for export subsidies of manufactures and primary products. Though the original GATT subjected both primary and manufactured-product export subsidies to the same notification and consultation procedures, in 1955 it was agreed to add an explicit prohibition on export subsidies on manufactured goods (Article XVI). Agricultural export subsidies were constrained only by the obligation not to use such subsidies to capture "more than an equitable share" of world markets. Successive GATT panels failed to come up with a satisfactory definition of this concept, and agricultural export subsidies in effect escaped any disciplines (Josling and Tangermann, 2003).

The result of these two exceptions was that many instruments used by countries in support of their domestic agricultural sectors escaped effective scrutiny and discipline in the GATT. But this was exacerbated by the request by the USA in 1955 to be granted a waiver from the provisions of Article XI:2 (c) so that quantitative restrictions could be imposed regardless of whether there were internal supply control programs in place.[14] By the 1980s it was clear that world markets were being distorted by the competitive subsidization of temperate zone farm products. A number of attempts to discipline export subsidies, particularly those employed by the EEC, by challenging such policies under the weak provisions of Article XVI failed. Moreover, it was increasingly clear that no discipline in the GATT would be effective if they did not constrain domestic price support policies. So the USA, along with other exporting countries, insisted that the rules negotiated in the Uruguay Round of GATT trade negotiations (1986–94) included more enforceable and coherent constraints on agricultural trade instruments and those aspects of domestic farm policy that distorted agricultural trade.

The URAA Rules

The URAA came into effect in 1995 as a part of the Marrakesh Agreement that established the WTO. The URAA modifies and elaborates on those Articles of the GATT that specifically deal with agricultural trade.[15] The Agreement also includes the country schedules that were appended to the WTO Treaty. These schedules contained maximum permitted levels for export subsidies and for certain types of domestic subsidies, as well as commitments for the reduction of bound tariffs.

The central elements of the URAA are often referred to as the three "pillars"—market access, domestic support, and export competition. In all three areas, new rules were added and reductions in trade barriers were agreed. Together they form a comprehensive framework for the regulation of measures that restrict trade in agricultural products. The full impact of the URAA includes the benefits that any country might get from the restraint on other country's policies as well as the restraints that are accepted for their own policy.

Market access rules include the conversion of all non-tariff import barriers (quotas and restrictive licenses) to tariffs. Moreover, it was agreed that tariff levels were to be bound and that TRQs—quantities that can be imported at a zero or low tariff) were to be established to maintain market access as "tariffication" took place. These TRQs were to represent "current access" in cases of existing trade or a "minimum access" of 3 per

---

[14] The EEC also avoided GATT disciplines by choosing as their main instrument of border protection a "variable levy" (a tariff that changed frequently depending on the level of import prices, so as to stabilize domestic markets). Countries were unable to agree whether or not this constituted a customs duty, and it was never bound in the GATT. The EU also called its export subsidies "export restitutions" and for many years claimed that they were not covered by the GATT.

[15] The scope of the URAA covers products in HS Chapters 1–24, excluding fish and fish products but including cotton, wool, hides, flax and hemp, and a few other products.

cent of domestic consumption (rising to 5 per cent over the implementation period) in cases where there were no imports in the base period. Tariffs were to be reduced from the base period (1986–90) by an (unweighted) average of 36 per cent, with a minimum cut of 15 per cent for each tariff line, over a six-year period (1995–2000).[16] In addition, the Agreement established a special safeguard (SSG) regime that countries could use to counter import surges or price drops in markets where they had newly established tariffs.

Domestic support was defined to include payments to farmers in addition to the transfers from consumers through border policies. These included deficiency payments, direct income supplements, administrative price systems and subsidies tied to research and extension, conservation compliance, and other programs that benefited farmers directly. These elements of domestic support were put into three categories, which have become known as the Amber Box, the Blue Box, and the Green Box.

Amber Box measures were those tied to output or input prices or to current output levels. These were to be reduced by 20 per cent (in aggregate) relative to the base period (1986–90) subject to *de minimis* amounts that were excluded from the commitment.[17] The Blue Box contained subsidies that were tied to supply control programs: such subsidies were regarded as less obviously output increasing.[18] There was no reduction obligation for Blue Box policies, but such subsidies were restricted to payments based on fixed acreage and yield or paid on a maximum of 85 per cent of production. Green Box subsidies were defined as those unrelated to price and output ("decoupled") and included research and extension, payments designed to compensate farmers for the cost of compliance with environmental regulations), and domestic food assistance programs. Both the general criteria (that they be provided from public funds and not act as price supports) and the specific criteria for each type of subsidy identified have to be met. Those subsidies that qualified as Green Box payments were not constrained, though they had to be notified.

The rules regarding export competition included a prohibition on new export subsidies and a reduction of existing subsidies by both volume and expenditure. A list of export subsidy practices that are covered is given in Article 9.1. Following the agreed Modalities, country schedules were drawn up that provided for reductions relative to the base period of 36 per cent by expenditure and 21 per cent by quantity subsidized. In addition, rules were made more explicit with regard to food aid and countries agreed to negotiate limits on export credit guarantees (government underwriting of sales to purchasers that might lack creditworthiness).

---

[16] The levels of tariff reduction and the requirements for market opening were included in the "Modalities" document that formed the basis for offers (draft schedules). This document ceased to be relevant after the schedules themselves had been agreed.

[17] The Amber Box is here used to refer to all subsidies not in the Blue and Green Boxes, and therefore includes the *de minimis* payments that are excluded from AMS reduction commitments.

[18] The Blue Box category of subsidies was an outcome of the Blair House discussions between the EU and the USA in November 1992, and was designed to cover the case of US deficiency payments and EU compensation payments both of which were tied to acreage limitation programs (set-asides).

Monitoring Compliance

The constraints on policies related to market access are relatively easily monitored. Tariff schedules are the most transparent means of protection, and it is rare that countries violate their obligations in this regard. Tariff rate quotas and the use of the special safeguard mechanism are somewhat more difficult to track, but have not been the subject of great controversy. Somewhat less transparent, but nevertheless monitorable, are the constraints on export competition, in particular the quantitative limits to export subsidies. Both the expenditure on export subsidies and the volume of goods that could be exported with the aid of those subsidies were limited in the schedules.

WTO constraints on domestic farm policy are of a quantitative kind: any kind of domestic (non-border) subsidy is allowed but they are subject to quantitative limits. These quantitative constraints are built in to schedules that were agreed in the Uruguay Round. Policy developments are monitored: violations of constraints can be subject to the dispute settlement regime, and thus may entail considerable political and financial costs. Economic costs could also mount if a dispute was not resolved and countries were allowed to "withdraw concessions" by raising tariffs in retaliation.

The monitoring is implemented through the Agriculture Committee of the WTO, and is based on "notifications" by members. On the face of it, there has been essentially full compliance with the quantitative constraints built in to the schedules agreed in the UR, both by the USA and other OECD countries. WTO members accepted an obligation to notify annually the payments made on domestic support under the Agreement on Agriculture. Early notifications were prompt, but after a few years they became somewhat tardy, impairing the usefulness of the Committee as a place for timely challenges and the exchange of information. When the agricultural negations started in 2000, and particularly after the Doha ministerial that launched the Doha Round in November 2001, notifications virtually halted.[19] The notifications for the years up to 2006 have now been submitted by the USA and the EU but many developing countries are still behind and so the notifications give an imperfect view of current conditions.

The Doha Round

The WTO Doha negotiations on agriculture are premised on the notion that the constraints introduced in the Uruguay Round on domestic agricultural policy and on trade policy in agricultural products, though useful in themselves, need to be strengthened if the trade system for these goods is to become fully responsive to the needs of the global marketplace (Blandford and Josling, 2009). The most significant advance, from the point of view of opening up agricultural trade,

---

[19] A more effective if less formal monitoring process is carried out for the OECD countries through the annual monitoring and evaluation process, as discussed above with respect to the PSEs. Indeed the OECD has remained the preferred location for debate about agricultural policy changes.

would be the tariff cuts. The current "Chairman's draft" of the modalities (mechanisms for implementing the aims of the agreement) captures what appears to be a broadly acceptable outcome—subject to agreement in other areas (WTO, 2008). Agricultural tariffs would be cut according to a formula, which prescribes steeper cuts on higher tariffs. For developed countries the cuts would rise from 50 per cent for tariffs below 20 per cent, to 70 per cent for tariffs above 75 per cent, subject to a 54 per cent minimum average, with some additional constraints on tariffs above 100 per cent. For developing countries the cuts in each tier would be two-thirds of the equivalent tier for developed countries, subject to a maximum average of 36 per cent. However, some products would have smaller cuts as a result of several flexibilities designed to take into account various domestic concerns and the status of certain countries. These include sensitive products (available to all countries), the smaller cuts being offset by tariff quotas allowing more access at lower tariffs, and special products (for developing countries only) for specific situations related to development. The least-developed countries are encouraged to lower tariffs but not obliged to do so.

As to contingent tariffs, developed countries would lose the protection of the existing "special safeguard" (available to products "tariffied" in the Uruguay Round). The need for a special safeguard mechanism for developing countries has been agreed, but this is one of the few issues where there are still disagreements on the nature of an acceptable compromise. The disagreement over the form of the special safeguard mechanism (SSM) was one of the main reasons for the failure of the talks in July 2008. Technical discussions have progressed in the past year, but no political agreement has been found. The issue is considered critical, as many developing countries see the SSM as a necessary way to defend their vulnerable farm sectors against import surges: the developed country exporters view it as a method of preventing the opening up of markets and even regressing from the market opening of the Uruguay Round.

Negotiations on export competition have proved somewhat easier, as fewer countries have a vital interest in the topic. The EU is the main WTO member that would be affected, and there is a strong likelihood that the EU will in fact phase out export subsidies within the next few years for budgetary reasons. The main issues have been agreed for some months and the Chairman's Draft Modalities has widespread support. The modification to the URAA would be to eliminate all export subsidies and measures that have equivalent effect, namely the payments to marketing boards to cover export losses, the provision of credit and credit guarantees to exporting firms at below market rates, and the sales of food under the heading of food aid that neither meet emergencies nor are in the form of grants. Indeed, this question of the ways in which food aid can be disbursed has perhaps been the main cause of disagreements in the export competition talks.[20]

---

[20] Another source of contention was whether the new text should prohibit the monopoly sales of agricultural products by state trading export agencies (such as the Canadian Wheat Board). The text does not at present resolve this issue.

One interesting feature of the proposed modalities text is the development of further disciplines on domestic support, in particular to encourage countries to move to less trade disruptive instruments. Negotiations have made substantial progress in identifying improvements in the way in which domestic support must be constrained if it threatens to distort trade. Among the changes has been the introduction of a measure of the "Overall Trade-Distorting Domestic Support" (OTDS) to complement the AMS that had been defined and constrained in the Uruguay Round.[21] In addition, the AMS itself would be complemented by product-specific AMS limits. The Blue Box, currently encompassing policies that are linked to supply control, would be expanded to embrace payments made on a fixed area and yield (or the equivalent for livestock) but that do not require supply control. Total Blue Box payments would also be limited for the first time, and product-specific Blue Box caps would be introduced. The amount of *de minimis* support that is excluded from notified support in the URAA would be reduced and certain provisions in the Green Box would be modified (Blandford and Josling, 2009).

Of course, it may be the case that the Doha Round is never completed, in which case the exiting arrangements (including the bindings of support and export subsidies) would continue to apply. But the tensions that are still present in agricultural markets could lead to new attempts to improve the operation of the URAA and members may be tempted to explore further the option of challenging current practices (such as the notification of subsidies as "Green Box" when some productive activity is still required). Such litigation may clarify the meaning of the URAA but at considerable political cost. This could itself drive members back to the bargaining table. Or countries may find that they can achieve their agricultural and food policy objectives through regional and bilateral trade agreements. The next few years will tell in which direction agricultural policy rules will go.

VII. GAINERS AND LOSERS: STUDIES OF THE EFFECTS OF PROTECTION AND TRADE LIBERALIZATION

This section looks at the expected gains and losses from border protection and subsidies in agriculture, specifically by summarizing the results of some of the main studies on the

---

[21] The base period OTDS is defined as the sum of the "final bound" total AMS from the Uruguay Round agreement, 10 per cent of the value of production in the 1995–2000 base period (to match the current product-specific and non product-specific *de minimis* amounts that are excluded from the total AMS), and the higher of the Blue Box support in the base period or 5 per cent of the base period value of production.

incidence of agricultural protection and subsidies, both those using general equilibrium models and those focusing on particular sectors. These include

- Studies of the gains from tariff reductions in the Uruguay Round and from the further reductions envisaged in the Doha Development Agenda.
- Studies on the impact of export subsidies and of the proposals for elimination of such subsidies in DDA.
- Studies of specific trade impacts of subsidies, in particular the categories of subsidies notified to WTO, and of the proposals for domestic support reduction in DDA.

There has been considerable effort by academic researchers and intergovernmental institutions to calculate the gains and losses that one might expect from a new trade agreement. Individual governments also make these estimates, but their results are generally not distributed widely for comparison. Empirical results differ markedly, depending on the model and data used and in the specific assumptions made about the outcome of the round. As no one knows what the shape of the final package will be, no current estimates can give more than an indication of the economic benefits. And the economic benefits themselves are only the most quantifiable aspects of what is essentially a political decision.

The World Bank, in particular, has done some comprehensive work on the twin issues of the benefits from total trade liberalization and the extent to which the Doha Round promises to achieve those benefits. Recent results have become available from the use of the LINKAGE model (an economy-wide CGE model) widely used for a decade by the World Bank. In addition, estimates have been made by Hertel and his colleagues at Purdue using a widely known CGE model, GTAP.[22] Both these models use essentially the same database (GTAP 6) but differ in other ways. The GTAP model is essentially a comparative static exercise indicating the difference that trade liberalization would make with other things remaining the same. Growth rates are set exogenously. The LINKAGE model incorporates more dynamic responses and is extended out for a longer period, allowing other factors to change over time.

Another approach to modeling policy changes is to focus on a set of product markets and calculate the change on equilibrium values (price and traded quantities) in those markets arising from trade liberalization. The ERS and Penn State have developed such a partial equilibrium model (PEATSim) that has the capability of quantifying the impact of particular policy instruments in the developed countries. The partial equilibrium analysis simulates new market clearing prices and quantities, and is useful for detailed policy evaluation.

---

[22] IFPRI has reported some results from a similar CGE model (Bouet et al., 2005).

There are well-known strengths and weaknesses of these two types of models. CGE models incorporate linkages and feedbacks from the rest of the economy, and are particularly appropriate when considering non-agricultural policy changes as well as those for agriculture. On the other hand, it is less easy to specify complex policy changes in particular products, as aggregation of commodities and the simplification of policy instruments are inevitable in economy-wide models. Moreover, the information needed to build CGE models is extensive and the price of comprehensiveness is arbitrary decisions on the process of restoring equilibrium after a policy change. Nevertheless, there is no satisfactory alternative to a CGE analysis for assessing the overall benefits of trade policy changes implied by the Doha Round.

The World Bank study referred to above, as reported in Anderson and Martin (2006) estimated the total welfare (real income) impact of total liberalization of merchandise trade at $287 billion each year by the year 2015. This can be considered a "ballpark" potential gain if the liberalization is undertaken in all countries over a period 2005–10. Such a gain may be an underestimate if there is endogenous productivity growth over the period linked with trade expansion and increased competition.[23]

The gains are, as one would expect, unevenly distributed. Two-thirds of the benefit ($201.6 billion) goes to high-income countries, $69.5 billion to middle-income countries and $16.2 billion to low-income countries. However as a share of GNP, the benefits are more evenly distributed. High-income countries gain 0.6 per cent of income, while middle-income and low-income countries gain 0.8 per cent of their income. Though these gains may seem modest when compared to total income, they are persistent and may stimulate other gains through structural changes and investment opportunities.

Gains from Agricultural Liberalization

A useful study by the Congressional Budget Office (CBO, 2006) has attempted to collate the various studies that estimate the benefits of multilateral trade liberalization in agricultural goods. The main results of this comparison are given in Table 11.5. The 2006 World Bank study shows static gains of about $100 billion by 2015. When the policy scenario is paired with the LINKAGE model, the gains increase, as investment and productivity improvements are taken into account. The results show some decline from the 2002 version of the World Bank model: the earlier version did not include the impact of Chinese accession to the WTO and other developments in the past few years.

The regional distribution of the gains is shown in Table 11.6. With just the high-income countries liberalizing their agricultural markets, most of the benefit stays with

---

[23] This estimate is considerably larger than the comparative static estimate from the GTAP model, of $85 billion, indicating the significance of the dynamic recursive nature of the LINKAGE model, as well as some differences in parameter values.

Table 11.5 Estimated effects of full agricultural trade liberalization (US$ billion)

Study	Static effect	With investment	With productivity
2006 World Bank LINKAGE model		182	292
2006 World Bank GTAP-AGR model	102		
2002 World Bank		182	431
ERS	41	50	75
Roberts et al.	102–167		
Buetre et al.		60–122	
Beghin et al.		81–146	

Source: CBO (2006: 26). Estimates have been made as comparable as possible.

Table 11.6 Estimated welfare effects of full agricultural liberalization, by region (billion 2001 US$)

	Liberalizing region		
	High-income countries	Developing countries	All regions
High-income countries	109	19	128
Developing countries	26	28	54
All regions	135	47	182

Source: Anderson, Martin, and van der Mensbrugghe (2006: 349).

them. Developing countries gain from their own liberalization, accounting for one half of the total gains from trade liberalization.

The contribution of the major sectors to the benefits of liberalization are also explored in the World Bank study. Table 11.7 shows the importance of various sectors to the benefits from liberalization.

Agricultural liberalization yields 62 per cent of the total gains from free merchandise trade, dwarfing its share in current trade and in global GDP.[24] This is due to the high level of tariffs in agricultural markets, as well as the prevalence of subsidies in that sector.

Although three-quarters of the gains from full liberalization are from reducing developed country tariffs and farm support, developing countries get five-sixths of their total benefits from agricultural liberalization (as compared to only one tenth from textiles

---

[24] A similar estimate using the GTAP model indicated that agricultural liberalization accounted for 66 per cent of the (somewhat smaller) gains from total liberalization. Most of the benefits accrued to developed countries. For all merchandise trade, developing countries achieved 26 per cent of the total gains, reflecting their greater interest in other areas such as textiles.

Table 11.7 Effects on economic welfare of full trade liberalization from different groups of products, 2015 (per cent)

From fullliberalization of:	Agriculture and food	Textiles and clothing	Other manufactures	ALL GOODS
Percentagedue to:				
Developed countries policies	42	6	20	68
Developing countries' policies	20	8	4	32
All countries' policies	62	14	24	100

Source: Anderson, Martin, and van der Mensbrugghe (2006).

and clothing). So the emphasis of developing countries on agriculture within the Doha Round seems appropriate. Much of the developing country gains are from South–South trade, a growing but still small element of global agricultural sales. It is also important to point out that adding non-agricultural liberalization doubles the benefits of trade liberalization for developing countries. In other words, the importance of agriculture should not cloud the fact that freeing up other sectors is a vital part of allowing the economy to adjust and make use of trading possibilities.

Gains by Country

It is no surprise that significant differences in the benefits from liberalization exist. In the World Bank study cited above, the region that gains the most as a percentage of income is South East Asia, where Vietnam (5.2) and Thailand (3.8) can expect significant gains. Their export prospects increase considerably (for rice among other exports). But high protection importers such as Korea and Taiwan (3.5) also get significant percentage gains. Large countries gain relatively less (but often more in absolute terms) and those that currently have good access to markets also stand to gain less. Thus both China and Bangladesh are estimated to gain 0.2 per cent of their national income.

In terms of the more competitive exporters in Latin America, the absolute gains are substantial. Countries such as Brazil ($9.9 billion) and Argentina ($4.9 billion) stand to gain from more open markets. So does the USA ($16.2 billion), though as a percentage of national income the gain is small (0.1 per cent). One group has relatively little to gain in absolute terms: Sub-Saharan Africa already has access into the EU market and increasingly into the USA, and would tend to lose from that preferential access. Net gains to the region are calculated at $3.5 billion, but this is higher as a proportion of income than in more developed countries. Though these figures may seem modest, it is important to remember the unquantifiable nature of some of the gains that could emerge from deeper integration with the world economy and greater investment flows.

Gains and Losses by Groups Within Countries

In all models of trade liberalization consumers of highly protected products come out the winner. Trade expands choice and lowers costs. Though protected producers have to modify their enterprises, or even move sectors, in order to gain, consumers get the results more quickly.[25] The biggest gainers from agricultural trade liberalization are consumers in developed countries, who get cheaper food. Consumers in developing countries, however, may suffer from higher food prices if world markets react to the lower levels of subsidies and tariffs. Producers in exporting countries gain from better market access and from terms of trade gains. Farmers in temperate zone exporting countries gain from curbs on domestic support in other countries. Governments (taxpayers) gain from subsidy cuts but lose tariff revenue as tariffs are reduced. So the "political economy" of trade reform is a mix of actors and motives. The gains and losses for particular groups are much higher than the overall income figures given above.

One group is particularly sensitive to changes in food prices and farm receipts. The poor have much more at stake than middle income or affluent families. Much of world poverty is in rural areas, so agricultural market conditions are vital to them. Reduction in tariff protection in food-importing countries could lower domestic prices and hurt farmers who sell to the cities, but lower prices help city-based poverty. Higher prices to local farmers for export crops helps reduce poverty with less impact on consumers. So the net impact on poverty depends on specific conditions in the country.

The World Bank has published a further study (using the same modeling framework mentioned above) to elucidate the likely impact on poverty of a WTO agreement of the type under discussion (Hertel and Winters, 2006). The results show that there could be a net reduction in the number of people in poverty (measured by incomes of $1 per day) of 44 million for full merchandise trade liberalization and 6.3 million from the more ambitious of the Doha Round outcomes. So as with income impacts, the Doha agenda moves towards the benefits that are possible with total trade liberalization, but in a modest rather than dramatic step.

Additional studies on the impact of further reductions in domestic support and improvements in market access include that by researchers at IFPRI. The study is notable for its consideration of two different scenarios of liberalization in the Round: an ambitious outcome and an unambitious one, chosen largely as the maximum cuts being called for by the agricultural exporters and the minimum cuts that the more reluctant countries have suggested might be possible (Bouet et al., 2005). The results of this study show how much is at stake in the negotiations: the benefits can range from a minimal gain for developed country consumers and small losses to developing countries to significant gains for all groups of countries if the more ambitious outcome is achieved.

Partial and general equilibrium models can also be used to calculate world price changes arising from trade liberalization. CGE models tend to give smaller effects, not

---

[25] Of course, in practice, it may take time, and the workings of competition, for the price advantages to permeate to the consumer level.

Table 11.8 Estimated impact on world prices of
elimination of export subsidies

	Percentage increase
Butter	26
SMP	9
WMP	15
Beef	1
Beef	-1
Wheat	-1
Maize	1
Oilseeds	-4

Source: OECD, based on Aglink model.

only because of larger commodity aggregates but also because of the assumption that goods from different countries are imperfect substitutes. Nevertheless the over-riding conclusion is consistent: prices of temperate zone products will generally rise with liberalization, but not by a dramatic amount. Some commodities have always been considered exceptions to this rule, as policies are more distorting in those markets. These markets include cotton, rice, sugar, and milk (including products), sometimes referred to as the "white" commodities. Estimates of 20–30 per cent price increases have been common on the past for these commodities if protection levels were lowered and subsidies reduced.

The World Bank model, and the GTAP model discussed above give the change in import and export prices for these goods in the process of calculating income effects, as the changes in the price of imports and exports is an important aspect of real income. Hertel and Ivanic (2006: 57) report these price changes for their "total liberalization" and "Doha Outcome" scenarios. Prices of rice, oilseeds, grains, and bovine meat are the most sensitive to trade policy reform. Export prices for rice could increase by 24 per cent with total trade liberalization, and 8 per cent with the Doha Round. Oilseeds could increase by 16 per cent and grains by 13 per cent with free trade, but the Doha Round only promises increases of 4 per cent for these products. Sugar and dairy products would rise by somewhat less but still be significant for importers and exporters (Table 11.8).

Other studies have focused on the price impact for particular commodities.[26] It is generally found that the price of cotton on world markets will increase substantially with the reduction of domestic supports and the elimination of export subsidies on that crop. Tropical product prices will, on the other hand, not be greatly influenced by trade liberalization.

[26] A partial equilibrium estimate of world price impacts of liberalization can be found in Aksoy and Beghin (2004).

Table 11.9 Estimated effects on real returns to land from full liberalization of all goods trade (selected countries)

Australia and New Zealand	17.4	Brazil	32.4
Western Europe	-45.4	South Africa	5.7
United States	-11	Thailand	11.4
Canada	22.8	Turkey	-8.1
Japan	-67.4	Vietnam	6.8
S. Korea and Taiwan	-45	Other LAC	17.8
Argentina	21.3	Rest of World	6.3

Source: Anderson, Martin, and van der Mensbrugghe (2006: 356).

Impact on Land Prices

Finally, it is interesting to note the impact of trade liberalization on the value of farm-land. The benefits of the farm policy are usually assumed to be captured in land prices, so the owners of the land at the time when support is reduced may be expected to suffer a capital loss. This is indeed the result suggested by the CGE models. Significant reductions in the rate of return to land would be expected as a result of support reductions (Table 11.9). So perhaps this may be the most difficult policy problem facing reformers of developed country farm policies.

VIII. Conclusions

The main conclusions of the chapter can be summed up as follows:

- Agricultural tariffs are several times the level of those in the manufactured sector. This causes significant distortions to trade in agricultural and food products, and indeed to the world economy.
- Export subsidies, now used primarily by the EU, distort particular commodity markets and reduce the export earnings of more efficient producers. Export subsidies have a beneficial impact on countries that import such products, though their variable nature makes them less useful as a regular food source than they may appear.
- The level of domestic subsidies has remained high over the past decade though the nature of those subsidies has been changing in a way that should reduce the trade impacts. The impact of these subsidies on other countries varies by commodity but in general is not so great as the high levels of tariffs.

- Protection has also come from regulations introduced ostensibly to prevent the importation of agents that could spread disease in plants or animals or harm human health. Such regulations are of course a normal aspect of trade but on occasions can be used to protect the incomes of local producers rather than the health and safety of consumers, animals and plants.
- Multilateral rules governing agricultural trade were introduced in the Uruguay Round, in 1995 to replace the unsatisfactory treatment of the sector in the GATT Articles. These rules have made the types and levels of protection more apparent: the reduction of the protection is one of the main tasks of the current Doha Round.
- Over the years there has been an increased effort to measure the impact of the protection afforded to developed country agriculture on trade flows and on developing countries. Partial and general equilibrium models differ in these estimates but in ways that one would expect from their different assumptions.
- The finding of most empirical studies on the benefits of trade liberalization (or the costs of protection) is that a significant part of the gains from further liberalization would come from lowering tariffs in the agricultural sector and a smaller part from the removal of subsidies. The benefits are concentrated in those countries with the highest tariffs, where consumers stand to gain from lower prices.
- Benefits to developing countries are most apparent for those countries that are exporters of temperate zone products (or substitutes for those products) and that can expand production to take advantage of the greater market access. Exporters that currently have preferential access into industrial countries can either gain or lose, depending on whether the general opening of trade compensates for their loss of preference.
- Developing country importers of temperate zone agricultural products can lose from the removal of subsidies and the reduction in tariffs in industrial countries, but the nature of that loss and its incidence is a function of country specific policies and market situations.
- The Doha Round is currently stalled because the major countries disagree on the balance between the reduction of agricultural tariffs and domestic support required of developed countries—particularly the USA and the EU—and the opening up—in the agriculture, manufactured goods, and service sectors—of the markets in the emerging countries such as Brazil, India, and China. Most of the text of the necessary revisions to the agricultural agreement is in place, but some movement by the major countries will be needed to complete the deal.

References

Abbott, P. and Morse, B. A. (2000), 'Tariff Rate Quota Implementation And Administration By Developing Countries' *Agricultural and Resource Economics Review,* Northeastern Agricultural and Resource Economics Association, 29(1): 115–124.

Aksoy, M. A., and Beghin, J. C. (eds.) (2004), *Global Agricultural Trade and Developing Countries.* Washington, DC: World Bank.

Anderson, K., Martin, W., and van der Mensbrugghe, D. (2006), 'Distortions to World Trade: Impacts on Agricultural Markets and Farm Incomes' *Review of Agricultural Economics*, 28(2): Summer. (Download at <www.worldbank.org/trade/wto> [accessed February 2013].)

Anderson, K., Martin, W., and Valenzuela, E. (2006), 'The Relative Importance of Global Agricultural Subsidies and Market Access' *World Trade Review*, 5(3): November. (Download at <www.worldbank.org/trade/wto> [accessed February 2013].)

Anderson, K., and Martin, W. (eds.) (2006) *Agricultural Trade Reform and the Doha Development Agenda*. Basingstoke, UK: Palgrave Macmillan and the World Bank.

Anderson, K., Will M., and van der Mensbrugghe, D. (2006), 'Market and Welfare Implications of Doha Scenarios' in Anderson, K. and Martin, W. (eds) (2006), *Agricultural Trade Reform and the Doha Development Agenda*. Basingstoke, UK: Palgrave Macmillan and the World Bank.

Blandford, D., and Josling, T. (2009), 'The WTO Agricultural Modalities Proposals and their Impact on Domestic Support in the EU and the US' (Unpublished paper).

Bouet, A., Mevel, S., and Orden, D. (2005), 'More or Less Ambition? Modeling the Development Impact of US-EU Agricultural Proposals in the Doha Round' Working Paper, IFPRI, Washington, DC.

CBO (2006), 'The Effects of Liberalizing World Agricultural Trade: A Review of Modeling Studies' Congressional Budget Office (CBO), June

FAO (1973), 'Agricultural Protection: Domestic Policy and International Trade' International Agricultural Adjustment Supporting Study No. 9, FAO Conference Document C 73/LIM/9, Food and Agriculture Organization, Rome, November.

FAO (1975), 'Agricultural Protection and Stabilization Policies: A Framework of Measurement in the Context of Agricultural Adjustment' 18th Session of the FAO Conference, Food and Agriculture Organization, 8–27 November.

GATT (1958), *Trends in Agricultural Trade: Report by a Panel of Experts* (The Haberler Report), Geneva.

Gibson, P., Wainio, J., Whitley, D., and Bohman, M.. 2001, 'Profiles of Tariffs in Global Agricultural Markets' AER 796. US Department of Agriculture, Economic Research Service, Washington, DC.

Hertel, T. (ed.) (1997), *Global Trade Analysis: Modeling and Applications*, Cambridge and New York: Cambridge University Press.

Hertel, T. W., and Winters, L. A. (2006), 'Poverty Impacts of a WTO Agreement: Synthesis and Overview' in Hertel, T. W., and Winters, L. A. (eds.) (2006), *Poverty and the WTO: Impacts of the Doha Development Agenda*. Basingstoke, U. K.: Palgrave Macmillan and the World Bank.

Hertel, T. W., and Ivanic, M. (2006), 'Assessing the World Market Impacts of Multilateral Trade Reforms' in Hertel, T. W., and Winters, L. A. (eds.) (2006), *Poverty and the WTO: Impacts of the Doha Development Agenda*. Basingstoke, UK: Palgrave Macmillan and the World Bank.

Josling, T., Roberts, D., and Orden, D. (2004), *Food Regulation and Trade*. Washington, DC: Institute for International Economics.

Josling, T., and Tangermann, S. (2003), 'Production and Export Subsidies in Agriculture: Lessons from GATT and WTO Disputes Involving the US and the EC' in Petersmann, E. U., and Pollack, M. (eds.) *Transatlantic Economic Disputes*. Oxford: Oxford University Press.

Legg, W. (2003), 'Agricultural Subsidies: Measurement and Use in Policy Evaluation' *Journal of Agricultural Economics*, 54(2): 175–201.

OECD (1987). *National Policies and Agricultural Trade* Paris: OECD.

OECD (2000), 'An Analysis of Officially Supported Export Credits in Agriculture' OCOM/AGR/TD/WP(2000)91/FINAL. Paris.

OECD (2004), '*Agricultural Policies in OECD Countries: Monitoring and Evaluation*' Paris: OECD, March.

OECD (2009), Producer and Consumer Support Estimates (online database accessed at <www. oecd.org> for 1986–2008 estimates).

Jean, S., Laborde, D., and Martin, W. (2006), 'Consequences of Alternative Formulas for Tariff Cuts' in Anderson, K., and Martin, W. (eds.) *Agricultural Trade Reform and the Doha Development Agenda.* Basingstoke, UK: Palgrave Macmillan and the World Bank.

UNCTAD (2006), 'Changes in the Trends in the External Environment for Development' UNCTAD Report.

WTO (1995), 'Notification Requirements and Formats' G/AG/2, Committee on Agriculture, 30 June.

WTO (2008), *Revised Draft Modalities for Agriculture*, TN/AG/W/4/Rev.4, December 6.

CHAPTER 12

THE ECONOMICS OF SERVICES TRADE: AN OVERVIEW

AADITYA MATTOO AND GIANNI ZANINI

I. INTRODUCTION

INTERNATIONAL trade and investment in services are an increasingly important part of global commerce. Advances in information and telecommunication technologies have expanded the scope of services that can be traded cross-border. Many countries now allow foreign investment in newly privatized and competitive markets for key infrastructure services, such as energy, telecommunications, and transport. More and more people are traveling abroad to consume tourism, education, and medical services, and to supply services ranging from construction to software development. In fact, services are the fastest growing components of the global economy, and trade and foreign direct investment (FDI) in services have grown faster than in goods over the past two decades.

International transactions, however, continue to be impeded by policy barriers, especially to foreign investment and the movement of service-providing individuals. All countries, and developing countries in particular are likely to benefit significantly from further domestic liberalization and the elimination of barriers to their exports. Indeed, income gains from a reduction in protection to services may be multiples of those from trade liberalization in goods. The increased dynamism of open services sectors can make the difference between rapid and sluggish growth.

The benefits from services liberalization, however, are by no means automatic. Significant challenges exist in introducing genuine competition, building the regulatory institutions that are needed to remedy market failures, appropriately sequencing service sector reforms, and establishing mechanisms that promote the availability of essential services especially among the poor.

Even though governments can initiate reforms of services unilaterally, international agreements can play an important catalytic role. In recognition of their rising role in international trade and the need for further liberalization, services were included in the multilateral trade architecture of the World Trade Organization (WTO) in the form of the General Agreement on Trade in Services (GATS). Services have featured prominently as well in the process of WTO accession. And services are increasingly important in the large and growing network of North–South bilateral and South–South regional trade agreements concluded of late or still under negotiation. The rules governing services trade under multilateral and regional agreements and the state of services negotiations are addressed in a separate chapter.

This chapter largely summarizes the relevant content of *A Handbook of International Trade in Services* (Mattoo, Stern, and Zanini, eds., 2008) and also draws on *International Trade in Services: New Trends and Opportunities for Developing Countries* (Cattaneo, Engman, Saez, and Stern, eds, 2010) and on the *Measuring Trade in Services: a Training Module* (WTO, 2010, and United Nations Statistics Division (UNSD), 2012).

We first discuss how international transactions are conducted in services and the sources of data on these transactions. We then present some evidence on the pattern of services trade, which launches a conceptual discussion on what we can say about the determinants of the pattern of services trade. After this we turn to the normative economics of services trade. We first discuss how services reform can promote efficiency and growth at the sectoral level and economy-wide, and note that the benefits of services liberalization may be diminished by flaws in reform programs. We argue that domestic reforms should recognize the critical importance of increasing competition, strengthening regulation to remedy market failure, appropriate sequencing of reforms, and putting in place policies that widen access to services for the poor and remote.

II. A Conceptual Framework for Services Trade[1]

What are Services and How are They Traded?

Services are often seen as intangible, invisible, and perishable, requiring simultaneous production and consumption. Goods, in contrast, are tangible, visible, and storable—and hence do not require direct interaction between producers and consumers. However, there are exceptions to each of these characteristics of services. For example, a software program on a diskette or an architect's design on paper are both tangible and storable, many artistic performances are visible, and automated cash-dispensing machines make

---

[1] Much of this section draws from Copeland and Mattoo (2008).

face-to-face contact between producers and consumers unnecessary. But these exceptions do not detract from the usefulness of the general definition of services presented above.

Service trade differs from goods trade in two major ways. First, goods trade involves shipping goods from one country to another, but cross-border trade is not the most important way of conducting international transactions in services. For services which require personal contact between customers and clients, trade is possible only via sales through a foreign affiliate or if either the customer or producer travels across borders. While foreign investment and labor mobility are also issues affecting goods trade, they are fundamental aspects of trade for some services. Second, services tend to be highly regulated. This latter aspect will be elaborated in the section below on barriers to services trade.

Instead of worrying about a precise definition of what a service is, it may be more useful to follow the GATS in simply listing all the important services sectors, with an "other" category to deal with those left out:

1. Business services
2. Communication services
3. Construction services
4. Distribution services
5. Educational services
6. Environmental services
7. Financial services
8. Health-related and social services
9. Tourism and travel-related services
10. Recreational, cultural, and sporting services
11. Transport services
12. Other services not elsewhere included.

Since the conventional definition of trade—where a product crosses the frontier—would miss out on a whole range of international transactions, negotiators took an unusually wide view of services trade, which is defined (in GATS Article I) to include four modes of supply, as follows (see Figure 12.1 and Box 12.1):

- *Cross-border (Mode 1):* services supplied from the territory of one member into the territory of another. An example is software services provided by a supplier in one country through mail or electronic means to consumers in another country.
- *Consumption abroad (Mode 2):* services supplied in the territory of one member to the consumers of another. Examples are where the consumer moves, for example, to consume tourism or education services in another country. Also covered are activities such as ship or aircraft repair abroad, where only the property of the consumer (the owner of the ship or aircraft) moves.
- *Commercial presence (Mode 3):* services supplied through any type of business or professional establishment of one member in the territory of another. An example

is an insurance company owned by citizens of one country establishing a branch by means of FDI in another country.

- *Presence of natural persons (Mode 4):* services supplied by nationals of one member in the territory of another. This mode includes both independent service suppliers and employees of the services supplier of another member. Examples are a doctor of one country supplying through his physical presence services in another country, or the foreign employees of a foreign bank providing services on a temporary basis.

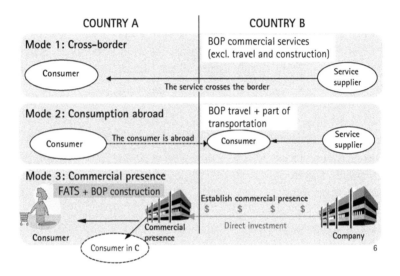

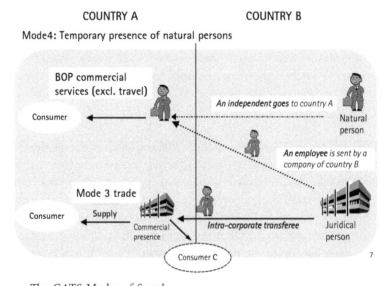

FIGURE 12.1 The GATS Modes of Supply

Source: WTO, Services Trade Division.

Box 12.1 Motorcycle Racing: An Example of Trade in Services

Motorcycle racing at the top level is a good example of international trade in services, via all modes. A for-profit international sports management and marketing company like Dorna Sports has the right to the MotoGP and World Superbike names and stages all the international championship racing events in various developed and developing countries. The company is headquartered in Madrid, with offices in Barcelona, London, and Tokyo (M3), from where it manages and facilitates all angles and steps of the two championships. It rents racetracks around the globe or enters into profit-sharing arrangements with racetracks owners (M1); deploys its own staff to supervise racing events in the different countries (M4); sub-contracts to a specialized global company the video recording of all events (M1); and streams via the Internet for a fee or sells the right to broadcast all live and archived championship racing events to national television channels. Racing teams employ pilots, technicians, mechanics, and so on, from various foreign countries (M4), fly from one foreign venue to the next (M2), ship bikes, tools, and equipment to the next race location ((M1), and are paid by advertisers around the world whose logos they prominently display on their gear (M1) and by Dorna Sports a share of ticket sales and associated revenues (M1). Some foreign fans travel to the country of the race venue and buy airline tickets as well as local lodging, food, and drinks (M2).

Can We Measure Services Trade?[2]

Following the entry into force of GATS, there has been an increasing demand for detailed, relevant, and internationally comparable statistical information on trade in services. It would be also useful if trade statistics for each service sector were available according to the modes of supply. This would enable an assessment both of the relative importance of different modes of supply in a particular sector and the impact of measures affecting each mode of supply. Trade negotiators also require statistics to evaluate market access opportunities, compare liberalization commitments, assess the extent of liberalization reached in specific sectors/markets, and provide statistical background for the settlement of disputes.

As a first step to respond to these needs, an inter-agency Task Force on Services Statistics (which included representatives from UNstats, Eurostat, International Monetary Fund (IMF), Organisation for Economic Co-operation and Development (OECD), and WTO) produced a *Manual on Statistics of International Trade in Services* (MSITS). It identifies the severe limitations of the existing statistical domains in providing information on trade by different modes of supply. It also provides guidelines and recommendations on how to use existing sources and develop new ones to measure trade in services, building upon internationally agreed standards. Its latest revision (UNSD, 2012) provides an even more detailed classification of services delivered through conventional trade

---

[2] Much of this section draws from WTO (2010).

between residents and non-residents than is contained in the Balance of Payments Manual vers. 6 (BPM6). This Extended Balance of Payments Services (EBOPS, 2010) classification has been revised in line with existing statistical frameworks.[3]

The only services trade statistics currently available on a global basis are the IMF Balance of Payments (BOP) Statistics, which register transactions between residents and non-residents. According to BOP conventions, if factors of production move to another country for a period longer than one year (sometimes flexibly interpreted), a change in residency is deemed to have occurred. The output generated by such factors that is sold in the host market is not recorded as trade in the BOP. Therefore, transactions involving commercial presence and stay of natural persons for durations of more than one year are not covered by the BOP statistics. Nonetheless, the BOP statistics include supplementary indicators for Mode 3 like FDI.

While many developed countries' statistical agencies currently provide adequately detailed BOP statistics, at present only a few developing countries collect and even fewer publish BOP statistics by origin and destination (which would allow analysis of the direction of services exports and imports) and also at the sectoral subheading detail beyond the broad eleven main BOP sectoral headings. The United Nations Statistical office (UNstats) disseminates on its website (<http://unstats.un.org/unsd/servicetrade>) the services trade statistics at whichever level of detail they are made available by its member countries.

The Manual also recommends the measurement of local delivery of services through foreign commercial presence (which are not captured by BOP statistics) under the Foreign Affiliates Trade in Services (FATS) statistical framework, by providing clarifications on inward and outward FATS and describing the links between FATS and the international supply of services. The situation regarding current data availability for FATS statistics, where demanding expanded enterprise surveys are essential, is similar to that described above. Moreover, no international organization disseminates global FATS data but the OECD for its (full and associate) members. Thus, technical assistance to non-OECD countries is badly needed to overcome their capacity constraints to produce detailed sectoral EBOPS and FATS and to facilitate access to domestic, partner country, and global databases.

Why do Services Matter for Development?

The share of services in Gross Domestic Product (GDP) has increased between 1965 and 2008 from below 40 per cent on average in developing countries to 54 and 47 per cent respectively in middle- and low- income countries, while in the OECD countries,

---

[3] The most significant change was the introduction of *manufacturing services on physical inputs* owned by others and *maintenance and repair services* as two new components and the removal of *merchanting* from other business services. The Manual includes a new chapter discussing "modes of supply" described in GATS through which services can be delivered, and elaborates recommendations for a statistical treatment of these modes, including the difficult-to-disentangle Mode 4.

the average share increased over the same period from 54 to over 73 per cent on average and 77 per cent in the USA. Trade in services is still a very low percentage of total trade, but it grew from 16 per cent in 1980 to 19 per cent by 2008. Among the fastest growing sectors in world trade during the pre-global crisis period of 2000–07 were commercial services "other" than transport and travel, like computer and information services (19 per cent annually), insurance and financial services (17 per cent), and other business services (15 per cent, reflecting the rapid shift towards outsourcing).

While developed countries still dominate world services trade, an increasing number of developing and transition countries are hosting successful service companies that export within their own regions and also to the developed countries. China, Egypt, India, Indonesia, Israel, Malaysia, Russia, Thailand, and Turkey, for instance, host large international construction companies. In the distribution service sector, Chilean, Mexican, and South African companies are big players in their respective regions. India's computer and information service and business service exports are valued at tens of billions of dollars, and there are many successful and rapidly growing exporters in these sectors from China, Egypt, Israel, Kenya, Nigeria, and South Africa. Other export success stories include Tunisia with engineering services; Brazil, Kenya, and Malawi with legal services; and Cyprus, the Czech Republic, and Hungary with accountancy services. Brazil, Cuba, India, Jordan, Malaysia, and Thailand are some of the countries whose doctors and hospitals treat large numbers of foreign patients, and the Caribbean countries, Ghana, and the Philippines are other countries that send large numbers of health professionals to serve abroad (Cattaneo et al., 2010; Goswami et al., 2012).

Efficient services not only provide a direct benefit to consumers, but also help shape overall economic performance. For example, an efficient and well-regulated financial sector leads to the efficient transformation of savings to investment, ensuring that resources are deployed wherever they have the highest returns; and facilitates better risk-sharing in the economy. Improved efficiency in telecommunications generates economy-wide benefits, as this service is a vital intermediate input to the dissemination and diffusion of knowledge—the spread of the Internet and the dynamism provided to economies around the world is telling testimony to the importance of telecommunications services. Similarly, transport and logistical services contribute to the efficient distribution of goods, and are very important in influencing a country's ability to participate in global merchandise trade.

Although these are the more prominent services, others are also crucial. Business services such as accounting and legal services are important in reducing firms' transaction costs, the high level of which is considered one of the most significant impediments to economic growth in Africa. Education and health services are necessary in building up the stock of human capital. Retail and wholesale services are a vital link between producers and consumers, and influence the efficiency with which resources are allocated to meet consumer needs. Software development is the foundation of the modern knowledge-based economy. Environmental services contribute to sustainable development by helping to alleviate the negative impact of economic activity on the environment.

III. Determinants of Trade in Services[4]

There are two major explanations for trade between countries: comparative advantage and gains from specialization arising from increasing returns to scale or agglomeration effects.

The first explanation relies on fundamental differences between countries in generating trade. The second approach can explain trade between similar countries: differences may emerge because of trade, but the differences need not have been present at the outset to generate trade. Both of these explanations apply to service trade as well as to goods trade. Moreover, both explanations apply not only to cross-border trade, but also to other modes of trade, including commercial presence and movement of natural persons. As these general determinants of trade are covered elsewhere in this course, we will only mention briefly some applications to services.

Comparative Advantage

Consider the following examples of comparative advantage in service trade: call centers in India provide customer contact services for US firms; nannies from the Philippines move to Canada temporarily to provide childcare services; Europeans travel to Peru for a week in the jungle as part of an eco-tourism package; middle-age, wealthy Westerners go to Brazil for a tummy tuck which is not covered by their home country national health systems or insurance companies. In each of these examples, trade takes place via a different mode: the call center services are sent across border using the telephone (M1); the nannies travel to a foreign country to provide their services (M4 or movement of natural persons); the eco-tourism consumers and plastic surgery patients engage in consumption abroad (M2). However, each of these examples has something in common: trade is driven by differences between countries. The trade in both child care and call center services is driven by differences in labor costs across countries; the Amazon has unique attributes that are not available at home to the European tourists; and Brazil has access to sophisticated medical technology and an abundance of skilled plastic surgeons meeting a large domestic demand for such services.

Differences in technology, natural resources, land/labor ratios, government policies, institutions, and other factors can all lead to differences in the prices of both inputs and outputs in the absence of trade. Differences in institutions and legal systems can also be important, as they affect the degree of confidence that a foreign client has in a firm, and this can affect its export success. Services such as insurance, for example, require that clients trust that contracts will be honored if a claim is made. Differences in regulatory systems can also affect the speed and flexibility with which service providers can respond to customers' needs, and this too will generate differences between countries that affect

---

[4] Much of this section draws from Copeland and Mattoo (2008).

trade patterns. The resulting price differences create incentives to trade. Some differences, such as skill levels and technological knowledge, are not innate characteristics of countries but evolve over time in response to economic decisions made by policymakers and individuals within a country. It is therefore useful to distinguish between short-run differences between countries and those that persist in the long run. Knowledge of new technology will diffuse across countries. Hence specific technologically-based differences may only provide short-run explanations of trade in specific goods and services. However, countries that have institutions that encourage and reward innovation should on average be expected to export innovation-intensive products or processes even in the long run.

One of the major differences between the services trade and goods trade is that much service trade must take place via movements of factors—such as movement of labor or foreign investment. If trade must take place through the movement of factors, are the basic propositions of trade theory—based on the notion of cross-border trade—put into question? One problem does arise from the point of view of positive theory: if different modes of supply are close substitutes, it is not easy to predict whether comparative advantage will manifest itself as a trade flow, investment flow, or labor flow. However, from the point of view of normative theory there is no obvious problem: a country gains from the import of services, irrespective of the choice of mode, if the terms at which international transactions take place are more favorable than those available on the domestic market.

The argument for gains from trade from comparative advantage applies to goods and services destined directly for final consumers as well as to those used as an input into production (Markusen, 1989). However, there is an important added twist when trade in inputs is concerned. Imports of producer services can lower costs of firms in the export sector and thereby stimulate exports. An example would be a country with untapped oil reserves. Access to foreign engineering services could lower the cost of developing oil extraction facilities that could then lead to increased exports of oil. That is, the benefits of allowing increased imports of producer services can be potentially magnified via their effects on improving production and trade in other sectors of the economy.

Increasing Returns to Scale as Another Determinant of Trade in Services

While differences between countries are one of the major explanations for trade, particularly between countries with very different income levels, they cannot account for all trade. Much of the world's trade occurs between high-income countries, suggesting that similarities between countries need not deter trade. In fact, there is some evidence that the more similar are countries, the greater is the volume of trade between them. Moreover, much of the trade between similar countries is in similar products. For example, Canadian engineers work on construction projects in the USA, and US engineers work on similar projects in Canada.

There are several theories that explain why trade occurs between similar countries. As these same explanations for trade often apply also when countries are different, they complement and interact with the standard comparative advantage approach discussed above. Think of two students starting university who are equally bright and talented. At this point their productive capacities may seem indistinguishable. However, suppose one chooses to study medicine and the other chooses to study architecture. If we revisit these same students ten years later, they will have very different skills, and they can trade with each other via the labor market, with the doctor selling the architect medical services and the latter selling the doctor architectural services.

This example highlights certain key processes related to scale effects, which are only mentioned here briefly as they have been covered extensively in other chapters (e.g. chapters 4 and 5). First, there are gains from *specialization*. However, specialization did not initially occur because of comparative advantage. That is, the students were assumed to be initially identical so there was no comparative advantage at the outset. Instead, comparative advantage evolved over time because of the opportunity to trade. Instead of trading with each other, the two students could have each decided to spend part of their time being an architect and part of their time being a doctor. However, because there are large upfront investments in education and experience required to excel in each of these fields, the students can avoid paying these fixed costs twice if they each specialize in different fields. Finally, there is an element of lock-in to this example. At the beginning of university education, each student could have gone down a different path. But once the investments in education and experience have been made, it is very costly to switch fields. History matters, and decisions made in the past (including past government policies) have a large influence on current patterns of trade and apparent comparative advantage. For many goods and services, these features give rise to the phenomenon of increasing returns to scale, which manifests itself in product variety (or market niche effect), the development of firm-specific intangible assets, agglomeration, and networks.

If *product variety* is valued either by producers purchasing services as inputs or by final consumers, then firms have an incentive to carve out their market niche and produce a specialized variety of a good or service. As in most cases there are fixed costs to establishing a market niche or developing a new variety, larger economies can be expected to supply more product variety. Examples of product variety in the service sector include entertainment (movies, television programs, music), tourism (consumers gain a wider choice of destinations), restaurants (cities that are open to a lot of foreign visitors can support a wider variety of restaurants), architecture and engineering services (a larger market allows firms or individual producers in these sectors to specialize in different types of projects), and many others. In fact since many types of services are tailored to individual customer needs, product variety is a major aspect of service trade. Trade driven by the market-niche effect will potentially generate three types of gains. First, the total variety of products available to consumers in any given market will increase because consumers gain access to both domestic and foreign varieties of the products. Second, each individual producer will have access to a larger market, and this can allow them to expand their output and reduce costs due to scale economies. Third, a specialized service that might not be economically viable in a small country might become viable as a result of the market expansion effects of trade. That is, a larger market will allow the development of new goods and services that might not have otherwise been available. The income distributional effects of trade driven by the market-niche effect are likely to be less significant than when trade is driven by differences between countries. Because product variety is valued, and because trade can increase both imports and exports within the same sector, it provides both countries with increased opportunities at the same time as it increases competition in any given sector.

Product variety alone, however, cannot explain why a foreign firm might be better able to more profitably a run-of the-mill retail store or a power plant. Many firms exist because they have developed *specialized firm-specific assets,* such as specialized knowledge of organizational and production processes, distribution and supply networks, and reputations for quality and reliability. This can explain the success of large firms in many different industries, such as financial institutions, construction firms, and courier companies. Successful large firms can potentially provide services to foreign markets via each of the four modes. However the notion of intangible firm-specific assets is particularly helpful in explaining FDI. Once the investment in firm-specific assets is made, the firm's knowledge and reputation can then be exploited in each of the plants or branches that a firm sets up (see for example, Markusen and Venables, 2000). By setting up branches in various countries, a services firm-level fixed costs need only be paid once, and each branch can be set up by paying only branch-level fixed costs. This creates gains to the host country as consumers gain access to a wider variety of specialized services at lower prices than otherwise would be available.

Increasing returns to scale can also lead to *agglomeration,* which can take two forms. A particular industry can concentrate in one area, such as the concentration of financial services in cities like New York, London, Honk Kong, and Singapore and of computer programming, back-office services, and call centers in Bangalore. Or there can be a general concentration of a wider variety of economic activity in cities, regions, or countries. That is, trade can lead to the emergence of "cores" and "peripheries." Agglomeration arises from the presence of spillover effects across firms or from the interaction between scale economies and transportation costs or trade barriers. The welfare effects of trade in the presence of agglomeration are complicated. For the purpose of this overview of the determinants and gains from services trade, it suffices to note that while completely free trade in the presence of agglomeration effects could potentially benefit all countries, partial trade liberalization could hurt the periphery. Often the core does not have an incentive to eliminate all barriers to trade, because then the advantage of being in the core is reduced.

Another scale-related motive for trade arises from access to *networks.* This motive for trade is at root driven by economies of scale that are not specific to an individual firm or even a given country. In many sectors, such as telecommunications, shipping, financial services, and transportation, the efficiency, quality, and benefits to consumers of the services provided depend on access to networks of other consumers and producers. For example, a phone system is only useful if many other people have phones; email became a standard form of communication after a critical mass of people had access to it; and the value of having a debit or credit card increases with the number of places that have access to a network that accepts the card. In such cases, the gains from trade arise from the increased market size. If two countries of similar size each had their own Internet network, then establishing a connection between the two networks would roughly double the number of sites that can be accessed, and double the number of people who can be contacted by email. This scale effect generates gains from trade.

In the case of shipping and transportation, where regulatory barriers often limit the connection points between domestic and foreign networks, allowing smooth connection and integration of systems can generate large gains from trade. For example, if three neighboring countries have customers who want to send packages to Peru, each country could have an airplane that carries packages to Peru, or they could all send their packages to a hub in one of the three countries, from which a single airplane would carry the cargo to Peru. Integration of the shipping network generates economies of scale that in turn can generate gains from trade (e.g. in the form of lower costs and prices or faster, more frequent deliveries).

The analysis of the benefits of liberalization to allow smoother access to international networks is complicated by two important factors. First, because of the economies of scale that arise from having a large integrated network, some networks can become dominated by a small number of large firms. Therefore, there can be a trade-off between the advantages of economies of scale and the costs of the concentration of power. Second, in part because of the issues of concentration of power, networks are publicly owned in some countries, run by monopolies in other countries, and subject to various entry and regulatory constraints in still other countries. These differences across countries lead to barriers to trade that can be difficult to circumvent.

Why Firms Choose Particular Modes to Supply Services to Foreign Customers

For many types of services, the costs of provision vary substantially across the different modes of supply, and for some services, supply is essentially not feasible via some modes.

Foreign tourism, for example, cannot take place unless consumers are free to travel and spend their money abroad. Fast food restaurant services cannot be provided without a commercial presence in the country where the food is served. Construction workers have to be able to move across borders for construction services to be traded.

Rules that allow trade via some modes but not others will favor some countries over others. A set of rules that allows FDI, direct cross-border export of services, and movement of customers between countries, but which does not allow labor movement across countries, will preclude certain types of services from being traded at all. The services that cannot be traded in such a regime are labor-intensive services that require physical contact between the customer (e.g. a builder) and service provider (e.g. an architect or a roofer). Hence countries that have a comparative advantage in such services (labor abundant countries) will be seriously constrained in their ability to export these types of services. Although there are many potential gains from importing services (especially via increased productivity in goods production), the gains from trade will generally be larger when foreign barriers to exporting services are removed as well. Consequently, the rules affecting different modes of supply can be critically important both in determining which services will be traded, and in determining the distribution of the gains from trade across countries.

For some types of services, different modes of supply are substitutes, in the sense that if one mode is not available, firms will use a different mode to supply their service to foreign customers. For example, consider an insurance firm. A foreign customer could buy an insurance contract by mail or electronically. That is, the insurance services could be directly exported (M1). Alternatively, the insurance company could set up a branch office in the foreign country to serve its foreign customers (M2). In that case, the foreign client would deal with the local office of the foreign insurance company. When it becomes time to settle claims, the insurance company could send agents from the home office to assess the claim; that is, it could rely on temporary movements of personnel for assessments of claims (M4). Or, if it set up a branch office, then local personnel in the foreign branch office could assess the claims (M3). Another example is medical services. A specialized surgical team could come from a foreign country to perform surgery in the home country (M4); or the patient could go to the foreign country to receive treatment (M2). If the different modes of supply are substitutes, then in some cases virtually all of the gains from trade can be realized by opening up just one mode of trade. This is the basis of Mundell's (1957) observation that under some conditions, trade in goods and services and trade in factors are perfect substitutes. That is, a country with an abundance of skilled workers can either export goods and services directly produced by these workers; or the workers themselves can move to produce in other countries. In both cases, gains from trade will be realized.

However, even when modes of supply are substitutes, restrictions on which modes are available to firms can have important implications. First, modes are typically not perfect substitutes. In the example of the surgeon above, hospital facilities will differ across countries and so the success rate and cost of the surgery will differ depending on where it is performed. Travel costs for patients and surgeons will differ. The health of a seriously ill patient may be jeopardized by travel; and the opportunity costs of travel for a surgeon may be high because of the needs of other patients. In the case of the insurance company, the reliance on a foreign branch office may increase overhead expenses, but it might allow the firm to better deal with the needs of local clients. At one extreme, if a service (e.g., road construction) can only be supplied through one mode (e.g., movement of asphalt machine operators), then a prohibitive trade restriction on that mode shuts out foreign supply completely. At the other extreme, if modes (say cross-border and movement of individuals) are substitutes for the supply of a service (e.g., standardized software development), then the impact of a restriction on one mode is diluted. Nonetheless, if firms are free to choose their modes of supply, one would expect that they would choose the most cost effective mix. Restrictions on access to foreign markets via some modes but not others can therefore lead to increased costs of provision of the services and therefore potentially reduce the gains from trade.

Second, different modes of supply will have different effects on income distribution. For example, consider the insurance example again. Suppose that a developed country has a comparative advantage in the provision of insurance services. Suppose also that FDI in insurance services is liberalized but insurance agents are not allowed temporary access to a developing country to assess claims and serve the local needs of their clients. In this case, insurance firms from the developed country are likely to set up branch offices in the developing country to serve local clients. This will increase the demand for skilled insurance agents in the developing country and may push up wages. On the other hand, if FDI is not allowed and developed country insurance personnel are allowed temporary access to the developing country of our example, this can reduce the demand for labor in the insurance sector in the developing country and may push down wages.

Complementarities may also occur across similar types of factors. For example, if a large foreign engineering firm has a contract to build a bridge, then allowing temporary access for foreign engineers can increase the productivity of local engineers who also work on the project and may increase the incomes of local engineers (Markusen, Rutherford, and Tarr, 2000). As another example, allowing foreign movie stars into a country to make a film can increase the demand for local actors who will work on the film as well. More generally, allowing FDI will have different effects on wages and employment than will policies that allow labor to move across countries. Even if the efficiency effects of the two different modes of supply are not very different, the effects on income distribution may be important in determining political support for the different modes.[5]

In many cases the different modes of supply will be complementary. For example, if a firm chooses to have a physical presence in a foreign market (M3), then the effectiveness of their operation may be enhanced if personnel are allowed to move between the home and foreign establishments (M4). As well, there will likely be direct intra-firm trade in services, with for example, research services concentrated in one location, accounting services in others, and so on (M1). A policy that restricted any of these three modes would affect either the cost or quality of the service provision. In cases where there are strong complementarities across different modes of supply, fully effective liberalization of service trade requires that all modes be opened up.

Services may also be complementary with goods trade. Export of goods requires transportation and insurance services, but it may also require the establishment of distribution networks, facilities to deal with repairs or with training of customers in the use

---

[5] In models with agglomeration effects, the choice between FDI and direct exports of services can affect the incentives to agglomerate. If direct trade is the only mode permitted, this tends to favor the country with a larger market because its larger size allows it to take advantage of the agglomeration effects. On the other hand, if direct trade is restricted, and governments require a local presence as a condition for local provision of the service, then the smaller market is favored, because such a policy will encourage FDI, which can increase the demand for local producer services, and thereby transfer some of the agglomeration benefits from the larger market to the smaller one.

of products, and so on. Hence in some cases the potential gains from goods trade cannot be fully realized without liberalization of service trade. Conversely, liberalization of goods trade, for example in computers, may well be a condition for the realizing the benefits of services trade.

IV. SERVICES TRADE POLICY

Identifying Services Trade Barriers

In contrast to goods, relatively few services are subject to simple discriminatory taxes on trade. Instead barriers to trade in services arise from non-tariff barriers. Many types of services are publicly provided or are produced by regulated monopolies or professionals. For example, because of issues in asymmetric information, doctors must be certified to protect patients, engineers need certification to ensure that bridges they build do not collapse, and insurance companies have to be regulated to ensure their solvency. However, these same rules can be manipulated to protect local suppliers. A rule requiring an engineer graduate from a domestic university might ensure that quality standards are met, but would prevent consumers from having access to the services of highly qualified foreign engineers.

The regulatory apparatus may therefore serve the dual purpose of responding to market failures (such as ensuring quality standards for medical practitioners) and protecting local suppliers from foreign competition at the expense of consumers. This means that identifying and measuring the regulatory trade barriers in the service sector is very complex. It also means that simple rules for trade liberalization that have worked for the goods trade (such as reducing all tariffs by 30 per cent) are not available as an option for service trade liberalization. Instead service trade liberalization is organized around the notion of non-discrimination and is often linked with domestic regulatory reform. A challenge for trade policy analysis is to isolate the protective effect of regulatory policy from the beneficial effects, and to suggest rules for liberalization that provide the benefits of increased trade while ensuring that other legitimate policy objectives are achieved. In many cases, trade liberalization may not be possible or viable unless it is accompanied by domestic regulatory reform. Four types of regulatory barriers on services trade are usually found in the real world.

- Tariff-like, revenue-generating discriminatory taxes whose implications are the same as for goods trade, but are less common for services trade.
- Discriminatory regulations which add to the cost of trading services, but which do not yield any direct benefits to local consumers, are a very common form of trade barrier. Examples include delays in crossing the border, country-specific standards

for trucks (such as differing weight and trailer length regulations) that add to the cost of cross-border transport services, preferential government procurement policies, and lack of transparency of domestic regulations.

- Licensing and certification requirements which inhibit trade in professional services. Doctors, engineers, architects, lawyers, accountants, and other service providers typically need to satisfy local regulations for certification. In some cases, compliance may be very costly (a domestic residence or graduating from a domestic educational institution may be required). These types of regulations can be justified by the need to protect consumers by ensuring that quality and safety standards are met. However, they can also protect local service providers from foreign competition, which can lead to higher prices and reduced choice for local consumers.

- Quotas which are pervasive and have similar implications as for goods trade. On cross-border trade, they are common in the transport sectors. Foreign providers are either completely shut out (i.e., a zero quota) of certain segments, such as transport within a country; or only provided limited access, as in international transport. On consumption abroad, quotas are sometimes implemented through foreign exchange restrictions; for example the ability of citizens to consume services, such as tourism and education, abroad is limited by limits on foreign exchange entitlements. On commercial presence, quotas are imposed on the number of foreign suppliers who are allowed to establish in sectors like telecommunications and banking. Quotas on foreign participation also take the form of restrictions on foreign equity ownership in individual enterprises. Restrictions on FDI assume particular significance in the case of services where cross-border delivery is not possible, so that consumer prices depend completely on the domestic market structure. In many service sectors, such as in communications and financial services, there are restrictions both on entry and on foreign ownership. This is despite the fact that a basic conclusion from the literature on privatization is that larger welfare gains arise from an increase in competition than from simply a change in ownership from public to private hands. Finally, quotas are perhaps most stringent in the case of movement of service-providing personnel, and affect trade not only in professional services, but also in a variety of labor-intensive services.

The Economic Analysis of Services Trade Barriers

Here we only summarize the results of the economic analysis of these barriers, which is similar to that for goods and which is presented in more detail in an Appendix to this chapter. Because trade protection is often inextricably linked with domestic regulation, our analysis is not exhaustive. The trade-related implications of regulations will depend on the special characteristics of the service industry in question, and the types of market failures that the regulations are designed to correct.

For those familiar with the analysis of trade barriers on goods, the analysis of the welfare effect of the introduction of an import tariff on goods applies equally to the case of a tax on imported services compared to the free trade base case. Part of the loss suffered by consumers (due to the tax-induced higher prices) is offset by the gains to domestic providers (due to the higher prices thanks to the protection afforded from imports) and by the government's revenue. However, the import tax-induced distortions in domestic consumption and in the (higher cost) provision of services generate a real net loss to the economy.

As mentioned above, the most common restrictions applicable to foreign-provided services (or foreign providers of services) raise prices in (and the costs of serving) the domestic market but do not generate any revenue for the government. These are akin to quotas on goods, and can be outright limitations on licensing foreign providers and on foreign equity shares, or bureaucratic measures that generate delays, restrictions on travel, requirements, inspections, and so on. Without the partially compensating gain of tariff revenue, the total social cost of such quantitative restrictions is much greater for the country that adopts them than for a tariff.

Trade liberalization, accompanied by domestic regulatory reform, raises welfare. But trade liberalization in a poor regulatory environment likely might not be welfare improving. The interaction of trade policy and regulation is a complex issue, as in the case of professional services, and in particular where low quality service providers generate negative externalities.

Sometimes, certification requirements are just disguised trade barriers, as for example in Italy where the rents consequent to highly restrictive entry qualifications, regulations, and quotas have made local notaries and pharmacists among the country's highest income earning professional categories and fiercely adverse to even the most modest liberalization proposals. However, in other sectors and in other countries, certification requirements cannot simply be dismissed as a trade barrier because often they are a response to problems of asymmetric information in those markets. Prospective clients often do not have enough information to judge the safety and quality of the service on offer. Even if the client could determine quality and safety at some cost, it can be more efficient to require certification to economize on screening costs. For example, if a bridge collapses or if a public building is not constructed safely, then there will be costs to society at large, not just to the contractor. Similarly, in countries with public medical systems, the cost of bad medical treatment will fall not just on the patient and, via malpractice awards, on the negligent doctor, but also on taxpayers.

Screening of Foreign Service Providers

Where the domestic regulatory system is inadequate, screening is imperfect and customers face in practice a mix of good and bad service providers. In this case, as shown in the Appendix to this chapter, trade liberalization without improvements to the domestic certification system can lower welfare. Under a well-functioning certification system, instead, free trade is unambiguously welfare improving, though the magnitude of the gains depends on the way in which foreigners are screened.

Trade liberalization in many service industries and especially in professional services requires both that foreigners be given market access, and that they not be subject to discriminatory barriers. There are several ways of implementing non-discrimination rules.

In a national treatment regime, governments have the flexibility to implement their own regulations subject to the requirement that the same regulations apply to domestic and foreign suppliers. That is, a national treatment regime essentially requires non-discrimination. Such a rule does not completely eliminate discrimination, however. For example, an insurance company might be required to establish a local office before it can sell insurance. While both domestic and foreign firms are subject to the same requirement, it may be much easier for local firms to meet the requirement— such a rule imposes a fixed cost that excludes foreign firms who might want to do only a small amount of business locally. Similarly, a requirement that engineers, doctors, or truck drivers obtain domestic licensing and certification can impose additional costs on foreigners who have already gone through a similar certification process in their own country.

In a mutual recognition regime, each country agrees to accept service providers who meet the certification requirements of their home country. For example, under a mutual recognition agreement (MRA), a US resident can be permitted to drive in Canada as long as he holds a valid US driver's license. Under a national treatment rule, the US resident could be permitted to drive in Canada only if a Canadian driver's license is obtained. The advantage of mutual recognition regimes is that they can economize on regulatory costs. The disadvantage is that it can be more difficult for a government to meet its regulatory objectives. If the trading partner has weaker certification requirements, then the average quality of service provision may fall when imports increase. For this reason, mutual recognition is not appropriate for many types of services and often may also only be feasible and recommended for countries with similar approaches to regulation. Between countries with very different standards, the country with the weak standard can agree to recognize certification from the country with the high standard, but not vice versa.

Harmonization of regulatory standards is another option. In this case, countries agree on common regulatory standards. For example, countries may agree on a common set of rules to regulate insurance companies, and this then may facilitate easy access by insurers to markets in each country. The advantage of harmonization is that it removes the ability of governments to unilaterally adjust standards to favor local suppliers. The disadvantage is that it can add inflexibilities into the system that make it more difficult to change regulations when conditions merit changes. Additionally, harmonization by its nature eliminates diversity in regulatory approaches. Regulations appropriate for one country need not be the best solution for other countries.

Each of these approaches constrains government flexibility in some way. They may also conflict with other government objectives. For example, a government may choose to have an exclusively public education or health system. In cases of cultural services, a government may prefer to favor explicitly local providers. For some types of services, governments may see value in having them provided by producers with a long-term vested interest in a local community. The literature on social capital suggests that this can strengthen communities and provide both economic and non-economic benefits. Consequently, for some types of services, social or other legitimate regulatory objectives may well be incompatible with full trade liberalization.

Empirical Analysis of Barriers to Services Trade

For all four modes of the supply of services, one objective of empirical measurement has been to deduce some sort of tariff equivalent of the barrier to trade in particular services. Since direct price comparisons seldom serve that purpose, however, researchers have pursued other means of inferring the presence and size of barriers to trade.

Some of these methods have been quite direct: they simply ask governments or participants in markets (or legal firms or think tanks) what barriers they impose or face. The answers are usually only qualitative, indicating the presence or absence of a particular type of barrier, but do not take into account its implementation and its economic impact. Such qualitative information can take on a quantitative dimension when it is tabulated and aggregated, often with subjective weights by types, modes, and/or sector. The result is a set of frequency measures of barriers to trade, recording where the barriers are, and perhaps also the fraction of trade within a sector or country that is subject to them. Alternatively, indexes of restrictiveness for either commitments or (but much more demanding) for actual policy can be constructed, typically measured on a scale of zero to one, such as the World Bank Services Trade Restrictions Index (STRI) (see World Bank, 2012 and Borchert et al., 2012). Neither frequency or index measures, however, purport to say how much a barrier either raises price or reduces quantity.

Even though such frequency or index measures do not translate directly into the tariff equivalents of trade barriers, in order to use them for quantitative analysis, researchers have often converted them to that form in rather ad hoc ways. For particular industries, moreover, the construction of such measures requires considerable industry-specific knowledge, since each industry has, at a minimum, its own terminology, and often also its own distinctive reasons for regulatory concern.

Other, more indirect measurements of trade barriers in service industries have also been used, alone or in combination with frequency and index measures. These may be divided into two types: measurements that use information about prices and/or costs; and measurements that observe quantities of trade or production and attempt to infer how trade barriers have affected these quantities. In both cases, if one can also measure or assume an appropriate elasticity reflecting the response of quantity to price, a measured effect on either can be translated into an effect on the other. Thus both price and quantity measurements are also often converted into, and reported as, tariff equivalents.

Simple price comparisons are seldom of much use. This is because many services are differentiated by location in a way that renders comparison of their prices inside and outside of a country meaningless. For example, the cost of providing telephone service to consumers on the Texas side of the USA–Mexican border need bear no particular relationship to the cost, for the same firm, of providing it across the border in Mexico, where wages are much lower but costs of bank loans and of infrastructure may be much higher. So even if trade in the service were completely unimpeded, we would not expect these prices to be the same and thus we cannot infer a trade barrier in either direction from the fact that prices are not the same. Similar arguments can be made about most traded services. Indirect measurements of barriers to trade in services are therefore less common than for trade in goods, although they do exist. There has been some success using the so-called gravity model as a benchmark for quantities of trade in services, and the results of these models have therefore been the basis for indirect measurement of barriers in the quantity dimension. Financial data have also been the basis for inferring barriers from differences in the markups of price over cost.

Some guidelines for assessing services barriers and their liberalization are provided in Box 12.2.

Box 12.2. Guidelines for Assessing Services Barriers and Their Liberalization

Principles

1. Most barriers to trade and investment in services take the form of domestic regulations, rather than measures at the border.
2. No single methodology is sufficient for documenting and measuring barriers to trade in services. Instead, investigators need to draw upon all available information, including both direct observation of particular barriers and indirect inference of barriers using data on prices and quantities.
3. Because of the special role of incumbent firms in many service industries, regulations do not need to be explicitly discriminatory against foreign firms in order to have discriminatory effects.

Procedures

1. Collect the details of domestic regulations and related policies affecting services firms in the countries and/or sectors being examined, including the manner in which they apply to foreign vs. domestic firms, plus quantitative details of their application, such as any percentage or value limits that they impose.
2. Ideally, this information should be collected by systematic surveys of governments and/or firms. However, it may also be possible to infer it less directly from documents

Box 12.2 *Continued*

prepared for other purposes, such as the commitments that governments made to the GATS in the Uruguay Round and subsequent negotiations.

3. For each type of regulation or policy, define degrees of restrictiveness and assign scores to each, ranging from zero for least restrictive to one for most restrictive.

4. Construct a measure of restrictiveness by: weighting the scores from step 3 based on judgments of the relative importance of each policy; using a statistical methodology such as factor analysis that will serve to identify the weights; or designing proxy measures, such as dummy variables, to represent particular restrictions. The resulting measures can then be used directly for reporting the presence and importance of barriers across industries and countries, as well as for providing an input to subsequent analysis.

5. Convert the measures of restrictiveness from step 4 into a set of tariff equivalents by one or more of the following methods. Depending on the quality of information that goes into their construction, these tariff equivalents may be superior to the restrictiveness measures themselves for reporting about barriers and analyzing their effects.

   a. Assign judgmental tariff-equivalent values to each of the component measures, representing the percentage taxes on foreign suppliers to which each component is thought to correspond at their most restrictive levels (index = 1).

   b. Use data on prices and their determinants as the basis for a regression model that includes an index or other measures of restrictiveness and that estimates the effect on prices.

   c. Use data on quantities produced or traded as the basis for a regression model that includes an index or other measures of restrictiveness and that estimates the effect on quantities. This estimate can then be converted to tariff equivalents using an assumed or estimated price elasticity of demand.

6. Use an index or other measures of restrictiveness or the tariff equivalents constructed above as inputs into a model of production and trade in order to ascertain the effects of changes in the barriers to which they correspond. The appropriate model for this purpose depends on whether sectoral or economy-wide policy changes are to be analyzed. For economy-wide policy changes, the model should be a general equilibrium one, incorporating the full effects of barriers across sectors and countries. Ideally, too, the model should be designed to capture the effects of service regulations in the form that they have been observed and quantified as above

Source: Deardorff and Stern (2008).

V. SERVICE REFORMS CAN PROMOTE EFFICIENCY AND GROWTH

A vast cross-country and country-specific literature has shown that liberalization of trade in services, when accompanied by reform of inadequate regulation and supported by complementary and pro-competition policies, has led to significant sectoral and economy-wide improvements in performance.

Removing barriers to trade in services in a particular sector is likely to lead to lower prices, improved quality, and greater variety. As in the case of trade in goods, restrictions on trade in services reduce welfare because they create a wedge between domestic and foreign prices, leading to a loss to consumers that is greater than the gain to producers and in government revenue. Several empirical sectoral studies support this contention. Since many services are inputs into production, the inefficient supply of such services acts as a tax on production and prevents the realization of significant gains in productivity. As countries reduce tariffs and other barriers to trade in goods, effective rates of protection for manufacturing industries may become negative if they continue to be confronted with input prices that are higher than they would be if services markets were competitive.

A major benefit of liberalization is access to a wider variety of services whose production is subject to economies of scale. Consumers derive not only a direct benefit from diversity in services such as restaurants and entertainment, but also an indirect benefit because a wider variety of more specialized producer services, such as telecommunications and finance, can lower the costs of both goods and services production (Ethier, 1982; Copeland, 2001). In such circumstances, smaller markets can be shown to have a strong interest in liberalizing trade in producer services, since this can offset some of the incentives that firms have to locate in larger markets (Markusen, 1989).

Estimates of benefits, especially for FDI in services, vary for individual countries— from around 1 per cent to over 50 per cent of GDP—depending on the initial levels of protection and the assumed reduction in barriers. For example, a study of the impact of FDI services liberalization on manufacturing productivity of 350 Czech firms based on a 2004 firm-level survey estimated that a 10 per cent increase in FDI implies a 3 per cent increase in total factor productivity (Arnold et al., 2011). Similarly, significant impacts were found for a large sample of European and Central Asian countries (Ana Fernandes, 2007) and India (Arnold et al., 2010) that had undertaken ambitious liberalization programs in services.

In simulations of global service-trade liberalization, developed countries gain more in absolute terms—which is not surprising given the relative size of their economies—but developing countries also see significant increases in their GDP. One model predicted gains of between 1.6 per cent of GDP (for India) to 4.2 per cent of GDP (for Thailand) if tariff equivalents of protection were cut by one-third in all countries (Chadha et al., 2003). The gains from liberalizing services are likely to be substantially greater than those from liberalizing trade in goods, because current levels of protection in services are higher than in goods and because liberalization of services would also create spillover benefits from the required movement of capital and labor. For instance, another model finds that the welfare gains from a 50 per cent cut in services sector protection would be five times larger than the gains from non-services sector trade liberalization (Robinson et al., 1999). These results are particularly striking because they are derived from models that assume only very limited or no temporary movement of individual service suppliers—potentially a major source of gain.

Temporary movement of workers offers arguably the neatest solution to the dilemma of how international migration is best managed, enabling the realization of gains from trade while averting social and political costs in host countries and brain drain from poor countries. Researchers find that if OECD countries were to allow temporary access to foreign workers equal to just 3 per cent of their labor force, the global gains would be over $150 billion—more than the gains from the complete liberalization of all trade in goods (Walmsley and Winters, 2005). Both developed and developing countries would share in these gains, and they would be largest if both high-skilled mobility and low-skilled mobility were permitted (see Figure 12.2).

Fink et al. (2002) find that international variations in communication costs indeed have a significant influence on the composition of bilateral trade patterns and in particular that their impact on trade in differentiated products is larger than on trade in homogenous products—by as much as one third. The implication is that lower communication costs can shift a country's comparative advantage towards more sophisticated communication-intensive differentiated goods and away from more standardized primary goods.

Box 12.3 details how services reform benefits Mauritius. Box 12.4 cites Zambia's experience with services trade and development.

Certain services industries clearly possess growth generating characteristics. Furthermore, barriers to entry in a number of services sectors, ranging from telecommunications to professional services, are maintained not only against foreign suppliers but also against new domestic suppliers. Full liberalization can, therefore, lead to enhanced competition from both domestic and foreign suppliers. Greater foreign participation and increased competition together imply a larger scale of activity, and hence greater scope for generating scale and growth enhancing effects. Even without scale effects, participation by foreign providers in services sectors liberalization could still have positive effects, because foreign services companies are likely to

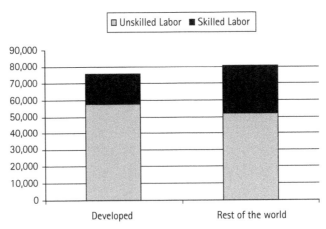

FIGURE 12.2 Welfare gains from a 3 per cent increase in developed countries' temporary quotas on foreign workers

Note: Data in US$ million.

Source: Adapted from Walmsley and Watson (2002).

Box 12.3 Mauritius—Unshackling New Sources of Growth Through Services Reform

By the mid 2000s, Mauritius was facing a sharp transition from dependence on trade preferences to open competition in the global economy. A necessary element of the reform program to reignite growth was upgrading services that are crucial inputs into internationally competitive sectors, together with encouraging private investment flows into dynamic activities. Among services, tourism, outsourcing, ICT, and cargo trans-shipment were recognized to have potential for exports, and in merchandise, fish processing and non-sugar agricultural production to have potential for efficient substitution of imports. One other source of growth was in small and medium enterprises (SMEs) that were largely relegated to the informal economy and, by virtue of their isolation from the system of laws, were unable to take advantage of financial services and export opportunities.

For the tourism sector, air fares that were high cost, even controlling for distance, raised the price of tourist packages and discouraged tourist arrivals. High telecommunications charges, often 2–4 times higher than comparator countries, hobbled the offshoring and ICT industries, and discouraged essential internet access for businesses trying to sell Mauritian products in export markets. They limited access to the global information so essential to businesses wishing to adopt the latest technologies, to say nothing of their crippling effect on education of the citizenry. Electricity also cost more than in comparator countries, was unreliable and imposed additional costs on firms and households for maintaining back-up systems. Even if not a major cost for most industries, poor quality professional services also were driving down average productivity.

A service activity of far-reaching importance is the education and training of new professionals and workers. Mauritius was turning out too few workers and professionals with the world-class skills needed to staff new opportunities in tourism and hotel management, offshoring and ICT industries, and other dynamic businesses competing effectively in the global market. While Mauritius was doing well at the primary school level, its secondary schools were performing at a rate comparable to countries with only 60 per cent of its living standard and its colleges and universities had enrollment rates equal to countries with half its per capita income. Left unattended this constraint would have increasingly undermined the country's needed adjustment towards global competitiveness.

Other selected public services such as customs, investment, and tourism promotion agencies, and agricultural extension also required reform to promote competitiveness. In particular, the government was advised to strengthen its important role in disseminating knowledge of food and hygiene standards among farmers and small enterprises to facilitate linkages between the expanding tourism sector and local horticulture and food processing. Ensuring compliance with those standards remains critical in protecting the reputation of the Mauritian tourism sector.

---

bring new technology and management techniques with them. If greater technology transfer accompanies services liberalization—either embodied in FDI or disembodied—the growth effect will be stronger.

There is econometric evidence—relatively strong for the financial sector and less strong but nevertheless statistically significant for the telecommunications

Box 12.4 Services Trade and Development: The Experience of Zambia

Zambia is a least-developed country (LDC) which derives nearly two-thirds of its output from services (much higher than the LDC average) and which has seen significant services liberalization since the 1990s. Nonetheless, Zambia has so far under-performed both in terms of its services exports and in widening access to services for its firms, farms, and households. Tourism export services have grown, but at one-tenth of the rate in Botswana and Tanzania.

Most sectors, including banking, mobile telephony, distribution and tourism, are characterized by a high degree of openness, with foreign investors holding dominant or significant shares, unlike in some other LDCs whose open markets they have largely ignored. Nonetheless, from finance and accounting to telecommunications and transport, despite a significant degree of liberalization and even after allowing for the low income levels in Zambia, access to services remains low and highly unequal—being available at affordable prices primarily to the affluent in urban areas and to the larger firms. Upon the government's request, a team of World Bank economists assessed the country's services reform experience, priorities ahead, and how to leverage international agreements to achieve them.

In Zambia's Investment Climate Surveys, a large share of firms identifies inadequacies in finance, telecommunications, and transport as a major or severe obstacle to their operations. A study of 42 countries found that Zambian firms had the second highest share of "indirect" costs, most of which were attributable to services related inputs into production—energy, transport, telecom, water, insurance, marketing, travel, independent professionals, and accounting. If Zambian firms had access to banking services at the same average level as their South African counterparts, their productivity would have been 6 per cent higher, and if they were also to enjoy the access to telecommunications services that South African firms currently have, they could be 13 per cent more productive. In this situation, any competitive advantage that Zambian firms derive from the country's low labor costs was being eroded by the high level of indirect costs attributable to the high prices of services inputs.

By the mid 2000s, the crisis of access in Zambia, and hence the diminishing faith in reform, were attributable to the fact that the government and donor organizations behaved as if they had complete faith in the power of markets. They moved aggressively, but unevenly, on the elimination of barriers to entry, sluggishly on the development of regulations to deal with market failure, and only notionally on the implementation of access widening policies. The end result was that access had been undermined by the persistence of barriers to competition, the weakness and inappropriateness of regulation, and the absence of meaningful access policy. The government and donors were not naïve and did appreciate the importance of the latter two dimensions, but they did what they could do quickly and relatively easily, which was to privatize and allow entry in some sectors. It is nonetheless ironic that only limited liberalization was accomplished in precisely those sectors (e.g., telecommunications, as an influential incumbent was not equipped to survive under competitive conditions) where successful outcomes could have been achieved even without progress in the other dimensions of reform, whereas barriers had been completely eliminated in sectors (e.g., financial services) where successful outcomes depended critically on complementary reforms.

(Continued)

Box 12.4 *Continued*

Zambia has continued to implement services reform and is actively engaged with services trade negotiations in the WTO under the GATS, with the EU in the context of the EPAs, and within regional blocs (COMESA and SADC). Such international engagement can be a powerful instrument of reform, by helping to mobilize assistance for, and lend credibility to, domestic reform, deliver improved access to foreign markets, and foster deeper regional integration. As to reform priorities, competition itself is a powerful instrument to widen access in sectors like transport and telecommunications. In these sectors, the case for introducing meaningful competition immediately by eliminating barriers at home and abroad is overwhelming. A quite different type of problem arises in a service sector like tourism where Zambia has a comparative advantage but is unable to exploit it because regulatory barriers impede entry by domestic and foreign services providers. Good regulation is a pre-condition for efficient competitive markets, and Zambia faces contrasting challenges: in a number of sectors, from telecommunications to transport, the regulatory framework is weak; in some others, such as financial services, auditing, and accounting, it is inappropriately strong. Both problems need to be remedied in order to widen access. Finally, even an open, efficient, competitive market will not deliver socially desirable levels of access to services, so a policy priority must be the institution of effective and efficient access widening policies.

Source: Adapted from Mattoo and Payton (2007: ch. 1).

---

sector—that openness in services influences long-run growth performance. After controlling for other determinants of growth, countries that fully liberalized the financial services sector (in terms of the three dimensions noted above) grew, on average, about 1.0 percentage point faster than other countries. An even greater impetus on growth was found to come from fully liberalizing both the telecommunications and the financial services sectors. Estimates suggest that countries that fully liberalized both sectors grew, on average, about 1.5 percentage points faster than other countries (see Mattoo et al. 2006; and Figure 12.3).

While the estimates above indicate that there are substantial gains from liberalizing key services sectors, it would be wrong to infer that these gains can be realized by a mechanical opening up of services markets. We may note that regulation in services, as in goods, may be purely due to rent-seeking behavior, but it often arises essentially from market failure attributable to three kinds of problems: natural monopoly; inadequate consumer information; and considerations of equity and protecting the poor. A flawed reform program on either of these fronts can undermine the benefits of liberalization.

Importance of Increasing Competition

For example, if privatization of state monopolies is conducted without concern for creating conditions of competition, the result may be merely transfers of monopoly

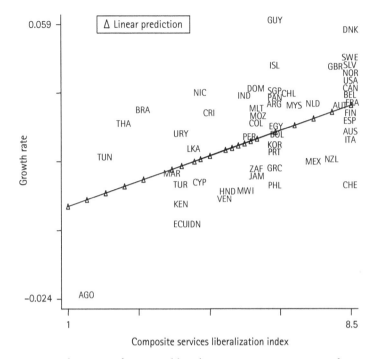

FIGURE 12.3 Estimated impact of services liberalization on economic growth

Source: Adapted from Mattoo, Rathindran, and Subramanian (2006).

rents to private owners (possibly foreigners). Similarly, if increased entry into financial sectors is not accompanied by adequate prudential supervision and full competition, the result may be insider lending and poor investment decisions. Also, if policies
to ensure universal service are not put in place, liberalization may not improve access
to essential services for the poor. Managing reforms of services markets therefore
requires integrating trade opening with a careful combination of competition and
regulation.

South Africa's experience in the late 1990s with liberalizing telecommunications services is instructive. The government recognized the need for a more efficient supply of
services. It decided to sell a 30 per cent equity stake of the public incumbent, Telkom, to
a strategic investor and to grant the newly privatized entity a five-year monopoly period
for fixed-line telephone services. It was hoped that market exclusivity would facilitate
rapid infrastructure roll-out to previously under-serviced areas. But the program has
had mixed results. Even though network growth picked up, Telkom did not meet its
roll-out obligations and sought to renegotiate the targets specified in its monopoly
license. The cost of the fixed-line monopoly was also reflected in Telkom's rising price–
cost margin, with gains in productivity leading to higher margins rather than lower
prices (Hodge, 1999). Finally, despite some improvement, labor productivity was only
a quarter of that of leading international operators, with the lack of competition in the

domestic market identified as a major contributing factor. Continued restrictions on domestic and foreign entry appear to have prevented the realization of the full benefits of competitive markets.

Many developing countries have moved away from public monopolies in sectors such as communications, financial, and transport services, but are still reluctant to allow unrestricted new entry. Privatization does not axiomatically mean greater competition. Restrictions on foreign presence assume particular significance in the case of services where cross-border delivery is not possible, because consumer prices then depend completely on the domestic market structure. Several studies have concluded that larger welfare gains arise from an increase in competition than from simply a change in ownership from public to private hands (Armstrong, 1997). Foreign investment clearly brings benefits even in situations where it does not lead to enhanced competition. Foreign equity may relax a capital constraint, help ensure that weak domestic firms are bolstered (e.g., via re-capitalizing financial institutions), and serve as a vehicle for transferring technology and know-how, including improved management. However, if restrictions on competition artificially inflate the returns on investment, the net returns to the host country may be negative.

Are there good reasons to limit entry? In some cases, technical limitations may prevent competition, such as those imposed by the scarcity of radio spectrum needed for the provision of mobile telecommunications services, and scarcity of space for department stores or airports in a city. More generally, entry restrictions might be justified by the existence of significant economies of scale, for example, if there are substantial fixed costs of networks, competitive entry could lead to inefficient network duplication.

However, entry restrictions are increasingly difficult to defend in principle, in the face of the mounting evidence that competition works and of rapid technological change. Entry restrictions change the nature of interaction between incumbents and may well make collusion more likely. Such restrictions dampen the impact of competition on productive efficiency, and the regulator is usually not better placed than the competitive process to determine the optimal number of firms in the market, especially given the difficulty of obtaining information about the cost structure of firms and other sources of regulatory failure. Furthermore, technological advances have significantly lowered network costs in sectors like telecommunications, and vertical separation (e.g., through network unbundling) has widened the scope for competitive entry (Smith and Wellenius, 1999). Therefore, inefficiencies introduced by duplication of networks may be small compared to operational inefficiencies that can result from a lack of competitive pressure. For example, countries in Latin America that granted monopoly privileges of six to ten years to telecom operators in privatized state enterprises saw connections grow at 1.5 times the rate achieved under state monopolies. That higher average rate was, however, only half the rate of growth of connections experienced in Chile, where the government retained the right to issue competing licenses at any time (Wellenius, 2000).

Institutional Framework and Regulatory Quality

In addition to competition, the institutional framework and regulatory quality play a critical role. For example, in the 1990s, financial reforms were introduced in many African countries but have been less successful than expected (World Bank, 2001). Some of the reasons for the disappointing results are directly related to the financial system, while others pertain to the more general economic environment. The restructuring of state owned banks was not sufficient to change the behavior of the financial institutions. Public authorities still pressured these institutions to lend money to loss-making public enterprises. Liberalization failed to trigger competition in the banking sector, and governments were mostly reluctant to close down distressed state banks. Furthermore, liberalization of interest rates in a setting characterized by uncontrolled fiscal deficits had a pernicious effect on domestic public debt, which in turn led to larger deficits. Finally, and crucially, there was a lack of adequate regulation and supervision mechanisms to monitor the functioning of the financial system.

The collapse of the Korean economy in 1997 also reveals the precariousness of financial liberalization in an imperfect policy environment. Korea did liberalize its financial markets substantially, but it encouraged the development of a highly fragile financial structure. By liberalizing short-term (but not long-term) foreign borrowing, the Korean authorities made it possible for the larger and better-known domestic banks and chaebols to assume heavy short-term foreign currency debt. Meanwhile, the second tier of large chaebols greatly increased their short-term indebtedness in the domestic financial markets (funded indirectly through short-term foreign borrowing of the banks). The funds borrowed were being invested in over-expansion of productive capacity. At the same time, financial regulation and supervision were fragmented with responsibilities spread unclearly between the Bank of Korea and several parts of the Ministry of Finance. In addition, Korea had a restrictive regime in terms of foreign bank entry. Until the 1997 financial crisis, the Korean banking system was virtually closed to foreign banks, in contrast to some other East Asian countries, such as Hong Kong, which was almost completely open for all financial services. This restrictive regime impeded the development of the local institutions and contributed to the large capital outflows as foreign creditors refused to roll-over their loans.

Liberalizing Prices of Services and the Poor

Opening up essential services to foreign or domestic competition can have an adverse effect on the poor—which is often cited as a reason for the persistence of public monopolies. However, a more efficient solution is to have regulations with a social purpose. If a country is a relatively inefficient producer of a service, liberalization and the resultant foreign competition are likely to lead to a decline in domestic prices and improvement in quality. But there is a twist. Frequently, the prices pre-liberalization are not determined by the market but are set administratively and kept artificially low for certain categories of end users and/or types of services products. Thus, rural borrowers may pay lower interest rates than urban borrowers, and prices of local telephone calls and public transport may be kept lower than cost of provision. This structure of prices is often sustained through cross-subsidization within public monopolies or through government financial support.

Liberalization threatens these arrangements. Elimination of restrictions on entry implies an end to cross-subsidization because it is no longer possible for firms to make extra-normal profits in certain market segments. New entrants may focus on the most profitable market segments ("cream-skimming"), such as urban areas, where network costs are lower and incomes higher. And privatization could mean the end of government support. The result is that even though the sector becomes more efficient and average prices decline, the prices for certain end-users may actually increase and/or availability decline.

The evidence on the relationship between competitive market structures and wider access to services is mixed. In some cases, a positive relationship has been observed in services like basic telecommunications, especially in countries where initial conditions are feeble, as exemplified by a low teledensity or service rationing (long waiting lists for obtaining connections). However, there is also evidence that financial services liberalization in some countries has had an adverse effect on access to credit for rural areas and the poor. There is a need accordingly to create mechanisms to ensure that the poor have adequate access to services in liberalized markets.

Factor Adjustment to Services Liberalization

Different modes of supply have different effects on factor markets. Cross-border trade and consumption abroad resemble the goods trade in their implications. The impact of the movement of factors depends critically on whether they are substitutes for or complements to domestic factor services. Given the structure of factor prices in poor countries, we would typically expect liberalization to lead to an inflow of capital and skilled workers. Such inflows would tend to be to the advantage of the unskilled poor—increasing employment opportunities and wages. Interestingly, it has been shown that even when foreigners compete with local skilled workers in a services sector, the productivity boost to the sector from allowing foreigners access could lead to an increase in the demand for domestic skilled workers—the scale effect could outweigh the substitution effect (Markusen, Rutherford, and Tarr, 2000). Given these predictions, why are workers in developing countries sometimes skeptical about the benefits of liberalization? One concern is the possible reduction in employment in formerly public monopolies that have frequently employed surplus labor. For example, Alexander and Estache (1999) find that the privatization of electricity distribution in Argentina led to a 40 per cent reduction in the workforce after privatization.

But there is also evidence that pessimism may not always be justified. For example, a number of developing countries have managed to maintain or even increase employment in their liberalized telecommunications sectors. Since many developing countries have low teledensities (in the vicinity of 5 lines per 100 people), roughly 70 per cent of telecom investment in developing countries is directed towards building wire line and mobile networks that are labor intensive and hence help to maintain or raise employment levels. Petrazzini and Lovelock (1996) find in a study of 26 Latin American and Asian economies that telecom markets with competition were the only ones that consistently increased employment levels, while two thirds of the countries with monopolies saw considerable declines in their telecom work force.

The Sequence of Reform Matters

Fink et al. (2003) analyzed the impact of policy reform in basic telecommunications on sectoral performance, using a panel dataset for 86 developing countries across Africa, Asia, the Middle East, Latin America, and the Caribbean in the period 1985 to 1999. It was found that both privatization and competition can independently lead to significant improvements in performance. But a comprehensive reform program, involving both policies and the support of an independent regulator, produced the largest gains: an 8 per cent higher level of mainlines and a 21 per cent higher level of labor productivity compared to of partial and no reform (see Figure 12.4). Mainline penetration was found to be lower if competition was introduced after privatization, rather than at the same time.

This result suggests that delays in the introduction of competition—for example due to market exclusivity guarantees granted to newly privatized entities—may adversely affect

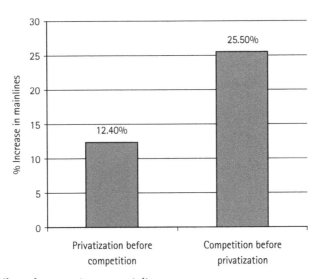

FIGURE 12.4 Effect of sequencing on mainlines

Source: Adapted from the World Bank/ITU Telecommunications Policy Database in Fink, Mattoo, and Rathindran (2003).

performance even after competition is eventually introduced. This could happen for three reasons. First, the importance of location-specific sunk costs in basic telecommunications suggests that allowing one provider privileged access may have durable consequences because sunk costs have commitment value and can be used strategically (Bös and Nett, 1990). Second, allowing privileged access creates vested interests that may then resist further reform or seek to dilute its impact. For example, in South Africa, private shareholders (national and foreign) in the incumbent successfully lobbied to reduce the number of entrants that the government was planning to allow from two to one (Lamont, 2001).

Finally, sequence matters because of the implied changes in the post-liberalization regulatory environment: before, the incumbent is a relatively inefficient public operator but the regulator is usually well informed about the cost structure; afterwards the incumbent is a relatively efficient private operator and the regulator is less well informed. It is obvious that that new entry by multiple private operators is easier to accomplish in the former situation.

A Services Reform Agenda

Policymakers should conduct regulatory audits, encompassing all stakeholders like the relevant government agencies, industry associations, consumer groups, and labor representatives to identify key constraints and priorities for reform. Professional bodies can help raise standards, but policymakers must avoid regulatory capture, as for instance has been the case in Italy until the most recent economic crisis in late 2011. They should also consider that most services sectors are knowledge intensive and often require rethinking of education policies to foster local service providers and improve their workers' prospects (Cattaneo et al., 2010).

Trade policymakers at the OECD have identified six principles that are key to market-oriented and trade- and investment-friendly regulation (OECD, 2005):

- Transparency and openness in decision making.
- Non-discrimination.
- Avoidance of unnecessary trade restrictions.
- Application of competition principles from an international perspective.
- Use of internationally harmonized measures.
- Streamlining of conformity assessment procedures.

Regulation to Make Competition Work

The existence of natural monopoly or oligopoly is a feature of the "locational services." Such services require specialized distribution networks: roads and rails for land transport, cables and satellites for communications, and pipes for sewage and energy distribution (United Nations Conference on Trade and Development (UNCTAD) and World Bank, 1994).

Many countries have instituted independent regulators for basic telecommunications services to ensure that monopolistic suppliers do not undermine market access by charging prohibitive rates for interconnection to their established networks. A similar approach is being taken in a variety of other network services, including transport (terminals and infrastructure) and energy services (distribution networks).

Regulation of the interconnection price may not, however, be sufficient. Small markets may not be able to create conditions for effective competition in the supplies of certain telecommunications, transport, and financial services, even if they eliminate all barriers to entry. This is the case for two related reasons. First, unlike in the case of goods, national markets are often segmented from the international market due to the infeasibility of cross-border delivery. Second, changing technologies may have reduced the optimal scale of operation as well as sunk costs in these sectors, but not enough for small markets to sustain competitive market structures. Some form of final price regulation may, therefore, be unavoidable. In some cases, such regulation can, at least in principle, be implemented at the national level although, in practice, many developing countries today lack the means to do so. In other cases, the limited enforcement capacity of small states strengthens the case for multilateral initiatives.

Regulation to Remedy Inadequate Consumer Information

In many intermediation and knowledge-based services, consumers have difficulty securing full information about the quality of service that they are buying (UNCTAD and World Bank, 1994). Consumers cannot easily assess the competence of professionals such as doctors and lawyers, the safety of transport services, or the soundness of banks and insurance companies. When such information is costly to obtain and disseminate and consumers have similar preferences about the relevant attributes of the service supplier, the regulation of entry and operations in a sector could increase social welfare. However, the establishment of institutions competent to regulate well is a serious challenge, as is revealed by the difficulties in the financial sector—not only in a number of developing countries but also in the USA, Sweden, and Finland in the 1980s, 1990s, and 2007–09. The fact that regulatory inadequacies cannot be quickly remedied raises the issue of how different elements of reform—particularly prudential strengthening and trade and investment liberalization—are best sequenced.

A separate problem is that domestic regulations to deal with the market failure may themselves become impediments to competition and trade, as a result of differences across jurisdictions in technical standards, prudential regulations, and qualification requirements in professional, financial, and numerous other services. In many cases, the impact on trade is an incidental consequence of the pursuit of a legitimate objective, but in some cases regulation can be a particularly attractive means of protecting domestic suppliers from foreign competition. The issue of how multilateral trade rules might shift the legitimate from the protectionist is an issue to which we return in the final section below.

Regulation to Widen Access to Services

Reform programs can accommodate universal-service obligations by imposing this requirement on new entrants in a non-discriminatory way. Thus, such obligations were part of the license conditions for new entrants into fixed network telephony and transport in several countries. However, subsidies have often proved more successful than direct regulation in ensuring universal access (Estache et al., 2001). For example, in 1999, Peru adopted a universal-service levy of 1 per cent to finance a fund dedicated to providing universal access in remote areas. Funds were allocated through a competitive bidding process that encouraged operators to adopt the best technology and other cost saving practices at minimum subsidy. The Chilean government adopted a similar scheme that permitted it to leverage over $2 million in public funds into $40 million in private investment; this resulted in installation of telephones in 1,000 localities at about 10 per cent of the costs of direct public provision. In Chile, household ownership of a telephone increased from 16 to 74 per cent in 1988–2000, and all but 1 per cent of the remaining households were provided with public access to a telephone.

Public subsidies also should be directed to the consumer rather than the provider (Cowhey and Klimenko, 1999). Governments have experimented with various forms of vouchers from education to energy services. This last instrument has at least three advantages. First, it can be targeted more directly at those who need the service and cannot afford it; second, it avoids the distortions that arise from artificially low pricing of services to ensure access; and finally, it is an instrument that does not discriminate in any way between providers.

VI. Conclusion

In this chapter, we have presented a conceptual framework for services trade, including what are services and how they are traded, the measurement of services trade, and why services matter for development. We also have discussed the determinants of services trade in terms of comparative advantage and increasing returns to scale, and why firms choose particular modes of supplying services. Issues of services trade policy were covered in detail, including identifying, analyzing, and measuring the effects of service trade barriers. The effects of services reform on efficiency and growth were considered, with examples drawn from the experiences of Mauritius and Zambia. The emphasis was on the importance of increasing competition, the critical importance of the institutional framework and regulatory quality, the effects of services liberalization on the poor, factor adjustment to services liberalization, and the importance of sequencing of services reform. Finally, an agenda for services reform was presented.

For the benefit of the more technical reader, the Appendix to this chapter contains a graphic presentation of the economic effects of barriers on trade in services.

Appendix: Economic Analysis of Barriers on Trade in Services

Tariffs and Quotas

We begin by reviewing the analysis of a tariff to use as a benchmark. For those familiar with the analysis of trade barriers on goods as set out in detail in Chapter 7, the analysis of the welfare effect of an import tariff on goods is the same as that of a tax on imported services.

Many types of quantitative restrictions apply to service trade. For example, Canada and Australia have restrictions that require that foreign content in broadcasting (such as popular music or television programs) does not exceed some limit. There are also many types of licensing restrictions that put explicit quantitative limits on the number of foreign suppliers who are permitted to compete in a local market.

It is noteworthy that a tariff and quota have similar effects. That is, if markets are competitive, producer surplus will rise by the same amount in both cases, and consumer surplus will fall by the same amount. But there are some differences. The first difference is that a tariff generates tax revenue, while a quota does not. The quota rents generated accrue to the individuals who have the right to import services into the domestic economy. If the government auctioned off the rights for foreigners to provide units of services to the economy, then the government would collect rents equal to the revenue that it would have collected from tariffs. However, such auctions typically do not occur. In the case of quotas on both goods and service imports, the quota rents typically accrue to domestic agents who have import licenses.

In practice, however, quota rents are often dissipated by rent-seeking activities. That is, because those who obtain import licenses can earn quota rents, there is an incentive to spend resources on lobbying and other activities (some possibly involving corruption) to try to acquire import licenses. Since these activities consume real resources and are unproductive, they are a cost, and tend to push the social costs of quotas above tariffs.

There is an even more compelling reason to expect that the quota rents will be lost. Because services are provided directly by foreign providers, they are typically not imported by middlemen, as in the case of goods. That is, those foreign service providers who are allowed to operate in the domestic economy will sell their services directly to domestic consumers. Hence, the foreign service providers will typically collect the quota rents. In this case (that is, unless the government auctions off quota licenses for the right to provide services), there will be a loss in consumer surplus that accrues to foreigners and so counts as a loss to the domestic economy.

Quotas fare even worse when markets are not competitive, as was pointed out by Bhagwati (1965). The key difference between a tariff and quota is that in a tariff regime the domestic monopolist faces potential foreign competition on every unit that it sells. But under a quota, there is competition only for the first units imported. Once the quota is filled, the monopolist faces no more competition. That is, an import quota gives the monopolist power that it does not have in a tariff regime. This means that quotas are significantly inferior to tariffs in markets where there are not very many local firms.

The other major benefit of tariffs over quotas is the added transparency of tariffs. Consumers may not be aware of the extent to which quotas are pushing up domestic costs. However, if they have to pay a tax on foreign services, then the magnitude of the tax is a useful index of the stringency of protection. Moreover tariffs can simplify negotiations over trade liberalization, in part because of the added transparency. An agreement to reduce tariffs by 30 per cent is easier to implement that one that requires the import quotas be relaxed.

Are there any cases where a quota might be better than a tariff? If the government wants to completely exclude foreigners, then an import ban (a prohibitive quota) and a prohibitively high tariff will have the same effect, except that the ban will be more certain in its effects. Also, producers often prefer quotas. Quotas help to insulate the domestic market from price changes occurring in foreign markets. This can reduce uncertainty for domestic producers. However, as discussed above, this added benefit for producers can come at a high cost to consumers.

Restrictions on FDI in Competitive Markets

If markets are competitive, the benefits of FDI are similar to the standard gains from trade. Figure 12.A1 illustrates a case where a service (X) can be provided only via

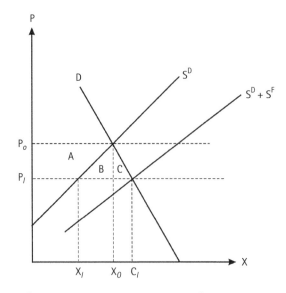

FIGURE 12.A1 Foreign direct investment: competitive market

commercial presence. Domestic supply is SD and demand is D. In the absence of foreign investment, output is x_o and price is p_o. If FDI is allowed, the supply of service providers will shift out. We denote the expanded supply as the sum of supply from domestic and foreign firms: SD + SF. With the foreign presence in the local market, price falls to P_1 and output increases to C_1. There is a gain in consumer surplus (A+B+C), and a loss in producer surplus (A), which yields a net social gain of B+C. FDI increases welfare by increasing competition, lowering prices, and increasing consumer choice. Conversely, restricting FDI would shift in the foreign supply curve and lead to social costs as the area B+C is eroded.

There are also many other potential benefits from FDI—through joint ventures, local firms may gain access to improved technology and financing. For some services such as insurance and finance, there can be increased risk pooling. There may also be spillover effects: local workers employed in foreign owned firms may receive knowledge, experience, and training that might otherwise be unattainable. Taking these effects into account would increase the measure of social costs of restricting FDI.

Analyzing the Interaction of Trade Policy and Regulation

To illustrate the interaction between trade policy and regulation, we consider the example of professional services, and in particular where low-quality service providers generate externalities. We consider two scenarios. First we consider a case where the domestic regulatory system is initially inadequate. That is, screening is imperfect, and there is a mix of good and bad service providers in practice. In this case, we show that trade liberalization without reforms of the domestic certification system can lower welfare. Next we consider the effects of trade under a well-functioning certification system. In this case, trade will be welfare improving. However, the magnitude of the gains depends on the way in which foreigners are screened.

Figure 12.A2 illustrates a market for professional services. There are two types of service providers: qualified (Q) and unqualified (U). Unqualified providers make mistakes that cause external harm. The demand for services is denoted by D. SQ is the (long run) domestic supply of qualified personnel (this takes into account training costs). These providers do not generate external harm. SQ+U is the combined domestic supply of qualified and unqualified personnel. The curve E(MSCQ+U) measures the expected marginal social cost of service provision by the mix of qualified and unqualified personnel.

If initially there is no trade, the price is P_o and output is Q_o. Now consider the effects of allowing foreigners to provide services under the same rules affecting local providers. For simplicity, we have assumed that the mix of qualified and unqualified personnel is the same among foreigners as among domestic suppliers, so that the expected external costs are the same.

When trade opens up, price falls to PU+Q, and consumption rises to Q2. Domestic output falls to Q1 because of increased competition from foreigners. Consumers gain

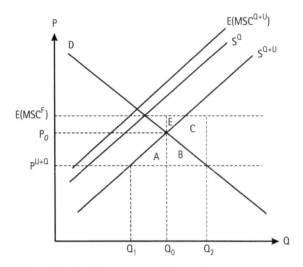

FIGURE 12.A2 Trade in professional services with imperfect screening

from lower prices and domestic producers lose. The net gain in consumer and producer surplus (ignoring the external harm caused by bad screening) is A+B. However, the increase in service provision caused by trade also generates more harm as more mistakes are made by unqualified service providers (domestic and foreign, see curve E(MSCF)).

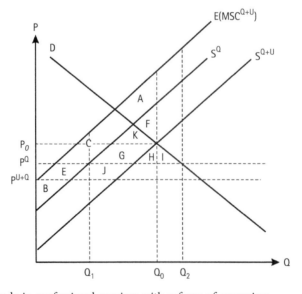

FIGURE 12.A3 Trade in professional services with reform of screening

The increase in external harm after trade opening is measured by B+C+E. Hence the net social gain from trade is A − (E+C). Welfare could rise or fall: in the example here it falls.

The point of this example is similar to the point raised in our discussion of entry barriers. If the domestic regulatory system is initially inadequate, then liberalizing trade can exacerbate the problems arising from imperfect regulation. The ensuing social costs can potentially more than offset the gains from trade liberalization.

This does not mean, however, that trade liberalization is a bad policy. However, on the contrary, if domestic regulatory reform accompanies trade liberalization, then gains can be assured. To see this, consider Figure 12.A3. Now suppose that the government introduces a certification requirement that fully screens both domestic and foreign personnel. Let P^Q be the price of services provided by qualified foreign service personnel. If trade opens, price falls from P_0 to P^Q, consumption rises to Q_2, and domestic output falls to Q_1 (since now only qualified domestic agents supply services). In this case, in addition to the net gain in consumer and producer surplus, there are additional gains as the external harm from mistakes is eliminated. Social gains are therefore B+E+C+A+F+K+G+H+I; these are unambiguously positive. Trade liberalization, accompanied by domestic regulatory reform, raises welfare.

References

Alexander, I., and A. Estache. (1999). 'The Role of Regulatory Reform and Growth: Lessons from Latin America.' Paper presented at TIPS Annual Forum, Johannesburg, South Africa (September).

Armstrong, M. (1997). 'Competition in Telecommunications.' *Oxford Review of Economic Policy,* 13(1): 64–82.

Arnold, Je. M., B. Javorcik, M. Lipscomb, and A. Mattoo (2010). 'Services Reform and Manufacturing Performance: Evidence from India.' CEPR Discussion Papers 8011, C.E.P.R. Discussion Papers.

Arnold, J. M., B. S. Javorcik, and A. Mattoo (2011). 'Does Services Liberalization Benefit Manufacturing Firms? Evidence from the Czech Republic.' *Journal of International Economics,* 85(1): 136–46.

Bös, D., and L. Nett (1990). 'Privatization, Price Regulation, and Market Entry: An Asymmetric Multistage Duopoly Model.' *Journal of Economics (Zeitschrift für Nationalökonomie),* 51(3): 221–57.

Cattaneo, O., M. Engman, S. Saez, and R. M. Stern (2010). *International Trade in Services: New Trends and Opportunities for Developing Countries.* Washington, DC: The World Bank.

Chadha, R., D. Brown, A. Deardorff, and R. Stern (2003). 'Computational Analysis of the Impact on India of the Uruguay Round and the Forthcoming WTO Trade Negotiations.'In Mattoo, A., and R. M. Stern (eds.) *India and the WTO.*Washington, DC: Oxford University Press and The World Bank.

Copeland, B. R. (2001). 'Benefits and Costs of Trade and Investment Liberalization in Services: Implications from Trade Theory.' A paper prepared for the Department of Foreign Affairs and International Trade, Government of Canada.

Copeland, B. R., and A. Mattoo (2008). 'The Basic Economics of Services Trade.' In Mattoo, A., R. M. Stern, and G. Zanini (eds.) *Handbook of International Services Trade.* Oxford: Oxford

University Press.

Cowhey, P., and M. M. Klimenko (1999). 'The WTO Agreement and Telecommunication Policy Reforms.' A draft report for the World Bank, Graduate School of International Relations and Pacific Studies, University of California at San Diego (March).

Deardorff, A. V., and R. M. Stern (2008). 'Empirical Analysis of Barriers to International Services Transactions and the Consequences of Liberalization.' In Mattoo, A., R. M. Stern, and G. Zanini (eds.) *Handbook of International Services Trade*. Oxford: Oxford University Press.

Estache, A., Q. Wodon, and V. Foster (2001). 'Accounting for Poverty in Infrastructure Reform: Learning from Latin America's Experience.' Washington, DC: The World Bank.

Ethier, W. (1982). 'National and International Returns to Scale in the Modern Theory of International Trade.' *American Economic Review*, 72(June): 492–506.

Fernandes, A. M., (2007). 'Structure and Performance of the Services Sector in Transition Economies,' Policy Research Working Paper Series 4357, The World Bank.

Fink, C., A. Mattoo, and I. C. Neagu (2002). 'Assessing the Impact of Communication Costs on International Trade.' World Bank Policy Research Working Paper No. 2929.

Fink, C., A. Mattoo, and R. Rathindran (2003). 'An Assessment of Telecommunications Reform in Developing Countries.' *Information Economics and Policy*, 15: 443–66.

Goswami, A. G., A. Mattoo, and S. Saez (eds.) (2012). *Exporting Services: A Developing Country Perspective*, Washington, DC: The World Bank.

Hodge, J. (1999). 'Liberalizing Communications Services in South Africa.' Trade and Industrial Policy Secretariat, Johannesburg.

Hoekman, B. (ed.) (2006). *Trade in Services at 25: Theory, Policy and Evidence*. Cheltenham: Edward Elgar.

Lamont, J. (2001). 'South Africa U-turn on Telecoms Competition.' *Financial Times*, August 15.

Markusen, J. R. (1989). 'Trade in Producers Services and in Other Specialized Intermediate Inputs.' *American Economic Review*, 79: 85–95.

Markusen, J., T. F. Rutherford, and D. Tarr (2000). 'Foreign Direct Investment in Services and the Domestic Market for Expertise.' Policy Research Working Paper No. 2413. Washington, DC: The World Bank.

Markusen, J. R., and A. J. Venables (2000). 'The Theory of Endowment, Intra-industry and Multi-national Trade.' *Journal of International Economics*, 52: 209–34.

Mattoo, A., R. Rathindran, and A. Subramanian (2006). 'Measuring Services Trade Liberalization and Its Impact on Economic Growth: An Illustration.' *Journal of Economic Integration*, 21(1): 64–98.

Mattoo, A., and L. Payton (eds.) (2007). *Services Trade and Development: The Experience of Zambia*. Washington, DC: The World Bank, and Palgrave McMillan.

Mattoo, A., R.M. Stern, and G. Zanini (eds.) (2008). *A Handbook of International Trade in Services*. Oxford: Oxford University Press.

Mundell, R. (1957). 'International Trade and Factor Mobility.' *American Economic Review*, 67: 321–35.

OECD (2005). *Taking Stock of Regulatory Reform: A Multidisciplinary Synthesis*. OECD Reviews of Regulatory Reform. Paris: OECD.

Petrazzini, B. A., and P. Lovelock (1996). 'Telecommunications in the Region: Comparative Case Studies.' Paper presented at the International Institute for Communication Telecommunications Forum, Sydney, Australia, April 22–3.

Robinson, S., Z. Wang, and W. Martin (1999). 'Capturing the Implications of Services Trade Liberalization.' Paper presented at the Second Annual Conference on Global Economic

Analysis, GL Avernaes Conference Center, Ebberup, Denmark, June 20–2.

Smith, P. L., and G. Wellenius, (1999). 'Mitigating Regulatory Risk in Telecommunications.' *Public Policy for the Private Sector*, Note 189 (July). The World Bank.

UNCTAD and World Bank (1994). *Liberalizing International Transactions in Services: A Handbook*. New York and Geneva: United Nations.

United Nations Statistics Division (UNSD) (2012). *Manual on Statistics of International Trade in Services* (MSITS). Washington, DC: United Nations, and others.

Walmsley, T. L., and L. A. Winters (2005). 'Relaxing the Restrictions on the Temporary Movement of Natural Persons: A Simulation Analysis.' *Journal of Economic Integration*, 20(4): 688–726.

Wellenius, B. (2000). 'Extending Telecommunications beyond the Market: Toward Universal Service in Competitive Environments.' *Public Policy for the Private Sector*, Note 206, Finance, Private Sector, and Infrastructure, The World Bank.

World Bank (2001). *Can Africa Claim the 21st Century?* Washington, DC: The World Bank.

World Bank (2006). 'Mauritius—From Preferences to Global Competitiveness: Report of the Aid for Trade Mission.' April 26, pp. 1–6.

World Bank. (2012). Services Trade Restrictions Database, The World Bank. Washington, D.C., available at: <http://iresearch.worldbank.org/servicetrade/>.

World Trade Organization (2010). 'Measuring Trade in Services: A Training Module.' December, related paper and slide presentation available at: <http://www.wto.org/english/res_e/statis_e/services_training_module_e.htm> (accessed April 2013).

CHAPTER 13

MIRACLES AND DEBACLES: AN EXTENSION*

ARVIND PANAGARIYA

A key policy question confronting developing countries today is whether to opt for outward oriented trade policies or yield to protectionism. I will demonstrate below that the last 50 years of experience overwhelmingly favors the former option. Virtually all growth miracles involving sustained rapid growth in the developing world have taken place in the presence of low or declining barriers. Moreover, there are few growth debacles involving stagnant or declining per capita incomes that can be attributed to sustained import surges. Before I turn to the evidence, however, it is useful to sort out a series of confusions that have plagued the debate on this important subject.

I. NON-SEQUITURS: CRITICISMS THAT WON'T DO

Free trade critics often offer arguments that seem superficially plausible but fail to stand up to closer scrutiny. For example

- Some critics cite countries that opened to trade and failed to achieve higher growth to make a case in favor of protectionism. Others argue that the existing

* This is an updated version of my paper "Miracles and Debacles: In Defense of Trade Openness" published in the World Economy 27, No 8, (special issue on Global Trade Policy), August 2004, 1149–71. © John Wiley & Sons.

econometric evidence fails to persuasively establish a *causal* link between barriers to trade and growth. But such criticisms miss the point that the policy choice must be based not on whether openness by itself leads to higher growth but on whether it is more *conducive* to sustained growth. Few serious advocates of free trade argue that openness is by itself sufficient for growth. They fully recognize that in the absence of macroeconomic stability, policy credibility, and enforcement of contracts, it is unlikely that a country will be able to register significantly high growth rates for a sustained period. But these policies yield the high-growth dividend only in an open trading environment.

- Critics also attack the case for liberal trade policies on the ground that certain successful experiences of sustained growth were actually catalyzed by alternative policies such as a government engineered increase in investment demand or innovation. But these critics fail to distinguish between initial catalysts to growth and policies necessary to *sustain* it. Even if growth is initially stimulated by increased investment demand or innovation, growth is unlikely to be sustained if the trading environment is autarkic and continues to be autarkic. Of course, if openness also serves as a direct stimulus to growth, it is an added advantage. A careful study of the successful cases reveals that whatever the source of the initial stimulus, increased growth often leads to increased trade liberalization and vice versa. The recent successful experiences of China and India graphically illustrate the process of growth and openness feeding on each other.

- Critics also like to cite examples of countries that managed to register high growth rates behind high walls of protection to conclude that protectionism works. Again, high *initial* trade barriers do not preclude the *onset* of rapid growth, especially in countries such as Brazil, China, and India that have potentially large internal markets. Indeed, the growth process itself may sometimes be kicked off by gradual liberalization of an initially highly protected regime. But such growth will be sustained only if the country responds by undertaking liberalization that accommodates the necessary expansion of trade. Evidence pointing to the fact that a country grew rapidly while still behind a high protectionist wall does not prove the efficacy of protection! The critical question for such an economy is whether it was lowering or further raising the protectionist wall during the period of rapid growth.

- Critics also like to cite examples of countries that managed to register high growth while raising barriers to trade. But pro-free trade economists have often recognized that in an *initial* phase of development and starting with relatively low barriers to trade, increased protection need not preclude fast growth as long as protection remains moderate and short lived. Even the late Bela Balassa, one of the early advocates of outward oriented policies—who was sometimes regarded as a free trade ideologue by the devotees of import substitution industrialization— recognized that the *first* stage of import substitution may have played a positive role in the development of South Korea, Taiwan, and Singapore. He defined this stage as the period during which imports of non-durable consumer goods such as textiles and apparel and the intermediate inputs used in them are replaced by domestic production. In the present context, this qualification is largely academic since the time for such import substitution is now behind virtually all developing countries.

- Finally, though pro-free trade and pro-market policies often go hand in hand and reinforce each other, the necessity of trade openness for growth is not inconsistent with the use of industrial policy. Critics sometimes challenge the case for openness by pointing to what they regard as the success of interventionist industrial policies in the high growth economies of the Far East. While the efficacy of industrial policies itself constitutes a separate subject of debate among economists, the success of an activist industrial policy does not prove the failure of outward oriented policies.

The contrasting experiences of South Korea and India during the first three decades (1950–80) of their development vividly illustrate these points. Therefore, I next discuss these experiences. Before I do this, however, let me clarify one definitional issue. An exchange rate that errs on the side of under-valuation rather than over-valuation is an integral part of an outward oriented policy regime. If the exchange rate is over-valued, discrimination against the traded goods sector emerges even with low formal trade barriers such as tariffs. Avoiding an over-valued exchange rate is not merely good for macroeconomic stability but is an essential condition for maintaining openness itself.

II. A Tale of Two Countries: South Korea and India

Rodrik (1995) has questioned the importance of openness in Korea's growth experience during the 1960s and 1970s arguing that the country grew rapidly because its government "managed to engineer a significant increase in the private return to capital" by "subsidizing and coordinating investment decisions." He views the expansion of trade as merely a passive outcome of the process unleashed by this expansion of investment: new investments required machinery that had to be imported and increased imports necessitated increased exports.[1]

To be sure, one can question the basic premise underlying this simplistic story. During 1961–80, Korea's exports grew at an annual rate of 23.7 per cent in real terms.[2] Even though Korea began at a relatively low exports-to-Gross Domestic Product (GDP) ratio of 5.3 per cent in 1961, by 1980, that ratio had reached 33.1 per cent! This dramatic

---

1 I offer a more detailed comparison of the experiences of India and Korea between 1950 and 1980 in chapter 6 of my recent book, *India: The Emerging Giant* (Panagariya, 2008).

2 Unless otherwise noted, export figures reported in this chapter include both goods and services and are measured at the 1995 constant prices.

growth in exports, which came in large part after 1965, had to be the outcome of active policy changes rather than a passive response to the government coordinated investment boom. More importantly, the dramatic growth in exports had to be a significant stimulus to the economy at the margin. The efficiency gains that accrue from competing against the most efficient producers in the world and from accessing state-of-the-art technology via imports of new products and machinery had to be of primary importance.

Indeed, Larry Westphal and Kwang Suk Kim (1982), who have diligently studied the Korean experience during the first three decades of its development and strongly believe in the efficacy of industrial policy, assign the central role in stimulating growth in Korea to activist trade policy. Thus, consider the following statement from the concluding section of their long and careful study (p. 271):

> The growth of manufactured exports over the fifteen years from 1960 to 1975 contributed to Korea's industrial development in various ways. Export expansion was directly responsible for more than one quarter of the growth of manufactured output and for an even larger fraction of the increase in manufactured employment. In turn, the manufacturing sector has accounted for almost 40 % of the growth in both GNP and employment. These figures understate the contribution of export growth. They do not reflect the backward linkages to domestically produced intermediate inputs, the multiplier effect resulting from increased consumption and investment resulting from additional income earned, or the increase in economic efficiency that results from exporting in accordance with a country's comparative advantage.

Thus, Westphal and Kim turn the Rodrik story almost on its head attributing partially the growth in investment itself to export growth and the income increase accompanying it. Subsequently, in his review article in the *Journal of Economic Perspectives* entitled "Industrial Policy in an Export-Propelled Economy: Lessons from South Korea's Experience," Westphal (1990) notes, "Korea's industrial performance owes a great deal to the government's promotional policies toward exports and to its initiatives in targeting industries for development. If nothing else, policies towards exports have created an atmosphere—rare in the Third World—in which businessmen could be certain that the economic system would respond to and subsequently reward their efforts aimed at expanding and upgrading exports." Exports were not a passive response to the import demand generated by the investment boom but one of the "propellers" of the investment activity itself.

But suppose we grant Rodrik the point that it was the successful coordination of the investment decisions by the government that triggered Korea's growth. Does this diminish the importance of outward oriented trade policies that Korea pursued? In other words, what would have happened if Korea had chosen to continue raising trade barriers and moved deeper into import substitution by attempting to produce its own machinery to undertake the investments? After all, if import substitution works at all stages of development, as Rodrik seems to believe, domestic machinery production was an option that could have been exercised.

Some insight into this question can be obtained by studying the experience of India during the same time period. India tried to solve the investment coordination problem through explicit investment planning during the 1950s and beyond. By the standards applied by Rodrik to Korea, public interventions in India were surely successful, with total investment as a proportion of the GDP rising from 15.7 per cent in 1960–61 to 22.7 per cent in 1980–81.[3] Public investment consistently accounted for more than a third of this investment. Through macroeconomic stability, policy credibility, and legal institutions capable of enforcing contracts, India was successful in pushing its GDP growth rate from less than 1 per cent during the first half of the twentieth century to the 3–4 per cent range during 1950–80. But it came nowhere near the ultra-high growth rates experienced by Korea during the 1960s and 1970s principally because it opted for an increasingly protectionist trade policy regime with nearly all imports coming under strict licensing by the early 1970s. By the mid 1970s, India's trade regime had become so repressive that imports (other than oil and cereals) had fallen from the already low level of 7 per cent of the GDP in 1957–58 to 3 per cent in 1975–76.[4] Whereas Korea recognized the importance of competing against the world's most efficient producers and the need for importing state-of-the-art machinery from abroad, India chose to hide behind a steel wall of protection, manufacturing its own machinery (and steel!). The result was an annual *per capita* GDP growth of 6.3 per cent in Korea and 1.1 per cent in India during 1961–80. Thus, Rodrik's conclusion that outward orientation of the Korean economy was merely "the result of the increase in the demand for imported capital goods" misses the important point that ultimately such openness was the result of a conscious policy choice made by the country. Had Korea chosen to take the same path as India, its miraculous growth would have been choked despite its presumed success in coordinating the investment decisions.

Differences between the experiences of Korea and India during the first three decades of development are to be seen not just in terms of the outcome variables such as growth in trade and GDP but also policies and policy changes. Whereas Korea consciously moved away from an import substitution to outward oriented trade regime relatively early in the game, India became progressively protectionist. In the case of Korea, it is once again instructive to quote Westphal and Kim (1982: 214):

> Until the early 1960s, Korea followed a protectionist strategy of import substitution for non-durable consumer goods. Once import substitution could go no further in these areas, the government had to decide whether to continue with an inward-looking strategy but shift to import substitution for intermediate and durable goods, or whether to adopt an outward-looking strategy providing equal incentive to exports and import substitution. On the whole, it opted for the latter.

Kim (1985), who offers a lucid account of the policy changes in Korea, divides its policy regimes in the post-Korean War era (1953–78) into three phases. During the first

---

3 India's financial year begins on April 1 and ends on March 31. Therefore, year 1957–58 refers to April 1, 1957, to March 31, 1958.

4 Comparable data for India during 1960s are not available.

phase, which lasted from the end of the Korean War to 1960, Korea pursued the policy of import substitution of non-durable consumer goods and their intermediate inputs. During this phase, the real exchange rate was over-valued, foreign exchange controls were widely practiced, finished consumer goods were subject to high tariffs and the government relied progressively on quantitative import controls. The main incentive to exporters was the sale of foreign exchange in the free market.

In the second phase, 1961–65, Korea switched from the import substitution to export oriented strategy. The Korean won was devalued first in 1961 to 130 won per dollar and then in 1964 to 256 won per dollar. During these years, preferential export credit for exporters; tariff and indirect domestic tax exemptions on inputs used in exports; direct tax reductions on income earned on exports; and accelerated depreciation allowances for the fixed assets of major export industries were also introduced. In 1962, an export targeting system was set up.

In the last phase, 1966–78, the export oriented strategy was institutionalized with relatively minor changes in the export policy regime. The government did gradually relax the quantitative restrictions on imports and reduce tariffs on imports through several reforms during this third phase, however. Moreover, it roughly maintained the real exchange rate at the 1965 level through periodic adjustments of the nominal exchange rate and/or adjustment in export subsidies.

The history of trade policy in India, documented systematically in Bhagwati and Desai (1970), Bhagwati and Srinivasan (1975), and most recently Panagariya (2008), shows a sharp contrast to that of Korea. India started with a relatively open trade regime in 1950 and did not turn inward until a foreign exchange crisis led to the adoption of foreign exchange budgeting in 1958. Tariffs were low; quantitative import restrictions, though present, were not onerous; and foreign exchange reserves being comfortable there was no evidence of foreign exchange controls being practiced. But following the adoption of foreign exchange budgeting, quantitative restrictions on imports, industrial licensing, and foreign exchange controls were progressively tightened and expanded. This process continued till 1966 though some export subsidization schemes were introduced in 1962 and expanded subsequently to partially offset the discrimination against exports. Bhagwati and Srinivasan (1975) describe the regime during 1957–66 thus: "The import and exchange policy regime, throughout this period, aimed at comprehensive, direct control over foreign exchange utilization. Thus administrative decisions had to be made over the allocation of foreign exchange for practically all uses in the economy…Reliance on the direct allocative mechanism was thus almost complete during this period."

For each six-month period, the Ministry of Finance prepared an estimate of the available foreign exchange. In the first stage, debt repayment, Embassy expenditures, food, fertilizer, petroleum, oil and lubricant (POL), and defense needs were netted out from the estimated reserves. At the next stage, allocations were made to (1) different public sector undertakings for their raw material and machinery imports, (2) iron and steel controller, and (3) commerce ministry for private sector imports of raw materials and machinery. A large multiplicity of licensing agencies was involved in the allocation process before foreign exchange reached the actual user. Typically, imports of raw materials were not permitted if domestic substitutes were available. The burden of proof that no domestic substitute was available also fell upon the potential importer.

According to Bhagwati and Srinivasan (1975: 46), the effective export exchange rate was uniformly less than effective import exchange rate across industries. This was partially redressed starting in 1962 through export subsidization schemes but the change did not go far enough. One of the important side effects of the requirement that domestically produced inputs be used when available was that exportable items had to be manufactured with inferior quality inputs and capital equipment. In turn, this had a detrimental effect on product quality and placed exporters at considerable disadvantage in the highly competitive world markets.

During 1966–68, India went through a brief liberalization episode. In June 1966, the rupee was devalued by 37.3 per cent from 4.7 rupees to 7.5 rupees per dollar. The devaluation was accompanied by some liberalization of import licensing, cuts in import tariffs and export subsidies. Because the devaluation turned into a serious political liability (in part due to the widespread impression that the World Bank, prompted by the United States, had forced it), the process of liberalization was quickly reversed. According to Bhagwati and Srinivasan (1975: 30), by 1969–70, the liberalization had been largely reversed with the import premium back to 30–50 per cent. Almost all liberalizing initiatives were reversed and import controls tightened. This regime was consolidated and strengthened in the subsequent years and remained more or less intact until the beginning of a period of phased liberalization in the late 1970s.

To sum up then, both Korea and India started with import substitution policies. India intervened at least as much as Korea, perhaps more, to boost investment and was even successful in it. But after a short phase that was limited to the production of non-durable consumer goods and their inputs, Korea shifted to an export oriented policy. India, on the other hand, continued to go deeper towards import substitution extending it to consumer durables, raw material, and machinery. The policies had vastly different outcomes. GDP and trade in Korea grew at astronomical rates while those in India did so at a snail's pace.

III. Miracles and Debacles

The experience of Korea is not unique. We now have considerable systematic evidence supporting the hypothesis that openness is a necessary condition for fast growth. Specifically, the Global Development Network Growth Database provides growth rates for approximately 200 countries over a period of 38 years from 1961 to 1999. Despite missing entries in a number of cases, the database is sufficiently comprehensive to allow a systematic analysis of the issue at hand.

Since the precise division of data over time turns out not to matter, I divide them into two equal periods: 1961–80 and 1980–99. For each 19-year period, I identify countries that grew at 3 per cent or more in per capita terms as "miracles" and those that declined in per capita terms as "debacles." I then look at how the growth in per capita income correlates with growth in exports and imports for miracles and debacles. Since trade is an endogenous variable and is likely to respond positively to GDP growth, this is only the first step toward establishing the necessity of outward oriented policies for sustained rapid growth. I later return to the issue of the link between trade *policies* and growth.

Table 13.1 shows all non-oil exporting developing countries that grew at 3 per cent or more in per capita terms during 1961–80 in declining order of growth rates. Alongside, the third and fourth columns show annual growth rates of exports and imports. The last column shows the population of the country at the beginning of the period. The most remarkable point to note in Table 13.1 is that even though the 1960s and 1970s are commonly identified with the import substitution phase in developing countries, virtually all countries that grew rapidly did so while rapidly expanding their exports and imports. The countries in this group come from virtually all continents in the South including, especially, Latin America, which is often described as having led the developing world in the pursuit of import substitution. Brazil, which grew at the impressive rate of 4.6 per cent, expanded its exports and imports at 8.1 and 7.6 per cent, respectively, during the period. Among countries that grew at 3.6 per cent or more in per capita terms, the lowest recorded growth rate of imports was 7.2 per cent for Tunisia, which grew at 4 per cent in per capita terms. Even as we go down the growth rate column, there are only two countries that register relatively low growth rates of imports: Mauritius and Kenya with import growth of 3.8 and 3.6 per cent, respectively.

In addition to arguing that openness is not necessary for growth, some critics of free trade go so far as to contend that it actually leads to declining incomes. To examine this contention, Table 13.2 lists all countries that experienced a growth debacle during 1961–80. For the purpose of the table, a growth debacle is defined as a reduction in the per capita income on a sustained basis. It is evident that the weight of evidence is hugely against trade openness being responsible for the debacles. Out of the seven debacle cases in which we have data on both growth rates of per capita income and trade, only two show significant growth in imports. In the other cases, declines in per capita incomes are accompanied by import growth of less than 2 per cent.

This experience is repeated during the second period under study: 1980–99. Tables 13.3 and 13.4 show growth rates of per capita incomes and trade for the miracle and debacle countries, respectively. As in Table 13.1, leaving aside a handful of the cases, the miracle countries in Table 13.3 experience very substantial growth in imports and exports. The two largest countries in the world, China and India, join the club of miracle growth countries in this period and they both show respectable rates of growth of both exports and imports. In turn, Table 13.4 provides more substantial evidence that debacles are rarely accompanied by import surges. We now have as many as 65 countries in this category and in no case does the rate of growth of imports reach even 6 per cent. And in many cases, it is actually negative and large in absolute terms.

If we go by the *number* of countries that grew at 3 per cent or more in per capita income terms, performance during 1961–80 is clearly superior to that during 1980–99. As many as 33 non-oil exporting developing countries grew at this high rate during

Table 13.1 Miracles of 1961–80*

Country	Growth rates			Population in millions (1961)
	GDP per capita	Exports	Imports	
Botswana	8.5			0.5
Malta	7.3			0.3
Singapore	7.2			1.5
Hong Kong, China	6.9	10.8	10.6	3.2
Gabon	6.6	10.6	12.1	0.5
Taiwan, China	6.4			11.0
Korea, Rep.	6.3	23.7	18.0	25.7
Lesotho	4.8	7.6	11.8	0.9
Trinidad and Tobago	4.7	3.8	9.1	0.9
Thailand	4.6	9.3	9.6	27.2
Brazil	4.6	8.1	7.6	75.0
Malaysia	4.4	6.9	7.2	8.4
Barbados	4.4			0.2
Israel	4.2	10.8	8.1	2.2
Georgia	4.1			4.2
Cote d'Ivoire	4.1	7.6	7.9	3.9
Seychelles	4.0			0.0
Tunisia	4.0	8.3	7.2	4.3
Bermuda	4.0			0.0
Ecuador	3.7	8.2	8.0	4.6
Dominican Republic	3.6	5.6	10.6	3.3
Ireland	3.6	8.0	7.8	2.8
Egypt, Arab Rep.	3.5	5.4	8.1	26.5
Indonesia	3.5	6.5	10.2	95.9
Paraguay	3.5	3.0	10.6	1.9
Mauritius	3.5	2.4	3.8	0.7
Mexico	3.4	8.6	7.8	38.1
Panama	3.4			1.2
Belize	3.4			0.1
Togo	3.2	9.9	8.8	1.5
Fiji	3.0	7.6	7.7	0.4
Mauritania	3.0	11.3	7.7	1.0
Kenya	3.0	3.3	3.6	8.6

*Non-oil exporting developing countries with per capita GDP growth rate of 3 per cent or more (33 countries with a combined population of 356.5 million people in 1961).

Source: Author's calculations based on the World Bank GDN database.

Table 13.2 Debacles of 1961–80*

Country	Growth rates GDP per capita	Exports	Imports	Population in millions (1961)
Central African Republic	-0.1			1.6
Zambia	-0.3	1.0	0.4	3.2
Somalia	-0.4			2.9
Madagascar	-0.4	1.2	1.8	5.5
Dominica	-0.4			0.1
Ghana	-0.4	-2.7	-3.0	7.1
Guinea-Bissau	-0.5			0.5
Niger	-0.5	3.5	7.8	3.1
Senegal	-0.6	-0.1	1.2	3.3
Iran, Islamic Rep.	-0.7			22.1
Congo, Dem. Rep.	-0.9	2.8	5.7	15.7
United Arab Emirates	-1.0			0.1
Chad	-1.9	1.4	0.8	3.1
Kuwait	-3.6			0.3

*All developing countries with negative growth rates (14 countries with a total population of 68.6 million). Exports and imports include goods and services and are measured at constant prices.

Source: Author's calculations from the World Bank GDN databases.

Table 13.3 Miracles of 1980–99*

Country	Growth rates GDP per capita	Exports	Imports	Population in millions (1980)
China	8.3	10.4	8.0	981.2
Korea, Rep.	6.6	12.9	10.5	38.1
Equatorial Guinea	6.4			0.2
Taiwan, China	6.1			17.6
Singapore	5.9			2.3
St. Kitts and Nevis	5.9	2.9	2.9	0.0
Thailand	5.5	11.9	8.0	46.7
Indonesia	4.7	2.6	3.7	148.3
Botswana	4.7			0.9
Hong Kong, China	4.5	11.0	10.8	5.0
Antigua and Barbuda	4.4	5.4	4.8	0.1
Dominica	4.2	9.1	1.8	0.1

Table 13.3 *Continued*

Country	Growth rates			Population in millions (1980)
	GDP per capita	Exports	Imports	
Bhutan	4.1			0.5
Malta	4.1			0.4
Chile	3.9	7.7	5.5	11.1
Malaysia	3.9	11.1	9.6	13.8
India	3.8	8.5	6.5	687.3
St. Vincent and the Grenadines	3.7	4.4	2.6	0.1
St. Lucia	3.7	4.0	3.1	0.1
Mauritius	3.7	7.4	6.8	1.0
Grenada	3.4	6.0	3.8	0.1
Maldives	3.3			0.2
Vietnam	3.2			53.7
Sri Lanka	3.1	6.0	5.6	14.7
Cape Verde	3.1			0.3
Pakistan	3.0	5.8	1.4	82.7

* Non-oil exporting developing countries with per capita GDP growth rate of 3 per cent or more (26 countries with combined population of 2106.5 million in 1980). Exports and imports include goods and services and are measured at constant prices.

Source: Author's calculations based on the World Bank GDN database.

Table 13.4 Debacles of 1980–99*

Country	Growth rate			Population in Millions (1980)
	GDP per capita	Exports	Imports	
Afghanistan	-0.1			16.0
Gambia, The	-0.1	2.7	-1.1	0.6
Estonia	-0.1			1.5
Guatemala	-0.2	1.5	3.4	6.8
Ecuador	-0.2	4.9	-1.7	8.0
Samoa	-0.2			0.2
Namibia	-0.2	2.5	2.6	1.0
El Salvador	-0.3	3.6	5.7	4.6
Latvia	-0.3			2.5
Gabon	-0.3	2.8	0.1	0.7
South Africa	-0.4	2.9	2.5	27.6

Continued

Table 13.4 *Continued*

Country	Growth rate GDP per capita	Growth rate Exports	Growth rate Imports	Population in Millions (1980)
Honduras	-0.5	0.8	1.6	3.6
Bolivia	-0.5	2.7	4.3	5.4
Netherlands Antilles	-0.5			0.2
Croatia	-0.5			4.6
Togo	-0.5	-0.8	0.0	2.6
Yemen, Rep.	-0.6			8.5
Sao Tome and Principe	-0.6			0.1
Rwanda	-0.7	-1.0	5.5	5.2
Albania	-0.7			2.7
Algeria	-0.7	3.5	-2.1	18.7
Suriname	-0.7	-5.6	-6.4	0.4
Cameroon	-0.7	4.8	4.0	8.7
Romania	-0.8			22.2
Mali	-0.9	6.9	4.0	6.6
Somalia	-0.9			5.9
Nigeria	-0.9	0.0	-3.0	71.1
Vanuatu	-0.9			0.1
Comoros	-1.0	11.3	0.1	0.3
Lithuania	-1.0			3.4
Micronesia, Fed. Sts.	-1.0			0.1
Belarus	-1.0			9.6
Russian Federation	-1.1			139.0
Bahrain	-1.1			0.3
Burundi	-1.2	7.7	2.6	4.1
Venezuela, RB	-1.2	3.3	2.1	15.1
Uzbekistan	-1.2			16.0
Central African Republic	-1.3			2.3
Angola	-1.4			7.0
Kuwait	-1.5			1.4
Zambia	-1.6	-0.1	-2.3	5.7
Djibouti	-1.6			0.3
Madagascar	-1.9	0.8	-1.9	8.9
Nicaragua	-1.9	2.7	3.2	2.9
Kyrgyz Republic	-1.9			3.6

Continued

Table 13.4 *Continued*

Country	Growth rate			Population in Millions (1980)
	GDP per capita	Exports	Imports	
Cote d'Ivoire	-1.9	2.9	0.1	8.2
Liberia	-2.0			1.9
Marshall Islands	-2.1			0.0
Armenia	-2.2			3.1
Haiti	-2.2	2.7	5.6	5.4
United Arab Emirates	-2.4			1.0
Kiribati	-2.4			0.1
Kazakhstan	-2.5			14.9
Saudi Arabia	-2.6			9.4
Niger	-2.6	0.1	-5.1	5.6
Brunei	-2.8			0.2
Sierra Leone	-2.9	-4.8	-5.2	3.2
Moldova	-3.6			4.0
Tajikistan	-4.1			4.0
Ukraine	-4.3			50.0
Libya	-4.5			3.0
Congo, Dem. Rep.	-4.5			27.0
Georgia	-4.7			5.1
Azerbaijan	-5.1			6.2
Iraq	-9.5			13.0

*Developing and transition economies with negative growth rates (65 countries with combined population of 621.4 million). Exports and imports include goods and services and are measured at constant prices.

Source: Author's calculations from the World Bank GDN database.

the first period compared with 26 in the second. Yet, if we go by the *population* in the developing countries experiencing the high growth rates, it is the second period that stands out. Whereas the population of the countries growing at 3 per cent or more at the beginning of the period was only 356.5 million during the first period, it was at a high of 2.1 billion during the second period. Those who have chosen to characterize the 1980s and 1990s as the lost decades of development have often overlooked this crucial fact.

The explanation for why the period 1980–99 has been viewed unfavorably relative to the prior two decades, especially the 1960s, is that this period produced a very large number of debacles that also impacted on a very substantial proportion of the world's population. Thus, during 1961–80, debacles were limited to 14 developing countries with a total population of 68.6 million at the beginning of the period. But during 1981–99, there were as many as 65 debacle countries accounting for 621.4 million people at the beginning of the period. Not only did a large number of tiny countries in Africa do poorly during this latter period, the large majority of the former Soviet republics, some with sizable populations, also joined the ranks of the debacle countries. It is the coincidence of this fact with a series of financial flow crises in Latin America and East Asia that fueled the anti-globalization movement, victimizing liberal trade policies in the process despite the fact that trade had little to do with either of the phenomena.

IV. Trade Volumes versus Trade Barriers

Before I turn to some additional, country-specific evidence, let me address an important criticism of the link between growth and openness offered by free trade skeptics (Rodriguez and Rodrik, 1999). Observing that the cross-country regression studies linking growth and *direct* measures of trade policy such as tariff and non-tariff barriers offer at best weak evidence, these skeptics also reject the link between growth and openness.

For one thing, the evidence from cross-country regression studies is not as weak as critics would have us believe. Following the Rodriguez-Rodrik critique, Greenaway, Morgan, and Wright (2002) have taken another look at the relationship between growth and trade liberalization using panel data. They disentangle the short and long run effects of liberalization and conclude that while the former may be negative, the latter are positive.

Wacziarg and Welch (2003) offer even more compelling evidence linking openness and growth. Interestingly, in the first part of their paper, they themselves begin by rejecting the Sachs–Warner approach that Rodriguez and Rodrik criticize. They then construct a panel dataset that allows them to exploit within and between country variations. They base their openness indicators on the date at which individual countries liberalized their import policies. In a panel of countries extending from 1950 to 1998, they find that on average, a country grows at 1.5 per cent per annum higher rate in the liberalized phase than in the protected phase, controlling for country and year effects. Because trade reforms sometimes occur during periods of macroeconomic instability, the authors also experiment with excluding the three years surrounding the reform but find the results robust to this modification.

A recent paper by Romalis (2006) goes one step further by explicitly addressing the endogenous nature of the openness variables. He uses the opening up by the United States under the multilateral trade negotiations as the instrument for estimating the openness variable for the developing countries and uses the estimated values of the latter to estimate the effect of openness on growth.[5] Romalis finds that the expansion of trade "induced by greater market access appears to cause a quantitatively large acceleration in the growth rates of developing countries."

This evidence notwithstanding, suppose for the sake of argument that we grant critics the point that evidence to date does not conclusively establish a positive link between growth and trade openness. But this is hardly sufficient to choose protectionism over outward oriented policies. Once we agree that fast growth in per capita GDP strongly correlates with fast growth in trade, the rejection of a link between low or declining trade barriers and growth in per capita incomes is equivalent to the rejection of a link between low or declining trade barriers and growth in *trade*. Admittedly, trade barriers are not the only determinant of growth in trade. But they are hardly irrelevant to the latter. In the extreme case, we cannot expect trade to grow rapidly if a country adopts autarkic or near autarkic trade policies.

An analogy may help put the matter in perspective. The speed with which water flows through a tap depends on water pressure as well as how far the tap is open. Rising water pressure will not translate into commensurate rise in water flow if the tap is not sufficiently open. Increased GDP growth can raise the growth in trade flows but only if trade barriers do not suppress the pressure created by the former. The experience of India until the late 1970s, discussed earlier, illustrates this point. It will be a stretch to argue that India's trade failed to grow rapidly because India's GDP failed to grow rapidly during that period. India consciously chose to suppress the growth in trade through draconian physical restrictions on trade flows. Additionally, if free trade skeptics truly believe that growth in trade is unrelated to the level of trade barriers, they should be indifferent to their removal. But the fact that they oppose such removal suggests they view the barriers as positively conducive to growth.[6]

In large part, the controversy surrounding the econometric evidence in support of the positive link between low or declining trade barriers and growth in per capita income is the result of our inability to accurately measure the protective effect of a given set of trade barriers. Difficulties in measuring the effects of non-tariff barriers are well known. For example, the effect of import licensing depends crucially on the severity with which it is enforced. Traditionally, developing countries have not explicitly specified the quantities permitted under licensing. Instead, they stipulate conditions under which an import license can be obtained. A license may be issued depending on the desired use of

[5] Given that the developing countries did not actively participate in the multilateral trade negotiations until the Uruguay Round, it can be reasonably assumed that the developed country liberalization prior to the Uruguay Round was independent of the policies of the developing countries. This assumption justifies the use of developed country liberalization as an instrument for estimating the openness variable for the developing countries.

[6] Rodrik (2001) goes so far as to offer a graph showing a *positive* association between growth rates and average tariffs with the title "Low import tariffs are good for growth? Think again." Evidently, in relying on such a graph to question the wisdom of openness, Rodrik does not hold himself to the same standards of rigor he applies to the defenders of openness in the Rodriguez–Rodrik (1999) critique.

the product, its proposed user, availability of like domestic products, and the availability of foreign exchange. Under such a regime, even without any formal change in the policy regime, imports can be permitted in smaller or larger quantities through a more or less strict administration of the existing rules.

Even when restrictions take the form of tariffs, aggregating them into a single measure that is comparable across countries is difficult. A 15 per cent uniform tariff has a very different effect from a two-part tariff regime that subjects one half of the imports to 10 per cent duty and the remaining half to 20 per cent duty. Yet, when aggregated for purposes of regressions, they are both set equal to 15 per cent. More dramatically, a two-part tariff consisting of 20 and 10 per cent tariff rates can have a *more* protective effect than even a single 20 per cent tariff rate. Thus, starting with a 20 per cent tariff on auto parts as well as automobiles, a reduction in the tariff on the former increases the effective protection to the latter. If domestic output of auto parts is small, this will likely result in increased overall protection in the economy. Not surprisingly, in his provocative paper "Measuring outward orientation in LDCs [Least-Developed Countries]: Can it be done?" Pritchett (1996) finds that some of the measures of openness used in cross-country growth regressions are actually negatively correlated with each other. This means that if one measure yielded a positive correlation between growth and trade barriers, the other one would do exactly the opposite.

Also important in assessing the impact of openness on growth is the real exchange rate. Even when countries liberalize trade but leave the real exchange rate over-valued, discrimination against traded goods remains. In this respect, the Rodriguez–Rodrik criticism of Sachs and Warner (1995) that posits that once the black market premium is taken out of their index, the link between openness and growth disappears, is itself problematic. The black market premium can be a measure of the over-valuation of the exchange rate and the resulting discrimination against traded goods and therefore arguably belongs in the openness index.

V. Import Substitution: Is Latin America an Exception?

Going by the *number* of countries experiencing rapid growth, Rodrik (1999) characterizes the years 1960–73 as the golden period of growth for developing countries. Per capita incomes in as many as 30 countries grew annually at rates equaling or exceeding 3 per cent during this period. In comparison, growth rates plummeted in most developing countries during 1973–84 to 1984–94. Noting that 1960–73 was the period of import substitution industrialization (ISI) and 1984–94 that of liberalization, Rodrik concludes that this suggests the triumph of ISI.

Much is wrong with this story. To begin with, the proposition that 1960–73 defined the golden period of growth for developing countries is itself questionable. For it is based on counting the *number* of countries that grew rapidly. But most of these countries were tiny in terms of population as well as GDP. As already emphasized above, if we choose to count the number of people in the developing countries impacted by high growth, we get a very different picture. With more than 2 billion people in China and India benefiting from rapid growth during the 1980s, 1990s, and 2000s, one can as easily argue that it is these decades that define the golden period. Put differently, if we consider developing countries as a single unit, their growth rate turns out to be higher in the 1980s and 1990s than during 1960–73.

But let us set aside this qualification and consider Rodrik's case. How is ISI to be defined? Rodrik offers no definition. Nor does he make the case that the fast growing countries during 1960–73 were import substituting and doing so more vigorously than the slow growing countries during the same period. Indeed, he does not even look at growth rates of exports and imports or trade policies. The reader must simply accept his word that the period in question was one of ISI.

But detailed country studies conducted over the last three decades provide substantial evidence that sheds light on this issue. Two large scale projects, one directed by Little, Scitovsky, and Scott (1970) at the Organisation for Economic Co-operation and Development (OECD) and the other by Bhagwati and Krueger (1974) at the National Bureau of Economic Research (NBER), offer detailed documentation of the success achieved during the 1960s and 1970s by countries that adopted outward oriented policies and the general failure of those that did not. In addition, we have the important study of a large number of semi-industrialized economies edited by Balassa (1982) that provides systematic evidence in favor of the superior performance of outward-oriented economies. Greenaway and Nam (1988) provide further evidence demonstrating that industrialization and growth have progressed farther in the more open economies.

While I have already noted that import substitution may have a role to play for a short period in the early stage development, if we take a close look at the experience, it still remains true that typically truly rapid growth is associated with phases characterized by low or declining barriers to trade. According to the study by Westphal and Kim (1982) in Balassa (1982), Korea's per capita GNP at 1970 prices grew at rates of 0.7, 3.6, 8.8, and 7.5 per cent per annum during 1955–60, 1960–65, 1965–70, and 1970–75, respectively. Thus, the performance during the core import substitution period, 1955–60, was not as spectacular as one might think. By 1961, Korea had already begun to move toward outward oriented policies. A similar story holds for Singapore, which went through a truly brief import substitution phase during 1965–67 and with relatively low protection and Taiwan, which perhaps had the best performance under import substitution during 1952–60 but even then not nearly as good as under outward orientation (see Augustine Tan and Ow Chin Hock (1982) on Singapore and T. H. Lee and Kuo-Shu Liang (1982) on Taiwan, both in Balassa (1982)).

Perhaps *prima facie* one would expect the greatest scope for making a case in favor of import substitution in Latin America. After all, this is where much of the intellectual stimulus for the desirability of import substitution policies had originated. But even here closer examination reveals a different picture than painted by Rodrik. Thus, the case of Brazil, by far the largest country on the continent and the star performer of 1960–73, fails to fit the ISI model. Its exports and imports in constant 1995 dollars grew at the impressive annual rates of 7.8 and 8.9 per cent, respectively, during this period. With imports rapidly substituting for domestic production and exports accounting for an increasingly larger share of GDP, *prima facie* Brazil cannot be characterized as succeeding through import substitution.

But this is not all. Even if we consider policies rather than trade outcomes, the Brazilian growth experience during the post 1960 era fails to fit the ISI story. Thus, consider Brazil's growth rates during 1961–68, 1968–75, and 1975–80. During 1961–68, the average growth rate was 1.6 per cent followed by 8.3 and 3.5 per cent, respectively, in the subsequent periods. It turns out that thoughtful trade policy specialists on Brazil describe the period 1965–73 as one of "cautious outward-looking trade policy liberalization" and 1974–80 as one of "renewed inward-looking policies."[7] During the former period, Brazil adopted a number of policy measures aimed at integrating itself into the global economy. On the exchange rate front, it undertook several devaluations to correct the over-valuation of the real exchange rate and later adopted the crawling peg to ensure its stability. It also introduced several export incentives to reduce the anti-export bias. Finally, it lowered the average legal tariff (including surcharges) for manufacturing from 99 to 57 per cent and for agriculture from 53 to 34 per cent.

This still leaves the question of why Latin America failed to grow during the 1980s despite substantial trade liberalization. Here we must recall the qualification that trade openness is an important necessary ingredient in the fast growth recipe but not the only ingredient. Therefore, the 1980s debacle in Latin America is to be attributed not to sustained import surges that did not happen, but to macroeconomic instability that resulted from short-term capital mobility, which most Latin American countries had embraced by then. The 1970s had been characterized by rising foreign debt in many Latin American countries with debt service as a proportion of exports rising to 30 per cent or more by the early 1980s in many cases. On top of that came the Volcker era interest rate increases in the United States, which led capital to flow out of Latin America abruptly and choked all growth potential.

But even from the 1980s onward Latin America offers an example that supports the hypothesis that trade openness is necessary for growth. During the past two decades, Chile is perhaps the only major country in Latin American that has registered sustained rapid growth. Its GDP grew at annual rates of 5.3 and 5.9 per cent respectively during 1981–91 and 1991–2001. During the same periods, its exports of goods and services grew annually at 8.6 and 9 per cent, respectively with the imports to GDP ratio rising from 26.8 per cent in 1981 to 32.7 per cent in 2001.

Like many other Latin American countries, Chile opened up its economy to trade by slashing tariffs and undertook reforms such as privatization. What distinguished it

---

[7] See Braga and Tyler (1992). Rodrik has suggested in personal correspondence that most accounts place Brazil's turn to outward orientation in 1968. Fortuitously, that date brings liberalization even closer to 1969, the year in which growth rate takes off.

from others, however, was the management of macroeconomic affairs. For example, on average, Chile had a balanced budget during the 1980s and a fiscal surplus during 1990s. Through prudent management of monetary policy, Chile also brought inflation down to 3 per cent in 1999 from 21 per cent in 1989. Above all, Chile has avoided financial capital-flow crises through a credible policy regime in general and judicious use of capital controls in particular.

VI. Additional Country Evidence: Vietnam, India, and China

Three examples from recent times offer further evidence in favor of the hypothesis of this chapter: Vietnam, China, and India. Because free trade skeptics also like to claim these examples as supporting their view, they require careful scrutiny.

According to a story by Larry Eliot in the *Guardian* (December 12, 2005) Dani Rodrik sees Vietnam as supporting the position of the skeptics.[8] "Take Mexico and Vietnam, he [Rodrik] says. One…has had a free-trade agreement with its neighbor across the Rio Grande. It receives oodles of inward investment and sends its workers across the border in droves. It is fully plugged in to the global economy. The other was the subject of a US trade embargo until 1994 and suffered from trade restrictions for years after that. Unlike Mexico, Vietnam is not even a member of the WTO [World Trade Organization]."

Eliot continues,

> So which of the two has the better recent economic record? The question should be a no-brainer if all the free-trade theories are right—Mexico should be streets ahead of Vietnam. In fact, the opposite is true. Since Mexico signed the NAFTA (North American Free Trade Agreement) deal with the US and Canada in 1992, its annual per capita growth rate has barely been above 1%. Vietnam has grown by around 5% a year for the past two decades. Poverty in Vietnam has come down dramatically: real wages in Mexico have fallen.

To be sure, Vietnam has achieved a major success in stimulating growth and alleviating poverty in recent years. Its GDP grew at 5.2 per cent during the three year period spanning 1989–91. In the following six years, 1992–97, the growth rate jumped to 8.8 per cent. The Asian crisis saw the rate decline some but the economy still managed to clock a rate of 5.8 per cent during 1998–2000. As one would expect, this rapid growth helped "pull-up" vast numbers out of poverty. The proportion of those living in absolute poverty fell from 78 to 37 per cent between 1988 and 1998.

If Vietnam had achieved this impressive growth in the absence of low or declining protection, it would indeed offer an indictment of the position of pro-free trade

---

[8] My discussion of Vietnam below draws heavily on Panagariya (2006a).

economists. But it did no such thing: Vietnam's exports of goods and services as a pro-portion of the GDP grew from 31 per cent in 1991 to 55 per cent in 2000. Because the rise took place during a period of very high GDP growth, the growth rate of exports of goods and services was truly impressive: 28 per cent during 1991–2001.

Economic policies in Vietnam underwent significant liberalization along virtually all dimensions including external trade and investment during this period of high growth in the GDP and trade. Under the old regime, trade was primarily with the Soviet bloc countries. And it was regulated by shipment-by-shipment licences and import and export quotas using a multiple exchange rates system. Reforms resulted in all foreign transactions being done in convertible currencies by 1993. The multiple exchange rates were unified in 1989 and a series of devaluations helped eliminate the general bias against traded goods. Import and export controls were relaxed and trade progressively moved from the licence-based to tariff-based regime. By 1995, export quotas had been removed on all products except rice and import quotas were limited to six items. Steps were taken to liberalize foreign investment throughout the 1990s.

What do we make of the lack of WTO membership and the US trade embargo? Traditionally, the large majority of the WTO members have granted their most favoured nation (MFN) tariffs to non-members in the expectation that the latter would eventu-ally become WTO members. As a result, non-members have not been unduly disadvan-taged as long as they themselves play by the WTO rules. The main exception for Vietnam was the USA, which subjected it to a trade embargo until 1994. But such embargoes are almost never successful in containing determined exporters unless they are applied by virtually all countries, as was done against South Africa under the apartheid. With the large European and Asian markets open to them, Vietnamese exporters could hardly be constrained on the demand side.

The experiences of China and India from the early 1980s to date lend further sup-port to the view taken in this chapter. In Panagariya (2006b), I discuss these two cases in detail. Here let me just note that starting in the late 1970s, China gradually began to open its economy to both trade and foreign investment side by side with other market-friendly policy measures. The results were spectacular. China's GDP grew at near double digit rates during both the 1980s and 1990s with per capita incomes more than quadru-pling over the two decades. This was accompanied by the annual growth in imports of goods and services at 10.3 per cent during the 1980s and 16.3 per cent during the 1990s. The corresponding growth rates of exports of goods and services were 12.9 and 15.2 per cent.

India's experience is slightly more complicated. As I document in Panagariya (2004), the country undertook several liberalizing steps during the 1980s, especially in the lat-ter half of the decade, which allowed a more liberal flow of foreign raw materials and machinery. Faster expansion of exports stimulated by a steady depreciation of the rupee and several pro-export policy measures complemented by expanded borrowing abroad helped this expansion of imports. India also expanded domestic demand through fiscal stimuli supported by large deficits. This strategy allowed the country to achieve a growth rate of 4.8 per cent during 1981–88 and 7.6 per cent during 1988–91.

But the expansionary fiscal policy and borrowing abroad also led to a macroeconomic crisis in 1991 that triggered more systematic reforms including orderly liberalization of trade. In a little more than one and a half decades, import licensing, which had covered around 80 per cent of the tariff lines, was entirely abolished and the highest tariff rate came down from 355 to 10 per cent where it currently stands. The result was a growth rate of 6.3 per cent during 1988–2006. During 2003–07, the growth rate shifted to above 8 per cent. Simultaneously, the Indian economy has become far more integrated into the world economy. Exports of goods and services as a proportion of the GDP have risen from just 7.2 per cent in 1990–91 to 20.5 per cent in 2005–06. Foreign investment and remittances together exceeded $40 billion in 2005–06.

VII. What do Free Trade Skeptics Recommend?

As a final point, let me note that despite their *apparent* difference of opinion, the bottom line drawn by free trade skeptics is so close to the position taken by many pro-free trade economists as to be virtually indistinguishable from it.[9] Thus, in public perception, foremost among skeptical economists today is the Nobel Laureate Joseph Stiglitz. Yet a careful pro-free trade economist finds very little in his widely publicized book *Globalization and its Discontents* (Stiglitz, 2002) with which to disagree.[10] When it comes down to putting down their ideas on the paper, skeptics end up singing the free trade economist's song!

In *Globalization and its Discontents*, Stiglitz never questions the importance of liberal trade policies for development. On the contrary, he explicitly recognizes their role in all successful cases of sustained growth. His beef with free trade hovers around two propositions: trade liberalization must be gradual and rich countries need to do their part by removing trade barriers on products of interest to developing countries, especially agriculture where domestic and export subsidies further undermine the interests of developing countries.

Pro-free trade economists have written extensively and affirmatively on both issues. Indeed, since the Kennedy Round of negotiations, gradualism has been an integral part of all liberalization under the General Agreement on Tariffs and Trade (GATT)/WTO auspices. As regards liberalization in agriculture and industrial products of interest to developing countries, the problem has been recognized for decades. The lack of progress, however, has much to do with the absence of developing countries from the negotiating table until the Uruguay Round. This absence has meant that developed countries

---

[9] See the provocatively entitled paper by Deardorff (2003) in this context.
[10] See Freeman (2004) in this context.

negotiated principally on products that they traded with one another. In fact, when developing countries did at last join the negotiations in the Uruguay Round, agreement to end the import quotas in developed countries on textiles and apparel was actually reached and agriculture appeared on the liberalization agenda.

But let us return to what Stiglitz has to say about the role of liberal trade policies themselves in the process of development. On the second page of Chapter 1 of his book appears the following statement (Stiglitz, 2002: 4):

> Opening up to international trade has helped many countries grow far more quickly than they would otherwise have done. International trade helps economic development when a country's exports drive its economic growth. Export-led growth was the centerpiece of the industrial policy that enriched much of Asia and left millions of people there far better off.

This assertion is not only consistent with what the present author has said earlier in this chapter but is actually stronger. Stiglitz sees a causal link between growth and low or declining trade barriers and, contrary to Rodrik (1995), assigns the *central* role to the latter for the success of Asia. Later in the chapter (p. 6), he turns to one of his two central criticisms of free trade:

> The critics of globalization accuse Western countries of hypocrisy, and the critics are right. The Western countries have pushed poor countries to eliminate trade barriers, but kept up their own barriers, preventing developing countries from exporting their agricultural products and so depriving them of desperately needed export income.

In so far as Stiglitz implies here that developing countries have now liberalized their markets and developed countries have not or that developing countries have liberalized more than the latter, he is factually incorrect. In Bhagwati and Panagariya (2002), we have documented this fallacy systematically. But in so far as Stiglitz makes a case for more, not less, liberalization by developed countries and argues that such liberalization is beneficial to developing countries, few trade economists would have a reason to disagree with him. The latter disagree with him only in so far as he implies that developing countries should have chosen to keep higher trade barriers because of continuing agricultural protectionism in the rich countries. For, as Stiglitz himself concedes in the last quotation, the countries in East Asia could successfully penetrate rich country markets because they themselves chose to be more outward oriented.

Subsequently, in Chapter 3, Stiglitz complains about the unemployment caused by trade liberalization and cites East Asian economies as having been successful because they liberalized "slowly and in a sequenced way." Again, most trade economists recognize that trade liberalization, like any other effective policy change, leads to reallocation of resources and in the process may cause dislocation in the short run. There are generally two solutions to this problem: creation of adjustment programs and gradualism in policy change. Often developing countries lack resources for adjustment programs so that gradualism is the main option. Recent experiences of China and India suggest that gradualism can indeed allow countries to accomplish substantial liberalization relatively painlessly.

Stiglitz reiterates the gradualism theme in Chapter 7, entitled "Better Roads to the Market," of his book. The title of this chapter is itself revealing: in so far as the ultimate destination is concerned, Stiglitz is in agreement with the mainstream economists that countries must eventually reach a market based economy. Citing the successful cases of China and Poland, he once again makes a pitch for gradualism. Here, in so far as Poland is concerned, he is wrong to assert that the country moved gradually in the area of trade. Soon after it broke away from the Soviet Union, Poland quickly adopted a very liberal trade policy regime and proceeded in quick succession to sign a free trade area agreement with the European Union. Most developing countries have been in the business of trade liberalization much longer and have substantially more protected trade regimes than Poland today. Thus, if Poland passes the test of gradualism in trade policy, most other developing countries pass it as well.

More recently, Stiglitz has adopted a more mainstream protectionist view, however. Referring to the status of the Doha negotiations in a column with Andrew Charlton (Charlton and Stiglitz, 2005) in the *Financial Times*, he writes, "[European Union Trade Commissioner] Mr. Mandelson's deal is also based on the assumption that poor countries should satisfy themselves with being agricultural suppliers to rich nations. It asks developing countries to expose their manufacturing industries to competition from more advanced and larger economies, potentially throwing those workers into unemployment, and it asks them to forgo attempts to promote their own service sector industries. A trade agreement that would restrict the policy options of developing countries is not the best to promote long-term industrialization."[11] Here Stiglitz clearly contradicts his emphasis on the benefits of outward orientation reaped by East Asian tigers in his 2002 book. Unsurprisingly, in a letter to the *Financial Times* Gary Hufbauer (2005) was quick to remind, "No country has achieved prosperity through enduring protection, though many have tried. Trade barriers are the proven mother of distortion, monopoly and corruption." Consistent with the systematic evidence provided in the earlier sections of this chapter, he also noted, "Developing countries that integrated their economies with world markets have prospered; others have not. Contrast Korea versus Egypt; Chile versus Argentina; Thailand versus Burma."

Most of the prominent free trade skeptics echo the Stiglitz view on trade policy as articulated in his 2002 book. Generally speaking, serious economists critical of globalization rarely take a firm stand against free trade. Much of the discomfort of these economists with globalization derives from the injury inflicted by financial crises that followed the embrace of short-term capital mobility by Latin America and East Asia. Free trade has simply turned into an innocent victim of that discomfort.

Thus, consider a recent paper by the Harvard University economist Richard Freeman (2002) on why and how to raise labor standards around the world. In the early part of this paper, Freeman expresses deep admiration of anti-globalization demonstrators and mercilessly attacks various forms of globalization including trade liberalization. To quote him, "While orthodox policies have a certain logic inside simple Macro and Trade models, whether they are right for real economies is less clear. Cross-country evidence

---

[11] Also see Stiglitz and Charlton (2005) in this context.

shows that policy measures relating to openness such as tariffs and trade barriers have little link to growth."

Yet, in the later part of the paper, when Freeman draws up his own list of steps that may be taken to promote labor standards in the poor countries, liberal trade policies occupy a place of pride on it. "Elimination of tariffs and other barriers to LDCs, particularly in agriculture, and reduction of huge debt burdens almost certainly can create more good for more people than improved labor standards for workers in the export sector or even more broadly," he writes.

One might still argue that skeptics do not advocate liberalization by the poor countries themselves. Instead, their recommendations are limited to the removal of trade barriers imposed against their products by rich countries. But such a position would be logically inconsistent. If skeptics believe that the removal of rich country barriers stimulates poor country exports by making the latter more profitable, they cannot simultaneously argue that poor country liberalization, which also makes their exports more profitable by lowering the relative price of import-competing goods, does not accomplish the same objective.

Indeed, if the poor country barriers are high, they are likely to fail to take advantage of even the rich country liberalization. For example, during the 1960s and 1970s, while the more open Far Eastern economies took advantage of the progressive opening and expansion of the rich country markets and managed to register spectacular export growth, autarkic India failed to register rapid growth of exports as well as GDP. Symmetrically, the poor country liberalization will fail to bear fruit if their rich country counterparts are autarkic. The poor country door must be open to let the goods out and the rich country door to let them in.

Rodrik seems to recognize at least some of the logic behind a country's own liberalization more explicitly when confronted with the choice between liberal and protectionist trade policies. Thus, in his famous critique of econometric studies linking growth and trade, written jointly with Francisco Rodriguez, he states in the second to last paragraph, "We do not want to leave the reader with the impression that we think trade protection is good for economic growth. We know of no credible evidence—at least for the post-1945 period—that suggests that trade restrictions are systematically associated with higher growth rates."

The paper goes on to conclude, "The effects of trade liberalization may be on balance beneficial on standard comparative-advantage grounds; the evidence provides no strong reason to dispute this. What we dispute is the view, increasingly common, that integration into the world economy is such a potent force for economic growth that it can effectively substitute for a development strategy." But few thoughtful trade economists consider free trade as sufficient for fast growth. On the contrary, many of them also happen to be serious development economists. As an example, the early advocacy of freer trade policy in India by Bhagwati and Desai (1970) carried many more chapters on domestic policy and institutional reforms than on the advocacy of liberal trade policies.

VIII. Concluding Remarks

The central theme of this chapter is that sustained growth cannot be achieved without rapid growth in trade, which requires either low or declining barriers to trade. The experience of the past four decades offers virtually no examples of sustained rapid growth—termed miracles in this chapter—with high and non-declining barriers to trade. Simultaneously, the claim that opening to trade leads to sustained income losses is unfounded. A review of the experience of the countries that have faced stagnation or declining per capita incomes—termed debacles in this chapter—reveals no connection to sustained import surges.

I have also argued that many of the so-called criticisms offered by free trade skeptics fail to support their skepticism towards outward oriented trade policies. For instance, the claims such as those by Rodrik that growth in Korea during the 1960s was triggered by a successful coordination of investment activities by the government, even if accepted as valid, do not undermine the importance of outward oriented trade policies. India also successfully raised investment in the 1960s but failed to grow rapidly because, unlike Korea, it chose a very inward-looking trade policy.

Indeed, a close and critical examination of the writings of skeptics reveals that when faced with choosing between freer trade and protection, they almost always choose freer trade. Neither of the two leading skeptics—Rodrik and Stiglitz—recommends protectionism so that one is hard pressed to understand precisely what to make of their criticisms. They argue against freer trade but wind up concluding in favor of it!

References

Balassa, B. (1982), 'Development Strategies and Economic Performance: A Comparative Analysis of Eleven Semi-industrialized Economies' in Balassa, B. (ed.), *Development Strategies in Semi-industrialized Economies,* Baltimore, MD: Johns Hopkins University Press, 38–62.

Bhagwati J., and Desai, P. (1970), *India: Planning for Industrialization,* London: Oxford University Press.

Bhagwati, J., and Krueger, A. (eds.) (1974), *Foreign Trade Regimes and Economic Development: A Special Conference Series on Foreign Trade Regimes and Economic Development,* New York: Cambridge University Press.

Bhagwati, J., and Panagariya, A. (2001), 'The Truth about Protectionism' *Financial Times,* March 29.

Bhagwati, J., and Panagariya, A. (2002), 'Wanted: Jubilee 2010: Dismantling Protection' *OECD Observer,* No. 231/232, May, 27–29.

Bhagwati, J., and Srinivasan, T. N. (1975), *Foreign Trade Regimes and Economic Development: India,* New York: National Bureau of Economic Research.

Braga, H. C., and Tyler, W. G. (1992), 'Trade Policies in Brazil' in Salvatore, D. (ed.), *National Trade Policies: Handbook of Comparative Economic Policies, Volume 2,* New York: Greenwood Press, 337–59.

Charlton, A and Stiglitz, J. (2005), 'The Doha Round is Missing the Point on Helping Poor Countries' *Financial Times*, December 13, p. 19.

Deardorff, A., (2003), 'What Might Globalization's Critics Believe?' *World Economy*, 26(5): 639–58.

Freeman, R., (2002), 'The Battle over Labor Standards: A Report from the Front' presented at the IADB-LATN 'First Roundtable: Labor Standards', Buenos Aires, September 20.

Freeman, R., (2004), 'Trade Wars: The Exaggerated Impact of Trade in Economic Debate' *World Economy*, 27(1): 1–23.

Greenaway D., Morgan W., Wright P. (2002), "Trade Liberalisation and Growth in Developing Countries," *Journal of Development Economics* 67: 229–44.

Greenaway, D. and Nam C. H. (1988), "Industrialisation and Macroeconomic Performance in Developing Countries under Alternative Trade Strategies," *Kyklos*, 41: 419–35.

Hufbauer, G., (2005), 'Belief in these Myths Can Damage Developing Nations' *Financial Times*, December 15, p. 14.

Kim, K. S. (1985), 'Lessons from South Korea's Experience with Industrialization' in Corbo, V., Krueger, A.O., and Ossa, F. (eds.), *Export-Oriented Development Strategies: The Success of Five Newly Industrialized Countries*, Boulder, CO, and London: Westview Press, 57–78.

Lee, T. H. and Liang, K., (1982), 'Taiwan: Incentive Polices for Import Substitution and Export Expansion' in Balassa, B. (ed.), *Development Strategies in Semi-industrialized Economies*, Baltimore, MD: Johns Hopkins University Press, 310–83.

Little, I., Scitovsky, T., and Scott, M. (1970), *Industry and Trade in Some Developing Countries*, London: Oxford University Press

Panagariya, A., (2004), 'India in the 1980s and 1990s: A Triumph of Reforms' Paper presented at the NCAER-IMF conference on 'A Tale of Two Giants: India's and China's Experience with Reform and Growth' New Delhi, India, November 15-16, 2003; also IMF Working Paper WP/04/43.

Panagariya, A., (2006a), 'Free Trade Skeptics: Wrong Again' *Economic Times*, January 25.

Panagariya, A., (2006b), 'India and China: Trade and Foreign Investment' Working Paper No. 302, Stanford Center for International Development, Stanford University.

Panagariya, A., (2008), *India: The Emerging Giant*, New York: Oxford University Press.

Pritchett, L. (1996), 'Measuring Outward Orientation in LDCs: Can it be Done?' *Journal of Development Economics*, 49(May): 307–35.

Rodriguez, F., and Rodrik, D. (1999), 'Trade Policy and Economic Growth: A Skeptic's Guide to Cross-National Evidence' NBER working paper no. W7081.

Rodrik, D. (1995) 'Getting Interventions Right: How South Korea and Taiwan Grew Rich' *Economic Policy*, 20: 55–107.

Rodrik, D. (1999), *The New Global Economy and Developing Countries: Making Openness Work*, Washington, DC: Overseas Development Council.

Rodrik, D. (2001) "Trading in Illusions," *Foreign Policy*, 123 (March/April): 54–62.

Romalis, J. (2006) 'Market Access, Openness and Growth' University of Chicago, mimeo.

Sachs, J., and Warner, A. (1995), 'Economic Reform and the Process of Global Integration' *Brookings Papers on Economic Activity*, 1, 1–118.

Srinivasan, T. N. and Bhagwati, J. (20010, 'Outward Orientation and Development: Are Revisionists Right?' in Lal, D., and Snape, R. (eds.), *Trade, Development and Political Economy. Essays in Honor of Anne O. Krueger*, London: Palgrave.

Stiglitz, J. (2002), *Globalization and its Discontents*, New York: W. W. Norton & Company.

Stiglitz, J. and Charlton, A. (2005), *Fair Trade for All: How Trade Can Promote Development*, New York: Oxford University Press.

Tan, A. H. H., and Ow C. H. (1982), 'Singapore: Incentives to Industrialization: A Historical Perspective' in Balassa, B. (ed.), *Development Strategies in Semi-industrialized Economies*, Baltimore, MD: Johns Hopkins University Press, 280–309.

Wacziarg, R., and Welch, K. H. (2003), 'Trade Liberalization and Growth: New Evidence' mimeo, Stanford, CA: Stanford University.

Westphal, L. E. (1990), 'Industrial Policy in an Export-Propelled Economy: Lessons from South Korea's Experience' *Journal of Economic Perspectives*, 4(3): 41–59.

Westphal, L. E. and Kwang S. K. (1982), 'Korea: Incentive Policies for Exports and Import Substitution' in Balassa, B. (ed.), *Development Strategies in Semi-industrialized Economies*, Baltimore, MD: Johns Hopkins University Press, 212–79.

CHAPTER 14

....

POLICY PRACTICES AND INSTITUTIONS FOR SUCCESSFUL EXPORT DEVELOPMENT AND DIVERSIFICATION IN DEVELOPING COUNTRIES[*]

....

SALOMON SAMEN

I. INTRODUCTION

....

DRAWING upon the lessons of experience of the most successful exporters in the developing world,[1] this chapter provides an overview of institutions and policy practices successfully experienced for the development and diversification of exports in some developing countries.

As is now well established, openness to trade has been a central element of successful growth strategies, and higher and sustained economic growth is associated with export growth (Dollar and Kraay, 2001). Defined as the expansion of exports in volume and value, export growth has been recognized since the mercantilist era as critical for any

[*] The author wishes to thank Wendy Takacs, Rao Viriyala, Luc de Wulf, Gianni Zanini, Raj Nallari, and members of the School of International and Public Affairs–SIPA/Columbia University for their thoughtful comments on an earlier version of this chapter. The views expressed here are exclusively those of the author and should not be attributed in any way to the World Bank or affiliates.

[1] The most successful exporters of the developing world include: the "original Asian tigers" (Hong Kong, South Korea, Singapore, and Taiwan), the "New Asian tigers" (Indonesia, Malaysia, and Thailand), as well as China, India, Argentina, Brazil, Chile, Mexico, and Turkey. Some authors refer to these countries as the "Rest" in contrast to the "West" in relation to their late industrialization (Amsden, 2001).

country for a variety of macro and microeconomic reasons including the: (1) need to generate foreign exchange vital to finance imports; (2) need to exploit larger scale economies that can be achieved by producing for export markets, given the small size of many developing countries and their negligible purchasing power; and (3) potential contribution to employment and growth of national product. Increasing exports is therefore a key concern for development economists and policymakers in all developing countries. Integration to global markets brings with it exposure to new technologies, new designs, and new products while enhancing production efficiency and competitiveness. Because heavy dependence on a small number of primary commodity products exposes a country to the negative effects of unfavorable characteristics of world demand and negative supply-side features of these primary products, export diversification is equally critical. It has implications in the expansion of opportunities for export and improvement of backward and forward linkages to domestic inputs and services. For a country to expand and diversify, export competitiveness is therefore essential.

Although the policy practices of the most successful exporters in the developing world are now quite well known, many developing countries are still struggling with the challenge of expanding and diversifying their export baskets of goods beyond primary products bases. However, learning from the lessons of the most successful exporters of the developing world, it is now clear that to enhance their competitiveness and improve export diversification of their economies, these countries have over time tested and experienced a variety of institutions and policy practices with significant government intervention.

The first section of this chapter examines the rationale, role, and usefulness of active export-oriented trade policy measures and selective industrial interventions policies in the context of developing countries. The second section reviews policy practices and institutions that have played a critical role in export development and industrialization of the most successful exporters in the developing world. The last section concludes with some suggestions for policymakers seeking guidance for a successful export development and diversification strategy.

II. Theoretical Rationale, Role, and Usefulness of Selective Government Interventions in Support of Export Development and Diversification

In the Import Substitution strategy era that prevailed in many developing countries from the 1950s to the 1980s, trade regimes were significantly distorted. There were relatively high import duties on intermediate inputs used by exporters, high import duties on final goods, escalated tariff structures with lower tariffs on intermediate goods than on goods at later stages of processing quantitative import restrictions and other non-tariff barriers to imports, and so on. These distortions created significant levels of anti-export bias, that is, disincentives to export.

Against the background of such distorted trade regimes with dramatic implications for exporters, a look at the experience of successful exporters in the developing world indicates that over time they implemented a variety of government policy interventions aimed essentially at improving the environment for export growth. As access to imported inputs at world prices was essential for export growth, many policy measures including duty drawback and special import licenses for exporters, bonded manufacturing and export processing zones, focused initially on measures to reduce anti-export bias and make exports more competitive.

Anti-export bias arises whenever the relative profitability of home-market goods as opposed to export sales is raised, as a result of policy interventions and excessive regulations restricting the growth effects of trade liberalization. In the case of anti-export bias created by high protection against imports, such a bias will be inevitable unless explicit measures of export subsidies, export rebates, or special import regimes are used. Because detailed empirical work carried out in earlier Newly Industrialized Economies (NIE, including Korea, Taiwan, and Singapore) in the early 1960s (Balassa, 1982) indicates that there was in a fact a strong bias in favor of exports, this suggests that, at the minimum, neutrality of incentives or proactive support were explicit policy objectives critical to export success in NIE countries. Hence, the growing consensus that complementary policies and reforms in the form of special import regimes or other trade incentives can enhance the growth effects of trade openness (Lall, 2002; and Chang, Kaltani, and Loayza, 2005).

This section analyses the rationale, role, and usefulness of selective government intervention for export development and diversification and summarizes what the literature says about government intervention in export development and diversification.

The role of intervention in export promotion and diversification performances has resurged in economic policy debates in recent years. Although the controversy is not new and can be traced back to decades or centuries (Reinert, 1995), and as faster growth happens in developing countries with structural transformation from low productivity of traditional sectors to high productivity of modern/industrial activities (Lewis, 1954), the central questions remain the same. That is, how do countries transit from production of low value added primary products to production of high value added manufactured products? How do countries achieve international industrial competitiveness? Two schools of thought, neoclassical and structuralist/revisionist, stand out in the literature to address these complex questions (Lall, 1997, 2000; Mkandawire and Soludo, 2003).

The Neoclassical Approach

For several decades, the prevailing intellectual consensus has been heavily influenced by the neoclassical approach, which is based on a mixture of theoretical, empirical, and political considerations. According to this school of thought based on the original classical model developed by Smith (1776), Ricardo (1817), and Mill (1848), the best strategy for all countries and in all cases is simply to liberalize with the hope that their natural comparative advantage will be realized with resource allocation driven essentially by free markets. Although the neoclassical approach has evolved in recent decades (Balassa, 1982) to recognize that there is a role for the state provision of basic public goods, law and order, and a sound legal system, the state also has a role in providing non-selective or functional support for health, education, and infrastructure. But the neoclassical approach still defends the idea that any policy intervention that affects prices will, by definition, be distorting and move the overall society away from optimal resource allocation permitted essentially by free markets.

On theoretical grounds, if markets worked perfectly, resource allocation would be optimal and there would be no grounds for government intervention. However, it is now well established that export promotion and industrial policy like all government interventions is justified by the presence of market failures (Rodrik, 2009). A market failure is a departure from Pareto optimality, which would, in theory, occur in a market clearing equilibrium under conditions of perfect competition. The particular set of market failures and related remedies is an empirical issue depending on the country and time. In many cases, factor market failures are likely in physical infrastructure, labor markets, capital markets, technology imports, and various institutions. Product market failures can be related to lack of information and high transaction costs in marketing, oligopolistic market structures, and effects of international competition on new market entrants. Market failures highlighted in the neoclassical approach that justify selective interventions include: capital market deficiencies caused by information gaps, asymmetries, and moral hazard; lumpiness of investments (i.e., scale economies), and inability of individual actors to invest rationally when there are interdependent investments. In the presence of significant scale economies and learning externalities, other theoretical justifications for industrial policy include the: need to coordinate competing investments not only between complementary projects but also between competing projects; need for organization of domestic firms in their interactions with foreign firms or foreign governments; need to provide some "social insurance" for firms in temporary difficulties; or need to promote structural changes or technology upgrades for structurally depressed industries (Chang, 2006). Based on the neoclassical position, and assumptions that markets are efficient and that getting prices right is necessary and sufficient for an economy to achieve optimality in world trade, functional policies[2] are all that is required for export promotion. The government should therefore implement free trade and avoid interventions in resource allocation.

Information economics (Stiglitz, 1996), however, indicates that in the case of developing countries characterized by widespread asymmetries and imperfect information markets, diffuse and rife externalities, and highly imperfect and incomplete markets, free markets may not meet the requirements for optimality in resource allocation. Costs of market or institutional failures are borne disproportionally by the modern/industrial

---

[2] Functional interventions (or market friendly policies) are aimed at remedying market failures without influencing resource allocation between specific activities.

sector that is subject to learning spillovers and coordination failures, externalities in knowledge, and high costs imposed by weaknesses in legal and regulatory institutions (Rodrik, 2009). Hence, because markets work poorly in developing countries, there is need for an alternative approach.

The Structuralist/Revisionist Approach

As none of the countries that successfully integrated into world markets in the last 30 years (i.e., the original Asian tigers and new tigers, as well as China, India, and Brazil) is an unambiguous story of export growth achieved exclusively by unequivocal trade openness and free markets, it is increasingly being recognized that the success achieved by the most successful exporters in the developing world, particularly the original East Asian Tigers and new Tigers, was based on unconventional combinations of both permissive and positive policies, both functional and selective, to promote export growth and export diversification.

Depending on the nature of market failures, the structuralist/revisionist theoretical literature (Westphal, 1982, 1990; Amsden, 1989, 2001, 2007; Wade, 1990; Lall, 1997, 2000) distinguishes between "permissive" policies and "positive policies."

Permissive policies are aimed at "removing" distortions that deter exporting in order to "permit" better resource allocation. These policies are generally uncontroversial and accepted by almost everyone. They are achieved mostly through a combination of price, fiscal, exchange rate, and monetary policy tools. Offered essentially via special import regimes described below, permissive policies aim at removing distortions and include: removing high rates of domestic protection; removing high inflation; removing high interest rates; removing price controls or taxes; removing cumbersome procedures at entry or exit; removing policy volatility and uncertainty; removing or reducing macro-policy mismanagement; removing over-valued exchange rates; and removing or reducing biases against exports, to make exporting profitable and minimize transaction costs to exporters without influencing resource allocation.

Positive policies are aimed at tackling the costs and deficiencies in stimulating new areas of export activities. These add another policy tool to the battery of measures to boost export performance and include: raising the quality or improving competitiveness cost of existing or new activities; supporting small enterprises to enter export markets; lowering informational costs, as well as costs for setting up distribution systems in foreign markets; enhancing domestic content, and so on. Positive policies can in turn be subdivided into functional and selective policies. Functional policies are across the board measures with no intent to shift resource allocation, while selective policies are targeted to specific firms, sectors, or activities with clearly declared and deliberate intent to shift resource allocation.

Functional interventions, also coined market friendly policies, are aimed at remedying market failures without influencing resource allocation between specific activities and without targeting particular activities or firms. They include, for example: actions to improve physical infrastructure and general skills/human capital; provision of export market information and technical support to help potential exporters overcome cost and risks of unfamiliar and risky international markets; and actions to favor small and medium enterprises (SMEs) over larger enterprises. While there is less controversy on the role and effectiveness of functional policies, selective policies trigger the most controversy.

Selective interventions aim at influencing resource allocation, or remedying market failures for specific activities while favoring selected activities over others. These policies, also dubbed productivist policies (Rodrik, 2009), have been followed by all successful countries. They attempt to enhance relative profitability of non-traditional products and modern industrial activities and accelerate movement of resources towards industrial activities facing large information externalities or coordination failures or poor institutional environments. In recognition that, in the absence of selective policies, export growth and diversification are likely to be quite slow, policymakers in the successful exporters in the developing world promoted various forms of industry-specific policies via measures such as: outright protection; industry specific promotion via investment, productions, and export subsidies; creation of specific skills or technology support to upgrade quality, design, productivity, and R&D; directed or subsidized credit allocations to promote specific firms (e.g., large firms) or particular types of firms and industries (i.e., industrialization based on SMEs or heavy industries and high tech); and policies towards attracting specific foreign direct investment (FDI) investors, human resource development, technology support, and export marketing. Selective intervention policies target specific firms or sectors and privilege some at the expense of others. They entail explicit industrial policies in support of new activities, including trade protection, subsidies, tax and credit incentives, special government attention, and under-valued currencies to promote tradables; and eventually subsidized credit and supportive development banking (Rodrik, 2009).

The role of selective industrial policy has been one of the most controversial dimensions of the debate on the experience of the most successful exporters of the developing world. Until the end of the 1980s, many neoclassical economists still doubted the effectiveness of selective industrial policy. In the light of the experience of the East Asian successful exporters, it is now generally accepted that selective industrial policies make theoretical sense and can be successful in certain circumstances.

Nonetheless, while the distinction between functional and selective export-promotion policies appears to be useful in theory, that distinction may not always be crystal clear, and may be difficult to apply in practice.

III. Policy Practices and Institutions for Export Development and Diversification

This section summarizes policy practices and institutions used extensively in the most successful exporters of the developing world to promote the growth, diversification, and upgrading of their manufactured exports. Overall, using the classification described above, successful exporters used a mixture of permissive and positive policies to accelerate their export growth and diversification.

The gamut of policy practices and institutions that led to rapid skill formation and industrialization in successful exporting countries was carefully built, diligently developed, and tested over many years (Amsden, 2007). In the early years of this effort, where prices were significantly distorted to allow production of competitive exports, the first experiments in the 1950s and 1960s focused on getting the price right by allowing manufacturers exporters, located on a geographically limited space, to buy their imported inputs at world prices. This explains the focus in earlier stages on export processing zones (EPZs). But despite the installation of EPZs, only a few firms geographically located in the EPZs took advantage of duty free concessions offered. Policymakers, in their drive to boost exports by all means, went a step further and offered duty drawback on imported inputs used for exports for all firms in the country. However, the results of duty drawback continued to be mixed, and policymakers went even further by offering subsidies in various forms to exporting firms. Together with duty free taxes on imported inputs, export subsidies—started in the textiles industries in the 1950s—were systematized in almost all successful exporting developing countries with the exception of Argentina in the 1960s and expanded to other sectors. The result was the strengthening of the array of policy tools of special import regimes for exporters. Hence, free access to imported inputs to exporting firms and subsidies and various other complementary measures formed the basis of the standard permissive and positive policies used to accelerate export growth and diversification.

Permissive Policies in Practice

As tariff and non-tariff barriers (NTBs) significantly distort prices and hinder imports and exports as well as industrial production, access to imports at world prices for exporters was the central pillar of permissive policies. Permissive policy measures were usually achieved by means of tax privileges and subsidies through special import regimes to grant duty free access to imported inputs for exporters, hence removing or reducing price distortions and correcting anti-export bias. Special import regimes were supplemented by other measures to encourage exporters, including: measures to remove/reduce high transactions costs for exporters through efficient streamlined admissions of imports/customs clearance and shipping facilities; both long and short-term financing with across the board programs to facilitate access to credit via central bank monetary policy and effective use of exchange rate policies; market penetration, with institutional support to exporters to overcome hurdles on foreign markets; and flexibility with pragmatism to adapt to changing conditions.

Free Access to Imports for Exporters/Special Import Regimes

Access to imports at reduced cost for exporters in the form of special import regimes makes it possible to shift relative incentives in favor of tradables and particularly exports. This allows export oriented firms to import their manufacturing inputs without paying the applicable duties or taxes. Special import regimes were granted mostly through: duty drawback; bonded manufacturing or warehousing; duty/tax exemptions; and EPZs or temporary admissions.

These regimes were designed to remove or reduce the tariff burden to give export-ers access to their inputs at world prices and make exports more competitive in foreign markets. Exempting duty/tax on inputs or refunding the duty paid when the inputs were incorporated into the finished goods and exported helped to reduce capital costs and enhance competitiveness. Special import regimes helped to remove the anti-export bias arising whenever the relative profitability of home market goods as opposed to export sales was due to policy interventions and excessive regulations restricting the growth effects of trade liberalization. When anti-export bias is created by high protection against imports, this bias can therefore be corrected by the explicit measures noted as follows.

Duty drawbacks

Traditionally used in highly protected economies as a means to provide exporters of manufactured goods with imported inputs at world prices, duty drawback schemes increase exporters' profitability, while maintaining the protection for domestic indus-tries that compete with imports. In practice, duties are initially paid as goods are landed. Duty drawback refunds are subsequently provided upon shipment of export goods that include dutiable components. Contrary to duty/tax exemptions, duty draw-back procedures by and large do not necessarily require firms to submit any applica-tion and pre-approval by customs. Following the exports, beneficiary firms submit a drawback claim requesting a specific amount of drawback refund of duty or tax, show-ing what was imported and exported. Upon verification and cross-check of the claim, customs will refund the duty or tax. Modes of drawback operations include: direct identification of manufacturers; substitution drawback; same condition drawback; shipment-by-shipment based on predetermined input/output standard; and pre-agreed fixed drawback schedule whereby a list of the fixed money value of duties is refunded for one unit of an export commodity based on input/output coefficients. Countries using such schedules usually revise them on a periodic basis.

When poorly designed and implemented with inefficient procedures and burden-some requirements, duty drawbacks can be costly for an economy in terms of loss of government revenue, greater opportunities for cheating and abuses, and high admin-istrative implementation costs. For example, the impact expected by exporters on their imported input will be mitigated or diluted when NTBs such as prohibitions, quantitative restrictions, or exchange controls are the really binding constraints on inputs. Elements to improve efficiency and effectiveness of drawback include: (1) sim-plification of procedures and documents to make them easily understandable by the users; (2) involvement of high-level committees representing all stakeholders (treasury, customs, tax authorities, industry, and trade) at all stages from the devel-opment of procedures with time limits for processing of refund, and eventual revi-sions; (3) payment of 100 per cent of the duties paid on imported inputs by direct and indirect exporters; (4) automatic payments and periodic replenishment of the budget required for payments of refunds; and (5) use of pre-tabulated input/output coefficients.

Bonded Manufacturing or Warehousing

Bonded manufacturing (BM) is a form of temporary admission, which is equivalent to suspended import duty for specified imported goods for a limited period of time, normally until goods are either re-exported or entered into home use at which time duty/tax becomes payable. The term used varies from country to country: Export Only Units in India; Special Bonded Warehouses in Bangladesh; and Bonded Manufacturing Warehouses in Malaysia. The benefits are at the discretion of the governments that grant them, and the rules under which they operate vary substantially from country to country and also over time in individual countries.

As a status given to firms that export 100 per cent of their output, BM status allows specified firms to bring imported goods into their warehouses without paying import duty, use the goods in their production, and export the output. They can usually also import machinery and replacement parts and other supplies duty free, and buy from domestic suppliers free of domestic excise, sales, and other taxes. The factories operate under the supervision of customs authorities, who check the import and export containers going to and from the bonded factory, or in some cases, rely on spot checks of the factory's inventories. These inventory checks may be assisted by pre-tabulated input–output coefficients.

Because Bonded Warehousing requires extensive physical customs controls over the movement of the container from the port or airport to the warehouses and from the warehouses to the production units, dedicated customs officers may need to be permanently posted to the warehouses, but should be rotated regularly to limit collusion with manufacturers. Poorly designed and poorly controlled bonded warehousing can be exploited fraudulently by smuggling goods into the country. This situation may occur in case of non-automated inventory controls. Improved computerization of recording systems and customs administrations could help improve controls of inventory balances kept in the bond, unauthorized operations while in the bond, and inspection of goods removed from the bond. Transition from physical controls to audit control has proved to be effective in reducing opportunities for corruption and for enhancing customs enforcement effectiveness. Freedom to choose location is the key feature distinguishing Bonded Warehousing from EPZs, although bonded warehouses lack the benefits of the infrastructure and services sometimes provided in EPZs.

Export Processing Zones

In recent decades, EPZs have become increasingly popular. Today, there are over 3,000 EPZs or other types of Free Zones in 135 countries around the world, accounting for over $500 billion in total trade. Many developing countries have been using them as the ideal vehicle to achieve multiple objectives including: (1) enhancement of foreign exchange earnings by promotion of exports of non-traditional manufactured goods; (2) creation of jobs and generation of income; (3) improvement of competitiveness of exporters; and (4) attraction of FDI with its attendant technology transfer, knowledge spillover, demonstration effects, and backward linkages.

By and large, EPZs are spatially confined areas where governments experiment with a set of fiscal and regulatory requirements and infrastructure that are different from the domestic economy. In compliance with Article 2.9 of World Trade Organization (WTO) agreement,[3] EPZs have in recent years been shifting the emphasis from tax benefits towards infrastructure and regulatory frameworks, particularly in middle-income countries. Today's EPZs have evolved from their original definition as "an industrial estate, encompassing an entire area of a country or entire city, all or part of an airport, all or part of an industrial park, usually a fenced-in area of 10–300 hectares that specializes in manufacturing for export." However, most EPZs normally have a secure perimeter under customs control. EPZs range greatly in size and structure and have been undergoing substantial changes recently. Although EPZs can be publicly or privately owned or managed, in the past 10–15 years, the number of privately owned or managed zones has grown substantially because they are believed to achieve superior results. Hence, EPZs are increasingly developed and run by the private sector as opposed to the State, which is calling for new applications of public–private partnerships.

Benefits granted to EPZ firms (which can be domestic, foreign, or joint ventures) include: (1) duty free imports of raw and intermediate inputs and capital goods for export production; (2) streamlined government procedures allowing "one-stop shopping" for permits, investment applications, and so on; (3) more flexible labor laws compared to most firms in the domestic market; (4) generous, long-term tax concessions; (5) more advanced communications services and infrastructure than firms have in other parts of the country; and (6) utility and rental subsidies. Many firms, so-called export processing firms, now also benefit from the incentives offered in the zones without being physically fenced in. In addition, countries have liberalized restrictions on domestic sales of products produced in EPZs. Colombia for example, imposes no limits on serving the domestic market on a secondary basis. Mexico, also, allows 20–40 per cent of its zones' output to be sold domestically.

In the years ahead, the success of EPZs will depend on the extent to which they are integrated with their host economies through backward and forward linkages, the transparency and responsiveness of the regulatory framework, as well as infrastructural efficiency.

Duty Relief and Tax Exemptions

Duty relief and tax exemption regimes allow for full or partial exemption of duty/tax on specific imported raw materials integrated into finished goods to be exported. Such exemptions are normally granted to firms that are primarily export oriented and which then must export a very high percentage of their finished production (in general, at least

---

[3] It should also be noted that the practice of not imposing duties or taxes on goods not intended for entry into the commerce of a country and not going to physically remain in the country is entirely consistent with WTO rules, provided that amounts that are refunded (if any) do not exceed the duties or taxes that would be normally payable. This is recognized by the World Customs Organization in annexes B, D, F, and G of the revised Kyoto Convention.

80 per cent of production). Because export-oriented firms' capital is not tied up by payment of duty/tax at the time of import, this provides beneficiary firms with a significant competitive advantage.

Although exemptions are comparatively easy to administer, they can represent significant revenue risk when not coupled with effective customs audit systems to ensure that exempted inputs are not diverted to local markets. In some cases, duty relief and tax exemptions can be geared towards non-exporting firms (e.g., call centers, computer and electronic imports, as in the WTO ITA agreement[4]). But the net effect of such policies can be indeterminate when tariff exemptions on inputs, while good for final products, can have negative effects for local producers of inputs.

See Box 14.1 for a description of Duty Rebates in Taiwan.

Temporary Imports for Re-Exporting Unaltered Products

Under this import regime, full or partial relief from import duties/taxes on goods imported for specific purposes is granted for a limited period of time to exporting firms under the condition that the goods will be re-exported in the same state (other than normal depreciation due to usage) within the prescribed period. A security is generally posted to cover the duty/tax liability, and once exported, the security posted is released immediately. Products often subject to temporary admissions include: vehicles of experts temporarily working in a country; equipment used temporarily for construction purposes; and goods for display in fairs, exhibitions, meetings or similar events.

Logistics and Trade Facilitation Practices to Encourage Exports

Poorly functioning logistic environments—including cost of clearing customs, transport costs, and transit for landlocked countries, non-customs trade documentation requirement, and unenforceability of legal trade documents—significantly hinder successful integration into the global market. Measures may be needed to reduce transaction costs via streamlined administration of imports, exports, and customs clearance complemented with special import regimes in many successful exporters in the developing world.

Under-valued Exchange Rate and Monetary Policy as Tools in Support of Exporters

The exchange rate is central to a country's monetary policy by making domestic goods cheaper or more expensive as needed, and setting the relative price of tradables vis-à-vis non-tradables. Poorly managed exchange rates and particularly excessive and sustained

---

[4] The Information Technology Agreement (ITA) is an agreement under the WTO, establishing the elimination of tariffs for Information and Communication Technology (ICT) products. It entered into force on July 1, 1997, and now counts 70 WTO Members, including the EU, United States, Japan, China, and India. Some ICT producing countries in South America and Russia are excluded. The aim of the ITA is to encourage trade and thus the availability and use of ICT worldwide by eliminating tariffs.

Box 14.1 Duty Rebates in Taiwan

Since 1955, Taiwan's support for exports has included rebates of import duties and other indirect taxes on inputs used directly or indirectly to produce manufactured exports. A firm that is a major, regular, law-abiding manufacturer exporter is allowed to put its duty liabilities "on account," to be canceled against evidence of subsequent exports. Firms must furnish a bank guarantee that the duty plus penalties will be paid if the exports are not produced within 18 months. Since 1965, exporting firms have had the further option of locating in an export processing zone or becoming in-bond manufacturers, but these schemes account for only modest shares of the economy's exports. Firms (including trading firms) not involved in either of these schemes must pay duties on their imported inputs. These duties are reimbursed or canceled for exporters by the customs administration following presentation of documentation showing completed exports, receipt and appropriate disposition of foreign exchange proceeds, and the amount of the rebate to which the firm is entitled. The customs administration handles more than half a million rebate applications a year with a staff of about 200.

Either the direct exporter or one indirect exporter collects the entire rebate. The indirect exporter (for example, a firm supplying inputs for exports) can collect the rebate only if the direct exporter signs over the necessary documents. Often, a large supplier of inputs that is dependent on imported raw materials systematically acquires these documents from its small exporter customers and collects the rebates. Typically, it sells to direct exporters (or extends them credit by accepting postdated checks) at a duty free price, but it also requires a post-dated check covering the duty. This check is returned uncashed once the exporting firm signs over its documents.

Rebates on new products are calculated on a case-by-case basis, whereas rebates for established products are determined on the basis of published fixed rates. Both methods involve the systematic application by customs rebate officials of pre-established input coefficients for each physical unit of output.

To export a product not previously exported, an exporter must obtain an export license and a list of the product's physical input–output coefficients. To work out the coefficients, government staff or consultants visit the factory, inspect its records, and examine or test the product. The list is then certified and supplied to the customs administration within a month of the exporter's application. To get a rebate, the exporter must then provide evidence on the source and quantity of all imported and dutiable inputs used. To save administrative time, any input valued at less than 1 per cent of the value (FOB) of the exported product is dropped from the calculation of the rebate.

Once a product has had a long enough production history for its input and output coefficients to be fairly stable, it is switched over to the fixed rate method. To work out the fixed rate, the customs administration calculates the duties rebated on all inputs (direct or indirect) into the product over the previous 12 months compared with the combined value or volume of the corresponding exports for all makers of the product. The result is a standard rate based on value or a physical unit such as weight. Where technical processes and input coefficients of different firms vary widely, their exports are defined as different products with their own fixed rates. Fixed rates on about 6,000 products are published each July, reflecting changes since the previous year in prices, duties, and sources of inputs.

Continued

> **Box 14.1** *Continued*
>
> Once a fixed rate is in effect, exporters receive the stipulated amount of rebate only after providing evidence that they paid (directly or indirectly) duties and indirect taxes equal to that amount. Otherwise, they receive rebates equal only to the amount they actually paid. However, details are no longer examined. If an exporting firm shows that its actual payments were more than 20 per cent higher than the standard rebate, and it can give good reasons why it needs these extra imported inputs, it can apply to an inter-agency committee for a redefinition of its export as a separate product eligible for a higher rebate.
>
> The system described began to be partly dismantled, along with protective tariffs, after the mid 1980s. The description is of the system in operation around 1984.
>
> _____
> *Source*: Robert Wade, "Taiwan, China's Duty Rebate System". Trade Policy Division, Country Economics.

currency over-valuation can seriously damage domestic and international competitiveness. Although the use of the exchange rate as a policy tool for export competitiveness is still very controversial in view of the considerable disagreement on the effectiveness of devaluation as a tool for improving trade balance (Tochitskaya, 2007), and although conventional trade theories in the new classical tradition do not stress any role of the exchange rate policy in improving international competitiveness, it has been established (Dornbusch, 1996; and Rodrik, 2007), that under-valued exchange rates were part of the gamut of policy tools used to assist exporters in successful exporting countries. Rodrik asserts that while over-valuation hurts growth, under-valuation facilitates it by increasing the relative profitability of tradables, including exports, without discrimination across the board. For most successful exporting countries, high growth periods were clearly associated with under-valued currencies, as evidenced by the experience of China, India, South Korea, and Taiwan.

Positive Policies

To complete the battery of policy tools used to accelerate their export growth and diversification, the permissive policies described below are important to consider.

Functional Policies

As noted above, functional policies are not meant to shift resource allocation. They are policies of a general kind, providing general resources that all firms or industries use, but are not provided adequately by the market. The key functional policies experienced in successful exporting countries included policies to improve physical infrastructure for transportation, communication and information transmission, general skills, and technology. These policies generally require investments in infrastructure, support for R&D, or investments in education/general skills.

Physical Infrastructure

As market failures in the provision of public goods like infrastructure are one of the major constraints to exports, many exporting countries have invested heavily in the provision of public infrastructure in support of their export activities. Earlier support was provided by concentrating limited resources on EPZs, which serves to explain the popularity of EPZs in many countries.

General Skills

Against a background of lower education base in developing countries, and as low literacy and poor general skills are not propitious for industrialization, many developing countries have invested heavily in education over time by upgrading general education and worker training. Countries that did not invest in advance skills saw their exports concentrated in simple technology production so that, over time, they may require significant improvement in their skills base to move towards more complex and sophisticated exports.

Selective Policies

Selective policies with an impact on export performance used in successful exporting countries were centered not only on trade policies affecting selected exporters directly, but were also focused on industrial policies aimed at impacting industrial structures and capabilities.

Selective Intervention for Promotion of Industrialization

It is now generally accepted that successful exporting countries practiced extensive selective trade interventions from the start of their industrialization process. They promoted areas of activities considered to be in their long-term national interest, focusing on products with maximum export potential, domestic linkages, and local capabilities. Selective trade interventions were offered in various forms. These included extensive infant industry protection (except for Hong Kong), tariff and NTB-based measures shielding domestic producers from competition, and subsidies tied to export performance. These protective measures were implemented flexibly, changing with changing circumstances. In some cases, there was a strengthening of existing mature industries facing growing competition from new entrants and using selective measures to assist firm restructuring, improve technological levels, raise quality and design, and enhance skills. Negative effects of protection were systematically offset by export orientation with rigorous performance indicators to be met as a counterpart to privileges received for duty free imported inputs. No incentive was given away without obligation. When a government gave an incentive such as protection, subsidies, or credits, the beneficiary firm had to comply by reaching specific export targets, output levels, investment rates, or management practices (Amsden, 2007).

Box 14.2 provides a description of South Korea's selective policies. The focus in South Korea on heavy and chemical industry was the most intensive form of intervention,

Box 14.2 Selective Industrial Policies in South Korea

The Republic of Korea is the most successful of the Bank's borrowers in terms of industrial development and is widely regarded as a role model by other developing countries. Prior to 1963, Korea pursued a predominantly import substitution strategy that covered some heavy as well as labor-intensive light industry. From 1963, it switched to a primarily export oriented strategy, providing strong incentives and support for exports while pursuing import substitution in a range of new, increasingly complex, industries. Its drive into these new industries, while largely in the private sector, was strongly directed by the government. Its policies to this end included high and variable rates of effective protection, central allocation of credit, a deliberate policy to create large conglomerate enterprises, minimal reliance on foreign direct investment, and close coordination by the government on the pace and direction of industrial development. It is generally agreed that the government's interventions played a central role in guiding, shaping, and promoting Korea's industrial development.

The drive was supported by a rapid build-up of skills at all levels and by extensive development of the science and technology infrastructure. Firms were required to invest heavily in worker training and encouraged to launch R&D. They were given liberal access to foreign technologies but primarily in the form of new equipment and licensing rather than the setting up of foreign controlled ventures. Interventions in the technology markets were designed to strengthen local absorptive and later innovative capabilities. Unlike most 'classic' import substituting regimes, however, Korea applied protection selectively, encouraged domestic competition, and forced early entry into export markets. It maintained a distinction between a relatively mature, competitive sector, which operated in export markets under near free trade conditions, and a set of new activities that were more highly protected, undergoing "learning," and aimed primarily and initially at domestic markets.

Source: World Bank, Support for Industrialization in Korea, India, and Indonesia, OED, 1992.

which, despite difficulties at the beginning, formed the foundation of industrial deepening and upgrading. This was done in a range of industries, including electronics, steel, chemicals, heavy engineering, and automobiles, built behind high and variable import protection and export subsidies tied to export performance. However this protection was pragmatic, non-ideological, flexible, and tied to export performance, in contrast to the experience of some Latin American countries where infant industry protection was non-selective, open ended, and inflexible.

Selective Intervention to Orient Industrial Structure

Selective intervention to change industrial structure was a deliberate and integral part of export strategies in successful countries. In many cases, the objective was to move progressively from SMEs to high tech and heavy industry, particularly in South Korea, and to coordinate technological activities. In the belief that large size mattered and that development of their own local production of input and machinery equipment locally was essential, South Korea focused on building their own know-how capabilities and technological leaders. Singapore targeted foreign investors/multinational corporations (MNCs). Taiwan and South Korea maintained a relatively tight control over MNCs by imposing restrictions on the areas where MNCs could enter. When MNCs were allowed, joint ventures were strongly encouraged to facilitate transfer of core technologies and managerial skills to national firms. These measures were designed to affect industrial structure for FDI in the long term. They were aimed at building the foundation for local linkages to other industries, utilization of domestic raw materials, increased technological knowledge, and upgrading of comparative advantage that would pull the economy ahead in the future.

Selective Interventions in Human Resource Development

With the aim of developing more specialized skill formation, selective intervention policies have encouraged funding science and engineering, public and private provision of specialized industrial training, and the introduction of skills certification systems as an incentive for workers to acquire continued higher specialized skills. In order to upgrade skills in selected areas, investments in education have been highly selective and aimed in some cases at creating high level technical capabilities in activities targeted by the government concentration on technical education and setting up of high level technical institutions as the Korean Advanced Institute Technology.

Selective Intervention for Technology Support and Upgrading/Innovation

Because enhancing the level of technology to improve competitiveness of a country is crucial, selective interventions have been used to encourage and facilitate technology inflows, adoption, adaptation, and absorption. In order to facilitate assimilation of technologies, policies that regulated the inflow of technology and enhanced abilities to absorb them were critical to raise domestic capabilities and capacities of domestic firms to import, absorb, and adapt existing and new technologies. This was achieved essentially by government funding of general education. In the light of frequent technology changes and the enhanced technology sophistication of imported technology, absorbing new technologies required scaling up R&D with a focus on improving the quality, design, and productivity of firms.

Selective Intervention for Trade Finance/Credit Allocation and Subsidization

Limited access to adequate financing, high financing costs, and lack of insurance or guarantees are equivalent to trade barriers and seriously challenge exporters on a day-to-day basis. Firms need access to disposable resources to respond to increased international demands and meet the costs of international market research and innovation. Because one of the most important challenges for exporters is to secure financing to ensure that the transaction will actually take place, exporters usually require financing to process or manufacture products for export markets before receiving payment. Export opportunities of firms also largely depend on access, domestically or abroad, to appropriate financial instruments for developing export transactions. Buyers in many cases need a line of credit to buy goods overseas and sell them in the domestic market before paying for imports. Trade finance supplies the liquidity necessary for efficient trade and can be provided by a variety of sources including: commercial banks; official export credit agencies; multilateral development banks; insurance firms; suppliers; and purchasers.

The faster and easier the process of financing an international transaction, the more trade will be facilitated. Hence, in countries with poor financial markets, market failures and information asymmetries, a proactive role of government in trade finance, with assistance and support in terms of export financing and development of efficient financial markets, would alleviate the lack of trade finance and contribute to trade expansion and facilitation. In the long term, the first-best solution is to encourage the growth and development of a vibrant and competitive financial system, preferably with strong private sector players.

Trade transactions can be facilitated by a variety of financial tools, including trade financing instruments, export credits insurance, and credit guarantees. Firms can choose to finance their transactions through a variety of instruments including: captive financing; factoring; or independent credit collection agencies.

Given the under-developed status of financial and money markets in many developing countries, and in light of the experience of the most successful exporters of the developing world, trade finance is an area in which the government can play a direct role, with provision of trade finance or credit guarantee, or an indirect role by facilitating establishment or development of trade financing enterprises. In some cases, selective interventions are justified to extend support for cheaper credit through central bank favorable terms and conditions for refinancing of commercial banks and loans for export. Specialized financing institutions such as an export–import bank, factoring houses, export credit insurance agencies may also be helpful. In case of significant information asymmetry giving rise to funding gaps between innovators and mainstream financial intermediaries, the funding gaps could be addressed through: (1) matching grants with direct or indirect support of the government; and (2) venture capital with development of the private sector.

A major controversial issue in developing countries is whether or not firm export finance should be publicly subsidized. Based on lessons of experience, it is now established that public subsidies for export can work when they are mediated by competent and financially sounds banks, and when these banks overcome the issue of moral hazard. It has also been established that export credit guarantee schemes need a certain time threshold before they can build the trust that is essential to maintain the productive harmony between the lenders and guarantors. Many Organisation for Economic Co-operation and Development (OECD) countries effectively promote export credit agencies.[5]

---

[5] The following link provides some background information on officially supported Export Credit Financing Systems in OECD member countries and non-member economies. <http://www.oecd-ilibrary.org/trade/export-credit-financing-systems-in-oecd-member-countries-and-non-member-economies_17273870>.

Selective Interventions for Trade Promotion Organizations/Export Marketing

Although there are many support institutions needed for export development, such as standards bureaus or packaging institutions, support institutions for basic infrastructure, customs, transport, air, and sea ports, market access and so on, trade promotion organizations (TPOs) or export promotion agencies (EPAs) are the most comprehensive bases for export development. While in the mid 1980s and early 1990s TPOs were considered ineffective as mechanisms for delivery of export support, with the radical change in the international trade environment, TPOs have evolved considerably in recent years (Reynolds, 2005; and Williams, 2005). The initial criticisms of the 1980s have been considerably toned down.[6] Recent World Bank research on the impact of existing EPAs and their strategies, based on a new dataset covering 104 developing and developed countries, suggests that on average they have a strong and statistically significant impact on exports (Lederman, Olarreaga, and Payton, 2006).

Given significant asymmetric information and other market failures, as well as the public good nature of export support institutions, the role of TPOs has become increasingly recognized. Although TPOs may not be the best form of intervention to overcome the information asymmetries that justify some government action, government funded and independently managed agencies for trade support services, including TPOs, can play a key role to help deliver such services on a long term basis.

Global experience suggests that because developing countries have little TPO management capacity, they should share export promotion activities with other activities, such as investment promotion or export financing. So far, TPOs worldwide have been offering a variety of services, including: country image building; training and capacity building on logistical and regulatory issues; and market research and promotion. Looking forward, and as few people now question the need for a focal point for export development, countries should focus their activities on specialized assistance tailored to their domestic firms' specific needs, providing these firms with services that add value to their operations, and providing assistance that firms cannot readily obtain by using the Internet, a private consultant, or some other readily available resource. A large share of TPO executive boards should also clearly be in the hands of the private sector, while use of public sector funding, as is the case in many OECD countries, can be justified on several grounds.

Selective Intervention in Support for Marketing Boards

Marketing boards in developing countries mostly began during colonial times to facilitate the export of agriculture products to Europe, stabilize prices, and carry out other key functions such as quality control, access to seasonal credits, access to inputs, strategic food or grain reserves, insurance against extraordinary price fluctuations,

---

[6] Criticisms include: lack of strong leadership and strategies; wrong attitudes; poorly paid staff and bloated bureaucracies; confusion of purpose resulting from the assumption of regulatory and administrative roles; failure to develop the range of necessary commercial support services; and outdated information and little ability for TPO staff to provide firm-specific suggestions on improving efficiency in production processes, product design, packaging, and marketing in importing countries.

bulk inter-seasonal storage, and long-haul motorized transport. Marketing board systems have been prevalent in most parts of Africa (Anglophone, Lusophone, and Francophone), South Asia, and Latin America. Following decades of mixed results due to mounting deficits, poor management and perverse incentive systems created by anti-competitive behavior, state owned and funded marketing boards went through significant liberalization reforms in the 1980s and 1990s throughout the developing world. These reforms were aimed at reducing the role of the public sector and encouraging private sector participation to let markets allocate scarce resources more efficiently. Despite widespread liberalization in many countries, the impact was mixed and formal, and informal private traders, who took over many activities previously performed by state owned marketing boards, did not, in many cases, fill the voids left by the withdrawal of the marketing boards from core commodity market functions, such as quality control, provision of seasonal credits, or crop inputs. Moreover, with the withdrawal of state owned marketing boards, private monopolies or monopsonies emerged, and serious contract enforcement issues, unreliable physical security, and poor communications and transport infrastructure created hurdles in market integration and price transmission. Hence, there is a need to consider efficient and selective government intervention in such critical areas.

Although some countries have been able to use selective intervention successfully, government intervention is extremely vulnerable to corrupt practices, inefficiency, and abuses by ruling classes, ethnic, or vocal lobbying groups. The risks of government failures are very high for various reasons, including: lack of clarity or conflicting objectives of governments; lack of sufficient information, inadequate technical, and administrative skills; agency problems; resource constraints; poor coordination with the private sector; inflexibility of interventions; sectional interests; and corruptibility of public officials. Governments cannot be trusted with selectivity, and cannot improve the information processing capabilities of markets. Because government failures are bread and butter issues in development, these risks could be mitigated through carrots and sticks and greater accountability (Rodrik, 2009). Challenges arising from international agreements, particularly for non-LDCs countries, could over time be mitigated in the context of the negotiations of international agreements, such as the ongoing Doha Round or the Economic Partnership Agreement between the EU and ACP countries that are assigned to help developing countries adjust and be better prepared for international competition with more advanced countries.

IV. Conclusions: How to Diversify Exports and Enhance Export Competitiveness?

There is no simple and unique response to these challenging questions. Building on the experience of several countries in Asia and Latin America, it is now clear that when appropriate policies are in place, low skills manufacturing can be a viable option in countries in which human capital is not the major driver of comparative advantage. However, diversifying towards manufacturing may not necessarily be the only alternative for developing countries. Despite impressive increases of manufactured export goods in successful developing countries in recent decades, with shares of world manufacturing exports from developing countries increasing (from 10.6 per cent in 1980 to 26.5 per cent in 1998), the value added in manufacturing from developing countries did not increase as much (from 16.6 per cent in 1980 to 23.8 per cent in 1998), possibly due to the fallacy of composition, namely that: "What may be good and possible for one exporting country may be less attractive when done by all countries." Also, there is evidence that most dynamic agricultural commodities have outperformed most manufactured goods in terms of export volumes and values (e.g., silk, beverages, prepared cereals; preserved food; sugar preparation; manufactured tobacco; chocolate; and fish and sea food).

The discussion suggests that, rather than following the exclusive route of low skills manufacturing based on relocative FDI and exports relying on labor intensive manufacturing processes—which may not necessarily yield sustained benefits in the long term, pursuing different alternatives combining resource based manufacturing and commodity processing could be a viable option. Expanding non-traditional primary exports can be achieved, for example, by increasing the efficiency of firms operating in the agriculture and natural resources sectors; building on recent technological advances in food packaging and transportation; producing new types of commodities such as off-season specialty, fresh vegetables, cut flowers; and trade in services. Hence, for a country to achieve sustainable long term growth, it should not only diversify from the primary sector into high value added manufactured goods, but combine wherever possible actions to expand the manufacturing sector with measures to strengthen the primary sector, as Chile did.

Overall, for policymakers seeking good practice and guidance for diversification of their economies, the policy package should be multifaceted and comprehensive, covering constraints at the borders, behind the borders (supply side), and beyond the borders (market access issues). Drawing on the experience of successful exporting countries, it is now very well established that good macroeconomic policy, including limited government deficits, low rates of inflation, and adequate real exchange rates in support of exports may explain the many successful export-led experiences (Noland and Pack, 2004).

Addressing constraints at the borders implies a focus on tariffs and NTBs, as well as better customs facilitation, against a background of an appropriate macroeconomic framework, including low inflation, a realistic exchange rate, and low fiscal and external deficits. Measures to mitigate anti-export bias and adverse social consequences of reforms are also needed to align domestic and international prices.

Addressing constraints behind the borders implies addressing supply-side barriers affecting infrastructure and institutional constraints and incentives.

Addressing constraints beyond the borders implies addressing market access impediments to export growth. Effective negotiating skills can be useful in this context to enhance the benefits of bilateral, regional, and multilateral negotiations. By and large, expanding exports to respond to increased regional and global market demands requires increased production (supply) of goods and services in many sectors (i.e., agriculture, industry, services), and, in turn, requires not only adequate infrastructure (telephone, services, electricity, water), but also adequate trade-related institutions and good policies. Hence, a multifaceted approach is essential for a successful export development strategy.

A successful export development and diversification strategy should also build on the lessons of experience of successful exporting countries. From these experiences, it is now recognized that

- Besides "getting the fundamentals right," successful exporting countries adopted a wide range of selective measures (e.g., fiscal and direct credit incentives and selective subsidies), which can, under the right conditions help firms to improve their export competitiveness by solving coordination failures and providing services that have the nature of public goods.
- Trade reform alone will not by itself be sufficient to deliver sizable supply responses in terms of expanding trade volumes, increasing export varieties, and attracting FDI inflows. There may be other considerations, such as including lack of adequate infrastructure, that can prevent local farmers or producers from expanding production of raw material materials for export. The lack of an enabling environment can also stifle entrepreneurship and innovation.
- Reducing transaction costs and improving local business conditions can help firms to expand more quickly to emerging opportunities and challenges coming from ongoing policy reforms.
- A flexible combination of state intervention and market forces, open trade and selective transitional protection, micro and macro-policies, and public and private partnerships can play a key role in the improvement of developing country export competitiveness and integration of their industries and SMEs into regional and global production and distribution chains.
- International trade negotiations at the bilateral, regional, and multilateral levels could also help reduce market access constraints and open opportunities to tap into regional and global markets.

Enhancing export competitiveness will remain the major challenge for the acceleration of growth in the developing world for many more years to come. Although competitiveness is created at the firm level (Meyer-Stamer, 1995), it emerges from complex interactions between several stakeholders, including the government, private sector, and other institutions. Given the multifaceted nature of competitiveness, the policy package for enhanced export competitiveness requires actions at the level of each key stakeholder (UNCTAD, 2004). Actions by the government may include: declaration of a political commitment to export competitiveness at the highest country level; a coherent policy framework in attracting FDI, with an adequate macroeconomic framework, adequate taxation, trade liberalization, and a business-friendly environment; incentives to support exporting SMEs; measures to improve exporting SMEs access to finance; and measures to enhance backward and forward linkages. Actions by the private sector include: promotion of associations with renowned trading houses and linking with Transnational Corporations; establishment of clusters to allow for proximity to sources of raw materials; availability of suitably customized business development services; presence of a skilled labor force; abundance of clients attracted by the cluster tradition; and development of financial and non-financial business services.

References

Amsden, A. H. (1989), *Asia's Next Giant*, Oxford: Oxford University Press.

Amsden, A. H. (2001), *The Rise of the Rest: Challenges to the West from Late-Industrializing Countries*, New York: Oxford University Press.

Amsden, A. H. (2007), *Escape from Empire: The Developing World's Journey from Heaven to Hell* Cambridge, MA: MIT Press.

Balassa, B. A. (1982), 'Development Strategies and Economic Performance' in Balassa, B., (ed.) *Development Strategies in Semi-Industrial Economies*, Baltimore: The Johns Hopkins University Press.

Chang, H.-J. (2006), *The East Asian Development Miracle: The Miracle, Crisis, and the Future*, London: Zed Books and Third World Network.

Chang, R., Kaltani, L., and Loayza, N. (2005), 'Openness Can be Good for Growth: The Role of Policy Complementarities' World Bank Research Policy Research Paper No. 3763, October.

Dollar, D., and Kraay, A. (2001), 'Trade, Growth, and Poverty' mimeo, Washington, DC: World Bank.

Dornbusch, R. (1996), 'The Effectiveness of Exchange-Rate Changes' *Oxford Review of Economic Policy*, 12(3): 26–38; doi: 10.1093/oxrep/12.3.26.

Lall, S. (1997), 'Selective Policies for Export Promotion: Lessons from the Asian Tigers' Research for Action 43, UNU/ World Institute for Development Economics Research.

Lall, S. (2000), 'Selective Industrial and Trade Policies in Developing Countries: Theoretical and Empirical Issues' QEH Working Paper Series, Working Paper No. 48, August.

Lall, S. (2002), 'Selective Policies for Export Promotion: Lessons from the Asian Tigers' in Helleiner, G.K. (ed.), *Non-Traditional Export Promotion in Africa: Experience and Issues*, Basingstoke, UK: Palgrave.

Lederman, D., Olarreaga, M., and Payton, L. (2006), 'Export Promotion Agencies: What Works and What Doesn't' World Bank, Policy Research Working Paper Series 4044.

Lewis, W. A. (1954), 'Economic Development with Unlimited Supplies of labor' *The Manchester School*, 22(2): 139–91.

Meyer-Stamer, J. (1995), 'Micro-Level I innovations and Competitiveness' *World Development*, 23(1): 143–48.

Mill, J. S. (1848), *Principles of Political Economy*, London: Longman, Green and Co. 7th edition, 1909.

Mkandawire, T., and Soludo, C. (2003), 'African Voices on Structural Adjustment: A Companion to Our Continent Future' Council for the Development of Social Science Research in Africa (CODESIRA), International Development Research Centre, Ottawa, Canada.

Noland, M., and Pack, H. (2004), 'Islam, Globalization, and Economic Performance in the Middle East.' Available at: <http://works.bepress.com/marcus_noland/12> (accessed April 2013).

Reinert, E. S. (1995), 'Competitiveness and its Predecessors: A 500 Year Cross National Perspective' *Structural Change and Economic Dynamics*, 6(1): 23–42.

Reynolds, A. (2005), 'Have TPOs Moved on Since the 1990s? A View from Western Europe' International Trade Forum, Issue 1/2005, International Trade Centre, Geneva.

Ricardo, D. (1817), *Principles of Political Economy and Taxation*, London: John Murray; 3rd edition, 1821.

Rodrik, D. (2007), 'Normalizing Industrial Policy' prepared for the Commission on Growth and Development.

Rodrik, D. (2009), 'Growth after the Crisis', prepared for the Commission on Growth and Development.

Smith, A. (1776), *An Inquiry into the Nature and Causes of the Wealth of Nations*, Edward Cannan (ed.), London: Methuen; 5th edition, 1904.

Stiglitz, J. (1996), 'Some Lessons from the East Asian Miracle' *The World Bank Research Observer*, 11(2): 151–77.

Tochitskaya, I. (2007), 'The Effect of the Exchange Rate Changes on Belarus's Trade Balance', *Problems of Economic Transition*, 50(7): 46–65.

UNCTAD (2004), 'Promoting the Export Competitiveness of SMEs: Issues Note by the UNCTAD Secretariat' October 20.

Wade, Robert (1990), *Governing the Market,* Princeton: Princeton University Press.

Westphal, L. (1982), 'Fostering Technological Mastery by Means of Selective Infant Industry Protection' in Syrquin, M., and Teitel, S. (eds.) *Trade, Stability, Technology, and Equity in Latin America*, New York: New York Academic Press.

Westphal, L. (1990), 'Industrial Policy in an Export Propelled Economy: Lessons from South Korea's Experience', *Journal of Economic Perspectives*, 4(3): 41–59.

Williams, P. (2005), 'Have Trade Promotion Organizations (TPOs) Changed?' International Trade Forum, Issue 1/2005, International Trade Centre, Geneva.

......

CHAPTER 15

TRADE, POVERTY, INEQUALITY, AND GENDER

......

FRANCISCO L. RIVERA-BATÍZ

I. INTRODUCTION

......

THE surge of international trade flows in the last 25 years is well known and is the backbone of globalization. But how has globalization influenced inequality in the world? How have developing countries been affected: has poverty declined or increased as a result of trade flows? There are widely divergent opinions on this subject.

A number of prominent economists have argued that trade reduces poverty and inequality. For instance, Dollar and Kraay (2002: 195) conclude in a wide-ranging study of the links between trade, poverty, and inequality: "We provide evidence that, contrary to popular beliefs, increased trade has strongly encouraged growth and poverty reduction and has contributed to narrowing the gaps between rich and poor worldwide." And Bhagwati (2004: 66) has argued that:

> when we have moved away from the anti-globalization rhetoric and looked at the fears, even convictions, dispassionately with the available empirical evidence, we can conclude that globalization (in shape of trade and ... equity investments as well) helps, not harms the cause of poverty reduction in poor countries ... globalization cannot be plausibly argued to have increased poverty in the poor nations or to have widened world inequality. The evidence points in just the opposite direction.

But others appear to contradict these claims, arguing instead that there is no evidence that trade reduces poverty or inequality and that, in fact, the opposite may be true (see Aisbett, 2007). Wade (2004: 579) concludes that: "globalization has been rising while poverty and income inequality have not been falling." And Goldberg and Pavcnik (2007: 76–77), in their extensive review of the literature go further: "the substantial amount of evidence we reviewed in this article suggests a contemporaneous increase in globalization and inequality in most developing countries." In another study, Weller, Scott, and Hersh (2001: 1) review the research and conclude that despite the increased trade observed over the last 20 years, "the empirical evidence suggests that reductions in poverty and income inequality remain elusive in most parts of the world, and... while many social, political, and economic factors contribute to poverty, the evidence shows that unregulated capital and trade flows contribute to rising inequality and impede progress in poverty reduction."

Who is right? What does the evidence show? This chapter examines the impact of international trade in goods and services on poverty and income distribution. It studies the theories establishing various connections between trade, poverty, and inequality and then presents the available evidence. The chapter further examines the diverse effects that trade and trade policy may have on the socioeconomic status of various groups in society, looking as well at the different experiences around the world.

II. The Impact of Trade on Poverty and Income Distribution: Theory

The impact of international trade is examined by looking at what happens to economies whose barriers to trade decline, opening their borders to international trade in goods and services. Historically, transportation and communications costs were a major barrier to trade. But these barriers have been sharply reduced over many decades, and it is government-imposed trade barriers that have remained as the most significant block to international trade. The move from a closed economy to an open economy is therefore, in most cases, a move to eliminate tariffs and customs duties, quotas, licensing requirements, and other government policies restricting trade.

The benchmark framework used in international trade theory is the Hecksher–Ohlin model. What does this model say about the effects of trade liberalization on income distribution and poverty? The theory begins by postulating that when domestic markets are opened to international trade, countries will export those goods and services in which they have a relative comparative advantage in producing. And, according to this approach, comparative advantage is determined by the relative abundance of inputs or factors of production in the economy. Consider, for example, the case of a developing country, which has abundant endowments of unskilled workers relative to other inputs, such as capital or skilled labor. These countries can produce cheaply goods and services that require the intensive use of unskilled labor. As a result, when trade is liberalized, these are the goods and services that will be exported. On the other hand, goods and services that require intensive use of physical and human capital will be relatively costly to produce in a poor country and, with an opening to trade, they will be imported from high-income countries.

The impact on income distribution is determined by noting that, as a developing country shifts to manufacture and export unskilled labor-intensive products, the impact will be to raise the demand for unskilled workers and increase the relative wages of these workers. Similarly, as production of goods and services that are intensive in the use of skilled labor and physical capital contract due to competition from imports, the demand for human and physical capital will decline. This will induce a relative drop in the wages of skilled workers and in the cost of physical capital in developing countries. Since unskilled workers are usually poor while the owners of both physical and human capital tend to be richer, the impact of international trade and globalization in the Hecksher–Ohlin framework is to reduce poverty and improve income distribution in developing countries.

In high-income economies, trade is expected to have the opposite impact. According to the theory, trade liberalization will lead to a rise in the exports of skilled intensive, high-tech products in these countries, raising the demand for—and the wages of—the skilled workers used in these sectors. At the same time, trade liberalization will lead to a flood of cheap imports of textiles, shoes, and other products that use unskilled labor. Sectors that manufacture these goods in high-income countries will contract, leading to a reduction in the employment—and salaries—of unskilled workers. In addition, since exports tend to be relatively capital intensive in these economies, the rate of return to capital will increase. The impact is to sharpen income inequalities.

This impact of trade on income distribution, as derived from the Hecksher–Ohlin model, is known as the *Stolper–Samuelson theorem* (see Stolper and Samuelson, 1941). Of course, the Hecksher–Ohlin model is a simple one, and it has been analyzed in more comprehensive theoretical frameworks over the years (see Bhagwati, Panagariya, and Srinivasan, 1998). These frameworks either do not have the strong predictions noted above or otherwise establish a number of nuances on the original theory (as Davis and Mishra, 2007, emphasize). Still, the Stolper–Samuelson theory remains the benchmark that economists use in identifying the effects of international trade on income distribution.

Are the predictions of the Stolper–Samuelson theorem correct? What is the evidence on the impact of trade liberalization on income distribution and poverty?

III. Measuring Trade Liberalization, Poverty, and Income Distribution

In order to examine how the liberalization of international trade has led to changes in poverty and income distribution, one must first determine the extent to which countries have opened or liberalized their domestic markets to trade over time, and, secondly, one must be able to measure changes in poverty and income distribution. The third step is then to confidently establish causality between greater trade on the one hand and changes in poverty or income distribution on the other hand.

Measuring Protectionism and Trade Liberalization

One of the most popular barriers to trade is in the form of tariffs or customs duties. To measure the extent to which a country imposes these trade barriers, economists calculate *tariff rates*, defined as the value of the customs duties imposed on a unit of an imported product expressed as a percentage of the price of that product. Average tariff rates have generally declined sharply since the 1980s, especially for manufactures. For this group of products, the reductions in barriers to trade have been remarkable. For instance, in Bangladesh, the average tariff rate dropped from 106.6 per cent in 1990 to 14 per cent in 2008. For India, the drop was from 79 per cent in 1990 to 7.8 per cent in 2009 and for Brazil from 42.2 to 13.4 per cent in 2011.

But tariff rates are limited as a measure of barriers to trade. Customs duties are only one of many restrictions imposed on exports and imports. There are also non-tariff barriers to trade, including quotas on imports, subsidies to domestic producers competing with foreign suppliers, license requirements, and so on. Consider, for example, the subsidies given by high-income countries to their agricultural producers. The United States provides each year over $30 billion in subsidies to agricultural producers, the European Union over $100 billion to its farm industry, and Japan close to $60 billion (OECD, 2012). Given that these subsidies are not in the form of customs duties, the tariff rates above do not reflect them. In addition, countries that control tightly their foreign exchange markets often have under-valued exchange rates that make foreign goods and services comparatively expensive compared to domestic products. This fixing of exchange rates can serve to protect domestic industries and it constitutes a barrier to trade. Governments can also intervene directly in the trade arena by nationalizing major industries, such as minerals, oil, natural gas, and other natural resources. Since nationalized firms can be heavily subsidized, this is another way of erecting barriers to foreign imports.

Based on the variety of barriers to trade just noted, Sachs and Warner (1995a) constructed a comprehensive index of openness to trade that includes them. This so-called *Sachs–Warner index* defines an economy to be open if

1. average tariff rates are less than 40 per cent
2. non-tariff barriers cover less than 40 per cent of trade
3. any black market premium on the exchange rate is less than 20 per cent
4. government has no monopoly of major exports
5. the government is not a centrally planned socialist economy.

They compiled data for 93 countries and calculated whether these economies were open or not in the period from 1970 to 1990. In a more recent and comprehensive paper, Wacziarg and Horn (2008) extended the series up to 2000 and expanded the sample to 141 countries.

Figure 15.1 shows the proportion of countries catalogued as open by the Sachs–Warner approach and the share of the world population accounted for by open economies. The diagram shows clearly the increased trade liberalization the world has seen, especially since the 1980s. According to the data, less than 30 per cent of all economies were open economies in the period 1970–89, while in the period 1990–98 more than 70 per cent of all countries were open.

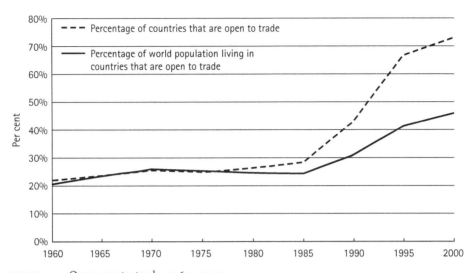

FIGURE 15.1 Openness to trade, 1960–2000

Note: Openness is defined according to the Sachs and Warner (1995) criteria. Sample includes 141 countries

Source: Wacziarg and Horn (2008: 188).

Although the Sachs–Warner index is not without its shortcomings (see, for example, Rodrik and Rodriguez, 2001), it remains the most widely used measure of openness of an economy to international trade in goods and services.

Measuring Poverty

Poverty refers to a situation of scarcity or need on the part of a household, family, or person. Whether or not someone is catalogued as poor is determined by social criteria of what constitutes living at or below a very basic level of subsistence. These criteria may vary over time, historically, in a given country, and different countries may have different criteria about what constitutes being poor.

Although poverty has many dimensions, everyone would agree that the economic dimension is essential: the poor are those who have the lowest consumption or income in society. For measurement purposes, most experts and statistical agencies adopt concepts of poverty that establish thresholds of income, consumption, or other indicators, below which a person or a household is said to be in poverty. More than one threshold may be established, with a lower income or consumption level used to measure extreme poverty. The World Bank, for example, has adopted two benchmark thresholds for a person to be poor: one and a quarter dollars and two dollars a day, but others are calculated as well (Chen and Ravallion, 2013). The one and a quarter dollars a day figure really reflects extreme, abject poverty and is based on estimates of the cost needed for a person to consume the minimum amount of food required to live with a minimum level of nutrition and health. The two dollars a day figure allows greater consumption, satisfying some basic needs above the bare minimum sufficient to merely survive.

Usually, poverty is measured by estimating the income or consumption available to a household. People in the household are poor if the per capita income or consumption in the household lies below the poverty line. The number of people found to be under the poverty threshold is the estimate of the poor in a country. The percentage of the poor in the population is the *headcount poverty rate* or simply the *absolute poverty rate*. Poverty rates are adjusted for inflation, to take into account changes in the cost of living over time. Many governments also adjust poverty rates in a household depending on the composition of adults and children.

How the number of poor people in a country—and the poverty rate—are calculated can be described diagrammatically by showing the income distribution of a country. The distribution of income shows the variation in income received by different households or persons in a country, in a ranking from the lowest to the highest levels of income. A diagrammatic representation of this distribution of income can be obtained by counting the number of people that receive each level of income and then plotting the results of this calculation in a diagram, from the lowest income levels to the highest in the economy.

Figure 15.2 shows the distribution of income for China, plotted for four decades, from 1970 to 2000, as calculated by Sala-i-Martin (2006). The horizontal axis measures income of a person per year and the vertical distance at any point along the various distributions represents the number of people receiving that income level, in thousands. As can be seen, the income distribution in China shifts towards higher income levels substantially over time. This is reflected in the rising value of the mode of the distribution. The mode shows the value of income that has the largest frequency or number of people. For 1970, the mode in China was $750 a year while in 2000 it was $2,400.

Also shown in Figure 15.2 is the value of income in China corresponding to a one dollar a day international poverty level established by the World Bank. Clearly, over time, the proportion of the population living under that poverty line has declined sharply. This is diagrammatically represented by the portion of the distribution in Figure 15.1 that lies to the left of the poverty line. In addition, another phenomenon that can be seen clearly is that the distribution of income also becomes more spread-out as time passes. This issue, dealing with the emerging inequality in China, will be examined in detail later.

How does one compare poverty rates across countries? This is not an easy measurement task. Most critically, one needs to adjust the poverty-income threshold levels in different countries for cost of living differences. The international standards ($1, $1.25, and $2) used by the World Bank, for example, are adjusted country by country, in order to convert them to the local purchasing power of the domestic currency. Of course, the so-called PPP indices that adjust for cost of living differences are difficult to compute since different people consume different baskets of goods across countries and comparable data on prices are often difficult to obtain, among other problems (Wade, 2004; and Chen and Ravallion, 2013). In any case, the calculation of these conversion indices has become more sophisticated over time, more countries have been included, and inaccuracies have diminished (see Chen, Ravallion, and Sagraula, 2009).

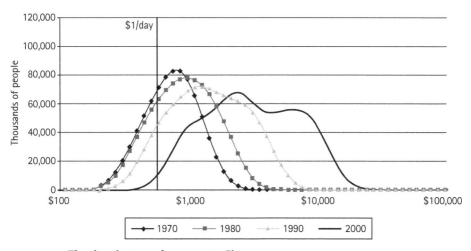

FIGURE 15.2 The distribution of income in China, 1970–2000

Source: Sala-i-Martin (2006: 363).

A second measurement issue is whether to use consumption or income to measure poverty. Strictly speaking, consumption is a more direct indicator of the standard of living and the needs of a person than income. Income can be used to satisfy consumption needs, but it may also have to be used for other purposes, such as paying-off debts. There are also alternative sources of data for income and consumption, each with pros and cons in terms of their reliability (Deaton, 2005). Sources of information for income and consumption levels can be broadly obtained from national income accounts statistics. Government authorities invest heavily to collect such data from individuals and households, whether through tax returns or surveys connected to national income accounts. But detailed information on the distribution of consumption and income in a country can also be obtained from household surveys. Over time, the World Bank—through its Living Standards Measurement Surveys (LSMS)—and many national authorities around the world have invested heavily in implementing household surveys designed to measure poverty. But household surveys are costly to carry out and are sometimes unavailable for rural or isolated regions of a country. In addition, survey response rates may be low among certain groups of the population (Deaton, 2005).

Table 15.1 shows the latest World Bank estimates of world poverty among developing countries. In 2008, there were 1,289 million people living in households that had consumption per capita of less than one and a quarter dollars a day, equivalent to a 22.4 per cent poverty rate. With a threshold of two dollars a day, the world poverty rate was much higher, equal to 43.0 per cent in 2008, which means that 2.5 billion people were living under the poverty line. The highest poverty rates are in South Asia and in Sub-Saharan Africa.

Despite the wide availability of data on poverty at the present time, there are serious conceptual issues involved in their interpretation, in addition to the measurement problems noted earlier. Poverty is a relative concept and different countries may adopt

Table 15.1 Poverty rates in the world, 2008

Region	Poverty in poverty at $1.25 a day	Number of people rate below $1.25 a day	Poverty $2 a day	Number of people in poverty at below $2 a day
Rate of				
Developing World	22.4%	1,289	43.0%	2,471.4
East Asia and Pacific	14.3	284.4	33.2	659.2
Europe and Central Asia	0.5	2.2	2.1	10.4
Latin America and The Caribbean	6.5	36.8	12.4	70.5
Middle East and North Africa	2.7	8.6	13.9	44.4
South Asia	36.0	570.9	70.9	1,124.6
Sub-Saharan Africa	47.5	386.0	69.2	562.3

Source: Chen and Ravallion (2012).

different poverty thresholds. What constitutes a minimum standard of living is a societal concept and rises with the average wealth of the community. By adopting a common international poverty standard (one dollar a day or two dollars a day), one is ignoring the problems associated with assessing poverty among different cultures and societies (see Reddy and Pogge, 2005, and Ravallion, 2006, for a debate on these issues). As a result, poverty rate estimates provided by national statistical offices may diverge from those published by international organizations.

Measuring Inequality

Poverty is concerned with who is at the bottom of the distribution of income or consumption. Inequality is a measure of the disparity between those who are at the top of the distribution and those at the bottom. Let us consider the case of a specific country and examine various measures of inequality.

Within-Country Inequality

The distribution of income shows the variation in income received by households or persons in a country, in a ranking from low to high levels of income. A common

Table 15.2 The distribution of income, selected countries

Country	Poorest quintile(A)	Second lowest quintile	Third lowest	Fourth lowest quintile	Richest quintile(B)	Disparity index(B/A)	Gini coefficient
Brazil (2009)	3%	7%	12%	19%	59%	19.7	55
China (2009)	5	10	15	23	47	9.4	42
Finland (2000)	10	14	17	22	37	3.7	27
Honduras (2009)	2	6	11	20	60	30	57
India (2009)	9	12	16	21	42	4.7	34
Jordan (2010)	8	12	16	21	43	5.4	35
Mexico (2009)	5	9	13	20	53	10.6	47
Russia (2009)	7	10	15	21	47	6.7	40
Sweden (2000)	9	14	18	23	37	4.1	32
S. Korea (1998)	8	14	18	23	37	4.6	25
Uganda (2009)	6	10	14	20	50	8.3	44
USA (2010)	3	9	15	23	50	16.7	47

Source: World Bank (2013) and U.S. Bureau of the Census (2011).

presentation of these data is to separate the population into equal groups of people (five, ten, or more) and then calculate the total share of the country's income received by each group. For instance, if the distribution is separated into five groups or quintiles, then this presentation of the distribution of income would show the percentage of total income in the country received by the bottom 20 per cent of the households in the country (those with the lowest income), the percentage received by the second lowest 20 per cent of the population, as well as the percentages received by the remaining quintiles. Note that if there is absolute equality in the country, then all five quintiles would receive an equal share of the income pie (20 per cent for each group).

Table 15.2 displays the income distribution by quintile for a selected sample of countries. As can be seen, Brazil's income distribution in 2009 was such that the bottom or poorest 20 per cent of the population received only 3 per cent of the country's income while the richest 20 per cent of the population received 59 per cent of all income. By contrast, in a country like Finland, the bottom 20 per cent of the population received 10 per cent of all income while the richest 20 per cent had 37 per cent of income. Clearly, Finland represents a more equal distribution of income than Brazil. But how can we develop an index of inequality?

The simplest indicator of inequality is the *disparity ratio* between what the top and bottom groups in the population receive in income. If the distribution is separated into quintiles, this index would be equal to the percentage of total income obtained by the top 20 per cent divided by the percentage of total income obtained by the bottom 20 per cent. If the country has absolute equality, this index is equal to one, while the more unequal the distribution is in favoring the rich, the higher the value of the index.

The sixth column of Table 15.2 displays the disparity ratio for the selected countries. Brazil had a ratio equal to 19.7, showing that the top 20 per cent of the population in that country received about 20 times the share of income than the bottom 20 per cent. This can be compared to the most equalitarian country in the table, which is Finland, where the top 20 per cent received only 3.7 times the share of income of the bottom 20 per cent.

The disparity index involves a simple calculation, but it is only a measure of the income gap between the top and bottom of the distribution and does not consider at all the middle of that distribution. A more complex index that involves the whole distribution in the calculation of inequality is called the *Gini* coefficient. The value of this index ranges from 0 for complete equality to 100 for complete inequality, with a higher value of the coefficient implying a more unequal distribution of income. Table 15.2 presents Gini coefficients for a set of countries using data for the 2000s. The highest values are for Brazil (55), Honduras (57), Mexico (47), and the United States (47). The lowest values are for Sweden (25) and Finland (27).

Multi-Country and World Inequality

Up to this point the discussion has been about measuring inequality within a country. But what if we wanted to examine the disparities that exist among people in different countries? In this case, one needs first to convert incomes in various countries to a common denominator, say dollars adjusted for cost of living differences (international dollars), just as was discussed earlier in reference to comparing poverty rates. One then joins together the various income distributions in different countries into a joint distribution. Using this multi-country distribution, one can then calculate an overall Gini coefficient or other indicator of inequality for the various countries under consideration. One could do this calculation regionally as well as for the whole world (see Dikhanov, 2005; and Milanovic, 2005).

Overall, the world is much more unequal than any countries or regions. The Gini coefficient for the world ranges around 70, which sharply exceeds the Gini for most countries or regions of the world (Milanovic, 2012). Of course, this is to be expected: the disparity between someone in the lowest and highest income quintiles in Brazil or in India is not that large compared with the disparity between someone at the lowest income quintile in Nepal or Burkina Faso and the highest quintile in Switzerland or Singapore.

World inequality is a mixture of the inequality that exists within countries and among various countries. If, for example, everyone within a country had the same income per capita, then disparities in income among different countries in the world would be determined solely by the distribution of average per capita income across countries. On the other hand, if every country in the world had the same average income per capita, then the world distribution of income would be determined by differences in the distribution of income within each country.

One can decompose empirically the joint income distribution for several countries into a component that is connected to *within-country inequality* and a second component that relates to *cross-country inequality*, as represented by the differences in mean per capita income across countries (Ferreira and Ravallion, 2008; Milanovic, 2009, 2012). In fact, one can calculate a Gini coefficient that reflects overall inequality among a group of countries and decompose this Gini coefficient into a part that reflects within-income inequality and a second one that measures cross-country inequality. Estimates available of this decomposition show that most of the world inequality is due to between-country inequality. In 2002, for example, over 80 per cent of the world income inequality was due to between-country inequality (Milanovic, 2009: 14).

IV. Empirical Evidence on Trade, Inequality, and Poverty

Having discussed indicators of trade and trade liberalization, poverty, and inequality, this section presents the evidence on the connection between these variables. The simplest relationship that can be drawn between increased trade on the one hand and poverty and inequality on the other is looking at a simple correlation between the two. Since, as established in the previous section, trade has increased so sharply in the last 20 years, the question is then: how have poverty and income distribution changed during this time period?

Globalization and Poverty

Has the increased globalization since 1980 been associated with a reduction or an increase in poverty? Table 15.3 shows the behavior over time of extreme poverty, measured as people with consumption below the one and a quarter dollars a day level. The table depicts a sharp overall reduction in extreme world poverty rates, from 52.2 per cent in 1981 to 43.1 per cent in 1990 and then to 22.4 per cent in 2008. This represents a cut in poverty rates of more than one half and has meant a reduction in the number of the poor in the world from 1,937,800 in 1981 to 1,289,000 in 2008. But despite this overall result, it is important to differentiate among countries and regions. A major reason why absolute poverty declined in the world between 1981 and 2008 is because of the success of China in cutting their poverty rates. As Table 15.3 shows, the poverty rate in China (on the one dollar a day basis) declined from 84 per cent in 1981 to 13.1 per cent in 2008. But even excluding China from the calculation, world poverty (at $1.50 a day) still dropped, from 40.5 per cent in 1981 to 25.2 per cent in 2008. On the other hand, poverty in Sub-Saharan Africa did not change as much in the period between 1981 and 2008 and, in fact, there was an increase in poverty between 1981 and 1990.

Table 15.3 The drop in global poverty, 1981–2008

Country/Region	$1.25 a day poverty rates		
	1981	1990	2008
Overall	52.2%	43.1%	22.4%
Excluding China	40.5	37.2	25.2
China	84.0	60.2	13.1
India	42.1	33.3	24.3
East Asia Pacific	77.2	56.2	14.3
Europe Central Asia	1.9	1.9	0.5
Latin America Caribbean	11.9	12.2	6.5
South Asia	61.1	53.8	36.0
Sub-Saharan Africa	51.5	56.5	47.5

Source: Chen and Ravallion (2012).

The drop in world poverty since the 1980s coincides with the rise of globalization and appears to be consistent with a negative impact of increased trade on poverty. Furthermore, the two economies that have seen some of the sharpest increases in openness, China and India, are also the two economies where poverty has dropped the most. To cap off all of this, the region that has been the slowest to drop trade barriers, Sub-Saharan Africa, is also the region where poverty failed to drop during the period. Indeed, using the Sachs–Warner method, less than 50 per cent of all Sub-Saharan African countries were considered open in 2000, and many of those that were open had liberalized their international trade only in the 1990s. From Nigeria to Zimbabwe, Sub-Saharan Africa remains a relatively closed environment in terms of international trade. It is also the region of the world where poverty is the highest and rising.

But despite the clear, simple negative correlation between trade and poverty, there are a number of important caveats. First of all, globalization is not the only major economic change that has occurred in the world since the 1980s. Many economies have undergone major social and economic reforms at the same time as globalization. Both China and India undertook major changes in public governance before or during the time that they underwent trade reforms. In order to examine the specific impact of trade on poverty, one needs to hold constant the effects of these other changes.

Consider the case of China, used earlier as an example of the impact of increased trade in reducing poverty. Poverty in China dropped sharply in the early 1980s. This change was spearheaded by a drop in the rural poverty rate, which fell from 76 per cent in 1980 to 23 per cent in 1985. During those years, however, trade in China was only beginning to expand, and it was not the main force linked to reduced rural poverty. Instead, during those years China was already implementing a comprehensive land reform program that allowed greater diversity in the use of land, a move that led to sharp increases in agricultural productivity and output. There were also agricultural sector reforms that resulted in the growth of local agricultural markets, which stimulated production and income in rural areas. Chen and Ravallion (2007) have argued that these reforms—more than trade—were behind the reduced poverty in China in the 1980s.

Research carried out using multivariate analyses of the effects of trade liberalization on poverty, which hold constant other variables, are mixed (see, for example, the survey by Harrison, 2007). However, there are a number of careful studies documenting reductions in poverty with trade liberalization. Consider the case of Mexico, which engaged in drastic elimination of trade barriers in the 1980s and early 1990s. Hanson (2007) examines the impact of trade liberalization on poverty in Mexico. He separates regions of Mexico that had greater exposure to globalization and trade from those that had less exposure. He finds those Mexican states with high exposure to globalization had greater income growth and reduced poverty. Similar results are found by Wei (2002) and Luo and Zhu (2008) for China, and Porto (2003) for Argentina's trade liberalization under Mercosur.

A second issue to consider is that although the data show a sharp drop of extreme poverty during the period of globalization since the 1970s, as measured by the $1.25 a day threshold, many of those who moved above the poverty line barely did so, suggesting that the impact of trade on less stringent measures of poverty may not have been as significant. Table 15.4 presents figures for poverty rates using the two dollar a day threshold income level. As can be seen, the data do show again that poverty has dropped sharply, from 69.5 per cent in 1981 to 43 per cent in 2008. Note, however, that this result is moved mostly by the huge drop in poverty in China (from 97.8 per cent in 1981 to 29.8 per cent in 2008). Once China is removed from the analysis, poverty for the rest of the world drops over time, but not as precipitously. In Sub-Saharan Africa, poverty remains close to 70 per cent in both 1981 and 2008. All of this leads to the fact that—using the two dollar a day poverty level—the number of poor people did not drop at all between 1981 and 2008, remaining at about 2.5 billion people during the time period.

The much more modest results regarding changes in poverty between 1981 and 2008, when measured using the two dollar a day measure, suggest that although extreme poverty has dropped during the period of increased globalization, a substantial amount of poverty remains, and many of those who abandoned extreme levels of poverty remain at income levels that are below less stringent poverty measures. Their economic situation thus remains fragile.

Trade and Income Inequality: The Failure of the Stolper–Samuelson Theory

In contrast to the drop of poverty noted in the last section, most of the recent estimates available suggest that the recent expansion of international trade in the world has been associated with a period of increased inequality. This inequality is displayed in both

Table 15.4 Global poverty changes, two dollars a day indicator, 1981–2008

Country/Region	Two dollars a day poverty rates		
	1981	1990	2008
Overall	69.5%	64.6%	43.0%
Excluding China	59.3	57.7	47.0
China	97.8	84.6	29.8
India	86.6	82.2	68.8
East Asia Pacific	92.4	81.0	33.2
Europe Central Asia	8.3	6.9	2.1
Latin America Caribbean	23.8	22.4	12.4
South Asia	87.2	83.6	70.9
Sub-Saharan Africa	72.2	76.6	69.2

Source: Chen and Ravallion (2012); data for India is for 2010.

greater within-country inequality and higher cross-country inequality. Figure 15.2, for example, showed increased within-country inequality in China between 1970 and 2000. It is an experience that other countries of the world have experienced also, from the USSR/Former Soviet Union to the United States. In addition, world inequality has risen as well. The global Gini coefficient rose from 65.7 in 1980 to 70.7 in 2002 (Milanovic, 2009).

These findings appear to be consistent with the Stolper–Samuelson theory as it applies to industrialized countries. But the simple correlation between increased trade and greater inequality in high-income countries over the last 20 years may not hold when other forces affecting inequality are considered as well. In a number of OECD countries, for example, there has been a retrenchment from government income redistribution programs and social safety-net policies that protected workers and low-income populations. These and other policies have had a tendency to increase inequality. Furthermore, there have been major technological developments sweeping through the economies of high-income countries ever since the early 1980s, when the development and growth of computers, the information sector, electronics and telecommunications drastically altered the economic landscape, leading to expanding exports of these goods and services. These technological developments have increased the demand for skilled workers and could be the main reason for the rising inequality in high-income countries. Finally, another possible major factor is the expansion of immigration. Those countries that have attracted a large fraction of unskilled workers may have seen the wages of low-income, unskilled workers drop as a result of immigration; although the evidence shows only small effects for this impact (see Rivera-Batíz, 2008).

Given the various phenomena occurring simultaneously, in order to determine the impact of international trade on inequality one needs to utilize a multivariate framework where a variety of factors are tested as possible determinants of inequality. The goal is to determine which one(s) are the most significant. Studies of high-income economies that have used such an approach find that, although trade may explain some of the rising inequality (see Burtless, 1995), for most countries the role played by trade has not been that significant (see Lawrence and Slaughter, 1993; Johnson and Stafford, 1999; and Katz and Autor, 1999). Instead, they almost uniformly agree that it has been the wave of technological changes sweeping through high-income countries, not rising trade, that explains the increased inequality. This is an issue that will be discussed in more detail in a later section.

Turning now to the evidence on developing countries: the absence of any significant trend for inequality to decline since the 1980s contradicts the results of the benchmark theory of international trade examined earlier. According to the Stolper–Samuelson theory, in low-income countries globalization should have increased the demand for unskilled workers (their relatively abundant factor of production) raising their relative wages and inducing a drop of income inequality. But this has not generally happened. There are two possible interpretations of this result. First, it is possible that trade liberalization had some additional economic impacts that the Stolper–Samuelson theory missed. Second, is it possible that there is another economic force that has emerged since the early 1980s that has counteracted the effects of trade as indicated by Stolper–Samuelson? The answer to both of these questions is yes, as the next sections discuss.

V. Trade, Growth, and Poverty

The mechanisms through which trade liberalization affects an economy are many and complex. In addition to the effects that trade liberalization may yield directly on the distribution of income, as identified earlier, the theoretical literature in this field has also discussed extensively how trade may accelerate economic growth.

The Hecksher–Ohlin framework itself suggests that the opening of an economy to international trade should provide a short-run spurt to economic growth. The reason is that the specialization of the economy according to its comparative advantage makes it relatively more productive, resulting in a real income gain (Bhagwati, Panagariya, and Srinivasan, 1998: chapters 18–19). This is, however, a short-run gain in income. It happens immediately after the trade liberalization, and it gradually disappears as an independent effect on income growth.

But there are other effects of trade on long-run growth. Since Solow (1957), economists have understood that technological change and innovation are intimately connected to economic growth. How does trade liberalization affect technical change? One theory is that the increased competition and rivalry generated by the foreign competition forces domestic firms to increase their innovative efforts (Porter, 1998). A second theory suggests that trade liberalization allows domestic producers to sell new products to an increasing foreign consumption base, providing an incentive for the creation and design of new consumer and durable goods for sale domestically and abroad (see Rivera-Batíz and Romer, 1991). This approach emphasizes that a significant fraction of international trade does not occur along the lines of traditional comparative advantage, but rather involves the sale and purchase of differentiated products within the same industry, sometimes called intra-industry trade. Trade liberalization provides incentives for intra-industry trade to flourish, providing the incentives for domestic producers and entrepreneurs to innovate, generating economic growth in the process (Rivera-Batíz, 1996).

Although not without its detractors, the balance of the evidence provides some support for the positive effects of international trade liberalization on economic growth. The early research by Edwards (1991, 1993) and Sachs and Warner (1995a) carried out a multivariate analysis where international trade—measured through the indices discussed earlier—was included as one of the variables explaining economic growth. The openness index turns out to be positively connected to growth during 1970–90, and the results are statistically significant (see, however, Harrison and Hanson, 1999, for different results using these data).

While Sachs and Warner (1995a) and other studies used a cross-section of countries to examine the association between openness and long-run growth, Wacziarg and Horn (2008) used time-series data, to determine whether trade liberalization in a country increased economic growth after the liberalization when compared to the situation before. Figure 15.3 presents the results for the sample of countries available. As can be seen, economic growth after the period of trade liberalization, T, is on average substantially higher than that prevailing before the liberalization, perhaps as much as two percentage points higher on average.

Additional support for the positive association of trade liberalization and economic growth is provided by Dollar and Kraay (2002). These authors catalog developing countries into two groups: globalizers and non-globalizers. Globalizers are developing countries that have had an increase in the trade (exports plus imports) to GDP ratio after 1980 while non-globalizers are developing countries that have had a decline in that ratio. They find that the globalizers also had much lower barriers to trade than the non-globalizers. They then examine the economic growth experience between 1980 and 1999 of the globalizers and non-globalizers. The globalizers have had rising growth rates, from 1.8 per cent per year in the 1970s to 2.5 per cent in the 1980s and 5.1 per cent in the 1990s. By contrast, the growth rates of the non-globalizers actually declined from 2.6 per cent per year in the 1970s to –0.1 per cent in the 1980s and –1.1 per cent in the 1990s.

Having established the theory and evidence supporting a significantly positive link between trade liberalization and economic growth, the second stage is to connect increased economic growth to lower poverty and to increased inequality. Dollar and

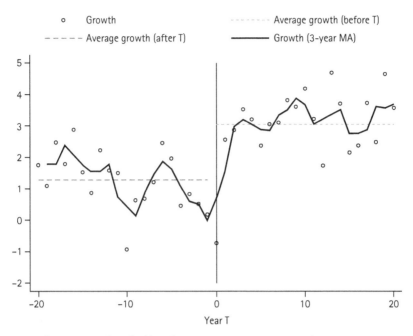

FIGURE 15.3 The impact of trade liberalization on economic growth

Source: Wacziarg and Horn (2008: 203).

Kraay (2002) examine the simple connection between growth and poverty, finding a strong negative relationship between the two. Overall growth of income per capita spills over into growth of income per capita of the poor, thus reducing poverty. This result has been shared by other studies, which control for other variables. As Rodrik (2000) concludes: "Is growth good for the poor? Generally yes. All developing countries that have experienced sustained high growth over the last few decades have reduced their absolute poverty levels."

To summarize: the discussion in this section suggests that trade can reduce poverty through its effects on technical change and growth. But there are reasons to suspect that these same mechanisms—while reducing poverty—may at the same time generate inequality.

VI. Trade, Technical Change, and the Rising Wages of Skilled Workers

If trade liberalization fosters economic growth by inducing the adoption of new technologies and accelerating the process of innovation in developing countries, what impact would such a process have on income distribution?

At the theory level, the answer depends on the nature of the technological change that occurs as a result of trade. If the technical change is what economists call skill-biased technical change, it will tend to increase the demand for skilled labor at the expense of unskilled labor. Such a shift in demand would then have the effect of raising the wages of skilled labor relative to unskilled workers. Since skilled labor has substantially higher wages than unskilled workers, the result would be an increase of inequality.

The evidence from studies in the United States and other high-income countries is that technological change has been connected to a sharp increase in the wages of skilled workers and in the rate of return to education in the United States since the early 1980s. The trend continues to the present time, although in recent years the demand for workers at the very lowest levels and at the very highest levels of the educational distribution may be increasing relative to workers in the middle, thus still maintaining the rising trend in inequality but now also leading to a polarization of the labor market (see Goldin and Katz, 2007).

A number of hypotheses have been postulated to explain these changes, including de-unionization, the collapse in the real value of minimum wages, and increased immigration, among others. But the evidence suggests that it was skill-biased technical change that increased the relative demand for highly educated workers (Katz and Autor, 1999; and Acemoglu, 2002). The clearest indication that technological change and the rising demand for skills in the US economy are connected is the fact that the introduction of computers in the early 1980s coincides almost precisely with the beginning of the increase in the demand for skilled workers in the US labor market. Indeed, research on the issue shows that the growing use of computers in the workplace has been closely linked to the rising demand for more-educated labor and the relatively higher pay of these workers (see, for instance, Levy and Murnane, 2004).

For the United States, and other high-income countries, the creation of the personal computer and the technological changes associated with a new generation of electronics, information and communications equipment and products was the outcome of decades of research and development efforts. At the same time, some authors have suggested that increased international competition was the spark that led to flexible production techniques and to the just-in-time inventory delivery systems that have resulted in a greater use of electronics, communications, and robotics, all of which are complementary to skilled workers (see Lindert and Williamson, 2003).

For those developing countries that proceeded to adopt the new, more productive technologies based on computers, electronics, and informatics, trade was also intimately connected to this process. Globalization and trade facilitated the transmission of the new technologies to developing countries. This is not a new development since economists have examined for decades the process of transmission and adoption of new technologies from high-income to developing countries and how trade stimulates this transmission (Vernon, 1966; and Krugman, 1979). What has been different in recent years, however, is that the new technologies appear to have systematically increased the relative demand for skilled labor in developing countries as well as in the high-income economies. Hence, trade, by inducing technological change, may have spurred growth and reduced overall poverty in many developing countries, but it also may have contributed to increased labor market inequalities.

What evidence is there that trade has resulted in increased wage inequality in developing countries? Early studies showing the impact of increased trade on the relative wages of skilled and unskilled workers in the East Asian miracle economies did not find any skill bias. Instead, the increased trade was linked to a reduction in wage inequality. Following the Stolper–Samuelson conclusions, wages in South Korea and other East Asian miracle countries rose more sharply among unskilled workers, leading to wage contraction and maintaining what was already a relatively equitable distribution of income in these economies. The Gini coefficient in South Korea, for example, has been estimated at 34.4 in 1965 and 32.3 in 1990 (see Ahn, 1997; and Almeida, 2009).

But the experience of globalizing countries since the 1980s has been different. There is widespread evidence that increased trade and trade liberalization have been associated with an increase in the wages of skilled relative to unskilled workers in these countries (see Harrison, 2007). Among the first studies on this issue, Robbins (1995) found that the returns to education and the relative salaries of skilled workers rose sharply in Chile after trade liberalization. Similarly, Robbins and Gindling (1999) looked at the impact of trade on relative wages in Costa Rica, finding again that skilled wages rose relative to those of unskilled workers. In Mexico, Hanson and Harrison (1999) found as well an increase in the wages of skilled workers, a result that is also obtained by Feliciano (2001). In Colombia, Attanasio, Goldberg, and Pavcnik (2004) find a 20 per cent increase in the skilled wage premium between 1990 and 1998, following trade liberalization in that country. For Brazil, Arbache et al. (2004) find increased inequality associated with rising trade, and test whether the evidence is consistent with skill-biased technical change. They conclude (p. 96): "Our findings are consistent with theories which imply that trade liberalization unleashes a period of intensified competition and technical innovation that is complementary with high-level skilled labour. Trade and technology are thus intimately linked as sources of change in wages in the case of developing countries." The more recent work of Helpman et al. (2013) finds that Brazilian trade liberalization increased wage inequality through the expansion of export-oriented firms, which paid higher relative wages when compared to closed-economy firms.

Although the association of increased trade with skill-biased technical change partly explains the rising inequality associated with trade liberalization in a number of countries, other phenomena may be at hand as well. In some countries, for example, sectors intensively using unskilled labor are heavily protected from foreign competition. These sectors could be producing agricultural goods considered essential for local food security, or they could be manufacturing industries whose workers have been successful in lobbying for protection. But the Stolper–Samuelson theory itself would then suggest that trade liberalization in this context would lead to a rise in the skill premium, as employment and wages of unskilled workers in the previously protected sector decline. Within this context, trade liberalization also leads to greater inequality. Evidence of this phenomenon has been documented for Colombia (Attanasio, Goldberg, and Pavcnik, 2004); Mexico (Hanson and Harrison, 1999); and Argentina (Galiani and Porto, 2006), among others.

VII. TRADE AND INEQUALITY ON THE BASIS OF GENDER

Trade can have divergent economic effects on men and women. These effects can be positive or negative and may increase or decrease gender inequities. As a result, there is no systematic pattern of change in poverty or inequality on the basis of gender, whether at the theory level or in the empirical evidence available (see, for example, Seguino, 2006).

Consider labor force participation rates, that is, the proportion of the economically active population (the working-age population) that is in the labor force, whether employed or seeking employment. This is a significant indicator because labor force participation allows individuals to earn income, and it thus reflects earnings potential. Among unmarried persons, labor force participation is essential in ensuring economic survival in periods of economic stress. Among married persons, the ability to earn is a significant factor in reducing dependence on other household members and may increase individual power to shift household resources in its favor. All of these would be connected with increased economic welfare.

Overall, the labor force participation rates of men and women have not changed much in the developing world during the recent period of globalization between 1980 and 2005. The labor force participation rate of women aged 25 to 64 in developing countries has actually slightly declined, from 59 per cent in 1980 to 57 per cent in 2005. Among men, labor force participation rates have also slightly declined, from 87 per cent to 84 per cent. In high-income economies, on the other hand, the labor force participation rates of women have risen from 53 per cent in 1980 to 64 per cent in 2005, compared to declining labor force participation rates among men, from 84 per cent in 1980 to 80 per cent in 2005.

But the overall relative stability of labor force participation rates in the developing world does not mean that major changes have not occurred in some countries. In fact, since 1980 there has been a massive entry of women into the labor force in a variety of countries. In the case of Colombia, for example, labor force participation rates of women increased from 26 per cent in 1980 to 66 per cent in 2005 while for men they have been relatively stable. In Mexico, the increase in the female labor force participation rate was from 31 per cent in 1980 to 43 per cent in 2005 and in Brazil from 41 per cent to 61 per cent. In these countries, the rising female labor force participation rates reflect a variety of forces, including domestic economic forces, such as the expansion of the service sector, increased educational attainment, legislative changes, and so on. Globalization, however, has been a force as well. Women have been a major source of employment in the export-oriented assembly plants that have sprouted in many developing nations as a result of trade and investment liberalization policies. From electronics firms in Mexico and Central America to textiles, clothing, and footwear producers in Asia, women now constitute a large share of the labor force in the export-oriented sectors of a number of developing countries. For instance, a 2011 study conducted by the International Finance Corporation found that 63 per cent of the workforce in export processing zones in Bangladesh were women; in El Salvador it was 70 per cent, and in the Philippines as much as 75 per cent of workers in some export zones were female (see also Tran-Nguyen and Beviglia Zampetti, 2004).

Despite these gains, there does not appear to be a systematic impact of trade on gender inequities. Although female participation in export sectors may have spearheaded improvements in the standard of living of women in some countries, the fact is that in other countries trade may have hurt them. In agricultural sectors, for example, the evidence available is that trade has been associated with a deterioration of the relative economic situation of women. Women constitute a significant portion of the agricultural work force, equal to 50 per cent worldwide and 60 to 80 per cent of the labor force in the food crops sector. In Asia, in countries such as Bangladesh, Bhutan, Cambodia, and others, the percentage of women in the agricultural labor force ranges from 60 to 98 per cent. But the impact of trade liberalization on the agricultural sector is complex, sometimes displacing the small-scale, import-competing producers where many women are employed. Only in cases where women are employed in non-traditional agricultural export sectors, such as the flower industry, has there been a clear-cut, positive impact observed in the relative socioeconomic status of women (see Standing, 1999; and Fontana and Wood, 2000).

There is also no evidence that increased trade has reduced the gender gap in wages. Worldwide, the higher earnings of men relative to women has been a persistent characteristic of labor markets. Trade does not appear to have any substantial impact on reducing these pay gaps (Oostendorp, 2004). In fact, the evidence on trade liberalization in manufacturing is mixed, with some countries appearing to have narrowing gender gaps in wages with trade and others having the opposite effect (Berik et al., 2003). Indeed, many of the employment opportunities offered in export-processing zones are relatively unskilled, offering low wages often under strenuous working conditions. Opportunities for upward mobility are thus limited. The main impact appears to be long term, as the savings obtained through employment in these industries allow workers to move later to other sectors of employment, or to seek greater educational attainment, either for themselves or their children.

VIII. Regional Effects of Globalization

Trade liberalization can be expected to have serious regional effects, and these effects may leave certain regions with lower income and higher poverty. At the theory level, the Hecksher–Ohlin framework clearly suggests that trade liberalization induces major real-locations of production activity in a country, leading to the decline of import-competing industries and the expansion of export industries. If the import-competing industries are in poor, rural areas and exports are in richer, urban locations, then trade will widen the gap between urban and rural areas. But the opposite will happen if the exporting regions are also poor.

In many developing countries, exports of agricultural goods are subject to domestic policies that either directly tax their proceeds or otherwise reduce their revenues indi-rectly (such as price ceilings on food items). How trade liberalization affects the agricul-tural sector and rural dwellers depends on the exact nature of these policies.

In a number of countries, agricultural exports are heavily taxed and the revenues used to finance domestic government, whose expenditures then fall heavily in urban areas. In addition, prices of food exports are often controlled by the government, which helps the urban poor to have a supply of relatively cheaper food, but which hurts the income opportunities of agricultural producers in rural areas. These poli-cies in effect constitute an income redistribution scheme, transferring resources from the relatively poor to the relatively rich. In this context, trade liberalization would raise the incomes of the rural poor, reducing inequality (see Sahn, Dorosh, and Younger, 1996).

But in other countries, the opposite may hold. Trade may generate greater employ-ment opportunities in urban—often coastal—areas, having a negative economic impact on rural areas, which see their population dwindle in response to rural–urban migration. Evidence on the deleterious effects of trade on regional poverty and income distribution exists for a variety of countries. In the case of China, inequality has increased between the coastal areas, where the majority of trade-related indus-trialization has been established and many inland areas, which have not benefited as much from trade and growth (see Kanbur and Zhang, 2003). This is a pattern that holds more generally around the world. As trade expands, areas that have a geograph-ical advantage for trade, due to their coastal location or along rivers or other central locations, will grow faster than regions not so favored by nature (Gallup and Sachs, 1999). But as trade and growth increase, the advantages of locating near these foci rises, leading to an agglomeration of economic activity around them. Locations that are not favored by this process are gradually left behind, unless active development policies are implemented to revive them.

The regional effects of trade are complex and predicting the regional consequences of trade policy reforms requires a framework that considers the general equilibrium inter-actions among various sectors of the economy, determining impacts on various groups of consumers, producers and workers, and modeling factor mobility (see Kehoe and Kehoe, 1994; and Hertel et al., 1998).

IX. Governance and the Impact of Trade on Poverty and Inequality

Previous sections have shown that trade can reduce poverty through its impact on growth. But there is an important caveat to this result. The evidence also tends to show that the growth benefits of trade are limited in countries with poor public sector governance.

Consider the case of countries that have increased their international trade on the basis of the exploitation of natural resources. Have these countries become richer? Have poverty rates dropped as a result of this type of trade? Surprisingly, despite the wealth associated with the exploitation and export of natural resources, countries that have greater trade in natural resources are not richer nor do they have lower poverty rates, holding other things equal.

Consider the case of Nigeria, one of the largest oil exporters in the world. Oil reserves were discovered in Nigeria in 1965, and the sum of oil revenues received by that country since that time has been over $400 billion. What has been the economic growth of Nigeria? In 1970, the GDP per capita was $1,113 but by 2000 it was $1,084, where the figures are adjusted for inflation. There was, therefore, no growth in Nigeria between 1970 and 2000. And poverty? In 1970, the poverty rate in Nigeria (using the one dollar a day measure) was 36 per cent, but by 2000 it was almost twice as high: 70 per cent. In 2000, there were 90 million people in Nigeria living in households that had consumption below the poverty line, compared to 19 million in 1970.

Cross-country evidence of a lack of a positive association of increased trade in natural resource products and economic growth has been provided by Sachs and Warner (1995b) in an analysis that is multivariate and thus considers the various possible factors connected to economic growth. In fact, their analysis indicates that countries that have a greater ratio of natural resource exports as a fraction of GDP also tend to have *lower* growth rates, holding other things constant. This connection has become known as the "natural resource curse."

What explains the lack of impact of natural resource exports on growth and poverty? One possible explanation is that as countries pull resources into the exploitation of natural resources, they withdraw resources from other sectors, including manufacturing, which may have provided the bulk of exports in the past. As a consequence, there is a crowding-out effect, with natural resource output crowding-out manufacturing output, leaving no net impact on GDP and even a net reduction in employment and rising poverty. This type of effect has been called the *Dutch disease* and originated in the case of natural gas exploitation in the Netherlands, which—as is typical in so many other countries—failed to generate sustained economic growth.

A second explanation links with the earlier discussion on technical change. As noted, one of the key determinants of economic growth is technological change. But increased specialization in exporting natural resources may in fact act to constrain technical change in an economy. The rewards for working in the natural resource industry are high, and therefore a significant portion of a country's talent may be employed in this industry. But the natural resources sector is not itself one that leads to great innovations or that will stimulate entrepreneurship in the economy. Since trade in new goods and services is one of the main engines of economic growth, countries specializing in the production of natural resources may in fact face lower economic growth in the long run.

The fact that international trade may promote specialization in the export of goods that may be dynamically weak, with few possibilities for future technological change, is an issue that extends further than just natural resources. Thus, Rodrik (2006) argues that the important question to ask in developing countries is not "how much to export" but "what you export." Rodrik argues that one of the reasons China has been so successful in its export-led growth is the fact that the technological sophistication of its export industries is very high compared to those of other developing countries.

But for the case of Nigeria and many other countries, there is another culprit behind the lack of impact of natural resource exports on economic growth: poor public sector governance. Corruption and poor governance have been found by a number of studies to be essential in undermining the process of economic growth and in allowing trade and growth to raise poverty and inequality (see Rivera-Batíz, 2002, and Kaufmann et al., 2009). An analysis of the history and political economy of the specific institutions that disrupt growth and promote inequality and poverty has been addressed in Acemoglu et al. (2006).

The significance of governance also emerges in the fact that, for openness and trade to generate sustained economic growth, domestic investment rates must be sufficiently high for a country to generate the funds required to develop new export industries. The evidence available suggests that, from South Korea to China, government policies to stimulate physical and human capital investment have been essential in allowing trade liberalization to generate growth and reduce poverty (see Rodrik, 1995; and Rivera-Batíz, 2009). As countries liberalize their trade regimes, other policy changes may be required in order for the reforms to be effective (see Le Goff and Singh, 2013).

X. Conclusions

What is the impact of increased international trade in goods and services on poverty and income distribution? How does trade liberalization affect different groups in a country, regionally, by gender, and so on? This chapter has considered the latest theories and evidence available on these issues.

The recent period of increased international trade and globalization coincides with a significant drop in world poverty, which appears to be consistent with a negative impact of increased trade on poverty. Furthermore, the two economies that have seen some of the sharpest increases in openness, China and India, are also those where poverty has declined the most. The region that has been the slowest to drop trade barriers, Sub-Saharan Africa, is also the region where poverty failed to drop during the last 25 years.

But this simple association between rising trade and lower poverty must be interpreted carefully. Although the data show a sharp drop of extreme poverty during the period of globalization since the 1980s, as measured by a $1.25 a day poverty threshold, many of those who moved above this poverty line barely did so. The impact of trade on poverty using a two dollar a day threshold income level is much less significant and declined mostly because of the huge drop in poverty in China. Furthermore, despite the simple negative correlation between trade and poverty, there is not as much evidence that trade itself caused the drop in poverty. Most countries have undertaken a variety of social and economic reforms since the 1980s, some of which have been connected to the drop in poverty as well. Indeed, research carried out for specific countries seeking to establish a direct causality of the impact of trade on poverty, using multivariate regression analyses or even natural experiments, is mixed and cannot provide a conclusive link.

Most of the recent estimates available suggest that the recent expansion of international trade in the world has been associated with a period of increased inequality, although again the research is mixed and must be interpreted carefully. The rising inequality is displayed in both greater within-country inequality and higher cross-country inequality. This increased inequality is inconsistent with what the benchmark theory of international trade says should have happened in developing countries. That is, according to the Stolper–Samuelson theory, as a developing country shifts to manufactures and exports unskilled labor-intensive products in which it is has a comparative advantage in producing, the demand for unskilled workers and their relative wages will increase. Globalization, according to theory, should reduce inequality. But this has not happened.

The increasing inequality and declining poverty associated with globalization can be reconciled by noting that the evidence indicates that trade liberalization is generally associated with greater economic growth. And this economic growth in the last 25 years has been associated with both a reduction of poverty and increased inequality. The reason is that the main mechanism through which trade liberalization increases growth is by stimulating innovation and technological change. But most of the technical change affiliated with trade recently has been skill biased, so that it will tend to increase the demand for skilled labor at the expense of unskilled labor. Since skilled labor has substantially higher wages than unskilled labor, the result is an increase in inequality.

Trade can have divergent economic effects on various groups within a country. The evidence shows that trade liberalization may increase or decrease gender inequities, depending on the country, region, and so on. Although female workforce participation in export sectors may have spearheaded improvements in the standard of living of women in some countries, in others trade may have severely hurt the standard of living of women, especially rural women and those working in agricultural sectors. Serious regional effects of trade liberalization have also been observed, with urban and coastal areas receiving the greater benefits while rural areas stagnate.

Despite the fact that greater international trade tends to be associated with increased economic growth, this relationship must be interpreted carefully. Consider the case of countries that have increased their trade on the basis of the exploitation of natural resources. Have these countries become richer? Have poverty rates dropped? Surprisingly, despite the wealth associated with the exploitation and export of natural resources, countries that have greater trade in natural resources are not richer nor do they have lower poverty rates, holding other things equal. They have also generated greater inequality.

In order for openness and globalization to be clearly associated with a reduction of poverty and inequality, the process of trade liberalization must be accompanied by a set of complementary policies. These policies vary across the various sectors of the economy and include, among many others, earmarking the revenues obtained from natural resource exports for social investments; engaging in land reform and agricultural sector diversification policies; controlling corruption and improving public sector governance; adopting tax subsidy policies to stimulate investment in physical and human capital and promote exports; establishing research and development funds and other mechanisms to facilitate entrepreneurship, product development, and technical change; and establishing trade adjustment assistance policies that compensate those who are clearly hurt and displaced by international competition. Without at least some of these policies being carefully implemented, it is unlikely that trade liberalization will be associated with significant social and economic progress.

REFERENCES

Acemoglu, D. (2002), 'Technical Change, Inequality and the Labor Market' *Journal of Economic Literature*, 40(1): 7–72.

Acemoglu, D., Johnson, S., and Robinson, J. (2006), 'Understanding Prosperity and Poverty: Geography, Institutions and the Reversal of Poverty' in Banerjee, A.V. Benabou, R., and Mookherjee, D. (eds.) *Understanding Poverty*. New York: Oxford University Press, 19–35.

Ahn, K. (1997), 'Trends in and Determinants of Income Distribution in Korea' *Journal of Economic Development*, 22(2): 27–56.

Aisbett, E. (2007), 'Why are the Critics so Convinced that Globalization is so Bad for the Poor?' in Harrison, A. (ed.) *Globalization and Poverty*. Chicago: University of Chicago Press, 33–86.

Almeida, R. (2009), 'Openness and Technological Innovation in East Asia: Have They Increased the Demand for Skills?' IZA Working Paper No. 4474. Berlin: Institute for the Study of Labor.

Arbache, J. S., Dickerson, A., and Green, F. (2004), 'Trade Liberalization and Wages in Developing Countries' *Economic Journal*, 114(1): F73–F96.

Attanasio, O., Goldberg, P., and Pavcnik, N. (2004), 'Trade Reforms and Wage Inequality in Colombia' *Journal of Development Economics*, 74(2): 331–66.

Berik, G., van der Meulen Rodgers, Y., and Zveglich, J. (2003), 'Does Trade Promote Gender Wage Equity? Evidence from East Asia' Working Paper No. 373. New York: The Levy Economics Institute.

Bhagwati, J. N. (2004), *In Defense of Globalization*. New York: Oxford University Press.

Bhagwati, J. N., Panagariya, A., and Srinivasan, T. N. (1998) *Lectures on International Trade*, Second Edition. Cambridge, MA: The MIT Press.

Burtless, G. (1995), 'International Trade and the Rise in Earnings Inequality' *Journal of Economic Literature*, 33(2): 800–16.

Chen, S. and Ravallion, M. (2012), 'Global Poverty Update' World Bank Research Report. 'China is Poorer than we Thought but no Less Successful in the Fight Against Poverty' Policy Research Working Paper No. 4621. Washington, DC: The World Bank.

Chen, S. and Ravallion, M. (2013), 'More Relatively-Poor People in a Less Absolutely-Poor World' *Review of Income and Wealth*, 59(1): 1–28.

Chen, S., Ravallion, M., and Sagraula, P. (2009), 'Dollar a Day Revisited' *The World Bank Economic Review*, 23(2): 163–84.

Davis, D. and Mishra, P. (2007), 'Stolper-Samuelson is Dead: And Other Crimes of Both Theory and Data' in Harrison, A. (ed.), *Globalization and Poverty*. Chicago: University of Chicago Press, 87–108.

Deaton, A. (2005), 'Measuring Poverty in a Growing World (or Measuring Growth in a Poor World)' *Review of Economics and Statistics*, 87(2): 353–78.

Dikhanov, Y. (2005), 'Trends in Global Income Distribution: 1970-2000 and Scenarios for 2015' Human Development Report Occasional Paper. New York: United Nations.

Dollar, D and Kraay, A. (2002), 'Growth is Good for the Poor' *Journal of Economic Growth*, 7(3): 195–225.

Edwards, S. (1991), 'Trade Orientation, Distortions and Growth in Developing Countries' Working Paper No. 3716. Cambridge, MA: National Bureau of Economic Research.

Edwards, Sebastian (1993), 'Openness, Trade Liberalization, and Growth in Developing Countries' *Journal of Economic Literature*, 31(3): 1358–93.

Feliciano, Z. (2001), 'Workers and Trade Liberalization: The Impact of Trade Reforms in Mexico on Wages and Employment' *Industrial & Labor Relations Review*, 55(1): 95–115.

Ferreira, F., and Ravallion, M. (2008), 'Global Poverty and Inequality: A Review of the Evidence' Policy Research Working Paper 4623. Washington, DC: The World Bank.

Fontana, M., and Wood, A. (2000), 'Modeling the Effects of Trade on Women, at Work and at Home' *World Development*, 28(7): 1173–90.

Galiani, S., and Porto, G. (2006), 'Trends in Tariff Reforms and Trends in Wage Inequality' Policy Research Working Paper No. 3905. Washington, DC: World Bank.

Gallup, J. L., and Sachs, J. D. (1999), 'Geography and Economic Development' Center for International Development Working Paper. Cambridge, MA: Harvard University.

Goldberg, P., and Pavcnik, P. (2007), 'Distributional Effects of Globalization in Developing Countries' *Journal of Economic Literature*, 45(1): 39–82.

Goldin, C., and Katz, L. F. (2007), 'Long-Run Changes in the Wage Structure: Narrowing, Widening, Polarizing' *Brookings Papers on Economic Activity*, (2): 135–65.

Hanson, G. (2007), 'Globalization, Labor Income and Poverty in Mexico' in Harrison, A. (ed.) *Globalization and Poverty*. Chicago: University of Chicago Press, 417–56.

Hanson, G., and Harrison, A. (1999), 'Trade and Wage Inequality in Mexico' *Industrial and Labor Relations Review*, 52(2): 271–88.

Harrison, A. (2007), 'Globalization and Poverty: An Introduction' in Harrison, A. (ed.), *Globalization and Poverty*. Chicago: University of Chicago Press, 1–32.

Harrison, A., and Hanson, G. (1999), 'Who Gains From Trade Reform? Some Remaining Puzzles' *Journal of Development Economics*, 59(1): 125–54.

Helpman, E., Itskhoki, O., Muendler, M. A., and Redding, S. (2013), 'Trade and Inequality: From Theory to Estimation' Department of Economics Working Paper. Cambridge, MA: Harvard University.

Hertel, T. W., Masters, W. A., and Elbehri, A. (1998), 'The Uruguay Round and Africa: A Global, General Equilibrium Analysis' *Journal of African Economies* 7(2): 208–34.

Johnson, G., and Stafford, F. (1999), 'The Labor Market Implications of International Trade' in Ashenfelter, O., and Card, D. (eds.) *Handbook of Labor Economics*. Amsterdam: North Holland, Volume 3: 2215–88.

Kanbur, R., and Zhang, X. (2003), 'Fifty Years of Regional Inequality in China: A Journey through Central Planning, Reform and Openness' World Institute for Development Economics Research. New York: United Nations.

Katz, L., and Autor, D. (1999), 'Changes in the Wage Structure and Earnings Inequality' in Ashenfelter, O. and Card, D. (eds.) *Handbook of Labor Economics*. Amsterdam: North Holland, Volume 3A: 1463–555.

Kaufmann, D., Kraay, A., and Mastruzzi, M. (2009), 'Governance Matters VII: Aggregate and Individual Governance Indicators for 1996-2008' Policy Research Working Paper 4978. Washington, DC: The World Bank.

Kehoe, P., and Kehoe, T. (1994), 'Capturing NAFTA's Impact with Applied General Equilibrium Models' *Minneapolis Federal Reserve Bank Quarterly Review*, 18(1): 1–20.

Krugman, P. (1979), 'A Model of Innovation, Technology Transfer and the Distribution of World Income' *Journal of Political Economy*, 87(2): 253–66.

Lawrence, R. Z. and Slaughter, M. J. (1993), 'International Trade and American Wages in the 1980s: Giant Sucking Sound or Small Hiccup?' *Brookings Papers on Economics Activity*, 2: 161–26.

Le Goff, M. and Singh, R. (2013), 'Can Trade Reduce Poverty in Africa?' Policy Research Working Paper No. 6327. Washington, DC.: The World Bank.

Levy, F. and Murnane, R. (2004), *The New Division of Labor: How Computers are Creating the Next Job Market*. Princeton, NJ: Princeton University Press.

Lindert, P. H. and Williamson, J. G. (2003), 'Does Globalization Make the World More Unequal?' in Bordo, M. D., Taylor, A. M., and Williamson, J. (eds.) *Globalization in Historical Perspective*. Chicago: University of Chicago Press, 227–75.

Luo, X. and Zhu, N. (2008), 'Rising Income Inequality in China: A Race to the Top' Policy Research Working Paper 4700. Washington, DC: The World Bank.

Milanovic, B. (2005), *Worlds Apart: Measuring International and Global Inequality*. Princeton, NJ: Princeton University Press.

Milanovic, B. (2009a), 'Global Inequality Recalculated: The Effect of New 2005 PPP Estimates on Global Inequality' Policy Research Working Paper 5061. Washington, DC: The World Bank.

Milanovic, B. (2009b), 'Global Inequality and the Global Inequality Extraction Ratio: The Story of the Past two Centuries' Policy Research Working Paper 5044. Washington, DC: The World Bank.

Milanovic, B. (2012), 'Global Income Inequality by the Numbers: In History and Now' Policy Research Working Paper 6259. Washington, DC.: The World Bank.

Oostendorp, R. H. (2004), 'Globalization and the Gender Wage Gap' Policy Research Working Paper No. 3256. Washington, DC: The World Bank.

Organization for Economic Cooperation and Development (2009), *Agricultural Policies in OECD Countries Monitoring and Evaluation*. Paris: OECD.

Porter, M. (1998), *The Competitive Advantage of Nations*. New York: The Free Press.

Porto, G. (2003), 'Trade Reform, Market Access and Poverty in Argentina' Policy Research Working Paper No. 3135. Washington, DC: The World Bank.

Ravallion, M. (2006), 'How Not to Count the Poor: A Reply to Reddy and Pogge'. Washington, DC: The World Bank.

Ravallion, M., and Chen, S. (2007), 'China's Uneven Progress Against Poverty'. *Journal of Development Economics*, 82 (1): 1–42.

Reddy, S. G., and Pogge, T. W. (2005). 'How Not to Count the Poor', working paper, New York: Barnard College, Columbia University.

Rivera-Batíz, F. L. (1996). 'The Economics of Technological Progress and Endogenous Growth in Open Economies' in Koopmann, G. and Scharrer, H. E. (eds.), *The Economics of High-Technology Cooperation and Competition in Global Markets*. Baden-Baden, Germany: Nomos Verlagsgesellschaft, 31–63.

Rivera-Batíz, F. L. (2002), 'Democracy, Governance and Economic Growth: Theory and Evidence' *Review of Development Economics*, 6(2): 225–47.

Rivera-Batíz, F. L. (2008), 'International Migration, the Brain Drain and Economic Development' in Dutt, A. K., and Ros, J. (eds.) *International Handbook of Development Economics*. Cheltenham, UK: Edward Elgar, 119–36.

Rivera-Batíz, F. L. (2009), *Education as an Engine of Economic Development: Global Experiences and Prospects for El Salvador*. San Salvador: Fundación Salvadoreña para el Desarrollo Económico y Social, FUSADES.

Rivera-Batíz, L. A., and Romer, P. (1991), 'Economic Integration and Endogenous Growth' *Quarterly Journal of Economics*, 6(2): 531–55.

Robbins, D. J. (1995), 'Trade Liberalization and Earnings Dispersion—Evidence from Chile' mimeo, Cambridge: Harvard University Institute for International Development.

Robbins, D. J., and Gindling T. H. (1999), 'Trade Liberalization and the Relative Wages for More-Skilled Workers in Costa Rica' *Review of Development Economics*, 3(1): 140–54.

Rodrik, D. (1995), 'Getting Interventions Right: How South Korea and Taiwan Grew Rich' *Economic Policy*, 10(1): 55–107.

Rodrik, D. (2000), 'Growth and Poverty Reduction: What are the Real Questions?' mimeo, JFK School of Government, Cambridge, MA: Harvard University

Rodrik, D. (2006), 'What's So Special about China's Exports?' *China & World Economy*, 14(5): 1–19.

Rodrik, D and Rodríguez, F. (2001), 'Trade Policy and Economic Growth: A Skeptics Guide to the Cross-National Evidence' in Bernanke, B., and Rogoff, K. (eds.) *NBER Macroeconomics Annual 2000*, Cambridge MA: MIT Press, 261–338.

Sachs, J. D., and Warner, A. M. (1995a), 'Economic Reform and the Process of Global Integration' *Brookings Papers on Economic Activity*, (1): 1–118.

Sachs, J. D., and Warner, A. M. (1995b), 'Natural Resource Abundance and Economic Growth' Working Paper No. 5398. Cambridge, MA: National Bureau of Economic Research.

Sahn, D. E., Dorosh, P., and Younger, S. (1996), 'Exchange Rate, Fiscal and Agricultural Policies in Africa: Does Adjustment Hurt the Poor?' *World Development* 24(4): 719–47.

Sala-i-Martin, X. (2006), 'The World Distribution of Income: Falling Poverty and… Convergence. Period' *Quarterly Journal of Economics*, 121(2): 351–97.

Seguino, S. (2006), 'The Great Equalizer? Globalization Effects on Gender Equality in Latin America and the Caribbean' in Shaik, A. (ed.), *Globalization and the Myth of Free Trade*. London: Routledge, 177–214.

Solow, R. M. (1957), 'Technical Progress and Productivity Change' *Review of Economics and Statistics*, 39(3): 312–20.

Standing, G. (1999), 'Global Feminization through Flexible Labor: A Theme Revisited' *World Development*, 27(3): 583–602.

Stolper, W., and Samuelson, P. A. (1941), 'Protection and Real Wages' *Review of Economic Studies*, 9(1): 58–73.

Tran-Nguyen, A.-N., and Beviglia-Zampetti, A. (2004), *Trade and Gender: Opportunities and Challenges for Developing Countries.* New York: United Nations.

U.S. Bureau of the Census (2011), *Income, Poverty and Health Insurance Coverage in the U.S.: 2010.* Washington, D.C.: U.S. Department of Commerce.

Vernon, R. (1966), 'International Trade and International Investment in the Product Cycle' *Quarterly Journal of Economics,* 80(2): 190–207.

Wacziarg, R. and Welch, K. H. (2008), 'Trade Liberalization and Growth: New Evidence' *The World Bank Economic Review*, 22(2): 187–231.

Wade, R. H. (2004), 'Is Globalization Reducing Poverty and Inequality?' *World Development*, 32(4): 567–89.

Wei, S.-J. (2002), 'Is Globalization Good for the Poor in China?' *Finance and Development*, 39(3): 26–29.

Weller, C., Scott, R., and Hersh, A. (2001), 'The Unremarkable Record of Liberalized Trade: After Twenty Years of Global Economic Deregulation'. Washington, DC: Economic Policy Institute.

World Bank (2013), *World Development Indicators.* Washington, DC: The World Bank.

CHAPTER 16

MIGRATION: THE GLOBALIZATION OF INTERNATIONAL LABOR FLOWS, ITS CAUSES AND CONSEQUENCES

FRANCISCO L. RIVERA-BATÍZ

I. INTRODUCTION

JUST as international trade in goods and services has expanded by historical proportions in recent decades, so has the movement of people. In 1960, there was a stock of about 75 million people residing in countries other than their birthplace. By 2010, this number was estimated to have grown to close to 214 million (United Nations, 2010). Most of these migrants—65 per cent of them—were born in developing countries, and they were spread all over the world. The United States is the largest country of immigration, and a number of European countries follow, including Germany, the United Kingdom, France, and Spain. But some of the major importers of labor are in the developing world. Indeed, half of all migrants born in developing countries have moved to other developing countries, such as India, Pakistan, and Saudi Arabia.

There are many reasons for the rising globalization of labor flows. Some recipient countries relaxed their immigration policies. But economic forces as well as social and political upheavals have created a tide of migrants that governments often find difficult to control. Undocumented migration has proliferated. From the northern states of Mexico to the western and northern coasts of Africa, thousands of potential migrants struggle every day to undertake perilous trips north, to the United States, Spain, Italy, and beyond. For many developing countries, international labor-migration flows have become an integral part of their economic life, as much as trade and investment flows. For some countries, the income received from the services of workers abroad is now a major item in their balance of payments. But these flows are not without costs. For many years, the so-called brain drain has been studied by international economists. Whether it involves software engineers in India, doctors in the Philippines, or nurses in Sub-Saharan Africa, the exodus of skilled migrants has been a source of concern for many. The impact on the skilled labor forces of some countries has been substantial, especially in Sub-Saharan Africa. In Ghana, for example, over 40 per cent of persons with a college degree or more have migrated to other countries. In Gambia, the corresponding proportion is close to 65 per cent, and in Somalia it is 59 per cent. But in recent years, substantial research has emerged, documenting the benefits that skilled emigrants are providing to developing countries. This "brain gain" is not only in the form of remittances, but also through return migration and the experience gained abroad by workers, as well as increased international trade and network formation between host and source countries, among other effects.

What are the consequences of international labor migration flows? How do they benefit or hurt the recipient countries? And what benefits or costs do they impose on the sending nations? This chapter seeks to answer these questions, presenting the existing literature by experts and practitioners in the field of international migration. The chapter begins with a discussion of the recent trends in global migration flows. It then proceeds to examine the causes of these migration flows and the consequences for the migrants themselves as well as the source and recipient countries. The chapter concludes with a discussion of migration policies, including an analysis of the current and potential future role played by the World Trade Organization in the management of labor flows, as part of the General Agreement on Trade in Services (GATS).

II. Global Migration Trends

The volume of world migration flows in the last century has generally followed the same pattern as those of international trade in goods and services. From a period of significant openness in the early twentieth century, migration flows dropped precipitously in the 1920s and 1930s, gradually rising after World War II and gathering a strong momentum in the last decades of the twentieth century and the first decade of the twenty-first. This section documents the trends in the magnitude of world migration, by type of migrant, by country and region of origin and destination, and by occupation or skill.

Data on international migration are available directly from immigration authorities in recipient countries. However, these figures are sketchy and difficult to compare due to differences in migration policies, definitions, and so on. Some international organizations gather cross-country information on migration and seek to provide more uniform, comparable statistics. The Organization for Economic Cooperation and Development (OECD) collects information on the migration of OECD countries (see, for example, OECD, 2009). The United Nations has the most comprehensive worldwide database on the number of migrants residing in different countries (see United Nations, 2010). There are also data collection efforts supported by the World Bank (Docquier and

Table 16.1 Estimates of the stock of international migrants in the
world: 1960–2010

Year	Stock of migrants	Change between years
1960	75,463,352	2,980,581
1965	78,443,933	2,891,846
1970	81,335,779	5,453,525
1975	86,789,304	12,486,594
1980	99,275,898	11,737,332
1985	111,013,230	44,504,835
1990	155,518,065	10,450,713
1995	165,968,778	12,529,785
2000	178,498,563	16,756,844
2005	195,245,407	18,698,405
2010	213,943,812	

Source: United Nations (2010).

Marfouk, 2006; and Beine, Docquier, and Rapoport, 2007), the International Monetary
Fund (Carrington and Detragiache, 1998), and the Development Research Centre on
Migration, Globalization and Poverty at the University of Sussex (see Parsons, Skeldon,
Walmsley, and Winters, 2007).

Table 16.1 shows the massive growth in the number of international migrants in the
world over the last 45 years. In 1960, there was a stock of slightly over 75 million people
residing in countries other than their country of birth. By 1990, this number had grown
to about 155 million, and for 2010 it was approximately 214 million.

The great majority of migrants move to rich countries. In 2010, 127 million migrants
were residing in high-income economies, representing about 60 per cent of the total.
Many of these migrants came from developing countries with about 68 million people
born in developing countries residing in high-income nations in 2010. In addition to these
migrants, high-income economies had significant intra-regional migration, with 59 million migrants from high-income countries residing in other high-income economies.

International migration within the developing world is substantial as well. Estimates
are that in 2010, as many as 86 million migrants were residing in developing countries.
There were 16 million persons born in high-income countries who had migrated to
developing nations and 70 million migrants from developing nations residing in other
developing nations. Some of these are refugees and asylum-seekers, forced out of their
home countries by civil strife or wars, but a large fraction consists of migrants seeking improved economic opportunities. Resource-rich developing countries—such as
Saudi Arabia or Qatar—and other newly-industrialized developing countries—such
as Malaysia or South Africa—can offer improved employment opportunities to their
poorer neighbors.

Countries of Immigration

Table 16.2 shows the countries with the largest immigrant populations in 2010 and the change between 2005 and 2010. The United States had by far the largest group of immigrants in the world, with over 38 million in 2005 and 43 million in 2010. The countries sending the largest number of migrants to the USA in 2010 included Mexico (11.7 million migrants), India (1.8 million), China (1.6 million), Vietnam (1.2 million), and El Salvador (1.2 million). As these numbers attest, the great majority of migrants residing in the USA come from just two regions: Latin America and the Caribbean (53.3 per cent) and Asia (25 per cent).

The second largest country of immigration is the Russian Federation, which hosted 12 million migrants in 2010. Note, however, that a significant fraction of these migrants moved into Russia during the Soviet Union era. The approximately

Table 16.2 Countries receiving the highest number of international migrants, 2010

Estimates of the stock of international migrants as a Percentage of host		
	2005	2010	Country population
Overall migrants	195,245,407	213,943,812	3.1
United States	38,400,000	42,813,281	13.5
Russian federation	12,100,000	12,270,388	8.7
Germany	10,100,000	10,758,061	13.1
Saudi Arabia	6,400,000	7,288,900	27.8
Canada	6,100,000	7,202,340	21.3
France	6,500,000	6,684,842	10.7
United Kingdom	5,400,000	6,451,711	10.4
Spain	4,800,000	6,377,524	14.1
India	5,700,000	5,436,012	0.4
Australia	4,100,000	4,711,490	21.9
Italy	2,500,000	4,463,413	7.4
Pakistan	3,300,000	4,233,592	2.3
United Arab Emirates	3,200,000	3,293,264	70.0
Kazakhstan	2,500,000	3,079,491	19.5
Jordan	2,200,000	2,972,983	45.9
Israel	2,700,000	2,940,494	40.4
Cote D'Ivoire	2,400,000	2,406,713	11.2

Source: United Nations (2010).

3 million persons born in the Ukraine who now reside in Russia, or those from Kazakhstan, Georgia, and Belarus, were to a large extent originally internal migrants, only considered international migrants after the breakup of the Soviet Union. A similar situation holds for two other countries listed in Table 16.2: the Ukraine and Kazakhstan.

Among the labor importers in the developing world, Saudi Arabia stands out, with 7.3 million in 2010. The largest migrant populations in Saudi Arabia come from India (1.2 million), Egypt (1.2 million), Pakistan (779,000), the Philippines (451,000), Yemen (424,000), and Indonesia (349,000). Other Middle Eastern countries with large immigrant populations include the United Arab Emirates, with 3.2 million immigrants in 2010, Jordan, which had 2.2 million immigrants in 2010, Iran, with close to 2 million, Kuwait with 1.7 million, Oman with 628,000, and Qatar with 637,000 migrants.

Another major country of immigration is India, which had 5.7 million immigrants in 2010. The largest migrant populations in India include persons from Bangladesh (3.7 million), Pakistan (1.3 million), Nepal (641,000), and Sri Lanka (183,000).

The large magnitude of the migration flows just described has led to significant increases in immigration rates, that is, the percentage of immigrants relative to the national populations of the host countries. In the United States, immigrants accounted for 5.2 per cent of the population in 1960, but by 2010 this had risen to 13.5 per cent. In Germany the immigration rate rose from 7.5 per cent in 1990 to 13.1 per cent in 2010, in Italy it increased from 1.5 per cent in 1960 to 7.4 per cent in 2010, and in Spain from 0.8 per cent in 1960 to 14.1 per cent in 2010.

But despite these increases, immigration rates for most recipient countries remain comparatively low. For most host countries, immigration rates lie well below 10 per cent. There are, however, some countries that stand out for the significant importation of migrants. The country with the highest immigration rate in the world in 2010, according to the United Nations database, was Qatar, where immigrants accounted for 86.5 per cent of the population. Other countries in the region also had major immigrant populations in 2010, including the United Arab Emirates, with an immigration rate of 70 per cent, Kuwait (68 per cent), Israel (40.4 per cent), Jordan (45.9 per cent), Saudi Arabia (27.8 per cent), and Oman (28.4 per cent). Other countries with high immigration rates include Luxembourg (35.2 per cent), Switzerland (23.2 per cent), and Australia (21.9 per cent).

Countries of Emigration

Table 16.3 displays the countries that had the largest emigrant populations in 2005. Mexico had the highest number of persons residing abroad, equal to over 11 million in 2005, largely in the United States. This was followed by India and China, which had close to 10 million persons residing abroad.

Table 16.3 Countries sending the highest number of international
migrants, 2005

	Stock of emigrants, 2005
Overall migrants	195,245,407
Mexico	11,502,616
India	9,987,129
China	7,258,333
Bangladesh	4,885,704
United Kingdom	4,158,909
Germany	4,095,015
Philippines	3,631,405
Pakistan	3,415,952
Italy	3,459,027
Turkey	4,402,914
Afghanistan	2,031,678
Morocco	2,718,665
Egypt	2,399,251
Colombia	1,969,282

Source: World Bank (2008).

How does emigration affect the labor force of the sending countries? Although the figures that have just been presented measure the magnitude of the exodus of workers from a country, they do not tell us much about the importance of the emigration relative to the labor force of the source country. For instance, India is one of the countries with the highest emigration levels, with close to 10 million. But this is a small number relative to India's population of 1.1 billion people. Furthermore, overall migration figures, which include children and retirees, do not tell us the number of working-age persons within the emigrant contingent.

Labor emigration rates are defined as the people in the labor force of a country who have migrated to other countries, calculated as a percentage of the total labor force in the source country augmented by the migrants themselves. This shows the percentage of workers born in a country that is residing outside its borders and is a measure of the relative impact of the emigration on the sending-country labor market.

Suriname and Guyana have the world's highest labor emigration rates, with 43.3 per cent of Suriname's labor force residing outside its borders and 34.5 per cent of Guyana's. This is followed by Jamaica, with a 30 per cent labor emigration rate, and the West Indies (such as Grenada and Barbados), where 28.7 per cent of the labor force is living outside. In Africa, Cape Verde and Somalia have the highest emigration rates (23.5 and14.6

percent, respectively); in Asia and the Pacific, the Pacific islands have the greatest emigration rate (16.4 per cent), in Western Europe it is Malta and Ireland (with 23.9 and 22.8 per cent, respectively) and in East-Central Europe it is Bosnia/Herzegovina (with 15.9 per cent).

Measuring the Brain Drain

The emigration of skilled workers has been one of the major concerns for developing countries, especially with regard to the emigration of doctors and nurses. In 2005, as many as 41.4 per cent of all physicians born in Jamaica were residing abroad, 35.4 per cent of those born in Haiti were located abroad, 30 per cent of Ghanaian physicians, and 19.3 per cent of Lebanese physicians, among many others (Mullan, 2005).

To measure the magnitude of skilled emigration or brain drain, economists subdivide a country's labor force into those who are skilled—generally considered to be those who have some tertiary education, that is, 13 years of schooling or more—and those who are less skilled, who have achieved less than tertiary education. The *skilled emigration rate* is then defined as the stock of skilled migrants from a country (all persons with tertiary education living abroad) calculated as a percentage of the total skilled labor force in the source country augmented by the skilled migrants themselves. This shows the percentage of workers with tertiary education who were born in a country but reside outside its borders. Hence, it is a measure of the relative impact of the emigration on the sending country's skilled labor market.

Table 16.4 shows the highest skilled emigration rates in the world in 2000. The highest rate prevails in the Caribbean, where as much as 42.8 per cent of the region's tertiary labor force resides outside its borders. Within the Caribbean, the brain drain is the most significant in Jamaica, where 85.1 per cent of the skilled workforce has emigrated, Haiti, with an 83.6 per cent emigration rate, Trinidad and Tobago, where 79.3 per cent of the skilled labor force is abroad, and the Minor Antilles, with a 57.4 per cent emigration rate.

There are also relatively high rates of skilled emigration from East Africa, where 18.6 per cent of the skilled labor force lives outside the countries of origin. Central Africa, has a 16.1 per cent skilled emigration rate, and in West Africa it is 14.8 per cent. African countries with the highest skilled emigration rates include Cape Verde, where 67.5 per cent of the skilled workforce are abroad, Gambia, with a 63.3 per cent skilled emigration rate, Somalia (58.6 per cent skilled emigration rate), Eritrea, and Ghana.

The emigration of the skilled has been rising sharply. In OECD countries, for example, there were 12.5 million skilled immigrants of working age in 1990, but by 2000 the number had risen to 20.4 million. In the United States, the number of skilled immigrants rose from 6.2 million in 1990 to 10.3 million in 2000; in Australia, from 1.1 to 1.5 million, in Canada from 1.8 to 2.7 million, and Germany from 0.5 to 1.0 million.

Table 16.4 Regions and countries with highest tertiary emigration rates

Region/country	Tertiary emigration rate 2000
Caribbean	42.8
East Africa	18.6
West Africa	14.8
Central America	16.9
Central Africa	16.1
Suriname	89.9
Guyana	89.0
Jamaica	85.1
Haiti	83.6
Trinidad & Tobago	79.3
Cape Verde	67.5
Gambia	63.3
Somalia	58.6
Malta	57.6
West Indies/Minor Antilles	57.4
Belize	51.0
Eritrea	45.8
Ghana	42.9
Mozambique	42.0
Sierra Leone	41.0
Vietnam	39.0
Madagascar	36.5
Nigeria	36.1
El Salvador	31.5
Nicaragua	30.9
Lebanon	29.7
Croatia	29.4
Cuba	28.9
Papua New Guinea	28.2
Sri Lanka	27.5
Kenya	26.3

Source: Beine, Docquier, and Rapoport (2007); and Docquier and Marfouk (2006).

Undocumented Migration

International migration laws are the institutional framework within which global migration flows occur and the single most important factor determining those flows. However, the reality is that a rising number of migrants are persons who have crossed the border into a country without any legal visa or immigration documents.

Since by definition the undocumented immigrant population cannot be officially counted, one must rely on indirect methods to estimate its size. The most reliable estimates of undocumented workers have been obtained in recent years using the so-called *residual methodology*. This methodology calculates the number of illegal immigrants present in a country as the difference between the total number of immigrants who are counted in the recipient country at any given moment in time and the number of legal immigrants residing in the country. The first step, therefore, is to identify the overall immigrant population in the country, which is usually done by means of national surveys of the population, such as a decennial census. These surveys are able to provide a count or estimate of the overall population residing in the country, including the total immigrant population residing at the time. What few if any of these surveys do, however, is to specify the legal status of the immigrants, which means that they cannot separate this population into legal and illegal components. This is where a count or estimate of the number of legal immigrants, from other sources, becomes necessary. But most immigration authorities do provide estimates of the number of legal immigrants who are residing in the country at any given moment in time. An estimate of the number of undocumented immigrants is then provided by the difference, or residual, between the total number of immigrants counted or estimated by using census-type data and the number of legal immigrants counted through the use of immigration data.

This methodology has been applied to obtain estimates of the illegal immigrant population in the United States, Europe, and other countries (see OECD, 2006, Kovacheva and Vogel, 2009, and Warren and Warren, 2013). The United States has by far the highest number of undocumented immigrants, equal to 11.7 million in 2010, up from 3.5 million in 1990. Note that undocumented or irregular migration is not only a characteristic of industrialized economies. Developing countries that are recipients of migrants are also subject to such migration flows. Reliable estimates of these populations, however, are not widely available.

III. The Determinants of International Migration Flows

What has caused the mass migration documented in the previous sections? This section presents the main forces and conceptual approaches that seek to explain migration flows.

International Migration Policies

International migration policies are the single most important factor determining those flows. Restrictive migration policies—whether in the form of stringent exit requirements from a sending country or strict immigration quotas in the recipient countries—are usually one of the strongest factors reducing migration flows. Changes in these policies can then lead to massive migration movements. Part of the explanation behind the rise of global migration flows in the 1980s and 1990s was the elimination of emigration restrictions in communist countries as a result of the break-up of the Soviet Union.

But what factors influence migration policies? The literature on the determinants of migration policies follows a growing literature in political economy that seeks to answer the question of how the policies of a country are generated through the interaction of economic, political, and social forces (see Mayda and Patel, 2006). There are two sides to the process. First are individual and societal attitudes and opinions towards immigrants. These attitudes may be based on economic forces. For instance, if immigration reduces wages and raises the profits of employers and owners of capital, then persons who own firms or farms or own relatively large amounts of capital will be in favor of immigration, but those who do not have wealth and only have their labor will be against immigration (see Benhabib, 1996). But if the distribution of capital in a country is highly concentrated, with a great part of the workforce laboring at low wages, then there may be very few persons supporting immigration and many opposing it. As a result, if immigration policy is determined by the influence of voters, immigration restrictions may be enacted. This force may be magnified if the immigrants are unskilled, since in this case they may appear to be competing for jobs with the poor masses of the country, generating stronger opposition (Hatton and Williamson, 2005).

Studies examining the determinants of the attitudes of natives in recipient countries towards immigrants confirm the important role that economic forces (unemployment, education, etc.) have in affecting the opinions of individuals towards immigration. Often, attitudes towards immigrants are based on the perceived labor-market competition that the immigrants may generate against natives (see Gang and Rivera-Batíz, 1994a; Scheve and Slaughter, 2001; and Mayda, 2006). But there may be other economic aspects involved. For instance, it is often the case, whether correctly or incorrectly, that natives see immigrants as over-using domestic government transfer programs or other fiscal expenditures. They favor immigration restrictions on this basis. This may explain why natives in many high-income countries tend to be pro-trade but against immigration: although migrants may be seen as seeking welfare state benefits, increased international trade is not seen to have this type of effect (see Hanson, Scheve, and Slaughter, 2007; and Mayda, 2008).

Political processes often do not reflect individual preferences but the power of specific groups in society to lobby the government to their advantage. In the case of immigration, for example, the agricultural lobby in the United States is extremely powerful, and has heavily influenced immigration policies. Throughout the years, this lobby has ensured that a supply of farm workers is available to the industry. In fact, labor shortages in general, through their devastating economic impact on various industries, represent one of the most influential forces moving countries to relax their immigration policies, especially those regarding temporary labor migration. It was the accelerated economic recovery in Europe after World War II that generated labor shortages and led to the massive guest-worker programs of the 1960s.

Perhaps unfortunately, economic forces are not the only ones affecting attitudes towards immigrants. Xenophobia and bias against foreigners can have a major influence on immigration policies. In a sense, as immigration flows grow, anti-immigrant sentiments grow as well. As the stock of foreign migrants rises, cultural clashes and ethnic and racial conflicts may emerge that give rise to anti-foreigner attitudes. Often, those feelings are aggravated by conditions of social and economic distress in the recipient countries. The immigrants are an easy target to blame for the deterioration of local economic conditions that may in fact have nothing to do with them (see Gang, Rivera-Batíz, and Yun, 2010, 2013).

The impact of individual and social preferences towards immigrants may influence the extent to which a country uses temporary versus permanent migration. Countries where the population has fears about the absorption of large numbers of immigrants may prefer temporary migration. The naturalization of immigrants and their children is also a policy variable. And in countries where immigrants are permanent and allowed to naturalize, the growth of a block of second generation immigrants may itself influence immigration policies (see Ortega, 2005).

The Economic Determinants of Migration Flows

At the theory level, the classical economic model of the decision to migrate was formalized by Sjaastad (1962) and has been extended in a number of directions (see, for example, Lucas, 1985 and Borjas, 1987). In the economic approach, the decision to migrate is seen as an investment decision that depends on individual assessments of the net balance of the present and future costs and benefits of migration. The benefits are generally in the form of higher wages in the destination country, higher likelihood of employment, improved occupational possibilities, and so on. The costs involve the sacrifice of wages at home (the foregone earnings), transportation costs, and so on. The larger the net benefits of migrating, the more likely the person will wish to move.

Note that this framework can incorporate the economic as well as the non-economic costs and benefits of migration. For instance, the psychological costs of leaving family members at home could be considered as part of the costs of migration. Similarly, for those who are unable to obtain legal migration documents, the cost of immigration restrictions may be in the form of not only the monetary costs of entering the country without documents (the payments to the smugglers), but also the psychological costs of illegally entering and staying in the recipient country without being detected, costs that may be prohibitively high for many. For some migrants the non-pecuniary forces behind migration may dominate the economic forces (see Gibson and McKenzie, 2009).

Overall, the evidence on the importance of economic factors in motivating migration flows is extensive. Both documented and undocumented migration flows have been found to be strongly correlated to the relative economic conditions in recipient and source countries (see Hanson and Spilimbergo, 1999, and Castaldo et al., 2007).

However, despite the widespread support for the hypothesis that increased income differentials between recipient and source countries stimulate migration, there is also ample support for the view that this connection does not always work and may actually hold in reverse (see Massey, 1988, and Waddington and Sabates-Wheeler, 2003). For instance, in recent research seeking to determine the impact of differences in income per capita on migration flows in the world, Hatton and Williamson (2005: 240) find that in Sub-Saharan Africa, increases in income at home *increase* migration: "for a typical West European country, a 10% rise in GDP per capita (holding education constant) reduces migration to the US by 12.6 %...A ten percent increase in income reduces migration from the typical East Asian country by 4.3 % and that from the typical South American country by 3.7 %...For the typical African country, however, a ten percent rise in income per capita *increases* migration to the US by 0.3 %." What explains this paradoxical result?

The evidence suggests that the relationship between income per capita in source countries and emigration has an inverted-U shape. For poor countries, as income rises, migration actually *increases*. But as the wealth of a country grows, at some point, further increases in income per capita actually reduce emigration. One explanation for this behavior is the fact that, at low levels of income per capita, a large part of the population just simply cannot afford the monetary costs of migrating (Mayda, 2010). However, as per capita income rises, this allows some people to save enough to pay for the transport and other costs of migration (Hatton and Williamson, 2005).

An additional explanation is that the massive structural changes occurring in the early industrialization of an economy (the shift from agriculture to industry and services, from urban to rural areas, etc.) leads to a dislocation of the population that fosters international migration. As the economic development process matures, however, these changes diminish and migration declines.

The impact of structural economic changes on labor migration flows is not circumscribed to sending nations. Economic forces in recipient nations can be the motor behind more permissive immigration policies. Whether one speaks of highly unskilled jobs in agriculture or in service sectors, software engineers in high-tech sectors, or managers and engineers in oil industries, the fact is that destination countries around the world face rising demands for workers in specific sectors of the economy. As a result, the recipient countries allow employers to recruit migrant labor to satisfy the unfilled demand for labor. There may be sectors that have a persistent need to import foreign workers, such as agriculture and other low-wage service sectors in the USA (see Piore, 1979).

A third hypothesis for the paradoxical rise of migration flows as income increases in source country economies is based on *relative deprivation theory*. It suggests that, as inequality rises in the early years of economic development (a trend first noted by economist Simon Kuznets), those who become relatively poor will find themselves increasingly dissatisfied with their relative standing in the community. This will stimulate them to emigrate (see Stark and Taylor, 1991).

Despite its powerful role in explaining migration flows, another problem of using a simple economic approach based on income differences across countries is that it cannot explain temporary migration. If there is a significant and persistent wage and employment differential between origin and destination regions, why do so many migrants wish to stay in the destination only for short periods of time? This can be understood if one recognizes that migration decisions are often made by families and households, not individuals (see Stark and Bloom, 1985). As such, families may see the migration of some household members as part of their saving and investment decisions. The idea is that, if low-income households encounter capital market imperfections at home, which exclude them from access to the financing of investments in housing, durable goods, or in self-employed businesses, migration abroad may lead to the accumulation of remittances that can then be used to finance these purchases and investments. Migration becomes a short-term activity needed by households to raise funds in the absence of local financing.

Demographics and International Migration

Migrants tend to be relatively younger than both the population in the sending country and the recipient economy (McKenzie, 2008). The economic approach explains this by noting that the younger the worker, the longer the expected years of labor force participation that the migrant can have in the destination, and the higher the expected returns from migration will be. But this point also suggests that the demographic composition of a country can have a major impact on its migration patterns. If younger people tend to have a stronger propensity to migrate, then countries that have a higher proportion of young people will also have greater migration.

Indeed, one of the reasons for the mass migration surge originating in developing countries in recent years is the fact that many of these countries have had a sharply rising population of young people. The case of the Middle East and North Africa (MENA) stands out. These countries have faced sharply lower death rates but relatively high birth rates, which have led to a population explosion. As a result, labor markets have been flooded with young, new entrants, which the supply of jobs has not been able to match. The unemployment rate in a number of non-oil exporting countries in the MENA region lies above 20 per cent, and migrants emerge from this pool of workers

There are also demographic changes in recipient countries that may pull migrants into high-income countries. The theory of the demographic transition suggests that, over time, as countries increase their per capita income and become more developed, birth rates will eventually drop. Population growth rates will decline and may become negative. In many high-income countries, as a matter of fact, population growth has been declining in recent years and in some the growth has been negative. For instance, the average fertility rate (number of children ever born to women) in Europe among native, non-immigrant populations was 1.4 children in 2005, but the number of children needed to keep the population constant is 2.0. Immigration is seen as a solution for a range of problems partially connected to lower labor supply, from labor shortages in key economic sectors to the viability of public social security and retirement funds (European Commission, 2006).

Social and Political Conflicts, Refugees and Asylum Seekers

International migration flows have at periods been heavily influenced by refugees and asylum seekers seeking safety from political persecution, civil wars, armed conflicts, ethnic and racial violence, and natural disasters. Compared to the 1960s and 1970s, recent decades have seen a surge of refugees and asylum seekers. The United Nations estimates that, from 2–3 million in the 1960s and 1970s, the numbers rose to a peak of over 18 million in the late 1980s and 1990s, declining to about 14 million in 2005, when refugees and asylum seekers accounted for 7.1 per cent of all international migrants in the world. The data, however, show a rebound, and it is estimated that in 2010 there were over 16 million refugees and asylum seekers.

Geography and Proximity in International Migration Flows

Most migration flows occur among geographically close, often neighboring, countries. This is the case for the United States, where most immigrants originate in Mexico, Central America, and the Caribbean. In Western Europe, international migrants move from Eastern and Central Europe as well as from the Middle East and North Africa. In South Asia, migrants move from Pakistan and Bangladesh to India, and from the Philippines, Indonesia, and other countries to Japan. And in Africa, most of the countries sending migrants to South Africa are from neighboring countries, including Lesotho, Swaziland, Mozambique, and Zimbabwe.

The role of distance and proximity in migration movements is emphasized by the *gravity theory of migration flows* (see Lowry, 1966; and Kamemera, Oguledo, and Davis, 2000). Based on the renowned Newtonian model, the theory argues that the magnitude of labor flows between any two countries is proportionally related to the population or labor force of the two countries (their "mass") and the distance between them. The distance can be geographical distance as well as cultural distance. That is, countries with the same language and culture will tend to have greater flows, holding everything else constant. The gravity model has been tested empirically and its hypotheses are supported by the evidence from a wide array of countries (see Ortega and Peri, 2009, and Mayda, 2010).

Networks and Trans-nationalism

Studies of the determinants of international migration from a country X to another country Y find that one of the major factors accounting for such flows at any given time is the stock of immigrants from country X already residing in country Y. One approach that explains this result is *network or chain migration theory* (see Piore, 1979; Rivera-Batíz, 1986; Massey, Alarcon, Durand, and Gonzalez, 1987; and Bauer, Epstein, and Gang, 2009). This theory suggests that some migration flows are self-sustaining. According to the theory, an initial, contained migration flow—a movement that in fact may have been random—may lead to mass migration eventually.

The explanation lies in the presence of imperfect information about job opportunities in the destination region. The absence of that information may prevent migrants from moving. But once a few migrants have made it to the host location, they can monitor more carefully employment vacancies and inform members of their home communities about those opportunities. This leads to greater flows from the same origin region to the same destination region. Furthermore, as some of the migrants and their families accumulate wealth, this demonstrates to other migrants the success of the migration process, further increasing migration from the origin to destination. A network thus develops between the sending and recipient communities, effectively reducing the costs of moving across the border, leading to an acceleration of the migration process.

Circular migration occurs when migrants move back and forth between source and destination countries. In fact, families or households may become trans-national in that some members will be abroad and others at home. The result is that the migrants become attached economically, socially, and culturally to both host and sending countries. For instance, in the case of Mexican migration to New York City, the network process of migration has led to a majority of migrants that originate in the state of Puebla, forging a close relationship between the two communities (Rivera-Batíz, 2004).

IV. MIGRANTS AND THEIR SOCIOECONOMIC SITUATION

What are the economic consequences of mass migration? What changes in the source and destination countries are generated by migrants? In analyzing these issues, one can separate the impacts on: the migrants themselves, the remaining population in the source country, and the population in the recipient economy. This section begins with a survey of the impacts on the migrants.

A large body of research has now accumulated, studying the labor market outcomes of immigrants (see, for example, the collection of research in Zimmermann and

Constant, 2004, as well as Borjas, 1999a, and Hanson, 2006 and 2010). This section summarizes the pertinent research. Because of data availability, most of the studies are about
migrants moving to high-income countries.

The economic returns to migrating are substantial for most workers. For example, the
average wage received by Mexican workers aged 23 to 27 in the United States (adjusted
for differences in the cost of living between the two countries) varies from close to six
times the equivalent wages in Mexico for workers with four or less years of schooling
to 2.5 times for workers with 16 or more years of schooling. Even after discounting any
transportation costs (including the costs of the smugglers for undocumented workers),
the gains remain large. Other studies find similar results. Clemens, Montenegro, and
Pritchett (2008) find that the wage gap between workers with the same characteristics
in source and host countries can be enormous, even after correcting for possible unobserved differences in these workers, including the fact that workers who move across
borders are not the typical workers in developing countries (an issue to be discussed
below). On this basis, Pritchett (2006) believes that just as trade policy is often associated with improved development prospects in developing countries, greater openness
towards immigrants would have a much stronger effect.

Notwithstanding the generally substantial economic gains obtained by most migrants
relative to their standard of living at home, a second question to consider is how the
migrants fare relative to the non-immigrants in the recipient countries. This is an essential issue to determine since it responds to the question of whether immigrants can
stagnate economically in the host countries. Policymakers in recipient countries may
be particularly concerned with the extent to which immigrants are able to assimilate
into the labor market, thus avoiding the possibility of becoming an economic underclass
(Constant and Zimmermann, 2009).

The economic progress of migrants relative to natives varies by country and over
time. Unexpected shifts in the demand for labor can have deep impacts on immigrants,
such as in the 2007–09 global economic collapse. But the relatively poor labor market
outcomes of immigrants relative to natives are partly related to education, language and
other skills (see Rivera-Batíz, 1990 and 2007; Schmidt, 1997; Chiswick and Miller, 2004;
Borjas and Katz, 2007; and Basilio and Bauer, 2010). They are also linked to legal status,
with undocumented immigrants receiving substantially lower wages than legal migrants
with similar characteristics (see Rivera-Batíz, 1999). But even legal immigrants may be
subject to labor market discrimination, receiving lower wages than natives with identical characteristics (Kaas and Manger, 2010). On the other hand, as time in the host
country passes, the labor market outcomes of migrants tend to become closer to those of
natives, as discussed below (see Peracchi and Depalo, 2006).

The duration of stay of the migrants in a country is highly correlated with their economic progress. The research of Chiswick (1978, 2000) and Duleep and Regets (2000)
has suggested that immigrants face an initial shortfall or dip in their labor market performance after they arrive in a recipient country. This dip is the result of the adjustment
costs that immigrants experience as they enter the country. With limited knowledge

about labor market institutions in host countries—and a compelling need to obtain employment—recent migrants may accept jobs with wage offers lower than those they would otherwise accept given their skills. As their stay in the recipient country passes and they are able to search for better paying jobs, earnings will rise and they will be paid wages that correspond more closely to their skill endowments.

But what determines the skill composition of a migration flow? One of the most discussed issues in the international migration literature is whether or not emigrants are the most qualified, skilled workers in the origin economy. If migrants are positively selected, then they will be more likely to succeed abroad, but their exit from the source country will drain the most capable, most skilled population from the nation, with a potentially negative impact on its economy and society.

What determines whether migrants are positively or negatively selected? There are forces that favor a positive selectivity and others that encourage a negative selectivity. The best known hypothesis is that emigrants tend to be positively selected because, in order to compensate for the substantial costs of migration, only those who have the strongest drive and motivation—and the expectations of great rewards—will actually undertake the migration process (see Chiswick, 2000). Of course, if costs of migration decline, then this aspect of selectivity will tend to become less significant. In addition, the impact of motivation on migration depends on whether motivational skills are more strongly rewarded in the destination region. Indeed, one suspects that holding constant the distribution of motivational skills in a population, if these skills are poorly rewarded at home but richly rewarded abroad, the incentives to migrate from source to destination regions will increase.

A second hypothesis (referred in the literature as the *Roy model*) is that the inequality in the distribution of income in the source and destination countries is essential in determining whether there are incentives for skilled or unskilled migrants to migrate. For instance, the more unequal the income distribution in the origin area as compared to the destination, the more likely that the highly skilled will be more richly rewarded in the source country relative to the destination and the lower the incentives for the highly skilled to emigrate relative to the less skilled. On the other hand, if employers in the destination region cannot assess well the skills of the migrants (such as when different languages are involved, different educational systems, etc.), they may offer lower wages to the highly skilled migrants, whereas employers in the source country would be able to assess more accurately the potential migrants' skills and pay them wages more consonant with their skills. The result is a reduction in the incentive to migrate of the highly skilled relative to the unskilled (Stark and Taylor, 1991).

Some evidence appears to support the implications of the Roy model (see Borjas, 1987 and 1999a). Recent research finds a negative selectivity in the migrant contingent from Mexico to the United States (that is, the emigrant group tends to have lower average skills than the population left behind), as would be expected from the relatively more unequal distribution of income in Mexico relative to the United States (see Fernandez-Huertas Moiraga, 2011, for this analysis and Chiquiar and Hanson, 2005, for alternative results).

In addition, the patterns of migration of highly skilled workers suggest that they tend to move to countries that reward education more strongly (Grogger and Hanson, 2008.

V. The Consequences of International Migration: Host Countries

The economic consequences of migration in the host countries has been one of the most debated topics in the area of international migration (see the surveys by Borjas, 1999a and Hanson, 2009). This literature focuses on the distributional effects of immigration, particularly the labor market consequences, as well as the effects of the migrants on the public sector.

The Labor Market Effects of Immigration

The simplest theoretical framework within which one can examine the effects of immigration is one that focuses on the demand for and the supply of labor as determinants of employment and wage opportunities. In this model, an inflow of immigrants raises the supply of labor and thus tends to generate a surplus of workers in the labor market that pushes down wages and reduces the employment opportunities of natives. As a result, the immigration reduces the economic welfare (the standard of living) of the non-immigrants in the recipient economy.

Do the results of this model hold? The research in this area is vast and includes: Altonji and Card, 1991; Rivera-Batíz and Sechzer, 1991; Gang and Rivera-Batíz, 1994b; Card, 2005; and Chojnicki, Docquier, and Ragot, 2011). The results of these studies are mixed, but the predominance of the evidence is that the impact of immigrants on the overall wages and employment of natives is small. For example, Rivera-Batíz and Sechzer (1991), in their simulation of Mexican migration to the USA, find that a 10 per cent increase in the US labor force owing to an inflow of Mexican immigrants would have the strongest negative effect on the wages of Mexican workers already in the country; but even this impact is small, equal to a less than 1 per cent drop in wages.

Why this lack of impact? Partly, the explanation is that immigrants generate their own demand for labor. As immigrants place downward pressure on wages, this makes employment in labor intensive sectors, such as agriculture or textiles, more profitable. As a result, employers will have an incentive to increase their employment of labor intensive products (agricultural production and textile production rise), which raises the demand for labor. This demand for labor places upwards pressure on wages and increases employment opportunities for domestic workers as well. In international economics, this situation, where an influx of labor leads to no change in wages, is called the

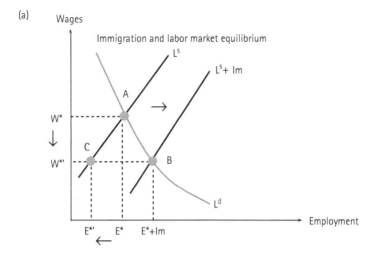

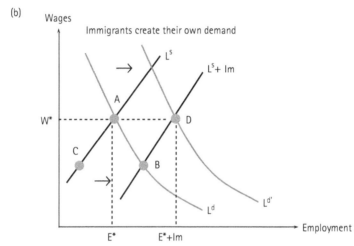

FIGURE 16.1 The effects of immigration in a simple labor demand and supply model

Rybczyinski effect, in the name of the economist that first postulated it (see Bhagwati, Panagariya, and Srinivasan, 1998 and Rivera-Batíz, 1983).

These effects of immigration can be depicted diagrammatically. Figure 16.1 shows first a labor demand curve represented by L^D, which is downward-sloping and reflects the fact that, as wages rise, employers will reduce the number of workers they hire. The diagram also shows a labor supply curve, depicted by L^s, which is upward-sloping and reflects the fact that, as wages increase, domestic workers will increase their labor supply, whether because labor force participation increases or through longer hours of work each day or week. The labor market is in equilibrium when labor demand and supply are equal, which occurs at point E, with domestic wages given by W* and domestic employment E*.

In this model, immigration increases the labor supply in the economy by supplementing the domestic labor supply by Im, which represents the number of workers (or hours of work) that the immigrants bring to the host-country labor market. As the diagram shows, the impact of the immigrants is to reduce the labor market equilibrium wage, from W^* to $W^{*\prime}$. This drop in wages also discourages domestic workers from seeking employment and their employment also drops from E^* to $E^{*\prime}$.

But this is not the end of the story. Figure 16.1(b) shows the effects of immigration when the immigrants act to generate employment in the host country, either by reviving decaying industries, serving as a magnet for new industries, or by providing their own investment and employment opportunities through self-employment. In this case, the immigrants still raise labor supply, but they also lead to an increase in labor demand, from L^D to $L^{D\prime}$. As shown in the diagram, in this situation, it is possible for immigration to have no impact on the wages or employment of natives (which remain at W^* and E^*).

Evidence of the impact of immigrants in raising employment opportunities in recipient regions is substantial. Probably the best known of these studies is Card (1990), who examined the impact of the 1980 Mariel Cuban immigrant influx on wages and employment in the Miami area. Card found that, despite the substantial inflow of workers, the labor market trends in Miami between 1980 and 1985 were no different from those in other cities that did not experience the influx. Other studies also find no negative impact of immigration on wages or employment (see Card, 2005 and Ortega and Peri, 2009), among others). These studies suggest that the increased supply of labor induced by immigration generates increased investment and sectoral adjustments that create employment opportunities and offset any significant negative effects of the immigrants on wages and employment of natives. There are caveats, however, to these results. If the migration influx is massive and the host country or region is incapable of generating the physical capital and sectoral adjustments necessary to generate employment growth, due to capital market imperfections or other constraints, then the impact of the immigrants may be negative, especially in the short run. There is also some evidence of such an impact (see, for example, Ortega (2008), who studies the impact of immigration in Spain).

A second explanation for the lack of empirical evidence showing a significant impact of immigration on wages lies in the fact that immigrants are concentrated in very specific sectors of the labor market that do not compete with the native-born. This point suggests that immigrants may actually have a positive impact on the labor market outcomes of natives. This issue is examined in the next section.

The Effects of Skilled vs. Unskilled Immigration

When one considers the impact of immigration in a context where immigrants and natives belong to different segments of the labor market, there is a strong possibility that immigration can have a positive impact on natives. Suppose, for example, that the immigration is composed predominantly of unskilled workers while the native workers are predominantly skilled. What is the impact of immigration in this context?

Unskilled migrants tend to raise the wages and employment opportunities of workers that are *complementary* to them (such as skilled workers) but may reduce the wages and employment of workers that are *substitutes* or compete with them in the same labor market (i.e., other unskilled workers). If skilled and unskilled workers are complements, then an influx of unskilled workers will raise the demand for skilled workers. If the skilled workers are natives, this means that immigration will increase the wages and employment opportunities of natives. In other words, immigration will raise the economic welfare of the nationals.

Evidence that immigrants are complements with natives in the case of the United States has been provided recently by Peri (2006) using data for immigration to California (see also Ottaviano and Peri, 2005 and 2008; Card and Shleifer, 2009; and Peri and Sparber, 2009). At the same time, other researchers have found different results on this issue (Borjas, Grogger, and Hanson, 2008).

The Effects of Immigrants on Public Finances

A second major area of concern regarding the impact of immigration in host countries has involved the effects on government expenditures and revenues. Those critical of lax immigration policies have argued that immigrants raise government expenditures by more than they do tax revenues, causing natives to bear an increasing tax burden. Others, however, argue that the opposite holds, with immigrants actually alleviating the tax burden of the native population. The evidence on this issue is, once again, mixed (see, for example, Smith and Edmonston, 1995; Gustman and Steinmeier, 2000; and DeVoretz and Werner, 2002). There are a number of reasons for the complexity in the results of these studies.

The impact of immigrants on government public finances depends on the relative significance of a wide array of effects. On the revenue side, immigrants pay taxes, but the magnitude of these taxes depends on the tax system in the host country, including the type of taxes used, the average and marginal tax rates, and the progressivity of the system, as well as the characteristics of the immigrants themselves (their skills, income, etc.). From the expenditure side, immigrants will be raising government expenditures, but the magnitude of the impact depends on the safety nets present in the country (the generosity of welfare or other public assistance programs and the participation and/or eligibility of immigrants to receive payments from those programs), as well as the cost of the services provided by the government (such as the cost of educating the children of immigrants or the cost of free public health services), and the usage of those services by immigrants. Different groups of immigrants, depending on their age, gender, marital status, location of residence, skills, income, regular versus irregular status, temporariness of their migration, and so on may have widely different effects on government finances (see OECD, 2013).

(a)

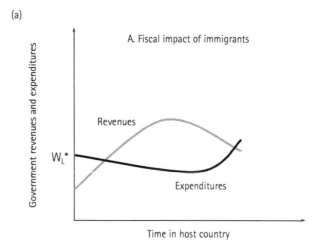

(b)

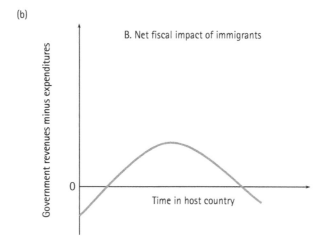

FIGURE 16.2 The impact of migration on government revenues and expenditures

One issue that becomes very clear is that the time horizon used to measure the impact of immigration on the public sector matters. Studies that focus on the short-run effects of immigration generally obtain negative (or more negative) impacts while studies that incorporate medium-run and long-term effects of immigration generally obtain positive (or more positive) results. The reason is illustrated through the use of Figure 16.2. As shown in Figure 16.2a, at the time of arrival, and for a number of years after that, immigrants are more likely to generate an excess of government expenditures over the tax revenues they provide (this excess, of course, would have to be filled by non-immigrants, who would face higher taxes). The main reason is because of the costs of educating the children of the young immigrants. But in addition, as was noted earlier, recent immigrants have both lower wages and lower likelihood of employment, and this reduces the taxes they generate. As time passes, the wages received by immigrants will increase and, as their children age and complete their schooling, the net impact of the immigrants on government finances will turn positive. Eventually, as workers retire, they may again constitute a drain on government resources, depending on their access to social security and other safety nets for senior citizens. Figure 16.2b shows that in these conditions, immigrants will have a negative impact on the fiscal situation of the government in the short run, but a positive impact in the medium and long run.

In order to weigh short-run versus long-run effects, economists evaluating the fiscal effects of immigration make an assessment of the time profile of the costs and benefits of the immigrants, considering the fact that any future effects should be discounted relative to the present, and that the long-run effects last for a longer period of time than the short-run effects. They refer to these calculations as the *net discounted value* of the contribution of immigrants to the fiscal situation of the government. Although the results vary depending on the assumptions made about the future, most studies find that the net discounted value of the fiscal impact of immigrants is positive. For instance, the US National Academy of Sciences conducted a comprehensive study of the fiscal effects of immigration (Smith and Edmonston, 1995). They found the short-run effects to be significantly negative, but positive in the long run (see also DeVoretz and Werner, 2002, on the Canadian case).

It should be emphasized that not only do immigrants affect public finances, but also government transfer and spending policies can influence immigration. More generous transfer programs may attract greater inflows of immigrants, which may then magnify the fiscal costs of immigration to natives. Evidence on the issue is mixed, with some studies finding that immigrants are attracted to "welfare states" and others finding no such relation (see Borjas, 1999b , and Cohen and Razin, 2008).

The Impact on the Economic Welfare of Natives

As has been examined in this section, the impact of immigration on the economic welfare of natives in the host country may be quite complex to identify. Immigration may have a negative short-run impact on the workers in the recipient economy (lower wages and employment) as well as on public finances, but this may be ameliorated or even compensated by a number of other forces, particularly over the long run. At the same time, if wages do go down, this will benefit employers and the owners of those firms in the economy, as their production and profits rise. This explains why sectors which employ immigrants in recipient countries constantly lobby for relaxed immigration restrictions.

Overall, given the variety of results obtained in assessing the impact of immigration in host countries, both in terms of the labor market and the fiscal effects, one may share economist George Borjas' conclusion about the USA that "after accounting for the impact of immigration on the productivity of native workers and firms and on the fiscal ledger sheet, immigration probably has a small net economic impact on the United States" (Borjas, 1999a: 126).

VI. The Impact of Emigration in the Source Countries

This section begins by examining the labor market effects of emigration on those left behind. Later sections look at other consequences of emigration, including the impact on remittances.

Labor Market Effects of Emigration

At the theory level, the analysis of the labor market consequences of emigration for the population left behind in the source countries can go along lines similar to those followed by the discussion about the effects of immigration. Instead of examining an increase in the labor force, one could identify the opposite happening: a reduction in the domestic labor supply. As implied from the previous section, the direct impact of a reduced labor force in the source country would be to generate labor shortages and to increase wages. However, as was also noted before, there are a number of economic adjustments that can ameliorate or compensate the effects of the emigration. For instance, the higher wages might induce some local workers to increase their labor supply, thus softening the shortages of labor induced by the emigration.

The evidence suggests that the impact of emigration on home country labor markets may be substantial. Mishra (2007: 195) finds a significant impact of emigration on wages in Mexico. She concludes: "I find a strong and positive impact of the outflow of workers on wages in Mexico. A 10 % decrease in the number of Mexican workers due to emigration in a skill group (defined by schooling and experience), increases the average wage in that skill group by about 4 %. The estimates suggest that the outflow of Mexican workers to the United States between 1970 and 2000 has increased the wage of an average Mexican worker by about 8 %."

This impact means that workers left behind gain while employers using them lose. Is there any net impact from these distributional changes? In her paper, Mishra concludes that "the gain to the workers who have stayed behind is 5.9 % of GDP and the loss to the owners of fixed factors is 6.4 % of GDP." The net impact in the economic welfare of those left behind is, therefore, negative but comparatively small. On the other hand, there are other potential impacts of emigration, as discussed next.

Table 16.5 International migrant remittances, 2009

Country/Region	Remittances in current $ (millions)	Remittances in PPP-adjusted $ (millions)
Overall	420,210	648,320
High-income countries	102,873	94,239
Low- and middle-income countries	317,237	554,081
East Asia and Pacific	84,785	148,373
Latin America and the Caribbean	58,481	102,342
South Asia	71,955	125,921
Europe and Central Asia	48,279	84,787
Middle East and North Africa	32,212	56,740
Sub-Saharan Africa	20,525	35,918

Source: Data for remittances in current $ are taken from Ratha et al. (2009); other indicator is author's calculations using PPP adjustments from World Bank (2010).

Remittances and the Impact of Emigration

One of the most visible impacts of the migrants on source countries is connected to the remittances that they send back home. A vast literature has grown examining the effects of remittances on development (see Asian Development Bank, 2006, and United Nations, 2009).

Table 16.5 presents the value of migrant remittances in 2009. That year, source countries in the world received $420 billion in remittances from their migrants abroad. But the real value of these remittances is greater since each dollar buys much more in most countries than in the USA. Therefore, when one adjusts the $420 billion for differences in purchasing power, the value of the remittances in 2009 was $648 billion. Most of these remittances are being received by developing countries. In fact, in 2009, developing nations received $554 billion in remittances in purchasing power-adjusted dollars. The regions receiving the most remittances were South Asia and East Asia.

Remittances have been growing rapidly since 1980. Developing countries received close to $50 billion in migrant remittances in 1980 (in 2010 international dollars), but by 2009 this had multiplied to over $600 billion. The significance of remittances in many developing countries can be seen by comparing the value of remittances with the value of the merchandise goods exported by the source countries. Table 16.6 shows this calculation. In India, for instance, migrant remittances are equal to 26.2 per cent of merchandise exports. In the Philippines, the comparable figure is close to 38.7 per cent, in Egypt it is 60.4 per cent, and in Lebanon, it is over 155 per cent.

Table 16.6 Migrant remittances in developing countries, largest recipients, 2009

Country/Region	Remittances in Current $ (millions)	Remittances in PPP-adjusted $ (millions)	Remittances in merchandise as a % of exports
Developing countries	317,237	554,081	6.3%
India	47,000	136,147	26.2%
China, People's Republic	46,989	85,880	5.8
Mexico	22,870	32,566	7.8
Philippines	19,411	36,919	38.7
Bangladesh	10,431	28,019	67.9
Nigeria	9,585	14,685	11.7
Pakistan	8,619	22,073	42.3
Romania	8,000	11,569	23.4
Egypt	7,800	21,253	60.4
Lebanon	7,000	11,986	155.5
Vietnam	6,901	18,380	11.0
Indonesia	6,639	11,806	8.5
Morocco	5,720	8,806	28.5
Russian Federation	5,506	7,409	1.2
Serbia	5,438	8,426	49.5
Brazil	4,910	6,166	2.5
Colombia	4,273	6,940	11.1
Guatemala	4,065	6,794	52.3
El Salvador	3,460	6,525	76.1
Dominican Republic	3,344	5,937	48.4
Jordan	3,650	5,556	46.9

Source: Data for remittances in current $ are taken from Ratha et al. (2009); other indicators are author's calculations using PPP adjustments and exports from World Bank (2010).

Remittances clearly constitute an improvement in the standard of living for family members who are recipients of such income. Recent evidence suggests that remittances are connected to lower poverty levels (see Adams, 2007, and Acosta et al., 2008). Some questions have been raised over the years as to the extent to which the remittances simply raise current consumption instead of stimulating investment and future economic growth. However, the fact is that a significant portion of so-called consumption spending consists of household investments in housing, automobiles, and durable goods, whose long-term wealth-raising capacities are substantial; second, the use of remittances for community investment projects is not insignificant and also acts to stimulate local development; and, third, the multiplier effects of the increased consumption spending in generating local economic activity may be substantial (see Adams, 2007 and Yang, 2008).

The Impact of Skilled Emigration and the Economics of the Brain Drain

The positive contribution of migrant remittances for economic development must be weighed against the potentially negative consequences of the migration flows. In countries where emigration leads to the loss of the most talented and skilled, the so-called brain drain, migration can have negative externalities (for analyses of the effects of the brain drain, see Bhagwati and Rodriguez, 1975; Bhagwati, 1979; and Docquier, Lohest, and Marfouk, 2007).

If the emigration of skilled labor is substantial and these workers are employed in local service sectors, the result can be acute shortages in the supply of essential services, from school teachers and doctors to professors and nurses. Note that the emigration of workers employed in sectors that produce exports and imports is not subject to these effects because local consumers can import these products from abroad when the laborers leave the country. But when the workers are employed in service sectors that produce internationally non-traded goods, the impact of emigration is more significant and potentially disastrous because domestic consumers can only obtain those services locally (see Rivera-Batíz, 1982). If doctors and nurses emigrate, the supply of health services can collapse, resulting in higher prices and acute shortages. A brain drain can therefore reduce sharply the economic welfare of those left behind. Remittances may or may not offset these negative effects (Djajic, 1986).

The potentially negative effects of skilled emigration, combined with the fact that many developing countries pay dearly for their investments in the schooling of workers who emigrate, has generated a set of policy proposals seeking to remedy the situation. The so-called Bhagwati tax seeks to impose a duty on the income earned by emigrants abroad (Bhagwati, 1979). The flow of revenues missing from the coffers of developing countries may be substantial (Desai et al., 2009). Some, however, have questioned whether such a policy provides disincentives for emigration and whether it can be managed effectively.

Skilled emigration can have a number of additional effects. First, demographers have argued that the emigration of workers from an economy has a deep, negative impact on savings and the accumulation of physical capital. Emigration of working age people tends to reduce the share of the population that is productively engaged. This means that the dependency rate in the economy—the proportion of senior citizens and children in the population—rises, which tends to absorb resources that would otherwise be dedicated to the accumulation of capital and economic growth. A second phenomenon is that working age people tend to have higher savings rates than other people. The reason is that they wish to accumulate funds for their later years, when they may retire. As emi-grants move out of an economy, therefore, the savings rate may decline, thus reducing economic growth. These effects appear to be significant since the available empirical evidence suggests that the emigration of economically active workers reduces economic growth in the sending countries (Bloom and Williamson, 1998).

Another issue is that the emigration of skilled labor directly reduces the human capi-tal available to those left behind in source countries. This can potentially have a devastat-ing effect on economic growth. The reason is that one of the main sources of economic growth is technological change. The innovation of new products and new technologies is what lies behind a significant part of both trade and economic success in a modern economy. But if human capital flees, then the ability of those left behind to sustain inno-vation and technical change may be compromised, thus reducing an economy's growth. On the other hand, there are important caveats to this point. The evidence shows that public sector governance is central in the process of generating long-run economic growth. If, because of poor governance, domestic skilled workers end up employed in low productivity sectors, then the emigration of these workers may have a minimal impact on local growth

In addition, there may be reasons to expect some positive externalities of skilled emi-gration on source countries. First of all, some researchers have recently suggested that a brain drain may actually lead to a brain gain by raising the level of schooling of the population in the source country, at least in the long run. One hypothesis is that the emi-gration of skilled workers will raise the wages of the workers that remain at home, thus increasing the rate of return to education. As a result, more young people in the country will decide to pursue higher education, raising educational attainment. Another mecha-nism may be linked to remittances. If the remittances are used by households to offset local capital market imperfections (credit constraints) that have not allowed them to invest in human capital, then the emigration will stimulate the school enrollment of the children of migrants (Amuedo-Dorantes and Pozo, 2006). Although a brain drain will directly reduce the stock of human capital (negative effect), it may lead to an increase in the level of schooling of the population left behind (positive effect). And by fostering financial sector development, the remittances may have a further positive effect on local growth (Giulano and Ruiz-Arranz, 2009).

Despite the recent research on the positive effects of remittances on education in source countries, there is still a question of how much skilled emigrants remit, when compared to other migrants (see Faini, 2007) and the empirical evidence on the brain gain is mixed (see Schiff, 2005, and Beine, Docquier, and Rapoport, 2008).

Finally, the brain drain may result in a loss of economies of scale among scientific and technological communities at home. But, on the other hand, they may generate interna-tional networks that could enhance the scientific and technological capacities at home. Evidence on the relative significance of these two effects is mixed. There is significant evidence that the presence of scientific and technical networks, developed on the basis of ethnicity—combining source and host countries—has developed and contributed to business creation, innovation, international trade, and foreign direct investment in a number of developing countries, including China and India among others (see Gould,

1994; Combes et al., 2005; Burns and Mohapatra, 2008; Kerr, 2008; Docquier and Lodigiani, 2010; and Javorcik et al., 2011). There may be, hence, a strong complementarity between international labor, trade, and capital flows, all integrated by diaspora networks (see Rauch and Trindade, 2002; Pandey et al., 2006; Kugler and Rapoport, 2007; and Kuznetsov and Sabel, 2006).

VII. INTERNATIONAL MIGRATION AND THE WORLD TRADE ORGANIZATION

The international movement of workers is not an area of international trade that is under the general jurisdiction of the World Trade Organization (WTO). However, the WTO does consider specific migration flows as part of its GATS. The GATS is a multilateral, voluntary, and legally enforceable agreement covering international trade in services. International migration flows enter as part of GATS so long as the workers are producing or consuming a service.

Both conceptually and statistically, a sharp distinction exists between goods and services. Goods relate to tangible products that are usually produced in one location at a certain point of time, and then later transferred and sold in other locations. Services generally involve outputs that are more intangible and tend to be produced, transferred, and consumed at the same time and in the same location. The international Standard Industrial Technical Classification (SITC) system of economic sectors considers services to include: wholesale and retail trade; transportation, storage, and communications; finance, real estate, and insurance; business, professional, and technical services; travel and tourism services; and personal, community, and social services. Educational services are included as part of the last category, which also includes health services, cultural services, and so on.

Any transactions that occur between residents of a country and non-residents are considered to be international transactions. Historically, international trade has consisted mostly of trade in merchandise goods. Whether in the form of agricultural products, mining, or manufacturing, world trade has been dominated by trade in goods. In 2000, for example, trade in merchandise goods accounted for 82 per cent of all world trade. Over the last 20 years, however, trade in services has been rising rapidly. In recent years, the value of trade in services has been increasing at a growth rate of close to 10 per cent per year. Higher education services constitute one of the categories of greatest growth.

There are four modes of international trade in services considered by GATS:

Mode 1: Cross-border supply focuses on the service crossing the border, but does not require the consumer to move physically. Examples include distance education and e-learning.

Mode 2: Consumption abroad refers to the consumer migrating or moving to the country of the supplier, which is the case of students pursuing all or part of their education in another country, as has been documented above.

Mode 3: Commercial presence involves a service provider establishing a commercial facility in another country to provide a service. Examples include a US software developer setting up a branch in China.

Mode 4: Presence of natural persons, means persons traveling to another country on a temporary basis to provide a service, which may be in the form of contract labor, consulting services, technical assistance, educational services, and so on.

Temporary labor migration flows are clearly included as part of the GATS Mode 4 trade in services. The migration of people to buy educational services, that is, the flow of international students, is included as part of Mode 2 trade.

The presence of barriers to trade in services acts to severely restrict temporary migration across borders. The impact of trade liberalization in this area would thus serve to increase migration flows. The impact of such liberalization on host and source countries is a policy issue that is currently being discussed as part of the Doha Round of GATS negotiations. The discussion of the impact of GATS-related migration flows can be discussed using the same methodology developed earlier to examine the effects of other migration flows (see Winters, 2002).

VIII. Conclusions

This chapter has provided a detailed discussion of the key recent trends in international migration, the determinants of migration flows, the consequences for the source and host countries, and the relationships between migration flows and international trade in services. The most recent theory and evidence available on the globalization of labor flows has been presented.

The globalization of labor flows has proceeded in the same direction as the globalization of trade flows. Migration flows have accelerated since the 1990s. Even developing countries themselves have become substantial recipients of immigrants. Some of the major importers of labor in the developing world include India, Russia and other former Soviet Republics, Saudi Arabia, Pakistan, and Iran.

The growth of migration flows in recent years responds to a variety of forces. Some of these are: the relaxation of immigration policies in high-income economies; the sustained and sometimes widening gaps in income and employment opportunities between high-income and developing countries; demographics that cause low or negative population growth rates in recipient countries and high rates in source countries; reduced transport costs and rising regional economic integration; and the growth of closely knit networks of household members across source and destination countries.

The economic returns to migration are substantial and a vast literature has developed calculating those returns. But there are a number of forces that can depress the labor market outcomes of migrants relative to non-immigrants in host countries. One of them is the duration of stay of the migrants in the country: immigrants generally face an initial shortfall or dip in their labor market performance after they arrive in a recipient country. A second force that may explain a shortfall in the economic performance of immigrants relative to non-immigrants is the selectivity of the migration process. Given the effort required by the emigration process, migrants are generally positively selected, displaying unusual motivation and drive. But if emigrants are negatively selected out of the source country population, they will have lower skills and may not perform as well in the host countries.

Mass immigration flows often generate fears among natives in immigration countries. Concerns arise about potentially negative effects on wages and employment possibilities. Some fear that immigrants overuse public services and may in fact move to countries or regions that have a more generous welfare state. The evidence presented in this chapter on these issues is mixed. In countries with flexible labor and capital markets, immigration does not appear to generate significant negative effects on wages or employment, especially over the long run. Immigrants tend to cluster in specific occupations and sectors, with relatively little competition with natives. In some cases, the migrants may in fact be complementary with natives, raising their wages and employment opportunities. Employers that utilize immigrants may not survive international competition without the availability of the migrants and both their income as well as the earnings of the natives they employ is positively affected by immigration. On the other hand, in economies where domestic capital mobility is sluggish, and goods and labor markets are rigid, immigration may have a significant negative labor market effect, especially in the short run.

Although the majority of migrants from developing countries are relatively unskilled, skilled emigration is significant, and its impact remains a matter of serious debate. The highest skilled emigration rates in the world are in the Caribbean, where as much as 42.8 per cent of the region's tertiary labor force resides outside its borders. There are also relatively high rates of skilled emigration in Africa.

When emigration leads to the loss of the most skilled, as in the so-called brain drain, it can have substantial negative externalities. If the emigrants are employed in local service (non-traded goods) sectors, the result can be acute shortages in the supply of essential services, from school teachers and nurses to professors and doctors, having a devastating effect on those left behind. But in recent years, it has been recognized that what appears as a brain drain may also generate a brain gain, whether because remittances are used to raise the schooling of children back home, or by generating business ties and greater trade and investment between source and recipient economies.

But any potentially negative effects of emigrants must be weighed against the benefits of the remittances sent by the migrants to their families back home. In 2009, developing nations received $554 billion worth of remittances. For some countries, remittances are a major component of the balance of payments. Although remittances are often used for purely consumption purposes, in many countries they are used for wealth-enhancing activities, such as to develop a small business, for construction purposes, to buy automobiles or consumer durables, or to invest in the schooling of children.

The international movement of workers is not an area of international trade that is under the general jurisdiction of the WTO. However, the WTO does consider temporary migration flows as part of its General Agreement on Trade in Services (GATS). International migration enters as part of GATS so long as the workers are producing or consuming a service. But WTO involvement with migration issues remains in its infancy.

The rising trend in global migration flows as well as the presence of substantial movements of undocumented immigrants suggests that global coordination of these flows is needed. Most high-income countries seek to reform their immigration laws without collaboration with sending countries, a strategy that has often led to failure. The same can be said of taxation policies affecting migrants. There is therefore substantial room for coordinated international migration policies to emerge as a major topic in global international trade and development discussions.

References

Acosta, P., Calderón, C., Fajnzylber, P., and López, H. (2008), 'What is the Impact of International Remittances on Poverty and Inequality in Latin America?' *World Development*, 36(1): 89–114.

Adams, R. (2007), 'International Remittances and the Household: Analysis and Review of Global Evidence' Policy Research Working Paper No. 4116. Washington, DC: The World Bank.

Altonji, J. G., and Card, D. (1991), 'The Effects of Immigration on the Labor market Outcomes of Less Skilled Natives' in Abowd, J. M., and Freeman, R. (eds.) *Immigration, Trade and the Labor Market*. Chicago: University of Chicago Press, 201–34.

Amuedo-Dorantes, C. and Pozo, S. (2006), 'Remittances as Insurance: Evidence from Mexican Immigrants' *Journal of Population Economics*, 19(2): 227–54.

Asian Development Bank (2006), *Workers' Remittances Flows in Southeast Asia*. Manila: Asian Development Bank.

Basilio, L., and Bauer, T. (2010), 'Transferability of Human Capital and Immigrant Assimilation: An Analysis for Germany' IZA Discussion Paper No. 4716 Bonn: Institute for the Study of Labor.

Bauer, T., Epstein, G., and Gang, I. N. (2009), 'Measuring Ethnic Linkages among Migrants' *International Journal of Manpower*, 30(1): 56–69.

Beine, M., Docquier, F., and Rapoport, H. (2007), 'Measuring International Skilled Migration: a New Database Controlling for Age of Entry' *World Bank Economic Review*, 21(2): 249–54.

Beine, M., Docquier, F., and Rapoport, H. (2008), ' Brain Drain and Human Capital Formation in Developing Countries: Winners and Losers,' *Economic Journal*, 118(528): 631–53.

Benhabib, J. (1996), 'On the Political Economy of Immigration' *Economic European Review*, 40(9): 1737–43.

Bhagwati, J. N. (1979), 'International Migration of the Highly Skilled: Economics, Ethics and Taxes' *Third World Quarterly*, 1(3): 17–30.

Bhagwati, J. N., and Rodriguez, C. (1975), 'Welfare-Theoretical Analyses of the Brain Drain' *Journal of Development Economics*, 2(3): 195–221.

Bhagwati, J. N., Panagariya, A., and Srinivasan, T. N, (1998), *Lectures on International Trade*, Second Edition. Cambridge, MA: The MIT Press.

Bloom, D. E., and Williamson, J. (1998), 'Demographic Transitions and Economic Miracles in Emerging Asia' *World Bank Economic Review*, 12(3): 419–55.

Borjas, G. J. (1987), 'Self-Selection and the Earnings of Immigrants' *American Economic Review*, 77(4): 531–53.

Borjas, G. J. (1999a), *Heaven's Door: Immigration Policy and the American Economy*. Princeton, NJ: Princeton University Press.

Borjas, G. J. (1999b), 'Immigration and Welfare Magnets' *Journal of Labor Economics*, 17(4): 607–28.

Borjas, G. J., and Katz, L. (2007), 'The Evolution of the Mexican-Born Workforce in the United States' in Borjas, G. J. (ed.), *Mexican Immigration to the United States*. Chicago: University of Chicago Press, 13–56.

Borjas, G. J., Grogger, J., and Hanson, G. H. (2008), 'Imperfect Substitution Between Immigrants and Natives: A Reappraisal' Working Paper No. 13887. Cambridge, MA: National Bureau of Economic Research.

Burns, A., and Mohapatra, S. (2008), 'International Migration and Technological Progress' Migration and Development Brief No. 4. Washington, DC: The World Bank.

Card, D. (1990), 'The Impact of the Mariel Boatlift on the Miami Labor Market' *Industrial and Labor Relations Review*, 43(1): 245–57.

Card, D. (2005), 'Is the New Immigration Really So Bad?' *Economic Journal*, 115(4): F300–F323.

Card, D., and Shleifer, A. (2009), 'Immigration and Inequality' *American Economic Review*, 99(2): 1–21.

Carrington, W. J., and Detragiache, E. (1998), 'How Big is the Brain Drain?' Working Paper No. 98/102. Washington, DC: International Monetary Fund.

Castaldo, A., Litchfield, J., and Reilly, B. (2007), 'Who is Most Likely to Migrate from Albania? Evidence from the Albania Living Standards Measurement Study' *Eastern European Economics*, 45(5): 69–94.

Chiquiar, D., and Hanson, G. (2005), 'International Migration, Self-Selection, and the Distribution of Wages: Evidence from Mexico and the United States' *Journal of Political Economy*, 113(2): 239–81.

Chiswick, B. (1978), 'The Effects of Americanization on the Earnings of Foreign-Born Men' *Journal of Political Economy*, 86(5): 897–922.

Chiswick, B. (2000), 'Are Immigrants Favorably Selected?' *American Economic Review*, 89(3): 181–85.

Chiswick, B. and Miller, P. (2004), 'Language Skills and Earnings among Legalized Aliens' in Zimmermann, K., and Constant, A. (eds.), *How Labor Migrants Fare*. Berlin: Springer-Verlag, 279–306.

Chojnicki, X., Docquier, F., and Rago, L. (2010), 'Should the U.S. Have Locked Heaven's Door? Reassessing the Benefits of Post-War Immigration' *Journal of Population Economics*, 24(1): 317–59.

Clemens, M., Montenegro, C., and Pritchett, L. (2008), 'The Place Premium: Wage Differences for Identical Workers across the U.S. Border' Policy Research Working Paper No. 4671. Washington, DC: The World Bank.

Cohen, A., and Razin, R. (2008), 'The Skill Composition of Immigrants and the Generosity of the Welfare State: Free vs. Policy-Controlled Migration' Working Paper 14459. Cambridge, MA.: National Bureau of Economic Research.

Cohen, A. and Razin, A. (2008), 'The Skill Composition of Immigrants and the Generosity of the Welfare State: Free vs. Policy-Controlled Migration' Working Paper 14459. Cambridge, MA: National Bureau of Economic Research.

Combes, P. P., Lafourcade, M., and Mayer, T. (2005), 'The Trade-Creating Effects of Business and Social Networks: Evidence from France' *Journal of International Economics*, 66(1): 1–29.

Constant, A. F., and Zimmermann, K. (2009), 'Migration, Ethnicity and Economic Integration' IZA Discussion Paper No. 4620. Bonn: Institute for the Study of Labor.

Desai, M. A., Kapur, D., McHale, J., and Rogers, K. (2009), 'The Fiscal Impact of High-Skilled Emigration: Flows of Indians to the U.S.' *Journal of Development Economics*, 88(1): 32–44.

DeVoretz, D., and Werner, C. (2002). 'Canada: An Entrepot Destination for Immigrants?' in Rotte, R., and Stein, P (eds.), *Migration Policy and the Economy: International Experiences.* Muenchen, Germany: Hanns-Seidel Foundation, 37–56.

Djajic, S. (1986), 'International Migration, Remittances and Welfare in a Dependent Economy' *Journal of Development Economics*, 21(2): 229–34.

Docquier, F., Lohest, O., and Marfouk, A. (2007), 'Brain Drain in Developing Countries' *World Bank Economic Review*, 21(2): 193–218.

Docquier, F., and Marfouk, A. (2006), 'International Migration by Educational Attainment: 1990–2000' in Özden, C., and Schiff, M. (eds.), *International Migration, Remittances and the Brain Drain.* Washington, DC: The World Bank, 151–99.

Docquier, F., and Lodigiani, E. (2010), 'Skilled Migration and Business Networks' *Open Economies Review*, 21(4): 565–88.

Duleep, H. and Regets, M. (2000), 'Immigrants and Human-Capital Investment' *American Economic Review*, 89(2): 186–91.

European Commission (2006), *The Demographic Future of Europe: Challenges and Opportunities.* Brussels: European Commission.

Faini, R. (2007), 'Remittances and the Brain Drain: Do More Skilled Migrants Remit More?', *World Bank Economic Review* 21(2): 177–91.

Fernandez-Huertas Moraga, J. (2011), 'New Evidence on Emigrant Selection' *Review of Economics and Statistics*, 93(1): 72–96.

Gang, I. N., and Rivera-Batíz, F. L. (1994a), 'Unemployment and Attitudes towards Foreigners in Germany' in Steinmann, G., and Ulrich, R. (eds.), *The Economics of Immigration in Germany.* Berlin: Springer-Verlag, 121–54.

Gang, I. N., and Rivera-Batíz, F. L. (1994b), 'The Labor Market Effects of Immigration in the United States and Europe: Substitution vs. Complementarity' *Journal of Population Economics*, 7(2): 157–75.

Gang, I. N., Rivera-Batíz, F. L. and Yun, M.-S. (2010), 'Changes in Attitudes towards Immigrants in Europe: Before and After the Fall of the Berlin Wall' in Epstein, G., and Gang, I. N. (eds.), *Migration and Culture*, (Frontiers of Economics and Globalization Volume 8). Bingley, UK: Emerald Group Publishing.

Gang, I. N., Rivera-Batíz, F. L. and Yun, M.S. (2013), 'Economic Strain, Education, and Attitudes towards Foreigners in the European Union', *Review of International Economics*, 21(2): 177–90.

Gibson, J., and McKenzie, D. (2009), 'The Microeconomic Determinants of Emigration and Return Migration of the Best and Brightest: Evidence from the Pacific', IZA Discussion paper No. 3926. Bonn: Institute for the Study of Labor.

Giulano, P., and Ruiz-Arranz, M. (2009), 'Remittances, Financial Development and Growth' *Journal of Development Economics*, 90(1): 144–52.

Gould, D.M. (1994), 'Immigrant Links to the Home Country: Empirical Implications for U.S. Bilateral Trade Flows' *The Review of Economics and Statistics*, 76(2): 302–16.

Grogger, J., and Hanson, G. H. (2008), 'Income Maximization and the Selection and Sorting of International Migrants' Working Paper No. 13821. Cambridge, MA: National Bureau of Economic Research.

Gustman, A., and Steinmeier, T. (2000), 'Social Security Benefits of Immigrants and U.S. Born' in Borjas, G. (ed.) *Issues in the Economics of Immigration.* Chicago: University of Chicago Press, 309–50.

Hanson, G. (2006), 'Illegal Migration from Mexico to the United States' *Journal of Economic Literature*, 44(4): 869–924.

Hanson, G. (2007), 'Emigration, Labor Supply and Earnings in Mexico' in Borjas, G. (ed.), *Mexican Immigration.* Chicago: University of Chicago Press, 289–328.

Hanson, G. (2009), 'The Economic Consequences of the International Migration of Labor' *Annual Review of Economics*, 1: 179–207.

Hanson, G. (2010), 'International Migration and the Developing World' in Rodrik, R., and Rosenzweig, M. (eds.) *Handbook of Development Economics*, Vol. 5. The Netherlands: North-Holland, 4363–4414.

Hanson, G. and Spilimbergo, A. (1999), 'Illegal Immigration, Border Enforcement, and Relative Wages: Evidence from Apprehensions at the U.S.-Mexico Border' *American Economic Review*, 89: 1337–57.

Hanson, G., Scheve, K., and Slaughter, M. (2007), 'Public Finance and Individual Preferences over Globalization Strategies' *Economics & Politics*, 19(1): 1–33.

Hatton, T., and Williamson, J. (2005), *'Global Migration and the World Economy: Two Centuries of Policy and Performance.* Cambridge, MA: The MIT Press.

Hoefer, M., Rytina, N., and Baker, B. (2010), *Estimates of the Unauthorized Immigrant Population Residing in the United States: January 2009.* Washington, DC: United States Department of Homeland Security Office of Immigration Statistics.

Javorcik, B, Özden, C., Spatareanu, M., and Neagu, C. (2011), 'Migrant Networks and Foreign Direct Investment' *Journal of Development Economics*, 94(2): 231–41.

Kaas, L. and Manger, C. (2010), 'Ethnic Discrimination in Germany's Labor Market: A Field Experiment' IZA Discussion Paper No. 4741. Bonn: Institute for the Study of Labor.

Kamemera, D., Oguledo, V., and Davis, B. (2000), 'A Gravity Model Analysis of International Migration to North America' *Applied Economics*, 32(13): 1745–55.

Kerr, W. R. (2008), 'The Ethnic Composition of U.S. Inventors' Working Paper No. 08–006. Cambridge, MA: Harvard Business School.

Kovacheva, V. and Vogel, D. (2009), 'The Size of the Irregular Foreign Resident Population in the European Union in 2002, 2005 and 2008: Aggregated Estimates' Working Paper No. 4/2009. Hamburg: Hamburg Institute of International Economics.

Kugler, M. and Rapoport, H. (2007), 'International Labor and Capital Flows: Complements or Substitutes?' *Economics Letters*, 92(2): 155–62.

Kuznetsov, Y., and Sabel, S. (2006), 'International Migration of Talent, Diaspora Networks and Development: Overview of Main Issues' in Kuznetsov, Y. (ed.), *Diaspora Networks and the International Migration of Skills.* Washington, DC: World Bank, 3–20.

Lowry, I. S. (1966), *Migration and Metropolitan Growth: Two Analytical Models.* San Francisco: Chandler Publishing Company.

Lucas, R. E. B. (1985), 'Migration among the Batswana' *Economic Journal*, 95(2): 358–82.

Massey, D. (1988) 'Economic Development and International Migration in Comparative Perspective' *Population and Development Review*, 14 (3): 383–413.

Massey, D., Alarcon, R., Durand, J., and Gonzalez, H. (1987), *Return to Aztlan: The Social Process of International Migration from Western Mexico.* Berkeley: University of California Press.

Mayda, A., M. (2006), 'Who Is Against Immigration? A Cross Country Investigation of Individual Attitudes towards Immigrants' *Review of Economics and Statistics*, 88(3): 510–30.

Mayda, A. M. (2008), 'Why are People More Pro-Free Trade than Pro-Migration?' *Economics Letters*, December, 101(3): 160–63.

Mayda, A. M. (2010), 'International Migration: A Panel Data Analysis of Economic and Non-Economic Determinants' *Journal of Population Economics*, 23(4): 1249–74.

Mayda, A. M., and Patel, K. (2006), 'International Migration Flows: The Role of Destination Countries' Migration Policies' Working Paper. Washington, DC: Center for Strategic and International Studies.

McKenzie, D. J. (2008), 'A Profile of the World's Young Developing Country Migrants' *Population and Development Review*, 34(1): 115–35.

Mishra, P. (2007), 'Emigration and Wages in Source Countries: Evidence from Mexico' *Journal of Development Economics*, 82(1): 180–95.

Mullan, F. (2005), 'The Metrics of the Physician Brain Drain' *New England Journal of Medicine*, 353(17): 1810–18.

Organization for Economic Cooperation and Development (2006), *International Migration Outlook 2006.* Paris: OECD.

Organization for Economic Cooperation and Development (2009), *International Migration Outlook 2009.* Paris: OECD.

Organization for Economic Cooperation and Development (2013), *International Migration Outlook 2013.* Paris: OECD.

Ortega, F. (2005), 'Immigration Quotas and Skill Upgrading' *Journal of Public Economics* 89(9–10): 1841–63.

Ortega, F. (2008), 'The Short-Run Effects of a Large Immigration Wave: The Case of Spain 1998-2008' Working paper. Barcelona: Universitat Pompeu Fabra.

Ortega, F., and Peri, G. (2009), 'The Causes and Effects of International Labor Mobility: Evidence from OECD Countries1980-2005' Human Development Research Paper. New York: United Nations Development Program.

Ottaviano, G. and Peri, G. (2005), 'Rethinking the Gains from Immigration: Theory and Evidence from the US' Working Paper 11672. Cambridge, MA: National Bureau of Economic Research.

Ottaviano, G. and Peri, G. (2008), 'Immigration and National Wages: Clarifying the Theory and the Empirics' Working Paper 14188. Cambridge, MA: National Bureau of Economic Research.

Pandey, A., Aggarwal, A., Devane, R., and Kuznetsov, Y. (2006), 'The Indian Diaspora: A Unique Case?' in Kuznetsov, Y. (ed.), *Diaspora Networks and the International Migration of Skills.* Washington, DC: The World Bank, 71–97.

Parsons, C., Skeldon, R., Walmsley, T., and Winters, L. A. (2007), 'Quantifying the International Bilateral Movement of Migrants' in Özden, O., and Schiff, M. (eds.) *International Migration Policy and Economic Development: Studies Across the Globe.* Washington, DC: The World Bank, 17–58.

Peracchi, F. and Depalo, D. (2006), 'Labor Market Outcomes of Natives and Immigrants: Evidence from the ECHP' Social Protection Working Paper. Washington, DC: The World Bank.

Peri, G. (2006), 'Immigrants' Complementarities and Native Wages: Evidence from California' Working Paper. Cambridge: National Bureau of Economic Research.

Peri, G. (2009), 'Migration and Trade: Theory with an Application to the Eastern–Western European Integration' *Journal of International Economics*, 79 (1): 1–19.

Peri, G. and Sparber, C. (2009), 'Task Specialization, Immigration and Wages' *American Economic Journal: Applied Economics*, 1(3):135–69.

Piore, M. J. (1979). *Birds of Passage: Migrant Labor and Industrial Societies*. New York: Cambridge University Press.

Pritchett, L. (2006), *Let Their People Come: Breaking the Gridlock on Global Labor Mobility*. Washington, DC: Center for Global Development.

Ratha, D., Mohapatra, S., and Silwal, A. (2009), 'Migration and Remittance Trends 2009' Migration and Development Brief No. 11. Washington, DC: The World Bank.

Rauch, J. and Trindade, V. (2002), 'Ethnic Chinese Networks in International Trade' *Review of Economics and Statistics*, 84(1): 116–30.

Rivera-Batíz, F. L. (1982), 'International Migration, Nontraded Goods and Economic Welfare in the Source Country' *Journal of Development Economics*, 11(1): 81–90.

Rivera-Batíz, Francisco L. (1983), 'Trade Theory, Distribution of Income, and Immigration' *American Economic Review*, 73(2):183–87.

Rivera-Batíz, F. L. (1986), 'Can Border Industries Reduce Immigration to the U.S.?' *American Economic Review*, 76(2): 263–68.

Rivera-Batíz, F. L. (1990), 'English Language Proficiency and the Economic Progress of Immigrants' *Economics Letters*, 34(2): 295–300.

Rivera-Batíz, F. L. (1999), 'Undocumented Workers in the Labor Market: An Analysis of the Earnings of Legal and Illegal Mexican Immigrants in the United States' *Journal of Population Economics*, 12(1): 91–116.

Rivera-Batíz, F. L. (2004), 'NewYorktitlán: The Socioeconomic Status of Mexican New Yorkers' *Regional Labor Review*, 6(1): 33–45.

Rivera-Batíz, F. L. (2007), 'How Do Migrants from Latin America and the Caribbean Fare in U.S. Labor Markets?' *The World Economy*, 30(9): 1399–1429.

Rivera-Batíz, F. L., and Sechzer, S. L. (1991), 'Substitution and Complementarity Between Immigrant and Native Labor in the United States' in Rivera-Batíz, F., Sechzer, S., and Gang, I. (eds.), *U.S. Immigration Policy Reform in the 1980s: A Preliminary Assessment*. New York: Praeger Publishers, 89–116.

Scheve, K., and Slaughter, M. (2001), 'Labor Market Competition and Individual Preferences Over Immigration Policy' *Review of Economics and Statistics*, 83(1): 133–45.

Schiff, M. (2005), 'Brain Gain: Claims about its Size and Impact on Welfare and Growth are Greatly Exaggerated' in Özden, C., and Schiff, M. *International Migration, Remittances and the Brain Drain*. Washington, DC: The World Bank, 201–26.

Schmidt, C. (1997), 'Immigrant Performance in Germany: Labor Earnings of Ethnic German Migrants and Foreign Guest Workers' *The Quarterly Review of Economics and Finance*, 37(2), 279–397.

Sjaastad, Larry (1962), 'The Costs and Returns of Human Migration' *Journal of Political Economy*, 70(5, Part 2): S80–S93.

Smith, R. S., and Edmonston, B. (1995), 'Panel on the Demographic and Economic Impacts of Immigration' in National Research Council (eds.), *The New Americans: Economic, Demographic and Fiscal Effects of Immigration*. Washington, DC: National Academy Press.

Stark, O., and Bloom, D. E. (1985), 'The New Economics of Labor Migration' *American Economic Review*, 75(2): 173–78.

Stark, O., and Taylor, J. E. (1991), 'Migration Incentives, Migration Types: The Role of Relative Deprivation' *Economic Journal*, 101(408): 1163–78.

United Nations (2009), *Human Development Report 2009: Overcoming Barriers: Human Mobility and Development*. New York: United Nations.

United Nations (2010), 'World Migrant Stock: the 2009 Revision Population Database' New York: The United Nations.

Waddington, H. and Sabates-Wheeler, R. (2003), 'How Does Poverty Affect Migration Choice?' Development Research Centre on Migration, Globalization and Poverty, Working Paper. Sussex: University of Sussex.

Warren, R. and Warren, J. R. (2013), 'Unauthorized Immigration to the U.S.: Annual Estimates and Components of Change, by State, 1990 to 2010', *International Migration Review*, 47(2): 296–325.

Winters, L. A. (2002), 'The Economic Implications of Liberalizing Mode 4 Trade' Paper presented at the joint WTO/World Bank Conference on The Movement of Natural Persons (Mode 4) under the GATS. Washington, DC: The World Bank.

World Bank (2008), *Migration and Remittances Factbook*. Washington, DC: The World Bank.

World Bank (2010), *World Development Indicators*. Washington, DC: The World Bank.

Yang, D. (2008), 'International Migration, Remittances, and Household Investment: Evidence from Philippine Migrants' Exchange Rate Shocks'. *Economic Journal*, 118(528): 591–630.

Zimmermann, K. and Constant, A. (2004), (eds.) *How Labor Migrants Fare?* Berlin: Springer-Verlag.

PART IV

IMPLEMENTING AND NEGOTIATING TRADING ARRANGEMENTS FOR THE TWENTY-FIRST CENTURY

CHAPTER 17

....

DEEP INTEGRATION IN PREFERENTIAL TRADE AGREEMENTS*

....

JEAN-CHRISTOPHE MAUR

I. INTRODUCTION

REGIONAL agreements are today less about preferential tariffs than they used to be and more about other market access, cooperation, and even non-economic dimensions. This is partly the outcome of a wave of regionalism that is fueled by North–South agreements (Acharya et al., 2011) and the evolution of the global economy towards more integrated markets, including in their regulatory dimensions.

What are the implications for policymakers of this shift from goods towards non-goods and regulatory dimensions, or in other words deep integration? What are the sources of economic gains, if any, by liberalizing these policies areas? Do the traditional results and policy lessons of economic and political economic theory still hold in that context? Are trade creation and diversion concerns and, if so, what are the new barriers to trade? Does preferential liberalization create a stumbling or building block for further liberalization?

The basic answer to these questions provided in this chapter is that, indeed, different outcomes hold in the context of deep integration. This chapter offers an introduction into some of the reasons for this and the specific economic and policy questions that may be raised by the deep integration dimensions of preferential trade agreements (PTAs).

At the heart of the inquiry is the essentially different nature of liberalization at work with deep integration dimensions compared to tariff elimination. This difference in the nature of liberalization explains why different modalities of liberalization may be

* This chapter is adapted from Chauffour and Maur (2011: chapter 1). It reflects the sole views of the author and should not in any way be attributed to the World Bank.

needed, and also why PTAs may offer a possible answer. There are also different challenges posed by deep integration that policymakers should be well aware of before
entering into demanding liberalization commitments.

II. Analyzing the Evolution of PTAs: From Negative to Positive Integration

The Increasing Relevance of Deep Integration in Preferential Agreements

In the last 20 years, the growth in the number of PTAs has been unabated. Even
more strikingly, their scope has broadened while their number has increased.
The ambition of recent PTAs beyond tariff liberalization is illustrated by the general growth of agreements that include deep integration provisions. These provisions
include "traditional" ones like competition, investment, trade facilitation, standards, intellectual property (see Figure 17.1), but also procurement, labor, or environment.[1] In a recent study of US and EU PTAs, Horn et al. (2009) identify no less than

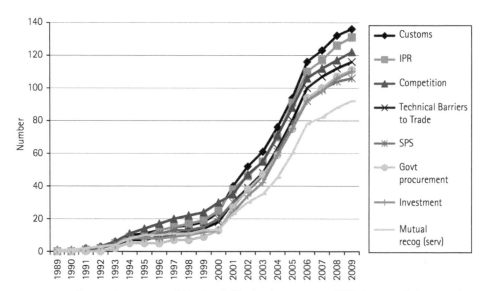

FIGURE 17.1 Deepening scope of Regional Trade Agreements (RTAs): cumulative number
of PTAs

Source: Acharya et al. (2011).

[1] The WTO RTA database currently includes only the commitments undertaken in PTAs notified
to the WTO following the introduction of the Transparency Mechanism in 2006 and to a lesser extent
agreements notified before December 2006. As a result, the sample covers currently about 45 per cent

38 areas in US and EU PTAs that aim to go beyond World Trade Organization (WTO) disciplines. While negotiations under the WTO have also pursued a similar path (for instance with the agreement on Trade-Related Aspects of Intellectual Property Rights (TRIPS) in 1995), nowhere is the ambition as high as in PTAs with the spreading of regulatory disciplines to non-trade areas such as environment and labor. This encompasses what has been call a WTO-plus agenda, on disciplines already included in the WTO, but often expanding on them in depth and breadth and seeking enforceability. A second and important dimension is that PTAs also incorporate numerous areas that are not covered by the WTO ("WTO-extra" measures), or are covered very imperfectly. In practice, PTAs often pursue both objectives but to a varying degree: US and Canadian PTAs for instance focus more on WTO-plus disciplines, adding a few WTO-extras to the mix. The EU on the other hand includes numerous WTO-extra aspects in its agreements. Thus, PTAs play both a substitute and complementary role in the WTO negotiations.

If Northern countries are leading the way into these new areas, there is also a general tendency to include commitments that go beyond tariffs, as is demonstrated by notifications of agreements to the WTO. Figure 17.1 shows the importance of these new areas.

A higher number of PTAs to manage with more disciplines is not the only problem that a country must face. It is apparent that the new measures are quite different in nature compared to traditional trade barriers (i.e., tariffs or quotas):

- they concern not solely traded goods and services, but also domestically produced ones;
- elimination of offending practices is not necessarily the main objective;
- their objective might be to protect the domestic market in some way, although not always, and in these instances is not systematically to protect domestic industries; their objective is not necessarily economic;
- there is not necessarily one universal way to liberalize;
- they are not necessarily in force in developing countries.

Thus, the growth of deep integration in both quantity and scope is posing a challenge for policymakers as they must cover an increasingly large and complex set of issues—of different natures—with limited administrative resources, both for negotiation and implementation.[2] This means that countries should either increase their negotiating capacity or prioritize the areas where they want to see reform (or likely both). A second point is that PTAs increasingly address policy areas that are entirely new to many developing countries

of PTAs notified to the WTO. The Authors complement the WTO information with other sources to provide a more accurate picture of the basic trends in the inclusion of additional commitments in PTAs. While the cumulative rise of agreements including such commitments is partly the outcome of the sample composition, the sheer volume of agreements with such provisions (compared with the total number of PTAs) in recent years indicates the level of interest in deeper integration in the context of preferential trading (Acharya et al., 2011).

[2] It is not uncommon that secretariats of PTAs among developing countries have only a handful of staff to deal with trade-related issues (as often agreements cover much more than just trade and economic cooperation).

signing up to them. This is a sharp difference from traditional trade agreements, which are chiefly about dismantling barriers to trade (in a way making it actually easier to administer trade policy). Third, these are areas of reform where there is no simple and single template as is the case for tariff elimination. This raises questions as to what should be the content of agreements: should they restrict themselves to common universal principles or explore specific solutions to the issues that signatories face?

While offering opportunities for countries wishing to reform their trade and business environment, this set of new issues also raises numerous challenges and policy dimensions that did not exist before. This will be especially the case when commitments included in agreements are not a priority interest of the conceding partner. To take an example, it is possible that the inclusion of advanced forms of intellectual property rights (IPRs) protection may not only be welfare decreasing for developing countries, but also may require an alternative economic development model. This may involve acquisition of knowledge and know-how that is not achieved through imitation and reverse engineering, thus diverting administrative resources towards the setting up of new agencies, but also perhaps fostering investment and growth of new industries that would not have been able to exist without IPR, and so on.

Negotiating PTAs thus requires significant effort, and knowledge of issues that for poor countries may be areas with no pre-existing practice.

Deep Integration: Concepts

It is useful to try to capture the essence of the difference in nature of the liberalization challenge posed by the new disciplines in PTAs. The trade literature uses several roughly equivalent terminologies to characterize variations in the process of integration. These include *deep vs. shallow*, *positive vs. negative*, and *behind the border vs. at the border*, as the most frequently used.

Positive Integration

The first Nobel Prize winner in economics, Jan Tinbergen (1954) proposed the notions of *positive* and *negative integration* to characterize the process of international economic integration. Negative integration refers to the removal of trade barriers and the principle of non-discrimination. This is the traditional remit of trade negotiations.[3] As to positive integration, Tinbergen (1954: 79) defines it as follows.

---

[3] The General Agreement on Tariffs and Trade (GATT) architecture has been historically built essentially around the notion of negative integration and the prohibition of the most detrimental policies through elimination of border trade barriers and non-discrimination principles (Hoekman and Kostecki, 2001). Recently, however, new forms of economic integration have been included in the multilateral trade framework, starting with the Kennedy Round and services under the General Agreement on Trade in Services (GATS) in 1979, and continuing with the WTO (and the incorporation of TRIPS in particular). The WTO incorporates many more significant elements of positive integration than previously. PTAs follow the exact same trend, going even further in many instances.

[the] creation of new institutions and their instruments or the modification of existing instruments. [...] More generally, positive integration should consist of the creation of all institutions required by the welfare optimum which have to be handled in a centralized way.

Analysts have often retained the first aspect of the definition, the notion according to which integration is not just about removal of barriers to trade flows, but that it also requires the creation of new measures to facilitate these flows. Interestingly though, Tinbergen offers in the second part of the definition a vision that suggests that the creation of intergovernmental public goods is also needed. This is an important aspect which we will come back to later in this chapter.

Various interpretations of the Tinbergen characterization have survived. But the basic intuition remains that some processes of trade liberalization involve abstaining from protectionist policies, thus not changing the basic legal framework (negative integration), while others require active development of new policies or the modification of actual policies.

The distinction between positive and negative integration implies substantive differences in the process of integration. Negative integration would be mainly about the prohibition of a narrow set of policies, joint surveillance, and eventually mechanisms of redress, while positive integration requires taking active steps towards integration by defining common policies and setting up the legal and administrative framework to implement them. This difference is, however, not as clear-cut as it appears at first.[4] In both cases of integration a certain degree of legal alignment is required as is the setting up of a minimum of common institutions. For instance, agreeing on new rules that limit the way governments can intervene in markets could be seen alternatively as an instance of positive or negative integration. Nevertheless the distinction remains useful to broadly think about important characteristics of deep integration, as new dimensions of PTAs imply clearly more "retooling" of legal frameworks at the domestic level.

Positive integration thus has several implications in terms of how trade liberalization is conducted. First, positive integration can be conducted in various ways, depending on how it is legally instrumented. Torrent (2007) notes the substantive different between US and EU agreements regarding procurement. Whereas the US approach is more normative with insertion of the rules in the agreement, the EU adopts a more progressive approach by defining the rules through specialized organizations (such as expert committees). Relative to negative integration, positive integration entails

---

[4] Torrent (2007) provides the following example: "The European Community directives on the liberalization of movements of capital seem to be a clear example of 'negative' integration, but they were enacted according to what, in Tinbergen's terms, would be a clear example of 'positive integration' (and they would be defended in this way by many in the European Commission). In political terms, NAFTA's Chapter XI on investment would be looked at as a typical example of "negative integration" that sharply reduces the capacity of governments to intervene in the economy. But nobody can deny that it is an excellent example of common rules that go much further than liberalization of access (for example on protection of investments). Therefore, it could also be an excellent example of 'positive integration.' "

substantial differences with respect to drafting language in agreements—the instruments of implementation being more complex—and therefore negotiations, as well as probably predictability with regard to implementation. For instance, when tackling trade facilitation issues, it is not sufficient to agree on rules that should be prevented (e.g., the use of consular fees), or on simple positive obligations such as transparency. Countries must also agree on standards of procedures, such as using risk management screening at borders and monitoring agency conduct. These obligations cannot be easily—and should not at all, according to some (Messerlin and Zarrouk, 2000)—be incorporated into normative commitments in trade agreements. A second aspect of positive integration, beyond adopting new policies to open markets, is also about coordination of policies with trading partners, which may imply some form of institutional arrangement to that end.

Behind the Border Policies

Torrent (2007) points to another dimension, which relates to whether legal obligations affect international or internal transactions.[5] This is characterized in the literature as *behind the border* vs. *at the border measures*. National Treatment and uniform obligations indeed differ in substance from Most Favored Nation (MFN) obligations in that they require that countries change policies that also affect internal transactions that are not necessarily trade related.

The trade implications of domestic regulations are not new and, for instance, are well recognized in the WTO (Article III) as domestic policies that have the potential to be designed to discriminate against foreign producers.[6] Beyond addressing discrimination per se—the National Treatment principle—there is also the objective of reducing the costs of compliance with multiple and heterogeneous requirements. As the world economy becomes more integrated and supply chains incorporate sourcing from many countries, the calls for some uniformity are growing. This is an area where PTAs play an increasing role.

With behind the border policies, domestic transactions are also directly affected; this has obvious direct welfare implications that differ from the indirect effect through trade goods prices and volumes. This also involves a different political economy equilibrium.

Finally, as we will see later, the notion of behind the border measures could be expanded to include those measures that are included in trade agreements, not because

---

[5] Torrent (2007) distinguishes between three main approaches to promote integration: "The first is to impose obligations on liberalization and access to markets. The second is to impose certain obligations of nondiscrimination on the legal framework applicable to transactions and operations covered by the agreements—basically MFN status or national treatment (NT) obligations—while leaving domestic legislation intact. The third is to create uniform legislation establishing a common legal framework for transactions and operations covered by the agreement."

[6] Think for instance of an *ad hoc* standard requirement that has the effect of barring foreign imports while still allowing domestic producers or procurement rules that favor domestic sourcing.

of their direct or indirect effects on trade, but merely because trade agreements provide a convenient vehicle of international negotiation or enforcement.

III. Understanding the Rationales Driving Deep Integration

The reality of the new PTA landscape requires us to revisit the motives for entering into regional agreements. The important conclusion behind this reexamination is that one should look simply beyond market access for goods. This was foreseen by Krugman (1993) who assumed that one cause of the success of PTAs is because it should be easier to deal with the variety, complexity, and opacity of modern trade barriers in their setting rather than in the GATT. Schiff and Winters (2004) surveyed alternative rationales for regional integration spanning from policy lock to foreign policy consideration, importing good regulatory practices, hegemons exporting regulatory standards, and supra-national coordination to achieve regional policy goals. Recent negotiations of US and European PTAs point, for instance, to new motives for preferential trade agreements (Schott, 2003; European Commission, 2007).

We propose in the following section to review the alternative motives (i.e., other than traditional market access and barrier reduction) that may help explain the growth of deep integration provisions in modern PTAs. We separate these rationales into three broad categories: economic or efficiency motives; value-related demands (according to the expression coined by Bhagwati, 2008); and institutional motives. The first category identifies traditional and more recent economic rationales according to which preferential liberalization provides clear welfare-enhancing outcomes. The second describes mostly non-economic and more ideological sources of motivations to use PTAs to advance given international agendas. Finally, the third relates more to political economy motives, where PTAs provide the most opportune way of reaching agreement compared to other institutional solutions.

Economic Motives or Achieving Efficiency Through PTAs

New Dimensions of Market Access

Market access conditions are not only determined by tariffs. A range of other domestic policies, such as standards and customs procedures, may affect foreign exporters' access to the market. Traditional mercantilist market-access motives provide an incentive to look also at domestic regulations, as lower tariffs have increased the visibility of their role as domestic regulations. As noted by Bagwell and Staiger (2001), when governments choose these policies unilaterally, there is a possibility that market access might be set at a lower and non-optimal level than it would be under reciprocal liberalization negotiations.

Second, the market access question is not limited to goods only. Foreign investment decisions are another way to gain access in foreign markets, and therefore the inclusion of disciplines relating to investment in PTAs can be an additional motive for reciprocal liberalization commitments.[7] Many PTAs now include disciplines that go beyond the WTO. That is, WTO rules are limited to the supply of services following an investment ("commercial presence") in the GATS and to trade-related investment measures (the Trade Related Investment Measures (TRIMs) agreement). Moreover, the GATS relies on an "enterprise-based" definition of investment, while bilateral rules generally refer to a broader "asset-based" definition that covers portfolio investment and different forms of tangible and intangible property (Miroudot, 2011).

The traditional analysis of market access focuses on goods trade. Services trade is often omitted from this discussion. At a time when the services sector represents an increasingly higher share of value added (50 per cent in developing countries), when many services (electricity, telecom, transport) are key inputs into the production of goods and other services, and when the IT revolution has increased their tradability, the scope for gains from services liberalization might be considerable. Furthermore, in instances where preferential integration in goods may bring few benefits because of lack of complementarity of production structures or absence of effective liberalization, looking at other integration dimensions such as services, investment, and labor might be desirable. Jensen, Rutherford, and Tarr (2008) show that gains from services liberalization rival those of goods trade in magnitude.

Notwithstanding the market access considerations, PTAs also have a role to play when it comes to trans-national regulation. This reflects the standard economic efficiency motive for regulation, which is to address three types of market imperfections: (1) tackle monopoly power; (2) externalities and public goods; and (3) information asymmetries. There is a fourth category, which involves the societal choice motives of regulation (e.g., redistributive motives such as universal services provisions, or moral choices such as prohibition of child labor).

Monopoly Power and Supranational Competition

With the existence of economies of scale and more generally market failures, the possibility of monopoly power and abusive conduct by private firms arises. Trade liberalization may go some way to create competition by opening markets, but this will not always be sufficient. In such instances, competition policy should complement trade liberalization in order to secure the gains from the opening of markets. This rationale is the market access one described earlier.

This by itself is not sufficient to justify the inclusion of competition law disciplines in a PTA on economic motives alone. After all, countries can opt to implement competition

---

[7] According to Ethier (1998) attracting Foreign Direct Investment (FDI) is one of the main attractions of entering into PTAs.

policy individually. Arguably, the same market access mercantilist motives could suggest that commitments about competition law enforcement in the agreement are required for the same reason as commitments on tariff reform are.

The second reason to include competition rules is that there is also a risk of a cross-border externality as large domestic producers' conduct may affect trading partners either because of foreclosure of access to foreign competitors of domestic markets or because of abuse of conduct in export markets.

For competition rules to be relevant in a PTA context presupposes that the abuse of market power or collusive practice takes place in more than one national jurisdiction or that international legislation and cooperation are required to put an end to or sanction it. For instance, a firm may use its market power in one market to extract monopoly rents in another, a dominant position may span several countries (e.g., Microsoft), potentially leading to anti-competitive market conduct, or firms may have agreed in one jurisdiction to collude in another, therefore requiring cooperation between authorities in order to collect evidence. Arguably, the need for such international competition arrangement will depend on the size of individual economies and the extent of their enforcement capacity.

Externalities and Public Goods

Externalities arise when the behavior of one agent spills over positively or negatively to other agents without them having any involvement in the transaction. Externalities are not necessarily confined within the borders of given countries (climate change, for instance), and in some cases may be best tackled by a small group of countries. For instance river management should involve neighboring countries, as do some transport issues. Externalities are closely related to the need to provide public goods, that is, benefits that markets would not otherwise supply. The presence of externality is one of two reasons, along with indivisibility.

Addressing regional externalities should logically be a priority of regional PTAs given the need for some form of supra-national coordination to help internalize the externalities. Coordination can take several forms, as noted below.

- **Alignment and harmonization of policies to avoid "leakage."** This is, for instance, when one jurisdiction in the PTA has lower regulatory standards, thus possibly undermining regulatory efforts of its neighbors or trade partners. One example is deficient control of animal epizooties in one country that spill over to neighbors as animal border crossings cannot be totally controlled.
- **Alignment and harmonization of policies to create networks** and facilitate information exchange. This essentially relates to the adoption of common standards and regulatory language in order to facilitate flows within the region (for instance, ensuring interoperability of national networks at a regional level). Sectors where this seems of particular relevance are services sectors such as financial and insurance, IT, professional services, transport, and electricity.
- **Pooling of efforts** to create infrastructure, or of resources (financial, human) to provide a regional public good. Large infrastructure serving a region, such as a

hydroelectric dam or a large port, are examples where pooled financing might be needed.

- **Joint decision making** to ensure that national policies are coordinated at the regional level.
- **Transfer of resources** to solve externality problems when the contribution of individual member states is required. A common instance is when institutions are weak and capacity building is required to bring a partner country to a higher standard for the regional common good (e.g., customs enforcement).

However, it is not entirely clear whether the need to address regional externalities (good or bad) is very present when signing PTAs. Also there is always the possibility (as for all commitments agreed in PTAs) to address these issues through dedicated agreements and trans-national institutions such as bilateral customs or water management agreements. Historically, many of these problems have been addressed this way (we discuss this below).

Information Asymmetries

Product characteristics are often discernible to buyers before consumption takes place. Such goods are called experience or credence goods. While experience goods reveal their characteristics upon consumption (e.g., the quality of a product will be experienced over time), credence goods do not do so (e.g., chemicals may be harmful to health, unbeknownst to people exposed to them). The same applies to services, in particular, because of their intangibility, which makes it difficult for the buyer to learn about their quality prior to consumption (Hoekman, Mattoo, and Sapir, 2007). Finally, information asymmetries may also affect producers themselves when consumer characteristics are hidden (e.g., the problem of insurance). In the latter case one talks of moral hazard, while in the former one talks of adverse selection. While in most instances the market itself tackles these information asymmetries through information and brand signaling, when the asymmetries are not addressed the market outcome is suboptimal.

Regulation may then be called for, for instance, through licensing or imposing compulsory standards. International cooperation can help reduce the overall complexity of the regulatory framework for international traders by aligning and harmonizing regulations. It may also be the case that failing to tackle some of these issues in a coordinated fashion may generate negative externality effects.

In the specific PTA context, the test will then be to assess whether information asymmetry problems are best tackled at that level, rather than in other international fora. In most instances, this will be a question of judging the trade-offs between the transaction costs of cooperating with a given number of countries (or the international community) and the benefits of coordination at the global or PTA level. Taking the example of regional standards, there is a clear risk that such standards may exclude third non-adhering countries. However, it may be much easier to agree on a common approach with a small number of countries and with countries with similar preferences. Finally, in some cases the problem is purely regional in nature (e.g., regional epizooties).

Value Related Demands

Beyond the economic motives of addressing bad regulations impeding market access and market failures, an additional motive for regulatory intervention relates to societal choices or value related demands, as Bhagwati (2008) calls them.

Each society has moral and social preferences that may be undermined by market forces if left to their own devices. For instance the trading of dangerous weapons or morally/religiously reprehensible material needs to be restricted. What is considered dangerous or morally reprehensible will vary for each country.

National moral and social preferences may be undermined by trade liberalization. That is, it is still easier to control borders than a whole territory, and foreign producers may not hold themselves up to the same standards as the nationally chosen ones. This has long been recognized in trade agreements by the possibility of safeguard provisions and general exceptions, (such as on moral grounds). At the same time, the mechanisms of safeguards and the language of general exceptions may be found to be insufficient, and therefore sector specific provisions are added, such as reservations in the opening of services sectors to meet universal provision.

What is then the specific value added of PTAs in helping to achieve these objectives? A first explanation might be that the threat to societal preferences is localized in a limited number of partners, and thus it makes more sense to deal with them directly. Narcotics production is one such instance and explains why some PTAs have been specifically linked to measures to fight against production and trafficking such, as CAFTA in the United States (see e.g., Hornbeck, 2003).

A second motivation relates to the choice of the best available forum for promoting the international sharing of such values, either focusing on issues that are not already present in other agreements such as the WTO (for instance on labor or environment), or pushing for higher standards than currently exist in the international community. This is, for example, a clear objective of the new US trade policy of pursuing PTAs that was initiated under the Bush administration. In a 2001 speech, then Ambassador Robert Zoellick said: "... we need to align the global trading system with our values. [...] We can encourage respect for core labor standards, environmental protection, and good health [...] And we must always seek to strengthen freedom, democracy and the rule of law."

Related to this is the desire to use every trade forum to reaffirm these choices with a view to mutual complementarity and reinforcement between these different instruments.

Political Economy Motives or the Opportunistic Use of PTAs

Beyond the need for coordinated policymaking with trading partners, PTAs also serve a function as forums for policy objectives that are either not strictly related to exchanges or not to the preferential nature of PTAs. PTAs can be seen as efficient forums to achieve these other objectives, and therefore PTAs have evolved beyond their initial mission by having their agenda loaded with this other set of objectives. In what follows, we evaluate the institutional characteristics that may render PTAs attractive for policymakers.

Geostrategic Motives

Geostrategic considerations have historically been involved in the formation of PTAs. There are numerous examples of trade agreements that have been used to promote peace. Chief among the agreements is the European Union, which was borne from the desire to prevent war. Winston Churchill called in 1946 for a "United States of Europe," but it is through economic integration and the 1951 European Steel and Coal Community that European integration actually started.

Others examples of agreements used for stability purposes include Mercosur and APEC (Bergsten, 1996). More recently, the push by the United States to conclude PTAs has also been motivated by foreign policy considerations (Bhagwati, 2008).

Thus, PTAs can serve to delivering peace and stability as a regional public good (see Schiff and Winters, 2004: chapter 7, and World Bank, 2005: box 2.6). Two mechanisms may come into play. First, trade exchanges increase economic interdependence and thus act as a disincentive for conflict. They may also contribute to increasing familiarity and trust and help diffuse trade related disputes. Second, and more specific to PTAs, institutions themselves serve as a conduit for diplomacy, allowing for frequent and repeated official interaction, and better exchange of information.

While previous research has examined the role of membership in a PTA on the decreased likelihood of armed conflict and found a significant effect (Mansfield and Pevehouse, 2003), the precise channels through which this occurs were left unexplored. In recent research, Lee and Pyun (2009) provide statistically significant evidence that PTA institutions decrease the probability of conflict between members. WTO membership on the other hand seems only marginally significant.

PTAs as Institutions

The geopolitical dimension explored above offers an insight into the possible broader relevance of institutions as an incentive to sign PTAs. By offering a different set of institutions, and related services, than other forms of international agreements, do PTAs provide an infrastructure that is well suited to the policies pursued under the deep integration agenda? As noted by the World Bank (2005), many issues covered by PTAs (such as the externality problems described above), could well be handled without a trade agreement. But if they are, it must be because PTAs offer a good framework to make progress on them.

PTAs are relatively flexible instruments in so far as they allow for various levels of legal commitments and nearly infinite ways of creating policy space. Taking the specific case of dispute settlement (Porges, 2011), the options are numerous: no mechanism at all, or one or several dispute settlement mechanisms. Each PTA can come with its own ad hoc mechanisms, including using external mechanisms such as international arbitration or WTO dispute settlement. Before dispute settlement per se, various ways of reaching settlement are provided from good offices, and include third-party mediation and conciliation. Indirect evidence of legal flexibility is also provided by Horn et al. (2009), who show that binding and non-binding provisions coexist in agreements in nearly all issues covered. Note that such flexibility might appear as a virtue to policymakers but may not necessarily achieve factual reform.

Innovative institutions are also a feature of many PTAs, not found in particular in the multilateral forums. Involvement of the private sector is one of them, from involvement in stakeholder forums to the ability for private parties to lodge complaints, as in the case of the European Court of Justice, the General Secretariat of the Andean Community, or the North American Free Trade Agreement (NAFTA) investment provisions. Some PTAs also offer more substantial transfers of sovereignty. Governments may opt to transfer or devolve some of their authority to institutions created by PTAs, such as regional competition authorities.

Transaction costs of agreement are lower in PTAs where the number of participating countries is small. This also makes free riding more difficult and is a key obstacle to successful global liberalization (Krugman, 1993). Lower transaction costs both allow for more binding constraints for each partner (non-cooperation is more difficult), as well as allowing for further legal flexibility with the possibility to amend and to revisit PTAs more frequently than multilateral agreements, as the numbers required to reach consensus are lower. A smaller number of participant countries enables more frequent and probably less formal interactions, which can contribute to problem solving and deeper interactions. This seems an important feature for regulatory dimensions, which require agreement on complex issues, such as mutual recognition agreements, and the setting up of expert bodies. This is the road followed by the European Union under the Florence process.

Resource transfers are more likely to occur in the framework of PTAs than in other international agreement settings. Many PTAs, North–South in particular, incorporate such transfers.

Finally PTAs may offer innovations in terms of monitoring and transparency mechanisms.

Policy Anchoring

A traditional political economy explanation for binding international trade commitments is the pursuit of a domestic reform agenda and the use of external commitments to "lock-in" the progress and prevent future reversals. The possibility of lock-in is also a motive for including behind the border aspects in agreements. There are several recent examples of countries that have used PTAs to pursue an ambitious domestic agenda. For instance, Mexico and Chile (Schott, 2003) or more recently Peru, used their FTA negotiations with the United States to push domestic reforms or lock-in recent reforms.

In Europe, Eastern European countries used the process of accession to the EU to consolidate market reforms after the fall of communism.

Various explanations have been put forward to suggest when PTAs may offer good lock-in opportunities. On the one hand, PTAs may be more effective lock-in mechanisms than other international agreements. On the other hand, PTAs may complement other instruments in the process of external lock-in of reforms.

By extending their reach to regulatory issues, PTAs offer a way to improve policy credibility. What are the differences then between the sort of anchor offered by PTAs and the one provided by the WTO? Aside from the obvious point that PTAs may offer commitments in WTO-plus and WTO-extra areas, other aspects may point to other specific advantages. The possibility of picking a partner may help reinforce the credibility aspect, as the partner of choice may be perceived as a strong proponent of reform (think for instance that the EU, the United States, and other developed countries promote different agendas through their respective PTAs). It may also signal a preference for a certain regulatory approach. Additionally, lock-in by the means of PTAs can be complemented by transfers of finance and knowledge that often take place between North and South partners.

The higher cost of free riding in PTAs advanced by Krugman (1993) is a powerful rationale for preferring them as international lock-in mechanism. Also, add Schiff and Winters (1998), there is more scope for retaliation as concessions may go beyond just tariffs in a PTA. Schiff and Winters, however, note that the disciplining effect is only limited to the extent of partner countries in the PTA, not third country members. These dynamics are echoed by the conclusion reached by Prusa (2011) that PTAs tend to discipline the use of contingent protection measures among partners, while at the same time there seems to be an increase in the use of protection against third countries.

Finally, another way in which PTAs can affect other negotiating forums is by increasing the bargaining power of groups of countries vis-à-vis third countries or on the multilateral stage (Fernandez and Portes, 1998). The EU, for instance, negotiates as one entity in the WTO negotiations, and Caribbean countries do too. In the EU PTAs, the objective to influence multilateral regulatory forums is also present, with clauses of cooperation defining common positions in international organizations being spelled out.

IV. HOW DIFFERENT ARE DEEP INTEGRATION PTAS? EVIDENCE

The expansion of PTAs in scope and depth creates new dimensions to the challenge that faces policymakers. New rationales for deep integration translate into specific characteristics of PTA disciplines that should induce policymakers to rethink their approach when considering preferential liberalization policies. Does the deepening and popularity of PTAs create new challenges to the multilateral order? To what extent are the multiple motives pursued by PTAs congruent? Do new disciplines incorporated in PTAs create a different category of obligations?

Several recent studies have sought to investigate how deep integration agreements are designed (Baldwin et al., 2009). A comprehensive review of the evidence across sectors can be found in Chauffour and Maur (2011), on which we largely base this section. We provide below the key conclusions of these studies in seven of the most frequent deep integration sectors: services; investment; competition; procurement; trade facilitation; standards; and intellectual property rights.

Services

In practice, PTAs tend to show broad commonality, both among each other and vis-à-vis the GATS, using a broadly similar standard panoply of disciplines. Liberalization in PTAs tends to follow two approaches: replicate the GATS positive list or a hybrid approach to market opening or otherwise pursue a negative-list methodology.[8] The positive-list method lists sectors that are scheduled for opening. All sectors that are not listed are thus excluded from liberalization commitments. In practice, positive lists are combined with across the board liberalization commitments (such as National Treatment) to which reservations in selected areas can be added.[9] Alternatively, negative lists mention the sectors that will not be liberalized; therefore the default assumption is that all other sectors will be liberalized.

Both approaches should in theory generate broadly equivalent outcomes. However, a negative-list approach can be more effective in locking in the regulatory status quo. Also a number of good governance-enhancing features are associated with negative listing, most notably in transparency terms. Studies suggest that North–South PTAs based on a negative-list approach tend to achieve deeper liberalization (see Mattoo and Sauvé, 2011). PTAs are also becoming more flexible: for instance, they increasingly mix positive- and negative-list approaches under the same agreement.[10]

A small number of governments (particularly when the negative list is used) have shown a readiness to subsequently extend regional preferences on an MFN basis under the GATS. This may reflect a realization that preferential treatment may be difficult to achieve in services trade (and is indeed perhaps economically undesirable). Also, PTAs covering services typically extend preferential treatment to all legal persons conducting

---

[8] More than half of all PTAs featuring services provisions concluded to date proceed on the basis of a negative list approach. Such agreements are more prevalent in the Western hemisphere, reflecting the influence of the NAFTA, as well as in agreements conducted along North–South lines (with the exception of the EU and European Free Trade Association (EFTA) agreements).

[9] Hence the mention of the hybrid approach.

[10] For example, positive listing for cross-border trade and negative listing for commercial presence; or negative listing for banking services and positive listing for insurance services.

business operations in a member country, either by featuring a liberal[11] "rule of origin" or denial of benefits clause.[12] Both cases would tend to demonstrate that discrimination is not systematic in PTAs covering services.

Recent agreements have looked towards complementing the GATS. An increasing number of PTAs have sought to complement disciplines on cross-border trade in services,[13] with a more comprehensive set of parallel disciplines on investment (both investment protection and liberalization of investment in goods- and services-producing activities)[14] and the temporary movement of business people (related to goods and services trade and investment in a generic manner).

PTAs (with considerable variations and diversity) also go beyond existing GATS commitments and WTO negotiations in terms of sector coverage. This is especially the case for developing countries, which have low sector coverage in the GATS. WTO-plus advances are evident both in sectors that have attracted low interest under the GATS— such as audiovisual services—and more "popular" sectors in the GATS (computer, tourism, or telecom services). PTAs (North–South in particular) nonetheless encounter resistance to market opening in services sectors that have proven difficult to address at the multilateral level (e.g., air and maritime transport; audiovisual services; movement of service suppliers; energy services).

Finally, market-opening progress in PTAs is also notable in sectors where new (post-Uruguay Round) pro-liberalization constituencies have emerged. Among these are rules governing digital trade, pro-competitive disciplines in the tourism sector, express delivery services, as well as greater advances on freeing up temporary movement of persons.[15] A number of PTAs have also begun to address the issue of aid-for-trade in services trade, albeit through non-binding provisions. In so doing, PTAs serve as useful "laboratories" for innovative approaches to rule making or market opening likely to inform the development of similar provisions at the multilateral level.

However, PTAs have generally made little progress in tackling the rule making interface between domestic regulation and trade in services. This is most notably the case for disciplines on an emergency safeguard mechanism and subsidy disciplines for services trade. Governments confront the same conceptual and feasibility challenges, data limitations, and political sensitivities at the regional level as they do on the multilateral front. Indeed, many PTAs feature provisions in this area that are no more fleshed out and, in some instances, weaker or more narrowly drawn (i.e., focusing solely on professional

---

[11] That is, non-restrictive.

[12] Denial of benefit clauses specify who cannot benefit from the liberalized regime.

[13] Modes 1 and 2 of the GATS.

[14] PTAs featuring comprehensive or generic investment disciplines typically provide for a right of non-establishment (i.e., no local presence requirement as a pre-condition to supply services) as a means of encouraging cross-border trade in services. Such a provision, for which no GATS equivalent exists, might prove particularly well suited to promoting digital trade.

[15] Several recent PTAs have made headway on temporary movement of persons (Mode 4), including South–South agreements such as Mercosur or AFAS (Association of South East Asian Nations (ASEAN)), which have reached trade-facilitating mutual recognition agreements, notably in selected regulated professions and highly skilled occupations.

services) than those arising under Article VI of the GATS (including the Article VI:4 work program).

The relationship between PTAs and the WTO is not unidirectional in character but involves iterative, two-way, interaction between the two layers of trade governance in ways that can inform subsequent patterns of rule making and market opening at both the PTA and WTO levels. Examples of such interaction can notably be found in areas where WTO jurisprudence has clarified or interpreted the scope of key provisions governing services trade that are typically found both in the WTO-GATS and in the services and investment chapters of PTAs.

Standards

Standards is another well surveyed area. The summary of the key dimensions of standards provisions below is based on Maur and Shepherd (2011) and Stoler (2011).

Standards matter in PTAs, just like they do in the WTO, since governments seek to act on their PTAs in order to protect human, animal or plant life, or health. In a number of instances, PTA members seek to go beyond the approach followed in the WTO to reduce the differences in national standards and certification processes that impede trade.

There are broadly two different models. Where the EU is involved, the agreement often expects the partner country to harmonize its national standards and conformity assessment procedures with those of the EU. PTAs in the Asia-Pacific region and those in which the United States is a partner typically aim to address problems resulting from different national standards and conformity procedures through a preference for international standards or the use of mutual recognition agreements. Legally, there is an important difference between the ways in which the two types of obligations tend to be structured. Agreements to pursue harmonization can sometimes impose relatively few up-front obligations. It is common for the parties to commit to ongoing negotiations with a view to harmonization. The devil is thus in the details, since the extent of harmonization that in fact takes place depends on the outcome of a long and complex process.

Mutual recognition agreements (MRA) are an essential and distinguishing feature of PTAs (relative to multilateral-type agreements). Mutual recognition is the process by which two countries agree that their rules and/or procedures, although different, achieve the same objective. It allows avoiding a process of strict harmonization. As Baldwin et al. (2009) note, liberalizing product regulation without lowering regulatory quality requires trust; governments must believe that the other government is capable of establishing and enforcing highly technical rules in a transparent and credible manner. This makes deep liberalization at the multilateral level impossible. The WTO's Technical Barriers to Trade (TBT) Agreement recognizes this by encouraging MRAs among members. However, whereas harmonization to international standards automatically extends the preference to third-party members, mutual recognition has the potential to exclude them. It is therefore important that an MRA does not contain an exclusionary rule of origins (Baldwin et al., 2009).

In a study by Budetta and Piermartini (2009) of 58 agreements with provisions on standards, harmonization appears to be much more common than mutual recognition for standards. Some 29 agreements provide for harmonization of mandatory standards, and 25 provide for harmonization of voluntary standards. By contrast, only 5 agreements provide for mutual recognition of voluntary standards, and 15 provide for mutual recognition of mandatory standards.

Mutual recognition is, on the other hand, the most frequent approach for conformity assessment. This may reflect the fact that mutual recognition of conformity is easier to achieve than for standards. The reason might be that instead of implying equivalence of regulatory objectives, which is a sensitive issue in many cases, it requires equivalence of how tests are performed and certification granted.

Another key component of provisions is usually a cluster of obligations relating to the transparency of standards and their administration. For instance, Budetta and Piermartini (2009) find that 21 of the 58 PTAs dealing with product standards impose a requirement of prior (entry into force) notification on the parties; in many cases, there is also an obligation to allow some time for comments. Another common example of a transparency obligation is the creation of a national contact point, or putting in place a consultation system.[16]

Some PTAs go even further in their treatment of product standards, and incorporate institutions designed to make the process of standard-setting and administration work more smoothly between trading partners. Of the agreements reviewed by Budetta and Piermartini (2009), 34 created some kind of regional administrative body to deal with the administration of standards systems. Twenty-four agreements included a dispute settlement mechanism. Interestingly, 22 agreements have provisions relating to technical assistance.

PTAs tend to converge with, and support, the multilateral trading system. Budetta and Piermartini (2009) find that out of 58 PTAs with TBT provisions, 30 (51 per cent) refer to the WTO Agreement on TBTs. Lesser (2007) finds that 86 per cent of 24 PTAs reviewed make a reference to the WTO Agreement. Also, on the whole, PTAs look by and large as a potential complement to international initiatives. For instance, when PTAs seek harmonization of standards, technical regulations, and certification procedures among partners (about half of PTAs reviewed do so), promotion of the use of international standards is made in about 60–70 per cent of cases (Lesser, 2007). Likewise transparency measures often echo those contained in the WTO, such as advance notification of new regulations. However, this is far from being systematic. Regional standards are promoted alongside or instead of international ones (the EU promotes the use of its standards in several agreements[17]); in 2004, Mercosur had developed around 370 regional voluntary standards and 407 regional technical regulations (TBT and SPS);

---

[16] Based on 20 of the 58 agreements surveyed by Budetta and Piermartini (2009).

[17] The diffusion of EU standards is clearly advocated in one document: "… to promote where possible, the adoption of overseas standards, and regulatory approaches based on, or compatible with, international and European practices, in order to improve the market access and competitiveness of European products" (European Commission, 1996).

another example is the Andean Community, which has harmonized technical regulations for 31 agricultural products representing around 60 per cent of intraregional trade (Aldaz-Carroll, 2006).

Harmonization where one partner is less developed than the other will call for the incorporation in the PTA of technical assistance and capacity-building measures. Governments should also recognize that the resolution of standards related problems will take time and require considerable bilateral work. Thus, argues Stoler (2011), a PTA that aims to be effective should incorporate bilateral institutions (committees, working groups, notifications, etc.) mandated to deal with standards related questions over time. Ideally, the institutions established in the PTA should also be capable of helping to resolve trade related problems arising out of exporters' need to comply with private standards in an importing country's market. But it is not clear whether this is factually the case in many instances.

PTAs also offer additional venues of "soft" dispute resolution through dialog and information sharing at the expert level that can help avoid many disputes. In some cases, PTAs offer more stringent arbitration rules than the WTO, for instance, foreshadowing the repeal of offending standards. In NAFTA the possibility of resorting to both the WTO and the PTA dispute settlement mechanisms is explicitly made (Budetta and Piermartini, 2009).

Procurement

Baldwin et al. (2009) and Dawar and Evenett (2011) offer a recent review of the treatment of procurement in PTAs. Two-thirds of the PTAs notified to the WTO since 2000 include some form of provision relating to government procurement.

Government procurement provisions in PTAs may offer better prospects for reforming national procurement systems, given the longstanding difficulties in accomplishing unilateral reform and the absence of a multilateral accord on government procurement. Provisions vary considerably across agreements in detail and content (Baldwin et al., 2009), but they typically cover a dozen aspects of procurement policies, including non-discrimination provisions, procedural rules, dispute settlement mechanisms, commitments to cooperation and further negotiations, state entities and sectors covered, as well as so-called "offsets" (Dawar and Evenett, 2011).

All the PTAs including government procurement provisions acknowledge and share a common aim of transparent, non-discriminatory, and competitive procurement markets. Where they differ is in terms of the scope and strength of their commitment to progressive liberalization of procurement markets. North–South PTAs can be considerably less comprehensive than North–North or South–South agreements.[18]

---

[18] For instance, the EC–Cariforum Economic Partnership Agreement (EPA) only contains binding commitments to ensure transparency in procurement markets; conversely the USA–Jordan PTA simply indicates both parties' commitment to Jordan's accession to the WTO's Government Procurement Agreement (GPA).

In many PTAs, a particular focus of attention has been on eliminating the more transparent forms of discrimination (such as price preferences) which, in turn, may have had the unintended consequence of driving more discrimination into non-transparent forms, such as contract thresholds, limitation on number of bidders, exclusion of sensitive sectors, and so on. Another focus of attention in PTAs has been on improving the transparency of the public institutions responsible for state purchasing in signatories.

Despite being discussed in preferential negotiations, the procurement provisions in PTAs do not seem to create much discrimination against non-members. A first reason—specific to procurement—is because the government is only one of numerous national buyers. This limits the impact of its decisions to award specific preferences on market outcome. A second reason—common to other regulatory reforms—arises from the consideration that, having improved national procurement procedures and complied with PTA provisions, a government may decide not to retain separate processes for dealing with bids from PTA signatories and non-signatories. In short, PTA government procurement provisions offer the prospect of being implemented across the board, more formally, on an MFN basis.

Third-party MFN rules are an important mechanism to further non-discriminatory liberalization and diffuse good practices over time and across trading partners. The initial objective is merely to limit the extent to which preferential procurement is undermined by subsequent PTAs. But this has also the fortunate consequence to extend the more generous (i.e., liberal) treatment. Baldwin et al. (2009) explain this as follows: "this implies that if nations A and B sign a PTA with such a provision and B subsequently signs a PTA with nation C that grants the latter's firms more generous access to B's procurement market, B must unconditionally extend the more generous access to firms in A."[19] These clauses have been used by middle-sized trading nations and blocs, notably EFTA and Mexico.

Turning to implementation, even in the most advanced PTAs, such as the Australia–New Zealand agreement, government procurement provisions leave implementation to national entities rather than a regional body.

Improvements to procurement regimes, such as transparency, could be costly for a small and poor country. This expense could be mitigated by technical assistance and capacity building programs signed as part of the PTA. There are flexibilities available to negotiators, including exclusion of certain entities from the agreement, the level of the thresholds set for procurement to be covered by the agreement, the exclusion of sectors such as defense or financial services, and the use of offsets or set asides to allow for domestic policies such as the promotion of indigenous communities or small businesses.

---

[19] As in services FTAs, there is also a "soft" variant of the most preferential access clause. This implies that the better access is not automatically granted, but rather negotiated.

Investment

This section is based on detailed analysis of preferential investment provisions by Baldwin et al. (2009) and Miroudot (2011). As trade and investment are more and more intertwined in the context of international supply chains and firms' strategies of vertical specialization, countries are increasingly incorporating investment provisions in PTAs. Most of the innovation in designing international disciplines is taking place in preferential agreements such as Bilateral Investment Treaties (BITs) and PTAs rather than at the multilateral level.

By combining trade liberalization provisions with investment liberalization and protection, these agreements emphasize the complementary relationship between trade and FDI and are empirically found to have a stronger impact on investment than sole BITs. Importantly PTAs are not limited to disciplines on investment in the post-establishment phase (as with most BITs). They also deal with market access, national treatment, and most-favored treatment in the pre-establishment stage, thus providing economic incentives for investors (i.e., access to the market) in addition to legal incentives (the protection of investment once established).

Because of liberal rules of origin, market opening PTAs have not introduced severe distortions among investors, and developing countries have been able to maintain some of the restrictions needed for legitimate policy considerations.

Two models of PTAs can be identified, one inspired by the provisions found in the NAFTA that deals in the same chapter with investment in goods and services industries, and one following the GATS model for part of the provisions on investment in services. Despite important differences, these two types of agreements offer the same degree of protection for investment and can equally liberalize investment, even if empirically NAFTA-inspired agreements are found to be more ambitious in their scope and sectoral coverage.

A consequence of PTAs is the spreading of certain investment provisions. There are reasons to believe that the diffusion of these provisions is contributing to liberalization and even non-discriminatory liberalization. Baldwin et al. (2009) examine how NAFTA's MFN restrictions on the use of performance requirements (i.e., including on third parties not originating from the PTA) have been adopted by 14 other countries. Also, a further 36 countries have banned such requirements on a preferential basis only. As the authors note, preferential liberalization of investments might not be welfare optimal as it distorts investment patterns. But it is also likely to help eliminate egregious measures (at least partially).

For developing countries, North–South PTAs with substantive investment provisions are found to positively impact FDI flows. They can also offer an opportunity to address concerns with respect to dispute settlement for countries that are not ready to face commercial arbitration.

With the shift of demand and production networks to the South, investment provisions in South–South PTAs should be further developed, as observed in recently signed PTAs in Asia. The multilateralization of investment disciplines, through strengthened MFN provisions and liberal rules of origin or consolidation of PTAs in larger regional trade agreements, can help the least developed countries who lack resources and may be at a disadvantage in bilateral negotiations.

Trade Facilitation

Trade facilitation is a relatively recent aspect of PTAs. Current approaches to trade facilitation are extensions of earlier customs cooperation provisions with some variations depending on signatory countries. Trade facilitation provisions are also closely related to the proposals in the current Doha Round of WTO negotiations.

Trade facilitation is a domain of international trade cooperation where countries are still very much in the process of learning how to design the best approach.[20] Current provisions in PTAs often revolve around best practices in the area of customs administration, and do not venture beyond the sole remit of customs to include other border agencies, services, and standard dimensions, which are often treated separately.

Recent PTAs incorporate more advanced trade facilitation provisions—yet still often related to customs administration—which demonstrates the increased interest of using preferential agreements to reduce transaction costs. Generally, the purpose of these provisions is to advance a customs modernization agenda, reflecting multilateral standards developed in the World Customs Organization (and the revised Kyoto Convention). The agenda in these agreements is largely driven by the most developed partners, which tend to set terms of agreement that do not necessarily reflect the needs and capacity, especially of their developing country partners. There are, for instance, few examples of special and differential treatment by trading partner. Demanding reforms, such as risk management, authorized economic operators, or electronic based systems, are often part of recent PTAs when one might perhaps expect more attention and detail given to more achievable reforms. Furthermore, and contrasting with the relative sophistication of provisions relating to customs modernization (including harmonization with international standards), provisions dealing with cooperation and intra-regional efforts are relatively few and modest. Mutual recognition measures do not seem explored, and mutual assistance provisions seem modest.

This can be contrasted with notable efforts of trade facilitation reform to be found in certain South–South agreements, such as Comesa and West African Economic and Monetary Union (UEMOA), with innovative common regional policies such as harmonized transport insurance and regional carrier licensing.

It thus seems that trade facilitation provisions that focus on reform on the ground, implementation, and monitoring of measurable objectives such as in APEC seem to deliver more effective and successful reforms. Such agreements tend to be pragmatic, flexible, and country-specific, and are generally well suited to the type of reforms required in the context of trade facilitation.

---

[20] A review of issues of trade facilitation in a regional context can be found in Maur (2008).

Intellectual Property Rights

Rules for the protection of IPRs have become a common feature of PTAs, especially involving Northern partners. According to the survey by Fink (2011), on which this section draws, these rules seek to deepen and update pre-existing multilateral IPRs rules, as embedded in the WTO's TRIPS Agreement. The adoption of TRIPS-plus standards is often an important element in the overall package of "quid pro quos" necessary to conclude a trade deal, reflecting the importance of IPRs as a market access concern for developed countries. The two chief promoters of TRIPS-plus PTAs are the United States and Europe: Horn et al. (2009) show that nearly all of their PTAs include legally-binding provisions that commit partner members to rules not covered by the WTO TRIPS agreement. However, the US and European approach differ substantially.

The US has negotiated 12 FTAs over the past decade with ambitious IPRs chapters. These chapters introduce TRIPS-plus standards of protection for all types of IPRs. The most prominent—and sometimes most controversial—ones include: patent-term extension, patenting of life forms, patent-registration linkage for pharmaceutical products, exclusive rights to test data, prolonged copyright protection, rules on technological protection measures and the liability of Internet service providers, and more stringent requirements for the enforcement of IPRs. In 2006, following the US Congressional elections, a new framework rolled back some of the TRIPS-plus provisions as they relate to pharmaceutical products. While the Agreement was limited to only three FTAs, it marks an important shift in US trade policy towards more sensitivity of public health concerns in global IPRs rules.

Until recently, the agreements concluded by the EU were less far-reaching, tending to commit partners to sign international IP conventions (although not all conventions are part of the TRIPS agreement), rather than incorporating formal IP provisions. The main TRIPS-plus element of the EU's FTAs with Chile, Mexico, and South Africa takes the form of separate agreements on wines and spirits, which establishes lists of geographical names to which signatories must apply rigorous GI protection. In 2006, the EU embarked on a new set of FTA negotiations demanding the inclusion of more comprehensive IPRs chapters. The EU–Cariforum EPA offers a window into this new EU approach. It shows TRIPS-plus provisions not only in the area of geographical indications, but also in other areas, notably IPRs enforcement (see Spence, 2009). Future EU agreements with more developed trading partners may well be more ambitious than the EU–Cariforum EPA.

TRIPS-plus standards of protection are also found in several PTAs not involving the USA or EU. Notably, several of the EFTA FTAs provide for patent term extension and pharmaceutical test data exclusivity. The recent Switzerland–Japan FTA has an ambitious IPRs chapter, with especially far-reaching obligations in the area of rights enforcement. While agreements among developing countries usually do not go beyond TRIPS, several of the FTAs signed by Chile and Mexico include lists of geographical indications that benefit from protection in the signatory countries.

Finally, IPRs have been included in the definition of investment in many PTA investment chapters and BITs. Such a broad definition of investment raises the possibility that private rights holders directly challenge government measures affecting IPRs under the terms of an investment accord. While there has been no investment dispute in this area so far, the rapid spread of PTAs and BITs may well lead to the initiation of arbitration claims in the future.

PTA provisions tend to be followed by IPR reform, which demonstrates the influence of PTAs in shaping the IP framework of developing countries with adoption of new IP laws, adhesion to new international conventions, and in some instances reform of the institutions administering IP. Biadgleng and Maur (2011) offer an analysis of the implementation of IPRs in PTAs.

Competition

For recent analysis of competition provisions in PTAs, see Evenett (2008) and Dawar and Holmes (2011).[21]

The lack of a multilateral competition framework has coincided with a surge in PTAs, including competition provisions to address market failures that national competition laws cannot address. There is resistance to including competition provisions in PTAs because any form of regionalism creates trade diversion and preferentialism, and because of the costs of negotiating and implementing the provisions despite the inconclusive evidence on their economic and welfare effects.[22]

Regional competition provisions can complement the incentives to implement national regimes with a view to creating policy lock-in, increasing FDI, and, in the case of North–South agreements, gaining technical assistance and the opportunity to learn by doing.

In some instances, the economic burdens of implementation can be alleviated by PTA cooperation if the parties are able to exchange information effectively and avoid duplication and conflicting decisions. If cooperation leads to a successful investigation, then the costs are justified by the access to greater data and avoiding conflicting enforcement activities. The Caribbean competition regime indicates potential economies of scale provided by regional cooperation because the provisions allow for resource pooling among neighboring countries when national capacity is not enough to implement and enforce the regional framework.

Competition measures in PTAs fall in the following broad categories:

- adopting, maintaining and applying competition measures;
- coordination and cooperation provisions (notification, exchange of evidence and/ or information, provisions relating to competition policy and enforcement, and provisions relating to negative and positive comity);
- provisions addressing anti-competitive conduct;

---

[21] This section draws on Evenett (2008) and Dawar and Holmes (2011).
[22] Evenett (2008).

provisions relating to the principles of non-discrimination, due process, and
transparency;
- provisions to suspend or limit trade remedies (anti-dumping measures,
  countervailing duties, and safeguards);
- dispute settlement with respect to the application of the competition provisions
  within a PTA; and
- special and differential treatment to developing country signatories.

The same authors find two broad families of agreements, modeled after the US and
European PTAs. Most of the agreements containing provisions addressing anti-competitive behavior have been concluded by the EC or among non-EC European countries
in Eastern and Southeastern Europe. On the other hand, agreements that focus more
on coordination and cooperation provisions have been concluded in the Americas (or
involving a North or South American party) and with some Asian countries.

Evenett (2008) draws three main conclusions from the examination of PTAs. First
competition measures in the agreements concern state behavior as well as firms. Second,
competition provisions create obligations to both enact competition law and implement
legislation and to effectively enforce competition law. Thus the impact of such provisions is not just on international trade but also national markets. PTAs can be an instrument for improving the governance of competition policy. Third, there are a number of
ways in which cross-border cooperation can be operationalized (cooperation between
authorities, on enforcement, notifications, positive comity, etc.).

The main defining characteristic of competition provisions in PTAs relates to how the
regional competition regime is designed. A comparative overview of competition provisions at the regional level indicates great diversity. Dawar and Holmes (2011) distinguish between four main models.[23] At one end of the scale are decentralized agreements
that only require the existence of a local competition law and authority to apply the law,
such as NAFTA or SACU. At the other end of the scale, are regimes that establish a fully
centralized law with a supporting regional authority, such as the EC or Comesa. Such
regimes establish a regional authority and regional legislation that supersedes national
law. Partially decentralized regimes, such as in the Australia–New Zealand agreements
and Caricom, also rely on supra-national authority and rules, but leave enforcement to
national authorities. Finally, partially decentralized regimes, although without regional
authority, incorporate regional laws (for instance, Mercosur). Competition provisions
included in customs union agreements are, in general, more specific and demand higher
commitments.

Economic and human resources necessary to implement even a minimal decentralized competition regime are significant for both developed and developing countries.

---

[23] This taxonomy can be reconciled with the two broad models of Solano and Sennekamp (2005) by
noting that three of the four models tend to follow a European-type approach (with supra-national rules
and in some instance supra-national authority). Only the decentralized model can be identified with the
US approach.

For instance, an obligation to effectively enforce competition law can have implications for the powers, human resources, and budget of a competition authority.[24] Evenett (2008) argues, however, that emerging evidence on the costs associated with cross-border anti-competitive practices outweighs those of implementation.

North–South PTAs will have greater development benefits and better implementation records if the more developed party offers appropriate technical assistance, capacity building, and effectively enables the less developed regional partner to benefit from the provisions. For those countries with little experience in implementing competition, it may be more beneficial initially to focus on establishing a culture that values competition at the national or subregional level in the region. The provisions should be limited to the exchange of information, technical assistance, and capacity building. Subsequent negotiations can expand the agreement. Soft law can be more beneficial if governments are uncertain of the underlying technical issues and consequences of the provisions. Other non-judicial mechanisms may also be more appropriate, such as voluntary peer review and consultations.

Finally, in practice, competition laws look unlikely to discriminate against third parties. And while cooperation provisions and agreements could be seen to exclude third parties, they are unlikely to have any significant trade diverting impact. Indeed, there is very little scope for third-party discrimination in regional competition provisions, in law and in practice, and therefore they are unlikely to create any significant trade diversion. While competition commitments, such as non-discrimination, due process, and transparency are made on a regional basis, they generate positive multilateral spillover. Where a PTA competition chapter tackles cartels, the publication and notification of cartel enforcement actions in one country will generally stimulate enforcement efforts in other countries. This provides a positive demonstration effect to other jurisdictions, which can serve as competition advocacy.

V. CONCLUSION: A CHANGE OF PARADIGM

Deep integration differs from traditional integration agreements both in its motives and modalities of implementation. This has been long understood and the notion of "deep" integration captures intuitively the fact that the external dimension (chiefly market access, but also access to efficient inputs) is only one part of the picture. The domestic dimension is the other paramount facet of the integration challenge of modern PTAs.

In reviewing both the rationales and the realities (for seven sectors) of deep integration and attempting to provide a clearer understanding about the specific nature of deep

---

[24] Of course, this can go further, in so far as competition provisions can mandate the legal independence of a competition authority.

integration, this chapter identifies several important general characteristics of modern PTAs that should be taken into account by policymakers.

The first and main message is that *mercantilism is not the right way to think about deep agreements*. Whereas the focus on market access has the unintended consequence of leading to an optimal and mutually beneficial free trade outcome when tariffs are concerned, this is largely insufficient when dealing with the regulatory policies found in modern PTAs. One reason is that deep integration is not achieved through the complete elimination of trade barriers since other regulatory objectives must be met—the mercantilist logic does not pay heed to them, just market access. The usual reciprocity mechanism of trade liberalization may not work any longer because it becomes very difficult to separate clearly measures that promote market access and measures that pursue legitimate regulatory objectives. A second reason is the different nature of the political economy considerations when regulatory issues are at stake as consumers may fear that liberalization will affect their wellbeing (Hoekman et al., 2007).

A second consideration is more positive as it relates to *the discriminatory aspects of preferential integration*. Disentangling the domestic from the global aspects is complex when regulations are concerned, which in effect means that MFN treatment is generally provided. Thus, when liberalization occurs and National Treatment is given in the context of a PTA, it is not infrequent that this is extended to all partners. We have witnessed this in several instances, from customs reform to competition policy. Even in sectors where discrimination could be enforced more easily, such as with investment or procurement, the experience of PTAs shows that MFN liberalization is not uncommon. One should, however, not forget that regulatory issues are by nature complex and offer scope for hidden forms of protection and discrimination.

Since deep integration tends to be multilateral in nature, pursuing liberalization through PTAs, which may be faster and deeper than doing so multilaterally, should then be beneficial and should provide a building block towards free multilateral trade. Evidence also shows that PTAs contribute to the diffusion of liberal regulatory practices to other PTAs. This is either through the imbedded mechanism of a third-party MFN clause or through the diffusion of templates, generally initiated by the two large Northern trade partners, the EU and the USA. Replication of model provisions may be motivated by the desire to keep complexity at manageable levels.

The regulatory issues involved in the new wave of PTAs are complex for countries with weak capacity. *Flexibility is an important feature of deep PTAs*, by tailoring the level of ambition of given disciplines according to the trading partners (Heydon, 2003).[25] While special and differential treatment and policy space are important features of modern trade negotiations involving developing countries, we take the logic further here, arguing that it is not only the nature of partner countries and their capacity that dictates the need for such flexibility, but the regulatory issues themselves. Provisions in PTAs are only one of the elements of broader cooperation that may include institutional

---

[25] One exception is IPRs.

arrangements, hard (e.g., a common institution) or soft (e.g., expert consultations), as well as technical assistance and capacity building; gradual implementation as reform will not be completed overnight and will present unique challenges in a given country context. Areas of cooperation may have to be revisited as regulatory needs and understanding of how to address them change over time (e.g., with technology). The implementation must be monitored and if needed adjusted. Finally institutional mechanisms to build understanding and deal with misunderstandings and disputes must be varied and combine soft and hard law. As noted by Hoekman (2011) the flexibility of approach is required for reasons of practicality, but also because of the inherent uncertainty that surrounds regulation and political economy. Uncertainty is caused because finding the optimal regulation is a discovery process and depends on specific country circumstances such as the nature of the national legal framework and national preferences about regulatory objectives. A flexible and gradual approach to liberalization in the context of a PTA can thus serve this process. Likewise, flexible arrangements can help with the political economy process and the inclusion of a broader and more diverse set of stakeholders (relative to shallow forms of liberalization). Finally, flexibility should also enable PTAs to continue as "laboratories" of innovation for new ways of regulatory liberalization and cooperation.

A fourth observation is that *policymakers must think holistically*. The first aspect of the broader agenda is of course the regulatory one. The reason why such policies are included in PTAs is at least in part because trade liberalization interacts with the objectives pursued under these policies. The regulatory objectives of policies covered in PTAs are numerous: redistribution (services provision obligations); guaranteed standards levels and prudential requirements (services, product standards, environment, labor rights); migration control (labor movement, border management); enforcement of prohibitions and restrictions (border controls, intellectual property); fiscal revenue (border management); and competition (competition law, procurement, investment).

Thus trade policies can no longer be conceived by assuming separability from other policies.[26] Deep integration is as much about trade as it is about other dimensions of economic management and public policy. Starting with liberalization of services, all the deep integration policies meet specific objectives. The liberalization question cannot be divorced from the consideration of these objectives. Thus policymakers should carefully think about *why* and *how* trade agreements should serve these objectives in the specific context of PTAs.

Moreover, policymakers do not only have to deal with multiple policies with different classes of objectives, they must also think about the interaction of these various objectives. In essence, new PTAs capture a broader paradigm than traditional ones. Evans et al. (2006) point out that, unlike traditional trade liberalization that focuses chiefly on goods trade, deep integration aims at broad factor mobility, including investment (capital movement) liberalization, services, migration, and labor

---

[26] While this was never really the case in practice, the traditional approach to trade policy was to consider it in relative isolation of other policies (including other economic policies).

standards dimensions (labor movement). Perhaps nowhere more than in PTAs are all these dimensions explored as deeply and comprehensively. The complementarities thus created might then explain their attraction (Mattoo and Sauvé, 2011). Take for instance the trade facilitation agenda, which requires the streamlining of numerous border measures. All have specific regulatory objectives in many sectors (health, immigration, security controls for instance), the inclusion of services sectors that facilitate trade (transport, logistics, insurance, etc.), the consideration of movement of persons, standards policies, etc.

All these consideration have important implications on how developing countries should approach and implement deep PTAs. This leads to our fifth point: *countries ought to pursue deep rather than broad integration and be strategic about partner choices.* The reason behind prioritization is straightforward as deep integration issues are complex and resource intensive. It seems preferable to invest scarce resources on a few specific areas of priority interest and seek genuine deep cooperation and results rather than having multiple sectors of shallow engagement. By initially focusing efforts on selected sectors, PTAs could achieve results faster as well as possibly making future reform in other areas easier. Deeper rather than broader integration would indeed contribute to strengthen the institutional machinery of agreements, as well as creating demonstration effects of the *possibility* and *how* of reform.

The importance of partner choice is vividly illustrated in the differences among categories of PTAs. North–South agreements are a recent phenomenon, characterized by the push for WTO-plus rules and asymmetric relations. In such agreements, it is difficult for the smaller partner to negotiate on much of the deep integration agenda. Prospects for developing countries revolve more around the import of regulatory rules and templates, and the receipt of technical assistance. Upward harmonization is the option. Prospects for active cooperation on regulatory issues are at best limited. Prospects beyond goods market access have been limited, although in recent agreements with the EU, some headway has been made on services. The generic designation of South–South PTAs masks a diversity of situations. Not all are symmetric (e.g., SACU). They differ greatly in the nature of their institutions from highly integrated institutions (e.g., UEMOA) to partial FTAs (e.g., FTAs involving China). Some are regional in nature and others are not. Some have relatively important intra-regional trade, others not; and so on. Thus, the potential for deep integration must be tested against these realities. Examination of South–South arrangements reveals, however, plenty of scope for deep integration, especially in the more symmetric groupings, where common policies can arise, facilitated by similarities of legal systems (e.g., in West African countries), common borders and trans-border issues (externality problems that need addressing), or the need to pool resources together in the face of low capacity and size. In these instances, putting in place sound institutions and processes and political commitment matters much more than paper agreements. We should also acknowledge that in many cases countries may not be ready to go all the way. It can be recommended then to ensure that PTAs commit to an inbuilt work plan of reform over time and allow for the agreement to be augmented and amended regularly.

Finally, a *focus on implementation is vital*. Deep integration agreements should be understood as "living agreements," where the process of integration is as important as agreeing on rules of liberalization. First, because of the attention that must be devoted to enforcement questions as, in many cases, enacting the legislation is only a start. Compliance with law requires a regulatory infrastructure (such as patent offices, standards and metrology laboratories), a legal infrastructure (with specialized professional bodies, administrative and judicial courts), and information systems. Second, regulatory practice tends to evolve with business practices, technology evolutions, and improvements over time. Third, since the text of the PTAs is only one starting element of the process of integration, implementation aspects must also be carefully examined to see whether or not liberalization is effective. Monitoring and accountability matter. This is a more complex process than verifying that trade barriers are effectively dismantled, and one for which information is often not readily available. In general, implementation in PTAs is not a very transparent process. Fourth, the nature and operation of common institutional arrangements that will govern the PTA and their relation to national ones should be as much a part of the design as negotiations over rules.

REFERENCES

Acharya, R., Crawford, J.-A., Maliszewska, M., and Renard, C. (2011), 'Landscape.' In Chauffour, J.-P., and Maur, J.-C. (eds.) *Preferential Trade Agreements Policies for Development: A Handbook*. Washington, DC: The World Bank, chapter 2.

Aldaz-Carroll, E. (2006), 'Regional Approaches to Better Standards Systems' Policy Research Working Paper No. 3948, The World Bank.

Bagwell, K. and Staiger, R. (2001), 'The WTO as a Mechanism for Securing Market Access Property Rights: Implications for Global Labor and Environmental Issues.' *Journal of Economic Perspectives*, 15(3): 69–88.

Baldwin R., Evenett, R., and Low, P. (2009), 'Beyond Tariffs: Multilateralizing Non-Tariff RTA Commitments.' In Baldwin, R., and Low, P. (eds.) *Multilateralizing Regionalism: Challenges for the Global Trading System*. Cambridge: Cambridge University Press, Chapter 3.

Bergsten, F. (1996), 'Globalizing Free Trade.' *Foreign Affairs*, 75(3): 105–20.

Bhagwati, J. (2008), *Termites in the Trading System*. Oxford: Oxford University Press.

Biadgleng, E. and Maur, J.-C. (2011), 'The Influence of Preferential Trade Agreements on the Implementation of Intellectual Property Rights in Developing Countries: A First Look.' UNCTAD–ICTSD Project on IPRs and Sustainable Development; Issue Paper No. 33; International Centre for Trade and Sustainable Development and United Nations Conference on Trade and Development, Geneva, Switzerland.

Budetta, M. and Piermartini, R. (2009), 'A Mapping of Regional Rules on Technical Barriers to Trade.' In Estevadeordal, A., Suominen, K., and Teh, R. (eds.) *Regional Rules in the Global Trading System*. Cambridge: Cambridge University Press.

Chauffour, J.-P. and Maur, J.-C. (2011), 'Beyond Deep Integration.' In Chauffour, J.-P. and Maur, J.-C. (eds.) *Preferential Trade Agreement Policies for Development: A Handbook*. Washington, DC: The World Bank, chapter 1.

Dawar, K. and Holmes, P. (2011), 'Competition.' In Chauffour, J.-P. and Maur, J.-C. (eds.) *Preferential Trade Agreement Policies for Development: A Handbook*. Washington, DC: The World Bank, chapter 16.

Dawar, K. and Evenett, S. (2011), 'Government Procurement.' In Chauffour, J.-P. and Maur, J.-C. (eds.) *Preferential Trade Agreement Policies for Development: A Handbook*. Washington, DC: The World Bank, chapter 17.

Ethier, W. J. (1998), 'The New Regionalism.' *Economic Journal*, 108(449): 1149–61.

European Commission (1996), 'Community External Policy in the Field of Standards and Conformity Assessment', Communication from the Commission, COM(96) 564 final, 13 November 1996, Brussels: European Commission.

European Commission (2007), 'A Strong Neighborhood Policy', Communication COM(2007) 774 final, Brussels: European Commission.

Evans, D., Holmes, P., Iacovone, L., and Robinson, S. (2006), 'Deep Integration and New Regionalism.' In Evans, D., et al. (eds.) Assessing Regional Trade Agreements with Developing Countries: Shallow and Deep Integration. Trade, Productivity, and Economic Performance. Report prepared for DFID, chapter 2.

Evenett, S. (2008). 'Incorporating Competition Principles into Regional Trade Agreements: Options for Policymakers.' Paper prepared for the Latin American Competition Forum, September 10–11, 2008, Panama City.

Fernandez, R. and Portes, J. (1998). 'Returns to Regionalism: An Analysis of Nontraditional Gains from Regional Trade Agreements.' *World Bank Economic Review*, 12(2): 197–220.

Fink, C. (2011), 'Intellectual Property Rights.' In Chauffour, J.-P. and Maur, J.-C. (eds.) *Preferential Trade Agreement Policies for Development: A Handbook*. Washington, DC: The World Bank, chapter 18.

Heydon, K. (2003), 'Regionalism: A Complement, not a Substitute.' In *Regionalism and the Multilateral Trade System*. Paris: OECD.

Hoekman, B. (2011), 'North South PTAs.' In Chauffour, J.-P. and Maur, J.-C. (eds.) *Preferential Trade Agreement Policies for Development: A Handbook*. Washington, DC: The World Bank, chapter 4.

Hoekman, B., and Kostecki, M. (2001), *The Political Economy of the World Trading System*, Second edition. Oxford: Oxford University Press.

Hoekman, B., Mattoo, A., and Sapir, A. (2007), 'The Political Economy of Services Trade Liberalization: A Case for International Regulatory Cooperation?' *CEPR Discussion Papers* No. 6457.

Horn, H., Mavroidis, P. C., and Sapir, A. (2009), 'Beyond the WTO? An Analysis of EU and US Preferential Trade Agreements' *CEPR Discussion Papers* No. 7317.

Hornbeck, J. F. (2003), 'The U.S.-Central America Free Trade Agreement (CAFTA): Challenges for Sub-Regional Integration.' Report for the US Congress, RL31870.

Jensen, J., Rutherford, T. F., and Tarr, D. G. (2008), 'Modeling Services Liberalization: The Case of Tanzania.' World Bank Policy Research Working Paper Series, No. 4801.

Krugman, P. (1993), 'Regionalism Versus Multilateralism: Analytic Notes.' In De Melo, J., and Panagariya, A. (eds.) *New Dimensions in Regional Integration*. Cambridge: Cambridge University Press.

Lee, J.-W. and Pyun, J. H. (2009), 'Does Trade Integration Contribute to Peace?' Asian Development Bank Working Paper on Regional Integration, No. 24.

Lesser, C. (2007). 'Do Bilateral and Regional Approaches for Reducing Technical Barriers to Trade Converge towards the Multilateral Trade System?' OECD Trade Working Paper No. 58, TAD/TC/WP(2007)12/FINAL.

Mansfield, E. D. and Pevehouse, J. C. (2003), 'Institutions, Interdependence, and International Conflict.' In Gleditch, N., Schneider, G., and Barbieri, K. (eds.), *Globalization and Armed Conflict*. London: Routledge.

Mattoo, A. and Sauvé, P. (2011), 'Services.' In Chauffour, J.-P. and Maur, J.-C. (eds.) *Preferential Trade Agreement Policies for Development: A Handbook*. Washington, DC: The World Bank, chapter 12.

Maur, J.-C., and Shepherd, B. (2010), 'Product Standards.' In Chauffour, J.-P. and Maur, J.-C. (eds.) *Preferential Trade Agreement Policies for Development: A Handbook*. Washington, DC: The World Bank, chapter 10.

Maur, J.-C. (2008), 'Regionalism and Trade Facilitation: A Primer.' *Journal of World Trade*, 42(6): 979–1012.

Messerlin, P., and Zarrouk, J. (2000), 'Trade Facilitation: Technical Regulations and Customs Procedures.' *The World Economy*, 23(4): 577–93.

Miroudot, S. (2011), 'Investment.' In Chauffour, J.-P. and Maur, J.-C. (eds.) *Preferential Trade Agreement Policies for Development: A Handbook*. Washington, DC: The World Bank, chapter 14.

Porges, A. (2011), 'Dispute Settlement.' In Chauffour, J.-P. and Maur, J.-C. (eds.) *Preferential Trade Agreement Policies for Development: A Handbook*. Washington, DC: The World Bank, chapter 22.

Prusa, T. (2011), 'Trade Remedies.' In Chauffour, J.-P. and Maur, J.-C. (eds.) *Preferential Trade Agreement Policies for Development: A Handbook*. Washington, DC: The World Bank, chapter 9.

Schiff, M. and Winters, L. A. (1998), 'Regional Integration as Diplomacy.' *World Bank Economic Review*, 12(2): 271–95.

Schiff, M. and Winters, L. A. (2004), *Regional Integration and Development*. Oxford: Oxford University Press.

Schott, J. J. (2003), 'Assessing US FTA Policy.' In Schott, J. (ed.), *Free Trade Agreements: US Strategies and Priorities*. Washington, DC: Institute for International Economics, chapter 13.

Solano, O. and Sennekamp, A. (2005), 'Competition Provisions in Regional Trade Agreements.' OECD Trade Policy Working Paper No. 32, COM/DAF/TD(2005)3/FINAL.

Spence, M. (2009), 'Negotiating Trade, Innovation and Intellectual Property: Lessons from the CARIFORUM EPA Experience from a Negotiator's Perspective.' *UNCTAD—ICTSD Project on IPRs and Sustainable Development, Policy Brief* No. 4.

Stoler, A. L. (2011), 'TBT and SPS.' In Chauffour, J.-P. and Maur, J.-C. (eds.) *Preferential Trade Agreement Policies for Development: A Handbook*. Washington, DC: The World Bank.

Tinbergen, J. (1954), *International Economic Integration*. Amsterdam: Elsevier.

Torrent, R. (2007), 'The Legal Toolbox for Regional Integration: A Legal Analysis from an Interdisciplinary Perspective.' Paper prepared for the ELSNIT Conference, October 26–27, 2007, Barcelona.

World Bank (2005), *Global Economic Prospects: Trade, Regionalism, and Development*. Washington, DC: The World Bank.

CHAPTER 18

RULES OF ORIGIN[*]

PAUL BRENTON

"Rules of Origin are very, very complex. You don't want to know about them. They are terrible things to deal with."

Canadian Finance Minister, Hon. Michael H. Wilson, February 12, 1992[1]

I. INTRODUCTION

ASCERTAINING the country of origin or "nationality" of imported products is necessary to be able to apply basic trade policy measures such as tariffs, quantitative restrictions, anti-dumping and countervailing duties, and safeguard measures as well as for requirements relating to origin marking, public procurement, and for statistical purposes. Such objectives are met through the application of basic or *non-preferential* rules of origin.

Countries that offer zero or reduced duty access to imports from certain trade partners will apply another and often different set of *preferential* rules of origin to determine the eligibility of products to receive preferential access. The justification for preferential rules of origin is to prevent trade deflection, or simple trans-shipment, whereby products from non-preferred countries are redirected through a free trade partner to avoid the payment of customs duties. Hence the role of preferential rules of origin is to ensure that only goods originating in participating countries enjoy preferences. Therefore, preferential rules of origin are integral parts of preferential trade agreements (PTAs) such as bilateral and regional free trade agreements and the non-reciprocal preferences that industrial countries offer to developing countries.

The nature of rules of origin and their application can have profound implications for trade flows and for the work of customs. Rules of origin can be designed in such a way as

---

[*] This chapter is a revised and updated version of Brenton and Imagawa (2005). It reflects the views of the author and should not in any way be attributed to the World Bank.

[1] This quote is provided in Clark-Flavell (1995).

to restrict trade and therefore can and have been used as trade policy instruments. The proliferation of free trade agreements (FTAs) with accompanying preferential rules of origin is increasing the burdens on customs in many countries with consequent implications for trade facilitation. Perhaps surprisingly, given their potential to influence trade flows, rules of origin are one area of trade policy that has been subject to very little discipline during the almost 50 years of the multilateral rules based system governed by the General Agreement on Tariffs and Trade (GATT) and more recently the World Trade Organization (WTO). It is also worth noting that, during this period, the determination of the country of origin of products has become more difficult as technological change, declining transport costs, and the process of globalization have led to the splitting-up of production chains and the distribution of different elements in the production of a good to different locations. The issue becomes which one or more of these stages of production define the country of origin of the good. This chapter concludes that complex rules of origin, which differ across countries and agreements, can be a significant constraint on trade and a substantial burden on customs and the improvement of trade facilitation. The nature of the rules of origin can act to undermine the stated intentions of PTAs.

    Section II explains what is meant by origin and examines methods for determining substantial transformation. Section III discusses the current situation with regard to non-preferential rules of origin, where a concerted attempt, although one which has yet to bear fruit, has been made to harmonize the rules regarding wholly obtained products and substantial transformation. Section IV elaborates on the definition of preferential rules of origin for which, to date, there has been no attempt to achieve harmonization and for which there are no real and effective multilateral disciplines, and then looks at the rules of origin in existing free trade and preferential trade agreements. Section V reviews the economic implications of rules of origin, discusses the links between rules of origin and the utilization of trade preferences, and estimates of the costs of complying with rules of origin. This section also analyses the use of the rules of origin as a tool of economic development. Finally, Section VI provides some conclusions.

II. Defining Origin

When a product is produced in a single stage or is *wholly obtained* in one country, the origin of the product is relatively easy to establish. This applies mainly to "natural products" and goods made entirely from them, and hence products that do not contain imported parts or materials. Proof that the product was produced or obtained in the preferential trade partner is normally sufficient. For all other cases in which two or more countries have taken part in the production of the good, the rules of origin define the methods by which it can be ascertained in which country the particular product has undergone *sufficient* working or processing or has been subject to a *substantial* transformation (in general these terms can be used interchangeably). A substantial transformation is one that conveys to the product its essential character. Unfortunately, there is no simple and standard rule of origin that can be identified as identifying the "nationality" of a product. The International Convention on the Simplification and Harmonization of Customs Procedures (the Kyoto Convention) defines (in Annex D1) the three main techniques for the determination of origin: change of tariff classification, value added, and specific manufacturing process.

Methods for Determining Substantial Transformation

Change of Tariff Classification

Origin is granted if the exported product falls into a different part of the tariff classification to any imported inputs that are used in its production. This "tariff-shift" method forms the basis of the efforts by the World Customs Organization (WCO) to harmonize non-preferential rules of origin discussed below. Application of this approach has been facilitated by the widespread adoption of the Harmonized System (HS), whereby the majority of countries throughout the world (over 190) are now classifying goods according to the same harmonized categories. There is, however, the issue of the level of the classification at which change is required. Typically it is specified that the change should take place at the heading level (that is at the 4-digit level of the HS).[2] Examples of simple HS headings are:

- "Beer made from malt" (HS 2203) and "umbrellas and sun umbrellas" (HS 6601).

An example of a more sophisticated heading would be:

- "Machinery, plant or laboratory equipment, whether or not electrically heated (excluding furnaces, ovens and other equipment of heading 8514), for the treatment of materials by a process involving a change of temperature such as heating, cooking, roasting, distilling, rectifying, sterilizing, pasteurizing, steaming, drying, evaporating, vaporizing, condensing or cooling, other than machinery or plant of a kind used for domestic purposes; instantaneous or storage water heaters, non-electric" (HS 8419).

However, the HS was not designed specifically as a vehicle for conferring country of origin; its purpose is to provide a unified commodity classification for defining tariff schedules and for the collection of statistics. Thus, in particular cases, it can be argued that change of tariff heading will not identify substantial transformation, whilst in other cases it can be that substantial transformation can occur without change of tariff heading. As a result, schemes utilizing the change of tariff heading criterion usually provide for a wide range of exceptions whereby other criterion must be satisfied to confer origin.

---

[2] The HS comprises 96 chapters (2 digit level), 1,241 headings (4 digit level), and around 5,000 subheadings (6 digit level).

The change of tariff classification can provide both a positive test of origin, by stating the tariff classification of imported inputs that can be used in the production of the exported good (for example, those in a different heading), and a negative test by stating cases where change of tariff classification will not confer origin. For example, in North American Free Trade Agreement (NAFTA), the rule of origin for Tomato Ketchup states that a change to Ketchup (HS 210320) from imported inputs of any chapter will confer origin except subheading 200290 (Tomato Paste). In other words any Ketchup made from imported fresh tomatoes will confer origin but Ketchup made from tomato paste imported from outside of the area will not qualify for preferential treatment even though the basic change of tariff classification requirement has been satisfied.[3] In EU preferential rules of origin, bread, biscuits, and pastry products (HS 1905) can be made from any imported products except those of chapter 11, which includes flour, the basic input to these products.

The WTO Agreement on Rules of Origin (ARO) (the "Origin Agreement") stipulates that preferential and non-preferential rules of origin should be based on a positive standard. However, it allows the use of negative standards (a definition of what does not confer origin) if they "clarify a positive standard." The latter is sufficiently vague as to have had very little impact, such that EU and NAFTA rules of origin, for example, are rife with negative standards (see Box 18.2 below).

Thus, whilst in principle the change of tariff classification can provide for a simple uniform method of determining origin in practice, instead of a general rule there are often many individual rules. Nevertheless, the change of tariff classification rule, once defined, is clear, unambiguous, and easy for traders to learn. It is *relatively* straightforward to implement. In terms of documentary requirements it requires that traders keep records that show the tariff classification of the final product and all the imported inputs. This may be undemanding if the exporter directly imports the inputs but may be more difficult if they are purchased from intermediaries in the domestic market.

Value Added

When the value added in a particular country exceeds a specified percentage, the goods are defined as originating in that country. This criterion can be defined in two ways: either as the minimum percentage of the value of the product that must be added in the country of origin or as the maximum percentage of imported inputs in total inputs or in the value of the product.

As in the case of change of tariff classification, the value added rule has the advantage of being clear, simple, and unambiguous in its definition. However, in actual application, the value added rule can become complex and uncertain. First, there is the issue of the valuation of materials, which may be based upon ex-works, fob, cif, or into-factory prices. Each method of valuation will give a different, here ascending, value of non-originating materials. Second, the application of this method can be costly for firms that

---

[3] The apparent reason for this rule in the NAFTA is to protect producers of tomato paste in Mexico from competition from producers in Chile (Palmeter, 1997).

will require sophisticated accounting systems and the ability to resolve often complex accounting questions. Finally, under the value added method, origin is sensitive to changes in the factors determining production cost differentials across countries, such as exchange rates, wages, and commodity prices. For example, operations that confer origin in one location may not do so in another because of differences in wage costs. An operation that confers origin today may not do so tomorrow if exchange rates change.

Specific Manufacturing Process

This criterion delineates for each product or product group certain manufacturing or processing operations that define origin (positive test) or manufacturing or processing procedures that do not confer origin (negative test). The formulation of these rules can require the use of certain originating inputs or prohibit the use of certain non-originating inputs. For example, EU rules of origin for clothing products stipulate, "manufacture from yarn," whilst the rule for sodium perborate requires manufacture from disodium tetraborate pentahydrate.[4]

The main advantages of specific manufacturing process rules is that, once defined, they are clear and unambiguous so that, from the outset, producers are able to clearly identify whether or not their product is originating. However, there are also a number of drawbacks with this system, including obsolescence following changes in technology and the documentary requirements, such as an up-to-date inventory of production processes, which may be burdensome and difficult to comply with.

Table 18.1 summarizes the main advantages and disadvantages of these different methods of determining sufficient processing or substantial transformation. No one rule dominates others as a mechanism for formally identifying the nationality of all products. Each has its advantages and disadvantages. However, it is clear that different rules of origin can lead to different determinations of origin. For example, in the case of non-preferential rules of origin, the United States changed its rules for textile and clothing products in 1996 in a way that changed the origin or products previously deemed as being of European origin as originating in Far Eastern countries and hence subject to quantitative restrictions under the Agreement on Textiles and Clothing. These changes also required that products such as silk scarves previously labeled as "made in Italy" had to be relabeled as "made in Pakistan," with implications for the purchasing decisions of consumers who take the country of origin indicated on such labels as an indicator of quality (Dehousse, Ghemar, and Vincent, 2002).

In the late 1980s, the EU changed its non-preferential rules of origin for photocopiers to ensure that the operations carried out in the United States by a subsidiary of a Japanese company did not confer origin to the United States. The products concerned were deemed to be originating in Japan and subject to anti-dumping duties.[5] Under preferential schemes, producers who are eligible for preferential access to different markets

---

[4] The EU rule of origin for sodium perborate also allows satisfaction of a maximum import content rule of 40 per cent.

[5] As described in Hirsch (2002).

Table 18.1 Summary of the different approaches to determining origin

Rule	Advantages	Disadvantages	Key issues
Change of tariff classification in the Harmonized System	Consistency with non-preferential rules of origin.Once defined, the rule is clear, unambiguous and easy to learn.Relatively straightforward to implement.	Harmonized System not designed for conferring origin, as a result there are often many individual product specific rules, which can be influenced by domestic industriesDocumentary requirements maybe difficult to comply with.Conflicts over the classification of goods can introduce uncertainty over market access.	Level of classification at which change required—the higher the level the more restrictive. Can be positive (which imported inputs can be used) or negative (defining cases where change of classification will not confer origin) test[a]—negative test more restrictive.
Value added	Clear, simple to specify and unambiguous. Allows for general rather than product specific rules.	Complex to apply—requires firms to have sophisticated accounting systems. Uncertainty due to sensitivity to changes in exchange rates, wages, commodity prices etc.	The level of value added required to confer originThe valuation method for imported materials—methods which assign a higher value (e.g., cif) will be more restrictive on the use of imported inputs
Specific manufacturing process	Once defined, clear and unambiguous.Provides for certainty if rules can be complied with.	Documentary requirements can be burdensome and difficult to comply with. Leads to product specific rules.Domestic industries can influence the specification of the rules.Can quickly become obsolete due to technological progress and therefore require frequent modification.	The formulation of the specific processes required—the more procedures required the more restrictive. Should test be negative (processes or inputs which cannot be used) or a positive test (what can be used)—negative test more restrictive.

[a] A positive determination of origin typically takes the form of "change from any other heading," as opposed to a negative determination of origin, such as "change from any other heading except for the headings of chapter XX." It is worth noting that change of tariff classification, particularly with a negative determination of origin, can be specified to have an effect identical to that of a specific manufacturing process.

under different schemes with different rules of origin may find that their product qualifies under some schemes but not others. For example, a company in a developing country may find that the product that it produces qualifies for preferential access to the EU market under the EU's GSP scheme, but that the exact same product does not satisfy the rules of origin of the US GSP scheme.

Whilst it is difficult to derive specific recommendations with regard to the best practice approach to the design of rules of origin, certain general propositions can be made which apply to both preferential and non-preferential rules of origin:

- The rules of origin should be simple, precise and easy to understand, transparent, predictable, and stable. Rules of origin should avoid or minimize scope for interpretation and administrative discretion.
- They should be designed to have the least trade distorting impact and should not become a disguised non-tariff barrier (NTB). Protectionist lobbying should not compromise the specification of the rules of origin.
- As much as possible, the rules should be consistent across products and across agreements. The greater the inconsistencies, the greater the complexity of the system of rules of origin both for companies and for officials administering the various trade schemes.

III. Status of the Harmonization Work Program for Non-Preferential Rules of Origin

Harmonization of rules of origin has long been a "dream" of customs and trade officials. Under the GATT (1947) the Contracting Parties were free to determine their own rules of origin. Nevertheless, records show that the GATT first considered the harmonization of rules of origin in 1951. Two years later, in 1953, following a recommendation from the International Chamber of Commerce for the adoption of a common definition of nationality of manufactured goods, a GATT working party was established on the "Nationality of Imported Goods" and examined both the definition of origin and proof of origin.

Despite the fact that these early GATT attempts were not successful, the WCO took a significant step forward through the establishment of the International Convention on the Simplification and Harmonization of Customs Procedures (the "Kyoto Convention") that came into force in 1974. Annexes D.1 to D.3 to the Kyoto Convention deal with rules of origin, including administrative matters. Although not many members have ratified these Annexes,[6] they have been influential because they set out the

---

[6] There are 31 Annexes to the Kyoto Convention. Contracting parties to the Convention do not have to accept all the Annexes, but they are required to notify the Secretary General of the WCO that they accept one or more Annexes. Out of the 63 current contracting parties to the Convention, 26 members have accepted Annex D.1, 25 Annex D.2, and 8 Annex D.3). A particular Annex enters into force when at least five members ratify or accede to that Annex.

first international standards or models in the field of origin. For instance, a number of existing preferential and non-preferential rules of origin, including those of non-contracting parties to the Kyoto Convention, have adopted similar or almost identical definitions of wholly obtained goods as those set out in Annex D.1. But with regard to manufactured goods, the Annex does not provide a single set of standard rules of origin concerning the criteria for identifying a "substantial transformation." Instead, it explains the most commonly used criteria: (a) change in tariff classification; (b) value added; and (c) specific manufacturing or processing operations, and suggests "recommended practices" with regard to their use. Nevertheless, each administration has remained free to choose any one or combination of those criteria and to specify those criteria how they wish.

With regard to the change of tariff classification rule, the underlying technical constraint to harmonization in the past was the absence of a common, internationally agreed tool for classifying products. Different countries could classify the same good in different ways. A major breakthrough came in 1988 with the entry into force of the Harmonized System such that all major trading nations now use the same classification system for coding products for customs and statistical purposes.[7] However, because of the trade policy implications, in terms of policies such as anti-dumping measures, attempts to harmonize rules of origin only occurred following inclusion of the issue on the negotiating agenda of a large-scale multilateral trade negotiation, the Uruguay Round of GATT negotiations.

The Uruguay Round and the Agreement on Rules of Origin

During the June 1989 Uruguay Round meetings, Japan proposed to negotiate the harmonization of preferential and non-preferential rules of origin, as well as a mechanism for notification, consultation, and dispute settlement. This was motivated, among other things, by a series of trade disputes during the 1980s between Japan and other East Asian countries, on the one hand, and their major trading partners, on the other. Some of these trade disputes stemmed from the application of rules of origin in conjunction with anti-dumping proceedings. While the United States endorsed the idea to include this issue on the Uruguay Round agenda, the European Community and the EFTA countries were initially reluctant. They considered the issue better suited to the more technical WCO and believed that the discussion should not address the rules of origin used under preferential arrangements.

In February 1990, agreement was reached that the negotiating group should define policy principles (e.g., non-discrimination, transparency, predictability) to govern the application of rules of origin. Another compromise agreement was

---

[7] The HS is used by over 190 countries and customs or economic unions (including 112 contracting parties to the HS Convention), representing about 98 per cent of world trade.

reached prior to the Brussels Ministerial Meeting in December 1990 that the harmonized rules of origin should cover non-preferential trade only. A non-binding common declaration with regard to preferential rules of origin was agreed at this meeting. This contained a number of general exhortations to members to make their preferential rules clear, base them on a positive standard, publish them in accordance with GATT rules, that changes should not be applied retroactively, and that judicial review be available.

The outcome of these negotiations was compiled as an Agreement on Rules of Origin annexed to the Marrakech Agreement Establishing the World Trade Organization, which entered into force in January 1995. The Origin Agreement mandated the Technical Committee on Rules of Origin (TCRO) under the auspices of the WCO and the Committee on Rules of Origin (CRO) under the WTO to undertake a Harmonization Work Program (HWP) for non-preferential rules of origin, to be completed within a three-year period. Under the Origin Agreement, members are obliged to adhere to the following disciplines after the implementation of the results of the HWP (Article 3: Disciplines after the Transition Period):

- Rules of origin are applied equally for all purposes (e.g., application of most favorite nation (MFN) treatment, anti-dumping and countervailing duties, and safeguard measures, origin marking requirements, any discriminatory quantitative restrictions or tariff quotas, government procurement, trade statistics).
- Rules of origin determine origin of goods either by definitions of wholly obtained goods or the substantial transformation criteria.
- Rules of origin observe national treatment and MFN obligations.
- Rules of origin must be administered in a consistent, uniform, impartial, and reasonable manner.
- Laws, regulations, judicial decisions, and administrative rulings of general application relating to rules of origin must be published.
- Origin assessments must be provided, upon request, within 150 days (valid for three years).
- Changes in rules of origin are not to be applied retroactively.
- Any administrative action regarding the determination of origin is subject to possible review.
- Confidentiality of information must be observed.

The HWP and the Draft Harmonized Non-Preferential Rules of Origin

From its inaugural session in February 1995, the TCRO undertook technical work, developing definitions of wholly obtained goods and minimal operations or processes and elaborating upon substantial transformation criteria. At the same time, the Geneva-based CRO has carried out the policy work, including endorsing the results of the TCRO's technical review. It took nearly four years (and 20 formal and informal sessions) for the TCRO to complete its technical review. A key feature of this process was discussion of the rules on a product-by-product basis, as dictated by the Origin Agreement.[8] The work of the TCRO was submitted to the CRO in May 1999. The TCRO agreed to product-specific rules for over 500 out of 1,241 headings; 486 issues[9] were referred to the CRO. The CRO has continued the HWP based on the results of the TCRO's technical review and has substantially narrowed the number of outstanding issues.[10] In September 2002, 94 core policy issues were referred to the WTO General Council and negotiations at the ambassadorial level still continue to date.[11] The General Council has mainly argued about the so-called "implications issue" as to whether the harmonized, non-preferential rules of origin (HRO) should be applied mandatorily to other WTO instruments, in particular anti-dumping and countervailing duty proceedings.

Which are the underlying factors that have hindered the completion of the HWP? The process of harmonization has required the standardization of definitions, rules, and practices, which differ across countries and regions. This has required a consensus building approach that has been time consuming since: (a) the issues were highly technical and the work involved was extremely voluminous and labor intensive; and (b) the disparity among delegations with regard to technical arguments on certain crucial product-specific and other issues was deeply rooted in national industrial and trade policy and, as such, Members had to be ready to change the national policy concerned if they accepted an alternative position. The Origin Agreement itself (Article 9.2c) required that the harmonization work of the TCRO be "conducted on a product-sector basis, as represented by various chapters or sections of the HS nomenclature." This reflects the view of those who believe that such an approach is necessary to achieve non-preferential origin rules that are "objective, understandable and predictable," the objectives defined in the Origin Agreement. On the other hand, it appears that, when negotiations are conducted on a product-by-product basis, it is inevitable that specific domestic interest groups will become involved, ensuring that different countries adopt different and often entrenched positions.

It is important to note that most of the core problems relating to product-specific rules that are still to be resolved relate to products of particular relevance in the exports of developing countries. Of the 94 remaining key product-specific issues, 69 (or 75 per cent) are concerned with agricultural products (45) and textiles and clothing (24). These are products that are subject to the highest levels of protection in developed countries.

---

[8] The Origin Agreement denies the possibility of a conceptual definition of substantial transformation on the basis of a simple rule. Instead the TCRO is mandated to "consider" use of change of tariff subheading or heading on a product basis (Art. 9.2(c)(ii)).

[9] The scope of an issue varies from one subheading to several HS Chapters. Consequently, the fact that 486 issues exist does not mean that there are unresolved product-specific rules for 486 headings.

[10] By end 2002, 349 issues out of 486 had been resolved by the CRO (WTO Doc. G/RO/52).

[11] The CRO was to complete its work by end 2001. The deadline was initially extended to July 2003 for 94 core policy issues and December 2003 for the remaining technical work. These deadlines have subsequently been extended several times.

Only 10 per cent of the outstanding issues concern engineering products, which dominate the exports of the developed countries.

The draft HRO consists of Definitions, General Rules, and two appendices. When
the HWP is completed, the results will be annexed to the Origin Agreement as an integral part thereof (Article 9.4). Definitions and General Rules are general provisions
governing the entire HRO. Appendix 1 sets out two Rules and Definitions for wholly
obtained goods, which evolved from the current Kyoto definitions. It consists of two
parts: goods wholly obtained in one country and products taken from outside the
country (such as from the high seas). It is the latter group that is still under discussion
in the WTO. Appendix 2 consists of product-specific rules of origin for goods that are
not wholly obtained (there is a sequential application of these two appendices with
Appendix 1 having precedence over Appendix 2). Seven Rules, which are to be applied
for the purposes of Appendix 2 only, have been proposed and largely agreed. Rule 3 is
the core (Determination of Origin) and sets out a series of provisions to be applied in
sequence.

In these rules product-specific requirements are set out for each HS heading or subheading. Two types of rules are specified, primary and residual rules. Primary rules, in
the form of change in tariff classification, value added, or specific process rules, or a
combination of these rules, are applied first (there is a sequential application between
the primary and residual rules). There is no precedence amongst these different primary
rules, that is, the primary rules are considered to be "co-equal." Regardless of the place-
ment of the rules, that is, at the chapter, heading, or subheading level of the Harmonized
System, there is no hierarchy among them. The residual rules determine the country of
origin of a good that fails to meet the primary rule, such as a change of heading rule. It
is worth noting that whilst preferential rules of origin lead to either a "yes" (qualified)
or "no" (not qualified) answer, under the HRO a decision defining the country of origin
must ultimately be made, there will be no good for which the country of origin cannot
be determined. Residual rules do have a hierarchical structure, with those defined for
specific products at the chapter level taking precedence over the general residual rules.

The Harmonization of Non-Preferential Rules of Origin: Conclusions

The benefits of harmonized rules of origin to the globalized world economy cannot be
overstated. The application of a single set of rules of origin for the various non-preferential purposes would save time and cost to traders and customs officers all over the world.
It would add to the certainty and predictability of trade by ensuring consistency of origin determination across countries and across time. Harmonized non-preferential rules
of origin would also help to avoid potential trade disputes arising from uncertainties in
the determination of the country of origin with regard to anti-dumping and countervailing duties, safeguard measures, origin marking requirements, quantitative restrictions or tariff rate quotas, and government procurement decisions.

After more than a decade of negotiations, an increasingly defined shape of the HRO has emerged. The HRO are guided by the clear principles laid down in the ARO. From the technical point of view, it has been observed that members cannot pursue absolute consistency between product-specific rules of origin as long as the results of the HWP are the fruit of compromise. However, such a fact does not undermine the benefit of having *harmonized* non-preferential rules of origin. Transparency and consistency in origin determination cannot be ensured without a clear standard. Nevertheless, the existence of a "far from perfect" standard is better than the absence of any standard whatsoever, as shown by the benefits of introducing the Harmonized System that has led to the benefits of a "common language" for purposes of classification. Thus, whatever the applicable rules of origin are, once harmonized, those rules are the same both in the exporting and in the importing country. In a highly interconnected world, there can be substantial benefits from having a single set of rules applied in all WTO members.

A further advantage of harmonized, non-preferential rules of origin would be that they would provide a benchmark by which to assess rules of origin applied on preferential trade flows. Countries seeking rules of origin that deviate from the non-preferential rules could be asked by partners to explicitly justify why the non-preferential rules of origin are insufficient. It is in this context that we now proceed to a more detailed discussion of the preferential rules of origin and their impact on trade and customs.

IV. The Definition of Preferential Rules of Origin

Preferential rules of origin define the conditions that a product must satisfy to be deemed as originating in a country that is eligible for preferential access to a partner's market, and that it has not simply been trans-shipped from a non-qualifying country or been subject to only minimal processing. In practice, the greater the level of work that is required by the rules of origin, the more difficult it is to satisfy those rules and the more restrictive those rules are in constraining market access relative to what is required simply to prevent trade deflection. This is particularly true for small, less-diversified developing economies. Thus, the higher the amount of domestic value added required by a value added rule, the more difficult it will be to comply with since there will be less scope for the use of imported parts and materials. A rule of origin that prevents the use of imported flour in the production of pastry products such as biscuits, for example, will be very restrictive for countries that do not have a competitive milling industry.

Preferential rules of origin often differ from non-preferential rules. In the main, it is the requirements relating to specific processing that vary and are usually more demanding in PTAs. However, there are also cases, some of them initially rather surprising, where rules relating to what would appear to be wholly obtained products are more restrictive in PTAs. (See Box 18.1 below for such an example.)

Box 18.1 Example of Restrictive rules of Origin: The Case of EU Imports of Fish

On the face of it determining the origin of fish, fresh or chilled, would appear to be straightforward with origin being conferred to the country whose trawler caught the fish, there is after all no apparent import content in the fish. However, in practice the determination of origin for fish caught outside of territorial waters but within the exclusive economic zone of a country can be very complex. To receive preferential access to the EU under the Generalized System of Preferences (GSP), all of the following conditions must be satisfied:

The vessel must be registered in the beneficiary country or in the EU.

The vessel must sail under the flag of the beneficiary or of a member state of the EU.

The vessel must be at least 60 per cent owned by nationals of the beneficiary country or the EU or by companies with a head office in either the beneficiary country or a EU state of which the Chairman and a majority of the board members are nationals of those countries.

The master and the officers must be nationals of the beneficiary country or an EU member and at least 75 per cent of the crew must be nationals of the beneficiary country or the EU.

Under the EU's Cotonou agreement, which gives preferential access to the EU market to countries in Africa, the Caribbean, and the Pacific (ACP), the rules of origin for fish are slightly different and a little more liberal than those for GSP countries.

The vessel must be registered in the EU or any ACP state.

The vessel must sail under the flag of any ACP country of the EU.

The vessel must be at least 50 per cent owned by nationals of any ACP or EU state and the Chairman and the majority of the board members must be nationals of any of those countries.

Under certain conditions the EU will accept vessels chartered or leased by the ACP state under the Cotonou agreement.

Under Cotonou 50 per cent of the crew, the master, and officers must be nationals of any ACP state or the EU.

So identifying the nationality of a fish can be complex task!

With regard to requirements relating to sufficient processing, change of tariff classification is used in the vast majority of current PTAs and features in both EU agreements and NAFTA. WTO (2002) shows that of 87 FTAs and other PTAs investigated, 83 used change of tariff classification in the determination of origin. Most agreements specify that the change should take place at the heading level (that is at the 4-digit level), although in many agreements, especially those involving the EU and in the NAFTA, the tariff shift requirement varies across different products. Estevadeordal and Suominen (2003) show that in NAFTA, whilst around 40 per cent of tariff lines require a change of tariff heading, for most tariff lines (54 per cent) it is a change of chapter (2-digit level) that is required. The requirement of change of chapter is more restrictive than change of heading. For a small number of products in NAFTA, it is only change of subheading that is required.

Whilst change of tariff heading is used in the majority of PTAs, it is seldom the only method applied. It is also important to note that in some agreements, such as those involving the EU, change of tariff classification is applied to some products while the other methods, value added rules and specific technical processes, will be applied to other products. In the NAFTA rules of origin, all rules tend to require at least change of tariff classification, but the level at which change is required varies across products. This typically leads to considerable complication for customs officials in the determination of origin in PTAs. In contrast, many of the agreements involving developing countries tend to provide general rules of origin and eschew the detailed product-by-product approach adopted by the EU and NAFTA. Further, in EU agreements and in NAFTA for certain products, rules will be stipulated that require satisfaction of more than one method to confer origin. This is clearly more restrictive than a requirement to satisfy a single method. For example, in NAFTA rules of origin the requirement for passenger motor vehicles (HS 870321) is

- A change to subheading 8703.21 from any other heading provided there is a regional value content of not less than 50 % under the net cost method.

In some agreements for certain products, two or more methods will be stipulated and satisfaction of any one of the methods will be sufficient to confer origin. For example, in the EU rules of origin, the requirements for wooden office furniture (HS) 940330) are

- manufacture in which all the material used is classified within a heading other than that of the product, or
- manufacture in which the value of all the materials used does not exceed 40 per cent of the ex-works price of the product.

Providing alternative means of satisfying origin requirements is more liberal and will facilitate trade under preferential trade agreements.

With regard to the value added requirements, the WTO concludes that on average a threshold on domestic content of between 40 and 60 per cent is the norm, with the average import requirement of between 60 and 40 per cent. In the EU agreements, there are various thresholds on import content ranging from 30 to 50 per cent. In NAFTA, there is a domestic content requirement of either 50 or 60 per cent according to the method used to value the product. A value added requirement of 50 per cent can be very demanding in the globalized world of today in which production has become split across, often many, countries. A further feature of globalization is that in a range of products such as clothing products, computers, and telecommunication equipment, much of the value added lies in the intermediate products. High value added requirements therefore become particularly difficult for developing countries to satisfy since it is the final labor intensive stage that they host. It is in this way that restrictive rules of origin act to con-strain specialization at the country level.

In general these percentage value rules are rarely applied as the sole test of origin and are typically applied with the change of tariff classification. Exceptions are ANZCERTA, SPARTECA, and AFTA, which have percentage requirements without any additional need for change of tariff heading, although all three agreements do require that the last process of manufacture be undertaken in the exporting country.

As noted above, under the value added method, origin is sensitive to changes in fac-tors such as exchange rates, wages, and commodity prices. This means that the value added method will tend to penalize low labor cost locations that will find it more dif-ficult to add the necessary value relative to higher cost locations, and it is likely to cause particular problems of compliance for companies in developing countries that lack the sophisticated accounting systems necessary under this method.

Rules based upon specific manufacturing processes are widely used (in 74 of the 83 PTAs analyzed by the WTO), often in conjunction with change of tariff classification and/or the value added criterion, and are a particular feature of the rules applied to the textiles and clothing sectors.

Examples of rules of origin and their implications for conferring origin:

- A producer imports cotton fabric (HS5208), which is then dyed, cut, and made-up into cotton shirts (HS6105). The value of the imported materials amounts to 65 per cent of the value of the shirts. In this case, the product would be originating under the change of tariff heading rule. The product would not be originating under a value added rule requiring an import content of no more than 60 per cent (or a domestic content of more than 40 per cent). A specific manufacturing process requirement that the product be manufactured from yarn (the production stage before fabric) would entail that the product would not be originating.[12]
- A doll (HS9502) is made from imported plastics and imported ready-made garments and footwear. The value of the imported materials amounts to 50 per cent of the value of the doll. In this case, the doll would be originating under a value added rule requiring an import content of no more than 60 per cent, but would not be originating under the change of tariff heading since garments and accessories for dolls are normally classified under the same tariff heading as dolls.

Most PTAs also specify a range of operations that are deemed to be insufficient work-ing or processing to confer origin. Typically these include: simple packaging operations, such as bottling, placing in boxes, bags and cases, and simple fixing on cards and boards; simple mixing of products and simple assembly of parts; and operations to ensure the

---

[12] This yarn-forward rule is common in EU agreements for all clothing products. The USA typically applies an even stricter process rule that the clothing be made from fibers, entailing that both spinning into yarn and weaving into fabric as well as the making up into clothing are required in the exporting country to confer origin on the product.

preservation of products during transport and storage. These requirements act to ensure that these basic operations do not confer origin even if the basic rule of origin, such as change of tariff heading, has been satisfied.

There are several other typical features of the rules of origin of preferential trade schemes, which can influence whether or not origin is conferred on a product and hence determine the impact of the scheme on trade flows. These are cumulation, tolerance rules, and absorption. The treatment of duty drawback and of outward processing outside of the free trade or preferential trade partners can also be important.

Cumulation

The basic rules of origin define the processing that has to be done in the individual beneficiary or partner to confer origin. Cumulation is an instrument allowing producers to import materials from a specific country or regional group of countries without undermining the origin of the final product. In effect, the imported materials from the identified countries are treated as being of domestic origin of the country requesting preferential access. There are three types of cumulation, bilateral, diagonal (or partial), and full.

The most basic form of cumulation is *bilateral cumulation*, which applies to materials provided by either of two partners of a PTA. In this case, originating inputs, that is materials, which have been produced in accordance with the relevant rules of origin, imported from the partner, qualify as originating materials when used in a country's exports to that partner. For example, under the EU's GSP scheme, the rule of origin for cotton shirts states that origin is conferred to a beneficiary country if the shirt is manufactured from yarn. That is, non-originating yarn may be imported, but the weaving into fabric and cutting and the making up into a shirt must take place in the beneficiary. The EU's GSP scheme allows for bilateral cumulation, so that fabric, which originates in the EU (that is fabric that has been produced in accordance with the rule of origin for fabric, in the case of the EU scheme this is that it has been produced from the stage of fibers) can be treated as originating in the beneficiary country. Thus, originating fabrics can be imported from the EU and used in the production of shirts, which will qualify for preferential access to the EU. However, the EU is often not the least-cost supplier of inputs, and so the benefits of this type of cumulation can be limited. If the extra cost of using EU sourced inputs rather than the lowest-cost inputs from elsewhere exceeds the available benefit from preferential access, then cumulation will have no effect and there will be no improvement in market access.

Second, there can be *diagonal cumulation* on a regional basis, so that qualifying materials from anywhere in the specified region can be used without undermining preferential access. In other words, parts and materials from anywhere in the region that qualify as originating can be used in the manufacture of a final product that can then be exported with preferences to the partner country market. Diagonal cumulation is widely used in EU agreements but is not applied by NAFTA. In Europe, a pan-European system of rules of origin with diagonal cumulation has been developed that governs EU FTAs with the EFTA countries and countries in Central and Eastern Europe. Diagonal cumulation is allowed under the EU's GSP scheme, but within a limited set of regional groups that have pursued their own regional trade agreements. For example, under the EU's GSP scheme, diagonal cumulation can take place *within* four regional groupings: ASEAN, CACM, the Andean Community, and SAARC. Diagonal cumulation allows *originating* materials from regional partners to be further processed in another country in the group and treated as if the materials were originating in the country where the processing is undertaken.[13] However, this flexibility in sourcing is constrained by the further requirement that the value added in the final stage of production exceed the highest customs value of any of the inputs used from countries in the regional grouping. Thus, for example, with diagonal cumulation, shirt producers in Cambodia can use fabrics from Indonesia (providing they are originating, that is, produced from the stage of fibers) and still receive duty free access to the EU. But the value added in Cambodia must exceed the value of the imported fabric from Indonesia. Similarly, producers in Nepal can import originating fabric from India and still qualify for preferential access to the EU if the value added in Nepal is sufficient.

However, UNCTAD (2001) shows how the value added requirement mentioned above can render regional cumulation of little value. For example, value added in the making up of clothing in Bangladesh ranges from between 25 and 35 per cent of the value of the product so that the import content of the fabrics from India is around 65 to 75 per cent. In this case, the value added requirement placed on regional cumulation is not met, and origin of the made-up clothing is not conferred on Bangladesh but on India. Regional cumulation still allows clothing produced in Bangladesh from Indian fabrics preferential access to the EU, not at the zero rate (for which Bangladesh is eligible) but at the rate for which India is eligible, which is a 20 per cent reduction from the MFN rate. Thus, instead of the zero duty, which is in principle available to Bangladesh under the EBA, a tariff of over 9 per cent would be levied on these exports from Bangladesh to the EU.

Finally, there can be *full cumulation* whereby any processing activities carried out in any participating country in a regional group can be counted as qualifying content regardless of whether the processing is sufficient to confer originating status to the materials themselves. In certain GSP schemes, cumulation is permitted across all developing country beneficiaries. Full cumulation allows for more fragmentation of production processes among the members of the regional group, and so stimulates increased economic linkages and trade within the region. Under full cumulation, it may be easier for more developed higher labor-cost countries to outsource labor-intensive, low-tech production stages to less-developed, lower-wage partners whilst maintaining the preferential status of the good produced in low-cost locations. Diagonal cumulation, by requiring more stages of production and/or higher value added to be undertaken in

---

[13] For both bilateral and regional cumulation, there can be an additional requirement that the processing carried out be more than "insufficient working or processing." This is typical in EU agreements but not those of other countries, and requires that more than packing, mixing, cleaning, preserving, and simple assembly of parts take place.

the lower-cost country, may make it more difficult for the products produced by out-sourcing to qualify for preferential access. However, the documentary requirements of full cumulation can be more onerous than those required under diagonal cumulation. Detailed information from suppliers of inputs may be required under full cumulation, whilst the certificates of origin, which accompany imported materials, may suffice to show conformity under diagonal cumulation. For this reason, it is desirable that traders be offered the opportunity to use either diagonal or full cumulation.

Under full cumulation, all of the processing carried out in participating countries is assessed in deciding whether there has been substantial transformation. Hence, full cumulation provides for deeper integration amongst participating countries. Full cumulation is rare and is currently applied in the EU agreements with the EFTA countries, in the EU agreements with Algeria, Morocco, and Tunisia, and under the Cotonou Agreements between the EU and the ACP countries. It is also available in the GSP schemes of Japan and the United States, amongst countries within specified groupings, and on a global basis amongst all developing country beneficiaries in the schemes of Australia, Canada, and New Zealand, as well as in the following regional agreements, ANZERTA, and SPARTECA.

For example, a clothing product made in one country from fabric produced in a regional partner that in turn was made from non-originating yarn would be eligible for duty free access to the EU under full cumulation but not under diagonal cumulation, since the fabric would not be deemed to be originating (the rule of origin for the fabric requires manufacture from fibers).

A second example is given whereby country A provides parts (say chassis for bicy-cles) to country B that are then processed (painted and prepared) and sent to country C for final assembly using other locally produced parts (tires and seat) before being exported to Country D. Countries B, C, and D participate in the same FTA; Country A is not a member. The value of the final product (bicycle) exported from Country C to Country D comprises 25 per cent of parts from Country A, 25 per cent of value added in Country B, and 50 per cent of parts and value added in Country C. The value of parts from Country A comprises 50 per cent of the value of the intermediate product exported from Country B to Country C. If there were a 40 per cent maximum import content for all products, the bicycle exported from Country C to D would qualify for preferential access under full cumulation (only the 25 per cent of parts from Country A is non-originating). However, it would not qualify under diagonal cumulation (the value of non-originating materials in the product exported by Country B exceeds 40 per cent). This intermediate product would not be treated as originating, and the total of non-originating materials in the final product is now calculated as 50 per cent of the final price of the bicycle (the value from both countries and B).

Tolerance or De Minimis

Tolerance or *de minimis* rules allow a certain percentage of non-originating materials to be used without affecting the origin of the final product. Thus, the tolerance rule can act to make it easier for products with non-originating inputs to qualify for preferences under the change of tariff heading and specific manufacturing process rules. This provision does not affect the value added rules. The tolerance rule does not act to lower the limitation on the value of imported materials. The non-originating materials will always be counted in import value content calculations.

Under the NAFTA, non-originating materials can be used even if the rule on sufficient processing is not fulfilled provided their value does not exceed 7 per cent of the value of the final product. Under the EU's GSP scheme, the threshold is 10 per cent, but under the Cotonou Agreement between the EU and the ACP countries, the tolerance rule allows 15 per cent of non-originating materials that would otherwise not be acceptable to be used. For example, in the case of the doll given above in which the use of dolls clothing accessories denied origin to the final product under the change of heading rule (since the accessories are classified under the same heading), origin would have been conferred under the EU GSP, for example, if the value of the dolls clothing and accessories was less than 10 per cent of the value of the doll.

Thus, the tolerance rule can act to make it easier for products with non-originating inputs to qualify for preferences under the change of tariff heading and specific manufacturing process rules. However, the tolerance rules applied to the textiles and clothing sector are often different and generally less favorable than the general rules on tolerance. In many cases, the rule is applied in terms of the maximum weight rather than value of non-originating materials that are tolerated, and in cases where the value threshold is maintained, it is set at a lower level than in the general rule.

Absorption (or Roll-Up) Principle

The absorption principle provides that parts or materials that have acquired originating status by satisfying the relevant rules of origin for that product can be treated as being of domestic origin in any further processing and transformation. This is of particular relevance to the value added test. For example, in the production of a particular part, origin is conferred since imported materials constitute 20 per cent of the final price of the part and are less than the maximum 30 per cent import content rule of origin. This part will then be treated as 100 per cent originating when incorporated into a final product. The 20 per cent import content of the part is not taken into account when assessing the import content of the final product. The converse of this is that, if the part does not satisfy the relevant rule of origin, then it is deemed to be 100 per cent non-originating (so-called 'roll-down'). Ideally, if the part or materials do not satisfy the relevant rule of origin then the portion of value added domestically should still be counted in the determination of the origin of the final product.

Duty Drawback

Provisions relating to duty drawback can lead to the repayment of duties on non-originating inputs used in the production of a final product exported to a freetrade or preferential trade partner. Some agreements contain explicit no drawback rules that will affect decisions relating to the sourcing of inputs by firms exporting within the trade area and will reduce the previous incentives towards the use of imported inputs from non-participating countries towards the use of originating inputs from participating ones. Increasingly important are rules concerning *territoriality* and the treatment of outward processing by companies located within the FTA to locations outside it. These rules determine whether processing outside of the area undermines the originating status of the final product exported from one partner to another.

Rules of Origin in Existing Free Trade and Preferential Trade Agreements

Table 18.2 below provides a simplified look at the key features of the rules of origin applied in a number of regional and bilateral trade schemes. The table contrasts the nature of the rules applied as well as the use of cumulation mechanisms, tolerance rules, and absorption.

Table 18.2 shows that all three methods of determining origin are employed in agreements involving the EU and NAFTA. A key feature of the EU and NAFTA models of rules of origin is that the rules are specified at a very detailed level on a product-by-product basis. The Japan–Singapore agreement also follows this approach. The USA–Singapore FTA has rules of origin that are very similar to those of the NAFTA, which means that product specific and sometimes very complex rules are specified. The annex specifying these rules of origin can be very large. In the USA–Singapore agreement, there are over 240 pages of product-specific rules of origin. Box 18.2 provides a further example of complex and restrictive rules of origin from the NAFTA rules of origin for clothing products.

This detailed product-specific approach to rules of origin of the EU and NAFTA can be contrasted with most of the agreements involving developing countries, such as AFTA, COMESA, and Mercosur, where general rules are typically specified and there are no, or very few, product-specific rules of origin. This is suggestive that domestic industry did not play a significant role in the specification of these rules. Some agreements, such as AFTA, rely solely on the value added method. The COMESA rules of origin require satisfaction of a value criterion (either the cif value of imports must not exceed 60 per cent of the value of all materials used or domestic value added should be at least 35 per cent of the ex-factory cost of the goods[14]) *or* a change of tariff heading.[15]

What are the merits of these different approaches to the specification of preferential rules of origin? Specifying detailed product-by-product rules can lead to precise rules that leave very little scope for interpretation. Indeed, some argue that a product-by-product approach based upon input from domestic producers is the best way to deal with the specification of rules of origin. However, as the examples in this chapter show, product-specific rules can become very complex and restrictive, reflecting the fact that

---

[14] The COMESA agreement also specifies that a range of goods deemed to be of particular importance to economic development need only satisfy a 25 per cent domestic value added criterion.

[15] At the present time, however, the change of tariff heading provision is not being implemented.

Box 18.2 More Restrictive Rules of Origin: The Case of Clothing under NAFTA Rules

The following example is for men's or boys' overcoats made of wool (HS620111).

A change to subheading 620111 from any other chapter, except from heading 5106 through 5113, 5204 through 5212, 5307 through 5308 or 5310 through 5311, Chapter 54 or heading 5508 through 5516, 5801 through 5802 or 6001 through 6006, provided that:

The good is both cut and sewn or otherwise assembled in the territory of one or more of the Parties...

The basic rule of origin stipulates change of chapter, but then provides a list of headings and chapters from which inputs cannot be used. Thus, in effect, the overcoat must be manufactured from the stage of wool fibers forward since imported woolen yarn (HS5106-5110) or imported woolen fabric (HS5111-5113) can be used. However, the rule also states that neither imported cotton thread (HS5204) nor imported thread of manmade fibers (HS54) can be used to sew the coat together. This rule in itself is very restrictive; however, the rule for this product is further complicated by requirements relating to the visible lining:

Except for fabrics classified in 54082210, 54082311, 54082321, and 54082410, the fabrics identified in the following sub-headings and headings, when used as visible lining material in certain men's and women's suits, suit-type jackets, skirts, overcoats, car coats, anoraks, windbreakers, and similar articles, must be formed from yarn and finished in the territory of a party: 5111 through 5112, 520831 through 520859, 520931 through 520959, 521031 through 521059, 521131 through 521159, 521213 through 521215, 521223 through 521225, 540742 through 540744, 540752 through 540754, 540761, 540772 through 540774, 540782 through 540784, 540792 through 540794, 540822 through 540824 (excluding tariff item 540822aa, 540823aa or 540824aa), 540832 through 540834, 551219, 551229, 551299, 551321 through 551349, 551421 through 551599, 551612 through 551614, 551622 through 551624, 551632 through 551634, 551642 through 551644, 551692 through 551694, 600110, 600192, 600531 through 600544 or 600610 through 600644...

This stipulates that the visible lining used must be produced from yarn and finished in either party. This rule may well have been introduced to constrain the impact of the tolerance rule that would normally allow 7 per cent of the weight of the article to be of non-originating materials. In overcoats and suits, the lining is probably less than 7 per cent of the total weight. Finally, it is interesting to note that the rules of origin also provide a number of very specific exemptions to the rules of origin for materials in short supply or not produced in the United States and reflects firm-specific lobbying to overcome the restrictiveness of these rules of origin when the original NAFTA rules of origin were defined. The most specific example is where apparel is deemed to be originating if assembled from imported inputs of

Fabrics of subheading 511111 or 511119, if hand-woven, with a loom width of less than 76 cm, woven in the United Kingdom in accordance with the rules and regulations of the Harris Tweed Association, Ltd., and so certified by the Association...

So, the job of business and the relevant official to check consistency with such rules is clearly not a simple one!

Table 18.2 Rules of origin in selected free-trade and preferential trade agreements

	Change of tariff classification (principal, secondary level)	Value added (in per cent)		Specific manufacture process	Cumulation	Tolerance (in per cent)	Absorption
		Domestic or import content	Implied import content				
A. Agreements involving the EU							
EU Pan Euro	Yes (4,2)	Yes–Import (50–30)	50–30	Yes	BilateralDiagonal	Yes 10[b]	Yes
EU GSP	Yes (4,2)	Yes–Import (50–30)	50–30	Yes	Bilateral, diagonal[a]	Yes 10[b]	Yes
EU Cotonou	Yes (4,2)	Yes–Import (50–30)	50–30	Yes	Full	Yes 15[b]	Yes
EU–Chile	Yes (4,2)	Yes–Import (50–30)	50–36	Yes	Bilateral	Yes 10	Yes
EU–Mexico	Yes (4,2)	Yes–Import (50–30)	50–30	Yes	Bilateral	Yes 10	Yes
EU–South Africa	Yes (4,2)	Yes–Import (50–30)	50–30	Yes	Bilateral, Diagonal (ACP)Full (SACU)	Yes 15[b]	Yes
B. Agreements in the Americas and with the USA							
NAFTA	Yes (2,4,6)	Yes–Domestic (60–50)	50–40	Yes	Bilateral	Yes 7[b]	Yes[e]
Canada–Chile	Yes	Yes–Domestic (60–25)	75–40	Yes	Bilateral	Yes 9	Yes
US–Israel		Yes–Domestic (35)	65		Bilateral[c]	NA	Yes
C. Agreements in Asia/Pacific and with Asian countries							
AFTA		Yes–Import (60)[d]	60		Diagonal	NA	Yes
ANZERTA		Yes–Domestic (50)[d]	50		Full	NA	Yes

Agreement							
Singapore–Japan	Yes (4)	Yes–Domestic (60)	40	Yes	Bilateral	Yes	Yes
Singapore–New Zealand (ANZSCEP)		Yes–Domestic (40)[d]	60		Bilateral	NA	No
Singapore–US	Yes (2,4,6)	Yes–Domestic (55–35)	65–45	Yes	Bilateral	Yes 10[b]	No
D. Agreements amongst developing countries							
CACM	Yes (4)				Bilateral	Yes	Yes
CARICOM	Yes (4)				Bilateral	No	No
COMESA	Yes (4)	Yes–Import (60), Domestic (35)	60		Full	No	Yes
Mercosur	Yes (4)	Yes–Domestic (60)	40		Bilateral	No	Yes[e]

[a] Within Andean, ASEAN, CACM, SAARC only and subject to a 50 per cent value added requirement in the country of export

[b] Alternative rules for textiles and clothing products, often in terms of weight rather than value. Sectoral exemptions are common. For example, the EU–South Africa agreement excludes certain meat products, fish and alcoholic beverages, and tobacco from the general tolerance rule. Under NAFTA, tolerance does not cover dairy produce, citrus fruits and juices, and certain machinery, such as air conditioners, amongst others.

[c] Up to a maximum of 15 per cent of the value of the product, with the additional requirement that the last stage of manufacture be performed in the exporting country, excluding automotive products.

Sources: WTO (2002), Estevadeordal and Suominen (2003), and individual agreements.

a product-by-product approach offers opportunities for sectoral interests to influence the specification of rules of origin in a way that is not directly related to their function of identifying the nationality of products and of preventing trade deflection.

The more complex and the more technical the rules become, the greater the scope for the participation of domestic industries in setting restrictive rules of origin (Hoekman, 1993). Indeed "the formulation of product specific rules of origin is, by its nature, very much out of the practical control of generalists, which is to say government officials at the policy level, and very much in the practical control of specialists, which is to say the representatives of concerned industries" (Palmeter, 1997). Other interests, such as consumers of the relevant product, are effectively excluded from discussion concerning the rules of origin. Those who lobby hardest for trade policy interventions are not altruistic; and their objectives with regard to rules of origin are likely to be to restrict competition from imports and to expand their own exports within an FTA at the expense of third-country suppliers. Such objectives can be more effectively pursued when policy is determined in an environment that lacks transparency and openness, as can easily occur when rules of origin are determined in a product-by-product manner.

From a trade policy perspective, the restrictiveness of a value added rule, in terms of its impact on trade, is clearer and more apparent than the change of tariff classification and specific manufacturing process rules. It is relatively straightforward to compare alternative proposals concerning a value added rule. The extent of protection engendered by complex and technical rules of origin that differ across products is much more difficult to detect. This asymmetry of information is one reason why those groups seeking protection will push for complex rules of origin, and why the change of tariff classification and specific manufacturing process rules may be more susceptible to capture by protectionist, domestic interest groups (Hirsch, 2002).

Thus, it is apparent that adopting a product-by-product approach to rules of origin will tend to lead to rules that are more restrictive than is necessary to prevent trade deflection, that is, protectionist rules of origin, and can lead to an overly complex system that is difficult to implement by traders and adds considerably to the burden of customs.

On the other hand, it appears that more general rules of origin can lead to greater scope for interpretation, as noted by Izam (2003), for example, with regard to the rules of origin in the Latin American Integration Association. In Asia, there are some suggestions of under-utilization of AFTA preferences, reflecting uncertainties concerning the rules of origin. It appears that the rules of origin may be subject to different interpretations in different ASEAN countries, leading to inconsistent application of the rules throughout the region.[16] Nevertheless, this suggests the need for more effective coordination between customs and other relevant authorities in different partners to clarify existing rules and regulations rather than more restrictive rules of origin. However, it is also important that alternative rules be considered so that producers are allowed some flexibility in proving origin. Hence, providing producers with the option of satisfying

---

[16] <http://www.us-asean.org/ctc/thai_Customs_workshop/pwc.ppt>.

either a value added rule or a change of tariff classification rule is likely to be trade facilitating.

In Table 18.2, the column showing the use of the value added methods highlights the variation in the permitted amount of non-originating import content across the different agreements. In the Canada–Chile agreement, for example, products are typically subject to a change of tariff classification (the level of change required varies by product) and a domestic value added requirement that varies between 25 and 60 per cent (according to the product and the method of valuation used). In the USA–Chile agreement, where the rules are similar to those of NAFTA but are not identical for all products, the required domestic content is between 35 and 55 per cent. Under the Canada–Chile agreement, for example, plastic products (HS39) must satisfy requirements of change of tariff heading and between 50 and 60 per cent of domestic value added (depending on the method of valuation). Under the USA–Chile agreement, most plastic products need only satisfy the requirement of change of subheading to be originating. To be originating under the USA–Chile agreement, non-electrical engineering products (HS84) must satisfy a change of subheading and a domestic value content of between 35 and 45 per cent (according to method of valuation), whilst under the Canada–Chile agreement, such products need to satisfy change of subheading but only a 25 to 35 per cent content requirement (depending on valuation method). Thus, certain products produced in Chile that are granted duty free access to Canada may not receive such treatment in the United States due to the more liberal rules of origin applied in the Canada–Chile agreement for those products, whilst other products may satisfy US rules of origin requirements but not those of Canada.

Table 18.2 also shows that all the agreements contain provisions regarding cumulation, but also that there is considerable variation in the nature of cumulation. For example, the EU allows for diagonal cumulation in the Pan-European Area of Cumulation encompassing the EFTA, Central and Eastern European, and the Balkan countries, whilst there is full cumulation amongst the African and Caribbean countries under the Cotonou agreement. Similarly, for tolerance rules, which are widely applied in agreements that are not based on the sole use of the value added method, there are considerable differences across agreements, even those involving the same country. Under the EU–Mexico Free Trade Agreement, non-originating materials up to 10 per cent of the value of the final product can be used, whilst under the agreement between the EU and South Africa, the level of tolerance is set at 15 per cent. Different rules of tolerance are often established for certain sectors, especially textiles and clothing. Table 18.2 also shows the widespread use of the absorption principle.

Thus, this simple and brief look at the nature of the rules of origin applied in a number of existing FTAs and PTAs highlights that the methods of defining origin and provisions relating to cumulation, tolerance, and absorption are widely applied. However, there is little commonality across agreements in the precise nature of the rules that are adopted. In general, recent agreements involving the EU and the United States are based upon detailed, often complex, product-specific rules of origin. The restrictiveness of these rules would appear to vary across sectors. For example, the rules for clothing products requiring production from yarn can be particularly difficult to satisfy for small, less-developed economies. As such the impact of these agreements will not be uniform across sectors.

V. The Economic Implications of Rules of Origin

Rules of Origin and Trade Preferences

The specification and implementation of rules of origin can be a major determinant of the impact of FTAs and PTAs. Compliance with rules of origin entails costs that can affect the sourcing and investment decisions of companies. If the optimal input mix for a firm involves the use of imported inputs that are proscribed by the rules of origin of an FTA in which the country participates, then the rules of origin will reduce the value of the available preferences. The firm will have to shift from the lowest to a higher cost source of inputs in the domestic economy that will reduce the benefits of exporting under a lower tariff. In the extreme, if the cost difference exceeds the size of the tariff preference, then the firm will prefer to source internationally and to pay the MFN tariff. The ability to cumulate inputs from a partner under bilateral, diagonal, or full cumulation will tend, in increasing order, to open the possibilities for identifying low cost sources of inputs that do not compromise the qualifying nature of the final product. Nevertheless, if the lowest-cost supplier is not a member of the area of cumulation, then the benefits of the preferential scheme will always be less than indicated by the size of the preferential tariff.

The key initial contributions on the economics of rules of origin are Krishna and Krueger (1995) and Krueger (1997) who demonstrate how rules of origin can act as hidden protectionism and induce a switch in demand in free-trade partners from low-cost external inputs to higher-cost partner inputs to ensure that final products actually receive duty free access. Falvey and Reed (1998) show how rules of origin can be used to protect a domestic industry from unwanted competition from a partner, even in conditions where trade deflection is unlikely.

Rules of origin can also distort the relative prospects of similar firms within a country. For example, a clothing producer in, say, Moldova may have established an efficient manufacturing process on the basis of importing fabrics from Turkey. A less efficient producer who uses imported EU fabrics may be able to expand production on the basis of preferential access to the EU market under the GSP (with bilateral cumulation). The more efficient firm may not be able to expand since its product does not qualify for preferences due to the use of non-qualifying fabrics, and there may be substantial costs in changing suppliers of fabrics.

These problems will be exacerbated in sectors where economies of scale are important. A producer that supplies both preferential and non-preferential trade partners, or faces different rules of origin in different preferential partners, will have to produce with a different input mix for different markets if they are to receive preferential access. This may undermine the benefits from lower average costs that would arise if total production were to be based on a single set of material inputs and a single production process.

Rules of origin may be an important factor determining the investment decisions of multinational firms. Such firms often rely on imported inputs from broad international networks that are vital to support the firm-specific advantages that they possess, such as a technological advantage in the production of certain inputs. More generally, if the nature and application of a given set of rules of origin increases a degree of uncertainty concerning the extent to which preferential access will actually be provided, then the level of investment will be less than if such uncertainty were reduced.

For companies, there is not only the issue of complying with the rules on sufficient processing, but also the cost of obtaining the certificate of origin, including any delays that arise in obtaining the certificate. The costs of proving origin involve satisfying a number of administrative procedures so as to provide the documentation that is required and the costs of maintaining systems that accurately account for imported inputs from different sources to prove consistency with the rules. The ability to prove origin may well require the use of, what are for small companies in developing and transition economies, sophisticated and expensive accounting procedures. Without such procedures, it is difficult for companies to show precisely the geographical breakdown of the inputs that they have used.

The costs of complying with the certification requirements of rules of origin will tend to vary across different agreements, depending upon the precise requirements that are specified. With regard to the issuing and inspection of the preferential certificate of origin, EU agreements, Mercosur, AFTA, and Japan–Singapore all mandate that certificates must be verified and endorsed by a recognized official body, such as customs or the Ministry of Trade. In certain cases, private entities can be involved, provided that they are approved and monitored by the government. In contrast, agreements involving the United States provide for self-certification by the exporter. The authorities of the exporting country are not involved and are not responsible for the accuracy of the information provided in the certificates. In principle, this should reduce the administrative burden of complying with the rules of origin. Further, under NAFTA, a certificate of origin is valid for multiple shipments of identical goods within a one-year period, whilst, in most other agreements, a separate certificate of origin is required for each shipment. EU agreements, however, do allow for exporters whom the authorities approve and who make regular shipments to make an invoice declaration of origin.

An important feature of most preferential trade schemes is the requirement of direct consignment or direct transport. This stipulates that goods for which preferences are requested are shipped directly to the destination market, and that, if they are in transit through another country, then documentary evidence may be requested to show that the goods remained under the supervision of the customs authorities of the country of transit, did not enter the domestic market there, and did not undergo operations other than unloading and reloading. In practice, it may be very difficult to obtain the necessary documentation from foreign customs.

Finally, it is important to note that it is the customs authorities that are typically responsible for implementing the system of rules of origin. Customs usually has the responsibility to check the certificate of origin; customs can also be involved in the issuing of origin certificates for local exporters. Rules of origin, while an essential element of FTAs, add considerable complexity to the trading system for traders, customs officials, and trade policy officials.

Implementing PTAs increases the burden on customs. Limited resources and weak administrative capacity in many developing countries mean that there are inevitable repercussions for trade facilitation arising from these trade agreements. At the very least, when designing trade agreements, the participants should bear in mind the implications for customs, and that, if such agreements are to be effective in stimulating trade, then issues of administrative capacity in customs need to be borne in mind. Complicated systems of rules of origin increase the complexity of customs procedures and the burden upon origin certifying institutions. In a period where increasing emphasis has been placed upon trade facilitation and the improvement of efficiency in customs and other trade related institutions, the difficulties that preferential rules of origin create for firms and the relevant authorities in developing countries is an important consideration.

In general, clear, straightforward, transparent, and predictable rules of origin that require little or no administrative discretion will add less of a burden to customs than complex rules. In this regard, the use of general rather than product-specific rules appears to be most appropriate for preferential rules of origin applied by and applied to developing countries. Less complicated rules of origin stimulate trade between regional partners by reducing the transaction costs of undertaking such trade relative to more complex and restrictive rules of origin.

WTO members have recognized that rules of origin are an important factor affecting the ability of exporters to exploit market access opportunities. At the 6th Ministerial meeting in Hong Kong in December 2005, Ministers declared that "developed-country Members, and developing-country Members declaring themselves in a position to do so, agree to implement duty-free and quota-free market access for products originating from LDC" and that "Members shall take additional measures to provide effective market access, both at the border and otherwise, including simplified and transparent rules of origin so as to facilitate exports from LDCs."

Quantifying the Costs Associated with Rules of Origin

As discussed above, the costs of complying with rules of origin can be decomposed into distortionary costs (caused by changes in the production structure to be able to comply) and administrative costs (to prove origin). There is limited information on these costs. Early studies suggested that the costs of providing the appropriate documentation to

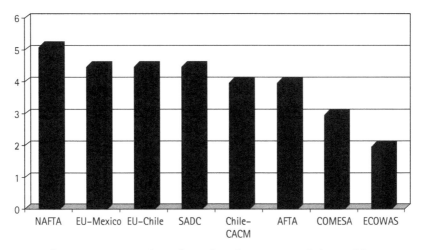

FIGURE 18.1 The restrictiveness of R-index rules of origin around the world

Source: Derived from Estevadeordal and Suominen (2006).

prove origin could be around 3 per cent or more of the value of the export shipment for companies in developed countries.[17]

It is difficult to identify the magnitude of the economic impact of rules of origin because these costs of compliance cannot be directly observed. Efforts have been made to derive estimates of costs of different product-specific rules of origin by linking an index of the restrictiveness of rules of origin to rates of utilization of preferences after controlling for the size of the preferential margin. Estevadeordal (2000) first introduced an ordinal index (the R-index) of rules of origin computed at the tariff line level based on an observation rule with the following two assumptions:

1. For a change of tariff classification (CTC), change at the chapter level (CC) is more difficult to satisfy than a change at the heading (CH) level; a change at the heading level is stricter than at the subheading (CS) level, and a change at the subheading level more stringent than at the tariff line or item level (CI).
2. More criteria usually imply a more restrictive rule. When a CTC is accompanied by the requirement to satisfy other criteria, then the rule is more difficult to meet. On the other hand, allowances (tolerance) and cumulation will tend to diminish the restrictiveness of a given rule.

Higher values are assigned more demanding rules with a maximum value of 7. Figure 18.1 provides a simple summary of the outcome of applying this index to a number of FTAs using information presented in Estevadeordal and Suominen (2006). In general, agreements involving the United States and the EU tend to have more restrictive rules

---

[17] See Herin (1986). This study also found that the costs for EFTA producers of proving origin led to one-quarter of EFTA exports to the EU paying the applied MFN duties.

of origin according to the R-index than do agreements between developing countries such as COMESA (Common Market for Eastern and Southern Africa) and ECOWAS (Economic Community of West African States). Agreements involving the EU and United States tend to have complex product-specific rules of origin. The COMESA and ECOWAS agreements have more simple rules that are common across products.

While the agreements between developing countries often have less restrictive rules of origin on paper, in practice their implementation can be highly restrictive. For example, to be able to use the ECOWAS Trade Liberalization Scheme, companies must obtain approval for each and every product that they wish to export from both their national Ministry and then from ECOWAS. This is in addition to requiring a certificate of origin for each shipment. However, the whole process apparently takes between four to six months. Indeed, an exporter registering for the first time is advised to state the names of future products to be exported under the scheme. If not, they will have to apply again for each new product they wish to export!

Cadot et al. (2006) find utilization rates of preferences to be positively related to preferential margins and negatively related to the restrictiveness of the rules of origin, as proxied by the R-index. They then proceed to use the R-index and the information on utilization of preferences to carry out non-parametric estimation of the upper and lower bounds of the costs of complying with the rules of origin. By revealed preference, when utilization rates are 100 per cent then the preference margin provides an upper bound for compliance costs. When utilization rates are zero, the preference margin provides a lower bound of the costs of complying with the rules of origin. For intermediate rates of utilization, the average rate of preference is taken to capture the costs of compliance. The trade weighted average of compliance costs is found to be 6.8 per cent for NAFTA and 8 per cent for EU rules of origin.

These authors also use the information of utilization rates to break down the estimate of compliance costs into the element that is due to the costs of administration and due to the distortionary element. They assume that low values of the R-index will tend to be associated with low administrative costs (for example the requirement to satisfy only change of tariff heading will require little paperwork). Hence, preference margins for high utilization rates and a low value of the R-index will give an upper bound on the distortionary element of the compliance costs. They conclude that administrative costs for NAFTA are around 2 per cent and those for EU rules around 6.8 per cent, reflecting the more demanding certification procedures of EU schemes.

Using the R-index, Portugal-Perez (2009) distinguishes the impact of "justifiable" determinants of rules of origin, for which the rationale is to prevent trade deflection, from determinants associated with "political economy" forces on the restrictiveness of rules of origin under the NAFTA. Political economy forces, especially from the United States, are found to have strongly influenced the restrictiveness of the NATFA rules of origin. In industries where political economy forces were strong or Mexico had a revealed comparative advantage, more stringent rules of origin were introduced.

Estevadeordal and Suominen (2006) include the R-index in a standard gravity model of bilateral trade flows. Their econometric analysis leads them to conclude that restrictive product specific rules of origin undermine overall trade between the partners to an

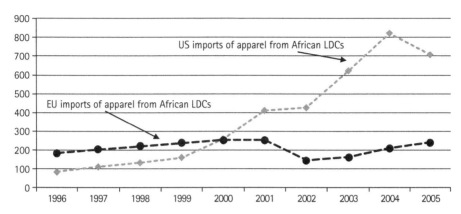

FIGURE 18.2 Non-restrictive rules of origin have strongly stimulated US imports of apparel from African LDCs; but EU imports have stagnated in the face of strict rules

Source: Brenton (2006).

FTA, and that provisions such as cumulation and *de minimis* rules, which act to increase the flexibility of application of a given set of processing requirements, serve to boost intra-regional trade. Applying this approach at the sectoral level finds support for the hypothesis that the restrictiveness of rules of origin for final goods stimulates trade in intermediate products between preferential partners.

The welfare effects of rules of origin should also factor in the rent associated with preferences and their distribution between the exporting and importing country. This implies estimating the extent to which preferences translate into a higher producer price for exporters. If there is little effective competition among importers of the product, then the exporters may be unable to acquire much of the price premium. Ozden and Olarreaga (2005) find evidence that only one-third of the available rents for African exports of apparel to the United States under AGOA actually accrue to the exporters.

It is useful to complement these econometric studies with case studies, and there is one product-specific case that clearly highlights how restrictive rules of origin can constrain the ability of beneficiaries to exploit trade preferences.[18] Both the EU and the United States have schemes that offer duty free access to low-income countries in Africa. A key sector is clothing. Most developed countries of today and newly industrialized countries have used the clothing sector as a gateway to industrial development. The sector has very low entry barriers—it is labor intensive, technology is relatively simple, start-up costs are comparatively low, and scale economies are negligible. Thus, it generates employment for large magnitudes of unskilled labor. Finally, the clothing sector is still subject to high tariffs in rich countries, so that there are large margins of preference for low-income countries in Africa.

Exports of apparel from African LDCs to the EU and United States were almost equal in 2000, but the value of exports to the United States in 2004 was almost four times greater than the value of exports to the EU (Figure 18.2). The key factor explaining why

---

[18] The following is based on Brenton (2006).

exports to the United States have grown much faster than to the EU is the rules of origin. EU rules stipulate production from yarn. This entails that a double transformation process must take place in the beneficiary, with the yarn being woven into fabric and then the fabric cut and made up into apparel. These rules prohibit the use of imported fabric, although cumulation provisions allow for the use of inputs produced in other ACP countries. To obtain preferences, apparel producers must use local, EU, or ACP fabrics. They may not use fabrics from the main fabric producing countries in Asia and still qualify for EU preferences—a binding restriction, since few countries in Africa have competitive fabric industries. The rules of origin under the US scheme allow African clothing exporters to use fabrics from any country (so-called third-country fabric rule). The EU rules do not allow producers in African LDCs the flexibility they currently have under AGOA to source fabrics globally.

De Melo and Portugal-Perez (2008) find that, after controlling for other factors, while Sub-Saharan African countries were offered similar preferential margins of around 10 per cent in both the EU and US markets under EBA and AGOA, the third-country fabric rule of AGOA was associated with an increase in apparel exports from the seven main African exporters of about 300 per cent. On the other hand, the removal of tariffs on imports of apparel from Sub-Saharan African countries was estimated to have led to a 96 per cent increase in exports.

These authors also find that the less restrictive rules of origin under AGOA are associated with an expansion of the range of exported apparel products. Thus, preferential market access with non-restrictive rules of origin can encourage export diversification. This also suggests that strict rules of origin can be prohibitive and prevent firms from exploiting tariff preferences for particular products. For this reason, rates of utilization of preferences may not be a good indicator of the relative restrictiveness of the rules of origin for a particular product group or preference scheme. The most restrictive and prohibitive rules will not be given any weight in such a measure.

It is worth remembering that the EU has granted preferences to African countries for apparel subject to these strict rules of origin for more than 20 years under the Lomé and then Cotonou agreements. However, these strict rules have done little to encourage the development of an efficient fabric industry in Africa and are likely to have severely constrained the impact of preferences in stimulating the apparel industry.[19]

The specific justification for constraining access to third-country fabrics through the use of restrictive rules of origin is to encourage the expansion of fabric production in Africa, consistent with the view that vertical integration in Africa is crucial to survival in a world in which competitors in Asia are no longer constrained by quotas. However, the basis for this view is not well-founded,[20] since restrictive rules of origin will not lead to the emergence of competitive textile producers in Africa, and actually undermine the prospects of the sector. Textile capacity will only emerge if production of apparel

---

[19] See Brenton and Ozden (2009) for a more detailed analysis of the impact of the EBA and AGOA on apparel exports from African LDCs and the role of the rules of origin.

[20] See also Stevens and Kenan (2004).

continues. Lack of access to competitively produced fabrics undermines the viability of the apparel sector, so that there will be no demand for locally produced yarns and fabrics. Substantial improvements in infrastructure, especially power and transport, together with a better climate for investment, are essential requirements for significant investments in textile production.

The EC Commission now appears to have accepted the need for less restrictive rules of origin for clothing in its negotiations of Economic Partnership Agreements with countries in Africa, the Caribbean, and the Pacific. In the interim, in EPAs that have been signed with African countries, the rules of origin for clothing have been relaxed to allow African exporters to use imported fabrics from any country and qualify for preferential access to the EU market. The EU also accepted to amend the rules of origin for fish products in the interim EPAs, removing the nationality requirements for the crew and officers. Nevertheless, the strict ownership and registration requirements remain and will continue to limit the ability of countries to attract FDI into their fisheries sector.

Rules of Origin and Economic Development

Can and should rules of origin be used as tools to stimulate economic development within a regional grouping? The Draft Ministerial Text for the Cancun meeting of the WTO members as part of the Doha Development Round of trade negotiations proposes, under provisions for special and differential treatment, that "developing and least-developed country Members shall have the right to adopt preferential rules of origin designed to achieve trade policy objectives relating to their rapid economic development, particularly through generating regional trade." Strict rules of origin are viewed by some as a mechanism for encouraging the development of integrated production structures within developing countries to maximize the impact on employment, and to ensure that it is not just low value added activities that are undertaken in the developing countries.

There are problems with this view. First, such rules discriminate against small countries where the possibilities for local sourcing are limited or non-existent. Since most developing countries are small countries, they are particularly disadvantaged by restrictive rules of origin relative to larger countries. Second, there is no evidence that strict rules of origin over the past 30 years have done anything to stimulate the development of integrated production structures in developing countries. In fact, such arguments have become redundant in the light of technological changes and global trade liberalization that have led to the fragmentation of production processes and the development of global networks of sourcing. Globalization and the splitting up of the production chain do not allow the luxury of being able to establish integrated production structures within countries. Strict rules of origin act to constrain the ability of firms to integrate into these global and regional production networks and, in effect, act to dampen the location of any value added activities. In the modern world economy, flexibility in the sourcing of inputs is a key element in international competitiveness.

Thus, it is quite feasible that restrictive rules of origin rather than stimulating economic development will raise costs of production by constraining access to cheap inputs and undermine the ability of local firms to compete in overseas markets. By limiting the viability of final goods producers, restrictive rules of origin will do nothing to support the development of input producing activities. Rather an approach to rules of origin that allows for global sourcing of inputs and provides the initial base for a viable export sector is more likely to allow for subsequent domestic investment in activities that substitute for imported inputs. Trade preferences provide a window of opportunity for the export sector to become viable and for the government to put in place an investment and business climate that encourages firms to exploit opportunities for new higher value added activities.

Flatters (2002) and Flatters and Kirk (2003) highlight these points in their documentation of the evolution of the rules of origin in the South African Development Community (SADC). They show that the adoption of restrictive rules of origin is more likely to constrain than to stimulate regional economic development. This example provides a salutary lesson of how sectoral interests and misperceptions of the role and impact of rules of origin can act to undermine regional trade agreements.

SADC initially agreed to simple, general, and consistent rules of origin similar to those of neighboring and overlapping COMESA. The initial rules required a change of tariff heading, a minimum of 35 per cent of value added within the region or a maximum import content of 60 per cent of the value of total inputs. Simple packaging and so on were defined to be insufficient to confer origin. However, subsequently, these rules were revised and are now characterized by more restrictive sector- and product-specific rules with the change of tariff heading requirement being supplanted by detailed technical process requirements and with much higher domestic value added and lower permitted import contents. The rules became much more similar to those of the EU and of NAFTA, reflecting in part the influence of the recently negotiated EU–South Africa agreement and the rules of origin governing EU preferences to ACP countries: "The EU-South Africa rules were often invoked by special interests in South Africa as models for SADC. Such claims were too often accepted at face value and not recognized as self-interested pleading for protection by already heavily protected domestic producers. There were few questions about the appropriateness of the underlying economic model (whatever it might be) for SADC."[21]

Flatters (2002) also points out that, in the SADC case, it has also been argued that customs administrations in the region are weak, and this makes it likely that low-cost products from Asia could enter through porous borders and then claim tariff preferences when exported to another member state. It is then suggested that restrictive rules of origin are required to prevent this happening. However, there is no reason to expect that weak customs administrations should be better able to enforce strict rules of origin than less restrictive rules. In fact, in many cases, the rules of origin become so strict that no producers in the region can satisfy them so that no discretion from customs

---

[21] Flatters and Kirk (2003: 7).

is required—preferences are not granted. This of course entails that the PTA has no impact. Of course, a better approach is to adopt economically sensible rules of origin and a program to improve administrative capacities in customs. Clearly designed safeguard measures can also be adopted to deal with surges of imports entering via partner countries.

To conclude, rules of origin are an inefficient tool in achieving development objectives. Better policies are available. Rules of origin should be used as a mechanism for preventing trade deflection. Restrictive rules of origin that go beyond this function and which seek to force use of local content are more likely to be counterproductive by undermining the competitiveness of downstream industries. If the objective is to stimulate regional trade, then this is best achieved by adopting simple, clear, consistent, and predictable rules of origin that avoid administrative discretion and onerous burdens on customs and minimize the costs to businesses in complying with them.

VI. Conclusions

The nature of rules of origin will typically reflect the purpose that is set for them, the transparency of the process by which they are determined, and the composition of the groups involved in that process. Within PTAs, complex and restrictive rules of origin act to dampen the increase in competition for final producers within a country from suppliers in partner countries and stimulate intra-area exports of intermediate products by diverting demand away from third-country suppliers. Such rules typically emerge when the process by which they are determined lacks transparency and openness and does not have widespread participation and, in particular, is dominated by input from domestic industry. If the purpose set for preferential rules of origin is simply to prevent trade deflection, then a simple and more liberal set of rules of origin implemented through general rather than product-specific rules would be the result. In the current globalized world market, such rules are more likely to stimulate trade and investment in the region by providing producers with as much flexibility as possible in sourcing their inputs without compromising the ability to prevent trans-shipment of goods from third countries that are not members of the agreement.

What is important is that the purpose set for the rules of origin is clearly specified and is consistent with the objectives that have been set for the particular trade agreement or policy. If the objective is to foster trade and development, then this is best achieved through simple and liberal rules of origin rather than using rules of origin as opaque measures of trade protection. In this way, the rules of origin are a key trade policy issue, and their determination should be open and transparent with participation from all affected groups. The rules of origin are a major factor determining whether PTAs work in achieving their objectives. The analysis of this chapter leads to the following broad conclusions.

Restrictive rules of origin constrain international specialization and discriminate against small low-income countries where the possibilities for local sourcing are limited. Simple, consistent, and predictable rules of origin are more likely to foster the growth of trade and development. Rules of origin that vary across products and agreements add considerably to the complexity and costs of participating in and administering trade agreements. The burden of such costs falls particularly heavily upon small and medium-sized firms and upon firms in low-income countries. Complex systems of rules of origin add to the burdens of customs and may compromise progress on trade facilitation.

Cumulation mechanisms may be important. Full cumulation provides for deeper integration and allows for more advanced countries to outsource labor-intensive production stages to low-wage partners. Full cumulation allows low-income countries the greatest flexibility in sourcing inputs. Nevertheless, the sometimes onerous documentary requirements and administrative difficulties that can be associated with full cumulation suggest that diagonal cumulation should also be permitted.

The value added criterion appears to be particularly difficult to implement from the perspective of customs. Agreement on a standard formula for calculation would be particularly helpful. Providing traders with alternative means of proving origin could be an important way of increasing flexibility in trade agreements.

Harmonization of non-preferential rules of origin and consolidation, if not harmonization, of preferential rules would bring substantial gains in terms of increasing the predictability of conditions under which companies trade and in reducing the burden on customs in administering both the multilateral and PTAs.

The above analysis leads to the following key conclusions:

- Specifying generally applicable rules of origin, with a limited number of clearly defined and justified exceptions, is appropriate if the objective is to stimulate integration and minimize the burdens on firms and customs in complying with and administering the rules. Unnecessary use of a detailed product-by-product approach to rules of origin is likely to lead to complex and restrictive rules of origin and to constrain integration.
- Producers should be provided with flexibility in meeting origin rules, for example by specifying that *either* a change of tariff requirement *or* a value added rule can be satisfied.
- When change of tariff classification is used, the level of the classification at which change is required should, as much as possible, be common across products. Change at the heading level seems most appropriate as a principal rule.
- Preferences granted by OECD countries would be more effective in stimulating exports from developing countries if they were governed by less restrictive rules of origin. Ideally, rules of origin for these schemes should be common. Producers in developing countries should be able to gain preferential access to all developed country markets if their product satisfies a single origin test.
- Restrictive rules of origin should not be used as tools for achieving economic development objectives, as they are likely to be counterproductive. The potential

benefits of trade agreements amongst developing countries can be substantially undermined if those agreements contain restrictive rules of origin.

- Bilateral agreements between a member of an existing regional trade agreement and a third country should provide for an alternative approach to allow for the benefits of both diagonal and full cumulation with the other members of that regional group.

References

Brenton, P. (2006), 'Enhancing Trade Preferences for LDCs: Reducing the Restrictiveness of Rules of Origin.' In Newfarmer, R. (ed.) *Trade, Doha and Development*. Washington DC: World Bank.

Brenton, P. and Imagawa, H. (2005), 'Rules of Origin, Trade and Customs.' In De Wulf, L. and Sokol, J. (eds.) *The Customs Modernization Handbook*. Washington DC: The World Bank.

Brenton, P., and Ozden, C. (2009), 'Trade Preferences for Apparel and the Role of Rules of Origin: The Case of Africa.' In Hoekman, B., Martin, W., and Braga, C. P. (eds.) *Trade Preference Erosion: Measurement and Policy Response*. Washington DC: Palgrave Macmillan and World Bank, 401–24.

Cadot, O., Carrère, C., de Melo, J., and Tumurchudur, B. (2006), 'Product Specific Rules of Origin in EU and US Preferential Trading Arrangements: An Assessment.' *World Trade Review*, 25: 199–225.

Clark-Flavell (1995), 'Canadian Rules of Origin.' A Joint Study Prepared by Grey, Clark, Shih and Associates, and Flavell Kubrick LLP, Barristers & Solicitors for the Japan Machinery Exporters' Association, <http://www.greyclark.com/index2.php?page=61> (Accessed April 2013)

Dehousse, F., Ghemar, K., and Vincent, P. (2002), 'The EU-US Dispute concerning the new American Rules of Origin for Textile Products.' *Journal of World Trade*, 36:67–84.

De Melo, J. and Portugal-Perez, A. (2008), 'Rules of Origin, Preferences and Diversification in Apparel: African Exports to the US and to the EU.' CEPR Discussion Paper 7072.

Estevadeordal, A. (2000), 'Negotiating Preferential Market Access: the Case of NAFTA.' *Journal of World Trade*, 34(1): 141–66.

Estevadeordal, A. and Suominen, K. (2003), 'Rules of Origin in FTAs in Europe and the Americas: Issues and Implications for the EU-MERCOSUR Inter-Regional Association Agreement.' In Valladao, G., and Bouzas, R. (eds.) *Market Access for Goods and Services in the EU-Mercosur Negotiations*. Paris: Chaire Mercosur de Sciences Po.

Estevadeordal, A. and Suominen, K. (2006), 'Rules of Origin: A World Map and Trade Effects.' In Estevadeordal, A., Cadot, O., Suwa-Eisenmann, A., and Verdier, T. (eds.) *The Origin of Goods: Rules of Origin in Preferential Trade Agreements*. Oxford: Oxford University Press.

Falvey, R. and Reed, G. (1998), 'Economic Effects of Rules of Origin.' *Weltwirtschaftliches Archiv*, 134: 209–29.

Flatters, F. (2002), 'SADC Rules of Origin: Undermining Regional Free Trade.' Paper presented at the TIPS Forum, Johannesburg, September.

Flatters, F. and Kirk, R. (2003), 'Rules of Origin as Tools of Development? Some Lessons from SADC.' Presented at INRA conference on Rules of Origin, Paris, May.

Herin, J. (1986), 'Rules of Origin and Differences Between Tariff Levels in EFTA and in the EC.' EFTA Secretariat, Geneva.

Hirsch M. (2002), 'International Trade Law, Political Economy and Rules of Origin: A Plea for a Reform of the WTO Regime on Rules of Origin.' *Journal of World Trade*, 36: 171–88.

Hoekman, B. (1993), 'Rules of Origin for Goods and Services: Conceptual and Economic Considerations.' *Journal of World Trade*, 27: 81–99.

Izam, M. (2003), 'Rules of Origin and Trade Facilitation in Preferential Trade Agreements in Latin America.' Paper presented at International Forum on Trade Facilitation, Geneva, May, <http://www.unece.org/trade/forums/ forum03/presentations/ventura_en.pdf> (Accessed April 2013).

Krishna, K. and Krueger, A. (1995), 'Implementing Free Trade Areas: Rules of Origin and Hidden Protection.' Working Paper 4983, NBER.

Krueger, A. (1997), 'Free Trade Agreements Versus Customs Unions.' *Journal of Development Economics*, 54: 169–87.

Ozden, C. and Olarreaga, M. (2005), 'AGOA and Apparel: Who Captures the Tariff Rent in the Presence of Preferential Market Access?' *World Economy*, 28:63–77.

Palmeter D. (1997), 'Rules of Origin in Regional Trade Agreements.' In Demaret, P., Bellis, J.F., and Garcia Jimenez, G. (eds.) *Regionalism and Multilateralism after the Uruguay Round: Convergence, Divergence, and Interaction.* Brussels: European Interuniversity Press.

Portugal-Perez, A. (2009), 'Assessing the Impact of Political Economy Factors on Rules of Origin under NAFTA.' World Bank Policy Research Working Paper 4848.

Stevens, C., and Kenan, J. (2004), 'Comparative Study of G8 Preferential Access Schemes for Africa' Institute of Development Studies. <http://www.ids.ac.uk/files/CSG8PrefsFinal_Report_Phase_IandII.pdf> (Accessed April 2013)

UNCTAD, Commonwealth Secretariat (2001), 'Duty and Quota Free Market Access for LDCs: An Analysis of Quad Initiatives.' <http://unctad.org/en/docs/poditctabm7.en.pdf> (Accessed April 2013)

WTO (2002), 'Rules of Origin Regimes in Regional Trade Agreements.' WT/REG/W/45.

CHAPTER 19

REGIONALISM IN THE AMERICAS AT THE TURN OF THE TWENTY-FIRST CENTURY: NAFTA AND MERCOSUR*

EDWARD D. MANSFIELD

I. INTRODUCTION

DURING the period since World War II, there has been a rapid proliferation of preferential trading arrangements (PTAs). Dozens of these arrangements have been formed and almost every country now belongs to at least one of them. PTAs are a broad class of economic institution that can be distinguished by the extent of integration and policy coordination among member states. Free trade areas (FTAs) eliminate trade barriers among members; customs unions (CUs) eliminate internal trade barriers and impose a common external tariff (CET) on the products of third parties; common markets are CUs that coordinate a wide range of policies and permit the free movement of factors of production and finished products across national borders; and economic unions are common markets in which members also adopt a common currency. Despite the differences among these arrangements, however, all of them grant each member state preferential access to the other participants' markets. This preferential access has stimulated a rise in flow of trade and investment within many PTAs, leading to the widespread view that these groupings have become increasingly important features of the international political economy (Mansfield and Solingen, 2010).

* I am grateful to Rosella Cappella and Matthew Tubin for research assistance.

Since PTAs tend to be composed of states located in the same geographical region, the spread of these arrangements has led many observers to conclude that economic regionalism is on the rise (World Bank, 2005). Over the past half-century, there have been two "waves" of regionalism (Bhagwati, 1993; Mansfield and Milner, 1999). The first began in the 1950s, with the advent of the European Coal and Steel Community (ECSC), the European Economic Community (EEC), the European Free Trade Association (EFTA), and the Council for Mutual Economic Assistance (CMEA). As this initial wave continued, developing countries (especially in Africa and Latin America) rushed to establish their own PTAs.

Developing countries chose to enter these arrangements for various reasons (Schiff and Winters, 2003). Chief among them, however, was a desire to reduce their dependence on the advanced industrial countries. Many of these groupings were formed as part of import substitution industrialization (ISI) strategies, which aimed to develop domestic industries by shielding them from foreign competition. As such, this set of PTAs involving developing countries was marked by the imposition of extensive trade barriers on goods produced in third parties. In general, these arrangements failed to achieve their stated goals. Many of them did little to improve the economic welfare of participants and were beset by severe political problems, including conflicts over how to distribute the costs and benefits of regional integration among member states.

The second wave of regionalism in the period since World War II began in the 1980s and has continued for more than two decades. It emerged for different reasons than the earlier wave. Particularly important in this regard was the decision by the United States to launch a series of PTAs, as well as the collapse of the Soviet bloc and the ensuing rush by its former members to join preferential groupings. It also seems to have been more benign from an economic standpoint. Although opinion remains divided on this issue, many observers conclude that the recent wave of regionalism has promoted greater economic openness and has helped to bolster the multilateral trading system (Krueger, 1999).

In this chapter, I analyze two of the largest PTAs formed during the second wave of post-war regionalism, the North American Free Trade Agreement (NAFTA) and Mercosur. In my analysis of both cases, I begin by examining the run-up to the agreement and the factors that prompted its establishment. I then discuss the institutional design and the effects of each arrangement. I conclude by addressing some future challenges facing NAFTA and Mercosur and by using these cases to draw some more general lessons about the political economy of PTAs.

II. The North American Free Trade Agreement

NAFTA entered into force on January 1, 1994. Composed of Canada, Mexico, and the USA, it immediately became the world's largest FTA, encompassing almost 365 million people, about one third of the world's gross domestic product (GDP), 19 per cent of world exports, 25 per cent of world imports, 24 per cent of global inward foreign direct investment (FDI), and 25 per cent of global outward FDI. The arrangement was especially significant because it represented Mexico's initial effort to promote extensive integration with its North American neighbors.

The history of regional integration in North America is dominated by US–Canadian relations. The first major initiative in the region was the Canada–United States Automotive Agreement. Launched in 1965, it liberalized bilateral trade in cars and auto parts. But the most important agreement between these countries prior to NAFTA was forged in 1988 and came into effect the next year. Concluded on the heels of the 1987 Canadian elections that were in some ways a referendum on open trade with the USA, the Canada–USA FTA was designed to eliminate tariffs on all trade between these countries and to reinforce their already close economic relationship.

In contrast to the USA and Canada, Mexico spent much of the period after World War II trying to shelter its economy from foreign competition and limit its exposure to global markets. During the 1980s, however, President Miguel de la Madrid decided to abandon Mexico's ISI strategy and to encourage trade liberalization and export promotion in an effort to modernize and expand the Mexican economy. As a result, average tariffs dipped from 100 per cent to 10 per cent during this decade (Ready, 1993). Various sectors of the economy were protected by import permits rather than tariffs. But whereas 92 per cent of domestic manufacturers were covered by such permits in 1985, only 11 per cent were in 1990 (Tornell and Esquivel, 1995). Moreover, as a centerpiece of its trade liberalization program, Mexico acceded to the General Agreement on Tariffs and Trade (GATT) in 1986.

These measures had a marked impact. Between 1975 and 1994, for example, Mexican exports grew more than tenfold. The expansion in oil revenues accounts for much of this growth over the first decade, but trade liberalization was the root cause of export growth during the second decade.

The Rationale for NAFTA

The initial inquiry about creating a North American FTA was made by Mexican President Carlos Salinas de Gortari, who broached this subject with US Trade Representative Carla Hills at a 1990 conference in Davos, Switzerland. Salinas was concerned that Mexico's trade liberalization during the 1980s would be insufficient to guarantee success in international markets since many other developing countries were taking similar steps (Cameron and Tomlin, 2000; Hufbauer and Schott, 2005). Equally, the pace at which PTAs were forming had picked up substantially. Mexico was not a party to any PTA at that time and Salinas feared that it would be locked out of key foreign markets unless it entered arrangements with its core trade partners. The Canadian market was not terribly important in this regard since relatively little trade was conducted between Mexico and Canada at the time. The US market, however, was of crucial importance to Mexico, and Salinas wanted to ensure that US–Mexican economic relations would not be disrupted in the event that protectionist sentiment took hold in either country.

Moreover, Salinas was concerned about the lack of FDI in Mexico. Historically, Mexico had been reluctant to accept FDI. That began to change in 1989, when Salinas repealed a regulation that prohibited foreign entities from holding majority owner-ship of Mexican firms in certain sectors and enacted policies that limited the gov-ernment's ability to take advantage of foreign investors (Tornell and Esquivel, 1995). NAFTA was designed as much to promote overseas investment in Mexico as it was to promote trade.

Not only did NAFTA hold out the promise of greater and more secure access to the North American market, this arrangement also helped Salinas to lock in the economic and political reforms that he had championed. Although Salinas had made considerable headway in enacting such reforms, he faced influential segments of Mexican society that were likely to be harmed as a result and therefore had a strong incentive to roll-back reform. Unions, for example, feared that liberalization would stimulate a flood of imports into Mexico, leading to rising unemployment. Business interests in central Mexico (especially those in textile and leather goods) and firms providing financial ser-vices were also concerned about their ability to compete with foreign firms. The tra-ditional farming sector was a particularly outspoken opponent of trade liberalization, since it expected cheap imports to pose a substantial threat. Furthermore, the politi-cal support of this sector was important to the ruling Institutional Revolutionary Party (PRI). Salinas worried that the withdrawal of its support could either prompt future PRI governments to jettison reforms or precipitate the election of a government led by a party (for example, the leftist Party of the Democratic Revolution) with an interest in overturning them. Partly to address this issue, NAFTA called for the liberalization of Mexican agriculture over a fifteen-year period, creating time for the traditional farming sector to adjust to foreign competition.

But NAFTA also was an institutional device for locking in Mexican reforms that set up explicit targets for liberalization and left member governments little discretion in various policy arenas. As such, future Mexican governments would have difficulty dismantling economic reforms without violating the agreement. Further, since liber-alization measures in some of the most sensitive and politically important sectors were slated to be phased in over a five-year, ten-year, or fifteen-year period, Salinas calculated that they were unlikely to jeopardize the PRI's hold on power. It would take time for any erosion of the party's control of the government to occur, at which point groups within Mexican society benefiting from economic liberalization would have emerged. These groups would fight any subsequent efforts to derail liberalization. As Tornell and Esquivel (1995: 22) argue,

> NAFTA is the commitment device that will ensure that ... [delays in implementing reforms] will not occur and reform will continue. This will happen in two ways. First, there are huge political and economic costs associated with breaching an international agreement such as NAFTA. Second, NAFTA will consolidate the power of the new export groups that will have in their interest to defend the new set of property rights.

For various reasons, Salinas's initial overtures about establishing a North American integration agreement were received warmly by President George H. W. Bush. First, by 1990 the Uruguay Round of the GATT had ground to a halt and the view that the USA should focus on forming regional and bilateral trade agreements was gaining popularity within the Bush Administration. This negotiating round had been launched in Punta del Este, Uruguay, in September 1986 and was scheduled to conclude in December 1990. But the round had been marked by heated disagreement, especially over trade in services and agricultural products. When Salinas broached the idea of negotiating NAFTA, the Uruguay Round seemed hopelessly deadlocked. Secretary of State James Baker and various other senior officials in the Bush Administration believed that it would be easier to conclude regional integration agreements than a multilateral agreement, since the latter involved coordination among a much larger and more heterogeneous group of countries (Cameron and Tomlin, 2000). Equally, they felt that creating a regional agreement would enhance the bargaining power of the USA in GATT negotiations, since the regional agreement would ensure the liberalization of trade with key US trade partners even if the multilateral negotiating round collapsed.

Second, Bush viewed NAFTA as a way to improve US–Mexican relations and to promote peace and stability within Mexico. Improving these relations was seen as an important first step in combating the flow of illegal drugs and illegal immigration into the USA. Mexico was in the process of making a series of democratic and economic reforms that the USA was anxious to encourage. And the Bush Administration hoped that a regional economic agreement would stimulate economic growth in Mexico, thereby helping to dampen domestic unrest and violence, especially in the southern part of the country.

Third, the Bush Administration considered NAFTA to be in the economic interest of the USA. Mexico was a lucrative market for US exporters; the growth of that market would increase the demand for US goods. In addition, NAFTA would help US industries by giving them both greater access to relatively cheap Mexican labor and preferential access to the entire North American market, thereby helping to generate economies of scale in production and enhancing their competitiveness.

With these aims in mind, Bush announced plans to negotiate NAFTA in 1991. He also requested that Congress grant him "fast track" approval. Such approval would require Congress to vote on any trade agreement, without amending it, within 90 days of the president submitting the agreement to the legislature. In May 1991, Congress granted this approval and then subsequently extended it for two years.

NAFTA negotiations heated up as the 1992 US presidential race was starting. Trade, globalization, and NAFTA became key issues in the election. Patrick Buchanan unsuccessfully challenged Bush for the Republican Party's presidential nomination on a platform that emphasized economic nationalism and opposed PTAs like NAFTA. Ross Perot, a third-party candidate, made ominous predictions that NAFTA would produce a "great sucking sound," prompting firms to move from the USA to Mexico in order to gain access to lower cost labor and threatening massive job losses in the USA. In fact, most analyses found that NAFTA was likely to have only a modest impact on wages or employment, except in a few industries (namely, textiles, household appliances, and sugar). However, a portion of the US public clearly worried about the economic implications of greater North American integration.

These concerns posed a problem for Bill Clinton, who emerged as the winner of the 1992 presidential election. Clinton supported NAFTA, but many of his key constituents did not. Some groups viewed NAFTA as potentially trade diverting and protectionist. They worried that the agreement could damage the multilateral trading system, further imperil the Uruguay Round, and harm the US economy. Many unions (led by the American Federation of Labor and Congress of Industrial Organizations (AFL-CIO)) despised NAFTA, anticipating that it would precipitate the loss of jobs for their rank and file and place downward pressure on wages. They were also concerned that NAFTA would be the first in a series of PTAs that the USA would conclude with developing countries. The likely upshot, in their view, was a flood of cheap imports that would create even more sizable job losses. Environmental groups also worried about NAFTA. They feared that maquiladoras (factories in Mexico located just south of the US border) would expand production in an environmentally harmful way and that US firms would relocate to Mexico because of its lax environmental standards.[1]

Realizing that NAFTA faced substantial opposition on the part of these groups and in Congress, Clinton convinced Salinas and Canadian Prime Minister Brian Mulroney to accept side agreements on labor standards (the North American Agreement on Labor Cooperation), environmental standards (the North American Agreement on Environmental Cooperation), and safeguards against a spike in imports from Mexico. Clinton also included a provision in the NAFTA legislation for assistance to US workers who were displaced as a result of this arrangement. As Destler (1995: 217) points out, "NAFTA set off the most prominent and contentious domestic debate on trade since the Smoot-Hawley Tariff Act of 1930." These agreements and provisions did not mollify many of the fiercest opponents of NAFTA, but they did create the political cover that Clinton needed in order to gain Congressional approval for the agreement (Hufbauer and Schott, 2005). On November 17, 1993, the House of Representatives voted 234 to 200 to ratify NAFTA. Three days later, the Senate followed suit, 61 to 38.

Of the three member states, Canada was by far the least enthusiastic participant in NAFTA.[2] Since Mexico was not an important trade partner, Canada saw little reason to create an institutional firewall against any future rise in Mexican protectionism. Furthermore, Canada already had a successful FTA with the USA. As such, Canada expected to realize few additional benefits from NAFTA. Other Canadian objections to NAFTA were similar to those raised in the USA. Some observers feared that Canadian firms would relocate to Mexico and that cheap imports from Mexico would threaten Canadian jobs in sensitive sectors, such as textiles. Canadian critics of NAFTA also worried about Mexico's lax labor and environmental standards. Also voiced were broader concerns about Canada's growing dependence on the USA and the need to maintain its economic sovereignty.

---

[1] On these concerns, see Destler (1995) and Hufbauer and Schott (2005).
[2] On Canada's position, see McConnell and MacPherson (1994), Cameron and Tomlin (2000), and Hufbauer and Schott (2005).

In the end, though, Mulroney could not stand by while the USA and Mexico negotiated an agreement with potentially adverse consequences for the Canadian economy. A bilateral pact between the USA and Mexico would vest US goods with preferential access to the Mexican market, furnishing them with a competitive advantage over Canadian goods. At the same time, the existing Canada–USA FTA provided US goods with preferential access to the Canadian market, helping them compete with Mexican goods. Ottawa wanted to avoid this type of "hub-and-spoke" arrangement (McConnell and MacPherson, 1994). Once it became clear in 1990 that the USA and Mexico were committed to striking a regional accord, Canada agreed that the arrangement should span all of North America.

NAFTA's Institutional Design

The text of NAFTA contains almost 300 articles in 22 chapters. The agreement immediately eliminated tariffs on roughly half of all import categories. Most of the rest were to be removed over the next five years. As noted earlier, however, some sectors were accorded special treatment, especially those where a member state feared that open regional trade would dislocate a substantial number of workers or have other severe distributional consequences. Textile quotas, for example, were scheduled to be eliminated over ten years. Protection on agriculture was slated to be phased out over fifteen years. The automobile sector was also accorded special treatment. Nonetheless, all tariffs were eliminated by January 1, 2008.

In addition to reducing trade barriers, NAFTA includes rules of origin to ensure that only goods produced in member states receive tariff preferences. It also established a set of institutions, led by the Free Trade Commission, to implement the agreement and help address disputes among member states. Based on the model created by the USA–Canada FTA, NAFTA put bi-national panels in place to deal with anti-dumping (AD) and countervailing duty (CVD) disputes (Goldstein, 1996; Abbott, 2000). These panels were designed to determine whether AD or CVD rulings were in accordance with countries' domestic law and were in lieu of judicial review at the domestic level. The existence of bi-national panels has had an important effect on the behavior of member states. Goldstein (1996: 555), for example, argues that these panels have enabled Canada and Mexico to gain considerable relief from US laws regarding unfair trade.

Besides its agreement on trade, NAFTA includes an extensive investment agreement. It also set up a series of working groups to supervise emergency actions, as well as issues concerning investment and services. These groups are designed to facilitate cross-national communication on a range of technical issues.

Taken as a whole, though, NAFTA's institutional super-structure is relatively spare. In part, this reflects the fact that the USA has long expressed a particularly strong aversion to supra-national institutions with the authority to regulate its behavior. Canada and Mexico were in accord on this point: neither country wanted its sovereignty compromised by a regional organization. NAFTA's sparse institutional design also stems from the fact that it is an FTA and was not created to achieve deeper or broader integration

(Abbott, 2000; Fernandez de Castro, 2004). In this sense, it stands in contrast to the European Union (EU), which is a common market and therefore aims to foster political integration as well as much greater economic integration than NAFTA. Each member of NAFTA was expected to adhere to its own laws and norms. No NAFTA laws were established. Even the labor and environmental side agreements to NAFTA avoided the creation of any supra-national law; instead these agreements simply affirmed that each country will apply their own laws in both areas.

More broadly Abbott (2000: 519) argues that "NAFTA embodies a high degree of precision and obligation." However, "it involves only a moderate degree of delegation of decision-making authority." NAFTA has no judicial or legislative bodies. Alternatively, the EU involves greater delegation of authority and obligation to supra-national institutions but less precision in the content of its charter (Abbott, 2000: 521). Both the EU and the NAFTA model contrast with PTAs like the Asia-Pacific Economic Cooperation (APEC) group, which have low levels of obligation, precision, and delegation.

The Effects of NAFTA

By most standards, NAFTA has been a qualified success. Since the agreement went into effect, intra-regional trade has tripled. Mexico's share of US imports rose by roughly 50 per cent from 1993 to 2008. During this time, Mexico's exports to the USA grew by almost 400 per cent. By 2002, 87 per cent of Canadian exports, 90 per cent of Mexican exports, and 36 per cent of US exports were sold within NAFTA. Many observers argue that these developments reflect the fact that NAFTA has been "trade-creating" and therefore welfare enhancing (Weintraub 2004: xii). Equally, NAFTA has succeeded in promoting foreign investment. United States FDI in Canada and Mexico has more than doubled. On average, annual real GDP grew 3.6 per cent in Canada, 3.3 in the USA, and 2.7 in Mexico since NAFTA's inception. North American integration probably would have deepened even in the absence of NAFTA; but in all likelihood, it would have occurred at a noticeably slower pace (Abbott 2000; Hufbauer and Schott 2005: 2).

One of the most telling indicators of rising North American integration is the growth in intra-industry trade. Especially in the automobile sector, computers, office and electrical machinery, and other manufactured goods, there has been a marked increase in such trade since NAFTA went into effect. As Weintraub (2000: 9) notes, heightened intra-industry trade has been spurred by product differentiation, as well as NAFTA's open trade regime. As a general rule in the automobile sector, for example, "Mexico produces smaller cars, the United States intermediate and specialty vehicles, and Canada larger autos and light trucks."

NAFTA established a number of dispute settlement procedures. Hufbauer and Schott (2005: 55) point out, however, that these procedures have had a mixed record of success. They "have worked relatively well in cases where the NAFTA obligations were clearly defined (including most Chapter 19 cases involving AD and CVD) but poorly in big cases where domestic politics have blocked treaty compliance (notably, US-Mexico trucking, Canada-US softwood lumber, and US-Mexico sugar and high-fructose corn syrup)." The record in some other areas has been equally mixed. Overall, NAFTA has not produced the job losses that some of its critics predicted. Nor has it created the large number of jobs that some of its chief advocates anticipated. Instead, its impact on employment is generally regarded as positive, though modest. So too has been NAFTA's influence on labor and environmental standards, issues that the side agreements Clinton insisted upon were designed to address. It is important to recognize, however, that even these modest gains in environmental and labor standards are more than just about any PTA except the EU can claim. In large measure, this reflects the fact that Canada and the USA are wealthy states with fairly stringent labor and environmental regulations. States like Mexico that that want to enter their lucrative markets have to abide by these standards.

Earlier, we discussed the reasons why Salinas approached the USA about forming NAFTA. In light of these objectives, how has Mexico fared under this arrangement? From the standpoint of promoting trade and investment, the agreement has been a success (Weintraub, 2000 and 2004; Zepeda et al., 2009). Mexican exports to the USA almost quadrupled from 1993 to 2008; US exports to Mexico almost tripled over the same period. The average annual flow of FDI to Mexico was about $3 billion in the five years prior to NAFTA, a figure that has spiked to $12 billion since the agreement went into force. Various observers attribute this rise to the fact that NAFTA reduced foreign firms' uncertainty about whether the Mexican government would treat FDI unfairly. Some of the growth in trade and investment growth probably would have happened regardless of whether NAFTA was formed, but this institution nonetheless played an important role. Mexico has also experienced a significant increase in productivity in its manufacturing sector since NAFTA went into effect, suggesting that the arrangement has helped to promote efficiency.

In addition, NAFTA helped Mexico recover from its so-called "peso crisis" of 1994–95. Between December 1994 and April 1995, the value of the peso collapsed as Mexico became unable to pay its dollar-denominated debt, precipitating a massive increase in inflation. The Clinton Administration responded to the crisis with a bailout package that included roughly $20 billion in immediate US assistance and $30 billion from other foreign sources. Largely as a result, the Mexican economy was back on stable footing by 1996. There was no single impetus for the bailout, but a key influence was exerted by US firms that had a stake in the Mexican economy due to NAFTA. As Hufbauer and Schott (2005: 11) argue, "If NAFTA had not been in place, the United States would surely have mounted financial assistance for Mexico, but the NAFTA partnership very likely enlarged the size of the rescue package and accelerated the speed of its delivery." Furthermore, NAFTA prompted Mexico to respond to the crisis using export-led measures and "fiscal constraint, tight money, and currency devaluation, rather than trade and capital controls" (Hufbauer and Schott, 2005: 11).

Despite the gains that Mexico has made since 1994, however, problems remain. Since the turn of the century, Mexico's exports and overall economic performance have slumped. Equally, critics of NAFTA have charged that the agreement has done little to create jobs in Mexico, to reduce income inequality, or to forestall the country's current economic crisis (Zepeda et al., 2009). These problems were exacerbated by the slowdown of the US economy after 2000: indeed, one of the adverse consequences of heightened integration has been that Mexico (and Canada) is especially vulnerable to fluctuations in the US market. Further, while the flow of FDI has increased, the overall rate of investment has not, contributing to Mexico's economic slowdown. However, Tornell et al. (2004) maintain that these troubles would have been far worse in the absence of NAFTA. The source of the problem is not NAFTA, they argue, but rather a lack of structural and judicial reform, as well as a credit crunch. The low rate of tax collection has created pressure to heavily tax the state oil company, reducing its ability to explore and develop new sources of petroleum. The educational system is in bad shape, creating a poorly trained and inflexible labor force. Contracts are weakly enforced and the courts cannot be counted on to render fair and impartial decisions. Banks are saddled with too many non-performing loans, hampering their ability to provide credit.

Both Salinas and Bush hoped that NAFTA would improve US–Mexican relations. It is difficult, however, to determine whether these hopes have been realized. Weintraub (2000) argues that NAFTA has improved US–Mexican relations by facilitating cooperation on issues regarding the environment and illegal drugs, as well as helping to lock in democratic reforms in Mexico. Still, some observers feel that Mexican policy changes in these areas would have occurred regardless of NAFTA (Toro, 2004). Further, there is little doubt that US–Mexican relations have been strained of late. President Vincente Fox came to office in 2000 eager to establish a North American Economic Community that would deepen regional integration. But his seemingly close relationship with President George H.W. Bush deteriorated after the terrorist attacks on 9/11. Fox became angry when Bush appeared to back away from the idea of striking an agreement on immigration to the USA. Bush was upset when Mexico failed to support US policy on Iraq in the United Nations (UN) Security Council. Since then, the Obama Administration has made some attempt to repair this relationship, but it is hard to say whether the strains on US–Mexican relations will ease in the future.

Immigration from Mexico to the USA is an important issue for both countries. In addition to its economic and social implications, immigration has taken on heightened prominence since 9/11, as the USA has grown increasingly concerned about terrorists entering its borders (Bailey, 2004). There is little evidence that NAFTA has had much effect on immigration, although it may have produced a short-term increase in migration to the USA soon after the agreement went into effect. Instead, Bean and Lowell (2004) conclude that migration to the USA rose rapidly throughout the 1990s because the expanding Mexican economy made it more affordable to travel to the USA.

Strategic interaction has long guided the formation of PTAs (Mansfield and Milner, 1999). The creation of a PTA can arouse fears in third parties that their competitiveness in international markets or their bargaining power will erode, leading them to respond by forming a PTA of their own. NAFTA gave rise to this type of strategic integration, stimulating the establishment of other PTAs throughout the Western hemisphere and in the Asia-Pacific region (Baldwin, 1995). One of the most important agreements of this sort is Mercosur, the second PTA examined in this chapter.[3]

III. MERCOSUR

Mercosur is composed of Argentina, Brazil, Paraguay, and Uruguay. It entered into force on March 26, 1991, when these countries signed the Treaty of Asuncion. Since then, Bolivia, Chile, Columbia, Ecuador, Peru, and Venezuela have been added as associate members. Mercosur and the Association of Southeast Asian Nations (ASEAN) are currently the two largest PTAs in the developing world.[4]

As noted in the introduction to this chapter, various efforts to promote Latin American integration were made during the first wave of regionalism after World War II.[5] None of them were particularly successful. The Latin American Free Trade Association (LAFTA) formed in 1960, the Andean Pact was established in 1969, and the Latin American Integration Association entered into force in 1980. These arrangements were characterized by an emphasis on discriminating against imports from third parties in order to promote the development of industry in member states. They were also marked by conflicts among member states over how to distribute the costs and benefits stemming from regional integration.

However, events in the Southern Cone soon precipitated a revival of interest in Latin American integration. During the 1980s, Argentina and Brazil experienced democratic transitions. Nascent democratic regimes in both countries were anxious to make sure that the military would not return to power. Both governments wanted to promote political–military cooperation and avoid the re-emergence of conflicts like their 1979 dispute over the Plata Basin. Elites in Argentina and Brazil believed that closer economic ties would reduce the prospect of interstate hostilities and would limit the military's ability to reassert itself in the domestic affairs of either state. They also believed that integration would contribute to regional economic stability and end repeated bouts of hyperinflation and economic mismanagement in the region.

As a result, these countries established the Program for Integration and Economic Cooperation in 1986. This agreement aimed to foster economic cooperation between Argentina and Brazil, including the elimination of all bilateral trade barriers within ten years. In 1988, they signed the Treaty on Integration, Cooperation, and Development, which was designed to be the first step toward the establishment of a common market. As Pereira (1999: 9) notes, this agreement was a reaction to "the worldwide trend toward

---

[3] For an analysis of what lessons the members of Mercosur (and the rest of Latin America) can draw from NAFTA, see Lederman et al. (2005).

[4] For more general analyses of regionalism in the developing world, see Schiff and Winters (2003) and World Bank (2005).

[5] On these efforts, see Nogues and Quintanilla (1993) and WTO (1995).

regionalization, the notion that Latin American countries were outside the area of economic interest to the developed countries, and the choice to open trade in Brazil and Argentina." It also laid the basis for Mercosur.

Decision makers in Brazil and Argentina were of the opinion that previous efforts to promote Latin American integration had been hampered by overly ambitious goals and by an excessively large number of participating states with heterogeneous interests. Consequently, they attempted to keep Mercosur's goals and membership limited. Mercosur's original members agreed to eliminate internal tariffs within four years and to enact a CET, thereby forming a customs union. At some later date, it was hoped that the customs union would evolve into a common market.

The Rationale for Mercosur

There are at least six reasons why the leaders of Argentina, Brazil, Paraguay, and Uruguay decided to form Mercosur: (1) to consolidate and lock in the democratic transitions that had occurred in these states, (2) to foster political–military cooperation in the Southern Cone, (3) to promote economic liberalization, especially in the area of international trade, (4) to more fully integrate the Southern Cone into the global economy, (5) to promote industrial restructuring and generate economies of scale in production, and (6) to obtain greater bargaining leverage in negotiations with the USA and the EU.

Earlier, we briefly discussed the first two reasons. In 1983, Argentina elected a civilian government, replacing the military junta that had ruled the country. Similarly, democratically elected governments came to power in Uruguay in 1984 and in Brazil in 1985. As Roett (1999: 3) points out, "for the political leadership of [these] countries, the decision to seek new levels of regional integration was fundamental in securing the fragile democratic regimes." Indeed, like the EU, Mercosur has placed a premium on the consolidation of democracy since its inception. Argentina and Brazil, for example, required Paraguay make democratic reforms before it was granted membership (Birch, 1996).

Mercosur also made the preservation of peace in the Southern Cone a high priority (Hirst, 1999). Historically, both Argentina and Brazil have sought the mantle of leadership in South America. During the 1970s, this rivalry came to a head, highlighted by a series of disputes over waterways and an arms race that threatened to turn nuclear. In both countries, the democratic governments that came to power in the 1980s saw a need to promote political–military cooperation in order to avert inter-state conflict that could serve as a pretext for the military to seize power and jeopardize the economic relationship between these countries. Furthermore, as the Cold War came to an end, there were increasing similarities in the foreign policy goals of Argentina and Brazil. Each country had an interest in fostering stability in Central America, non-proliferation, a successful conclusion to the Uruguay Round, and peace in the South Atlantic. In addition, while Argentina had established a close relationship with the USA during the 1980s, Brazil valued its autonomy in international relations and had resisted what it perceived as US efforts to influence Latin American affairs. By the early 1990s, however,

Brazil's relationship with the USA had improved, another indication of the growing similarity of Argentine and Brazilian foreign policies as they prepared to launch Mercosur.

The need to address a set of political challenges was a key impetus to Mercosur. However, this arrangement also aimed to achieve various economic goals. Both Argentina and Brazil viewed regional economic cooperation as a means to consolidate domestic economic reforms and adjustments. After various failed attempts to foster integration through PTAs that were designed to promote industrialization by walling Latin America off from foreign competition, countries in the Southern Cone concluded that they needed to become more fully integrated in the global economy. Mercosur was considered crucial to this end. In addition, like many other PTAs, Mercosur was intended to generate economies of scale in production by expanding the size of the market to which member states' firms had duty free access, thereby enhancing their competitiveness worldwide. This was an especially important consideration for Paraguay and Uruguay, small economies that stood to generate sizable gains from having unfettered access to the Brazilian and Argentine markets. In the same vein, the members of Mercosur envisioned creating a number of bi-national joint ventures, especially between Argentina and Brazil.

Finally, Mercosur was an effort to enhance the bargaining power of member states in international negotiations with the USA and the EU. Of particular importance were negotiations in the GATT and the World Trade Organization (WTO), as well as negotiations with the USA over the proposed Free Trade Area of the Americas (FTAA). Indeed, Pascal Lamy—the EU's Commissioner for External Trade—acknowledged that "consolidating Mercosur will give Brazil and its partners...more political weight in international negotiations" (European Commission, Trade DG, Information Unit, July 10, 2001). And in the run-up to Mercosur's entry into force, a Brazilian official similarly remarked that "Dealing directly with the U.S. on international trade issues is like getting into a cage with a tiger. Only if we have others in with us do we stand a better chance of getting some satisfactory results" (*Financial Times*, July 2, 1985, p. 5).

Mercosur's Institutional Design

Unlike earlier regional institutions that aimed to promote Latin American integration, Mercosur has a weak and sparse framework (Bouzas and Soltz, 2001; Preusse, 2004). This arrangement, for example, is much less detailed and rules based than the framework underlying NAFTA, not to mention the EU. All of Mercosur's institutions are inter-governmental and decision-making authority lies in the hands of state leaders. Its two major bodies are the Council of the Common Market, which is made up of foreign affairs ministers, and the Common Market Group, which is made up of high ranking government officials. In principle, all decisions are consensual. In practice, however, major decisions are often made by the presidents of Brazil and Argentina alone.

Mercosur has no jurisdictional body and a weak dispute settlement system. Furthermore, while decisions taken by its key organs are considered binding, they are neither "immediately applicable" nor do they have "direct effect." Consequently, members may or may not actually enforce these decisions (Bouzas and Soltz, 2001).

At its inception, Mercosur focused largely on liberalizing intra-regional trade, although exceptions were made for the computer industry, automobiles, sugar, and a number of other sensitive sectors. As noted earlier, Mercosur called for the elimination of internal trade barriers and the formation of a CU over a four-year period. Later, it was hoped, the CU would evolve into a common market. Political issues were not addressed in the Treaty of Asuncion since the participants worried that these issues could generate friction and derail the agreement.

The Effects of Mercosur

During the first five to six years of Mercosur's existence, the arrangement was widely considered a success. Since then, however, there have been various strains on the grouping and tensions among its members. Consequently, Mercosur has not met many of its core objectives, especially on the economic front.

From a political standpoint, Mercosur has generated a number of benefits. As Manzetti (1993/94: 110) observes, this arrangement "has provided its member states with a forum for discussion of sensitive policy issues, such as those in relation to transport and communications, nuclear proliferation...environmental protection, military cooperation, illegal immigration, and the drug traffic." Furthermore, it has made a number of changes to advance key political goals. In 1996, for example, Mercosur added a clause committing each member to maintain a democratic government and calling on participants to sanction any government that deviated from democratic rule. The next year, Argentina and Brazil signed the Rio Declaration and created a Permanent Commission for Coordination. These developments led to the coordination of political–military affairs, joint military consultations, and an agreement to ban nuclear weapons. In 1995, Mercosur intervened in a war between Peru and Ecuador. It helped to enforce a cease fire and—together with the USA and Chile—placed pressure on the combatants to craft a peace treaty. There is considerable evidence that, taken as a whole, PTAs inhibit political–military conflict between member states (Mansfield, Pevehouse, and Bearce, 1999; Mansfield and Pevehouse, 2000). Mercosur is exemplary in this regard: especially during the 1990s, it made an important contribution to peace and stability in the region. Mercosur also enhanced the bargaining power of member states in their negotiations with the EU and the USA, a key objective noted earlier.

From an economic perspective, most observers seem to view Mercosur's initial phase as relatively successful, although the evidence is not clear cut. Intra-regional trade barriers were slashed during the first five years of its existence. Largely as a result, the ratio of intra-regional exports to total exports for the members of Mercosur jumped about two and a half fold, from 8 per cent to roughly 20 per cent. Equally, FDI in the region almost tripled during this period. A number of firms established subsidiaries in member states and various joint ventures were forged. In this vein, Bouzas (1997: 66) points out that "By late 1994 there were 215 bilateral inter- and intra-firm initiatives, 43 per cent of which had direct production implications... More than 300 Brazilian firms had some kind of investment commitment in Argentina, in contrast to just over 30 Argentine firms in Brazil." And as the arrangement's first five years wound down, Mercosur started to expand, adding Bolivia and Chile as associate members.

Nonetheless, Mercosur's initial phase was not an unqualified economic success. Member countries had trouble coordinating policies along the lines that would be needed to establish a common market. Indeed, they were not even able to conclude a CET during the arrangement's "transition phase." Moreover, while the Argentine economy performed well, the Brazilian economy did not, contributing to economic tensions between these countries. In 1992, Argentina raised its surcharge on imports, angering its partners in Mercosur. Argentina responded by exempting Paraguay and Uruguay from these charges, but Brazilian goods were granted no such relief (Bouzas, 1997: 61). In 1993 and 1994, Argentina imposed trade barriers on paper and textile products; it also levied AD charges against Brazil. These events and Brazil's domestic economic problems dampened its enthusiasm for regional integration. By 1995, Brazil began contemplating the roll-back of regional integration and trade liberalization, while the other members were pressing for more extensive integration (Veiga, 1999). In that year, for example, it raised tariffs in its already highly protected automobile sector to 70 per cent on certain imports.

More generally, there has been considerable debate over the welfare effects of Mercosur. In a well-known study based on Mercosur's initial phase, Yeats (1998) concluded that the arrangement was trade diverting. Critics, however, charged that Yeats's analysis focused on exports and that the corresponding results based on imports are less conclusive. They also claimed that imports by Mercosur members from third parties rose just as quickly as intra-regional imports (Eichengreen and Frankel, 1995; Markwald, 2003). Thus, it remained unclear whether Mercosur was actually creating or diverting trade.

During its initial phase, Mercosur had some significant achievements. Many were political, but some were economic. Since then, however, this PTA has been marked by a series of severe problems and strains (Hurrell, 2001). In the late 1990s, intra-regional trade started to drop and economic growth in the region began to lag. Eventually, as Preusse (2004: 149) observes, "the region itself tumbled into a severe depression."

A key source of strain within Mercosur grew out of Brazil's financial crisis. In January 1999, Brazil decided to float its currency, the real, leading to a substantial depreciation. This episode, in the opinion of Markwald (2003: 84), precipitated "the most serious crisis in Mercosur since the start of the integration project." The Argentine peso had appreciated over the second half of the 1990s, and the combination of a rising peso and falling real undercut the competitiveness of Argentine producers in the important Brazilian market. Further, Argentina, Paraguay, and Uruguay faced the specter of a surge in imported Brazilian goods, prompting a rise in protectionist sentiment throughout the Southern Cone. Firms and workers who were adversely affected by these developments discovered that Mercosur provided them with no recourse, sparking widespread dissatisfaction.

The real crisis also highlighted the extensive macroeconomic differences among member states. Argentina, for example, relied on a Currency Board to establish the peso's value, whereas Brazil, Paraguay, and Uruguay relied on some variation of a managed float. Lack of coordination over foreign exchange and macroeconomic policy reduced the attractiveness of foreign investment in tradable sectors of members' economies. Instead, FDI was primarily funneled into the non-tradable sector (Preusse, 2004: 168).

Throughout the first decade of the twenty-first century, Mercosur faced a series of additional problems. Although trade within the region was fairly open, plenty of exceptions remained for sensitive sectors, such as sugar. In the automobile sector, there is a steep external tariff and Mercosur's automotive industry, led by Brazil, remains largely uncompetitive outside the Southern Cone. More generally, the hopes for promoting economies of scale in key industries and improving member firms' competitive position in global markets have not been realized. By 2003, Preusse (2004: 181) characterized Mercosur as "paralyzed and near to failure."

Mercosur has also encountered political challenges over the past decade. Whereas Argentina and Brazil's foreign policy goals started to converge in the immediate aftermath of the Cold War, relations between them deteriorated as the twentieth century came to a close (Llana, 2003: 172). Argentina's opposition to the Brazilian bid for a permanent seat on the UN Security Council created friction between these countries. At the same time, Brazil worried that Argentina's political relationship with the USA was becoming too close. Brazil feared that this development might precipitate a rise in USA influence in South America, threatening its preeminence in the region. Brazil has increasingly opted for a unilateral foreign policy, rather than one based on coordination with its neighbors. As illustrated by its efforts to gain a permanent seat on the UN Security Council, Brazil views itself as a world power that should be accorded corresponding status. Such goals are unlikely to be advanced by strengthening and working through regional institutions, like Mercosur. This, in turn, has fueled resentment by other Mercosur participants, which feel that Brazil has reaped a disproportionate share of the economic benefits generated by the organization. To be sure, the resulting political tensions within the Southern Cone have not overheated, but they nonetheless have been a source of concern (Hirst, 1999: 43).

IV. Conclusions

The purpose of this chapter has been to trace the causes and consequences of NAFTA and Mercosur. Having done so, I conclude by laying out some of the future challenges facing the members of each PTA. I then suggest some broader implications that can be drawn from these arrangements about the political economy of PTAs.

Within NAFTA, Canada, Mexico, and the USA face ongoing problems with illegal immigration and illegal drug trafficking. In the wake of 9/11, these issues have become linked to national security concerns, making them even more sensitive. For all three NAFTA members—but especially the USA—there is a need to address the security of national borders, intelligence sharing, and other issues related to terrorism. These countries also face a series of environmental challenges, including US–Mexican water allocation issues, problems associated with deforestation, soil erosion, and the water supply in Mexico, and logging and energy issues in the USA and Canada.

From an economic standpoint, the looming problem facing NAFTA is agriculture. On January 1, 2008, the member states eliminated all remaining trade barriers on farm products. Mexican farmers are deeply concerned about the effect of this development on the price of beans and corn, two staples of the Mexican diet. In recent years, Mexico has experienced a substantial decline in agricultural employment. This is partly a result of productivity increases, but it also stems from a surge in lower priced agricultural imports from the USA. The removal of all trade barriers on agricultural products threatens to place an even greater strain on Mexican farmers. There also continues to be a dispute between these countries over sugar, which has led Mexico to take steps to make it extremely costly for US producers to sell high fructose corn syrup to Mexico for use in soft drinks. The agricultural challenges facing NAFTA are hardly unique. In almost every major regional and multilateral forum, they are crucially important. But these issues could be a source of considerable stress on the arrangement.

More generally, Barack Obama made promises to renegotiate key features of NAFTA with Canada and Mexico during the 2008 presidential campaign. Since taking office, Obama has backed away from that position. It remains to be seen whether he will face domestic political pressure to make changes to NAFTA that could ultimately weaken the arrangement.

Mercosur faces important challenges as well. One concern is its institutional form. Writing in the late 1990s, Veiga (1999: 25) observed that Mercosur is "halfway between a free trade area and a customs union with few mechanisms for institutionalization." There continues to be debate within Mercosur about whether the institution should be scaled back to an FTA or whether the CU that was called for in the Treaty of Asuncion should be consolidated with an eye toward eventually establishing a common market. The latter aspiration, however, has been frustrated by the lack of an institutional foundation that is robust enough to facilitate the coordination of members' policies on a wide range of issues. This institutional weakness is a problem. Various observers have argued that Mercosur needs to do a better job of coordinating and regulating the macroeconomic policies of member states if the organization is to meet its objectives.

Mercosur faces a number of internal challenges as well. Compared to the hopes of its founders, for example, firms within the bloc have experienced relatively few gains in competitiveness and have undertaken little restructuring. Furthermore, Argentina, Paraguay, and Uruguay remain highly dependent on the Brazilian market. Import competing interests remain politically powerful, especially in Brazil, and will need to be kept at bay for the arrangement to succeed.

Mercosur is in the process of trying to expand. Bolivia and Venezuela have applied for full membership. However, there are concerns among the existing member states about the undemocratic and economically nationalist policies of Bolivia and especially Venezuela. Adding states with policy positions that diverge significantly from the four original members could damage the PTA. At the same time, the failure to expand could undermine Mercosur's position in the global economy.

In the same vein, Mercosur must address its economic relationship with the USA and the EU, the two largest economic actors in the world. At the Summit of the Americas in 1994, President Clinton called for a hemispheric-wide FTA by 2005. President George W. Bush repeated this call when he entered office. At the same time, the EU and Mercosur stepped up efforts to negotiate an FTA. Neither of these initiatives has yielded fruit to date. However, both of them are important. There are concerns within Latin America that the failure to establish an FTAA has led the USA to start forming bilateral agreements with countries in the region, such as Chile. This approach could weaken the economic influence of Brazil in particular and Mercosur in general. At the same time, however, Mercosur is a relatively small market, especially for Brazil, which may create a need to expand economic relations with other regions. Partly as a result, Mercosur has started negotiating PTAs with the members of the Southern African Customs Union, Egypt, Israel, Jordan, Morocco, and Turkey, among others.

The experiences of NAFTA and Mercosur also suggest various broader lessons about the political economy of PTAs. First, both of these institutions have been marked by the existence of one particularly large country, the USA in the case of NAFTA and Brazil in the case of Mercosur. These regional hegemons have provided various benefits, helping to address collective action problems and facilitating the coordination of members' policies. Equally, the large markets of hegemons made it especially attractive for smaller states to join NAFTA and Mercosur. Nonetheless, smaller participants have bridled at their dependence on the US and Brazilian markets and the tendency for these regional hegemons to discount the interests of other member states, creating strains on each of the arrangements.

Second, despite these strains, the experiences of NAFTA and Mercosur suggest that PTAs help to defuse conflicts and stabilize political relations among members. This has been most evident in the case of Mercosur, which has promoted peace in the Southern Cone and helped to improve political–military relations between Brazil and Argentina. Third, both NAFTA and Mercosur illustrate how PTAs can be used to foster economic and political reform in participating countries. Mexico, Argentina, Brazil, and Paraguay have successfully consolidated democratic regimes since entering these arrangements, although the political situation in Venezuela is a worrisome exception to this tendency. Further, NAFTA and Mercosur have limited the ability of member states to roll back various economic reforms, since doing so would violate the regional agreements.

Fourth, while these PTAs have reinforced certain economic reforms, they have also been marked by various industries (for example, agriculture in NAFTA and autos in Mercosur) that were initially granted exceptions to the open trade regime. Such exceptions are commonplace in PTAs. They help shield politically potent sectors that might otherwise try to derail an arrangement. Even when an arrangement calls for the exceptions to be phased out, however, doing so can be painful and difficult, which is one reason why most PTAs ultimately liberalize only a fraction of the trade conducted by members.

Fifth, both arrangements illustrate how states can use PTAs to improve their bargaining position in international negotiations (Mansfield and Reinhardt, 2003). It is widely argued that the decision by the Bush Administration to start negotiating NAFTA enhanced the bargaining power of the USA in the GATT and led states that had been holding up the Uruguay Round to return to the bargaining table. In the same vein, by forming Mercosur, countries in the Southern Cone improved their leverage in negotiations with both the USA and the EU, even though these negotiations have yielded few tangible results.

Finally, these cases illustrate the importance of a PTA's institutional design. Both NAFTA and Mercosur have fairly sparse designs. Mercosur's institutions are especially weak. This feature has preserved the autonomy of member states, since they do not answer to a regional authority. However, this design feature has also limited the effectiveness of both PTAs in responding to certain intra-regional issues. The problem is especially acute for Mercosur. It is hard to see how this arrangement will become an effective customs union, much less a common market, with such a thin and weak set of institutions.

References

Abbott, F. M. (2000), 'NAFTA and the Legalization of World Politics: A Case Study.' *International Organization*, 54(3): 519–47.

Bailey, J. (2004), 'Security Imperatives of North American Integration: Back to a Future of Hub and Spokes.' In Weintraub, S. (ed.), *NAFTA's Impact on North America: The First Decade*, Washington, DC: Center for Strategic and International Studies Press.

Baldwin R. E. (1995), 'A Domino Theory of Regionalism.' In Baldwin, R., Haaparanta, P., and Kiander, J. (eds.), *Expanding Membership of the European Union*. New York: Cambridge University Press.

Bean, F. D. and Lowell, B. L. (2004), 'NAFTA and Mexican Migration to the United States.' In Weintraub, S. (ed.), *NAFTA's Impact on North America: The First Decade*. Washington, DC: Center for Strategic and International Studies Press.

Bhagwati, J. (1993), 'Regionalism and Multilateralism: An Overview.' In de Melo, J., and Panagariya, A. (eds.), *New Dimensions in Regional Integration*. Cambridge: Cambridge University Press.

Birch, M. H. (1996), 'Economic Policy and the Transition to Democracy in Paraguay.' In Morales, J. A., and McMahon, G. (eds.), *Economic Policy and the Transition to Democracy: The Latin American Experience*. New York: St. Martin's Press.

Bouzas, R. (1997), 'Mercosur and Preferential Trade Liberalization in South America: Record, Issues, and Prospects.' In Lipsey, R. G., and Meller, P. (eds.), *Western Hemisphere Trade Integration: A Canadian-Latin American Dialogue*. New York: St. Martin's Press.

Bouzas, R. and Soltz, H. (2001), 'Institutions and Regional Integration: The Case of Mercosur.' In Bulmer-Thomas, V. (ed.), *Regional Integration in Latin America and the Caribbean: The Political Economy of Open Regionalism*. London: Institute of Latin American Studies.

Cameron, M. A. and Tomlin, B. W. (2000), *The Making of NAFTA: How the Deal was Done*. Ithaca, NY: Cornell University Press.

Destler, I. M. (1995), *American Trade Politics*, 3rd edition. Washington, DC: Institute for International Economics.

Eichengreen, B. and Frankel, J. A. (1995), 'Economic Regionalism: Evidence from Two 20th Century Episodes.' *The North American Journal of Economics and Finance*, 6(2): 89–106.

Fernandez de Castro, R. (2004), 'The Functioning of NAFTA and its Impact on Mexican-US Relations.' In Weintraub, S. (ed.), *NAFTA's Impact on North America: The First Decade*, Washington, DC: Center for Strategic and International Studies Press.

Goldstein, J. (1996), 'International Law and Domestic Institutions: Reconciling North American 'Unfair' Trade Laws.' *International Organization*, 50(4): 541–64.

Hirst, M. (1999), 'Mercosur's Complex Political Agenda.' In Roett, R. (ed.), *Mercosur: Regional Integration, World Markets*. Boulder, CO: Lynne Rienner.

Hufbauer, G. C. and Schott, J. J. (2005), *NAFTA Revisited: Achievements and Challenges*. Washington, DC: Institute for International Economics.

Hurrell, A. (2001), 'The Politics of Regional Integration in Mercosur.' In Bulmer-Thomas, V. (ed.), *Regional Integration in Latin America and the Caribbean: The Political Economy of Open Regionalism*. London: Institute of Latin American Studies.

Krueger, A. O. (1999), 'Are Preferential Trading Arrangements Trade-Liberalizing or Protectionist?' *Journal of Economic Perspectives*, 13(4): 105–24.

Lederman, D., Maloney, W. F., and Servén, L. (2005), *Lessons from NAFTA for Latin America and the Caribbean*. Stanford, CA: Stanford University Press and the World Bank.

Llana, C. P. (2003), 'Mercosul: An Interpretation of the Past and a View to the Future.' In Jaguaribe, H., and Vasconcelos, A. (eds.) *The European Union, Mercosul, and the New World Order*. Portland, OR: Frank Cass.

Mansfield, E. D. and Milner, H. V. (1999), 'The New Wave of Regionalism.' *International Organization*, 53(3): 589–627.

Mansfield, E. D., and Pevehouse, J. C. (2000), 'Trade Blocs, Trade Flows, and International Conflict.' *International Organization*, 54(4): 775–808.

Mansfield, E. D., Pevehouse, J.C., and Bearce, D. H. (1999), 'Preferential Trading Arrangements and Military Disputes.' *Security Studies*, 9(1–2): 92–118.

Mansfield, E. D. and Reinhardt, E. (2003), 'Multilateral Determinants of Regionalism: The Effects of GATT/WTO on the Formation of Preferential Trading Arrangements.' *International Organization*, 57(4): 829–62.

Mansfield, E. D. and Solingen, E. (2010), 'Regionalism.' *Annual Review of Political Science*, 13:145–63.

Manzetti, Li. (1993/1994), 'The Political Economy of MERCOSUR.' *Journal of Interamerican Studies & World Affairs*, 35(4): 101–41.

Markwald, R. (2003). 'Mercosul: Beyond 2000.' In Jaguaribe, H., and Vasconcelos, A. (eds.) *The European Union, Mercosul, and the New World Order*. Portland, OR: Frank Cass.

McConnell, J. and MacPherson, A. (1994), 'The North American Free Trade Agreement: An Overview of Issues and Prospects.' In Gibb, R., and Michalak, W. (eds.) *Continental Trading Blocs: The Growth of Regionalism in the World Economy*. New York: John Wiley.

Nogues, J. J. and Quintanilla, R. (1993), 'Latin America's Integration and the Multilateral Trading System.' In de Melo, J. and Panagariya, A. (eds.), *New Dimensions in Regional Integration*. Cambridge: Cambridge University Press.

Pereira, L. V. (1999), 'Toward the Common Market of the South: Mercosur's Origins, Evolution, and Challenges.' In Roett, R. (ed.), *Mercosur: Regional Integration, World Markets*. Boulder, CO: Lynne Rienner.

Preusse, H. (2004), *New American Regionalism*. Cheltenham, UK: Edward Elgar.

Ready, K. J. (1993), 'NAFTA: Labor, Industry, and Government Perspectives.' In Bognanno M. F., and Ready, K. J. (eds.), *The North American Free Trade Agreement: Labor, Industry, and Government Perspectives*. Westport, CT: Quorum Books.

Roett, R. (1999), 'U.S. Policy Towards Mercosur: From Miami to Santiago.' In Roett, R. (ed.), *Mercosur: Regional Integration, World Markets*. Boulder, CO: Lynne Rienner.

Schiff, M. and Winters, L. A. (2003), *Regional Integration and Development*. Washington, DC: World Bank.

Tornell, A. and Esquivel, G. (1995), 'The Political Economy of Mexico's Entry to NAFTA.' Cambridge, MA: National Bureau of Economic Research Working Paper.

Tornell, A., Westermann, F., and Martinez, L. (2004), 'NAFTA and Mexico's Less-Than-Stellar Performance.' Cambridge, MA: National Bureau of Economic Research Working Paper.

Toro, M. C. (2004), 'Mexican Policy Against Drugs: From Deterring to Embracing the United States. In Weintraub, S. (ed.), *NAFTA's Impact on North America: The First Decade*. Washington, DC: Center for Strategic and International Studies Press.

Veiga, P. da Motta (1999), 'Brazil in Mercosur: Reciprocal Influence.' In Roett, R. (ed.), *Mercosur: Regional Integration, World Markets*. Boulder, CO: Lynne Rienner.

Weintraub, S. (2000), 'NAFTA Evaluation.' *Issues in International Political Economy*, 8: 1–16.

Weintraub, S. (2004), 'Trade, Investment, and Economic Growth.' In Weintraub, S. (ed), *NAFTA's Impact on North America: The First Decade*. Washington, DC: Center for Strategic and International Studies Press.

World Bank (2005), *Global Economic Prospects: Trade, Regionalism, and Development*. Washington, DC: World Bank.

World Trade Organization (WTO) (1995), *Regionalism and the World Trading System*. Geneva: WTO.

Yeats, A. J. (1998), 'Does Mercosur's Trade Performance Raise Concerns about the Effects of Regional Trade Arrangements?' *The World Bank Economic Review*, 12(1): 1–28.

Zepeda, E., Wise, T. A., and Gallagher, K. P. (2009), 'Rethinking Trade Policy for Development: Lessons from Mexico under NAFTA.' Washington, DC: Carnegie Endowment for International Peace.

CHAPTER 20

SAFEGUARDS, ANTI-DUMPING, AND SUBSIDIES IN INTERNATIONAL TRADE LAW

JOEL P. TRACHTMAN

I. Introduction: Mercantilism and Contingent Protection

In responding to pressures of free trade, states have devised three main types of measures to reduce market access conditional on determination of specified phenomena. These three types of measures are: (1) safeguards measures, (2) anti-dumping duties, and (3) countervailing duties in response to subsidies. These measures are all predicated on determinations that imports are causing injury to a domestic industry, as well as other factors.

Contingent Derogation from Liberalization Commitments and Efficient Breach

While states have liberalized in significant measures since the establishment of the General Agreement on Tariffs and Trade (GATT) in 1947, states have determined that it is desirable to maintain the right to impose "contingent protection" in order to reverse their liberalization under certain circumstances. Obviously, if the right to engage in contingent protection is not constrained enough—if it is too easy to rightfully apply safeguards, anti-dumping duties, and countervailing duties—then the concessions made by states in international trade negotiations would have little value.

So the international system is finely balanced—some would say it is unbalanced in one direction or the other—between enforcement of liberalization commitments and permission to derogate from liberalization commitments.

It might be argued that the permission to derogate from liberalization commitments under appropriate circumstances may play a role in inducing greater liberalization commitments. That is, trade negotiators may be willing to make greater liberalization commitments under conditions of uncertainty regarding the effects of liberalization, when they know that they can derogate from these commitments in the event that they turn out to be unexpectedly burdensome. It might further be argued that at least the safeguards mechanism represents a kind of international law facility for "efficient breach." That is, it allows states to determine to back away from their commitments, if they are willing to provide compensation (under certain circumstances).

Finally, these measures tend to ignore the consumer benefits that may arise from the imported goods at issue. Especially in the case of dumping and subsidization, there may be a transfer of economic welfare from the exporting state to the importing state, with consumers in the importing state experiencing the greatest benefit.

Yet attitudes towards dumping, subsidization, and safeguards tend to assume that imports of inexpensive goods cause harm that is greater than the benefits that accrue. They also tend to assume, without necessarily finding empirical or theoretical support, that dumping or subsidization may allow exporters to capture market share that will be difficult to regain. This is a mercantilist perspective. In some contexts, it is possible that the mercantilist perspective may be validated by a strategic trade theory analysis.

Free Trade and Fair Trade

In connection with anti-dumping and countervailing duties, it is argued by proponents that these measures are responses to "unfair trade:" to dumping and subsidization. According to this perspective, anti-dumping and countervailing duties function to "level" the playing field. Indeed, this is how they are designed to operate: to charge an additional tariff that is set by reference to a calculation of the extent of dumping and/or subsidization.

Hidden Protectionism and the "Law" of Conservation of Protection

On the other hand, it may be argued by some that these three types of measures are simply different names for a technique of defection from trade liberalization commitments. To the extent that contingent protection measures are less visible, or easier to legitimate, than normal tariffs, they may be a preferred form of protectionism from a political standpoint. This type of protectionism may be more difficult to identify, and to address through negotiated limits. In fact, observers have suggested that as explicit protection in the form of tariffs and quotas have been reduced, states have made greater use of hidden protection, including contingent protection.

Core Definitions and Concepts

This section presents several core definitions and concepts that will be useful to understand prior to proceeding to subsequent sections.

Of course, free trade involves competition, including "creative destruction" in the sense that some producers will be harmed, or will not survive. As liberalization has progressed—as tariff barriers and quotas have been dismantled or reduced—states have found that some of their domestic industries have been harmed or driven out of business. Indeed, one explanation of the role of GATT and later the World Trade Organization (WTO) is to allow states to reciprocate in liberalization, in order to allow domestic coalitions of consumers and exporters to overcome the fears and protectionism of producers for the domestic market.

However, as noted above, import surges that cause serious injury to domestic industries, and dumping and subsidization that cause material injury to domestic industries, are explicitly not part of the WTO bargain. Rather, the WTO bargain includes authorization for states to respond to these phenomena with renewed trade barriers.

Legal Setting

It is important to note that safeguards, anti-dumping, and countervailing duties actions are never required under international law. The role of international law in this setting is to restrain, and set conditions for, national action. Each type of contingent protection is permitted, subject to satisfaction of the relevant conditions, under GATT 1994.

Additional requirements for each type of contingent protection are set under the WTO Agreement on Safeguards (Safeguards Agreement), the WTO Agreement on Implementation of Article VI of the GATT 1994 (Anti-dumping Agreement), and the WTO Agreement on Subsidies and Countervailing Measures (SCM Agreement). In order for a national measure to be permitted, it generally must comply with all of the requirements of applicable law, including both the GATT 1994 requirements and the requirements of the other applicable agreements. WTO law imposes both substantive and procedural requirements—conditions—for application of contingent protection measures. Finally, these legal rules do not apply directly to individuals or firms. Rather, they apply to imported goods.

Dumping and subsidization are addressed under some jurisdictions' competition laws. For example, for a number of years, the United States maintained a criminal anti-dumping law as part of its competition (or anti-trust) laws. The European Community imposes legal disciplines on subsidies by its member states under its competition laws. Actions against foreign states' firms or goods under these types of competition laws may be constrained under WTO law.[1]

Safeguards

Safeguards measures respond to "serious" injury to a domestic industry caused by increased imports. Safeguards measures are permitted by Article XIX of GATT 1994, sometimes known as the "escape clause." Safeguards are not based on allegations of "unfair" trade, but simply respond to increased imports resulting from earlier trade concessions. Safeguards actions are dependent upon a finding that the increased imports "caused" serious injury. Safeguards measures may take the form of increased tariffs (above the otherwise applicable bound level) or quotas. Importantly, safeguards measures are generally to be applied to all imports of like products, regardless of source: they are to be applied on an most favored nation (MFN) basis.

Dumping

Dumping involves the sale of goods at prices below the home market price of like products, or if no such price exists, below either (1) the cost of production plus a reasonable addition for selling cost or profit, or (2) the price of like products when sold to a third country. Thus, dumping may be understood as either: (a) international price discrimination, or (b) sales of goods below cost. The latter definition is related to the competition law concept of predatory pricing.

Importantly, dumping involves private sector activity; so if a private company "cross-subsidizes" one product with profits from another, and sells the "cross-subsidized" product below cost, this would be evaluated as "dumping," rather than subsidization. Importantly, it is possible that the private sector entity that dumps could achieve the ability to dump by virtue of profits earned in a protected home market, where it can charge higher prices than would be possible in a liberalized home market.

Anti-dumping duties are permitted under WTO law when dumping exists, and it is found to cause "material injury" to a domestic industry. As dumping is in theory a private enterprise act, anti-dumping duties are not applied on an MFN basis. Indeed, they are generally applied to producers of a specific good from a specific state. Producers may seek exclusion from the group of producers subject to anti-dumping duties, on the basis that they do not dump. Anti-dumping duties are additional tariffs on goods found to

---

[1] Appellate Body Report, *United States—Anti-Dumping Act of 1916*, WT/DS136/AB/R, WT/DS162/AB/R, adopted September 26, 2000 (finding this additional set of disciplines illegal under the Anti-Dumping Act (ADA)).

be dumped, charged over and above existing tariffs. They are calculated by reference to the "dumping margin" found: the difference between the export price and the "normal value," which is the home market price or, if that is not available, either the cost of production or third country price.

Subsidies

Subsidization involves a government financial contribution that confers a benefit on the producer of exported goods. As with dumping, countervailing duties are permitted when subsidization exists and is found to cause "material injury" to a domestic industry. Countervailing duties are additional tariffs on goods found to be subsidized, charged over and above existing tariffs.

Serious Injury

"Serious injury" is a required condition for the initiation of safeguards actions. There is no quantitative definition of "serious injury" under WTO law, but it is understood to be a greater threshold than "material injury," discussed below. However, WTO law specifies certain factors that national authorities must evaluate in order to make a finding of serious injury. Without such a finding, safeguards measures are not permitted.

Material Injury

"Material injury" is a required condition for either anti-dumping or countervailing duty actions. Similarly to "serious injury," there is no quantitative measure by which to determine the existence of "material injury." However, as with "serious injury," WTO law specifies factors that national authorities must evaluate in their determination.

Causation

Determinations of causation, especially of serious injury or material injury, play an important role in each area of contingent protectionism. As each of them requires a causal nexus between the imported goods at issue and a specified level of injury, it is initially up to national authorities to make findings of causation (except in certain cases of "serious prejudice" subsidies). Economic analysis of causation in this context is difficult and contentious.

Box 20.1 Summary: Matrix of Contingent Protection Measures

Form of contingent protection	Import characterization	Injury threshold	Authorized response
Safeguards	Surge in quantity	Serious injury	Tariff or quota
Dumping	Dumped	Material injury	Anti-dumping duty
Subsidies	Subsidized	Material injury	Countervailing duty

II. Practice of Safeguards, Anti-Dumping Duties, and Countervailing Duties

In this section, we describe the existing terrain of import surges, dumping and subsidization, and responses in the form of safeguards, anti-dumping duties, and countervailing duties.

Origins of Import Surges, Dumped Exports, and Subsidized Exports

It is difficult to speak in a methodologically sound way of the actual origins of import surges, dumped exports, and subsidized exports, because there is no consensus method by which to define and measure these phenomena. WTO law provides *limits* on national measures *responding* to these phenomena, and it requires national authorities to identify these phenomena. However, it allows significant discretion in the way that national authorities identify these phenomena.

Moreover, in reality, national actions for safeguards, anti-dumping duties, and countervailing duties cannot be the measure, as the decision to commence an investigation is dependent on a number of other factors. As we will see below, the legal basis for these actions provides a large degree of flexibility. Furthermore, the raw numbers of contingent protection measures listed below should be normalized against a measure of trade in order to determine the relative proportionality of actions by or against particular states.

Pursuant to Article 2.2 of the Safeguards Agreement, safeguards measures are generally applied irrespective of the source of the relevant goods, and so it is difficult to obtain data on the extent of investigations of surges from particular countries. However, the WTO has gathered some sectoral data for the period since January 1, 1995 (the date of formation of the WTO): "The most frequent subject of investigations since 1995 were chemical products (26 initiations), metals and metal products

(21 initiations), foodstuffs (16 initiations), and ceramics and vegetables (14 initiations each)."[2]

During the period from January 1, 1995 to June 30, 2006 the following states were the leading targets of anti-dumping duty investigations: China (500 investigations), Korea (223), United States (169), Taiwan (167), Japan (129), India (124), Indonesia (123), Thailand (117), Russia (99), and Brazil (87).[3]

There were far fewer countervailing duty investigations. During the period from January 1, 1995 (the formation of the WTO) to June 30, 2006, the following states were the leading targets of countervailing duty investigations: India (42 investigations), Korea (15), Italy (13), European Community (10), Indonesia (10), Thailand (9), and Canada (8).[4] The WTO Annual Trade Report for 2006 focuses on subsidies, and includes extensive data on the incidence of subsidies.[5]

Countries Using Contingent Protection

During the period from January 1, 1995 to June 30, 2006, the following states were the leading initiators of safeguards investigations: India (15), Chile (11), Jordan (11), Czech Republic (9), Turkey (10), and United States (10).[6]

As of 2003, 98 countries had anti-dumping laws (Zanardi, 2004, 2005).[7] During the period from January 1, 1995 to June 30, 2006, the following states were the leading initiators of anti-dumping duty investigations: India (448), United States (336), European Community (345), Argentina (209) and South Africa (199).[8]

During the same period, the following states were the leading initiators of countervailing duty investigations: United States (72), European Community (45), Canada (18), South Africa (11).[9]

Perspective of Developing Countries

The data summarized above suggest that contingent protection is not a tool only of wealthy countries, although the largest users of countervailing duty actions appear to be developed countries. Furthermore, the targets of contingent protection include

---

[2] <http://www.wto.org/english/news_e/news06_e/sfg_29nov06_e.htm>.

[3] <http://www.wto.org/english/tratop_e/adp_e/adp_stattab1_e.xls>.

[4] <http://www.wto.org/english/tratop_e/scm_e/scm_stattab1_e.xls>.

[5] See Section E of the World Trade Report 2006, especially Appendix Table 1 http://www.wto.org/english/res_e/booksp_e/anrep_e/wtr06-2e_e.pdf.

[6] <http://www.wto.org/english/tratop_e/safeg_e/safeg_stattab1_e.xls>.

[7] For Zanardi's tables, including a table listing states that have anti-dumping laws, and the dates of adoption, see <http://center.uvt.nl/staff/zanardi/ADdoha.xls>.

[8] <http://www.wto.org/english/tratop_e/adp_e/adp_stattab2_e.xls>.

[9] <http://www.wto.org/english/tratop_e/scm_e/scm_stattab2_e.xls>.

both developing and developed countries, although the majority of frequent targets of anti-dumping actions appear to be developing or emerging market countries. For more information on the use of anti-dumping by developing countries, see Bown (2006) and the World Bank database.

III. Basic Political Economy of Safeguards

The political economy explanation of safeguards is very similar to the political economy explanation of anti-dumping duties and countervailing duties. All three are explained as providing contingent protection: conditional defection from WTO commitments. While the conditions for application of anti-dumping duties and countervailing duties include the identification of dumping and subsidization, it will be seen below that these additional conditions may be met more frequently than might be expected. In fact, as to dumping, Finger (1993: vii) suggests that "[w]hen the politics of the matter compel action against imports, the legal definition of dumping can be stretched to accommodate it."

Economic Rationales for Safeguards

There is no generally accepted economic rationale for safeguards measures: most explanations of the role of safeguards propose political rationales. Of course, the political context of liberalization is a real, and significant, constraint. Safeguards provisions—specifically, Article XIX of GATT 1994 as supplemented by the Safeguards Agreement—serve as a limit on the scope of political action to withdraw liberalization commitments. They serve as a limit by setting certain conditions for access to this type of withdrawal of commitment, and by establishing a requirement for compensation to states harmed by the withdrawal, under specified circumstances.

The main argument for safeguards is that a domestic industry needs a period of protection to shield it from a surge in imports, and that after a period of protection the domestic industry will be able to compete globally. Horn and Mavroidis (2003) have argued that safeguards measures may serve an efficient temporizing function, by allowing more gradual and therefore (under specific and limited circumstances) less costly reallocation of resources, especially labor. However, economists are broadly distrustful of the ability of governments to sort between valid claims along these lines, and invalid claims that will result in a chronic need for protection.

Sykes (1991) evaluates and rejects a number of possible economic justifications for the existence of a safeguards provision in GATT. He concludes that safeguards measures are inconsistent with economic efficiency, for the same reasons that other trade barriers are inconsistent with economic efficiency: they impede the operation of comparative advantage, impeding the transfer of resources from less efficient industries to more efficient industries. In fact, safeguards are interposed precisely where this transfer seems to be occurring due to market forces.

Conservative Social Welfare Function and Compensation of Injured Persons

One quasi-economic explanation of safeguards law is Corden's "conservative social welfare function," which embodies Corden's notion (1974: 107) that "…any significant absolute reductions in real incomes of any significant section of the community should be avoided" (Deardorff, 1987). This early concept is consistent with modern behavioral economics insights regarding individual preferences to avoid risks of loss in favor of obtaining risks of gain. As discussed below, it is also consistent with a pragmatic political approach to significant disruptions in incomes.

Deardorff extends Corden's analysis, suggesting that safeguards may serve as a technique by which to compensate persons injured by trade liberalization. In this sense, safeguards may be consistent with "embedded liberalism." This is the concept first formulated by Karl Polanyi and applied to trade by John Ruggie, suggesting that liberalization must be "embedded" in a regulatory mechanism that can serve to accomplish sufficient redistribution to compensate those harmed by liberalization. However, Sykes (2005: 18) suggests that protection arising from safeguards is an "extremely costly and clumsy device for compensating the 'losers' from trade liberalization."

Politically Efficient Breach

The best way to understand safeguards measures is as a facility for politically efficient breach. The leading work in this area is Sykes (1991). Under this explanation, the WTO tariff commitments are understood as "contractual" commitments made by governments at particular points in time. At those points in time, governments are not able to predict accurately the competitive effects of their liberalization commitments. However, governments recognize that, for political reasons (as suggested by Corden), "any significant absolute reductions in real incomes of any significant section of the community should be avoided." Under uncertainty, governments include the "escape clause" in order to provide the possibility for derogation from commitments, with compensation to harmed states. This type of facility is known in domestic legal analysis as a facility for "efficient breach." Interestingly, efficiency is measured according to this analysis in the political welfare of governments, rather than in the public interest welfare of citizens.

Sykes' argument is predicated on the assumption that declining domestic industries have made sunk investments, and that these sunk investments serve to deter domestic entry. At the same time, foreign exporters have less at stake, especially as they are assumed to be efficient and therefore profitable. Sykes does not assume that domestic persons have greater political influence than foreign exporters, but this may also affect political decisions.

Bagwell and Staiger (2005) suggest that politically efficient breach may be permitted, but that it must be constrained in order to induce member states to exercise restraint in their use of the facility for breach. And so, for Bagwell and Staiger, it is critical that the Safeguards Agreement (as discussed below) restricts the repeated use of safeguards measures.

IV. BASIC ECONOMICS OF DUMPING AND ANTI-DUMPING

We will discuss both the economics of dumping, and the economics of anti-dumping. A discussion of the economics of dumping requires a definition of dumping. However, there is no economic definition of dumping, as dumping is not a discrete economic phenomenon and it has little separate economic significance. Therefore, we begin with a legal definition of dumping, in order to be able to discuss the economics of this phenomenon. The legal definition of dumping contained in Article VI of GATT (see Box 20.2) will suffice for our purposes at this point (it has been supplemented in Article 2 of the Anti-dumping Agreement).

Box 20.2 Article VI GATT 1994

The contracting parties recognize that dumping, by which products of one country are introduced into the commerce of another country at less than the normal value of the products, is to be condemned if it causes or threatens material injury to an established industry in the territory of a contracting party or materially retards the establishment of a domestic industry. For the purposes of this Article, a product is to be considered as being introduced into the commerce of an importing country at less than its normal value, if the price of the product exported from one country to another

(a) is less than the comparable price, in the ordinary course of trade, for the like product when destined for consumption in the exporting country, or,

(b) in the absence of such domestic price, is less than either

(i) the highest comparable price for the like product for export to any third country in the ordinary course of trade, or

(ii) the cost of production of the product in the country of origin plus a reasonable addition for selling cost and profit.

Due allowance shall be made in each case for differences in conditions and terms of sale, for differences in taxation, and for other differences affecting price comparability.

Under subclause (a), which has priority, "dumping" occurs when like products are sold at lower prices in the export market than in the home market: a type of international price discrimination (hereinafter referred to as "Price Discrimination Dumping"). Where Price Discrimination Dumping cannot be found due to lack of like products being sold in the ordinary course of trade in the home market, WTO law allows states to choose between two alternative benchmarks. The first available benchmark is to use an alternative market as a "deemed" home market, and to compare the export price to the importing market to the export price to the deemed home market (hereinafter referred to as "Third Country Price Discrimination Dumping"). The second alternative, equal in priority to Third Country Price Discrimination Dumping, compares the export price to the cost of production ("Cost of Production Dumping"). We will focus on Price Discrimination Dumping and Cost of Production Dumping.

Political Economy of Dumping and Anti-Dumping

According to Finger, anti-dumping is merely "protectionism with good public relations" (Mastel, 1998: 5). Finger views anti-dumping measures as ordinary protection, subject to the same economic analysis as ordinary protection (Finger, 1993). Similarly, Hoekman and Kostecki state that anti-dumping "constitutes straightforward protectionism that is packaged to make it look like something different (Hoekman and Kostecki, 2001: 322)."

As suggested above, anti-dumping can also be subject to the same political analysis as safeguards or other conditional or contingent protection. Furthermore, as anti-dumping measures are subject to fewer constraints than safeguards, in the form of requirements of compensation and restrictions on the duration and renewal of protection, anti-dumping may have different political economy characteristics.

That is, it is more difficult to argue that anti-dumping duty facilities provide a mechanism for efficient breach, when no compensation is required to be made to harmed states. It is also more difficult to argue that the anti-dumping facility forces states to be selective in their use, as in addition to there being no requirement for compensation, there is no restriction on duration of anti-dumping measures and no restriction on renewal. Furthermore, anti-dumping measures may be used selectively: they are not subject to a requirement, as safeguards measures generally are, to apply the measure to goods irrespective of their source country.

The reason why Finger was able to suggest that anti-dumping is protectionism with good public relations is because dumping is commonly portrayed as unfair. In fact, anti-dumping duties and countervailing duties in response to subsidization are both viewed as responses to unfair trade practices. In the case of dumping, the unfairness arises from an assumption that exporters intend to drive domestic producers out of business, and then charge supra-competitive prices to recoup the cost of dumping. It can readily be seen that this perception of unfairness is dependent upon the definition of dumping. To the extent that the definition of dumping includes parameters that indicate this type of intent, it seems appropriate to understand dumping as unfair. However, the definition of dumping generally does not require showings of unfairness.

It is important to state here that, even if there were a plausible argument that dumping causes injury to the importing state, or that it causes political harm to the government of the importing state, the legal tests that serve as conditions for invocation of anti-dumping duties are so imprecise, and so incongruent with the likely genesis of these concerns, that anti-dumping actions in the real world may still be subject to significant criticism. As a leading trade lawyer, David Palmeter (1991: 66), has stated,

> The standards of the day, the procedures it uses and the implementation of these standards and procedures by the [U.S.] Department of Commerce increasingly ensure that, at the end of the day, an exporter determined to have been selling in the United States below fair value probably has been doing no such thing in any meaningful sense of the word "fair." On the contrary, rather than being a price discriminator, a dumper is more likely the victim of an anti-dumping process that has become a legal and an administrative non-tariff barrier.

The international legal disciplines on anti-dumping law contained in the WTO treaty generally have been fiercely restricted by lawyers and lobbyists for protection-seeking US firms, in order to ensure that they provide little discipline on anti-dumping actions as carried out under US law. In this context, it is worth noting that the European Community, in connection with its *internal* trade, does not permit anti-dumping actions. That is, for example, Italian goods cannot be subjected to anti-dumping actions in Germany. Rather, European Community competition law is deemed sufficient to police similar conduct.

Market Effects of Dumping

Dumping is commonly portrayed as "unfair" under an assumption that the dumping has the intent and the ability to drive domestic producers of like products out of business. However, the legal definition of dumping in WTO law requires no finding of intent, and states generally require no finding of intent. The next question is whether dumping may be successful: whether the pricing practices defined as dumping have the capacity to drive domestic competitors out of business in a way that provides a source of market power and resulting profit durable enough to compensate the dumper for the losses incurred by dumping. This latter question depends importantly on the competitive structure of the relevant market, as well as the ability of domestic producers to obtain financing sufficient to endure the price pressure of dumping, and/or on the height of barriers to new entrants that could enter the market after successful dumping drives domestic producers out of business.

The market effects of dumping in the international context may usefully be compared to the market effects of predatory pricing domestically. Predatory pricing occurs when a competitor sets its prices at a level lower than it would otherwise set under perfect competition, so as to drive its competitors out of business, with the expectation that it will be able to raise prices later to recoup losses from earlier low pricing.

Again, anti-dumping laws generally do not require tests for intent and effects that would make them congruent with predation.

An Economic Defense of Anti-Dumping Duties

For a period, economists were skeptical of the possibility of rational predatory pricing, and were equally skeptical of the possibility of rational international predatory pricing. However, modern economic theory, utilizing dynamic and strategic models, and supported by more refined empirical analysis, is no longer skeptical (Bolton, Brodley, and Riordan, 2000). This modern economic theory has not yet infused US domestic competition law, and may not yet be fully recognized in commentaries on anti-dumping duties.

The main argument in favor of anti-dumping duties from a neoclassical economic standpoint is the same as the main argument for competition laws. According to this argument, anti-dumping laws are necessary in order to prevent the formation of monopolies that would reduce welfare (Mastel, 1998: 65). Mastel refers to the history of Japanese economic development in the late twentieth century, when Japan protected domestic markets and Japanese producers began to export at prices below home market prices. Sectors in which this occurred include semiconductors, photographic film, bearings, steel, and automobiles. Profits due to supra-competitive pricing in the domestic market were often devoted to improving manufacturing processes. It should be noted that a closed home market is not only useful to allow supra-competitive pricing at home in order to fund dumping abroad, but also to prevent flow of dumped exports back into the home market. During the early periods of export, products were dumped because they would not be competitive at home market prices (Mastel, 1998: 67–69).

Mastel develops a "strategic trade theory" argument regarding the rationale for dumping. By allowing domestic firms to benefit from a protected home market, and allowing them to undercut the pricing of foreign firms, a state may establish a competitive position, or may even deter entry by other firms. Similar analyses have been suggested with respect to predatory pricing (Milgrom, 1987). Under this analysis, dumping may be rational even though predatory pricing generally is not. "[D]umping can force marginal competitors without secure home markets to exit the industry. If dumping is severe and continuing, even established competitors can be driven from the industry..." (Mastel, 1998: 70). Mastel further argues that the "high fixed costs for entry into many manufacturing industries and the continued threat of dumping would pose substantial reentry barriers." Thus, to the extent that dumping may be successful in allowing the establishment of a globally competitive industry, or may be successful in allowing subsequent supra-competitive pricing, dumping may be rational and may indeed occur.

Beyond these strategic trade effects, dumping may artificially depress market prices and take sales away from otherwise efficient companies.

Thus, to the extent that it appears that a particular state's economic welfare will be diminished by dumping originating in another state, anti-dumping duties may serve to protect against these effects. Anti-dumping duties are definitely a "second-best" solution compared to an open home market and resulting competitive pricing.

Furthermore, it is worthwhile to point out that to the extent that the scope of legitimate concern regarding dumping is limited to predatory pricing, domestic competition laws may provide a sufficient response.

International Price Discrimination and Segmentation

It is easy to see that there is nothing necessarily unfair, or irrational, about international price discrimination, whether in the form of Price Discrimination Dumping or Third Country Price Discrimination Dumping. Thus, as Sykes points out, "anti-dumping law is not simply redundant of antitrust policy" (Sykes, 2005: 44).

> From an economic standpoint, selling at prices below "fair value" can be considered normal business practice. If competition in the U.S. market is fiercer than competition in a foreign market, for example, a foreign firm might be able to maximize profits by selling its products in the United States at lower prices than in its home country. Rather than the result of predatory practices by foreign firms, lower prices are often the result of healthy competition.... (Mankiw and Swagel, 2005)

Indeed, anti-dumping duties will only make sense to the extent that it is possible to distinguish between rational price discrimination and predatory pricing. WTO law does not require national authorities to discern between rational price discrimination and predatory pricing: they are only required to find a difference in prices.

However, to the extent that WTO law diminishes barriers to trade, predatory pricing will become less rational. This is because there will be fewer international barriers to entry, and diminished possibilities of rational predatory pricing.

Furthermore, under reduced barriers to trade, Price Discrimination Dumping and Third Country Price Discrimination Dumping will become less attractive, because of the possibility of parallel importation. Parallel importation is effected by arbitrage between markets where identical products are priced differently. So, if Nike prices identical sneakers at a higher price in China (where they are produced) and a lower price in the Philippines, then an entrepreneur may, subject to transport costs, trade barriers and possible intellectual property restrictions, transport these sneakers back to China, raising the prices in the Philippines and reducing the prices in China.

Market Effects of Anti-Dumping Duties

As suggested above, the market effects of anti-dumping duties are the same as the market effects of other protection. However, to the extent that it is possible to limit anti-dumping duties to the situations and amounts where it responds to true predatory pricing, then the market effects of anti-dumping duties could be to reduce the anti-competitive effects of predatory pricing.

V. BASIC ECONOMICS OF SUBSIDIES

States provide subsidies for a variety of legitimate reasons, and it is important to point out that subsidization alone is generally not illegal under WTO law. (Export subsidies and import substitution subsidies are illegal, and subsidies that cause "serious prejudice" must be withdrawn or their adverse effects must be removed.) Furthermore, subsidies that are provided to protect a domestic industry from import competition may be found to "nullify or impair" WTO concessions, and may therefore be subject to a requirement of compensation.

Unless a subsidy responds accurately to a market failure, it will reduce welfare, as it will cause a misallocation of resources compared to a perfect market without the intervention. Relevant market failures may include the possibility of increasing returns to scale or externalities. For example, a certain high technology industry might provide learning or other externalities.

Of course, the most important question regarding subsidies in international economic relations is how a national subsidy may harm other states. First, as suggested above, State A may use domestic subsidies to protect its domestic industry against imports from State B. Second, subsidies provided by State A may have adverse competitive effects on producers in State B. These adverse competitive effects would normally result from increased production in State A, with adverse effects on pricing in State B (from the standpoint of State B producers). Of course, subsidies by State A that reduce prices in State B transfer welfare from State A to the consumers of State B.

Thus, while a national subsidy may often confer welfare benefits on foreign consumers at least initially, it may also diminish the welfare of foreign producers. For the same reasons relating to the greater political influence of producers compared to consumers that we observe with protectionism generally, states may tend to discount the beneficial welfare effects on their consumers and respond more to the detrimental effects on their producers.

Market Effects of Subsidization

The primary market effect of subsidization is on quantities produced. The subsidy reduces the cost of production to the producer.[10] This change is likely to shift the supply curve to the right, where it intersects with the demand curve at what is likely to be a

---

[10] Of course, "[w]hen a firm receives untied funds from the government, it faces a variety of expenditure options. Possible trade effects depend on the commercial possibilities that recipient firms can exploit with those funds. It is not clear that such funds will be put to immediate use to gain an advantage in international markets" (WTO, 2005: note 41).

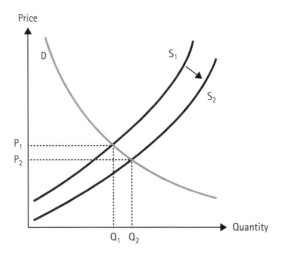

FIGURE 20.1 Market effects of a subsidy[11]

reduced price. That is, as supply is increased, it is likely that price will decline. This effect is illustrated in Figure 20.1.

There is a difference between an export subsidy, which is a subsidy that is conditional upon exportation, and a domestic subsidy, which is not. An export subsidy will be likely to restrict domestic supply and therefore cause domestic prices to rise, as it will increase sales abroad. At the same time, it will cause world prices to fall. This assumes that imports from abroad cannot readily replace the exported supply.

Of course, much depends on whether the subsidizing state is large enough so that its production affects world prices. If we assume perfect competition in a closed market, subsidies will result in increased output and reduced consumer prices. Once we relax the assumption of a closed market, if the subsidized industry is an import-competing industry, it will expand output and imports will be reduced, assuming that world prices are unaffected. Assuming a price-taking small country, then, "quantities adjust in response to the subsidy intervention. In the domestic production subsidy case, imports contract or exports expand, whereas in the export subsidy case exports expand. Inefficiencies arise in both cases since a portion of domestic output is determined by the subsidy-inclusive price, as opposed to the world price" (WTO, 2006).

With a larger country, holding the power to affect world prices, if a subsidy results in greater exports, it will reduce world prices.

The Polite Response to Subsidies: Send a "Thank You Note"

Thus, on first analysis, an economist would recommend a polite "thank you" as a response by State B to subsidies provided by State A (attributed to Paul Krugman). This

[11] Source: <http://en.wikipedia.org/wiki/Image:Supply-demand-right-shift-supply.svg>.

is similar to an initial response to dumping, and is also true of both export subsidies and domestic subsidies. Subsidies that have price effects on exports confer welfare on consumers in importing states.

Subsidization and Strategic Trade Theory

However, of course, subsidies that have price effects on exports also impose competitive pressure on producers in importing states, as well as on third states that compete for import markets. In the same way that, as discussed above, dumping may be used strategically in order to dissuade foreign firms from remaining in or entering a particular market, subsidization may also be used strategically. In imperfectly competitive markets, government policy measures may alter the strategic relationship between firms, and may thereby provide an advantage to national firms compared to foreign firms.

While economists are skeptical of the ability of governments to "pick winners," and therefore to choose accurately an industry to subsidize in order to achieve strategic benefits, states nevertheless seem to attempt to do so. The commercial aircraft industry is a good example, involving disputes between Canada and Brazil, on the one hand, and the United States and the European Community, on the other hand.

Just as there may be rational dumping in the sense of predation, there may be rational subsidization that has similar effects. Although it may be rational from a firm or subsidizing state standpoint, it may harm others, and may be globally irrational. So, it is not easy to argue that states should eliminate their countervailing duty responses to certain subsidies. However, as with dumping, we may examine the structure of states' countervailing duty responses in order to determine whether they are likely to be congruent with concerns regarding predatory subsidization.

Countervailing Duties and Terms of Trade Theory

Countervailing duties, like other tariffs, may allow a larger state to use its terms of trade power to extract monopsony rents on its imports. While this activity may provide gains to the importing state, it would harm the exporting state.

VI. Basic Economics of Injury and Causation

WTO law requires as a condition for the implementation of safeguards, anti-dumping duties, and countervailing duties that the increased imports, dumping, and subsidies, respectively, "cause" a specified level of injury. In connection with safeguards, the requirement is "serious injury," while in connection with dumping and subsidies, it is "material injury." Determination of injury is less difficult than determination of causation of injury.

Conceptually, the requirement of a specified level of injury may be justified on the basis that if the domestic industry is not being injured, then there should be no basis for a trade restriction. This justification seems to accord with a political economy analysis: unless a domestic industry is being injured, there is not likely to be a political problem for the importing government. However, it might be argued that the correct concern from a political economy standpoint for the importing government is not injury in the sense of debilitation, but injury in the sense of reduction of profitability. This would also seem to be the correct concern from a welfare economics standpoint. However, in WTO law, it is not clear whether a healthy industry may be considered "injured."

We may also understand the injury requirement as a parameter that serves simply to limit the scope of possible contingent protection. Even if the injury requirement had no other rationale, it seems useful to avoid the complete breakdown of liberalization. This understanding may be reconciled with the political economy justification mentioned above if we consider that the injury requirement gives the domestic government a basis for rejecting certain requests for protection from some domestic industries.

Defining and Determining "Injury"

Interestingly, WTO law does not specify quantitative benchmarks or indicia of injury for purposes of safeguards, anti-dumping, or countervailing duties. Under this discretionary legal environment, WTO panels and the WTO Appellate Body have focused in their review on whether national agencies have examined the requisite factors, rather than engaging in an *ab initio* review of the national agencies' determination.

For example, under Article 4.1(a) of the Safeguards Agreement, "serious injury" is defined as "a significant overall impairment in the position of a domestic industry." Article 4.2(a) provides a list of considerations in determining serious injury:

> In the investigation to determine whether increased imports have caused or are threatening to cause serious injury to a domestic industry under the terms of this Agreement, the competent authorities shall evaluate all relevant factors of an objective and quantifiable nature having a bearing on the situation of that industry, in particular, the rate and amount of the increase in imports of the product concerned in absolute and relative terms, the share of the domestic market taken by increased imports, changes in the level of sales, production, productivity, capacity utilization, profits and losses, and employment.

Article 3.1 of the Anti-dumping Agreement provides that:

> A determination of injury for purposes of Article VI of GATT 1994 shall be based on positive evidence and involve an objective examination of both *(a)* the volume

of the dumped imports and the effect of the dumped imports on prices in the domestic market for like products, and *(b)* the consequent impact of these imports on domestic producers of such products.

Article 3.4 of the Anti-dumping Agreement does not provide a definition of "material injury," but provides that:

> The examination of the impact of the dumped imports on the domestic industry concerned shall include an evaluation of all relevant economic factors and indices having a bearing on the state of the industry, including actual and potential decline in sales, profits, output, market share, productivity, return on investments, or utilization of capacity; factors affecting domestic prices; the magnitude of the margin of dumping; actual and potential negative effects on cash flow, inventories, employment, wages, growth, ability to raise capital or investments. This list is not exhaustive, nor can one or several of these factors necessarily give decisive guidance.

Similarly, Article 15.1 of the SCM Agreement provides that:

> A determination of injury for purposes of Article VI of GATT 1994 shall be based on positive evidence and involve an objective examination of both *(a)* the volume of the subsidized imports and the effect of the subsidized imports on prices in the domestic market for like products and *(b)* the consequent impact of these imports on the domestic producers of such products (footnote omitted).

Article 15.4 of the SCM Agreement tracks fairly closely Article 3.4 of the Anti-dumping Agreement:

> The examination of the impact of the subsidized imports on the domestic industry shall include an evaluation of all relevant economic factors and indices having a bearing on the state of the industry, including actual and potential decline in output, sales, market share, profits, productivity, return on investments, or utilization of capacity; factors affecting domestic prices; actual and potential negative effects on cash flow, inventories, employment, wages, growth, ability to raise capital or investments and, in the case of agriculture, whether there has been an increased burden on government support programmes. This list is not exhaustive, nor can one or several of these factors necessarily give decisive guidance.

Injury to a "Domestic Industry"

In order to determine injury, it is first necessary to determine the relevant industry for purposes of the determination. Complainants generally wish to argue for an industry definition that will support a positive determination of the requisite level of injury, but that will be large enough to provide the greatest scope of protection. Respondents wish to argue for an industry definition that will result in a negative determination. The concept of "like products" is used here to determine the relevant industry: the relevant industry is the domestic producers of like products.

How Do Increased Imports, Dumping and Subsidization "Cause" Injury?

It may seem strange to separate the determination of the requisite level of injury from the determination that this level of injury is caused by the relevant trade phenomenon: increased imports, dumping, or subsidization. We discuss below the question of how to separate out different causal factors for the purposes of determining the causation of injury.

It may also seem strange to examine at all the role in causing injury of dumped or subsidized imports, as opposed to the dumping or subsidization itself. For example, in the dumping context, with relatively small dumping margins and relatively large import market share, it may be that the dumping itself causes little injury, while the dumped imports cause material injury. Article 3 of the Anti-dumping Agreement seems to leave it open to national authorities to focus on either dumping or dumped imports.

Injury Caused by Imports from Various Sources

As mentioned above, safeguards measures are not country-specific, and relate to increased imports from all sources. So the question in safeguards investigations is whether imports generally cause serious injury. In dumping and subsidies cases, investigations relate to goods from specific countries, but it is possible that several specific countries are the source of dumped or subsidized goods at the same time. Under these circumstances, investigating authorities are permitted to "cumulate" the injury caused by goods from different sources, and may "cross-cumulate" injury from subsidized goods and injury from dumped goods, in order to make a finding of material injury.

VII. INTERNATIONAL LEGAL REGULATION OF SAFEGUARDS

National safeguards measures are regulated by WTO law. The most relevant sources of WTO law in this context are Article XIX of the GATT and the Agreement on Safeguards. Importantly, these legal rules are broadly cumulative: a national measure must comply with the requirements of both. The international law in this area sets certain substantive and certain procedural requirements that national authorities must follow as a condition for their right to impose safeguards measures.

The procedural requirements specified by the Safeguards Agreement include notice to interested parties, an investigation by national "competent authorities," and published findings stating "reasoned conclusions" as to matters of fact and law. Furthermore, the national competent authority must provide a "reasoned and adequate explanation" of how the facts support their determination under Article 4.2 of the Safeguards Agreement.[12]

GATT Article XIX

GATT Article XIX contains a number of important interpretative issues (see Box 20.3). We explain above that Article XIX is intended to provide conditional exceptions to—relief from—liberalization commitments made elsewhere in GATT. To the extent that Article XIX is read too broadly to allow too many exceptions, it would eviscerate GATT. On the other hand, if Article XIX were read too narrowly, states would not have sufficient flexibility. In the following box, we present the text of Article XIX, highlighting eight interpretative issues.

Unforeseen Developments and Effect of the Obligations

The "unforeseen developments" and "effect of the obligations" implement the concept, described above, that the safeguards facility is intended to protect against unexpected results of liberalization commitments. So, of course, the reduction of a tariff would be expected to produce more imports, but the "unforeseen developments" requirement establishes that there must be some factor that causes a larger increase in imports than expected.

Interestingly, toward the end of the pre-WTO period (the WTO, including the Safeguards Agreement, was established on January 1, 1995), the requirement for

---

Box 20.3 Article XIX GATT 1994

If, as a result of (1) **unforeseen developments** and of the (2) **effect of the obligations** incurred by a contracting party under this Agreement, including tariff concessions, any product is being imported into the territory of that contracting party in (3) **such increased quantities** and under such conditions as to (4) **cause** or threaten (5) **serious injury** to (6) **domestic producers** in that territory of (7) **like or directly competitive products**, the contracting party shall be free, in respect of such product, and (8) **to the extent and for such time as may be necessary** to prevent or remedy such injury, to suspend the obligation in whole or in part or to withdraw or modify the concession.

---

[12] Appellate Body Report, *United States—Safeguard Measures on Imports of Fresh, Chilled or Frozen Lamb Meat from New Zealand and Australia*, WT/DS177/AB/R, WT/DS178/AB/R, adopted May 16, 2001, para. 103.

unforeseen developments was diplomatically "dropped" from the agreement. By implicit consensus, states were not required to make a finding of unforeseen developments as a condition for use of the safeguards mechanism. And, indeed, the WTO Safeguards Agreement does not contain a requirement for a finding of unforeseen developments. However, the Appellate Body has found that since Article XIX of GATT continues to require a finding of "unforeseen developments," this requirement must be satisfied in the case of all safeguards measures.[13] The concept is that the developments must be subsequent to the relevant tariff concession, and must not have been reasonably anticipated. Furthermore, note that the unforeseen developments must cause the increased imports. However, this concept raises difficult problems of proof.

Increased Quantities

For some time, it was debated whether the increased quantities must be absolute increases, or relative (percentage) increases. Article 2.1 of the Safeguards Agreement made clear that the increased quantities may be either absolute or relative to domestic production. However, if there is no absolute increase, an immediate obligation to provide compensation to affected member states arises. (Under Article 8.3 of the Agreement on Safeguards, the obligation to provide compensation may be delayed for three years, provided that the safeguard measure relates to an absolute increase in imports and is in conformity with the Agreement on Safeguards.)

Of course, when one speaks of "increased quantities," it is necessary to establish a baseline: over what period will increase be measured? The Appellate Body has held that the phrase "is being imported" indicates that the increase must be "recent enough, sudden enough, sharp enough, and significant enough, both quantitatively and qualitatively, to cause or threaten to cause 'serious injury.'"[14] While this leaves some uncertainty, it provides a broad standard for national competent authorities.

Causation

Article XIX requires a determination that the increased quantities of imported goods cause serious injury. However, as Sykes (2005: 13) points out, "[t]he difficulty with this inquiry from the standpoint of economic logic is that import quantities are not a causal or exogenous variable—they are endogenous and *result* from other forces." That is, the quantity of imports will generally equal the difference between domestic demand and

---

[13] Appellate Body Report, *Korea—Definitive Safeguard Measure on Imports of Certain Dairy Products*, WT/DS98/AB/R, adopted January 12, 2000; Appellate Body Report, *United States—Safeguard Measures on Imports of Fresh, Chilled or Frozen Lamb Meat from New Zealand and Australia*, WT/DS177/AB/R, WT/DS178/AB/R, adopted May 16, 2001.

[14] Appellate Body Report, *Argentina—Safeguard Measures on Imports of Footwear*, WT/DS121/AB/R, adopted January 12, 2000, para. 131.

domestic supply at the equilibrium price. In the Argentina–Footwear decision, the Appellate Body used simple correlation between increases in imports and indicia of injury in the domestic industry.[15]

Putting this important conceptual difficulty aside, causation is, as mentioned above, a difficult *legal* issue in this area of WTO law. There are always other factors that may be contributing to injury. When lawyers discuss causation in this type of context, there are three possibilities: (1) that the increased quantities are sufficient, by themselves, to cause serious injury; (2) that the increased quantities are necessary, but not sufficient by themselves, to cause serious injury; and (3) that the increased quantities are neither necessary nor sufficient, but add to the injury. Article 4.2(b) specifies that the determination that increased imports cause serious injury shall not be made unless the investigation by the national authority demonstrates "the existence of the causal link between increased imports of the product concerned and serious injury or threat thereof. When factors other than increased imports are causing injury to the domestic industry at the same time, such injury shall not be attributed to increased imports."

The Appellate Body has implicitly held in the safeguards context that if increased imports are merely a contributory cause of the "seriously injured" state of an industry (possibility (3) above), they can be understood as satisfying the requirement for a causal link between increased imports and serious injury under Article 4.2(b) of the Safeguards Agreement.[16] However, to the extent that the existence of serious injury is dependent on another causal factor—say, change in demand patterns— it seems inconsistent to find actionable serious injury in one context of increased imports but not in another otherwise identical context, that is, where increased imports contribute equally, but other factors are not sufficient to bring the injury up to the "serious" level. Given this position, and despite the attention to causation in Article 4.2(b) of the Agreement on Safeguards, we might argue that safeguards law is responding not so much to causation as to existence of serious injury. In the context of anti-dumping duties, the Appellate Body has made a similar determination,[17] but has not yet had an opportunity to address this issue in the countervailing duties context.

Safeguards Actions

Safeguards actions may take the form of either quantitative restrictions or duties.

    [15] Appellate Body Report, *Argentina—Safeguard Measures on Imports of Footwear*, WT/DS121/AB/R, adopted January 12, 2000.

    [16] Appellate Body Report, *United States—Safeguard Measures on Imports of Fresh, Chilled or Frozen Lamb Meat from New Zealand and Australia*, WT/DS177/AB/R, WT/DS178/AB/R, adopted May 16, 2001; Appellate Body Report, *United States—Definitive Safeguard Measures on Imports of Wheat Gluten from the European Communities*, WT/DS166/AB/R, adopted January 19, 2001.

    [17] Appellate Body Report, *United States—Anti-Dumping Measures on Certain Hot-Rolled Steel Products from Japan*, WT/DS184/AB/R, para. 223, adopted August 23, 2001.

Duration and Review

Although Article XIX provides that safeguards measures may be applied for only such time as may be necessary to remedy injury, during the GATT period safeguards actions tended to mutate from emergency actions to permanent actions. The Safeguards Agreement responds to this concern in Article 7, by providing that safeguards measures have a maximum duration of four years, unless an additional determination of continued necessity is made by the national competent authority. However, the total period of application of safeguards measures is not permitted to exceed eight years. In addition, there is a requirement of degressivity: any safeguard measure lasting more than one year must be reduced at regular intervals. Furthermore, no safeguard measure may be reasserted until after the passage of a period of time equal to that during which it was originally applied.

Compensation

Article XIX:3 of GATT provides that safeguards actions are not costless to the protecting state. Rather, under Article XIX:3, member states affected by a safeguards action may suspend the application to the acting state of substantially equivalent concessions or other obligations.

During the GATT period, Article XIX was seldom used. It is thought that the requirement of compensation provided a disincentive for the use of safeguards, and an incentive to structure contingent protection as anti-dumping or countervailing duties, where no requirement of compensation applies. As noted above, under Article 8.3 of the Agreement on Safeguards, the obligation to provide compensation may now be delayed for three years, provided that the safeguard measure relates to an absolute increase in imports and is in conformity with the Agreement on Safeguards. This provides a greater incentive to use safeguards measures, and thereby supports the prohibition on grey area measures provided by the Agreement on Safeguards.

Prohibition of Grey Area Measures

As part of the "bargain" in establishing the Agreement on Safeguards, member states agreed to prohibit so-called "grey area measures." Article 11.1(b) of the Safeguards Agreement provides that members "shall not seek, take or maintain any voluntary export restraints, orderly marketing arrangements or any other similar measures on the export or the import side."

Regional Agreements and MFN Application of Safeguards

According to Article 2.2 of the Agreement on Safeguards, safeguards measures shall be applied to a product being imported irrespective of its source. Thus, with a few exceptions, safeguards are required to be applied on an MFN basis. This raises a number of problems. The most difficult involves the treatment of free trade areas (FTAs) and customs unions (CUs). Under Article XXIV of GATT, regulating the formation of FTAs and CUs, it is not clear whether states are prohibited to apply safeguards to imports from its partners in FTAs and CUs. It is also not clear whether Article 2.2 of the Safeguards Agreement *requires* states to apply their safeguards measures to imports from FTA and CU partners. Although the WTO Appellate Body has been presented with this issue, it has avoided speaking on it by finding that the investigation at hand was faulty because it did not exclude from its assessment of injury imports from those states that would be excluded from the safeguards measures (a failure of "parallelism").

VIII. International Legal Regulation of Anti-Dumping Duties

As we discussed in connection with safeguards, the function of WTO law (and other international law) in connection with dumping is to restrain national anti-dumping measures. In this connection, we consider Article VI of GATT as well as the Anti-dumping Agreement. Dumping, by definition, is an action of a particular enterprise: it is a pricing action. Importantly, international law does not require states to restrain dumping by its nationals or residents. A multilateral competition law treaty, if it were entered into, might address these types of issues.

Under Article VI of GATT and the Anti-dumping Agreement, a member state may only apply an anti-dumping measure if, pursuant to an investigation in compliance with these rules, a determination is made that (1) dumping is taking place, (2) a domestic industry producing the like product is injured, and (3) there is a causal link between the dumping and the injury.

Anti-Dumping Investigations

Anti-dumping investigations generally involve private producers, or sometimes groups or producers, on both sides. Even labor unions may participate as petitioners. Petitioners argue that there is both dumping and material injury, each as defined. Respondents argue that neither condition is met. The magnitude of dumping identified is critical, as it determines the amount of the anti-dumping duty that may be levied. The calculation of the magnitude of dumping—of the dumping "margin"—is extremely complicated and involves complex issues of pricing, accounting, and comparison. There is much room for argument regarding these issues, and for measures that may distort the calculation.

After a preliminary determination of the existence of both dumping and injury, exporters may enter into "price undertakings" under Anti-dumping Agreement Article 8.

Pursuant to a price undertaking, the exporter will raise its prices to a level that elimi-nates the dumping or removes its adverse effects. Of course, a price undertaking allows the exporter to retain the increased price, as compared to an anti-dumping duty, which flows to the importing government.

After dumping and injury are established, the investigating state will levy an anti-dumping duty equal to the margin of dumping. This anti-dumping duty will be sub-jected to a "sunset review" after five years. The purpose of the sunset review is to determine whether the removal of the duty would be likely to lead to continuation or recurrence of dumping and injury.[18]

It should be noted here that investigations will generally aggregate exporters from a single country for purposes of examining the volume of dumped imports and injury, although each exporter may be examined individually in order to assign it an individual dumping margin and anti-dumping duty.

Normal Value

As suggested above, there are three possible references for the "normal value." The pre-ferred reference is the comparable price for like products sold in the home market. However, this price might not be available, for example, because the producer does not sell like products in its home market.[19] It may be possible to make price adjustments for some dissimilarities. In addition, the home market price may not be available because sales are not made in large enough numbers to be representative, or are made to related companies. Finally, it may be that sales are not made in the ordinary course of trade under Article 2.2.1 of the Anti-dumping Agreement, meaning that the prices charged are "below per unit (fixed and variable) costs of production plus administra-tive, selling and general costs," are made to related parties, or are at abnormally high or low prices.

If the comparable price for like products sold in the home market is unavailable, then national authorities may use either: (1) the comparable price for like products sold in a third country selected by the investigating authority, or (2) a constructed value. The Anti-dumping Agreement does not express a preference between third country pricing and constructed value.

Each price comparison must be made at the same level of trade, meaning, for exam-ple that wholesale prices must be compared with wholesale prices, rather than with retail prices. Furthermore, in any price comparison, the goal of investigation is to make adjustments so as to achieve an ex-factory price on each side of the comparison. Where

---

[18] Anti-dumping Agreement, Article 11.3.

[19] "Like products" are defined by Anti-dumping Agreement Article 2.6 as "a product which is identical, i.e., alike in all respects to the product under consideration, or in the absence of such a product, another product which, although not alike in all respects, has characteristics closely resembling those of the product under consideration."

there are sales to related parties, it may be necessary to look through the related party to the first independent purchaser.

For investigations regarding allegations of dumping from non-market economies, national authorities have a great deal of discretion to use other methods to determine normal value, because the home country prices may not be deemed appropriate for use in comparison.[20]

The constructed value is comprised of two components: (1) cost of production, and (2) selling, general and administrative expenses, plus profit. The calculation of cost of production can be very complex for modern production, especially involving large companies. It involves nuanced decisions regarding the allocation of costs among production activities.

Export Price

The export price is generally the transaction price at which the subject goods are exported. However, where the export sale is to an affiliate of the producer, these prices may be artificially controlled: they may be made at a high (non-dumping) price, and the affiliate may then resell the goods at a low (dumping) price. Under these types of circumstances, the Anti-dumping Agreement allows the use of a constructed export price based on the price at which the good is first sold to an unaffiliated buyer. Complex adjustments may be necessary to reflect differences in the level of sale, and value that may be added by the affiliated distributor.

Comparing Normal Value to Export Price

In order to determine the existence and magnitude of dumping, it is necessary to compare the normal value to the export price. In order to provide a fair comparison, Article 2.4 of the Anti-dumping Agreement provides that:

> Due allowance shall be made in each case, on its merits, for differences which affect price comparability, including differences in conditions and terms of sale, taxation, levels of trade, quantities, physical characteristics, and any other differences which are also demonstrated to affect price comparability.

Prior to the establishment of the WTO, it was common in some states' investigations to compare weighted average home market prices with individual export market transactions. This method would result in findings of dumping wherever there was price variation, even if it was identical in both markets. Under Article 2.4.2 of the Anti-dumping

---

[20] See the second Supplementary Provision to paragraph 1 of Article VI of GATT, referenced in Article 2.7 of the Anti-dumping Agreement.

Agreement, states must compare weighted averages to weighted averages, or individual transactions to individual transactions.[21]

Another practice that was common prior to the establishment of the WTO, and which some states have continued to practice, is "zeroing." See Box 20.4. The practice of zeroing has now been found to be illegal by the Appellate Body, in the instances and configurations in which it has been litigated.[22] Zeroing may take several different forms, but is generally characterized by a determination to ignore home market sales that are made at less than average export prices. If low home market prices are ignored, the average home market price will be higher, leading to an artificially increased dumping margin. In *EC—Bed Linen*, the Appellate Body explained zeroing as in Box 20.4:[23]

Box 20.4 Zeroing

The practice of "zeroing," as applied in this dispute, can briefly be described as follows: first, the European Communities identified with respect to the product under investigation—cotton type bed linen—a certain number of different "models" or "types" of that product. Next, the European Communities calculated, for each of these models, a weighted average normal value and a weighted average export price. Then, the European Communities compared the weighted average normal value with the weighted average export price for each model. For some models, normal value was higher than export price; by subtracting export price from normal value for these models, the European Communities established a "positive dumping margin" for each model. For other models, normal value was lower than export price; by subtracting export price from normal value for these other models, the European Communities established a "negative dumping margin" for each model. Thus, there is a "positive dumping margin" where there is dumping, and a "negative dumping margin" where there is not. The "positives" and "negatives" of the amounts in this calculation are an indication of precisely how much the export price is above or below the normal value. Having made this calculation, the European Communities then added up the amounts it had calculated as "dumping margins" for each model of the product in order to determine an overall dumping margin for the product as a whole. However, in doing so, the European Communities treated any "negative dumping margin" as zero—hence the use of the word "zeroing." Then, finally, having added up the "positive dumping margins" and the zeroes, the European Communities divided this sum by the cumulative total value of all the export transactions involving all types and models of that product. In this way, the European Communities obtained an overall margin of dumping for the product under investigation.

---

[21] Appellate Body Report, *European Communities—Anti-Dumping Duties on Imports of Cotton-Type Bed Linen from India*, WT/DS141/AB/R, adopted March 12, 2001.

[22] For example, Appellate Body Report, *European Communities—Anti-Dumping Duties on Imports of Cotton-Type Bed Linen from India*, WT/DS141/AB/R, adopted March 12, 2001. Appellate Body Report, *United States—Laws, Regulations and Methodology for Calculating Dumping Margins*, WT/DS294/AB/R, adopted May 9, 2006.

[23] Appellate Body Report, *European Communities—Anti-Dumping Duties on Imports of Cotton-Type Bed Linen from India*, WT/DS141/AB/R, adopted March 12, 2001, para. 47 (footnotes omitted).

IX. THE INTERNATIONAL LAW OF SUBSIDIES

The international trade system's approach to subsidies reflects the problem of "interface" as Jackson (2006: 230) has discussed. Different states have different economic systems, including different degrees of state intervention in the economy. As these states engage in trade, their subsidies may have external effects.

Certain subsidies may be "neutralized" as the subsidized goods are imported, through the operation of countervailing duties equal in value to the subsidy. Other subsidies—specifically export subsidies and import substitution subsidies—are prohibited. Still other subsidies—those that cause "serious prejudice"—must be withdrawn or their adverse effects removed. Finally, subsidies that have the effect of "nullifying or impairing" liberalizing concessions may give rise to a requirement of compensation.

The main sources of international law in this field are Article XVI of GATT, and the SCM Agreement.

Defining and Calculating Subsidization

The term "subsidy" was not defined in the GATT. However, many different types of governmental action could be understood as a subsidy. There were several disputes during the GATT period over whether a particular government action should be considered a subsidy. In the SCM Agreement, member states provided a definition that includes two main parameters: (1) governmental financial contribution, and (2) benefit to the recipient. Furthermore, only subsidies that are "specific" to an enterprise or industry or group of enterprises or industries may be countervailed. In other words, subsidies that are generally available are not countervailable.

The parameter of "financial contribution" contained in Article 1.1(a)(1) of the SCM Agreement includes both direct transfers and foregone revenues, as well as the provision of goods or services. The parameter of "benefit" means that even if government provides goods or services, for example, there is no subsidy unless they are provided at a price below the market price.[24] The difference between the actual price and the market benchmark equals the amount of the subsidy. For benefits in the form of foregone revenue, it has been difficult to define the benchmark "normal case" from which the state has departed in "foregoing" revenue.[25]

---

[24] Appellate Body Report, *Canada—Measures Affecting the Export of Civilian Aircraft*, WT/DS70/AB/R, adopted August 20, 1999.

[25] See Appellate Body Report, *United States—Tax Treatment for "Foreign Sales Corporations"*, WT/DS108/AB/R, adopted March 20, 2000; Appellate Body Report, *United States—Tax Treatment for "Foreign Sales Corporations"—Recourse to Article 21.5 of the DSU by the European Communities*, WT/DS108/AB/RW, adopted January 29, 2002; Appellate Body Report, *United States—Tax Treatment for "Foreign Sales Corporations"—Second Recourse to Article 21.5 of the DSU by the European Communities*, WT/DS108/AB/RW2, adopted March 14, 2006.

Benefits may also be difficult to calculate in cases of "upstream" subsidies: where, for example, a subsidy may be granted on primary goods which are then transferred at arm's length prices to a separate person, which subjects them to manufacturing processes. Under these circumstances, a member state must conduct an analysis of the extent to which the upstream subsidy persists in the downstream good.[26] A similar issue arises in connection with subsidies paid to state-owned enterprises that are subsequently privatized. Does the subsidy persist after a privatization at arm's length prices? In a 2002 decision, the Appellate Body found instead that privatization at arm's length and for fair market value "may result in extinguishing the benefit." Furthermore, there is a "rebuttable presumption" that a benefit ceases to exist after such a privatization.[27]

Specificity

The function of specificity appears to be to limit the scope of application of possible countervailing duties. For example, where the government provides public education, police services, or general infrastructure, these "subsidies" are not intended to be countervailed. However, where the government builds a road to serve a particular factory, or trains workers in skills specific to a particular industry, these may be specific. The specificity requirement may serve as a proxy for intent: for generally available subsidies, there may be no intent to benefit a particular industry.

Export Subsidies and Import Substitution Subsidies

Export subsidies—subsidies contingent upon export performance—and import substitution subsidies—subsidies contingent upon the use of domestic over imported goods—are prohibited by Article 3 of the SCM Agreement. Contingency in this context may be either *de jure* or *de facto*. However, the Appellate Body has held that the provision of subsidies to an industry that exports a large proportion of its production, alone, does not constitute *de jure* contingency, and so does not constitute an export subsidy.[28]

Serious Prejudice

Article 5 of the SCM Agreement prohibits WTO member states to cause "serious prejudice" through the use of a subsidy. Article 7.8 of the SCM agreement requires states to either remove the adverse effects or to withdraw the subsidy.

---

[26] See Appellate Body Report, *United States—Final Countervailing Duty Determination with Respect to Certain Softwood Lumber from Canada*, WT/DS257/AB/R, adopted February 17, 2004.

[27] Appellate Body Report, *United States—Countervailing Measures Concerning Certain Products from the European Communities*, WT/DS212/AB/R, adopted January 8, 2003.

[28] Appellate Body Report, *Canada—Measures Affecting the Export of Civilian Aircraft*, WT/DS70/AB/R, adopted August 20, 1999.

X. WTO DISPUTE SETTLEMENT AND THE CAPACITY OF THE INTERNATIONAL SYSTEM TO POLICE CONTINGENT PROTECTION

It is difficult to say empirically whether most member states' contingent protection rules now comply with WTO law and are administered in accordance with WTO law. There seem to be frequent allegations of violation, and these complaints are generally successful. Appellate Body and panel decisions have been criticized from time to time. The most vociferous criticism seems to come from US trade remedies lawyers and industry lobbyists, who argue that the Appellate Body is exceeding its mandate in finding violations, especially in the field of safeguards. However, other instances can be identified where it appears that the Appellate Body has provided liberal interpretations allowing contingent protection measures that might otherwise be found illegal.

So far, the remedies for violation of WTO law have generally been prospective in nature, after a violation has been fully adjudicated, and after a reasonable period of time has elapsed for compliance. This structure provides a weak incentive for compliance with WTO law. Generally, the measure of authorized retaliation is set at an amount equivalent to the "nullification or impairment" caused by the violation. In cases of violation of the prohibition of export subsidies, WTO arbitration panels have set greater authorized retaliation, pursuant to a questionable interpretation of the SCM Agreement.

Although WTO dispute settlement is formally intended to settle immediate disputes, and not to set precedents to resolve future disputes, states have been frustrated by the fact that users of contingent protection have often maintained domestic laws that result in contingent protection measures that violate WTO laws. More recently, litigation has attacked these rules "as such," arguing that the rules violate WTO law independent of their application.

XI. CONCLUDING PERSPECTIVES: POLICY AND NEGOTIATING IMPLICATIONS FOR DEVELOPING COUNTRIES

In the Uruguay Round, the dumping negotiations were polarized between those participants, including the United States and the European Community (EC), wishing to facilitate the taking of anti-dumping actions, and those participants that had been frequent targets of anti-dumping actions, including Japan, Korea, and Hong Kong. The Anti-dumping Agreement represents a compromise between facilitation and restriction, and depended to some extent on compromises elsewhere.

In the Doha Round, developing countries have diverse negotiating goals. It is likely that developing countries as a group would benefit from broad liberalization in the developed world, and so one possible goal would be to negotiate strengthened disciplines on safeguards, anti-dumping duties, and countervailing duties imposed by developed countries. As Stiglitz (1999) stated:

> As developing countries do take steps to open their economies and expand their exports, in too many sectors they find themselves confronting significant trade barriers—leaving them, in effect, with neither aid nor trade. They quickly run up against dumping duties, when no economist would say they are really engaged in dumping, or they face protected or restricted markets in their areas of natural comparative advantage, like agriculture or textiles.[29]

Developing countries would also be likely to benefit from tools that would allow them selectively to refuse to provide protection to their own industries, and so some disciplines applicable to developing countries may also be beneficial to developing countries. Finally, developing countries carry on significant trade with other developing countries, making it potentially useful to develop stronger constraints on contingent protection by developing countries.

REFERENCES

Bagwell, K. and Staiger, R. W. (2005), 'Enforcement, Private Political Pressure, and the General Agreement on Tariffs and Trade/World Trade Organization Escape Clause.' *The Journal of Legal Studies*, 34:2, 471–513.

Bolton, P., Brodley, J. F., and Riordan, M. H. (2000), 'Predatory Pricing: Strategic Theory and Legal Policy.' *Georgetown Law Journal*, 88: 2239–429.

Bown, C. P. (2006), The WTO and Anti-Dumping in Developing Countries, July. Available at: <http://people.brandeis.edu/~cbown/papers/AD_developing.pdf>.

Corden, M. (1974), *Trade Policy and Economic Welfare*. Oxford: Clarendon Press.

Deardorff, A. (1987), 'Safeguards Policy and the Conservative Social Welfare Function.' In Kierzkowski, H. (ed.), *Protection and Competition in International Trade: Essays in Honor of W. M. Corden*. Oxford: Blackwell, 1987, pp. 22–40. Available at: <http://www.fordschool.umich.edu/rsie/workingpapers/PPP1-25/ppp2.pdf>.

Finger, J. M. (1993), *Antidumping: How it Works and Who Gets Hurt*. Ann Arbor: University of Michigan Press.

Hoekman, B. M., and Kostecki, M. M. (2001), *The Political Economy of the World Trading System*. Oxford: Oxford University Press.

Horn, H., and Mavroidis, P. C. (2003), 'United States—Safeguard Measures on Imports of Fresh, Chilled or Frozen Lamb Meat from New Zealand and Australia: What Should be Required of a Safeguard Investigation?' Horn, H. and Mavroidis, P. C. (eds.), *The WTO Case Law of 2001*, American Law Institute Reporters Series. Cambridge: Cambridge University Press.

Jackson, J. H. (2006), *Sovereignty, the WTO and the Changing Fundamentals of International Law*. Cambridge UK: Cambridge University Press.

---

[29] See Stiglitz (1999).

Mankiw, N. G., and Swagel, P. L. (2005), 'Antidumping: The Third Rail of Trade Policy.' *Foreign Affairs,* July/August.

Mastel, G. (1998). *Antidumping Laws and the U.S. Economy.* Armonk: M.E. Sharpe.

Milgrom, P. (1987), 'Predatory Pricing' Eatwell, J., et al. (eds.), *The New Palgrave Dictionary Of Economics,* pp. 937–8. Basingstoke, UK: Palgrave Macmillan.

Palmeter, N. D. (1991), 'The Antidumping Law: A Legal and Administrative Trade Barrier.' In Litan, R. E., and Boltuck, R. D. (eds.), *Administration of the Trade Remedy Laws.* Washington, DC: Brookings.

Stiglitz, J. E. (1999), 'Two Principles for the Next Round, or, How to Bring Developing Countries in from the Cold' September 21, 1999. Available at: <http://www.worldbank.org/knowledge/chiefecon/articles/geneva.htm>.

Sykes, A. O. (1991), 'Protectionism as a 'Safeguard': A Positive Analysis of the GATT 'Escape Clause' with Normative Speculations.' *University of Chicago Law Review,* 58: 255–303.

Sykes, A. O. (2005), 'The Economics of WTO Rules on Subsidies and Countervailing Measures.' In Appleton, A., Macrory, P., and Plummer, M. (eds.), *The World Trade Organization: Legal, Economic and Political Analysis,* Volume II. New York: Springer.

World Trade Organization (WTO) (2005), 'Quantitative Economics in WTO Dispute Settlement', in World Trade Report 2005. Available at: <http://www.wto.org/english/res_e/booksp_e/anrep_e/wtr05-3a_e.pdf>.

World Trade Organization (WTO) (2006), 'The Economics of Subsidies', in World Trade Report 2006: Subsidies, Trade and the WTO. Available at: <http://www.wto.org/english/res_e/booksp_e/anrep_e/wtr06-2c_e.pdf>.

Zanardi, M. (2005), 'Anti-Dumping: A Problem in International Trade.' Centre Working Paper No. 2005-85, at<http://arno.uvt.nl/show.cgi?fid=53783>

Zanardi, M. (2004), 'Anti-Dumping: What Are the Numbers to Discuss at Doha?' *The World Economy,* 27:403–33.

CHAPTER 21

SERVICES TRADE AGREEMENTS AND NEGOTIATIONS: AN OVERVIEW

AADITYA MATTOO AND GIANNI ZANINI

I. INTRODUCTION

IN recognition of their rising role in international trade and the need for further liberalization, services were included in the multilateral trade architecture of the World Trade Organization (WTO) in the form of the General Agreement on Trade in Services (GATS). Services have also featured prominently in the process of WTO accession. And services are increasingly important in the large and growing network of regional, and especially North–South, trade agreements.

Services have assumed added significance from a broader global policy perspective in the aftermath of the recent global financial and economic crisis. Expanding the scope for international trade and investment in services can complement the required other structural and macroeconomic changes to rebalance global demand and production between countries with major current account surpluses and deficits. As services account for most non-labor costs of production, action to improve the efficiency of services must be a major focus of policy in deficit countries, complementing policies to switch the pattern of expenditure and reduce net consumption. Expanding domestic consumption and investment in surplus countries must also involve a focus on services such as financial intermediation, insurance, and retail distribution and related logistics (Hoekman and Mattoo, 2011).

In the multilateral negotiations under the Doha Development Agenda and also in most regional agreements, however, services have received surprisingly little attention. The neglect of services can be costly. The potential gains from recipro-cal liberalization of trade in services are likely to be substantial, as discussed in Chapter 12, and progress in services is necessary for a positive negotiating outcome in other areas. For international negotiations to be fruitful, however, countries must recognize mutual interests in reciprocal liberalization, supported by broader interna-tional cooperation.

First of all, developing countries must see the advantages of international agreements to increase competition in services, enhance credibility of potential domestic reform, and strengthen domestic regulation. But developed countries need also to provide sup-port to developing countries in devising sound policy, strengthening regulatory insti-tutions, enhancing participation in the development of international standards, and in ensuring access to essential services in the poorest areas.

Second, both developed and developing countries must see advantages to allowing the temporary movement of individual service providers. Facilitating such movement will require greater cooperation between source and host countries than agreed upon so far. Realistically, this may be more feasible in bilateral and regional contexts than at the WTO.

Third, all countries must lock in the current openness of cross-border trade in a range of services. Such trade is the most dynamic dimension of international trade, in which both advanced and developing countries have a growing stake, but over which looms the specter of protectionism provoked by the potential costs of adjustment.

Finally, there is a strong case for regional cooperation in services. Most regional agreements in services have focused principally on the preferential elimination of explicit barriers to the entry of service providers, but the required legislative changes are usually easier and more desirable to accomplish on a non-preferential basis. This traditional approach has diverted attention and negotiating resources away from an area of much greater potential benefit: regional cooperation on infrastructure services and regulation.

In what follows we cover the GATS' scope, general obligations, rules on protection, and the unfinished agenda related to safeguards, subsidies and government procure-ment. This and the other sections on the GATS are largely drawn from Adlung and Mattoo (2008). We also address the growing trend towards preferential agreements, which may provide greater opportunities for achieving deeper integration of particu-lar services sectors. This section is largely drawn from Mattoo and Sauvé (2011) and Chaffour and Maur (2011). A subsequent section provides a brief overview of the achievements to date (or lack thereof) of the current negotiating round. Finally, we assess what international negotiations have to offer with respect to unilateral liberaliza-tion, and the context—multilateral, regional, bilateral—in which they are most likely to produce outcomes that support economic development. These two sections are largely drawn from Adlung and Mattoo (2008), Borchert, Gootiiz, and Mattoo (2011), and Hoekman and Mattoo (2011).

II. The Scope of the GATS

Definition of Services and Modes of Supply

As already anticipated in the chapter on the economics of services trade (Chapter 12), there is no explicit definition of services in the GATS, which went into effect in January 1995. Instead of worrying about precise terminology, negotiators opted for an open-ended classification of services by 12 main sectors and by four modes of supply. Activities under various modes may be closely related in practice, for example, a US-owned hospital established in Australia (mode 3, commercial presence) may employ foreign doctors and nurses (mode 4, presence of natural persons), receive medical advice through the Internet from a US-based specialist (mode 1, cross-border trade), and attract patients from small islands in the Pacific Ocean (mode 2, consumption abroad). Nonetheless, the market access and national treatment obligations that a country may want to commit to could vary widely across the individual sub-sectors and modes.

Comprehensiveness and Flexibility

Although a number of terms and concepts in the GATS have been borrowed from the General Agreement on Tariffs and Trade (GATT), the older agreement covering merchandise trade, there are important differences. For example, the GATS is more comprehensive in coverage. Its definition of trade in services (see below) extends beyond the traditional notion of cross-border exchange to cover also consumer movements and factor flows (investment and labor): the reach of relevant disciplines is not confined to the treatment of products, that is, services, but extends to measures affecting service suppliers (producers, traders, and distributors). Its rules are also more flexible, as they have been designed to accommodate the diversity of sector-related objectives and concerns among WTO members. For example, unlike under the GATT, the use of quantitative restrictions is legitimate under the GATS, unless explicitly foregone by the member concerned, and national treatment is not a general obligation, but a negotiable commitment. There are no common templates and country-specific schedules of commitments instead define the extent to which these rules apply to individual service sectors (see Adlung, 2006a).

Measures Covered

Articles I:1 and 3 confine the scope of the Agreement to (policy and regulatory) measures affecting trade in services taken by governments and public authorities, at all federal levels, as well as by non-governmental bodies in the exercise of delegated powers (e.g., government-mandated regulators or licensing bodies). In turn, this implies that purely commercial decisions or measures by individual consumers and producers or their associations (e.g., a consumer boycott) without government interference are beyond the scope of the Agreement.

The concept of measures affecting trade in services is very broad. First, according to Article XXVII(a), a "measure" could take virtually any form, including that of law, regulation, rule, procedure, decision, or administrative action. Second, "affecting" is wider in reach than, for example, "regulating" or "governing" trade in services.[1] For instance, the mere fact that a particular measure is essentially intended to govern merchandise trade does not preclude the possibility that it also affects trade in services. In assessing the relevance of the GATS for a particular policy or policy proposal, government officials are thus well advised to use a broad interpretation. Table 21.1 gives examples of various types of measures that affect services trade under different modes.

Exclusions

The GATS provides for two deliberate sector- and policy-specific exclusions. First, there is the so-called governmental service carve-out under Article I:3. It stipulates that, for the purpose of the Agreement, services supplied in the exercise of governmental authority are not considered to be services. The definition of such services rests on a twin criterion: they are supplied neither on a commercial basis, nor in competition with one or more suppliers.

Examples of "governmental services" excluded from the GATS include fire protection, primary education, police and security services, or the operations of central banks. Other cases are less clear, however. For example, while some governments provide free basic health services via a public monopoly, others rely primarily on private commercial entities, that is, medical practices and hospitals, among which patients are allowed to choose (such systems tend to be complemented by subsidized health insurance schemes to ensure a degree of social equity, see Box 21.1). Although there may be little doubt that the former systems are beyond the scope of GATS, questions may arise in countries where free public provision, for example, through government hospitals, co-exists with a commercial market segment.

Economists normally tend to associate the existence of competition with attempts of rival operators who may use various marketing instruments (advertisements, price, and/or quality differentiation) to attract customers. Accordingly, if a "governmental supplier" does not behave like a rival, it might not be deemed to be in competition

---

[1] WTO document WT/DS27/AB/R of September 9, 1997 (Report of the Appellate Body: European Communities—Regime for the Importation, Sale and Distribution of Bananas).

Box 21.1 Liberalization of Health Services under Trade Agreements to Benefit Poor People

Services of many kinds play important roles in the protection of public health (e.g., sanitation services) and the delivery of health care to individuals (e.g., hospital services). The GATS (and liberalizing trade agreements in general) creates both health-related opportunities and challenges, especially for developing countries, that are essential for health policymakers to comprehend.

Smith et al. (2008) caution that any liberalization under international trade agreements should aim to produce better quality, affordable, and effective health-related services, leading to greater equity in health outcomes. Liberalization should also ensure the necessary policy and regulatory space that governments require to promote and protect the health of their populations, particularly those in greatest need. Recognizing that the GATS accords countries considerable choice and flexibility as to the process, pace, and extent of liberalization of trade in health-related services, they encourage countries to embed the following health-policy principles to protect health adequately:

- Liberalized trade in health-related services should lead to an optimal balance between preventive and curative services.
- Involvement of both private industry and civil society is important to ensure that liberalization of health-related services promotes participatory health policy towards achieving national goals.
- Improving access and affordability of health-related services should be a goal of liberalization of trade in health-related services.
- Developing countries, and least-developed countries, in particular, deserve special consideration in the process of liberalizing trade in health-related services.
- The status of health as a human right should inform and guide proposals to liberalize trade in health-related services.

Other economists are more critical of the developing countries' reluctance so far to commit to health-services liberalization under the GATS or other regional or bilateral trade agreements. Many, if not most, governments today in the developing world are failing to meet the health needs of poor people. Moreover, trade agreements are unlikely to have a direct effect on the health of poor people because the health services they receive are not the ones actually being liberalized. This is a pity, notes Devarajan (2008), currently Chief Economist for the Africa Region at the World Bank and formerly Chief Economist for the South Asia Region and Director of the 2004 World Development Report dedicated to making public services work for poor people. Liberalization under trade agreements and the competition it would introduce could have indirect, beneficial effects by helping poor countries break out of the trap of capture of the fiscal expenditures on health by the rich and by the health-service providers, thus releasing resources for improving the health of the poor.

Source: Smith et al. (2008) and Devarajan (2008).

(Adlung, 2006b). Additional questions may arise in cases where the relevant service is provided in return for a certain fee or charge. If it is low in comparison to production cost, one might still be inclined to infer that no commercial interest is involved. Again, however, there may be borderline cases. Thus, for example, although a highly profitable telecom monopoly would certainly be considered as operating on a commercial basis, is this equally true for the exclusive provider of local voice services that is kept afloat only through high (cross-) subsidies?

The second full-fledged exclusion from the GATS is sector-specific. Pursuant to the Annex on Air Transport Services, the Agreement does not apply to measures affecting air traffic rights and services directly related to the exercise of these rights. Nevertheless, three sub-segments are explicitly mentioned as being covered: aircraft maintenance and repair; selling and marketing of air transport services; and computer reservation system services.[2] In addition, the WTO's Council for Trade in Services is mandated to review developments in the sector at least every five years with a view to considering the further application of the Agreement. The first two such reviews in 2003 and 2008 did not produce any results. The persistence of the special status of this sector might be attributed, on the one hand, to domestic commercial interests and, on the other hand, to the apparently smooth functioning of the existing system of bilateral air traffic arrangements under the Chicago Convention. Like any bilateral system, it tends to benefit countries with large home markets, which have stronger negotiating leverage than would be the case under conditions of non-discrimination.

Domestic Policy Implications

The broad reach of the GATS appears breath-taking at first glance and outside observers might wonder whether members have any possibilities left—for whatever political, cultural or historical reasons—to pursue non-trade and non-commercial objectives as they see fit. Concerns about undue external encroachment upon national policy makers, for example in health, are a major source of public criticism. However, there is little in the GATS (or other trade agreements) that would justify such concerns (see for instance Box 21.1 on GATS commitments to health liberalization, as well as Adlung, 2009).

The GATS does not entail any constraints on a government's ability to pursue the regulatory objectives that it deems appropriate. The Preamble explicitly recognizes the right of members to regulate and introduce new regulations on the supply of services in order to meet national policy objectives. These basic principles have since been reiterated in the Trade Ministerial Declarations in Doha (2001) and Hong Kong (2005).

The drafters of the GATS had the option of creating either a broad framework—in terms of sectors and permissible trade measures—that is very flexible in application or,

---

[2] The commitments and MFN exemptions concerning "air transport services" that are recorded in Figures 21.1 and 21.2 thus relate exclusively to these three types of ancillary services.

rather, a system of tight disciplines for a limited number of sectors and circumstances. The Agreement that ultimately emerged from the Uruguay Round is clearly based upon the first option: an almost comprehensive system of rules combined with almost unlimited flexibility. There are virtually no policy regimes that would be GATS-inconsistent per se or, at least, that could not be accommodated under exception provisions. Typically, all measures listed in Table 21.1 are perfectly legitimate for WTO members to maintain or to introduce. Some measures might even prove compatible with the guarantee of unfettered market access and full national treatment under relevant treaty provisions. An indicative list of relevant examples from Table 21.1 includes A.3(c), B.3(c), B.4(a) and (b), and C.3(d).

Table 21.1 Service trade restrictions under the four modes of supply

Mode of supply	A. Hotel services	B. Hospital services	C. Insurance services
Cross-border trade (Mode 1)	[Feasible?*]	B.1 Hospitals not allowed to contract foreign suppliers of tele-health services	C.1(a) Car and fire insurance may be provided only by domestic companies
Consumption abroad (Mode 2)	A.2 Exit charge for nationals traveling as tourists abroad	B.2 No cover of treatment abroad under public health insurance scheme	C.2 Life insurance policies purchased abroad are subject to a tax of […] %
Commercial presence (Mode 3)	A.3(a) Foreign equity ownership limited to X% A.3(b) Investment grants of up to Y% for new constructions A.3(c) Local zoning rules must be respected A.3(d) Foreigners are not allowed to own land	B.3(a) Total number of hospital beds limited to […] until [date], and […] thereafter B.3(b) Approval of new hospitals only in regions with less than X beds per Y people B.3(c) Obligation to comply with hygiene standards issued by Ministry of Health	C.3 (a) Number of foreign non-life insurers limited to ten C.3(b) Establishment only as a joint-stock company C.3(c) No more than five branches per company C.3(d) Minimum equity: US$ 1,000,000
Presence of natural persons (Mode 4)	A.4(a) Number of work permits for foreign staff limited to […] A.4(b) Skilled foreign employees must provide training to nationals	B.4(a) Doctors must pass a test of competence with the Ministry of Health B.4(b) Foreign degrees are recognized only if issued in countries with whom recognition agreements exist	C.4(a) No more than 10% of staff may be foreign nationals. C.4(b) Language requirement for board members

*Many members have not undertaken commitments on hotel services under mode 1 since they considered cross-border trade of such services not to be technically feasible. However, according to Article XXVIII(b) of the GATS, the "supply" of a service does not comprise only production and delivery, but includes activities such as distribution, marketing and sale. It may be argued that these are tradable across borders.

III. The General Obligations of the GATS

The GATS rules operate at two levels. First, there is a set of general rules that apply across the board to measures affecting trade in services, and then there is a set of sector-specific commitments that determine the extent of liberalization undertaken by individual countries. The most important of the general rules are transparency and the most-favored-nation (MFN) principle (see for more details the Framework Disciplines section below). The former requires that all measures of general application affecting trade in services be published by a member, and that other members be informed of significant changes in trade policy. The latter prevents members from discriminating among their trading partners. Other general rules on market access, national treatment, additional commitments, and the scheduling of commitments are covered below. Note, however, that the specific commitments on market access and national treatment are the core of the GATS, and the impact of the Agreement depends to a large extent on the substance of the commitments made by members.

Market Access (Article XVI)

Article XVI provides an exhaustive list of restrictions that a member is not allowed to operate in a scheduled sector, unless it has inscribed the relevant limitation in its schedule of commitments. These limits may also be expressed in the form of an economic needs test, in which case members are expected to specify the approval criteria that are being applied. The six types of restrictions are: (i) the number of service suppliers; (ii) the total value of services transactions or assets; (iii) the total number of services operations or the total quantity of service output; (iv) the total number of natural persons that may be employed in a particular sector; (v) specific types of legal entity through which a service can be supplied; and (vi) foreign equity participation (e.g., maximum equity participation).

Three aspects of Article XVI should be noted. First, Article XVI does not include all types of measures that could restrict market access. Perhaps most significantly, fiscal measures are not covered. Thus, a member could maintain, without being obliged to schedule, a high non-discriminatory tax on a particular service that severely limits market access. Similarly, although minimum capital requirements (C.3(d)) or tight environmental, professional and other standards (A.3(c), B.3(c) and B.4(a)) listed in Table 21.1 might deter many potential entrants from seeking market access, such measures do not fall under the purview of Article XVI.[3] Second, Article XVI has been interpreted to cover both discriminatory and non-discriminatory measures, that is, measures of the type "only five new foreign banks will be granted licenses" and also measures such as

---

[3] However, other GATS provisions, in particular Article VI on domestic regulation, may prove relevant.

"only ten new [foreign and domestic] banks will be granted licenses." Finally, the limitations must be read as "minimum guarantees" rather than "maximum quotas," that is, a country that has promised to allow five foreign banks entry is free to grant entry to more than five.

National Treatment (Article XVII)

While the GATT guarantees full national treatment to duty-paid merchandise imports under all trade-related laws and regulations, national treatment under the GATS applies only to the sectors inscribed in the commitment schedules and to the extent that no limitations have been attached. Article XVII:1 states the basic national treatment obligation as follows: "In the sectors inscribed in its Schedule, and subject to any conditions and qualifications set out therein, each Member shall accord to services and service suppliers of any other Member, in respect of all measures affecting the supply of services, treatment no less favorable than that it accords to its own like services and service suppliers." It should be noted that the national treatment standard hinges on the effects of a measure (modification of conditions of competition), and not on the direct modal context in which the measure is being implemented. For example, domestic subsidies may well be granted regardless of the nationality of the supplier and, thus, would not constitute a national treatment problem under mode 3. Another peculiarity is that, unlike Article XVI on market access, Article XVII provides no exhaustive list of measures inconsistent with national treatment. Nevertheless, Article XVII:2 makes it clear that limitations on national treatment cover cases of both *de jure* and *de facto* discrimination.

Consider two examples of limitations on national treatment. If domestic suppliers of audiovisual services are given preference in the allocation of frequencies for transmission within the national territory, such a measure discriminates explicitly on the basis of origin of the service supplier and thus constitutes formal or *de jure* denial of national treatment. Alternatively, consider a measure stipulating that prior residency is required for the issuing of a license to supply a service. Although the measure does not formally distinguish service suppliers on the basis of national origin, it *de facto* offers less favorable treatment to foreign suppliers because they are less likely to be able to meet a prior residency requirement than like national service suppliers.

Additional Commitments (Article XVIII)

Article XVIII provides a framework for undertaking commitments with regard to measures not falling under market access or national treatment. The Article only provides some examples—qualifications, standards, licensing issues, and so on—to which many more could be added. Additional Commitments currently play a particular role in telecommunications, where some 70 members have inscribed a so-called reference paper in the relevant column. This paper defines a range of regulatory disciplines, competitive safeguards, transparency, and institutional obligations (e.g., independence of regulator) that go beyond the GATS rules discussed above. The reference paper was developed by an informal group of countries and the original WTO members were free to inscribe it, with or without modifications, in their schedules of commitments (new members, however, were not given such freedom). Once inscribed, however, the ensuing obligations are as legally binding as any other specific sectoral and modal commitments laid down in the schedule. Members have also used the relevant column to foreshadow liberalization initiatives—for example the preparation and submission to parliament of a law that would terminate a monopoly regime—when their governments are able to commit only to the procedural steps, but not yet to a final outcome.

Scheduling Commitments

All WTO members are signatories to the GATS and, thus, are legally required to submit a schedule of commitments (Article XX:1). The schedule serves to specify a set of access and other commitments that a member undertakes in individual sectors. As noted above, given the diversity of the WTO membership and the flexibility of the Agreement, it might be impossible to find members with identical schedules.

The identification of limitations in law, administrative regulations, and practice, the policy decision about which substantial limitations or future policy space to retain, and their proper scheduling are challenging for most members, but in particular for new and inexperienced WTO members. Services schedules may need to be prepared in consultations with far more ministries and agencies (e.g., finance, justice, communication, construction, transport, tourism, education, health) than is the case with tariff concessions on merchandise trade. The Scheduling Guidelines list close to 40 examples of limitations that members have actually inscribed in their schedules. These include restrictions on foreign land ownership, discriminatory training requirements, and discriminatory tax treatment. Additional examples, listed in Table 21.1, are exit visa requirements on tourists traveling abroad under mode 2, exclusion of consumption abroad from domestic support schemes in areas such as health or education, as well as language requirements that are not directly related to the exercise of a profession. For example, a requirement of proficiency in the local language for a bank's board members would affect the conditions of competition in favor of nationals, and thus ought to be listed in the schedule of commitments. A language requirement for interpreters, instead, would be considered a core, necessary job qualification criterion that all interpreters, regardless of their nationality, can reasonably be expected to meet and thus, no member was expected to schedule it for translation and interpretation services.

All schedules have a common format, consisting of four columns. The first column is used to indicate the sector covered, while the second and the third columns serve to specify the trade commitments, by mode of supply, assumed by the member concerned. These relate to two distinct sets of obligations laid down in Part III of the Agreement, market access (Article XVI) and national treatment (Article XVII). Given the existence

Table 21.2 Structure of a schedule of commitments

Sector or Sub-sector	Limitations on market access	Limitations on national treatment	Additional commitments
Hotels and restaurants	(1)...	(1)...	...
	(2)...	(2)...	
CPC 641-643	(3)...	(3)...	
	(4)...	(4)...	

of four modes of supply, there are at least eight entries per sector, four each in the market access and national treatment column. A fourth column might be used to undertake any additional commitments not falling under these provisions (see Table 21.2).

The scheduling of commitments under the GATS is based on a so-called "positive list approach." Market access and national treatment commitments are undertaken only in those sectors that a member has listed in its schedule ("bottom-up"). The GATS, in Article XX:1, requires all WTO members to set out in a schedule the commitments they undertake, but does not further prescribe any particular sector focus. There are thus no requirements in the Agreement to ensure a balance in sector coverage. As shown in Figure 21.1, there are vast differences in the extent to which individual sectors have been committed. Members' "scheduling preferences" may have been influenced, first, by the degree to which particular segments have traditionally been open to foreign participation. Tourism is a typical example of an area in which virtually all countries have

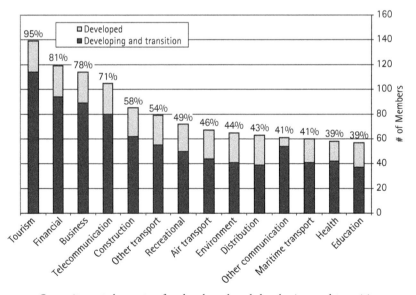

FIGURE 21.1 Commitments by sector for developed and developing and transition economies

Note: The vertical axis displays the number of members that have scheduled at least one sub-segment out of the large services sectors, from tourism to education, listed horizontally. EC members are counted individually.

Source: Adapted from Adlung and Roy (2005).

long maintained comparatively liberal investment regimes. Second, there is an apparent concentration of commitments (likely indicating openness) in sectors of general infrastructural importance, whose related flows of services, investment, skills, and expertise, promote growth and efficiency across many user industries.

The legal scope of the commitments, as specified in Articles XVI and XVII respectively, applies in full unless a member inscribes one or more limitations under a particular mode ("top-down"). The absence of limitations is indicated by the entry "none." However, members remain free to completely exclude one or more modes in either column from commitments, thus retaining policy discretion. In this case, the entries would read "unbound." The implications of "unbound" entries across all modes and under market access and national treatment are comparable to the situation in which that specific sector has not been inscribed at all.

Although there is no uniform classification of service sectors, similar to the Harmonized System used for tariff concessions under the GATT, the sector definitions underlying most current schedules of commitments display a large degree of commonality. Quite a number of members have worked with a Sectoral Classification List that was developed by the previous GATT Secretariat during the Uruguay Round. It consists of 11 broadly defined sectors (plus one residual category), which are further divided into some 160 sub-sectors.[4]

Schedules are legal instruments that guarantee, as a minimum, the specified access conditions. Enforceable via the WTO's dispute settlement mechanism, they create an element of transparency and predictability in services trade that did not previously exist. However, as mentioned before, the number of sectors inscribed and the depth of the commitments undertaken vary widely among members (Table 21.3). In non-scheduled sectors, or for all "unbound" entries, governments remain free at any time to grant or withdraw market access and national treatment as defined in the relevant Articles. By the same token, if a sector has been liberalized beyond the scheduled level, nothing in the Agreement would prevent a member from withdrawing the additional liberalization elements. The government concerned is thus able to explore the implications of a more liberal environment, while at the same time retaining the possibility of policy corrections. On the other hand, such non-scheduled liberalization may prove less attractive for potential market entrants, and therefore generate more modest trade and investment effects, than would be the case under corresponding bindings under the GATS. Potentially interested suppliers will consider the risk of policy slippages and reversals, since governments remain more susceptible to pressure from sector incumbents and their lobbies.

Many schedules contain a horizontal section that specifies limitations and/or additional commitments that apply across all services contained in the sector-specific part

---

[4] Excluding exceptions in financial and telecommunication services, the sub-sectors concord to a considerable degree to categories contained and described in a classification list developed by the UN in the early 1990s for mainly statistical purposes (provisional UN Central Product Classification). To enhance clarity, many members have added in their schedules the respective CPC numbers to the sector names. A recent dispute case, revolving inter alia around the classification of gambling services, suggests that members are well advised either to base themselves explicitly on the relevant CPC categories or, if a CPC category is deemed inappropriate, to specify clearly an alternative definition.

Table 21.3 Commitments by country group, November 2005

Countries	Average number of sectors included in schedules	Range(Lowest/highest number of sectors scheduled by individual countries)
Least-developed economies	24	1–111
Developing & transition economies	52 (104)*	1–147 (58–147)*
Developed economies	105	86–115
Accessions since 1995	102	37–147
ALL MEMBERS	50	1–147

*Transition economies only.

Notes: Total number of sectors: 160. Total number of members: 146.

Source: Adapted from WTO.

that follows. The sole purpose of this section is to facilitate the readability of schedules and avoid unnecessary repetition. Horizontal limitations may well coexist with a sector-specific "none", which implies, in the absence of additional clarification, that the limitation prevails. In contrast, if a sector entry (e.g., 25 per cent foreign capital ceiling) is more restrictive that the horizontal limitation (e.g., 75 per cent), the former applies.

Services liberalization is often more difficult to implement domestically than tariff reductions under the GATT. Thus, even if a country is prepared in principle to open a sector to competition in view of expected efficiency effects and budget savings, it may take years for the necessary legal and institutional changes to be implemented in full. And often these changes are staged over time, for example, in the form of an increasing number of licenses being auctioned off in subsequent years. In fact, a government may want to use external policy bindings to advance internal reforms and, if assumed during services rounds, as negotiating coinage to prod other members to move along as well. The GATS offers sufficient flexibility to accommodate such intentions. Nonetheless, such phase-in commitments (e.g. B.3(a) in Table 21.1 above) are as legally valid and enforceable as any other commitments inscribed in schedules. They have been used for instance by a number of African, Latin American and Caribbean countries that have bound themselves to introduce competition at precise future dates in telecommunication services (see Table 21.4 below).

Modification or Suspension of Commitments

As mentioned before, the very purpose of commitments is to enhance the stability and predictability of trade and investment conditions. It would contradict such intentions if commitments could be modified or reversed easily. This does not imply, however, that

Table 21.4 Examples of pre-commitments to liberalization in basic telecommunications (mode 3)

LATIN AMERICA	
Argentina	No restrictions as of November 8, 2000.
Grenada	Reserved for exclusive supply until 2006. No restrictions thereafter.
Venezuela	No restrictions as of November 27, 2000.
AFRICA	
Côte d'Ivoire	Monopoly until 2005, no restrictions thereafter.
Mauritius	Monopoly until 2004, no restrictions thereafter.
South Africa	Monopoly until December 31, 2003; thereafter duopoly and authorities will consider the feasibility of more licenses.
ASIA	
India	Review the subject of opening up national long-distance services in 1999, and international services in 2004.
Korea, Rep. of	Will raise in stages foreign equity participation in facilities-based supplier.
Pakistan	Proposes to divest 26% to a strategic investor who will have an exclusive license for the operation of basic telephonic services for seven years.
Thailand	Will introduce revised commitments in 2006, conditional upon the passage and coming into force of new communication acts.

Source: Adapted from WTO.

governments are locked in for good, should something have gone wrong in the scheduling process or initial expectations fail to materialize. In such cases, Article XXI offers the possibility to modify or withdraw existing commitments. The member concerned would need to notify the Council for Trade in Services of its intentions and be prepared to negotiate compensatory adjustments with affected members. Should such attempts fail, Article XXI provides for arbitration. Only once all procedural steps have been completely exhausted, which may take several months, can the commitment concerned be modified or withdrawn.

In addition, members are allowed to restrict trade, even in circumvention of existing specific commitments, in the event of serious balance-of-payments and other financial difficulties. The relevant conditions—temporary application, avoidance of unnecessary damage, and so on—are laid down in Article XII.

Broader exception clauses, which could provide an override over all provisions of the Agreement, are contained in Article XIV. Modeled on Article XX of the GATT, they provide cover for measures necessary to protect public morals and/or human, animal or plant life and health, and to accommodate some other situations. The measures must not be applied so as to constitute "a means of arbitrary or unjustifiable discrimination between countries where like conditions prevail, or a disguised restriction on trade in services." The security exceptions of Article XIVbis allow members, *inter alia*, to take any action considered necessary for the protection of their essential security interests.

Framework Disciplines

Part III of the GATS ("Specific Commitments"), comprising the provisions governing the scheduling of commitments (Articles XVI to XVIII) and discussed above, may be viewed as the centerpiece of the Agreement. All the access and country-specific trade obligations under the GATS are specified in and assumed under these three Articles. Nevertheless, their full implications can only be properly understood in the context of a broader framework of disciplines that are laid down in Part II. These disciplines essentially fall into two groups. First, there are those that must be respected by all members in all sectors covered by the GATS, regardless of the existence of specific commitments ("unconditional obligations"). Second, there are disciplines ("conditional obligations") whose scope is confined to those sectors and modes for which a member has undertaken specific commitments. Both sets apply as they are and cannot be modified by way of scheduling limitations.

The unconditional obligations contained in Part II can be grouped into three broad categories, requiring all members in all sectors: (a) not to discriminate among other members (most-favored-nation or MFN treatment); (b) to ensure transparency in the use of measures (publication and information requirements, including establishment of enquiry points); and (c) to comply with some additional duties, mostly procedural in nature, vis-à-vis other members and their suppliers (e.g., access to domestic judicial mechanisms; consultation requirements concerning restrictive business practices and trade-distorting subsidies).

Given the relatively modest levels of many market access commitments, it is probably fair to say that the most immediately palpable result of the Uruguay Round was the entry into force of the MFN requirement. All like foreign services and service suppliers must be treated on a par. As in merchandise trade, the MFN requirement is a powerful instrument in particular from the perspective of small countries that do not have the economic leverage and administrative resources to negotiate effectively with large trading partners. It ensures that the "mice" are able to share automatically—"immediately" and "unconditionally" in the terms of Article II:1—any trade benefits that the "elephants" may be able to extract from, or otherwise extend to, each other. If there is a continued disadvantage of small members, it is not rooted in discriminatory treatment, but unequal agenda-setting power.

Nonetheless, even for such core obligations as MFN treatment, the GATS offers more scope for accommodating country- and sector-specific peculiarities than is the case with the GATT. This was necessary due to the Agreement's broad policy coverage, including investment-related issues under mode 3, which extends its reach into areas with a long tradition of bilateral accords. Sector-specific bilateral concessions are particularly widespread in services trade, and especially in professional services and transport, as governments have found it easier to overcome domestic resistance to foreign competition if access remains confined to countries that offer comparable conditions. The GATS drafters thus allowed (in Article II:2) the grandfathering of existing MFN-inconsistent measures, not to exceed a period of ten years in principle and subject to review, although this limitation was softened by the insertion of "should" and "in principle." The possibility of listing MFN exemptions still exists for new members at accession time, but not for current members.[5]

About two-thirds of WTO members considered it necessary to attach a list of MFN exemptions to their services schedules in order to obtain legal cover. In total, more than 470 MFN-inconsistent measures have been listed, indicating the sector concerned, the relevant measure and its inconsistency with the MFN obligation, affected countries, intended duration, and the underlying policy needs. In over 90 per cent of all cases, the listed exemptions were intended to apply for an indefinite or otherwise non-specified period.

The general exceptions contained in Article XIV, already referred to above, allow members to disregard the MFN obligation, if necessary, for the attainment of the specified policy objectives, including protection of life and health. Additional provisions allow members to facilitate exchanges of locally produced and consumed services in frontier zones (Article II:3); to conclude economic integration agreements (Article V) and labor market integration agreements (Article Vbis); and to recognize educational degrees, licenses, certificates, and so on from particular countries (Article VII).

Unlike the time frame for MFN exemptions, application of the additional provisions above is not subject to any time limits. However, there are other constraints to prevent abuse. Article II:3, by its very nature, is limited in its geographic application; Article V requires an economic integration agreement, *inter alia*," to ensure "substantial sectoral coverage" and the elimination of "substantially all discrimination" between participants; and recognition agreements under Article VII must be open in principle for third countries to join.

The Unfinished GATS Agenda: Conditional Obligations

While unconditional obligations apply across all sectors falling under the Agreement, the scheduling of commitments triggers an additional range of (conditional) obligations that apply only to sectors and modes for which bindings are being assumed. The basic purpose of these obligations is to protect the commercial value of what has been inscribed in schedules and prevent commitments from being gradually undermined, intentionally or otherwise, by ongoing policy changes.

---

[5] The only option for them to obtain cover for additional measures would be a waiver under Article IX:3 of the WTO Agreement. However, no such waivers have been sought to date for MFN-inconsistent measures.

The related "regulatory disciplines," however, apply to the measures that may be taken in pursuit of any legitimate policy objective, not to the objective per se. The intention is to have members choose among alternative implementing measures (qualification and licensing requirements, technical standards and qualification procedures) those that avoid unnecessary trade restrictions. However, except for the accountancy sector where an agreement on disciplines has been put on hold pending completion of the ongoing services negotiations, other relevant disciplines are rudimentary at present. The GATS merely contains a negotiating mandate to develop disciplines to ensure, *inter alia*, that regulatory requirements are based on objective and transparent criteria, no more burdensome than necessary to ensure the quality of the service, and not in themselves a trade restriction (in the case of licensing procedures). These rule-making negotiations are sometimes referred to as the "built-in agenda," since the respective mandates are self-contained and not directly connected with the new round of services negotiations under the Doha Development Agenda.

Negotiations under Article VI:4 are going on within the framework of the Working Party on Domestic Regulation. So far they have revolved around four core elements and concepts: necessity in view of a specific legitimate objective; transparency of regulatory principles and processes; equivalence (including recognition of relevant foreign qualifications); and international standards and their possible role as benchmarks. As long as the negotiations are underway, Article VI:5 imposes some relatively soft stand-still obligations. Accordingly, members should refrain from applying measures (qualification and licensing requirements, etc.) that would nullify or impair a specific commitment, are incompatible with the above set of criteria, and could not reasonably have been expected of them at the time when they made the commitment.

Because of its immediate impact on trade, market failure due to natural monopolies or oligopolies may need to be addressed directly by multilateral disciplines. However, the GATS provisions applying to monopolies, in Article VIII (see below), are limited in scope. They only deal with monopolistic and exclusive suppliers established or enabled under government legislation and only with resulting domestic distortions that are inconsistent with the MFN principle or specific commitments in relevant sectors. Other monopoly situations that may be attributable, for example, to the existence of network effects (electricity grids, public transport, etc.) and/or economies of scale in markets of limited size, are not covered. Nor could Article VIII be used to challenge competition-related access problems that affect all potential market entrants, whether domestic or foreign, to the same extent. As a consequence, in the context of the telecom negotiations, negotiators developed the so-called reference paper to ensure that such problems would not undermine market access. The question arises, and may need to be addressed by WTO members, whether there is a similar rationale for pro-competitive disciplines in other network services, including transport (terminals and infrastructure), environmental services (sewage), and energy services (distribution networks).

In other cases of market failure, future multilateral disciplines may not need to target the problem per se, but rather to ensure that any domestic regulatory response does not unduly restrict trade (the same is true for measures designed to achieve social policy objectives). Such trade-restrictive effects can arise from a variety of technical standards, including prudential regulations, and qualification and licensing requirements in professional, financial and numerous other services. The GATS contains other conditional obligations such as notification requirements to ensure transparency and prohibitions to restrict payments and transfers for transactions falling under specific commitments. All such multilateral disciplines are to be addressed in the negotiations mandated under Article VI:4.

In addition to the negotiating mandate on regulatory disciplines under Article VI:4, the GATS contains three further rule-making mandates, namely on emergency safeguard measures (Article X), government procurement (Article XIII), and subsidies (Article XV). The fact that these issues were not solved during the Uruguay Round may not only be attributable to time constraints, but also to the structural peculiarities of the GATS (four modes of supply, right to operate quota-type, and other limitations) and lack of empirical experience. Negotiators thus sought to avoid a final decision on the need for, and shape of, particular rules and disciplines. Even after several years of negotiations, there is no consensus yet in the Working Party on GATS Rules on how to address these areas.

IV. Preferential Trade Agreements (PTAs) in Services

The proliferation of trade agreements featuring detailed disciplines on trade and investment in services is evidence of heightened policy interest in the contribution of efficient service sectors to economic development and a growing appreciation of the gains likely to flow from the progressive dismantling of impediments to trade and investment in services. For many countries, preferential negotiations offer the opportunity to pursue, deepen, or lock in some (or much) of the policy reforms put in place domestically in recent years and to reap the benefits, notably in terms of improved investment climates, likely to flow from such policy consolidation.

Because they have typically been negotiated in a concurrent fashion, preferential and multilateral efforts at services rule-making have tended to be closely intertwined processes, with much iterative learning by doing, imitation, and reverse engineering.

As the main economic implications of PTAs were already considered in other chapters of this volume, the following sub-sections focus on three issues. The first issue relates to the practical feasibility of preferential liberalization in services. The second addresses the political economy of regionalism in services trade, highlighting a number of patterns and lessons for negotiators and policymakers arising from the practice of preferential liberalization in services. The third issue addresses the legal dimension of this policy interface, focusing on a number of aspects of rule-design, including the strengths and weaknesses of existing multilateral disciplines on preferential approaches to services trade and investment liberalization. A brief discussion of issues that parties to prospective PTAs in services will likely need to confront and seek novel solutions to in advancing the process of services liberalization and rule-making is at the end of the chapter.

Is Preferential Liberalization in Services Trade Feasible?

At first sight, it is not obvious how a preferential agreement in services would be implemented. The benefits of any reduction in domestic subsidies cannot be denied to any exporter. On the other hand, the preferential use of explicit or implicit quantitative restrictions in air and road transport and in professional services and the allocation of licenses in other areas, like certain segments of telecommunications and financial services, is certainly feasible.

Domestic regulations like educational qualification requirements can be made less stringent, and national-treatment provision more liberal for certain professionals and business people from a preferred partner, as is indeed the case in Brazil for service providers from Mercosur. Restrictions on foreign ownership in a variety of transport services for nationals of certain countries can also be easily relaxed—as Mexico did in the context of North American Free Trade Agreement (NAFTA) and Vietnam in that of Association of South East Asian Nations (ASEAN). And service providers from certain countries can be exempted from the requirements on the legal form of commercial presence (i.e., through local incorporation) or the restrictions on branching in financial services. All these measures certainly are amenable to preferential elimination in many services sectors.

Similarly, in government procurement, certain transparency disciplines have a public good aspect—everyone benefits from the requirement that the intention to procure be publicly announced. But the benefit of other deeper non-discriminating disciplines could be provided more selectively, as is happening currently between parties to the WTO's plurilateral Agreement on Government Procurement.

Finally, there is a more subtle way in which preferences can be extended, as discriminatory commitments can create a more certain environment for suppliers from particular countries even though the actual policy environment does not discriminate. For example, although all foreign providers enjoy the same access to the Brazilian telecommunications market, Mercosur providers have the security of binding commitments, despite Brazil having made none in this sector under the GATS.

The Practice of Preferential Liberalization in Services

Several studies have reviewed how deep and comprehensive regional or bilateral integration agreements are designed across sectors (Baldwin et al., 2009, and Chauffour and Maur, 2011). A review of the evidence for services can be found in Marchetti and Roy (2008) and Mattoo and Sauvé (2011) and an updated dataset of services commitments in PTAs is in Roy (2011). This section provides the key conclusions of these studies (see also the services trade section of J. C. Maur's Chapter 17 in this volume).

PTAs tend to show broad commonality, both among each other and vis-à-vis the GATS, as regards the standard panoply of disciplines directed towards the progressive opening of services markets. In some instances, however (e.g., non-discriminatory quantitative restrictions, domestic regulation), GATS disciplines go further than those found in a number of PTAs.

Starting with the NAFTA in 1994, an increasing number of PTAs have in recent years sought to complement disciplines on cross-border trade in services (modes 1 and 2 of the GATS) with a more comprehensive set of parallel disciplines on investment (both investment protection and liberalization of investment in goods- and services-producing activities) and the temporary movement of business people (related to goods and services trade and investment in a generic manner).

PTAs featuring comprehensive or generic investment disciplines typically provide for a right of non-establishment (i.e., no local presence requirement as a pre-condition to supply services) as a means of securing the right to cross-border trade in services. Such an explicit provision is particularly well suited to promoting e-commerce, although the same result can be achieved by entering "none" under mode 1 in the GATS schedule of commitments.

With generally few exceptions (of a mainly sectoral nature), PTAs covering services typically feature a liberal rule of origin/denial of benefits clause, that is, extend preferential treatment to all legal persons conducting substantial business operations in a member country. In practice, the adoption of a liberal stance in this regard implies that the post-establishment treatment of what in many instances represents the most important mode of supplying services in foreign markets—investment—may be largely akin to non-preferential treatment insofar as third country investors are concerned. A liberal rule of origin minimizes the costs of trade diversion and is economically efficient. But it creates the same problems for bargaining as negotiations under the MFN rule: partners' willingness to pay for preferential access is dampened because they will be subject to greater competition from third countries; and the country itself loses future negotiating leverage vis-à-vis third countries. These considerations are going to be particularly important for a country like Brazil in the Free Trade Area of the Americas (FTAA) and in the EU–Mercosur negotiations, because the United States and the European Union already host most major service suppliers. Full access to either with liberal rules of origin (Mexico's choice under NAFTA) would approximate MFN liberalization.

Liberalization in PTAs tends to follow two approaches: replicate the GATS positive list or a hybrid approach to market opening; others pursue a negative-list methodology.[6]

---

[6] More than half of all PTAs featuring services provisions concluded to date proceed on the basis of a negative list approach. Such agreements are more prevalent in the Western hemisphere, reflecting the influence of the NAFTA, as well as in agreements conducted along North–South lines (with the exception of the EU and European Free Trade Association (EFTA agreements)).

The positive-list method lists sectors that are scheduled for opening. All sectors that are not listed are thus excluded from liberalization commitments. In practice, positive lists are combined with across-the-board liberalization commitments (such as National Treatment) to which reservations in selected areas can be added.[7] Alternatively, negative lists mention the sectors that will not be liberalized; therefore the default assumption is that all other sectors will be liberalized.

Both approaches should in theory generate broadly equivalent outcomes. However, a negative-list approach can be more effective in locking in the regulatory status quo. Also a number of good governance-enhancing features are associated with negative listing, most notably in transparency terms. Studies suggest that North–South PTAs based on a negative-list approach tend to achieve deeper liberalization in practice (see Mattoo and Sauvé, 2011). PTAs are also becoming more flexible: for instance, they increasingly mix positive and negative list approaches under the same agreement.[8]

Some governments (particularly when the negative list is used) have shown a subsequent readiness to extend regional preferences on an MFN basis under the GATS. This may reflect a realization that preferential treatment may be difficult to achieve in services trade (and is indeed perhaps economically undesirable). Also, PTAs covering services typically extend preferential treatment to all legal persons conducting business operations in a member country, either by featuring a liberal[9] "rule of origin" or denial of benefits clause.[10] Both cases would tend to demonstrate that discrimination is not systematic in PTAs covering services.

With considerable variations and diversity PTAs also go beyond existing GATS commitments and WTO negotiations in terms of sector coverage. This is especially the case for developing countries, which have low sector coverage in the GATS. WTO-plus advances are evident both in areas that have attracted low interest under the GATS—such as audiovisual services and skilled labor mobility—and more "popular" areas in the GATS (computer, express delivery, tourism, and telecom services).[11]

North–South PTAs nonetheless encounter resistance to market opening in services sectors that have proven difficult to address at the multilateral level (e.g., air and maritime transport; audio-visual services; movement of service suppliers; energy services). Financial services liberalization, instead, is mainly covered in PTAs involving at least

---

[7] Hence the mention of the hybrid approach.

[8] For example, positive listing for cross-border trade and negative listing for commercial presence; or negative listing for banking services and positive listing for insurance services.

[9] That is, non-restrictive.

[10] Denial of benefit clauses specify who cannot benefit from the liberalized regime.

[11] Several recent PTAs have made headway on temporary movement of persons (mode 4), including South–South regional agreements such as Mercosur and ASEAN, whose members have reached trade-facilitating mutual recognition agreements, notably in selected regulated professions and highly skilled occupations.

one northern partner (e.g., Australia–USA Free Trade Area (FTA), South Korea–EU FTA, or Chile–USA FTA) rather than in PTAs among southern partners. For instance, ASEAN had by mid-2013 yet to implement most of its ambitious services liberalization agenda to achieve its goal of an ASEAN Economic Community (AEC) by 2015. And while financial services were included in 16 PTAs involving Latin American and Caribbean countries (out of a total of 34 PTAs), only Mexico (primarily in the immediate post-NAFTA period) and Panama (an offshore financial center) included them in their South–South trade agreements (Goncalves and Stephanou, 2010). The Central American countries also liberalized financial services trade among themselves, but under the framework of the CAFTA-DR-US, a regional agreement whose agenda was largely set by their powerful northern neighbor (Echandi 2010). For an overview and case studies of the experience and lessons of financial services liberalization in PTAs, see Box 21.2 below and Marchetti (2008) and Haddad and Stephanou (2010).

PTAs are commonly viewed as offering greater scope for making speedier headway on matters relating to regulatory cooperation in services trade, notably in areas such as services-related standards and the recognition of licenses and professional or educational qualifications. Despite the greater initial similarities in approaches to regulation and greater cross-border contact between regulators that geographical proximity can afford, however, progress in the area of domestic regulation has been slow and generally disappointing even at the regional level. This is most notably the case for disciplines on an emergency safeguard mechanism and on subsidies for services trade, where governments confront the same conceptual and feasibility challenges, data limitations, and political sensitivities at the regional level as they do on the multilateral front.

In recent years, however, an increasing number of South–South PTAs, as in the case of a few Asian and Caribbean PTAs, have incorporated mutual recognition agreements for certain professions, in some cases along with harmonized qualification standards, and soft-law provisions encouraging regulators to facilitate the movement of professionals, such as across-the-board necessity tests for domestic regulations, as in the Trans-Pacific Economic Partnership Agreement. In addition, a large number of North–South agreements have detailed regulatory disciplines on telecommunications, e-commerce, and maritime transport (Fink and Molinuevo 2007, and Marchetti and Martin 2008). Some progress has also been made at the regional level in opening up procurement markets for services, though such advances have tended to be made in procurement negotiations rather than in the services field.

The relationship between PTAs and the WTO is not unidirectional in character but involves iterative, two-way interaction between these layers of trade governance in ways that can inform subsequent patterns of rule-making and market opening at both the PTA and WTO levels. Examples of such interaction can be found where WTO jurisprudence has clarified or interpreted the scope of key provisions governing services trade that are typically found both in the WTO-GATS and in the services and investment chapters of PTAs.

Box 21.2 Financial Services Trade in Latin America and the Caribbean

An analysis of the treatment of financial services in trade agreements involving Latin America and Caribbean (LAC) countries and of the regulations governing trade in financial services in three selected country case studies (Chile, Colombia, and Costa Rica) reached a number of interesting conclusions.

- First, the proliferation of PTAs has contributed to greater financial services liberalization commitments and led to an increasingly complex regional "commitments map" (or financial services "spaghetti bowl"). Most progress in financial services rule-making and market opening—typically via a stand-alone financial services chapter—has been achieved via North–South FTAs; by contrast, LAC countries that have relied on the GATS and on sub-regional customs unions for trade commitments in financial services have not made much progress. This reflects the fact that the majority of foreign financial institutions in LAC countries are headquartered in developed countries, as well as the relative bargaining powers between the negotiating counterparts. Only two LAC countries have tended to include financial services chapters in South–South agreements—Mexico (in the post-NAFTA period) and Panama (which is an offshore financial center and a net exporter of financial services).
- Second, PTAs reflect significant deeper liberalization commitments when compared to the GATS. Additional commitments tend to span all financial sub-sectors, including those that were not well covered in the first GATS round, such as insurance, securities-related and other financial services. The same is true in modal terms, with significant new commitments particularly in mode 2 (consumption abroad). Mode 1 commitments, while better than under the GATS, remain relatively more timid.
- Fourth, *de novo* liberalization—which has chiefly taken the form of pre-commitments to future market-opening—is relatively modest. With a few exceptions, PTAs are primarily used to consolidate and "lock in" existing unilateral liberalization rather than as means to promote actively further market opening and the process of domestic regulatory reform. Apart from the opening of Costa Rica's insurance sector under the CAFTA-DR-US FTA, real liberalization appears to have mostly taken place in the cross-border provision of some insurance services, as well as in asset management and auxiliary financial services, which are relatively less important modes and sub-sectors than "core" banking services. However, the abolition of numerical quotas (e.g. economic needs test) and certain juridical restrictions on forms of entry (e.g. insurance branching) might also contribute to further liberalization in other sub-sectors under mode 3.
- Fifth, consolidation of the regulatory status quo and the application of certain disciplines in FTAs, by limiting the arbitrary use (and abuse) of "policy space" by the authorities, enhance predictability, prevent potentially costly policy reversals, and benefit both domestic and foreign financial services providers and local consumers.
- Sixth, many *de novo* liberalization commitments in FTAs are actually not preferential in nature. While some commitments are country-specific and benefit the financial services providers of the FTA counterpart, others require new "horizontal" regulations or laws that would presumably apply to the entire industry and could actually benefit financial service providers from third countries. Thus, there might not be important first-mover

(Continued)

Box 21.2 *Continued*

advantages or serious economic distortions created by using PTAs to promote market opening in financial services.

- Seventh, it is unclear how critical GATS- or NAFTA-type "architectural" models actually are to greater liberalization in financial services. The negative list approach and broader rules and disciplines embedded in NAFTA-type agreements (the most widely used in LAC) has been more effective, primarily on grounds of heightened regulatory transparency, but this can be largely attributed to the involvement of the USA in them. In addition, one could argue that the direction of causality between scheduling approaches and the level of liberalization commitments can run both ways. Finally, both models have introduced new features in recent years that borrow from each other, revealing signs of convergence around a more hybrid-type approach.
- Finally, it is too early to judge the outcomes of PTAs on domestic financial systems and overall welfare in LAC countries. Even if a commonly accepted methodology for quantifying impact was established and relevant data were available, the short time span since the negotiation or entry into force of PTAs under review means that their contribution still cannot be fully assessed.

Source: Goncalves and Stephanou (2010).

Multilateral Constraints on Preferential Services Liberalization

The need for clarity in respect of the relationship between preferential and multilateral disciplines on services has assumed heightened importance given the large number of PTAs that have been signed or extended to the services area since the conclusion of the Uruguay Round. As with goods trade under Article 24 of the GATT, Article V of GATS allows a derogation of the MFN obligation of GATS Article II, on the assumption that preferential arrangements can contribute to the further liberalization of the multilateral trading system. However, Article V imposes three conditions on economic integration agreements among WTO members for the latter to be deemed WTO-compatible. First, such agreements must have "substantial sectoral coverage" (Art. V:1(a)). Second, regional agreements are to provide for the absence or elimination of substantially all discrimination between or among the parties to the agreement in sectors subject to multilateral commitments. Third, such agreements are not to result in higher trade and investment barriers against third countries.

As with the GATT, under the GATS compensation of non-members is only foreseen for increases in explicit discrimination (i.e., the raising of external barriers), and not for increases in implicit discrimination. But Article V of GATS features a number of loopholes for the formation of agreements that do not fully comply with multilateral disciplines. In particular, Article V:3(b) allows developing countries particular flexibility in according more favorable treatment to firms and services whose ownership or control are in countries that are parties to an integration agreement. The greater policy flexibility shown by WTO members towards preferential liberalization in services may in part reflect the novelty of the subject matter at the time of the Uruguay Round as well as the policy preferences of a number of important WTO members that were negotiating (or contemplating future) PTAs in services at the time that GATS Article V was being drafted. In any case, implementation of Article V of the GATS is likely to be more straightforward than that of Article 24 of the GATT, largely because GATS disciplines are weaker with respect to internal liberalization.

V. SERVICES TRADE IN THE NEW MULTILATERAL NEGOTIATING ROUND

The Mandate and (Slow) Progress

Unlike the GATT, the GATS explicitly provides for future trade negotiations. This mandate reflects the recognition that while the Uruguay Round proved a milestone in the history of services trade, because it helped create a multilateral framework of rules and disciplines and the architecture for future rounds, it was certainly not a milestone in actual services liberalization, judging by the breadth and depth of most current commitments. Today, virtually all current GATS schedules of commitments offer significant scope for improvement even if members were to confine themselves only to bind the currently prevailing access conditions across the same or a wider range of sectors or extend the benefits exchanged in a recent tide of preferential agreements to all WTO members.

According to Article XIX:1, WTO members are committed to enter into successive rounds of such negotiations "with a view to achieving a progressively higher level of liberalization." After the failure of the Seattle Ministerial Meeting in late 1999, however, it took more than one year until delegations in Geneva were able to agree upon a negotiating mandate for services. In March 2001, the WTO Council for Trade in Services, in a special session, finally approved the "Guidelines and Procedures for the Negotiations on Trade in Services," which were endorsed later that same year by the Doha Ministerial Conference and whose content may be summarized as follows:

1. *Objectives and Principles*. Confirmation of the objective of progressive liberalization as enshrined in relevant GATS provisions; appropriate flexibility for developing countries, with special priority to be given to least-developed countries; reference to the needs of small and medium-sized service suppliers, particularly of developing countries; and commitment to respect "the existing structure and principles of the GATS" (e.g., the bottom-up approach to scheduling and the four modes of supply).

2. *Scope*. No sectors or modes are excluded *a priori*; special attention to be given to export interests of developing countries; (re-)negotiation of existing MFN exemptions.

3. *Modalities and Procedures.* Negotiations shall start from current schedules (rather than actual market conditions); request–offer approach to remain the main negotiating method; credit for autonomous liberalization to be agreed upon based on common criteria; ongoing assessment of trade in services; and mandate for the Services Council to evaluate the results of the negotiations, prior to their completion.

The Doha Declaration contained target dates for the circulation of initial requests (June 30, 2002) and initial offers (March 31, 2003) of specific commitments, and envisaged all negotiations to be concluded not later than January 1, 2005. However, the failure of the Ministerial Conference in Cancun in November 2003 marked a first serious setback and it was not until 2004 (after the "July Package") that services negotiations resumed.

The circulation of requests was essentially a bilateral issue and not subject to any further information or notification requirements, let alone guidelines concerning structure or content. It was left to the individual members to decide whom to approach and what issues to raise under relevant GATS provisions (Annex on Article II Exemptions, Articles XVI, XVII and XVIII). Anecdotal evidence suggests that large developed countries circulated requests to almost all other members, covering a wide range of services, and that most middle-income developing countries actively participated in this process as well. With the possible exception of some recently acceded transition economies, every WTO member received at least a handful of requests. But while the request-and-offer process advanced smoothly in procedural terms, the overall momentum was not impressive.

Renewed Impetus and Stalling After Hong Kong

The services-related sections of the Hong Kong Ministerial Declaration of December 2005 set a new standard. The negotiating objectives contained in the relevant Annex were far more detailed and ambitious than those listed in any preceding Declaration (see Table 21.5). This was true not only for the definition of mode-specific objectives, but also for the language on MFN exemptions and the proclaimed need to improve the quality and accuracy of the schedules. Other new elements in the Declaration were provisions governing collective exchanges of request and offers (plurilateral request–offer negotiations) and an obligation to develop guidelines for the implementation of Least-Developed Countries (LDC) modalities. At the same time, the Declaration exempted LDCs, in recognition of their "particular economic situation," from the expectation to undertake new commitments.

In the aftermath of the Hong Kong Ministerial Conference, many members engaged intensively in the plurilateral request-offer process. By mid-April 2006, however, the 22 plurilateral requests and the very few bilateral offers (70 initial and 30 revised offers) that had been tabled did not translate into an agreement. Moreover, such discussions showed an uneven geographic participation. While a relatively large number of countries from the Americas and Europe and, with some gaps, from Asia had made contributions, Sub-Saharan Africa had remained largely on the sidelines.

Possibly more important, there was deep disappointment concerning the "quality" of the offers, both in terms of new sector inclusions and improvements of existing

Table 21.5 Overview of mode-specific objectives in the Doha Round

Mode 1
(i) Commitments at existing levels of market access
(ii) Removal of existing requirements of commercial presence

Mode 2
(i) Commitments at existing levels of market access
(ii) Commitments on mode 2 where commitments on mode 1 exist

Mode 3
(i) Commitments on enhanced levels of foreign equity participation
(ii) Removal or substantial reduction of economic needs tests
(iii) Commitments allowing greater flexibility on the types of legal entity permitted

Mode 4
(i) New or improved commitments on Contractual Services Suppliers, IndependentProfessionals and Others, delinked from commercial presence [...]
(ii) New or improved commitments on Intra-corporate Transferees and Business Visitors
[...]These commitments are to reflect, *inter alia*:
- removal or substantial reduction of economic needs tests
- indication of prescribed duration of stay and possibility of renewal. if any

Source: Adapted from WTO, Hong Kong Trade Ministerial Declaration in November 2005.

commitments. The WTO estimated that on average for all members, if current offers had entered into effect, the share of service sectors subject to commitments would have increased only by two or three percentage points to reach some 36 per cent. The overall emphasis was on the services and modes that already dominated existing schedules, with relatively little innovation in "sensitive" areas (education, health and other social services, as well as mode 4). The picture for MFN exemptions did not look brighter either. Less than 7 per cent of the 480-odd exemptions had been earmarked for removal, with many of the proposed changes being only by-products of the European Union's enlargement to EU-25 and the re-organization of preferential relations in Europe.

A second round of revised offers was due to be submitted by July 2006, but fell victim to the suspension of the Doha Round negotiations, announced by the WTO's Director General on July 27, 2006 in view of the stalemate in agriculture. When services negotiations resumed in 2008, three landmarks were achieved:

- a services text, attached to the July 2008 Report by the Chairman of the Council for Trade in Services in Special Session, which set out the elements required for the completion of the negotiations;

- a signaling conference among selected countries, which yielded some indication of what members would be willing to include in their revised services offers; and
- successive rounds of bilateral and for the first time plurilateral consultations and meetings.

In the most recent five years through mid-2013, however, little or no further progress towards a services agreement has been once again made. In 2011, two reports by the Chairman of the WTO Council for Trade in Services on the achievements and remaining gaps in all areas of the services negotiations acknowledged that on:

- Market access: limited progress had been achieved since July 2008.
- Domestic regulation: recent intensification of negotiations has produced notable progress, even if disagreement persists on important and basic issues.
- GATS rules: while technical work continues, there does not seem to be any convergence regarding the expected outcome in any of the three negotiating subjects (safeguards, government procurement and subsidies).
- Implementation of LDC modalities: members had been supportive of a waiver permitting preferential treatment toward LDCs, but disagreements mainly regarding the scope of the waiver and rules of origin for services and service suppliers were only resolved in November 2011, when the Council finally approved the waiver.

Services in Doha: Quantifying What's on the Table

As requests and offers made by countries are confidential, it is difficult to accurately assess what little additional market access has been offered so far. It is also difficult to measure their "value-added" compared to actual policies and regulations that have been adopted from unilateral reform programs or preferential free-trade agreements. Borchert, Gootiiz and Mattoo (2011) used available public information on the best offers by 62 WTO members that had been put on the table in the Doha Round and information from the 2007–08 surveys commissioned by the World Bank of applied trade policies in the major services sectors of 102 industrial and developing countries in selected sectors. They then scored GATS commitments, best offers so far, and actual policies and regulations for the surveyed countries and in the selected sectors to compute synthetic indexes of services trade restrictivenesses (STRIs). Database and background papers are available at <http://iresearch.worldbank.org/servicestrade/home.htm>.[12]

Borchert, Gootiiz and Mattoo (2011) and Hoekman and Mattoo (2011) concluded that the ambitious goals adopted at the WTO's Hong Kong Ministerial in 2005 were still remote. Little has changed in the past eight years regarding GATS commitments and Doha Round negotiations.

---

[12] The most restrictive actual policies are observed in the Middle East and North African (MENA) and Asian countries, while policies are much more liberal in Latin America, Africa, Eastern Europe and the OECD countries (see World Bank 2012 and Borchert et al. 2012).

At this stage, the Doha Round promises somewhat greater security of access to services markets, but not one iota of liberalization. Ironically, two of the most protected sectors, transport and professional services (involving the international mobility of skilled people), are either not being negotiated at all or are not being negotiated with any degree of seriousness. As Figures 21.2 and 21.3 show for 62 countries that submitted offers, Uruguay Round commitments inscribed in the GATS are, on average, 2.3 times more restrictive than current policies. The best offers submitted so far as part of the Doha negotiations improve on Uruguay Round commitments by about 10 per cent but are still, on average, twice as restrictive as actual policies.

At present, the Doha negotiations offer not greater access to markets but only the prospect of a weak assurance that current access will not get worse. The "request–offer" negotiating process has resulted in a low-level equilibrium trap, with services not been given the political attention that their economic significance deserves.

Even major private sector associations from key developed and middle-sized emerging economies appear to have grown skeptical that the services negotiations in the Doha Round will ever produce real liberalization, and have turned their focus more and more towards bilateral and regional agreements (e.g., the 2009 EU-South Korea and 2012 US-South Korea FTAs, and the proposed Transatlantic Trade and Investment Partnership or T-TIP or the Trans-Pacific Partnership or TPP currently still being negotiated). This does not mean that they are ready to accept an overall Doha agreement

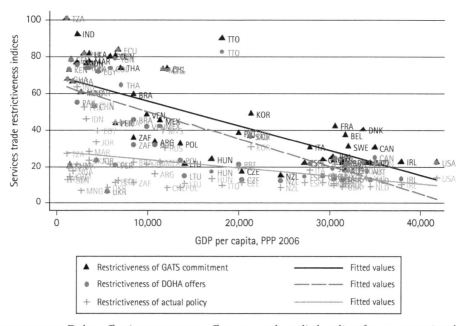

FIGURE 21.2 Doha offer improvement, offer gap, and applied policy for 62 countries, by GDP per capita

Source: Borchert, Gootiiz and Mattoo (2011).

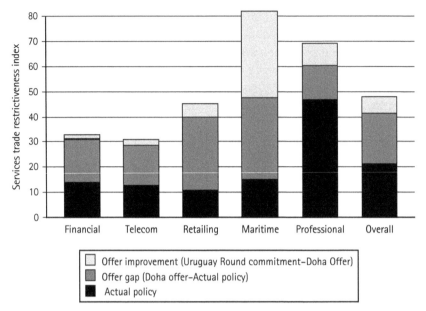

FIGURE 21.3 Offer improvement, offer gap, and applied policy for 62 countries, by sector

Source: Borchert, Gootiiz and Mattoo (1).

without significant and real new market access in services for their members. The final communiqués of the Global Services Summit (2010, 2011 and 2012) show clearly the private sector dissatisfaction with what is on the table and its views on what is required to move negotiations forward and to obtain the support of the national coalitions of service industries: "On services, what is on the table falls far short of providing the substantial and meaningful improvements in market access, especially by the large emerging countries, that are needed to create the new business opportunities essential for economic growth, development, and job creation." They also support strongly a move to a bolder plurilateral approach to the negotiations as an alternative to the ineffective bilateral request-offer approach.

Hoekman and Mattoo (2011) also suggest that a bolder approach than has been followed so far is required to strike a meaningful agreement on services in the Doha Round, involving a subset ("critical mass") of the major players on services and spanning three elements:

- A pledge not to impose any new restrictions, especially on cross border trade (mode 1) and FDI (mode 3), by inscribing binding language to this effect in the schedules of specific commitments in the GATS.
- Pre-commitments—inscribed again in each country's specific schedules—to implement reforms by a certain future date (to be negotiated) to liberalize trade in services, especially on FDI and in the transport sector.
- Agreement to expand the scope for temporary movement of services suppliers with source country obligations, specified in a model schedule.

Such a package, to be supported by an expanded aid-for-services trade agenda (see below), would offer benefits for established services exporters and also to developing countries. The occupational shifts in importing countries and adjustment costs associated with increased trade in services are increasingly raising the specter of protectionism. This specter may never materialize because of the triumph of good sense. But it would still be wise to preempt protectionism, by ensuring that any adjustment pressures created by international competition are dealt with through domestic assistance rather than by discrimination against foreign services providers. More important, fully locking—in applied policies would send a strong signal that governments are willing to use the GATS as a mechanism to enhance the predictability and transparency of policy.

VI. International Negotiations on Services Trade: Why and Where?

Most developing countries are today engaged in services trade negotiations in one or more fora: in the WTO under the General Agreement on Trade in Services (GATS); bilaterally with a large trading partner like the United States or the European Union, for example, in the context of the Economic Partnership Agreements (EPAs); and regionally, e.g., in the context of Mercosur, ASEAN and COMESA. See Boxes 21.3 and 21.4 for guidelines on negotiating services liberalization in either multilateral or preferential trade agreements. For a more in-depth treatment of negotiating rationales and guidelines, see Adlung and Mattoo (2008) and also Saez (2010).

Historically, most international services trade negotiations have not been powerful instruments of reform, and that remains especially true for the least-developed countries (see Box 21.4). Governments have been opening up their markets to foreign service providers on a unilateral and MFN basis for a long time, under structural reform programs often spurred by macroeconomic crises or loss of international competitiveness.

There are a number of agreements, however, both historic (the EU Single Market, the Australia–New Zealand Agreement and to a more limited extent, NAFTA) and recent ones (e.g., USA–Singapore, Japan–Singapore, China–Macao, China–Hong Kong, USA–Chile, USA–South Korea, CAFTA, USA–Colombia, EU–South Korea), that have achieved significant liberalization outcomes for services trade, proving the potential for beneficial engagement in bilateral, regional and (potentially) multilateral fora.

Reciprocity vs. Unilateral Liberalization

A major advantage of reciprocal trade agreements is that they can ensure that each country gains increased access to the other's market. In the local context, the advantage of signing a trade agreement is that it helps a domestic government stand up to local protectionist interest groups. This commitment effect has two advantages: trade barriers stay lower because the government caves in less often; and fewer resources are wasted because the lobbyists know the payoff on wasteful lobbying has fallen.

Box 21.3 Guidelines for Services Negotiations

Face-to-face trade negotiations, whether for the Doha Round or for a PTA, are or certainly should be the culmination of a long and extended process of preparation. While many think that the outcome of negotiations depends largely on the negotiating skills of individual negotiators at the bargaining table, other dimensions are often just as important, if not more important: good research and analysis, skillful shaping of a policy or negotiating issue, persuasive oral and written communication skills, the ability to build alliances, and buy-in by the relevant sectoral ministries.

Because barriers to trade in services are enmeshed in domestic regulations, the challenges involved in services negotiations are greater than for goods, as they inevitably touch on issues considered the sovereign prerogative of any national government to protect its consumers and national development objectives. Thus, it is especially important in services to follow an orderly process for sorting out the issues and building consensus about policies and negotiating mandates.

Collecting information. The first task for diligent negotiators is to assemble and compile background information on their own country's exports and imports of services, competitive strengths and weaknesses of domestic industries, and foreign regulatory barriers that inhibit national exports to other markets.

Sectors that export are likely to be relatively competitive, while sectors with large imports are likely to be competitively weak. Trade data, however, do not tell the full story. The reasons why a sector in which a country has potential comparative advantage may not show many exports could well be due to foreign trade barriers or domestic regulatory constraints inhibiting such trade or simply because the industry has not yet explored export opportunities. Additional insights into a country's competitive strengths can be found in economic studies carried out by academic experts, assessments provided by industry experts, and a review of the export performance of other countries at a similar stage of economic development and similar economic circumstances. Such studies are often available from academic sources and from intergovernmental organizations such as the World Bank and the International Trade Centre.

Information about foreign trade barriers is best provided by industry. The necessary canvassing of the industry can be done either by the trade negotiators themselves, by consultants hired for the task, or by industry associations. Insights into trade barriers can also be found in the surveys done by third countries, particularly developed countries with large human and financial resources, or by international organizations. Many such surveys and updated inventories of trade barriers are increasingly available on the Internet.

Negotiators also have to collect information about how the negotiating partners and other third-party but major trading partners are likely to be affected by reforms under negotiation. They need to understand the strengths and weaknesses of those countries' industries, their stakeholders and their interests, in order to anticipate any negative reactions that could lead to a trade dispute. And they need to understand in advance the difficulties foreign governments are likely to face in meeting requests for liberalization, and also what they are likely to request in return.

Analyzing the information. Some trade officials think they have completed their work when they have compiled voluminous information on trade and barriers with the negotiating partner(s). But real analysis consists of using such information to shed light on the economic interests of stakeholders affected by a measure, the potential interpretations

Box 21.3 *Continued*

that can be given to relevant laws and regulations, the policy issues that may have to be addressed and ultimately how the issue can be shaped to maximize the chances for a successful reform or negotiation.

Clarifying policy and negotiating objectives. Only the technical details of a trade agreement should be left to the negotiators' responsibility. The country's broad strategic policy and negotiating objectives should have been set out in a statement and approved by the political leadership, well before technical negotiating meetings begin. And the country's negotiating objectives should be formulated by government as part of a broader domestic economic development strategy, a task beyond the scope of responsibilities of trade officials and therefore requiring leadership by the country's top political leaders and key economic ministers and agency heads.

Stakeholder consultations. Once negotiators have developed a policy or negotiating proposal, they must both verify with and persuade stakeholders at home and abroad on the merits of the proposal. In part this is done through meetings with stakeholders and conferences as well as the preparation of position papers, published statements, press releases, and websites. Documents can be targeted either at the general public through the mass media or at targeted groups through specialized publications serving particular services industries or professions. Policymakers and negotiators might also make public speeches to stakeholder groups, testify at legislative hearings, and post white papers on the organization's web site. Following such consultations, revisions are made to the country's proposed policy and negotiating position to correct mistakes and ensure broad ownership and support.

Source: Feketekuty, Geza (2008). See also Saez, Sebastian (2010).

Domestic services providers gain from protection, and, although the barriers may lower social welfare, its costs are widely dispersed across consumers. Consequently, producer lobbies for protection will often be stronger than consumer lobbies for free trade. For example, a proposed policy change to allow foreign engineers into the country may well benefit local consumers, but is likely to encounter resistance from local engineering professional associations. But if it is coupled with a bilateral, regional, or multilateral

Box 21.4 The LDC and the WTO Services Negotiations

To say that the LDCs have a major stake in services trade is to invite either incredulity or derision. The first comes from those who see services trade as largely irrelevant to the LDCs development agenda. The second comes from those who see few benefits from past market-opening by LDCs. These views have had a powerful influence on international services trade negotiations. Over the last decade, the international trading community has made fewer and fewer demands for liberalization of the LDCs. Are these developments a sensible policy or a recipe for further marginalization of LDCs?

In the services negotiations at the WTO, the least-developed countries have pursued three goals: retaining flexibility in making liberalizing commitments, obtaining assistance

(Continued)

Box 21.4 *Continued*

---

to enhance the capacity of their services sectors, and securing commitments from other countries in sectors and modes of export interest to them. They have so far succeeded in achieving the first two goals, but not the third.

On the issue of increasing the participation of developing countries, Article IV of the GATS states that "particular account shall be taken of the serious difficulty of the least-developed countries in accepting negotiated specific commitments in view of their special economic situation and their development, trade and financial needs." In September 2003, WTO members adopted the "Modalities for the Special Treatment for Least-Developed Country Members in the Negotiations on Trade in Services" (henceforth, LDC Modalities), which accepted that "there shall be flexibility for LDCs for opening fewer sectors, liberalizing fewer types of transactions, and progressively extending market access in line with their development situation. LDCs shall not be expected to offer full national treatment, nor are they expected to undertake additional commitments under Article XVIII of the GATS on regulatory issues which may go beyond their institutional, regulatory, and administrative capacities." The December 2005 Hong Kong Ministerial Declaration went even further, stating, "We recognize the particular economic situation of LDCs, including the difficulties they face, and acknowledge that they are not expected to undertake new commitments." The right to hold back in most cases has been exercised.

Zambia, for example, had committed in the Uruguay Round to openness only in a few business services, construction, health, and tourism, but not in communications, finance, or transport. In the current round of negotiations, it has so far offered no improvements on its GATS commitments (Mattoo and Payton, 2007). For another case study highlighting the contrast between the high level of actual liberalization of FDI and the detailed services reform plans of Mali and its GATS commitments, see Honeck, 2011.

Pascal Lamy in his previous role as EU commissioner for trade said that the EU would make no market-opening demands of LDCs at the WTO. And as a condition of accession, LDCs have been asked to bind their existing policies and regulations as they affect market access and national treatment, but hardly to commit to any significant new liberalization. In the case of Cambodia, which acceded in 2004, for example, the government was only asked to liberalize audio-visual and distribution services.

With respect to the third goal, however, the LDCs have had no success. Beginning with GATS Articles IV and XIX, and continuing with the LDC Modalities and the Hong Kong Ministerial Declarations, there have been exhortations to members to "give special priority to providing effective market access in sectors and modes of supply of export interest to LDCs, through negotiated specific commitments". In the LDC Modalities, "It is recognized that the temporary movement of natural persons supplying services (mode 4) provides potential benefits to the sending and recipient Members. LDCs have indicated that this is one of the most important means of supplying services internationally. Members shall to the extent possible ... consider undertaking commitments to provide access in mode 4, taking into account all categories of natural persons identified by LDCs in their requests." WTO members, however, have largely ignored these exhortations (see Figure 21.4) and have promised little in the Doha negotiations in the area of greatest export interest for the LDCs, that is, the provision of services through the movement of unskilled workers.

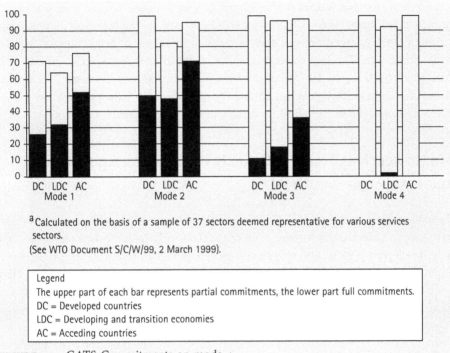

^aCalculated on the basis of a sample of 37 sectors deemed representative for various services sectors.
(See WTO Document S/C/W/99, 2 March 1999).

Legend
The upper part of each bar represents partial commitments, the lower part full commitments.
DC = Developed countries
LDC = Developing and transition economies
AC = Acceding countries

FIGURE 21.4 GATS Commitments on mode 4

agreement that includes increased access for domestic engineers to the foreign market, then the gains from increased trade will be greater and domestic resistance will be lessened.

The second commitment effect is in the international context. Service providers often have to invest in fixed costs to serve a foreign market, either through direct investment or in obtaining certification or developing local knowledge. If firms face high risks of being shut out of the foreign market, they may be reluctant to make such investments and a country that wants to attract foreign service providers may fail to do so. Even if foreign providers will not be shut out, they may feel vulnerable because of what is known as the hold-up problem. Once foreigners have invested in country-specific skills, they may still be concerned that the host government will try to extract rents from them by imposing discriminatory taxes or other requirements. A formal trade agreement can help to increase the credibility of a commitment either to not cut off access once investments have been made, or to not arbitrarily change the rules to extract rents.

Note that a country's commitment to a trade agreement also fosters its internal trade. Much of the success of internal trade within a country relies on confidence that contracts will be enforced and rules will be applied in a predictable manner. International trade agreements lead to the development of institutions and rules-based systems that can help settle disputes more rapidly and fairly and increase the consistency with which rules are applied to resolve even purely domestic business disputes.

Reciprocity can also help avoid trade wars. It is well known that governments can get into self-defeating trade wars, as for example happened during the Great Depression in the 1930s. Each government may face pressure to protect local firms. But if all governments do this, then overall economic activity is lower and all countries are worse off than if they trade freely. The situation is much like a prisoners' dilemma. The optimal strategy for an individual government may be to protect, but if they all do it, they are all worse off. Coordinated liberalization can circumvent the problem.

Aid for Services Trade: A Priority in the Doha Agenda and Bilateral North–South PTAs

The poorer developing countries are currently well placed to mobilize international assistance to facilitate adjustment to services trade reforms, improve regulation, and institute effective policies for universal access (Hoekman and Mattoo, 2011). The multilateral aid-for-trade initiative that was launched at the 2005 WTO Ministerial in Hong Kong provides a mechanism through which low-income developing country governments can obtain ample financial and technical assistance to implement regulatory improvements.

Sub-Saharan Africa by 2009 was the largest recipient of total aid for trade among the different regions, with commitments to Africa increasing by 40 per cent to reach US$13 billion and those to the Latin America and the Caribbean region by almost 60 per cent to US$3 billion. Low income countries and regional programs increased their share. Driving this shift in regional distribution has been the increased focus of aid for trade on the low-income countries, which saw their share of commitments increase by 26 per cent in 2009. Global and regional programs also continued to grow, receiving 18 per cent (US$7 billion) of total commitments in 2009 (see WTO and OECD, 2011). The evidence to date is that most aid for trade assistance has focused on infrastructure investments and trade facilitation—not on regulation or service sector policies. But there is no reason why aid for trade would not be provided for services policy reforms which are identified as priorities by developing country governments (Hoekman and Mattoo, 2007).

Beyond international services negotiations, aid-for-trade support is needed at four levels: in devising sound policy, strengthening the regulatory environment, enhancing developing country participation in promoting international standards, and ensuring access to essential services in the poorest areas.

While there is growing consensus on the benefits of liberalization, there is less agreement on the precise route to liberalization. Certain issues have prompted differing strategies. Should all barriers to entry be eliminated in sectors with significant economies of scale? How far should trade and investment liberalization be conditioned on strengthened prudential regulation? Developing countries in particular could benefit from the experience of other countries on these issues—but poor experiences with liberalization of electricity in California and rail transport in Britain suggest that there is scope for learning even by developed countries.

Sound domestic regulation—ranging from prudential regulation in financial and professional services to pro-competitive regulation in a variety of network-based services—is critical to realizing the benefits of services liberalization. Devising and implementing such regulation is not easy, and there are acute regulatory problems in many developing countries. Regulatory institutions can be costly and require sophisticated skills. To some extent, such costs can be recovered through fees or regional cooperation—but external assistance can help ensure that adequate regulation is in place.

Improvements in domestic standards and qualifications are also needed in order to be able to export services. For example, in the case of professional services, low standards and disparities in domestic training and examinations can become major impediments to obtaining foreign recognition and can legitimize external barriers to trade. If national standards are not optimal or insufficiently developed, then regional and/or international harmonization or standardization can be a way of improving such standards. In such situations, the best partners for regulatory cooperation are likely to be those with the soundest regulatory frameworks. Such partners may not always be found within regional compacts. At the same time, developing countries need to participate more actively in the development of international regulations and standards, especially in new areas like electronic commerce. Otherwise, standards will evolve to reflect the concerns only of developed countries and impede the participation of developing countries in services trade.

There will remain certain poor countries, or certain regions within poor countries, where improvements in services policy and regulation will not be sufficient to ensure access to essential services. The criterion for determining whether assistance is needed could be the absence of private-sector provision despite comprehensive policy reform. The effectiveness of international assistance could be maximized by allocating it in a manner similar to that used domestically by countries like Chile and Peru to achieve universal service. For instance, once a country (or a region within a country) has been selected for assistance, funds—such as those provided by certain countries to bridge the digital divide—could be pooled and allocated through international competitive tenders to the firm that offers to provide the necessary infrastructure at least cost. Providing international assistance in meeting the costs of the required subsidy programs could increase the benefits of, and facilitate, liberalization by ensuring that the needs of the poor would be met.

Deeper Regional Cooperation to Create Single Markets

In order to create stronger incentives for investment and to reap the benefits of economies of scale in a competitive environment, small countries need to be part of a more integrated market. Integration often requires deep regulatory harmonization, which has benefits but also costs. The former will dominate where national regulation can be improved, as is often the case in areas like transport and telecommunications. But where national regulations are already adequate, the benefits of international harmonization in terms of greater competition in integrated markets must be weighed against the costs of departing from nationally appropriate regulations. For example, harmonizing accounting standards with the European Union (EU) may give a developing country's accountants access to the larger EU market, but it may require more demanding standards than if they were harmonized with neighboring countries. The choices are simpler where it is possible to have separate standards, for example, one for exporters and one for those who serve the domestic market, as may be feasible in accountancy.

Regulatory cooperation and standards harmonization may be more feasible—and likely more desirable—among neighboring countries at a similar level of development than in the multilateral or North–South preferential context. Some of the more obvious priorities are cooperation on telecom and transport infrastructure, air and road transport liberalization, and the development of regionally appropriate professional standards in areas like accountancy, as well as the enforcement of competition policy. At the next stage, countries may consider exploiting economies of scale in regulation by creating common regulators and pursuing deeper integration in other ways. Another promising area for cooperation at the regional and bilateral levels is on mode 4 (see below). Table 21.6 below summarizes how developing countries may decide on priorities in the different negotiating contexts. For examples of pre-commitment to reforms see Table 21.7.

Cooperation on Temporary Labor Mobility of Unskilled Service Providers

In practice, all WTO members have been unwilling to grant greater access for foreign individuals except for the limited class of skilled intra-corporate transferees. A trade-off among modes of delivery simply has not occurred in the Uruguay Round and, while desirable, will be difficult to achieve in the Doha Round. And also in regional (e.g. ASEAN) and bilateral agreements (e.g., USA–Chile FTA) countries have shown so far little interest in liberalizing the inward flow of the unskilled, while being relatively more open to temporary entry of the skilled.

The very heart of international trade, however, be it in goods, services, or in factors, lies in exploiting differences. The larger the differences, the larger the potential gains from opening up international trade. In the case of temporary mobility, potentially very large returns would be feasible if medium and less skilled workers, who are relatively abundant in developing countries, were allowed to move and provide their services in developed countries. The fears of most countries over the erosion of their cultural identity, problems of assimilation, and the drain on the public purse associated with mass permanent migration of less skilled workers ought to be much less pressing with temporary mobility, providing that governments correctly inform their citizens and take steps to make "temporary" credible. The other major domestic concern with unskilled

Table 21.6 Developing country priorities in alternative negotiating fora[a]

	WTO	Bilateral with the USA and/or EU (e.g. EPA)	Regional, (e.g. ASEAN, COMESA, Mercosur)
Reciprocal market opening	Abroad: Locking in openness of cross-border trade, seeking greater scope for temporary migration and transport liberalization desirable but all except the first probably infeasible in the short run.Home: Desirable and feasible to open telecom, banking, etc. on an MFN basis	Abroad: Locking in openness of cross-border trade, cooperation on temporary migration and transport liberalization desirable and may be feasible. Home: Preferential opening not necessarily desirable	Home and abroad: Reciprocally liberalizing access is desirable and may be feasible, but opening is ideally on an MFN basis.
Credibility of own reforms	Binding existing openness and pre-committing to future opening is feasible and desirable	May be feasible	May be feasible
External assistance	"Aid for trade" is desirable and may be feasible	Desirable and most likely to be feasible	Limited feasibility
Deeper integration	Infeasible in the foreseeable future	Relatively feasible but not always desirable	Regulatory cooperation in professional, financial, telecom and transport sectors, is desirable and feasible.

[a] The assessment of desirability is based on economic considerations; the assessment of feasibility, by our view of the broad political environment.

workers' mobility of any kind (permanent or temporary) is its competitive challenge to local less skilled workers. This is similar to the challenge posed to such workers in developed countries by imports of labor-intensive goods and services (e.g. online or telephone customer service) from developing countries, which has been overcome by the realization of the economic gains that trade can deliver and by policies to ease adjustment among local less skilled workers. Clearly, opening up to foreign mobile service providers needs to be carefully managed with the same sensitivity and the same sort of supportive policies that trade policy reform in goods received in the past.

A development-friendly policy and negotiating outcome regarding mobility of service providers at either the bilateral, regional, or multilateral levels would strive to ensure temporariness. On the one hand, industrial countries may be willing to accept higher numbers of unskilled workers (service providers and also others) if they could be certain that their stay was temporary. On the other hand, concerns about brain drain in

Table 21.7 Examples of pre-commitment to market reforms

Country	Pre-commitment to Liberalization in GATS schedules
LATIN AMERICA	
Argentina	No restrictions as of November 8, 2000
Grenada	Reserved for exclusive supply until 2006. No restrictions thereafter.
Venezuela	No restrictions as of November 27, 2000.
AFRICA	
Cote d'Ivoire	Monopoly until 2005, no restrictions thereafter,
Mauritius	Monopoly until 2004, no restrictions thereafter.
South Africa	Monopoly until December 31, 2003: thereafter duopoly and authorities will consider the feasibility of more licenses
ASIA	
India	Review the subject of opening up of national long-distance service in 1999, and international services in 2004.
Korea	Will raise foreign equity participation in facilities based suppliers.
Pakistan	Proposes to divest 26% to a strategic investor who will have an exclusive license for the operation of basic telephonic services for seven years.
Thailand	Will introduce revised commitments in 2006, conditional upon the passage and coming into force of new communication acts.

developing countries from the current more liberal rules for skilled labor mobility by a number of developed countries would be greatly alleviated if their move was temporary rather than permanent. The problem is that host countries cannot unilaterally ensure temporariness of unskilled mobility because repatriation cannot be accomplished without the cooperation of the source. And source countries cannot unilaterally ensure temporariness of their skilled emigration, because repatriation cannot be accomplished without the cooperation of the host—today most temporary migration mobility schemes in the OECD countries are in fact stepping stones to permanent migration.

Hence, there is a strong case for cooperation between source and destination countries in the design and implementation of migration policies, so that unskilled mobility becomes more acceptable to developed countries and skilled mobility more desirable for developing countries. The source country would need to agree to help with the selection and screening of migrants, provide necessary pre-departure training and cooperate to ensure timely return. And the host country would need to agree to repatriate (especially the skilled) by issuing visas that are not renewable except after a certain period spent back in the home country. Bilateral agreements on these lines have been successfully implemented between the Caribbean and Canada, Ecuador and Spain, and Poland and Germany.

As noted above, negotiations on the "temporary presence of natural persons" (mode 4) under the GATS have not been successful in the past and prospects in the current Doha Round are not bright. In the absence of a dramatic change in the multilateral framework that would allow addressing and agreeing on the issues discussed above, a development-friendly approach to manage service labor mobility is more easily developed in a regional or bilateral context.

VII. Conclusion

In this chapter, we have covered the scope, general obligations, rules on protection, and the unfinished agenda of the GATS. We have also addressed the growing trend towards preferential agreements, which may provide greater opportunities for achieving deeper integration of particular services sectors. Further, we have provided a brief overview of the achievements and difficulties to date of the Doha Negotiating Round. Finally, we have assessed what international negotiations may have to offer with respect to unilateral liberalization, and the context in which they are most likely to produce outcomes that support economic development.

References

Adlung, R. (2006a), 'Services Negotiations in the Doha Round: Lost in Flexibility?' *Journal of International Economic Law*, 9(4): 865–93.

Adlung, R. (2006b), 'Public Services and the GATS.' *Journal of International Economic Law*, 9(2): 455–85.

Adlung, R. and Mattoo, A. (2008), 'The GATS.' In Mattoo, A., Stern, R. and Zanini, G. (eds.) *Handbook of International Services Trade*. Oxford: Oxford University Press.

Adlung, R. (2009), 'Trade in Healthcare and Health Insurance Services: The GATS as a Supporting Actor.' WTO Staff Working Paper ERSD-2009-15.

Baldwin, R., Evenett, S. and Low, P. (2009), 'Beyond Tariffs: Multilateralizing Non-Tariff RTA Commitments.' In Baldwin, R. and Low, P. (eds.), *Multilateralizing Regionalism: Challenges for the Global Trading System*. Cambridge: Cambridge University Press.

Borchert, I. S., Gootiiz, B. and Mattoo, A. (2011), 'Services in Doha: What's on the Table? In Martin, W. and Mattoo, A. *Unfinished Business? The WTO's Doha Agenda, 2011*. Washington DC: The World Bank.

Borchert, I. and Gootiiz, B. and Mattoo, A. (2012), 'Guide to the services trade restrictions database' Policy Research Working Paper Series 6108. Washington DC: The World Bank.

Chauffour, J. P. and Maur, J. C. (eds.) (2011), *Preferential Trade Agreement Policies for Development: A Handbook*, Washington DC: The World Bank.

Devarajan, S. (2008), 'The GATS and the Health of Poor People.' In Mattoo, A., Stern, R. and Zanini, G. (eds.) *Handbook of International Services Trade*. Oxford: Oxford University Press.

Echandi, R. (2010), 'The CAFTA-DR-US Negotiations in Financial Services: The Experience of Costa Rica.' In Haddad, M.and Stephanou, C. (eds.) *Financial Services and Preferential Trade Agreements: Lessons from Latin America*. Washington, DC: The World Bank.

Feketekuty, G. (2008), 'A Guide to Services Negotiations.' In Mattoo, A., Stern, R. and Zanini, G. (eds.) *Handbook of International Services Trade*. Oxford: Oxford University Press.

Fink, C. and Molinuevo, M. (2007), *East Asian Free Trade Agreements in Services: Roaring Tigers or Timid Pandas?* Washington, DC: The World Bank.

Goncalves, M. P. and Constantinos S. (2010), 'Financial Services and Preferential Trade Agreements: An Overview'. In Haddad, M. and Constantinos, S. *Financial Services and Preferential Trade Agreements: Lessons from Latin America*. Washington, DC: The World Bank.

Global Services Coalition (2010). 'Final Communique.' Global Services Summit, Sept. 22, 2010. Available at: <http://globalservicesnetwork.com>.

Global Services Coalition (2011), 'Final Communique.' Global Services Summit, July 20, 2011. Available at: <http://globalservicesnetwork.com>.

Global Services Coalition (2012), 'Final Communique.' Global Services Summit, September 19, 2012. Available at: <http://servicescoalition.org/about-csi/global-services-summit-2012>.

Haddad, M. and Constantinos, S. (2010), *Financial Services and Preferential Trade Agreements: Lessons from Latin America*. Washington, DC: The World Bank.

Hoekman, B. and Mattoo, A. (2007), 'Regulatory Cooperation, Aid for Trade and the GATS.' *Pacific Economic Review*, 12(4): 399–418.

Hoekman, B. and Mattoo, A. (2011), 'Services Trade Liberalization and Regulatory Reform: Re-invigorating International Cooperation.' Policy Research Working Paper No. 5517. The World Bank, Washington, DC, and CEPR Discussion Papers No. 8181, London.

Honeck, D. (2011), 'Expect the Unexpected? LDC GATS Commitments as Internationally Credible Policy Indicators? The Example of Mali.' WTO Staff Working Paper ERSD-2011-07, Geneva: World Trade Organization.

Marchetti, J. A. (2008), 'Financial Services Liberalization in the WTO and in PTAs.' In Marchetti, J. A. and Martin, R. *Opening Markets for Trade in Services: Countries and Sectors in Bilateral and WTO Negotiations*. Geneva: World Trade Organization.

Marchetti, J. A. and Martin, R. (2008), *Opening Markets for Trade in Services: Countries and Sectors in Bilateral and WTO Negotiations*. Geneva: World Trade Organization.

Mattoo, A. and Payton, L. (eds.) (2007), *Services Trade and Development: The Experience of Zambia*. Washington, DC: The World Bank. Available at: <http://documents.worldbank.org/curated/en/2007/01/7572927/services-trade-development-experience-zambia> (Accessed April 2013).

Mattoo, A. and Sauvé, P. (2011), 'Services.' In Chauffour, J. P. and Maur, J. C. (eds.) *Preferential Trade Agreement Policies for Development: A Handbook*. Washington DC: The World Bank.

Mattoo, A., Stern, R. and Zanini, G. (eds.) (2008), *Handbook of International Trade in Services*. Oxford: Oxford University Press.

Roy, M. (2011), 'Services Commitments in Preferential Trade Agreements: An Expanded Dataset.' WTO Staff Working Paper ERSD-2011-18, Geneva: World Trade Organization.

Saez, S. (ed.). (2010), Trade in Services Negotiations: A Guide for Developing Countries, Washington, DC: The World Bank.

Smith, R., Blouin, C., Drager, N. and Fidler, D. (2008), 'Trade in Health Services and the GATS.'

In Mattoo, A., Stern, R. and Zanini, G. (eds.) *Handbook of International Trade in Services*. Oxford: Oxford University Press.

World Bank. (2012), Services Trade Restrictions Database. Washington, DC: The World Bank. Available at: <http://iresearch.worldbank.org/servicetrade/> (Accessed April 2013).

World Trade Organization (WTO) and Organization for Cooperation and Development (OECD) (2011), 'Aid for Trade at a Glance 2011,' *Showing Results*. Geneva: WTO/OECD.

World Trade Organization (WTO). (2011), 'Negotiations on Trade in Services,' Report by the Chairman, Amb. De Mateo, to the Trade Negotiations Committee, WTO.

CHAPTER 22

PUBLIC AND PRIVATE FOOD SAFETY STANDARDS: COMPLIANCE COSTS AND STRATEGIC OPPORTUNITIES[*]

SPENCER HENSON AND STEVEN JAFFEE

I. INTRODUCTION

THIS chapter explores the role that public and private standards play in influencing exports from developing countries, with a particular focus on the impact of food safety standards on trade in agricultural and food products. Food safety standards have been chosen because they have been the subject of considerable interest and concern as potential constraints on the efforts of developing countries to access higher value markets for agricultural and food exports and illustrate the ways in which the World Trade Organization (WTO) Agreements have attempted to discipline the use of standards as non-tariff barriers to trade (NTBs).[1] More generally, by focusing on a particular sub-set of standards, this chapter can explore the complex and interrelated ways in which standards influence trade, and the particular issues and concerns for developing countries.

The scope and focus of this chapter differ from much of the common discourse on standards and developing countries, especially in the area of food safety. Indeed, the aim is to provide a new or "fresh" perspective on this topic. To guide the reader through the arguments that are presented, the key content and messages are made clear up-front:

- Standards have become a critical institutional mechanism through which markets are governed and increasingly form a basis of competitive strategies among

[*] Prepared by Spencer Henson, University of Guelph, Canada, and Institute of Development Studies, UK and Steven Jaffee, East Asia and Pacific Sustainable Development Department, World Bank.

[1] Here "higher value" markets refer to quality-differentiated markets for agricultural and food products as distinct from traditional commodity markets for more homogeneous products.

market participants. This is particularly evident with food safety standards in both national and international markets for agricultural and food products. Thus, food safety standards are associated with modes of quality-based competition, while compliance has become a critical capacity at the firm and national levels.

- In many high value markets for agricultural and food products, food safety standards are evolving rapidly due to a wide range of interrelated demand and supply-side drivers. In particular, there is a shift towards quality meta-systems that define broad parameters for effective food safety controls and that are associated with systems of certification. At the same time, private food safety standards have come to play a more prominent role, working alongside and sometimes interrelated with public standards. Thus, for many agricultural and food products, compliance with prevailing food safety standards is the predominant challenge for developing countries attempting to maintain and/or enhance exports of agricultural and food products.

- The predominant paradigm in discourse on food safety standards and trade is based on "standards as barriers," whereby the costs of compliance and associated impacts on competitiveness act to prevent market entry and/or exclude developing country exporters from high value markets. While acknowledging the scope for food safety standards to act as barriers to trade and that developing countries are often "standards takers" rather than "standard makers," this chapter contends that standards can be catalysts for processes of capacity upgrading and form the basis of competitive positioning in high value markets.

- The challenges faced by developing countries in the context of evolving food safety standards relate to weaknesses in prevailing food safety management capacity. The sheer scale of the upgrading needed, especially in most low-income countries, suggests the need to prioritize. In many cases there is a hierarchy of food safety management functions that are most efficiently established and enhanced in an iterative manner. Indeed, the chapter defines a pyramid that distinguishes between lower and higher levels of capacity; in many cases the predominant challenge for developing countries is to put in place the lower level functions (for example establishing recognition and understanding of the role and importance of food safety standards to trade performance), on which "higher" level functions can be established. Even in countries where overall capacity is weak, however, we can often observe "islands" of enhanced capacity that support internationally competitive exports of particular agricultural and food products.

- A strategic framework is proposed for analyzing the responses of developing countries to changing standards, which is specifically applied to food safety standards. The framework suggests that the scope for "standards as catalysts" is greatest where countries, and exporters therein, are proactive in responding to the changing standards landscape. Thus, compliance is seen as both a challenge and opportunity to upgrade capacity and gain competitive advantage in key markets. Even where the associated costs of compliance are significant and have the potential to undermine established market positions, proactivity is considered the optimum strategic response; in this context; being proactive is likely to minimize compliance costs and threats to competitiveness. The notion of proactivity in compliance extends across the public and private sectors. Such a perspective suggests a new focus in capacity-building towards enhancing the scope for strategic choices.

The chapter starts by outlining the nature of standards and the institutional forms they take, before focusing specifically on food safety standards. It then describes the ways in which food safety standards are evolving and the drivers that are directing such changes. Alternative perspectives on the trade effects for developing countries of food safety standards are then examined, before proceeding to the related challenges for developing countries in the areas of establishing associated management capacity, costs of compliance, and scope for SPS diplomacy. Finally, the scope and need for a strategic perspective on compliance with standards in international trade is explored. Throughout, country- and product-specific examples are provided as illustration.

II. What are Standards?

A "standard" can be defined as a specification (or a set of specifications) that relates to a product's attributes (Sykes, 1995). The International Organization for Standardization (ISO) defines the role of a standard as "providing for common and repeated uses, rules guidelines, or characteristics for activities or their results, aimed at the achievement of the optimum degree of order in a given context" (Bureau, 2004). A broad definition of standards includes mandatory technical regulations as well as voluntary agreements on the quality characteristics of goods and services. The WTO's Agreement on Technical Barriers to Trade (TBT), on the other hand, makes a clear distinction between mandatory technical regulations and standards that are voluntary.

Standards can take a variety of forms according to their purpose/focus and the administrative form in which they are constituted. A typical classification is as follows:

- **Terminology:** Define terms used in technical and legal documents. For example, units of measurement.
- **Basic standards:** Form the basis for products and activities. For example, tolerances on limits and fits in the field of mechanical engineering, packaging materials, and so on.
- **Dimensional standards:** Allow for the compatibility and interchangeability of products and services. For example, components and units of electric motors.
- **Performance standards:** Define performance of product in terms of certain defined criteria. For example, minimum durability of light bulbs.
- **Variety reduction:** Provide for a limit in the variety of components in terms of diameter, strength, and so on. For example, standard screw sizes.
- **Testing and quality control:** Define standard methods of testing and quality control. For example, methods to determine the protein content of animal feed.

FIGURE 22.1 Forms of standards

A distinction can also be made between standards that relate to process and production methods (PPMs) and products (Bureau, 2004). Product standards focus on the characteristics of the final product (for example, size, composition, function, safety etc.), while PPM standards address the way in which a product is made. Further, PPMs encompass environmental and labor standards, as well as a host of other ethical and social issues.

Standards can be promulgated in a variety of forms that differ in the extent to which users have freedom of choice and action regarding compliance (Figure 22.1). They can be mandatory in a legal sense or required in practice because of the sheer proportion of buyers that adopt them. Alternatively, standards can be voluntary such that potential users can decide whether to comply or not and take the economic consequences associated with this decision. In reality, the distinction between these three categories is rather "fuzzy" and is thus delineated by dashed lines in Figure 22.1.

Mandatory standards, also termed technical regulations, are standards set by public institutions (in particular regulatory agencies) with which compliance is legally required. In some areas, mandatory standards predominate, particularly related to health and safety where the buyer is unable to assess reliably the safety of the product prior to purchase/use and/or the cost of doing so is high. Examples include food, drugs, toys, fire prevention, building materials, electrical appliances, gas appliances, and protection of the environment. However, even in these areas, voluntary standards are becoming more important, for example, as a means to achieve compliance with mandatory requirements and/or to demonstrate compliance.

Mandatory standards fall within the purview of the WTO, specifically the Agreements on Sanitary and Phyto-sanitary (SPS) measures and on TBT. These agreements have established international rules that aim to prevent mandatory standards from impeding trade unless they are required to achieve a legitimate objective and, in such circumstances, to ensure that the measures applied are least trade distortive.

Voluntary consensus standards arise from a formal coordinated process involving participants in a market. Members of the group attempt to achieve consensus on the best technical specifications to meet their collective needs. A variety of private organizations are involved in the establishment of voluntary consensus standards, including industry and trade organizations, professional societies, standards-setting membership organizations, and industry consortia. Use of the resulting standard is voluntary.

In many cases, voluntary consensus standards are applied by the majority of suppliers. This reflects the economic advantage associated with standardization and also customer requirements. Further, the collaborative and consultative processes through which standards are promulgated in many industrialized countries promote the use of standards.

De facto mandatory standards arise from an uncoordinated process of market-based competition. When a particular set of products or specifications gains market share, such that it acquires authority or influence, the set of specifications is then considered a *de facto* standard. Standards promulgated by private institutions, unless referenced by regulations, cannot be legally mandated. However, through market transactions, such standards can become involuntary in practice. Firms must comply with these standards if they wish to enter or remain within a particular market.

In many markets, voluntary and mandatory standards co-exist and there can be considerable interrelationships and dependencies between them. First, voluntary standards can evolve as a mechanism to facilitate compliance with mandatory standards and/or to demonstrate compliance. For example, compliance with voluntary standards can be used to demonstrate "due diligence" with respect to legal liability standards. Second, mandatory standards can reference private standards as part of their requirements. The use of standards as points of reference in regulations reinforces the voluntary use of standards, giving them additional weight. Further, it increases the responsibility of standards institutions and ensures active participation of industries in the standards setting process. When the use of voluntary standards becomes widespread, they may become embedded in mandatory standards. Thus, voluntary and mandatory standards should be seen as complementary and equal components of systems of standardization. There are strong arguments for these elements to be coordinated in order to prevent duplication of efforts and to ensure compatibility.

A further distinction can be made between the standards developed by countries, domestically, and standards developed by countries on a collective basis, whether internationally or regionally. International and regional standards can be a time and cost-effective manner in which to upgrade domestic standards and comply (at least in part) with international market requirements.[2] Thus, in a developing country context, the use of international and regional standards can be an effective strategy to meet the needs of local industries, in particular those that are exporting. However, their efficacy at the national level is dependent on the extent to which they reflect domestic needs and circumstances. In cases where international and regional standards fail to take adequate account of local conditions, costs of compliance can be greater than for standards promulgated domestically.

---

[2] This is dependent, however, on the extent to which other countries, and in particular industrialized countries, adopt international standards rather than their own domestic standards. Further, private buyers may themselves impose additional requirements over and above regulatory requirements.

Turning now to food safety in the context of international trade specifically, three broad categories of policy instruments can be employed by governments to achieve food safety protection (Figure 22.2) (Roberts et al., 1999). First, import bans prohibit the entry of a product entirely. These can apply to a product category as a whole or be restricted to supplies from particular countries/regions and/or imports at particular times of the year. These are most widely applied to products that pose a great risk to human health and where alternative methods of control are technically or economically infeasible.

Second, technical specifications define requirements that products must satisfy in order to be permitted entry. These can encompass the characteristics of the product itself, the process by which it is produced, and the manner in which it is packaged. Predefined methods of conformity assessment are specified to determine whether the product is in compliance and can be permitted to enter. Examples include maximum bacterial counts for milk and dairy products, minimum heating times in the processing of meat or fish, maximum residue levels (MRLs) for pesticides in fresh fruit and vegetables, and restrictions on the types of material that can be used when packaging comes in direct contact with the food product.

Third, information measures require certain information to be disclosed on the product label and/or control the claims that can be made about the characteristics of the product. These are most commonly applied when the risk is relatively low, can be controlled easily through the actions of the consumer, or the risk is confined to a sub-set of the population (for example in the case of allergies). Examples include instructions on how a product should be stored and prepared.

Closely associated with standards are the processes of quality assurance employed by users in order to effect and manage compliance. Indeed, a "new" category of standards has evolved that define and describe these so-called food safety management meta-systems. Most notable, in the standards regime more generally, are the ISO 9000 series of standards on quality management systems and the ISO 14000 series on environmental management systems. In certain industries, compliance with these standards is itself becoming *de facto* mandatory alongside more traditional product and process standards, such that certification to ISO 9000 and ISO 14000 is becoming widespread in both industrialized and developing countries. Specific to food safety, such meta-standards include hazard analysis and critical control point (HACCP), good manufacturing practices (GMP), good agricultural practices (GAP), and ISO 22000.

Import bans		Technical specifications			Information requirements	
Total ban	Partial ban	Process standards	Product standards	Packaging standards	Labeling requirements	Controls on voluntary claims

FIGURE 22.2 Classification of food safety measures

III. EVOLUTION OF FOOD SAFETY STANDARDS

Consumers in industrialized countries, in particular, have well-established concerns about food safety. A seemingly persistent series of "scares" over the safety of food, amplified by the media and compounded by poor risk communication, have served further to challenge the confidence of consumers in the efficacy of prevailing food safety controls (Henson and Reardon, 2005). Simultaneously, broader demographic and social trends have changed the nature of food markets in industrialized countries and altered expectations and demands with respect to the food safety and quality attributes of food (Buzby et al., 2001; Caswell, 2003; Jaffee and Henson, 2004; FAO, 2005). In response, governments and commercial firms have implemented enhanced and new forms of food safety controls, resulting in a complex and dynamic standards "landscape" that continues to evolve over time, often rapidly, and through periods of intense activity punctuated by periods of relative quiet over time. Both the extent and speed of these changes have undoubtedly posed challenges for developing countries.

Developments in the scientific understanding of food-borne hazards have changed or (maybe more accurately) added to the focus of public food safety managers. While there has been heightened attention to well-established food safety concerns (for example, microbial pathogens), measures have been implemented to address emerging hazards (for example, Bovine Spongiform Encephalopathy (BSE)), or at least hazards that have become of heightened importance on the political "radar screen" (for example, avian influenza). The efficacy of traditional approaches to food safety control, based predominantly on product standards and focusing almost entirely on the processing sector, has also been challenged. Today, there is greater scrutiny of the production or processing techniques employed along the length of supply chains (Buzby, 2003; Unnevehr, 2003) and a number of performance-based meta systems, for example HACCP, have increasingly become global food safety norms. Further, product liability has come to play a more prominent role, both through tort liability standards (Buzby et al., 2001) and the legal "duty of care" required of food sellers with respect to their legal food safety obligations, most notably the concept of "due diligence" (see, for example, Henson and Northern, 1998).

National food safety regulations are promulgated and applied within the context of the rights and obligations defined by the WTO's Agreement on SPS Measures. The objectives of the SPS Agreement are to: (1) protect and improve the current human health, animal health, and phyto-sanitary situation of all member countries; and (2) protect the members from arbitrary or unjustifiable discrimination due to different sanitary and phyto-sanitary standards. The SPS Agreement acknowledges the right of WTO members to apply measures in pursuit of food safety objectives, but aims to guard against the discriminatory and unjustified application of public standards that have the potential to impede trade in agricultural and food products. The Agreement thus permits individual nation states to take legitimate measures to protect the life and health of consumers, given the level of risk that they deem to be "acceptable," provided such measures can be justified scientifically and do not unnecessarily impede trade. However, they are required to recognize that measures adopted by other countries, although different, can provide equivalent levels of protection.

The specific rights and obligations of the SPS Agreement are detailed below:

- **Harmonization:** In many circumstances, the harmonization of SPS standards can act to reduce regulatory trade barriers. Therefore, members are encouraged to participate in a number of international standards setting organizations, most notably Codex Alimentarius, the International Office of Epizootics (OIE), and the International Plant Protection Convention (IPPC). Members are expected to base their SPS measures on the standards, guidelines, or recommendations set by these organizations, where they exist. They are, however, entitled to adopt measures that diverge from these, provided they can be justified scientifically.
- **Equivalence:** Members are required to accept the SPS measures of other members where they can be demonstrated to be equivalent, such that they offer the same level of protection. This protects exporting countries from unjustified trade restrictions, even when these products are produced under simpler and/or less strict SPS standards. However, in practice, the right of the importing country to test imported products limits the right of equal treatment.
- **Assessment of risk and determination of the appropriate level of sanitary or phyto-sanitary protection:** Members are required to provide scientific evidence when applying SPS measures that differ from international standards. This evidence should be based on a risk assessment, taking into account, when possible and appropriate, risk assessment methodologies developed by the international standards organizations. Further, members are obliged to achieve consistency in the application of SPS measures, and to avoid arbitrary or unjustifiable distinctions in the levels of protection it considers to be appropriate if the distinctions which result act to distort trade.
- **Adaptation to regional conditions, including pest- or disease-free areas and areas of low pest or disease prevalence:** The Agreement recognizes that SPS risks do not correspond to national boundaries; there may be areas within a particular country that have a lower risk than others. The Agreement, therefore, recognizes that pest- or disease-free areas may exist, determined by factors such as geography, ecosystems, epidemiological surveillance, and the effectiveness of SPS controls.
- **Transparency:** The Agreement establishes procedures for enhanced transparency in the setting of SPS standards amongst members. Member States are required to notify the SPS Secretariat of all proposed and implemented SPS measures. This information is relayed to the National Notification Authority of Member Governments. Moreover, members are required to establish an Enquiry Point, which is the direct point of contact for any other member regarding notifications of SPS measures.

- **Consultation and dispute settlement:** The Agreement establishes detailed and structured procedures for the settlement of disputes between members regarding the legitimacy of SPS measures that distort trade. An SPS Committee meets on a regular basis (three times per year) and provides a forum through which issues relating to the SPS measures applied by WTO members can be raised. More formally, members can refer issues to the WTO's dispute settlement mechanism.

Given that developing countries typically implement quantitatively lower SPS standards than developed countries, in principle the SPS Agreement should help to facilitate trade from developing to developed countries by improving transparency, promoting harmonization, and preventing the implementation of SPS measures that cannot be justified scientifically. Much of this is dependent, however, on the ability of developing countries to participate effectively in the Agreement. The Agreement itself tries to facilitate this by acknowledging the special problems that developing countries can face in complying with SPS measures and allowing for special and differential treatment.[3]

There is evidence that the SPS Agreement has had some positive impacts on the application of SPS measures by WTO members and their governance internationally. For example, it has enhanced transparency, encouraged the use of risk assessment techniques in the development of national SPS measures, and emphasized the importance of pest- and disease-free areas, both within and across national boundaries (IATRC, 2000). However, in other areas, for example equivalency, there has been less success. Whilst the SPS Committee has established general guidelines on the assessment of equivalency, there are few concrete examples of equivalency having been established between trading partners. Arguably, the equivalency provision is one of the most valuable elements of the SPS Agreement to developing countries.

In parallel with the evolution of public regulations have been moves by the private sector to address consumer concerns about food safety and to harness these concerns as a means to differentiate their products and to compete in quality-defined markets. Much of the motivation for the promulgation of private food safety standards has been the mitigation of reputational and/or commercial risks associated with the safety of food products, related in part to the level and nature of public regulatory requirements and media interest in food safety "stories," alongside quality-based modes of product differentiation (Henson, 2006a). More broadly, a wide range of market and firm-level factors motivate the implementation of enhanced food safety and quality controls (see, for example, Segersen, 1999; Henson and Caswell, 1999).

Thus, there is a rapidly increasing plethora of private "codes of practice," standards schemes and other forms of supply chain governance (Jaffee and Henson, 2004; Henson

---

[3] For example, the Agreement makes provision for the phased or time-delayed implementation of SPS measures by developing countries. And members are encouraged to provide technical assistance to developing countries to better enable the latter to upgrade capacities.

and Reardon, 2005), promulgated by private firms in the form of business-to-business standards and/or by collective private entities (Fulponi, 2005). These efforts have been especially prominent among large food retailers, food manufacturers, and food-service operators, reflecting both their considerable market power and competitive strategies based around "own" or private brands that tie a firm's reputation and performance to the safety and quality attributes of its products (Berges-Sennou and Réquillart, 2004). Thus, contemporary agri-food systems are increasingly governed by an array of interrelated public and private standards, both of which are becoming *a priori* mandatory, especially in supply chains for high value agricultural and food products.

Implicit in the trends highlighted above is significant variation in food safety standards across countries and products, and between supply chains. It is perhaps this variation that is of greatest concern to developing countries; exporters often face distinct standards in each of the markets they supply that require particular skills and competences. There are legitimate reasons why food safety standards may differ between countries (Unnevehr, 2003; Jaffee and Henson, 2004). First, distinct tastes, diets, income levels, and perceptions influence the tolerance of populations towards the risks associated with food. Second, differences in climate and the application of production and process technologies affect the incidence of particular food safety hazards. Food safety standards, in turn, reflect the feasibility of implementing alternative mechanisms of control, which itself is influenced by legal and industry structures as well as available technical, scientific, administrative, and financial resources.

At the same time, however, established control systems coupled with policy inertia may mean that countries apply differing controls in pursuit of similar objectives. For example, Henson and Mitullah (2004) contrast the varied standards that low and middle-income countries must meet in order to gain and maintain access to the US, EU, and Japanese markets for fish and fishery products. While there are some overlapping requirements, especially the increasing emphasis on application of HACCP, there remain significant differences in the food safety standards and (more profoundly) conformity assessment procedures between these markets.

Overlaid on the inter-country variation in food safety standards are the private standards of buyers that may lay down distinct requirements in terms of food safety controls and conformity assessment procedures for particular supply chains. For example, private standards regimes are interconnected with systems of second and third-party certification (Busch and Bain, 2004; Henson, 2006a). Further, exporters may face requirements beyond food safety, including official plant and animal health controls and a range of food quality standards. On the one hand, this means that developing country exporters attempting to access high value markets for agricultural and food products face a web of (sometimes interconnected or even conflicting) dynamic standards across food safety, plant and animal health, and food quality attributes within a particular export market. On the other hand, the range and stringency of these standards is likely to differ significantly between markets, perhaps affording choices to exporters in the food safety and other standards with which they must comply in the short to medium term.[4]

The overall picture, therefore, is of a multilayered food safety standards landscape with public and private modes of governance, in some cases interacting and in others applying distinct requirements. While the overall level of oversight and the number and range of standards has increased, requirements differ between countries and distinct product markets therein. Such variation can even be observed in the context of concerted attempts towards harmonization, of which the EU is perhaps the most prominent example. Thus, across EU member states a multilayered web of mandatory and voluntary standards can be observed that differ not only between countries but also between value chains within and across member states. This sets the context for concerns about the trade effects of food safety standards, to which we now turn.

IV. IMPACT ON DEVELOPING COUNTRIES IN THE CONTEXT OF TRADE

The proliferation and evolution of public and private food safety standards in industrialized countries has raised concerns about the impact on global trade in agricultural and food products (Baldwin, 2001; OECD, 2003; Josling et al., 2004). Indeed, a growing number of analytical studies have highlighted the trade reduction and/or diversion effects associated with food safety and quality standards (Beghin and Bureau, 2001; Maskus and Wilson, 2001). A specific concern, and the issue of importance here, is the potentially adverse impact on the ability of developing countries to exploit potentially lucrative markets for high-value agricultural and food products and/or their continued competitiveness in markets where they have already made inroads (Henson et al., 2000a; Unnevehr, 2000; Wilson and Abiola, 2003; Otsuki et al., 2001a, 2001b; Jaffee and Henson, 2004; World Bank, 2005). Indeed, there is a widespread presumption that food safety standards are used as a protectionist tool, providing "scientific" justifications for prohibiting imports of agricultural and food products or discriminating against imports by applying higher and/or more rigorous regulatory enforced standards than on domestic suppliers. Such concerns have become heightened as traditional barriers to trade have been reduced through progressive rounds of multilateral trade negotiations and/or preferential trading arrangements have been put in place, at least for the least-developed countries.

While there is general agreement that food safety and agricultural health measures do, indeed, strongly impact international agro-food trade, there is no consensus on the

---

[4] Elsewhere (Jaffee, 2003; Henson, 2006b) illustrate this by highlighting the diverse landscape of regulatory requirements and private standards applicable within different segments of the European market for fresh fruit and vegetables.

relative importance of individual measures in relation to other trade distorting measures, or their aggregate net effect. Indeed, enormous difficulties are involved in empirical testing of the impact of such standards on trade, for example:

- What assumptions are made about how the broad array of measures is actually enforced and how this deters or encourages potential export suppliers? Depending upon the enforcement regime, the adjustments needed by different suppliers may be either significant or modest. This variable cannot be aggregated and differs from country to country and among different industries.
- There may be many secondary and tertiary effects as a result of food safety and agricultural health requirements, for example leading to shifts in sourcing, affecting complementary and competitive goods, the spread of regulations and restrictions to other countries, and so on.
- Specific measures are frequently not a dominant determinant of observed trade flows, or lack thereof. There is a risk to ascribing shifts in trade to agro-food standards that are more fundamentally driven by other economic or technical factors.
- There are problems in defining the counterfactual situation. What would have happened in the absence of the measure? Would trade have been unimpeded or would distributors and consumers have sought product from other suppliers instead? In the absence of a (trade restricting) measure, might overall demand have declined for a product for which certain problems were identified?
- Many food safety and agricultural health measures will affect domestic suppliers as well, with varied outcomes in terms of shifts in the relative competitiveness and market share of the different players.

These and other empirical problems have led researchers to devote more attention to specific cases and to attempt to highlight the role played by (changing) food safety and agricultural health requirements on bilateral or broader multi-country patterns of trade. A discussion of some such cases is provided below.

In extreme cases, food safety standards can exclude exports from an entire country. Explicit prohibitions can be applied because an acute food safety hazard is associated with an entire sector, or because key elements of an effective food safety management system are not in place, especially within the public sector. For example, systems for the inspection and certification of product consignments may be inadequate to provide the level of assurance required by an importing country. More commonly, however, food safety standards act to preclude (or exclude) elements of a country's export sector. Most frequently, the negative effects of stricter standards are observed among smaller and more marginal agri-business firms and producers, for example, those having weak food safety controls, facing other market supply or demand-side challenges, or having difficulty raising the required capital to upgrade, especially in the context of a supply sector that is itself under-developed. More dynamic exporters and those with more developed food safety controls may be in a better position to meet the challenges of evolving food

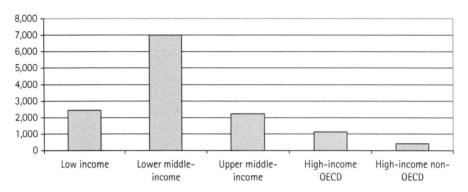

FIGURE 22.3 Number of EU border rejections of food and feed products from third countries, 2002–08

safety standards in their key export markets. However, even leading exporters can be excluded from export markets, often to the wider detriment of the sector as a whole, if the required public sector capacity is not in place or the required changes impose costs that jeopardize market competitiveness.[5]

An explicit (although admittedly crude) indicator of the ongoing difficulties faced by developing country exporters in meeting food safety standards in industrialized countries is the level of border rejections. Indeed, arguably the ultimate risk faced by exporters is that their consignments will be turned back at the border, necessitating that the implicated products are destroyed or that the additional transport costs are incurred to bring the products home or diverted them to an alternative market. For example, Figure 22.3 presents data on the number of border rejections of Third Country food and feed imports to the EU over the period 2002 to 2008. Of a total of 13,335 rejections, lower-middle income countries alone accounted for 53 per cent, most notably a relatively small number of large agricultural and food exporters to the EU including China, India, Thailand, and Vietnam (UNIDO, 2011). These countries faced rejections across many of their agri-food exports to the EU including fish and fishery products, fruit and vegetables, nuts and seeds, and herbs and spices. Other countries faced product- and hazard-specific issues, most notably Iran which had the largest number of border rejections of any developing country, most of which related to aflatoxins in nuts. Developing countries as a whole accounted for 87 per cent of EU border rejections of food and feed

---

[5] The case of Kenyan fish and fishery exports to the EU, which we explore in some detail below, provides an example of the dramatic and significant impact that food safety standards can have (Henson and Mitullah, 2004). Here, lengthy periods of restrictions were applied to exports of Nile perch over the period 1997 to 2001, related to concerns about pathogens and residues of pesticides. For example, exports of fish filets were subject to a rigorous program of microbiological tests in 1997, and subsequently an outright ban on exports to the EU. As a result, exports collapsed from in excess of 30 million euros in 1996 to less than seven million euros in 1998. Further restrictions over the period 1998 to 2001 meant that exports became virtually zero by 2000. Exports recommenced when these restrictions were finally removed in 2001 but have not recovered to the levels experienced in the mid 1990s.

products from Third Countries over the period 2002 to 2008, but only 75 per cent of imports (UNIDO, 2011).

Border rejections due to food safety or related technical compliance issues, however, account for only a modest impact on *overall trade* in agricultural and food products, including that of developing countries(Jaffee and Henson, 2004; UNIDO, 2011). Indeed, the proportion of agri-food trade that encounters official rejections is, for most agri-food commodities, probably lower than the proportion of sales that are subjected to price discounts by private buyers because of issues related to quality defects, lack of timeliness, and poor presentation. Further, the products with the highest estimated proportion of rejections are also among those for which there have been proportionally the highest rates of growth in international agricultural trade.[6]

Even within individual industries, there may be a diverse range of impacts associated with non-compliance with trade partner requirements. Thus, a blend of the effects outlined above can be observed, even in a specific context, as indicated in Box 22.1.

Figure 22.4 provides a summary of the impacts that food safety and other SPS measures have had on Indian horticultural exports during the last five years. It also notes several "looming threats" that present potential challenges for the future. The range of current and future impacts makes it extremely difficult to discern the impacts of food

Binding constraint	Temporary losses	High compliance costs	Defensive commercialization	'Looming threats'
Fresh mango entry into USA, Japan and Australia	Grape consignment rejections in Europe	Pesticide monitoring program for grapes	Processed fruit & vegetables sales by SMEs	Heavy metals in fresh & processed vegetables
	Border rejections of many small consignments of processed fruit & vegetables	Fumigation of cut flowers in Japan	Grape export strategies	Pesticides in pomegranate
		Stalled upgrading of mango pulp operations	Onion export strategies	Requirements for traceability in processed fruit & vegetables
	Onion consignment rejection in Europe	EUREPGAP and smallholder vegetable growers	Avoidance of certain cut flower markets	
	Periodic price discounts by private buyers			Environmental & social requirements in cut flowers

Source: World Bank (2007)

FIGURE 22.4 Impacts of SPS measures and challenges on Indian horticultural exports

---

[6] While the overall impact on trade from border rejections may not be very significant, for individual suppliers (or countries), the costs may be considerable, both in terms of the value of lost product and any adverse effects on the supplier's reputation.

Box 22.1 India's Horticultural Exports

World Bank analysis of India's horticultural exports (World Bank, 2007) noted that the challenges posed by standards have manifested themselves as:

- *Absolute barriers or binding constraints for accessing particular markets.* The most prominent case of this involves fresh mango and the plant health concerns of the US, Japanese, and Australian authorities.
- *Temporary losses due to rejected (and sometimes destroyed) consignments of fresh or processed product.* The most high-profile incident was the rejection of some 28 containers of grapes consigned to Holland in 2003 due to violative pesticide residues. Less visible yet more common have been the rejection of numerous (small) consignments of processed horticultural products entering the USA due to improper labelling, poor packaging, inclusion of illegal additives, and so on. In other markets, there have been a sporadic episodes of fresh produce rejections.
- *Higher consignment-specific or recurrent transaction costs* due to duplicative testing, high levels of entry point inspection, or the further treatment of goods upon overseas market arrival. This has affected the profitability of India's cut flower trade into Japan and the Netherlands and provided added costs to exporters of other products.
- *Patterns of "defensive commercialization,"* whereby firms fail to pursue opportunities for remunerative trade with certain countries or types of buyers as a result of concerns about their inability to ensure compliance with regulatory or private standards in those markets. This pattern is common in Indian horticulture, although additional factors have also weighed on these commercial strategies.

safety standards in international trade, even within one distinct product sector within one country.

An alternative and less pessimistic view, however, emphasizes the potential opportunities provided by evolving food safety standards and the likelihood that developing countries may be able to utilize these to their competitive advantage (Jaffee and Henson, 2004; World Bank, 2005). From this perspective, public and private standards are viewed, at least in part, as a necessary bridge between increasingly demanding consumers and the participation of international suppliers. Many food safety standards provide a "common language" through the supply chain and across international markets (Henson, 2006a), in turn reducing transaction costs and promoting consumer confidence in food product safety without which the market for these products cannot be maintained and/or enhanced.

The costs of complying with food safety standards (see below) may also provide a powerful incentive for the modernization of export supply chains in developing countries. Compliance with stricter food safety standards can also stimulate capacity building within the public sector and enhance the efficacy of associated institutional structures. Further, through increased attention to the spread and adoption of "good practice" in the supply of agricultural and food products, spillovers can occur into domestic food safety systems, to the benefit of the local population and producers supplying domestic and/

or regional markets, in turn promoting enhanced and wider human development in the exporting country. Thus, the associated costs of compliance are offset (at least in part) by an array of benefits, not all of which may be foreseen and easily measurable, flowing from the more general enhancement of food safety management capacity. Therefore, rather than degrading the competitiveness of developing countries, the enhancement of capacity needed to meet stricter food safety standards can potentially induce new forms of competitive advantage. While there will inevitably be losers as well as gainers, with inevitable distributional consequences that undoubtedly are cause for concern, this view suggests that the process of standards compliance can conceivably provide the basis for more sustainable and profitable agricultural and food exports in the long term. In turn, this "standards as catalysts" perspective redirects the debate to the conditions and capacities needed for developing countries to gain from evolving food safety standards and to exploit the potential opportunities in high value agricultural and food markets.

V. The Challenges for Developing Countries

The picture painted so far is that, while high value agricultural and food products may present potentially lucrative opportunities for developing countries to enhance their trade performance, complex and dynamic food standards regimes can mitigate market access. The "standards as barrier" perspective suggests that food safety requirements, predominantly in industrialized countries but increasingly also a facet of south–south trade, can act as an absolute constraint that excludes developing countries (in particular poorer and/or smaller countries) and more vulnerable supply chain actors therein. Alternatively, seeing "standards as catalysts" suggests that strict food safety standards can induce the very reforms and upgrading required to exploit high value market opportunities and can be the basis of competitive positioning in exacting markets. Regardless of the perspective adopted, however, the challenge for developing countries, and producers and agri-business firms therein, is to develop the required food safety management capacity in order to achieve compliance in a manner that preserves (or enhances) market competitiveness. From the "standards as barrier" viewpoint, the prevailing food safety management capacity in many developing countries is an "insurmountable" constraint, while the "standards as catalysts" outlook suggests that food safety standards provide the very stimuli needed to upgrade this capacity.

Food Safety Capacity

Food safety management in the context of trade involves an agglomeration of basic and more sophisticated technical and administrative functions, requiring a broad

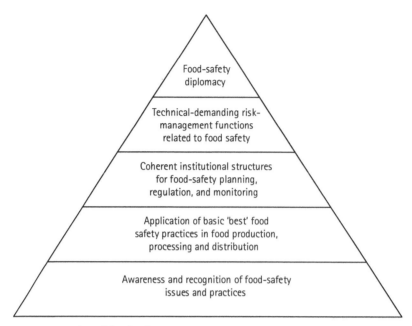

FIGURE 22.5 Hierarchy of food safety management capacity

range of skills, physical infrastructure, institutional structures and procedures, and financial resources (World Bank, 2005). It is possible, however, to cluster these functions into a pyramid-shaped hierarchy (Figure 22.5) that recognizes the dual role of capacity in the public and private sectors, and that the enhancement of capacity needs to proceed sequentially with "lower" level functions put in place ahead of those further up the pyramid (Jaffee and Henson, 2004). Functions toward the base of the pyramid represent the foundations of food safety management capacity, while those towards the top are more sophisticated functions. Further, functions higher up the pyramid gain in importance as an industry matures and encounters increasingly complex technical, administrative, and political challenges as higher value and more exacting markets are accessed.

The foundation of a system of food safety management in the context of trade, as well as more generally, is broad awareness and recognition among stakeholders of the relevance and importance of food safety to the competitiveness of the country, industry, and firm or farm, while appreciating their own role in the system. Where this awareness is weak, any attempt at regulatory enforcement will almost certainly be overwhelmed. Awareness of major food safety challenges and opportunities is needed at several levels. First, among senior agricultural and trade officials, in order to assign appropriate priorities for public programs and expenditures. Second, among the owners and managers of agricultural and food processing and exporting firms, in order to make appropriate investment decisions at the enterprise level, as well as in the industry organizations that represent them. Finally, among farmers and their employees involved in the production and handling of agricultural raw materials.

Further up the hierarchy, is the application of risk management good practices by agri-business firms and producers along the supply chain for export products, including implementation of GAP and GMP, HACCP, and so on. Positioning this element of food safety management as a critical foundation serves to emphasize the importance of the private sector in the enhancement of capacity. Too often, food safety management is regarded as primarily a public sector responsibility. At the most basic level, implementation of risk management practices along the supply chain involves training of food handlers in basic hygiene, appropriate use of chemical inputs, record-keeping, and so on. However, as supply chains become more sophisticated, capital investments in upgraded production or processing facilities may be required.

With broad awareness and the widespread application of good hygiene practices, many potential food safety risks can be managed in an effective and efficient manner. However, certain hazards cannot be controlled through and across supply chains without more systematic and broader oversight and/or collective action on the part of the public and private sectors. This includes the implementation of monitoring and surveillance systems, quarantine procedures, and emergency responsiveness, among others. Further, external systems may be needed to ensure that controls at the firm level operate effectively, and are recognized by others as efficacious. This can take the form of public regulation or certification by the public or private sectors. Such higher level functions require more sophisticated technical skills, clear and coherent procedures and administrative structures, regulatory and institutional frameworks, physical infrastructure, etc. The associated financial and human investments required to establish and maintain such systems can be considerable.

At the peak of the pyramid is food safety diplomacy. In the context of international trade, the ability to engage with trading partners is critical in order to address ongoing concerns with food safety standards. Such diplomacy can take place bilaterally, or through multilateral institutions such as the WTO. Further, engagement in the setting of international food safety standards is critical, most notably through Codex Alimentarius. While the preceding commentary suggests that private standards are becoming a more dominant mode of regulation in global supply chains, especially for high value agricultural and food products, international standards have become of much greater importance with the implementation of the SPS Agreement. Further, the Codex Alimentarius Commission has devoted more of its attention and resources to the development of common approaches to risk identification, assessment, and management in the form of meta-standards than to international standards per se. It is crucial that developing countries are engaged in these processes as they participate more actively with international high-value markets.

Costs of Compliance

It is evident that many developing countries face considerable weaknesses at all levels of the pyramid in Figure 22.5 and across both the public and private sectors (Jaffee and Henson, 2004; World Bank, 2005). In some cases, prevailing capacity may be so weak as to require very substantial human and financial resource investments in order to comply with export market food safety standards and to keep abreast of these standards over time. In other cases, the associated recurring costs may undermine exporter competitiveness. Indeed, for the poorest and smallest countries, and for small producers and agri-businesses or those who struggle to gain access to credit, these costs can be prohibitive, giving credence to the "standards as barrier" perspective. At the same time, however, it is possible to observe investments being made and institutional structures reformed as part of efforts to gain access to, or retain established positions in, high-value agricultural and food markets. Here, exacting food safety standards are acting as catalysts for the enhancement of capacity.

The trade and other economic impacts of food safety standards are related to the incidence and level of "compliance costs" incurred by the government and the private sector. Such costs are the focus of concern that developing countries are disadvantaged in complying with these standards. In some cases, the prevailing capacity may be so weak as to require very substantial investment to attain compliance. In others, incremental recurrent costs can undermine exporter competitiveness. In practice, however, the costs of compliance for developing countries are estimated.[7] This lack of data reflects the considerable difficulties associated with undertaking such calculations.

In the context of trade, compliance costs are defined as the additional costs necessarily incurred by government and/or private enterprises in meeting the requirements to comply with a given standard in a given external market. This refers not only to the costs associated with compliance per se, but with the range of strategic responses (see below) to evolving food safety standards (see World Bank, 2005). There are two key elements to this definition. First, it covers the costs that are "additional" to those that would have otherwise been incurred by the government and/or the private sector in the absence of the standard. Second, it refers to those costs that are "necessarily" incurred in complying with the standard. It is these two key concepts that create some of the problems associated with estimation of compliance costs.

In the case of regulatory requirements in international trade, costs are imposed on both the public and private sectors. In order to establish a "competent authority" recognized by trading partners, government controls may need to be strengthened and institutional structures reformed. Processors may have to upgrade their procurement systems or hygiene controls in their food processes. In some cases, the actions of the public and private sectors may substitute for one another (for example, private laboratory testing instead of public testing). In other cases, they may complement each other (for example, improved public sampling and testing procedures alongside improved safety management systems at the processing level). The costs and benefits associated with both public and private actions need to be ascertained.

---

[7] In industrialized countries, a much more extensive literature estimates the costs and benefits associated with various food safety, environmental, and other standards. See, for example, OECD (2003) and Unnevehr (2000). The one type of food safety standards where estimates of compliance costs (in particular) have been made relate to GAP.

An important distinction is made according to the level of recurrence of compliance costs. Non-recurring costs are the one-off or time-limited investments made in order to be able to achieve compliance. Typically, these include the upgrading of laboratory infrastructure and processing facilities, establishing new procedures and the associated training of personnel, and the costs of designing new management systems such as implementation of HACCP. Some of these are "lumpy" investments for which there may be significant economies of scale. Conversely, recurring costs are borne over time and include the costs of maintaining regular surveillance and laboratory testing programs and the additional production costs associated with enhanced food safety controls. For some functions, non-recurring and recurring costs are substitutes for one another. For example, an individual exporter can choose between using an external laboratory to undertake routine product and input testing, or establishing its own laboratory facilities that permit such tests to be undertaken at a lower unit cost.[8]

Recurring and non-recurring costs can impede trade in a somewhat different manner and also influence the potential benefits that might flow from alternative strategic choices related to compliance. For example, "first movers" might realize significant advantages if non-recurring costs are high and they have the resources to make needed investments ahead of their competitors. Yet, significant recurring costs can impede competitiveness by increasing unit production costs, especially where significant cost variations are borne by individual suppliers owing to local conditions.[9]

There have been a limited number of attempts to quantify the costs of compliance with export market, food safety standards faced by developing countries (see, for example, Cato and Limos dos Santos, 1998, 2000; Cato and Subasinge, 2004; Henson et al., 2000b; Herath, 2001), reflecting the inherent difficulties of deriving reliable estimates. These analyses have predominantly focused on compliance with regulatory standards, often in the context of changes in requirements that cause acute compliance problems and threaten market access. For example, as noted in Box 22.2, Henson and Mitullah (2004) and Henson et al. (2005) examine the costs incurred by the public and private sectors in complying with EU hygiene standards for fish and fishery products in Kenya and India (and specifically the state of Kerala), respectively.

In contrast to the cases of fish and fishery product exports, it is evident in some instances that compliance costs are substantial, and raise pertinent questions about the sustainability of the established capacity and longer-term industry competitiveness. An example is the efforts of the Indian grape sector to achieve compliance with stricter controls on pesticide residues in the EU (World Bank, 2007). Substantively, attempts by the Indian government and grape exporters to implement controls on pesticide

---

[8] The distinction between recurring and non-recurring costs suggests that account must be taken of the stage in the compliance process that costs are measured. Costs can be significantly underestimated if an attempt is made to estimate costs at an early stage in the compliance process at which only non-recurring costs have been borne. Conversely, there is a tendency to overestimate costs if recurring costs decline significantly over time as exporters, for example, learn to adapt to the required controls.

[9] Pertinent factors can be quite varied and include differences in infrastructure conditions and the availability of local technical and administrative services.

Box 22.2 Costs of Complying with EU Hygiene Standards for Fish and Fishery Products in Kenya and Kerala, India

During the later 1990s and early 2000s, weaknesses in hygiene standards within the fish and fishery products sectors in Kerala and Kenya cut across the public and private sectors. Common deficiencies included inadequate legislation relating to hygiene controls in fish processing, poorly defined administrative responsibilities for the approval and inspection of processing facilities and certification of exports, weak inspection systems for processing facilities (including lack of documented procedures, insufficient inspection staff, limited skills, and weak reporting), inadequate laboratory testing capacity for microbiological and chemical contaminants, and poor hygiene controls through the supply chain, including low levels of HACCP implementation. Given these prevailing weaknesses, both countries struggled to comply with stricter controls on the hygiene in the value chain for fish and fishery products implemented by the EU, and indeed faced periods during which imports were prohibited and/or enhanced border controls were applied to their products.

In India, the Export Inspection Council (EIC), the recognized competent authority for the regulation of fish exports to the EU, upgraded its laboratory facilities at a cost of around US$345,000 and implemented a rigorous inspection and laboratory-testing regime to monitor EU-approved processing facilities. It is estimated that the ongoing cost per plant of this regime was around $6,444 per annum, with most of this cost associated with ongoing testing of product samples. This implies a total annual cost of monitoring EU-approved plants in Kerala of around $341,000 in 2003, and a cost for all of India of around $876,000. As a proportion of the value of exports to the EU, however, this represents only 0.3 per cent per annum, much of which is borne by the public sector.

Within the Keralan fish-processing sector specifically, significant investments had to be made in basic infrastructure and the implementation of HACCP. The required changes varied significantly between individual processing facilities. In extreme cases, plants had to be extended or the entire layout was changed. Many plants also installed ice-making and laboratory facilities, upgraded water treatment systems, and increased chill-room capacity. Some facilities were unable to raise the capital needed to fund these investments and ceased operations. In other plants, however, prevailing hygiene standards were relatively high, and only minimal changes were needed to comply with EU requirements. Non-recurring costs of compliance ranged from US$51,400 to US$514,300, with a mean cost (weighted by volume of production) of $265,492. As a proportion of annual firm turnover in the period immediately preceding these changes, non-recurring costs ranged from 2.5 per cent to 22.5 per cent, with a weighted mean of 7.6 per cent. In 2001, there were 51 EU-approved facilities in Kerala, suggesting an overall non-recurring cost across the sector of US$13.5 million, corresponding to around 4.6 per cent of annual exports of fish and fishery products.

In Kenya, substantial investments were also required to comply with the EU's hygiene standards for fish and fishery products. Non-recurring costs borne by processing firms ranged from US$8,500 to US$128,000, reflecting the varying standards of hygiene that prevailed in the sector. As in Kerala, costs were greatest where processing facilities required major structural change in order to implement effective hygiene controls. The total costs of compliance for the fish-processing sector were estimated to have been US$557,000, with an average cost per facility of around US$40,000. While the total investments needed to comply with EU requirements only represented 1.7 per cent of annual exports valued at

Box 22.2 *Continued*

US$33.5 million, a significant number of facilities have since ceased their operations and have not managed to recoup the investments that they made.

In both the Keralan and Kenyan cases, the recurring costs of compliance with the EU's hygiene standards for fish and fishery products were significant. In Kerala, production costs increased by between 5 and 15 per cent, with a mean cost (weighted by volume of production) of 11.7 per cent. In Kenya, production costs increased by between 5 and 25 per cent, with a weighted mean of 15 per cent. Across processing operations, the highest recurring costs of compliance were typically found in facilities that also had significant non-recurring costs, suggesting that these plants had lower prevailing hygiene controls. In extreme cases, these additional costs compromised market competitiveness to the extent that firms exited the sector. There is also evidence of significant economies of scale in compliance, such that a disproportionate cost burden was imposed on smaller exporters, bringing about rationalization and concentration of the processing sector in both cases.

Table 22.1 Estimated annual cost of compliance with EU food safety requirements for Indian table grapes, 2005

Expense	Public sector	Private sector	Total
Laboratory equipment*	50,000	75,000	125,000
Pack-house upgrades*	62,500	187,500	250,000
NRC Pesticide Monitoring Management**	115,000		115,000
Pack-house approval		5000	5000
Farmer registration	32,500	32,500	65,000
Field inspector farm visits	97,500	97,500	195,000
Pesticide residue testing	341,860	341,861	683,721
Certification		25,000	25,000
Total***	699,360	764,361	1,463,721

Notes:
*Amortized over ten years & assuming only 50 per cent of costs could be attributed to residue testing for grapes.
**Excluding capital investments.
***Assuming exports of 15,000 tons, then the SPS compliance cost is US $98/ton. Assuming average FOB price is US$1.0/kg. Therefore, the cost of SPS compliance is 10 per cent. Simply the cost of residue testing not including any capital expenditures is $45/ton or 4.5 per cent of FOB value.

Source: NRC (1995).

residues were induced by a warning under the EU's Rapid Alert System for Food and Feed (RASFF) in 2003. In response, the Agricultural Product Export Development Authority (APEDA) implemented an integrated system of oversight through the grape supply chain. Significant resources were expended in implementing this system which, arguably, applied an onerous system of checks and controls on the sector. Indeed, the related costs of compliance are enormous and way out of line with broader international experience (see Table 22.1). For example, the cost to government and the private sector of pesticide residue testing alone is equivalent to 7.9 per cent of the FOB value of India's grape trade to Europe. Considering the investments that have gone into the pesticide monitoring program as well as other costs associated with the oversight of the grape supply chain, compliance costs are estimated to account for 13 per cent of this FOB value.

The overall picture presented by the studies highlighted above is of significant upfront investment that varies widely between firms according to prevailing standards and firm size. At the same time, there are examples of very major costs which threaten the long-term competitiveness of exports. While these may be the exception rather than the rule, they do have profound implications for developing countries. A critical factor influencing the level of compliance costs is the level of public food safety capacity. In some cases, firms make investments to offset weaknesses in public infrastructure, for example, lack of accredited laboratory facilities. While these costs are typically quite low as a proportion of the value of exports, suggesting a considerable potential payoff in terms of continued market access, they can act as an absolute barrier to compliance and pose a significant risk of exclusion from markets, especially for smaller producers and agri-businesses and/or firms that have problems accessing the necessary finance. At the same time, however, the impact of food safety standards needs to be examined alongside the wider constraints and problems that exporting firms face. In both the Keralan and Kenyan fish and fishery products cases discussed above, firms were already contending with excess installed capacity, constraints on supplies of raw materials, enhanced competition in export markets, and so on. Thus, the imposition of stricter food safety standards served to enhance the challenges that exporters were already facing.

A second series of studies focuses on the costs of compliance faced by exporters in supply chains that are predominantly governed by private standards regimes (see, for example, Jaffee, 2003; Garcia-Martinez and Poole, 2004). Here, the predominant focus is on firms that have already penetrated supply chains to high value markets for agricultural and food products, or that are making efforts to reposition themselves towards higher-value markets, in the context of evolving standards. In such contexts, however, distinguishing the costs of compliance with food safety standards per se from wider efforts to upgrade quality and add value, and to satisfy exacting logistics and supply requirements on the part of buyers, is problematic. Certainly, estimates of the costs of installing the necessary physical infrastructure, for example in the form of packing facilities, can be enormous. For example, Jaffee (2003) suggests that the "high-care" packing facilities of the leading fresh vegetable exports in Kenya have involved investments of up to US$5 million. It is difficult to say, however, what proportion of these costs is directly related to the food safety standards that exporters face. Indeed, this question in itself may be of little value in the context of the overall competitive positioning and challenges faced by these leading firms.

Food Safety Diplomacy

The hierarchy of food safety management functions presented in Figure 22.2 suggests that, beyond implementation of food safety management capacity within the public and private sectors in order to comply with food safety standards in international trade per se, a critical function is the ability to engage in food safety diplomacy. Indeed, the capability to engage in bilateral and multilateral relations with trading partners and in the establishment of international standards is increasingly critical for developing countries as efforts are made to gain access to high value agricultural and food markets. It is evident, however, that many developing countries are unable to participate consistently in institutions such as the WTO and Codex Alimentarius and, even where they are able to attend meetings, support their negotiating positions with the necessary scientific evidence and reasoning (Henson et al., 2001).

Perhaps a more detailed picture of the ability of developing countries to engage in SPS diplomacy, and how this has changed over time, is provided by the level of participation in the Codex Alimentarius Commission. The limited participation of developing countries in Codex has been widely documented (see, for example, Henson et al., 2001; Jensen, 2002; Walkenhorst, 2003) and indeed was recognized by the review of the Codex Alimentarius Commission in 2002 (Traill, 2002). There are some indications that levels of participation have increased over time, although they still remain worryingly low for low-income countries. At the same time, while a number of developing countries are making efforts to be "at the table" in institutions such as Codex, it is not evident that they are actively engaged in the business of these institutions in a manner through which they can represent their national interests in an effective manner (Henson and Humphrey, 2009).

VI. Exploiting Opportunities

The previous section highlighted the challenges faced by developing countries in complying with food safety standards for high value agricultural and food products. Examples were provided of countries and exporters therein that have addressed the challenges they face and managed to achieve compliance in a manner that maintains market competitiveness. On the other hand, there are countless instances where exporters have been pushed out of lucrative export markets as food safety standards are "ratcheted-up," or even prevented from getting into these markets in the first place. In many cases, both of these processes are seen to occur side-by-side. The general picture in many developing countries is of weak food safety management capacity in both the public and private sectors. At the same time, it is possible to discern "islands" of elevated (and often high level) capacity, especially within the private sector. Often such enhanced capacity has been induced by the requirements of critical export markets, giving credence to both the concepts of "standards as barriers" and "standards as catalysts," operating in proximate contexts.

Regardless of the perspective adopted on the impact of food safety standards on developing countries, the critical factor mitigating the exploitation of potentially lucrative opportunities in high-value agricultural and food markets is the establishment and maintenance of food safety management capacity. In turn, it is necessary for developing country governments and exporters to recognize effective food safety management as a core competence in competitiveness, and to consider the costs and benefits of standards compliance in their decisions over what to produce and export, and which markets to target, in the context of evolving standards and prevailing competencies and capacity. Further, the challenges posed by food safety standards in exploiting the opportunities provided by high-value agricultural and food markets must be viewed from a strategic perspective, alongside other business decisions (Jaffee and Henson, 2004; Henson and Jaffee, 2005, 2006). In many developing countries, this requires an attitudinal shift in the way agricultural and food export decisions are made, although one that is necessary more generally in the context of high value, but also very competitive, international markets.

Embedded within the challenges of complying and then "keeping up" with a highly dynamic food safety standards landscape are a plethora of strategic decisions that policymakers and agri-business firms need to make in order to manage the associated threats or opportunities (Jaffee and Henson, 2004; Henson and Jaffee, 2005, 2006; World Bank, 2005). In so doing, they must trade off the available options through which compliance can be achieved and manage the chosen processes of capacity building and adjustment. The notion of strategic options is admittedly rather novel when considering the impact of food safety standards on developing countries in the context of trade, especially if a "standards as barriers" perspective is adopted. However, in most situations developing countries and exporters do have at least some "room for maneuver" in meeting the challenges posed by food safety standards and, in turn, this provides scope for strategic decision-making. Indeed, compliance with food safety standards needs to be considered from a strategic perspective if developing countries are to exploit the opportunities provided by high value agricultural and food markets or, at the other extreme, to minimize the associated threats.

Developing countries (suppliers) can pursue one or a combination of the following types of strategies in the context of evolving standards (Figure 22.6) (Henson and Jaffee, 2008):

- *Compliance*: adopting measures to meet international standards or the requirements of one's trade partners. This might involve some combination of legal/regulatory change, the application of certain technical or other risk management approaches, implementation of testing, certification, and/or other conformity-assessment measures, and so on.
- *Voice*: seeking to influence the "rules of the game" and/or how they are implemented via participation in international standard-setting fora, communications with the

	Reactive	Proactive
Exit	Wait for standards and give up	Anticipate standards, leave particular markets or market segments, and make other commercial shifts
Loyalty	Wait for standards and then adopt measures to comply	Anticipate standards and comply ahead of time
Voice	Complain when existing standards are applied or new measures are adopted	Participate in standard creation and/or negotiate before standards are applied

FIGURE 22.6 Strategic response to food safety standards

WTO, negotiations with bilateral or regional trading partners, and/or business planning with downstream clients.

- *Redirection and exit*: altering commercial strategies to encompass sales to different countries or market segments, changes in the mix or form of products, and other maneuvers taking into account the costs and benefits of complying with different standards.

The timing and mode of strategic response, of course, can vary. Actions may be taken on a proactive or reactive basis. In the former, future requirements are anticipated and measures taken ahead of time in a manner that minimizes costs or maximizes benefits. In the latter, the players wait until the requirements are put in place and only then adopt responsive actions, perhaps hoping to limit action or at least learn from the mistakes of the "first movers." The strategy can be either defensive or offensive; the former involves measures designed to minimize the changes required; the latter involves trying to exploit an opportunity created by standards (i.e., a price premium prevailing for organic products). Box 22.3 provides an illustration of this strategic perspective on compliance with agri-food standards.

The locus of strategic response may also vary (Henson and Jaffee, 2008). Some responses may be taken by individual firms, farms, or government agencies. Other responses involve collective action, perhaps through producer or industry organizations, or inter-ministerial task forces. There is scope also for strategic response which involves public–private collaboration, or collaboration between developing country stakeholders in multiple countries.

More often than not, the strategic response by developing countries to emerging trade-related standards takes the form of reactive-defensive responses, frequently made in the context of a crisis (i.e., a trade ban or outbreak of disease). The necessary public systems and private investments are frequently not made until there is a threat of trade interruption to an important market. This is most unfortunate since, in this mode of response, both the government and the private sector will typically have fewer technical or administrative options to order to achieve compliance with the required standard,

Box 22.3 Strategic Responses of India and Kenya to EU Restrictions on Exports of Fish and Fishery Products

To illustrate how the framework presented in Figure 22.6 highlights the scope for strategic responses to evolving food safety standards, and how the application of a strategic "lens" can aid understanding of the opportunities and challenges faced by developing countries in this context, we return to the cases of fish and fishery products exports from Kerala and Kenya introduced above. Although it is not evident that a strategic approach was adopted by decision-makers in these cases, at least explicitly, it is apparent that the alternative responses to the challenges presented by stricter hygiene requirements for exports to the EU, especially within the private sector, had profoundly different outcomes.

As described above, both India and Kenya were faced with restrictions on exports to the EU because of non-compliance with hygiene standards which, although they were introduced in the early 1990s, were not rigorously enforced in both cases until the mid to late-1990s (Henson and Mitullah, 2004; Henson et al., 2005). Indeed, while some improvements had been made to hygiene controls in India, standards were significantly below those required by the EU across both countries, suggesting at the outset that the public and private sector responses as a whole were reactive. The end result in both cases was a period in which exports to the EU were restricted and longer periods of enhanced oversight of consignments at the EU border. However, while India reformed its food safety controls within the sector rapidly and exports reopened within five months, the process of upgrading controls in Kenya was protracted, and long periods of restrictions were imposed on exports (on and off) over the period 1997 to 2001. Subsequently, shrimp exports from Kerala (as well as India as a whole) have generally thrived, despite enhanced international competition, while Nile perch have continued to be challenged by on-going food safety issues alongside supply constraints and enhanced competition from neighboring countries, as well as new international competitors.

In both the Indian and Kenyan cases, it is evident that the imposition of stricter food safety standards has had a profound impact on the structure of the respective fishery export sectors, predominantly at the level of processor/exporter firms. Overall, there has been a net decline in the number of processing facilities, with significant rates of plant closure. However, at the same time competitive leading firms, most of which were proactive in responding to the imposition of stricter hygiene standards for fish and fishery products, have increased their share of exports and—at least in the case of Kerala—expanded their operations, including the installation of new processing facilities. While more marginal (and usually smaller) processors were excluded from the sector, larger and more proactive firms took advantage of their better competitive position and expanded production. Such firms poisoned themselves as "high-end" on the safety spectrum in key international fish and fishery product markets, supporting more general strategies aimed at value addition.

There was evidence of attempts at voice in both the Indian and Kenyan cases, although with very different outcomes. Having taken rapid and highly transparent actions to address the concerns of the European Commission over standards of hygiene, the Indian government was well positioned to enter into a dialogue with the EU as and when new food safety concerns arose. It is evident that the Indian government used this opportunity to good effect through its delegation in Brussels; when new concerns arose about antibiotic residues in shrimp exported from a number of Asian countries, India was one

Box 22.3 *Continued*

of the few countries that was not subject to restrictions. While Kenya responded to the initial imposition of restrictions on exports to the EU by sending a delegation of government officials and industry representatives to Brussels, the lack of concerted action to upgrade capacity in both the public and private sectors meant that this attempt at voice "fell on deaf ears."

The case of fish and fishery exports from India and Kenya illustrates the benefits of a strategic and more proactive response to food safety standards in the context of international trade at both a country and firm level. On the one hand, the aggressive response by the Indian government to achieve compliance with EU requirements, that contrasts starkly with the delayed and more defensive action of the Kenyan government, is a major factor explaining its more rapid regaining of market access. On the other hand, in both countries, it is the firms that took proactive actions to achieve compliance that have maintained and/or gained market leadership. Firms that delayed actions to achieve compliance and responded defensively have tended to perform less well and have lost their market position. At the extreme, a number of such firms exited the sector altogether.

and one's credibility in the exercise of voice may be undermined by weaknesses in the basic regulatory and private management systems for compliance.

The predominant dialogue on food safety standards with respect to developing countries—implicit in the "standards as barrier" perspective—presents a single strategic option in compliance. This can take a variety of forms, including regulatory reform, changes in production technologies, shifts in the structure of supply chains, upgrading of conformity assessment, and so on. However, all are driven by the standards that exporters are being required to meet. This approach to compliance can be implemented at the time a standard comes into force, that is, "reactively," or ahead of time in view of expectations as to how standards are likely to evolve in the future, that is "proactively." Everything else being equal, a "proactive" approach is likely to provide greater scope for the management of compliance in a manner that brings about strategic gain and minimizes any detrimental spillovers, for example in terms of industrial restructuring or associated loss of employment. This relates to the existence of "first mover" advantage, for example through earlier sunk costs or reputational effects, as well as the greater flexibility afforded by a longer compliance period (Henson and Jaffee, 2006). Further, proactive compliance provides greater scope to test and apply alternative technologies and employ varied administrative and institutional arrangements.

In practice, however, there are other strategic options beyond compliance, although these may not always be readily apparent. On the one hand, countries and/or exporters can either exit a market (i.e., choosing not to comply with the food safety standards applied in that market) or redirect commercial efforts. This implies switching customers, in the case of a private standard, or exiting particular export markets altogether. The producer and/or exporter may choose to switch to different products for which the food safety standards are less onerous. Even in the context of the overall "ratcheting-up" of food safety standards within a sector, this can afford vital additional time in which to upgrade food safety management capacity. Such a strategy might be employed where compliance will yield a fundamental loss of competitiveness and/or where profitable alternative markets exist that have less demanding standards. At the country level, it might also reflect the prioritization of resource use where more competing uses are considered of greater importance. Such a perspective regards exit or redirection not as a loser's strategy per se, but as strategic redirection in the face of institutional and competitive pressures.

In parallel with strategies of compliance and redirection, developing country governments and/or exporters can seek to influence prevailing rules or respond to new standards by negotiating or complaining. In Figure 22.6, this represents voice. This is a critical element of food safety diplomacy as depicted in Figure 22.5. For example, WTO members may raise their complaints through a counter-notification in the SPS Committee (Roberts, 2004) or engage in bilateral negotiations with their trading partners regarding the specific actions required to achieve compliance. Individual exporters may question the food safety standards being imposed by their customers and attempt to come to some compromise between their own competencies and competitive position and customer demands. As with compliance, it is more strategically advantageous to approach re-direction and voice proactively.

In the context of the two-dimensional strategic framework presented in Figure 22.6, it is argued that the most potentially advantageous strategy combines voice and proactivity. Everything else being equal, this approach is most likely to turn the challenges associated with evolving food safety standards into a competitive opportunity and to yield positive competitive gains. Conversely, the weakest approach is a combination of exit and reactivity. Indeed, there may be considerable costs associated with such an approach where sunk costs and the gains from being a "first mover" are significant.

A variety of factors will influence the viability of alternative strategic responses to evolving food-safety standards in export markets. A summary of these factors is provided in Figure 22.7 (World Bank, 2005; Henson and Jaffee, 2006). Most developing

Factor	Re-direction	Voice	Compliance
Size of firm or industry	−	++	+
Share of target market (segment)	−	++	+
Reputation for quality/safety	+	++	+
Suitability of legal/regulatory framework		++	+
Leadership/coordination within private sector		+	++
Private sector management/technical capacity	+	+	++
Clarity of institutional responsibilities/procedures		+	+
Geographic/agro-climatic factors	−/+		−/+
Circumstances (for example 'crisis' event)	++	−	−/+

FIGURE 22.7 Factors influencing availability and choice of strategic options

countries will undoubtedly be constrained in their strategic choices but, at the same time, are likely to face some degree of choice as to response.

Across countries, strategic options in the face of evolving food safety standards vary according to economic, political, and social systems, institutional structures, geographical size, and so on. More specifically, prevailing food safety management capacity will determine the speed with which public and private decision-makers can respond to new standards and the viability and cost-effectiveness of alternative responses. A country (and the exporters therein) may have very limited scope for proactivity if functions towards the base of Figure 22.5 are not in place. More generally, there are potentially significant gains to be made from generating a reputation for rigorous food safety management. Trading partners are unlikely to negotiate with suppliers that are not seen as legitimate in terms of the food safety controls they have in place. This is likely also to extend to multilateral institutions.

For individual exporters, enterprise size is a key variable in the ability to be proactive and offensive. There are frequently significant economies of scale and scope in compliance, such that unit costs are lower for larger enterprises. Economies of scale, however, are likely to be less significant for firms that are highly diversified by products and/or markets. Large enterprises may also have greater scope to negotiate on the standards they face, especially the requirements of customers, and may have easier or lower-cost access to capital. At the same time, however, the strategic options of all enterprises will be influenced by levels of managerial and technical capacity and overall organizational objectives. The reputation of the firm, the level of value-addition of products, and the degree to which products are branded are also critical factors influencing the viability of alternative strategic choices.

The size and structure of an industry and the competitive environment in which it operates will influence the strategic options that exporters face, especially their scope to be proactive. Key factors include the size of the sector, levels of integration and coordination along supply chains, level and modes of competition, installed capacity relative to operational levels, and the degree and form of industry cooperation. Even industries with a large supply base of small and medium-sized enterprises (SMEs) may be able to exert voice if there is a well-established and effective industry or trade organization. The share of key export markets commanded by the sector and existence of alternative sources of supply are also key, in that they affect the ability of government or customers that set standards to "go elsewhere" should critical suppliers choose not to comply. A key issue is also the level and effectiveness of industry leadership at the firm and industry levels. For example, leading exporters and/or producers can set an example, test newer technologies or organizational approaches, and apply pressure for overall standards in the sector to be enhanced.

The plethora of factors outlined above suggests that the strategic choices available to any one country, and to any sector or firm within that country, will vary widely. At the same time, the choices that are made within this constrained strategic environment will reflect attitudes toward standards, levels of risk adversity, and other factors, which will be reflected in strategic objectives at the country, industry, and/or firm levels (Box 22.4).

Box 22.4 Objectives in Strategic Response to Emerging Food Safety Standards

In considering possible responses to the emerging complex of food safety standards, what objectives are private entities and policymakers pursuing? Alternatively, one can ask what parameters define the "success" or "failure" of efforts to achieve compliance or otherwise respond to emerging standards. There are a number of possibilities, more than one of which may be pursued simultaneously. In the context of export-oriented horticulture, the following parameters are important:

Market access: The most obvious success measure for efforts to comply with evolving standards is the level of access to existing or new markets for agricultural and food products. This might include the value or volume of trade over time compared to some benchmark. In the case of existing markets, the benchmark might be the level of exports or market share prior to the imposition of the standard or the level of exports that is estimated to have occurred in the absence of the standard. With new markets, it might be the level of exports or market share in a comparable market for which there is a history of trade.

Benefits exceeding costs: To be considered successful, the benefits from compliance measures or other responses should clearly exceed the associated direct and indirect costs. Compliance should not be sought "at any cost." Both the non-recurring and recurring costs of compliance need to be compared with the expected flow of benefits over some defined time period in terms of the economic value of exports, spillover effects, and so on. Cost-effectiveness might be used as an alternative metric, whereby differing approaches to maintaining or achieving market access are compared against the value of a defined unit of exports. This cost/benefit calculus might vary among different private stakeholders and between these and policymakers, depending upon which costs and benefits are included as being relevant to their own decision making.

Long-term competitiveness: Aside from short and medium-term impacts on market access, it is important to recognize the effects of compliance efforts on the long-term competitiveness of an industry and the different participants therein. Indeed, a more strategic perspective on food safety standards would suggest that this is the most appropriate metric to use. Thus, compliance efforts should be judged in terms of the extent to which the compliance acts to enhance competitiveness, on a sustainable basis, in the context of prevailing competitive forces and trends.

Social inclusion/exclusion: Beyond the trade effects of efforts to comply with new food safety standards, it is important to recognize that the resultant changes to the structure and *modus operandi* of supply chains can result in the inclusion or exclusion of particular groups. Of greatest concern is the impact on vulnerable groups, for example smallholder farmers and small and medium-sized enterprises (SMEs), especially where these have become dependent on export-oriented supply chains and may have limited alternative livelihood opportunities.

Spillover effects: Efforts to comply with food safety standards for external markets can have both positive and negative spillover effects for domestic consumers and producers. These may include impacts on food safety itself, but also agricultural productivity, worker safety, and rural livelihoods. The extent of these spillovers will depend on the level of integration of supply chains and regulatory systems for international and domestic markets. Although rarely considered, the existence of such social and economic spillovers can have a significant impact on the balance of costs/benefits associated with capacity building and compliance efforts.

Box 22.4 *Continued*

These points suggest that food safety standards need to be considered from a wider strategic perspective that pervades many elements of development. Compliance decisions can have wide-ranging implications not only for market access and the efficiency of resource use, but also for the livelihood of vulnerable social groups and wider processes of economic and social change.

It is also evident that there may be trade-offs among the above objectives. Certain approaches may result in a rapid resumption of market access, yet entail considerable costs and require the exclusion of some or numerous producers and firms. In making strategic decisions regarding compliance with new food safety standards in, inevitably choices have to be made regarding the relative importance of these parameters and the trade-offs among them. To reiterate one point, maintaining and/or gaining access to lucrative export markets cannot be pursued at all cost! There is also a time element. Further, it is imperative to consider both short and long-term impacts, examining not only immediate trade flows but longer-term competitive issues and implications for social change. This suggests that a "good practice" model for standards- related capacity building should take account of all of these elements, with explicit recognition of the trade-offs that exist and are deemed acceptable/unacceptable.

This strategic approach to food safety standards in international trade is distinct from short-term "fire fighting" in response to immediate problems. While immediate problem solving is inevitable in certain contexts, for example where a new food safety risk emerges that threatens market access, all too often developing countries adopt a "fire fighting" approach when a more strategic perspective is more appropriate and might yield competitive gains that offset the associated costs of compliance. This suggests that standards-related compliance should be incorporated into broader policymaking and capacity building decisions, forming part of wider efforts to promote competitiveness in international markets. This requires that efforts to respond to food safety standards be proactive, looking ahead to how requirements are likely to change in the future and incorporating responses to longer-term development efforts.

Indeed, in the short term many developing countries may lack the confidence to move away from their more traditional compliance-based strategies and to become proactive and exhibit voice. It is only though positive experiences, perhaps shared among countries, that public and private decision-makers will recognize that they do indeed have choices, and that the most advantageous way in which to respond to the opportunities and challenges presented by food safety standards in the context of high value agricultural and food markets is to act strategically.

VII. Conclusions

This chapter has set out the challenges and opportunities related to evolving food safety standards faced by developing countries in attempting to gain and/or maintain access to high value markets for agricultural and food products. The key message is that, while food safety standards, predominantly in industrialized countries but increasingly also in the context of south–south trade, can act as a barrier to participation in high value markets, both for entire countries and for more marginal exporters therein, the challenges posed by stricter standards can be both a catalyst for the upgrading of key capacities and the basis for the competitive positioning in quality-driven markets. This is not to downplay the challenges faced by developing countries. In many countries, prevailing levels of food safety management capacity in both the public and private sectors are low, and the investments needed to achieve the standards required to access the more exacting high value markets clearly stretch (and may well exceed) limited financial and human resources. However, even where levels of capacity are generally weak, it is frequently possible to observe "islands" of highly sophisticated food safety controls, the development of which has almost always been driven by market demands. The challenge is to harness these "islands" as leaders of capacity development more generally.

A key implication of adopting the "standards as catalysts" perspective is the need to see compliance as a strategic issue, such that the opportunities and challenges are managed to competitive advantage, or at least minimum competitive disadvantage. In turn, this suggests that the focus of capacity building efforts should focus on maximizing the strategic options for developing countries and, more particularly, enhancing the scope to implement strategies that are proactive and involve voice. Arguably, however, this contrasts with the predominant approach of many donors that focuses on overcoming the immediate problems that developing countries face in complying with strict food safety standards, casting them as inevitable "standards takers." There is a need for donors, and their public and private sector counterparts in developing countries, to fundamentally rethink the ways they approach capacity development in this context.

A remaining question is what countries and agri-business firms should do if they find themselves excluded from high value markets due to weaknesses in food safety management capacity. Given the diversity of food safety standards applied within and between countries and supply chains, there is scope for the development of capacity at different speeds according to local realities and priorities. In most instances, developing country suppliers do not face an "all or nothing" choice when determining the investments or other changes they must make in order to conform with evolving food safety standards in alternative markets. Significant markets remain where food safety standards are less onerous, even in industrialized countries where in some value chains the strictest standards are applied which offer market opportunities for countries (and agri-businesses and producers therein) with lower levels of food safety management capacity. Choices then need to be made about which of these markets can and should be targeted in ways that offer the greatest competitive opportunities given food safety standards and prevailing capacities. In the longer term, however, such market opportunities are likely to diminish. They should be used by public and private decision-makers to "buy time" rather than to avoid the ultimate need to upgrade food safety management capacity.

REFERENCES

Baldwin, R. E. (2001), 'Regulatory Protectionism, Developing Nations and a Two-Tier World Trade System.' *Brookings Trade Review,* 3: 237–80.

Beghin, J. and Bureau, J. C. (2001), 'Quantitative Policy Analysis of Sanitary, Phytosanitary and Technical Barriers to Trade.' *Economie Internationale,* 87: 107–30.

Bergès-Sennou, F., Bontems, P., and Réquillart, V. (2004), 'Economics of Private Labels: A Survey of Literature.' *Journal of Agricultural and Food Industrial Organization,* 2(3): 1–23.

Bureau, J-C. (2004), *Raising the Bar on Product and Process Standards: Economic Principles.* Washington, DC: The World Bank.

Busch, L. and Bain, C. (2004), 'New! Improved? The Transformation of the Global Agri-Food System.' *Rural Sociology,* 69(3): 321–46.

Buzby, J., Frenzen, P. D. and Rasco, B. (2001), *Product Liability and Microbial Food-Borne Illness.* Washington, DC: Economic Research Service, US Department of Agriculture.

Buzby, J. (ed.) (2003), *International Trade and Food Safety: Economic Theory and Case Studies.* Washington, DC: United States Department of Agriculture.

Caswell, J. (2003), 'Trends in Food-Safety Standards and Regulation: Implications for Developing Countries.' In Unnevehr, L. (ed.) *Food Safety in Food Security and Food Trade.* Washington, DC: International Food Policy Research Institute.

Cato, J. C. and Lima dos Santos, C. A. (1998), 'European Union 1997 Seafood Safety Ban: The Economic Impact on Bangladesh Shrimp Processing.' *Marine Resource Economics,* 13(3): 215–27.

Cato, J., and Lima dos Santos, C. A. (2000). 'Costs to Upgrade the Bangladesh Frozen Shrimp-Processing Sector to Adequate Technical and Safety Standards and to Maintain a HACCP Program.' In Unnevehr, L. (ed.) *HACCP: New Studies of Costs and Benefits.* St Paul: Eagen Press.

Cato, J., and Subasinge, S. (2004), *An Overview of the Bangladesh Shrimp Industry with Emphasis on the Safety and Quality of Exported Products.* Washington, DC: The World Bank.

FAO (2005), *The State of Food and Agriculture 2005.* Rome: Food and Agriculture Organisation.

Fulponi, L. (2005), 'Private Voluntary Standards in the Food System: The Perspective of Major Food Retailers in OECD Countries.' *Food Policy,* 30(2): 115–28.

Garcia-Martinez, M. and Poole, N. (2004, 'The Development of Private Fresh Produce Safety Standards: Implications for Developing Mediterranean Exporting Countries.' *Food Policy,* 29: 229–55.

Henson, S. J. (2006a), 'The Role of Public and Private Standards in Regulating International Food Markets.' Paper presented at Summer Symposium of International Agricultural Trade Research Consortium, University of Bonn, May.

Henson, S. J. (2006b). 'Market Access and Private Standards: Case of Ghana Fruit and Vegetable Market' Paper prepared for Organisation for Economic Cooperation and Development, Paris.

Henson, S. J., and Caswell, J. (1999), 'Food Safety Regulation: An Overview of Contemporary Issues.' *Food Policy,* 24: 589–603.

Henson, S. J. and Humphrey, J. (2009), 'The Impacts of Private Food-Safety Standards on the Food Chain and on Public Standard-Setting Processes.' Report for annual meeting of Codex Alimentarius, May. Food and Agriculture Organization, Rome.

Henson, S. J., Loader, R. J., Swinbank, A., et al. (2000a), *Impact of Sanitary and Phytosanitary Measures on Developing Countries* Reading: Department of Agricultural and Food Economics, The University of Reading.

Henson, S. J., Brouder, A. and Mitullah, W. (2000b), 'Food-Safety Standards and Exports of Perishable Products from Developing Countries: Fish Exports from East Africa to the European Union.' *American Journal of Agricultural Economics*, 82(5): 1159–69.

Henson, S. J., Preibisch, K. L. and Masakure, O. (2001), *Enhancing Developing Country Participation in International Standards-Setting Organizations*. London: Department for International Development.

Henson, S. J., and Mitullah, W. (2004), *Kenya Exports of Nile Perch: Impact of Food-safety Standards on an Export-Oriented Supply Chain*. Washington, DC: The World Bank.

Henson, S. J. and Northern, J. R. (1998), 'Economic Determinants of Food-Safety Controls in the Supply of Retailer Own-Branded Products in the UK.' *Agribusiness*, 14(2): 113–26.

Henson, S. J. and Reardon, T. (2005), 'Private Agri-Food Standards: Implications for Food Policy and the Agri-Food System.' *Food Policy*, 30(3): 241–53.

Henson, S. J., Saqib, M. and Rajasenan, D. (2005), *Impact of Sanitary and Phytosanitary Measures on Exports of Fishery Products from India: The Case of Kerala*. Washington, DC: The World Bank.

Henson, S. J. and Jaffee, S. (2005), 'The Public and Private Responses to Food Safety and Quality issues and Supply Chain Governance: Implications for Developing Countries.' Paper presented at the conference 'The Role of Labelling in the Governance of Global Trade: The Developing Economy Perspective,' University of Bonn.

Henson, S. J. and Jaffee, S. (2006), 'Food Safety Standards and Trade: Enhancing Competitiveness and Avoiding Exclusion of Developing Countries.' *European Journal of Development Research*, 18(4): 593–621.

Henson, S. J. and Jaffee, S. (2008), 'Understanding Developing Country Strategic Responses to the Enhancement of Food-Safety Standards.' *The World Economy*, 31(1): 1–15.

Herath, A. (2001). *Costs of Compliance of Sanitary and Phytosanitary Requirements for Beverages and Spices in Sri Lanka*. Jaipur: CUTS.

IATRC (2000). 'The Economics of Food Safety in Developing Countries' by Spencer Henson, ESA Working Paper No. 03–19.

Jaffee, S. (2003). *From Challenge to Opportunity: Transforming Kenya's Fresh Vegetable Trade in the Context of Emerging Food Safety and Other Standards in Europe*. Washington, DC: The World Bank.

Jaffee, S. and Henson, S. J. (2004), *Standards and Agri-Food Exports from Developing Countries: Rebalancing the Debate* Policy Research Working Paper 3348. Washington, DC: The World Bank.

Jensen, M. F. (2002), *Reviewing the SPS Agreement: A Developing Country Perspective*. Copenhagen: Centre for Development Research.

Josling, T., Roberts, D. and Orden, D. (2004), *Food Regulation and Trade: Toward a Safe and Open Global System*. Washington, DC: Institute for International Economics.

Maskus, K. E. and Wilson, J. S. (2001), 'A Review of Past Attempts and the New Policy Context.' In Maskus, K. E. and Wilson, J. S. (eds.) *Quantifying the Impact of Technical Barriers to Trade: Can it be Done?* Ann Arbor: University of Michigan Press.

NRC (1995), Standards, Conformity Assessment and Trade. Washington, DC: National Research Council.

OECD (2003), *Trade Effects of the SPS Agreement*. Paris: Organisation for Economic Cooperation and Development.

Otsuki, T., Wilson, J. and Sewadeh, M. (2001a), 'Saving Two in a Billion: Quantifying the Trade Effects of European Food-safety standards on African Exports.' *Food Policy*, 26(5): 495–514.

Otsuki, T., Wilson, J. and Sewadeh, M. (2001b), 'What Price Precaution? European Harmonization of Aflatoxin Regulations and African Groundnut Exports.' *European Review of Agricultural Economics,* 28(2): 263–83.

Roberts, D. (2004), *The Multilateral Governance Framework for Sanitary and Phytosanitary Regulations: Challenges and Prospects.* Washington, DC: The World Bank.

Roberts, D., Josling, T. and Orden, D. (1999) *A Framework for Analyzing Technical Trade Barriers in Agricultural Markets.* Washington, DC: Economic Research Services, United States Department of Agriculture.

Segersen, K. (1999), 'Mandatory vs. Voluntary Approaches to Food Safety.' *Agribusiness* 15(1): 53–70.

Sykes, A. O. (1995), *Product Standards for Internationally Integrated Goods Markets.* Washington, DC: Brookings Institution.

Traill, W. B. (2002), *Report of the Evaluation of the Codex Alimentarius and other FAO and WTO Food Standards Work.* Rome: Codex Alimentarius Commission.

Unnevehr, L. (2000). 'Food Safety Issues and Fresh Food Product Exports from LDCs.' *Agricultural Economics,* 23: 231–40.

Unnevehr, L. (2003), 'Food Safety in Food Security and Food Trade: Overview.' In Unnevehr, L. (ed.) *Food Safety in Food Security and Food Trade.* Washington, DC: International Food Policy Research Institute.

UNIDO (2011), *Meeting Standards, Winning Markets. Trade Standards Compliance 2010* Vienna: United Nations Industrial Development Organization.

Walkenhorst, P. (2003), 'The SPS Process and Developing Countries.' Paper presented at the conference Agricultural Policy Reform and the WTO: Where are we Headed? Capri, Italy.

Wilson J. and V. Abiola. (2003), *Standards and Global Trade: A Voice for Africa.* Washington, DC: The World Bank.

World Bank (2005), *Challenges and Opportunities Associated with International Agro-Food Standards* Washington, DC: The World Bank.

World Bank (2007), India's Emergent Horticultural Exports: Addressing Sanitary and Phytosanitary Standards and Other Challenges. Report # 36178-IN. South Asia Region.

CHAPTER 23

....

INTELLECTUAL PROPERTY RIGHTS: ECONOMIC PRINCIPLES AND TRADE RULES[*]

....

CARSTEN FINK

I. INTRODUCTION

....

ONE of the most significant developments of the Uruguay Round of Trade Negotiations (1986–94) was the inclusion of intellectual property rights (IPRs) issues on the agenda of the multilateral trading system. The resulting Agreement on Trade-Related Aspects of Intellectual Property Rights (TRIPS) is one of three pillar agreements, setting out the legal framework in which the World Trade Organization (WTO) has operated since the end of the Uruguay Round.[1]

For the multilateral trading system, TRIPS marked the departure from narrow negotiations on border measures such as tariffs and quotas toward the establishment of multilateral rules for trade-affecting measures beyond borders. This move reflected underlying trends in international commerce. Due to the growth of trade in knowledge and information-intensive goods, the economic implications of imitation, copying, and counterfeiting had in many industries become at least as relevant for international commerce as conventional border restrictions to trade.

[*] Senior Economist, World Bank Institute, World Bank Office in Geneva (at the time of writing this paper). This module is an expanded and updated version of Fink (2006). Comments from Steve Charnovitz, Philip English, Roumeen Islam, Gianni Zanini, and an anonymous reviewer on an earlier draft are gratefully acknowledged. The views expressed here are personal and should not be attributed to the World Bank.

[1] The other two pillar agreements are the Multilateral Agreement on Trade in Goods and the General Agreement on Trade in Services (GATS).

Yet the TRIPS negotiations on intellectual property were marked by significant North–South differences. Developed countries, which host the world's largest intellectual property-producing industries, were the key advocates for comprehensive minimum standards of protection and enforcement of IPRs. By contrast, many developing countries, which saw themselves mostly as a consumer of intellectual property, felt that stronger standards of protection would serve to limit access to new technologies and products, thereby undermining poor countries' development prospects.

Not surprisingly, IPRs remain one of the most controversial topics in the WTO. The implementation of the TRIPS standards of protection has raised concerns about adverse development implications, particularly in the area of pharmaceuticals. These concerns have prompted WTO members to clarify and amend certain TRIPS rules. At the same time, the new generation of free trade agreements (FTAs) concluded in the past ten years has led to the adoption of new IPRs standards, especially in agreements involving the USA. In addition, technological developments and new business models are challenging the premise of the traditional intellectual property regime, leading to a continuous adaptation of policies at the national level.

What are the key economic trade-offs related to the protection of IPRs? How has policymaking evolved since the end of the Uruguay Round? This chapter offers a short introduction into the economics and law of intellectual property protection. [2] In particular, the chapter will review the main instruments used to protect intellectual property (Section II), the key economic trade-offs of stronger IPRs (Section III), the basic provisions of the TRIPS Agreement (Section IV), recent IPRs developments affecting access to medicines in developing countries (Section V), and the intellectual property disciplines found in free trade agreements (Section VI). Section VII summarizes the key messages.

II. WHAT ARE INTELLECTUAL PROPERTY RIGHTS?

Intellectual property broadly refers to creations which result from intellectual activity in the industrial, scientific, literary, and artistic fields. Over the course of history, different legal instruments for protecting intellectual property have emerged. These instruments differ in their subject matter, extent of protection, and field of application, reflecting society's objective to balance the interests of creators and consumers for different types of intellectual works. Table 23.1 provides an overview of the different IPRs instruments.

---

[2] Several sections of this chapter draw from Primo Braga, Fink, and Sepulveda (2000), Fink and Primo Braga (2001), Fink (2005a, 2005b), and Fink and Reichenmiller (2005). These papers as well as Maskus (2000) and World Bank (2001) offer a more extensive treatment of the material covered in this chapter.

Table 23.1 IPRs: Instruments, subject matter, fields of application, and related international agreements

Type of IPR	Instruments of protection	Subject matter	Main fields of application	Major international agreements
Industrial property	Patents, utility models	New, non-obvious inventions capable of industrial application.	Manufacturing, agriculture	Paris Convention (1883), Patent Cooperation Treaty (1970), Budapest Treaty (1977), Strasbourg Agreement (1971), TRIPS
	Industrial designs	Ornamental designs	Manufacturing, clothing, automobiles, electronics, etc.	Hague Agreement (1925), Locarno Agreement (1979), TRIPS
	Trademarks	Signs or symbols to identify goods and services	All industries	Madrid Agreement (1891), Nice Agreement (1957), Vienna Agreement (1973), TRIPS
	Geographical indications	Product names related to a specific region or country	Agricultural products, foodstuffs, etc.	Lisbon Agreement (1958), TRIPS
Literary and artistic property	Copyrights and neighboring rights	Original works of authorship	Printing, entertainment (audio, video, motion pictures), software, broadcasting	Berne Convention (1886), Rome Convention (1961), Geneva Convention (1971), Brussels Convention (1974), WIPO Copyright Treaty (1996), WIPO Performances and Phonograms Treaty (1996), Universal Copyright Convention (1952), TRIPS
Sui generis protection	Plant breeders' rights	New, stable homogenous, distinguishable plant varieties	Agriculture and food industry	Convention of new Varieties of Plants (UPOV, 1961), TRIPS
	Integrated circuits	Original layout designs of semiconductors	Microelectronics industry	Washington Treaty (1989), TRIPS
Trade secrets		Secret business information	All industries	TRIPS

Note: All international treaties except TRIPS and the Universal Copyright Convention are administered by the World Intellectual Property Organization. Years shown refer to the year in which an agreement was first adopted.

Source: Primo Braga et al. (2000).

Patents are legal titles granting the owner the exclusive right to make commercial use of an invention. To qualify for patent protection, inventions must be new, non-obvious, and commercially applicable. The term of protection is usually limited to 20 years, after which the invention moves into public domain. The patent system is one of the oldest and most traditional forms of IPRs protection. Almost all manufacturing industries make use of the patent system to protect inventions from being copied by competing firms. Since the early 1980s, patents have also been granted for agricultural biotechnology products and processes and for certain aspects of computer software. The United States has granted patents for business methods, though the limits to what type of business methods may be eligible for patent protection are legally uncertain.[3]

As an adjunct to the patent system, some countries have introduced *utility models* (or petty patents). The novelty criteria for utility models are less stringent. They are typically granted for small, incremental innovations. Their term of protection is far shorter than for "regular" invention patents (typically four to seven years). Similarly, *industrial designs* protect the ornamental features of consumer goods such as shoes or cars. To be eligible for protection, designs must be original or new. They are generally conferred for a period of five to fifteen years.

Trademarks are words, signs, or symbols that identify a certain product or company. They seek to offer consumers the assurance of purchasing what they intend to purchase. Trademarks can endure virtually indefinitely provided they remain in use. Almost all industries use trademarks to identify their goods and services. The use of trademarks has turned out to be of high significance in certain consumer goods industries, such as clothing and watches. Similar to trademarks, *geographical indications* identify a product (e.g., wine or olive oil) with a certain city or region.[4]

Copyright protects original works of authorship. Copyright protection differs from patent protection in that copyright solely protects the expression of an intellectual creation, whereas the ideas or methods advanced in the title can be freely copied. Copyright protection typically lasts for the life of the author plus 50 to 70 years. It is applicable to literary, artistic, and scientific works. During the past decade, copyright protection has also developed as the main form of protection for computer software. Rights related to copyright—sometimes referred to as *neighboring rights*—are accorded to phonogram producers, performers, and broadcasting organizations. Their term of protection typically varies between 50 and 95 years (see Box 23.1 below). Limits to copyright and neighboring rights exist in certain "fair use" exemptions, such as educational or library use or for purposes of criticism and scholarship.

---

[3] In June 2009, the United States Supreme Court agreed to hear a case that is set to clarify what types of business methods will qualify for protection. See "High Court to Hear Case on Patent Limits," *Bloomberg News*, June 2, 2009.

[4] Geographical indications and trademark typically do not involve any inventive or creative input. They therefore do not fall within the definition of intellectual property as a product of intellectual activity. As will be further explained below, the protection of these two types of IPRs is also rooted in a different economic rationale.

Box 23.1 Should the Copyright Term for Sound Recordings be Extended from 50 to 95 years?

In anticipation of a review by the European Commission on the length of copyright protection, a policy debate emerged in the United Kingdom in 2005 on the desirability of extending the copyright term for sound recordings from 50 to 95 years. Members of the UK music industry called on the UK government to support such an extension. They further demanded that the extended copyright term apply prospectively (to any future sound recordings) as well as retrospectively (to past sound recordings eligible for protection under the new rules).

The arguments advanced by the supporters of an extended copyright term included the following:

(1) *Parity with other countries.* In particular, in the United States, the 1998 Copyright Act extended the term of protection for sound recordings to 95 years.

(2) *Incentives to invest in new music.* Increasing the copyright term would encourage more investments, because performers and producers would have more time to recoup any initial outlay.

(3) *Maintaining the UK's positive trade balance.* In 2004, the UK sound recording industry showed a trade surplus of £83.4 million, earning £238.9 million in export incomes. Stronger copyright protection would solidify the UK's competitiveness in this industry.

How convincing are these arguments? An independent inquiry into the UK intellectual property regime requested by the UK Treasury was charged to consider these arguments and offer policy recommendations. The inquiry was led by Andrew Gowers—the former editor of the *Financial Times* newspaper—and its final report was published in December 2006.

Drawing on economic analysis, the Gowers report rejected each of the arguments in support of copyright term extension. With respect to the first argument, the report noted that the term of copyright protection is only one factor determining the royalties that artists and recording companies receive. Equally important is the breadth of protection. In the US, certain exceptions to copyright law allow 70 per cent of eating and drinking establishments and 45 per cent of shops to play music royalty free, generating no income for performers and producers. The report conjectures that total royalties received in the EU may be no less than, and may even be more than, those received in the USA.

More fundamentally, the report sheds serious doubts on the hypothesis that copyright term extension would create significant incentives for the supply of new music. Additional royalty flows from extended protection would only materialize after 50 years. To measure their incentive effect today, these flows must be discounted. Estimates suggest that prospective term extension would increase the net present value of total royalty flows by less than 1 per cent. Moreover, retrospective extension of the copyright term would not add any additional investment incentive whatsoever. Investment decisions are made on the basis of expected future returns rather than those already received. Where producers have access to capital markets, future investment decisions will be unaffected by the length of protection of current works.

Finally, the report disbelieved that term extension would serve to strengthen the UK's positive trade balance and, in fact, argued that extension would have a negative effect on the trade balance. Due to the territorial nature of copyright, term extension would not

Box 23.1 *Continued*

apply to music produced in the UK but performed abroad. However, it would apply to music produced abroad and performed in the UK. Even though the UK sound recording industry is extremely successful, 43 per cent of the UK market consists of international repertoire. In combination, term extension in the UK would cause little additional inflows, but would increase remittances abroad.

In light of these considerations, the Gowers report recommends that the European Commission retain the length of protection on sound recordings and performers' rights at 50 years and that intellectual property rights should not be altered retrospectively. Notwithstanding this recommendation, the European Commission pushed ahead with a proposal for copyright extension. Following several years of debate, the European Parliament approved in April 2009 a compromise proposal that foresees the extension of copyright for sound recordings from 50 to 70 years. However, as of May 2009, this legislation was not yet adopted by the Council of Ministers and, according to press reports, still faces opposition from a number of EU member states.

Source: Gowers Review of Intellectual Property (2006), available at <http://www. hm-treasury.gov.uk/media/583/91/pbr06_gowers_report_755.pdf>; "MEPs back 70-year copyright" EuropeanVoice.com (<http://www.europeanvoice.com/article/2009/04/meps-b ack-70-year-copyright/64701.aspx>).

Besides these traditional forms of IPRs, ongoing technological change and the unique characteristics of certain industries and products have led to additional, so-called *sui generis* forms of protection. *Layout designs for integrated circuits* protect producers of semiconductors. Protection is limited to the design of an integrated circuit and does not restrict reverse engineering of a semiconductor. In this regard, protection of layout designs is similar to copyright. However, the term of protection is shorter than under copyright—typically ten years. Title holders have the right to prevent unauthorized reproduction, importation, sale, or other distribution of the layout design for commercial purposes. *Exclusive rights to test data* submitted to regulatory agencies have been granted in the pharmaceutical and chemical industries. Companies that first submit these data can, for several years, prevent competing firms from using the same data to obtain own marketing approval.

Plant breeders' rights (PBRs) protect new plant varieties that are distinct from existing varieties, uniform, and stable. Exclusive rights, in principle, include the sale and distribution of the propagating materials for a minimum of 15 years. PBRs are typically subject to two general exemptions: the *research exemption*, which permits the use of a protected variety as a basis for the development of a new variety; and the *farmers' privilege*, which gives farmers the right to reuse seeds obtained from their own harvests. With the advent of biotechnology, however, many breeders in industrial countries are increasingly using the regular patent system for protecting agricultural products and processes. Breeders enjoying patent protection can not only prevent their competitors from using their protected material for breeding purposes, but can also prevent farmers from reusing harvested seed.

Finally, the protection of *trade secrets* is part of many countries' IPRs systems. Trade secret protection differs from other forms of protection in that it does not grant an explicit title to the creator of an original work. Instead, it protects businesses from the unauthorized disclosure or use of confidential information. Such confidential information includes inventions not yet at the patenting stage, ways of organizing business, client lists, purchasing specifications, and so on. In agriculture, breeders rely on trade secrets to protect hybrid plant varieties, if they can be kept secret. Copying through reverse engineering does not infringe trade secret laws. In essence, all industries possessing secret business information rely on trade secret protection to guard their intangible assets.

These legal instruments are just one of the pieces that form a national system of intellectual property protection. Also crucial to the system's overall effectiveness are the institutions administering these instruments, the mechanisms available for enforcing IPRs, and the rules regarding the treatment of non-nationals.

The administration of IPRs is most significant in the area of patents, industrial designs, trademarks, and plant breeders' rights. To obtain protection for these types of intellectual property, applicants have to submit their intellectual creations to a national IPRs office, which examines their eligibility for protection. Copyright and neighboring rights protection typically applies automatically upon creation of the intellectual work, although for evidentiary purposes authors may choose to register their works at copyright offices.

The enforcement of IPRs relies on a country's judicial system. Title holders fight infringement of their exclusive rights in front of courts. To immediately stop infringing activities, they can request seizures or preliminary injunctions. If the claim of infringement is verified by trial, courts can demand the payment of punitive charges to the infringed title holder (or secret holder in the case of trade secrets).

IPRs are created by national laws and therefore apply at the level of each jurisdiction, independent of such rights granted elsewhere. Accordingly, nations must reach accommodation as their residents seek protection for their intellectual works abroad. Numerous international treaties to promote cooperation among states in the protection of intellectual property have been negotiated over the last 100 years (see Table 23.1). These treaties are administered by a specialized agency of the United Nations—the World Intellectual Property Organization (WIPO). They typically require their signatories to follow national treatment in the protection of IPRs (equal treatment of nationals and non-nationals) and facilitate the registration of intellectual property titles in foreign jurisdictions. But for the most part they do not promote harmonized standards of protection.

III. The Economics of Intellectual Property Protection

Why do governments extend legal protection to intellectual property? From an economic perspective, one can broadly classify the various forms of IPRs into two categories: IPRs that stimulate inventive and creative activities (patents, utility models, industrial designs, copyright, plant breeders' rights, and layout designs for integrated circuits) and IPRs that offer information to consumers (trademarks and geographical indications). IPRs in both categories seek to address certain failures of private markets to provide for an efficient allocation of resources.

Patents, Copyright, and Related Rights

IPRs in the first category resolve inefficiencies in markets for information and knowledge. As opposed to, say, an automobile, information and knowledge can be copied easily once first put on the market. This characteristic is inherent in what economists refer to as "public goods." As the name suggests, public goods are usually not provided by private markets. Profit-oriented firms have little incentive to invest in the production of public goods, as third parties can free ride on the good once it is first produced. In the specific case of information and knowledge, if creators of intellectual works cannot protect themselves against imitation and copying, they have little economic incentive to engage in inventive or creative activities, as they cannot recoup any expenditure incurred in the process of creating new information and knowledge.

Patents and copyrights offer a solution around this dilemma, as they prevent freeriding on intellectual assets by third parties and thereby create an incentive to invest in research and development (R&D) and related activities. Because the fruits of inventive and creative activities—in the form of new technologies and new products—push the productivity frontiers of firms in an economy, patents and related instruments are often seen as important policy tools to promote economic growth.

At the same time, IPRs in this first category are considered as only "second-best" instruments of economic policy. This is because the exclusive rights of patents and copyrights confer market power in the supply of the protected good to the title holder, which poses a cost to society in that firms can charge prices above marginal production costs. In theory, governments can adjust the length and breadth of protection such as to maximize the net benefit that accrues to society from new knowledge and literary and artistic creations, while taking into account the distortion that arises from imperfectly competitive markets. In practice, such a welfare maximization exercise is complicated by the fact that the societal value of new intellectual creations is typically not known in advance and different sectors may require different levels of protection. Actual patent and copyright regimes are often the outcome of history, rules of thumb, and the influence of vested interests. Still, economic analysis can play an important role in decisions on the strength of IPRs—as illustrated by the recent debate in the UK on the extension of the copyright term (see Box 23.1).

Even though patents and copyright are only considered second-best, policymakers see these instruments as superior to government-funded research and artistic creation, as decisions about inventive and creative activities are decentralized and market driven. Government bureaucrats are only imperfectly informed about society's technology needs, whereas such information is conveyed by market signals. Notwithstanding these considerations, the public sector in middle- and high-income countries does finance and conduct R&D in areas ignored or neglected by private markets. In particular, this is the case for basic scientific research and areas of technology to which societies attach special importance despite the lack of private demand (for example, aerospace, defense, or neglected diseases).

Patents and copyrights also impact on the diffusion of new knowledge and information. On the one hand, patent and copyright protection has a negative effect on diffusion to the extent that third parties are prevented from using proprietary knowledge. For example, some commentators argue that companies with strong intellectual property portfolios in the electronics and biotechnology industry may stifle follow-on research, as competing innovators cannot—or only at a high cost—access key technologies and fundamental research tools.

At the same time, IPRs can play a positive role in diffusion. Patents are granted in exchange for the publication of the patent claim. In return for temporary exclusive rights, inventors have an incentive to disclose knowledge to the public that might otherwise remain secret. Although other agents may not directly copy the original claim until the patent expires, they can use the information in the patent to further develop innovations and to apply for patents on their own. Moreover, an IPRs title defines a legal tool on which the trade and licensing of a technology can be based. Protection can facilitate technology disclosure in anticipation of outsourcing, licensing, and joint-venture arrangements. The IPRs system can thus reduce transaction costs and help create markets for information and knowledge.

Governments and academics have long thought to assess how effective the patent system really is in promoting industrial innovation and technology diffusion. In 1958, an economist named Fritz Machlup (1958) conducted an investigation on behalf of the US Congress into the functioning of America's patent system and concluded:

> If we did not have a patent system, it would be irresponsible, on the basis of our present knowledge of its economic consequences, to recommend instituting one. But since we have had a patent system for a long time, it would be irresponsible, on the basis of our present knowledge, to recommend abolishing it.

The effectiveness of the patent system remains a controversial topic to date. Few economists would disagree that the patent system has been a stimulus to innovation over the past decade. At the same time, few economists would say with confidence that today's patent system strikes the optimum balance between innovation incentives and competitive access to new products and technologies.

Trademarks and Geographical Indications

Trademarks and geographical indications resolve inefficiencies that result from a mismatch of information between buyers and sellers on certain attributes of goods and services. Nobel Prize-winning economist George Akerlof (1970) first pointed out that markets may fail when consumers have less information than producers about the quality of goods. Uncertainty about quality will make consumers reluctant to pay for high quality goods, eroding incentives for companies to invest in quality. Trademarks can help reduce—though not completely eliminate—this uncertainty. They identify a product with its producer and its reputation for quality, generated through repeat purchases and word of mouth. Trademarks thus create an incentive for firms to invest in maintaining and improving the quality of their products. Trademarks can be considered as first-best tools of economic policy, in the sense that they do not confer any direct market power and can co-exist with competitive markets. The presence of a trademark does not restrict imitation or copying of protected goods as long as they are sold under a different brand name.

Advertising-intensive consumer products, or so called status goods, constitute a special group within products bearing trademarks. For these types of goods, the mere use or display of a particular branded product confers prestige on their owners, apart from any utility derived from their function and physical characteristic. Since in this case the brand name plays a central role in firms' product differentiation strategies, it is no surprise to find that owners of well-known brands often register up to 40 or more different trademarks to deter competing firms from entering their "brand space." Market research reports regularly put the value of well-known brands at billions of dollars. For instance, in a 2008 ranking published by *Business Week*, Coca-Cola was estimated to be the most valuable brand, estimated to be worth $67 billion, followed by Microsoft, IBM, General Electric, and Intel.[5] Status value is also associated with certain agricultural products protected by geographical indications, such as sparkling wine from the French Champagne region or ham from the Italian city of Parma.

In the case of status goods, brands can confer substantial market power to producers. In contrast to patents and copyrights, however, market power is not created by trademark ownership per se, but rather by heavy investments in marketing and sales promotion. In addition, firms with valuable brands may not necessarily generate "supernormal" profits. Even though prices may be above marginal production costs, firms have to bear the costs of fixed marketing investments. Typically, the resulting market structure for many status goods industries can be characterized as monopolistically competitive: firms have a monopoly within their brand space, but have to compete with the brands of close substitute products.

The welfare consequences of status value associated with certain goods are complex, and few generalizations can be made. For example, status value may stem from exclusive consumption, or, in other words, from the fact that only a selected group of consumers enjoys them. This interdependency between consumers inside and outside the exclusive group suggests that firms' marketing activities can make some consumers better off and others worse off (Grossman and Shapiro, 1988).

---

[5] See < http://www.businessweek.com/magazine/toc/06_32/B399606globalbrands.htm>.

IPRs in Open Economies

If one moves from a closed economy to an open economy, additional considerations arise. Consider the case of a small economy, in which most intellectual property titles are owned by foreign residents. This economy may be better off by weak standards of protection, if this leads to lower prices for goods and technology and the global incentives for the creation of new products and technologies are not much reduced (Deardorff, 1992). To put it differently, if a hypothetical small economy with little intellectual property ownership introduced patent rights from one day to another, the main effect would be a transfer of rents to foreign title holders, with little benefit to the local economy. At the same time, if a small country has special technological needs not present in other countries, such as drugs to fight country-specific diseases, it has a stronger incentive to protect foreign intellectual property (Diwan and Rodrik, 1991).

An additional consideration is that IPRs are likely to affect the international diffusion of new technologies. On the one hand, one might argue that countries that host few creative industries may benefit from weak IPRs protection, as it would allow them to imitate foreign technologies and thus build technological capacity. For example, in the early 1970s India abolished patent protection for pharmaceutical products and subsequently experienced rapid growth of its pharmaceutical industry (Fink, 2001). On the other hand, it is not always possible to imitate a technology without the participation of the firm that originally developed it. In these cases, countries may be compelled to protect IPRs to offer incentives for technology transfer to foreign intellectual property holders.

International technology transfer occurs through a variety of channels: trade, foreign investment, and international licensing. Economists have in recent years attempted to empirically link the extent of trade, investment, and licensing activities to the degree of intellectual property protection in developing countries. While measurement problems are inherent in any such assessment, several empirical patterns have been established.[6] First, international trade generally seems to respond positively to the degree of IPRs protection and more so in the case of middle-income countries than low-income countries. However, this effect is surprisingly absent in the case of high technology products. One explanation is that high technology products may be more difficult to imitate than other products. Another is that high technology companies may choose to invest in countries with stronger protection rather than export to these countries.

Second, and confirming the last point, firm-level studies suggest that intellectual property policies affect the extent and nature of investments undertaken by multinational enterprises. At the same time, relative to other factors determining foreign

---

[6] Fink and Maskus (2004) review the empirical literature on the linkages between IPRs and trade, investment, and licensing decisions in greater detail. See also Branstetter et al. (2006) for a prominent recent study on the link between IPRs reforms and the activity of multinational enterprises. Note that most of the arguments on the open economy effects of IPRs presented here apply mainly to patents, copyrights, and related forms of protection.

investment decisions, IPRs seem to be of relatively minor importance. To illustrate, China has attracted vast amounts of foreign investment, even though multinational companies and foreign governments regularly complain about weak intellectual property enforcement in the country. Finally, the cross-border licensing of technology is found to respond positively to the degree of IPRs protection in the destination country. This is not surprising, given the central importance legal protection for firm-to-firm technology transactions. At the same time, little is known about how the formal transfer of IPRs affects knowledge diffusion and productivity growth in the receiving countries.

IV. The TRIPS Agreement

The TRIPS Agreement is a multilateral WTO agreement and, as such, is applicable to all 153 members of the WTO.[7] It is also binding for every country that accedes to the WTO. The Agreement's general obligations require countries to apply the principles of national treatment (same treatment of foreign title holders and domestic title holders) and most favored nation treatment (same treatment of foreign title holders regardless of their country of origin).

Unlike the IPRs treaties administered by WIPO (see above), TRIPS sets minimum standards of protection with respect to all forms of intellectual property: copyright, trademarks and service marks, geographical indications, industrial designs, patents, layout designs of integrated circuits, and trade secrets.[8] In respect of each of these areas of intellectual property, the Agreement defines the main elements of protection, namely, the subject-matter to be protected, the rights to be conferred, and permissible exception to those rights. For the first time in an international agreement on intellectual property, TRIPS addresses the enforcement of IPRs by establishing basic measures designed to ensure that legal remedies will be available to title holders to defend their rights. The approach taken by the Agreement is to set general standards on, among other things, enforcement procedures, the treatment of evidence, injunctive relief, damages, and provisional and border measures. The TRIPS Agreement also requires WTO members to make publicly available all laws, regulations, final judicial decisions, and administrative rulings related to the Agreements' subject matter.

In principle, the provisions of TRIPS became applicable to all signatories by the beginning of 1996 and are binding on each WTO member. Certain transition periods applied to developing countries and economies in transition, but those expired on January 1, 2005. Many developing countries (e.g., Mexico, South Korea) strengthened their intellectual property regimes before the coming into force of the TRIPS

---

[7] As of June 2009.

[8] The Agreement makes reference to several of the conventions listed in Table 23.1, requiring WTO members to adhere to certain principles of these conventions.

Agreement, such that no or only few adjustments were necessary to comply with its provisions. For others (e.g., Brazil, India) certain changes to intellectual property laws have been made since 1996, as these countries have faced the end of the transition periods outlined above.

Least-developed countries (LDCs) still receive special treatment under TRIPS. The original agreement granted them a ten-year transition period that was to expire at the end of 2005. However, recognizing the economic, financial, and administrative constraints of LDCs, WTO members in 2005 agreed to extend the implementation deadline for LDCs until July 1, 2013.[9]

TRIPS has made disputes between WTO members with respect to the Agreement's obligations subject to the WTO's integrated dispute settlement procedures. WTO disputes are always state-to-state disputes. In other words, disputes are not about individual IPRs infringement cases, but are about disagreements between governments on whether a country's laws and regulations meet the TRIPS requirements. In case a WTO member is found to violate its obligations, complaining governments obtain the right to impose trade sanctions in the form of punitive tariffs. Since 1996, there have indeed been more than 20 TRIPS-related disputes between WTO members. Interestingly, only around one-third of these disputes involved a defendant from a developing country. Most disputes are between developed country members, especially between the United States and the European Union.[10]

Economic Benefits and Costs of TRIPS

As mentioned at the outset, the signing of TRIPS has generated much controversy about its economic implications for developing countries. Proponents of the Agreement have argued that stronger IPRs will stimulate creative industries in developing countries and promote foreign direct investment, with an overall positive development outcome. Opponents of TRIPS have claimed that the Agreement will forestall developing countries' access to new technologies, lead to higher prices and rent transfers from poor to rich countries, and impose high implementation costs in resource-constrained environments. As always, the truth lies somewhere in between these two polar views.

Developing countries indeed host inventive and creative industries that stand to benefit from stronger IPRs. However, these industries can mostly be found in middle-income countries, rather than the least-developed countries.[11] The empirical evidence discussed above on the link between Foreign Direct Investment (FDI) and IPRs,

---

[9] Notwithstanding this transition period, LDCs are required to meet the national treatment and most favored nation treatment obligations of TRIPS. In addition, as will be discussed in Section V, a longer transition period for LDCs applies to patents for pharmaceutical products.

[10] See <http://www.wto.org/english/tratop_e/dispu_e/dispu_subjects_index_e.htm>.

[11] The TRIPS Agreement requires developed country WTO members to provide incentives to enterprises and institutions in their territories for the purpose of promoting and encouraging technology transfer to least-developed countries. However, the Agreement does not spell out the nature and extent of such incentives.

suggests that the mere strengthening of an intellectual property regime is unlikely to result in a dramatic increase in inflows of foreign investment. At the same time, past reform experiences suggest that stronger IPRs can positively impact on domestic enterprise development and foreign investment, if they are complemented by improvements in other aspects of the investment climate.[12] By signaling a country's commitment to internationally binding rules, TRIPS can make a positive contribution in this regard—though it is difficult to assess the quantitative importance of this contribution.

Turning to the costs of TRIPS, it is first important to point out that the Agreement, in principle, did not require the extension of patent protection to products and technologies that did not receive protection prior to the Agreement's implementation. Information and knowledge that were in the public domain at the time TRIPS requirements became effective will continue to be in the public domain.[13] The implementation of the Agreement has therefore not led to actual price rises of previously existing products and related rent transfers, because patent protection only applies to new products and technologies entering the market.[14] Still, as the market share of newly protected products and technologies increases over time, prices above marginal production costs and associated rent transfer are a cause for concern—especially in the case of pharmaceutical products, as will be further explained in the next section.

As for the implementation of the Agreement, a number of commentators have argued that TRIPS poses significant institutional and financial challenges for developing countries. For example, based on figures from World Bank assistance projects, Finger and Schuler (1999) put the cost of upgrading intellectual property laws and enforcement in Mexico at $30 million. For many resource-constrained governments in poor countries, implementation costs of this magnitude would likely impose a significant burden on public sector budgets and draw away resources available for other development priorities.

At the same time, it can be questioned whether the $30 million figure from Mexico is a realistic estimate of TRIPS-related implementation costs. The underlying World Bank project in Mexico was not aimed at implementing the TRIPS Agreement (the project was completed before the coming into force of TRIPS) and mostly consisted of activities not directly mandated by TRIPS, such as staff training, computerization of the patent and trademark office, and the creation of a specialized intellectual property court. Indeed, it is important to point out that the institutional obligations of TRIPS accommodate the weaker institutional capacities of developing countries. For example, while TRIPS sets certain principles on rights enforcement, it does not require members to redistribute scarce law enforcement resources towards the enforcement of IPRs. Similarly, in the area of rights administration, TRIPS only requires that IPRs are administered such as to

---

[12] See the review by Fink and Maskus (2004).

[13] Certain exceptions to this principle apply in the case of copyright and neighboring rights.

[14] The World Bank (2001) presents estimates of rent transfers associated with the TRIPS Agreement. However, they should be regarded as hypothetical and interpreted with caution, as they do not take account of the fact that knowledge related to products and technologies for which patents were previously unavailable will remain in the public domain.

avoid "unwarranted delays" in the grant or registration of an IPR. Finally, the Agreement calls on developed country WTO members to provide technical and financial assistance to developing and least-developed countries to support the development of IPRs laws and institutions.

Importance of Flexibilities

Although the TRIPS Agreement lays the foundation toward higher standards of protection for intellectual property rights on a global scale, it leaves its signatories with important flexibilities in designing national IPRs regimes. It is important for governments to carefully consider alternative ways of implementing provisions in the TRIPS Agreement that only set a broad standard of protection and choose the options that are most suited to domestic needs.

For example, the criteria used for determining the novelty, non-obviousness, and usefulness of patentable inventions can be defined differently across countries. Thus, a WTO member may deny patent protection for, say, business methods that are frequently claimed to involve only a minor inventive step. TRIPS also does not require countries to extend patent protection to computer software, and it expressly allows for the exclusion of plants and animals from patentability.[15]

Countries are free to override the exclusive rights of patents by granting so-called compulsory or government use licenses (government authorizations to use a patent without the patent holder's consent). TRIPS only imposes certain conditions on the use of such licenses, including that they be considered on their individual merits, that "adequate remuneration" be paid to rights holders, and that prior efforts are undertaken to obtain a voluntary license from the right holder. Importantly, the latter requirement can be waived " ... *in the case of a national emergency or other circumstances of extreme urgency or in cases of public non-commercial use.*"[16]

In the area of copyright, TRIPS allows for important leeway in defining fair use exemptions to strike a balance between the interests of copyright producers and the interests of the general public.

TRIPS does not address the question of so-called parallel trade. In some jurisdictions, IPRs holders have the right to block the importation of products that they have placed for sale in a foreign market. In other jurisdictions, IPRs holders do not have such a right and parallel imports can be an important means of creating price competition for products such as books, CDs, or pharmaceuticals. Under TRIPS, countries are free to allow or disallow parallel importation.

Additional flexibilities exist in many other areas of TRIPS. As already pointed out, bilateral FTAs or WTO-plus commitments in accession agreements may reduce these

---

[15] Article 27.3(b) exempts "plants and animals other than micro-organisms, and essentially biological processes for the production of plants or animals other than non-biological and microbiological processes."

[16] See TRIPS Article 31.

flexibilities. It is important for governments to carefully assess whether the benefits of "TRIPS-plus" standards outweigh their costs and defend their interests in the course of trade negotiations.

TRIPS in the Doha Development Agenda

Several intellectual property issues are the subject of discussions in the current multilateral trading round—the Doha Development Agenda (DDA). The three most prominent discussion areas relate to IPRs and public health (see next section), geographical indications, and bioresearch.

In the area of geographical indications (GIs), the TRIPS Agreement has already established certain standards of protection. WTO members must prevent GIs from being used by non-original producers in a way that would mislead the public as to the geographical origin of a good or would constitute an act of unfair competition. A higher level of protection is reserved for GIs relating to wines and spirits, for which members have to prevent the use by non-original producers of a GI even where the true origin of the good is made clear. At the same time, the TRIPS Agreement allows for certain exceptions to these rules, notably when a GI has become part of the common language in a certain member country—such as the term "china" for porcelain wares.

Discussions on GIs in the DDA have consisted primarily of two elements: the establishment of a multilateral system of registration for GIs and the extension of the higher level of protection to products other than wines and spirits. The main demandeurs for stronger disciplines include the European Union and Switzerland. But several developing countries also see themselves as having "offensive" interests in this area—including Bulgaria, Georgia, India, Kenya, Mauritius, Sri Lanka, Thailand, and Turkey. Members with less ambitious interests in strengthening GI protection are often associated with the "New World"—which refers primarily to countries in the Western hemisphere.

WTO members have put forward several explicit negotiating proposals on the design of a multilateral GI register. However, deep divisions remain on the scope of the new registration system and the legal effect registered GIs would have in the national jurisdiction of member countries. Even less progress has been made on the question of GI extension, where WTO members still disagree on whether there exists a negotiating mandate for such a move in the first place.

In the area of bioresearch, DDA discussions have centered on the proper use of genetic resources and traditional knowledge. The TRIPS Agreement came into force four years after more than 160 countries signed up to the UN Convention on Biological Diversity (CBD)—an outcome of the 1992 Earth Summit in Rio de Janeiro. That Convention calls for the conservation of biological diversity and the fair and equitable sharing of the benefits from the use of genetic resources. Ever since, there have been concerns about possible tensions between these two treaties.

Genetic resources can serve as inputs for research and development of new products and production methods. Some WTO members worry that the TRIPS Agreement has inadequate safeguards against so-called "bio-piracy"—the acquisition of patent rights for biological material (and related traditional knowledge) simply taken from one country's biological resources and without inventive effort. In addition, they argue that TRIPS insufficiently promotes the fair and equitable sharing of benefits when bio-prospecting activities lead to the commercialization of new products. The 2001 Ministerial Declaration launching the DDA calls for a review of the relationship between the TRIPS Agreement and the Convention on Biological Diversity (CBD). The scope of this review also extends to the protection of traditional knowledge.

Since then, discussions at the WTO have gone into considerable detail. A group of developing countries (Brazil, Cuba, Ecuador, India, Pakistan, Peru, Thailand, Venezuela, and others) have argued for a requirement to disclose the source and origin of genetic resources and traditional knowledge in patent applications. This group also calls for patent holders to submit evidence that they have obtained "prior informed consent" for using genetic resources and traditional knowledge and that benefits are shared in a fair and equitable manner. Where non-compliance with these requirements is discovered after the grant of patents, those patents should be revoked.

Developed countries stress that they do not see a conflict between the TRIPS Agreement and the CBD. Still, the European Union has come out to support an international disclosure requirement of the source and origin of genetic resources and traditional knowledge, but opposes patent revocation in case of non-compliance. The United States, in turn, opposes a disclosure obligation, claiming that such a move would introduce uncertainty into the patent system. It argues that there are other mechanisms to prevent the erroneous grant of patents, including the use of searchable databases of genetic resources and the examination of relevant information already submitted by patent applicants. The United States also opposes the submission of evidence proving "prior informed consent" in patent applications, favoring instead a contractual approach outside the patent system to promote the fair and equitable sharing of benefits.

In an important negotiating development, proponents of stronger GI protection and advocates of a disclosure requirement for genetic resources formed a coalition in advance of the "mini"-ministerial meeting in July 2008. They put forward a set of 'draft modalities' that pool the negotiating demands in the two areas. Even though more than 100 WTO members support these "draft modalities," they face stiff opposition from other members—led by the United States—and the outcome of these discussion remains uncertain.

V. IPRs and Access to Medicines

In few other sectors is the role of patents as important—and as controversial—as in the pharmaceutical industry. Research-based pharmaceutical companies invest heavily in the development of new drugs, which is a risky and lengthy process. At the same time, new chemical entities can easily be imitated by competing firms, unless these chemical entities are protected by patent rights.

The extent to which innovative drug companies have pricing power depends critically on the therapeutic efficacy of a new medicine and the availability of substitute products that compete with this medicine. For some drugs, the pricing power can be substantial. This is revealed when drug patents expire and competing producers—so-called generics companies—enter the market. For example, the wholesale price of Pfizer's blockbuster drug Prozac fell from $240 to less than $5 per bottle within six months after patent expiry in the United States in 2001.[17]

The TRIPS Agreement requires WTO members to protect patents without discrimination as to the field of technology, which means that countries are obliged to grant 20-year patent protection for pharmaceutical products and processes. This represented a significant shift in a number of developing countries such as Brazil, India, and Thailand that previously allowed generics producers to freely copy medicines protected by patents in other countries. Those medicines—including important drugs classified by the WHO as essential medicines—will continue to be available generically at competitive prices. However, the share of patented drugs that has been or will be introduced to developing country markets is bound to increase, though the effect will only be felt gradually. Even though TRIPS came into force in 1996, it usually takes 8–10 years from the grant of the patent for a new medicine to be introduced to the market.[18]

The shift in global pharmaceutical patent rules has raised concerns that greater pricing power by pharmaceutical companies would adversely affect access to medicines in poor countries. These concerns were brought to the fore by the spreading HIV/AIDS pandemic in large parts of the developing world. Treatments in the form of anti-retroviral drugs became available in the second half of the 1990s, but initially these drugs were priced at levels unaffordable to poor people and health systems in the developing world. However, the introduction of generic versions of these drugs— marketed by producers in developing countries in which they were not patent protected—contributed to a steep price decline, starting in 2000 (see Figure 23.1).

Responding to concerns that the TRIPS patent rules could undermine access to medicines in poor countries, members of the WTO issued a Declaration at the Ministerial Meeting in Doha, Qatar in 2001. In this Declaration, WTO Members agreed that "*the TRIPS Agreement does not and should not prevent members from taking measures to protect public health.*" It reaffirms the right of WTO members to employ compulsory

---

[17] As reported by Frontline documentary "The other drug war," June 19, 2003.

[18] In principle, the TRIPS Agreement allowed developing countries to delay the introduction of pharmaceutical product protection until 2005. However, a convoluted negotiating compromise during the Uruguay Round required countries—such as India—that chose to make use of this transition period to grant "exclusive marketing rights" to patent application filed in the interim. Effectively, most pharmaceutical products that were at the stage of patenting between 1996 and 2005 benefit from TRIPS-style patent protection in developing countries.

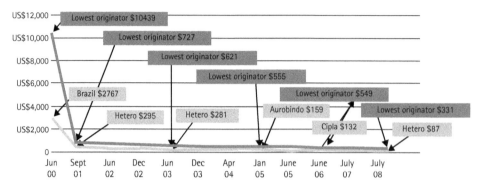

FIGURE 23.1 The effects of generic competition
Price for sample of anti-retroviral triple-combination

Notes: Sample combination consists of stavudine (d4T), lamivudine (3TC), nevirapine (NVP). Originator refers to the patent holding company or its licensee. Cipla, Aurobindo, and Hetero are generic pharmaceutical manufacturers based in India.

Source: Doctors without Borders, "Untangling the Web of Price Reductions." 11th Edition. Available at <http://www. doctorswithoutborders.org>.

and government-use licenses to override the exclusive rights conferred by patents. Moreover, for least-developed countries, it delayed the implementation of TRIPS with respect to pharmaceutical patents until 2016 (with the possibility of further extensions).

Granting a compulsory license to a local producer may be an effective strategy to promote generic competition in developing countries that have the capacity to manufacture pharmaceuticals. For example, well-developed pharmaceutical industries can be found in Brazil, China, India, or Thailand. Yet many other developing countries—especially the least developed countries in Africa—do not possess pharmaceutical manufacturing capabilities. These countries can effectively use the compulsory licensing option only if they are allowed to import generic drugs. Yet there was legal uncertainty in the original TRIPS Agreement over whether such importation would be allowed if the drug were patented in the exporting country. The "Doha Declaration" acknowledged the difficulties countries with insufficient or no manufacturing capacity face in effectively using the compulsory licensing mechanism and called for negotiations " ... *to find an expeditious solution to this problem.*"

After almost two years of negotiations, WTO Members decided in August 2003 on a mechanism that creates a framework for the importation of generic drugs produced under a compulsory license. This mechanism includes several safeguards intended to minimize the risk that drugs destined for poor countries leak into rich countries' pharmaceutical markets. The 2003 Decision was formally integrated into the TRIPS Agreement in 2005.[19] Several developing and developed country WTO

[19] The amendment of the TRIPS Agreement will only take legal effect once two thirds of WTO members have formally accepted it. As of May 2010, 29 countries have notified their acceptance (see <http://www.wto.org/english/tratop_e/trips_e/amendment_e.htm>). In any case, until the TRIPS amendment comes into force, the August 2003 Decision has full legal effect.

members have implemented legislative changes that allow for the export of generic drugs under terms consistent with the amended Agreement. The new system has only been used once in 2007 for exports from Canada to Rwanda. This seemingly rare use of the system has generated debate on whether its safeguards and procedural requirements are too onerous, thus deterring companies and member states from using it.[20]

As pointed out above, most medicines in developing countries have been free of patents, such that there has been little need to issue compulsory licenses. More recently, however, several developing and least-developed countries have issued compulsory or government use licenses on selected anti-retroviral drugs, including Brazil, Ecuador, Ghana, Malaysia, Mozambique, Thailand, and Zambia. In early 2007, Thailand also issued a government use license for a drug fighting heart disease.[21] In addition, the threat of permitting the production of competing generic medicines has led pharmaceutical companies to offer the drugs at cheaper prices themselves. This was arguably the case when some in the US government advocated the grant of a compulsory license on the patented drug Ciprofloxacin during the 2001 anthrax crisis. Similarly, the pharmaceutical company Roche offered a 40 per cent price reduction on its AIDS drug Viracept to Brazil, after the government publicly announced in 2001 that it would issue a compulsory license to a local laboratory (Fink, 2005a).

The dilution of patent rights through the exercise or threat of compulsory licenses invariably reduces incentives for research-based pharmaceutical companies to invest in new drugs—particularly those fighting diseases mostly found in poor countries. At the same time, this reduced incentive effect is arguably small. In 2003, North America, the European Union, and Japan alone accounted for 88 per cent of the $466 billion of global pharmaceutical sales. The low-income countries with the heaviest disease burden probably account for less than 1 or 2 per cent of global sales (Fink, 2005a). It is therefore important to find alternative incentive mechanisms and funding sources to encourage more developing-country specific R&D.

The World Health Organization took up this issue in 2006 by forming a special Working Group on Public Health, Innovation and Intellectual Property, charged with finding ways to promote research into diseases disproportionately affecting developing countries. After much deliberation, the Sixty-First World Health Assembly approved a "Global Strategy and Plan of Action" in May 2008, which sets forth a number of recommendations to policymakers. These recommendations range from strengthening public sector research to the adoption of more novel tools such as innovation prizes. Subsequent discussions at the WHO have focused on the implementation and monitoring of the Global Strategy.[22]

[20] See <http://www.wto.org/english/news_e/news10_e/trip_02mar10_e.htm>.
[21] See <http://www.cptech.org/ip/health/cl/recent-examples.html>.
[22] See <http://www.who.int/phi/en/>.

VI. TRIPS-Plus Provisions in Recent FTAs[23]

Since the end of the Uruguay Round, there has been a rapid proliferation of bilateral and regional FTAs. From 1950 to 1995, less than three of these agreements were on average notified annually under the General Agreement on Tariffs and Trade (GATT). Since 1995, this number has jumped to 11 agreements per year. Between January 2004 and February 2005 alone, the WTO received 43 notifications, setting a historical record.[24]

A number of the "new generation" FTAs have established rules for the protection of intellectual property that go beyond the minimum standards set by the TRIPS Agreement. These so-called TRIPS-plus provisions have to date been most ambitious in FTAs negotiated by the United States, though certain TRIPS-plus elements can also be found or are envisaged in FTAs negotiated by the European Union (EU) and the European Free Trade Association (EFTA).[25]

TRIPS-Plus Provisions in US FTAs

For the US, the establishment of strong rules for the protection of IPRs is a key offensive market-access interest—supported by private-sector constituents for whom the export of intangible assets is commercially gainful. Indeed, the Trade Promotion Authority, under which these agreements were negotiated, explicitly states as a negotiating objective to promote intellectual property rules that "… *reflect a standard of protection similar to that found in United States law.*" US trading partners generally have more defensive negotiating interests in intellectual property, but are willing to commit to stronger intellectual property rules as a quid pro quo for concessions in other areas—most notably, preferential access to US markets for agricultural and manufactured goods.

Table 23.2 offers an overview of the US FTA landscape, focusing on the new generation of agreements negotiated after 2000. The 12 agreements negotiated so far include provisions on all types of intellectual property instruments and the mechanisms available to enforce exclusive rights. Even though the detailed TRIPS-plus elements differ from agreement to agreement, there are certain common elements.[26]

All US FTAs contain provisions that strengthen the protection of IPRs for pharmaceutical products. Most agreements include a requirement to extend the patent term for

---

[23] For a more detailed treatment of this subject, see Fink (2009).

[24] See Crawford and Fiorentino (2005). These figures underestimate the number of concluded FTAs, as numerous agreements have not (or not yet) been notified to the WTO.

[25] In a related development, requests for stronger IPRs protection have been placed on countries that are negotiating accession to the WTO (e.g., Russia and Ukraine). Even though TRIPS is the primary WTO benchmark on IPRs, existing members of the WTO have demanded in the past TRIPS-plus commitments—similar to what is found in FTAs—as a condition of entry into the WTO.

[26] See Fink and Reichenmiller (2005) for a more detailed overview.

Table 23.2 Recent US free trade agreements

FTA signed and approved by US Congress	FTA signed, but not yet approved by US Congress	FTAs currently being negotiated
Jordan (2001)	Colombia Korea Panama	Malaysia
Singapore (2003)		Thailand
Chile (2003)		Southern African Customs Union
Morocco (2004)		(SACU)
Australia (2004)		United Arab Emirates
DR-CAFTA (Dominican Republic,		Free Trade Agreement of the
Costa Rica, El Salvador, Guatemala,		Americas
Honduras, Nicaragua, 2005)		Trans-Pacific Strategic Economic
Bahrain (2006)		Partnership (Brunei, Chile, New
Oman (2006)		Zealand, Singapore)
Peru (2007)		

Source: United States Trade Representative (<www.ustr.gov>).

delays in obtaining authorizations to market new drugs and to make patents available for new uses of known products. In addition, several TRIPS-plus provisions limit the ability of governments to introduce competition from generic producers. First, some agreements limit the use of compulsory licenses to emergency situations, anti-trust remedies, and cases of public non-commercial use. Second, most FTAs prevent marketing approval of a generic drug during the patent term without the consent of the patent holder—an issue on which TRIPS does not impose any obligation. Such a rule may render compulsory licensing ineffective as patent holders could still object to a competing generic drug being marketed. Third, most FTAs mandate the protection of test data submitted to regulatory agencies through exclusive rights. Again, such exclusive rights may pose an obstacle for governments to effectively use compulsory licensing, because generic suppliers may find it prohibitively expensive to generate their own test data for seeking marketing approval. Finally, several agreements introduce restrictions on the parallel importation of pharmaceutical products, effectively preventing the import competition from patented medicines sold more cheaply abroad.

In the area of copyright, most US FTAs extend the copyright term from life of author plus 50 years to life of author plus 70 years. They also include provisions governing the protection of literary and artistic works in digital form, largely based on the US Digital Millennium Copyright Act of 1998. Thus, FTA signatories must have measures against circumventing so-called technological protection measures—devices and software developed to prevent unauthorized copying of digital works. In addition, FTAs establish rules on the liability of Internet Service Providers (ISPs) when copyright infringing content is distributed through their servers and networks.

US FTAs expand on the enforcement obligations of the TRIPS Agreement. To begin with, most US FTAs do not allow countries to invoke resource constraints as an excuse to not comply with specific enforcement obligations (a flexibility available under TRIPS).

At the same time, some of the specific enforcement requirements of the FTAs create additional institutional obligations. For example, as in the case of TRIPS, the FTAs require customs authorities to stop trade in counterfeit and pirated goods. But TRIPS only requires these measures for imported goods, whereas most FTAs mandate border measures for imported and exported goods and, in some cases, even transiting goods. Moreover, several FTAs mandate a stronger deterrent against IPRs infringement—for example, by considering certain forms of end-user piracy a criminal offense.

In addition to the rules contained in the intellectual property chapters of the FTAs, IPRs are subject to separate investment disciplines. As no multilateral agreement on investment exists at the WTO or elsewhere, these bilateral investment rules break new ground. IPRs are explicitly included in the definition of investment under these rules. Thus, the agreements' specific investment disciplines apply, in principle, to government measures affecting the intellectual property portfolios of foreign investors. A special feature of bilateral investment disciplines is that they allow for direct investor-to-state dispute settlement, whereby investors can seek arbitration awards for uncompensated expropriation (though no investment dispute involving intellectual property has been initiated so far).

An important shift in the US negotiating stance towards FTAs took place in 2007. Over time, the adoption of TRIPS-plus standards in US FTAs received much criticism by Non-governmental Organizations (NGOs) and selected US lawmakers, particularly in the area of pharmaceuticals. With Democrats winning both houses of Congress in the November 2006 elections, the Administration and Congressional leadership started to negotiate a new trade framework. The resulting May 2007 Bipartisan Agreement sets out flexibilities that roll back some of the pharmaceutical TRIPS-plus provisions outlined above.

Specifically, it turns the obligation to grant patent term extension for delays in obtaining marketing authorization into a voluntary option that governments "may" choose to adopt. Similarly, drug regulators would not be required any more to deny marketing approval based on a drug's patent status. Governments would only be required to make available certain mechanisms to allow patent holders to effectively enforce their rights.[27] Crucially, the Agreement creates an express exception to test-data exclusivity rules for measures to protect public health. In other words, it removes any legal uncertainty about countries' ability to make effective use of compulsory licensing.[28]

The Bipartisan Trade Deal only applied to those US FTAs that had been signed by the Administration, but not yet ratified by Congress. In May 2007, these were the FTAs with Colombia, Korea, Panama, and Peru. However, only the US–Peru FTA has since then gained congressional approval. That said, the Deal marks an important shift in US trade policy towards more sensitivity of public health concerns in global IPRs rules.

---

[27] For instance, drug regulators need to give general notice of submissions of applications for marketing approval, so that patent holders have the opportunity to discover products that may infringe on their products.

[28] See Roffe and Vivas-Eugui (2007) for a more detailed review of the May 2007 Bipartisan Agreement.

TRIPS-Plus Provisions in FTAs Negotiated by the EU and EFTA

As is the case for US FTAs, there is no single IPRs model in the agreements negotiated by the EU and European Free Trade Association (EFTA).[29] Nevertheless, one can broadly discern three areas of emphasis in the IPRs obligations established by these agreements. First, they require signatories to ratify a number of WIPO administered treaties—notably those that are not incorporated into the TRIPS Agreement. Second, most of the EU and EFTA agreements include provisions on the reciprocal protection of geographical indications related to wines and spirits. These agreements often contain comprehensive lists of geographical names that can only be used by original producers in the concerned jurisdictions.[30] Third, some of the EFTA agreements feature exclusive rights for pharmaceutical test data submitted to regulatory agencies—similar to what is found in US FTAs (see above).

Fourth, the recent EU-CARIFORUM EPA agreement introduces new obligations on IPRs enforcement that go beyond the TRIPS Agreement. Interestingly, many of these obligations are rooted in the EU's internal approach towards upholding IPRs, notably Directive 2004/48 on the Enforcement of Intellectual Property Rights and two Regulations dealing with border measures.[31] The EU has put forward even more ambitious proposals on enforcement in its current negotiations with the Association of South East Asian Nations (ASEAN) bloc and the Andean Community, though one has to await the outcome of these negotiations for a definite assessment (Fink, 2011).

Finally, the EFTA–Colombia FTA sets new ground by incorporating, for the first time, a mandatory disclosure requirement in patent applications of the origin or source of genetic material (see the discussion in Section IV). This agreement shows that the negotiation of IPRs chapters in FTAs can also advance the interests of developing countries.[32]

Economic Considerations

What are the economic benefits and costs of TRIPS-plus standards of IPRs protection? It is difficult to assess this question without considering the broader package of commitments embedded in an FTA, including preferential market access for agricultural and manufactured goods. Nonetheless, a number of observations can be made.

[29] EFTA comprises Iceland, Liechtenstein, Norway, and Switzerland.

[30] The recent EU-CARIFORUM and Japan–Switzerland agreements also establish the higher level of geographical indication protection for all products, not just wines and spirits, as discussed in the Doha Development Agenda (see above).

[31] See Council Regulation (EC) #1383/2003 concerning customs action against goods suspected of infringing certain IPRs and the measures to be taken against goods found to have infringed such rights, and Commission Regulation (EC) #1891/2004 laying down provisions for the implementation of Council Regulation (EC) #1383/2003.

[32] It is also worth noting that Chile and Mexico have signed a considerable number of FTAs that include provisions for the protection of GIs, expressly listing "Pisco" (or "Pisco Chileno") in the case of Chile and "Tequila" and "Mezcal" in the case of Mexico (Fink, 2009).

First, it is important to discern the changes in laws and regulations required by FTAs that do not already reflect actual legal practice in the countries concerned. In many cases, countries already had TRIPS-plus standards in their domestic laws before signing an FTA. To be sure, trade agreements are still relevant even if they do not require changes in laws, because they make it difficult for countries to change their minds and amend laws. But FTAs that simply lock in the domestic policy status quo will have fewer implications than an FTA that requires far-reaching IPRs reforms.

Second, as discussed in Section III, IPRs that protect inventive and creative activities imply a trade-off between incentives for innovation and competitive access to new technologies. There is no assurance that stronger intellectual property rules will always be welfare-enhancing, and the direction and size of the welfare effect will depend on a country's level of economic development. In the particular case of pharmaceutical products, concerns about adverse effects of stronger IPRs on access to medicines are frequently voiced and have led WTO members to clarify and amend certain TRIPS rules.

Third, improved access to developed country markets for agricultural and manufactured goods is of a preferential nature. These preferences are time-bound because they will be eroded once the trading partner in question reduces remaining tariffs and quotas on a non-discriminatory basis in the current or future multilateral trading rounds (or signs additional FTAs). By contrast, a commitment to stronger IPRs rules is permanent and likely to be implemented on a non-preferential basis. Even if preferential treatment in the area of IPRs were technically feasible, it would likely be inconsistent with the TRIPS Agreement which mandates most favored nation (MFN) treatment of IPRs holders.

Fourth, it is inherently difficult to quantify the implications of changing intellectual property standards, let alone to compare them in monetary values to the gains derived from improved market access abroad. Certain effects of stronger IPRs are conceptually not well-understood. But even where they are well-understood, the direction and size of net welfare changes depend on future developments that are difficult to predict—such as the nature of future innovations and their relevance to the country concerned.

Fifth, in contrast to the enforcement obligations of the TRIPS Agreement, the implementation of FTA enforcement standards may be costly—both in terms of budgetary outlays and the employment of skilled personnel. For developing countries that face many institutional deficiencies, a critical question is whether stronger enforcement of IPRs would draw away financial and human resources from other development priorities.

VII. Summary of Key Messages

This chapter has offered an introduction to the main instruments used to protect intellectual property, the key economic trade-offs of stronger IPRs, the basic provisions of the TRIPS Agreement, recent TRIPS developments affecting access to medicines in developing countries, and the TRIPS-plus standards of IPRs protection in FTAs. The key messages can be summarized as follows:

- IPRs protect creations that result from intellectual activity in the industrial, scientific, literary, and artistic fields. IPRs instruments encompass patents, copyrights and neighboring rights, trademarks, geographical indications, layout designs for integrated circuits, plant breeders' rights, and trade secrets.
- IPRs seek to resolve certain failures of private markets. Patents, copyrights, and related forms of protection aim at stimulating inventive and creative activities. Trademarks and geographical indications offer information about the origin of goods to consumers.
- For developing countries, stronger IPRs bring about benefits in terms of increased trade, foreign direct investment, and technology transfer. However, these benefits mainly accrue to middle-income countries and the size of benefits depends on complementary policy reforms, notably improvements in other aspects of the investment climate.
- The main cost of stronger patents, copyrights, and related rights is the market power conveyed to IPRs holders, leading to prices above marginal production costs for the duration of protection. For small developing economies with little inventive and creative capacity, stronger IPRs may lead to rent transfers to foreign title holders.
- The TRIPS Agreement is the most important international agreement for the protection of intellectual property. It is binding on all members of the WTO and enforceable through the WTO's dispute settlement system. It sets minimum standards of protection for all IPRs instruments, but also leaves governments important flexibilities to design IPRs regimes to suit domestic needs.
- Stronger pharmaceutical patent rights required by TRIPS have raised concerns that greater pricing power by pharmaceutical companies would adversely affect access to medicines in poor countries. To address these concerns WTO members have reaffirmed the right of governments to use compulsory licenses to override the exclusive rights conferred by patents. In addition, a special importing mechanism was created in 2003 that allows developing countries with insufficient pharmaceutical manufacturing capabilities to import generic drugs.
- Discussions on TRIPS in the DDA have focused, among other things, on strengthening the protection of geographical indications and promoting the appropriate use of genetic resources and traditional knowledge. However, disagreements among WTO members have so far prevented the adoption of new rules or mechanisms in these two areas.
- Many "new generation" FTAs negotiated in the past 14 years—especially by the United States, the EU, and EFTA—feature TRIPS-plus standards of IPRs protection. TRIPS-plus provisions relate to all of the different IPRs instrument

and the mechanisms available to enforce exclusive rights. Their acceptance by developing countries cannot be explained by expected economic benefits, but has to be understood as a quid pro quo for preferential market access in developed country markets for agricultural and manufactured goods.

References

Akerlof, G. A. (1970), 'The Market for Lemons: Qualitative Uncertainty and the Market Mechanism.' *Quarterly Journal of Economics*, 84: 488–500.

Branstetter, L., Fisman, R., and Foley, F. C. (2006), 'Do Stronger Intellectual Property Rights Increase International Technology Transfer? Empirical Evidence from U.S. Firm-Level Panel Data.' *The Quarterly Journal of Economics*, 121(1): 321–58.

Crawford, J.-A. and Fiorentino, R. V. (2005), 'The Changing Landscape of Regional Trade Agreements.' WTO Discussion Paper No. 8. Geneva: World Trade Organization.

Deardorff, A. V. (1992), 'Welfare Effects of Global Patent Protection.' *Economica*, 59: 35–51.

Diwan, I. and Rodrik, D. (1991), 'Patents, Appropriate Technology, and North-South Trade.' *Journal of International Economics*, 30: 27–47.

Finger, M. J. and Schuler, P. (1999), 'Implementation of Uruguay Round Commitments: The Development Challenge.' Policy Research Working Paper No. 2215. Washington, DC: The World Bank.

Fink, C. (2001). 'Patent Protection, Transnational Corporations, and Market Structure: A Simulation Study of the Indian Pharmaceutical Industry.' *Journal of Industry, Competition and Trade,* 1(1): 101–21.

Fink, C. (2005a). 'Intellectual Property and Public Health: The WTO's August 2003 Decision in Perspective.' In Newfarmer, R. (ed.). *Trade, Doha, and Development: Window into the Issues.* Washington, DC: The World Bank.

Fink, C. (2005b). 'Shifting Tides: TRIPS in the Doha Round.' *The World Trade Brief.*London: Haymarket Management.

Fink, C. (2006). 'Intellectual Property and the WTO.' In Tarr, D. (ed.) *Trade Policy and WTO Accession for Economic Development in Russia and the CIS: A Handbook.* Washington, DC: World Bank Institute.

Fink, C. (2011). 'Intellectual Property Rights.' In Chauffour, J.-P. and Maur, J.-C. *Preferential Trade Agreement Policies for Development: A Handbook* Washington, DC: The World Bank.

Fink, C. and Primo Braga, C. A. (2001). 'Trade-Related Intellectual Property Rights: From Marrakech to Seattle.' In Deutsch, K. and Speyer, B. (eds.) *Freer Trade in the Next Decade: The Millennium Round and the World Trade Organization.* London: Routledge, pp. 180–98.

Fink, C. and Maskus, K. E. (2004), *Intellectual Property and Development: Lessons from Recent Research.* Washington, DC: The World Bank and Oxford: Oxford University Press.

Fink, C. and Reichenmiller, P. (2005), 'Tightening TRIPS: the Intellectual Property Provisions of Recent US Free Trade Agreements.' Trade Note. Washington, DC: The World Bank.

Grossman, G. and Shapiro, C. (1988), 'Foreign Counterfeiting of Status Goods.' *Quarterly Journal of Economics*, 103(1): 79–100.

Machlup, F. (1958), 'An Economic Review of the Patent System.' Study No. 15, Subcomm. Patents, Trademarks and Copyrights of the U.S. Senate Judiciary Commission.

Maskus, K.E. (2000), *Intellectual Property Rights in the Global Economy* Washington, DC: Institute for International Economics.

Primo Braga, C. A., Fink, C., and Sepulveda, C. P. (2000), 'Intellectual Property Rights and Economic Development.' World Bank Discussion Paper No. 412. Washington, DC: The World Bank.

Roffe, P. and Vivas-Eugui, D. (2007), 'A Shift in Intellectual Property Policy in US FTAs?' *Bridges*, Year 11, No. 5, International Center for Trade and Sustainable Development, pp. 15–16.

World Bank. (2001), *Global Economic Prospects 2001*.Washington, DC: The World Bank, Chapter 5.

CHAPTER 24

INTERNATIONAL INVESTMENT AGREEMENTS: INVESTOR PROTECTIONS AND FOREIGN DIRECT INVESTMENT[*]

ANA FRISCHTAK AND RICHARD NEWFARMER

I. INTRODUCTION

INVESTMENT provisions in bilateral investment treaties and reciprocal preferential trade agreements (PTAs) are intended to promote investment flows by granting investors greater predictability on the policy framework regulating foreign investment. These agreements typically provide for transparency, non-discrimination among foreign and domestic investors, and guarantees against expropriation. Some agreements may prevent contracting parties from imposing trade related investment measures (TRIMS) on foreign investments, such as local content requirements and local hiring requirements. Finally, nearly all provide for some sort of dispute settlement. Provisions contained in US bilateral investment treaties, for example, are also found in its preferential free trade agreements, such as the North American Free Trade Agreement (NAFTA), the US free trade agreement (FTA) with Chile and with Singapore, among others. For these reasons, this chapter reviews recent trends regarding Bilateral Investment Treaties (BITs) and

* Ana Frischtak is Associate, Debevoise & Plimpton, and Richard Newfarmer is Country Director, International Growth Centre. The views expressed are solely those of the authors and should not in any way be attributed to their respective institutional affiliations. The authors wish to thank Grace Muhimpundu for her help with research assistance, and Joerg Weber and James Zhan of United Nations Conference on Trade and Development (UNCTAD) for their helpful comments.

investment provisions in PTAs, enumerates purported benefits of increased investment flows, and considers the costs associated with disputes lodged under these agreements.

II. The Rising Tide of Bilateral Investment Treaties

BITs are the primary vehicle for international cooperation on the regulation of investment flows. They customarily provide a definition of investment coverage, include rules of origin to determine the nationality of investors, and specify the treatment of inward investment and investors, either once established and/or in pre-establishment phase. Most BITs do not deal with market access restrictions per se—such as restrictions on sectoral entry or equity ownership limitations—although some do impose disciplines on performance requirements and similar TRIMs. Often the treatment that is guaranteed to foreign investors in BITS is better than that accorded to domestic investors, for example, in terms of access to foreign exchange or ability to transfer capital outside of the country, or in terms of investor protection/rights.

Standard provisions in most BITs include the obligation to provide most favored nation (MFN) and national treatment. These provisions guarantee, respectively, that foreign investors are treated as favorably as investors from non-contracting parties and as favorably as domestic investors are treated in "like" circumstances. Other standard provisions found in BITs include the obligation to provide foreign investors with "fair and equitable treatment" and "full protection and security." Since a major function of BITs is to provide investor protection against property takings, almost all BITs include a standard provision prohibiting expropriation of foreign investments unless it is for a public purpose, non-discriminatory, in accordance with the due process of law, and adequately compensated for in a timely manner (Cosbey, 2005). The expropriation provision is usually specified to include both direct (i.e., the direct transfer of property) and indirect expropriation. The latter often involves the host state's passage of a series of measures that, over time, deprive the investor of use and/or enjoyment of the property.

A significant aspect of most BITs is the provision of an investor–state dispute resolution mechanism for enforcement of the treaties' substantive provisions. Dispute settlement provisions usually provide that arbitration disputes will be governed according to pre-existing rules under a supervisory institution such as the World Bank Group's International Center for Settlement of Investment Disputes (ICSID) or the United Nations Commission on International Trade Law (UNCITRAL), where a set of procedural rules are to be followed, but no supervisory institution is provided (Cosbey et al., 2004). By allowing private investors to bring cases against host country governments, BITs remove any foreign policy-driven uncertainty regarding the willingness of an investor's home country government to defend its rights. And because most BITs lack a domestic judicial-exhaustion requirement, they allow foreign investors to bypass the host state's judicial system altogether, removing any risk of bias or discrimination in favor of the home country.

Significantly, recent treaties have begun to clarify the scope and meaning of some substantive provisions, particularly those that have been widely, and often divergently, interpreted by tribunals. For example, the Mexico–Singapore BIT (2009) specifies that the concept of "fair and equitable treatment" does not require treatment in addition to, or beyond, that which is required under customary international law. The Australia–Chile FTA (2008) clarifies that "full protection and security" encompasses only physical security as opposed to other forms of security, such as legal and economic security. With regard to the MFN principle, because this provision has sometimes been used by tribunals to import a more favorable standard of treatment accorded to investors from third countries, some treaties are now explicitly prohibiting application of the MFN principle to particular treaty obligations. For example, the Ethiopia–UK BIT (2009) clarifies that the MFN principle does not apply to dispute settlement provisions, thereby prohibiting an investor from invoking more favorable dispute settlement provisions from treaties with a third country. And other agreements are also tackling the definition of expropriation, carefully distinguishing between compensable indirect expropriation and the adverse effects endured by a foreign investor as a result of bona fide regulation in the public interest (Common Market for Eastern and Southern Africa (COMESA)) as well as specifying that the issuances of compulsory intellectual property licenses do not amount to expropriation (Malaysia–New Zealand FTA (2009)) (UNCTAD, 2010a: 87).

BITs have proliferated sharply since the 1980s. The total number of BITs in force has risen from 355 in 1990 to 2,750 by the end of 2009 (UNCTAD, 2006: 81). The pace of new annual signings has attenuated—from over 200 in the mid 1990s to 82 in 2009 as the pool of countries willing to enter into agreements began to reach full coverage (see Figure 24.1). In the first five months of 2010, 46 new international investment agreements were concluded, six of which were BITs (UNCTAD, 2010a: 81). While the majority of agreements are North–South arrangements, recent signings feature agreements among developing countries. Nineteen of the 82 BITs signed in 2009 were between developing countries and South–South agreements now constitute 26 per cent of the total (UNCTAD, 2009c). Amongst developing countries, those from Asia and Oceania led the conclusion of BITs in 2008. They signed 31 new BITs, bringing the total of their agreements to 1,112 or 41 per cent of all BITs (UNCTAD, 2009c). Additionally, apart from BITs, 2009 witnessed the conclusion of 129 other treaties, 109 of which were double taxation treaties (DTT) and 20 other international investment agreements (IIAs), such as free trade agreements (FTAs) bringing the total number of the latter to 295 (UNCTAD, 2010a: 81).

The top 10 signatories of BITs included seven from Europe (Germany, France, the United Kingdom, Italy, Belgium, the Netherlands as well as Switzerland), with China, Egypt, and Korea rounding out the top 10 (UNCTAD, 2009c). BITs now cover a substantial share of foreign direct investment (FDI) flows from OECD countries to developing countries. In 1990, we calculate some 9 per cent of investment flows were covered (though data in the early years are somewhat understated). By 2004, 43 per cent of investment was covered. Many of the new BITs follow the post-establishment model,

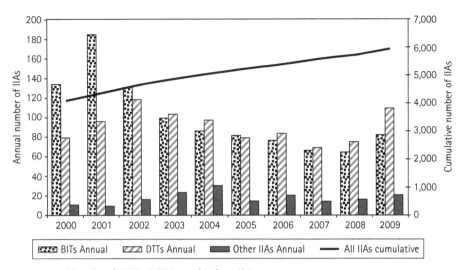

FIGURE 24.1 Trends of BITs, DTTs, and other IIAs, 2000–09

Source: UNCTAD 2010a: 82. By kind permission of UNCTAD.

which includes dispute resolution provisions, and a few also include pre-establishment rights, such as the Canada–Jordan BIT (2009) and Canada–Romania BIT (2009) (UNCTAD, 2010a: 82).

III. PREFERENTIAL TRADE
AGREEMENTS: INVESTMENT PROVISIONS

PTAs, like BITs, have multiplied in the years since 1990. UNCTAD reports that 232 PTAs were signed (not all of which were necessarily in force) at the end of 2005, 86 of which were purely South–South arrangements and, as shown above, by the end of 2009, there were 295 such agreements. Many of these agreements, particularly the North–South agreements, now cover investment and contain substantive investment provisions similar to those found in most BITs (UNCTAD 2010a: 82, 83).[1]

---

[1] UNCTAD (2010a: 82, 83) reports that these agreements fall into three types. The first type are broader economic cooperation agreements that nonetheless include investment chapters with substantive investment provisions, similar to those found in BITs, such as national treatment, MFN treatment, and fair and equitable treatment, while also providing recourse to dispute settlement. The second type are those with much more limited investment related provisions, focusing more on granting market access to foreign investors than to the protection of their investments once the investment is made, such as the Albania–European FTA. The third type only deals with investment cooperation, often providing for the creation of a consultative committee to pursue common initiatives to encourage an open and transparent investment climate and may commit the parties to enter into future negotiations.

PTAs involving the United States and the EU have been important drivers. As of the fall of 2010, the United States had in force FTAs with investment provisions involving 16 countries, including Australia, Mexico, Chile, Morocco, and Singapore, with three more signed and awaiting Congressional approval (i.e., Panama, Korea, and Colombia) (Office of USTR, 2010).

The EU engagement in PTAs is even more extensive, with more than 100 PTAs, and investment is more frequently on the agenda. Thus, for example, investment policies are being discussed as part of the Economic Partnership Agreement negotiations with Africa, the Caribbean, and the Pacific (ACP) countries and the recent agreements with Southern Mediterranean countries. Often investment policies are addressed through parallel investment treaties. Because these agreements involve stricter disciplines on governments and have wider coverage than South–South PTAs, they merit more detailed review.

US FTAs

Recent US FTAs include pre-establishment rights of market access. This implies opening services markets to competition from foreign suppliers—or locking in prior autonomous liberalization—except in those sectors excluded (through a negative list). This therefore may expand on the coverage of commitments in the GATS, where a positive list is used, and greatly enhances the transparency of prevailing policies. Since most of the countries with which the United States has concluded bilateral PTAs are already open in most sectors, as a general statement the agreements lock in prevailing openness and effect changes in only a few still-restricted activities. Common provisions range from inclusion of insurance, financial advisory services, and selected telecommunications services to arguably relatively inconsequential changes to already open regimes, such as the commitment of Singapore to cease cross-subsidies in express mail delivery or the commitment of Chile in insurance services and a few other sectors. The exclusion of labor services is notable, except provisional visas for professionals associated with investing firms.

All US FTAs provide for national treatment and MFN treatment. For many of the initial FTA countries, these had long been included in national legislations and/or have been incorporated into bilateral investment treaties on a post-establishment basis. The US FTAs have subsumed pre-existing BITs and provided new measures covering investment. Agreements, especially post-NAFTA ones, include broad definitions of investment, including not only FDI, but also portfolio flows, private debt, and even sovereign debt issues as well as intellectual property (see Cosbey et al., 2004). The inclusion of short-term debt, together with pre-establishment rights, led the US Treasury to demand that Chile modify its controls on capital inflows that were designed to curtail destabilizing short-term capital inflows. Such broad definitions of investment policies can expose countries to dispute settlement across a wide range of assets.

The inclusion of intellectual property rights (IPRs) in the definition of assets covered by the investment provisions creates a potential liability for signatory governments. Not only are the IPRs far more extensive under the recent PTAs than under the WTO (TRIPS), the dispute settlement provisions are more powerful. For example, if a government decides to issue a compulsory license to control drug prices and the patent owner disputes this action under the terms of the US PTA, the patent holder can take the claim to commercial arbitration under the PTA's investment provisions. This instrument is considerably more powerful for IPR enforcement than the state-to-state provisions under the TRIPS Agreement (see Abbott, 2004; Fink and Reichenmiller, 2005).

Another area of discipline on government that is more expansive than under the WTO concerns TRIMs—government policies that require foreign companies to export in a certain portion of its sales or balance trade and use local inputs to achieve value added objectives. All of the bilateral US PTAs ban TRIMs. The US bilateral agreements have in effect established a "WTO TRIMs PLUS" set of obligations that include outright bans on certain performance requirements, including management restrictions and export, minimum domestic content, domestic sourcing, trade balancing and technology transfer requirements. In general, government procurement, environmental standards, and requirements for local R&D are not covered (te Velde et al., 2003).

A key feature of US agreements is the use of "negative lists" that exclude sectors or industries from coverage. This implies that all other sectors not mentioned—including, importantly, new economic activities—would be included; this is distinct from the "positive list" approach typically found in EU agreements and most South–South agreements. Related to this are "ratchet provisions," also a feature of US agreements; these bind liberalizing policies enacted subsequent to the agreement's entrance into force, intended to lock the policy framework progressively into ever greater openness and certainty.

Finally, with the exception of the Australian FTA, all the US agreements contain an investor–state dispute resolution provision that permits investors to take foreign governments to dispute resolution for violation of the treaty's substantive provisions, such as national treatment, non-discrimination, or expropriation provisions, among others. NAFTA's Chapter 11 and Chile's Chapter 10 are the most widely known mechanisms, but they are also contained in the other bilateral agreements.

European Union Agreements

Prior to the entering into force of the Lisbon Treaty on December 1, 2009, which shifted competence over FDI to the EU, investment was solely the competence of EU member states. Accordingly, EU PTAs have treated investment only generally or indirectly. The earliest (and least comprehensive) are the Euro-Mediterranean

Partnership agreements (starting in 1995) and the South African agreement (1999), and contain virtually no investment provisions. Thus, the market access provisions are general, directed mainly at services, and contain only the promise of potential liberalization after discussions to transpire some five years after the entry into force of the agreement. In the EU–Mexico PTA, several general provisions were included, many ratifying GATS arrangements, as well as specific liberalization commitments in the financial sector. The EU–Chile agreement goes further by additionally locking in some liberalization of telecommunications and maritime services (Ulrich, 2004: 3–7).

The EU agreements with Mexico and Chile, though more comprehensive than earlier agreements, do not have the same strength of disciplines of the US agreements. The trade provisions are phrased on the basis of a positive list, and implicitly exclude new products. The treatment of investment and capital flows in both agreements was not extensive. For example, the EU–Mexico agreement simply states that the existing restrictions on investment will be progressively eliminated and no new restrictions adopted, without specifying particular sectors or setting a timeline for liberalization. The language in the EU–Chile agreement is even more general, calling for "free movement of capital relating to direct investments made in accordance with the laws of the host country." In both cases, the agreements allow for use of safeguards in the event of monetary or exchange rate difficulties, and, although the time limit is set at 6 months for Mexico and 12 months for Chile, both agreements allow for continuation of the safeguard after the time limit through its formal reintroduction.

The treatment of dispute settlement involves state-to-state mechanisms rather than the investor–state provisions in US agreements that allow private companies to initiate arbitration cases against governments. The EU provisions pertaining to investment are subsumed in the general dispute settlement provisions for all matters in the PTA (Szepesi, 2004a, b). State-to-state dispute settlement is first attempted through consultations with a Joint Committee (Association Committee in the case of Chile and Mediterranean countries) within 30 days of a party's request. If this step of "dispute avoidance" proves unsuccessful, in the case of Chile, the concerned party can forward its request to an arbitration panel comprised of representatives of both parties. The arbitration panel's decisions are binding, and the panel can also rule on the conformity of any measures undertaken as a result of its decision with the original ruling. Both agreements provide extensive detail on the process of appointing members to the arbitration panel, timelines for the panel's ruling, and compliance with the panel's decisions. Still, companies in member states that have their own BITs with recipient countries can activate investor state arbitration through BIT mechanisms.

Most recently, the EU and Korea concluded negotiations on an FTA. The EU–Korea agreement is the most ambitious trade agreement ever negotiated by the EU and was expected to be signed by the two countries in Brussels on October 6, 2010 (European Commission, 2010). Nonetheless, the EU–Korea FTA does not provide investors with the substantive protections found in most BITs and in many

US FTAs, nor does it allow for investor–state dispute settlement. The effect of the Lisbon Treaty on these new agreements is still an open question. A number of issues remain to be sorted out, including how investor–state dispute settlement will be handled since the EU is not a member of ICSID and cannot become one pursuant to ICSID rules. It also remains to be seen how consistency will be ensured where the EU concludes an agreement with the same country as member states (UNCTAD, 2010a: 84).

Multilateral Initiatives

Since 1948, when the Havana Charter was created, governments in high-income countries have sought to weave investment provisions into international trade law. While selected investment issues were addressed with the creation of the UN Center on Transnationals and the OECD Guidelines for Multinationals, it was not until the OECD launched the Multilateral Agreement on Investment in 1995 that a full scale effort was resurrected once again. This effort eventually foundered in the face of resistance from labor and environmental groups, as well as developing countries that were largely excluded; when France withdrew from the negotiations in 1998 over the failure to protect its media and cultural interests, the negotiations collapsed.

With the launching of the Doha Development Agenda in the Ministerial meeting of the WTO in November 2001, it seemed that investment would once again be taken up as part of the negotiating mandate for the so-called Singapore issues. Discussions in the 20 subsequent months before the next Ministerial meeting in Cancun, Mexico, in 2003, focused on the definition of investment to be covered, whether to adopt positive or negative lists, and the type of dispute resolution to be adopted. In each of these areas, the contentious negotiations tended to gravitate toward outcomes favoring the lowest common denominator: narrowly focused definitions of investment, positive lists with abundant room for exclusions, and state-to-state dispute resolution.

However, progress in the Doha Round was painfully slow in the run up to the Cancun meeting, and disagreement on the Singapore issues was only one symptom. Including investment in the negotiations encountered vehement opposition from a coalition of developing countries, including most notably India and Malaysia. Negotiations were stymied over other major issues in agriculture and non-agricultural products, and many developing countries considered the heated discussions on the Singapore issues a distraction and of little value to their development.

Finally, in an ill-fated effort to move the discussions off dead center, the EU, the principal demandeur of Singapore issues, at the last minute offered to abandon investment and competition—and even cease future WTO activity in the Working Group. The Cancun Ministerial nonetheless broke down in acrimony. Only later when India offered to accept one of the four Singapore issues, trade facilitation, did this later became the accepted position in subsequent negotiations (Hoekman and Newfarmer, 2003). Investment in the WTO Doha Round was officially dead.

IV. Economic Effects: Increasing Investment

From a development point of view, a main objective of a BIT is to increase the flow of investment to signatory countries. Does the signing of bilateral investment treaties in fact increase the flow of FDI? Theory might suggest that it would: to the extent that investment rules and investor protections embodied in BITs credibly substitute for—or enhance—domestic legislation, one would expect that investment flows would increase. Hallward-Driemeier (2003), in one of the first systematic statistical analyses,[2] considered bilateral flows of Organisation for Economic Co-operation and Development (OECD) members to 31 developing countries over two decades. Her analysis found that, controlling for a time trend and country-specific effects, BITs had virtually no independent effect in increasing the share of FDI to a signatory country from a home country. Said differently, countries signing a BIT were no more likely to receive additional FDI than countries without such a pact. Even comparing flows in the three years after a BIT was signed to the three years prior, there was no significant increase in FDI.

Bilateral Investment Treaties

In the years since Hallward–Dreimeier's pioneering work, two things have happened. First, the number of BITS and PTAs with investor protections have skyrocketed. Second, the academic community has undertaken more than a score of studies of the relationship of investor protections to FDI flows.[3] Rose-Ackerman and Tobin (2005) analyzed the flows to 63 countries with data averaged over a five-year period, and found that only with countries at very low levels of risk was there any increase of investment from the signatory home country. In a detailed analysis of US FDI behavior, they failed to find any statistically significant effects on US FDI to 54 countries, irrespective of political risk.

---

[2] UNCTAD (1998), in an early study, found little evidence that BITs increased FDI. That work looked at a single year of investments and tested whether the number of BITs signed by the host was correlated with the amount of FDI it received.

[3] The studies summarized in this section are shown in Appendix Table 24.A1. For a thoughtful review of some of these studies, see UNTCAD, 2009d.

Neumayer and Spess (2005), using a larger sample over a longer period and considering simply the number of BITs signed, found robust and positive effects of the total number of BITs on total inflows of FDI. This finding relies heavily on the notion that signing a BIT signals to all would-be investors that the environment is more welcoming. In this model, the signal is more important than the specific investor protections. A series of other studies reached similar general conclusions, using different methodologies and often with different (and useful) nuances. By and large, the weight of the econometric evidence has now shifted in favor of the notion that bilateral investment treaties do—on average across many countries with wide variance—have a positive impact on foreign direct investment inflows.

Exceptions to this generalized finding can be found in both different econometric formulations and in sampling methods. Aisbett (2007) found that common specifications of models lacked robustness when she controlled for endogeneity. Indeed it is plausible that the causation runs in the other direction: foreign investors, once established and part of the domestic political process in host countries, could well pressure host governments to sign BITs to provide additional protection to their investments, Indeed, Swenson (2006) found that *previous* levels of FDI tend to explain the propensity for governments, particularly in Asia, to sign a BIT. On the other hand, Kerner (2009) uses a two stage least square procedure to control for endogeneity and finds that it heightens the significance of the BITs FDI relationship. In a recent paper, Busse et al. (2010), using a gravity model and adopting more exhaustive controls for endogeneity, conclude that indeed investment flows are positively correlated. For Latin America, Gallagher and Birch (2006) found that neither the total number of BITs, nor BITs with the USA, have an independent and positive impact on investment flows to Latin America. Similarly, Lesher and Miroudot (2006), looking at the investment provisions in detail in 24 PTAs found no effects of BITs on investment flows—but a strong effect of investment provisions in PTAs.

This literature also provides hints at other interesting findings. First, BITs seem to work differently in different environments. Those in less risky business environments have no independent effects, but in stable but higher-risk environments they do have a positive effect on increasing FDI (Rose-Ackerman and Tobin, 2005). Similarly, countries with strong political relations and low risk experience less benefit from BITs, whereas in risky but stable environments, BITS have greater effect (Desbordes and Vicard, 2009). It should be noted that the literature is far from definitive on this point: Yackee (2010b) in a creative test of the proposition (based on a small sample) found that the presence of a network of BITs had no significant impact on private rankings of political risk. There may also be declining marginal returns to signing additional BITs with additional source countries. This is because the very presence of a network of BITs is enough to convince unprotected as well as protected investors of the security of the investment climate. Indeed Rose-Ackerman and Tobin (2005) find that BITs appear to have no effect on the domestic business climate, and that poor countries cannot avoid the hard work of improving their own domestic environment as it affects the political risks of investment. In a corollary, Haftel (2009) finds that signed—but unratified—treaties have virtually no effect in increasing investment.

...and in PTAs?

Investment provisions are not limited to bilateral investment treaties and are increasingly found in PTAs, particularly in the US-model regime. US FTAs have generally supplanted any extant BITs with partner countries in favor of the (usually stronger) protections in the trade agreement. These are stronger insofar as they typically contain additional disciplines on pre-establishment rights for covered sectors and no expiration period, among other things. EU FTAs generally do not have investor–state dispute settlement protections because these are the province of the EU member states, and would otherwise be covered in bilateral investment treaties. Nonetheless, many PTAs among countries outside the EU have increasingly contained investor protections (Figure 24.2).

Assessing the evidence of investment provisions in PTAs is difficult because of the need to distinguish the effects on investment flows of creating a larger, single market from the effects of investor protections and other investment provisions in the trade agreement. Recent studies have, if anything, pointed out that the combined effects of free trade and investor protections have a positive effect

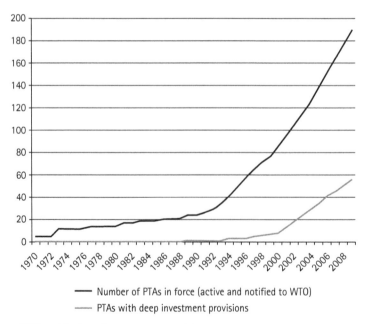

—— Number of PTAs in force (active and notified to WTO)
—— PTAs with deep investment provisions

FIGURE 24.2 PTAs with deep investment provisions

Source: Lesher and Miroudot, 2006; updated in Miroudot, 2011.

on increasing investment flows. The *Global Economic Prospects 2005* (World Bank, 2004) examined the effects of PTA membership and other variables on FDI inflows for a panel of 152 countries over the 1980–2002 period.[4] The study found that PTAs that result in larger markets do attract greater FDI. The interaction of signing a PTA and expanded market size associated with the integrated markets is significant and positively related to FDI. On average, a 10 per cent increase in market size associated with a PTA produces an increase in FDI of 5 per cent. Büthe and Milner (2008) similarly found that signing a PTA had a significant impact on inflows of FDI as did other indicators of willingness to subscribe to international rules and norms, such as membership in the WTO and signing many BITs. Adams et al. (2003) examined nine separate PTAs and found that non-trade provisions (i.e., investment provisions) had positive effects on investment flows in six. Miroudot (2011) stressed the complementarities between trade and investment in his review and found PTAs with investment provisions to be much more powerful in eliciting new investment flows than BITs—in large measure because of the pre-establishment provisions and trade commitments inherent in PTAs.

One example is NAFTA, which is a comprehensive arrangement that includes significant investor protections in combination with broad-based tariff reductions and border liberalizations. Chapter 11 of NAFTA allows investors to sue the government in the event of regulatory or other actions that might diminish the value of a foreign investment. Lederman, Maloney, and Serven (2003: chapter 4, p. 23) find that, in addition to positive forces in the global economy that propelled investment into Mexico and other emerging markets after 1994, "the trade opening and NAFTA accession also played a role in Mexico's FDI rise…." Firms, especially export oriented firms, appeared to take advantage of liberalized financial flows inherent in NAFTA to begin to use foreign equity and debt financing.

This study did not attempt to distinguish the role of enhanced investor protections from access to the Mexican market and its other resources in increasing the flow of FDI. It may be that simply liberalizing the investment law in 1993 and making it easier to take advantage of productivity-adjusted wage differentials in the NAFTA countries was sufficient to explain the difference. Indeed, Daude and Stein (2001) find that FTAs generally tend to increase FDI.[5] Lederman, Maloney, and Serven (2003) corroborate this when FTAs combine to form the largest markets. However, investor protections in Chapter 11 may have played an important independent role. This is because Mexico's legal and

[4] Some of the problems include the absence of data on implementation and the variable coverage of FDI provisions across agreements, making it difficult to distinguish the effects of investment rules from trade rules. Moreover, the absence of FDI data that allow the effects of PTAs on differing types of investment—vertical or horizontal—to be distinguished limits the analysis. Nonetheless, the regressions are robust to variations in specifications.

[5] They find that: "FTA provisions with a source country will receive 70- percent more FDI that a non-partner, other things being equal" (2001: 114), though it should be noted their regression coefficients are significant only at the 15 per cent level.

judicial framework is well below competing destinations (such as East Asia, the United States, and UK, and even the average for Latin America). In an analysis of shareholder rights, creditor rights, efficiency of judiciary, rule of law, and absence of corruption, Mexico scores *below* the Latin American average in 4 of 5 measures (La Porta et al., 2002, as cited in Lederman, Maloney, and Serven 2003: 24). To the extent that Chapter 11 provided investors with additional comfort over and above the existing investment climate, its protections would have offset these disadvantages. In any case, Lederman et al. (2003) conclude that "Mexico's entry into NAFTA led to an increase in annual FDI by around 40 percent" (2004: 130). Waldkirch (2001), with less complete annual data, also found that NAFTA increased FDI substantially, mostly from the United States and from Canada.

More recent studies have tried to tease out the differential effects of trade provisions and investment provisions on expanded FDI flows. Lesher and Miroudot (2006) take the analysis much farther. They create an index of the depth of investment provisions in PTAs and apply this in a gravity model to determine the effects on flows. Even though the effects of BITs in their study were not significant, they find a strongly positive effect of the presence of investment provision per se as well as their index of the extensiveness of investment provisions in PTAs. These results are similar to the findings of Te Velde and Bezemer (2006) which found that the common investment provisions heightened the attractiveness of PTAs to foreign investors.

Conclusions about Investment Provisions ... and Unanswered Questions

The literature on BITs and investment provisions in PTAs suggests several conclusions of policy consequence: countries seeking to attract FDI to promote development are best advised to focus as a first-best priority on the overall business environment because a stable macroeconomic context and a regime of enforceable property rights are clear determinants of investment decision-making. Absent this environment, investor protections are unlikely to have much effect—save possibly (and evidence on this point is scarce) in extractive enclave industries or in labor-intensive export industries with very low fixed investment. That said, in situations where the investment climate is in transition and relatively stable, BITS and investment provisions in PTAs may help at the margin. Moreover, linking these characteristics of a positive investment climate with an open trading system—either on an MFN basis or in the context of a PTA—and adding in investor protections is likely to have the greatest effects on attracting investment.

Several questions are now emerging that merit further investigation. First, the content of agreements varies widely (a point emphasized by Yackee, 2007), but few studies try to determine the consequences of differing investment provisions. Is it MFN treatment and other common provisions or is it investor recourse to arbitration panels that is most valued by investors and leads them to invest? Salacuse and Sullivan (2005) begin this effort by comparing the differential effects of US agreements with others from the OECD, and find that US agreements, with their usually stronger uniform provisions and dispute settlement rules, tend to have greater effect. A second question is whether the positive effects of BITs and investor protections would hold up once detailed descriptors of the investment climate—such as those in the World Bank's Doing Business data base—were included. It cannot be excluded that these are omitted variables and bias the regression estimations. A third question is whether investors in different activities respond differently to the presence of investor protections. It stands to reason that investors with large sunk capital commitments and few technological and other dynamic linkages—a situation that might tempt governments to seize associated rents—would value investor protections more than investors with limited capital commitments, such as in light manufacturing or services. Miroudot (2011) gives special weight to investment provisions in PTAs as a way of creating an attractive environment for the emergence of production chains.

One way to examine in greater detail the value of BITs is the creative exploration of Yackee (2010). After exploring the effects of BITs on political risk assessments—and finding no effects—he polled private insurers to see whether the presence of BITs affected their insurance premiums. His sample was too small to draw any firm conclusions, but the responses indicated that political risk insurers did not attach great and uniform weight to the presence or absence of a BIT. Further research on this point could potentially establish the market value of these commitments.

In another study, Yackee (2010b) tried a particularly novel approach to discern the impact of investor protections on the decisions of investors: he asked them. Based on a survey of General Counsels of 200 large multinational companies and 75 responses, Yackee found that most were relatively unfamiliar with BITs. On a five-point scale, ranging from "1" ("not at all familiar") to 5 ("very familiar"), the median response for General Counsels was "2," nearly identical to the score of non-lawyer senior executives. Only about 21 per cent indicated having high familiarity ("4" or "5"). Moreover, General Counsels did not view BITs as providing particularly effective protection against expropriation (median response of "3" on a 5-point scale where "5" means "very effective" and "1" means "not at all effective"), with only about 21 per cent rating BITs as highly effective ("4" or "5").

A final interesting question concerns whether the proliferation of an essentially bilateral system of investor protections undermines any impulse for multilateral protections in the WTO. Adlung and Molinuevo (2008) in their review of these issues as they pertain to services present a sanguine conclusion: unlike PTAs, BITs do not contain the same insider–outside problem because BITs do not provide for more favored operating conditions, and protections tend to provide positive spillovers to unprotected investors. Miroudot (2011) argues that the proliferation of investment provisions has not yet caused major difficulties, but suggests that further effort should be made to harmonize and multilateralize accords.

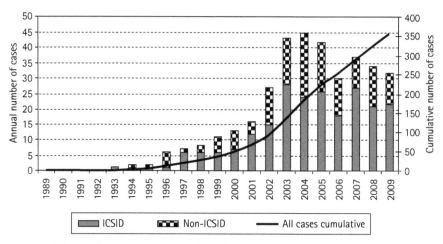

FIGURE 24.3 Known investment treaty arbitrations, 1989–2009

Source: UNCTAD, World Investment Report 2010. By kind permission of UNCTAD.

V. Dispute Settlement

Rising Case Load

Despite the benefits of BIT-type protections in the form of new FDI inflows, the costs of stronger protection arising from investor suits can be large. This is a growing phenomenon.[6] The number of cases brought under the various BITs and PTAs has risen dramatically. Though the absence of reporting data from all the dispute tribunals prevents full analysis, International Center for Settlement of Investment Disputes (ICSID) (2010-1: 7) reports a steady increase in the number of cases from an annual average of 1.5 cases in 1972–95 to 29 in 2003–04. In 2007, the number of ICSID cases peaked to a record 37, and then tapered off to an average of 23 in 2008–09, for a total of 305 cases through 2009 (ICSID, 2010-1: 7). However, UNCTAD (2011) has established a database that includes other sources, and it reports that some 32 cases were brought in 2009, bringing the total number of investor–state cases to 357 by the end of the year. (See Figure 24.3.)

The majority of ICSID registered cases has been brought against South American countries (30 per cent), followed by Eastern Europe and Central Asia (22 per cent), and Sub-Saharan Africa (16 per cent). Not surprisingly, Western European countries have faced the least amount of investment claims (1 per cent), followed by North America (6 per cent). The majority of investment claims registered under ICSID (62 per cent) have arisen under BITs. The largest number of ICISD disputes have arisen in the oil, gas, and

---

[6] For this reason, UNCTAD 2010b has made many useful recommendations to avoid formal dispute settlement processes.

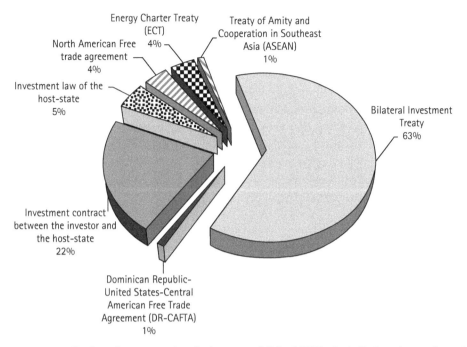

FIGURE 24.4 Basis of consent invoked to establish ICSID jurisdiction in registered ICSID cases

Source: ICSID, 2010-2: 10.

mining sector (25 per cent), followed by electric power and "other energy" (13 per cent), and transportation (11 per cent) (ICSID, 2010-1: 7, 10, 12).[7]

While a growing number of awards are being made public, the dispute settlement process is still largely cloaked in a veil of opaqueness. The ICSID registry contains only minimal information about the dispute, and thus it is generally not known whether a particular dispute arises from a BIT provision, an FTA provision, or some other state contract, and even less is known about the details of the dispute or the parties' claims and defenses. Information on a dispute is only made public by ICSID when both parties to the dispute agree to do so. Alternatively, each party can decide to publicize information on its own initiative. Outside of ICSID, however, many of the disputes are never made public, and even less is known about their resolution.

At least 81 governments—64 from the developing world (including transition countries)—have faced investment treaty arbitration (UNCTAD, 2011). More than 44 cases were lodged against the Argentine government after its devaluation of the peso in 2001 (UNCTAD, 2009c). Not all cases have emanated from BITs (see Figure 24.4).

---

[7] In 2009, the oil, gas and mining sectors continued to produce the largest amount of disputes (24 per cent) registered at the Centre, followed again by electric power and other energy (16 per cent) and transportation (16 per cent) (ICSID, 2010-1: 22).

Under NAFTA, which provides relatively greater transparency as compared to other international investment agreements, as of January 2009, 59 cases were brought under chapter 11.[8] Of these, 12 have been dismissed in favor of NAFTA members and 6 have been won by investors, with awards totaling $64 million.[9]

Causes of investor–state disputes have varied from traditional international law violations, such as expropriation without adequate compensation, to more subtle government conduct including the revocation of banking licenses, changes in the interpretation of tax laws, the passage of environmental regulations that adversely and disproportionally affect foreign investors, the failure to advise investors about the necessary licenses needed to operate an investment, and alleged breaches of commercial contracts with the host state (Franck, 2007: 4).

Rising Costs, Rising Awards

Awards can be sizeable. In February 2005, the Slovak Republic agreed to comply with an ICSID arbitral award of $830 million to CSOB, a Czech bank. This award surpassed that of a tribunal in Stockholm, which required the government of the Czech Republic to pay one company, Central European Media (CME), $350 million for violation of a BIT that deprived CME from a stake in an English language TV station in Prague. This amount was ten times higher than previously known awards under arbitration cases at the time, and about equal to the entire public sector deficit of the Czech Republic (Peterson, 2003). But the biggest case to date has been filed against the Russian Federation, involving a claim for more than $50 billion for the alleged expropriation of Group Menatep's majority shareholding in the Yukos oil firm under the 1994 Energy Charter Treaty (unratified by Russia) (*American Lawyer*, December 4, 2009). Parallel cases have been launched against Yukos by Spanish investor Renta 4 SVSA, and English investor RosInvestCo UK Ltd., whose claims against Russia are over $10 billion and $280 million, respectively (*IA Reporter*, November 30, 2009). Argentina in particular has been subject to a number of large awards (see Table 24.1), although an award has yet to be issued for the largest claim to date to arise out of the Argentine 2001 economic crisis. In *Giovanna a Beccara et al. (Italy) v. Argentine Republic*, more than 180,000 Italian holders of Argentine sovereign bonds, who declined to accept a 2005 settlement offered by the government, have brought a claim against the state for over $4.5 billion (*American Lawyer*, July 21, 2009).

Nonetheless, an empirical study of publicly available investment treaty awards before June 1, 2006 found that the average award in investor–state disputes was $10 million, indicating that even though awards remained high, those in the

[8] Table of NAFTA "Chapter 11" Foreign Investor-State Cases and Claims, January 2009 (available at <http://www.citizen.org/documents/Ch11CasesChart-2009.pdf>).

[9] *Id.*

Table 24.1 Monetary awards cast against Argentina, 2001–10

Claimant	Sector	Amount awarded	Date awarded	Date confirmed	Arbitral institution
CMS Gas Transmission Company	Gas transportation	$133.2 m	May 12, 2005	September 25, 2007	ICSID
Azurix Corp.	Water and sewer services concession	$165.2 m	July 14, 2006	Annulment proceedings pending	ICSID
Siemens A.G.	Informatic services contract	$237.8 m	February 6, 2007	Annulment proceedings pending	ICSID
LG&E Energy Corp., LG&E Capital Corp. and LG&E International Inc.	Gas distribution	$57.4m	July 25, 2007	Partial annulment proceedings pending	ICSID
Enron Corporation and Ponderosa Assets L.P.	Gas transportation	$106.2 m	May 22, 2007	Award annulled on July 30, 2010	ICSID
Compania de Aguas Del Aconquija S.A. and Vivendi Universal S.A.	Water and sewer services concession	$105 m	August 20,2007	August 10, 2010	ICSID
Sempra Energy International	Gas supply and distribution	$128.2 m	September 28, 2007	Award annulled on June 29, 2010	ICSID
BG Group Plc	Gas distribution	$185.2m	December 24, 2007	Challenge to the award pending before DC court	UNCITRAL
Continental Casualty Company	Insurance company	$2.8 m	September 5, 2008	Partial annulment proceedings pending	ICSID
National Grid plc	Electricity transmission	$54 m	November 3, 2008	Confirmed by DC court June 2010	UNCITRAL

Source: Lucy Reed, Scorecard of Investment Treaty Arbitrations Against Argentina Since 2001, KluwerArbitration, March 2, 2009 (available at <http://kluwerarbitrationblog.com/blog/2009/03/02/scorecard-of-investment-treaty-cases-against-argentina-since-2001/>); *IA Reporter*, 2010.

hundreds of millions were clearly outliers in the system (Franck, 2008b: 799).[10] Further, an analysis of the same awards found that the difference between the average amounts claimed and awarded was approximately US$333 million, indicating that investors rarely succeed in winning the full amount claimed at the start of proceedings (Franck, 2007: 59).

The magnitude of many arbitral awards won against host governments often obscures the fact that governments have defended suits with roughly the same success rate as investors have had in winning them, with the balance tilted slightly in favor of the host government. For example, UNCTAD (2011) reports that in 2009, of the 164 cases that were brought to conclusion, 38 per cent (62 cases), were decided in favor of the State, 29 per cent (47 cases) were decided in favor of the investor, and 34 per cent (55 cases) of cases settled. Unfortunately, the terms of these settlements are not completely transparent—and push evaluative conclusions toward agnostism. In 2007, the numbers are even closer: about 42 cases were decided in favor of the state compared to 40 cases decided in favor of the investor (37 cases settled) (UNCTAD, 2008: 3). These numbers are also consistent with Franck's empirical analysis of all final awards publicly available before June 1, 2006. In her study, 38.5 per cent (20) of awards were in favor of the investor, 57.7 per cent were in favor of the state (30), and 2 settled (Franck, 2007: 49). Even though the terms of the settled cases cannot be evaluated, the fact that the state wins a significant minority of cases may give comfort to critics of the system who claim that the process is biased towards investors.[11]

Nonetheless, even when states successfully defend arbitrations, they still face significant expenses emanating from the fact that tribunals generally hold each party responsible for their own legal fees and an equal portion of the tribunal costs. These expenses can be further aggravated if the tribunal decides to engage in some form of "cost shifting," that is, to allocate a higher percentage of the arbitration costs to the losing party (e.g., in *National Grid v. Argentina*, Argentina was ordered to pay 75 per cent of the arbitration costs, amounting to $1.3 million) or to order the losing party to reimburse a share of the winning party's legal fees (e.g., in *Rumeli Telekom v. Kazakhstan*, the state was ordered to pay 50 per cent of the claimants' legal fees and costs) (UNCTAD, 2009b: 10–11). Consequently, governments may have to pay costs

---

[10] Of significance, Franck does not include the $830 million CSOB award in her study on the grounds that, although the case was brought under both an investment and commercial agreement, the panel upheld jurisdiction only under the commercial agreement and thus the award is not investment treaty based.

[11] For example, Wells and Ahmed (2007: 289–90) argue that the investor–state arbitration system is inherently asymmetric, according investors a superior position in the resolution process, both in relation to governments (that cannot initiate a case against an underperforming investor) and to domestic investors (who cannot avail themselves of the system). Franck argues that the fact that neither party has had a disproportionate amount of victory over the other suggests "that the arbitration process itself does not necessarily disfavor [governments]" (Franck, 2007: 49).

well into the millions.[12] However, tribunals have also shifted costs to the investor, particularly when it has found that the claims filed against the host state were frivolous.[13] In these cases, unless the investor has gone bankrupt, governments are often able to recoup a portion of their expenses against foreign investors.[14] Finally, because the focus of investor–state arbitrations is often on a legislative or administrative act passed by the host state, an award in favor of a claimant may also create significant "policy costs" for the host government (Salacuse, 2007–08: 146). Investors, likewise, face high costs from engaging in arbitration. These include the opportunity cost of devoting significant executive time and attention to the arbitration as opposed to the investor's business, the financial costs of the proceedings,[15] and the relationship costs, that is, the potential damage to the investor's relationships with the government, business community, and the public of the host country in which it operates (Salacuse, 2007–08: 147).[16] The case of Indonesia after the East Asia crisis illustrates the ways that rigid contractual protections can eventually lead to unsatisfactory outcomes for both the country and investors (see Box 24.1).

Process

Arbitration under ICSID is commenced when the claimant files a request for arbitration pursuant to ICSID rules. The request must specify, *inter alia*, the nationality of the parties, basic information regarding the dispute, and the date and instrument (such as a BIT or investment contract) by which the parties consented to have their dispute arbitrated pursuant to the Centre. The case is subsequently registered by the ICSID Secretariat, and is followed by the creation of a tribunal. The tribunal is generally comprised of three arbitrators: two party-appointed arbitrators and the President of the tribunal, appointed

---

[12] In *Pey Casado v. Chile*, for example, Chile's costs totaled about $9.5 million, which included its own legal costs of $4.3 million (net of the legal costs of the current annulment proceeding underway), the majority of the tribunal's costs which amounted to $3.15 million, and all of the claimant's legal fees, which equaled $2 million (UNCTAD, 2009b: 11).

[13] See, for example, *Cementownia "Nowa Huta" S.A. v. Republic of Turkey*, ICSID Case No. ARB(AF)/06/2, (where the Tribunal awarded Turkey $5.3 million in costs because it found that the claimants' alleged claim to ownership of the shares at issue was fraudulent); and *Plama Consortium Limited v. Bulgaria*, ICSID Case No. ARB/03/24, (where an ICSID tribunal ordered the claimant to pay $7 million for a portion of Bulgaria's legal fees (in addition to $460,000 for a share of the tribunal's procedural costs) after finding that the claimant had committed certain illegalities while investing in Bulgaria) (*IA Reporter*, February 10, 2009, and September 24, 2009).

[14] Both Turkey and Bulgaria are facing difficulties in collecting their cost awards as Plama Consortium Limited is believed to have no assets and Cementownia has gone out of business (*IA Reporter*, February 20 and September 24, 2009).

[15] An investor's financial costs will often include legal expenses and its share of the tribunal's expenses, with the possible addition of the host state's arbitral costs (assuming the tribunal engages in some sort of cost-shifting).

[16] See Box 24.1 for a description of Indonesia's experience involving the collapse of its electric power arrangements.

Box 24.1 The Collapse of Indonesia's Electric Power Arrangements

Indonesia's experience negotiating and arbitrating with foreign investors as a result of the 1998 East Asia economic crisis is worth highlighting. In the 1990s, Indonesia invited foreigners to invest in its electric power sector, which was facing serious problems. In particular, the sector was suffering from a largely underdeveloped distribution system, mediocre planning and management on behalf of the state, low electricity tariffs, and high collection losses. Foreign investors rushed into Indonesia and began operating electricity distribution companies in the country. However, when the East Asia currency crisis hit, and the value of the rupiah and growth in electricity demand collapsed, the government could no longer honor its commitments to the investors. Accordingly, similar to what transpired in Argentina in the wake of the 2001 financial crisis, Indonesia suddenly found itself in the middle of various international disputes with foreign investors who were trying to collect damages for losses on their Indonesian investments. However, given the magnitude of the economic crisis at hand and the conditions under which the contracts at issue were negotiated, one wonders whether they should have been so rigidly upheld at all. In Wells and Ahmed's illuminating history of the collapse of these arrangements and subsequent dispute resolution, the authors conclude that the arbitration process "served the host countr[y] poorly" and that companies found the promised protections were "largely illusory."

Source: Wells and Ahmed (2007: 278, 285–7).

by agreement of the parties (ICSID, 2006: Art. 37). The vast majority of arbitrators appointed in ICSID cases are Western European (48 per cent) and North American (23 per cent); South Americans constitute 10 per cent of arbitrators in ICSID disputes (ICSID, 2010-1: 15).

There have been increasing challenges to arbitrator independence (UNCTAD, 2011). Of particular concern has been the risk of "issue conflicts" or "role confusion," whereby lawyers, as advocates, take certain positions regarding questions that, as arbitrators, they are asked to adjudicate or vice versa (Park, 2009: 648).[17] In other words, "[t]he arbitrator might be tempted, even subconsciously, to add a sentence to an award that could later be cited in another case [that] might lead to disparaging or approving some legal authority or argument regularly presented in similar disputes... The flip side of the coin might also present itself, with an arbitrator influenced by his or her position while acting as counsel in another case" (Park, 2009: 648). Nonetheless, commentators have argued that any incentives that may exist to produce biased decisions are outweighed by an even

[17] Other allegations of conflicts of interests have concerned, *inter alia*, an arbitrator's prior academic writings (see *Urbaser S.A. and Consorcio de Aguas Bilbao Biskaia, Bilbao Biskaia Ur Partzuergoa v. Argentine Republic*, ICSID Case No. ARB/07/26, where the claimant argued that Argentina's nominee, an academic, had expressed views contained in his prior writings that touched upon the matter in dispute); the fact that an arbitrator attended law school with claimant's counsel (see *Alpha Projektholding GMBH v. Ukraine*, ICSID Case No. Arb/07/16); and online blog postings by an arbitrator's law clerk (see *Tanzania Electric Supply Company Ltd. V. Independent Power Tanzania Ltd.*, ICSID Case No. ARB/98/8) (*IA Reporter*, April 9, 2009, and March 15, 2010).

stronger incentive to safeguard professional status (Park, 2009: 653). Further, the fact that arbitral institutions also need to maintain a reputation for "evenhandedness" in order to compete for arbitration business discourages biased behavior on the part of arbitrators (Park, 2009: 658).

Conflicts of interest are currently dealt with under ethical standards and disclosure rules provided by the relevant administrating body, such as ICSID or UNCITRAL, for example, and often supplemented by the International Bar Association's Guidelines on Conflicts of Interest.[18] Under ICSID rules, conflicts of interest are dealt with under Article 14 of the Convention, which provides that arbitrators need to exercise "independent judgment," and under Article 57, which provides that a party to the arbitration may propose disqualification of an arbitrator on account of any fact indicating a manifest inability to meet that standard. Additionally, Rule 6(2) of the ICSID Arbitration Rules requires arbitrators to sign a certification of independence at the beginning of the proceedings.

Once an arbitral tribunal issues an award, neither ICSID rules nor those of other arbitral institutions provide for avenues for appeal on the merits. The absence of a formal appeals mechanism in investor–state arbitration is the main contributing factor to what UNCTAD (2011) has identified as "the trend of diverging—and sometimes conflicting—awards" across various tribunals. At the core of this issue is the question of what role, if any, precedent should play in an arbitrator's decision-making process and whether a system of *stare decisis*, which would harmonize and create law that would apply across all tribunals, can or should exist in the dispute settlement system. While arbiters will often look to other cases for guidance on how to interpret a particular domestic statute or to define key terms in the parties' treaty, they are not formally restrained in deciding what prior approach to endorse, if any. This flexibility has led to divergent results in cases raising similar claims (UNCTAD, 2008: 12).[19] Nonetheless, arbitrators and practitioners often cite and engage with awards rendered by other tribunals (Weidemaier, 2010: 1908).[20] Indeed, an analysis of ICSID awards issued between 1990 and 2006 found that tribunals cited awards rendered by other ICSID panels about

---

[18] For a recent example of the use of IBA guidelines to decide an arbitral challenge, see *ICS Inspection and Control Services Limited v. The Republic of Argentina*, Decision on challenge to Mr. Stanimir A. Alexandrov, December 17, 2009, at 4 (available at <http://ita.law.uvic.ca/documents/ICSArbitratorChallenge.pdf>), where Argentina successfully challenged the claimant's nominee because of his law firm's representation of Vivendi in its ongoing dispute with Argentina.

[19] Further, cases brought against Argentina as a result of the 2001 financial crisis are illustrative. For example, in *CMS Gas Transmission Company v. the Argentine Republic*, the tribunal rejected Argentina's invocation of the state of necessity principle as a defense to the events resulting from its 2001 financial crisis. However, in *LG&E v. the Argentine Republic*, the tribunal held that the state of necessity defense applied, exempting Argentina from liability for measures taken during the financial crisis. And in May 2007, another arbitral tribunal (in the case of *Enron Corp. v. Argentine Republic*) reverted back to the CMS tribunal's approach in rejecting Argentina's state of necessity defense (*Investment Treaty News*, May 27, 2007).

[20] Weidemaier notes that awards that are well-reasoned and accessible to the public are necessary conditions to developing a system of precedent (Weidemaier 2010: 1914).

80 per cent of the time, and that ICSID tribunals have gradually developed an investment treaty " 'case law or jurisprudence' " (Weidemaier, 2010: 1908, citing Commission, 2007: 149–50). As this system of jurisprudence develops, it will likely lead to the emergence of a more consistent body of case law, a phenomenon that will be aided by the greater publication of awards.[21]

Despite the lack of an appeals court, an aggrieved party can nonetheless challenge an award on annulment grounds. Under ICSID (2006: Art. 52) rules, an award can be annulled in one of five instances: the tribunal was not properly constituted; it manifestly exceeded its powers; corruption on the part of an arbitrator; that there was a serious departure from a fundamental rule of procedure; or that the tribunal failed to state the reasons on which its award was based. Once a party files for annulment, an ad hoc committee comprised of three members appointed by the ICSID Secretariat is formed. The committee hears from both sides and then issues a decision maintaining or overturning, in whole or in part, the tribunal's award. It is important to note that "[c]ase law has set a high threshold for annulment, and it has been emphasized that the annulment procedure should not be confused with an appeals procedure" (Fauchald, 2008: 305). Indeed, "the annulment procedure must be regarded only as an avenue for eliminating decisions based on clear violations of relevant rules, and not as an instrument for harmonizing the practice of ICSID tribunals" (Fauchald, 2008: 306).

If an award is not annulled, it is deemed final and can be automatically enforced against the host state. Specifically, the ICSID Convention (2006, Art. 54(1)) provides that "[e]ach Contracting State shall recognize an award rendered pursuant to this Convention as binding and enforce the pecuniary obligations imposed by that award within its territories as if it were a final judgment of a court in that State." However, the Convention also provides that the execution[22] of awards is subject to the laws of the state in which execution is sought (ICSID, 2006: Art. 54(3)). Significantly, this means that awards are subject to laws on state immunity (Bjorklund, 2009).[23] Laws on state immunity, which can vary greatly among different governments, pose the main obstacles to enforcement of arbitral awards against states. The rationale for maintaining this immunity (despite the fact that governments in investor–state cases have waived immunity from jurisdiction of an international tribunal) is because certain state assets, such as

---

[21] However, Weidemaier notes (p. 1921) that the development of a system of arbitral precedent does not depend on publication of the awards, so long as the "system participants have *access* to past awards and assign value to them as precedent" which is likely when arbitrators are "repeat players." Thus, Weidemaier argues that "arbitral precedent may evolve more readily in systems in which relatively few arbitrators capture a large share of the arbitration business."

[22] "Execution" refers to the mechanics of attaching assets to satisfy an award. In contrast, "recognition" of an award refers to the process by which a municipal court confirms that the award is authentic and thus has legal consequences (also known as exequatur). "Enforcement" may refer to both recognition and/or execution (Bjorklund, 2009).

[23] Non-ICSID cases are subject to the enforcement provisions of the New York Convention on the Recognition and Enforcement of Arbitral Awards. While the Convention does not provide that state immunity is an explicit ground to refuse enforcement of an award, immunity nonetheless can arise through one of the limited grounds to refuse enforcement, such as the public policy exception.

central bank reserves and military and diplomatic property, are essential to government business and therefore should not be subject to seizure (Bjorklund, 2009). Accordingly, an investor confronting an explicit refusal from a state to pay an award can have it executed only if he can locate state assets and successfully persuade a court that these are properly classified as "commercial" (Bjorklund, 2009). This can be a challenging task. For example, German businessman Sedelmayer, in his quest to enforce a $2.35 million award won against Russia in 1998, spent about ten years attempting to locate Russian "commercial" assets abroad.[24]

Nonetheless, even though states can avoid honoring arbitral awards by invoking state immunity as a defense, doing so is a clear violation of their international obligations. Indeed, the majority of investor–state awards have been honored by host governments. A non-exhaustive study found that only about half a dozen awards are outstanding[25] and that countries including Ecuador, Canada, Chile, Czech Republic, Hungary, South Africa, Lebanon, Latvia, Mexico, and Poland have paid awards or reached a settlement.[26] This is consistent with Parra (2007: 9–10) who found that almost all of the 23 ICSID awards (issued on or before October 2, 2007) ordering the host state to compensate the investor had been honored. This is a positive development from the perspective of the legitimacy of the system, since a dispute settlement system with no teeth is no dispute settlement system at all. And if investors are by and large unable to collect on their awards, they are less likely to be willing to invest in countries where the probability of breach is significant, thereby effectively undermining the investment provisions of BITs and other investment treaties. See Box 24.2 for Argentina's experiences with honoring arbitral awards.

The Likelihood of Negotiated Settlements

The shortcomings exposed above shed light on the costs of the system for both the investor and the state. To these must be added the significant relationship costs of arbitration,

---

[24] In doing so, Sedelmayer brought more than 20 different execution cases against Russia, including an attempt to impound Lufthansa Airlines' payments to Russia for overflights of Russian airspace. Eventually, Sedelmayer was able to convince a Cologne court to order an apartment complex that had been formerly the Soviet trade mission to be auctioned off so that he could collect his award, which by March 2008, had grown to 4.9 million euros (Bjorklund, 2009).

[25] These include, *inter alia*, German businessman Franz Sedelmayer's quest to enforce a 1998 award against Russia, in what is apparently the longest-running refusal to pay a BIT award, Thailand's refusal to pay a July 2009 award of $29 million plus interest in favor of German toll highway investor, Walter Bau AG, and Zimbabwe's refusal to honor a $8.2 million euro ICSID award rendered last year in favor of a group of Dutch farmers who sued the state for confiscation of Zimbabwean farms (*IA Reporter*, May 7, 2010).

[26] Luke Peterson's non-exhaustive study of award compliance and the authors' own difficulty in finding accurate information on the same adds credence to Franck's call for more empirical studies in this area. (See generally Franck, 2008b: 795–801, arguing that there have been very few empirical studies in the international investment law field to date that can paint a truly accurate picture of the gains and losses of the system.)

Box 24.2 Chasing Argentina

Argentina has become the most notorious exception to the rule that most host governments honor arbitral awards. Argentina has taken the position that Article 54 of the ICSID Convention entitles it to subject award compliance to review by local courts before they can be enforced, if at all (ICSID, 2008a).[1] As a result, most claimants are hesitant to pursue enforcement, as they fear years of ultimately unsuccessful litigation in the Argentine court system. Indeed, there is a high likelihood that arbitral awards reviewed by local Argentine courts will be deemed unconstitutional (Mazorati, 2006: 241).[2] Unsurprisingly, CMS Gas Transmission Company, the only claimant to date to fully pursue enforcement, declined to go to local courts when Argentine officials told it to do so. With little hope that it would ever collect on its award, CMS ultimately transferred its rights to a third party (*American Lawyer*, June 25, 2009). In 2009, as the successor in interest to CMS, Blue Ridge Investments sought confirmation of the award in the Southern District of New York. The case was subsequently dismissed in August 2009 when the parties informed the court that they had reached a settlement. However, the parties' settlement apparently fell through as evidenced by Blue Ridge's filing of a new petition to the court in January 2010 (*IA Reporter*, June 16, 2010). Accordingly, as of September 2010, the CMS award continues to be outstanding and the authors do not know of any settlement reached between the parties. Similarly, the French water services company, Vivendi, is also seeking to enforce its $105 million plus interest award against Argentina (ICSID, 2007). Even prior to the confirmation of the award, the annulment committee had permitted Vivendi to pursue enforcement after Argentina failed to provide financial insurance to the claimant that it would pay the award should it be confirmed (*IA Reporter*, February 28, 2009).

Nonetheless, the majority of claims against Argentina are still in the midst of the arbitral process (*IA Reporter*, December 17, 2008). Given the challenges with enforcement, it remains to be seen whether investors who are in the midst of proceedings will insist on pursuing their claims or whether they will seek other avenues of relief, such as a negotiated settlement. Significantly, many investors appear to be doing so. Indeed, at least 16 claims against Argentina have already been settled,[3] suggesting that investors are seeking alternative solutions to their dispute, even when awards have already been rendered in their favor.[4]

---

[1] See also ICSID, 2008b, at pp. 5–6, where an ad hoc committee in *Enron v. Argentina* explicitly disagreed with Argentina's position, stating that "it would be inconsistent with the purpose of the ICSID Convention if an award creditor had to bring proceedings pursuant to national-law-enforcement mechanisms established under Article 54(1) as a prerequisite for compliance with the award by the award debtor."

[2] See Marzorati, 2006: 241, stating that ICSID "awards may be deemed to be unconstitutional for overlooking the provisions of section 27 of the Argentinean Constitution and certain principles of Argentinian public law such as the representative, republican and federal form of government, the guaranty of equality under the law, the division of powers, the non-absolute nature of laws, and the like."

[3] For a list of cases that have settled, see Lucy Reed, Scorecard of Investment Treaty Cases Against Argentina Since 2001, KluwerArbitration, March 2, 2009 (<http://kluwerarbitrationblog.com/blog/2009/03/02/scorecard-of-investment-treaty-cases-against-argentina-since-2001/>).

[4] For example, despite having won an award of $57.4 million in 2007, US-based energy company LG&E is currently in settlement discussions with Argentina (*IA Reporter*, December 17, 2008).

effectively "destroy[ing] whatever business relationships remain between the aggrieved investor and host country" (Salacuse 2007–08: 153). Accordingly, "a rational investor will not lightly resort to th[e] dispute settlement process and will examine other options for redress of its grievance before doing so" (Salacuse 2007–08: 153). Indeed, most parties are likely to procure some form of settlement before resorting to arbitration. It is estimated that about 30 per cent of ICSID cases settle (Coe, 2005–06: 35) a percentage which is likely to be greater if one considers the number of non-ICSID disputes that must inevitably settle before arbitration. Since "an improvement in the use of negotiation as an alternative dispute-settlement process requires a better understanding of how investor-State negotiations take place" (Salacuse, 2007–08: 167), it is critical to identify the factors that play a role in parties' settlement calculations. As the Argentine cases illustrate, whether a host state is likely to honor an award is one such factor. But given that the costs and risks of arbitration go well beyond the risk of default on an eventual award, there are clearly a host of other determinants to the settlement equation.[27]

Given the likely destruction of the business relationship between investor and the host state, whether the investor has intentions of investing in the host country in the future is likely to influence its decision to settle. If an investor has a long-term investment horizon in the country, its business relationship with the host state will be of supreme importance and, accordingly, greater efforts are likely to be spent on finding an alternative solution to the dispute. For example, in a dispute pinning Enron against the Indian government over electricity power tariffs in the early 1990s, one of the factors that influenced the successful negotiation of the parties' dispute was the fact that Enron's business strategy in India contemplated undertaking numerous energy projects in the country over the long run. "Enron judged those potential future investments to be worth more than winning an arbitration award in a case that would certainly be a protracted struggle and that might ultimately destroy its opportunities to undertake other power projects in the country" (Salacuse, 2007–08: 167).

The opposite is also true. "If the lead investor is exiting the business involved or the developing world, it is likely to turn heavily to the new international system of property rights—in particular, to insurance or arbitration, or both" (Wells and Ahmed, 2007: 267). Likewise, the more long term and complex the investment, as is often the case with the privatization of public services, such as water, gas, or telecommunications, the more likely it is that a negotiated solution to the dispute will be procured. "In such cases, the host country is dependent on the continued provision by the investor of the needed public service and at least in the short run has no option but to continue to deal with the investor. Similarly, the investor, having committed substantial capital to the

---

[27] The remarks of Grant Kesler, Metalclad's former CEO, concerning his experience arbitrating a NAFTA claim against Mexico are of interest. Despite winning a $17 million award, Kesler regretted pursuing arbitration (particularly the length, cost, and uncertainty of the process) and instead "wished he had merely entrusted his company's fate to informal mechanisms" (Coe, 2005–06: at pp. 8, 9 citing Grant Kesler). However, given that the award was only 20 per cent of the amount Metalclad believed it was owed, disappointment with the award amount must have also contributed to Kesler's general disillusionment with the investor–state dispute settlement mechanism.

privatized enterprise, is dependent on the host country for continued reserves and at least in the short run has few options with respect to settling its investment" (Salacuse, 2007–08: 141). Finally, the extent and size of investments in *other* countries may also impact the investor's decision to arbitrate since filing for arbitration against a particular host government can be a negative signal to future hosts. In this regard, it is interesting to note that subsequent to CMS's difficulties in Argentina, CMS sold all its investments in Brazil, Chile, and Venezuela, as well as in the Middle East, Africa, and India (CMS News Release, 2007).

Another important factor affecting the parties' chances of settlement is the fact that investor–state disputes are often political in nature, and as such usually involve a public good. For the host state, this means that the public, media, and political groups will often have, and voice, a specific position on the dispute in question, inevitably constraining the government's ability to negotiate, particularly if doing so will make the state appear weak vis-à-vis the foreign investor (Salacuse, 2007–08: 149–50). In such instances, it may be politically easier for the government to justify an unfavorable result from foreign arbitrators, a process it does not control, than a negotiated solution that it fully participated in (Salacuse, 2007–08: 169). Similarly, corporate executives may also prefer "imposed outcomes" to avoid being punished by dissatisfied shareholders for any eventual financial liability resulting from the dispute (Coe, 2005–06: 29). Additionally, another factor negatively affecting settlement is the fact that no single government agency is authorized to conduct negotiations on behalf of the government, thereby making the negotiations between the parties extremely difficult (Legum, 2006: 23).

Finally, the fact that many BITs and other investment treaties do not effectively promote alternatives to arbitration may have an effect on settlement rates. While most treaties call for parties to attempt to resolve their disputes through consultation and negotiation for a specified period of time (usually about three or six months) before arbitrating, Franck (2008a: 153) notes that the "lack of a clear consent to procedural parameters and the lack of substantive obligations leave[s] the [call for an amicable resolution] with little force." Accordingly, commentators have begun to explore how alternatives to arbitration, such as conciliation and mediation, might be better applied to the investor–state context.[28] A greater emphasis on ADRs has been touted as a possible solution to overcome the perceived shortcomings of the system as well as an efficient way to relieve the increasing pressure on the system from the rising number of arbitrations (Coe, 2005–06: 12).[29] Indeed, the ICSID Secretariat now routinely alerts disputants to the conciliation alternative and is exploring ways to increase access to conciliation (Boralessa, 2009: 4). Commentators have suggested, *inter alia*, designating a specific government agency to manage investor–state disputes and for negotiating settlements, adding specific treaty language encouraging or authorizing the use of ADRs to signal to the parties

---

[28] See generally, Salacuse, 2007–08; Coe, 2005–06; Franck, 2008a; and Boralessa, 2009.

[29] Coe (2005–06: 12) observes that the number of investor–state cases in recent years is "unprecedented" and that this "amplified roster of cases has both placed pressure on the institutions to handle such disputes (principally ICSID), and fueled interest in questions of reform and process design."

that the states intended for disputants to have access to ADR (Salacuse, 2007–08: 166, 170), and implementing treaty mechanisms that would allow for automatic conciliation, "so as to remove the onus of suggesting it from the party" (Coe, 2005–06: 37).

Improving the Dispute Settlement Process: The Way Forward

This analysis has attempted to shed light on the current dynamics of the system with a view to providing a useful framework through which to think about how to elicit better outcomes. The increasing popularity of treaties with dispute settlement provisions has led to a surge in investor–state arbitration over the past 13 years (ICSID, 2010-1: 7). In this time, what has emerged is a sophisticated dispute settlement system that has allowed investors to bring grievances against host states for alleged mistreatment of substantive rights (Franck, 2008a: 149). This phenomenon has marked a shift away from the "gunboat diplomacy" approach to resolving investment disputes that often left the investor without a proper forum to redress its grievances. Overall, the system has succeeded in providing a forum for the parties to resolve their disputes. Further, the general success in the enforcement of arbitral awards means that the dispute settlement has real teeth. Indeed, the Argentine cases are clearly outliers in the system. These two factors are important and significant for both the healthy functioning of the system as a whole and its legitimacy in the eyes of its users and the international community.

But serious challenges remain. Significantly, the system still suffers from a lack of transparency. Making the system more transparent would help increase the overall legitimacy of the system, both in the countries where the investors operate and on an international level. This in turn would make awards appear more legitimate and further facilitate enforcement against defendant states. Finally, greater transparency would also help to create a more robust and consistent case law which in turn would produce more reliable and predictable results.

The system also needs to find a way to moderate conflict of interest claims, so that these do not risk undermining its legitimacy. One possible solution might be to forbid the practice of allowing each side to appoint its own arbitrator. Paulsson (2010: 8, 9) notes that the vast majority of dissenting opinions are written by the arbitrator nominated by the losing party, which although does not necessarily imply that the arbitrator did not arrive at an unbiased opinion of the case, certainly instills less confidence in the neutrality of unilaterally appointed arbitrators and is thus "inconsistent with the fundamental premise of arbitration: *mutual* confidence in arbitrators." Paulsson (2010:11) suggests that an even more effective mechanism to moderate conflict claims would be to require arbitral appointments to be made from a pre-existing list of qualified arbitrators from the administrating institution. "When composed judiciously by a reputable and inclusive, international body, with in-built mechanisms of monitoring and renewal, such a restricted list may have undeniable advantages as a fairly intelligent compromise." Even though each party would still be allowed to appoint its own arbitrator, the fact that each potential nominee has been vetted by the arbitral institution means that they are less likely to be biased, or at the very least, less likely to be perceived as biased, in favor of the appointing party.

Further, many of the system's shortcomings might be addressed through refining current treaty language in order to fully protect the state's right to regulate in the public interest and to better clarify the scope and meaning of specific treaty provisions, in an effort to reduce the risk of divergent, and perhaps erroneous, interpretations of these by future tribunals. As the experiences in Indonesia and Argentina show, a more flexible approach to contract interpretation and enforcement, that is, one that appropriately takes into account changed circumstances, the role of corruption, and reasonable expectations from public policy, would help to ensure better and fairer results. (Wells and Ahmed, 2007: 293). One way this could be achieved is through the inclusion of broader force majeure clauses in investment treaties. These would also help to minimize the "moral hazards" created by the system. Specifically, as Wells and Ahmed (2007: 290) point out, by effectively discouraging companies, based on rigidly interpreted rights, from seeking resolution through renegotiating contractual arrangements, the system encourages possible moral hazards. Finally, the current effort to promote settlement and alternative dispute resolution mechanism needs to continue and to further develop so as to provide a real, attractive alternative to the parties.

Recent international investment agreements, such as the recently concluded US FTAs,[30] are addressing some of the system's shortcomings. In an effort to reach a better balance between investor protections and the preservation of state sovereignty these treaties narrow the scope of specific substantive obligations, such as expropriation and the minimum standard of treatment, and also modify important procedural rules (Gagne and Morin, 2006: 369–78). The latter includes providing preliminary procedures to deter the filing of frivolous claims and exempting certain claims entirely from adjudication, such as treatment in cases of strife, measures regarding payments and transfers, and disputes already submitted to a national court. These agreements also make significant progress with regards to transparency and enhancing public participation in the dispute settlement process. In particular, they require that the hearings and the main documents of the proceedings are made public and explicitly provide tribunals with the authority to accept and consider amicus submissions. Another major development of the recently concluded FTAs is the anticipation of an appellate body. Although the agreements themselves do not establish an appellate mechanism, they provide that if a separate multilateral agreement establishes one, the parties should strive to reach an agreement that would allow this appellate body to review the awards.

With regards to refining the treaty language to allow sufficient room for legitimate state regulation, some new treaties, such as the Canada–Jordan BIT (2009) and Peru–Singapore FTA (2008), have introduced general exceptions that exempt measures necessary to protect human, animal, or plant life or health, or for the conservation of exhaustible natural resources and public morals, for example. Other treaties

---

[30] These are US FTAs with Singapore, Chile, Central American countries (CAFTA), and Morocco.

have also carved out exceptions for national security (e.g., Ethiopia–United Kingdom BIT (2009) and those involving the stability of the financial system (Rwanda–USA BIT (2008)). Further, new agreements have also sought to clarify their intended scope by excluding certain areas of regulation from the agreement altogether, such as taxation and government procurement, or excluding specific assets from the definition of investment and including objective criteria as to what constitutes an investment (UNCTAD, 2010a: 87).

To these developments must also be added the current efforts to increase the role and use of ADRs in investment treaties, as discussed above, which will also benefit from expanded research and technical assistance for developing countries provided by UNCTAD in this area, and the ongoing revision processes of international arbitration rules, such as those of UNCITRAL and the ICC (UNCTAD, 2011).

Taken together, these reforms would help correct the perceived imbalances of the system.

VI. Conclusions

Investment provisions in BITs and reciprocal PTAs are rapidly putting in place a worldwide network of basic regulation covering a sizeable portion of FDI. Ironically, many of these agreements contain far more ambitious provisions—such as investor–state dispute resolution—than those proposed at the outset of the Doha Round and that countries collectively have resisted. There is some evidence that provisions in these arrangements have on average contributed to increased investment flows, but these findings are by no means universal. Studies indicate that investment provisions can help some stable countries with otherwise less developed property rights or those initiating reforms, and they appear to be most helpful in attracting foreign investment when undertaken in combination with multilateral or preferential trade agreements. The mixed results of the evidence and the several unanswered questions underscore the wisdom of avoiding sweeping assertions of benefits and instead tailoring the policy recommendations to each country.

One reason is that according investor protections under these agreements has come at considerable cost for some countries. The number of cases that investors lodge against governments in developing countries has risen geometrically along with the size of damages claimed. That said, actual awards have typically been a fraction of total claims, and governments have won a significant minority of dispute cases. The process of investment dispute resolution could be made more efficient and equitable through reforms that improved transparency, appointment of arbitrators, and more tightly worded rights and obligations under the contracts. The situation in Indonesia after the East Asia crisis of 1997–98 and of Argentina in 2001–02 underscore the need to include provisions that accommodate unanticipated macroeconomic shocks through more flexible force majeure arrangements.

APPENDIX

Table 24.A1 Selected Econometric Studies of FDI Response to Investor Protections

Authors–study	Dependent variable	Years	Host and home countries	Main results
Adams, Dee,Gali, and McGuire, 2003	Share of outward FDI stock located in host country	1970–97	116 countries and 18 PTAs examined; 9 with investment provisions	Of 9 PTAs, 6 had positive effects of investment provisions. FDI responds significantly to the non-trade provisions of PTAs—but not to bilateral investment treaties
Aisbett, 2007	Bilateral (log) inflows of FDI	1980–99	28 DCs. 29 OECD countries. Less than 672 observations per year	BITs are positively and significantly correlated with FDI inflows. Endogeneity of BITs mutes association
Banga, 2003	FDI inflows	1980–2000	15 host developing countries from South, East and SE Asia	FDI policies and BITS are an important determinant of FDI inflows, especially removal of restrictions
Busse, Koeniger, and Nunnenkamp, 2008	Three-year averages of bilateral FDI flows measured as a share of a host country in the outflows of a home country	1978–2004	83 host developing countries and transition economies and 28 home countries, including 10 developing countries	BITs promote FDI inflows to developing countries from developed countries. BITs may substitute for weak local institutions
Busse, Koniger, and Nunnenkamp 2010	Bilateral FDI flows	1978–2004	28 source countries; 83 developing countries	BITs help attract FDI to developing host countries
Buthe and Milner 2008	FDI inflows calculated as a percentage of GDP.	1970–2000	122 developing countries	WTO and PTAs have a significantly positive effect on inward FDI flows
Desbordes and Vicard, 2009	FDI stock (current USD)	1991–2000	30 OECD countries and 62 OECD and non-OECD countries	BITs have greater effect when implemented between countries with political tensions while they have no significant effect between friendly countries. BITs *do* work as a commitment device. Entry into force of a BIT increases bilateral FDI stocks by 16%, on average, after taking into account its indirect effects

Table 24.A1 *Continued*

Authors–study	Dependent variable	Years	Host and home countries	Main results
Egger and Merlo, 2008	Nominal bilateral stocks of FDI	1980–2001	24 home and 28 host in mainly transition countries	Short-run effect of BITs that amounts to 4.8%, and the long run effect amounts to 8.9%
Gallagher and Birch, 2006	Total FDI inflows; FDI inflows from the US	1980–2003	24 host countries from Latin America	Neither the total number of BITs nor BITs with the US have an independent and positive effect on total FDI inflows or inflows from the USA
Haftel, 2009	FDI flows	1977–2004	Large sample of developing countries	Mutually ratified treaties increase FDI flows, in contrast to signed treaties that have no effect on FDI flows
Hallward-Driemaier, 2003	Bilateral flows of FDI ; inflows/GDP; and share of home country outflows	1980–2000	31 host developing countries. 20 OECD countries. 537 pairs of countries	No statistically significant effect of BITs on FDI inflows
Hufbauer and Schott, 2007	One-way or two-way bilateral merchandise trade flows	1976–2005	13 regional agreements–15 countries (Americas, East and South Asia, and Oceania)	The growth of trade often leads the growth of FDI–trade is the "mother" of inward direct investment, with an elasticity estimate of 0.52–when a country increases its trade with the world by 10%, its inward FDI stock also increases by 5%
Kerner, 2009	Total FDI flows	1982–2001	FDI flows from OECD countries to developing countries	BITs attract significant amount of investment from protected and unprotected investors. This needs to be corrected in statistical methods applied
Lesher and Miroudot, 2006	Total FDI flows (net)	1990–2004	177 countries (34 North–North and South–South RTAs in total)	Investment provisions are positively associated with trade and to an even greater extent, investment flows–suggesting either that substantive investment provisions in RTAs impact trade and FDI flows more profoundly, or that the combination of substantive investment provisions rules and provisions liberalizing other parts of the economy jointly impact trade and investment more significantly

Continued

Table 24.A1 *Continued*

Authors–study	Dependent variable	Years	Host and home countries	Main results
Neumayer and Spess, 2005	FDI inflows into a host country in constant 1996 US$; share of a host country's total inflows of developing countries	1970–2001	119 DCs; OECD countries	Positive effect of BITs with developed countries on FDI. A one standard deviation increase in BITs may increase FDI inflows by between 44% and 93%
Salacuse and Sullivan, 2005	Total FDI inflows (% changes) Bilateral FDI flows from US	1998–2000. 1991–2000	100 developing countries31 developing countries, USA. 300 observations	US BITs have a large, positive and significant association with a host country's overall FDI inflows. Impact of other OECD BITs is weaker
Swenson, 2006	Number of new BITs signed	1990–94 and 1995–9	Africa, CEE, Asia, and South America	In 1990s, high-income countries and "risky" countries showed a propensity to enter new BITs—this was especially true for Asian countries. Data for the 1990s show that signing of the BITs was positively correlated with previous investment levels
Tobin and Busch, 2010	PTA formation	1960–2004	132 low and middle income countries, and 23 OECD partner countries	BITs between developed and developing country increases the predicted probability that this dyad will subsequently form North–South PTAs
Tobin and Rose-Ackerman, 2006	Total FDI inflows into DCs in constant 2000 dollars OECD outflows to DCs in constant dollars Five-year averages	1980–2003	137 developing countries	Number of BITs with a high-income countries has a positive and significant effect on FDI inflows. More worldwide BITs reduce the marginal benefit of an extra BIT to a host country

Table 24.A1 *Continued*

Authors–study	Dependent variable	Years	Host and home countries	Main results
UNCTAD 2009 (a)	Dependent variables in the studies the report uses are: IIAs (BITs and PTIAs)	1998–2008	Developing countries	There is no mono-causal link of IIAs and FDI. IIAs can influence the company's decision on where to invest, and this impact is stronger in PTIAs—more than for BITs. Strength of impact varies and depends on market size
	BITs signed	2005–08		BITs do not change the key economic determinants of FDI, but they improve policy and institutional determinants, and in so doing increase the likelihood of developing countries involved in BITs receiving more FDI
UNCTAD, 1998	1. Bilateral FDI flows; share of host country in home country's total outflows; share of home country in total host country's FDI inflows	1971–94	72 host developing countries. 14 OECD countries	BIT could cause small increase of FDI from a home partner country. But results are not robust. Small redirection of FDI to BIT partners
	2. Total FDI inflows into a host country; FDI stocks; FDI/GDP	1995	133 host developing countries	BITs found to have a positive and statistically significant effect in three out of nine regressions
Yackee 2007 (a)		1970–2000	1,000 BITs	Significant variation in extent to which treaties might meaningfully serve to credibly commit host states to treat investors favorably. BITs are not solution to the "obsolescing bargain"
Yackee 2007 (b)	FDI share	1984–2003	119 developing countries and OECD countries	The effect of BITs on FDI is largely insignificant. BITs are statistically significant predictors of FDI in low-risk countries

REFERENCES

Abbott, F. (2004), 'The Doha Declaration on the TRIPS Agreement and Public Health and the Contradictory Trend in Bilateral and Regional Free Trade Agreements.' Occasional Paper 14, Quaker United Nations Office.

Adams R., Dee P., Gali J., and McGuire G. (2003), 'The Trade and Investment Effects of Preferential Trading Arrangements—Old and New Evidence.' Productivity Commission Staff Working Paper. Canberra: Productivity Commission.

Adlung, R. and Molinuevo, M. (2008), 'Bilateralism in Services Trade: Is There Fire Behind the (BIT-)Smoke' NCCR Trade Working Paper 2008/6 and WTO Staff Working Paper ERSD 2008-01, January.

Aisbett, E. (2007), Bilateral Investment Treaties and Foreign Direct Investment: Correlation versus Causation. Berkeley: University of California Press.

Bjorklund, A. K. (2009), 'State Immunity and the Enforcement of Investor-State Arbitral Awards.' In Binder, C., et al. (eds.) International Investment Law for the 21st Century: Essays in Honor of Christoph Schreuer. Oxford: Oxford University Press.

Boralessa, A. (2009), 'Reconceptualizing the Mediation of Investor State Disputes.' Rutgers Conflict Resolution Law Journal, 7(1): 4.

Busse, M., Königer J., and Nunnenkamp P. (2010)). 'FDI promotion through bilateral investment treaties: more than a bit?' Review of World Economics, 146(1):147–77 and Kiel Institute for the World Economy working paper 1403.

Büthe T. and Milner H. (2008), 'The Politics of Foreign Direct Investment into Developing Countries: Increasing FDI through International Trade Agreements?' American Journal of Political Science, 52(4): 741–63.

CMS News Release, (2007), 'CMS Energy and CMS Electric and Gas Close Sale of CMS Energy Brasil fro $211.1 Million.' CMS Energy: <http://www.cmsenergy.com/MediaCenter/> (Accessed April 2013)

Coe, J. Jr (2005-2006), 'Toward a Complementary Use of Conciliation in Investor-State Disputes—A Preliminary Sketch.' U.C. Davis Journal of International Law and Policy, 12(7): 35.

Commission, J. P. (2007), 'Precedent in Investment Treaty Arbitration: A Citation Analysis of a Developing Jurisprudence.' Journal of International Arbitration, 24(2): 129–58.

Cosbey, A. (2005). 'International Investment Agreements and Sustainable Development: Achieving the Millennium Development Goals'. Winnipeg: International Institute for Sustainable Development.

Cosbey, A., Mann, H., Peterson, L., and Von Moltke, K. (2004), Investment and Sustainable Development: A Guide to the Uses and Potential of International Investment Agreements. Ottawa: International Institute for Sustainable Development.

Desbordes, R. and Vicard, V. (2009), 'Foreign Direct Investment and Bilateral Investment Treaties, an International Political Perspective.' CES Working Papers. Journal of Comparative Economics, 37(3): 372–86.

Egger, P. and Merlo, V. (2007), 'The Impact of Bilateral Investment Treaties on FDI Dynamics.' The World Economy. Oxford: Blackwell.

European Commission (2010), 'Council authorises signature of EU-Korea Free Trade Agreement.' September 16. Available at <http://trade.ec.europa.eu/doclib/press/index.cfm?id=619> (Accessed April 2013).

Fink, C. and Reichenmiller, P. (2005), 'Tightening TRIPS: Intellectual Property Provisions of U.S. Free Trade Agreements.' In Newfarmer, R. (ed.) Trade, Doha, and Development: A Window into the Issues. Washington, DC: The World Bank.

Fauchald, O. K. (2008), 'The Legal Reasoning of ICSID Tribunals—An Empirical Analysis.' *European Journal of International Law*, 19(2): 301–64.

Franck, S. (2007), 'Empirically Evaluating Claims About Investment Treaty Arbitration.' *North Carolina Law Review*, 86(1): 4–59.

Franck, S. (2008a), 'Challenges Facing Investment Disputes: Reconsidering Dispute Resolution in Investment Agreements.' In Sauvant, K. P. (ed.) *Appeals Mechanisms in International Investment Disputes*. Oxford: Oxford University Press.

Franck, S. (2008b), 'Empiricism and International Law: Insights for Investment Treaty Dispute Resolution.' *Virginia Journal of International Law*, 48(4): 767.

Gagne, G. and Morin, J.-F. (2006), 'The Evolving American Policy on Investment Protection: Evidence from Recent FTAs and the 2004 Model BIT.' *Journal of International Economic Law*, 9(2): 357–82.

Gallagher, K. and Birch, M. (2006), 'Do Investment Agreements Attract Investment? Evidence from Latin America.' *Journal of World Investment and Trade*, 7(6): 961–74.

Haftel, Y. Z. (2009), 'The Effect of U.S. Investment Treaties on FDI Inflows to Developing Countries: Signaling or Credible Commitment?' Paper prepared for presentation at the *ISA 50th Annual Convention*, New York City, February 15–18.

Hallward-Driemeier, M. (2003), 'Do Bilateral Investment Treaties Attract FDI? Only a bit...and they could bite.' World Bank Policy Research Paper 3121. Washington, DC: The World Bank.

Hoekman, B. and Newfarmer, R. (2003), 'After Cancun: Continuation or Collapse.' *Trade Note* No. 13. Washington, DC: The World Bank.

Hufbauer, G. C. and Schott, J. J. (2007), 'Fitting Asia-Pacific Agreements into the WTO System.' Presented at a Joint Conference of The Japan Economic Foundation and Peterson Institute for International Economics on "New Asia-Pacific Trade Initiatives" November 27. Washington, DC: Peterson Institute for International Economics.

IA Reporter (2007–2010), Various. Available at <http://www.iareporter.com>. (Accessed April 2013)

ICSID (2006), Convention, Regulations and Rules, Articles 36 and 37, April 2006. Available at <http://icsid.worldbank.org/ICSID/StaticFiles/basicdoc/CRR_English-final.pdf> (Accessed April 2013).

ICSID (2007), *Compañia de Aguas del Aconquija S.A. and Vivendi Universal v. Argentine Republic,* ICSID Case No. ARB/97/3, Award, August 20, 2007.

ICSID (2008a), *Siemens v. Argentina,* ICSID Case No. ARB/02/8, Argentina's Response to US Department of State Letter, June 2, 2008.

ICSID (2008b), *Enron Corporation Ponderosa Assets, L.P. v. The Argentine Republic,* ICSID Case No. ARB/01/3, Annulment Proceeding, Decision on the Argentine Republic's Request for a Continued Stay of Enforcement of the Award (Rule 54 of the ICSID Arbitration Rules), 7 October 2008.

ICSID (2010a), *ICSID Caseload—Statistics,* Issue 2010-1. Available at <http://icsid.worldbank.org/ICSID/FrontServlet?requestType=ICSIDDocRH&actionVal=CaseLoadStatistics> (Accessed April 2013).

ICSID (2010b), *The ICSID Caseload—Statistics,* Issue 2010-2. Available at <http://icsid.worldbank.org/ICSID/FrontServlet?requestType=ICSIDDocRH&actionVal=CaseLoadStatistics> (Accessed April 2013).

ICS Inspection and Control Services Limited v. The Republic of Argentina, Decision on challenge to Mr. Stanimir A. Alexandrov, December 17, 2009 at 4. Available at <http://ita.law.uvic.ca/documents/ICSArbitratorChallenge.pdf> (Accessed April 2013.)

Kerner, A. (2009), 'Why Should I Believe You? The Costs and Consequences of Bilateral Investment Treaties.' *International Studies Quarterly,* 53: 73–102

La Porta, R., Lopez de Silanes, F., Shleifer, A., and Vishny, R. (2002), 'Investor Protection and Corporate Valuation.' *Journal of Finance,* LVIII(3): 1147–58.

Lederman, D., Maloney, W., and Serven, L. (2003). *Lessons from NAFTA for Latin America and Caribbean.* Washington DC: World Bank.

Legum, B. (2006), 'The Difficulties of Conciliation in Investment Treaty Cases: A Comment on Professor Jack C. Coe's Toward a Complimentary Use of Conciliation in Investor-State Disputes A Preliminary Sketch.' *International Arbitration Report* 21(4).

Lesher, M. and Miroudot S. (2006), 'Analysis of the Economic Impact of Investment Provisions in Regional Trade Agreements.' OECD Trade Policy Working Papers, No. 36.

Marzorati, O. J. (2006), 'Enforcement of Treaty Awards and National Constitutions (the Argentinian Cases).' *Business Law International,* 7(2): 226–41.

Miroudot, S. (2011), 'Investment' In Chauffour J.-P. and Maur, J.-C. (eds.) *Preferential Trade Policies for Development: A Handbook.* Washington DC: The World Bank.

Neumayer, E. and Spess, L. (2005), 'Do Bilateral Investment Treaties Increase Foreign Direct Investment to Developing Countries?' *World Development,* 33(10): 1567–85.

Office of the United States Trade Representative (2010), Free Trade Agreements. Available at <http://www.ustr.gov/trade-agreements/free-trade-agreements> (Accessed April 2013).

Paulsson, J. (2010), 'Moral Hazard in International Dispute Resolution.' Inaugural Lecture as Holder of the Michael R. Klein Distinguished Scholar Chair, University of Miami Law School, April 29.

Park, W. W. (2009), 'Arbitrator Integrity: The Transient and the Permanent.' *San Diego Law Review,* 46(62): 651–53.

Parra, A. R. (2007), The Enforcement of ICSID Arbitral Awards, 24th Joint Colloquium on International Arbitration: Session on Specific Aspects of State-Party Arbitration. Paris, November 16.

Peterson, L. E. (2003), 'Czech Republic Hit With Massive Compensation Bill in Investment Treaty Dispute.' *Investment News Bulletin,* March 21, 2003.

Reed, L. (2009), 'Scorecard of Investment Treaty Cases Against Argentina Since 2001.' KluwerArbitration, March 2. Available at: <http://kluwerarbitrationblog.com/blog/2009/03/02/scorecard-of-investment-treaty-cases-against-argentina-since-2001/ (Accessed April 2013).

Rose-Ackerman, S. and Tobin, J. (2005), 'Foreign Direct Investment and the Business Environment in Developing Countries: The Impact of Bilateral Investment Treaties.' (May 2, 2005). Yale Law & Economics Research Paper No. 293.

Salacuse, J. W. (2007–08), 'Is There A Better Way? Alternative Methods of Treaty-Based, Investor-State Dispute Resolution.' *Fordham International Law Journal,* 31(1): 138.

Salacuse, J. W. and Sullivan, J. P. (2005), 'Do BITs Really Work? An Evaluation of Bilateral Investment Treaties and Their Grand Bargain.' *Harvard International Law Journal,* 46(1): 67–130.

Stein, E. and Daude, C. (2001), 'Institutions, Integration and Location of Foreign Direct Investment.' In *New Horizons for Foreign Direct Investment.* Paris : OECD, pp. 101–28.

Swenson, D. L. (2006), 'Why Do Developing Countries Sign BITs?' *U.C. Davis Journal of International Law and Political Economy,* No.131. Berkeley: University of California Press

Szepesi, S. (2004a), 'Coercion or Engagement? Economics and Institutions in ACP-EU Trade Negotiations.' European Center for Development Policy Management, ECDPM Discussion Paper 56. Maastricht, Netherlands.

Szepesi, S. (2004b), 'How Did David Prepare to Talk to Goliath? South Africa's experience of trade negotiations with the EU.' European Center for Development Policy Management, *ECDPM Discussion Paper* 53. Maastricht, Netherlands.

te Velde, D. W. and Fahnbulleh, M. (2003), 'Investment Related Provisions in Regional Trade Agreements.' Paper prepared for the project on Regional Integration and Poverty. UK Department for International Development (DFID). London, October.

te Velde D. W. and Bezemer, D. (2006), 'Regional Integration and Foreign Direct Investment in Developing Countries.' *Transnational Corporations*, 15(2): 42–69.

Tobin, J. L. and Busch, M. L. (2010), 'A BIT is Better Than a Lot. Bilateral Investment Treaties and Preferential Trade Agreements.' *World Politics*, 62(1): 1–42.

Tobin, J. L. and Rose-Ackerman, S. (2011), 'When BITs Have Some Bite: The Political-Economic Environment for Bilateral Investment Treaties.' *The Review of International Organizations*, 6(1): 1–32.

Ulrich, H. (2004), 'Comparing EU Free Trade Agreements: Services.' *ECDPM in Brief*. Maastricht: ECDPM, pp. 3–7.

UNCTAD (1998), *Bilateral Investment Treaties in the mid-1990s.* New York: United Nations.

UNCTAD (2006a), Entry into Force of Bilateral Investment Treaties (BITs). *IIA Monitor* No. 3. Geneva: UNCTAD.

UNCTAD (2008), 'Latest Developments in Investor-State Dispute Settlement.' *IIA Monitor*, 1: 3–12.

UNCTAD (2009a), *World Development Report: Transnational Corporations, Agricultural Production, and Development.* Geneva: United Nations.

UNCTAD (2009b), 'Latest Developments in Investor-State Dispute Settlement.' *IIA Monitor*, 1: 10–11.

UNCTAD (2009c), 'Recent Developments in International Investment Agreements, 2008–June 2009.' *IIA Monitor* 3. Available at <http://www.unctad.org/en/docs/webdiaeia20098_en.pdf> (Accessed April 2013).

UNCTAD (2009d), 'The Role of International Investment Agreements in Attracting Foreign Direct Investment to Developing Countries.' UNCTAD Series on International Investment Policies for Development. New York and Geneva: United Nations.

UNCTAD (2010a), World Investment Report 2010: Chapter 3, *Recent Policy Developments*, at p. 87. Available at <http://unctad.org/en/Docs/wir2010_en.pdf> (Accessed April 2013).

UNCTAD (2010b), *Investor–State Disputes: Prevention and Alternatives to Arbitration.* Geneva: UNCTAD.

UNCTAD (2011), 'Latest Developments in Investor-State Dispute Settlement.' *IIA Issues Note 1* Available at <http://www.unctad.org/en/docs/webdiaeia20113_en.pdf> (Accessed April 2013).

Waldkirch, A. (2001), 'The New Regionalism and Foreign Direct Investment: The Case of Mexico.' Working Paper, Oregon State University.

Weidemaier, W. M., 2010. 'Toward a Theory of Precedent in Arbitration.' *William and Mary Law Review*, 51: 1895–1958.

Wells, L. and Rafiq, A. (2007). *Making Foreign Investment Safe: Property Rights and National Sovereignty.* New York: Oxford University Press.

World Bank (2004), *Global Economic Prospects 2005 Trade, Regionalism, and Development.* Washington, DC: The World Bank.

Yackee, J. W. (2007a), 'Conceptual Difficulties in the Empirical Study of Bilateral Investment Treaties.' *Brooklyn Journal of International Law*, 32(2): 444–53.

Yackee, J. W. (2007b), 'Do BITs Really Work? Revisiting the Empirical Link between Investment Treaties and Foreign Direct Investment.' Legal Studies Research Paper Series Paper, No. 1054. University of Wisconsin.

Yackee, J. W. (2010a), 'Do Bilateral Investment Treaties Promote Foreign Direct Investment? Some Hints from Alternative Evidence.' Legal Studies Research Paper Series Paper, No. 1114, University of Wisconsin.

Yackee, J. W. (2010b), 'How Much do U.S. Corporations Know (and Care) About Bilateral Investment Treaties? Some Hints from New Survey Evidence.' In Sauvant, K. P. (ed.) *Columbia FDI Perspectives*. Vale Columbia Center on Sustainable International Investment No. 31, November 23.

CHAPTER 25

DISPUTE SETTLEMENT IN THE WTO: A MANUAL[*]

ROBERT HOWSE

I. Introduction

The Legacy of the GATT

THE General Agreement on Tariffs and Trade (GATT) was originally intended as just one element of what was supposed to be a much more ambitious institutional structure. By 1950, it was clear that the US Congress would not accept the International Trade Organization, with the result that the 1947 GATT was the sole result of the Bretton Woods negotiations on international trade. Unlike the International Trade Organization (ITO) draft charter, the 1947 GATT made no provision for formal, legal dispute settlement, nor was there any explicit provision for recourse to the International Court of Justice in resolving disputes.

Article XXII provided for consultations where representations were made by one Contracting Party to another "with respect to any matter affecting the operation of this Agreement." Article XXIII provided for the possibility of an investigation, recommendations, and rulings by the CONTRACTING PARTIES (in effect, the GATT Council consisting of all member states) in a case where a Contracting Party considered that a benefit under the GATT was nullified and impaired. This applied not only in the case where the nullification and impairment flowed from a violation of a provision of the GATT, but in other circumstances as well (which gave rise to what are referred to as non-violation nullification and impairment complaints, discussed later in this chapter). Article XXIII also permitted the CONTRACTING PARTIES to authorize a Contracting Party to suspend concessions under the GATT with respect to another Contracting Party, where it considered that "the circumstances are serious enough to justify such

---

[*] This chapter draws extensively from M. J. Trebilcock, R. Howse, and A. Eliason (2012) and collaborations with Petros Mavroidis.

action." This was the treaty basis for the evolution of dispute settlement practice in the GATT. With the creation of the World Trade Organization (WTO) in 1995, Article XXIII was retained as part of the GATT while also forming the "core" as it were of the new detailed code on dispute settlement, which, (along with various Agreement-specific provisions, discussed below) governs dispute settlement practice not only with respect to the 1994 GATT but also for all the "covered agreements" under the WTO umbrella.

In the early years of the GATT, dispute settlement under Article XXIII was pursued through "working parties." These were ad hoc groups of diplomatic representatives to the GATT, including those from the parties to the dispute itself, who were charged with investigating the dispute, particularly the "factual evidence," with a view to making recommendations of a solution. In the 1950s, this practice was largely overtaken by the use of "panels" under Article XXIII, which continued until the adoption of the Dispute Settlement Understanding in the Uruguay Round.

The essential features of panel dispute settlement in the GATT as it evolved up to the Uruguay Round were as follows:

- A panel was struck by consensus of the GATT membership (the CONTRACTING PARTIES) upon the request of the Complaining Party or parties; the consensus requirement meant that any single Contracting Party, including the defending one, could block the establishment of a panel.
- The panelists were usually trade officials, either in Geneva missions or in national governments, or sometimes retired officials; they were rarely lawyers; in the later years of the GATT, academics and distinguished legal practitioners were occasionally appointed as panelists; nationals of the disputing parties were disqualified from serving as panelists, giving the process the character of independent, impartial, third-party dispute settlement.
- The panelists were charged with making "recommendations" to the membership as to how the dispute should be resolved; typically these included findings of fact and also legal rulings on whether the measures complained of were consistent with the obligations of the GATT.
- Adoption of the "recommendations" by consensus of the GATT membership gave the panel ruling the character of a legally binding settlement of the dispute at hand, although not a binding precedent for use in future disputes.
- As the legal affairs division of the GATT developed, it began to play an important role in the panel process, in both identification and selection of panelists, as well as in providing assistance to the panelists in drafting of reports. A "jurisprudence" or interpretative approach to the legal text of the GATT evolved largely through the participation of the legal affairs division in the panel process.
- In theory, it was possible under Article XXIII for the winning party in a dispute to suspend concessions under the GATT in retaliation if the losing party did not implement the adopted recommendations of the panel; in practice, this was authorized only once by the membership of the GATT (against the United States in a dispute with the Netherlands concerning dairy products in 1952).

In the Tokyo Round, a Dispute Settlement Understanding (DSU) was negotiated, which in many respects codified and clarified GATT practice as it had evolved to that point, with some relatively minor reforms that addressed some of the concerns that had been raised about the effectiveness of the process.

Key Elements of the WTO Dispute Settlement Understanding[1]

The DSU negotiated in the Uruguay Round (1986–94) reflects a response to many criticisms of the GATT dispute settlement process:

- Delay and uncertainty in the process, given the absence of a genuine legal right to a panel (this being dependent on a consensus of the GATT membership to establish a panel, including therefore the non-objection of the erstwhile defendant), absence of hard time limits on consultations, responses to requests for panels, and panel proceedings and rulings.
- An absence of legal rigor and clarity in the panels' rulings.
- The uncertainty of a panel ruling being adopted, given the consensus rule for adoption (which demanded the acquiescence of the losing party).
- Delay in and partial or non-complete compliance with panel rulings.

The DSU key elements are listed below, many of which can be seen as responses to the abovementioned shortcomings of the GATT process:

- A negative consensus rule for establishment of panels, such that a panel must be struck within a certain period of time if requested by a complaining member, unless there is a consensus of the membership *against* the establishment of a panel; in practice, this means a legal right to a panel since such a negative consensus would only occur in the contradictory situation of the very member asking for the panel objecting to its establishment! (However, it is possible for a defending member to block the establishment of a panel for a certain period of time by keeping the question of the agenda of the Dispute Settlement Body for one particular meeting).
- A series of detailed, legally required deadlines applying to various stages of the proceedings.
- The establishment of an Appellate Body (AB), with a right of appeal by the parties to any panel of any question of law; the Appellate Body members being distinguished legal experts appointed for a once-renewable term of four years.

---

[1] In what follows in the chapter, references referring to official documents and other official reports and to WTO cases are available on the WTO website—WTO.org. The DSU text is at: <https://www.wto.org/english/docs_e/legal_e/28-dsu_e.htm>. See the Appendix for additional resources.

- A negative consensus rule for the adoption of panel reports, as modified by the Appellate Body, and Appellate Body reports, such that these are adopted unless there is a consensus of the membership against adoption.
- A formal mechanism, with precise deadlines, for referral to a panel of any disagreement as to whether the losing member has adequately implemented an adopted panel and/or Appellate Body report.
- A detailed institutional structure for the authorization of suspension of concessions in the case that a member fails to implement recommendations within a reasonable period of time, including arbitration concerning the appropriate level and kind of retaliation.
- With some clearly specified variations, the same structure and procedures for dispute settlement apply with respect to all the "Covered Agreements," the main WTO treaties that bind all members, including those in new areas such as intellectual property and services.

The Purposes of WTO Dispute Settlement

Some of the objectives of the WTO dispute settlement system can be discerned through Article 3.2, which lists very general objectives of the dispute settlement system:

- The clarification of the rights and obligations in the WTO agreements.
- "Prompt settlement" of disputes.
- "Satisfactory settlement of the matter in accordance with the rights and obligations" of the WTO treaties.

It is sometimes suggested that there may be a tension between the objective of clarification of the law through highly legalized "judicial"-style rulings on the one hand, and prompt or satisfactory settlement on the other, which would put a premium on compromise—on settling the matter at hand rather than affirming or applying the rule of law as such. In reality, such a tension may be very much overstated. As Ronald Coase famously observed, in a world where transaction costs of bargaining are significant, parties will always bargain in the shadow of the law as they understand it. Clear, consistent legal rulings, with transparent and detailed reasons, help to prevent disputes by providing some certainty about the "rules of the road" that all WTO members must follow, and can also, where disputes do arise, reduce the transaction costs of a negotiated or political agreement or settlement by giving the disputing parties a sense of the likely scenarios that would arise if negotiations were to fail to produce such a settlement.

An issue that has arisen is whether it is appropriate for dispute settlement in the WTO to serve the function of addressing "gaps" or ambiguities in WTO treaty texts, especially in politically controversial matters. Here there is some ambiguity built into the DSU as well, for it envisages as noted that the dispute settlement organs will not only simply apply the rights and obligations in the covered agreement but will also engage in the clarification of these rights and obligations, while on the other hand also stating that dispute settlement rulings may not add to or diminish the rights and obligations in the covered agreements. Where a provision seems to leave a situation unaddressed, or where there seem to be tensions between different provisions of the covered agreements, where is the appropriate borderline between "clarifying" the law on the one hand and stepping into the impermissible territory of adding to or diminishing it on the other? Consider the following two often noted examples where commentators have been divided as to whether the AB inappropriately crossed that borderline.

Softwood Lumber

In the long-lasting softwood lumber dispute between Canada and the United States, the United States had been imposing countervailing duties against imports of Canadian lumber; the grounds were that Canada subsidized softwood lumber through setting prices for access to timber on government lands at a level below what would prevail in a competitive market. The WTO Subsidies and Countervailing Measures (SCM) Agreement specifies that there must be a financial contribution by government in order for a measure to be a subsidy that can legally be countervailed, and further defines that financial contribution is to be determined, in the case of goods and services supplied by government (in this case timber), by the relationship of the price at which they are provided to the government and the prevailing market price in the country in question, in this case Canada. In the WTO case, the United States argued that the government dominated the timber market in Canada to such an extent that no market price existed that was not influenced or determined by the government prices; in the circumstances, the United States defended its decision to compare Canadian governmental prices to US private market prices as reasonable. The AB agreed in part with the United States, stating that it was possible to use an alternative benchmark price, where a true market price does not exist in the country of export (but the AB did not endorse the choice of the US market price as necessarily acceptable). However, the SCM Agreement provides no textual basis for allowing an alternative to the market price in the country of export. Here, the AB seems to have gone beyond the four concerns of the text of the relevant WTO treaty, since the objectives of the Agreement could be undermined if the pervasiveness of government intervention in the exporting country were, in effect, to deprive a WTO member of the ability to take action against subsidies because the deviance of the subsidized price from market price was unmeasurable in that market. Was this a reasonable judicial intervention or illegitimate judicial activism?

Shrimp–Turtle

In the *Shrimp–Turtle* case, the AB had to address the highly controversial question of the use of trade restrictions to influence other WTO members' environmental practices and policies. The United States was relying on Article XX(g) of the GATT to justify an embargo on shrimp from countries in Asia that did not require their fishers to adopt sea turtle-friendly fishing technology. The United States claimed that endangered species of sea turtles were at risk from shrimp fishing, where such technologies were not employed, and thus that its measures were "in relation to the conservation of exhaustible natural resources." Article XX(g) is silent on whether its scope extends to measures aimed at the policies of other WTO members as opposed to protecting resources within the domestic jurisdiction of the defending WTO member. In the old *Tuna–Dolphin* dispute in the GATT system, two panels had essentially read Article XX restrictively as not extending to such sanction-type trade restrictions. These rulings were very controversial and neither panel was adopted.

In *Shrimp–Turtle,* the AB took the opposite tack in the presence of textual silence; it assumed that in the absence of a textual limitation, Article XX allowed WTO members to condition imports on the policies of other members. Some commentators, for instance Jagdish Bhagwati, see inappropriate "judicial activism" in the AB's approach, given that these kinds of sanctions have been viewed by many WTO members as incompatible with the multilateral trading system. Others, such as the author of this chapter, see the *Tuna–Dolphin* rulings as inappropriate "judicial activism" in that they read into Article XX a legal restriction on sovereign rights that was unwarranted by the treaty text and its context. While the former experts appeal to background understandings within the trade policy and diplomatic community at the WTO, the latter invoke background understandings of public international law, which include the notion that, in the presence of ambiguity, a treaty interpreter should read a provision in the manner that least infringes sovereign rights of the state being bound, and the assumption that economic sanctions are not in principle incompatible with general international law (as the International Court of Justice ruled in the *Nicaragua v. USA* case).

II. A STEP-BY-STEP CHRONOLOGY OF A WTO DISPUTE SETTLEMENT PROCEEDING

This section provides an overview of all the individual steps or stages that can occur in a WTO dispute, from the commencement of proceedings to the enforcement stage, making reference to the relevant legal provisions, deadlines, and practices of the participating actors and institutions.

Request for Consultations

- All WTO dispute settlement proceedings begin by a complaining member requesting consultations with a responding member concerning measures of the responding member. These are measures that either are claimed to violate provisions of the WTO covered agreements; or (in some rare cases) are claimed even if they do not violate any specific provisions, to "nullify and impair benefits (i.e., market access)" that the complaining member could reasonably expect to have obtained from prior tariff negotiations.

- A member must reply to a request for consultations within 10 days of receiving it, and enter into "consultations in good faith" within 30 days thereafter. If a member of whom consultations have been requested fails to comply with either deadline, then the member so requesting may "proceed directly to request the establishment of a panel."
- If consultations fail to resolve the dispute within **60** days of the receipt of the request for consultations, the complaining member may request the establishment of a panel. A panel may be requested before this 60-day period has expired where both the complainant and the responding member consider that consultations have failed to solve the dispute.

Alternatives to Initiating a Panel: Conciliation, Mediation, and Arbitration

The DSU provides for several forms of alternative dispute resolution, that is, alternatives to contentious panel proceedings. Conciliation, mediation, and good office involve using the Secretariat and the office of the Director-General to assist the parties in coming to a negotiated solution of their dispute; this may entail the appointment of a mediator. But this does not prejudice or limit the ultimate right to resort to contentious proceedings should a negotiated solution not be found. Below, conciliation will be illustrated in a case study of Thailand's resort to this technique to resolve a dispute with the European Community concerning tuna exports. In addition, Article 25 of the DSU provides for "arbitration." In one dispute where this has so far occurred, the US Music or Juke Box case, the arbitration came *after* an adopted panel report, and concerned an alternative remedy to withdrawal of the measure, in this case monetary damages. As is illustrated by this example, arbitration allows the parties to define by agreement among themselves the question to be arbitrated and the kind of decision and relief that they are seeking from the arbitrator.

Request for a Panel

- The request for a panel must "identify the specific measures at issue and provide a brief summary of the legal basis of the complaint sufficient to present the problem clearly" (Article 6.2).
- At a minimum the Articles of WTO covered agreements that the complaining member seeks to rely on must be mentioned in the request for a panel (*Korea–Dairy* case).
- The level of detail must be sufficient for the defending member to understand the nature of the case against it, admittedly a very general standard, and so it is possible that a greater degree of specificity may be required in some disputes.
- Sometimes, the specificity of the claim can be, by implication, what the defending member can be reasonably expected to understand in the circumstances, given the

history and context of the dispute. However, different panels seem to take more or less liberal or strict views of the specificity requirement and the approach of the Appellate Body is not entirely clear, so it is prudent to spell out the details of the claim as precisely as possible in the Request for the Panel.

- This is all the more so because of the consequence of a panel finding lack of adequate specificity: the panel will consider itself without jurisdiction to adjudicate that claim and it will *not* be considered. While each claim must be specified, the AB distinguishes between claims and arguments. The latter do not need to be specified in the request. In the *EC–Customs* case, the AB observed: "Nothing in Article 6.2 prevents a complainant from making statements in the panel request that foreshadow its arguments in substantiating the claim. If the complainant chooses to do so, these arguments should not be interpreted to narrow the scope of the measures or the claims."

Establishment and Composition of a Panel

- **DSB Meeting:** Article 2 of the DSU establishes the Dispute Settlement Body (DSB), which is the collectivity of WTO members acting in their dispute settlement capacity and has a role parallel to that of the GATT Council in the pre-WTO multilateral dispute settlement arrangements. Thus, the DSB "shall have the authority to establish panels, adopt panel and Appellate Body reports, maintain surveillance of implementation of rulings and recommendations, and authorize suspension of concessions and other obligations under the covered agreements" (Art. 2.1). Article 6 provides that a panel shall be established at the latest at the DSB meeting following the meeting at which the request first appears as an item on the agenda. A member may request the convocation of a DSB meeting for these purposes, and one shall be held within 15 days of the request for the meeting, subject to a 10-day advance notice requirement.

- **Choosing the Panelists:** Panels are to be composed of three panelists, based on nominations from the Secretariat from its rosters. WTO members may from time to time propose additional names of qualified persons to add to the rosters. However, a Party to a dispute may not challenge the Secretariat's choice of panelists, except for "compelling reasons" (Art. 8.6). Panelists are to be "well-qualified governmental and/or non governmental individuals." These may include persons who have served as diplomatic officials at the GATT, in the Secretariat, or as senior trade officials in national governments. The only non-governmental category explicitly mentioned is that of persons who have "taught or published on international trade law or policy." In theory, a Party to a dispute may not challenge the Secretariat's choice of panelists, except for "compelling reasons" (Art. 8.6). In practice, the Parties tend to attempt to maintain close control over who serves as a panelist and it can take some time to settle on three persons acceptable to the Parties. One qualification is that, in some of the covered agreements, expertise in a substantive public policy area may be an additional criterion relevant to the establishment of the rosters—for instance, the *Decision on Certain Dispute Settlement Procedures for the General Agreement on Trade in Services*, which provides that a special roster of panelists be established for dispute settlement under the GATS, comprising persons who have expertise related to trade in services, "including associated regulatory matters" (Art. 3). There is supposed to be at least one developing country panelist on every panel in a dispute where a developing country is a party. Increasingly, failure of the parties to agree on the composition of panels has led to appointment of panelists by the WTO Director General.

- **Participants in the Panel Process:** The rules of conduct that apply to participants in the panel process are available at <http://www.wto.org/English/tratop_e/dispu_e/rc_e.htm>. These include matters of conflict of interest, disclosure, and confidentiality.

- **The Parties:** Only WTO members may be parties in a dispute settlement. There is no provision in the DSU that allows the WTO Secretariat or the membership to refer questions of law to a panel or indeed to the Appellate Body (unlike, for instance, the advisory jurisdiction of the International Court of Justice (ICJ)). Who can be a complaining party is defined by the nature of the complaint that may be the basis of a panel proceeding, that is, either the complaint must allege a violation of a provision of a WTO covered agreement that nullifies or impairs benefits, or they must allege non-violation nullification and impairment. However, there need not be any historical or current harm to the complainant's actual trade or commercial interests. It is enough that they have a "legal interest" in the complaint, according to the Appellate Body (*EC–Bananas*). The notion of "legal interest" is very broad. In the Bananas case, the USA had never exported any bananas. However, it might have opportunities to do so in the future. Moreover, its multinationals operating banana plantations in Latin America had a direct interest. Thus the US government was among the complaining parties, along with Ecuador, Guatemala, Honduras, and Mexico.

- **Multiple Complaints:** More Than One Complaining Party: Article 9 deals with a situation where more than one member wishes to complain about "the same matter." In this situation, a single panel may be formed to examine the multiple complaints, "taking into account the rights of all Members concerned." The proceedings are to be organized so that all members enjoy the same rights that they would have had in the case of separate panels being formed (Art. 9.2). A particular difficulty arises where a member or members seek to join a complaint as an additional Party or Parties, once a panel has been formed on the basis of an individual complaint. In such a case, the Terms of Reference will have been determined through the original individual complaint. Thus, in order to join a complaint and still enjoy the right to raise claims not initially raised by the original individual complainant, the other members would appear to have to do so before the panel's Terms of Reference (its "jurisdiction") have been determined. However, while a panel cannot amend its own Terms of Reference (Bananas), the DSB can. Thus, in Reformulated Gasoline, when Brazil requested a panel on US measures which were already the subject of a complaint by Venezuela, the DSB established new Terms of Reference for the joint panel. In this case, it was a particularly straightforward matter, since the original panel had standard terms of reference, which did not limit the panel's consideration of any provision in a covered agreement relevant to disposing of the complaint. In cases of a joint complaint, the panel may issue multiple reports, each of which addresses the particulars of the complaint of a single member (as for example occurred in Bananas) (Art. 9.2). It is to be emphasized that there is no requirement that complaints by two or more members concerning the same or similar measures of another member be consolidated in the same panel proceeding.

- **Representation:** Parties have the choice of what individuals will represent them before panel proceedings. Often a party's Ambassador to the WTO, or officials from its trade ministry or Geneva mission, will be involved in making oral argument before the panel. In other instances, and especially where in-house resources are lacking, counsel from private law firms may represent parties in the proceedings. In many instances both government officials and outside counsel play a role in the preparation and presentation of argument. Where the individuals in question are not governmental officials, the party in question is responsible for ensuring that their conduct (for instance in relation to confidentiality) is in compliance with the requirements of the DSU.

- **Third Parties:** Article 10 affords third party status to any member "having a substantial interest in a matter" (102). This entails the right to make both oral and written submissions to the panel, and to obtain the submissions of the Parties to the dispute for the first meeting of the panel. "Third party submissions are to be provided to the parties to the dispute and shall be reflected in the final report". In a number of cases, (such as Hormones, where the third party rights were those of other *parties* in a multiple complaint), panels have granted enhanced third parties rights, including the right to observe the entire proceedings, and to receive all of the parties' submissions (see United States-Anti-Dumping Act of 1916, WT/DS136/AB/R, September 26, 2000, para.150).

- **The Secretariat:** The Secretariat (in the guise of the legal affairs division) provides administrative and legal support to the panel. Administrative support includes travel and meeting arrangements in Geneva, organization of conference calls, and providing a clearing house for documentation in the proceedings. Legal support includes drafting parts of panel rulings, a controversial function, since, in some notorious cases, the Secretariat officials have apparently insisted on legal positions at odds with the deliberations of the panelists themselves. With respect to disputes that involve the WTO Anti-Dumping, Subsidies and Countervailing Duties and Safeguards Agreements, however legal support comes from the so-called "rules" division of the Secretariat, not the legal affairs division.

- *Amicus Curiae*: Private individuals, non-governmental organizations, or WTO members, who are neither parties nor third parties to a WTO dispute, may submit written views on any legal or factual aspect of the dispute to the panel. There is no legal obligation for a panel to consider such views. In some instances, a panel may determine that a submission is not admissible, for instance where it is submitted at a late stage in the panel proceedings. There are no formal rules concerning *amicus* submissions in the DSU, so this is largely a matter of the discretion of the individual panel. Panels have very rarely cited explicitly *amicus* submissions. Whether reading such documents may have a subliminal or indirect impact on how panelists view a given case is an open question.

- **Working Procedures of the Panel:** Some of the requirements of WTO panel proceedings are set out in the DSU itself; in addition, Appendix 3 of the DSU sets out Working Procedures for the panels. It is important to note that: (1) the timetable outlined can be deviated from "in light of unforseen developments"; (2) additional procedures can be established by the panel itself on other matters, as need be.
- **Terms of Reference of the Panel:** The panel's terms of reference are determined with the decision of the DSB to establish the panel. The terms of reference must be based on the request for a panel. The terms of reference in effect establish the jurisdiction of the panel; this is why it is so crucial, as discussed above, that the request for a panel contain all claims that the claimants wants adjudicated, described with adequate specificity.
- **Objections to Jurisdiction:** The panel has the inherent judicial competence to determine whether it has jurisdiction, subject to Appellate Body review of any such finding. Unlike some international courts and arbitral tribunals, there are not normally extensive preliminary jurisdictional proceedings in WTO disputes. Jurisdictional issues may be considered as appropriate at any point in the proceedings, although they should normally be brought up as soon as possible. Jurisdictional rulings are contained in the interim and final reports. Panels do not issue reports with preliminary jurisdictional rulings. Once the terms of reference have been established clearly, there are very few grounds on which a panel's jurisdiction can be challenged (although parties do argue sometimes about just what is or is not within the ambit of the terms of reference).

  In certain instances, a defending party has sought to advance a sort of "political question" or "institutional balance" argument to challenge the jurisdiction, or scope of jurisdiction of the panel, when the political branches of the WTO are also involved in the same or overlapping matters (*India–Balance of Payments; Turkey–Textiles*). In these cases, the panels and the Appellate Body found no clear basis in the DSU or other WTO treaties for declining jurisdiction. A right to a panel is regarded as a fundamental aspect of the Uruguay Round deal, and it is an uphill battle to convince a panel that it has the discretion or the duty not to take jurisdiction. In the *EC–Biotech* dispute, the panel took jurisdiction, despite the fact that the measures complained of by Canada, the United States, and Argentina had largely been withdrawn. In *India–Autos,* it was argued that aspects of the claim had already been decided by previous WTO proceedings. However, the panel found there that the parties and claims were not identical in the old and the new proceedings, and therefore it decided that it had jurisdiction to adjudicate.
- **Parallel Proceedings in Other Fora:** Facts and legal claims may overlap between WTO dispute settlement and proceedings in some other international forum. As a general matter, international law does not provide clear rules on how to deal with such a possibility. There is no rule excluding parallel proceedings unless such a

rule exists in a treaty establishing the jurisdiction of the one or the other forum, or both. Article 23 of the DSU provides that the WTO dispute settlement system is the exclusive means by which a violation of WTO law is to be determined. However, some regional agreements may require the claimant to proceed in the regional forum to the exclusion of the WTO one, where there are claims both under the WTO and the regional agreement in question. In a dispute between Brazil and Argentina concerning poultry, proceedings were first brought under Mercosur and then later in the WTO. The panel was invited to decline jurisdiction on the basis that the claimant was estopped from bringing proceedings before the WTO panel, having already chosen to litigate the matter in Mercosur. While not excluding that in some circumstances such an estoppel might apply, the WTO panel nevertheless chose to exercise jurisdiction, based on the fact that the Mercosur provisions that existed when those proceedings were filed did not exclude the possibility of multiple fora.

More recently, in another case that coincidently also concerned poultry (*EC–Chicken Cuts*), the issue was the EC customs classification of certain salted chicken imports from Brazil and Thailand. The Secretariat of the World Customs Organization argued that its specialized dispute settlement system for customs classification was binding on the parties and should be exhausted before any WTO claim was made. This argument was rejected by the panel, which argued that it had no basis in the DSU for declining jurisdiction once a valid issue of WTO law was raised. On balance, it seems that WTO panels are unlikely to decline jurisdiction (even temporarily) on account of the possibility of proceedings in other international fora.

In *Mexico–Soft Drinks,* the AB had to adjudicate Mexico's defense that its trade restricting measure was "necessary" to secure compliance with laws and regulations, within the meaning of GATT XX(d). The AB rejected Mexico's invocation of Article XX(d) on other grounds (that the phrase "laws and regulations" in XX(d) does not extend to international legal norms that have not been made effective in a member's municipal law). The essence of Mexico's argument, however, was that the USA had violated the NAFTA in its application of anti-dumping law to Mexico and had obstructed the dispute settlement process available to Mexico under NAFTA to enforce its rights. With respect to this argument, the AB found that the WTO dispute settlement organs lack jurisdiction to make determinations with respect to compliance with international legal norms outside the covered agreements, in this instance, the NAFTA (para. 56), apart, of course, from cases where there is some reference, implicit or explicit, to non-WTO law in the relevant WTO instruments.

Written Submissions of Parties and Third Parties to the Panel and *Amicus Curiae* Submissions

Each of the parties is entitled to two written submissions. Typically, the time frame will be such that, in their second submissions, the opposing parties have the opportunity to rebut arguments in each other's first submissions. The complainant's first submission should indicate the measures complained of, based on the request for a panel and the terms of reference, and *all* findings of facts and law that the complainant wishes the panel to make. It should be noted that while a party cannot introduce new "claims" that are not in the first written submission, it can add to or modify its arguments in favor of those claims during oral argument or in the second written submission. It is generally considered that, to be timely, *amicus curiae* submissions should be made no later than the first written submissions of the parties and certainly no later than the first oral hearing. Third parties are entitled to make written submissions, but there are no formal rules in the DSU governing the time frame for such submissions. Appendix 3 of the DSU provides that the panel may set deadlines for the written submissions of parties and Third Parties. Unless publicly released by the party making it, a submission is to be treated as confidential by all participants in the panel process. Third Parties are, however, entitled to see the written submissions of parties. In addition to written submissions, the panel may pose questions to the parties, and the parties to each other, to be answered in writing. This may occur as the issues become defined in the oral hearings. Also, further written submissions may be authorized or invited by the panel where new evidence is presented at later stages, such as the second oral hearing. The fundamental underlying principle is that the opposing party should be given an opportunity in writing to respond to any new facts or legal arguments introduced by a party.

Oral Hearings

While there may be additional hearings on matters of procedure, there are two substantive hearings before the panel. There is not a detailed code of procedure for the conduct of such hearings, of the kind that exists in most domestic judicial systems. The panel asks questions of the parties and the parties may pose questions to each other. Each of these hearings is likely to last only a few days. This may be far less than the amount of time devoted to proceedings on matters of equal factual complexity in domestic legal systems, which may last weeks or months. This suggests the cardinal importance of extremely concise, clear, and well organized presentation of all key facts. Traditionally, panel hearings have not been open to the public. More recently, in a number of disputes the parties have agree to open the hearings to the public (e.g., Hormones Suspension). This has occurred through members of the public who have registered with the WTO Secretariat viewing the proceedings on a live video feed in a room in the WTO headquarters. Where a third party objects to an open hearing that part of the proceeding involving the third party will not be broadcast to the public viewing room. The idea of webcasting open hearings is under consideration.

Fact-Finding In The Panel Process

- **Duties of the Parties to Provide Evidence:** In most domestic legal systems, and in some international tribunals as well, a process of "discovery" exists, whereby each party is entitled to demand of the other relevant documentary evidence. No comparable process exists in WTO panel proceedings and a panel has no power to require a party to release evidence to another party. However, there is a requirement of good-faith participation in dispute settlement and parties are under a duty to provide information requested by the panel itself.

- **Burden of Proof:** This is among the most complex and arcane areas of WTO law. The beginning point is the general principle that the complainant must prove all the facts required to make a *prima-facie* case of violation.[2] Once such a *prima-facie* case is made, the burden of proof shifts to the defendant to refute the *prima-facie* case of violation. Since there is no process of "discovery," it is often the case that many essential pieces of evidence for the complainant's case are in the hands of the other party. In such situations, the burden of proof may shift once the complainant has adduced the facts available to it. However, there is no clear pattern in WTO jurisprudence that would allow one to know just what level of proof is needed to make out a *prima-facie* case.[3] Fact-finding Powers of the Panel Itself: The panel is endowed with very extensive inquisitorial powers pursuant to DSU Article 13.1. A panel may seek information and technical advice from any individual or body it deems appropriate, and to 13.2 from any "relevant source." The panel's handling of the evidence is, however, subject to the duty on it under DSU 10 to "make an objective assessment of the matter."

- **Expert Evidence:** In some cases, expert evidence plays a large role, especially in disputes under the Sanitary and Phyto-sanitary (SPS) and Technical Barriers to Trade (TBT), which often deal with scientific matters. The panel may strike a panel of experts to which extensive questions are posed. In the Hormones–Suspension ruling, the AB clarified certain issues with respect to the selection and use of experts by WTO panels, especially the importance to due process within the meaning of Article 11 of the DSU of the experts selected being impartial and independent, and not having any vested interest in the scientific studies or viewpoints being assessed by the panel.

Proving the Law

- **The Applicable Law:** With the exception of "non-violation" complaints, in order for a panel to have jurisdiction, there must be an alleged violation of a provision of the covered agreements. As was underlined by the Appellate Body in the *Mexico–Soft Drinks* case, WTO panels and the Appellate Body have no jurisdiction to

---

[2] *Prima facie* is a Latin expression used in modern to signify that on first examination, a matter appears to be from the facts. In jurisdictions, *prima facie* denotes evidence that—unless—would be sufficient to prove a particular proposition or fact.

[3] Complicating this further is that there are some provisions of the WTO treaties that may be characterized as in the nature of exceptions or affirmative defenses. In such instances, it is the defendant that may be required to make a *prima-facie* case, then subject it to rebuttal by the complainant. However, the exact effects on the burden of proof of characterizing a provision as an exception may vary depending on the nature of the provision in question, thus adding further complexity yet to the matter (see the *EC–Preferences* case).

adjudicate a claim by the complainant that non-WTO rules of international law have been violated. But this does not mean that violation of other international agreements may not in some cases be relevant to disposing of claims that provisions of the covered agreements have been violated. By virtue of their status as part of the "universe" of international law, WTO rules are nevertheless applied in tandem with generally applicable international law, including *ius cogens,* which must be applied even where there is a conflict with treaty norms.[4] This includes a small number of international legal norms of surpassing force, such as the prohibition against torture, genocide and slavery, and the use of force, although all these will rarely be relevant to WTO disputes. Other general structural norms and principles of international law such as good faith, state responsibility, equity, estoppel, abuse of rights, and so forth are more relevant and are generally applicable to WTO disputes, except that they do not apply if they have been altered by specific rights and obligations in the WTO treaties concerned. For instance, the DSU itself considerably alters the general international law of state responsibility as it applies to remedies. Applicable law also includes any legal norm that has been incorporated directly or indirectly into the WTO provisions in question. For instance, many provisions of the WIPO intellectual property conventions are directly incorporated into the Trade-Related Aspects of Intellectual Property Rights (TRIPS) Agreement.

An example of indirect incorporation is the Lomé Waiver in the Bananas case, which was a basis for the EC's deviation from WTO rules—the Lomé Waiver implicitly incorporated the Lomé Convention itself as law to be applied in determining the scope of the Waiver. Similarly, rules on export subsidies in the WTO SCM Agreement refer to the Organisation for Economic Co-operation and Development (OECD) rules on export credits and make compliance with these norms a basis for the determination that certain measures are not prohibited export subsidies pursuant to WTO rules. Thus, a WTO panel would have to apply the OECD rules on export credit in order to determine a claim that WTO rules against export subsidies have been violated;

Rules and Sources of Interpretation (Vienna Convention on the Law of Treaties (VCLT)): By virtue of DSU Art. 3.2, the dispute settlement organs are required to apply the law of the WTO in accordance with "the customary rules of interpretation in public international law." These have been determined to include Articles 31 and 32 of the Vienna Convention. Any problem of legal interpretation in applying these rules will be analyzed by the panel, with attention to the hierarchy of interpretative sources specified in the rules themselves. In deciding the case, the panel is not limited to the legal reasoning provided by the parties (and third parties) to the dispute. It may rely on legal arguments and indeed legal provisions not invoked by the parties in their pleadings, as long as the panel limits itself to adjudicating the claims brought forth in the Request (US–Gambling, paras 280 and 281).

---

[4] *Ius Cogens* is a Latin expression that in modern English means peremptory norm. It is a fundamental principle of international law that is accepted by the international community of states as a norm from which no derogation is ever permitted.

III. Using the Vienna Convention to Make Legal Findings and Interpretations in the WTO

In the early years of the WTO, the Appellate Body tended to view the "ordinary meaning" provision of VCLT Art. 31.1 as requiring the WTO adjudicating body to begin its interpretative work by trying to establish dictionary definitions of the operative words in the WTO treaty provisions at issue. Only once this sort of "literal" meaning was established would the AB go on to consider "object, purpose and context."

This literal approach was widely criticized by academic commentators, even if may have reflected the justifiable caution of a new tribunal faced with applying many legal rules that had not before been judicially interpreted—rules binding a large number of countries with different cultures and political and social systems. More recently, the AB has displayed greater flexibility and subtlety in its approach, giving considerable importance to context, object, and purpose at all stages of interpretation

The Role of Non-WTO Legal Rules and Principles

We have already discussed how, in some instances, the law to be applied by the WTO panel may include international legal rules from outside the WTO Agreements, where these are directly or indirectly references in the WTO provisions at issue in the dispute or are background structural norms or principles of the international legal system. In addition, non-WTO legal rules may play a role in the interpretation of and even in the establishment of certain facts. The following are some examples of these kinds of uses of non-WTO legal rules from panel and Appellate Body rulings:

- In the *Shrimp–Turtle* case, the panel referred to the Convention on Trade in Endangered Species (CITES) to establish the fact that certain species of sea turtles were endangered.
- In *Shrimp–Turtle* as well, the Appellate Body referred to the Rio Biodiversity Convention, among other international environmental instruments, to support its interpretation that "exhaustible natural resources" within the meaning of Article XX(g) of the GATT include living resources.
- In interpreting the special provisions on remedies (countermeasures) in the SCM Agreement, the Arbitrator in the *US–Foreign Sales Corporation* case referred to the principle of proportionality in the Articles of State Responsibility of the International Law Commission (ILC).
- In the *EC–Meat Hormones* dispute, the Appellate Body found the Precautionary Principle to be relevant to interpreting obligations in the WTO SPS Measures Agreement, including the obligation to base measures on an assessment of risk, in

the case of potentially life threatening risks. Even though the Appellate Body was not prepared to conclude whether the Principle was "hard" international law, the AB felt it could nevertheless provide normative guidance to panels in applying the SPS Agreement.

- As noted above, in the *Mexico–Soft Drinks* case, the AB set certain limits with respect to its own authority to make legal determinations concerning provisions of non-WTO law that are not directly or indirectly referenced in provisions of WTO Agreements themselves. How this can be reconciled with the broad scope for using non-WTO law as an aid for interpretation of WTO rules in the instances discussed above is an open question.

IV. The Interim Panel Report

The Interim Report of the panel is issued to the parties on a confidential basis (although it may well be leaked to a wider community), with the intent that there should be an opportunity for the parties to raise with the panel any concerns they have with its findings of fact or law. This may result in changes that will be reflected in the final report. The practice of releasing an interim report dates from the GATT era, when there was no possibility of correcting panel findings through appellate review. It is rare that significant changes are made to a report in light of the concerns the parties raise concerning the interim report.

- In the China-Contervailing Duties case, the International Law Commission Articles on State Responsibility were used to interpret the applicability of the SCM Agreement to state enterprises.
- Finally, in the EC-Aircraft case, the AB made the important holding that for a norm in a non-WTO treaty to be taken into account as a relevant rule of international law applicable between parties under Vienna Convention Article 31:3(c), the non-WTO treaty did not have to be itself binding on all WTO Members.

V. Precedent in the WTO

In most domestic legal systems, prior decisions of an adjudicative body play a large role as precedent or "authority" to guide subsequent rulings. Indeed, in Anglo-American "common law" systems, prior rulings may formally bind a tribunal in its future interpretations, especially if they have been decided by the highest court in that system. As a general matter, in international law, this is not the case: rulings of domestic and international tribunals are merely secondary means of interpretation according to Article 38 of the ICJ Statute. In the WTO system, as already noted, one of the two central purposes of the dispute settlement is to "clarify the law," and predictability and security of rights and obligations are essential to the system functioning effectively to support global markets. Thus, not surprisingly, the AB has stipulated that panel and Appellate Body rulings should normally be followed in subsequent cases (*US–Shrimp*, para. 21.5). This was strongly reiterated by the AB in a recent dispute concerning zeroing, where a panel had quite explicitly refused to follow the legal interpretation of the AB in a prior ruling (*US–Stainless Steel (Mexico)*).

The creation of the Appellate Body by WTO members to review legal interpretations developed by panels shows that members recognized the importance of consistency and stability in the interpretation of their rights and obligations under the covered agreements. This is essential to promote "security and predictability" in the dispute settlement system, and to ensure the "prompt settlement" of disputes. The Panel's failure to follow previously adopted Appellate Body reports addressing the same issues undermines the development of a coherent and predictable body of jurisprudence clarifying members' rights and obligations under the covered agreements as contemplated under the DSU. Clarification, as envisaged in Article 3.2 of the DSU, elucidates the scope and meaning of the provisions of the covered agreements in accordance with customary rules of interpretation of public international law. While the application of a provision may be regarded as confined to the context in which it takes place, the relevance of clarification contained in adopted Appellate Body reports is not limited to the application of a particular provision in a specific case (paragraph 161).

A special case is panel rulings in the GATT prior to the establishment of the AB itself, where there was no central adjudicative body to ensure the consistency and coherence of ad hoc panel decisions. Here, the AB has made a distinction between adopted and unadopted GATT panel rulings. Adopted rulings form part of the legitimate expectations of WTO members, and while subsequent panels or the Appellate Body may deviate from them, such deviation would normally be expected to be accompanied by a reasoned explanation (*Japan–Alcoholic Beverages*). On the other hand, unadopted GATT panel reports (for example the *Tuna–Dolphin* reports), do not have such normative weight; still, they may be referred to for "guidance."

VI. PANEL FINDINGS AND RECOMMENDATIONS

The Duty to Provide Reasons

Article 12.7 of the DSU requires the panel to "provide the basic rationale behind any findings and recommendations it makes." By contrast, the panel is not required expressly to address all the claims and arguments of the parties.

Judicial Economy

In particular, where the panel has found that there is a violation of one or more provisions of the covered agreements, it may decide not to proceed to adjudicate the claims of the complainant that other provisions have been violated. But this is a matter of discretion. There is no requirement to exercise judicial economy, and no requirement to limit its use.

"Suggestions" and "Recommendations"

A finding that the defending member has violated one or more provisions of the covered agreements will normally trigger a "recommendation" that the defending member bring itself in conformity with the provisions in question. In addition a panel may make suggestions as to the modalities for implementing its ruling. Such suggestions are subject to the basic principle that it is up to the member to choose the means for complying with its WTO obligations. At the same time, whether what a member has done is adequate to implement the ruling and bring itself in conformity is subject, pursuant to DSU Art. 21.5, to further panel and Appellate Body review.

Other Remedies

Normally in international law, the winning party—in addition to a determination that the losing party cease its wrongful conduct—would be entitled to reparations, generally a monetary award, for the harm it suffered from the losing party's non-compliance up to the time of the ruling. One distinctive feature of the WTO dispute settlement system is that it makes no provision for such "retrospective" damages. In one, rather controversial instance, a panel has proposed as a remedy that the losing party have its producers repay a subsidy that was found to be illegal under the relevant WTO rules (*Argentina–Leather*). An unresolved issue concerns situations where anti-dumping or countervailing duties have been found to have been applied in contravention of WTO law that most duties (or "deposits" on duties) already taken be refunded. Is this a "retrospective" remedy not contemplated by the DSU? Or is continuing to hold moneys taken in contravention of WTO rules an *ongoing* violation, which would mean that to bring itself in conformity, the normal "prospective" remedy, the losing member would need to refund the duties?

VII. Review by the Appellate Body

Notice of Appeal

Either party may appeal findings of law in a panel report, including procedural rulings on matters of jurisdiction. While findings of fact are not as such subject to appellate review, fact finding has been challenged on the basis that a panel has violated its duty to make an objective assessment of the facts in Article 11 of the DSU. A Notice of Appeal must be filed within 60 days of the circulation of the final panel report. Otherwise, the panel report will be adopted automatically (i.e., based on the negative consensus rule) and will constitute a binding and final settlement of the dispute. The Notice must set out all of the errors of law and legal interpretations being appealed or cross-appealed. Cross-appeal simply refers to the case where, in response to a notice of appeal by the one party, the winning party at the panel level also chooses to appeal certain findings of the panel.

Composition of the Appellate Body Division

The Appellate Body members hear appeals in divisions of three. This is subject to the practice of collegiality where the members of the Division and the other AB members share their views on the appeal. The Appellant and Appellee have no say on which three AB members hear a particular appeal. Since AB members are independent adjudicators, they are not required to recuse themselves because their home state is an Appellant, Appellee, or Third Participant (known as the Participants in the Appeal). However, there are conflict of interest and disclosure rules that govern the possibility that an AB member could have a material or other personal interest in the appeal.

Written Submissions of Parties and Third Parties to the Appellate Body and *Amicus Curiae* Submissions

The Working Procedures for Appellate Review provide for written submissions for the parties. By virtue of the DSU itself, Third Parties are entitled to make written submissions to the AB. In *US–Shrimp* and *US–Carbon Steel,* the Appellate Body held that it has the discretion to accept and consider *amicus curiae* briefs from non-governmental persons. In *EC–Sardines,* the AB further held that it could accept and consider an *amicus curiae* brief from a WTO member that was neither a Party nor a Third Party to the dispute (in that case, Morocco). The AB has generally indicated that it has not had to rely on *amicus curiae* briefs submitted to it to decide the dispute. It is an open question whether these briefs have had a more subtle influence on AB members, that is, in terms of the framing of the dispute or the strengths and weaknesses of particular legal arguments.

   In the *EC–Asbestos* dispute, the AB created special procedural rules for submissions of *amicus* briefs, whereby an *amicus* would be required to seek leave for submission of the brief, providing detailed information of how it would assist in the resolution of the appeal, as well as disclosure concerning the nature of the organization submitting the brief and its material interest if any in the disposition of the dispute. The creation of this procedure was widely criticized by WTO members as beyond the authority of the AB and it has never been re-attempted in subsequent cases. The author of this chapter has succeeded in having an *amicus curiae* brief admitted by the AB through submitting it by email to the Director of the Appellate Body Secretariat, with copies by email to the Geneva missions of the disputing parties.

Oral Hearings

The Working Procedures for Appellate Review provide for an oral hearing. At the hearing, the division of the Appellate Body that hears the case will ask questions of the parties' representatives. Each party will be permitted to make a formal oral statement as well. Third parties are also allowed to appear at the hearing and to make oral statements. According to the revised version of the Working Procedures, they may do so even if they do not make written submissions. The DSU stipulates that AB "proceedings" are confidential (DSU Art. 17.10) but in certain recent cases the AB has opened up the hearing to the public where the parties requested it to do so. The Appellate Body may pose additional questions in writing after the hearing or require further submissions of law from the parties in writing. As with panel proceedings, parties and third parties have the sovereign prerogative to determine who will represent them at the hearing. In one instance, a former member of the Appellate Body, Claus-Dieter Ehlermann, represented a Third Party in an appellate proceeding (*EC–Tariff Preferences*). As with panel hearings, AB hearings have, with the agreement of the participants been opened to the public in the same manner.

Scope and Standard of Review of Appellate Review

Parties may only appeal or cross-appeal findings of law, but the Appellate Body may address the fact finding of the panel if a party claims that the panel has failed in its Article 11 obligation to make an objective assessment of the facts. In reviewing such Article 11 claims, the Appellate Body has displayed a very high degree of deference to the panel. Findings of fact have very rarely been impugned as violations of the obligation to make an objective assessment. The party claiming a failure to discharge the Article 11 obligation would have to show something amounting to bias or gross negligence or a complete lack of reasoned, objective analysis. Since very few panelists have experience as triers of fact, either from being judges or advocates in domestic or international tribunals, the virtual unavailability of appellate review to determine proper practices of fact finding is a problem. However, the Appellate Body must decide the appeal in a very tight time frame as already noted, and this does not practicably allow for detailed scrutiny of the factual analysis of the panel, especially in complex cases. One solution that has been suggested is to move to a professional standing corp of panelists. At the same time, the AB has itself noted that there are some legal findings that are very much informed by appreciations of the facts, such as for instance the determination of "like" product in Article III of the GATT, the National Treatment obligation, where the meaning and balance of the different considerations that inform a comparison of domestic and imported products as "like" may vary depending on the factual context. In these situations, where there is a mixed question of law and fact, the AB may reverse the panel's findings of law if these are incurably affected by its erroneous or inadequate appreciation of the factual context. However, this has only occurred once (*Canada–Periodicals*).

"Completing the Analysis"

In domestic legal systems, where an appellate tribunal has found errors of law in the judgment of a trial court, it may remand the matter to the trial level so that the trial court can apply the law as clarified by the appellate tribunal to the facts of the dispute. Under the DSU, the AB does not possess a comparable authority to remand a matter to the original panel. In these circumstances, the AB has engaged in a practice that it calls "completing the analysis." This means that, having found errors of law in the panel ruling, the AB will not simply leave matters at reversing or modifying the panel's legal findings, but will proceed to apply the law as the AB has clarified it to the existing factual record of the case, as developed in the panel proceeding. The AB will not "complete the analysis" if applying the law as corrected would require the finding of facts *outside* the existing record.

The case of the *US–Large Civil Aircraft (Second Complaint),* a complex dispute brought by the EU against the USA and focused on subsidy issues, illustrates well such practice. Dissatisfied on various counts, both the defendant and the complainant appealed in 2011 against the panel report findings. The AB report was circulated in March 2012 and adopted later that same month. Its key findings are detailed in the Appellate Body's 2012 Annual Report (WTO 2013).[5] The AB upheld a number of the panel findings, but also ruled that the panel had erred on a number of procedural, interpretative, and methodological issues that were critical to some other findings. For instance, it ruled that the panel had erred in its conclusions that "remaining" US subsidies had not been shown to have affected Boeing's prices in a manner giving rise to serious prejudice to the EU, because it failed to consider whether those subsidies had a genuine relationship to, and effects on, such prices. It also invalidated the corresponding finding. The AB then proceeded in some areas to complete the analysis and reached various factual findings, for instance, that the effects of such subsidies to Boeing caused serious prejudice to Airbus in the form of significant lost sales, within the meaning of Articles 5(c) and 6.3(c) of the SCM Agreement, in the 100–200 seat civil aircraft market.

Implementation Within a "Reasonable Period of Time"

Once the panel report as modified by the Appellate Body report, and the Appellate Body report itself, have been adopted, the losing member is required to implement within a "reasonable period of time" (DSU Article 21). Where there is disagreement between the parties to the dispute concerning what is a "reasonable period of time," this may be subject to arbitration under Art. 21.3 of the DSU. The arbitrator will normally be a single member of the Appellate Body. The DSU provides as a guideline for the arbitrator that the reasonable period of time should not normally exceed 15 months. The complexity of what is required for implementation, that could range from legislative changes to a complex

---

[5] They are also available in summary form at <http://www.wto.org/english/tratop_e/dispu_e/cases_e/ds353_e.htm>.

regulatory scheme to simply scrapping unjustified countervailing and anti-dumping duties, is an important factor in determining "a reasonable period of time" in arbitration In a recent May 2013 ruling concerning the *China–Grain Oriented Flat-Rolled Electrical Steel* dispute, for example, a WTO Arbitrator determined that the "reasonable period of time" for China to implement the recommendations and rulings of the DSB is 8 months and 15 days from the adoption on November 16, 2012, of the Panel and Appellate Body Reports (circulated to WTO members earlier that same year, in July and October, respectively).

Request for a Panel on Implementation

The winning and the losing parties may disagree concerning the adequacy of the actions that the losing party is prepared to take to implement the ruling. In such an instance, the implementing measures may be reviewed at the request of either party by an implementation panel, pursuant to Art. 21.5 of the DSU. An attempt is made to strike this panel with the same panelists as in the original panel ruling in the dispute, where they are available.

Scope and Standard of Review of the Implementation Panel

The implementation panel will above all consider the adequacy of the implementing measures in light of the original panel and Appellate Body reports. An implementation panel does not have the jurisdiction or mandate to reconsider *de novo* the findings in the panel and AB. On the other hand, the implementing measures may raise issues of WTO consistency that were not before the original panel. For example, the implementing measure may replace with a tax a regulatory requirement that ran afoul of the National Treatment obligation in Article III:4 of the GATT. There may now arise a question of whether the new tax is in compliance with Article III:2 of the GATT, which was not before the original panel. The implementation panel, according to the AB, may consider the issue of compliance with Art. III:2 in such an instance, even if that issue was not in the original proceedings.

Appeal of the Report of the Implementation Panel

There is a right of appeal of the findings of an Art. 21.5 report.

Relationship of Implementation Proceedings to Retaliation (Suspension of Concessions)

In the Bananas dispute, the United States argued that it had the right, once the reasonable period of time of implementation by the EC had expired without any remedial action, to proceed forthwith to retaliation under Art. 22.6, *without* the prior step of an Art. 21.5 panel on the issue of the adequacy of the EC actions to implement the original panel ruling. The DSU and Art. 22.6 in particular are silent on whether a party seeking DSB authorization for retaliation must first obtain a ruling by an Art. 21.5 panel that the violating party has failed to implement. This issue can only be clarified through changes to the text of the DSU, and this is indeed a topic of the current multilateral negotiations on dispute settlement reform. In the interim, in many instances the parties to the dispute have made an agreement among themselves as to the sequencing of actions envisaged under Articles 21.5 and 22.6. In the *US-Gambling* case the Arbitrator authorized Antigua to suspend intellectual property rights obligations to the United States as a response to the US failure to address violations of GATS found by the panel and AB.

Arbitration on Suspension of Concessions

Compensation and suspension of concessions are available to the complaining Party if the adopted panel or AB report is not implemented within a reasonable period of time. Compensation is a voluntary alternative to implementing a ruling. Suspension of concessions requires authorization by the DSB, subject to a number of conditions and criteria listed in Art. 22.3 and related provisions.

The suspension of concessions is to be equivalent to the nullification and impairment arising from the continued violation of the WTO provisions in question. Typically, the winning member that is seeking to suspend concessions will present a list of products with estimates of the value of the trade at issue. The arbitrator will seek to ensure that this amount does not exceed the value of the trade impeded due to the non-implementation of the dispute settlement ruling in question. The losing member may contest the estimates of both the effects of the proposed suspension of concessions as well as the effects of its non-implementation. Both parties should explain to the arbitrator the methodologies behind their calculations. The burden of proof, however, is on the member being retaliated against to make a *prima-facie* case that the level of suspension of concessions exceeds the amount of nullification and impairment (*European Communities-Measures Concerning Meat and Meat Hormones, Recourse to Arbitration by the European Communities under 22.6 of the Dispute Settlement Understanding*, WT/DS26/ARB, July 12, 1999as l).

Normally, retaliating members are expected to suspend concessions in the same sector or under the same Agreement as the violation. However, where this is not practical or effective, a member may retaliate in a different sector or under a different Agreement. Thus, in the Bananas case, Ecuador was permitted to withdraw concessions from the EC not only under the GATT but also under the TRIPs and GATS agreements. Ecuador had successfully argued before the arbitrator that retaliation in the goods sector alone would not be practical or effective, since it would involve suspending half of all EC exports to Ecuador, most of which were capital goods or inputs essential for the Ecuadorian economy (*European Communities—Regime for the Importation, Sale and Distribution of Bananas—Recourse to Arbitration By the European Communities under Article 22.6 of the DSU,* WT/DS/27/ARB/ECU, March 24, 2000).

More recently, an arbitrator has suggested that there are certain limits or constraints on the ability of a winning member to choose cross-retaliation (*United States–Cotton*). In particular, a member does not necessarily have a right to choose cross-retaliation in the sector where the cross-retaliation will cause the least harm to its own economy; also, the arbitrator will authorize cross-retaliation only for an amount that is net of the amount of retaliation the arbitrator thinks is practical and effective in the same sector.

Cessation of Retaliation Where the Losing Member has Subsequently Brought Itself into Compliance

A situation may arise where there is an active suspension of concessions, and the losing party takes some action that it believes puts it into compliance with the dispute settlement ruling in question. How then can the losing member ensure that the suspension of concessions is removed, especially if the winning party disagrees that what has been done is adequate for implementation? One route would be to ask for an Art. 21.5 panel (which can be requested by either side in the dispute. In the *EC Hormones–Suspension* case, the EC chose a different approach, which was to request a new panel. The AB, however, held that the duty to end the suspension of concessions is triggered through the determination in dispute settlement that there is compliance, not by a member's unilateral assertion that it has taken measures to bring itself into compliance. Therefore, a member that believes that it has brought itself into compliance should, if the retaliating member refuses to agree with this and continues to suspend concessions, make a request for an Art. 21.5 panel.

Negotiated Settlements

The DSU envisages the possibility that the parties can settle a dispute by negotiation among themselves ("mutually agreed solutions"). The question arises as to whether such agreements are binding, in the sense of precluding further WTO proceedings with respect to the original claims. In the 2007 *US–Bananas* ruling, the AB held that a negotiated settlement agreement does not preclude a member from recourse to further DSU proceedings with respect to the original claims of violation or non-implementation unless: (1) the negotiated agreement is a fully effective solution to the dispute; and (2) the parties have explicitly renounced their right to further recourse to DSU proceedings.

VIII. Using WTO Dispute Settlement Effectively: Challenges and Opportunities for Developing Countries[6]

A World Bank database provides information covering 1995 to 2011 on the participation in the WTO dispute settlement system of developing countries in relation to other groups of countries, on the type of dispute, and the legal provisions at issue.[7] It is clear that there is significant use by the system of developing countries (see also Torres, 2012), but equally clear that such use is generally far less pervasive than in the case of developed countries.

An increasing body of literature identifies the barriers for developing countries to make effective use of the system, including litigation costs that challenge the resources of poorer countries, lack of in-house governmental expertise in WTO law and dispute settlement, problems of coordination of private sector interests, effective mechanisms for partnerships between the government and the private sector in WTO litigation, and the limits of retaliation (withdrawal of concessions) as an effective means of achieving compliance. Withdrawing concessions increases the prices of imported goods and services to one's own industries and consumers, and even assuming that a small, poor country can inflict enough pain to pressure compliance through these limits on access to its market, it will be hurting its own people in attempting to do so. Of course, all developing countries are not the same, and some such as India and Brazil have been effective WTO litigants, with impressive internal expertise and domestic institutional mechanisms to facilitate WTO litigation.

In understanding how to effectively use WTO dispute settlement, it is necessary to begin with a fundamental characteristic of the system. Only governments can pursue WTO complaints, not the private sector, but it is the private sector that is affected by trade barriers in violation of WTO law. Thus, in order to generate appropriate WTO cases, it is necessary that private industry and government officials exchange information. In order for the private sector to identify situations where WTO legal rules can help them in improving market access abroad, the private sector must have knowledge of those rules, and on the other hand, for government officials to have a sense of where it may be fruitful to bring a WTO case, they must have some awareness of how the private sector is being affected.

---

[6] This section draws heavily from Shaffer (2003) and Bown and Hoekman (2005).

[7] The WTO Disputes Database (DSUD) is available at <http://econ.worldbank.org/ttbd/dsud/>, covering 1995–2011. Related databases on trade-restricting measures that are often the target of disputes can be found at <http://www.globaltradealert.org/> (covering most countries since the onset of the global financial crisis) and at <http://econ.worldbank.org/ttbd/> (covering more than 30 countries for the years 1980–2011). The WTO own database on the disputes is at <http://www.wto.org/english/tratop_e/dispu_e/dispu_status_e.htm>.

A preliminary challenge therefore is to figure out how government and the private sector can work together to identify those barriers to trade that are negatively affecting the country's economic interests, and how WTO dispute settlement could be used to challenge the barriers in question. This can involve solving a number of coordination- and collective-action problems. For example, a particular sector (say, fisheries) may consist of a large number of small economic actors, each of which alone would not easily be able to engage in a process of analyzing, in collaboration with government, foreign trade barriers. Thus, in some instances, it may be necessary to form or strengthen industry associations or alliances as a precondition to creating effective public–private partnerships.

WTO litigation can be costly. So it is important not only to identify the barriers, but also the economic value of having them removed. Is this likely to exceed the cost of litigating?

We have already noted that retaliation or threat thereof may not be an effective or viable means of ensuring compliance with a favorable ruling, particularly for small economies. Thus, the value of winning may have to be discounted not only by the chance that the legal outcome will not be favorable, but also by the risk that compliance will be difficult or impossible to achieve.

In thinking systematically about the steps involved in developing and implementing an effective WTO litigation strategy, Bown and Hoekman (2005) and Bown (2009) provide useful suggestions. Where there are effective mechanisms for overcoming

---

Box 25.1 Litigation costs

Litigation costs need to be estimated. These will vary considerably depending upon how much the complaining member relies on in-house governmental expertise and how much on private law firms or on the Advisory Centre on WTO Law (ACWL), which provides legal assistance at less than private market rates to developing countries in WTO litigation. Some figures that may be useful in estimating litigation costs when using ACWL are provided in Bown and Hoekman (2005: 870):

> Taking a conservative estimate of attorney fees in trade litigation cases at a billable rate of $350.00 per hour, one estimate of the average number of hours indicates that the bill for hourly legal services could run from $89,950 for a 'low' complexity DSU case to $247,100 for a 'high' complexity case. Nevertheless, these fees would not include the cost of litigation support through necessary data collection, economic analysis and hiring of expert witnesses for testimony, which may lead to another $100,000–$200,000. Furthermore, there are substantial overhead costs to the actual litigation process associated with travel, accommodation, communication, paralegal and secretarial assistance. Given market rates, a 'litigation only' bill of $500,000. is likely to be fairly typical. However, this would include neither the resources necessary to investigate potential claims in the pre-litigation phase, nor the resources necessary to engage public relations and/or political lobbying in the post litigation phase to generate compliance.

collective-action problems and organizing the economic actors who stand to benefit from a win at the WTO—or where the benefits are concentrated in one or a few
economic actors—having the private sector bear the bulk of litigation costs may be
a feasible option. Private firms, however, may be reluctant to put resources up front
when a final and fruitful outcome will depend on both a favorable panel ruling at the
WTO litigation stage and, on further actions by their own and the defending state's
government.

In the medium to longer term, affordable litigation resources can also be found among
NGOs, law schools, and the pro bono practices of private law firms, as well as creating
centers of expertise within government or public–private entities, such as think tanks
with both governmental and private sector participation. In their review of the experiences with dispute settlement of nine countries from South America, Asia and Africa,
with dispute settlement, Shaffer et al. (2006) and Shaffer and Melendez-Ortiz (2010)
have shown in detail how Brazil and others have effectively developed some of these
options. They also recommend to developing countries to build a strong institutional
structure with one coordinating focal point, effective public–private partnerships, and
a strategic, comprehensive approach to legal capacity building for WTO litigation and
international economic law disputes in general (see also ICTSD 2012).

Finally, a number of other hard questions need to be asked by any country, and especially a developing one, considering initiating a dispute at the WTO:

- If retaliation or the threat thereof is not likely to be effective, does the country have
  other means of achieving compliance such as political lobbying, leverage over the
  losing country in other policy areas (migration, security interests, anti-terrorism
  cooperation)? Could a favorable ruling be used as a "bargaining chip" in a WTO
  negotiating round, or even in bilateral trade and investment negotiations?
- Is bringing a dispute complaint likely to be perceived as a contentious or hostile
  act by the defending country? Might it retaliate in some way, cutting foreign aid or
  trade preferences?
- There is an old expression that "people in glass houses shouldn't throw stones."
  A country faced with a dispute complaint concerning trade barriers in a particular
  sector may respond by identifying policies of the complaining country that are
  arguably WTO-inconsistent and file a "counter-claim." This happened in the Brazil–
  Canada aircraft dispute, resulting in a proliferation of rulings against both countries,
  which made settlement of the problem very difficult and increased acrimony that
  spilled over to other areas of trade relations between Canada and Brazil.
- Because, as already noted, the WTO dispute settlement system does not provide for
  reparations—monetary compensation for past harm that the winning member has
  suffered from the losing member's violation—the economic value of a complaint
  is going to be limited to *future* market access. In some instances, the damage to
  an industry's competitiveness from trade barriers may have largely been done and
  be very hard to repair, even if the offending measure is removed in the future. It is
  important, therefore, that the focus be not on how much the industry has suffered
  in the past, but what it can gain in the future.

APPENDIX

Additional Resources

1. **WTO Dispute Settlement Course:** There is an on-line interactive introductory course on WTO dispute settlement available on the WTO website. There is a self-testing feature that allows the student to assess their progress through the course. The course is available at <http://www.wto.org/english/tratop_e/dispu_e/disp_settlement_cbt_e/signin_e.htm>.
2. **Glossary:** The Organization 3D has produced a glossary of commonly used terms in WTO law, which lists most of the expressions and concepts used in this chapter in relation to dispute settlement. The glossary has been reviewed by a variety of experts in WTO law. It is currently available at <http://www.3dthree.org/pdf_word/m311-D%20Glossary%20July%202004%20rev.pdf>.
3. **Advisory Centre on WTO Law:** The Advisory Centre provides legal advice to developing countries in specific disputes. In addition, the ACWL offers three annual training courses in WTO dispute settlement in Geneva. See <http://www.acwl.ch/e/training/reg_courses.html>.

REFERENCES

Bown, C., and Hoekman, B. (2005), 'WTO Dispute Settlement and the Missing Developing Country Cases: Engaging the Private Sector.' *Journal of International Economic Law*, 8(4): 861–90.

Bown, C., (2009), Self-Enforcing Trade: Developing Countries and WTO Dispute Settlement Washington, DC: Brookings Institution Press.

ICTSD (2012), Dispute Settlement at the WTO: The Developing Country Experience; ICTSD International Trade Law Programme; International Centre for Trade and Sustainable Development, Geneva, Switzerland, <www.ictsd.org> (information note prepared by Marie Wilke).

Shaffer, G. C. (2003), 'How to Make the WTO Dispute Settlement System Work for Developing Countries: Some Proactive Developing Country Strategies.' In Towards A Development-Supportive Dispute Settlement System in the WTO, Resource Paper No. 5, International Centre for Trade and Sustainable Development, Geneva.

Shaffer, G. C., Ratton Sanchez, M., and Rosenberg, B. (2006), 'Brazil's Response to the Judicialized WTO Regime: Strengthening the State through Diffusing Expertise.' ICTSD South America Dialogue on WTO Dispute Settlement and Sustainable Development, Sao Paolo, Brazil, June 22–23.

Shaffer, G. C., Ratton Sanchez Badin, M., and Rosenberg, B. (2011), 'Winning at the WTO: The Development of a Trade Policy Community Within Brazil' in Shaffer, G. C. and Meléndez-Ortiz, R. (eds.) Dispute Settlement at the WTO: The Developing Country Experience. Cambridge: Cambridge University Press, pp. 21–104.

Torres, R. (2012), Use of the WTO Trade Dispute Settlement Mechanism by the Latin American Countries Dispelling Myths and Breaking Down Barriers, Staff Working Paper ERSD-2012-03, February 2012, WTO, Geneva.

Trebilcock, M. J., Howse, R., and Eliason, A. (2012), *The Regulation of International Trade,* Fourth edition. New York: Routledge.

WTO (2013), Appellate Body Annual Report for 2012, Geneva, April 9, 2013.

CHAPTER 26

....

COMPETITION PROVISIONS IN REGIONAL TRADE AGREEMENTS: OPTIONS FOR POLICYMAKERS*

....

SIMON J. EVENETT

I. INTRODUCTION

....

DESPITE temporary setbacks during the recent global economic crisis, in many developing countries the integration of their markets for goods and services into the world economy continues apace. Along with this integration have been developments in national and international economic governance, which involve the enactment of competition laws for the first time in many jurisdictions, and their progressive strengthening in others, together with the proliferation of regional trade agreements (RTAs), with dozens coming into force since the year 2000. RTAs have grown in scope and are now vehicles for advancing state-to-state cooperation and shared values (such as the promotion of competition) across a wide range of commercial, scientific, and social matters of mutual interest. RTAs have thus moved well beyond their original goal, namely the mercantilistic exchange of access to the signatories' markets. Indeed, such is the expansion in scope of RTAs that referring to them as "trade agreements" risks becoming more and more misleading over time. However, labels matter to some, especially to those who fear that the imperatives of trade negotiations might color the manner in which cooperation between state bodies is codified in RTAs.

On the basis of detailed extensive research into the various ways in which competition-related matters and principles have been incorporated into RTAs, the purpose of this chapter is to identify and discuss a set of policy options available to decision-makers as

* An earlier version of this chapter was prepared for the Latin American Competition Forum 2008, organized by the Inter-American Development Bank or the Organisation for Economic Co-operation and Development. Funding from the Inter-American Development Bank is acknowledged with gratitude.

they contemplate their priorities for future international initiatives on competition law and policy. These policy options will be of interest to many developing countries formulating their negotiating strategies towards ongoing or planned RTA negotiations, including when facing demands from trading partners to include competition provisions in RTAs.

Some developing countries have signed RTAs with competition provisions in them and may want to conduct their own assessment of the proposed provisions or evaluate the analyses of others. For example, many of the Caribbean nations have initialed an Economic Partnership Agreement (EPA) with the European Union (EU). This agreement included specific provisions on competition law and policy and has led to a vibrant debate about the final agreed text. This was made all the more contentious by the considerable controversy surrounding the negotiation of this accord in the first place.[1]

It is important to state what this chapter is not about. While the chapter is about the options available to policymakers—many of which are not mutually exclusive—it would be getting too far ahead of the available evidence to rank those options in terms of impact, however conceived. On the basis of the available evidence, it is simply too early to come to a definitive judgment as to the efficacy of the different types of competition-related provision found in RTAs. As the next section makes clear, to the best of my knowledge there is only one econometric study of the impact of such provisions (Anderson and Evenett, 2006). The absence of a body of quantitative findings on these matters must surely qualify any assessment of the merits of competition provisions in RTAs. It is for this reason that the emphasis here is on the options available to policymakers, rather than on recommendations. Moreover, there is simply not enough known about the relative merits of measures to promote competition law and principles in trade agreements and in other international accords, such as bilateral agreements between competition agencies, for a definitive view to be advanced. Readers may wish to bear these points in mind.

This chapter thus focuses on the policy options relating to competition provisions in RTSs and not on the general efficacy of promoting competition in developing countries and the specific matter of whether enacting a competition law enhances the welfare of developing countries. Readers are referred to Evenett (2005a) for an account of the instruments of competition law and their relationship to competition policy and trade policy. This paper also contains a survey of the evidence concerning the intensity of inter-firm rivalry and economic development, finding that in general the former promotes the latter and, in the few instances where exceptions exist, there are legal means to restrict the application of competition law and policy. The argument that the pursuit of industrial policies provides a general argument against the promotion of competition and the enforcement of competition law is found wanting in an extensive analysis in Evenett (2005b). The general presumption, then, that intensified rivalry between firms is desirable from the development point of view is adopted in this chapter. Finally, the cross-border spillovers associated with enforcement and under-enforcement of competition laws are spelled out in Clarke and Evenett (2003), providing a rationale for international cooperation on competition law enforcement and associated matters.

---

[1] Dawar and Evenett (2008) includes an assessment of the competition provisions of this RTA.

The remainder of this chapter is organized as follows. In the next section the main findings of analyses of the competition-related provisions in RTAs are summarized, and certain types of provisions—each with different rationales—can be identified. This account provides the basis for the description in Section III of the various options for policymakers that are interested in including competition principles and measures into RTAs. As indicated earlier, this set of policy options is considerably richer than some might appreciate. Some concluding remarks are offered in Section IV of this chapter.

II. Discussion of Analyses of Competition-Related Provisions in RTAs

Unlike investment and certain other provisions of RTAs, only in the middle of the last decade did analysts begin to document systematically and assess the different competition-related provisions found in RTAs.[2] Silva (2004) provided an early discussion of these provisions; the contributions to Brusick, Alvarez, and Cernat (2005) are another source of information, especially on the experience with respect to certain RTAs. During 2004 and 2005, the author commissioned a number of studies of the competition provisions of specific RTAs (namely, Mercosur, ANZCERTA, Canada–Chile, Canada–Costa Rica, EU–Mexico, and EU–South Africa) as part of a larger project entitled "Competition Policy Foundations for Trade Reform, Regulatory Reform and Sustainable Development."[3] Before these analyses and their successors,[4] there was little information concerning the extent to which trade agreements had furthered, or even conflicted with, the proper enforcement of competition law and the advancement of sound competition principles.[5]

The first significant comparative analysis of competition-related provisions of RTAs was undertaken by two OECD staff members, Solano and Sennekamp (2006). These authors sought, amongst other goals, to "create a taxonomy to collect and classify existing agreements and the type of competition provision they contain" (p. 5). To do so, they carefully examined the competition law chapters of 86 RTAs, 59 per cent of which had

[2] In this chapter the term "regional trade agreement" is used rather than "free trade agreement" or "bilateral trade agreement."

[3] Copies of these studies are available from the author upon request. These papers were principally qualitative in nature.

[4] One such qualitative analysis of competition provisions in a selected number of RTAs can be found in Bourgeois, Dawar, and Evenett (2007).

[5] That is not to say that there was no information available about the form and consequences of cross-border anti-competitive practices (of which the evidence on international cartels is probably the strongest), or about the ways in which national enforcement of competition law can result in sub-optimal outcomes (from the perspective of the global allocation of resources), both of which provide in principle a rationale for further international measures on competition law and cooperation between enforcement agencies.

only developing country signatories and a further 27 per cent of which involved at least one developing country signatory and one industrialized country signatory. Without in any way implying that each RTA included every single type of competition-related provision, Solano and Sennekamp found that the competition chapters they analyzed included provisions on:

- Adopting, maintaining, and applying competition measures.
- Coordination and cooperation provisions, specifically, general cooperation provisions, notification provisions, provisions relating to exchange of evidence and/or information, provisions relating to competition policy and enforcement, and provisions relating to negative and positive comity.
- Provisions addressing anti-competitive behavior including anti-competitive agreements (horizontal and vertical), abuse of dominance or monopolization, state aids, or subsidies, anti-competitive mergers and acquisitions, and provisions relating to the potential for anti-competitive behavior by state enterprises or state monopolies.
- Competition-specific provisions concerning the principles of non-discrimination, due process, and transparency.
- Provisions not to apply so-called trade remedies (anti-dumping measures, countervailing duties, and safeguards).
- Provisions to limit the recourse to trade remedies.
- Provisions concerning dispute settlement that arise with respect to the application of the competition provisions within a RTA.
- Provisions that offer flexibility and progressivity—two forms of special and differential treatment—to developing country signatories to a RTA.

On the basis of this taxonomy, and analysis thereof, Solano and Sennekamp made a number of observations. The first observation concerns the rationale for including competition provisions in the RTAs. The authors argue (pp. 8–9) that "Trade is the overriding principle," by which they mean:

> While some agreements have more explicit language than others, in most of the analyzed agreements the parties emphasize that anti-competitive practices can undermine the trade objectives of the agreement. As such, parties express that measures adopted to combat anti-competitive behavior will enhance the trade objectives of the agreement.

With respect to the relative frequency of different types of competition provisions being included in RTAs, Solano and Sennekamp note (pp. 14 and 15):

> A first general observation is that RTAs take different approaches as to substantive competition rules and setting up of mechanisms on competition-related matters. Thus it is notable that agreements which contain more provisions addressing anticompetitive behavior tend to have fewer provisions concerning coordination and cooperation between national competition entities and vice versa.

Most of the agreements containing provisions addressing anticompetitive behavior have been concluded by the EC or among non-EC European countries in (South-) Eastern Europe. On the other hand, agreements that focus more on coordination and cooperation provisions have been concluded in the Americas (or involving a North- or South-American party) and with some Asian countries. Therefore, it is appropriate to distinguish between two 'families' of agreements, the EC-style agreements and the US-style agreements.[6]

Solano and Sennekamp note that relatively few RTAs contain competition provisions on anti-competitive mergers, due process, the elimination or application of trade defense measures, and flexibility and non-reciprocity towards developing countries. They further note that RTAs differ markedly in the manner in which disputes that arise from the application of competition provisions are treated, and in some cases the competition chapter is excluded from the application of any RTA-specific dispute settlement mechanism.

The study by Solano and Sennekamp broke important ground and helped identify a number of matters that they did not make much of. First, their study showed that competition provisions need not target only private anti-competitive practices, but also state measures that can distort market outcomes. These state measures can include direct steps, such as subsidization, but also indirect state influence over state-controlled enterprises and state monopolies. For this reason, it would be incorrect to conclude that competition provisions ostensibly target the private sector or are necessarily opposed to private sector development. It is perfectly possible to construct a set of competition provisions that "tame the state" or the application of state power.

Second, their study demonstrates that competition provisions in RTAs can create obligations to both enact competition law and implement legislation and to enforce competition law effectively. The impact of such provisions then is not just on international commerce and on domestic firms that face international competition, as a national competition law can apply to commercial transactions that involve only domestic (i.e., non-foreign) parties. To the extent that promoting competition in national markets is an ingredient for private sector development and for nurturing internationally competitive firms, then, RTAs can be an instrument for improving the domestic governance of markets—even if the apparent motivation initially was trade related. Moreover, an obligation to enforce competition law effectively could be drafted in such a way as to have implications for the powers, human resources, and budgets of a competition authority. In addition, nothing prevents competition provisions being drafted so as to mandate the legal independence of a competition authority (it being recognized that there are

---

[6] In fairness to these authors, they go on to argue (p. 15): "Furthermore it should be noted that, the denominations EC-style and US-style do not imply that the EC or US are a member of every agreement in that category. It rather describes the agreement as oriented either towards cooperation or towards substantive rules. While this distinction is true for many of the analyzed agreements it is not the case for all of the agreements in this study. There is overlap between these two 'families', especially in cross-regional agreements such as Chile-Korea, EC-Chile, EC-Mexico, EFTA-Mexico, or Korea-Singapore. Nevertheless, this categorization can provide a useful structure for further analysis."

many different facets to the independence of regulatory agencies). In which case, competition provisions in RTAs can have institution-building and institution-protecting components.

Third, Solano and Sennekamp's study shows that there are a number of different ways in which competition provisions in RTAs can be used to influence the form and extent of cross-border cooperation between competition authorities. Such cooperation need not be confined to discussions of general approaches to competition law and policy and, as a logical possibility, cooperation on the enforcement of competition law is possible. (Indeed, the positive comity provisions of some RTAs would suggest that some negotiating parties are open to certain types of enforcement-related cooperation.) Care is needed here as it may be impossible to mandate the degree of voluntary cooperation between enforcement agencies. However, mandating cooperation is not the only option available to RTA signatories. The question arises as to whether non-cooperation could be discouraged. Perhaps unfulfilled requests for cooperation could trigger an obligation to produce a public, written explanation from the uncooperative party. Or that party could forgo some benefits of the RTA. More generally, further attention could be given to the practicalities of strengthening cooperation between competition authorities on enforcement and non-enforcement matters and to the subtle incentives that could promote such cooperation.

An assessment of Solano and Sennekamp's study can be found in Anderson and Evenett (2006). While recognizing the breakthrough that this study represented, especially for those analysts and policymakers seeking a comprehensive overview of what might be called the landscape of competition provisions in RTAs, Anderson and Evenett expressed reservations concerning both the approach taken and the conclusions drawn. Anderson and Evenett first contend that the focus on the provisions in the competition chapters of RTAs may omit important ways in which competition principles and pro-competitive logic are incorporated into RTAs. Examples of competition-related provisions found in non-competition chapters of RTAs were provided, in particular examples drawn from chapters on certain service sectors (typically telecommunications and financial services), government procurement, and intellectual property. Moreover, it was pointed out that a number of RTAs include provisions that restrict state aid or restrict the behavior of state-owned or state-controlled enterprises in chapters other than the competition chapter. Overlooking the former may downplay the role that RTAs can play in "taming the state" or as some prefer to put it "leveling the playing field."

The second reservation is that, in some RTAs, agreement-wide obligations on non-discrimination, procedural fairness, and transparency apply to the provisions of the competition chapter without the former being mentioned in the latter chapter. Therefore, a general obligation not to discriminate against foreign commercial entities could limit or prevent outright a competition authority from treating a merger or acquisition that involved a foreign firm differently than a combination involving only domestic firms. An RTA, then, may have implications for the enforcement of competition law whether or not an RTA has a separate chapter on competition law and policy. Review of the general or "horizontal" principles included in an RTA and in the provisions for an

RTA to come into force is required to determine if this observation applies to a particular accord.

Anderson and Evenett's third reservation concerns the general conclusion that "trade is the over-riding principle" in shaping the competition provisions of RTAs. It is true that many competition chapters of RTAs state, as Solano and Sennekamp argue, that preventing anti-competitive acts eroding the potential benefits created by trade liberalization is an objective. However, Anderson and Evenett provide examples of RTAs that refer directly to the goals of promoting competition, consumer welfare, and economic efficiency. This is not a quibble as a growing number of the stated objectives in RTAs have nothing to do with trade liberalization per se, mercantilism, and its associated rhetoric (that many outside of the field of trade negotiations object to). Perhaps, then, it is better to characterize RTAs as state-to-state instruments to promote a number of common or shared goals and values, including those relating to competition.

Anderson and Evenett's critique was taken on board by Teh (2008) in his subsequent analysis of the competition-related provisions of 74 RTAs. Teh's analysis can, therefore, shed light on whether the examples provided in and the considerations raised by Anderson and Evenett (2006) are special cases or are of more general relevance. Teh devised a "mapping" of the many different ways in which competition-related provisions could enter a RTA and applied it systematically, in so doing compiling a large table that may be a useful reference guide for policymakers and analysts.[7] Teh's work contains a number of important findings including (p. 3):

> Whereas the OECD study suggests that competition provisions in RTAs are all about trade, the mapping suggests a much more nuanced relationship between trade and competition. While the competition principles are embedded in trade agreements, they are not necessarily subordinated to trade tests or concerns. This paper also emphasizes the non-preferential nature of a significant number of competition rules that are included in regional trade agreements, a feature that sharply distinguishes them for example from traditional RTA provisions on market access.

With respect to prominence given to competition principles in the general objectives of RTAs, Teh notes (p. 18):

> While one expects that removing obstacles to trade or expansion of trade would be universal, a surprisingly large proportion of the RTAs (42 % of the sample) see the promotion and advancement of 'conditions of competition' between the RTA partners as one of the principal objectives of the trade agreement. In addition, a number of RTAs (EU-Chile, Mexico-Japan, and Japan-Singapore) explicitly refer to the establishment of cooperation in the field of competition as an objective of the agreement. This appears to demonstrate that many RTAs place an intrinsic or independent value on the promotion of competition and do not consider it as necessarily subordinate to the trade goals of the agreement.

---

[7] Specifically table 2 of Teh (2008).

Moreover, Teh found that over half of the RTAs examined contained a general obliga-tion of transparency (that must be applied to all laws covered by the agreement) or a specific obligation relating to transparency in the competition chapter of the agree-ment. More generally, agreement-wide provisions on transparency were more prevalent than those relating to procedural fairness and far more prevalent than those relating to non-discrimination.

With respect to the inclusion of competition-related provisions in sectoral chapters of RTAs, Teh finds that 15 RTAs (accounting for just over 20 per cent of his sample) had investment chapters containing such provisions. Interestingly, in 12 RTAs, the very concept of National Treatment in chapters on trade in services is defined in terms of the "conditions of competition" facing domestic firms and their foreign rivals. Appeal then is made to a competition-based metric to interpret a major concept in international trade law, in which the competition horse then pulls the trade cart and not the other way around! Teh also found that the telecommunications chapters of 20 RTAs contained a number of provisions that seek to deter anti-competitive conduct by incumbent firms and to ensure that public obligations in this sector (such as Universal Service obliga-tions) do not have the effect of limiting competition unduly. Competition-related pro-visions were found in the maritime transport chapters of six RTAs and in the financial services chapters of five RTAs. Last but not least, Teh also describes a number of ways in which competition-related provisions enter into the government procurement chapters of 17 RTAs.

Taken together, Teh's findings imply that it is misleading to view RTAs solely through a mercantilist lens. For sure, today it is still possible to draft RTA provisions that seek only to liberalize trade between signatories. However, it ought to be recognized that many RTAs have gone beyond this point and other considerations have been invoked either as distinct objectives of RTAs or employed in the interpretation of trade concepts, such as National Treatment. Moreover, Teh's work also identifies circumstances when discrimination against a firm is permitted if a competition-related concern is present. That is, circumstances are envisaged when the objective of limiting discrimination in international commerce is subordinated to competition principles. In the light of these findings, no overarching conclusion about the prominence given to any one objective in RTAs seems tenable.

In addition to a discussion of Solano and Sennekamp's taxonomy of RTA provisions, Anderson and Evenett (2006) also contained an empirical analysis of the effects of dif-ferent types of competition provisions on the total value of cross-border mergers and acquisitions flowing into 116 countries during the years 1989 to 2004. Countries that already have a merger review law on the statute books were estimated conservatively to receive 43 per cent more inward mergers and acquisitions if they signed a RTA with a transparency-related provision in a competition chapter. Countries that signed RTA provisions on transparency, non-discrimination, due process, and on anti-competitive mergers were estimated (again conservatively) to receive 19 per cent more inward merg-ers and acquisitions. These findings suggest that certain competition-related provisions influence the pace of cross-border corporate consolidation, which tends to be triggered by trade liberalization and by international market integration more generally. Some caution, though, is needed as it would be unwise to base policy recommendations on one empirical study. Moreover, while Anderson and Evenett examined the impact of certain competition-related provisions (and controlled for other plausible determinants of the total value of inward mergers and acquisitions), they did not compare the impact of these provisions with other international initiatives that might improve the enforcement of competition law in a given jurisdiction. Policymakers may well be interested in the differential impact of international initiatives and not just the effects of any one instrument to promote inter-state cooperation. While this line of inquiry may be perfectly reasonable, unfortunately the paucity of empirical studies on related matters implies that it cannot be completed at present.

The last piece of evidence that will be discussed in this section relates to the spread of certain competition-related RTA provisions throughout the Americas and beyond. Baldwin, Evenett, and Low (2009) examined five areas of government policy covered by RTA provisions to see if more non-discriminatory norms were being adopted over time. One of the five areas of policy was competition law, and particular attention was given to three North American Free Trade Agreement (NAFTA) provisions, one of which was found in the competition chapter and two that were not. The latter two (specifically, Articles 1305.1 and 1305.2) proscribe anti-competitive conduct by state monopolies in the telecommunications sector and commit signatories to take steps to address anti-competitive conduct in that sector. Baldwin, Evenett, and Low found that, in the 10 years after the signing of NAFTA, identical or similar provisions had been incorporated into many other RTAs. Figures 26.1 and 26.2 summarize the spread of these two telecommunications-related provisions in the Americas and into East Asia. Provisions identical or very similar to Article 1305.2 were found in 16 subsequent RTAs, demonstrating that a non-discriminatory competition-related norm can spread through RTAs. It would seem that some degree of learning or benchmarking across agreements has taken place and that RTAs can be a vehicle for advancing non-mercantilist norms. Further research may be useful to examine the extent to which other competition principles have been adopted in RTAs, there being no reason to believe *a priori* that the NAFTA agreement is exceptional in this regard.

The purpose of this section has been to summarize and discuss the main findings of a number of detailed analyses of the content and spread of competition-related provisions in RTAs. While the research on these matters has added considerably to our understanding of the options available to policymakers and qualified some earlier perceptions of these RTA provisions, it should be noted that the evidential base is not sufficient to rank definitively the various ways in which international accords can strengthen national competition law and enforcement and cross-border cooperation. Clearly, this is an area of substantial innovation, and perhaps even experimentation, by policymakers, and future analysis will hopefully shed better light on the relative merits of alternative state initiatives in this field.

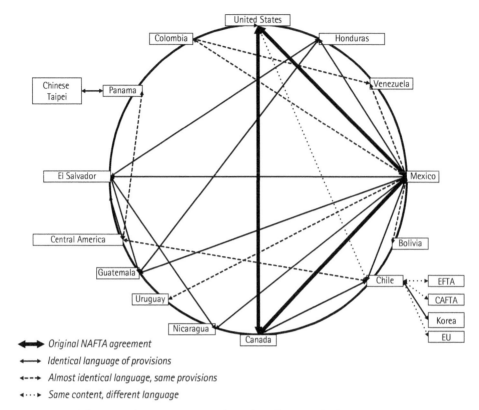

Original NAFTA agreement
Identical language of provisions
Almost identical language, same provisions
Same content, different language

FIGURE 26.1 Adoption of common or similar rules: the spread of NAFTA Art. 1305.1

III. Options for Policymakers

The research above allows for identification of the eight options for policymakers as they consider ways in which competition principles and related matters might be incorporated into RTAs. Unlike other taxonomies of related legal provisions, the purpose of each provision is stated explicitly so as to allow a better identification of ends and, then, of means. There is no suggestion here that every option below is relevant or of equal importance to every developing country. Surely, differences in national circumstances and priorities will determine largely whether any given provision is sufficiently important to be deemed a negotiating priority. Nor should it be forgotten that there may be non-RTA means to attaining any given end. Still, knowing the set of options available may inform decision-making and may motivate further proposals for different types of competition provisions in RTAs.

The eight options are:

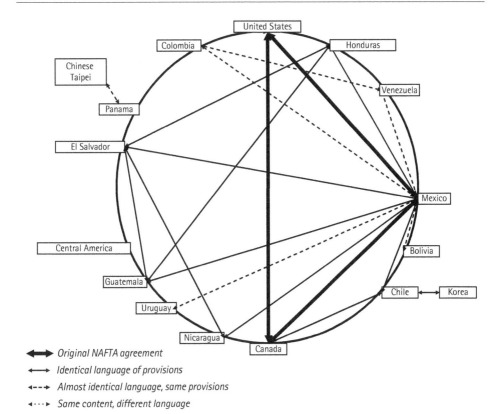

Original NAFTA agreement
Identical language of provisions
Almost identical language, same provisions
Same content, different language

FIGURE 26.2 Adoption of common or similar rules: the spread of NAFTA Art. 1305.2

1. The objectives of competition law (promoting efficiency, consumer welfare, and improvements in the allocation of resources) could be included in the overall goals of the RTA.[8]

   a. To the extent that a social or economic objective is stated as "trumping" competition-related objectives, then the state measures taken should be those that do the least harm to those competition objectives. Provisions could be included to ensure that such competition considerations be taken into account when those state measures are designed, when they are reviewed, revised, or challenged before any official body.

   b. The desire to enhance the welfare of RTA signatories could manifest itself in bans on provisions (including exemptions) from competition law and other economic laws that promote or facilitate anti-competitive practices in the jurisdiction of another party. Exemptions for competition law for export cartels could, thus, be banned.

---

[8] This option plus the option described in point 1a. below could be applied to each chapter that relates to a specific economic sector (e.g., telecommunications, financial services) or to specific government policies (e.g., government policy, investment policies, and intellectual property right policies).

2. The general principles of non-discrimination, transparency, and due process could apply to the content and enforcement of the signatories' competition law.

3. With respect to the RTA's dispute settlement provisions:

   a. Matters relating to the contents of a signatories' competition law and its enforcement could fall under the provisions of the RTA's dispute settlement provisions.

   b. Consistent with entrenching competition law objectives, a competition-related defense of any measure would be admissible in an otherwise trade-related dispute settlement proceeding and would, if established, take precedence over violations of national treatment or other pertinent non-discrimination clause.

4. Provisions in a RTA could be included that mandate that, over a specified period of time, signatories will adopt competition laws that can address the full range of private and state-created anti-competitive practices and outcomes.

   a. Signatories could be required to consider established international best practice with respect to investigative measures, transparency, due process, and sanctions before drafting of a competition law, or revising such a law. The competition authorities of RTA partners could be given rights to comment upon drafts of a signatory's competition law before submission is made to a legislature.

5. Provisions in an RTA could be included that mandate signatories to empower at least one national competition authority with powers relating to competition advocacy, including possibly the right to comment upon any governmental regulation that may have consequences for conditions of competition.

6. Provisions could be included in RTAs that strengthen the agencies responsible for enforcing national competition law, including provisions that each signatory must at all times provide:

   a. Each competition agency with independence, taken to mean at least the right to open an investigation and close an investigation without undue political or commercial interference.

   b. Each competition agency with the human resources and budget to undertake the agency's stated functions by employing international best practices. Insufficient human and budgetary resources could be a matter for state-to-state dispute settlement and comparisons with the resources received by peer agencies perceived to be operating at international best practices in comparable economic circumstances could be allowed.

7. Provisions in a RTA could be included that state the importance that the signatories attach to cooperation between competition authorities, and between

other state bodies that a competition authority chooses to seek assistance from. Furthermore, it could be specified that:

a. Cooperation on the enforcement of competition law is as important as cooperation between competition authorities.
b. Notification requirements and penalties could be triggered if a signatory fails to certify that a competition authority in another party has not undertaken cooperation consistent with the goals of the RTA. Such failure to certify could be taken to dispute settlement.

8. Review procedures could be incorporated into a RTA whereby reports are prepared by the competition authorities of the signatories on the degree to which experience since the RTA came into force has attained the specific and overall competition-related goals of the RTAs. Potential future reforms could be identified, including the negotiation of stronger inter-agency or inter-governmental accords. Such reviews could occur at regular intervals, such as every five years.

IV. Concluding Remarks

RTAs are not what they used to be. Their scope, the values advanced, and the measures and sectors covered have broadened considerably since 2000, so much so that characterizing RTAs as mercantilistic accords is incomplete and ultimately misleading. Why does any of this matter for competition authorities and associated practitioners? It transpires that many RTAs now include not just chapters devoted to competition law and its enforcement, but have sought to entrench competition principles in the overall objectives of such accords and in the implementation of a number of laws with potentially significant economic impact.

In general, establishing what opportunities are afforded by the recent proliferation of RTAs—and therefore what opportunities could be missed—requires appreciation of the options available to policymakers. The purpose of this chapter, therefore, was to summarize the latest findings of analyses of RTAs that contain competition-related provisions and to present a broad range of measures that could inform priority setting in RTA negotiations and in other international initiatives pertaining to competition law and its enforcement.

Of course, ideally one would like to conclude with evidence concerning the costs— implementation and, where relevant, any costs associated with inappropriate use of competition provisions in RTAs—and the benefits of these different options. Unfortunately, the evidential base does not support any sweeping statements in this regard. Much of the empirical evidence concerning competition law that does exist relates to the effects of national enforcement regimes. To the extent that competition provisions in RTAs plausibly improve the enforcement record and, therefore, the deterrent effect of national competition law, then an indirect case for competition provisions in RTAs can be made. It is simply far too early to defend or attack these provisions. Better instead to continue to explore what is feasible and commit to undertaking evaluations of existing competition provisions on a more regular basis so as to add to the empirical base to guide policymaking.

References

Anderson, R. D. and Evenett, S. J. (2006), 'Incorporating Competition Elements into Regional Trade Agreements: Characterization and Empirical Analysis.' Internet: <http://www.evenett.com/working/CompPrincInRTAs.pdf> (as of June 27, 2008).

Baldwin, R., Evenett, S. J., and Low, P. (2009), 'Beyond Tariffs: Multilaterizing Non-tariff RTA Commitments.' Chapter 3 of Baldwin, R., and Low, P. (eds.) *Multilateralizing Regionalism*. Cambridge: Cambridge University Press.

Bourgeois, J., Dawar, K., and Evenett, S. J. (2007), 'A Comparative Analysis of Selected Provisions In Free Trade Agreements.' Report prepared for DG TRADE, European Commission.

Brusick, P., Alvarez, A. M., and Cernat, L. (eds.) (2005), *Competition Provisions in Regional Trade Agreements: How to Assure Development Gains.* Geneva: United Nations Conference for Trade and Development.

Clarke, J. L., and Evenett, S. J. (2003), 'A Multilateral Framework for Competition Policy?' Chapter 2 in Evenett, S. J. and SECO (eds.), *The Singapore Issues and the World Trading System: The Road to Cancun and Beyond.* Bern: SECO.

Dawar, K., and Evenett, S. J. (2008), 'The CARIFORUM-EC EPA: An Analysis of its Government Procurement and Competition Law-Related Provisions.' Report prepared for GTZ. June.

Evenett, S. J. (2005a), 'What is the Relationship between Competition Law and Policy and Economic Development?' Chapter 1 in. Brooks, D. H., and Evenett, S. J. (eds.), *Competition Policy and Development in Asia* Basingstoke, UK: Palgrave Macmillan.

Evenett, S. J. (2005b), 'Would Enforcing Competition Law Compromise Industrial Policy Objectives?' Chapter 3 in Brooks, D. H., and Evenett, S. J. (eds.), *Competition Policy and Development in Asia* Basingstoke, UK: Palgrave Macmillan.

Solano, O., and Sennekamp, A. (2006), 'Competition Provisions in Regional Trade Agreements.' OECD Trade Policy Working Paper No. 31, COM/DAF/TD(2005)3/FINAL.

Silva, V. (2004), 'Cooperation on Competition Policy in Latin America and Caribbean Bilateral Trade Agreements.' Document presented at the APEC 2004 Economic Outlook Symposium, Santiago, Chile, 12–13 August.

Teh, R. (2008), 'Competition Provisions in Regional Trading Agreements.' Mimeo. World Trade Organization. April.

CHAPTER 27

INTERNATIONAL DISCIPLINES ON GOVERNMENT PROCUREMENT[*]

BERNARD HOEKMAN AND SIMON EVENETT

I. INTRODUCTION

THE growth of spending by central and local governments was one of the most profound economic changes of the twentieth century (Tanzi and Schuknecht, 2000). Although a large portion of government expenditures is devoted to social spending and redistribution (e.g., transfer payments), government entities of all types spend considerable sums on a wide range of products as inputs into the production of public goods and services—education, defense, utilities, infrastructure, public health, and so forth. According to one estimate, some 70 per cent of all central government expenditure is associated with a contract of some type (Transparency International, 2006).[1] As a consequence, the state has considerable influence over the allocation of resources in market-based economies. The purchases by the entities concerned are governed by various procedures and mechanisms that aim to ensure that the specific objectives of each agency or activity are achieved while minimizing costs to taxpayers. Such procedures and mechanisms constitute government procurement policy.

Given that government procurement often involves large projects and is an important interface between the public and private sectors, many countries have made attaining efficiency in public purchasing a priority. South Africa, for example,

---

[*] This chapter draws on previous work by the authors on government procurement, including Evenett (2010), Evenett and Hoekman (2005, 2006) and Hoekman and Kostecki (2009).

[1] <http://www.transparency.org/global_priorities/public_contracting>.

included a section on procurement principles in its 1996 Constitution. This requires that procurement be undertaken on the basis of a fair, public, and competitive process by independent and impartial tender boards that are to maintain records of decisions and motivate their decisions to interested parties. A common element of procurement systems that aim to ensure value for money is to mimic the working of the market by requiring that public entities seek competitive bids from potential suppliers of goods and services.

There is often a tension between the focus on efficiency ("value for money") and other policy objectives that are pursued by governments in the context of procurement. Throughout much of the post-World War II era, government entities tended to be supplied by domestic firms. Discrimination against foreign suppliers was rife. Two justifications were offered for this discrimination. First, the prevailing Keynesian macroeconomic orthodoxy emphasized that the increase in national income caused by a rise in government expenditures was greater the smaller was the share of each dollar spent on goods produced abroad (imports). Governments could reduce this share—what economists call the marginal propensity to import— by refraining from buying products from abroad. The second rationale for discrimination against foreign suppliers was protectionist, reflecting a desire that "our money" should be spent on "our goods" to keep "jobs at home," to safeguard national security, or to attain industrial policy objectives (e.g., to support strategic industries or to influence the geographic allocation of economic activity within the country).

Insofar as procurement policies favor domestic firms and products, they can impede international commerce. Such impediments can be prohibitive; for example, when there is an outright ban on purchases from foreign providers. Alternatively, they may be similar in some respects to an import tariff by the granting of a margin of preference to domestic bidders for state contracts. Effective market access could also be constrained if procurement rules prohibit sourcing from foreign owned firms, even if they have established a presence in the market through foreign direct investment (FDI). It is this market access dimension of discriminatory procurement practices that has generally provided the rationale for negotiating disciplines on government procurement policy in international trade agreements.

The desire to discriminate against foreign suppliers in public purchases was the major reason that government procurement was excluded from the original General Agreement on Tariffs and Trade (GATT) in 1947. It was not until the completion of the Tokyo Round of multilateral trade negotiations in 1979 that an agreement on disciplines for government procurement practices was introduced into the world trading system. This agreement bound only those countries willing to sign it—at the time only a subset of the Organisation for Economic Co-operation and Development (OECD) membership. During the Uruguay Round of multilateral trade negotiations, the coverage of the Agreement on Government Procurement (GPA) was expanded but participation remains voluntary and limited to mostly OECD countries.

A number of factors underlie the gradual shift towards greater acceptance of international rules on national procurement practices. First, since the mid 1970s, government budgets have come under increased pressure, especially in industrial nations. Spending on welfare states, health, education, and pensions has increased considerably. Stimulating competition between firms that bid for government contracts—including foreign suppliers—is one way of reducing costs. Directly subjecting production units to competitive forces is another—for example through privatization of state-owned enterprises, permitting entry of privately-owned firms into sectors traditionally reserved for public entities (such as utilities), and contracting out activities to independent suppliers. What was once produced "in-house" by government entities is increasingly supplied by private operators—resulting in a shift towards real market-based contracting as opposed to one where the focus was on mimicking the role of the market through competitive bidding for government contracts. Privatization reduces the size of the procurement market, but outsourcing of government activities increases it. Much of what is outsourced comprises services, resulting in new interest by foreign services firms to ensure that they are able to compete for the associated contracts.

Third, "export politics" are a major factor driving the interest of governments to negotiate rules for procurement policies. Domestic firms eye profitable opportunities in supplying foreign governments and press their own government to negotiate "access" to those overseas procurement markets. In industries where there are strong economies of scale—that is, average costs which fall as production levels increase—firms have an incentive to increase sales at home or abroad. Although one government could begin bilateral negotiations with another government to open the latter's procurement market, the most prevalent path to reform has been for nations in the same region to simultaneously increase the access to their procurement markets to firms from the same region. Reciprocity is at the core of such agreements to liberalize together, as contracts lost by domestic firms to foreign suppliers are compensated by an increase in contracts won in trading partners.

In this chapter, we discuss prevailing international disciplines on government procurement practices through the lens of economic analyses of the trade-related aspects of procurement reform; the political forces that encourage or retard such reforms; and developments in the WTO and in other international fora. The plan of the chapter is as follows. Section II discusses the size of public procurement "markets," the objectives of procurement policy, and the instruments that are used. In Section III, we briefly discuss negotiating incentives—why cooperate? Section IV describes the WTO Agreement on Government Procurement, which came into force on January 1, 1996 and currently has 40 signatories, and discusses the challenges of expanding its membership and the effort to define possible disciplines on procurement regimes in the WTO Working Group on Transparency in Government Procurement during 1997–2003. Section V briefly reviews the coverage of procurement-related disciplines in recent regional trade agreements. We focus in particular on agreements between Asian countries as many of these are of recent vintage and thus provide more information on what governments are willing to do in this area that is not feasible at the multilateral (WTO) level. Section VI offers some concluding remarks.

II. Procurement Markets: Size, Policy Objectives, and Instruments

There is little systematic cross-country analysis of the size of national procurement markets. OECD (2002) remains the only recent effort to quantify the magnitude of procurement contracts, using National Accounts data to compute the magnitude of government spending in the OECD member states and in 106 non-OECD economies in 1998. On average, government procurement of items other than defense and compensation for state employees in the OECD nations entailed outlays equivalent to 7.6 per cent of national income. These calculations imply that in 1998 approximately US$1.8 trillion of government expenditures were potentially contestable by firms located at home and abroad. Adjusting for the growth in GDP in current prices between 1998 and 2010 (which doubled for the OECD in this period), this suggests the total OECD government market is some $3.5 trillion. Between a quarter and a third of all outlays are undertaken by central governments, highlighting the importance of sub-national authorities as a source of demand. On average, contestable government expenditures in non-OECD countries were some 5–10 per cent of national incomes. The total amount of such expenditures in these non-OECD nations equaled $287 billion in 1998, approximately one-sixth of the size of the contestable procurement markets in OECD nations. Given a quadrupling of GDP in current prices between 1998 and 2010, this translates into over $1 trillion as of 2010, assuming ratios of procurement to national income did not change.

Targets and Instruments of National Procurement Policies

Jan Tinbergen, the Nobel-prize winning economist, introduced the distinction between a government's targets and instruments. The former are the objectives that the government wishes to achieve, and the latter are the means employed in attempts to meet those objectives. Government procurement policies tend to have multiple targets and numerous instruments. This reality complicates an analysis of procurement policies, and in part accounts for the multi-faced nature of international disciplines on the design and implementation of such policies.

Perhaps the most common objective of procurement policies is to obtain "value for money" for the government in its purchases. This objective in turn has many facets. It could mean the purchase of products that satisfy certain performance standards at lowest cost. Alternatively, it could mean choosing the highest quality product among a set of similarly priced goods. While value for money seems an obvious objective, from an economic perspective the appropriate metric is economic efficiency. Efficiency is attained when the price paid for a good (service) reflects the value to society of the resources used to produce the last unit of that good. A classic source of inefficiency occurs when a buyer with market power reduces the quantity purchased so as to induce suppliers to lower their prices. Therefore, it is important to bear in mind that attaining the lowest possible price, or "value for money," in government purchasing need not generate efficient economic outcomes.

A common element of procurement procedures is an effort to mimic the working of the market by requiring that public entities seek competitive bids from potential suppliers of goods and services. The cost-minimizing goal underlying competitive bidding requirements for purchases by public entities is frequently not attained because legislation requires procuring entities to pursue other objectives as well. These may include a desire to promote the development of domestic industry or technology, to support particular types of firms (such as small and medium-sized enterprises), to safeguard national security, or to favor certain groups or regions within a country. Economists refer to such policies as pursuing "non-economic" objectives, a term that does not imply that these objectives are misguided or unattainable, but that the objective is not economic efficiency. Often the pursuit of such objectives involves discriminating against foreign suppliers. Examples include outright prohibitions on foreign sourcing (civil servants must fly national airlines), threshold criteria for foreign sourcing to be permitted (minimum cost or price differentials compared to local suppliers), or offset and local content requirements. Chinese public procurement procedures, for example, require that purchasing entities give priority to products developed by domestic firms so as to help support the development of innovative capabilities of indigenous firms (OECD, 2010).[2]

The existence of multiple objectives implies that government procurement policies are often an exercise in "constrained cost minimization." The basic goal is value for money, subject to the other policy goals that need to be taken into account. In practice, these other goals often imply that, for all or part of any contract, the scope of competition is reduced to the set of firms that meet specific criteria laid out in legislation or procurement regulations. In some instances, there may not be any competition at all. For example, governments may use selective or single tendering procedures under which a procuring entity directly approaches a specific firm for a bid.

Research has shown that the pursuit of non-economic objectives by governments can have very different implications for the amount of economic efficiency sacrificed, depending on the instrument that is used. In general, the extent of the efficiency loss will

---

[2] The law requires that more than 30 per cent of technology and equipment purchased with public funds be for domestic equipment, and grants indigenous innovative products a price preference of 8 per cent (OECD, 2010).

be minimized if instruments target directly the source of problem at hand: lack of economic opportunities for minority groups; regional economic wealth differentials; and so on. For example, governments may want to promote the number and production levels of small firms by awarding these firms state contracts even though at least one large firm submitted a lower bid. An economic approach might point to a different course of action: first, the government should identify the impediments faced by small businesses and take measures that directly remedy them. If, for example, the critical impediment to the growth of small firms is access to financial credit, then policies should be directed towards bolstering the supply of credit to small firms—rather than using indirect means such as increasing the sales of small firms through government contracts that can then be used to obtain credit lines from banks.

These considerations have direct relevance for the design of government procurement policies. Governments may be more inclined to eliminate a procurement scheme that favors a certain industry if they know that other forms of state intervention can better attain this objective. Furthermore, if the chosen form of state intervention directly tackles the constraints confronting the favored industry's or group's performance, then economic efficiency can be improved also.

Economic Analysis of Discrimination in Procurement

Discriminatory public procurement practices are a major market access issue on the agenda of trade agreements. Given a global contestable market of some $5 trillion and procurement markets that account for 5 to 10 per cent of GDP or more, if many countries pursue discriminatory procurement practices, the end result for the world as a whole is likely to be inferior in welfare terms to a cooperative outcome where governments agree to refrain from using procurement as a tool to protect national industries or to pursue non-economic objectives.

Discriminatory procurement policies are often considered *prima facie* evidence of protectionism—after all, governments explicitly favor domestic suppliers of goods and services. The effect of discrimination depends on market structure and on the size of government demand. In general, a procurement policy that gives a price preference of 10 per cent to a local industry or to firms from a specific region or below a certain size will not be equivalent to a 10 per cent import tariff. This is because government demand is only a fraction of total demand for most goods and services. Baldwin (1970) and Baldwin and Richardson (1972) have pointed out that if domestic and foreign products are good substitutes, markets are competitive, and government demand is less than the initial domestic supply capacity, discrimination will have no effect on imports, prices, overall output, and welfare. Although discrimination results in increased demand by the government for domestic output, this will be offset by greater private-sector imports, so that the policy has no effect on equilibrium prices and production of the domestic industry. To see why, suppose originally the government bought 5,000 cars from abroad. Assume it then imposes a ban on foreign sourcing so as to support the domestic industry. After the ban, these 5,000 cars must be supplied by domestic firms, which in turn would have 5,000 fewer cars to supply to domestic private consumers. However, foreign firms have exactly 5,000 unsold cars which they can now supply to domestic consumers, making up any apparent shortfall. Therefore, when government demand is relatively small, goods are substitutes, and markets competitive, procurement discrimination merely reshuffles sales between domestic and foreign firms, with no effect on overall imports (market access), output, or prices.

If, however, government demand exceeded domestic supply at the prices that prevailed before the ban was imposed, the price of cars for the government must increase to encourage domestic supply to expand to meet government demand. The end result is that domestic sales to the government rise and imports fall. If the world price determined the pre-ban price for domestic private consumers, they will be unaffected by the procurement ban. After all, domestic consumers can buy all the cars they want on world markets at the world price. In contrast, if foreign producers customize their cars to the domestic market, the procurement ban leaves foreign producers with cars they used to sell to the domestic government but are now prevented from doing so. Since these cars were customized for a specific market (suppose they have steering wheels on the left hand side), then the possibility of selling these cars on the world market is remote. The foreign car suppliers are left with little choice but to offer additional cars to domestic consumers at lower prices. In this case, domestic consumers actually gain from a government ban on purchases from foreign cars—as the ban creates a temporary surplus of foreign goods which results in lower prices being paid by domestic consumers.

In the case where procurement discrimination raises the price paid by the government, domestic firms expand output and see their profits rise. New firms will want to enter this protected industry, driving down the price paid by the government until the incentive to enter this market (the higher than usual profits) has gone. The principal consequence of allowing free entry into the market is that the price paid by the government should fall to equal the world price—potentially eliminating any price wedge between that paid by private consumers and the government. Whether entry occurs depends on the prevalence of natural and policy-induced barriers to entry. Therefore, the long-term consequences of a procurement ban are determined in part by domestic competition policies and restrictions on FDI. This result continues to obtain if there is imperfect competition (oligopoly) as long as goods are perfect substitutes.[3]

Matters are different if the procurement is for products for which there are just a few suppliers. In such situations there may be a potential economic rationale for discrimination. Discrimination will increase domestic output and thereby can help local firms achieve economies of scale (lower unit costs of production) (Trionfetti, 2000). McAfee and McMillan (1989) show that if domestic firms have a competitive disadvantage in producing the product (are higher cost producers compared to foreign firms), and only a limited number of firms (foreign and domestic) bid for the contract, a price-preference

---

[3] See Evenett and Hoekman (2005a) for a more in-depth discussion.

policy may induce foreign firms to lower their bids. Even if the cost structures of domestic and foreign firms are identical and account is taken of the social cost of distortionary taxation, discrimination may be optimal simply because foreign firms' profits do not enter into domestic welfare (Branco, 1994; Vagstad, 1995). In the context of a small number of bidders, prices (bids) will exceed marginal costs, so that shifting demand to domestic firms may also reduce price–cost margins as domestic output expands (Chen, 1995).

If the products procured are intangible (services) or there are problems in monitoring and enforcing contract compliance, discrimination can increase the likelihood of performance by suppliers. The best (economic) case for discrimination revolves around situations where there is asymmetric information, for example, difficulties in monitoring the performance of a contractor if buyer and provider are located far from each other, or there is a need to offer a firm quasi-rents in order to increase the probability of contract compliance through the threat of losing repeat business (Laffont and Tirole, 1991).[4] Moreover, geographic proximity may be a precondition for effectively contesting procurement markets—making some products, in particular services, in essence non-tradable. Problems of asymmetric information and contract compliance may imply that entities can economize on monitoring costs by choosing suppliers that are located within their jurisdictions. In turn, this will make it more difficult for foreign firms to successfully bid for contracts, even if the goods or services involved are tradable and in the absence of formal discrimination. Such rationales have been explored extensively by Laffont and Tirole (1993); many of the underlying technical arguments are summarized and synthesized in Breton and Salmon (1995). The policy issue that arises in such situations is whether there are barriers against establishment (FDI) by foreign suppliers, as this is a precondition for them to bid for/supply contracts (Evenett and Hoekman, 2005a).

While discriminatory procurement may enhance national welfare by lowering procurement costs in small-number settings, simulation studies suggest that welfare gains are likely to be modest at best. Greater profits of domestic firms or cost savings to public entities will tend to be offset by increased prices. As a result, the potential cost savings are reduced (Deltas and Evenett, 1997). Given that in most instances the optimal discriminatory policy will be difficult to determine (it generally will vary depending on the specifics of the situation), in practice procurement favoritism can be expected to be more costly than a policy of non-discrimination. In many situations the information required to judge if diverging from non-discrimination is beneficial will not be available. Non-discrimination has therefore been argued to be a good rule of thumb (Hoekman, 1998).

The foregoing discussion has ignored the possible dynamic effects of alternative procurement procedures. From a governance perspective, if account is taken of the rent-seeking distortions that may be induced by discriminatory policies and the

---

[4] Discrimination is not necessarily the optimal instrument. Naegelen and Mougeot (1998) show that alternative instruments, such as cost targets, can be more efficient. Governments may also want to consider dual sourcing in such situations: see for example McGuire and Riordan (1995).

social cost of corruption and bribery, the case for non-discrimination is substantially strengthened. All of the above arguments regarding the economic pros and cons of discrimination cease to apply if government entities do not maximize social welfare. Non-discrimination will generally reduce discretion and enhance transparency of the procurement process and thus reduce the scope for rent seeking. Most important in this connection is transparency and a system of rules to impede corruption. Open and competitive bidding, whether or not there are preferences for domestic industry, is a key instrument in this regard.[5]

Such unambiguous conclusions may not apply if what is being procured has significant positive dynamic spillover effects. An example is procurement that seeks to encourage the development of new technologies. Geroski (1990) argues that targeted procurement in which the government creates demand for new or innovative technologies may be superior to policies that target the supply side, such as R&D subsidies, by both stimulating innovation and allowing firms to learn by doing through the process of producing associated products for the government.[6] Insofar as governments care about the nationality or ownership of the firms that acquire and control such technologies, discrimination will be a feature of the associated procurement process. However, it is not obvious that this will be optimal in terms of increasing the likelihood that the new desired technologies or products are in fact generated. If control is an objective then contracts can be structured so as to ensure that the government will be able to determine how the results of what is being financed can be used/made available. If one of the objectives is to utilize and develop local capacity and expertise, then this can be specified as well, implying that firms bidding for the contract need to have a local presence. As in other instances, therefore, per se discrimination against foreign firms in such "public procurement for innovation" is therefore neither needed nor likely to be desirable in attaining the innovation objective.[7]

III. Negotiating Incentives: Promoting International Cooperation

The "standard" rationale for small countries that cannot affect their terms of trade to engage in reciprocity in trade agreements is to break the political logjam that prevents policymakers from undertaking unilateral liberalization. By galvanizing domestic

---

[5] See Ades and Di Tella (1997), Auriol (2006), Auriol, Flochel, and Straub (2009), Borges de Oliveira (2010), Di Tella and Schargrodsky (2003), Hunja (2003), and Hyytinen, Lundberg, and Toivanen (2007) for studies that document the importance of procurement rules and transparency to reduce corruption.

[6] See Nelson (1982) for an early study of how government can use procurement among other instruments to stimulate technical progress.

[7] For discussions of the use of procurement to achieve innovation objectives, see Edler and Georghiou (2007) and European Commission (2004).

export interests seeking better access to foreign markets, a trade agreement can generate the political support needed to counter the opposition to reform by import-competing firms. Whether there is a case for international collective action on public procurement reform depends on the extent to which this political economy logic carries over to procurement policy.

Taxpayers have a clear stake in reforming state procurement systems to be more efficient. However, they are likely to be too dispersed to have enough at stake to organize politically on this issue. Domestic producer interests will have different incentives: those ready and able to supply government contracts will prefer exclusion of foreign competition; those that are "out of the domestic market" will not care—including firms that are able to supply foreign government contracts ("exporters"). Government officials and politicians will generally have preferences to allocate funds to local firms as this generates political support; an incentive that is bolstered if there is corruption. Overall, the support for unilateral reform of procurement discrimination may be weak.

Multilateral reform of discriminatory procurement practices can change the balance of interests as it offers the prospect of winning contracts abroad. The strength of that prospect will condition the degree of support that exporters provide for reform. Here, two considerations are pertinent. First, as was discussed above, economic analysis has shown that when a given foreign government's demand for a good is smaller than the amount actually supplied by that foreign nation's own firms, then there is no improvement in market access of reducing procurement discrimination. This consideration, therefore, reduces the number of domestic export sectors or industries that have an interest in supporting multilateral reductions in procurement discrimination. The second consideration is that a multilateral agreement to reduce foreign discrimination against bids from domestic exporters may encourage some foreign procuring entities to engage in covert *de facto* discrimination. In other words, a transparent form of discrimination might be substituted for a non-transparent form of discrimination. (There are parallels here to the case of trade in industrial goods where it has long been argued that falling tariffs have been replaced by less transparent, non-tariff barriers.) To the extent that domestic exporters believe that such a substitution will take place, their support for multilateral reform of discriminatory practices will be conditioned on the extent to which they are convinced that commitments are meaningful and can be enforced. Actions to ensure that procurement practices are transparent, subject to clear rules, and can be challenged will therefore be important.

This suggests that negotiation of procurement disciplines must include a focus on (enhancing) the transparency of procurement processes. Unilateral transparency reform may attract opposition from those firms that currently supply the government (that fear greater competition for state contracts), from inefficient officials (who oppose either greater workloads associated with more bidders or changes in their existing operating procedures), and from corrupt officials (if greater competition from state contracts reduces the total amount of inducements paid). Moreover, domestic exporters will not support unilateral reform as it offers no prospect of greater sales abroad. The only domestic producer interest to support unilateral reform will be those domestic firms that believe that, after transparency is improved, their prospects of winning a profitable government contract at home have increased. This support for unilateral reform will be attenuated to the extent that foreign firms are now more willing also to bid for domestic government contracts. These considerations suggest that the extent of domestic support for unilateral transparency reform may be weak. Worse still, in order to maximize support for unilateral transparency improvements, a government may be tempted to couple such reforms with greater discrimination against foreign bidders, hence reducing the likelihood that new domestic bidders for state contracts face stiffer competition from foreign rivals.

For a multilateral initiative to improve the transparency of government procurement practices to mobilize more political support than for unilateral reform, two additional factors need to be taken into account. To the extent that domestic exporters feel that a multilateral initiative increases the probability of them winning profitable contracts from foreign governments, then they will lend their support. However, the extent of that support will depend critically on domestic exporters' perceptions of the degree of existing foreign discrimination against their bids and whether more bids by domestic exporters in the future are likely to result in greater foreign discrimination against them. (A more transparent foreign procurement regime can still involve considerable *de jure* discrimination against domestic exporters.) Therefore, the extent of domestic political support for a multilateral initiative to improve the transparency of government procurement practices will be greater if such an initiative is coupled with measures to reduce discrimination against domestic bidders for foreign contracts. The case for international collective action to improve transparency and to reduce discrimination together is stronger than the case for collective action on either one alone.

IV. The WTO Agreement on Government Procurement

Article III:8 GATT excludes procurement from the national treatment obligation. Article XIII General Agreement on Trade in Services (GATS) does the same for services. The 1979 Tokyo Round GPA extended basic GATT obligations such as non-discrimination and transparency to the purchases of goods by selected government entities. The GPA has been renegotiated three times. The second, 1996 version of the Agreement, extended its reach to services. The most recent revision of the GPA was provisionally agreed in December 2006 (GPA/W/297). The periodic renegotiations are mandated by the Agreement itself. Although they have coincided with the Uruguay and Doha Rounds, as a plurilateral agreement, the (re-)negotiations were not formally part of the rounds.

The aim of the latest revision—which significantly rewrote and reorganized the 1996 version—was to make the GPA more attractive to non-signatories by simplifying the rules, to reflect advances in information technology and to expand the coverage of the Agreement (Anderson, 2007). Final agreement on the 2006 text is conditional on a mutually satisfactory outcome of parallel (and ongoing) negotiations to open up additional government procurement to international competition. A purported objective of the reorganization and redrafting of the text of GPA was simplification and making it reflect better the process that procuring entities go through. It is not clear that this objective was achieved—in our view, in some respects the 1996 text was more transparent and easier to understand.

As a result of the periodic renegotiations, the coverage of the GPA has expanded substantially over time to include services and more government entities, and its disciplines clarified and updated to reflect new technologies and procurement practices. Membership of the GPA is limited to mostly OECD countries. As of 2008 it comprised Canada, the European Communities, the 27 EU member states, the Netherlands with respect to Aruba, Hong Kong, Iceland, Israel, Japan, Liechtenstein, Norway, the Republic of Korea, Singapore, Switzerland, and the United States.[8]

The GPA applies to "any measure regarding covered procurement, whether or not it is conducted exclusively or partially by electronic means" (Article II:1). The concept of procurement covers all contractual options, including purchase, leasing, rental and hire purchase, with or without the option to buy.[9] A positive list is used to determine what procurement is covered. The GPA applies *only* to entities listed in Appendix I of the Agreement. There are three "entity annexes": Annex 1 lists cover central government entities; Annex 2 lists sub-central government entities; and Annex 3 lists all other entities that procure "in accordance with the provisions of this Agreement." Annex 3 is a catch-all category that includes bodies such as utilities. Entities listed in Annex 3 may be partially or totally private. What constitutes a government entity is nowhere defined in the Agreement, reflecting a lack of consensus on what constitutes a public undertaking—more specifically, whether a former state-owned or controlled enterprise that has been privatized or that is subject to competition should be required to follow GPA procurement practices. Instead a pragmatic approach is taken—governments negotiate which entities are listed.

The entities listed in the three annexes are subject to the rules and disciplines of the GPA with respect to their procurement of goods and services if the value of the procurement exceeds certain specified thresholds (see Table 27.1), and the goods or services involved are not exempted from the coverage of the Agreement. As far as goods are concerned, in principle all procurement is covered, unless specified otherwise in an annex. Procurement of services is subject to a positive list: only the procurement by covered

---

[8] The European Communities refers to the Community's institutions. Formally, there were 40 signatories to the GPA in 2008, as each EU member state has signed the Agreement individually in addition to the European Communities. This is because, in some dimensions of procurement, EU member states retain competence.

[9] The GPA applies to purchases of goods and services that are not intended for resale. If government entities engage in trade (buying and selling) Art. XVII GATT applies (Hoekman and Kostecki, 2009).

Table 27.1 GPA Thresholds for Coverage of Procurement Contracts (SDRs)

Category of procurement	Threshold
Central government entities	
Goods	130,000
Services except construction services	130,000
Construction services	5,000,000[1]
Annex 2: Sub-central government entities	
Goods	200,000[2]
Services except construction services	200,000[2]
Construction services	5,000,000[3]
Annex 3: All other entities whose procurement is covered by the Agreement*	
Goods	400,000[4]
Services except construction services	400,000[4]
Construction services	5,000,000[3]

* In general public enterprises or public authorities such as utilities.
[1] Israel: 8.5 million; Japan 4.5 million (with architecture services: 450,000).
[2] US and Canada: 355,000; Israel: 250,000.
[3] Israel: 8.5 million; Japan and Korea: 15 million.
[4] Canada and Israel: 355,000; Japan: 130,000.

Source: WTO Agreement on Government Procurement.

entities of services explicitly scheduled in Annexes 4 and 5 are subject to the GPA's rules, and then only insofar as no qualifications or limitations are maintained in the relevant annexes. To give an indication of the orders of magnitude involved in the 1995 extension of the GPA's coverage to sub-central entities and services—the offers made by the USA and the EU covered some US$100 billion of purchases, with care being taken to maintain reciprocity through addition of removal of specific entities (Schott and Buurman, 1994: 74).

The primary obligation imposed by the GPA on covered entities is non-discrimination—national treatment and MFN (Art. V). This extends not only to imports but also to subsidiaries of locally established foreign firms. The GPA thus goes beyond the GATT, which does not extend national treatment to foreign affiliates, and the GATS which does so only insofar as specific commitments to that effect have been made. Under the GPA, all foreign affiliates established in the country are to be treated the same as national firms. Local content, price preferences, and similar discriminatory policies are prohibited. Moreover, signatories may not discriminate against foreign suppliers by applying rules of origin that differ from those they apply in general to MFN-based trade.

Most of the provisions of the GPA concern transparency broadly defined. Thus, much attention is given to requiring signatories to specify where information on procurement systems and opportunities will be published (including through electronic means). These must be listed in Appendices II through IV to the GPA. There are detailed requirements for publication of notices of intended procurement, the conditions for participation and permitted systems to ascertain that suppliers are qualified, technical specifications and tender documentation, minimum time periods to allow bids to occur, and regular reporting of statistics on procurement activities of covered entities.[10]

The GPA does not explicitly require that procurement be competitive or that certain procurement methods be used. In this regard it is quite different from the procurement guidelines that international development organizations and national governments apply. Regarding conduct of procurement, signatories are simply required to "...conduct covered procurement in a transparent and impartial manner that is consistent with this Agreement, using methods such as open tendering, selective tendering and limited tendering; avoids conflicts of interest and prevents corrupts practices" (Art. V:4). Open tendering is any method that allows any supplier to bid (i.e., competitive tendering). Selective tendering is a method where only suppliers that satisfy specific criteria for participation may bid (usually prequalified suppliers). Limited tendering is non-competitive and usually involves a procuring entity approaching one or more potential suppliers of its choice.

The rules in the GPA regarding selective tendering are basically aimed at ensuring that foreign suppliers can demonstrate that they qualify and are not discriminated against in this regard (e.g., have the information needed). Limited tendering may only be used if no tenders were received or they were not responsive, only one supplier can provide the good or service (e.g., artwork, products protected by intellectual property rights), for additional, follow-on deliveries, in situations of extreme urgency, for commodities (the presumption being that there is a world price for standardized, homogenous goods), or for prototypes.

There is no explicit hierarchy of the three tendering methods mentioned in Art. V and governments are free to use others. The preference for competitive procurement methods is implicit in the Agreement, reflected in requirements that notices of intended or planned procurement be published (including information on the mode of procurement, its nature and quantity, dates of delivery, economic and technical requirements, and amounts and terms of payment), in the conditions that must be satisfied if governments use limited tendering, and in the disciplines on treatment of tenders and contract awards. Article XIII on limited tendering makes it clear that competition is preferred by making use of this method conditional on it not being used to avoid competition among suppliers, to discriminate or protect domestic suppliers. Article XV requires that entities award contracts to the supplier "determined to be fully capable of undertaking the contract" and who is either the lowest tender (if price is the sole criterion) or the tender

---

[10] The GPA does not define specific operational procedures such as whether bids should be assessed on price before determining whether bidders can satisfy technical requirements or whether technical selections should precede an assessment of price. In practice such matters can have an effect on expected procurement costs. See, for example, Blancas et al. (2011).

that is most advantageous (in terms of the evaluation criteria set out in the notices or tender documentation). It is rather surprising that the objective of competitive procurement is not embedded in the preamble of the Agreement. The "fuzziness" as regards the preference for competitive bidding may reflect the desire of signatories to see membership of the GPA expand to include developing countries.

Price preference policies, offsets, and similar policies that are widely used by governments are in principle prohibited for covered procurement as a result of the national treatment rule (Art. V). This has been a problem for developing countries, as these countries use procurement as an instrument to achieve objectives other than "value for money." Article IV of the 2006 GPA permits developing countries to negotiate the right to adopt or retain price preference policies and offset requirements on a transitional basis, and delay the implementation of any and all provisions other than MFN for up to three years (five years for a LDC). Moreover, after accession, the GPA Committee may extend the transition periods or approve the use of new transitional price preferences or offsets if there are "special circumstances that were unforeseen during the accession process" (Art. IV:7). Existing signatories also commit themselves to "give due consideration to any request by a developing country for technical cooperation and capacity building" (Art. IV:8). Some scope therefore exists for maintaining a price preference or offset policy—but it is time limited.

The nature of procurement is such that unless rapid action can be taken, firms may not have an interest in contesting violations of the rules of the game. Accordingly, the GPA supplements the right of signatories to invoke the WTO dispute settlement mechanism—which is too slow to be relevant for much real world procurement situations—with a requirement that members establish domestic review procedures. These bid-protest or challenge mechanisms should provide for rapid interim measures to correct breaches of the Agreement or a failure of a government entity to comply with the measures implementing the GPA (Art. XVIII). Measures to preserve commercial opportunities may involve suspension of the procurement process, or compensation for the loss or damages suffered. This may be limited to the costs for preparing the tender or the costs relating to the challenge, or both.

Articles IX and XVII GPA require each signatory, on request from another party, to promptly provide pertinent information concerning the reasons why the supplier's application to qualify was rejected, why an existing qualification was terminated, and information necessary to determine whether a procurement was conducted in accordance with the GPA, including pertinent information on the characteristics and relative advantages of the tender that was selected. The 2006 provisions in this area are weaker than those in the 1996 Agreement.

Operation of the GPA

The GPA requires signatories to report annual statistics on procurement by covered entities to the GATT Committee on Government Procurement. Such data reporting was intended to help parties determine how well the Agreement was functioning, in part by providing comparable cross-country information on sourcing practices. Signatories began reporting statistics for the year 1983. Unfortunately there has been little empirical research using these data, and it does not appear that signatories to the GPA have used the statistics as a way of monitoring the operation of the Agreement.

Data reported in Hoekman (1998) for the 1983–92 period—when only central government procurement of goods was covered by the GPA—revealed that the largest procurement market, by a substantial margin, opened up under the GPA was that of the United States, which accounted for almost half of the total procurement reported. Smaller countries, on average, procured much more on international markets than did large countries. If Canada, the EU, Japan, and the USA were excluded, about 60 per cent of purchases by covered entities exceeding the threshold went to national suppliers. This compared to more than 90 per cent for the large players. As EU statistics defined "domestic" as including intra-EU sourcing, reported self-sufficiency ratios for the EU-12 were above 90 per cent on average. In interpreting these statistics it should be noted that no distinction is made between domestic firms proper and foreign firms that have established a local presence. To the extent that large countries attract a greater amount of FDI, higher self-sufficiency ratios are not indicative of discriminatory policies.

In the EU, Japan, and the USA, the share of domestic firms in total above threshold procurement by covered entities remained virtually unchanged during 1983–92. For the smaller countries, however, with the exception of Singapore and Switzerland, the share of procurement from national sources declined over time. It is impossible to attribute such changes in sourcing patterns to the GPA—regional developments also played a role, such as the NAFTA in North America and efforts to liberalize EU procurement markets. Unilateral deregulation and privatization policies also must have had an impact. Nonetheless, the finding that smaller GPA members became less nationalistic in their purchasing decisions suggests that practices did become more open.

During the same period, the share of contracts that exceeded the threshold tended to increase. In 1983–85, some 39 per cent of all procurement by covered entities fell above the threshold. By 1991–92, it had risen to 49 per cent. This can be explained in part by a reduction in the threshold in 1988, from Special Drawing Rights (SDR) 150,000 to SDR 130,000. As of the early 1990s, the share of above threshold contracts for both EU and US entities averaged around 60 per cent.

Under the GPA, open competitive tendering procedures are in principle to be used for all contracts that exceed the relevant threshold. As noted earlier, limited tendering procedures involving an entity negotiating with potential suppliers individually is only allowed under certain conditions, and members are required to report data on their use of this method. The issue became important in USA–Japan trade relations in the 1980s, following US complaints that the use of limited tendering was excessive (Stern and Hoekman, 1987). In the period investigated by Hoekman (1998), the use of limited tendering varied from a reported low of zero (Singapore) to a high of over 30 per cent on average for France, Italy, Switzerland, and Hong Kong. Across all signatories the average share of limited tendering was about 13 per cent. As of 1992, both the EU and the USA used limited tendering for about 10 per cent of contracts. Japan's use of limited tendering rose from around 12 per cent during 1983–85 to 21 per cent during 1990–92.

Choi (2003) and Evenett and Shinghal (2006) have undertaken country-specific studies of the operation and impact of the GPA, focusing on Korea and Japan, respectively. Choi finds that accession to the Agreement by Korea was followed by a reduction in the share of procurement using limited tendering (which fell from 27 per cent in 1993–95 to 22.5 per cent in 1996–98. However, the share of foreign supplied goods during this period fell. Evenett and Shingal conclude that in 1999 in Japan more contracts fell below the GPA thresholds than in earlier years, and of the contracts that exceeded the threshold—and thus were covered by the GPA—a smaller share was awarded to foreign suppliers in 1998–99 than in 1990–91. Thus, during the 1990s, it appears that the GPA did nothing to increase the market access for foreign suppliers.

The limited evidence available for services procurement suggests the same conclusion applies. Shingal (2010) investigates whether the extension of the GPA to include services procurement has led to an expansion in purchases from foreign suppliers. Using data reported by Japan and Switzerland to the WTO Committee on Government Procurement, he concludes that the share of services contracts awarded to foreigners has declined over time for both countries. Indeed, he finds that in the absence of this decline, the value of services contracts awarded to foreign firms would have been more than 15 times higher in the case of Japan and nearly 68 times more in the case of Switzerland. Using a commonly used metric in the procurement literature—a comparison on the foreign share of purchases of a given product by government with that of the private sector (see, e.g., Francois, Nelson, and Palmeter, 1997), Shingal finds that, for the similar categories of services, the Japanese government purchased less from foreign suppliers.

The data reporting requirements of the GPA are not as useful or informative as they might be because most signatories do not report on a timely or comprehensive basis. One reason the studies just mentioned focus on Korea and Japan is that these countries report regularly. More regular reporting—and analysis of the reports by the WTO secretariat—would do much to improve knowledge regarding implementation of the Agreement. That said, what matters from an economic point of view is primarily the size of government demand for a good or service relative to total domestic supply. As discussed previously, it is especially in cases where the government is a big player relative to domestic supply that there can be significant effects on national welfare and foreign suppliers. Multilateral scrutiny will have potentially the largest payoff if it focuses on such situations. As the GPA reporting requirements are quite burdensome, an added benefit of a more focused approach to data collection would be a reduction in the costs of surveillance.

The Challenge of Expanding Membership

As mentioned above, membership of the GPA is quite limited. Indeed, not all OECD countries have signed it—for example, Australia and New Zealand are not members.

Despite longstanding efforts to expand the number of signatories, little progress in that direction has been achieved in the 30 years that the GPA has existed. The increase in membership since the early 1980s has predominantly been driven by the expansion of the EU from 12 to 27 members. Given that the EU is a signatory to the GPA and imposes procurement disciplines that are much more detailed and prescriptive than those of the GPA, the expansion of membership to date does not reflect well on the Agreement.

A number of countries that have acceded to the WTO since 1995 made commitments to negotiate accession to the GPA, with China being the most notable and important economy to have done so. Time will tell whether these accession promises will be realized. China has a clear interest insofar as membership in the GPA will give it access to the markets of signatories. One reason low-income countries have been reluctant to accede to the GPA is that they do not see reciprocal concessions from GPA members as having value. Negotiating leverage is a function of the size of the incremental market access that aspiring members can offer, and for most developing countries this tends to be small. Moreover, many developing countries are not players on the international procurement market, implying that the standard mercantilist bargain is not available to move things along.

Even if one abstracts from the skewed nature of the bargain from a (political) mercantilist perspective, what matters is whether adherence to the rules of the GPA will improve welfare. Taking a more "rational" economic perspective, the question confronting developing countries is whether the eventual loss of the ability to use procurement policy as an instrument of industrial, regional, or social policy is a good or bad thing.[11] And, if it is a bad thing, whether there are other sources of gain that offset the loss. There is little empirical research on the effectiveness of procurement discrimination in achieving the industrial and other policy objectives.[12] Tax/subsidy instruments are likely to be more efficient in assisting domestic target groups than procurement favoritism, but not necessarily. Governments may confront fiscal constraints that impede the use of such policies. Moreover, an advantage of procurement that favors specific domestic groups is that it can help the most efficient firms in that group (as they must compete for the contracts) (Watermeyer, 2004), whereas a subsidy to a region or a minority will be less selective.

Clearly, in practice, procurement has been and is used extensively by governments to promote innovation and more generally as a tool of industrial policy. The effectiveness of procurement as an instrument to achieve industrial policy objectives is a subject that should be the focus of much more targeted research, especially in developing countries. There is a conceptual and practical case to be made for using procurement to achieve industrial policy goals (e.g., Nelson, 1982; Edler and Georghiou, 2007), but the extant literature has focused on industrialized countries. Whether arguments for targeted

---

[11] See for example, Kattel and Lember (2010), McCrudden (2004), and Weiss and Thurbon (2006) for arguments in favour of using procurement to achieve such objectives.

[12] It is striking, for example, that in their comprehensive survey of the literature on trade and industrial policy, Harrison and Rodriguez-Clare (2010) do not discuss procurement discrimination.

procurement transfer to developing countries with weak governance and accountability systems, and how such approaches can be applied in a way that minimizes the scope for rent seeking, are important questions. A key feature of procurement is that the government is the buyer and thus in principle has greater control over outcomes than when "supply-side" industrial policies are used (e.g., subsidies of varying types). But in what types of situations does this ability/feature matter? More generally, from a trade rules/ negotiation perspective, research is needed into the question of whether discrimination should be an element of "industrial procurement policy." To us, the *prima facie* case for discrimination seems weak as much knowledge and know-how resides in foreign firms. This suggests a focus of policy should be to attract such firms into the market and seek to maximize the prospects of transfers of technology through learning, training, emulation, imitation, and so on. That in turn suggests promoting inward FDI, programs to support local suppliers and vertical linkages, incentives to transfer knowledge, and so on. As is true for traditional trade policies (tariffs), procurement discrimination is not likely to help in addressing the market failures that call for government intervention.

Whatever the case may be, in practice a large share of the procurement market where discrimination is now used to pursue equity and social objectives is unlikely to be of great interest to foreign suppliers: the average size of contracts is likely to be relatively small. Price preferences have the advantage of being transparent and less distortive than other types of discriminatory policies that are often pursued (such as bans on participation by foreign bidders or local content and offset requirements). Tariffying such policies through an agreement permitting the maintenance of price preference schemes by developing countries would provide a focal point for future multilateral negotiations to reduce discrimination. Such preferences are allowed subject to certain conditions and limits by multilateral development banks. Provisions for their use are also included in the United Nations Commission on International Trade Law (UNCITRAL) Model Law on Procurement. Many developing countries have incorporated such preferences into their legislation. Recognition of the legitimacy of price preferences for developing countries— without time limits and transition periods—could help alter the incentives for accession.

Many of the purchases by government entities comprise services or products where economic forces favor procuring from local suppliers. In such cases, procurement preferences will only be binding if foreign firms cannot contest the market through FDI, or if government entities differentiate across firms on the basis of their nationality. Outright market access restrictions that take the form of a ban on FDI are costly to the economy as a whole, and policy efforts that focus on elimination of such bans are likely to have a greater payoff than attempting to outlaw discrimination.

Transparency in Procurement

As noted above, discrimination is just one dimension of possible multilateral disciplines for government procurement. It is widely believed that there are significant potential gains from disciplines that promote transparent procurement mechanisms, thereby reducing the scope for corruption and rent seeking. There is an increasing body of evidence, mostly of a case study nature, that documents that the associated costs, both direct and indirect, can be large. For example, Auriol, Flochel, and Straub (2009) use on a database of some 50,000 procurement contracts in Paraguay over a four-year period in the mid 2000s to both document and estimate the effects of rent seeking in procurement in Paraguay. They show that corruption in procurement generated a far-reaching system of favoritism that inflated costs and created incentives to engage in directly unproductive rent-seeking activity: firms that obtained government contracts were estimated to have an average 35 per cent excess rate of return relative to competing firms that sold to private clients (did not get public contracts). They argue that procurement favoritism and corruption helps explain the bad growth and export performance of the Paraguayan economy.[13] Noteworthy is that discrimination against foreign suppliers was not a prominent feature of procurement favoritism in Paraguay as most goods were imported— what was at stake was the allocation of contracts and the associated rents generated by inflated markups resulting from bid-rigging and sole tendering (about a quarter of all contracts in 2004–05).

An important aspect of procurement reform therefore relates to the transparency of the numerous steps associated with the implementation of procurement law and regulation. Transparency, which refers to the publication, notification, and dissemination of pertinent information about a procurement regime to actual and potential bidders and to the public at large, is quite distinct from overt measures to discriminate against or in favor of one class of potential suppliers for state contracts. The absence of transparency is a precondition for corruption and similar practices. Even if procurement is not collusive or corrupt, a lack of transparency will reduce the number of firms able and willing to bid for state contracts, so reducing competition and increasing costs.

Corrupt government officials can solicit payments from actual and potential suppliers of goods and services to the public sector. A major rationale for efforts during the Doha Round to negotiate disciplines to increase transparency of government procurement was to reduce the scope for corruption, in the process increasing market access opportunities by "leveling the playing field." A growing body of evidence suggests that corrupt officials deliberately expand expenditures on goods and projects—such as aircraft and construction—which are highly differentiated and for which there are few, if any, comparable reference prices in world markets. Put simply, officials with an interest in personal rents will employ non-transparent procurement procedures to expand government spending where the opportunities for self-enrichment are greatest. Another consequence of having to pay bribes to bid for government contracts is to reduce the number of domestic bidders. That is, the result can be thought of as shifting outward the government demand curve for products where there are opportunities for corruption, and at the same time shifting in the supply curve of firms.

---

[13] Other contributions to this literature include Di Tella and Schargrodsky (2003), who assess the effects of reducing corruption in procurement in Argentine hospitals and Hyytinen, Lundberg, and Toivanen (2007), who analyze municipal cleaning contracts in Sweden.

The 1996 WTO Singapore Ministerial Conference established a working group to study "transparency in government procurement practices" and ways to develop "elements for inclusion in an appropriate agreement." Many developing countries perceived this to be a Trojan horse (a vehicle to start discussing discrimination and extend the coverage of GPA disciplines). However, given that discrimination is probably a second-order issue in comparison with corruption, there was a strong *prima facie* case to focus on transparency first and foremost.

The WTO working group proceeded by addressing the "Items on the Chairman's Checklist of Issues" relating to a potential agreement on transparency in government procurement. The checklist comprised such broad issues as the definition of government procurement and the scope and coverage of a potential agreement, the substantive elements of a potential agreement on transparency—including various aspects of access to general and specific procurement-related information and procedural matters, as well as compliance mechanisms of a potential agreement and issues relating to developing countries—including the role of SDT and technical assistance and capacity building. GPA members strongly supported negotiations on transparency, as did a number of non-GPA countries such as Australia. Several draft proposals for an agreement were submitted in November 1999, including by the EU, Japan, Australia, and a joint submission by Hungary, Korea, Singapore, and the USA. These countries sought to conclude an agreement at the Seattle Ministerial. Many developing countries emphasized that much more discussion was needed on the implications of transparency obligations in the procurement area.

At the Doha Ministerial Conference in 2001, Ministers agreed that negotiations of transparency in procurement would take place after the Fifth Ministerial Conference "on the basis of a decision to be taken, by explicit consensus, at that Session on modalities of negotiations." The Ministerial Declaration emphasized that "negotiations shall be limited to the transparency aspects and therefore will not restrict the scope for countries to give preferences to domestic supplies and suppliers." In line with the Doha Ministerial Declaration, which highlighted the need to "take into account participants' development priorities, especially those of least-developed country participants," the Working Group on Transparency in Government Procurement discussed extensively the development implications of a possible agreement in this area. The Doha mandate also recognized the need for enhanced technical assistance and capacity building and contained a commitment to provide such assistance both during any negotiations and after their conclusion.

No agreement on modalities for negotiations could be reached at the Fifth Ministerial Conference, held in Cancún in September 2003. On August 1, 2004, the WTO General Council adopted a decision that removed this subject, as well as competition and investment, from the Doha Work Programme. The decision did not indicate what might occur, if anything, following the completion of the Doha Round. The most compelling explanation of why there was resistance to negotiating an agreement on transparency in procurement is that many developing countries were not convinced that this would not end in a future discussion on market access. From a systemic perspective that is indeed what would be logical—given the size of procurement markets this is clearly an area where there is a rationale for WTO members to agree to mutual disarmament. In the absence of market access incentives and disciplines it is less obvious what the rationale is for discussing transparency in the WTO.[14]

V. Regional Trade Agreements

Despite the fact that most WTO members have not been willing to sign the GPA, there are dozens of regional trade agreements (RTAs) with developing country signatories that include chapters on government procurement policies.[15] Many of these are not far-reaching—they either simply reflect the prevailing status quo as regards procurement policy in signatories or limit commitments to best endeavor-type (non-binding, non-enforceable) language. However, many of the more recent vintage agreements include enforceable provisions—including through domestic bid-challenge type mechanisms—and some lay out a path for future reform, including in a few cases with the explicit aim to integrate government procurement markets along the lines of what has been achieved in the European Union.

The more ambitious agreements, many of which involve Asian-Pacific countries, go beyond commitments to remove discrimination in procurement and include language pertaining to the objectives of procurement policy (e.g., attaining best value for money); the use of new technologies, such as electronic procurement, provisions to create or strengthen national institutions that implement national procurement policies and associated reforms; how to address likely changes in the scope of transactions falling under the disciplines of the agreement as a result of privatization of government entities; and agreement to cooperate in the execution of national procurement policies and in the development of reform initiatives. Many of the more ambitious agreements also define the coverage of procurement disciplines to extend beyond central or national government. Noteworthy as well is that some agreements define circumstances under which non-trade objectives of government procurement policy dominate, or are subservient to, market access (national treatment) provisions/disciplines.

The creation of a Single Government Procurement Market in the New Zealand–Singapore Closer Economic Partnership Agreement is an example of a bilateral agreement with ambitious objectives. Article 46 of this agreement states that the parties agree

---

[14] Some of the economic dimensions of enhancing transparency of procurement processes are discussed in Evenett and Hoekman (2005a). They conclude that there is not necessarily a one-to-one mapping between more transparency and more market access.

[15] For example, most EU and US trade agreements include provisions on government procurement. Bourgeois, Dawar, and Evenett (2007) and Evenett (2010) discuss government-procurement provisions in regional agreements at greater length.

to establish a single New Zealand/Singapore government procurement market through implementation of the APEC Non-Binding Principles on Government Procurement (relating to transparency, value for money, open and effective competition, fair dealing, accountability and due process, and non-discrimination); ensuring that suppliers from both countries can compete on an equal and transparent basis for government contracts; and establishing a mechanism to work towards "achieving the greatest possible consistency in contractual, technical and performance standards and specifications, and simplicity and consistency in the application of procurement policies, practices and procedures."

Article 49 of the Agreement further specifies *inter alia* that all government bodies within their territories will "provide to services, goods and suppliers of the other Party equal opportunity and treatment no less favorable than that accorded to their own domestic services, goods and suppliers" (Art. 49:c) (i.e., national treatment applies); promote opportunities for their suppliers to compete for government business on the basis of value for money and avoid purchasing practices which discriminate or otherwise have the effect of denying equal access or opportunity to, their services, goods, and suppliers; and to use value for money as the primary determinant in all procurement decisions.

This example illustrates that greater ambition can be achieved through RTAs than through the WTO. Of course, this is nothing new—the EU has long been the foremost example of a subset of WTO members agreeing to far-reaching disciplines on the use of discrimination in procurement. Moreover, the most ambitious agreements on procurement involve high-income countries. What the recent agreements reveal, however, is that it is possible to go beyond the GPA approach, which is essentially limited to promoting foreign competition for state contracts. What the recent regional or bilateral agreements suggest is that complementary measures may be important in supporting international cooperation, and that an approach that allows governments to pre-commit to reforms may be seen as particularly useful. Recent agreements in Asia emulate earlier Association Agreements that the EU has concluded with neighboring states in that significant attention is paid to supporting efforts to build state institutions and expertise. Provisions in many North–South agreements that aim at fostering cooperation, information exchange, and training of staff strengthen the resources and the authority of state bodies. The newer RTAs also often establish future timetables for deliberation and review processes. What this suggests is that binding commitments on market access (non-discrimination) may be conditional on governments perceiving that the preconditions for effective implementation and "ownership" of the procurement disciplines— including by civil society and business—have been satisfied. This in turn can be pursued through technical assistance and capacity building and a sequenced approach to implementation of specific commitments. Rather than regarding trade agreements such as the GPA as an opportunity to generate one-off reforms, the review provisions that are found in some of the newer RTAs suggest a more dynamic approach is both feasible and desirable, one that revolves around helping partner countries achieve development objectives.

VI. CONCLUDING REMARKS

Public purchasing practices are one of the few major policy areas where WTO members continue to have discretion to discriminate at will against foreign suppliers. Limitations on the ability to discriminate only kick in if governments decide to sign the GPA. Even for signatories of the GPA, the proportion of goods and services contracts awarded to foreign firms is generally quite small. Thus, there is considerable room for expanding access to national procurement markets. How significant those opportunities are is not known, in part because *de jure* discrimination may not be binding: it may not negatively affect the actual access that foreign firms have to a country because government demand is relatively small. In practice much procurement involves goods and services that are either actually or effectively non-tradable (e.g., because the size of the contract is too small to be of interest to international bidders). But given the size of government procurement markets and the prevalence of discrimination, the potential for greater trade in this area is clearly substantial. This explains the interest that many current signatories of the GPA have in seeing membership expand.

The question then is whether there are situations where it makes economic sense to discriminate. If not, then engaging in multilateral negotiations has little downside, although it may also generate little upside insofar as the prospects of boosting exports to foreign government agencies are limited. But the fact that accession to the GPA is infrequent and has mostly been limited to countries that have joined the EU (so that there is no "additionality" associated with membership given that the EU's disciplines on procurement are more far-reaching for the countries concerned) suggests that governments do perceive the net gains from the GPA to be too small. The recent bilateral and regional trade agreements that cover procurement in a significant manner suggest that part of the problem may be that the GPA does not do enough to ensure that the preconditions are in place for governments to feel comfortable with making binding commitments. More ambitious bilateral and regional agreements go beyond a focus on discrimination and procedural rules to include mechanisms for technical assistance and capacity building, for cooperation aimed at convergence of procedures, for periodic review and allowance for adjustments in the rules of the game, and make better allowances for pursuit of the non-economic objectives of governments.

REFERENCES

Anderson, R. (2007), 'Renewing the WTO Agreement on Government Procurement: Progress to Date and Ongoing Negotiations.' *Public Procurement Law Review* 16: 255–71.

Ades, A. and Di Tella, R. (1997), 'National Champions and Corruption: Some Unpleasant Interventionist Arithmetic.' *Economic Journal*, 107: 1023–42.

Auriol, E. (2006), 'Corruption in Procurement and Public Purchase.' *International Journal of Industrial Organization*, 24(5): 867–85.

Auriol, E., Flochel, T., and Straub, S. (2009), 'La Patria Contratista: Public Procurement and Rent-Seeking in Paraguay.' Mimeo.

Baldwin, R. (1970), 'Non-Tariff Distortions in International Trade.' Washington DC: Brookings Institution.

Baldwin, R. and Richardson, J. D. (1972), 'Government Purchasing Policies, Other NTBs, and the International Monetary Crisis.' In English, H., and Hay, K. (eds.), *Obstacles to Trade in the Pacific Area.* Ottawa: Carleton School of International Affairs.

Blancas, L., et al. (2011), 'Do Procurement Rules Impact Infrastructure Investment Efficiency?' Policy Research Working Paper 5528, World Bank.

Borges de Oliveira, A. (2010), 'How Procurement Modernization Helped Improve Transparency and Efficiency in Minas Gerais, Brazil.' World Bank. Mimeo.

Bourgeois, J., Dawar, K., and Evenett, S. J. (2007), 'A Comparative Analysis of Selected Provisions in Free Trade Agreements.' Prepared for DG TRADE, European Commission.

Branco, F. (1994), 'Favoring Domestic Firms in Procurement Contracts.' *Journal of International Economics,* 37: 65–80.

Breton, A., and Salmon, P. (1995), 'Are Discriminatory Procurement Policies Motivated By Protectionism?' *Kyklos,* 49: 47–68.

Chen, X. (1995), 'Directing Government Procurement as an Incentive of Production.' *Journal of Economic Integration,* 10: 130–40.

Choi, I. (2003), 'The Long and Winding Road to the Government Procurement Agreement: Korea's Accession Experience.' In Martin, W., and Pangestu, M. (eds.), *Options for Global Trade Reform: A View from the Asia-Pacific.* Cambridge: Cambridge University Press.

Deltas, G., and Evenett, S. (1997), 'Quantitative Estimates of the Effects of Preference Policies.' In Hoekman, B., and Mavroidis, P. (eds.), *Law and Policy in Public Purchasing: The WTO Agreement on Government Procurement.* Ann Arbor: University of Michigan Press.

Di Tella, R., and Schargrodsky, E. (2003), 'The Role of Wages and Auditing during a Crackdown on Corruption in the City of Buenos Aires.' *Journal of Law and Economics,* 46(1): 269–92.

Edler, J. and Georghiou, L. (2007), 'Public Procurement and Innovation—Resurrecting the Demand Side.' *Research Policy,* 36: 949–63.

European Commission (2004), 'A Report on the Functioning of Public Procurement Markets in the EU: Benefits from the Application of EU Directives and Challenges for the Future.' <http://ec.europa.eu/internal_market/publicprocurement/docs/public-proc-market-final-report_en.pdf> (accessed April 2013).

Evenett, S. (2010), 'Improving National Procurement Regimes in the Asia-Pacific: What Role for FTAs?' Mimeo.

Evenett, S., and Hoekman, B. (2005), 'Government Procurement: Market Access, Transparency, and Multilateral Trade Rules.' *European Journal of Political Economy* 21(1): 163–83.

Evenett, S., and Shinghal, A. (2006), 'Performance Under Pressure: Japan and the Uruguay Round Agreement on Government Procurement.' In Evenett, S., and Hoekman, B. (eds.), *Economic Development and Multilateral Trade Cooperation.* Oxford: Oxford University Press and The World Bank.

Francois, J., Nelson D., and Palmeter D. (1997), 'Government Procurement in the U.S.: A Post-Uruguay Round Analysis.' In Hoekman, B., and Mavroidis, P. (eds.), *Law and Policy in Public Purchasing.* Ann Arbor: University of Michigan Press.

Geroski, P.A., 1990, 'Procurement Policy as a Tool of Industrial Policy.' *International Review of Applied Economics,* 4(2): 182–98.

Harrison, A., and Rodríguez-Clare, A. (2010), 'Trade, Foreign Investment, and Industrial Policy for Developing Countries.' In Rodrik, D., and Rosenzweig, M. (eds.), *Handbook of Development Economics,* Volume 5, chapter 63. Amsterdam: North Holland.

Hoekman, B. (1998), 'Using International Institutions to Improve Public Procurement.' *World Bank Research Observer*, 13(2): 249–69.

Hoekman, B., and Kostecki, M.. (2009), *The Political Economy of the World Trading System: The WTO and Beyond*. Oxford: Oxford University Press.

Hunja, R. R. (2003), 'Obstacles to Public Procurement Reform in Developing Countries.' In Arrowsmith, S., and Trybus, M. (eds.), *Public Procurement: The Continuing Revolution*. The Hague: Kluwer Law International.

Hyytinen, A., Lundberg, S., and Toivanen, O. (2007), 'Politics and Procurement: Evidence from Cleaning Contracts.' HECER Discussion Paper 196.

Kattel, R. and Lember, V. (2010), 'Public Procurement as an Industrial Policy Tool: An Option for Developing Countries?' *Journal of Public Procurement*, 10(3): 368–404.

Laffont, J., and Tirole, J. (1991), 'Auction Design and Favoritism.' *International Journal of Industrial Organization*, 9: 9–42.

Laffont, J., and Tirole, J. (1993), *A Theory of Incentives in Procurement and Regulation*. Cambridge MA: MIT Press.

McAfee, R. P., and McMillan, J. (1989), 'Government Procurement and International Trade.' *Journal of International Economics*, 26: 291–308.

McCrudden, C. (2004), 'Using Public Procurement to Achieve Societal Outcomes.' *Natural Resource Forum*, 28: 257–67.

McGuire, T., Riordan, M. (1995), 'Incomplete Information and Optimal Market Structure: Public Purchases from Private Providers.' *Journal of Public Economics*, 56: 125–41.

OECD (2002), *The Size of Government Procurement Markets*. Paris: OECD.

OECD (2010), *OECD Reviews of Innovation Policy: China*. Paris: OECD.

Naegelen, F., and Mougeot, M. (1998). 'Discriminatory Public Procurement and Cost Reduction Incentives.' *Journal of Public Economics*, 67: 349–67.

Nelson, R. R. (1982), *Government and Technical Progress*. New York: Pergamon Press.

Schott, J., and Buurman, J. (1994), *The Uruguay Round: An Assessment*. Washington DC: Peterson Institute for International Economics.

Shingal, A. (2010), 'Government Procurement of Services: Wither Market Access?' *World Trade Review*, 10(4): 1–23. Available at <http://papers.ssrn.com/sol3/papers.cfm?abstract_id=1564808> (accessed April 2013).

Stern, R.M., and Hoekman, B. (1987), 'The Codes Approach.' In Finger, J. M., and Olechowski, A. (eds.), *The Uruguay Round: A Handbook for the Multilateral Trade Negotiations*. Washington DC: The World Bank, 59–66.

Tanzi V. and Schuknecht, L. (2000), *Public Spending in the 20th Century: A Global Perspective*. Cambridge: Cambridge University Press.

Transparency International (2006), *Handbook for Curbing Corruption in Public Procurement*. Berlin: Transparency International. Available at <http://www.transparency.org/whatwedo/pub/handbook_for_curbing_corruption_in_public_procurement> (accessed April 2013).

Trionfetti, F. (2000), 'Discriminatory Public Procurement and International Trade.' *The World Economy*, 23: 57–76.

Vagstad, S., (1995), 'Promoting Fair Competition in Public Procurement.' *Journal of Public Economics*, 58: 283–307.

Watermeyer, R. (2004), 'Facilitating Sustainable Development Through Public and Donor Procurement Regimes: Tools and Techniques.' *Public Procurement Law Review*, 13(1): 30–55.

Weiss, L., and Thurbon, E. (2006), 'The Business of Buying American: Public Procurement as Trade Strategy in the USA.' *Review of International Political Economy*, 13(5): 701–24.

CHAPTER 28

TRADE FACILITATION AND DEVELOPMENT

ANDREW GRAINGER AND GERARD MCLINDEN

I. INTRODUCTION

As countries have come to realize the importance of trade in achieving sustainable economic growth, they have progressively lowered tariffs, established regimes to encourage foreign investment, and pursued opportunities for greater regional integration. This progress has, however, been undermined by the high costs and administrative difficulties associated with outdated and excessively bureaucratic border clearance processes, which are now often regarded as more important barriers to trade than tariffs. Inefficient border processing systems, procedures, and inadequate trade infrastructure result in high transaction costs, long delays in the clearance of imports, exports, and transit goods, and present significant opportunities for administrative corruption. They essentially undermine a country's competitiveness in the international marketplace.

Benefits to be derived from implementing trade facilitation measures are significant. For example, the economic model developed by the Organisation for Economic Co-operation and Development (OECD) suggests that a 1 per cent reduction in trade related transaction costs equates to a worldwide benefit of $43 billion dollars (OECD, 2003). Similar calculations emphasizing economic gains were also made by Wilson et al. (2003). Using gravity models, they calculate that if Asia-Pacific Economic Cooperation (APEC) members who perform below average on trade facilitation proxy indices[1] were able to improve their performance to half the APEC average, intra-APEC trade could increase by an impressive $254 billion and raise average GDP for the APEC region by 4.3 per cent. Later, Wilson et al. (2004) applied a similar methodology with a focus that extended from APEC to a representative mix of 75 countries, and calculated that the total gain in trade flow in manufacturing could be worth $377 billion.

---

[1] Proxy indices are calculated by the authors using datasets for port efficiency, customs environment, domestic regulatory environment, and e-business usage.

Trade facilitation has therefore become an important development issue in recent years, and this is reflected in increased levels of investment in trade facilitation reform by governments and donors alike. The importance of trade facilitation is also reflected in the numerous border management-related provisions incorporated in various bilateral and regional trading agreements. It is also reflected in a desire by many countries to seek enhanced multilateral rules on trade facilitation in the context of the World Trade Organization (WTO), as part of an overhaul of the now 50-year old trade facilitation provisions of the General Agreement on Tariffs and Trade (GATT). Trade facilitation has also become a key driver of the global "Aid for Trade" initiative. Essentially, there is now widespread agreement amongst all countries that trade facilitation reform is a win–win agenda. The importance of international trade as a catalyst for economic growth and national development is now well recognized. However, in recent years it has become increasingly clear that many developing and least developed countries face significant supply-side constraints that prevent them from participating effectively in the international trading system.

II. CONTEXT

The platitude "stuck at the border" is used all too often as an excuse for inefficient logistics that cost importers and exporters dearly. When interacting with officials and government authorities, traders (or their representatives) face all sorts of frustrations. Costs include the time, effort, and expense associated with preparing official declarations or presenting the cargo to the relevant executive agencies at the border. Costs also include those resulting from poor performance, such as missed business opportunities, contractual penalties, additional demurrage and storage charges, inhibited competitiveness, and failure to take advantage of market opportunities. Faced with uncertainty at the border, operators in many developing countries also need to deploy costly hedging strategies. One such strategy is to hold additional buffer stock (an inventory cost) to offset potential disruption to supplies. Another hedging strategy is to switch to more expensive transport modes (e.g., from shipping goods by sea to air or from rail to road) to offset—or even bypass—time penalties suffered at the border. These practices further undermine business competitiveness and the potential economic benefits derived from trade.

Inefficient border operations also have a cost for governments. Direct costs include the expense of enforcing trade and customs procedures as well as those expenses incurred in running cross-border infrastructure. Indirect costs might include the misallocation of resources, reduced revenue collection yields, vulnerabilities stemming from organized crime, denied access to preferential trade and customs arrangements, inhibited economic growth, and a stunted tax base. Moreover, where inefficiency gives rise to corruption, the overall integrity of the governing institutions is severely undermined.

III. Trade Facilitation

Sensible advocates of trade facilitation recognize that governments have legitimate policy objectives that need to be satisfied at the border and therefore seek to implement solutions that enable trade and border-management procedures to be administered effectively with minimal cost and disruption to the trading community. Both business and government stakeholders stand to gain. The topic of trade facilitation is very much reform orientated. Staples (2002) adeptly describes trade facilitation as the plumbing of international trade. Guiding principles tend to focus on the desire to simplify, harmonize, standardize, and modernize trade and customs procedures. For example, the WTO (1998), in an online training note published on its website, once defined trade facilitation as "the simplification and harmonization of international trade procedures," where trade procedures are the "activities, practices and formalities involved in collecting, presenting, communicating and processing data required for the movement of goods in international trade." Many trade facilitation advocates will also extend definitions to stress the commercial procedures between buyers and sellers, such as those necessary to make or receive payment.

Mustra (2010) notes that in recent years trade facilitation practitioners have tended to adopt a broader perspective of the supply chain and not simply to focus on trade procedures, but rather on the overall export and import supply chains and the associated physical movement of goods. Hence, in practice, a more comprehensive definition might describe trade facilitation as the process of identifying and addressing bottlenecks affecting the cost effective and timely movement of goods imposed by weaknesses in trade-related logistics and regulatory regimes This wider definition implies that trade facilitation covers issues such as logistics, trade-related infrastructure, and transport facilitation together, along with the simplification, rationalization of regulatory and commercial procedures, and the elimination of unnecessary red tape. This wider supply-chain focus is logical from the perspective of commercial competitiveness, since the ability of firms to connect effectively to regional and international markets depends in large part on the performance of the entire supply chain in terms of cost, time, and—above all—reliability and predictability.

Grainger (2011) identifies four interdependent elements that constitute the topic of trade facilitation. These relate to: (1) the simplification and harmonization of applicable rules and procedures; (2) the modernization of trade systems, in particular the sharing and lodging of information between business and government stakeholders; (3) the administration and management of trade and customs procedures; and (4) the institutional mechanisms to safeguard effective implementation of trade facilitation principles and the ongoing commitment to reform. See Table 28.1.

Several international institutions are actively championing trade facilitation (e.g., see UN/CEFACT and UNCTAD, 2002). The United Nations' Centre for Trade Facilitation and Electronic Business (UN CEFACT), has produced a catalog of recommendations

Table 28.1 The four interdependent topics that define trade facilitation

1. The simplification and harmonization of applicable rules and procedures

i. Harmonization of ProceduresFor example: the adoption of international conventions and instruments, and the harmonization of controls applied by the various different government agencies.

ii. Avoidance of DuplicationFor example: regional or bilateral agreements to recognize export controls in lieu of import control; shared inspection facilities, for instance for customs officers, veterinarians, plant health inspectors and health inspectors; and the formal recognition of private sector controls (e.g. in the area of security or quality) in lieu of official checks.

iii. Accommodate Business PracticesFor example: to accept commercial documents (such as the invoice) in lieu of official documents; and to allow goods to be cleared inland, away from the bottlenecks at ports and border-posts.

2. The modernization of trade compliance systems

i. SolutionsFor example: use of electronic information systems, the Single Window concept, electronic customs systems, port community systems, websites, and information portals.

ii. StandardizationFor example: electronic standards for the exchange of information between computers; paper document standards; barcode standards; document referencing conventions; and standards for the description of locations.

iii. Sharing of experiencesFor example: training and awareness building; development of toolkits and implementation guides; collaborative and open source systems developments.

3. Administration and standards

i. Service standardsFor example: public service level commitments; publish and make available applicable rules and procedures; produce plain language guides; develop online websites; keep the customs tariff up-to-date; provide for efficient appeal mechanisms.

ii. Management principlesFor example: enforcement of controls in proportion to the risk against which they seek to protect; selective (risk based) controls that reward compliant behavior (e.g. preferential treatment at the border).

4. Intuitional mechanisms and tools

For example: establishing a national trade facilitation body; produce and publish whitepapers setting out reform ambitions and inviting stakeholder comments.

Source: Adapted from Grainger (2011).

addressing issues as diverse as, for example, standards for sharing information between computer systems (EDIFACT), recommendations on capturing stakeholder requirements (UN/CEFACT, 1974), provisions for public electronic infrastructure (UN/CEFACT, 2004), and the layout and format of paper documents (UN/CEFACT 1981).

The World Customs Organization (WCO) also has a keen interest in trade facilitation, especially where it helps to align customs practice—for example by adopting the Revised Kyoto Custom Convention (WCO, 1999)—or improves the quality of control and brings about tighter security—for example by recommending the WCO's SAFE framework of standards to secure and facilitate global trade (WCO, 2007). Other trade facilitation measures include the Harmonized Commodity Description and Coding System for tariff classification (commonly referred to as the HS system)—which helps bring about uniformity in the classification of goods for establishing the correct customs duty. Likewise, on behalf of the WTO, the WCO also applies itself to the consistent interpretation of valuation rules and non-preferential origin rules.

At the WTO, trade facilitation is generally associated with GATT Articles V, VIII, and X, which relate to the freedom of transit, fees and formalities, and the publication and administration of trade regulations. Although trade facilitation has always been an implicit feature of the GATT, it was first specifically raised in 1996 as one of the four so called Singapore issues. Although transparency in government procurement, investment, and competition policy were ultimately dropped, there was general agreement that trade facilitation potentially represents a win–win for all nations. Formal negotiations on trade facilitation therefore commenced in November 2004 and are now reasonably advanced (WTO, 2010); closely linked to a successful outcome from the negotiations is the need for technical assistance and capacity building to ensure effective implementation of any new commitments agreed. Champions for development, such as the World Bank, have markedly stepped up their involvement in trade facilitation focused projects. In 2009, the World Bank provided $3.4 billion in trade-related support of which about 50 per cent was devoted to trade facilitation. Likewise, many bilateral donors have stepped up their support for trade facilitation-related reform and modernization. Such investments, as the case studies in Box 28.1 and 28.2 show, can produce significant benefits.

Box 28.1 Ghana and the Single Window

One of the more comprehensive trade facilitation concepts is the "Single Window," which aims to radically improve the exchange of information between business and government stakeholders in cross-border operations. Singapore, back in 1989, was one of the first countries to implement the single window concept on a nationwide basis, and has been the inspiration for many reformers since. The Singapore single window solution, TradeNet, has radically changed the nature of trade procedures in Singapore by reducing the documentary requirement from a range of 3–35 to just 1. Freight forwarders estimated that their costs for handling documents fell by 20–35 per cent; this figure includes the added expense associated with system implantation and submission fees.

With the help of the World Bank, the TradeNet system was also implemented in Ghana. To give a little background information, in 1998 Ghana had completed the implementation of several comprehensive reform packages. However, the expected inflow of foreign direct investment was still lacking. Ghana's government felt that this was due to structural investment constraints, particularly the need to improve the operational efficiency of frontline agencies such as customs. World Bank funds were used by the government to launch the Ghana Gateway Project. This project included the Ghanaian adoption of the TradeNet system—the Ghana Community Network (GCNet).

(Continued)

Box 28.1 *Continued*

Legacy procedures in Ghana were complex. For example, a carrier had to submit 13 copies of the shipping manifest to Ghanaian customs. The clearing of consignments involved an incredible 23 steps and included the involvement of many different regulatory bodies. The process of clearing consignments was described as time-consuming and an impediment to Ghana's competitiveness. Moreover, the situation also created many opportunities for soliciting "facilitation monies" to short-cut processes. The GCNet was held to be a remedy to these structural impediments.

The implementation of GCNet faced a number of problems. For example the change of government subsequent to elections in December 2000 delayed policy decisions on agreements made with the previous government. Laws needed to be amended to accommodate the electronic processing of information. Customs officers and other government agencies required hands-on training throughout the implementation.

Today, what used to be a matter of days is now a matter of hours at Kotoka airport. Traders are also less exposed to "facilitation monies." Transport operators, freight forwarders, and agents need to produce fewer documents in order to ship goods. Customs has been able to increase the efficiency of its revenue collection. For example at Kotoka Airport collection went up by 40 per cent even though estimated import volumes remained unchanged.

Irrespective of implementation difficulties, a number of benefits could be realized. Anecdotal estimates and research at Kotoka airport suggest that import times have come down significantly.

Source: edited extracts from DeWulf (2004).

Box 28.2 Russian Customs Modernization Project

In 2003, the Russian Federation's Federal Customs Service, with the support of the World Bank, launched the Russian Federation Customs Development Project, a reform and modernization project focused on achieving major improvements in the efficiency and effectiveness of customs operations in the central and northwest regions. The project aims to: promote internationally acceptable practices for processing of international trade flows by customs to further integrate the country into the world trading community; increase taxpayer compliance with the customs code; increase transparency; and increase timely transfer of collected revenues to the Federal budget.

In 2010, a comparative analysis of project indicators was completed as part of the Bank's ongoing monitoring and evaluation process. There were six primary project performance indicators agreed at the beginning of the project that were used to monitor progress. The indicators focus on the percentage of declarations selected for inspection; the average customs clearance times for vehicles and shipments; and the compliance gap and enforced compliance in tax/duty collection. As of 2010, the project has achieved:

- 75 per cent improvement in the percentage of import declarations selected for physical inspection;
- 88 per cent improvement in the percentage of (non-energy) export declarations selected for physical inspection;

Box 28.2 *Continued*

- 62 per cent reduction in the average customs clearance times at the border (vehicle customs checkpoints);
- 80 per cent reduction in the average customs clearance time;
- 58 per cent improvement in the compliance gap; and a
- 97 per cent improvement in the rate of enforced compliance in tax and duty collection.

Surveys of both stakeholders and customs employees revealed positive impacts of reforms. In addition, the results of the stakeholder survey showed users' assessment of customs work had improved since 2006. The stakeholder survey also revealed a steep decline in requests for additional payments during customs encounters. In an effort to validate the progress seen in the project indicators, a range of external sources of data was examined, including the Bank's Business Environment and Enterprise Performance Survey, the Logistics Performance Index (LPI),* the Doing Business Trading Across Borders Index, and the World Economic Forum's Enabling Trade Index (ETI). These sources measure customs efficiency and burden of regulation using varying definitions and methodologies.** Despite the differences in definitions and methods of measurement, overall, the external data sources show encouraging results over time, and reveal positive trends in the performance of the customs service and in customs regulations.

---

* The LPI includes two indices, an international ranking and a domestic index which includes specific indicators on institutions and performance, including indicators on clearance times and percentage of physical inspections.

** An important caveat to these indicators is that they are measured at the country level, whereas the project indicators only reflect the performance of the customs posts in the pilot regions.

Source: Original contribution by World Bank staff.

IV. THE CROSS-BORDER AND TRADE ENVIRONMENT

Probably one of the most defining challenges for implementation of trade facilitation-motivated reform is the operational complexity of international trade practices as well as the diversity of interests within business and government communities. Figure 28.1 shows some of the operational and regulatory steps necessary for moving goods between two contracting parties. These are likely to rely on a wide range of intermediaries, such as freight forwarders, logistics service-providers, airlines, and shipping lines. Additional service providers relied upon may include: those providing customs services; electronic IT infrastructure; insurance; and finance. Then there are also those operators managing the physical infrastructure, including handling operations at ports and borders. These groups of operators encompass the ports and airports, stevedores, cargo-handling agents, transit shed operators, inland clearance depot operators, and so on. Responsibility for physical and regulatory operations usually depends on the

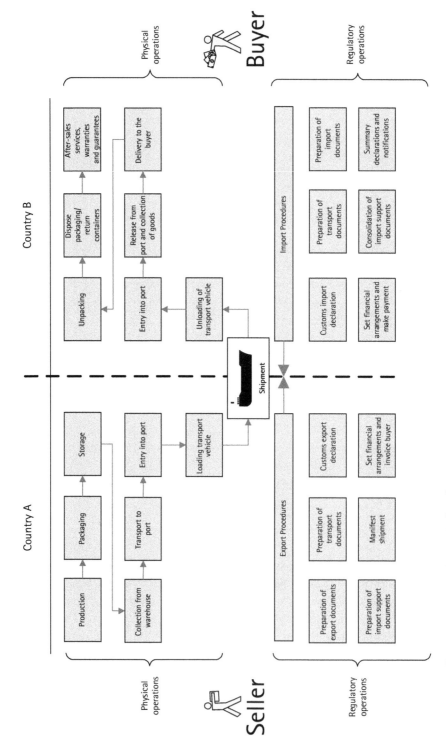

FIGURE 28.1 Business processes in a typical trade transaction

contractual arrangements between buyers and sellers, and may be split at any stage of the supply chain depending on the Incoterms used (ICC, 2010).

The number of government agencies with an interest in controlling the movement of goods and trade is equally diverse. Depending on the specific institutional arrangements, stakeholders might include (as suggested by Grainger, 2011): the revenue and customs authorities; the transport ministry; the port health authorities; the ministries for food and agriculture; the interior ministry; the immigration authority; trading standards; the ministry for inward investment together with collaborating sector-specific ministries; the ministry for trade; the finance ministry; the police; the border guards; and the maritime coast-guard agency. Their concerns will relate to: revenue collection (e.g., customs and excise taxes); safety and security (e.g., smuggling, dangerous goods, vehicle safety, anti-terrorism controls); environment and health (e.g., phyto-sanitary, veterinary and hygiene controls, endangered species (CITES) checks, and waste and pollution); consumer protection (e.g., labeling, marketing conformity checks, and product safety tests); and trade policy (e.g., the administration of quantitative restrictions and surveillance).

The potential for red tape and subsequent frustration can be extensive. In a typical developing country (and many developed nations, too), this may include anything from difficulties in obtaining the necessary paperwork, to institutionalized solicitation of "facilitation monies." Box 28.3 lists some illustrative examples of the problems operators may face. In reality this list is likely to be in excess of several hundred items, depending on the country concerned and the willingness of private sector operators to speak up.

Box 28.3 Examples of Operational Frustrations Suffered by Businesses

1. Excessive paperwork and authorization requirements.
2. Long queues at the government offices responsible for stamping paperwork.
3. Different ministries demand declarations that are similar or overlapping in content.
4. Checks at the border are unnecessarily long.
5. Border crossing may only be operational between 9:00 and 17:00—or even worse, have different operating hours to their counterparts across the border.
6. Border staff may decide to "close shop" during lunch breaks, causing backlogs and further delay.
7. Customs officers may be unnecessarily heavy handed in order to encourage payment for "special" treatment.
8. Government executives may display a lack of commercial awareness, failing to appreciate how their actions impact on the economy at large.
9. Operators may not be aware of the governing rules and procedures and have no place where they can go to obtain such information; often compliance requirements are established by costly trial and error.
10. Key publications such as the customs tariffs are not publically available.
11. Frontline staff may have not been briefed about new procedures; subsequently implementation may vary significantly throughout the country.

(Continued)

Box 28.3 *Continued*

---

12. Capacity at official labs to check health risk may be severely limited, leading to backlogs and very long delays (sometimes in excess of one or two months).
13. Government veterinary authorities may be deemed not suitably capable by their counterparts in key export markets, effectively rendering exports to these countries illegal.
14. Paper documents go missing, especially when traveling with the goods (for example in the driver's cab).
15. Rejected declarations because reference numbers in supporting documents contain errors (e.g. the number "8" can easily be confused with the letter "B").
16. Correction mechanisms to amend declarations or erroneous information may not exist—or are very cumbersome unless facilitation monies have been paid.
17. Appeal mechanisms to challenge decisions made by executive officers are non-existent or very time-consuming.
18. Delay because declarations are processed manually rather than electronically.
19. Procedures to enable inland clearance are unavailable.
20. The operational practices of one government agency contradict those of another.

Source: Examples based on the authors' work experience in the field.

V. Reform and Obstacles to Reform

Prudent reform to such challenges as outlined in Box 28.3 takes both a bottom-up and top-down approach (Grainger, 2008). The bottom-up approach considers experienced operational frustrations and seeks to find solutions. The top-down approach reflects upon international instruments and recommendations as well as perceived best practice (i.e., lessons learned from other countries). Reform projects often start with a trade diagnostic exercise, such as the Diagnostic Trade Integration Studies (DTIS) accessible via the World Bank website[2] and the Integrated Framework facility.[3] The WCO's Columbus program has also produced detailed diagnostic reports covering the development needs of over 100 national customs administrations.[4] Occasionally, governments will have commissioned their own national trade facilitation strategy, which is based on extensive research and consultation among all the key stakeholder groups in both the public and private sector. National trade facilitation bodies can play a particularly important role in translating those experienced (bottom-up) business frustrations and international recommendations (top-down) into successful trade facilitation initiatives

---

[2] <http://go.worldbank.org/ULW8UUZUТ0>
[3] <http://www.integratedframework.org/>
[4] The WCO Columbus program diagnostic reports are the property of the customs administration involved and are not published.

(Grainger, 2010). In reality, successful reform and modernization programs always involve a combination of both.

Although the rational for trade facilitation is very compelling, obstacles to reform are real and challenging. At the risk of oversimplifying the matter, obstacles to trade facilitation encompass conflicting interests, lack of knowledge, and institutional limitations (Grainger, 2008). Operational requirements by participants in international trade will vary significantly. Subsequently, their views about priorities, benefits, and preferred solutions will vary. It is not uncommon for interests to be conflicting. Occasionally, especially where simplification leads to greater efficiency, vested interests—such as those of licensed professions or government offices subject to review—come into play, too.

Considering operational practices in international trade, and the number of operators and service intermediaries, few individuals are able to take an umbrella view of the entire trade operation. For policymakers to take a system-wide perspective is challenging without the support and expertise found within a national trade facilitation body—as recommended by UN Recommendation 4 (UN/CEFACT, 1974). Moreover, given the operational nature of trade facilitation, evaluating specific practices and scope for reform can be somewhat difficult for policymakers in the capital city when they are one step removed from day-to-day operations. As described by Butterly (2003), trade facilitation is at once a political, economic, business, administrative, technical, and technological issue. Required skill sets and expertise are seldom found within one individual. Inevitably, trade facilitation is an interdisciplinary problem and requires the necessary supporting institutional environment.

While national trade facilitation bodies play a key role in filtering stakeholder specific interests, the "mainstreaming" of trade facilitation across line ministries and private sector interest groups (such as the Chamber of Commerce) is equally important. For example, to engage with trade facilitation initiatives meaningfully, it is essential that each ministry with a stake in cross-border operations has at least one "champion"; that is, an individual or a small group of "champions" that help raise awareness about trade facilitation-type issues and are able to drive reform within the ministry forward—often in collaboration with fellow champions in other ministries. In this endeavor the development of an overarching and clear vision for the future that all can agree to is a major ingredient necessary to establish the will to reform. One example of a vision prepared for an East Asian country as part of a World Bank project is outlined in Box 28.4.

In the absence of detailed diagnostic studies, lists, such as an expanded version of Box 28.4 can help focus discussion as well as consider reform priorities. However, one problem in most developing countries is that the cadre of policymakers is very thin. Trade facilitation is a technical subject and can be very time consuming in instances where consensus with multiple ministries and at different policy levels (local, national, regional, and international) is required. Moreover, it is often very difficult to secure the necessary ministerial attention to drive reform forward. Technical issues, such as operational practices at the border, are often delegated back down the hierarchies. This makes reform that is dependent on multiple ministries working together, or a rewrite of legislation, particularly difficult.

A further challenge for developing countries is that, in addition to trade facilitation, there are many other pressing reform requirements. These compete for resource and

Box 28.4 Example of a Vision for a Border Management Environment

The long term vision articulated by the Reform Team in an East Asian country described a border management environment characterized by the following:

- Implementation of a paperless trading environment in which 90–100 per cent of documentary requirements and approvals are transmitted to regulatory agencies electronically and where relevant government agencies share information and rationalize processes to eliminate duplication and overlapping mandates. The system would be compliant with all regional and internally agreed standards.
- Adoption of a clear, concise, and transparent legal framework in which traders know their rights and obligations and are able to challenge decisions through recourse to appropriate administrative and legal means.
- Adoption of a "single window" approach to allow traders to discharge all regulatory requirements through one central point of contact. This would involve the review and rationalization of all existing border management agency requirements and mandates.
- Adoption of a comprehensive risk management and compliance improvement philosophy leading to more focused targeting of high-risk shipments and a radically reduced need for intrusive and time-consuming routine physical verification of cargo.
- Development of close cooperation and partnership between government agencies and the private sector.
- Introduction of one WTO-compliant service fee to replace the current range of fees required by regulatory authorities.
- Adoption of appropriate organizational structures and human resource management approaches designed to rationalize and streamline operations and ensure officials are well trained, appropriately remunerated, and well regarded by the general public.

Source: Unpublished contribution based on research by McLinden.

policy attention. Many of them are likely to be equally or even more important in help-ing GDP growth—such as reliable electricity, working transport infrastructure, and access to a pool of skilled workers. Current trade facilitation definitions, which tend to be more narrowly focused on trade and customs procedures (Grainger, 2011), might be too restrictive for developing countries. The World Bank, recognizing the dependen-cies with transport, for example, considers trade and transport facilitation as one larger policy area.

VI. The Current State of Trade Facilitation and Development

Much of the reform effort for trade and customs procedures has been focused on cus-toms agencies. The wider trade environment and linkages with the non-customs border agencies has received little, if any, attention from the development community. Progress appears to have been patchy at best. There is a large knowledge gap in terms of diagnostic tools, reform, and modernization guidelines and international best practices—and even where such tools have been available (e.g., Raven, 2005; Mathur, 2006), they are typically confined to customs operations. Moreover, non-customs agencies typically do not have a single body such as the World Customs Organization to guide them in implementing appropriate trade facilitation-focused reform. Likewise, practical mechanisms that have proven effective in facilitating cooperation and information sharing between border management agencies are few, and little work has been done on analyzing the political economy issues and dynamics that impact on achieving meaningful cooperation.

While improving the performance of customs administrations remains a high priority for many countries, evidence suggests that it is often responsible for no more than a third of regulatory delays. In many cases, the level of satisfaction of logistics professionals with customs is much higher than with other border government agencies. Data from the World Bank's LPI[5] suggest that 32 per cent of logistics professionals in countries with high overall logistics performance are satisfied with customs, but only 13 per cent are satisfied with other border government agencies. This highlights the need to focus attention on reforming and modernizing border management agencies other than customs (including health, agriculture, quarantine, police, immigration, standards, etc.). Moreover, data from the LPI also suggest that, across the world, traders acknowledge customs agencies as improving at a greater rate than non-customs border management agencies. See Figure 28.2.

Time Release Studies (TRS) conducted using the WCO's TRS methodology[6] also suggest that, in many developing countries, improvements made by customs authorities to facilitate the speedy clearance of goods are undermined by the relatively static performance of other border management agencies that have failed to adopt similar contemporary approaches to regulatory reform and modernization. It is becoming increasingly clear that clearance times are largely determined by the performance of the weakest link in the border processing chain. Achieving meaningful trade facilitation gains therefore requires comprehensive "whole of border" reform initiatives and effective cooperation and information sharing among all border management agencies.

Many developing countries have now recognized the importance of addressing these issues and are keenly interested in trade facilitation (as opposed to just customs modernization). This has led to such initiatives as:

- Coordinated Border Management, which is based on approaches such as co-location of facilities, close cooperation between agencies, delegation of administrative authority, cross-designation of officials, and effective information sharing.

---

[5] <http://info.worldbank.org/etools/tradesurvey/mode1b.asp>.
[6] See <www.wcoomd.org>.

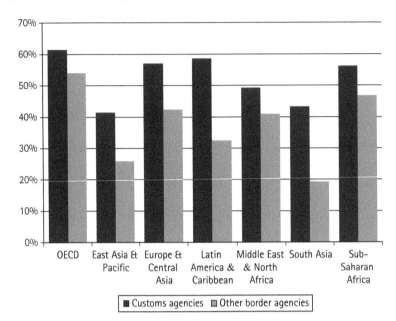

FIGURE 28.2 Percentage of LPI respondents claiming improvement in customs and other border agencies

Source: Li, et al. (2010).

- One-Stop Border Posts that allow neighboring countries to coordinate import, export, and transit processes to ensure that traders are not required to duplicate regulatory formalities on both sides of the same border.
- Single-Window Systems that allow traders to submit all import, export, and transit information required by regulatory agencies once via a single electronic gateway instead of submitting essentially the same information numerous times to different government entities.

While encouraging, such projects are unlikely to remedy the full list of issues suffered by business operators (e.g., as outlined in Box 28.3). Good trade facilitation practice requires policymakers to review and seek improvements to the trade environment on a continuous basis. At its worst, poorly implemented trade facilitation projects may even cause new kinds of problems—especially when functionality does not meet user requirements for cost and efficiency.

As outlined earlier, the obstacles to reform are significant and difficult to overcome. In fact, one of the big research questions is why trade facilitation has taken so long to establish itself as a mainstream trade policy agenda item and why trade facilitation-motivated reform proves so painfully slow. The current focus by the donor community on customs procedures alone—rather than wider dependencies with non-customs bodies as well as transport, energy, and human resources—may be something that needs to be revisited in the development context, too.

While the field of trade facilitation is rapidly evolving and progress in trade facilitation and development is being made, much more needs to be done. For traders, it matters little whether the problems they face are the result of poor customs procedures, inadequate infrastructure, or anti-competitive transport regulation. They all contribute to excessive transactions costs, delays, and unpredictability in the supply chain. And as all engineers understand well, any chain is only as strong as its weakest link.

References

Butterly, T. (2003), 'Trade Facilitation in a Global Trade Environment.' In *Trade Facilitation: The Challenges for Growth and Development.* UNECE. Geneva: United Nations, UNECE.

DeWulf, L. D. (2004), 'Tradenet in Ghana: Best Practice of the Use of Information Technology.' A background paper prepared for the *World Development Report 2005*, Washington: World Bank.

Grainger, A. (2007), 'Trade Facilitation and Supply Chain Management: A Case Study at the Interface Between Business and Government' Birkbeck, University of London, Ph.D. Thesis.

Grainger, A. (2008), 'Customs and Trade Facilitation: From Concepts to Implementation.' *World Customs Journal*, 2(1): 17–30.

Grainger, A. (2010), 'The Role of the Private Sector in Supporting Border Management Reform.' In McLinden, G., Fanta, E., Widdowson, D., and Doyle, T. (eds.), *Border Management Modernization.* Washington DC: The World Bank.

Grainger, A. (2011), 'Trade Facilitation: A Conceptual Review.' *Journal of World Trade*, 45(1): 39–62.

ICC (2010), *Incoterms 2010: ICC Official Rules for the Interpretation of Trade Terms.* Paris: International Chamber of Commerce.

Li, Y., McLinden, G., and Wilson, J. S. (2010), 'Building a Convincing Business Case for Border Management Reform.' In McLinden, G., Fanta, E., Widdowson, D., and Doyle, T. (eds.), *Border Management Modernization.* Washington DC: The World Bank.

Mathur, V. (ed.) (2006), *Reforming the Regulatory Procedures for Import and Export: Guide for Practitioners.* Washington DC: The World Bank.

Mustra, M. (2010), 'Border Management Modernization and the Trade Supply Chain.' In McLinden, G., Fanta, E., Widdowson, D., and Doyle, T. (eds.), *Border Management Modernization.* Washington DC: The World Bank.

OECD (Peter Walkenhorst, Tadashi Yasui) (2003). Quantitative Assessment of the Benefits of Trade Facilitation. Working Party of the Trade Committee. Paris: OECD. TD/TC/WP(2003)31/Final.

Raven, J. (2005), 'A Trade and Transport Facilitation Toolkit: Audit, Analysis and Remedial Action.' Washington DC: The World Bank.

Staples, B. R. (2002), 'Trade Facilitation: Improving the Invisible Infrastructure.' In Hoekman, B., Mattoo, A., and English, P. (eds.), *Development, Trade, and the WTO: A Handbook.* Washington DC: The World Bank, 139–48.

UN/CEFACT (1974), 'Recommendation No 4–National Trade Facilitation Bodies." Geneva: United Nations, ECE/TRADE/352, and CEFACT.

UN/CEFACT (1981), 'Recommendation No. 1: United Nations Layout Key for Trade Documents.' Geneva: United Nations, ECE/TRADE/137: 11, and CEFACT.

UN/CEFACT (2004), 'Recommendation No. 33: Single Window Recommendation.' Geneva: United Nations, ECE/TRADE/352: 37, and CEFACT.

UN/CEFACT and UNCTAD (2002), 'Compendium of Trade Facilitation Recommendations.' Geneva: United Nations, UN. ECE/TRADE/279, and CEFACT.

WCO (1999), 'Revised Kyoto Convention: International Convention on the Simplifications and Harmonization of Customs Procedures.' Brussels: World Customs Organisation.

WCO (2007), 'WCO SAFE Framework of Standards.' Brussels: World Customs Organisation.

Wilson, J. S., et al. (2003), 'Trade Facilitation and Economic Development: A New Approach to Quantifying the Impact.' *World Bank Economic Review,* 17(3): 367–89.

Wilson, J. S., et al. (2004), 'Assessing the Potential Benefit of Trade Facilitation: A Global Perspective.' *Policy Research Working Papers*, World Bank, WPS 3224.

WTO. (1998), 'WTO: A Training Package; What is Trade Facilitation?' Retrieved 2 August, 2006, from <http://www.wto.org/english/thewto_e/whatis_e/eol/e/wto02/wto2_69.htm#note2>.

WTO (2010), 'Draft Consolidated Negotiating Text. Negotiating Group on Trade Facilitation.' Geneva: WTO, TN/TF/W/165/Rev.4.

CHAPTER 29

···

TRADE AND ENVIRONMENT

···

STEVE CHARNOVITZ

I. INTRODUCTION

INTERNATIONAL policies on trade and on environment have always intersected.[1] The earliest multilateral environmental agreement (MEA), the Convention for the Protection of Birds Useful to Agriculture, signed in 1902, utilized an import ban as an environmental instrument.[2] The earliest multilateral trade agreement to pursue trade liberalization, the Convention for the Abolition of Import and Export Prohibitions and Restrictions, signed in 1927, contained an exception for trade restrictions imposed for the protection of public health and the protection of animals and plants against diseases and against "extinction."[3] As environmental regimes evolved over the twentieth century, trade instruments continued to be used by governments seeking workable environmental protection. When the post-war multilateral trading system was designed in 1947–48, governments recognized the need for some policy space to accommodate the use of trade measures as instruments to safeguard the environment and health. For example, the General Agreement on Tariffs and Trade (GATT) of 1947 contained provisions in Article XX (General Exceptions) to accommodate governmental measures necessary for the protection of life and health and measures relating to the conservation of natural resources.

In these first generation "trade and environment" policies, the two regimes recognized some linkage to the other, but did not actively look for ways to enhance each other's goals. For example, the Convention on International Trade in Endangered Species

---

[1] Some related material on the "trade and health" linkage will also be covered in this chapter. The "trade and health" linkage regarding generic drugs will not be covered. See the Appendix at the end of the chapter for definitions and discussion of core definitions and concepts pertinent to issues of trade and environment.

[2] Convention for the Protection of Birds Useful to Agriculture, March 19, 1902, 102 BFSP 969, Art. 2 (no longer in force).

[3] Convention for the Abolition of Import and Export Prohibitions and Restrictions, November 8, 1927, 97 LNTS 391, Art. 4, ad Art. 4 (not in force).

of Wild Fauna and Flora (CITES), signed in 1973, used trade bans as a central instrument for the management and enforcement of wildlife policies. For many years, however, CITES was not fully attentive to how controlled trade could enhance sustainable management. Similarly, the GATT system was often not attentive to how its normative activities to address non-tariff barriers were being perceived in the environmental community as a challenge to the legitimacy of environmental measures. With few exceptions, until the early 1990s, there was very little communication between trade officials and environment officials operating at the international level and not much more at the national level. As a result, the trade effects of environmental laws and regulations were often not considered by the governments imposing them. Similarly, the environmental effects of trade and investment liberalization and the impact of trade law disciplines were often not considered.

The private sectors of all countries want to export more, and governments share that goal in order to increase gross domestic product (GDP), create jobs, and satisfy political export interests. Although the products to be exported will typically satisfy the environmental and health regulations of the country of production,[4] there will be a great challenge in meeting the regulations of each of the potential importing countries. Some of the problems will be lack of transparency of regulations, the differences between various countries, and sometimes conflicts among those regulations. Exporters face an equally difficult challenge in meeting the non-governmental "standards" prescribed through market mechanisms. Such standards are not legally coercive, but voluntary markets are coercive in the sense that an exporter may only be able to sell its product to another country if it meets the private standards prescribed in that country. Privately prescribed standards are particularly extensive on matters of environment, safety, and health. The norms and perceptions in developed countries on some issues may be different from the norms and perceptions in developing countries.

As a result of the "trade and environment" debate beginning in the early 1990s, there is now much greater understanding of these linkages. Trade officials at the World Trade Organization (WTO) and in national capitals are much more aware of the links between trade and environment and say that they are committed to avoiding conflicts. Similarly, there is greater recognition by environmental officials as to how trade restrictions can be overused or misused in the pursuit of environmental goals. In the Doha Development Trade Round, two of the issues being negotiated have the potential for delivering benefits both to expand trade and to enhance environmental protection. The two issues are liberalization of environmental goods and services (EGS) and the development of disciplines for harmful fishery subsidies.

This maturation in "trade and environment" policy is owed to commitments by governments to address this policy linkage and was facilitated by analytical work and discussions occurring over many years in the GATT/WTO. Equally important, the progress made within the trading system is owed, at least in part, to the parallel efforts

---

[4] During the GATT era, there was attention to the phenomenon of export of domestically prohibited goods, but that concern has not been pursued in recent years.

in other international organizations to improve understanding of trade–environment linkages. Most noteworthy were the programs in the UN Environment Programme (UNEP), the Organisation for Economic Co-operation and Development (OECD), the UN Conference on Trade and Development (UNCTAD), and the World Bank, all of which have devoted resources to studying trade and environment linkages. Additionally, considerable credit should be given to many foundations, non-governmental organizations (NGOs), institutes, and business groups that devoted attention to these issues from the early 1990s forward.

Several initiatives have been undertaken to head off or resolve tensions between importing and exporting countries on the interface of environment or health, on the one hand, and trade on the other. For example, the UN Food and Agriculture Organization (FAO) and UNCTAD have teamed up with the International Federation of Organic Agricultural Movements to co-sponsor the International Task Force on Harmonisation and Equivalence in Organic Agriculture. Another fruitful collaboration involves UNCTAD and Brazil's National Institute of Metrology, Standardization, and Industrial Quality which have established a Consultative Task Force on Environmental Requirements and Market Access for Developing Countries. Still another is the Sustainable Trade and Innovation Centre co-sponsored by the European Commission, the French Ministry for the Environment, the Commonwealth Science Council, and the European Partnership for the Environment. The Centre has undertaken pilot projects on textiles and electronics.

Of course, the fact that international policy on "trade and environment" is more coherent and constructive now than it was in the 1980s and 1990s does not mean that this level of progress is sufficient or that the underlying problems have been solved. Environmental problems will always be a challenge on a planet where governmental units do not exactly match ecosystems. Another way of saying this is that, so long as the policies in one country can impose externalities on other countries, and so long as prices in the market are not fully reflective of environmental costs, there will be a need for international governance to manage the trans-border conflicts that will inevitably ensue. In a speech, WTO Director-General Pascal Lamy (2006) explained that governance "is a decision-making process that through consultation, dialogue, exchange and mutual respect, seeks to ensure coexistence and in some cases coherence between different and sometimes divergent points of view." This will be a key challenge for global governance in the twenty-first century

Because all major ecological problems affect the world economy—for example, climate change, biodiversity, forestry, fisheries, and pollution—linkages between the world trading system and environmental policies are inevitable. In Lamy's paradigm, there is a need for governance because individual governments acting alone will not, as a practical matter, adopt policies that are efficient on a global scale. Although individuals can act in a self-interested way in the market knowing that an invisible hand exists to help generate efficient outcomes, the same overall pro-efficiency dynamic does not automatically ensue in global politics if governments act only in a self-interested way toward other countries.

One of the contributions of the late environmentalist, Konrad von Moltke, about 20 years ago, was the axiom that "unmanaged environmental problems become trade problems." There are two insights in this axiom. The first is that major environmental problems can never be definitively solved; new developments will always spawn new problems that require new solutions and better management. The second insight is that governments need to cooperate to solve environmental problems, and when such cooperation is not forthcoming, a government stymied in getting the cooperation it seeks may resort to a trade measure. This dynamic of environmental problems spilling out into the trading system can be seen in all of the major trade–environment conflicts to date.

An example is the danger in the proposals being made for a climate tax or tariff to be imposed on imports from countries that did not ratify the Kyoto Protocol to the UN Climate Change Convention or are not controlling their greenhouse gas emissions.[5] Because many governments are not cooperating on addressing greenhouse-gas emissions and other energy conservation challenges, there is frustration spilling out into the trade arena. In the case of climate change, trade measures are being suggested as a way either to level the playing field between countries with different levels of energy tax or to induce free riding countries to better cooperate.[6]

Because the WTO is a functional international organization with a mandate for trade, WTO law does not generally address government policies beyond trade, but rather leaves those issues to environmental institutions. This approach has clear advantages and disadvantages. The advantage is that the WTO sticks to its technical competence and leaves environmental decisions to organizations with that technical competence. The disadvantage is that, in trade and environment, the WTO looks only at one side of a problem. For example, in the United States–Shrimp case, the WTO considered the appropriateness of the US import ban directed at countries that the US government believed were not adequately protecting sea turtles. But the WTO did not consider whether the complaining governments *were* adequately protecting sea turtles. Because it is partial rather than holistic, WTO dispute settlement may not be able to achieve a satisfactory solution to complex disputes that involve both trade and environmental values.

This legal point has an analog in the economic critiques of international trade law and WTO negotiations that point to the uncertainty as to whether trade liberalization will always benefit the participating countries. For example, the impact of services regulation on an economy will depend to some extent on whether the liberalizing government has an adequate regulatory regime in place. In other words, an adequate regulatory regime can be viewed as a precondition of fully benefiting from trade liberalization. The same point can be made regarding whether a government has in place an adequate legal system, effective competition policy, openness to investment, adequate assistance for workers and farmers, and well-administered environmental controls. All of these policy

---

[5] For example, see Bennhold (2007).
[6] See WTO and UNEP (2009), pp. 98–110; Houser et al. (2008).

preconditions have in common the fact that the WTO generally does not have rules assuring that non-trade policies are adequate for trade liberalization. In other words, the trade and environment regimes are not synchronized in law.

The same point can be seen in "trade distorting," a term used regularly in the WTO. For example, subsidies and non-tariff barriers are disciplined because they can be trade distorting. Yet, while the WTO disfavors trade-distorting governmental measures, the WTO has no rules about environment-distorting government policies (i.e., government policies that tolerate or cause harmful environmental change). The absence of rules in the WTO on environment (or "rights" to the environment) can be contrasted to the presence of positive rules in the WTO on intellectual property rights, namely the Agreement on Trade-Related Aspects of Intellectual Property Rights (TRIPS). As the WTO Secretariat has observed, the TRIPS Agreement "is to date the most comprehensive multilateral agreement on intellectual property."[7]

Seen against that WTO law backdrop, the inclusion of environmental issues in the Doha Round negotiations is especially noteworthy because negotiations are explicitly considering some environmental distortions. In the Rules negotiations, negotiators are considering disciplines on fisheries subsidies that weave in resource sustainability. In the Agriculture negotiations, the negotiators are considering "non-trade" concerns that include the protection of the environment. Unlike the proactive orientation of the fisheries negotiation, the Agriculture negotiations are more modest in seeking to preserve domestic policy space for environment-related subsidization.

Beginning with Agenda 21 (1992), governments have affirmed that trade and environment policies should be "mutually supportive in favour of sustainable development."[8] This mantra is inscribed in the Doha Ministerial Declaration where the WTO members state that "We are convinced that the aims of upholding and safeguarding an open and non-discriminatory multilateral trading system, and acting for the protection of the environment and the promotion of sustainable development can and must be mutually supportive."[9] This phraseology has been adoptable because there is something in it for all sides of the debate. Those who view the trading system as already supportive of the environment can point to the way that trade can positively contribute to environmental goals. On the other hand, those who are skeptical of the benefits of trade for the environment see the mutual supportiveness as a commitment by the WTO to carry out the Doha Agenda in a way that actually does deliver some environmental benefits. Of all trade officials, WTO Director-General Lamy has seemingly been the most committed to turning these pro-environmental aspirations in the Doha Declaration into reality. For example, in a February 2007 speech about the Doha Round, Lamy declared: "Trade, and indeed the WTO, must be made to deliver sustainable development. They are starting

---

[7] WTO, "Overview: the TRIPS Agreement," available at <http://www.wto.org/english/tratop_e/trips_e/intel2_e.htm>.

[8] UN Conference on Environment and Development, Agenda 21, para. 2.21(b).

[9] Doha Ministerial Declaration, WT/MIN(01)DEC/1, November 14, 2001, para. 6.

to."[10] In June 2010, Lamy reiterated that "Trade opening has much to contribute to the fight against climate change and to the protection of the environment...."[11]

A map of trade and environment issues would consider all the interconnections among international trade, the natural and human environment, governmental trade or environmental measures, international trade law, and international environmental law. Thus, it would consider markets, the physical world, and also the legal aspects on both the national and international planes. The optimal analytical tools for thinking through the challenges of trade and the environment would include theories and practice of trade economics, environmental economics, trade law, environmental law, public choice, international relations, and organizational behavior. This chapter emphasizes the legal dimension.

The economic perspective on trade and environment is important. Given capital mobility and open trade, concerns have been raised that investors will seek to move capital and production facilities to countries with lower environmental standards on the assumption that export opportunities can be most profitable when production occurs in countries with low production costs. This alleged phenomenon has been termed a "polluter haven," and critics see two problems. One is that the low standards in the host country will harm the environment in that country. The other is that exports produced under such standards are unfair trade because there is not a level playing field. Another allegation has been that some governments will seek to lower their standards as a means of attracting investment, and that will produce a dynamic that will artificially suppress environmental standards. This dynamic is called "race to the bottom." Considerable research has been done on both of these alleged problems, and some evidence exists to support these propositions. Yet most available evidence shows that working to achieve effective environmental standards is a good development strategy for governments.[12] A number of specific case studies confirm this conclusion. For example, a case study of Brazil, sponsored by the OECD, found that the stronger environmental legislation in the 1980s improved environmental enforcement in the early 1990s, and trade liberalization in the early 1990s has led to increased public and private investment in Brazil.[13]

Analysts of the impact of trade on the environment often distinguish between effects stemming from changes in production patterns and those stemming from changes in income. Production effects might arise, for example, when greater opportunities for trade boosts production and thereby increases pollution or deforestation. Income effects arise when trade leads to higher income for a country, and that induces greater consumption (which could put stress on the environment) and greater demand for environmental quality (which could translate into stronger environmental regulation).[14]

---

[10] WTO (2007).

[11] WTO (2010a).

[12] See Nordström and Vaughan (1999); Busse (2004); and Grether et al. (2006).

[13] See Lucon and Rei (2006).

[14] These and other potential effects of trade are carefully analyzed in Cosbey et al. (2005). The effect of higher income on pollution is sometimes seen as an inverted U curve, which is called an environmental Kuznets curve. (The Kuznets curve shows the effects of higher income on economic inequality.)

Many pathways of interaction have been identified. The structural and scale effects of trade on the environment involve the environmental benefits of greater specialization and the more efficient use of natural resources.[15] On the other hand, resource or pollution-intensive sectors may grow faster due to trade and investment, as they have in Vietnam.[16] The income effects of trade enable higher-income liberalizing countries to devote more financial resources toward environmental remediation.[17] The technology effects of trade involve the less costly availability of new pollution control technologies. In addition, there are physical effects of trade on the environment, such as the introduction of invasive species and the movement of hazardous waste. The net effect of trade on the environment depends on the interplay of the various factors (such as scale, structure, income, and technology). The induced effect also depends on the changes in environmental policy in the liberalizing country.

II. Guide to WTO Legal Provisions Addressing the Environment

This section provides background on the various provisions of WTO law that address the environment. The Marrakesh Agreement Establishing the World Trade Organization (WTO Agreement) mentions the environment in its Preamble. Specifically, the preambular language suggests that the parties recognize:

> …that their relations in the field of trade and economic endeavour should be conducted with a view to raising standards of living, ensuring full employment and a large and steadily growing volume of real income and effective demand, and expanding the production of and trade in goods and services, while allowing for the optimal use of the world's resources in accordance with the objective of sustainable development, seeking both to protect and preserve the environment and to enhance the means for doing so in a manner consistent with their respective needs and concerns at different levels of economic development.

The Appellate Body has stated that the WTO Preamble informs the interpretation of the WTO covered agreements, and the jurists used the language above in the US–Shrimp case to help interpret the WTO provisions at issue.[18] The Appellate Body has used other language in the WTO Preamble in two other cases.

[15] See, for example, Vilas-Ghiso and Liverman (2006). Scale effects are the increase in pollution, holding industrial structure constant; in reality, an economy always has structural/compositional changes.

[16] See Mani and Jha (2006), who note that trade liberalization has led to potentially adverse environmental consequences in toxic pollution intensive sectors.

[17] Greater trade openness will "help increase demand for environmental quality…" WTO (2010b).

[18] The WTO Appellate Body is the highest court in the WTO judiciary.

The foundational WTO agreement on trade in goods, the GATT, contains General Exceptions to all rules in that Agreement, including the disciplines governing import bans, domestic taxes, and border tax adjustments. Although most environmental measures can be carried out without infringing WTO rules, a trade-related environmental measure (TREM) may come into conflict with trade rules if the environmental regulatory distinction leads to different treatment when two products are "like." If two products are not like, then the GATT's non-discrimination rules do not apply.

With respect to the environment, Article XX (General Exceptions) states:

> Subject to the requirement that such measures are not applied in a manner which would constitute a means of arbitrary or unjustifiable discrimination between countries where the same conditions prevail, or a disguised restriction on international trade, nothing in this Agreement shall be construed to prevent the adoption or enforcement by any contracting party of measures:
> ...(b) necessary to protect human, animal or plant life or health;
> ...(g) relating to the conservation of exhaustible natural resources if such measures are made effective in conjunction with restrictions on domestic production or consumption;

The introductory paragraph to Article XX, known as the "chapeau" has been interpreted by the Appellate Body as a condition for the use of any of the Article XX exceptions. Under the chapeau, the challenged measure cannot be a disguised restriction on trade or arbitrary or unjustifiable discrimination between countries where the same conditions prevail. The contingent provision, "where the same conditions prevail," has received little attention in WTO jurisprudence so far and may loom more important in future cases.

The chapeau is examined after a disputed measure is found to qualify provisionally under one of the specific exceptions. Both the (b) and (g) exceptions would be usable for an environmental measure. A panel adjudicating Article XX should first consider the threshold question to see if the governmental measure being litigated fits within the range of policies covered by the exception. If so, then the specific discipline in that exception would be examined. The Appellate Body has allocated the burden of proof to the defendant government for most steps of the Article XX analysis.

For measures regarding human, animal, or plant life or health, the (b) exception requires that the measure be "necessary," and that term has been applied strictly. One early adjudication came in the *EC–Asbestos* case where the Appellate Body found that the XX(b) exception could justify the contested measure. According to the Appellate Body in that case, the term "necessary" in Article XX(b) requires that there be no reasonably available and WTO-consistent alternative measure that the regulating government could *reasonably be expected to employ to achieve its policy objectives. To determine whether a potential alternative is* reasonably available, a panel will engage in a "weighing and balancing process" that considers: (1) the extent to which the alternative measure "contributes to the realization of the end pursued," (2) whether the alternative measure would achieve the same end, and (3) whether the alternative is less restrictive of trade.[19] The relevance of the precautionary principle to Article XX(b) has not yet been addressed in dispute settlement.[20]

For measures regarding the conservation of exhaustible natural resources, the (g) exception requires that the disputed measure is "relating to" such conservation. In *US–Shrimp*, the Appellate Body ended the controversy as to whether "exhaustible" natural resources were distinguishable from renewable resources (such as turtles) by holding that exhaustible natural resources includes both living and non-living resources. The issue of whether there is an implied jurisdictional limit to Article XX(g), that is, whether the natural resources being protected by the contested measure must be within the territory of the defendant country, remains unresolved. In the *US–Shrimp* case, the Appellate Body seemed to suggest that there had to be a "sufficient nexus" to the defendant country.[21] The term "relating to" has been interpreted by the Appellate Body to require an examination of whether the general structure and design of the measure are reasonably related to the ends sought and are not disproportionately wide in scope. In addition, paragraph (g) further requires that a measure applying to imports be made effective in conjunction with restrictions on domestic production or consumption. In US–Gasoline, the Appellate Body held that this clause requires "even-handedness" in the imposition of restrictions, in the name of conservation, upon the production or consumption of exhaustible natural resources.[22]

The applicability of GATT Article XX to process related measures (PPMs) is controversial. In the *US–Shrimp* case, the Appellate Body ultimately ruled that a US import ban on shrimp from Malaysia was WTO consistent even though it was linked to Malaysia's conservation practices.[23] On the other hand, the WTO Secretariat continues to declare that: "trade restrictions cannot be imposed on a product purely because of the way it has been produced."[24] The issue of process related taxes can also raise questions regarding the exceptions in Article XX as well as the underlying GATT rules on the imposition of taxes on imported products and border tax adjustments on imported or exported products. If taxes get used more widely as an instrument to address climate change and to promote the use of clean energy, some tax disputes may be brought to the WTO. The availability of Article XX to justify measures against so-called eco-dumping or against MEA violations has not been litigated.

---

[19] Appellate Body Report, *EC–Asbestos,* paras. 162–72.

[20] Vranes (2009: 260–63).

[21] Appellate Body Report, *United States—Import Prohibition of Certain Shrimp and Shrimp Products,* WT/DS58/AB/R, adopted November 6, 1998, para. 133.

[22] Appellate Body Report, *United States—Standards for Reformulated and Conventional Gasoline,* WT/DS2/AB/R, adopted May 20, 1996, pp. 20–21.

[23] Appellate Body Report, *United States—Import Prohibition of Certain Shrimp and Shrimp Products—Recourse to Article 21.5 of the DSU by Malaysia,* WT/DS58/AB/RW, adopted November 21, 2001.

[24] WTO, "The Environment: A Specific Concern," available at <http://www.wto.org/english/thewto_e/whatis_e/tif_e/bey2_e.htm>. The Secretariat does not cite any legal authority for this assertion.

As for all WTO rules, the WTO dispute settlement system prescribes trade sanctions as an instrument to induce compliance when trade rules are being violated. Ironically, the WTO is the only international organization (other than the UN Security Council) to use trade sanctions in that manner. The implementation system for MEAs relies more on the soft powers of persuasion and capacity building. When MEAs use trade controls, the only trade blocked is the natural resource being regulated by the MEA. For example, a country violating CITES can see its exports of endangered species embargoed by CITES members.

The dispute settlement system in the WTO has adjudicated three environmental cases pursuant to the GATT (see Box 29.1).

Violations of GATT obligations were found in the *US–Gasoline* and *US–Shrimp* cases, and in the *Brazil–Tyres* case, and in all three instances, the offending government corrected the violation without sacrificing its environmental policies. The experience in all three cases demonstrates the focus of panels on the means used to achieve an environmental aim, not a second-guessing of the ends sought to be achieved. Of course, one should note that all three of these cases involved an Appellate Body decision that reversed the lower-level panel on key points. The original panel decisions, if carried to their logical conclusion, had seemed to undermine the right of a government to carry out environmental regulation that affected trade.

Besides the GATT, several other WTO agreements supervising trade in goods also include provisions pertaining to the environment:

• —The Agreement on Agriculture declares that fundamental reform is an ongoing process and committed parties to begin new negotiations in 2000. These negotiations are to take into account the so-called "non-trade concerns, including food security and the need to protect the environment."[25] The Agreement on Agriculture contains a so-called "green box" list of subsidies that have an exemption from reduction

Box 29.1 GATT–Based Trade and Environment Disputes in the WTO

Dispute	Parties	Disposition
Standards for Reformulated and Conventional *Gasoline*	Complainants: Brazil and Venezuela Defendant: United States	Complainants win case. US revises its clean air regulation
Import Prohibition of Certain *Shrimp* and Shrimp Products (the *Shrimp–Turtle* case)	Complainants: India, Malaysia, Pakistan, and Thailand Defendant: United States	Complainants win case. US revises its procedures for the import ban on turtles
Measures Affecting Imports of Retreaded *Tyres*	Complainant: EC Defendant: Brazil	Complainants win case. Brazil eliminates discrimination in favor of its Common Market partners

[25] Agreement on Agriculture, Preamble recital 6, art. 20 (c); Doha Declaration, para. 13.

commitments, so long as they have at most minimal trade-distorting effects or effects on production.[26] In this context, the color green is a traffic signal, not an environmental validator. The WTO Secretariat has opined that this green box enables governments to "capture positive environmental externalities."[27] Yet, there appears to be no research on the true value for the environment of green box subsidies.

- • —The Agreement on Technical Barriers to Trade (TBT) contains a complex set of rules regarding government and private regulatory systems. A central rule is that technical regulations not be more trade restrictive than necessary to fulfill a legitimate objective. The TBT Agreement includes, among an illustrative list of objectives, the "protection of human health or safety, animal or plant life or health, or the environment."[28] The TBT Agreement also has disciplines on how governments undertake conformity assessment procedures on imports. Governments are encouraged to negotiate mutual-recognition agreements. Another TBT rule requires governments to use international standards as "a basis for" technical regulations, except when such standards would be an ineffective or inappropriate means for the fulfillment of the legitimate objectives pursued.[29] The applicability of this requirement to international environmental standards has not been well defined. The TBT Agreement defines a standard as "rules, guidelines or characteristics for products or related processes and production methods."[30] Note for example that the International Organization for Standardization has adopted two standards (ISO 14064 and 14065) on the quantification and reporting of greenhouse-gas emissions. In 2012, the Appellate Body decided the first TBT environment case.

Despite the mention of PPMs, the extent to which PPMs come within the scope of the TBT Agreement remains unclear. For example, would the sustainable fisheries label devised by the Marine Stewardship Council be a TBT measure? Another ambiguity in the TBT Agreement is whether the rules for conformity assessment by nongovernmental bodies would apply to organizations such as the Forest Stewardship Council and Green Seal.

— The Agreement on the Application of Sanitary and Phytosanitary Measures (SPS) governs trade and domestic measures imposed to prevent risks to life or health from pests, diseases, additives, contaminants, toxins, and disease-causing organisms. The governmental responses to epidemics, insofar as the ensuing policies involve trade

---

[26] Ibid. Agreement on Agriculture, art. 6.1, Annex 2, paras. 2(a), 12. Among the listed subsidies are infrastructure works associated with environmental programs and payments under environmental programs. Eligibility for such payments has to be determined as part of a clearly-defined government environmental or conservation program and be dependent on the fulfillment of specific conditions. Moreover, the amount of payment has to be limited to the extra costs or loss of income involved in complying with the government program. No effort is being made in the Doha Round to regulate these subsidies.

[27] WTO, "Relevant WTO provisions: descriptions," available at <http://www.wto.org/english/tratop_e/envir_e/issu3_e.htm>.

[28] TBT Art. 2.2. See also TBT Art. 5.4. This requirement also applies to voluntary international standards.

[29] TBT Art. 5.4, para. 2.4.

[30] TBT Annex 1, para. 2.

in goods, are also governed by the SPS Agreement.[31] The SPS Agreement was written with a focus on food safety and veterinary concerns, and, at one time, trade law commentators thought that environmental regulations would be governed solely by the TBT Agreement rather than the SPS Agreement. Yet in 2006, the WTO panel in EC–Approval and Marketing of Biotech Products gave a broad interpretation to the scope of the SPS Agreement and emphasized that the Agreement could cover "certain damage to the environment other than damage to the life or health or animals or plants."[32] This precedent may mean that the disciplines of the SPS Agreement, which are among the most strict in the WTO, could collide more with TREMs in the future.

When a measure is covered by the SPS Agreement, then it will be subject to numerous rules. For example, SPS measures affecting trade have to be based on a risk assessment and cannot be maintained without sufficient scientific evidence.[33] SPS Article 3 directs governments to base their SPS measures on international standards, but allows governments to set a higher level of protection than exists in the international standard. The Appellate Body has taken note of the "the delicate and carefully negotiated balance in the SPS Agreement between the shared, but sometimes competing, interests of promoting international trade and of protecting the life and health of human beings."[34] In that holding, the Appellate Body seems to view the SPS Agreement as embodying a choice between trade and life/health. Another rule in the SPS Agreement is that regulatory measures (e.g., a maximum residue limit on pesticides) cannot be more trade restrictive than required to meet the importing government's appropriate level of protection.

—The Agreement on Subsidies and Countervailing Measures (SCM) supervises the use of domestic and export subsidies by governments, and the imposition of countervailing duties against subsidies. The SCM Agreement does not contain disciplines exclusively for environmental subsidies. Nor does the SCM Agreement incorporate the polluter pays principle. As negotiated in the Uruguay Round, the SCM Agreement contained an article (Article 8) making certain subsidies non-actionable. Listed among the non-actionable subsidies were financial contributions by governments for adapting existing facilities to new environmental requirement (subject to specified conditions). Insofar as these subsidies are used to address market failure, the SCM Agreement manifested sensitivity to the fact that some subsidies may be justifiable for economic reasons even if they distort trade. At the end of 1999, however, SCM Article 8 expired. With the expiration of this provision, an environmental subsidy can be "actionable," which means that if a subsidy is "specific" and causes "adverse effects" to the interests of other WTO members, then that subsidy would violate the SCM

---

[31] Measures to control cross-border travel of natural persons supplying or consuming services would be governed by the WTO Services Agreement. It is interesting to note that the World Bank (2007) counsels that trade and travel restrictions could be appropriate instruments to address an avian flu epidemic.

[32] Panel Report, EC—Measures Affecting the Marketing and Approval of Biotech Products, WT/DS291,292,293/R, para. 7.209, adopted November 21, 2006.

[33] SPS Arts. 2.2, 5.1. In instances where scientific evidence is insufficient, a government may provisionally impose SPS measures based on pertinent information. See SPS Art. 5.7.

[34] Appellate Body Report, EC–Asbestos, SPS Art. 5.7, para 177.

Agreement.[35] The remedy for such a violation would be for the subsidizing government to withdraw the subsidy or remove the adverse effects. The first green subsidy challenged under SCM was a Canadian feed-in tariff, but the WTO ruling in 2013 was inconclusive.

The foundational agreement on trade in services, the General Agreement on Trade in Services (GATS), contains General Exceptions to all rules in the Agreement. The structure of the GATS General Exceptions, found in GATS Article XIV, is similar to the structure of GATT Article XX in having a chapeau like the one in Article XX and a list of specific exceptions. The GATS includes an exception for measures necessary for the protection of life and health, but does not include an exception regarding conservation or the environment. So far, this omission has not proved significant because no environment-related service measure has been challenged in WTO dispute settlement. The Preamble to the GATS recognizes "the right of [WTO] members to regulate, and to introduce new regulations, on the supply of services within their territories. . . ."[36] Nevertheless, that language did not impede the finding of a violation in the US–Gambling case, which involves a US ban on Internet gambling without regard to whether the gambling services originate domestically or in other countries. In that dispute, the Appellate Body held that the challenged measure came within the scope of the GATS General Exception, but further held that the US measure did not qualify for an exception because the US government had not demonstrated that, with respect to horseracing, the regulations on remote gambling are not less favorable to foreign suppliers than to domestic suppliers.[37] If this decision means that governmental consistency is a precondition for a right to regulate, then that principle could work against many environmental regulations because governments may not regulate equivalent environmental risks symmetrically. One should also note that GATS Article VI contains disciplines on Domestic Regulation that could be applied to environmental measures. So far, Article VI has not been interpreted by the Appellate Body.

The foundational WTO agreement on intellectual property rights, the TRIPS Agreement, does not contain an overall environmental exception. Article 8 of the TRIPS Agreement states that WTO members "may" adopt measures necessary to protect public health and nutrition, provided that such measures are consistent with TRIPS. Thus, this provision is merely circular and may lack any content. The rules in TRIPS that would seem most likely to be in interface with environmental regulation are the requirements in Part II, Section 5, regarding the granting of patent rights to nationals of other WTO member countries. Section 5 provides that WTO members may exclude from patentability inventions if "necessary" to "protect human, animal or plant life or health or to avoid serious prejudice to the environment," and further provides that members may exclude from patentability plants and animals other than microorganisms provided

[35] SCM Arts. 1.2, 2, 5.

[36] GATS Preamble.

[37] Appellate Body Report, *United States—Measures Affecting the Cross-Border Supply of Gambling and Betting Services*, WT/DS286/AB/R, paras. 371–372, adopted April 20, 2005.

that plant varieties receive protection either through a patent or an effective *sui generis* system.[38] The meaning of these optional exclusions from patentability has not yet been explicated in WTO dispute settlement.

The Preamble to the TRIPS Agreement memorializes the desire of WTO members to "establish a mutually supportive relationship" between the WTO and the World Intellectual Property Organization (WIPO) "as well as other relevant international organizations." The WTO has moved to do so, for example, by signing a Cooperation Agreement with WIPO in 1996. In addition, the TRIPS Council has granted observer status to several international organizations such as the United Nations, the Food and Agriculture Organization, the World Bank, the International Monetary Fund, and the WIPO. Nevertheless, despite repeated requests for observer status from the Secretariat of the Convention on Biological Diversity (CBD), the TRIPS Council has not granted observer status to that Secretariat.[39] When the CBD Conference of the Parties meets, it gives observer status to the WTO, and WTO representatives do attend. The CBD welcomes the WTO and does not insist upon reciprocity.

The WTO Agreement establishes a Trade Policy Review Mechanism to examine the impact of a member's trade policies and practices on the multilateral trading system. This assessment is carried out "against the backdrop of the wider economic and development needs, policies and objective of the Member concerned, as well as of its external environment."[40] Many Trade Policy Reviews (TPRs) do take note of some ecological factors. The WTO Secretariat has not issued any analytical reports using the environmental information in TPRs.[41]

The WTO (2005) TPR on Nigeria can serve as an example. It notes that Nigeria promotes environmentally friendly farming practices, an environmental shrimp fisheries project, and has transport infrastructure policies seeking environmental sustainability.[42] On the other hand, the TPR notes that gas production leads to environmental pollution.[43] So far, however, the Secretariat has not made an effort to analyze the environment related constraints to Nigeria's trade competitiveness and its economic development. Nor does the TPR look systematically at how Nigeria's environment and trade policies support or undermine each other, and what potential there may be for new synergies in sustainable development. This omission seems a missed opportunity to put more substance behind the statement in the Doha Ministerial Declaration that "We strongly reaffirm our commitment to sustainable

---

[38] TRIPS Arts. 27.2, 27.2(b).

[39] WTO, Annual Report (2006) of the Council for TRIPS, IP/C/44, December 4, 2006, para. 3. Note that the Doha Ministerial Declaration states: "We welcome the WTO's continued cooperation with UNEP and other inter-governmental environmental organizations." Doha Ministerial Declaration, ibid. para. 6.

[40] WTO Agreement, Annex 3, Trade Policy Review Mechanism, Section A(ii).

[41] The most recent publicly released WTO Environmental Database goes back to 2003. See Environmental Database for 2007, WT/CTE/EDB/7, May 17, 2010. That Database excerpts the statements about the environment from several TPRs.

[42] WTO (2005: 55, 59, 80).

[43] WTO (2005: 66).

development, as stated in the Preamble to the Marrakesh Agreement."[44] Consider that in the latest Yale "Environmental Performance Index," Nigeria ranked in the bottom quarter for Sub-Saharan Africa (33 out of 41).[45]

III. GUIDE TO THE EMERGING ENVIRONMENTAL CHAPTER OF THE DOHA ROUND

The latest round of multilateral trade negotiations, the Doha Development Agenda, was launched in 2001, and the negotiations are still ongoing at the time of writing. The Doha Agenda contains several environmental elements, which the WTO Secretariat has called the "environmental chapter." It seems very likely that if the Doha Round is successfully brought to conclusion, the results will include an environmental dimension.

The Doha Declaration sets out a negotiating agenda and a forward work program for the WTO. Paragraphs 31–33 of the Ministerial Declaration address "Trade and Environment" and other several other paragraphs reference issues that come under the trade and environment rubric.

Box 29.2 summarizes the environment-related provisions in the Doha Declaration.[46] The negotiation on MEAs was explicitly limited in two important ways to keep the most difficult and challenging issues off the table. First, the negotiations were designed to exclude trade measures incorporated into MEAs that are *not* specific trade obligations (STOs). Trade measures that are not STOs occur when an MEA has language permitting or encouraging the use of trade measures, but not requiring them—for example, the Biosafety Protocol.[47] By contrast, some MEAs rely upon STOs; for example, the Montreal Protocol on ozone protection imposes trade controls against free riders not participating in the regime. Second, the negotiations were said to exclude disputes where one WTO member is a party to the MEA and the other WTO member is not. Despite the pre-commitment to leave some key MEA issues off the table, the European Communities has sought to revive them.[48] Perhaps it did so on the grounds that the

[44] Doha Ministerial Declaration, ibid. para. 6. The Marrakesh Agreement is the formal name of the WTO Agreement.

[45] Environmental Performance Index 2012, available at <http://epi.yale.edu/>. The Index was developed by the Center for Environmental Law and Policy at Yale University and the Center for International Earth Science Information Network at Columbia University in collaboration with the World Economic Forum and the Joint Research Centre of the European Commission.

[46] These environmental objectives are reiterated in the Hong Kong Ministerial Declaration, WT/MIN(05)DEC, paras. 30–32, December 22, 2005.

[47] Cartagena Protocol on Biosafety to the Convention on Biological Diversity, January 29, 2000, 39 ILM 1027 (2000), arts. 10.3(b), 10.6, 11.8, 12.1.

[48] See, for example, European Communities, "Proposal for a Decision of the Ministerial Conference on Trade and Environment," TN/TE/W/68, June 30, 2006.

Box 29.2 WTO Doha Agenda: Trade and the Environment

Paragraph	Goal for Negotiations or Related WTO Work
31(i)	Relationship between WTO rules and specific trade obligations in MEAs, but limited to matters involving parties to the MEA
31(ii)	Procedures for information exchange between WTO and MEAs, and criteria for granting observer status
31(iii), 32(i)	Reduction or eliminate of tariffs and non-tariff barriers to environmental goods and services.
31, 28	Clarify and improve WTO disciplines on fisheries subsidies
13	Environmental aspects of Agriculture negotiations
19, 32(ii)	Relationship between TRIPS Agreement and the Convention on Biological Diversity
32(iii)	Labeling requirements for environmental purposes
33	Technical assistance and capacity building in the field of trade and environment
6, 33	National environmental assessments of trade policies
51	Forum to identify and debate developmental and environmental aspects of negotiations in order to help achieve the objective of having sustainable development appropriately reflected

issues left off are those most likely to generate disputes at the WTO and therefore should be dealt with if possible.

The WTO-MEA issue has been discussed extensively, but apparently little progress has been made, beyond promoting a better understanding of the key issues. Many useful papers have been circulated, including, for example, the Matrix of Trade Measures, as prepared by the WTO Secretariat.[49] Although many leading MEAs make considerable use of STOs,[50] so far no trade dispute regarding an MEA has come to the WTO (or to the GATT). One theme in the discussions has been the need for better domestic coordination in the negotiation and implementation of MEAs, and for sharing of information among governments about national experiences with MEAs and good governance principles.[51]

With regard to information exchange with MEAs, the WTO has already taken action in holding MEA Information Sessions in the WTO Committee on Trade and Environment (CTE) and in the CTE negotiating sessions (CTESS). The WTO has also sponsored parallel events at intergovernmental environmental meetings. For

[49] "Matrix of Trade Measures Pursuant to Selected Multilateral Environmental Agreements," Note by the Secretariat, TN/TE/S/5/Rev.1, February 16, 2005.

[50] See, for example, UNEP, Governments to Consider New CITES Trade Controls, February 28, 2007.

[51] "Environmental Aspects of the Negotiations," Note by the Secretariat, WT/CTE/W/243, November 27, 2006, paras. 91, 92.

example, the WTO and UNEP cosponsored a High-Level Roundtable on Globalization and Environment at the February 2007 session of the UNEP Governing Council/ Global Ministerial Environmental Forum. In December 2009, the WTO cosponsored a Symposium for policymakers at the Copenhagen Climate Conference. The topic of the Symposium was "Trade, Technology and Climate Change Linkages: The Current Debate."

On the topic of observer status, the CTESS has invited UNEP and six major MEA Secretariats to CTESS sessions on an ad hoc basis. The issue of a formal observership of MEAs in regular WTO bodies has been discussed for years, but no decision has been made. The current talks are not aimed at making decisions to actually grant observer status.

Many relevant organizations continue to be excluded. For example, the oldest international organization on the environment, the World Conservation Union/IUCN, has not been invited despite its longtime interest in trade and headquarters near Geneva.[52] Similarly, the International Maritime Organization does not attend the WTO negotiations or the regular CTE meetings despite its recent work in drafting a convention on the recycling of ships.

The elimination or reduction of trade barriers to environmental goods and services (EGS) has been the most active negotiation in the field of trade and environment. Elimination of trade barriers to clean technologies could result in a 14 per cent increase in world trade, according to a recent World Bank study. This negotiation on market access is widely recognized to be win–win, that is, valuable for both trade and environment. Although environmental goods and services are interrelated, the negotiations have been bifurcated organizationally with environmental goods being addressed in the WTO negotiations on non-agricultural market access, and environmental services being addressed Council for Trade in Services Special Sessions. The CTESS has a monitoring role and has considered some conceptual issues relating to goods and services.

As in any WTO negotiation, definitional issues regarding environmental goods have been at the center of the talks. For example, what are environmental goods? At present, WTO tariff rules and the harmonized tariff nomenclature do not specifically address the end use of an item or its environmental footprint. Currently, there are at least nine different lists of environmental goods in play. Alternative approaches were suggested by India and Argentina—namely, a project-oriented approach suggested by India and an integrated approach suggested by Argentina to reconcile the two approaches. A challenging conceptual issue has been how to handle goods which are not used for pollution control or remediation, but rather are more energy efficient or less environmentally harmful than alternative goods. This category is called environmentally preferable products and some lists of those products include ethanol. In commenting on these negotiations, the

---

[52] For example, the IUCN has an ongoing Working Group on Environment, Trade and Investment. The IUCN is a hybrid international organization with a membership that includes 83 states, 116 government agencies, and hundreds of non-governmental organizations and affiliates. The IUCN was formed under Swiss law, not international law.

WTO Secretariat has noted that liberalizing trade in environmental goods can encour-age the use of new environmental technologies and make it easier for countries to obtain high quality goods. The Secretariat has suggested that the EGS negotiations can create a triple-win situation for trade, the environment, and development.

Considerable discussion has ensued about the modalities for the environmental goods negotiations and about the role of special and differential (S&D) treatment. No conclusions have been reached. Although some governments argue that environmental goods should be subject to the same modalities as non-environmental goods, other gov-ernments have argued for special treatment of environmental goods, meaning deeper cuts or tariff elimination. There have also been negotiations on non-tariff barriers to goods such as packaging, recycling, disposal, and various labeling regulations.

The GATS services sectoral classification list covers "Environmental Services" as Section 6 and the subsector categories are: sewage services (9401), refuse disposal ser-vices (9402), sanitation and similar services (9403), and other services. The Central Protection Classification (CPC) has additional relevant categories such as: cleaning of exhaust gases (9404), noise abatement services (9405), nature and landscape protec-tion services (9406), and other environmental services (9409). Of course, because of the pervasiveness of environmental considerations, any taxonomy is likely to be incom-plete, just as the CPC is. Thus, one can see that many other CPC categories can include environmental services—for example, natural water (180), engineering (8672), urban planning and landscape architectural services (8674), R&D on natural sciences (851), technical testing and analysis (8676), higher education (923), services incidental to energy distribution (887), travel agencies and tour operators (7471), transportation of fuels (7131), and so on. In the Uruguay Round and subsequent accession negotiations, about 50 WTO members made commitments in the environmental services classified in the 9400s, but the Secretariat has assessed these as "rather limited."[53] Most of the exist-ing commitments involve mode 3 (commercial presence).

One important service sector that has been highlighted is ecotourism where trade, investment, and ecological objectives can be mutually supportive. Green Globe, an NGO, has worked with major stakeholders in developing ecotourism labels that can help to bring transparency and accountability to this sector. Ecotourism consumption is mode 2. Although most regulation of ecotourism is by the host country, the WTO GATS commit-ments apply only to the home country.

So far, three themes reportedly have emerged in the environmental–services nego-tiations. First, governments see a need for better classification of services. Second, governments consider mode 3 the most important, followed by mode 4. Third, some regu-latory issues have been raised, particularly the recognition of professional qualifications. Government officials engaged in GATS negotiations can consult the Negotiating Checklist on environmental services prepared in the OECD.[54] More detailed discussion of these negotiations is hindered by the fact that the WTO Secretariat has classified some of the

---

[53] Environmental Aspects of the Negotiations, ibid. para. 58.
[54] OECD Trade Policy Working Paper No. 11, TD/TC/WTP(2004)/8/, February 15, 2005, para. 74.

documentation for this negotiation in its confidential JOB series, and therefore that documentation is not publicly available.

Besides EGS, the other major topic on which substantive progress has been made are disciplines for fisheries subsidies. The serious attention given to this issue has been a surprise to many observers as the WTO talks are considering detailed rule-making under the Doha mandate to "clarify and improve WTO disciplines on fisheries subsidies, taking into account the importance of this sector to developing countries."[55] Although at the advent of the negotiations, some governments were taking the position that the SCM Agreement should not have sector-specific provisions, this objection has seemingly diminished in recent years as the negotiators discuss the details of supervision proposals.

The concern about government subsidies for fisheries is that such subsidization leads to overcapacity of fishing and overfishing, and therefore to a depletion of world fish stocks. World fish stocks are currently threatened by overfishing and, despite a skein of international agreements governing fishing, there is still a great deal of illegal, unregulated, and unreported fishing.[56] Unless management improves, fish stocks could be severely depleted. The degree of fisheries subsidization is estimated to be about 20–25 per cent of total fisheries revenue.

At the Hong Kong Ministerial in December 2005, the WTO Declaration declared that there was broad agreement that the Negotiating Group on Rules "should strengthen disciplines on subsidies in the fisheries sector, including through the prohibition of certain forms of fisheries subsidies that contribute to overcapacity and over-fishing...."[57] The Declaration called on participants to undertake detailed work to "establish the nature and extent of those disciplines, including transparency and enforceability."[58] In addition, the Declaration calls for appropriate and effective S&D treatment for developing and least-developed WTO members.

Many proposals have been offered in the WTO, including proposals for a ban on fisheries subsidies that would be conditioned on certain fishery management indicators.[59] The conditioning of subsidy rules on management indicators would be an interesting development because it would provide a linkage between the WTO rules and the ongoing work of other international organizations, such as the regional fisheries-management organizations.[60] To the extent that fishery management programs allocate marketable rights, this could constitute a subsidy under the SCM agreement. At the end of 2007, the fishery negotiations led to a Chair's Text which would be a new set of

[55] Doha Declaration, ibid. para. 28.

[56] U.N. Food and Agriculture Organization, "Stopping Illegal, Unreported and Unregulated (IUU) Fishing," available at <http://www.fao.org/docrep/005/y3554e/y3554e01.htm>.

[57] Hong Kong Ministerial Declaration, ibid. Annex D, Part I, para. 9.

[58] Ibid.

[59] See, for example, Proposal from the United States, Fisheries Subsidies: Proposed New Disciplines, WTO Doc. TN/RL/GEN/145, March 22, 2007.

[60] Note that under the current WTO Agreement, new developments extrinsic to the WTO can lead to new obligations within the WTO. For example, TBT Art. 2.4 requires governments to use international standards as a basis for technical regulations.

rules governing fisheries management. The Text has no legal standing at this point and has been praised for concretely promoting sustainable development and environment within the framework of the WTO.[61]

As noted above, the environment is a topic in the agriculture negotiations and is characterized as a "non-trade issue." Both proponents and opponents of reducing (non-environmental) agricultural subsidies are marshalling green arguments for their positions. Those supporting reform emphasize how trade distorting subsidies for agriculture are now harming the environment by encouraging environmentally harmful agricultural practices, such as overuse or misuse of fertilizers and pesticides. Those opposing reform emphasize how subsidies can keep land from being developed in order to manage water resources and preserve biodiversity.

With regard to intellectual property, the Doha Declaration calls on governments to consider the relationship between the TRIPS Agreement and the Convention on Biological Diversity, and, in particular, the patenting process. The key issues are: (1) whether TRIPS should require that patents be available for genetic resources, (2) whether to require disclosure of the country of origin of genetic resources (and traditional knowledge), (3) whether to require "prior informed consent" by a government for the use of so-called sovereign resources, (4) whether to provide for "fair and equitable" benefit sharing, and (5) the legal approach to be used to achieve any agreed result (i.e., within TRIPS or beyond TRIPS). The Doha Declaration mandate for these discussions is bounded by the proviso that the negotiations "shall not add to or diminish the rights and obligations of Members under existing WTO agreements...."[62] In practice, however, such a pre-commitment could not prevent WTO members from agreeing to amend TRIPS, should there be a consensus to do so. WTO Director-General Lamy (2006) has stated that "it is incumbent on all countries to use intellectual property rights in a manner that fosters biodiversity—all countries have a responsibility."[63]

Two other matters are being addressed under the "Trade and Environment" mandate. The first is environmental labeling where the discussions are bounded by the same proviso not to alter WTO rules. So far, these discussions have been mainly informational. The second matter is technical assistance and capacity building for developing countries in the field of trade and environment, and in the Doha Declaration the WTO members have highlighted its importance. The Declaration also encourages governments with expertise in performing environmental reviews at the national level to share that expertise. Since 2001, the WTO has stepped up its capacity building on trade and environment. For example, in 2007, the WTO and UNEP held a joint Round Table on Globalization and the Environment as a side event to the Global Ministerial Environment Forum. In July 2009, the WTO held a Workshop on Environment-related Private Standards, Certification and Labeling Requirements. In February 2010, the WTO held a Regional

---

[61] Draft Consolidated Chair Texts of the AD and SCM Agreements, TN/RL/W/213, November 30, 2007, pp. 87–93; UNEP and WWF (2009); Moltke (2010).

[62] Doha Declaration, ibid. para. 32.

[63] WTO (2006).

Workshop on the Relationship between the Trade and Environment Regimes for Asia and the Pacific.

The last environment-related issue on the Doha Round agenda is the directive to the CTE and the Committee on Trade and Development to "each act as a forum to identify and debate developmental and environmental aspects of the negotiations, in order to help achieve the objective of having sustainable development appropriately reflected." This penultimate paragraph of the Doha Declaration is known as the "Paragraph 51" mandate. Director-General Lamy (2005) has explained that:

> In Paragraph 51, Ministers instructed us to change our frame of mind. In other words, to no longer compartmentalize our work; discussing environmental and developmental issues in isolation of the rest of what we do.[64]

Evaluating the progress on this objective is difficult for an outsider because none of these meetings are open to the public. But it appears that little progress has been made.[65] Certainly, the CTE is not conducting a real-time environmental impact assessment of the WTO negotiations.

Although climate change was not included in the Doha Declaration, the climate–trade linkage has become a *de facto* issue in the Doha Round.[66] There have been suggestions of a climate-related trade code to be agreed within Doha and of the possibility that political progress within the WTO could be linked to political progress in the UNFCCC negotiations. Many commentators continue to note that progress in the Doha negotiations could promote climate objectives, for example, on the liberalization of environmental goods and services.[67] In the run up to the Copenhagen conference in December 2009, there was hope in some quarters on reaching agreement on the misuse of border measures for climate purposes, but the minimal outcome at Copenhagen precluded environmental and trade negotiators from reaching those issues.

IV. An Introduction to Environmental Protection Provisions in Regional Trade Agreements

The WTO is in competition with other forums for the negotiation of new trade liberalization. In recent years, more progress has been made in achieving liberalization in bilateral free trade or regional agreements (RTAs). Many RTAs negotiated in the 2000s

---

[64] WTO (2005).

[65] Committee on Trade and Environment "Report of the Meeting Held on 17 February 2010, WT/CTE/M/49, para. 33.

[66] World Bank (2007); ICTSD (2008).

[67] Cosbey (2008) and Bacchus (2010).

embrace numerous "trade-and" issues beyond what is in the WTO. Investment is the most common WTO-plus issue in RTAs.

Many RTAs also have provisions regarding the environment. For example the China–Chile Free Trade Agreement states that the parties shall enhance their communication and cooperation on labor, social security and environment…."[68] The Japan–Mexico Agreement devotes an article to Cooperation in the Field of Environment.[69] The RTAs negotiated by the United States all contain a chapter on environment that commits parties to enforce their own environmental laws and provides for dispute settlement should that not occur. The RTAs also contain side agreements to effect environmental cooperation and capacity building. A detailed analysis of the current US model for incorporating environment into RTAs can be seen in the environmental review of a recent RTA conducted by a private sector advisory committee.[70] This model has been used in US trade agreements with Australia, Bahrain, Central America, Chile, Dominican Republic, Jordan, Morocco, Oman, and Singapore.

The most recent development in the United States is that after the 2006 elections, the new majority party (the Democrats) demanded stronger environmental provisions in pending RTAs. For example for the Peru–USA FTA, Peru agreed that the United States could restrict imports of products (such as mahogany) that are harvested and traded in violation of CITES. This FTA was approved by the US Congress. In 2011, the Obama Administration transmitted three RTAs to the Congress and they were quickly approved. The RTAs with South Korea, Panama, and Columbia contain environmental provisions.

V. Policy and Negotiating Implications for Developing Countries

The Doha Round negotiations have been stripped of investment, competition policy, and transparency in government procurement, and so it is an achievement for the WTO to have progressed this far on environmental issues. While the success of the Doha Round remains uncertain, if the issues being negotiated do coalesce, one can expect environment to be part of the final deal.

---

[68] Free Trade Agreement between the Government of the People's Republic of China and the Government of the Republic of Chile, November 18, 2005, Art. 108, available at <http://www.sice.oas.org/tradee.asp#CHL_CHN>.

[69] Agreement between Japan and the United Mexican States for the Strengthening of the Economic Partnership, September 17, 2004, Art. 147, available at <http://www.sice.oas.org/Trade/JPN_MEXDraftEPA_e/JPN_MEXind_e.asp>.

[70] "Final Environmental Review of the Dominican Republic—Central America—United States Free Trade Agreement, February 2005, available at <http://www.ustr.gov/Trade_Agreements/Bilateral/CAFTA/Section_Index.html>.

Trade and environment issues have many implications for developing countries. Given the consensus decision-making rule in WTO negotiations, it is hard to imagine any change in WTO rules that would be detrimental to developing countries. But how much positive gain the developing countries get on environment will depend in part on their understanding of the issues and their negotiating skills.

On the issue of MEAs, developing countries as a group do not have a distinctive interest in the WTO separate from others in the international community. MEAs are a response to environmental problems that cross borders or exist in the global commons, and are a way to enhance global public goods. Developing countries stand to gain from effective international environmental regimes. All recent MEAs contain provisions to assist developing countries. When such provisions are negotiated and carried out, developing countries should work within the environment regimes to secure phase-in times and technical assistance as needed. Developing countries can also work to improve transparency within MEAs.

On the EGS liberalization issues, the developing countries have a self-interest in improving trade in these vital services and technologies in order to get access at the lowest possible cost. This means that developing countries should be willing to make commitments on EGS in return for receiving reciprocal market access. Developing country governments that adopt competitiveness strategies should consider what opportunities exist for promoting exports of EGS. When developing countries are pressed to make commitments on environmental services, they should be careful in the details of their services commitments so that they do not inadvertently negotiate away the ability to regulate in a particular sector. That is the lesson to be drawn from the *US–Gambling* case, in which Antigua won a dispute against the United States because of a sloppily written US commitment on recreational services that was interpreted by the WTO panel as a commitment to open the US market to online gambling services, notwithstanding longtime US legal prohibitions on most remote gambling.[71]

Although energy trade is not specifically addressed in the Doha Declaration, that sector is especially important for energy importing and exporting countries.[72] According to Lamy, "While WTO rules have set the beginnings of an architecture to address the trade-related aspects of energy, these rules may need to evolve in [the] future to address energy trade more comprehensively."[73] The relationship between the WTO and the Energy Charter remains to be explored.[74]

One area of tension may be climate policy. The allocation of emission rights, if marketable, could constitute a subsidy under the SCM agreement. If so, the granting of such subsidies could be an illegal actionable subsidy under SCM rules if the subsidies cause adverse trade effects.[75]

---

[71] See Choueke (2007).

[72] See, for example, Rosen and Houser (2007).

[73] WTO, "Lamy Highlights Environmental Dimension of Trade Talks," May 10, 2006.

[74] Selivanova (2007).

[75] Hufbauer, Charnovitz, and Kim (2009: 61–64, 87–88).

On fisheries subsidies, the interests of a developing country will depend on whether fishing is a significant sector for that country. About half of world fish exports come from developing countries.[76] Although all countries have an interest in preventing overfishing from wasteful and unnecessary government subsidies, developing countries, where fishing is a significant export opportunity, may want to preserve some flexible special and differential treatment. Developing countries could also ask for compensatory programs if the ensuing regimes lead to higher costs for their fishery imports.

The debate on environmental subsidies in the agriculture negotiations is complex, and it is hard to generalize an interest for developing countries. As in all WTO issues, developing countries should partner with like-minded countries in order to deploy analytical resources in the most efficient way. Greater market access for developing countries to export agricultural products to the United States and Europe will be of benefit to developing countries, and so, when developing countries call for reduction in subsidies and other concessions, environmental arguments should be marshaled. In particular, developing countries can criticize the harmful environmental results arising from subsidy programs relied upon by many high-income countries. In the past few years, a series of WTO tribunals have criticized the US practice of granting WTO-illegal subsidies to cotton farmers. The complaint was brought by Brazil, which, in mid 2010, threatened trade sanctions against the United States because the Obama Administration had not fully complied with the WTO ruling.

The TRIPS and Biodiversity issues are complex. Because these issues are of great interest to the private sector in the high-income countries, the negotiators from those countries will be especially well prepared. In response, developing countries have engineered their own coalitions and have obtained technical help from NGOs and the academic community. The history of TRIPS in the trading system demonstrates that vigilance is always needed because, in the Uruguay Round, leading governments were focused mainly on gratifying the interest groups promoting rights for holders of intellectual property. At present, the WTO TRIPS Council has refused to give observer status to the Biodiversity Convention. This exclusion cannot possibly help developing countries, and they might consider being more vociferous in asking for greater WTO transparency and cooperation.

The WTO is carrying out significant capacity building on trade and environment, but these efforts can be stepped up. Developing countries should not hesitate to request technical assistance when they need it and should work to assure that WTO rules on the provision of technical assistance provide for some quantitative assessments of the need for assistance by country, perhaps carried out by the WTO Secretariat or a UN body.

The WTO capacity building on trade and environment is just one small part of what is being carried out in this field by other international organizations and many governments. For example, UNEP and UNCTAD have delivered technical assistance for over

---

[76] The leading exporters are China, Thailand, Norway, the United States, Canada, Vietnam, Chile, Taiwan, Indonesia, and the European Union. Japan is the largest importer.

a decade. The European Union's programs are wide-ranging—for example, the Forest Law Enforcement, Governance and Trade Program that helps countries control illegal logging and exports.

As noted above, while there has been very little progress made in implementing Paragraph 51 of the Doha Declaration, it is still important for developing countries to have a robust and open forum to analyze and debate the environmental and developmental implications of the Doha negotiations. The developing countries ought to consider promoting better implementation of Paragraph 51 and more attention in the WTO to developing ways to operationalize the concept of sustainable development.

On RTA environmental negotiations, developing countries should recognize that, in trade agreements with developed countries, there is a possibility of using the RTA negotiations to achieve effective environmental cooperation agreements with real commitments of financial resources and technical assistance. To use the United States as an example, at the outset of new RTA negotiations, developing countries should develop alliances with US environmental NGOs and work with them to put political pressure on US negotiators to improve the environmental cooperation provisions in the trade agreement or side agreements. In 2013, the ongoing negotiations for the Trans-Pacific Partnership include an environmental dimension.

APPENDIX

CORE DEFINITIONS AND CONCEPTS

Border tax adjustment. The imposition of a charge on an imported product equivalent to an indirect domestic tax being imposed on that product or on an article from which the imported product has been manufactured or produced. Such adjustments are permitted under WTO rules. WTO rules also permit the remission of indirect taxes on exported products; such rebates may not be in excess of the domestic tax.

Eco-dumping. A term referring to exports with prices that are artificially low because they have been produced under environmental regulations that are inefficient for the exporting country. Just as anti-dumping duties can be calculated based on hypothetical prices in a market economy, an eco-dumping duty could be based on the hypothetical prices that would ensue if all environmental externalities were internalized. Eco-dumping duties have been proposed but none have been imposed. Sometimes a claim of eco-dumping is used more broadly without reference to what is efficient for an exporting country.

Environmental goods and services (EGS). EGS are goods and services whose use or consumption is thought to promote better environmental outcomes. No universally agreed definition of EGS exists but some obvious products include wind turbines, solar cooking appliances, and photovoltaic cells. Although some environmental services are grouped within the services sectoral list, environmental technologies do not have separate tariff categories in the harmonized system. Some EGS trade liberalization has already occurred in bilateral and regional trade agreements.

Environmental harmonization. The use of international benchmarks for environmental regulations and standards by governments. The use of international standards in the production of goods is called for in the WTO TBT and SPS Agreements. Indeed, SPS Article 3 is captioned "Harmonization." The main purpose of such harmonization measures is to facilitate trade by preventing idiosyncratic trade restrictions. Harmonization to international standards also has the potential of raising standards in countries that do not have adequate regulatory systems appropriate to their level of development.

Environmental impact assessment. A principle of national and international environmental policy calling for an assessment of the risk to human health and/or ecological services of a project and calling for the consideration of alternatives. Environmental assessments can also be focused on government policies such as international negotiations. The WTO Doha Declaration (para. 51) calls for debate within the WTO on the "developmental and environmental aspects of the negotiations...."

Environmental services. In a trade context, "environmental services" refers to services traded via one of the four modes of the GATS. Many environmental services are grouped in the WTO Services Sectoral Classification List in Sector 6. In an environmental context, the term refers to services performed by nature itself, such as the protection of soil by trees and the natural filtration and purification of water. This is one of many terms that is used in different ways by the trade community and the environment community.

Free rider. In an environmental context, a free rider is a country that enjoys the benefits of an environmental regime without following the rules of that regime or contributing to its maintenance.

Level of protection. Not to be confused with the trade concept of effective protection, the "level of protection" in the SPS Agreement refers to the level of sanitary or phytosanitary protection that a WTO member government chooses to protect human, animals, or plants in its territory.[77] The SPS Agreement implies that a government may choose the "level" of protection that it wants, but the Appellate Body has held that governments do not have an absolute or unqualified right to do so.[78] By contrast, the Appellate Body has held that the concept of autonomous choice of a desired level of protection exists for the level of health protection sought under the GATT and the level of morality sought under the GATS.[79]

Level playing field. A normative claim that countries should compete in international trade fairly. In an environment context, a level playing field claim is that a country with stringent environmental regulations will suffer in competition against a country with less stringent regulations. The term "level playing field" is often used to describe trade relations that are perceived as fair. For example, the Brazil–Aircraft (Article 21.5—Canada) panel stated that the Agreement on Subsidies and Countervailing Measures "establishes a level playing field for all Members in respect of export credit practices...."[80]

Multilateral environmental agreements (MEAs). An international treaty or convention aimed at an environmental purpose that invites all governments to join as parties. Many environmental

---

[77] Agreement on the Application of Sanitary and Phytosanitary Measures (SPS Agreement), Annex A, para. 5 (definition of appropriate level of protection).

[78] Appellate Body Report, *EC Measures Concerning Meat and Meat Products* (Hormones), WT/DS26/AB/R, para. 173, adopted February 13, 1998.

[79] Appellate Body Report, *European Communities—Measures Affecting Asbestos and Asbestos-Containing Products*, WT/DS135/AB/R, para. 168, adopted April 5, 2001; Appellate Body Report, *United States—Measures Affecting the Cross-Border Supply of Gambling and Betting Services*, WT/DS285/AB/R, para. 308, adopted April 20, 2005.

[80] Panel Report, *Brazil–Export Financing Programme for Aircraft—Recourse by Canada to Article 21.5 of the DSU*, WT/DS46/RW, para. 6.107, adopted August 4, 2000 as modified by Appellate Body Report.

treaties are regional rather than multilateral. The UN Convention on Biological Diversity is an example of an MEA. Many MEAs have international secretariats that help coordinate efforts undertaken under the agreement.

Polluter havens (or pollution havens). A political unit that seeks to draw in foreign investment through lower environmental standards or that attracts investment for that reason. The identification of polluter havens is controversial. Indeed, the category may be a theoretical concept that is non-existent in practice.

Polluter-pays principle (PPP). The PPP, originally devised by the OECD in 1972, states that the polluter should bear the expenses for carrying out measures that governmental authorities determine are needed to ensure that the environment is in an acceptable state. The rationale for having the polluter bear these costs is that these costs will be passed forward to the ultimate users. The PPP acknowledges that there may be exceptions in which government subsidies can be used particularly for transitional periods, provided that the subsidies do not lead to significant distortions in trade or investment. The WTO has not explicitly endorsed the PPP.

Precautionary principle. A principle of international environmental law stating where there are threats of serious or irreversible damage, lack of full scientific certainty shall not be used as a reason for postponing cost-effective measures to prevent environmental degradation. Some commentators aver that the precautionary principle also counsels that the proponent of an activity, rather than a regulator, should bear the burden of proof. In the EC–Hormones case, the Appellate Body noted that the precautionary principle "finds reflection" in one provision of WTO law.[81]

Processes and production methods (PPMs). PPM is a term from the Agreement on Technical Barriers to Trade (and its Tokyo Round predecessor) that refers to the way that a product is produced. Some PPMs may be detectable in the product, such as whether milk or cheese is pasteurized. Other PPMs require information about the producer or the product chain, such as dolphin-safe tuna. The PPM concept is in use throughout the trading system—for example, with rules of origin, intellectual property, countervailing duties, and antidumping—where products that are intrinsically "like" are treated differently based on extrinsic factors. Many WTO agreements recognize, permit, and/or require non-product-related trade restrictions. Nevertheless, one should note that PPM-based trade restrictions relating to environment, labor, or human rights are very controversial, and their status under WTO law remains to be tested.

Sustainable development. Sustainable development is development that meets the needs of the present without compromising the ability of future generations to meet their own needs. To operationalize this amorphous term, environmentalists point to the need for sustainable production and consumption and the need for decision-making that seeks simultaneously to achieve economic and environmental (and sometimes also social) goals. In the *US–Shrimp* case, the panel stated that "sustainable development is one of the objectives of the WTO Agreement."[82] The goal of sustainable development is endorsed in the Doha Declaration.

"Trade-and" linkages. Trade-and linkages are the interconnections between international trade and labor," "trade and health," "trade and competition policy," "trade and investment," "trade and human rights," "trade and culture," and "trade and gender." Although not always

---

[81] Appellate Body Report, *EC–Hormones,* ibid. para. 124 (referring to SPS Article 5.7).

[82] Panel Report, *United States—Import Prohibition of Certain Shrimp and Shrimp Products—Recourse to Article 21.5 of the DSU by Malaysia,* WT/DS58/RW, para. 5.54, adopted November 21, 2001 as modified by Appellate Body report.

explicitly identified as such, the WTO has provisions addressing all of these "trade-and" linkages on this list except the last one. The linkages between "trade and development" are explicitly recognized in the WTO.

Trade-related environmental measures (TREMs). A measure in an environmental treaty, law, or regulation that affects trade. Disputes about TREMs can be lodged in the WTO. For example, the EC–Asbestos case involved a complaint by the Government of Canada about a French decree that banned the manufacture, sale, or importation of asbestos fibers and any product containing such fibers. The purpose of the decree was to prevent harm to human health. TREMs that inhibit trade are regularly used for environmental purposes. Of course, most measures that inhibit trade are trade measures, not environmental measures. For example, tariffs, quotas, and countervailing duties are trade related measures.

Win–win. A descriptor often used by government officials and the business community to suggest that coherent government policies can deliver victories for both the economy and the environment. Win–win is also used to connote a dual win for environment and development. Another descriptor is "win–win–win," which suggests that coherent policies can deliver wins for the economic, environmental, and social aspects of development. In the context of corporate responsibility, the term "triple bottom line" suggests business strategies that promote financial gains for the company, social gains for workers, and social and environmental gains for a broader community.

References

Note: The references referring to WTO cases and other official reports and documents are cited in the chapter footnotes.

Bacchus, J. (2010), 'Combating Climate Change. How WTO Rules Can Speed Up Global Action.' Forbes.com, April 26, available at <http://www.forbes.com/2010/04/26/climate-change-global-wto-opinions-contributors-james-bacchus.html>. (accessed April 2013).

Bennhold, K. (2007), 'France Tells U.S. to Sign Climate Pacts Or Face Tax.' *New York Times*, February 1, p. 10.

Busse, M. (2004), 'Trade, Environmental Regulations and the World Trade Organization.' World Bank Policy Research Working Paper 3361, July.

Choueke, M. (2007), 'Antigua Defeats US in Challenge to Gaming Law.' *Sunday Telegraph* (London), January 28, p. 1.

Cosbey, A., Peterson, L. E., and Pintér, L. (2005), Environmental Health and International Trade. Winnipeg: IISD. Available at <http://www.iisd.org/publications/pub.aspx?id=713> (accessed April 2013).

Cosbey, A. (ed.) (2008), *Trade and Climate Change: Issues in Perspective.* Winnipeg: International Institute for Sustainable Development.

Grether, J.-M., Mathys, N. A., and de Melo, J. (2006), 'Unraveling the Worldwide Pollution Haven Effect.' World Bank Policy Research Paper Working Paper 4047, November.

Houser, T., Bradley, R., Childs, B., Werksman, J., and Heilmayr, R. (2008), *Leveling the Carbon Playing Field.* Washington DC: Peterson Institute for International Economics.

Hufbauer, G. C., Charnovitz, S., and Kim, J. (2009), *Global Warming and the World Trading System.* Washington DC: Peterson Institute for International Economics.

ICTSD (2008), *Climate Change and Trade on the Road to Copenhagen*. Geneva: International Centre for Trade and Sustainable Development.

Lamy, P. (2006), 'The World Trade Organization: A Laboratory for Global Governance.' Malcolm Wiener Lecture, November, 1. Available at <http://www.wto.org/english/news_e/sppl_e/sppl47_e.htm> (accessed April 2013).

Mani, M., and Jha, S. (2006), 'Trade Liberalization and the Environment in Vietnam.' World Bank Policy Research Working Paper No. 3879, April.

Moltke, A. von (ed.) (2010). *Fisheries Subsidies, Sustainable Development and the WTO*. London: Earthscan.

Nordström, H., and Vaughan, S. (1999), 'Trade and the Environment.' WTO Special Studies 4, available at <http://www.wto.org/english/res_e/publications_e/special_studies4_e.htm> (accessed April 2013).

Rosen, D. H., and Houser, T. (2007), 'China Energy: A Guide for the Perplexed.' Washington DC: Peterson Institute for International Economics and Center for Strategic and International Studies, April.

Selivanova, J. (2007), 'The WTO and Energy: WTO Rules and Agreements of Relevance to the Energy Sector.' ICTSD Trade and Sustainable Energy Series Issue Paper No. 1.

UNEP and WWF (2009), The WTO Fishery Subsidies Negotiation: Update and Introductory Briefing for New Delegates', April 1, available at <http://www.unep.ch/etb/events/WTO%20FS%20workshop%201%20Apr%202009/Meeting%20Report%20UNEP-WWF%20Briefing%201April09.pdf> (accessed April 2013).

Vilas-Ghiso, S. J., and Liverman, D. M. (2006), 'Scale, Technique and Composition Effects in the Mexican Agricultural Sector: The Influence of NAFTA and the Institutional Environment.' Montreal: North American Commission on Environmental Cooperation.

Vranes, E. (2009), *Trade and the Environment*. London: Oxford University Press.

World Bank (2007), *International Trade and Climate Change: Economic, Legal and Institutional Perspectives*. Washington DC: The World Bank.

WTO (2005), 'Trade Policy Review Nigeria, Report by the Secretariat.' WT/TPR/S/xx147, April 13, 2005.

WTO (2005), 'Trade Can Be a Friend, and Not a Foe, of Conservation.' Pascal Lamy: speech at WTO symposium on Trade and sustainable Development within the framework of paragraph 51 of the Doha Ministerial Declaration. Geneva, October 10.

WTO (2006), 'Lamy Urges Members to Support Multilateral Environmental Accords.' May, 30.

WTO (2007), 'Lamy Urges Support for Environmental Chapter of the Doha Round.' February 5. Available at <http://www.wto.org/english/news_e/sppl_e/sppl54_e.htm> (accessed April 2013).

WTO (2010a), Lamy: 'Trade Opening has Much to Contribute to the Protection of the Environment', June 5. Available at <http://www.wto.org/english/news_e/news10_e/dgpl_05jun10_e.htm> (accessed April 2013).

WTO (2010b), 'DDG Yerxa Cites Benefits of More Open Trade on the Environment', March, 26. Available at <http://www.wto.org/english/news_e/news10_e/envir_26mar10_e.htm> (accessed April 2013).

WTO and UNEP (2009), 'Trade and Climate Change. A Report by the United Nations Environment Programme and the World Trade Organization.' Available at <http://www.wto.org/english/res_e/booksp_e/trade_climate_change_e.pdf> (accessed April 2013).

CHAPTER 30

INTERNATIONAL TRADE AND LABOR STANDARDS

T. N. SRINIVASAN[*]

I. INTRODUCTION

GLOBALIZATION, a process of integration of national economies, has gathered steam since the 1980s. The increase in exports of labor-intensive products from developing countries to developed countries that occurs with globalization is being viewed as a competitive threat by the producers of their substitutes in the latter countries. This has given a new lease on life[1] to the centuries-old pauper labor argument. Protectionist lobbies in developed countries argue that "low labor standards" in developing countries not only confer on them an unfair competitive advantage, but also competition from imports from such countries would erode their own high labor standards. In their view, imports from them constitute a form of dumping (i.e., social dumping). An implication of this argument is that since the rules of international trade incorporated in the General Agreement on Tariffs and Trade (GATT) and subsumed in the World Trade Organization (WTO) do not cover permissible actions against "social dumping," any future international trade agreements, bilateral, plurilateral, and multilateral, ought to include a "social clause" conditioning access to export markets to the exported products having been produced under suitably high "labor standards."

Besides protectionist lobbies, there are also well-meaning groups in developed countries genuinely interested in improving the living conditions of workers in poor countries. They view labor rights and standards as a part of *universal* human rights, and there

---

* Samuel C. Park, Jr. Professor of Economics, Yale University. This chapter draws extensively from Srinivasan (1996a, 1996b). I want to thank Kimberly Elliott for her comments though I did not agree with most of them! This version of the chapter was completed on June 15, 2007. Other than briefly taking into account some subsequent developments, till mid 2009 in a Postscript, I have left it as it was.

[1] This argument claims "that under conditions of free trade industries will relocate to countries with low wages [and] or firms will employ the very poorest people on very low wage rates, forcing down all wages as a result." (Meadowcroft, 2006: 1).

is therefore a moral obligation on their part to promote the spread of labor rights across the globe (Brown and Stern, 2007). They also see an opportunity for doing so in a social clause in trade agreements. Their reasoning is that since globalization enables poor countries to successfully pursue an export-led strategy of growth and development, they would be interested in improving labor standards at home if doing so becomes a precondition for the pursuit of the strategy. Thus these well-meaning groups view the social clause as an incentive or a carrot for poor countries to raise labor standards, in particular by eliminating child labor. In contrast, the protectionists view it as a stick to punish poor countries with low labor standards by denying them market access.

Various US administrations, Democrat and Republican, have proposed the inclusion of a labor standards article in the GATT, unsuccessfully as it turns out, during several rounds of multilateral trade negotiations. Thus the demand for formal inclusion of labor standards in the mandate of the WTO is not a surprise except in its timing, namely, that it was raised after the painful and lengthy Uruguay Round negotiations had been completed, almost holding the negotiated agreement hostage.[2] The agreement was signed, but not without an understanding that the topic of labor standards could be discussed by the preparatory committee that established the WTO in 1995.

At the first Ministerial meeting of the WTO in Singapore in 1996, the ministers declared:

> We renew our commitment to the observance of internationally recognized core labor standards. The International Labor Organization (ILO) is the competent body to set and deal with these standards, and we affirm our support for its work in promoting them. We believe that economic growth and development fostered by increased trade and further trade liberalization contribute to the promotion of these standards. We reject the use of labor standards for protectionist purposes, and agree that the comparative advantage of countries, particularly low-wage developing countries, must in no way be put into question. In this regard, we note that the WTO and ILO Secretariats will continue their existing collaboration.[3]

The Fourth Ministerial Conference at Doha in 2001 reaffirmed the Singapore declaration (WTO, 1996) on labor standards. The Ministerial Conference at Hong Kong in 2005 in turn reaffirmed the Doha Declaration. As of March 2007 there are no committees or working parties dealing with the issue in the WTO. However, the secretariats of

---

[2] Kimberly Elliott (hereafter, Elliott), in her comment, suggests that although US trade legislation as far back as 1974 called for US negotiators to include discussion of labor standards in trade negotiations, these calls were largely hortatory. This is not persuasive—negotiators from other countries normally took US demands seriously given the importance of the US in the world trading system. My use of the world "hostage" is not overblown: after all, the draft agreement concluding the negotiations did not mention labor standards, not because the US negotiators had not raised them earlier, but only because there was no consensus to include them. Hence raising it again after a consensus agreement had been drafted is indeed trying to hold it hostage.

[3] Elliott's comment that such cooperation was non-existent, even if true, is irrelevant: the only relevant point is that the ministers, from the Singapore Ministerial onward, were firmly committed to leaving labor standards in the ILO.

the WTO and ILO work together on technical issues under the banner of "coherence" in global economic policymaking.

Although the Ministerial Conference, the highest decision-making body of the WTO, is yet to change its consensus of Singapore to leave the setting of and dealing with labor standards to the ILO, it does not mean that the issue has been put to rest in international trade negotiations. It continues to be an item in preferential trade agreements in which the United States and European Union are signatories. From being included in a side agreement to the main trade agreement, as in the North American Free Trade Agreement (NAFTA), it has since been elevated to being a part of subsequent trade agreements themselves, as in the USA–Jordan, the USA–Morocco, and subsequent US free trade agreements. Indeed, the chances of renewal, after its expiry in June 2007, of the Trade Promotion Authority ceded to the President by the US Congress depends on whether the President will insist that a commitment to core labor standards is included in any future trade agreements, including any multilateral agreement from the Doha Round (*New York Times*, March 6, 2007, C1). Whether or not the Democratic majority in the US Congress would insist on such a commitment to include only bilateral, but not necessarily in multilateral, agreements as Elliott claims, is moot. If the majority was serious about the issue, drawing a distinction between bilateral and multilateral agreements would make no sense.

The literature on labor standards has grown enormously since the 1990s, with many theoretical and fewer empirical studies (Flanagan, 2003, 2006, and 2007). Basu et al. (2003) collected the papers (with comments) that grew out of a conference on international labor standards sponsored by the Ministry of Foreign Affairs, Government of Sweden. The conference papers cover the history, theory, and policy options relating to the topic. Another policy oriented study is Flanagan and Gould (2003). Studies by international institutions concerned with development (e.g., Organization for Economic Cooperation and Development (OECD) and The World Bank), international trade (e.g., The WTO), and labor (ILO) have also been published. I will not attempt to summarize this vast literature in a critical perspective. Instead, I will selectively draw on it for exploring some of the questions that have been raised on labor standards from several perspectives, *inter alia*, economic theory, national and international aspects, equity and fairness. The objective is to examine the strength of the case for inclusion of a social clause in the WTO or, more broadly, "whether trade actions could be used to impose labor standards or whether this would simply be an excuse for protectionism" (WTO, 2005). More specifically, I will address the following four broad questions raised in WTO (2005):

The analytical question: if a country has lower standards for labor rights, do its exports gain an unfair advantage? Would this force all countries to lower their standards (the "race to the bottom")?

The response question: if there is a "race to the bottom," should countries only trade with those that have similar labor standards?

The question of rules: Should WTO rules explicitly allow governments to take trade action as a means of putting pressure on other countries to comply?

The institutional question: is the WTO the proper place to discuss and set rules on labor—or to enforce them, including those of the ILO?

The chapter is structured as follows: Section II is devoted to definitions of labor standards in the literature ranging from the so-called "core" labor standards of ILO conventions to others that include hours of work, minimum wage, and other conditions of work. The question whether the standards should be viewed as *universal* and *eternal* norms that ought to apply *in any country* and *at any time* or whether they are spatial and temporal context specific, for example, the stage of economic development of a country will be examined for its implication for the choice of standards in international agreements. Section III is on the analytics of labor standards in economic theory. Appendix I starts from simple models of determination of labor standards in a competitive, but autarkic, market economy in equilibrium. It then moves on to the issue of appropriate interventions in the market if the standards obtaining in equilibrium are not deemed to be socially optimal. Ethical and moral issues will naturally arise in discussing individual and social optimality. Additionally, tradeoffs, if any are involved, between allocational efficiency and welfare optimum are discussed.

Appendix II introduces international trade and goods services. It is shown that there is no reason in general for labor standards to be uniform across countries in a global competitive market equilibrium under free trade. Ethical and moral considerations surface again, but this time also raising an additional issue, namely, the appropriateness or otherwise of one or more countries having a say on the ethical values of other countries, let alone their trying to impose their values on them. Section IV turns to the analytical and response questions of the WTO by asking whether there are cross-border spillovers and externalities with respect to labor standards that make it likely that non-cooperative unilateral exercise of policies regarding labor standards by each country would lead to an inferior equilibrium in a Pareto sense, compared to one that could be achieved with cooperation. This naturally leads to the questions of whether a "race to the bottom" is inevitable if countries do not cooperate, and if they do, whether the cooperative equilibria could be sustained through appropriate punishment of deviators from cooperation. In Appendix III, by means of a simple numerical illustration of equilibria of bilateral non-cooperative games, shows that although Pareto inferior equilibria of the so-called prisoner's dilemma situation can arise, they are not inevitable. Be that as it may, the use of trade policy interventions is inappropriate to prevent a race to the bottom. Section IV discusses this and the concerns in high-income countries about low labor standards in poor countries, particularly about child labor, from purely altruistic considerations. It argues that there are alternatives that are better from the perspectives of high-income countries and the workers in poor countries than the use of trade sanctions in expressing such concerns.Section IV concludes with a discussion of the empirical evidence on labor standards in international competition.

In the WTO there is a Dispute Settlement Mechanism (DSM) that enforces its rules and also allows for punishment of those who are held not only to have violated the rules, but also are not vacating the violation. The existence of DSM is one of the major considerations for proponents of the inclusion of a social clause in trade agreements concluded under the auspices of the WTO. Even if such a case for linking trade and labor standards can be made on a purely *instrumental*, rather than an *intrinsic* ground, still there could be more attractive alternatives to linkage for raising labor standards in poor countries. Section V discusses some of these alternatives. Section VI concludes the chapter with a statement of its key messages, and Section VII is a Postscript that discusses some significant recent developments since the chapter was initially written.

II. What are Labor Standards?

Alternative Definitions

The ILO's Governing Body has identified eight ILO conventions "as fundamental to the rights of human beings at work, *irrespective of the level of development of individual member states*" (ILO, 2002: 7, emphasis added) and view them "as a pre-condition for all the others in that they provide a necessary framework from which to strive freely for the improvement of individual and collective conditions of work" (ILO, 2002) . The set of "core labor standards or principles" was endorsed by the international community (i.e., members of the ILO) in the ILO's 1998 Declaration on Fundamental Principles and Rights at work (ILO, 2004). Specifically, the eight conventions, with the earliest, No. 29, on forced labor adopted in 1929 and the most recent, No. 182. on worst forms of child labor, adopted in 1999 cover four main areas: [4]

- Freedom of association and the effective recognition of the right to collective bargaining (conventions 87 and 98).
- The elimination of all forms of force or compulsory labor (conventions 29 and 105).
- The effective abolition of child labor (conventions 128 and 182).
- The elimination of discrimination in respect of employment and occupation (conventions 100 and 111).

Labor standards in the Fair Labor Standards Act in the United States also include a basic minimum wage and overtime pay. The Act covers most private and public employment. It requires employers to pay covered employees who are not otherwise exempt at least the federal minimum wage and overtime pay of one-and-one-half-times the regular rate of pay. For non-agricultural operations, it restricts the hours that children under age 16 can work and forbids the employment of children under age 18 in certain jobs deemed too dangerous. For agricultural operations, it prohibits the employment of children under age 16, during school hours and in certain jobs

---

[4] Elliott claims that the declaration focused on four principles but not the detailed obligations of the underlying conventions. This distinction between principles and obligations is not tenable since the principles have no force unless they are backed up by obligations.

deemed too dangerous (<http://www.dol.gov/compliance/laws/comp-flsa.htm>). The fact that the Act, strictly speaking, applies only to US domestic standards is not significant, since domestic standards, if they do override higher international standards, will rob any content of the latter.

In its free trade agreements (FTA) that were concluded prior to 2007, the US required its FTA partners to protect "international labor standards," namely, the Core Labor Standards of the ILO, even though the US has ratified only two (105 on Abolition of Force Labor and 182 on Worst Forms of Child Labor). Interestingly, while an overwhelming majority, namely 126 of 180 members of ILO, has ratified all the eight conventions, the USA is one of four who have ratified no more than one or two (<http://www.ilo.org/ilolex/english/docs/declworld.htm>).[5] Apparently, in its future FTAs, the USA will give its FTA partners the option of meeting the ILO's core labor standards or having labor laws that are generally equivalent to the rights and protections under US Federal Labor Standards. If the FTA partner chooses the first option, it commits itself to meeting standards set in ILO conventions that the USA is not required to meet since it has not ratified them. If it chooses the second option, it has to set and meet standards for minimum wage, overtime pay, and so on, that are yet to be recognized as international labor standards by the ILO. Moran and Hufbauer (2007) point out that "US labor laws are either openly inconsistent with core ILO standards or they could be challenged by lawyers if ILO standards trumped established statutes and longstanding interpretations. A trade agreement that enthroned ILO standards would not only alter federal law, it would also override state laws—triggering a constitutional [crisis]...The practical effect would be to stop US trade negotiations."[6] The authors conclude that including ILO standards in multilateral trade agreements would end up bringing an end to the entire trade negotiating process and thus hurting millions of poor around the world.

To be fair, it must be said that non-ratification of a convention by a member of ILO does not necessarily imply that the standards covered by the unratified conventions prevailing in that member state do not meet the levels set by the convention. Still, non-ratification by a member does raise the question of whether the member subscribes to

---

[5] Ratification of conventions is voluntary with no formal means in the ILO for ensuring that signatories of conventions also ratify them in a reasonable time. However, once a sufficient number of signatories of a convention notify it, the convention comes into force, and it has been suggested that it then becomes binding on all members of the ILO regardless of whether they have signed or ratified it. Whether this is correct or not, as Flanagan (2007) argues, ratification requires national leaders to take the possibly costly political action of bringing national laws to conform to standards specified in the relevant ILO conventions. On the other hand, non-ratification has virtually no costs. Presumably leaders derive some value from signing a convention while not necessarily committing to incurring the costs of ratification. Then ratification becomes an endogenous act requiring pre-existing labor conditions so that public costs of ratification are lower if pre-existing domestic standards are low enough to be international standards. Flanagan (2003) finds empirical support for endogeneity. See also Chau and Kanbur (2001) for an empirical model of adoption of ILO conventions.

[6] Elliott correctly points out that in US law treaties are not self-executing and implementing legislation has to be enacted to execute them. However, if negotiators of other countries anticipate such legislation is unlikely to be enacted, they would have no incentive to negotiate with the USA in the first place.

the universality and eternity claimed for the core standards, namely, they are "rights of human beings at work, irrespective of level of development of individual member states" (ILO, 2002: 7). Indeed, the Council of Economic Advisers to the President of the United States did claim that core labor standards represented "fundamental human and democratic rights that should prevail in all societies whatever their level of development" (CEA, 1995).[7]

International organizations such as the OECD and United Nations also claim that "core labor standards are a part and parcel of basic human rights, that the body of that should apply in all societies whatever their level of development" (CEA, 1995). Clearly the appeal of core labor standards lies in their being viewed as basic human rights. It is useful therefore to examine whether such a view is sound.

Basic Human Rights and Core Labor Standards

OECD (1996: 27) points out that a body of international law on human rights, including certain basic workers' rights, has evolved that "considers human rights as universal, transcending all political, economic, social and cultural situations. They are characterized as such because they involve the fundamental liberty, dignity and respect of the individual. Moreover, freedom of association, prohibition of forced labor, elimination of child labor exploitation and the principle of non-discrimination are well established elements of the human rights international jurisprudence; in fact these workers' rights are an inseparable part of human rights."

Sen (1999) identifies three broad critiques to the human rights approach—a legitimacy critique (a confounding of the consequences of legal systems with pre-legal principles), a coherence critique (rights do not mean much as long as there is no agency that has the duty to provide such rights), and a cultural critique (there are no universal values underpinning the rights)—only to argue against the significance of all three. I do not find his arguments, particularly the ones against legitimacy and coherence critiques, persuasive. For example, in dismissing the legitimacy critique, Sen argues that human rights are best seen as a set of ethical claims that must not be identified with legislated legal rights, and that their plausibility should be judged on the basis of ethical reasoning and as the basis of political demands. Clearly, the legitimacy critique is not about human rights as the basis for ethical reasoning (i.e., pre-legal principles), but rather about their status as entitlements sanctioned by law. Sen also dismisses the coherence critique on the ground that human rights are rights shared by all regardless of citizenship, the benefits of which rights everyone should

---

[7] Elliott claims that the fact that 89 per cent of ILO members have ratified eight core conventions *ipso facto*, this makes them universal and eternal. First of all, not all nations of the world are members of ILO, and, in any case, 89 per cent is not 100 per cent! Second, ratification essentially means that the content of the conventions represents at best universal aspirations to be attained sometime in the future.

have. It seems odd to claim that everyone should have a benefit, while it is not the duty of anyone to ensure that everyone does indeed enjoy that benefit. The cultural critique is also relevant since the values underpinning the core labor standards are not universally shared.[8]

Equally unpersuasive is an appeal to natural rights, that is, universal rights that are seen as inherent in the nature of human beings and not contingent on human actions or beliefs, as the foundation of core labor standards. Clearly labor standards, even as rights relating to human beings at work, cannot be divorced from how work is organized, and such organization is a consequence of human action. As such, they are contingent on such action. This in turn implies that the standards have to be contingent on the stage of development since organization of work depends on the stage of development.

Even if one were to deem core labor standards as basic human rights, one could still ask why one would have to go beyond the already existing conventions and charters on human rights. For example, ever since its creation, the United Nations (UN) has been concerned with human rights. Article 55 of the UN charter requires that countries should, *inter alia*, promote respect for human rights and basic liberties for all, without distinction of race, gender, language, or religion, not only as an end in itself, but also as a necessary condition for maintenance of peaceful relations between countries. The Universal Declaration of Human Rights of 1948, adopted by the UN General Assembly without dissent, gives an even more detailed description of human rights. These include

> civil and political rights (the right to life, liberty, freedom from torture, freedom of opinion and expression, freedom from slavery and servitude, right to peaceful assembly and association) and economic, social and cultural rights (right to join and form trade unions, right to work, right to equal pay for equal work, right to education). Again, the right to decent living standards is regarded as one important element. (OECD, 1996: 27)

The Declaration did not require ratification. It took nearly 20 years to transform the principles of the Declaration into treaty provisions establishing legal obligations on the part of each ratifying state. At the end of 1966, two covenants, one dealing with civil and political rights, the other with economic, social, and cultural rights, and an optional protocol were adopted by the General Assembly. Another 10 years elapsed

---

[8] Elliott suggests that the wide acceptance of the human rights declaration implies universality, and that governments of countries that either have not ratified or have abstained from voting on the declaration are not strong democracies and may not be representing the views of their people. The relevance of this comment is not apparent. The members of the UN who are signatories as well as non-signatories of the declaration are nation states. The UN membership does not require "strong democracy" as a pre-condition. As such, a government that has signed and ratified the declaration could well be non-democratic!

before the required minimum number of states ratified the two covenants and the optional protocol. As of 1998, a total of 132 states (including the USA) have ratified the covenant on civil and political rights, 133 the covenant on economic, social, and cultural rights, and 87 the optional protocol. The USA has signed, but not ratified, the covenant on economic, social, and cultural rights and is not a signatory of the optional protocol.[9]

An even larger number of states (168) has ratified the UN convention on the Rights of the Child adopted in 1989. Clearly the obligations of the Charter are binding on members of the UN and, as such, one does not need to include labor standards as obligations of trade agreements, if countries that enter into trade agreements are already obliged to meet them because they are members of the UN.

Besides international agreements, conventions, and covenants, the constitutions of some countries require their government to promote human rights. For example, the Constitution of India has a chapter entitled Directive Principles of State Policy that enjoins the state to strive to secure "a social order in which justice—social, economic, and political—shall inform all the institutions of national life" and "to minimize inequality in income, status, facilities and opportunities, amongst individuals and groups." Further, the state is required to ensure "that the ownership and control of the material resources of the community are so distributed as best to subscribe to the common good; that the operation of the economic system does not result in the concentration of wealth and means of production to the common detriment" (Basu, 1983). The constitution also protects the rights to work, to education, and to public assistance in case of unemployment, disability, or sickness. This review leads to two conclusions. First, except for a notable few, almost all states have signed and ratified a set of covenants that recognize an immense and overwhelming array of civil, political, economic, social, and cultural rights that go beyond the few so-called "core" labor standards selected by the proponents of the Social Clause, whether at the OECD or by the CEA in Washington. That selectivity must be explained and has to do, in all likelihood, with competitive pressures rather than human rights (Bhagwati, 1995). Second, almost none of the many rights are satisfied in reality, including in OECD countries. For example, discrimination on the basis of race and sex still exists even in the USA. This suggests that, at best, the rights recognized are universal aspirations, perhaps to be attained at some unspecified and distant future, though cynics might view them as empty rhetoric. Be that as it may, it is worth reiterating that the claim of universality and eternity, for a subset of rights covering the so-called "core" labor standards, is overblown.[10]

---

[9] I thank Bruce Russet for enlightening me on the history of human rights in the United Nations.

[10] Elliott argues that the issue is not one of universality but of enforcement of standards. But this distinction is not persuasive: insisting on enforcement of something that is not universally agreed as appropriate has no moral foundation. Of course, universality is meaningful only in the context of a multilateral agreement covering all countries. For bilateral agreements, it is not universality, but the two parties sharing the same values, that is relevant.

III. ANALYTICS OF LABOR STANDARDS

There is an extensive and growing literature on the economics (theoretical and empirical) of labor standards (see Brown et al. (1997) and references therein). I will leave it to interested readers to explore the major contributions in depth. [11] The model of Srinivasan (1996a) is reproduced in Appendix I. It demonstrates that diversity in labor standards among countries is not only legitimate but also does not detract from the case for free trade. In other words, such diversity, like diversity in tastes, technology, or factor endowments, is a source for gainful trade based on comparative advantage.

The model postulates, as Brown et al. (1996) do, that standards enter as arguments, in addition to inputs in production functions and also in utility functions of consumers, for the amounts consumed of various goods. The model begins with a simple world without international trade consisting of many autarkic economies. Each economy in this simple world produces and consumes two goods. Its convex production technology is represented by the production possibility frontier (PPF) of the technology with the two goods, and factor endowments could differ among countries. Consumer welfare is represented by a standard, concave Samuelson social utility function with the consumption of two goods and labor standards as arguments. Utility functions also could differ among countries. In a social welfare optimum, the production (and consumption) levels and labor standards will be functions of each country's factor endowments, and as such they will legitimately differ across countries.

In Appendix II the model of Appendix I is extended to a world of trading open economies by viewing each of them as small open economies taking the equilibrium relative price in world markets of one good in terms of the other as given, first leaving implicit how this global market-clearing equilibrium price is determined and then making it explicit as part of the determination of equilibrium levels of outputs, consumptions, and labor standards of each of the countries in a Global Pareto Optimum

---

[11] These include Anderson (1998), Bagwell (2000), Bagwell and Staiger (2002), Barry and Reddy (2006, 2008), Brown (2000), Brown et al. (1996, 1997, 2002), Dehejia and Samy (2004, 2006), De Waart (1996), Elliott and Freeman (2003), Enders (1996), Fields (1996, 2006), Freeman (1994), Genugten (2006), Golub (1997), Maskus (1997, 2002, 2004), Mishan (2005), Panagariya (2001a, 200b, 2002), Raynauld and Vidal (1998), Sensenberger and Campbell (1994), Singh (2003), Stern (1997), and Zhao (2006). Singh (2003), in particular, provides a comprehensive survey of alternative theoretical perspectives. Chapter 1 of Aidt and Tzannatos (2002) is entitled "Globalization versus International Labor Standards." The study is addressed to the economic effects of unions and collective bargaining in a global environment. It finds that adoption of freedom of association and collective bargaining do not adversely affect the costs and benefits of globalization. However, it does not take into account fully the fact that in many large developing countries, such as India, self-employment, rather than wage employment, is the dominant mode of employment. The relevance of this study for such countries is limited. I thank Kim Elliott for this reference.

(GPO) subject to market clearance. If the chosen GPO is not one that corresponds to a laissez-faire competitive market equilibrium (CME) with each country's trade being balanced, income transfer across countries would be needed to sustain it as a CME. In either case, the Pareto Optimum will be characterized by free trade and diversity in labor standards.

IV. Departures from the First-Best and Cross-Border Spillovers

The analyses of Appendices I and II show that diversity in labor standards or the implementation of a common minimal standard do not call for deviation from free trade as long as Global Pareto Optimality is the objective, and there is willingness not only to make income transfers between countries as necessary but also, to the extent standards in one country directly affect the welfare of another, such externalities are internalized in each country. What if this situation of "first-best" does not obtain? In answering this question, it is useful to distinguish between departures from first-best in a closed economy from those in an open economy. Obviously the possible use of trade policy to improve labor standards arises only in an open economy.

In a closed economy, labor standards could be sub-optimally low because of possible market failures. For example, if improving the safety of the work environment involves some initial investment that will pay off in terms of improved future worker productivity, and if capital markets are not efficient, the employer may not be able to obtain the resources for such investment. Suffice it to say that departures from first-best arising from domestic market failures do not raise new issues in the context of labor standards. And policies that address the failure at its source (the capital market in the above example) are the appropriate interventions. Even if there are no market failures, so that the prevailing labor standards are consistent with a domestic Pareto Optimum, still the real income distribution associated with the laissez-faire Pareto Optimum may be deemed unsatisfactory. In particular, the labor standards (along with factor and commodity prices) are also a reflection of the real income distribution. Changing the income distribution through policy will also change the equilibrium labor standards. Once again, there is nothing peculiar to labor standards in this and, as seen in the international context earlier, non-distortionary lump-sum income (or wealth) redistribution policy is the first-best to move the income distribution (and consequently the equilibrium labor standards) in the right direction. Of course the "unrealism" and/or infeasibility (for informational reasons) of lump-sum transfers can arise in this as well as myriad other contexts where such transfers are the first-best polices. But once you move away from first-best to what might be second-best, the answer invariably will be context specific. No general answers can be expected. If the first-best policy is infeasible, then other policies (such as, for example, commodity or factor taxes or subsidies) could in principle be used to achieve a better income distribution and labor standards, albeit at the cost of a dead-weight loss. In general, which taxes and what levels are to be used in achieving the desired change in labor standards while minimizing the dead-weight loss will vary across economies.

In open economies, it is clear that in the absence of a first-best non-trade related policy, trade policies could be used to change equilibrium labor standards. This can be seen simply in the case of trade in a two-country world, where one of the countries is "small" in that it behaves as if it has no influence on its terms of trade. As we saw earlier, a "small" open economy's optimal choice of its labor standard depends on its factor endowment and terms of trade. By exercising its own trade policy instrument, say tariffs or quotas, the large country can influence the terms of trade faced by the small country and thereby affect its choice of labor standards. If the small country's labor standard influences the welfare of the citizens of the large country (because of their humanitarian concerns), then the terms-of-trade effect of its choice of tariffs has two effects on the welfare of the large country. The first is the usual direct welfare effect of changes in terms of trade and the second is the indirect welfare effect arising from induced changes in the small country's labor standard. To the extent that a tariff shifts the terms of trade in favor of the large country, the first effect is positive. But the second effect could be negative since the adverse shift in terms of trade of the small country might induce a reduction in its labor standard. Depending on the balance between the two effects, it is possible that by choosing its welfare maximizing tariff, the large country could induce the small country to improve its labor standards relative to free trade.[12] But it could also deteriorate the standards if the balance between the two effects were different. The upshot is that if first-best policy instruments are unavailable, trade policy instruments could, though not necessarily would, help in raising labor standards in poor countries. However, the welfare of such countries need not rise.

Race to the Bottom and Non-Cooperative Equilibria

Is a Race to the Bottom Inevitable?

The analysis of Appendix II of Section III, by focusing on global Pareto Optimality supported by international transfers, assumes that nations cooperate with each other in settling globally optimal policies within and among nations. What if such cooperation is absent? One aspect of the absence of cooperation is the fear of a "race to the bottom."

---

[12] With spillover externalities, a laissez-faire free trade equilibrium is not Pareto Optimal. However with a one-way spillover effect (i.e., labor standards of the small country affect the welfare of the large country and not vice versa), with the unilateral exercise of market power by the large country, even though labor standards of the small country improve over its free trade value, the welfare of the small country need not.

It arises from the expectation that faced with competition from low cost (*because* of their low labor standards) developing countries, producers in countries with high labor standards would lobby for lowering labor standards at home by threatening to move production to low labor-standard countries. Those who harbor such fears have the option of not buying such imported products so that domestic producers will no longer face import competition.[13]

By not buying products of a firm or a country that does not observe what consumers view as acceptable labor standards, they can send a clear and effective signal to that firm or country to force it to choose between observing standards and retaining the market or losing the market altogether.[14] If it chooses to retain the market by observing acceptable labor standards, to the extent that the cost of the import goes up because of such observance, both the exporting country and the buyers of imports share the cost of improving labor standards. If it chooses to forego the market, then while workers in the exporting industry do not gain welfare through higher standards, there is a penalty to the firm in the form of lost exports. If the citizens of the developed countries are interested only in raising the welfare of the workers and not in penalizing the exporting firm, they will have to compensate the firm or make income transfer to workers. The basic point is that there is a real cost to raising labor standards, and that has to be incurred if the intended raise is to come about.

It should also be pointed out that the standard characterization of a "race to the bottom" as the unique non-cooperative equilibrium of a classic Prisoner's Dilemma game can be questioned. Appendix III illustrates this using a game of strategy between two countries with respect to their choice of labor standards, with a conventional payoff matrix in terms of real incomes and two alternative strategies of low and high labor standards.

---

[13] Elliott comments that "if consumer utility in the high standards country is affected by the level of standards associated with products they consume, then the cooperation problem could arise on the exporting country side. If the exporting-country government chooses to repress unions, for example, for either political or competitive reasons, then the utility-maximizing consumer would have no option but to avoid that particular product." I do not follow this. If the consumer in the high standards country derives utility from consuming products produced at home both from their consumption per se as well as from the high standards in their production, and derives utility from the consumption of imported product per se but either ignores the standards in their production or attaches disutility to it, there will be no competitive threat from lower labor standards embodied in the imported product.

[14] It might appear that consumers must have the information needed to distinguish the non-observing firms from observing ones to engage in such behavior. However, market forces might themselves generate such information as long as the consumers refuse to buy that product (or *all* products from a country) if they suspect *some* firms (or some *products* from that country) are being produced under unacceptable conditions. In such a case, producers (or countries) who maintain acceptable standards will have an incentive to invest in signaling (in a credible way) to the consumers that they in fact do so and thus distinguish themselves from those that do not.

Michiel Keyzer, in a private conversation, raised a troubling aspect of consumer boycott. Of course, boycott of products produced under working conditions that consumers deem unacceptable would seem appropriate. But how should one view boycott of products because they have been produced by particular groups in other countries that consumers in one country deem unacceptable for reasons of racial, ethnic, or other prejudices?

Trade Policy and Race to the Bottom

Rodrik (1996: 5) draws an analytical distinction between two arguments, which he claims "are often mixed-up," for the use of trade policy instruments for enforcing particular labor standards. The first is "that trade is a channel through which labor standards are arbitraged across countries towards the lowest level, requiring the use of trade policy to prevent a 'race to the bottom.'" The second is "that trade (and trade sanctions in particular) should be used to enforce internationally agreed standards such as ILO conventions, or to simply get trade partners to improve their labor standards" (p. 5). The distinction arises from the intended effect of trade policy. In the first case, the primary intention is to prevent a race to the bottom among countries in labor standards, so that they converge to a common low level, and not so much to change the labor standards in the poor countries themselves. On the other hand, in the second case, the primary goal is to enforce different, presumably higher, labor standards in poor countries than those prevailing in them through the threat of denial of access to markets of developed countries.

The "race to the bottom" referred to in the first argument is not that *between governments* in setting their mandatory labor standards. As argued earlier, a non-cooperative game between governments in setting labor standards need not necessarily result in a "race to the bottom." What Rodrik has in mind is competition among producers in different countries. Indeed, the ancient pauper labor argument claimed that trade with low-wage countries and the resulting competitive pressure on producers will lead wages in high-wage countries to converge to those of poor countries. Rodrik's "race to the bottom" argument for the use of trade policy in enforcing labor standards is the same old pauper labor argument, now couched in terms of competition in labor standards. The conventional answer to the pauper labor argument in the context of trade between rich North and poor South, as Rodrik himself points out, is "While unskilled labor may lose, the North is richer as a whole, and if governments in the North wished to do so they could compensate the losers and still come out ahead" (p. 8).

Thus in the absence of market failures[15] and any constraints on the ability of Northern governments to compensate potential losers from competition in trade with the South, comparative advantage, even if it reflects in part differences in prevailing labor standards, is legitimate and so are gains from trade based on it. Thus, there is no case for trade restrictions. Clearly, if such advantage is gained by flouting universal moral norms, it is

---

[15] It is not very difficult to construct theoretical examples of failures in the labor market and of the possibility of multiple equilibria, where the imposition of labor standards could alleviate the market failure or move the economy to a Pareto superior equilibrium. However, the issue is not one of theory but of its wide empirical relevance. Establishing the existence of a significant externality *empirically* in a convincing and econometrically sound fashion is more difficult and hence rare, than assertions of such existence. Also, it is not enough to show that mandating of labor standards would address the failure in labor markets. It has to be shown that there are no other more cost-effective means of addressing such failures. If everything else fails, a resourceful economist can always think up an un-internalized "externality" and the resultant market failure!

obviously illegitimate. For example, any cost advantage in products produced by prisoners could be *universally deemed illegitimate*. Indeed, it is for this reason that GATT–WTO allows countries to place otherwise disallowed quantitative restrictions on trade in such products. Put another way, unless core labor standards are universal and eternal, which they arguably are not, imposing restrictions on trade involving products embodying "low" labor standards would not be legitimate.

Concern in High Income Countries about Poor Labor Standards in Developing Countries

A concern about poor labor standards in general, and child labor in particular, has been expressed by various well-meaning groups in high-income countries. Groups in the USA such as "Save the Children," have raised funds to help poor children in less developed countries. It would indeed be wrong to dismiss such concerns out of hand since they could arise from *altruism*, for example, the welfare of workers and children in poor countries could be an argument in the utility functions of at least some individuals and groups in rich countries, so that their utility increases if the welfare of workers and children in poor countries increases. On the other hand, such concerns could also arise from purely *selfish* motives, that is, the fear of erosion of one's high standards through a "race to the bottom" in the global economy, with low labor standards in one country perceived as negative externalities on high standard countries.

Altruistic citizens of rich countries have, in principle, many ways of more efficiently and effectively expressing their concerns than through lobbying for imposing trade sanctions on countries with poor labor standards in the expectation that such sanctions would be effective in inducing the governments of such countries to institute policies for raising labor standards. First of all, it is not inconceivable that a country threatened with trade sanctions for failure to raise its labor standards might not respond by raising them but instead choose to forego gains from trade. Second, instead of relying on the *indirect means* through linkage which depends on the desired response by the developing country for its success, the citizens of the developed countries could adopt a more effective *direct means* of pressuring *their own governments* to lift any restrictions on immigration of workers from countries with poor labor standards. If they choose to migrate, such workers would enjoy higher labor standards prevailing in the country of immigration. Indeed there is support for lifting such restrictions on moral-philosophical grounds as in the writings of John Rawls (1993a). He views freedom of movement and freedom of choice of occupation as essential primary goods equivalent to other basic rights and liberties (as defined in Rawls, 1971), the entitlement to which is not open to political debate and allocation through the political process. While Rawls was writing about these freedoms in the context of constitutional essentials of a just society, implicit in the very expression of humanitarian concerns about others must be a view of the whole human race as one society. As such, a natural extension of Rawls' ideas would treat freedom of movement of humans across artificial political boundaries as a basic human right.[16]

Even if lifting immigration restrictions is deemed infeasible politically, still citizens of rich countries could make income transfers to the workers in poor countries. With higher incomes, it is reasonable to presume that the *supply* price (broadly defined to include labor standard) of their labor would rise and, to restore labor-market equilibrium, labor standards would have to rise. Indeed a test of the depth of their humanitarian concern is the price that citizens are willing to pay for translating the concern into an actual increase in welfare of workers in poor countries. Willingness to make needed income transfers is a demonstration of the willingness to pay the price.

Turning now to child labor,[17] excepting the abusive ones, most parents will weigh the welfare of their children significantly in making choices for them. And in making those choices, given their resources and opportunities, such parents could reasonably be expected to take into account the cost of putting their children to work in terms of their health and education relative to the income they bring in. As such, if some parents choose to put their children to work, it reflects more than anything else the limitations of their resources and opportunities, viz. their poverty. Once again, citizens of developed countries concerned with the welfare of such working children among the poor in developing countries could influence the choices of parents away from putting their children to work altogether or at least reduce the amount of work done by their children through income transfers to parents. Such transfers relax their resource constraints.

Many developing countries have ratified ILO conventions on child labor and indeed have domestic laws restricting it. Yet, it cannot be denied that the laws are not effectively enforced and children continue to be employed even in hazardous occupations and as "bonded" workers. This fact raises two related issues. First is whether legislation on labor standards including on child labor by themselves contributed to improvement in standards or in effective abolition of child labor. The works of Moehling (1999) on child labor in the USA and Engerman (2003) on the history of labor standards suggest that the contributions of laws are very modest, and economic development including changes in technology contributed most. Second, even if laws would contribute significantly were they to be enforced, is this an adequate reason to use denial of market access as a means of forcing developing countries to enforce their own laws on child labor? Even in the USA, the Department of Labor has confessed its inability to enforce its laws against so-called "sweat shops." After all, nations decide the allocation of limited resources of law

---

[16] By accepting existing political boundaries, Rawls himself does not make such an extension in his essay on "Law of Peoples" (Rawls 1993b) and is criticized for this failure by Ackerman (1994). In his earlier work, Ackerman (1971: 89–95, 256–57) argued that while there may be some grounds for restriction on immigration in real-world states, not only should such restrictions be exercised with great care, given the ease with which they may be abused, but also, such restrictions must be accompanied by a massive increase in foreign aid.

[17] There is a large body of theoretical and empirical literature on child labor. Basu (1999) is a good survey of the issues.

enforcement according to their own priorities. As such, forcing developing countries to alter their allocation of enforcement resources would constitute an unwarranted intrusion on their sovereignty.

Empirical Evidence on Labor Standards in International Competition

A number of empirical studies on various aspects of competitiveness in world markets, the flow of foreign direct investment, and labor standards are available. Serious data and econometric problems plague many of them. Most are based on multiple regressions usually estimated by ordinary least squares (OLS). Few of the regressions estimated are derived from any well-specified theoretical framework: the explanatory variables are often chosen based more on their plausibility than on theory. Proxies used, as for example by Rodrik (1996), for labor standards obtaining in a country (e.g., total number of ILO conventions ratified), statutory hours of work, etc.) are subject to significant measurement errors. Not all explanatory variables can be deemed truly exogenous. For example, whether to satisfy an ILO convention or not is a matter of choice. As is well known, if explanatory variables are either subject to measurement errors or endogenous or both, the OLS estimates of regression parameters will be inconsistent.

Stern (1997) and OECD (1996) summarize the results from many of the empirical studies.[18] The conclusions of OECD (1996) are worth excerpting:
On core labor standards and export performance:

> Within these limitations, empirical findings confirm the analytical results that core labor standards do not play a significant role in shaping trade performance. The view which argues that low-standards countries will enjoy gains in export market shares to the detriment of high-standards countries appears to lack solid empirical support... Moreover, the main result that emerges from a cross-country analysis of comparative advantage is that patterns of specialization are mainly governed by the relative abundance of factors of production and technology differences... These findings also imply that any fear on the part of developing countries that better core standards would negatively affect either their economic performance or their competitive position in world markets has no economic rationale. (p. 105)

---

[18] Their review does not include Chau and Kanbur (2001) who model the determinants of ratification of ILO conventions directly, and the determinants of labor standards indirectly. Surprisingly, they find that while economic variables such as real per capita income do not explain ratification, legal systems do. For some conventions, even after controlling for basic economic characteristics and domestic legal institutions, they find peer effects are significant—the probability of a country adopting standards depends on how many others in its peer group have already adopted that standard. It is unclear whether their legal system variable, such as Scandinavian, French, German, or a socialist system, in proxying other deeper factors such as social attitudes, reflects only the legal dimension.

On core labor standards and trade liberalization:

> The empirical results presented for the sample of 44 countries do not provide unambiguous support for one pattern of sequencing over the other as to whether trade liberalization or freer association rights come first. Rather, the clearest and most reliable finding is in favor of a mutually supportive relationship between successfully sustained trade reforms and improvements in association and bargaining rights. (p. 112)

On core labor standards and FDI:

> Empirical evidence on the direct relationship between FDI and core labor standards is scarce and remains open to different interpretations... According to reports by MNEs from OECD countries, core labor standards are not considered a factor in assessing investment opportunities in a potential host country. (p. 123)

On trade, employment and wages:

> Typically, analysts find that the impact of trade on employment and wage relativities has been significant in specific sectors. They also find that the measurable negative impact arising through increased import penetration is highest in sectors that employ relatively large numbers of low-skilled workers. Almost all studies find that the impact of trade on employment is small relative to changes in employment overall. (p. 125)

In sum, economic theory and empirical evidence confirm that the case for linking trade with observance of core labor standards is far from persuasive.

V. Linking Trade and Labor Standards

Linkage between trade and labor standards is commonly understood to mean that access to export markets is conditioned on or linked to the exporting country ensuring that core labor standards are met.[19] The linkage could come about through: (i) unilateral actions by a country as, for example, by it conditioning the *preferential* access to its markets, or (ii) through clauses in *preferential* (bilateral or plurilateral) as well as in non-discriminatory multilateral trade agreements. In either case, the mechanism of

---

[19] Barry and Reddy (2006, 2008) claim that linkage does *not necessarily* involve the application of trade sanctions against countries that fail to promote labor standards and could indeed involve *offers* of *additional* trading opportunities if they promote labor standards adequately without sanctioning them if they do not. For making such offers to developing countries, which presumably are the targets of linkage, Special and Differential Treatment provisions of GATT/WTO are adequate. However, whether such provisions themselves have served the interest of developing countries is arguable.

enforcement of labor standards is a trade sanction. In the first case, it is denial of prefer-ential access in case of failure to observe labor standards. For example, the USA denied Chile preferential access to its markets under the Generalized System of Preferences for Chile's failure to ensure human rights. In the second case, the enforcement process is through the Dispute Settlement mechanism in such agreements. Thus, the parties to the agreement commit themselves in the agreement to observing labor standards. If any party is alleged to have failed to meet its commitment, other parties could initiate pro-ceedings against the failing country in the Dispute Settlement Mechanism to investi-gate the allegation. The proceedings could end with either the dismissal of allegation or with it being substantiated. In the latter case, either the failed party agrees to meet its commitment or the other parties are allowed to withhold access to their markets to the party that continues to fail to meet its commitment. If this enforcement mechanism is credible, and the sanctions imposed on parties continuing to fail to meet their commit-ments even enough, then all parties will find it in their own interests to meet their com-mitments. Indeed, the perceptions that the ILO has no credible mechanism to enforce its conventions and the Dispute Settlement Mechanism of the WTO, on the other hand, is credible and effective lie behind the demand for linkage. In the US Congress the majority Democrats want *international conventions* (i.e., ILO conventions relating to core labor standards) with tough enforcement provisions to be added to all future agreements to be negotiated, as well as already concluded but not yet approved trade agreements with Peru, Colombia, and Panama and the negotiations towards an agree-ment with South Korea. Republicans have suggested the inclusion of relevant US laws as alternative standards (to ILO standards) with less scope for litigation (Callahan and Beattie, 2007).

The demand for linkage is not new. The deceptively appealing notion that lower labor standards in a country relative to its trading partners confer on it an *unfair* competitive advantage was already present in the charter of the International Trade Organization (ITO) negotiated by participant countries at Havana in 1948. Charnovitz (1987: 566–67), in his historical review of labor standards in the world trading regime, notes that Article 7 of the ITO stated that "The members recognize that unfair labor conditions, particularly in the production for export, create dif-ficulties in international trade, and accordingly, each member shall take whatever action may be appropriate and feasible to eliminate such conditions within its ter-ritory." The ITO did not come into being primarily because the United States did not ratify its charter. However, the General Agreement on Tariffs (GATT), consist-ing of tariff reductions and general clauses that themselves consist of a set of rules and obligations that have been negotiated earlier and are intended to operate under the umbrella of the ITO, came to be applied through its Protocol of Provisional Application. Except for allowing countries to prohibit trade in goods made with prison labor, the articles of GATT did not deal with labor standards. Various US administrations, Democrat and Republican, have proposed the inclusion of a labor standards article in the GATT, unsuccessfully as it turned out, during sev-eral rounds of multilateral trade negotiations. Similar proposals have been made by political parties in national parliaments in several European countries and also in the European Parliament.

The late Jan Tinbergen, Nobel Laureate in economics, pointed out that in general there must be at least as many instruments of policy as there are objectives and that in achieving any objective that policy instrument which has the most direct impact on that objective is most likely, though not always, to do so at the least social cost. His principle applies as well to the creation of agencies that set the rules governing international economic transactions and the specification of their mandates. Thus, the GATT and the United Nations Conference on Trade and Development were created as agencies specializing in issues relating to international trade; the World Bank and the International Monetary Fund were designed to deal respectively with financing long-term development and short-term stabilization. The Universal Postal Union covered postal and other matters of international communication. The Berne and Paris conventions addressed some aspects of intellectual property rights. The ILO deals with labor issues. Clearly such specialization makes eminent sense. Loading one specialized agency with matters that fall within the purview of another, such as including a social clause in the mandate of the WTO—rather than leaving labor standards within the purview of the ILO while ensuring consistency of actions of both through mutual consultation where appropriate, is not conducive to addressing them efficiently.

The above application of Tinbergen's approach of targeting policy instruments to specific objectives to assigning mandates of international institutions to specific global objectives is rather general, and its implication for the case of the WTO for achieving objectives relating to labor standards is not exact. Bagwell and Staiger (2002: chapter 8), note that this application may fail when policies enter the national (i.e., government) welfare function in an interdependent fashion. In such a case, if policies (say trade and labor standard policies) are strategic complements, a linked agreement (i.e., trade–labor standard linkage in the WTO) can generate additional cooperation in both. Leaving this aside, the main thrust of the analysis of the two authors is to answer the questions: (i) Is the GATT/WTO's traditional preoccupation with market access misplaced when the issue of labor standards is raised? (ii) Should WTO trade negotiations cover both international (i.e., trade) and domestic (labor standard) policies of governments? Using their powerful analytical approach to international agreements as a means to escape from the inefficiency (i.e., negative externality)[20] arising from unilateral exercise of policy, they conclude that the GATT/WTO agreement that focuses on the terms of trade externality does have other articles (such as on nullification and impairment) and general exceptions (Article XX) that are in principle adequate to answer both questions in the negative.

---

[20] Brown et al. (2002) who take on board the analysis of Bagwell and Staiger (2002) as well as the papers cited by them conclude that "On balance, our view is that dangers of using trade sanctions to enforce labor standards outweigh the benefits, both in terms of likely protectionism and in harm to affect to workers."

VI. Key Messages

The key messages of the previous sections are:

(1) The assertion that increasing competition from trade with developing countries with low labor standards is a threat to the prevailing higher labor standards in developed countries is yet another manifestation of the ancient pauper labor argument. It has weak analytical foundation and empirical support. The case based on it for including a social clause in trade agreements conditioning market access to enforce agreed labor standards has no merit.

(2) Most countries of the world have signed and ratified conventions covering the ILO's core labor standards. Expanding the definition of labor standards to go beyond these to include minimum wages and hours of works is not appropriate.

(3) Except for a notable few, such as the USA, almost all countries of the world have signed and ratified a set of covenants that recognize an immense array of civil, political, economic, social, and cultural rights that include and go beyond the labor standards proposed to be included in a social clause. Moreover, national constitutions of some countries have explicitly incorporated many of the rights. However, many of the rights are not at all satisfied in most countries, including developed countries that are proponents of social clause, and even those that are satisfied came to be so only after the latter became developed. Two insights flow from this: the claim of universality and eternity for a narrow set of rights proposed to be included in the social clause is not only overblown but is also ahistorical. It is most appropriate to view these and the broader rights in the covenants as *universal* in their aspiration, while their attainment would be conditional on national and temporal context including the stage of development of a nation.

(4) Labor standards can be modeled analytically as an activity that diverts resources from production from a producer perspective, while influencing welfare from a consumer perspective. It can be shown that labor standards will differ across countries in a competitive equilibrium. A global competitive trading equilibrium among small open economies under free and balanced trade will be Pareto Optimal. In such an equilibrium, labor standards will in general differ across countries. However, if the distribution of welfare across countries in such an equilibrium is deemed inequitable, an alternative Pareto Optimum that satisfies equity considerations can be sustained as a free trade competitive equilibrium with lump-sum income transfers across countries. A similar argument leads to the conclusion that if in the initial Pareto Optimum, labor standards in a subset of countries are below some commonly acceptable minimum standard, as long as there exists a non-empty set of Pareto Optima meeting such a minimum standard in all countries, once again it is feasible to sustain one of the Pareto Optima in this set with income transfers. If no Pareto Optimum meeting the

minimum standard exists, implementation of the minimum standard will require *domestic* taxes and subsidies in addition to *international* income transfers. Clearly as long as there is *international cooperation* in the sense of a consensus on minimum standard and a willingness to make income transfers and impose optimal domestic taxes and subsidies, there is no need for a social clause or for the departures from free trade. In the absence of cooperation, the social clause becomes moot anyway.

(5) If the use of first-best transfer tax-subsidy policies is precluded, a second-best role for trade policy could arise: trade policy instruments could be used to raise labor standards, if not welfare, in poor countries, as long as there is international cooperation. In the absence of cooperation, a race to the bottom could, though need not, arise. For example, consumers in countries with higher standards can attempt to protect their higher labor standard countries through market actions, such as refraining from purchases from countries known to be violating acceptable standards. Only in the absence of such means, could a race to the bottom emerge if low labor standards confer a competitive advantage. There is little empirical evidence for this.

(6) The demand for a social clause or a trade–labor standard linkage based on low labor standards conferring competition is not new. It can be traced to the Versailles Peace Treaty that led to the establishment of the ILO. The stillborn charter for an International Trade Organization adopted at the United Nations Conference on Trade and Employment in Havana in 1948 included an article (Article 7) that authorized members to take any appropriate and feasible action to eliminate "unfair labor conditions." The fact it is not new is no reason for entertaining it. The Governing Body of the WTO, namely, its biannual ministerial conference has thus far refused to entertain it and decided that the ILO is the appropriate forum for matters relating to labor standards. Yet the issue is alive, particularly in preferential trade agreements already negotiated. It is also a major issue in the debates in the US Congress on extending the President's authority to negotiate trade agreements. It has to be resisted.

(7) Efficiency in the assignment of mandates to international institutions would strongly suggest specialization: that the WTO's mandate is confined to trade matters and the ILO's to labor issues, with coordination, if needed, in dealing with any overlap. However, with the membership of WTO and ILO largely overlapping, the question of WTO permitting or not permitting something that ILO does or can do can arise only if the WTO and ILO agreements, that the same set of countries are parties to, contradict each other. Already, there is a committee in the WTO to ensure compatibility of international environmental agreements with the WTO. I suspect the Committee's mandate includes ILO agreements as well. If not, they could be added. Overloading the WTO with mandates on trade and labor is a prescription for achieving neither mandate efficiently. The existing rules and procedures of the GATT/WTO relating to market access are more

than adequate in general to address any actual or potential interdependence between trade and labor standard policies in the welfare function of national governments.

VII. Postscript

Since this chapter was completed in 2007, the literature on the impact of globalization labor and issues related to International Labor Standards has grown. The most recent publications include Brown et al. (2009), Brown (2009), Elliott (2011), and WTO (2009).[21] This literature importantly adds many new empirical studies. However, while appropriately qualifying and nuancing some of the conclusions of the chapter, it does not overturn any, and in some ways repeats the differences in perspectives noted. A brief review of the recent contributions follows.

Brown (2009), is a contribution to a World Bank Study that analyzes the link between globalization and working conditions in five low-income developing countries, one in Sub-Saharan Africa (Madagascar), two in Asia (Cambodia and Indonesia), and two in Latin America (El Salvador and Honduras). These countries vary substantially in their populations, economic structures, history, and institutions. But they have all experienced globalization since the 1980s. Among the few sectors in which globalization and foreign direct investment have played a significant role is the textile and apparel sector. In all five countries, the share of apparel in total merchandise exports was high, 82 per cent in 2003 in Cambodia and others. Moreover, the share of foreign owned firms in the apparel sector was also high.

The apparel sector is important for several reasons. First, it has been historically important as the first step on the ladder of industrialization and development. Second, since the 1990s this sector has streamlined and evolved highly efficient global supply chains and interacts with suppliers in poor countries. These suppliers operate in imperfectly competitive labor markets with workers with low literacy and market experience along with government failures. Third, it is a sector characterized by extremely fine divisions of labor. Fourth, and finally, textiles and apparel exports were governed by the Multifibre Arrangement (MFA) in the General Agreement and Tariffs and Trade (GATT), although the discriminatory bilateral quota system of MFA was itself an egregious violation of the non-discriminatory most-favored nation principle of GATT. The MFA was only phased out completely in 2005. Since it sheltered many inefficient exporters, its phase-out hit some developing countries very hard.

The studies suggest that the workers in the apparel sector earned a significant premium over each country's mean wage. However, they also suggest that the positive

---

[21] See also the selection of papers in Brown and Stern (2007) that covers: trade, labor, and labor markets; trade and the race to the bottom; labor protection and trade negotiations; and market-based mechanisms protecting labor rights.

impact of globalization might be short-lived, depending as it did on FDI. If FDI moves out, wage premiums fall. From the perspective of Brown's paper, the studies found an interesting and positive correlation between non-working conditions (which the adoption of international labor standards is meant to improve) and wages. For the three countries (Cambodia, El Salvador, and Indonesia) with data on non-wage working conditions, compared to the dominant default industry (i.e., agriculture) where non-wage working conditions were below country-wide averages, those in the FDI-intensive export industries were either at or above. Overall, the studies show that globalization has been associated with improvements in the working conditions in the exposed sectors.

Brown's own paper in the volume is very useful in referencing and surveying a large body of literature. It concludes that most of the studies undertaken in the 1990s, particularly by trade specialists, were optimistic on the impact of trade on labor. They found that globalization had a small, but still positive effect on workers, but had little impact on wages in the economy as a whole and on distribution of income, although there was some evidence that foreign-owned and export-oriented firms paid a wage premium. There was little or no evidence that global competition through trade has triggered a race to the bottom in labor standards.

Brown et al. (2009) is a very interesting quasi-experimental study of the role that buyers in global supply chains play in helping vendors uncover productivity-enhancing labor management innovations. They study a buyer-directed NGO-coordinated factory-based programme targeting intestinal parasites in seven apparel factories in Bangalore, India. Organizational changes had also been implemented in those factories in anticipation of the termination of the MFA that could confound the effects of targeted programming in pre- and post-productivity comparison, unless appropriate estimation techniques are employed to overcome possible confounding. Using the termination of MFA as a natural experiment, and applying a difference-in-difference estimator, the authors found that the full complement of medically appropriate treatments was found to increase individual productivity. If such individual productivity-enhancing effects could be associated with the adoption of improved labor standards, then the study would imply that such standards need not be imposed by law or international agreement, but would be adopted anyway by the firms. After all, the factories in Bangalore were not required by law to offer general healthcare, but they still did.

Since advocates of linking labor standards with trade have thus far not succeeded in including such linkage in multilateral trade agreements, they have tried and succeeded in including them in Regional Trade Agreements (RTAs). Barring the lone exception of a Free Trade agreement between Chile and Colombia, all such RTAs have been between industrialized and developing countries. The focus of Elliott (2011) is RTAs that create legal obligation at improving labor standards beyond hortatory language, reaffirming workers' rights. She finds it difficult to assess the implication of RTAs for developing countries because sustained attention to implementation is rare. She concludes that based on the experience to date, enforceable labor standards in RTAs have not been used for protectionist abuses as was feared, which means the developing countries need not fear entering into RTAs on this ground. In any case she finds that, as of mid 2009, in RTAs not involving the USA or Canada, labor provisions are unusual and rarely go beyond hortatory language to include largely binding and enforceable commitments.

WTO (2009) argues that the existence of large informal economies is one of the main reasons why developing countries do not fully benefit from their integration into the world economy, and they have to make serious efforts to adjust policies to tackle informal employment and establish decent working conditions in order to gain full benefits.

APPENDIX I

LEGITIMATE DIVERSITY OF LABOR STANDARDS

Consider first an autarkic economy producing and consuming two goods. Let Q_i and C_i denote respectively the production and consumption of good i (i = 1,2). Let S denote the level of *economy-wide* labor standards. Let $U[C_1, C_2, S]$ be the strictly concave Samuelson social utility function with $U_j > 0$, where U_j denotes the partial derivative U with respect to its jth argument. Let $Q_1 = F(Q_2, S; \bar{K}, \bar{L})$ denote the production possibility frontier denoting the efficient combination of Q_1, Q_2 that could be produced, given the level S of labor standard and inelastically supplied endowments of $\bar{K}$, $\bar{L}$ of capital and labor respectively. F is concave in Q_2 and S with F > 0, $F_1 < 0$, $F_2 < 0$, $F_3 > 0$, $F_4 > 0$, where F_j is the partial derivative of F with respect to its jth argument.[22] Under autarky, the economy's production of good i, Q_i, has to equal its consumption C_i. Taking this into account, the variables choice of C_1, C_2, and S are determined by maximizing

$$U[C_1, C_2, S] \qquad (30A.1)$$

subject to

$$C_1 = F[C_2, S; \bar{K}, \bar{L}] \qquad (30A.2)$$

$$C_i \geq 0, S \geq 0 \qquad (30.A3)$$

Substituting (30A.2) in (30A.1) the problem reduces to maximizing $U[F (C_2, S; \bar{K}, \bar{L}) C_2, S]$ with respect to C_2 and S. Assuming an interior maximum, the first-order conditions yield

$$U_2/U_1 = -F_1 \qquad (30A.4)$$

$$U_3/U_1 = -F_2 \qquad (30A.5)$$

The interpretation of (30A.4)–(30A.5) is straightforward. Equation (30A.4) states that the marginal rate of substitution in consumption of good 2 for 1 viz. U_2/U_1 equals the marginal rate of transformation of viz- F_1 in production. Equation (30A.5) states that the *marginal rate of substitution* (MRS) of labor standard for good 1 in *consumption* viz.

---

[22] The partial derivative F_2 should be viewed as the *net effect* of higher labor standards taking into account whatever positive effects they may have on labor productivity.

U_3/U_1 should equal the *marginal rate of transformation* (MRT) of labor standard and good 1 in production, that is, the cost of labor standard in terms of foregone output of good 1 in production viz. -F2. Since the exogenous variables of the problem are factor endowments $\overline{K}$, $\overline{L}$, the optimal values of the endogenous variables Ci and S will be functions of them. As such, the optimal values of endogenous variables, particularly the level of labor standards, would differ across countries. Under plausible assumptions on U and F, it can be shown that a richer country, that is, one with a greater endowment of one or both factors, will choose a higher standard. Clearly, there is nothing illegitimate or unfair about such diversity in labor standards across a cross-section of autarkic economies. If we generalize the model to allow for capital accumulation and labor force growth and solve its dynamic inter-temporal welfare maximization problem, in general labor standards will also vary over time along the optimal path. In other words, labor standards will depend on the stage of development of the economy.

It is well known that the social welfare optimum defined by solutions C_1^*, C_2^* and S^* equations (30A.2), (30A.4), and (30A.5) can be sustained as a decentralized competitive equilibrium, if we assume that (i) labor standards are set at its optimal value S^* by the society and (ii) all consumers and producers take S^* as beyond their control in their consumption, production, factor supply, and demand decisions and (iii) the policy instrument of lump-sum redistribution of incomes is available. In other words, given S^*, a relative price $P^* \equiv [U_2(C_1^*, C_2^*, S^*)] / [U_1(C_1^*, C_2^*, S^*)]$ for good 2 in terms of good 1, wage rate $\omega^* = [\partial F(C_1^*, C_2^*, \overline{K}, \overline{L})] / \partial t$ and rental rate $r^* = [\partial F(C_1^*, C \leq_2^*, \overline{K}, \overline{L})] / \partial K$ each consumer maximizes his/her utility subject to the budget constraint that expenditure on the two goods does not exceed his/her income from factor supplies, share in profits, if any, of producers, and transfers from government. Each producer maximizes profits given $p^*, w^* r^*$ and his production function. Government redistributes income so as to clear the market for goods and factors.

APPENDIX II

Open Economies

Instead of being autarkic, suppose the economy is open to international trade, and it is small in the sense that it takes the world relative price π of good 2 in terms of good 1 as beyond its control. Now with the possibility of trade, consumption C_i need not equal productions Q_i. Assuming trade is balanced, it follows that the value of the consumption bundle (C_1, C_2) has to equal that of the production bundle (Q_1, Q_2) at price π. Thus the economy will maximize social welfare.

$$U[C_1, C_2, S] \tag{30A.6}$$

subject to

$$C_1 + \pi C_2 = Q_1 + \pi Q_2 \tag{30A.7}$$

$$Q_1 = F[Q_2, S; \overline{K}, \overline{L}] \tag{30A.8}$$

$$C_i \geq 0, Q_2 \geq 0; S \geq 0 \tag{30A.9}$$

Substituting (30A.7) and (30A.8) in (30A.6) the problem reduces to maximizing U[F + $\pi(Q_2-C_2)$, C_2, S] with respect to Q_2, C_2 and S. Assuming an interior maximum, the first-order conditions yield

$$U_2/U_1 = \pi \qquad (30A.10)$$

$$F_1 = -\pi \qquad (30A.11)$$

$$U_3/U_1 = -F_2 \qquad (30A.12)$$

The interpretation of (30A.10)–(30A.12) is straightforward. Equation (30A.5) states that the marginal rate of substitution in consumption of good 2 for 1 viz. U_2/U_1 equals its world price π. Equation (30A.6) states that the marginal rate of transformation of good 2 into good 1 viz. $-F_1$ equals its world price π. Thus (30A.10) and (30A.11) together imply that both consumers and producers should face world prices were the social optimum to be implemented as a competitive equilibrium. *Thus free trade is the optimal policy.* Equation (30A.12) states that the *marginal rate of substitution* (MRS) of labor standard for good 1 in *consumption* viz. U_3/U_1 should equal the *marginal rate of transformation* (MRT) of labor standard and good 1 in production, that is, the cost of labor standard in terms of foregone output of good 1 in production viz. $-F_2$.

In the above discussion the determination of π through global market clearance was left implicit. To make it explicit and to explore other aspects of labor standards, it is useful to set up the problem as one of choosing Pareto Optimal (across countries) levels of output, consumption, and labor standards.

Let (C_i^j, Q_i^j, S^j) denote respectively the consumption of good i, production of good i (i = 1,2), and labor standard in country j (j = 1, ... N). Under appropriate assumptions on utility functions and production functions, any Pareto Optimum can be characterized as the solution to the maximization of a positively weighted sum of individual country utilities,

$$\sum_j \alpha^j U^j(C_i^j, S^j) \qquad (30A.13)$$

subject to

$$\sum_j C_i^j = \sum_j Q_i^j \, i = 1,2 \qquad (30A.14)$$

$$Q_i^j = F^j(Q_2^j, S^j; \overline{K}^j, \overline{L}^j) \, j = 1,2,...N \qquad (30A.15)$$

$$C_i^j \geq 0, Q_i^j \geq 0, S^j \geq 0 \, i = 1,2; j = 1,2,...N \qquad (30A.16)$$

Equation (30A.14) represents global market clearance for good i, and it replaces the balance of trade equation (30A.7) of the small-country problem.

Assuming that the non-negativity constraints (16) do not bind, the first-order conditions for the optimal choice of C_i^j, Q_i^j and S^j are:

$$\alpha^j \frac{\partial U^j}{\partial C_i^j} = \lambda_i \, j = 1,...N; i = 1,2 \qquad (30A.17)$$

$$\alpha^j \frac{\partial U^j}{\partial S^j} = -\mu^j \frac{\partial F^j}{\partial S^j} \, j = 1,...N \qquad (30A.18)$$

$$\lambda_1 = \mu^j \; j = 1,...N \tag{30A.19}$$

$$\lambda_2 = -\mu^j \frac{\partial F^j}{\partial Q_2^j} \; j = 1,...N \tag{30A.20}$$

In (30A.17)–(30A.20), λ_i is the Lagrangean multiplier associated with constraint (30A.14), which ensures that there is no excess supply or demand for good i in the world. μ^j is the Lagrangean multiplier associated with the production transformation constraint (30A.15) for country j. Taking (30A.17) and (30A.20) together, one gets:

$$\frac{\partial U^j}{\partial C_2^j} / \frac{\partial U^j}{\partial C_1^j} = \frac{\lambda_2}{\lambda_1} = -\frac{\partial F^j}{\partial Q_2^j} \tag{30A.21}$$

Thus the MRS is consumption of good 2 for good 1, viz. $[(\partial U^j / \partial C_2^j) / (\partial U^j / \partial C_i^j)]$ is the same in all countries j, with the common value being λ_2/λ_1. Also the MRT of good 2 for good 1 in production, that is, $- (\partial F^j / \partial Q_2^j)$, is the same in all countries j and its common value is also λ_2/λ_1. This in turn means that if the chosen Pareto Optimum (i.e., the one corresponding to a particular set of α^j) is implemented as a competitive equilibrium, then consumers and producers in all countries will have to face the same relative price of good 2 in terms of good 1. *In other words, a Pareto Optimum implemented as a competitive equilibrium will be characterized by free trade.*

It is seen from (30A.17)–(30A.20) that the MRS of labor standard for good 1 in country j, viz. $[(\partial U^j / \partial S^j) / (\partial U^j / \partial C_i^j)]$ equals the MRT of labor standards for good 1 in production in country j, viz. $-(\partial F^j / \partial S^j)$. However this common value of MRS and MRT can differ across countries. Once again such diversity is legitimate.

In the above analysis there was no requirement that each country's trade be balanced, only that globally there was no excess supply or demand for each commodity. Thus, given an *arbitrary choice* of α^j if the corresponding Pareto Optimum were to be implemented as a Pareto Optimum, the world market clearing relative price of good 2 in terms of good 1 will obviously be λ_2/λ_1. However, there is nothing to ensure that at these prices the value of the optimal consumption bundle of country j, that is, $C_j^i + (\lambda_2 / \lambda_1) C_2^j$, equals the value of its optimal production bundle, that is, $Q_1^j + (\lambda_2/\lambda_1) Q_2^j$ (i = 1,2). However, global clearance of the world market for each of the two goods ensures that for the world as a whole the value of its consumption equals value of production. In other words, while trade need not be balanced for any country, for the world as a whole it is balanced. Thus to implement any *arbitrary* Pareto Optimum, transfers to each country (equaling the excess of the value of its consumption bundle over the value of its production bundle) will in general be required. Of course some countries will *receive* and others *make* positive transfers. Because world trade is balanced, such transfers added over all the countries are zero. Thus making such transfers is feasible. However, following Negishi (1960), it can be shown that a set of positive α^j will in general exist such that the associated Pareto Optimum could be implemented without inter-country transfers. That is to say, a Pareto Optimum can be shown to exist that can be implemented as a competitive equilibrium at which the trade of each country is balanced. Let such a Pareto Optimum be denoted as No-Transfer Pareto Optimum or NTPO. For simplicity let us assume that NTPO is unique.

Clearly the analysis does not suggest that at such an NTPO the associated labor standard S^j is the same in all countries. Such diversity is legitimate. After all, the situation being characterized is a Pareto Optimum and it does not call for inter-country transfers. What if the vector $(S^1,... S^N)$ is deemed unsatisfactory in the sense that the standards in some country or countries are below some common minimum acceptable level $\bar{S}$?

Suppose for concreteness, let $S^j < \bar{S}$ for $j = 1, 2, ...M$ ($M < N$). Leaving aside the questions as to how the minimum $\bar{S}$ is set and, if there is a consensus on $\bar{S}$, how such a consensus came about, one could proceed as follows.[23] Suppose among the set of Pareto Optima (i.e., the set obtained as α^j are varied) there is a non-empty subset the elements of which satisfy $S^j > \bar{S}$ for all j. Then by definition any element of this subset will obviously meet the minimum standard criterion. However two points are noteworthy. First, by assumption, NTPO is not an element of the subset. As such, inter-country transfers would be necessary were any member of the subset to be implemented as a competitive equilibrium. Second, if there is more than one element in the subset, different elements will differ with respect to the distribution of welfare as well as transfers among countries. However, there is no way to choose among elements of this subset since the only requirement was that the minimal standard $\bar{S}$ be met. In a sense this is nice since additional criteria about the distribution of welfare and transfer could be brought to bear in making a choice. Be that as it may, *the important point is that as long as there exists a non-empty set of Pareto Optima meeting the minimal standards, it is feasible to meet such standards with income transfers but without departing from free trade. As such there is no need for a social clause or, to put it another way, the only rationale for a social clause has to be the odious one of protection of import competing industries.* I briefly discuss below the question of the consequences of possible infeasibility of income transfers.

What if there is no Pareto Optimum satisfying $S^j > \bar{S}$ for all j? *Suppose that the minimum $\bar{S}$ is the result of an international consensus as is the case with ILO conventions.* Then it is natural to look for Restricted Pareto Optima, that is, Pareto Optima subject to the additional restriction

$$-S^j < -\bar{S} \qquad (30A.22)$$

It can be seen that once (30A.17) is added to (30A.9)–(30A.11), the only first-order condition that is altered is (30A.13), which is replaced by

$$\alpha^j \frac{\partial U^j}{\partial S^j} = -\mu^j \frac{\partial F^j}{\partial S^j} - v^j \quad j = 1,2,...N \qquad (30A.23)$$

where v^j is the Langrangean multiplier associated with constraint (30A.23). Taking (30A.17), (30A.19), and (30A.23) together it follows that

$$\frac{\partial U^j}{\partial S^j} / \frac{\partial U^j}{\partial C^j_j} = -\frac{\partial F^j}{\partial S^j} - \frac{v^j}{\lambda_1} \qquad (30A.24)$$

Thus from (30A.19) it is seen that now there is a wedge between MRS in consumption of good 1 labor standard, viz. $[(\partial U^j / \partial S^j)/(\partial U^j / \partial C^j_i)]$ and MRT in production, viz.,

---

[23] Indeed with each country's labor standards entering only its production and utility functions, that is, with no international spillover effects on the other country's production or utility functions, one has to rationalize a common minimum standard, without viewing it as an implicit imposition of external ethical values on those countries in which the equilibrium labor standards are below in the NTPO equilibrium. One way to do so, which simultaneously rationalizes international transfers, is to argue that represents a universal minimum that all countries aspire to achieve, and some fail because their endowments of capital and labor do not permit them to succeed. Given international cooperation, other countries recognizing this make transfers to these countries to overcome the consequences of resource constraints. The case of spillover effects is considered below.

$-(\partial F^j / \partial S^j)$ the wedge being $- (\upsilon^j / \lambda_1)$. Now $\lambda_1 > 0$ and $\upsilon^j > 0$ (the reason being reducing $\bar{S}$ cannot reduce global welfare). As such (30A.19) implies that the shadow consumer relative price of labor standard in terms of good 1, namely the MRS, is lower than its shadow producer price, namely the MRT. Thus, in effect a consumer subsidy inducing demand for higher labor standards relative to goods, or equivalently a producer tax that induces a lower supply of goods relative to standards, is needed to sustain the optimum. *However, since the other first order conditions are unchanged, it is the case that restricted Pareto Optima are characterized by free trade.* Thus *international income transfers* (depending on α^j) and a *domestic tax or subsidy* to induce the appropriate level of standards are needed to sustain a Pareto Optimum. Indeed one could view the *international assistance* and *domestic compliance* measures associated with implementing ILO conventions as precisely the right approach.

APPENDIX III

BILATERAL GAMES OF STRATEGY IN LABOR STANDARDS

Two countries denoted by Home and Foreign play a game in setting labor standards, each with two possible strategies of setting them at "low" or "high" levels. There are thus four possible combinations of home and foreign labor standards. The pay-offs in real incomes associated with each combination (with the first (resp. second) component being the pay-off of the Home (resp. foreign) countries) are given by the following pay-off matrix:

		Foreign Strategy	
		Low	High
Home	Low	(-2,-2)	(2,-3)
Strategy	High	(-3, 2)	(1, 1)

It is easily seen that each country has a *dominant* strategy, viz. to set a low standard, because by doing so it maximizes its pay-off whether the other country chooses to set a high or low standard. Yet, compared to this *individually*-rational dominant-strategy Nash equilibrium with both countries setting low standards, the *collectively* rational strategy of each setting a high standard will yield a *higher* pay-off for *both*.[24]

---

[24] Aficionados of common-knowledge repeated game theory will point out that the collectively rational outcome could be sustained as an equilibrium through a suitable punishment strategy for deviation as long as both participants do not discount the future too heavily. Despite the fascination of political scientists for repeated Prisoner's Dilemma games, their relevance for real-life politics is dubious.

Of course competition need not necessarily lead to such a "prisoner's dilemma" type of Nash equilibrium. For example, if the pay-off matrix is as follows,

		Foreign Strategy	
		Low	High
Home	Low	(-4, -4)	(2, -3)
Strategy	High	(-3, 2)	(1, 1)

then (Low, High) and (High, Low) are both (pure strategy) Nash equilibria. In each of these, one jurisdiction sets a low standard while the other sets a high standard.

In both cases above, the Nash equilibrium is characterized by a "race to the bottom" in the sense that at least one country sets a low standard. But this need not be so, as consideration of the following pay-off matrix shows. Thus, consider:

		Foreign Strategy	
		Low	High
Home	Low	(-2, -2)	(2, -3)
Strategy	High	(-3, 2)	(3, 3)

It is readily seen that we have a unique Nash equilibrium where each country sets a high standard.

Of course, these are arbitrarily constructed pay-off matrices. While they are adequate to demonstrate that a destructive "race to the bottom" is not inevitable in the competition to set labor standards, we need to ground them in underlying models of economies to see whether such outcomes are sensible within them.

One such model is that of Chau and Kanbur (2006). The authors model competition among developing countries (South–South competition) to export to developed countries (North) and its impact on Southern standards. They demonstrate that whether a Southern "race to the bottom," in the sense that strategic responses to export competition induces southern countries to adopt lower standards, emerges in equilibrium, depends in a complex way on the Northern demand curve, the size of large exporters relative to each other, and the relative size of small exporters. In particular, their Proposition 6 states that "as the size of the competitive fringe of small Southern exporters grows, the likelihood of low standards equilibria *increases* if Northern demand is log convex (so that standards are complements) and *decreases* if Northern demand is log concave (so that standards are substitutes)" (Chau and Kanbur, 2006: 215). Moreover, even if the equilibrium is one of low standards, it need not necessarily mean that welfare is lowered as well, particularly when terms of trade adjustments and direct utility benefits are small, relative to the increase in production costs that higher standards necessitate. Accordingly, an equilibrium in which... countries select low standards need not necessarily imply a *coordination failure*" (Chau and Kanbur, 2006: 215, emphasis in original).

Clearly the rigorous analysis by Chau and Kanbur (2006) confirms the point of the numerical example that a "race to the bottom" is not inevitable. Their conditions for the existence of a "race to the bottom" in equilibrium is couched in terms of the properties of the Northern import-demand function, which is the difference between Northern domestic supply and domestic demand functions, and not in terms of the primitives of Northern Utility and Production functions. As such, the conditions are context (i.e., the forms of utility and production functions as well as factor endowments) specific. Moreover, their conclusion that there is no necessary connection between welfare and labor standards in equilibrium is very important.

References

Ackerman, B. (1994), 'Political Liberalisms.' *The Journal of Philosophy*, XCI7(4): 364–86.

Ackerman, B. (1971), *Social Justice in the Liberal State*. Cambridge MA: Harvard University Press.

Aidt, T. and Tzannatos, Z. (2002), *Unions and Collective Bargaining, Economic Effects in a Global Environment*. Washington DC: The World Bank.

Anderson, K. (1998), 'Environmental and Labor Standards: What Role for the WTO?' In Krueger, A. O. (ed.), *The WTO as an International Organization*. Chicago: The University of Chicago Press.

Bagwell, K. and Staiger, R. (2002), *The Economics of the World Trading System*. Cambridge, MA: MIT Press.

Bagwell, K. (2000), 'The Simple Economics of Labor Standards and the GATT.' In Deardorff, A. and Stern, R. (eds.), *Social Dimensions of US Trade Policies*. Ann Arbor: University of Michigan Press.

Barry, C. and Reddy, S. G. (2008), *International Labor Standards: A Proposal for Linkage*. New York: Columbia University Press.

Barry, C. and Reddy, S. G. (2006), 'International Trade and Labor Standards.' *Cornell International Law Journal*, 39(3): 545–640.

Basu, K., Horn, H., Roman, L. and Shapiro, J. (2003), *International Labor Standards*. Oxford: Blackwell.

Basu, K. (1999), 'Child Labor: Cause, consequences and cure, with remarks on International labor standards.' *Journal of Economic Literature*, 37(3): 1083–1119.

Basu, D.C. (1983), *Introduction to the Constitution of India,* 10th edition. New Delhi: Prentice Hall.

Bhagwati, J. (1995), 'Trade Liberalization and "Fair Trade" Demand.' *The World Economy*, 18(6): 745–59.

Brown, A. G. and Stern, R. M. (2007), 'What are the issues in using trade agreements for improving international labor standards?' Discussion paper #558, University of Michigan, Ann Arbor.

Brown, D. (2000), 'International Trade and Core Labor Standards: A survey of the Recent Literature.' Discussion Paper 2000–03, Department of Economics, Tufts University, Medford MA.

Brown, D. (2009), 'A Review of the Globalization Literature: Implications for Employment, Wages, and Labor Standards.' In Robertson, R., Brown, D., Pierre, G., and Sanchez-Puerta, M. L. (eds.), *Globalization, Wages and the Quality of Jobs*. Washington DC: The World Bank.

Brown, D., and Stern, R. M. (2007), *The WTO and Labor and Employment*. Cheltenham: Edward Elgar Publishers.

Brown, D., Downes, T., Eggleston, K., and Kumari, R. (2009), 'Human Resource Management Technology Diffusion through Global Supply Chains: Buyer Directed Factory-Based Health Care.' *World Development*, 37(9): 1484–93.

Brown, D., Deardorff, A. and Stern, R. M. (1996), 'International Labor Standards and Trade: A Theoretical Analysis.' In Bhagwati, J., and Hudec, R. (eds.), *Harmonization and Fair Trade*, Volume 1. Cambridge: MIT Press.

Brown, D., Deardorff, A., and Stern, R. M. (1997), 'Issues of Environmental and Labor Standards in the Global Trading System.' Paper presented at the Conference on 'Globalization, Technological Change, and the Welfare State', American Institute for Contemporary German Studies, The Johns Hopkins University, Washington DC, June 9–10.

Brown, D., Deardorff, A., and Stern, R. M. (2002), 'Pros and Cons of Linking Trade and Labor Standards.' Discussion Paper No. 477, School of Public Policy, University of Michigan, Ann Arbor.

Callahan, E. and Beattie, A. (2007), 'White House Ready to Force Trade Agenda.' *Financial Times*, March 8, p. 7.

CEA (1995), Economic Report of the President. Washington DC: Council of Economic Advisers.

Charnovitz, S. (1987). 'International Trade and Workers' Rights.' *The Johns Hopkins University SAIS Review, Winter–Spring*, 7(1): 185–98.

Chau, N. and Kanbur, R. (2006), ''. *Economica*, 73(290): 193–228.

Chau, N. and Kanbur, R. (2001), 'The Adoption of International Labor Standards Conventions: Who, When and Why.' Presented at Brookings Trade Forum, 2001, Washington, DC, Brookings Institute.

Dehejia, V. and Samy, Y. (2004), 'Trade and Labor Standards: Theory and New Empirical Evidence.' *Journal of International Trade and Economic Development*, 13(2): 177–96.

Dehejia, V. and Samy, Y. (2006), 'Labor Standards and Economic Integration in the European Union: An Empirical Analysis.' CESIFO Working Paper No. 1746, <www.cesifo-group.de> (accessed April 2013).

De Waart, P. (1996), 'Minimum Labor Standards is International from a Legal Perspective.' In Van Dijck, P. and Faber, G. (eds.), *Challenges to the New World Trade Organization*. Amsterdam: Kluwer Law International, 219–43.

Elliott, K. A. (2011), 'Labor Rights.' In Chauffour, J-.P., and Maur J. C. (eds.), *Preferential Trade Agreement Policies for Development: A Handbook*. Washington DC: The World Bank.

Elliott, K. A., and Freeman, R. B. (2003), 'Can Labor Standards Improve Under Globalization?' Washington DC: Peterson Institute for International Economics.

Enders, A. (1996), 'The Role of the WTO in Minimum Standards.' In Van Dijk, P. and Faber, G. (eds.), *Challenges to the New World Trade Organization*. Amsterdam: Kluwer Law International.

Engerman, S. (2003), 'The History and Political Economy of International Labor Standards.' In Basu, K., Horn, H., Roman, L. and Shapiro, J. (eds.), *International Labor Standards: History, Theories, and Policy Options*. Oxford: Blackwell.

Fields, G. (2006), 'The Role of Labor Standards in US Trade Policies.' In Deardorff, A. and Stern, R. M. (eds.), *Social Dimensions of US Trade Policies*. Ann Arbor: University of Michigan Press.

Fields, G. (1996), '"Trade and Labor Standards: Final Report on the Meeting." Working Paper No. 7, OECD, Paris.

Flanagan, R. (2003), 'Labor Standards and International Competitive Advantage.' In Flanagan, R., and Gould VI, W. (eds.) (2003), *International Labor Standards: Globalization, Trade and Public Policy*. Stanford: Stanford University Press.

Flanagan, R. (2006), *Globalization and Labor Conditions*. New York: Oxford University Press.

Flanagan, R. (2007), 'Globalization, Working Conditions, Labor Rights: Implications for Developing Countries.' Paper presented at the Eighth Annual Conference on Indian Economic Policy Reform, Stanford University, June 7–8.

Freeman, R. (1994), 'A Hard-headed Look at Labor Standards.' Sengenberger, W. and Campbell, D. (eds.), *International Labour Standards and Economic Interdependence*. Geneva: Institute for International Labour Studies, 79–92.

Genugten, W. van (2006), 'Linking the Power of Economics to the Realization of Human Rights: The WTO as a Special Case.' In Kumar, C.R. and Srinivastava, D.K. (eds.), *Human Rights and Development: Law, Policy and Governance*. Hong Kong: LexisNexis and School of Law, City University of Hong Kong.

Golub, S. (1997), 'Are International Labor Standards Needed to Prevent Social Dumping?' *Finance and Development*, 34(4): 80–83.

ILO (2004), 'A Fair Globalization: Creating Opportunities for All.' Report of the World Commission on the Social Dimension of Globalization, Geneva: ILO.

ILO (2002), *The International Labor Organization's Fundamental Conventions*. Geneva: ILO.

Maskus, K. (1997), 'Should Core Labor Standards Be Imposed Through International Trade Policy.' Washington DC: World Bank.

Maskus, K. (2002), 'Regulatory Standards in the WTO: Comparing Intellectual Property Rights with Competition Policy, Environmental Protection and Core Labor Standards.' *World Trade Review*, 1(2): 135–52.

Maskus, K. (2004), 'Global Labor Standards and the WTO: A Crack Opens?' *Labor History*, 45(4): 509–16.

Meadowcroft, J. (2006), 'Free Trade, 'Pauper Labor' and Prosperity: A Reply to Professor Mishan.' *Economic Affairs*, 26(1): 65–67.

Mishan, E.J. (2005), 'Can Globalization Depress Living Standards in the West?" *Economic Affairs*, 25(3): 66–69.

Moehling, C. 1999. 'State Child Labor Laws and the Decline of Child Labor.' *Explorations in Economic History*, 36(1): 72–106.

Moran, T. and Hufbauer. G. (2007), 'Why a 'Grand Deal' on Labor Could End Trade Talks.' *Financial Times*, March 13, p. 15.

Negishi, T. (1960), 'Welfare Economics and Existence of an Equilibrium for a Competitive Economy.' *Metroeconomica*, 12(2–3): 92–97.

OECD (1996), *Trade, Employment and Labor Standards*. Paris: OECD.

Panagariya, A. (2001a), 'Trade Labor Link: A Post-Seattle Analysis.' In Drabeh, Z. (ed), *Globalization Under Threat: The Stability of Trade Policy and Multilateral Agreements*. Cheltenham, UK: Edward Elgar, 101–23.

Panagariya, A. (2001b), 'Labor Standards and Trade Sanctions: Right End, Wrong Means.' <http://www.columbia.edu/~ap2231/Policy%20Papers/Hawaii3-AP.pdf> (accessed April 2013). Also in Mitra, D. and Hasan, R. (eds.), *The Impact of Trade on Labor: Issues, Perspectives and Experience of Developing Asia*. Amsterdam: North Holland.

Panagariya, A. (2002), 'International Trade and Labor Standards: Right End, Wrong Means.' In Mitra, D. and Hasan, R. (eds.), *The Impact of Trade on Labor: Issues, Perspectives and Experience of Developing Asia*. Amsterdam: North Holland.

Rawls, J. (1993a), *Political Liberalism*. New York: Columbia University Press.

Rawls, J. (1993b), 'Law of Peoples.' In Shuto, S., and Hurley, S. (eds.), *On Human Rights*. New York: Basic Books, 41–82.

Rawls, J. (1971), *A Theory of Justice*. Oxford: Oxford University Press.

Raynauld, A. and Vidal, J.-P. (1998), *Labor Standards and International Competitiveness: A Comparative Analysis of Developing and Industrialized Countries*. Northampton, MA: Edward Elgar.

Rodrik, D. (1996), 'Labor Standards in International Trade: Do They Matter and What Do We Do About Them?' In Lawrence, R. Z., Rodrik, D., and Whalley, J. (eds.), *Emerging Agenda for Global Trade: High Stakes for Developing Countries*. Overseas Development Council, Essay No. 20. Washington DC: John Hopkins University Press.

Sen, A. (1999), Development as Freedom, New York: Knopf.

Sensenberger, W. and Campbell, D. (eds.) (1994), *International Labor Standards and Economic Interdependence*. Geneva: International Institute for Labor Studies.

Singh, N. (2003), 'The Impact of International Labor Standards: A Survey of Economic Theory' In Basu, K., Horn, H., Roman, L., and Shapiro, J. (eds.) *International Labor Standards: History, Theories and Policy Options*. Oxford: Blackwell.

Srinivasan, T.N. (1996a), 'International Trade and Labor Standards from an Economic Perspective.' In Van Dijck, P., and Faber, G. (eds.), *Challenges to the New World Trade Organization*. Amsterdam: Kluwer Law International, 219–43.

Srinivasan, T.N. (1996b) "Trade and the Environment: Does Environmental Diversity Detract from the Case or Free Trade ?," coauthored by Jagdish Bhagwati, in Jagdish Bhagwati and Robert Hudec (eds.) *Fair Trade and Harmonization: Prerequisites for Free Trade?* Vol. 1 Cambridge, MA, MIT Press, 159–223.

Stern, R. M. (1997), 'Issues of Trade and International Labor Standards in the WTO System.' In *The Emerging WTO System and Perspectives from East Asia, Joint U.S.-Korea Academic Studies,* Vol. 7. Washington DC: Korea Economic Institute of America.

WTO (1996), 'Ministerial Declaration.' Singapore Ministerial 1996. <http://www.wto.org/english /thewto_e/minist_e/min96_e/wtodec_e.htm>

WTO (2005), 'Labor Standards: Consensus, Coherence and Controversy.' Section on Cross-Cutting and New Issues in Understanding the WTO. Geneva: World Trade Organization.

WTO (2009), *Globalization and Informal Jobs in Developing Countries*. Geneva: World Trade Organization.

Zhao, L. (2006), 'International Labor Standards and Southern Competition.' Research Institute of Economics of Business, Kobe University, (Mimeo).

Index of Names

General Index